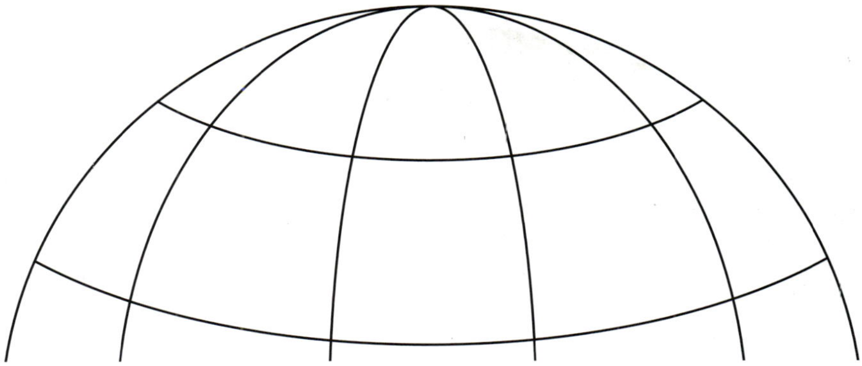

JOHN CATT'S GUIDE TO

International Schools 2022/23

20th Edition

Editors:
Jonathan Barnes and Phoebe Whybray

JOHN CATT

Published in 2022 by
John Catt Educational Ltd,
15 Riduna Park,
Melton, Suffolk IP12 1QT
Tel: 01394 389850 Fax: 01394 386893
Email: enquiries@johncatt.com
Website: www.johncatt.com

Designed and typeset by John Catt Educational Limited

A CIP catalogue record for this book is available from the British Library.

ISBN: 978 1 915261 35 9

Contacts

Editor
Jonathan Barnes
Email: jonathanbarnes@johncatt.com

Advertising & School Profiles
Tel: +44 (0) 1394 389850
Email: sales@johncatt.com

Distribution/Book Sales
Tel: +44 (0) 1394 389863
Email: booksales@johncatt.com

We are grateful to the many individuals and associations who helped with the production of this guidebook

Contents

continued on next page....

Appendices

How to use this guide

John Catt's Guide to International Schools has been specifically designed with the reader in mind. Now in its 19th year, this edition includes useful and informative information which is ideal for anyone looking for details of an international school, association, international curriculums, exams, tests and qualifications. There are clearly defined sections providing information for anyone looking at independent international education worldwide today.

Are you looking for help and advice? Take a look at our editorial section (see pages 7 to 41). Here you will find articles covering a wide variety of issues you are likely to come across when choosing a school for your child. Each year we try to find a differing range of topics to interest and inform you about the uniqueness of independent international education.

Perhaps you are looking for a school or college in a certain country? Then you need to look first in the directories (starting on page D289). Here you will find basic information about all the schools in each country (countries are featured in alphabetical order within their relevant continent), complete with contact details. From this section you will be directed to more detailed information in the guide, where this is available. An example of a typical directory entry is given at the end of this article. School profile information is written by the individual schools, outlining the reasons why you should choose their establishment.

Some of you may already be looking for a specific school or college. In which case, if you know the name of the school or college but are unsure of its location, simply go to the index at the back of the guide where you will find all the schools listed alphabetically. Page numbers prefixed with the letter D denote the directory section; those without, a full profile.

In the appendix you will find up-to-date information about international curriculums and the examinations, tests and qualifications available (see page 515), editorial about international schools associations (see page 485), and contact details for Ministries of Education worldwide (see page 495).

Key to directory

Country	**Whereford**
Name of school or college	**College Academy**
Indicates that this school has a profile	***For further details see p.12***
Address and contact number	Which Street, Whosville, Wherefordshire AB12 3CD **Tel:** 01000 000000
Head's name	**Head Master:** Dr A Person
Age range	**Age range:** 11–18
Number of pupils. B = boys G = girls VIth = sixth form	**No. of pupils:** 660 B330 G330 VIth 200
Fees per annum. Day = fees for day pupils. WB = fees for weekly boarders. FB = fees for full boarders.	**Fees:** Day £11,000 WB £16,000 FB £20,000
Curriculum	**Curriculum:** National, IBDP, ALevs
Language of instruction	**Language instr:** English, French
Memberships/Accreditation	(AISA) (COB) (EAR)

Key to icons

Key to symbols:

- Boys' school
- Girls' school
- Boarding accommodation

Member of:

- (AISA) Association of International Schools in Africa
- (CEE) Central and Eastern European Schools Association
- (EAR) East Asia Regional Council of Overseas Schools
- (ECIS) European Council of International Schools
- (RS) Round Square

Accreditation:

- (CIS) Council of International Schools
- (COB) Council of British International Schools

International education – life through a global lens

Nicholas Wergan, Global Education Director for Inspired Education Group, shares his thoughts on the benefits of an international education

Students attending an international school have the advantage of learning in an environment and community that is truly global – one that broadens their perspectives, outlook, and holistic development.

At international schools, students gain a head-start on the world stage. They learn to see life through a global lens and leave with a foundation for life: a deeply rooted inner confidence, a network of international contacts they can call on throughout their lifetime, and a mindset that sets them apart as the leaders of tomorrow. They develop an understanding of ethics and learn how to have a positive impact on their surroundings. By immersing themselves in other cultures there is a greater development of self-confidence and self-esteem.

The international curriculum builds on the core skills and knowledge all students need to learn and develop but is entwined with global perspectives, cultures and languages. This enables them to discover their unique individuality and become effective global citizens

The international curriculum builds on the core skills and knowledge all students need to learn and develop but is entwined with global perspectives, cultures and languages.

and leaders. The language immersion in international schools uniquely advantages students who learn in them, ensuring they flourish and succeed in their ambitious future pathways.

Students that attend a school that is part of an international group, such as Inspired Education Group, also benefit from global connectivity, which adds even more breadth and depth of opportunity.

From peer-led Global Student Leadership Conferences to the Inspired Builds Robotics competition, the Concours D'Arts Creative and Performing Arts competition, and international sports fixtures, tournaments, and tours. There is also an extensive global competition programme that includes sports from football to skiing, subjects from dance to history and interests from debating to chess – all designed to motivate and engage students' learning and deepen their development.

Inspired Global Camps provide an opportunity to develop life skills such as resilience, teamwork and

independence while building confidence, knowledge, and talent. The comprehensive programme of camps runs during school holidays and includes the Lake and Mountains Summer Camp, in the beautiful alpine setting of St George's International School in Montreux, Switzerland. Here students learn to sail, paddleboard, rock climb, wakeboard, and try canyoning.

A different type of experience is the Inspired Fashion, Art and Design Camp in the world's capital of fashion at the International School of Milan. Here the focus is on creativity and style, alongside iconic Italian fashion brands. Or students could take part in the Elite Tennis and Golf Sports Camp at Sotogrande International School in southern Spain – just a few examples of the enriching global student camps on offer.

Inspired's International Student Exchange Programme further adds to the benefits of attending an international school. They broaden students' horizons and give them access to enriching experiences in new and exciting environments that develop the lifelong skills required to truly flourish and succeed.

During exchange programmes, students are immersed in a different culture and country, discovering and learning new languages and ways of life that create international, globally-minded perspectives and aspirations. Inspired schools offer exchanges for four weeks up to a whole year, where students create lasting memories and make friendships that will last a lifetime.

For more information about Inspired, see inspirededu.com

International schools and when they pay off

accadis International School Bad Homburg (accadis ISB) in Germany provides a broad offering

The choice of school impacts on the everyday life of a family and on the learning experience of a child. It also affects the options available to a student after completing secondary school, for example in further education. Expat families in particular face the challenge to identify a school in a new country that meets the local regulatory requirements as well as leads to an internationally recognized university entrance qualification, allowing the student to study or pursue a career in a country of their choice. This is where international schools come in, often offering degrees that are recognized worldwide.

High School Diploma, A-Levels and the IB DP

Among the best-known school leaving certificates that open university doors worldwide are the US High School Diploma, the British A-Levels and the International Baccalaureate Diploma (IB DP). "The IB Diploma Programme is particularly highly regarded internationally," observes Professor Dr. Christoph Kexel, Managing Partner of accadis International School Bad Homburg (accadis ISB) in Germany.

Quality from Switzerland for educational success worldwide

Originally developed by the private International Baccalaureate Organisation (IBO) foundation in Switzerland for the children of diplomats, the IB Diploma Programme is now established worldwide. As of May 2022, more than 3500 schools in over 150 countries are offering this programme. "School leaders increasingly

recognize that IB graduates are ideally equipped for higher education," says Prof. Dr. Kexel, who led his school to accreditation as an IB World School.

Laying a strong academic foundation

"While graduates of other programs sometimes struggle with introductory courses to academic methodology in their first semester at university, IB DP graduates have already studied at this level while still in school," says Prof. Dr. Christoph Kexel. With the Extended Essay, they complete their first academic paper, developing research and writing skills. IB students apply their critical thinking skills across subjects, cultivate their curiosity and solve complex problems while still of school age. Students become independent learners, crucial for success at any university.

Hence, the quality of the programme of study and final qualification is a key factor in choosing an international school, according to education expert Prof. Dr. Kexel. "However, parents should also assess any potential schools against further criteria."

Growing and learning together

"In a learning environment, everything depends on the daily interactions between individuals. At international schools, children and teachers from numerous countries and cultures learn together, and the culture of a school is paramount in this context" emphasises Prof. Dr. Kexel. "Academic knowledge and skills can only be developed fully in a positive, constructive setting, in which the students' efforts are valued and all members of the school community interact with ease." accadis ISB applies a creative approach in order to communicate its core values. "We have matched the letters of our school name with our school values. This makes them easy to remember and helps everyone understand what our school community stands for."

a – ambition
c – compassion
c – courtesy
a – acceptance
d – dedication
i – integrity
s – service

Teachers at accadis ISB also form close partnerships with the parents of their students. "Only when parents and the school work together will the child develop in the best possible manner," adds Prof. Dr. Christoph Kexel.

Competence in language and strong communication skills are fundamental for the social

'In a learning environment, everything depends on the daily interactions between individuals. At international schools, children and teachers from numerous countries and cultures learn together, and the culture of a school is paramount in this context.'

interactions of all members of the school community. "So we would also recommend that parents consider carefully to what extent a school promotes languages and communication."

Globally recognized language development

The Immersion method is recognized worldwide as a successful approach to language learning from kindergarten age onwards and follows the principle of "one person – one language". Each educator or teacher speaks only in one language to the child, for example in either German or English. Spoken words are reinforced by facial expressions, gestures or pictorial support, allowing the child to learn the language naturally, from the context of the situation. In this way, each language, whether native or second language, naturally becomes a working and everyday language.

Well-structured teaching curricula and a careful staffing concept are of essence. "We employ teachers, social pedagogues and assistants with native language skills in either German or English, and who are not only skilled educators in a bilingual setting, but also capable of helping students developing their social skills in a multicultural environment," explains Prof. Dr. Christoph Kexel. Those who want to gain even more from a school education can seek out a multilingual international school for their child, he adds.

Multilingual is the new bilingual

A command of business English at a negotiating level is now a matter of course for success in studies and careers around the world. "English at a native-speaker level is no longer a unique selling point in the application process for a university place and on the job market," emphasizes Prof. Dr. Kexel. "In addition to English and German, we also offer Spanish as an additional language in the secondary school."

Staying one step ahead in teaching

"A good school continuously develops in order to support students in mastering tomorrow's challenges today. Our aspiration is to be one step ahead in teaching. We want our students to develop into responsible global citizens, equipped with problem-solving skills, with an open mind and a willingness to be lifelong learners." But how can parents determine whether a school is living up to such an aspiration?

According to Prof. Dr. Kexel, one indicator is the school's digital development. "As a result of digital transformation, the education sector also needs to be agile and respond to the fast-changing environment. Private international schools are ahead of the game in this regard in many countries." For years, accadis ISB has been using digitalized teaching with cloud-based learning via Google Workspace for Education, smart boards and laptops. For Prof. Dr. Kexel and accadis ISB, another advantage of digital instruction has emerged over the past two years. "Our concept has prepared us for crisis situations. Thanks to our experience in digital teaching, the pandemic changeover to home schooling was seamless. Our students and parents felt well-served by our thoughtful teaching approach."

Internationally recognized school leaving certificates, close and positive interactions between students, parents and teachers, language concepts, multilingual and digital teaching, and continuous improvement – paying attention to these aspects will certainly help a parent to identify a fitting (international) school for their child.

For more information about accadis International School Bad Homburg see page 121

Education is much more than academics

ES American School combines an innovative, inspiring programme that combines high-quality education with elite sports training

Providing world class, future focused and enriching education is the most important gift we can give to our children.

Preparing students to be confident, successful participants in the diverse, rapidly changing world is a responsibility that we, in education, take extremely seriously. Reviewing and adapting the experience our students have, ensuring we can give the very best opportunities possible is therefore of the utmost importance.

So what does outstanding education look like?

Personalization

As a leader in education, I came to the realization very early on that students thrive when they feel seen and heard. They flourish in a system where they feel highly involved in their learning instead of being a passive participant.

Personalization plays such a key role. Students only get one shot at growing up. Their formative school years should allow them to develop physically, emotionally, creatively, socially and cognitively. They should be encouraged to explore who they are and who they want to be.

Schools that have a focus on personalized learning employ teachers who care about each individual student. They do not allow students to get lost in a system. Students are never seen as just a class, they are seen as unique individuals, full of potential.

Outstanding education is flexible, adapting to meet the needs of each student. Outstanding education inspires, motivates, develops their talents and creates learners who love learning!

Internationally Minded Values

The world is becoming more and more connected and today's students increasingly will live and work in several different countries. Providing them with truly international experiences ensure they are open minded and culturally aware. These students embrace and learn from a range of cultures and styles, which sees them able to thrive wherever they choose to go.

Excellent education should prepare students to be confident and successful within their world, whatever path they decide to tread. They should leave school with highly developed key skills:

- Be excellent communicators who can work collaboratively and create strong networks.
- Have the confidence to use their initiative, give it a go and take the lead in order to achieve their goals.
- Be adaptable, think critically and act swiftly on feedback, realizing that failure is the next step towards success.
- Have developed curiosity and imagination, creating new thoughts and ideas that move the world positively forwards.

Choosing a school that promotes these strong values as well as excellent academics is key to their success.

Sports and Education

A world class education should also enable students to excel in a sport as well as in the arts.

The American educational system has always placed an importance on sports, from elementary right through to university. It enables and encourages students to succeed in their chosen sport as well as in their academic studies.

Flexibility is given for students to be able to attend sport tournaments and competitions, without their academics being penalized. This is helped these days by the increasingly effective use of online resources, whereby teachers and students can now communicate with ease, enabling quality learning experiences to be had, and assignments to be completed.

Apart from the clear health benefits of sport, there are many other advantages to linking sport and education. Sport motivates students to do well. Student athletes recognize that success comes from perseverance and putting in the required hours to gain mastery. Not to mention that many American universities give sports scholarships to high-achieving academic and athletic students.

Arts and Education

As well as sport, having opportunities to develop creatively is also an important aspect of any student's development. Whether this is studying the art of painting, playing a musical instrument or developing their acting skills, giving students time to develop in these areas teaches them so many skills for life.

Students learn that practice brings results and an enormous sense of achievement. They learn to manage their time more effectively. They have a greater appreciation of culture and a deeper understanding of the world around them.

Outstanding education is flexible, adapting to meet the needs of each student.

Creating the Dream

Having worked in several different education systems, I am delighted to have found a very special place in the campus of Emilio Sanchez Academy and American School. Bringing together students from over 30 different cultures, we provide a wide-ranging educational experience. Many of our students also take part in sport at a high level, with the majority choosing to take advantage of the world class tennis facilities and training provided within the campus.

Bringing all of the very best educational practices together, alongside giving students the opportunity to take their sport to the highest level was the dream realized by Emilio Sanchez Vicario, following his outstanding career as a professional tennis player.

With one campus in Barcelona, Spain and one campus in Naples, Florida, students have the opportunity to have a different experience, but with the same world class quality of education and tennis training in both continents.

"It was always clear to me that if I created something, it would have to be an Academy where the players could also study. I feel I have achieved something great: offering young people a program combining tennis and studying over two continents alongside the possibility to experience two cultures, two life experiences provided by the innovative and unique Emilio Sanchez Academy Intercontinental Program together with ES American School.

Every year, when I see not just the number of graduates, but the human quality of these young people who are going on to study at university in the United States, I realize that this initial idea was the right one. Even more so when the United States continues to set the standards for universities that combine sport and studies."

Emilio Sánchez Vicario

CEO & Founder at Emilio Sanchez Academy and American School

"Having a dream and turning it into a reality is something that every child should believe is possible. I urge all parents looking to choose a school to make sure it's a place where your child will thrive not only academically, but in all of these other ways that matter so greatly for their future success."

Mel Rose, Head of ES American School

For more information about ES American School see page 150

Innovative, immersive, international: The world's first online IB Diploma

King's InterHigh is working with the IB Organisation to explore the advantages of online learning and collaborate virtual communities.

King's InterHigh is proud to be the world's first and only school to offer the IB Diploma Programme entirely online – an innovative, immersive, and international option for students around the world.

The online Diploma Programme begins at King's InterHigh this September 2022, giving students a flexible path to an outstanding education. Bringing our experience and leadership in virtual education to a new partnership with the International Baccalaureate Organization (IBO), we are enriching the IB curriculum for the modern age.

Pioneering teaching, virtual reality classes, and a true global community: With all this and more, our young people are prepared for thriving futures in an ever-changing society.

Innovating the IB Diploma Programme

At its core, the IB Diploma Programme has always been ground-breaking. In the words of Haif Bannayan, the IBO's Global Director of Business Development, "*IB programmes are designed to be innovative from the ground up and ready to match the educational needs of today.*"

The world of today is increasingly online. With 5 billion internet users across the globe, leading organisations such as the United Nations say that digital intelligence is now a crucial skill for children to learn. There's also no doubt that the world of education has shifted following the pandemic, embracing the positive aspects that an online education can gift to our children ahead of a hybrid future.

To meet these advancing educational needs, King's InterHigh and the IBO are now innovating the International Baccalaureate® with a fully online Diploma Programme pilot.

As an Inspired school, our new IBDP pathway is backed by 40 years of experience delivering excellence in the IB across Inspired Education Group (with the highest-scoring Inspired school recording a 39-point average score in 2021). Combining this expertise with proven online teaching practices and the very best in educational technology, we bring a powerful edge to the IB curriculum.

Each school day, our students learn in live online classes with highly qualified and experienced teachers. Interactive tools and collaboration are part of every lesson, and students get round-the-clock access to all the learning materials they need, including recordings of past classes.

Our digital classrooms bring students a learning experience beyond what is possible in a traditional classroom setting. Virtual breakout rooms, for example, empower students to investigate topics independently with unlimited resources at their fingertips, while our learning platform's progress tracker ensures teachers can support or challenge students at the best possible level.

As leaders in online education, we make the most of modern technology to create a school environment where confidence, curiosity, and skill-building all come naturally.

There's also no doubt that the world of education has shifted following the pandemic, embracing the positive aspects that an online education can gift to our children ahead of a hybrid future.

Virtual reality for immersive learning

Uniquely immersive virtual reality (VR) is just one way we're bringing students an enhanced IB experience for the modern age. Using VR headsets, learners can interact with any simulated environment in first-person. This experiential way of learning plunges students into the content they're studying, with unmatched educational benefits that speak to the core of the IB's investigative, inquiry-driven learning model.

At King's InterHigh, we've conducted extensive research into VR learning with studies pioneered by our very own Learning Development Programme Champions, Anthony Peters and Nathan O'Grady. Results show that curriculum-aligned virtual reality has profound educational benefits that bolster traditional teaching, including stronger knowledge acquisition and understanding.

As part of our fully online IB Diploma at King's InterHigh, students will get to immerse themselves in these expert-designed VR experiences. Take, for example, our VR History lesson, where students toured Anne Frank's annex from their desks at home. Placing themselves in Frank's shoes, our learners were able to truly explore the thoughts and feelings of the time. In turn, this strong sensory experience gave our students a far deeper understanding of their key learning objective: contextualising historical events through written evidence.

While our students won't use VR headsets in every lesson, they'll have plenty of opportunity to experiment in Biology or Chemistry, evaluate the greatest artistic works up close in Visual Arts, and more – no matter where they are in the world.

Truly international education

King's InterHigh is also uniquely placed to give students the true international education the IB is named for.

Developing global mindedness is a core aim of all International Baccalaureate® programmes, which is why all IBDP students study a second language. Many IB subjects also use real international topics to contextualise learning, referring to sickle cell anaemia in Africa, for example, when studying genetics in IB Biology.

Furthermore, international thinking is an increasingly important skill for students with high-flying aspirations. Emily Tomlinson (Director of Admissions at Christ's College, Cambridge) notes that the global perspective students "*acquire while studying for the IB prepares them really well*" for university.

As a global school community of students and teachers, King's InterHigh adds an even greater international dynamic to IB learning.

One of the IBO's aims for the fully online Diploma Programme is to bring an IB education to more diverse cohorts of students, regardless of where they live. With a computer and internet access, students can learn with us from anywhere in the world, from the United Kingdom to South Africa to the UAE.

Learning with classmates from every continent, our students are exposed to a variety of backgrounds and cultures. As they interact and collaborate, learners get to share their unique perspectives, histories, and beliefs. In turn, our cohorts gain rich insights into how their knowledge applies across different countries worldwide.

Given that independent inquiry is a driving aspect of the IB Diploma Programme, we are delighted to bring students a rare opportunity to learn about the world from *each other* – not just from their teachers.

Leading the future of schooling

Through it all, King's InterHigh is also serving a greater educational mission. Together with us, the International Baccalaureate Organization seeks to explore all the advantages of online learning and collaborative virtual communities. For the first time, our partnership also brings the IB to students who cannot attend traditional schools, whether due to health, migration, or commitments to passions and careers.

As noted by the IBO, the online Diploma Programme will "*work alongside and inform the IB strategy*," showing how we can further empower students to succeed in a rapidly advancing global world.

For more information about King's InterHigh see page 195

How an innovative approach to STEAM education is key to delivering a 21st-century education that prepares students to shape the world

Daniel Jones, Chief Education Officer of Globeducate, one of the world's leading K12 education groups, shares the approach taken to STEAM education in the group's 55+ premium bilingual and international schools across nine countries

STEM (Science, Technology, Engineering and Maths) has been a topic of interest and priority for educators for just over 20 years, and most students and parents are familiar with how it links school curriculum choices and future careers. The focus now is on STEAM, with the "A" for Arts, and our ICS schools are leading the way, thanks to a variety of innovative and inspiring partnerships and projects.

We believe that present and future generations will need to be equipped with skills, knowledge and understanding to be able to face global challenges collaboratively. Education systems in different countries are under pressure to respond to a changing world where technology is overtaking the need for humans to perform knowledge-based, repetitive tasks. Future workforces will need the ability to solve problems, be agile, creative and flexible, and have a mindset and the ability to upskill themselves many times in their lifetime.

Project-based learning

Our teachers use a **project-based learning** approach that integrates the disciplines of science, technology, engineering, arts and maths and fosters a learning environment in which all students are able to engage and contribute. Unlike traditional models of teaching, the approach brings the disciplines together holistically. It prepares students for future life because, regardless of the career they choose, they learn to think more deeply, to challenge themselves and the accepted norm and to have the confidence to solve problems when they arise.

Creative Learning Spaces

Thanks to the existing culture of our ICS schools, where the IB Learner Profile was already strongly embedded, our STEAM approach gathered pace quickly, particularly in ICS Milan, ICS Côte d'Azur, and in ICS Paris. These schools have designated STEAM learning spaces or "Maker Spaces" to provide the spaces and resources for students to become hands-on, minds-on learners. Many other Globeducate schools are launching new campus extensions and upgrades, and new sites, which incorporate creative learning spaces to support our STEAM Agenda, such as ISN Nice, and Nobel Algarve British International School.

What is a Makerspace? It's a place to play, to create, to learn, to mentor, to invent; a place for learning and innovation, for design thinking, prototyping, electronics and robotics. The main aim of a School Maker Space is to empower young people with 21st Century skills and to improve the teaching of STEAM: Typically, a Maker Space will include affordable cutting-edge technology such as 3D printers, 2D and 3D laser cutters, vinyl cutters, milling machines and programmable microcontrollers.

Projects and partnerships adding value

In 2020, ICS Côte d'Azur, our bilingual international IB primary school in the south of France, was one of several Globeducate schools to participate in a pilot project bringing LEGO® Education into the classroom and integrating it into the STEAM curriculum with SPIKE™ Prime and WeDo 2.0 Robotic kits. This project has now been extended across many Globeducate schools.

Our colleague Amanda Scott, Head of School at ICS Côte d'Azur, an Apple Distinguished School, says: "It is hard to make concrete predictions about the world of tomorrow, but amongst all the uncertainties one thing becomes clear: we have to give students the tools and skills to navigate a future that will include lightning-speed changes and global challenges. Our students will be the designers and creators of tomorrow, and as such, they need to develop their design-process and critical thinking skills, as well as creativity and resilience, in collaborative environments."

New Models of Learning

ICS Milan is one of Globeducate's flagship schools for STEAM Education, the first school in the group to introduce three STEAM leadership positions – STEM Coordinator, Art and Design Coordinator and Performing Arts Coordinator. Rachel Fincken is our Art and Design Coordinator at the brand-new campus, ICS Milan Symbiosis. Being an educator in a city that is pivotal in design trends, she talks about needing to walk the walk, about all teachers being designers, saying "Our goal is to foster the true innovation that comes with combining the mind of a scientist or technologist with that of an artist or designer. Unlike traditional models of teaching, our STEAM Agenda strengthens the connections between the modelling process and computational thinking, for example. Students can exercise both sides of the brain at once."

Executive Head of School at ICS Milan, Antonia Giovanazzi, committed to making the STEAM approach part of the school´s DNA, not an add-on or a "strategy", introduced Arts International to the school and to other ICS schools - ISN Nice and ICS London. A team of West End stars have been working with students in these schools through a programme called "Finding your Voice", which has encouraged creativity and innovation in our students, and helped them to develop self-confidence and presentation skills, as well as empathy, compassion, cultural awareness and appreciation.

We know that students today rely increasingly on digital access to knowledge but their future success depends on how they apply their knowledge, skills, and character. Globeducate's key principles are delivering educational excellence, developing skills and competencies, building character and nurturing global perspectives, and our STEAM Agenda is one key element of bringing our principles to life for our 21st-century learners.

For more information about Globeducate, see globeducate.com

A decade after graduation

Suhail Bindra reflects on his time studying the IB Diploma at Hong Kong Academy and how it built the foundations for his career

I loved being part of the HKA community for twelve years, commencing my studies in Grade 1 (back in 2001) and graduating from the IB Diploma Programme in 2013 with a perfect score of 45 points. I obtained my LL.B. and PCLL from the University of Hong Kong as a HKSAR Government Scholar, being fortunate to receive over HK$400,000 in merit scholarships. After setting up my own consulting social enterprise and joining a startup, I worked in numerous not-for-profit organisations in the UK, Australia and Hong Kong, and also had a brief stint working in a private practice. With a passion for public interest litigation, I went on to obtain a Master of Public and International Law from the Melbourne Law School, graduating with First Class Honours. I had the chance to study under Professor Hilary Charlesworth, now a Judge at the International Court of Justice. Currently, I am a Legal Case Manager at Equal Justice Hong Kong, a not-for-profit community impact initiative that helps underserved people anticipate, prevent and solve their legal problems. In my free time I run legal education courses for ethnically diverse school children with an NGO called EmpowerU.

My IB Diploma was an important qualification which provided a stepping stone to where I am today. However, nearly a decade after graduating my certificate is a piece of paper which I rarely refer to, rather it is the skills,

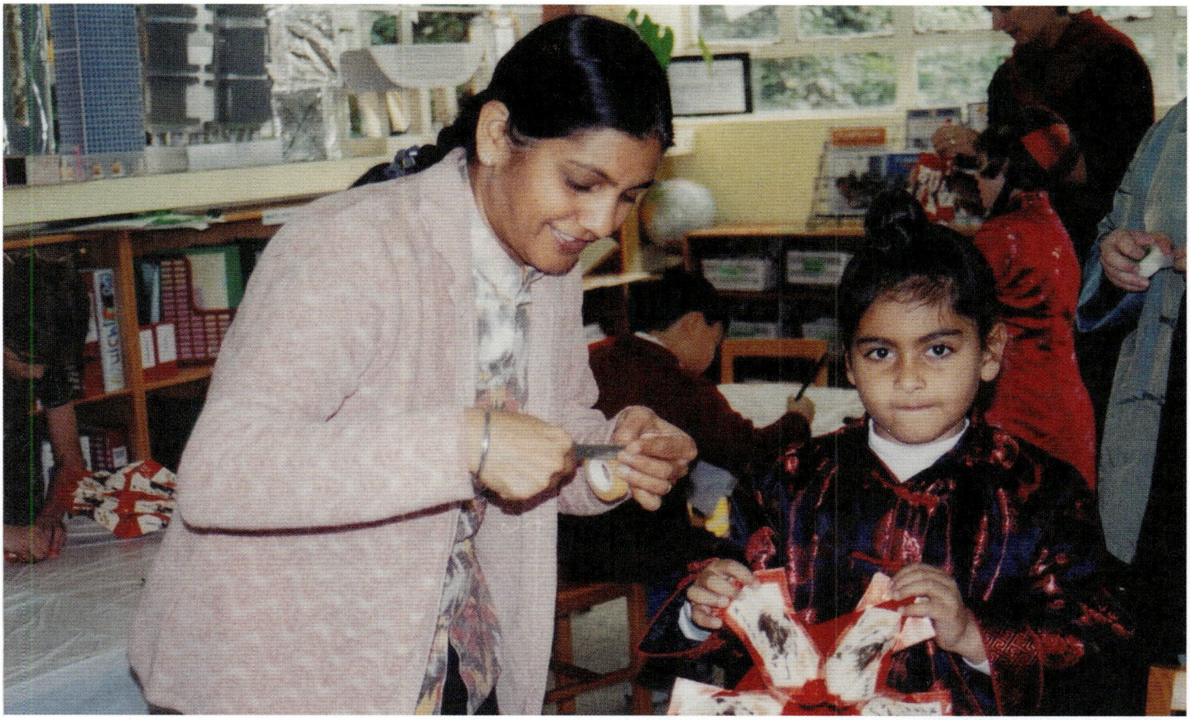

values and ideas that my education gave me which I regularly draw upon. HKA taught me to be organised. To be a leader. To speak up. To take initiative. To drive change. To volunteer. To live with integrity. To pursue what I wanted to pursue because I wanted to pursue it. To live authentically. To network. To create and build. To innovate. To imagine. To write concisely. To listen, not to what people say, but what people mean. To be curious. Read widely (and wildly). To take risks. Fail. Handle difficult situations. Adjust. Try again. Try differently. Innovate. Whilst I was busy learning all of that, I also learned how to study. Do past papers. To write exams and forge my own path.

I recently returned to HKA as an alumni volunteer and was honoured to watch this year's graduation. The traditions of the ceremony and the values of community, global citizenship, inclusion and pride were clearly evident just like they were for my cohort. Reflecting the wonderful international nature of the school's community, there were multiple graduates who had been students at HKA for their entire 15 years of education, and some who had joined HKA to commence their IB Diploma studies only two years prior.

All HKA students now graduate with two credentials and the majority receive three. The HKA Diploma and Global Citizen Diploma certificates were awarded during graduation, and students' IB results will come out in July. The Class of 2022 graduates have offers to study at leading colleges and universities all over the world, and the themes of graduation night speeches revolved around identity, making a positive impact on the world and a recognition that this cohort will be forever connected through their shared experiences at HKA. Students were recognised and in turn gave thanks to faculty, staff and parents who have supported them on their journey.

HKA is defined by its inclusiveness, its willingness to put people first, and teaches students to prioritise their education over their studies. This is a critical distinction, a point largely missed by many educational institutions. I learned this very early on. I'm so glad I did. It's made a difference. Looking back, I wish I could do it all over again, exactly the same way, with all of the same people.

Learn more about HKA on their website, www.hkacademy.edu.hk or contact Admissions at admissions@hkacademy.edu.hk.

For more information about Hong Kong Academy see page 76

Thinking internationally – preparing students as future leaders

High standards, international values and active citizenship are all core values of the International School of Milan

A school is more than just a place where students come to learn; it is the key to understanding how to build one's future. However, it must be a school that is ready to help young people embrace the commitment that managing change requires, and assist them in becoming the young leaders of the future.

International School of Milan in Italy has been dedicated to this for more than 60 years, for thousands of students from around the world. From Kindergarten to early years to high school, every young learner is supported in cultivating an attitude that enables them to find new solutions, adapt to new challenges, and invent new paths so they can create their own work for the future, particularly where the offer of work is found to be lacking. Alongside this, students also enhance and strengthen their communication skills quickly, especially in English, as well as learning the all-important skills of open-mindedness, academic rigour and intercultural awareness.

For each age group, IS Milan offers the globally recognised International Baccalaureate (IB) Programme. This is the gold standard that all the best international schools have chosen to adopt, and offers an outstanding level of inquiry-based learning that encourages students to become independent, internationally minded and lifelong learners. It is this consistent approach that helps to opens doors to not only some of the world's most renowned universities, but also prepares students for the future world of work.

So what differentiates the path of a successful young student after their school journey from any other student? Without doubt the international dimension. Those who

understand this element are able to appreciate the increasingly rapid evolution of society and anticipate what needs have yet to arise.

Francesca Arduini is one of many examples. She graduated in 2013, and eight years later began to teach Microeconomics at the prestigious University of Oxford in the United Kingdom. As soon as she graduated, Francesca was admitted to the same university, where the initial selection, as is well known, is very strict. "It was the teachers at IS Milan who made me dream of studying abroad, and they recommended Oxford to me. Then the flywheel started from there." says Francesca. Today, aged less than 30, she is on the other side of the chair as a Stipendiary Lecturer. "The other fundamental contribution from my point of view is how the IB Learner Profile pushes students to reflect on themselves and improve themselves, not only from a strictly academic point of view, but more broadly. In my opinion, this makes the difference between those who are good at school but struggle when moving forward, and those who are trained to be resilient in various work and personal contexts."

Alessandra Cestaro is another example of international learning. Graduating in 2010, in ten years he has been awarded two degrees at Bocconi - including 6 months at the University of California in San Diego (UCSD) - was part of an internship at Google in Dublin, has 3 years of professional experience at McKinsey as a Business Analyst, and has an MBA from the prestigious Columbia Business School in New York. Today at 28, while making a career as a Junior Manager at McKinsey, Alessandra has also created a successful startup business. In fact, he founded Holifya, a digital nutrigenetics platform that offers personalised nutrition plans based on DNA testing to consumers, companies and beyond. Alessandra says: "I am convinced when I say that without IS Milan I would not be where I am now, and above all I would not be who I am now. IS Milan shaped my personality and my ambition, and taught me to be a citizen of the world. The school also taught me to dream big - and then to roll up my sleeves to make those dreams come true."

High standards, international values and active citizenship are all core values of IS Milan. As part of the Inspired Group of schools, which educates over 50,000 students on 5 continents across 70 schools, it is the premium level of private education, caring and supportive teachers and a dedication to excellence that truly makes a difference to students. Francesca and Alessandra are just two of many former students who can attest to this. With thousands more students already on their educational journey, and those yet to begin, becoming one of tomorrow's leaders is easily within their reach.

For more information about International School of Milan see page 178

'The IB nourishes the way you look at things and it changes your perspectives'

The first cohort of IB students from King's College Madrid share their experience studying the Diploma Programme

In September 2020, true to its vision of being "at the forefront of British education at an international level", King's College extended its educational offer to introduce the International Baccalaureate Diploma Programme (IBDP) for students from 16 years old.

In combination with the British Curriculum, the world-renowned IBDP would offer students a unique learning pathway aimed to encourage international mindedness as well as intellectual rigour and academic flexibility.

We have spoken to the first cohort of IB students of the school, to learn about their experience.

"The IB really tries to push students forward to solving issues and complex problems and give them real case scenarios in which what we are learning applies," explains Gabriel, one of the first IB students at King's College Madrid. He decided to study the IB because, although his passion is Biology, he was looking for a programme that would allow him to study a wide range of subjects. "I wanted the opportunity to learn more things, to develop more knowledge, and I think the IB was really useful in that sense. In IB DP, they give you all the resources you need in order for you to really understand and get a feeling of what we are actually learning," he notes.

Marcos, who has been studying at King's College Madrid since he was 4 years old, felt that the IB Diploma Programme "nourishes the way you look at things and it changes your perspectives." He is preparing to study Medicine next year and is hoping to access a university in the UK. "I feel the IB has really helped me prepare for what university life will be like, because it has taught me how to be more organised and resourceful on my own, without needing that much help from my teachers," he explains.

Something similar happened to Sofia, who is a boarding student from Bulgaria: "I feel the IB really teaches you how to be independent and how to study in your own time as much as it gives you the resources and helps you throughout that journey that you're going through."

'I think the IB forces you to develop skills that robots, for example, can't replace.'

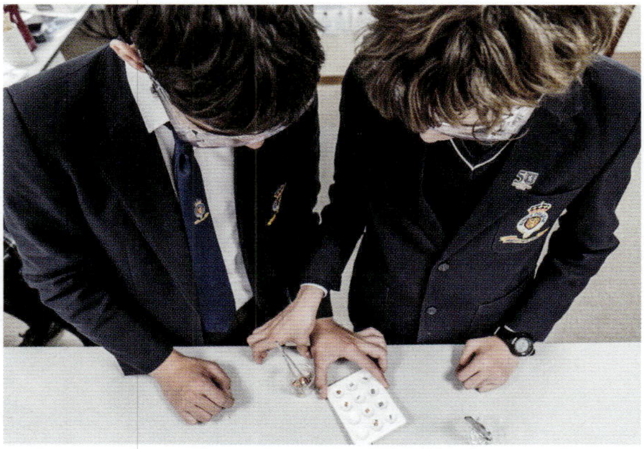

She decided to combine Film Studies and Biology for her IB DP, because she wanted to get deeper into both subjects before deciding which one to choose as a professional career. One of the things she especially liked about the IB was the "self-reflections". "I think that it's very important for you to take your time to write a reflection in everything you've done, because that allows you to understand better what you have learned, how you have learned it and what made you struggle the most," she adds.

Nadia, another IB student from King's College Madrid, decided to study the Diploma Programme because she felt that the IB would offer her a global perspective of "how the world works" and would help her progress her knowledge and learn "in a different way". "I would say the IB is as much challenging as it is fun. You need to be really organised and keep up with your studies, but you also get a chance to do a lot of debates in class, do interesting projects and open your mind to other perspectives," she comments.

For Valeria, who has been a student at King's College Madrid her whole life, the IB has given her a unique opportunity to develop her skills as a learner. "I think the IB forces you to develop skills that robots, for example, can't replace. The jobs of the future, that don't even exist now, will require skills like innovation, resilience, teamwork, those that IB helps us develop." Valeria wants to study Medicine, which is her passion, and she is preparing to access a university in the UK or The Netherlands.

"The IB is really helping me grow as a person because I feel way more challenged to manage my own time and be organized, but also to accept failure. Sometimes I've noticed myself struggle because of the workload. But to be able to accept that and be able to reflect on what have been my mistakes and how I can improve is a skill, self-awareness, that I value so much. And I feel like it's going to be useful for later years in my life," she explains.

The headmaster, Matthew Taylor, commented that "The IB at King's College is a great success. Students have thrived on the Diploma Programme and made great educational progress, achieving wonderful results, but also growing as intellectually curious, articulate, principled young people. The balance of academic work, alongside community action and service provides pupils with an all-round education. The IB at King's College prepares pupils for the future, in this digitally connected world where pupils are expected to work in jobs not yet invented. An extremely popular programme the IB Diploma continues to go from strength to strength at King's College."

For more information about King's College Madrid see page 194

What's right for my child?

Shaping your child's education journey – insights from Malvern College Hong Kong

Everyone understands that no two children are the same. Their interests, behaviour and academic abilities are all unique, which can make choosing the right school a difficult task for parents.

Malvern College Hong Kong has many years' experience in guiding parents to navigate what is one of the most important decisions they will make on behalf of their children. Our academic and admissions staff work closely with all prospective families offering tailored guidance and advice specific to each child's need.

We understand that the reality of a modern classroom can sometimes be daunting for parents who only have their own school experiences as a reference point. In our increasingly connected world, technology has vastly changed **what** and **how** children learn. In accepting that a child's school experience will be vastly different to their own, parents are often required to take a 'leap of faith' and need to trust that the chosen school will truly understand their child. However, once that hurdle is overcome, they can concentrate on deciding '**which school**?' can best meet their child's specific educational and developmental needs and best match their personality and learning style.

Schools strive to work in partnership with parents and understand all too well the need for them to find the 'best fit' for their child. To help in this process we believe that 'forewarned is forearmed'. We encourage families to equip themselves with as much information as possible before visiting a school and making a final decision, and whilst it's important to let a child feel involved in the decision-making process we recommend the ultimate decision should rest with the parents.

Schools provide extensive information on their websites and actively encourage questions via email, telephone or during school tours. Many offer 'meet and greets' or formal school tours which can be invaluable in

assessing a school's true character. In addition, parents should be prepared to share with prospective schools a full and honest assessment of their child's strengths and weaknesses, their interests, personality, and their preferred learning style. This will ensure that both parties can get a good understanding of each other before an offer or acceptance is made.

Important aspects to consider during a visit which will help in making a final selection include:

The School's Vision: What sort of pupils does the school develop? Is there a focus on becoming an international citizen, a leader of the future, and is the infra-structure there to enable that to happen?

The Calibre of Staff: Is there a good relationship between staff and pupils, do teachers seem engaged with their pupils, do they appear to understand their needs?

The Curriculum: Does it cater for your child's academic and developmental needs? What activities are offered beyond the curriculum, is there a strong extra curriculum activities programme, a pastoral care programme or additional learning support etc?

The Environment: Does the school have a vibrant and friendly atmosphere; does it feel like a supportive and nurturing place for your child? Do you sense children are pressured in their work or is there a more relaxed learning style in place?

Like many international schools, Malvern College Hong Kong places great importance on developing bright, self-assured, and resilient global citizens who will not shy away from leadership responsibilities, and who will proactively contribute to their chosen career, wherever they may decide to live in the future. Children spend a significant part of their lives in school so understanding how a school will impact their development is therefore vitally important.

In conclusion, we believe that in selecting the most appropriate school, parents are best guided by viewing their child's development as a partnership between the home and the school, rather than simply an extension of their own parenting efforts. By seeking to align their own vision and values with those of the framework of the chosen school, parents maximize the chances of success for their child in their educational journey.

For more information about Malvern College Hong Kong see page 86

Excellence in serving international sports talents

Interview with Mr. David Chapuis, Vice-Principal at St. George's International School, Switzerland, on the Sport Etudes programme

Sport Etudes at St. George's International School provides a balanced structure between the development of talents and academic life. Whilst sport is a key activity in the daily lives of all St. George's students, we recognise and support the commitment required from students in practising high-level sports.

How did the Sport Etudes programme come into being?
The programme was officially launched in 2019, but things originally got started some ten years back with Ralph Boschung, a student with a keen interest in Formula Two who has since turned professional. If he was going to compete on a regular basis, he really needed a lot of flexibility; that gave me the idea of setting up the programme.

In what way is the Sport Etudes programme at St. George's different from other schools?
Few private schools in Switzerland can offer such a full-scope, well-established sports programme; ours supports students in academic studies and sports training alike, giving them both time and plenty of flexibility in schoolwork so that they can practice their sport whilst ensuring a high level of academic achievement. We are the only school offering supervision that includes a Sport Etudes tutor in contact with outside institutions and our partners, along with a training centre that addresses these students' particular needs. What is more, St. George's International School has been accredited as an Athlete Friendly Education Centre by the World Academy of Sport (WAoS) – which has recognised no more than thirty or so schools in all.

How does this programme allow access to the best universities in the world?

St. George's International School prepares students for the International Baccalaureate, a gateway to leading universities and colleges in Switzerland and worldwide. In 2020, despite Covid-related restrictions, the school achieved a one hundred percent pass rate on this exam, putting us in first place among the World Academy of Sports (WAoS)-accredited schools in Europe. A university careers advisor also helps students determine appropriate universities, their admissions requirements, and who to contact, before putting together a portfolio summarising their tournaments and sporting achievements.

How many students have joined the programme? What sports are represented?

There are currently 12 students in the Sport Study programme, practising skiing, tennis, equestrianism, hockey, golf, and soccer. They include two skiers from the Danish national team, a girl in the process of joining the French Olympic equestrian team, a future Swiss golf champion who is about to make the national team, and a young team B soccer player from FC Stade Lausanne Ouchy, Switzerland..

How are the student-athletes supported?

We work with professional trainers and the coach of the Swiss golf team Billy Karageorgakis for all our targeted and personalised fitness sessions. Former professional Swiss golfer Christophe Bovet and Stan Wawrinka's former trainer Yannick Fattebert, also co-founder of the Sport Spirit, regularly give classes at the school. We also work with Marc-Henri Duc, head of the Villars ski school, and regularly welcome other athletes to share their experiences – one recent example is Croatian skiing champion Ana Jelušić.

For more information about St. George's International School, Switzerland see page 240

The benefits of international boarding

Boarding at Sotogrande International School creates a 'family-away-from-family'

"Never hesitate to go far away, beyond all seas, all frontiers, all countries, all beliefs." With these words, Amin Maalouf defined his vision of "travel", a concept that transcended the physical idea of moving to another place, and aimed more at the intellectual, experiential and emotional benefits of knowing and cohabiting with other ways of living and thinking. This experience is precisely one of the main advantages that young people find when they decide to study in an international boarding school. It is not only about studying in another country, but also about sharing unique experiences with colleagues from other parts of the world in a new, safe, vibrant, and enriching environment.

The benefits of studying at an international boarding school go far beyond the academic education. The experience in this type of schools has a number of benefits for students that are truly unique. To name just a few, we can refer to:

- Open-mindedness: living with peers from other parts of the world, in a different context from their own, helps young people to open their perspectives, learn about other ways of living and thinking, thus expanding their own criteria and ideas.
- Independence and autonomy: living away from home and having new responsibilities at an individual level, promotes in students a sense of autonomy and independence. This helps them to develop and grow, but also to gain self-confidence.
- Empathy and social responsibility: students who live together in a boarding house are part of a community. It is a group that they build themselves by sharing moments and routines. It helps them develop social skills and promotes respect and solidarity with one another.

Sotogrande International School: a new boarding house designed for and by students

Based on these ideas, the Sotogrande International School considered the construction of the new boarding house as an opportunity to elevate the experience it offered to its boarding students. With that purpose, the school decided to include the boarders in the design of the new building, called Templeton House.

Templeton House has been designed with students, nature and community at the centre of the decision-making process. Students from Sotogrande International School have had input into room design, colour schemes and communal space provision. All boarding students were approached to provide feedback before building work stated. This has allowed a design of inclusivity, care and attention to detail. The clean, modern furnishings will allow each individual to live in a comfortable environment where they are provided with the best chance of success.

The aim of this building work was to move boarding students on to the main school campus, increase boarding student numbers, cement boarding direction and philosophy as a central pillar at SIS, and provide SIS students with an exceptional boarding environment to thrive both academically and pastorally within.

Templeton House, which will be open in September 2022, will cater for 116 students predominantly in twin accommodation, with 3 small dorm rooms for junior boarders. The ensuite rooms will be climate-controlled, with wifi connectivity available.

SIS Boarding students will have evening onsite access to: indoor swimming pool, basketball courts, indoor sports centre, all weather pitches, library, kitchen, music rooms and recording studio.

"International boarding opens so many doors for students. Not only do they get to live and learn in a diverse and multicultural background, but they also get to experience a new culture and take part in activities that are connected with their boarding environment", explains James Kearney, Headteacher at Sotogrande International School.

"The benefits of boarding are great and wide ranging. Boarding provides students with exceptional memories, outstanding life skills, a great sense of personal and collective responsibility, resilience and significant amounts of fun and learning," commented Charles Debenham, Head of Boarding at Sotogrande International School.

"In my experience, international boarding adds layers upon this. Boarders at SIS come from over 30

different nationalities and this eclectic mix of cultures and backgrounds means that as much learning occurs outside of the classroom as within it. Living within such an international environment binds the students together, increases their worldview perspectives and creates a unique international environment in which to live and work.

"Many boarding provisions will use the phrase 'home-away-from-home' when describing their boarding programme but I think this oft-used phrase should be extended to, 'family-away-from-family' as the collegiate atmosphere and connections that boarders make are truly profound and lifelong. An international boarding environment extends this 'family' network across both countries and continents, and students at SIS will regularly spend time in the holidays visiting boarding friends in other countries both during and after their school days."

For more information about Sotogrande International School see page 231

International school students gain first-hand experience of international relations

Students from the International School of Düsseldorf gained huge benefits from their participation in the International Model United Nations conference

Fifteen senior students from the International School of Düsseldorf (ISD) took part in the 54th Hague International Model United Nations (THIMUN) conference early this year. The annual five-day event attracts over 3200 students and teachers from approximately 200 schools around the world, representing more than 100 different countries. An academic simulation of the real United Nations, the conference aims to educate students about current events, topics in international relations, diplomacy, and the role of the United Nations.

This year's theme was "One Planet, One World – Debate, Decide, ACT Now!", reflecting the concerns of young people around the world that action is not happening fast enough on the problems we all face: climate change, racial and social justice, and threats to democracy.

Each school is allocated a nation or NGO to represent. The participants research their country, take on roles as diplomats, investigate international issues, debate, deliberate, consult, and then develop solutions to world problems. This year, ISD was chosen to represent Afghanistan, which was a more challenging assignment than usual for the students.

ISD English Department Head, and Model United Nations coordinator, Claire Schwarting said: "The students' first question was "Are we representing the Taliban?". However, as the UN doesn't recognise the Taliban as the legitimate government of Afghanistan, this meant our delegates had to navigate their roles as ambassadors of an administration in exile, for whom the future is uncertain."

In their roles as international delegates, students are required to draw on a variety of communication and critical thinking skills – such as public speaking, group communication, research, policy analysis, active listening, negotiating, reaching consensus, conflict resolution, note taking, and technical writing – in order to best represent the policies of their country. The standard of the debates is high, and intense concentration is needed in order to follow the arguments being discussed.

In total, the conference passed 88 Resolutions, several of which were co-submitted by the ISD delegation. The most notable of these were: measures to increase youth participation to address climate change; measures to improve access to clean water for all; measures against fiscal fraud. These will be included in the 2022 conference record, which will be housed in the library of the United Nations Headquarters in New York.

The conference is organised by the THIMUN Foundation, whose mission is to "promote and foster collaborative solution-oriented discussion to important global issues by instilling a life-long passion in youth to take an engaging role in the future and become more responsible global citizens."

By researching and adopting views and attitudes other than their own, and by interacting with other young people from around the world, students not only gain a deeper insight into the causes of conflict between nations, but also a greater understanding of the interests and motivation of others.

'Students seem to grow before our eyes; they stand taller, speak with more empathy and authority, and carry themselves with more confidence.'

Ms Schwarting said: "During conference week, students seem to grow before our eyes; they stand taller, speak with more empathy and authority, and carry themselves with more confidence. Breathing the rarefied air of such weighty debate has a wonderful impact on them! Of course, this is exactly what we try to do at ISD each day; we believe that a "well-educated child" is one who can take his or her place among the future leaders of the world."

For more information about International School Düsseldorf see page 176

Getting to know English as a second language (EAL) program

Australian International School in Vietnam has developed a program to develop reading, writing, speaking and listening skills for language learners

Joining a new school can be a challenge. Making new friends, getting used to new teachers and language barriers can make things tricky. Because of this, the English as an Additional Language (EAL) program at Australian International School (AIS) aims to develop practical reading, writing, speaking and listening skills of students as quickly as possible so they can confidently and proficiently join mainstream classes.

As a leading international school, each of the school's subjects is taught in English. That means students who are not native speakers must take a language assessment upon enrolment. Those students who need additional support to access regular classes join the school's Intensive English Language Program (IELP) or afternoon EAL classes.

Garry Seabrook, the EAL program coordinator at AIS, has been teaching the subject for nearly 20 years and holds a Master's degree in EAL and a Doctorate in Philosophy. He is joined by eight staff members who are all committed to helping students develop the necessary language skills to prosper in all their subjects. Beyond the attention each teacher pays to personalizing the coursework, the program also uses the Cambridge curriculum. This involves a clear and accessible progression in coordination with the International General Certificate of Secondary Education (IGCSE) that all students prepare for and take as part of their AIS education in Year 11. This then leads to the IB Diploma Program in Years 12 and 13, which is the gateway to the world's leading universities.

The EAL program benefits from small class sizes and a high teacher-to-student ratio so individuals receive as much support as possible. "In Primary, the presence of support teachers allows for differentiation in class and

a lot of practice," Mr Seabrook explained. He added that the experienced teachers create a comfortable environment that encourages students to ask the questions and make the mistakes that are necessary to learn.

Language fluency involves far more than just being able to survive in formal settings. While AIS's EAL program uses materials relevant to regular coursework, it also prepares students for varied and nuanced social interactions as well by stressing collaboration with classmates and building relationships. Mr Seabrook also emphasized the value of English books, age-appropriate television shows and games that reinforce the idea that learning a new language can be fun and useful outside of the classroom.

Parents have an important role in the EAL program by encouraging English-based activities at home. Mr Seabrook noted that simply creating as many opportunities to encounter English by putting post-it notes on household objects or arranging casual visits with English-speaking friends and relatives can have a large impact. Moreover, teachers give parents regular progress reports so that they can take an active role in their children's development.

AIS's world-class education prepares students to excel in their future endeavors all around the world once they are supported by English fluency. One of the school's many advantages is its diverse student body which means many will arrive with limited English proficiency. The EAL program is designed exactly for this scenario so learners not only succeed in classes but develop language skills that will benefit them for the rest of their lives.

The EAL program benefits from small class sizes and a high teacher-to-student ratio so individuals receive as much support as possible.

For more information about Australian International School see page 55

One school, four values, endless possibilities

International School Ho Chi Minh City students and graduates have values strong enough to change the world

History and accreditation that make winners

More than 30 diploma subjects. A one-to-eight faculty to student ratio. Over 200 experienced IB educators. These are just some of the hallmarks that contribute to the 100% pass rate achieved by pupils at International School Ho Chi Minh City (ISHCMC).

ISHCMC is a school of many firsts: it is the city's first international school and first IB World School accredited to teach three IB programmes. Its pioneering spirit is matched by its prestige – ISHCMC has a long history of graduating students to top universities around the world and is fully accredited by the Council of International Schools (CIS), the most prestigious international accreditation organisation.

Where students achieve more than they believe they can

Hailing from over 55 countries, ISHCMC students enjoy the best of many worlds in harmony. Their school's location is steeped in history. ISHCMC is as well. However, while traditional approaches are appreciated, an academic journey here is as progressive as can be.

Modern environments abound for learners with their sights set on a lifetime of future-focused success. They are guided by expert IB educators who specialise in concept-driven, inquiry-based learning practices. Every member of ISHCMC's student body has a voice, and every question they have is answered.

This support is precisely why Akiko Motoki decided her Grade 9 journey had to begin at ISHCMC. "It is more inclusive than my previous school," she says. "There is definitely academic rigour and the teachers are really supportive of your wellbeing."

Their guidance gave her the confidence to explore. She joined the musical orchestra, competed in the intercity Battle of the Bands competition, was a member of the varsity soccer and basketball teams, and even led her CAS group for Operation Smile (a nonprofit service organisation providing free reconstructive surgery and dental care for patients with cleft lips).

"If I wanted a typical school with just academics, I could have gone to any other school here," she explains. "I wanted something different so I chose ISHCMC."

These opportunities helped her realise her passion for public health. Comprehensive lessons in the sciences were equally intriguing. The valedictorian is currently pursuing both disciplines at Brown University.

Such outcomes are typical of ISHCMC graduates. The school's core values play a fundamental role in ensuring it: Curiosity, Achievement, Resilience, and Empathy (CARE). Each was set in place to guarantee students are ready to thrive not just in 2022, but in 20 years from now as well – and beyond.

"They underpin our vision of enriching the lives of children to achieve more than they believe they can," says Mike Hebert, director of admissions and market growth. "They are our building blocks for our culture of CARE and enable our diverse, internationally-minded community to flourish as energised, engaged and empowered learners."

ISHCMC's life-enriching values

Diving into the unknown is compulsory at ISHCMC. In the process, they become self-motivated and self-efficient, and most importantly, ever keen on gaining an eventual understanding of the unfamiliar. Motoki's journey is a testament to this, and so is Silvia Familiari's.

She spent her IB Middle Years Programme as a volleyball champ and active member of the Student Council by leading a Welfare group – an opportunity that sparked her interest in Psychology. Soon, she will be attending Università Cattolica in Italy to advance her existing knowledge.

Every learner is encouraged to try a little bit of everything to determine their life's calling. Classrooms are just as powerful when it comes to inspiring aspirations. At ISHCMC, learning takes place in a safe, engaging environment. Each session is smooth, consistent, immersive, and sustained.

Achievement at ISHCMC extends beyond classroom successes. Here, character skills and in-demand competencies are causes for celebration as well. ISHCMC believes if students are versatile, multi-faceted, and truly interdisciplinary – there's no stopping them.

"We're looking at sports achievement, wellbeing achievements, and even their ability to achieve in terms of empathising with others," says Hebert. "Here, we see a full spectrum of achievement in a very big, broad sense."

Stroll ISHCMC's expansive campus and you'll notice that despite academic rigour, smiles are wide and giggles are contagious. All students are taught to be self-aware and confident in overcoming setbacks and tackling the challenges close to their hearts. This resilience helps them stay motivated, focused on their goals, and determined to live a happy life.

"Our students' achievements are representative of ISHCMC's strong academic programme that is grounded in a foundation of wellbeing and a culture of care that prepares students for outstanding performance, even in two abnormal years," enthuses head of school Kim Green.

Wellbeing experts and educational psychologists are plenty as well for students who could benefit from additional support. "We hold a principle of inclusion and differentiation," explains Hebert. "Every student has some sort of need. Some are gifted and need additional challenges. Some may feel like just getting to school is a challenge on its own. We have the resources to turn every negative into a positive."

At ISHCMC, all learners are encouraged to better themselves by bettering the world. Their school has the resources to teach them how. CAS, service learning and other community-based activities are frequent in ISHCMC's secondary school. Early Years and primary students are presented with many opportunities to get involved as well.

"Empathy is taught as a core value in every classroom," confirms Hebert. "Just last week, our Knitting Club knitted thousands of pieces to be sent to Vietnamese communities impacted by flooding. We are a country that is growing extremely fast, and while we have a large accumulation of wealth, there's still a lower class population that needs our help."

Thankfully, ISHCMC students and graduates have values strong enough to change the world.

Call the hotline at (+84) 28 3898 9100 or email admissions@ishcmc.edu.vn to learn more

For more information about International School Ho Chi Minh City see page 80

The questions you should ask

However much a school may appeal on first sight, you still need sound information to form your judgement

Schools, particularly independent schools, attract pupils by their reputations, so most go to considerable lengths to ensure that parents are presented with an attractive image. Modern marketing techniques try to promote good points and play down (without totally obscuring) bad ones. But every Head knows that, however good the school website/prospectus is, it only serves to attract parents through the school gates. Thereafter the decision depends on what they see and hear.

When you choose a school for your child, the key factor is that it will suit them. Many children and their parents are instinctively attracted (or otherwise) to a school on first sight. But even if it passes this test, and 'conforms' to what you are looking for in terms of location and academic, pastoral and extracurricular aspects, you will need to satisfy yourself that the school does measure up to what your instincts tell you.

Choosing an international school can prompt additional questions for parents and students alike. The international school's intake is not restricted by geographical or educational authority boundaries. International schools have the added benefit of being able to embrace a sense of national pride while encouraging a respect of and interest in international thinking, standards and cultures.

Research we have carried out over the years suggests that in many cases the most important factor in choosing a school is the impression given by the Head. As well as finding out what goes on in a school, parents need to be reassured by the aura of confidence that they expect from a Head. How they discover the former may help them form their opinion of the latter.

So how a Head answers your questions is important. Based on our research, we have drawn up a list of varied points on which you may need to be satisfied. The order in which they appear below does not necessarily reflect their degree of importance to each parent, but how the Head answers them may help you draw your own conclusions:

- How accessible is the Head, whose personality is seen by most parents as setting the 'tone' of the school?
- Will the child fit in?
- What is the overall atmosphere?
- To which organisations does the school belong?
- How has it been accredited?
- What is the ratio of teachers to pupils?
- What are the qualifications of the teaching staff?
- How often does the school communicate with parents through reports, parent/teacher meetings or other visits?
- What are the school's exam results? What are the criteria for presenting them? Are they consistent over the years?
- How does the school cope with pupils' problems?
- What sort of academic advice is available?
- What is the school's attitude to discipline?
- Have there been problems with drugs or sex? How have they been dealt with?
- What positive steps are taken to encourage good manners, behaviour and sportsmanship?
- Is progress accelerated for the academically strong?
- How does the school cope with pupils who do not work?
- What is the attitude to religion?
- What is the attitude to physical fitness and games?
- What sports are offered and what are the facilities?
- What are the extracurricular activities?
- What cultural or other visits are arranged away from the school?
- What steps are taken to encourage specific talent in music, the arts or sport?
- What is the uniform?
- What steps are taken to ensure that pupils take pride in their personal appearance?
- What are the timetable and term dates?
- What are the boarding facilities like?
- Is there a dedicated person to look after new international students?
- Does the school have a recommended guardian service?
- Does the school have a dedicated and strong pastoral team?
- Is it possible to be put in contact with parents with children at the school to approach them for an opinion?
- Does the school have a dedicated teacher for Mother Tongue languages or ESL?

International school profiles

International schools in Africa

Schools ordered A–Z by Name

Acorns International School (AIS)

ACORNS INTERNATIONAL SCHOOL
INSPIRING AND EMPOWERING

Plot 328, Kisota Road,
(Along) Northern Bypass,
Kisaasi Roundabout, Kampala, Uganda
Tel: +256 393 202 665
Email: admissions@ais.ac.ug
Website: www.ais.ac.ug
Head of School: Ameena Lalani

School type: Co-educational Day
Age range of pupils: 18 months–18 years
No. of pupils enrolled as at 01/09/2022: 500
Fees as at 01/09/2022:
$2,358 – $8,850
Average class size: 20
Teacher/pupil ratio: 1:3 (2yrs) to 1:12 (13yrs)

Encapsulating the adage, 'A tree with strong roots laughs at storms', Acorns International School (AIS) bears fruits that stand the test of time.

Nestled between the verdant folds of Kampala, the capital city of Uganda, AIS is sprawled over a 5-acre state-of-the-art, purpose-built campus, that nurtures the balance between academics and extracurriculars.

Over two decades in the field of education, we have grown to represent more than 50 nationalities. The AIS team strives to inspire and empower every student to achieve their personal best and become inquiring, knowledgeable, pluralists and lifelong learners, who create a better and peaceful world, through intercultural understanding and respect.

Admissions are open throughout the academic year, subject to availability. We have a limit to the number of students per classroom, for uncompromised quality. This interface gives teachers an edge to assess each student's area of strength, and improvement. Teachers are supported in this process, with timely professional development sessions, to ensure growth and excellence. Through an open-door policy, we ensure that our main stakeholders, our parents, are full partners in the decision-making process and voice concerns not only of their children, but their own too.

The language of instruction is English, with French and Kiswahili as part of our dynamic curriculum. Through our engaging and rigorous, inquiry-based environment, students reach their full academic potential and become responsible, caring, multilingual, and culturally-literate global learners.

Our teaching team is not just diverse, they epitomize academic excellence and have a penchant for pastoral care.

AIS is non-sectarian and co-educational institution, founded on strong partnerships between parents, teachers and learners.

A visit to AIS allows your family to experience the school in a relaxed environment, meet with the administration, as well as visit homerooms, the science lab, performing arts rooms, libraries, swimming pool, auditorium, soccer fields and the basketball courts.

AIS is an authorised International Baccalaureate (IB) Continuum School, offering the Primary Years Programme (PYP), the Middle Years Programme (MYP) and the Diploma Programme (DP).

AIS is an inclusive school that accepts students in the Early Childhood Department (Crèche to Reception Class), Primary (Years 1 to 6), and Secondary (MYP1 – DP2).

It is always onwards and upwards for us, and we would love for you to join us!

Ambrosoli International School

Plot 10-12 Binayomba Street, Bugolobi,
Kampala, Uganda
Tel: +256 414 220416
Email: admissions@ambrosolischool.com
Website: www.ambrosolischool.com

Head of School: Ms Emma Norris
School type: Co-educational Day
Age range of pupils: 3–11 years
Fees as at 01/09/2022:
Application Fee: $150

Ambrosoli is like no other school in Uganda. We have an outstanding reputation for our sense of family and community and we provide unique learning opportunities for all our pupils. We are an exciting, vibrant and inclusive school with something to offer to every child and family in our dynamic and diverse community.

We have 270 children from over 40 different countries. We encourage the children to be ambitious in their learning and believe there is no limit to what they can achieve. Our pupils are confident and successful because our approach encourages children to think for themselves, to question, to make mistakes and to be resilient – skills that will last a lifetime.

We currently follow the UK Early Years Foundation Stage, Key Stage 1 and 2 English National Curriculum and the International Primary Curriculum (IPC). Our high expectations are not limited to academic success. We want our students to develop a love for learning and the confidence, courage, compassion and conviction to look at the world around them and act to make it a better place.

We recruit outstanding teaching staff, specialists in their field, who support each student to achieve. Success takes many different forms and we celebrate them all; sportsmanship in competition, the courage to speak publicly and making friends. We also believe trying and failing are vital ingredients for success.

We are accredited by CIS and IPC and are members of AISA. We are located in a beautiful, quiet, green corner of Kampala. We have an excellent reputation as one of the most popular international schools in Uganda and are proud of the fact that all of the children at Ambrosoli are here because the school has been recommended to their families by existing or ex parents.

Glisten International Academy

Plot 1457 Cadastrial Zone B8,
Jahi District, Abuja, Nigeria
Tel: +234 90 3888 2824
Email:
info@glisteninternationalacademy.com

Website:
www.glisteninternationalacademy.com
Head of School: Mr. Eneh Charles Chibuzor
School type:
Co-educational Day & Boarding
Age range of pupils: 3–17 years

Glisten International Academy is committed to providing Early Years, Primary, Junior, and Senior Secondary education through quality teaching, continuous professional development of our members of staff, research, partnerships, and mentoring services that meet the expectation of all interested parties.

Our vision has a total commitment to developing the child's minds towards productivity for them to be of value to themselves, their immediate society, and the world at large. This is driven by conforming with ISO 9001:2015 and standards, a pledge to continually improve to meet the satisfaction of our valued partners and clients, through transparency, accreditations, and management reviews.

The policies of the organization support the vision of a school system with continuous nurturing of students in order to raise nation-builders that will influence our socio-cultural values in a positive way through services, commitment, and selflessness.

Our Curriculum

Glisten International Academy runs Nigerian and integrated curriculum with structures that support the personalization of learning, resulting in all-around success for our students' cognitive, emotional, and psychomotor development. Our aim is to go beyond the mere acquisition of knowledge to encourage character development, creativity, and innovation, based on higher-order thinking. Our curriculum is dynamic and it prepares learners for life, so that they can be productive and be of value to themselves, society, and the world at large.

Therefore, students and pupils will be guided to:

a. Acquire and apply knowledge,

b. Acquire transferable skills,

c. Acquire the orientation for a future career in the 21st Century workspace, productivity and find the right space in global citizenry.

Our curriculum is designed with content from Nigeria and other leading countries' curricula which includes preparations for the following:

- Diplome d'Etudes en Langue Francaise (DELF Prim)
- Cambridge Checkpoint – Primary/ Junior Secondary
- All local and National Junior and Secondary Certificate Examinations. (WASSCE)(NECO)(ERC)
- International University Preparatory Examinations (IGCSE) (SAT) TOEFL and IELT

Our Unique Added Value: Our learning experience offers 21st Century skill sets, like AI, robotics, internet of things, mechatronics, and embedded entrepreneurship and agropreneur programs, among others for learners.

Hillcrest International Schools

HILLCREST
INTERNATIONAL SCHOOLS

(Founded 1965)

PO Box 24819 -00502 Karen, Langata Rd,
Nairobi, Kenya
Tel: +254 733 255442
Email: admin@hillcrest.ac.ke
Website: www.hillcrest.ac.ke
Head of Secondary: John Eveson
Head of Prep & Early Years: Surbhi Vashisht

School type:
Co-educational Day & Boarding
Age range of pupils: 18 months–18 years
No. of pupils enrolled as at 01/09/2022: 570
Average class size: 17
Teacher/pupil ratio: 1:8

We are committed to inspiring, encouraging and empowering our students to achieve personal excellence. Guided by the British Curriculum, we cater for children aged 18 months to young adults aged 18 years. By stimulating everyone's abilities and talents within an atmosphere of mutual respect, we aim to ensure Semper Prospice (always looking forward) is a life-long quest.

Hillcrest Early Years

Offering young children a creative play-based learning environment in a caring, family-style atmosphere, we inspire and nurture a lifelong love of learning and sense of curiosity. We also empower our young children to grow in confidence, independence, determination and regard for each other.

Hillcrest Preparatory School

Recognising the uniqueness of each child, we provide pupils of every level with an individualized approach to learning that inspires and nurtures their talents while empowering them to do their best. Placing an emphasis on the development of the whole child within our mutually supportive community, our pupils develop confidence and determination as they work towards the Common Entrance Exam.

Hillcrest Secondary School

We nurture each student as they identify their strengths, and empower them to pursue these by providing a diverse and stimulating environment. We also motivate and guide each student to achieve their individual academic potential and grow into emotionally intelligent independent thinkers, effective young adults and world citizens. Sixth Form students have a choice of 19 A-Levels and 5 BTECs.

Hillcrest Boarding

Offering a safe and secure family environment, we offer Prep and Secondary students the opportunity to enhance their Hillcrest experiences while living in a caring, purposeful and multicultural community.

The RiverBank School

RAISING LEADERS
THE RIVERBANK SCHOOL

RCCG City of David, Didelou Estate,
Victoria Island, Nigeria
Tel: +234 (0) 909 859 872
Email: info@riverbankschools.org

Website: www.riverbankschools.org
Principal: Mrs. Regina Jemide
School type: Co-educational Day
Age range of pupils: 2–13 years

The Riverbank School is an independent co-educational school with well in excess of four hundred children presently on roll. It is situated in Victoria Island in Lagos, Nigeria. We are a Christian school currently accepting children from 3 months (Creche) to Year 8. Our curriculum is that of the English National Curriculum – Early Years Foundation stage (EYFS) through to Year 8. Admission to our school is by way of testing from Year 1.

We have a vision of raising God fearing child leaders and we operate on sound moral values, which are right standing, integrity, vision, excellence and refining.

The most important thing for us is that children enjoy spending their time at school. They look forward to coming to school each day and we seek to empower our children with the confidence to express themselves effectively in both their public and private lives. We foster an atmosphere in which mistakes are not reproached but seen rather as an essential part of a child's development. We believe in playing to pupils' strengths; in drawing out what is within each person rather than seeing a child as a vessel to be filled.

Our nursery provides a highly stimulating and welcoming environment for children to learn through interaction with one another and adults. They learn through play with songs, games and through the enthusiasm of their teachers. We work in small groups and one-on-one with each child at the younger end of the school to ensure that pupils moving to Year 1 are:

1) Able to read and enjoy reading
2) Able to write and enjoy writing
3) Are able to enjoy school and are confident in their abilities.

Our pupils in the primary school are taught the skills of critical thinking and problem solving in all aspects of the curriculum. They look forward to coming to school every school day of the week because of the positive treatment they receive from their teachers. The teachers are facilitators who create and ideal learning environment for our pupils to explore their potentials.

Assessments of and for learning are essential learning and teaching tools for us. This makes it more than necessary for us to inculcate effective classroom questioning into our positive classroom practices. Our systems of assessment enhances the use of information to bring about improved decision making which results into better learning experiences for our pupils.

Our pupils do not only excel academically, but also display outstanding

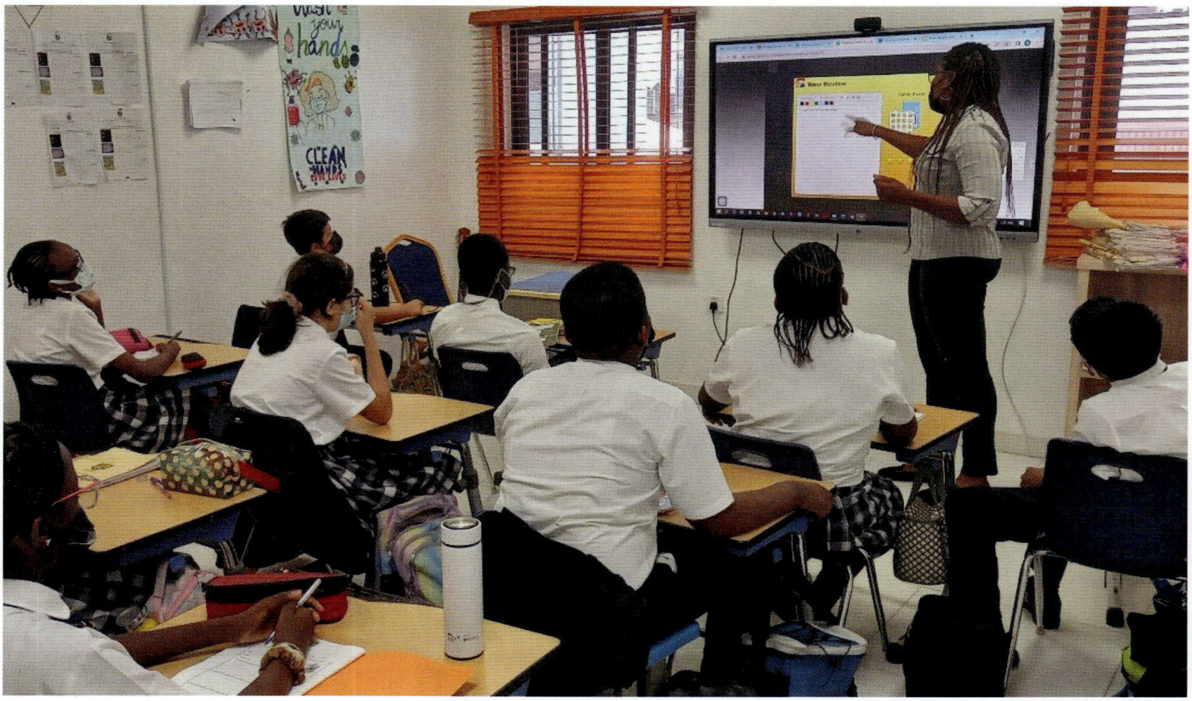

performances in music. It allows deep engagement and learning and sharpens the way students understand themselves and the world around them. Our school choir has performed excellently in both local and international choir games.

At Riverbank Secondary School our students mean everything to us. Our prime goal is to ensure that each one of them attains their full potential. The concepts of respect, motivation and achievement are fundamental and permeate every facet of life in our secondary school.

We know and accept that all of our students are unique individuals and consequently we keep our classes small enough to provide each with a child central balanced academic experience. Our learning is not confined to the classroom alone but students participate in a broad range of cultural and extra-curricular activities which complement and enrich their growth.

The success of our students is measured in a variety of ways, from their classwork, to homework, to computer based tests and of course the traditional end of term test.

At Riverbank Secondary each student is important and is carried along by our dedicated team. The development of a total child is our aim and we work towards equipping them with skills by offering a variety of extra-curricular activities based on the English National curriculum. We make provision for children with additional needs and the gifted and talented children.

Education is partial without sports. Therefore, sports at the Riverbank School helps children build character, improve their wellbeing and build their stamina. Team spirit and the self confidence of our children is also developed at the RiverBank School.

Our school is registered with Cambridge International Education UK, with whom our Year 6 (and soon to be year 9) students sit the Cambridge Checkpoint Examinations in English, Mathematics and Science. The RiverBank School is a member of the Council of British International Schools (COBIS), The Association of Christian Schools International (ACSI), The Association of International School Educators of Nigeria (AISEN) and we have the International Schools' Award (ISA).

Malvern College Egypt

MALVERN
COLLEGE EGYPT

B2-B3 South Ring Road, Investment Zone
Kattameya, Cairo, Egypt
Tel: +202 26144400
Email: info@malverncollege.edu.eg
Website: malverncollege.edu.eg
Headmaster and Head of Secondary School: Richard Moore

School type: Co-educational Day
Age range of pupils: 2.6–18 years
No. of pupils enrolled as at 01/09/2022: 920
Fees as at 01/09/2022:
Day: EGP130,000–EGP277,000

Malvern College Egypt (MCE) is the first British International School to be working in partnership with a leading British Independent School and is unique in having a teaching staff who have exclusively attended British Universities. Although MCE is a rather young school in Egypt, we are able to welcome over 150 years of experience in education from our mother school, Malvern College UK. Our aim is to provide an appropriate and balanced level of academic challenge, which will enable pupils to realize their potential while ensuring that they are happy and motivated.

MCE caters to pupils from pre-nursery to Sixth Form. We offer the International General Certificate of Secondary Education (IGCSE) as well as the International Baccalaureate Diploma Programme (IBDP). Additionally, MCE offers a full complement of A-level courses within our sixth form. At MCE we concentrate on four core areas: academic excellence, development of the performing arts, commitment to sports and engagement within our community.

We place great emphasis on ensuring that pupils develop humility and kindness. Our programme of community service projects helps pupils to develop this understanding through a variety of activities. Examples of such activities include visits to charities, bake sales, and donation appeals.

Performing Arts is at the heart of MCE and we provide every pupil with the opportunity to perform in choirs and musical groups. Involvement in sports is also important to us as it offers tremendous opportunities to develop social and leadership skills while promoting fitness and a healthy lifestyle for our pupils. We therefore encourage our pupils to participate in the extensive range of sporting co-curricular activities offered at MCE. We believe in the benefits of competitive sport where we play to win and give our all but we also believe in learning to accept defeat with dignity and respect befitting a Malvern pupil.

International schools in Asia

Schools ordered A–Z by Name

American School of Bombay

(Founded 1981)

SF 2, G-Block, Bandra Kurla Complex Road, Bandra East, Mumbai, Maharashtra, 400051 India
Tel: SS: +91 22 6772 7272
ES: +91 22 6131 3600
Email: inquiry@asbindia.org
Website: www.asbindia.org

Head of School: Dr. Paul Richards
School type: Co-educational Day
Age range of pupils: 3–18 years
No. of pupils enrolled as at 01/09/2022: 576
Fees as at 01/09/2022:
Day: US$20,000–US$35,020
Teacher/pupil ratio: 1:5

Celebrating 40 years of excellence in education in 2021, the American School of Bombay (ASB) is a beacon of schooling internationally. We are 'what school should be' and achieve this through modelling best practices and continually transforming the way we teach and learn. During the COVID-19 pandemic, our remarkable educators utilized the strength of their established relationships with students – and with each other – to create a world-leading virtual learning platform. Through positively engaging students in new ways of learning, our educators created a deep sense of trust with our parents and families. Now back on campus, we are continually assessing and adapting our approach to ensure continuity of learning within a safe environment.

The focus of our educational philosophy is our student body: students are at the center of the learning experience, they are empowered by dreams, and they are equipped with skills to become life-long learners. ASB's Mission is to inspire all of our students to continuous inquiry, empowering them with the skills, courage, optimism, and integrity to pursue their dreams and enhance the lives of others. Serving others, with a desire to make a positive impact in their world, underpins an ASB education.

With our home in India's vibrant cultural and financial capital, Mumbai, and a student population drawn from more than 50 countries, ASB is intentionally international. We identify the big issues that are affecting our students, and actively address equity, diversity and inclusion, both philosophically and through explicit teaching. We are committed to open dialogue with our students, parents and staff, to better educate ourselves and each other, and make a positive impact in our local and global community.

ASB is an accredited Middle States Association of Colleges and Schools (US) and IB World School, offering the Primary Years and Diploma Programs. Our graduates are awarded an American high school diploma and/or the IB Diploma. We are members of SAISA and ASIAC, offering opportunities for international inter-school collaboration and competition in sports and The Arts. ASB graduates are accepted at the world's finest colleges and universities, including MIT, Stanford, Johns Hopkins, Duke, University College London, Harvard, Princeton, University of Sydney, and the University of Paris, and contribute personally and professionally across a diversity of fields.

Australian International School (AIS)

AUSTRALIAN INTERNATIONAL SCHOOL
An inspired school

264 Mai Chi Tho Street, An Phu ward, Thu Duc City, Ho Chi Minh City, Vietnam
Tel: +84 28 3742 4040
Email: info@aisvietnam.com
Website: www.aisvietnam.com
Executive Principal: Ms Davina McCarthy

School type:
Co-educational Day & Boarding
Age range of pupils: 18 months–18 years
No. of pupils enrolled as at 01/09/2022: 1200
Fees as at 01/09/2022:
Day: VND 257,000,000 – 734,000,000

Leading to a bright future

At Australian International School (AIS), every action we take is designed to lead our students towards a bright future. Since our establishment in 2006, we have continued to achieve this aim by delivering high-quality international education. We are dedicated to creating an environment where we stimulate inquiry, creativity and innovation, to help our students embrace all opportunities that life brings them and to become global citizens.

Providing the IB curriculum

Understanding the significance of all that the IB curriculum offers, AIS has long identified its ability to foster both academic and personal success while challenging students to excel in their studies and their individual development. AIS was one of the first schools in Vietnam to become an authorised IB World School, and as such, we are now among the most experienced educators in the country to provide this curriculum.

Currently, AIS offers the IB Primary Years Programme (PYP) for both our Kindergarten and Primary School students and the IB Diploma Programme as part of its Senior School education. The University of Cambridge Secondary Programme with the International General Certificate of Secondary Education (IGCSE) is provided for our Lower Secondary School students.

For the IB Diploma, AIS has an extensive background in supporting and preparing students to study this acclaimed curriculum and develop real-world skills that extend beyond the classroom. Consequently, AIS graduates consistently obtain results above the world average, and students have gone on to gain places at leading universities around the globe, many with full or partial scholarships.

Exceptional education with modern facilities

Under the leadership and experience of AIS's Executive Principal, Ms Davina McCarthy, our team of enthusiastic, internationally-trained and qualified teachers are dedicated to challenging, inspiring, and supporting the individual needs of every student.

We support each child to reach their full academic potential, to nurture a love of arts, to become involved in and passionate about sport and to develop the resilience to overcome challenges. Our Australian values of fairness and a 'have a go' attitude, combined with a world-class curriculum, drive this ambition.

To aid our teaching staff, every classroom and learning environment is spacious, well-resourced, and technologically rich. Additionally, our students have access to an open garden style campus, swimming pools, a double gymnasium, an auditorium, soccer fields, a dedicated IB Centre, and much, much more.

Bangkok Patana School

Bangkok Patana School
The British International School in Thailand
Established 1957

PATANA

643 Lasalle Road (Sukhumvit 105), Bangna Tai, Bangna, Bangkok, 10260 Thailand
Tel: +66 2 785 2200
Email: admissions@patana.ac.th

Website: www.patana.ac.th
School type: Co-educational Day
Age range of pupils: 2–18 years

As the oldest British international school in Thailand, we are proud to embody the best of British values with an international outlook. The school has clear Guiding Statements that provide direction and purpose for the institution. Within our three values, Well-Being is intentionally first, followed by Learning and Global Citizenship. Our strong pastoral system supports student well-being and allows them to fulfil their potential.

Bangkok Patana is a not-for-profit school. The Board and management are the stewards of our organisation and they act on our core values of well-being, learning and global citizenship.

We are also a non-academically selective school, a fact that belies our history of excellent academic results and university matriculations.

Our curriculum is broad and balanced. From Nursery to Year 13, it links to the English National Curriculum with assessments taking place at key points. We are committed to the rigour of British education and emphasise hard work, integrity, strong moral principles and fairness. We provide diverse opportunities for our students to explore new areas and discover their passions. This includes more than 400 extra-curricular activities for students to choose.

We are a truly international school with a very diverse student body of students representing more than 65 nations. We develop global citizens and world perspectives are woven throughout the curriculum and extra-curricular programmes. We embrace the IB (International Baccalaureate) Learner Profile and students complete the IB Diploma Programme in their last two years at school. We are proud to see our students develop into respectful contributors to local and global communities.

At Bangkok Patana, we leverage our experience with the adoption of leading-edge pedagogical practices. More than 80% of our teachers are recruited from the UK or from British international schools. All our teachers are fully certified and we have a strong professional development culture to ensure they remain at the forefront of pedagogy. Our most recent

CIS accreditors noted that, "The quality of learning at Bangkok Patana School is clearly a strength....Parents and students were both highly complimentary about the teachers." Our teachers and students have been an integral part of campus development resulting in learning environments that are amongst the best in Asia.

Primary School children enjoy a 'neighbourhood', small-school environment within the larger community. They can feel confident and secure within their purpose-built "home", where their classrooms, collaborative learning spaces and playgrounds have been specially designed for their Year group. Secondary faculties also have purpose-built learning environments. The state-of-the-art Science Centre is well appointed, the Arts Centre boasts two theatres, sound-proofed music rooms, numerous Drama studios with mirrors and sprung floors and Art classes abundant in natural light. The Sports Complex has eight Tennis Courts and four full-size 11-a-side football pitches (in addition to the pitches on the school side).

Aside from the rigorous academic programme, the extra-curricular programme is second to none with more than 400 different activities being run each week. We have five academies: Swimming, Tennis, Gymnastics, Football and Dance and Drama. These academies offer specialised, focused training and competitive training. Our students benefit from this all-round development and supportive learning. Our graduates receive an incredible number of offers from top universities and programmes around the world. Our IGCSE and IB results are strong when compared with similar schools, and as a not academically selective school, this is the true test that shows we deliver on our mission to ensure that our students grow to their full potential as independent learners in a caring British international community.

British International School, Ho Chi Minh City

BRITISH INTERNATIONAL SCHOOL HO CHI MINH CITY
A NORD ANGLIA EDUCATION SCHOOL

(Founded 1997)

246 Nguyen Van Huong Street, Thao Dien, Thu Duc City, Ho Chi Minh City, Vietnam

Tel: +84 (0)28 3744 2335

Email: bis.admissions@bisvietnam.com

Website: www.bisvietnam.com

Principal: Mr. Anthony Rowlands

School type: Co-educational Day

Age range of pupils: 2–18 years

No. of pupils enrolled from August 2022: 2300

Fees per annum for 2022/23 academic year: US$12,300 – US$34,800

Average class size: 20

After its humble family beginning in 1997, The British International School, HCMC (BIS HCMC) has firmly established itself as the international school of choice in Ho Chi Minh City. It is a selective, independent and co-educational day school that provides a diverse international education measured by British standards. Twenty-four years on, they continue to be at the forefront of education, inspiring an international student body to achieve outstanding academic success in an innovative and dynamic environment.

BIS HCMC in one of the largest international schools in Vietnam and is part of the world's leading premium school's organization; Nord Anglia Education. It operates from three impressive campuses in the residential area of Thu Duc City (District 2), catering for students from 2 to 18 years of age. All campuses boast first class facilities and are staffed with internationally-trained teachers who are committed to nurturing and inspiring every child they care for.

The school provides a broad, balanced and differentiated curriculum to meet the wide-ranging needs of its students. At Primary level BIS HCMC operates within framework of the National Curriculum for England and the International Primary Curriculum whilst secondary students are prepared for both the International General Certificate of Secondary Education (IGCSE) and the International Baccalaureate Diploma Programme (IBDP). With these qualifications, BIS students have a well-established reputation of progressing into the top universities around the world.

BIS HCMC offers one-of-a-kind opportunities inside and outside the classroom, enhancing student learning through collaborations with the world's best organization. Their unique community service programme, extensive choice of co-curricular activities, and global expeditions provide students with a range of opportunities to develop life ready characteristics such as leadership, critical thinking, and empathy.

BIS HCMC has been inspected, approved and rated as 'Outstanding in all categories' by the British Government as detailed in their latest British Schools Overseas (BSO) Inspection Report.

BIS HCMC is fully accredited by the prestigious Council of International Schools (CIS) and the Western Association of Schools and Colleges (WASC). It is a registered centre for Cambridge International Examinations (CIE) and a designated IB World School. It is also recognised by the UK Government as an overseas school and is a full participating member of the Federation of British International Schools in Asia (FOBISIA).

British School of Beijing, Shunyi

THE BRITISH SCHOOL OF BEIJING, SHUNYI
A NORD ANGLIA EDUCATION SCHOOL

(Founded 2003)

South Side, No. 9 An Hua Street, Shunyi District, Beijing, 101318 China
Tel: +8610 8047 3558
Email: admissions@bsbshunyi.com
Website: www.bsbshunyi.com
Principal: Mrs. Jayne Needham
Appointed: July 2021
School type: Co-educational Day

Age range of pupils: 2–18 years
No. of pupils enrolled as at 01/09/2022: 1100
Fees as at 01/09/2022:
Day: RMB141,940–RMB318,790
Average class size: 15 (Early Years), 18 (Primary & Secondary)
Teacher/pupil ratio: 1:11

You want your child to excel. So do we. At The British School of Beijing (BSB) Shunyi, we promise to support your child to be their best and achieve more than they ever thought possible. We teach globally respected curricula to deliver excellent academic outcomes. Students follow an enhanced English National Curriculum and complete the IGCSE examinations at age 16. Senior students aged 17 & 18 study for the IB Diploma. Our German Primary Programme for our native German-speaking students study core subjects in German, integrating with non-core subjects. Our world-class teachers ensure your child experiences accelerated learning.

Established in 2003, our combined EYFS, Primary and Secondary campus is ideally situated within the very popular expatriate residential area of Shunyi and provides outstanding facilities to support your child's learning.

As part of a family of 70+ Nord Anglia schools in 31 countries with over 68,000 students, BSB Shunyi's global reach provides unique life and learning experiences for our students to develop into mature and successful global citizens. We benefit from collaborations with the best organisations including MIT, The Juilliard School and UNICEF.

Busan Foreign School

Busan Foreign School

Embracing Diversity, Striving for Excellence

The American International School of Busan, South Korea

45, Daecheon-ro 67 beon-gil, Haeundae-gu, Busan, 48084 Republic of Korea
Tel: +82 (0)51 747 7199
Email: bfs@busanforeignschool.org
Website: www.busanforeignschool.org
Upper School Principal:
Mr. Carl Brenneman

Early Childhood & Elementary School
Principal: Mrs. Lauren Harvey
School type: Co-educational Day
Age range of pupils: 3–18 years
No. of pupils enrolled as at 01/09/2022: 250
Fees as at 01/09/2022:
Please see our website
Teacher/pupil ratio: 1:8

Busan Foreign School is an international school with an American style educational philosophy and curriculum. Our mission is to inspire each learner by providing educational services that nurture their social, intellectual, emotional, and physical growth. Our students are prepared to enter top-tier universities worldwide as responsible citizens in a rapidly changing world. Our ongoing commitment to intercultural understanding and a strong partnership between students, parents/guardians, teachers and the community enable us to achieve this in a caring and supportive environment. Busan Foreign School has been fully WASC accredited (PreK-12th Grade) since 1998.

Busan Foreign School opened its doors in October of 1996. We are currently educating over 250 students from 25 different nations. The curriculum has developed into a highly rigorous American standards-based program that offers students a wide variety of courses and activities. Busan Foreign School provides additional student support services to best serve all student learning styles.

Over 95% of the teaching staff are either US or Canadian certified teachers, and all staff and administrators are trained in the most current research of best educational practices. The Common Core curriculum and other U.S. based national standards guide all classroom instruction. Staff members are required to professionally develop their skills. At the secondary level they apply their training in teaching rigorous Advanced Placement courses in the Maths, Sciences, English, Humanities, Languages, and the Arts. Busan Foreign School was accepted in the 2016 year to the AP Capstone Program, becoming the third school in Korea administering this Diploma. School-wide we subscribe to the Readers' and Writers' Workshop model to hone English literacy skills.

Busan Foreign School strives to offer a balanced program of academics, athletics, and arts. We believe that both academic and nonacademic life are equally important and help to shape our students into model citizens of the world. With a new building and grounds as of the fall of 2013 – including a STEAM (science, technology, engineering, arts, and mathematics) tower – Busan Foreign School is committed to continuing its strong tradition of providing a nurturing, yet rigorous academic experience for all learners. BFS is a member of ISS, Search Associates, KORCOS, EARCOS, NHS, and the National Association of Student Councils.

Chadwick International

45, Art center-daero 97 beon-gil,
Yeonsu-gu, Incheon,
22002 Republic of Korea
Tel: +82 32 250 5000
Email:
songdo-admissions@chadwickschool.org

Website: www.chadwickinternational.org
Head of School: Frederick T. "Ted" Hill
School type: Co-educational Day
Age range of pupils: 4–18 years
No. of pupils enrolled as at 01/09/2022: 1378
Teacher/pupil ratio: 1:8

Chadwick International is a PreK-G12 international school fully equipped with the state-of-the-art facility built in the Songdo International Business District, Incheon, Republic of Korea.

Chadwick International is the sister campus of Chadwick School, a K-12 school in the greater South Bay area of Los Angeles, which was founded by Margaret Lee Chadwick in 1935. The two campuses share the same mission that Chadwick Schools develop global citizens with keen minds, exemplary character, self-knowledge, and the ability to lead.

Chadwick International is an authorized four-programme International Baccalaureate (IB) World School, offering PYP, MYP, DP and CP. Chadwick International emphasizes experiential and inquiry-based learning both in and outside the classroom including Outdoor Education and Service Learning programs. The Outdoor Education allows students to develop conflict-resolution abilities and leadership skills through various outdoor experiences. Meanwhile, Service Learning program teaches students how to interact with both their local and international communities and problem solve on a deeper level. These fundamental programs assist students in transferring valuable lessons learned in the classroom and develop them as contributing members and leaders of tomorrow.

Physical Education plays an integral part of the Chadwick curriculum as it focuses on the promotion of good personal health and a holistic lifestyle for our students. Its activity-based program emphasizes the skill development that improves the fitness and well-being of the individual student as well as healthy and safe lifestyles.

Chadwick International has rich and diverse Visual and Performing Arts programs. In these classes, students develop their knowledge, skills, creativity and ability to respond to artistic ideas. Also, students are exposed to a variety of theatrical mediums to express themselves and heighten their awareness of themselves in relation to the people and culture around them.

Chadwick International helps to achieve its educational mission through recruiting and supporting highly experienced, dedicated, and diverse faculty members from around the world. With the support of the faculty, Chadwick International is capable of a low teacher to student ratio of 1:8.

Chadwick International's superior educational facilities include an aquatic center with scuba diving capabilities, two gymnasiums, two performing arts indoor theatres, a television studio that allows production up to eight channels, a working garden, purpose-built science laboratories and three design/maker spaces. These facilities permit the students to cultivate their intellectual, artistic and physical abilities based on Chadwick International's experience-based curriculum.

Chadwick International is accredited by Western Association of Schools and Colleges (WASC) and Council of International Schools (CIS).

Concordia International School Shanghai

Concordia
INTERNATIONAL SCHOOL SHANGHAI

(Founded 1998)

999 Ming Yue Road, JinQiao, Pudong,
Shanghai, 201206 China
Tel: +862 1 5899 0380
Email: admissions@concordiashanghai.org
Website: www.concordiashanghai.org
Head of School: Steve Winkelman
School type: Coeducational Day

Age range of pupils: 3–18 years
No. of pupils enrolled as at 01/09/2022: 1200
Fees as at 01/09/2022:
Preschool – Pre-kindergarten: RMB201,000
Kindergarten – Grade 4: RMB268,000
Grade 5-8: RMB273,000
Grade 9-12: RMB278,000
Average class size: 18 for ES/MS

Concordia International School Shanghai is a co-educational day school for students age 3 to 18, located on a 10-acre campus in the heart of Jinqiao – one of Shanghai's largest international communities. Known as the "green city", with its many open green spaces and family-oriented amenities, Shanghai's Jinqiao neighborhood is a destination for expatriate families from around the world. A diverse community made up of more than thirty nationalities is proud to call Concordia home. The school is welcoming and supportive, allowing expat students and families to successfully transition to their new environment.

Accredited by the Western Association of Schools and Colleges (WASC), Concordia is recognized for its dedication to academic excellence and for providing well-developed sports, arts, service and applied learning programs. Our caring, passionate faculty deliver a superior American-style curriculum and pioneer programs that guide students toward life success – no matter how they define it. The rigorous and holistic education offered at Concordia prepares our graduates for the world's top universities. Whether they are the youngest learners or soon-to-be graduates, our students are empowered to apply their learning to real-life challenges. Using an applied learning approach, purpose-built spaces and an age-appropriate integration of technology, our faculty provide authentic learning experiences that engage students in relevant and impactful ways.

Rather than simply focusing on the development of a student's intellect, we strive to develop the whole student within a unique global perspective. Encouraging fair play, good character and a heart for service is an important aspect of our holistic approach to education. We believe a child's education is a team effort among the parents, the student and the school. Together we prepare students for their future.

Dalian American International School

大连美国国际学校
DALIAN AMERICAN INTERNATIONAL SCHOOL
A NORD ANGLIA EDUCATION SCHOOL

(Founded 2006)
No. 2 Dianchi Road, Golden Pebble Beach National Resort, Dalian Development Area, Jinzhou District, Dalian, Liaoning, 116650 China
Tel: +86 411 8757 2000

Email: admissions@daischina.org
Website: www.daischina.org
Head of School: Dr. Richard Swann
School type: Co-educational Day
Age range of pupils: 4–18 years

Dalian American International School is situated in the Golden Pebble Beach National Resort, about 60 kilometers east of the center of Dalian, a city in Northeast China. It serves students of approximately 29 nationalities in Pre-K through 12th grade. The language of instruction is English for all classes except for proficiency leveled Mandarin classes.

Founded in 2006, DAIS was formed through the collaborative efforts of Intel Corporation, International School Services and Ms. Lisa Liang, CEO of the Honor Roll Company. Since its inception, our school has provided every student with an opportunity to achieve personal excellence and to contribute to the global community. From 2020, DAIS joined Nord Anglia Education and became part of its global family alongside with 70+ schools in 30 countries worldwide.

At Dalian American International School, students experience a broad range of academic subjects and co-curricular activities delivered by an experienced staff of international educators. DAIS is committed to providing a positive and nurturing environment that promotes learning and discovery. Optimum student/teacher ratios are maintained to give students the support they need to fully develop their skills and talents. Our graduates get offers from prestigious colleges and universities worldwide, and 70% of them are accepted into top 100 US universities.

Dalian American International School is housed in a purpose-built facility that provides over 8,000 sq. meters of learning space and enhances the delivery of high-quality programs in the arts and sciences.

We offer a wide range of athletics and extracurricular activities. The After School Activities program at DAIS is designed to allow students the freedom to discover and develop lifelong passions, maintain a healthy body and mind, extend and apply their classroom knowledge, and provide a link to give back to the community. Our students develop intellect, character, and health in a safe and welcoming environment.

Dalian Maple Leaf Foreign Nationals School

大连枫叶外籍人员子女学校
Maple Leaf Foreign Nationals School-Dalian

Downtown Campus: #78 Caiyunlu, Baiyunxincun, Xigang Distreet, Dalian, Liaoning, China
Tel: +86 411 82387757
Kaifaqu Campus: #4 Dongxing Street, Kaifaqu, Dalian, Liaoning, China
Tel: +86 411 39268103-0
Email: admin.mlfns@mapleleaf.net.cn

Website: www.mapleleafschools.com
Principal: Mr Jade Kersey
School type: Co-educational Day
Age range of pupils: 3–15 years
No. of pupils enrolled as at 01/09/2022: 200
Fees as at 01/09/2022:
Day: US$9,700–US$20,500

Introduction

Maple Leaf Foreign Nationals School-Dalian started in 2005, conducting the curriculum of BC, Canada. The school offers a full English teaching service and international education to Gr.P-9 foreign national children aged from 3-14. MLFNSD has also carried out three levels of courses authenticated by two countries so that students are able to function in and adapt to any of the educational model worldwide, to know China, to have the skills to be responsible citizens, and to make meaningful contributions to the global community.

International Curriculum

Canadian BC Curriculum has three key features that make up the foundation of learning: Content; Curricular Competencies; Big Ideas. Additionally, the Canadian BC Curriculum is student-focused and allows students to develop ownership over their own "Core Competencies". These areas include Communication, Thinking, and Personal & Social Responsibility.

Immersed Mandarin Class

The school offers students different levels of Mandarin and Chinese cultural classes according to their different Mandarin abilities using Maple Leaf Mandarin 1-9 developed by the Maple Leaf Educational System. Students who have great Mandarin abilities use the Mandarin Curriculum of China to meet their academic and language arts requirements. The school offers students Chinese Cultural classes which contain various topics like traditional skills, festivals, historical characters, traditional customs, national customs, food culture, etc. MLFNSD also offers students opportunities to take Mandarin tests of YCT and HSK.

International Qualifications

The School uses the Canadian BC curriculum and is accredited by the BC Ministry of Education. MLFNSD is a recognized BC Offshore School and undergoes rigorous annual inspection by the BC Ministry of Education. In addition, MLFNSD is also accredited by the world's largest accreditation organization: Cognia. The school is certified by the Duke Of Edinburgh Award scheme and hosts multiple international events.

Small class size

Respect individuals. Teach in accordance with student's aptitude. Multicultural environment. Care, Share and Dare.

Dulwich College (Singapore)

DULWICH COLLEGE
| SINGAPORE |

(Founded 2014)

71 Bukit Batok West Avenue 8, Singapore, 658966 Singapore
Tel: +65 6890 1003
Email: admissions.singapore@dulwich.org
Website: singapore.dulwich.org
Headmaster: Mr. Nick Magnus
Head of Senior School: Ms. Melanie Ellis

School type:
Co-educational Day & Boarding
Age range of pupils: 2–18 years
No. of pupils enrolled as at 01/09/2022: 2730
Fees as at 01/09/2022:
Day: S$17,780–S$49,310
Full Boarding: S$35,300
Average class size: 20
Teacher/pupil ratio: 1:4-22

Dulwich College (Singapore) opened its state-of-the-art campus in August 2014 and has since established a strong reputation. The College is an international school with a British independent school ethos which draws upon 400 years of excellence, innovation, tradition and values and is proud to welcome over 50 nationalities. It is a co-educational school, catering for students aged 2 to 18 in classes from Toddler to Year 13.

The College is academically selective and follows an enhanced version of the National Curriculum of England, adapted for the needs of our international student body. Students follow the IGSCE curriculum in Years 9, 10 and 11 followed by the IB Diploma Programme and IB Career-related Programme in Years 12 and 13. Continuing the tradition of excellence started by the founding school, Dulwich College in London, Dulwich College International graduates go on to study at leading universities in the UK, USA and around the world.

The College's holistic education is complemented by rewarding co-curricular programmes. Students are encouraged to participate in sporting competitions and every child from the age of seven is taught a musical instrument. Drama and opportunities for public speaking feature heavily from an early age with students using the 742-seat Alleyn Theatre daily for assemblies, performances and more.

The College offers a dual language programme in English and Mandarin for students in Toddler to Year 2 (aged two to seven) and daily Mandarin classes, streamed according to ability from the age of four. Additional modern foreign languages are offered in the Senior School. The close collaboration among the network of Colleges gives our students unique opportunities to participate in events and benefit from the group's relationships with leading educational and artistic organisations. The network enjoys an ongoing and strong partnership with Dulwich College in London.

Dulwich College Beijing

DULWICH COLLEGE
| BEIJING |
北京德威英国国际学校

(Founded 2005)
Address: 89 Capital Airport Road, Shunyi District, Beijing, 101300 China
Tel: +86 10 6454 9000
Email: admissions.beijing@dulwich.org
Website: beijing.dulwich.org
Head of College: Mr Anthony Coles
School type: Co-educational Day

Age range of pupils: 3–18 years
No. of pupils enrolled as at 01/09/2022: 1570
Fees as at 01/09/2022:
Day: RMB221,000–RMB332,000
Average class size:
20-22 (Dependent on year level)
Teacher/pupil ratio:
1:4-22 (Dependent on year level)

Dulwich College Beijing is an international school with British independent school ethos and values, which draws upon 400 years of excellence and tradition from Dulwich College, the founding College in London. Established in 2005, Dulwich College Beijing maintains strong ties with Dulwich College. We are proud to share a common heritage across the network of schools in Asia, and equally value the traditions, unique to our school, that we have created since we opened.

Our diverse student body is represented by more than 1,570 students from age 3 to age 18, with over thirty different nationalities. Holistic education is part of our identity and educational philosophy. We educate the whole child inside and outside the classroom. Starting from a young age, our students take ownership of their learning, achieving academic excellence, while at the same time engaging in sports, visual and performing arts, science and technology; engaging in community service, debating, leadership roles and anything else that they are passionate about.

Dulwich College Beijing has the honour and immense pleasure of receiving the British Schools 2021 Holistic Education Award and Science and Technology Award. These awards are a testament to our faculty's pioneering spirit in providing holistic education through innovative approaches and technologies. Dulwich College Beijing also received the 2022 International School Awards in the Pathways to Continued and University Education category. This award recognises our College's efforts to prepare students to Live Worldwise, and provide them with the opportunities and skills to make a positive impact on the world. Our graduating classes have consistently achieved IB results and university placements that place the College among the world's best.

Dulwich College Seoul

DULWICH COLLEGE
| SEOUL |

(Founded 2010)
6 Sinbanpo-ro 15-gil, Seocho-gu, Seoul, 06504 Republic of Korea
Tel: +82 2 3015 8500
Email: admissions@dulwich-seoul.kr
Website: seoul.dulwich.org

Head of School:
Gudmundur Hegner Jonsson
School type: Co-educational Day
Age range of pupils: 3–18 years
No. of pupils enrolled as at 01/09/2022: 700
Fees as at 01/09/2022:
Day: KRW: 34,500,000 – 37,000,000

Dulwich College is one of the UK's oldest independent schools, founded in South London as a boys' school in 1619. Dulwich College International (DCI) was established to bring the Dulwich education to students around the world and is now one of the fastest growing UK independent school networks.

Dulwich College Seoul offers an exemplary British-style international education for 700 expatriate students aged 3 to 18 from over 40 different countries. The curriculum follows the best practice of the Early Years Foundation Stage Framework and English National Curriculum. With our Cambridge International Examination (CIE) accreditation, we offer the IGCSE programme and our International Baccalaureate World School status enables students to proceed thereafter with the IB Diploma programme. Our College is accredited by the Council of International Schools (CIS) and the Western Association of Schools and Colleges (WASC).

Dulwich College Seoul is situated on a purpose-designed city campus just south of the Han River in the centrally located Seocho District. Our campus hosts outdoor play areas, an all-weather sports field, a futsal astro court area, an indoor gymnasium and a 25-metre indoor swimming pool. Facilities also include a 250-seat auditorium, a black box theatre, self-contained suites of music rooms, two fully stocked learning resource centres and libraries, science laboratories, an outdoor low ropes course, a food technology room, art and design workshops and a kiln room.

Dulwich College Shanghai Pudong

DULWICH COLLEGE
| SHANGHAI PUDONG |
上海浦东德威

(Founded 2003)

266 Lan An Road, Jinqiao, Pudong,
Shanghai, 201206 China
Tel: +8621 3896 1200
Email:
admissions.shanghaipudong@dulwich.org
Website: shanghai-pudong.dulwich.org

Head of School: Mr. Garry Russell
School type: Co-educational Day
Age range of pupils: 2–18 years
No. of pupils enrolled as at 01/09/2022: 1600
Fees as at 01/09/2022:
Day: RMB243,500–RMB357,100

Dulwich College Shanghai Pudong is an international school serving over 1,600 expatriate English-speaking students across three schools – DUCKS (Early Years and Year 1&2), Junior School (Years 3-6), and Senior School (Years 7-13).

Dulwich Pudong was founded in 2003 as the first independent British school in Shanghai. It is the founding school of Dulwich College International which now operates 14 schools in 5 countries. Dulwich Pudong graduates regularly score well above global averages on the IB exams and matriculate to the world's most selective universities.

Up to Year 9, our students follow the English National Curriculum. DUCKS Early Years students follow the UK Early Years Foundation Stage framework with a Dual Language approach. In Years 10 and 11 (Grades 9 and 10) students follow the International General Certificate of Secondary Education (I/GCSE) curriculum and in Years 12 and 13 (Grades 11 and 12) all of our students enter the International Baccalaureate (IB) Diploma Programme.

Dulwich College Shanghai Puxi

DULWICH COLLEGE
| SHANGHAI PUXI |
上海德威外籍人员子女学校（浦西）

(Founded 2016)

2000 Qianpujing Road, Maqiao, Minhang District, Shanghai, 201111 China
Tel: +86 21 3329 9310
Email: admissions.shanghaipuxi@dulwich.org
Website: shanghai-puxi.dulwich.org

Head of College: David Ingram
School type: Co-educational Day
Age range of pupils: 2–18 years
No. of pupils enrolled as at 01/09/2022: 500
Fees as at 01/09/2022:
Day: ¥126,200–¥357,100

Situated in the leafy and green west of Minhang district, Dulwich College Shanghai Puxi caters for families living in the west of Shanghai who are seeking the world-class holistic education that Dulwich College has become synonymous with.

Drawing on 400 years of rich Dulwich heritage, at Dulwich College Shanghai Puxi our curriculum is academically rigorous, yet the education of the whole child is seen as critical. Our wellbeing programme and range of co-curricular opportunities available to all children encourages academic, physical, social and emotional growth. Our robust Mandarin programme ensures that all students, regardless of background, can thrive in the local culture and context. Our curriculum is based on the British National Curriculum and is appropriately enhanced to meet the needs of our international student body, culminating in International Baccalaureate Diploma Programme in Years 12 and 13.

Committed to student leadership and service, our students uphold the College Values at all times: Aim High and Work Hard. Be Kind and Respectful. Make a Difference.

Dulwich College Suzhou

DULWICH COLLEGE
| SUZHOU |
苏州德威外籍人员子女学校

(Founded 2007)

360 Gang Tian Road, Suzhou Industrial Park, Suzhou, Jiangsu, 215021 China
Tel: +86 512 6295 9500
Email: admissions.suzhou@dulwich.org
Website: suzhou.dulwich.org
Head of School: David Massiah

School type:
Co-educational Day & Boarding
Age range of pupils: 2–18 years
No. of pupils enrolled as at 01/09/2022: 900
Fees as at 01/09/2022:
Tuition: RMB250,000
Boarding: RMB72,000

Dulwich College Suzhou was the third to join the Dulwich College International (DCI) family of schools, opening its doors in 2007. The College is made up of approximately 1000 students from age 2 to age 18, with over forty different nationalities represented in our diverse student body.

Our links to Dulwich College, founded in 1619, are strong and we collaborate closely with the other schools in the network to encourage an international outlook and create an extended community where academic ability is fostered, creativity is valued, and diversity is celebrated.

We are proud to share a common heritage with all the schools in the DCI network, and equally value the traditions, unique to our school, that we have created since we opened.

Dulwich International High School Suzhou

DULWICH INTERNATIONAL HIGH SCHOOL
| SUZHOU |
苏州工业园区德威联合书院

(Founded 2012)

Fangzhong Street, Near East Zhong Xin Avenue, Suzhou, Jiangsu, 215021 China
Tel: +86 512 6787 5003
Email: admissions.dhsz@dulwich.org
Website: suzhou-high-school.dulwich.org
Head of School: Sarah Tielman
School type:
Co-educational Day & Boarding

Age range of pupils: 14–19 years
No. of pupils enrolled as at 01/09/2022: 750
Fees as at 01/09/2022:
Day: RMB206,000
Weekly Boarding: RMB25,900
Full Boarding: RMB39,300

Dulwich International High School Suzhou (DHSZ), with a current enrolment of approximately 750 students, was founded in 2012 as a means for Chinese national students to have the opportunity to study a rigorous international curriculum based upon the Dulwich College London educational philosophy.

Dulwich International High School Zhuhai

DULWICH INTERNATIONAL HIGH SCHOOL
| ZHUHAI |
珠海德威国际课程高中项目

(Founded 2010)

No. 29 Hongjing Road, Guangdong-Macao in-depth cooperation zone in Hengqin, Zhuhai, Guangdong, 519060 China
Tel: +86 756 8693133
Email: admissions.dhzh@dulwich.org
Website: zhuhai-high-school.dulwich.org
Head of School: Matthew Conn

School type:
Co-educational Day & Boarding
Age range of pupils: 14–18 years
No. of pupils enrolled as at 01/09/2022: 300
Fees as at 01/09/2022:
Day: RMB180,000–RMB200,000
5-day Boarder: RMB210,000 – RMB230,000
7-day Boarder: RMB220,000 – RMB240,000

Dulwich International High School Zhuhai was co-founded by Education in Motion (EiM) and Zhuhai Huafa Education in 2010, offering authentic British international education to both Chinese and overseas students aged 14-18.

The three to four years' Cambridge Assessment International Education (CAIE) curriculum covers the IGCSE (International General Certificate of Secondary Education) and A-Level (AS and A2). With the mission of Graduate Worldwise, Dulwich Zhuhai provides a rigorous education that supports academic excellence through international curricula delivered in English, as well as focusing on the wellbeing of every student, developing individuals with outstanding capabilities and skills to become global citizens, Building Bridges to the World for each student.

European International School HCMC

EUROPEAN
International School
HO CHI MINH CITY

An inspired school

730 Le Van Mien Street, Thao Dien Ward, Thu Duc City, Ho Chi Minh City, 70000 Vietnam
Tel: +8428 7300 7257
Email: info@eishcmc.com
Website: www.eishcmc.com

Head of School: Mr. John Veitch
School type: Co-educational Day
Age range of pupils: 2–18 years
No. of pupils enrolled as at 01/09/2022: 600
Fees as at 01/09/2022:
VND 241,000,000 – 664,000,000

With possibly the most convenient location in Thao Dien, the European International School Ho Chi Minh City (EIS) is the only boutique international school, set in lush garden surroundings, offering the International Baccalaureate (IB) continuum of studies for children aged 2-18.

Our vibrant, unified campus is a place where students, teachers and parents of all grade levels and different backgrounds interact freely with each other within a home-from-home, tranquil village atmosphere. EIS offers a truly diverse 'melting pot' of 40+ nationalities and global cultures, where students are encouraged to find their unique voice, to pursue languages, and to contribute to all aspects of school life.

EIS teachers, with over 13 years' average experience, are well-practiced in individualized learning methods. With a very low student-to-teacher ratio, particularly in the middle-high school sections of the school, students benefit directly from more frequent access to teachers.

Graduating IB Diploma students consistently achieve well-above the world averages, and have achieved acceptances into prestigious universities worldwide, often with significant merit-based scholarships.

EIS provides an outstanding world-class education for students, evidenced by our full accreditation status with the Council of International Schools (CIS).

Being a medium-sized school, we are large enough to offer a wide range of educational opportunities, while also being intimate enough to provide the unique personal attention and care that each child deserves.

Green School Bali

(Founded 2008)
Jalan Raya Sibang Kaja, Abiansemal, Badung, Bali, 80352 Indonesia
Email: mads.hedegaard@greenschool.org
Website: www.greenschool.org/bali

Head of School: Sal Gordon
School type: Co-educational Day
Age range of pupils: 3–18 years
No. of pupils enrolled as at 01/09/2022: 375
Fees as at 01/09/2022:
Day: US$7,800–US$19,992

Green School Bali is a Pre-K to Grade 12 international school with 350 students from more than thirty different countries around the world, including 36 local scholarship students from Bali. Our mission is to nurture a global community of learners making our world sustainable. Green School's wall-less bamboo campus connects students to their natural environment, fostering empathy and a biocentric perspective. The curriculum focuses on experiential learning in nature, and empowers students to find creative, values-driven solutions to the problems they encounter in the world.

An education at Green School is co-created between students and their teachers. We believe in developing a new kind of IQ – Intelligent Questioning – and encouraging students to actively pursue the questions they have about the things that interest them the most. From there, teachers integrate foundational proficiencies in math, science and literacy into the projects students pursue. At every level, students are encouraged to find solutions to real-world problems and are empowered to affect change. Student empowerment is so essential because when students are in the driving seat, they are so much more invested. In this way, we foster a life-long love of learning that stays with our students long after they leave Green School.

We call our learning R.E.A.L – **R**elationship-driven, **E**ntrepreneurial, and evolving, **A**uthentic to real-world circumstances and grounded in the **L**ocal community and cultural context. In addition to adhering to the REAL approach, each class at Green School also incorporates our Three Frames of Learning. The **Experiential Frame** is simply 'learning by doing' rather than just through books and instructions. The **Proficiency Frame** refers to the strong Literacy, Mathematics and Science components we integrate into each lesson. And the **Thematics Frame** represents the themes around which lessons are planned each term. These themes are grounded in our iRespect values of integrity, responsibility, empathy, sustainability, peace, equality, community and trust.

Hoi An International School

24 Phan Ba Phien, Hoi An, Vietnam

Tel: +84 (0)235 651 8518
Email: admissions@hais.edu.vn
Website: www.hais.edu.vn
CEO & Founder: Ms. Tran Hanh An
Principal: Mr. Brett Macdoucll
International Vice Principal: Mr. Balint Kocsis
Bilingual Vice Principal: Ms. Ve Thi Hanh
School type: Co-educational Day
Age range of pupils: 2–18 years

Hoi An International School meets and nurtures our students' individual needs in a supportive, community-minded and responsible environment. Through the provision of well-rounded, high-quality education, HAIS is committed to cultivating creative opportunities and a range of age-appropriate activities so that our students develop as resilient, independent and lifelong learners. At HAIS, we create a great future for our students.

Hoi An International School's campus is an environment that is functional, environmentally friendly and sustainable. Our campus has been specially designed to incorporate spaces where students can gain hands-on experience in shaping their natural environment while focusing on their academics, creativity and living a healthy lifestyle. Our grounds are lined with lush gardens and feature large, open spaces, providing our students with a safe, spacious and healthy environment in which to learn. In addition to our separate, fully-equipped facilities for Early Years, Primary, and Secondary, our campus features a multilingual library, indoor and outdoor sporting facilities, a fine arts studio, a music studio, a performing arts studio, a computer lab, a science laboratory, and an aquatics facility. Furthermore, we have a beautiful garden on campus, providing opportunities for our students to interact with nature and take lessons outside of the classroom. Our campus is the perfect space to cater to every student's interests and passions.

Hoi An International School has two pathways of study: the International Programme and the Bilingual Programme. The International Programme is a learning pathway through Early Years, Primary, and Secondary education. In our Early Years Programme, we provide every child with the best possible start in life. HAIS uses the Early Years Foundation Stage (EYFS) curriculum, engaging children through activities that concentrate on social and emotional development, literacy, numeracy, creative skills, gross motor development and discovering the world. The Primary Programme then begins a more formalised approach to learning. The curriculum is broad and diverse, and whilst it is subject-based, there are many opportunities for a cross-curricular approach to learning. In addition to core subjects, specialist teachers teach Drama, Art, Music and Physical Education. In both the Primary and Secondary Programmes, HAIS uses the internationally recognised Cambridge Assessment International Education (CAIE) curriculum. The Secondary Programme provides a natural progression for children to move from primary education to lower secondary and prepare for higher secondary education programmes, leading to formal, international qualifications.

Starting August 2022, HAIS will offer an A-Levels Programme to enable our students to continue their studies in various subjects, while maintaining the strong student-teacher relationships we have built on campus through our Pastoral Programme.

The Bilingual Programme is a learning pathway moving from Early Years to Primary education. This pathway develops students' skills in mathematics, language and more while encouraging inquiry and enthusiasm for learning. Although the emphasis is given to global perspectives, our Bilingual Programme embraces Vietnamese values and culture. We offer a play and structured inquiry-based approach to teaching and learning. Our qualified and engaging Vietnamese teachers share the teaching of the Bilingual curriculum with our qualified native-English speaking teachers. While using traditional learning techniques alongside structured inquiry, we ensure that students learn and practice in both languages concurrently, without sacrificing their mother tongue.

At HAIS, all curriculum content is delivered in a way that inspires, motivates and challenges. With our teachers guiding, assisting and encouraging, all our students can strive for greatness and achieve their personal best. In short, they can 'Find their passion and realize their dream'.

Please follow us on Facebook for a 'sneak peek' into the daily life of our HAIS students. See our website for more information and to contact our Admissions Team, who will welcome any further inquiry.

Hong Kong Academy

HONG KONG ACADEMY

(Founded 2000)

33 Wai Man Road, Sai Kung, Hong Kong, SAR, Hong Kong, China

Tel: +852 2655 1111
Email: admissions@hkacademy.edu.hk
Website: www.hkacademy.edu.hk
Head of School: Stephen Dare
Primary School Principal: Virginia Hunt
Secondary School Principal: Teresa Tung
School type: Co-educational Day
Age range of pupils: 3–18 years
No. of pupils enrolled as at 01/09/2022: 500

Fees as at 01/09/2022:
PreK1-PreK2: HK$149,800
K-G5: HK$201,300
G6-G8: HK$221,600
G9-G10: HK$230,900
G11-G12: HK$240,300
Average class size: 18-24
Teacher/pupil ratio: 1:6

Founded in 2000, Hong Kong Academy (HKA) is a non-profit international school that provides a highly personalised and holistic education for students from 3-18 years old. HKA's educational programmes are designed to equip students with the skills and knowledge they need to thrive as thoughtful and successful individuals who meaningfully contribute to their local and global communities.

Three Diploma credentials

From our Early Childhood programme to the final years of Secondary School, teachers provide well rounded, student-centred experiences that encourage all learners to fulfill their greatest potential. All HKA graduates can earn up to three Diploma credentials; the HKA Diploma, Global Citizen Diploma (GCD) certificate, and IB Diploma or IB course certificates. HKA's IB Diploma pass rate has been 100% for the last two years and we are the only school in Hong Kong to offer the GCD.

A unique international education

Small class sizes and a low student to teacher ratio allow for individualised attention; within our classrooms, we have the ability to meet the needs of accelerated learners as well as students requiring learner support. We offer a wealth of curricular and co-curricular programmes on our award-winning campus and are home to the International Schools Theatre Association of Performing Arts, Hong Kong (ISTA).

Award-winning campus

In recognition of our mission as an innovative and future-focussed school, our campus is rated Gold BEAM by the Green Building Council of Hong Kong. Designed to operate as a sustainable learning lab, the campus employs durable materials and data collection systems which enable students to connect their learning to their surroundings. We encourage students to see themselves as custodians of our world and they work alongside faculty and staff on sustainability projects, giving them a voice in operational decisions which benefit our social and natural world.

Highly engaged community

A warm and engaging community, HKA parents are integral to the school as volunteers. Whether serving on the board of trustees, reading in the classroom, sharing their experience as industry experts and mentors, leading community events, supporting the theatre or coaching HKA athletes, parents are partners who enrich our school in many ways.

Global alumni network

HKA graduates are able to effectively apply research, critical thinking and communication skills precisely, flexibly and intentionally across subject areas. They pursue post-secondary degrees in a diverse range of disciplines, with the majority of our graduates entering their first-choice universities and successfully securing employment in a wide variety of professions all over the world. We are proud to be an inclusive, multicultural community and welcome new families all year round.

Contact us today to learn how your child could benefit from an HKA education.

Ibn Khuldoon National School

(Founded 1983)
Building 161, Road 4111, Area 841, P.O. Box 20511, Isa Town, Bahrain
Tel: +973 17780661
Email: k.algosaibi@ikns.edu.bh
Website: www.ikns.edu.bh

President: Dr Kamal Abdel-Nour D.Ed
Appointed: August 2008
School type: Co-educational Day
Age range of pupils: 4–18 years
No. of pupils enrolled as at 01/09/2022: 1700
Average class size: 18-22

Ibn Khuldoon National School (IKNS) is a non-profit, self-supporting, coeducational institution that is dedicated to providing high quality education for local and expatriate students. The school is licensed by the Ministry of Education to offer a bilingual programme of study for students from Kindergarten to Grade 12. A diverse faculty, whether teaching in Arabic or English, provides a rich and supportive learning environment for students. The faculty is supported by a dedicated team of administrative, IT and support staff.

IKNS has been affiliated with the International Baccalaureate (IB) since 1990, as an IB Diploma Programme provider. The first group of students sat for the IB Diploma examinations in 1992. Since then, the results of the students have been a great source of pride to IKNS.

In addition to the IB Diploma, IKNS offers an American high school diploma. Both are tertiary education preparatory programmes, and are considered to be equivalent to the Bahraini "Tawjihi".

The IB Diploma Programme and the American High School Diploma programme are offered in Grades 11 and 12. In Grades 6 to 10, IKNS offers the IB Middle Years Programme (MYP) and in KG1 to Grade 5, the IB Primary Years Programme (PYP).

The school received its full accreditation from the Middle States Association of Colleges and Schools (MSA) in 1994, and it continues to be in good standing with the association. The Accredited status of the school affirms that it provides the level of quality in its educational programmes, services, activities and resources expected by its stakeholders.

IKNS continues to be an "Outstanding" school as rated by "Bahrain Education and Quality Authority".

International School Bangkok

(Founded 1951)

39/7 Soi Nichada Thani, Samakee Road, Pakkret, Nonthaburi, 11120 Thailand
Tel: +66 2 963 5800
Email: admissions@isb.ac.th
Website: www.isb.ac.th
Head of School: Dr. Andrew Davies

School type: Co-educational Day
Age range of pupils: 3–18 years
No. of pupils enrolled as at 01/09/2022: 1700
Fees as at 01/09/2022: US$16,751 – US$30,441
Average class size: 20

International School Bangkok (ISB), widely recognized as one of the world's leading international schools, was the first to be established in Thailand. Opened on the grounds of the U.S. Embassy in 1951, ISB has proudly provided a high-quality international education to students from over a hundred nationalities and is the pioneer International Baccalaureate school in Thailand.

ISB is a learning-focused, US-accredited, IB authorized, independent Pre-K to Grade 12 school offering a challenging international curriculum to a multicultural and multilingual student body of over 1,700 students from 60 different nationalities. Learning at ISB is informed by leading educational research and global best practice, incorporated into North American and International Baccalaureate Diploma frameworks.

ISB has long valued its globally-minded, inclusive and vibrant community and its strong culture of care. ISB is committed to encouraging students to follow their passions in academics, the arts, athletics, and many other areas both in and out of school. ISB maintains a constant focus on quality with respect to learning, faculty, leadership, professional development, and facilities.

ISB graduates attend colleges and universities around the world. ISB takes great pride in the accomplishments of thousands of alumni who are enriching our local and global communities.

Located in the safe and beautiful community of Nichada Thani, ISB's 15-hectare campus houses world-leading facilities purpose built to align with the multitude of subjects and activities on offer for students. These include state-of-the-art performance venues and studios, international standard sports facilities, fully-equipped science and design labs, innovative libraries and learning spaces, and cutting-edge technology integrated across the school.

Through outstanding teaching and learning, ISB inspires students to achieve their academic and personal potential; be passionate, reflective learners; become caring, global citizens, and lead active, healthy, balanced lives. ISB's vision is *to enrich communities through the intellectual, humanitarian and creative thoughts and actions of our learners.*

International School Brunei

(Founded 1964)
Jalan Utama Salambigar, Kampong Sungai Hanching, Berakas 'B' BC2115, Brunei Darussalam
Tel: +673 233 0608
Email: admissionmgr@ac.isb.edu.bn
Website: www.isb.edu.bn
Headteacher: Mr Tony Macfadyen
School type:
Co-educational Day & Boarding
Age range of pupils: 2–18 years
No. of pupils enrolled as at 01/09/2022: 1200
Fees as at 01/09/2022:
Early Years: $6,840 – $11,700
Primary – Secondary: $11,700 – $15,450
IB: $18,150
Boarding fees per annum:
$16,500 (5 days)– $21,500 (7 days)
Average class size: 12
Teacher/pupil ratio: 1:6

International School Brunei (ISB) is one of the world's leading international schools with a very strong academic track record. Our results are consistently above world averages; the 2020 cohort of ISB Year 11 students gained 88 percent A*-C grades while Year 13 graduates celebrated exemplary IBDP results with a 96 percent pass rate. 2021 saw even better results as the school continues its upwards trajectory.

Accredited by the Council of International Schools, ISB is also one of the oldest and most distinguished schools in Southeast Asia, with 57 years of heritage in Brunei Darussalam. ISB now has three campuses: Bandar, Seria (Primary only), and our Centre for Inclusive Learning (CIL). Built on a strong reputation as a highly regarded, inclusive, Eco-school, where 'Everyone Excels', ISB provides a first-class international education for 2 to 18-year-olds across its Early Years Provision (Pre-Kindy to Reception), Primary School (Year 1 to Year 6) and Secondary School (Year 7 to Year 13).

The school offers an adapted England and Wales curriculum in the Primary and Lower Secondary sections followed by IGCSE and the International Baccalaureate Diploma Programme (IBDP) in Secondary. Our Primary campuses offer our younger students a warm, nurturing, friendly space, with specialist teachers and great resources that combine for exciting and engaging learning experiences. As a fully inclusive school, ISB provides education to all students regardless of their abilities. ISB is proud to have a learning support provision led by an experienced and highly qualified team. The school is committed to continued professional development and is forward-thinking in its approach. ISB values the contribution students make in performing arts, music, and sporting events where opportunities are almost limitless for all.

In ISB boarding facilities, The Residence, boarders are not only nurtured to achieve academically and be model global citizens, but also to be able to thrive in the increasingly competitive 21st Century. The Residence provides an environment where students are treated as individuals and receive a personalised experience with the opportunity to develop and grow in body, mind, and spirit. This ethos is reflected in the school as a whole.

International School Ho Chi Minh City (ISHCMC)

Primary campus: 28 Vo Truong Toan St., An Phu ward, Thu Duc City, Ho Chi Minh City, Vietnam
Secondary campus: 01 Xuan Thuy St., Thao Dien ward, Thu Duc City, Ho Chi Minh City, Vietnam
Tel: +84 28 3898 9100
Email: admissions@ishcmc.edu.vn
Website: www.ishcmc.com
Head of School: Ms. Kim Green
School type: Co-educational Day
Age range of pupils: 2–18 years

As the most established International School in Ho Chi Minh City (ISHCMC) represents a culturally diverse group of families and teachers from 60 countries. The community is united in the common purpose to build a Culture of Care (Curiosity, Achievement, Resilience, Empathy) that is Energized, Engaged and Empowered. As a leader in the field of international education with a renowned reputation, ISHCMC is proud to deliver three International Baccalaureate Programmes in its own unique manner. Students construct an understanding and knowledge of their world through carefully developed learning experiences and inquiries that develop a deep understanding of important concepts in global contexts.

Progressive in its view of education, ISHCMC is preparing students for their futures. Its educational approach is set within modern learning environments designed to develop both learning and social skills that have been identified as being important for the future. ISHCMC has built two outstanding campuses that encourage collaborative learning opportunities in state-of-the-art facilities that encourage the development of the whole child whilst encouraging students to explore their passions and find their identity.

ISHCMC is renowned for its approach to the social and emotional wellbeing of its students. Its welcoming and supportive community has developed and embedded a deep-rooted Culture of Care within the school. ISHCMC provides a very safe learning environment in which students flourish whilst being supported by experienced, qualified, caring teachers, and a team of dedicated counsellors and student support services. At ISHCMC we develop a love of learning in students that prepares them for the complex and unpredictable world beyond school.

Academic Accreditation

ISHCMC is fully accredited by the Council of International School (CIS), one of the most prestigious international accreditation organizations. In addition, ISHCMC was the first International School in Ho Chi Minh City and the first IB World School in HCMC accredited to teach three IB programs: Primary Years Programme, Middle Years Programme and Diploma Programme.

IB World School for ages 2 to 18

ISHCMC is authorized by the International Baccalaureate Organization (IBO) to teach all 3 of their programs. 2-year-old children join ISHCMC's Early Explorers, enjoying an inquiry-based curriculum to develop their language, cognitive, creative, social and motor skills, providing a seamless transition to the IB Primary Years Program, progressing to the rigorous IB Diploma Program from Grade 11 to 12. ISHCMC is proud to have 20 years' history of graduating IB Diploma candidates to top universities worldwide, including Yale, Harvard, and Stanford.

Arts, Sports & Community Service

ISHCMC offers over 40 after school activities every term for students to pursue their creative and sporting passions. As a member of several international sporting associations such as the South East Asia Student Activities Conference (SEASAC). These opportunities allow students to

enjoy athletic tournaments, cultural exchanges and leadership conferences with international schools in the region. 120 students across Grades 1-12 join the prestigious ISHCMC Stingrays Swim Team, competing internationally throughout the Asia region.

One community, two campuses

ISHCMC communities welcome the introduction of a state-of-the-art ISHCMC Secondary Campus located less than 5 km away from the ISHCMC Primary Campus. Both ISHCMC campuses are located in District 2. This campus offers great opportunities for student learning through technologically advanced classrooms, collaborative learning spaces and senior student study areas. Unique facilities such as Vietnam's first Innovation Center aim to prepare our students for the realities of the commercial world in the 21st century. Full-scale musical productions are hosted in our brand new 350-seat theater with professional lighting and sound equipment, extending opportunities into the technical aspects of theatre productions. In line with our goal of producing well-balanced and healthy students, our new facility provides ISHCMC Secondary-aged students with a wide range of facilities to support their wellbeing. Sports facilities include multi-purpose courts, a rooftop sports field and 25m – eight-lane competitive swimming pool with seating.

The new facility allows students of both primary and secondary age to flourish on campuses that suit their respective educational needs. The existing campus continues to undergo extensive renovations to meet the needs of younger learners by offering new learning suites including a Fab Lab, Food Tech, film studio and studio concept. Both campuses offer clean air through advanced purification systems. Although two campuses, ISHCMC remains one community.

Jerudong International School

(Founded 1997)
Jalan Universiti, Kampong Tungku, Bandar Seri Begawan, BE2119 Brunei Darussalam
Tel: +673 241 1000 (Ext: 1206/7100/1214)
Email: admissions@jis.edu.bn

Website:
www.jerudonginternationalschool.com
Principal: Nicholas Sheehan BSc. Geography, PGCE
Appointed: August 2019
School type:
Co-educational Day & Boarding
Age range of pupils:
2–18 years (Boarding from 8 years)
No. of pupils enrolled as at 01/06/2022: 1652

Sixth Form: 366
No. of boarders: 221
Fees as at 01/08/2022:
Day: B$18,108–B$26,952
Weekly Boarding: B$17,688–B$23,500
Full Boarding: B$23,688–B$29,500
Average class size: Years 7-9: 20; Years 10-13: 20 or less
Teacher/pupil ratio: 1:20 (maximum), IBDP classes are typically 1:15 or less

Founded in 1997, Jerudong International School (JIS) is located in Southeast Asia, in the small country of Brunei Darussalam, on the north coast of the island of Borneo.

Brunei has excelled in its management of COVID. It has a superb vaccination record with 72% of the population (age 12 Years +) having 3 doses and 83% of children ages 5-11 having 2 doses. A direct flight from major regional hubs, Brunei is easy to access, making it an ideal school of choice for parents seeking an outstanding school in a safe, secure environment. For full Boarders, the school is able to sponsor visas and arrange entry into Brunei.

The School aims are: **Communication, Engagement, Integration, Leadership, Resilience and Thinking**. Students are encouraged to Challenge Yourself, Respect Others and Inspire Change.

Academic Excellence

JIS is a fully accredited **'British School Overseas'**, a large, thriving school with 1660 students from 55 countries from 2 – 18 years in age. It is a leading British international school preparing students for I/GCSEs, A levels and the IB Diploma. We pride ourselves on providing an education that is not only academically challenging but also seeks to develop the whole student.

JIS examination results have been truly excellent with students entering the best Universities in the world every year. Current graduate destinations include: UK – Cambridge, University College London, Imperial College, London School of Economics. USA – Columbia University. Canada – University of British Columbia, The University of Toronto. Australia – Australian National University and Melbourne University. National University of Singapore.

JIS is an international member of the prestigious UK based HMC organisation, accredited by The Good Schools Guide as well as COBIS, FOBISIA and the BSA. JIS is proud to be an IB World School.

JIS has almost 200 highly qualified teachers primarily from the UK but also a small number from Australia, New Zealand. Our language teachers are native language speakers from China, France and Brunei.

The School is divided into two main sections: Junior School, for children ages 3 – 11 years and Senior School. Within Senior School, the Middle Years consists of students in Years 7 – 9 (ages 11 – 14 years) whilst students in the Upper Years, Years

10-13, follow the IGCSE, IB Diploma and A Level programmes.

Campus

The facilities on the120 acre single campus are exceptional. The purpose-built, fully WiFi and ICT networked school is located near the coast – a short drive from the capital city. Students can use the Arts Centre (725 seat auditorium, dance studio, black box theatre and rehearsal rooms), 27 science laboratories, extensive music faculty, art, design and technology and textile studios, libraries and traditional classrooms as well as the 2 swimming pools (50m and 25m), 3 large air-conditioned Sports Halls, outdoor netball/basketball and tennis courts and 3 soccer/rugby pitches. A well- equipped medical centre with 3 Nurses is on site to take care of students. An award winning Outdoor Discovery Centre – an eco-forestry initiative on tropical heathland on the campus is regularly used for activities and also as an Outdoor Classroom learning space. In January 2021, a refurbished and enlarged library and study area was opened. A Racquet Sports Centre for Tennis and Squash was also opened in 2021.

Boarding facilities

The recently inspected and accredited 'outstanding' Boarding facilities for students age 8 years + are purpose designed and built for the community of boarders. 221 girls and boys presently enjoy separate Boarding Houses cared for by experienced staff. A separate Junior Boarding House is for the Junior Boarders. The Boarding Housemaster or Housemistresses are all teachers in the School. Boarders can also use the school facilities. A programme of weekend activities is arranged for the boarders to fully embrace the wonderful environment of Brunei. A special partnership exists between the boarding staff and a student's family with mutual trust at the heart of the relationship between home and school.

Pastoral Care

All students and teachers in the School are members of a House (a community of about 70 students) which plays a vital role in establishing and maintaining a strong school spirit and enabling leadership opportunities. The 16 Houses in Senior School, named after birds in Borneo, provide leadership, mentoring

and teamwork opportunities. Weekly House sports competitions and other House Events including House Debates, House Music, 'JIS has Talent' and Spelling Bees are arranged as part of a busy programme.

Co-curricular programme

A strong co-curricular programme exists with almost 300 activities on offer including a wide range of sports and arts activities. JIS has a well-established International Award (DoE) programme – Bronze, Silver and Gold level. The Model United Nations club and chess club are particularly popular too. Eco JIS, a student led group has developed a number of school wide initiatives and leads Earth Day each year. The School takes full advantage of the wonderful unique tropical environment of Brunei.

Jakarta Intercultural School

(Founded 1951)
Jalan Terogong Raya No. 33, Cilandak, Jakarta Selatan, DKI, 12430 Indonesia
Tel: +62 21 50989555
Email: admissions@jisedu.or.id

Website: www.jisedu.or.id
Interim Head: Maya Nelson
School type: Co-educational Day
Age range of pupils: 3–18 years

After 70 years of pioneering international education in Indonesia and Southeast Asia, Jakarta Intercultural School (JIS) is proud to continue our mission to be "Best for the World" through joyful, rigorous learning.

Our diverse community of nearly 2,000 students and more than 200 teachers represents over 60 nationalities and a vibrant array of cultural backgrounds, all growing, teaching, and learning together across three expansive, garden-like campuses. Each is equipped with leading-edge facilities that support inquiry, critical thinking, problem-solving, and collaborative study. With access to a STEAM building, robotics lab, three extensive libraries/research centers, two world-class theaters, indoor and outdoor sports facilities, and much more, our students are encouraged to be creative and inquisitive as they explore both their academic and co-curricular interests.

From Early Years to High School, they are empowered with choice, responsibility, and balance to take charge of their own learning journey through programs derived from up-to-date research and best educational practices from around the world. Meanwhile, through the intentional and meaningful integration of service learning and environmental stewardship, JIS students develop a deeper understanding of what it means to be agents of change.

Our steady commitment to upholding the values of diversity, equity, and inclusion (DEI) is further strengthened this year with the opening of the JIS Learning Center, a specialized education program tailored to meet the needs of children with moderate to severe developmental delays. This life-centered program is the latest reflection of our school's mission to be "Best for the World", which goes beyond academics to embrace the values of diversity and inclusion, empower community members regardless of their background, and teach respect for others.

Léman International School Chengdu

No.1080 Da'an Road, Zheng Xing County, Tianfu New Area, Chengdu, Sichuan, 610218 China
Tel: +86 28 6703 8650
Email: admissions@lis-chengdu.com
Website: www.lis-chengdu.com

Principal: Tom Ferguson
School type: Co-educational Day
Age range of pupils: 2–18 years
No. of pupils enrolled as at 01/09/2022: 450
Fees as at 01/09/2022:
Day: RMB142,500–RMB249,000

Léman International School Chengdu (LIS) welcomes students from Pre-nursery to Year 13 on its 50 acre campus.

The Primary School uses the English National Curriculum for Maths, English, Computing and PSHE. This is integrated with the International Primary Curriculum (IPC), currently used in over 1000 schools in 65 countries, to give a truly international educational experience throughout the Primary years. The Secondary School, from Years 7 to 11, is based upon the International Baccalaureate Middle Years Programme, with Year 12 and 13 following the International Baccalaureate Diploma Programmme. LIS offers foreign languages including Mandarin and French. Korean is also offered to its native speakers.

LIS has world class facilities on an extensive campus, including fully equipped modern classrooms, science laboratories, an art studio, music studios, I.T. rooms, maker spaces, gymnasium, 25 meter indoor swimming pool and further outdoor sports facilities, including two full size football pitches; this allows us to offer an extensive extra-curricular activity program as well as comprehensive sports and arts programs.

We are proud that 3 out of 4 of our graduates have chosen, and been admitted to, the world's top universities (according to the QS World University Rankings 2020). Our graduates attend the very best universities in the world, including Oxford, Tsinghua, UCL, LSE, UBC and NYU. We have graduates attending top Art & Design Institutes, including University of Arts London, the School of Visual Arts, and the Fashion Institute of Technology.

LIS is accredited by the Council of International Schools (CIS) and the New England Association of Schools and Colleges (NEASC).

LIS is part of the global Nord Anglia Education family and this gives us a unique link to collaborate with schools and pursue opportunities worldwide. This includes the world leader of performing arts education, The Juilliard School, and the world's top university, MIT, as well as our collaboration with UNICEF, whereby students have their social consciousness raised so they care more deeply about the world and the people in it. Our unique online and classroom collaboration platform, Global Campus, connects more than 68,100 Nord Anglia students, and the Nord Anglia University platform enables the very best professional development for our staff.

Malvern College Hong Kong

MALVERN
COLLEGE HONG KONG
香港墨爾文國際學校

3 Fo Chun Road, Pak Shek Kok,
Hong Kong, China

Tel: +852 3898 4688
Email: admissions@malverncollege.org.hk
Website: www.malverncollege.org.hk
Headmaster: Dr Robin A. Lister
Head of Senior: Wayne Maher
Head of Prep: Maria Gebrial
School type: Co-educational Day
Age range of pupils: 5–18 years

No. of pupils enrolled as at 01/09/2022: 1000
Fees as at 01/09/2022:
Primary: HK$178,010
Secondary: HK$202,480
Annual Capital Levy: HK$42,000 (pupils covered by nomination rights are exempted from annual capital levy payments)

World-class education through the Five Centres of Excellence

Malvern College Hong Kong (MCHK) is an IB World School offering the PYP, MYP and DP curriculum. Following its successful launch in August 2018, primary and secondary classes now operate from Prep 1 (Y1) to Upper Sixth (Y13), with the first Sixth Form cohort graduating in May 2023. The school is looking forward to celebrating its 5th birthday at the same time.

Malvern's state-of-the-art campus facilities are located in Pak Shek Kok, New Territories, just adjacent to the Hong Kong Science Park. Small class sizes give teachers the chance to engage with pupils personally and differentiate within lessons according to individual aptitude, skill set and need. Dedicated tutor-time and a genuine concern for the individual, built around an active house system, are additional key features. The school is strongly committed to holistic education and offers an extensive co-curricular activities programme for pupils to build on their existing talents and to explore new activities.

MCHK is a member of the growing network of Malvern schools across the globe including the UK, Egypt, Qingdao, Chengdu, Hong Kong and Switzerland. Further school openings are planned for Barbados and Tokyo in 2023. Although each Malvern school has its own unique identity, they all share the same DNA and ethos built around the "Five Centres of Excellence", namely: British-style Pastoral Care, Enhanced Learning, Entrepreneurial Education, Outdoor and Environmental Education and a Global Network.

Malvern seeks to develop independent, forward-thinking individuals who demonstrate strength of character and responsibility. By providing a caring, supportive and ambitious learning environment, the school enables its pupils to maximise their academic potential, develop their talents and to flourish as individuals. The aim is for Malvern pupils to become truly open-minded, global citizens capable of building consensus, respect and an ability to collaborate with those from backgrounds different to their own.

NIST International School

NIST INTERNATIONAL SCHOOL

(Founded 1992)

36 Sukhumvit Soi 15, Wattana,
Bangkok, 10110 Thailand
Tel: +66 2 017 5888
Email: admissions@nist.ac.th
Website: www.nist.ac.th
Head of School: Dr James Dalziel
School type: Co-educational Day

Age range of pupils: 3–18 years
No. of pupils enrolled as at 27/05/2022: 1720
Fees as at 27/05/2022:
THB541,700 – THB975,800
Average class size: 23
Teacher/pupil ratio: 1:12

The first and only full, not-for-profit IB World School in Bangkok, NIST International School was established in 1992 with the guidance and support of the United Nations. The school now welcomes over 1,600 students representing more than 60 nationalities, and provides all three International Baccalaureate (IB) programmes: the Primary Years Programme, Middle Years Programme and Diploma Programme. NIST is governed by the parent-elected NIST International School Foundation and is accredited through the Council of International Schools and New England Association of Schools and Colleges.

Through the IB and its own unique programmes, NIST aims to inspire, empower and enrich lives. The academic structure emphasizes student-driven learning, exploration, risk taking and trans-disciplinary learning. Students engage in social entrepreneurship projects and develop their own service initiatives using professional needs analysis models. NIST partners with other top schools to offer the Global Citizen Diploma, an optional qualification that assesses graduates' leadership, service and community engagement. The school is also committed to IT excellence and innovation. All students receive MacBook Air computers and iPads that are connected through a completely wireless campus.

In addition to its rigorous academics, NIST offers an expansive World Languages Programme and over 500 extra-curricular activity options. As one of the founding members of the Southeast Asia Student Activity Conference, the NIST Falcons compete against their peers from other top schools in Southeast Asia. NIST represents the future of learning through its stellar academic achievements and expansive resources.

More importantly, the school is successful in fostering reflective, principled learners with a passion for making a difference in the lives of others. With its graduates attending the best universities around the globe and going on to become community leaders, NIST has become recognized as one of the world's leading international schools.

Nord Anglia International School Manila

NORD ANGLIA INTERNATIONAL SCHOOL MANILA

Bradco Avenue, Aseana, Paranaque City, Metro Manila, 1701 Philippines
Tel: +63 2 7987 7878

Email: admissions@naismanila.edu.ph
Website: naismanila.edu.ph
Head of School: Chris Pooley
Appointed: May 2021
School type: Co-educational Day
Age range of pupils: 2–18 years

No. of pupils enrolled as at 01/09/2022: 200
Fees as at 01/09/2022:
Day: Php427,919–Php1,475,588
Average class size: 22
Teacher/pupil ratio: 1:12

Nord Anglia International School Manila (NAIS Manila) is a community that supports our children's learning, growth and development from Early Years through to Secondary. Our inspirational and internationally diverse community of teachers, support staff, students and parents will make you and your family love being part of our school.

NAIS Manila is part of the Nord Anglia Education family, a growing global community of premium international schools currently with 73 schools, based in 30 countries around the world, offering personalised, inspiring learning to more than 69,000 students between 2 to 18 years old.

We educate your child for the future, enhancing learning through collaborations with the world's best organisations – MIT, Juilliard and UNICEF. Individually tailoring our approach to your child enables them to achieve outstanding academic results whilst developing the skills and mindset to thrive in a changing world.

Our school, and the one-of-a-kind opportunities we create for your child inside and outside the classroom, enrich learning, instil life-long memories and a deep sense of achievement. We welcome your family to become a valued member of our vibrant global community.

NAIS Manila accepts applications for enrolment year-round. Visit our website www.naismanila.edu.ph or email admissions@naismanila.edu.ph to receive Admissions information.

Nord Anglia International School Shanghai, Pudong

NORD ANGLIA INTERNATIONAL SCHOOL
SHANGHAI, PUDONG

(Founded 2002)

2888 Junmin Road, Pudong New District, Shanghai, 201315 China
Tel: +86 (0)21 5812 7455
Email: admissions@naispudong.com
Website: naispudong.com
Principal: Lesley-Ann Wallace
Appointed: January 2015

School type: Co-educational Day
Age range of pupils: 2–18 years
Fees as at 01/09/2022:
RMB117,370 – RMB333,680
Average class size: Max 22
Teacher/pupil ratio: 1:9

As a parent, you want your child to excel. So do we.

At Nord Anglia International School Shanghai, Pudong we are known for our warm and welcoming international community, whilst delivering excellent academic outcomes for our students. Our outstanding teachers, globally renowned curriculum and best-in-class teacher parent communications ensure that every child receives a world-class education.

One-of-a kind opportunities we create inside and outside the classroom enrich and amplify our academic offering, leading to outstanding academic results year after year. During the past five years, our students achieved an average score of 36 in IB and 95% earned 5 A* – C grades in GCSE. One in three of our students go on to attend universities ranked in the world's top 50. These are results of which we are truly proud.

As part of the Nord Anglia Education global family of over 70 schools, our curricula are enhanced by collaborations with preeminent organisations such as The Juilliard School, Massachusetts Institute of Technology, and UNICEF. These unique collaborations transform the learning experience for our students, helping them to develop global awareness and get ahead in the changing world of the future. Our students also have access to Global Campus, a platform connecting them with over 67,000 students around the world, further amplifying their learning potential.

We promise to support your child to be their best and achieve more than they ever thought possible.

Nord Anglia International School, Hong Kong

NORD ANGLIA INTERNATIONAL SCHOOL HONG KONG

(Founded 2014)

11 On Tin Street, Lam Tin, Kowloon, Hong Kong, SAR, China

Tel: +852 3958 1428

Email: admissions@nais.hk

Website: www.nais.hk

Principal: Mr Kenny Duncan

School type: Co-educational Day

Age range of pupils: 3–18 years

Fees as at 01/09/2022:

Pre-school: HK$83,430 – HK$175,100

Primary: HK$175,100

Secondary (Year 7 – 11): HK$195,895

Secondary (Year 12 – 13): HK$197,770

Teacher/pupil ratio: Nursery: 1:7, Reception 1:10, Primary/Secondary: 1:12

As a parent, you want the best for your child. So do we. That's why we enrich your child's learning experience with opportunities beyond traditional education and collaborate with world-leading organisations.

At Nord Anglia International School Hong Kong (NAIS Hong Kong) we promise to support your child to be their very best and achieve more than they ever thought possible. We provide more than just teaching. We take education beyond the classroom to transform and enrich learning, enabling students to be ambitious and inspired to do more. Every child is unique, and by individually tailoring our approach to your child's education, we ensure that they will be confident and ready to take on any challenge that they may encounter in our ever-changing world.

NAIS Hong Kong is part of a global family of over 77 premium international schools located in 31 countries across the world. Nord Anglia Education (NAE) teachers and school staff look after more than 68,000 students globally. Our global scale enables us to recruit and retain the best teachers in the world. The school's unique Global Campus allows students to connect with pupils from NAE's schools around the world through virtual learning and exchanges.

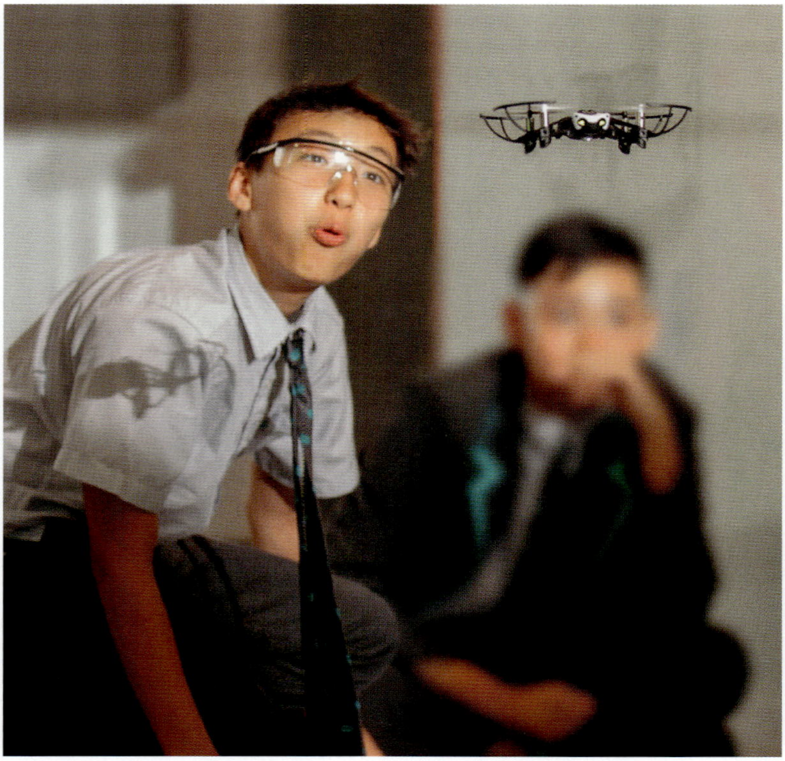

Nord Anglia holds exclusive collaborations with two of the world's most prestigious organisations, The Juilliard School – giving students a unique opportunity to learn about music through iconic works and regular connections with musicians; and the Massachusetts Institute of Technology (MIT) – bringing a new approach to learning the interdisciplinary subjects of Science, Technology, Engineering, Arts and Mathematics (STEAM). Groups of students visit MIT every year to meet leading researchers and take part in activities such as bio-engineering, coding and robotics. Furthermore, Nord Anglia's partnership with UNICEF enables students to take a leading role in the global discussion about key issues affecting our world.

NAIS Hong Kong offers an all-round through-train education for students aged 3-18, with specialist teachers in Art, Music, Drama, PE and Mandarin from the very start of a child's educational journey. With a focus on individualised learning, teachers ensure that all students have a creative and transformational learning experience.

We are ambitious for our students, believing there is no limit to what they can achieve – our approach supports and nurtures every child to succeed academically, socially and personally,

helping them go beyond what they thought possible. We encourage every student to love learning, to try something new, and, above all, to be ambitious.

All three campuses feature top-class facilities, including large multi-purpose indoor and outdoor spaces, outdoor play areas, library, and specialist music and art rooms. The Pre-school campus features specially-designed child-friendly furniture, purpose-built learning and play spaces, and amazing sea view of Sai Kung – sure to inspire learning and a love for nature.

Curriculum:
Early Years Foundation Stage framework, English National Curriculum, IGCSEs, IB Diploma Programme

Transport:
Comprehensive bus service available

Facilities (vary according to campus):
Multi-purpose hall, sports hall, performance hall, fitness suite, 25m swimming pool, large outdoor play areas, climbing walls, libraries, learning centre, drama and dance studios, Maker Space, space lab, science labs, music and art rooms, multi-media room, cafeteria.

North London Collegiate School Jeju

North London Collegiate School Jeju

(Founded 2011)

33, Global edu-ro 145beon-gil,
Daejeong-eup, Seogwipo-si, Jeju-do,
63644 Republic of Korea
Tel: +82 64 793 8001
Email: admissions@nlcsjeju.kr
Website: www.nlcsjeju.co.kr
Principal: Ms Lynne Oldfield

School type:
Co-educational Day & Boarding
Age range of pupils: 4–18 years
No. of pupils enrolled as at 01/09/2022: 1476
Fees as at 01/09/2022:
Day: KRW 31,808,331 – 44,584,739
Boarding: KRW 13,315,000 – 15,786,000
Teacher/pupil ratio: 1:7

North London Collegiate School Jeju is a boarding school for girls and boys aged 4 to 18. We provide a stimulating and diverse experience in which every child is challenged and supported to realise their potential. We send confident, successful and caring young people to the world's best universities.

Academic Excellence

Situated on UNESCO World Heritage island of Jeju, our proud history began in North London 170 years ago. Since 1850, NLCS UK has maintained its reputation for providing an outstanding education, consistently delivering some of the best academic results in the UK. Founded by Victorian pioneer of education, Frances Mary Buss, the vision of our founder remains true to this day and we are a school which believes fundamentally in what students 'can do'; we never place ceilings on them nor label them. Strong in tradition, yet forward-thinking and outward-looking, North London Collegiate Schools provide an ambitious academic education. NLCS Jeju's rigorous curriculum challenges students to think critically and to problem solve. We follow the NLCS model in its ethos and standards with a few small local differences.

We recruit some of the best teachers from around the world – they are highly qualified and inspire their students to discover a love of learning that will last a lifetime. Teachers are carefully selected for their love of their subject and spend time at NLCS UK to ensure they share the NLCS school ethos. They encourage students to explore beyond curriculum boundaries and discover their own passions.

We follow IGCSE and IB Diploma, which are two of the most globally robust academic examination programmes available worldwide. All studies throughout the school are designed to prepare all our children for success in both. In 2021, passing students achieved an average IB Diploma score of an incredible 39 points for the second year running. We are currently placed in the Top 25 Global IB Schools. This places us in the Top 25 Global IB Schools. This is an amazing achievement – and all the more so when you consider most of our students are non native English speakers. This is a true testament to the very high standards of teaching and learning.

Pastoral Care

We believe that by supporting students in every aspect of their lives, and removing all barriers to learning, they will perform to their full potential. We address any issue that can affect a child's learning with conviction, professionalism and purpose. We also ensure that our students have a balanced approach to their school years which includes appropriate levels of sleep, exercise, social activity and academic pursuits. We therefore advise against extra-tuition in evenings, weekends and holidays.

Our pastoral system is typical of

successful British boarding schools. Every student, day or boarder, is a member of a House that provides a sense of belonging and identity to all its members. All faculty staff are members of a House and support in the academic and pastoral development of students in that House. The House is the family that provides the opportunities, support and challenge for all NLCS Jeju students to be happy and successful. Positive, lifelong relationships are made in Houses that serve students during and beyond their time at NLCS Jeju.

NLCS Jeju is now offering a full boarding experience from Junior School onwards. The highest standards of pastoral care will be maintained. Our staff ensure that every child is happy, comfortable and nurtured.

Beyond The Classroom

In addition to the outstanding facilities we offer on campus, Jeju is home to a stimulating array of leisure activities. NLCS Jeju takes advantage of its rich, natural and cultural environment and students are encouraged to explore the fascinating island during school trips and co-curricular activities. We are very proud that each week a programme of more than 150 activities offers a wide variety of opportunities for all our students. In just one week students might participate in student led House competitions, after-school activities, Academic Societies, the unique Saturday morning 'Bryant' programme, ambitious school productions, successful sports squads and magical musical events. The opportunities to show commitment, leadership and to try out new things are never-ending.

Universities care about the character of the young people they admit – what students do outside the classroom tells them a lot about the kind of student who is applying. Co curricular activities are the best way students can demonstrate how unique, interesting and accomplished they are and showcase where their passions lie. Through our co curricular programme, NLCS Jeju gives our students opportunities to develop characteristics such as leadership, initiative, commitment and many more.

NLCS Jeju students embody the idea that they really can Start here. Go anywhere.

Regents International School Pattaya

REGENTS
INTERNATIONAL SCHOOL
PATTAYA
A NORD ANGLIA EDUCATION SCHOOL

(Founded 1994)
33/3 Moo 1, Pong, Banglamung,
Chonburi, 20150 Thailand

Tel: +66 (0)93 135 7736
Email: admissions@regents-pattaya.co.th
Website:
www.nordangliaeducation.com/our-schools/pattaya
Principal: Mrs. Sarah Osborne-James
School type:
Co-educational Day & Boarding

Age range of pupils: 2–18 years
No. of pupils enrolled as at 01/09/2022: 800
No. of boarders: 50
Fees as at 01/09/2022:
From: THB316,350
Average class size: 18
Teacher/pupil ratio: 1:8

About Regents International School Pattaya – A Day and Boarding School

Nord Anglia Education is the world's leading premium schools' organization, with campuses located across 31 countries in the Americas, Europe, China, India, Southeast Asia, and the Middle East. Together, our 77 schools educate more than 67,000 students from kindergarten through to the end of secondary/high school. We are driven by one unifying philosophy: we are ambitious for our schools, students, teachers, staff and communities, and we inspire every child who attends a Nord Anglia Education school to achieve more than they ever imagined possible.

Every parent wants the best for their child and so do we. Nord Anglia Education schools deliver high quality, transformational education and ensure excellent academic outcomes by going beyond the traditional learning. Our global scale enables us to recruit and retain world-leading teachers and to offer unforgettable experiences through global and regional events, while our engaging learning environments ensure all of our students love coming to school.

Regents is an exciting, vibrant day and boarding school that thinks beyond traditional education to transform learning. We focus on a holistic education as well as academic excellence. In Primary we teach the International Primary Curriculum (IPC) and in Secondary we offer the International GCSE (iGCSE). We are the only school in the area to offer our Sixth Form students the choice of either A Levels or the International Baccalaureate Diploma Programme (IBDP), ensuring access to the world's top universities.

We are part of Nord Anglia Education which means we can offer our students exclusive collaborations with Juilliard School of the Performing Arts, Massachusetts Institute of Technology (MIT), UNICEF, our Gap Programme and we are also the only Round Square school in our region. Being a Round Square school means we focus on internationalism, democracy, environmental awareness, adventure, leadership and service to the community. We have an extensive outdoor education program with national and international expeditions. We are also a Boarding school, with memberships to the British Boarders Association and the Australian Boarders Association.

Boarding at Regents

Regents has a well-established boarding community in beautiful surroundings, well away from the busy streets and pollution of Bangkok, yet still within easy reach of the main airport. We are ideally placed to offer fantastic imaginative supervised trips at weekends and our sporting facilities provide excellent opportunities after homework is complete each evening. Our boarders are encouraged to work hard and play hard – whilst they will be encouraged towards independence, they will also know that they have our staff's full support as they grow.

We offer girls and boys boarding from Year 3 to Year 13 (age 8 – 18).

There are many different options for boarders, from occasional boarding, part time and full-time boarding. We also offer boarder tasting sessions if you would like to try boarding as an option for your child. There are many benefits to boarding, including immersion in English language, set study (prep) time, no commute and use of school facilities.

SEK International School Qatar

(Founded 2013)
Onaiza 65, Doha, Qatar
Tel: +974 4012 7633
Email: info@sek.qa

Website: www.sek.qa
Head of School: Verónica Sánchez
School type: Co-educational Day
Age range of pupils: 3–18 years

SEK International School Qatar was founded in 2013 within the framework of the Outstanding Schools Programme of the Ministry of Education and Higher Education of the State of Qatar. The school today caters for students from over 60 nationalities. The teaching staff represents more than 25 different nationalities.

The school is an innovative coeducational, international and multilingual school in Qatar, with a cutting-edge learning campus located in the sophisticated West Bay district of Doha. English is the language of instruction, and the school also offers Spanish and Arabic courses for all students. Technology is embedded across the curriculum, supported by their staff as Microsoft Innovative Educators and a Bring your Own Laptop programme form Grade 4.

SEK-Qatar is an IB World School authorized to offer the IB Primary Years Programme (PYP), the Middle Years Programme (MYP) and the Diploma Programme (DP), from pre-school to grade 12. The IB offers high-quality and challenging educational programmes, with a reputation for their high academic standards. SEK-Qatar is also proud to be an accredited school by New England Association of Schools and Colleges (NEASC), one of the most prestigious international university and school accreditation agencies. It indicates that the school meets high standards of institutional quality through ongoing, independent, and objective process of peer-review.

Established in 1892, SEK International Schools are places where innovation and pedagogical leadership are combined with 120 years of tradition and history to offer educational programmes. The SEK Group has launched over a hundred pioneering initiatives introducing innovations such as the classrooms without walls, the SEKMUN Model United Nations and the International Baccalaureate Organisation programmes.

SEK-Qatar has a unique educational model, committed to offering quality education that promotes individualisation, places emphasis on learning rather than teaching, and fosters activity and effort, freedom, interaction and teamwork as well as transformational learning. Technology, sports, artistic and social activities also play a major role in the SEK educational model. The ultimate goal is for students to acquire skills, knowledge and understanding to become active citizens, committed and determined to build a better world.

In all SEK International Schools we are able to offer a quality online learning model in which students are able to continue their learning if necessary, with synchronous and asynchronous classes, and with personalized monitoring by teachers and tutors, which has proved successful with students and families.

SEK International School Riyadh

Al Toq Street, Ar Rabi, Riyadh,
13315 Saudi Arabia
Tel: +966 53 063 3295
Email: admissions@sek.sa

Website: www.sek.sa
Principal: Mr Ivan Martinez Pastor
School type: Co-educational Day
Age range of pupils: 3–12 years

SEK International School Riyadh opened its doors in September 2021, thereby establishing in the Middle East, the second international school from the prestigious SEK Education Group, which has 130 years of history and experience in national and international education in five countries.

SEK-Riyadh builds on the experience and legacy of our innovative group of schools. SEK Education Group has excelled in providing an outstanding international Education to the local and international communities in Spain, France, Ireland and Qatar, as will the new member of the group – SEK-Riyadh in Saudi Arabia.

We are a community of learners, working together to prepare young people for the challenges of tomorrow through a broad and engaging curriculum, effective use of learning technologies; an individualised programme to cover the educational needs of each student and challenging our students to think critically and independently. Our dedicated International and multicultural team of well trained teachers and support staff are highly motivated and engaged in helping each of our students reach their full potential.

The core of the SEK profile is to prepare our students to be capable of guiding their own futures and to becoming lifelong learners. To demonstrate our commitment towards this ambitious goal, SEK International School Riyadh is a candidate school* for the IB Primary Years Programme (PYP) and for the IB Middle Years Programme (MYP). There are plans to implement the Diploma Programme (DP) in the future. Language of instruction is English with additional languages, including Arabic and Spanish.

SEK-Riyadh has also started the process of International accreditation with the New England Association of Schools and Colleges (NEASC), to ensure we meet demanding international standards of education. NEASC accreditation is a highly valued globally recognized standard of excellence; we will be part of their network of over 2,000 schools, technical and career institutions, colleges and universities in New England and International schools spanning more than 65 countries.

** Only schools authorized by the IB Organization can offer any of its four academic programmes: the Primary Years Programme (PYP), the Middle Years Programme (MYP), the Diploma Programme (DP), or the Career-related Programme (CP). Candidate status gives no guarantee that authorization will be granted. For further information about the IB and its programmes visit www.ibo.org.*

Seoul Foreign School

SEOUL FOREIGN SCHOOL

CELEBRATING 40 YEARS OF THE BRITISH SCHOOL,
40 YEARS OF IBDP & THE 110TH ANNIVERSARY OF SFS

(Founded 1912)

39 Yeonhui-ro 22-gil, Seodaemun-gu,
Seoul 03723, Republic of Korea
Tel: +82 2 330 3100
Email: admissions@seoulforeign.org
Website: www.seoulforeign.org
Head of School: Mr. Colm Flanagan
Appointed: July 2014

Elementary School Principal: Damian Prest
Middle School Principal: Justin Smith
High School Principal: Dr. Nancy Le Nezet
School type: Co-educational Day
Age range of pupils: 2–18 years
No. of pupils enrolled as at 01/09/2022: 1500
Average class size: 17
Teacher/pupil ratio: 1:8

Seoul Foreign School Inspiring Excellence, Building Character – Since 1912

Seoul Foreign School is the longest established international school in Korea and one of the first 10 international schools in the world. Founded in 1912, it offers a community of teaching and learning excellence, coming together to educate children at all ages and stages. Seoul Foreign School inspires a passion for learning, pursues academic and creative excellence and is dedicated to the service of others.

An unrivalled legacy is combined with state-of-the-art facilities on our 25 acre campus in central Seoul. With a current population of over 1500 students from more than 50 countries and with many diverse backgrounds, our students are able to learn and grow as truly global citizens.

Four sections, Elementary School, Middle School, High School and the British School, are situated together on a world class campus benefitting from individual space but aligned with one purpose and ethos. Academic, physical and social needs are served across the facilities. Students have the opportunity to participate in various activities – within the school day and in extracurricular time – including many competitive sports, arts, sciences and holistic interests.

Seoul Foreign School is an IB continuum school – a Pre-K to Grade 12 IB World School and additionally Foundation to Year 9 British School. The IB Primary Years Programme and IB Middle Years Programme are offered along with the English National Curriculum delivered through the international framework of Fieldwork Education, and both lead into the IB Diploma Programme. Based on its history of 40 years of IB Diploma Programme, SFS High School provides students an outstanding flexibility allowing 160 combinations of subjects, including unique course offerings in Seoul such as Design & Technology.

Teachers are rigorously selected and their passion, inspiration and academic excellence ensure that students go on to attend prestigious universities and colleges and succeed in all walks of life. Seoul Foreign School is a Christian school for all. Students enjoy an education surrounded by rich heritage in preparation for a future as global contributors.

Shanghai Community International School – Hongqiao Campus

(Founded 1996)

1161 Hongqiao Road, Shanghai, 200051 China
Tel: +86 21 6261 4338
Email: admissions@scis-china.org
Website: www.scis-china.org
Director of Schools: Daniel Eschtruth
Appointed: 2016

School type: Co-educational Day
Age range of pupils: 2–18 years
No. of pupils enrolled as at 01/09/2022: 1550
Fees as at 01/09/2022:
Day: RMB126,500–RMB285,000
Average class size: 20
Teacher/pupil ratio: 1:20

Established in 1996 as one of Shanghai's first international schools, Shanghai Community International School (SCIS) is a non-profit educational day school, governed by a self-perpetuating board of directors and overseen by the International Schools Foundation.

With over twenty years of rich tradition, SCIS offers a truly unique international experience. The SCIS community is unparalleled, consisting of a diverse mix of outstanding teachers, students, and parents representing over sixty nationalities and thirty-five languages, across six continents. SCIS leverages this unique community to provide a personalized approach to holistic education, ensuring all students have the opportunity to be successful.

SCIS is one of the first international schools in Shanghai to become fully authorized as an International Baccalaureate (IB) Continuum World School, a world class academic program aimed at rigorous critical thinking and global citizenship. This accreditation extends across all SCIS Campuses, including Hongqiao and Pudong, providing a seamless program for students aged 2-18, and comprised of the Primary Years Programme (PYP), Middle Years Programme (MYP), and Diploma Programme (DP).

Primary Years Programme (PYP) prepares students to become active, caring, lifelong learners who demonstrate respect for themselves and others and have the capacity to participate in the world around them. It focuses on the development of the whole child as an inquirer, both within and beyond the classroom. (Age 2-10)

Middle Years Programme (MYP) is a challenging framework that encourages students to make practical connections between their studies and the real world. The MYP is a five-year programme, which can be implemented in a partnership between schools. Students who complete the MYP are well-prepared to undertake the IB Diploma Programme (DP). (Age 11-15)

Diploma Programme (DP) is designed as an academically challenging and balanced program of education with final examinations that prepares students for success at university and life beyond. (Age 16-17)

Shenzhen College of International Education

深圳国际交流学院
Shenzhen College of International Education
办中国最好的国际高中

(Founded 2003)
No. 3, Sixth Antuoshan Road, Futian District, Shenzhen, Guangdong, China

Tel: +86 755 8349 5025
Email: info@scie.com.cn
Website: www.scie.com.cn
Headteacher: Neil Mobsby
Appointed: July 2018
School type: Co-educational Day & Boarding

Age range of pupils: 14–18 years
No. of pupils enrolled as at 01/09/2022: 1800
Fees as at 01/09/2022: RMB248,000 (regular stream) – RMB278,000 (Arts Academy)

Founded in 2003, Shenzhen College of International Education (SCIE) was the first high school to offer an international curriculum in Shenzhen, China. It delivers (I)GCSE, AS, AL and AP courses to both day and boarding students who have undergone a rigorous and highly selective admissions process. In 2022, the Year 10 acceptance rate was 15%.

SCIE students are well-rounded, compassionate and highly-driven. They learn and thrive in an international and challenging environment, developing social responsibility, creativity, independence and enthusiasm during their four years at the College. Academically, their passion for learning, commitment and resilience have brought them the highest accolades in external examinations. In the Cambridge Assessment International Education IGCSE, AS and AL summer exams 2021, 14 SCIE students received 'Top in the World', 11 'Top in China' and one student received 'Best Across'. Together with the 'High Achievement' awards, SCIE received 31 awards in total, outperforming all other CAIE schools in China.

Beyond the classroom, SCIE students have equally impressive achievements, especially in competitive events that challenge them to contribute to the wider community. In the 2021 BPhO (British Physics Olympiad), 25 of SCIE participants received Top Gold. In the most recent American Mathematics Competitions, 18 of SCIE students won the Honor Roll of Distinction. SCIE Humanities students are as outstanding, regularly presenting at international forums and receiving top awards from competitions and research projects, like China Thinks Big, FOBISIA Humanities essay writing competition, and International Economics Olympiad.

SCIE graduates attend leading universities in the world. With 33 Oxbridge offers this year, the College has maintained its position as the school in China with the highest number of Oxbridge offers for 17 consecutive years. Along with top US university offers including from Stanford and Ivy League, SCIE celebrates another exceptional cohort that will join the alumni network: one that has been contributing to our world in both arts and sciences.

In 2021, we successfully obtained the accreditation from WASC and the re-accreditation from CIS, which marked another important milestone in SCIE's history.

St Andrews International School Bangkok

ST ANDREWS
INTERNATIONAL SCHOOL
BANGKOK
A NORD ANGLIA EDUCATION SCHOOL

(Founded 1997)

1020 Sukhumvit Road, Phra Khanong,
Khlong Toei, Bangkok, 10110 Thailand
Tel: +662 056 9555
Email: admissions@standrews.ac.th
Website: www.standrews.ac.th
Head of School: Mr. Paul Schofield
Appointed: 2003

School type: Co-educational Day
Age range of pupils: 2–18 years
No. of pupils enrolled as at 01/09/2022: 2000
Fees as at 01/09/2022:
Day: THB331,000–THB702,000
Average class size: 17
Teacher/pupil ratio: 1:7

St Andrews International School Bangkok was founded in 1997 on an attractive, conveniently located site, with excellent facilities and good access to local transportation. Today we are a school of more than 2,000 students representing some 50 nationalities ranging from Nursery (2 years) to Year 13 (18 years). In August 2017 we opened an additional campus at a nearby prime city centre location which delivers state of the art purpose-built learning facilities to our High School.

Our school provides a high quality, professional, well-resourced learning environment where each child's talents and abilities are recognised and nurtured, and their needs supported. Our teachers are professional and caring, selected for their awareness of the needs of a broad range of children who may come from different social, cultural, religious and educational backgrounds. They are capable educators who take care with their preparation of the curriculum, use a variety of strategies for its delivery and pay close attention to the progression of each individual.

We are an inclusive school that welcomes students of all abilities. To ensure that all our children have an equality of opportunity, we have a professional Learning Support Department. This team works with class teachers to identify and support children in their learning across the school, whether they need extra help with their studies or have been identified as gifted and talented.

The curriculum draws on the best UK practices, adapted to reflect the international context of the school. Students take IGCSE examinations at the end of Year 11 and then follow the Senior Studies Programme in Years 12 and 13. Our school offers the International Baccalaureate Diploma Programme, alongside an alternative school-based curriculum, both of which lead to graduation and provide the opportunity to apply to prestigious universities all around the world. As part of Nord Anglia Education, the world's leading premium schools organisation, we collaborate with the preeminent performing arts conservatory, The Juilliard School, and one of the world's leading universities, the Massachusetts Institute of Technology (MIT), to bring truly inspiring learning experiences to all of our students.

With high quality teaching, excellent facilities and small class sizes, St Andrews International School Bangkok offers students the opportunity to fulfil their academic potential in a stimulating, caring and nurturing environment. We are fully accredited by CfBT Education Trust and Thailand's Office for National Education Standards and Quality Assessment (ONESQA), the first school in Thailand to receive this joint accreditation award.

St. Joseph's Institution International

ST. JOSEPH'S INSTITUTION INTERNATIONAL

(Founded 2007)

490 Thomson Road, Singapore, 298191 Singapore
Tel: +65 6353 9383
Email: admissions.hs@sji-international.com.sg
Website: www.sji-international.com.sg
HS Principal: Mrs Roisin Paul
Appointed: June 2012

Elementary School Principal: Ms Catherine Nicol
School type: Co-educational Day & Boarding
Age range of pupils: 4–18 years
No. of pupils enrolled as at 01/09/2022: 2000
Fees as at 01/09/2022: S$32,978
Teacher/pupil ratio: 1:10

Established in 2007, St. Joseph's Institution International offers a holistic, values-driven and international educational experience to a diverse student body of 40 nationalities rooted in the context of Singapore.

As a school with a Lasallian Catholic foundation, our community welcomes students, teachers, parents, friends and supporters of all faiths and cultural backgrounds. Our mission is to enable students to learn how to learn and learn how to live, empowering them to become people of integrity and people for others. Our core Lasallian values are central to everything that we do: spirituality, mutual respect, internationalism, leadership, experiences and service.

Today, we celebrate a community of 2,000 students across two schools on one campus. The Elementary School offers the International Primary Curriculum for pre-school Prep 1 – 2 (ages 4 turning 5 – 6) and Grade 1 – 6 (ages 7 – 12), while the High School offers the IGCSE followed by the IB Diploma Programme in Grades 7 – 12 (ages 12 – 18).

The IB Diploma Programme

The attributes of the IB Learner profile underpin much of the teaching and learning throughout SJI International with a desire to develop curious, independent and confident learners. The most important principle within the school's educational philosophy is that of active learning. Crucially, active learning is about students doing. This involves a wide range of activities within the programme which will vary according to the subject: research, role plays, simulations, thinking exercises, decision-making exercises, debates, presentations and so on. These provide a stimulating educational environment and one that is intellectually challenging for the students.

Values, education and character-building are achieved through a range of challenging activities in sports, adventure and creativity, with a special emphasis on service, featuring weekly service activities and overseas projects that help students connect with and serve the local and global community.

We are justifiably proud of the outstanding achievements of our IB Diploma students. Many of our graduates have continued their studies at many of the top universities around the world. But outstanding academic results are only part of what we strive for. Our students leave SJI International ready for lifelong learning.

Stonehill International School

STONEHILL
INTERNATIONAL SCHOOL

An Embassy Group Education Initiative

(Founded 2008)

Near the International Airport,
No.259/333/334/335, Tarahunise Post, Jala Hobli, Bengaluru, Karnataka, 562157 India
Tel: +91 70 2666 6911
Email: admissions@stonehill.in
Website: www.stonehill.in
Head of School: Dr. Brian D. Brumsickle
Primary School Principal: Karen Crooke
Secondary School Principal: Joe Lumsden

School type:
Co-educational Day & Boarding
Religious Denomination:
Non-denominational
Age range of pupils: 3–18 years
No. of pupils enrolled as at 01/09/2022: 600
Average class size: 18
Teacher/pupil ratio: 1:7

Founded in 2008, Stonehill International School is one of the most widely reputed international schools in Bangalore, India. We were the first school in Bangalore to exclusively offer the International Baccalaureate (IB) curriculum from kindergarten all the way up to Grade 12 and continue to be a centre of IB excellence. We are accredited by the Council of International Schools (CIS), and the New England Association of Schools and Colleges (NEASC). Stonehill is also a member of the Australian Boarding Schools Association (ABSA).

The expansive 34-acre lush green campus, near the International Airport, offers ample space and infrastructure for sporting, cultural, and leisure activities. Besides state-of-the art classrooms, the world-class facilities include a 25-meter temperature-controlled pool, synthetic turf football field, tennis and volleyball courts, an Arts Centre, a STEM block, and a multipurpose sports hall. Stonehill also prides itself on modern boarding houses and a fully equipped cafeteria that serves nutritious and healthy meals.

Our students and faculty comprise 35 different nationalities. We are dedicated to our mission statement – "To provide stimulating, engaging academics integrated with enhanced opportunities for technological innovation, sports, and the arts."

University Placement Programme

Our College Counselling Department works with students from Grade 9 onwards to identify their aptitude, understand their interests, and guide them towards colleges that will help them meet their academic and personal goals. Students are assisted with scheduling of tests such as SAT, ACT, TOEFL, or IELTS.

Stonehill graduates have been accepted to some of the most prestigious universities across the globe, including Stanford University, MIT Boston, London School of Economics (LSE), Dartmouth College, University of Cambridge, Parsons School of Design, University of California, Los Angeles (UCLA), New York University (NYU), Sarah Lawrence College, University of Southern California (USC), University of British Columbia (UBC), LaSalle School of Arts, City University of Hong Kong, Essec University, Erasmus University, University of Sydney, Newcastle University and many more.

Sports

Through our sports programme,

importance is given to not just students' health and fitness, but also to developing skills, learning to work in teams and building leadership and personal growth. Stonehill students also compete regularly with teams from other schools in Bangalore, India, and Asia. Swimming, tennis, equestrian sports, basketball, football, volleyball, and cricket are just a few of our sports offerings.

Arts

Stonehill prides itself on a committed Arts department with a special focus on Visual Art, Drama, and Music. The transdisciplinary nature of arts gives them relevance throughout the curriculum. Stonehill uses the creative arts to promote attitudes such as empathy and appreciation, and skills such as analysis, that help see the uniqueness of each person as well as explore the commonalities that connect each other.

We also offer private music lessons for instruments such as piano, guitar, drums, violin and cello along with numerous opportunities to perform at concerts, assemblies and other gatherings.

Technology

At Stonehill, we have a 1:1 policy for devices and our students use a wide variety of technology tools to communicate, collaborate, research, and create.

In Primary School, the digital citizenship programme teaches students to be safe and responsible in the online world. Learning is supported through the Makerspace where digitally enhanced Lego and robotics work alongside the traditional elements of design, sewing, and construction.

Technology in the Secondary School is seamlessly integrated into all subjects.

Additionally, Product Design, Digital Design, and Computer Science are offered as subjects. In Design, students make digital and real products using 3D modelling and design technologies. They also design and develop applications using pure computer coding.

Boarding

Stonehill offers weekly and full time boarding options to students. The residential programme at Stonehill is for students from Grade 6 onwards, and is designed to extend IB learning through the social aspects of boarding. The small number of boarders provide a warm atmosphere and creates a sense of community.

The boarding houses at Stonehill feature twin and quad sharing rooms, a common lounge, and a study room. The houses are supported by a cafeteria, a fitness centre, and a 24-hour medical centre. Experienced House Parents, tutors, and service staff take care of children and their individual needs.

Tanglin Trust School, Singapore

(Founded 1925)

95 Portsdown Road, 139299 Singapore

Tel: +65 67780771

Email: admissions@tts.edu.sg

Website: www.tts.edu.sg

CEO: Mr Craig Considine BA MA

Appointed: 2018

School type: Co-educational Day

Age range of pupils: 3–18 years

No. of pupils enrolled as at 01/09/2022: 2800

Fees as at 01/09/2022:

Nursery to Reception: S$29,916 – S$36,696

Year 1 to Year 6: S$37,275 – S$38,910

Year 7 to Year 13: S$44,355 – S$48,126

Average class size: 24; Nursery: 20; Sixth Form: 15

Established in 1925 Tanglin Trust School is the oldest British international school in South East Asia. Tanglin provides the English National Curriculum with an international perspective to children from 3 to 18 years in Singapore.

Tanglin is a vibrant co-educational school of 2,800 students representing over 50 nationalities and provides a unique learning environment for children from Nursery right through to Sixth Form. As a not-for-profit school, tuition fees are devoted to the provision of an outstanding education.

As the only international school in Singapore to offer A Levels or the IB Diploma in Sixth Form, all of Tanglin's Sixth Formers study a programme that is tailored both to the subjects they are passionate about and to the style of learning that most suits them, ensuring they thrive and flourish.

Tanglin has an excellent academic reputation. Students' examination results consistently surpass Singapore and global averages, with around 95% of graduates typically receiving their first or second choice university, which are among the best in the world.

Tanglin is inspected every year within the British Schools Overseas (BSO) framework, recognised by Ofsted. All three schools have been repeatedly awarded 'Outstanding', the highest possible grade, including in their latest inspections (2017 – Senior, 2018 – Infant and 2019 – Junior).

Drawing on professional and dynamic staff, we strive to make every individual feel valued, happy and successful. Responsibility, enthusiasm and participation are actively encouraged, and integrity is prized. Working together in a safe, caring yet stimulating environment, we set high expectations whilst offering strong support, resulting in a community of lifelong learners who can contribute with confidence to our world.

What the inspectors say:

"Tanglin pupils talk with passion about their school because it is special. They say it makes them feel happy and valued, not just for what they can do, but for who they are." Junior School Inspection 2019

"A rich and diverse curriculum provides outstanding learning across the school. Leaders are relentless in their ambition to offer pupils not only breadth but also depth in their learning. As a result, stimulating opportunities are built into everyday lessons for all pupils." Infant School Inspection 2018

"The teachers' enthusiasm for learning is often infectious, leading to students seeing learning as a highly worthwhile and enjoyable process; students are highly motivated to succeed." Senior School Inspection 2017

The British International School of Kuala Lumpur

THE BRITISH INTERNATIONAL SCHOOL KUALA LUMPUR
A NORD ANGLIA EDUCATION SCHOOL

(Founded 2009)

No 1 Changkat Bukit Utama,
Bandar Utama, 47800 Petaling Jaya,
Selangor, Malaysia
Tel: +60 3 7727 7775
Email: admissions@britishschool.edu.my
Website: www.britishschool.edu.my
Principal: Dr Mike O'Connor
School type: Co-educational Day

Age range of pupils: 2–18 years
No. of pupils enrolled as at 01/09/2022: 1200
Fees as at 01/09/2022:
RM49,250 – RM107,070
Application Fee: RM1,500
Enrolment Fee: RM17,050
Average class size: 20

The British International School of Kuala Lumpur (BSKL) is a warm and welcoming international community. Our commitment to nurturing student happiness forms the foundation of student success and our 'be ambitious' philosophy.

Our school offers an early years programme featuring play-based learning for children as young as 2 and continues with primary school and secondary school programmes culminating with A-levels in Year 13. Students from more than 60 nationalities learn, collaborate and build together; making the school community authentically international.

Our teachers know each child and engage them in an exceptional learning environment. This results in happy children who look forward to coming to school each day and working to achieve more than they thought possible.

BSKL uses the English National Curriculum, with enhancements especially designed for an International school. On average, our Year 6 students score 10 points better than their international school peers on end of year assessments. Our IGCSE students perform well above the UK average with 81% of grades being A*-A last year. The programme delivered the Best Global IGCSE Results in Nord Anglia Education for an astounding three consecutive years. Our A-level students also perform extremely well with a 100% pass rate and 100% of students earning at least one university offer. Past graduates are attending universities all over the world, including Imperial College, University of Oxford, St. Andrew's University, University College London (UCL), London School of Economics (LSE), King's College London, and University of Edinburgh, as well as universities in the USA, Canada, Australia, The Netherlands, Hong Kong and Malaysia.

BSKL is proud to be part of the Nord Anglia Education (NAE) family, the world's leading premium schools organisation with 78 international schools located in 31 countries around the world.

The International Academy – Amman

الأكاديمية الدولية - عمان
THE INTERNATIONAL ACADEMY - AMMAN
Learners of Today - Leaders of Tomorrow

(Founded 2004)

PO Box 144255, King Hussein Parks, Sa'eed Khair Street, Amman, 11814 Jordan
Tel: +962 6550 2055
Email: info@iaa.edu.jo
Website: www.iaa.edu.jo
Director: Dr Hana Kanan
School type: Co-educational Day

Age range of pupils: 3–18 years
No. of pupils enrolled as at 01/09/2022: 1181
Boys: *626* ***Girls:*** *555*
IB Grade 12: *74*
Average class size: 22
Teacher/pupil ratio: 1:5 Early Years, 1:10 Primary, 1:18 Secondary

The International Academy – Amman is a place of vision, principle, and aspiration. Dedication to excellence propels it forward and upward year after year. The four IAA Pillars, Leadership, Duty, Cultural Heritage, and Acceptance, are the basis of a clearly defined mission: to make our Learners of Today, our Leaders of Tomorrow.

IAA is an inclusive, non-profit, non-commercial educational institution offering an acclaimed curriculum at a world-class standard. It is an international, day school existing within a Jordanian context, promoting both global perspective and national heritage. This defining principle is reflected in the diversity of IAA staff, representing more than ten countries around the world and instilling a robust spirit of interculturalism within the school.

Accredited by the Council of International Schools (CIS) and the New England Association of Schools (NEASC), IAA now offers a comprehensive program beginning in Pre-K and culminating with Grade 12.

Most IAA graduates enjoy placement at competitive or top-tier universities throughout the United States, Britain, and Canada.

The IAA curriculum is a rigorous symbiosis of the finest curricula from around the globe, employing modern and holistic educational approaches. At the Primary level, IAA utilises an eclectic program based on the British curriculum for literacy and the Australian curriculum for mathematics. The curriculum is further enhanced by the International Primary Curriculum (IPC) that is used for an integrated approach to learning, covering a range of subjects. The Jordanian Ministry of Education curriculum is used for the Arabic Language. At the Secondary level, IAA is an International Baccalaureate (IB) World School authorised for the Middle Years Programme (MYP) and the IB Diploma Programme (DP). IAA also offers a myriad of extra-curricular activities, and rich opportunities to exercise leadership, athleticism, artistry, oratory, citizenship, and more, providing every student with a chance to explore his/her unique talents.

The sky is the limit at IAA.

For information, please visit www.iaa.edu.jo.

The International School of Kuala Lumpur (ISKL)

THE INTERNATIONAL SCHOOL OF KUALA LUMPUR

(Founded 1965)
2, Lorong Kelab Polo Di Raja, Ampang Hilir, 55000 Kuala Lumpur, Malaysia
Tel: +60 3 4813 5000
Email: admissions@iskl.edu.my
Website: www.iskl.edu.my

Head of School:
Mr Rami Madani , MA, BSc
School type: Co-educational Day
Age range of pupils: 3–18 years
No. of pupils enrolled as at 01/09/2022: 1500
Fees as at 01/09/2022:
Day: RM59,000–RM120,400

The International School of Kuala Lumpur (ISKL) believes that its success today is based on how well it prepares its students for their future. Offering a diverse academic and co-curricular program, ISKL supports learners in exploring and developing the passions, skills, and competencies they need to be future-ready, not only for university and their career but for life itself.

The school is located on a 26-acre, state-of-the-art campus in the heart of Kuala Lumpur and is home to students representing more than 65 nationalities. Students benefit from its robust international curriculum that combines leading North American educational frameworks with global best practices.

ISKL is a fully inclusive school and offers the International Baccalaureate Diploma Programme (IBDP) on a non-selective basis. With IBDP results that are consistently above the world average, ISKL's 30-year pass rate of 98% is a testament to the strength of its program and expert international faculty. In 2021, 37% of ISKL students scored 40 or more points and 19% earned a bilingual diploma. Multilingual students have the opportunity to take IB Language and Literature courses in English, Chinese, Japanese, Korean, and Spanish.

ISKL is one of the only schools in Malaysia offering transdisciplinary pathways that are designed to enable every learner to choose a curriculum best suited to their abilities, interests, and aspirations. In addition to the IBDP, High School options include PRAXIS 2030 (Grade 9-10) and ISKL's Pursuits Program combining individual IB, Advanced Placement, and High School courses for students who want to deep-dive into a specific area. The flexibility of ISKL's academic program enables students to take advantage of higher education opportunities worldwide, as typified by the Class of 2020 which received more than 450 acceptances from over 200 universities in 13 countries spanning five continents.

As the longest-running World IB School in Malaysia, ISKL has seen more than 1,500 students graduate with an IB Diploma over the past 30 years, representing a 98% pass rate. This flexibility creates further education opportunities, with ISKL students receiving acceptance from leading universities worldwide.

ISKL is accredited internationally through the Council of International Schools (CIS), and in the United States through the Western Association of Schools and Colleges (WASC). ISKL has a strong focus on service and sustainability across its divisions and is a member of the Eco-Schools organization and the Green Schools Alliance. Past awards include Highly Commended in the Relocate Awards for School Providing Outstanding Relocation Support category.

TIPS Coimbatore

(Founded 2001)
193 Sathy Road, S.S.Kulam P.O.,
Coimbatore, Tamil Nadu, 641107 India
Tel: +91 42 2236 6666
Email: askcbemain@tipsglobal.net

Website: www.tipsglobal.org
Founder: Mr. Ashok Kumar
School type:
Co-educational Day & Boarding
Age range of pupils: 2.6–17 years

Established in 2001 The Indian Public School is the first of its kind to offer International Baccalaureate and IGCSE curriculum in Coimbatore. For more than a decade TIPS, as a global school has gained momentum for itself in fulfilling international standards accredited by both IB and Cambridge. Set in a sprawling campus the infrastructure offers complete boarding facilities and a broad range of curriculum to students, national and international. More than a decade the institution has gained prominence both with local and international students in offering academic commitment in overall educational endeavor in IB and Cambridge IGCSE.

The philosophy and mission of TIPS is woven in its everyday routine. Right from academic to co-curricular activities the range provides the apt environment to tap the energy and spirit of every aspiring student. The lessons are meticulously curated with integrated teaching methods extracted from various international curriculums to provide an ideal learning experience. Every student is at the heart of the teaching process. Students are encouraged to work independently and are encouraged to develop inquiry skills, scaffolded appropriately and aptly at every stage of progress. The Primary years, Middle School and High School stands testimony to this learning experience. The school curriculum assimilates IBPYP, Cambridge IGCSE, and IBDP to offer a broad range of challenge and opportunity to the student community to pursue their interests.

Students evolve into confident, respectful, digitally excelling, articulate individuals who actively collaborate in team efforts. Skill developments are tailor made in accordance with the latest global requirements. The classrooms and the sprawling infrastructure equipped with the state of art technology envisage an ideal environment to provide the appropriate academic progress required for every student. Thoroughly structured and consistently engaged Labs, Playgrounds, Swimming pool, Digital multimedia centres, Music halls, Theatres, Libraries, Seminar halls, Auditoriums and Gardens are few to mention.

Apart from a fully fledged contemporary and premium boarding facilities, the school has dedicated departments to look into health, hygiene and catering facilities. A 24x7 infirmary, in a tie up with a multi specialty hospital, is equipped with qualified medical staff with basic nursing facilities within the campus. The in house dining boasts an international menu specifically curated keeping in mind the nutritional value to promote a "eat healthy" lifestyle.

TIPS alumni spread across renowned Universities are a standing testimony to the school's mission and vision. Students over the years have evolved to be better versions of themselves as envisioned by their teachers within the global context.

It is our sole aim to provide the best academic experience to our students, to enable their dreams to come true one at a time!

TIPS Coimbatore in alliance with Globeducate – an international K12 education group, strives to provide a world class education by inculcating the four key principles of – Delivering Educational Excellence, Developing Skills & Competencies, Building Character and Nurturing Global Perspectives. A truly international experience offered by TIPS involves an international student exchange program to help students communicate with individuals on a global platform. This includes providing students with the opportunity to participate in the international exchange programmes and other academic events organised by Globeducate. TIPS – Special Wing was conceived with an intention to provide a specialized educational environment that will inspire and empower every student with a clear and well structured educational programme for children experiencing challenges such as Attention Deviation Hyperactivity Disorder (ADHD), Attention Deviation Disorder (ADD), Dyslexia. We also ensure a dynamic transition opportunity to the mainstream curriculums when the children are ready.

Having successfully established itself across cities in South India, TIPS has also spread its wings in Malaysia.

Wellington College International Hangzhou

WELLINGTON COLLEGE INTERNATIONAL HANGZHOU

(Founded 2018)
2399 Xue Zhi Road, Xiaoshan District, Hangzhou, Zhejiang, 311231 China
Tel: +86 (571) 8239 6366
Email: admissions.wcih@wellingtoncollege.cn

Website: hangzhou.wellingtoncollege.cn
Master: Ms Kathryn Richardson
School type: Co-educational Day & Boarding
Age range of pupils: 2–18 years

Wellington College International Hangzhou offers a world-class international education for children of expatriate families from the ages of 5 to 18, following a curriculum based on the English National Curriculum in Primary School, enhanced by the International Primary Curriculum (IPC). These naturally lead into the IGCSE and A Levels in Senior School. As with all Wellington College schools, the Wellington Values and Identities to ensure our well-rounded pupils will be ready for acceptance into the best universities around the world, leaving Wellington College Hangzhou prepared with the 21st century skills required for the future.

The Wellington College Hangzhou campus covers over 74,000 square meters and hosts a range of custom built, state-of-the-art facilities that provide pupils with access to the very best academic and co-curricular opportunities.

Wellington College International School Bangkok

WELLINGTON COLLEGE
INTERNATIONAL SCHOOL BANGKOK

18 Krungthep Kreetha Road, Saphan Sung District, Bangkok, 10250 Thailand
Tel: +66 2 087 8888
Email: admissions@wellingtoncollege.ac.th

Website: www.wellingtoncollege.ac.th
Master: Mr Christopher Nicholls
School type: Co-educational Day
Age range of pupils: 2–18 years
No. of pupils enrolled as at 01/09/2022: 640

Wellington College International School Bangkok is part of the prestigious Wellington College Family of Schools, whose founding school was established in England over 160 years ago, receiving a royal charter from Queen Victoria. The school offers its students the chance to develop their zest for life. Our students are hungry to learn, willing to challenge and be challenged and are open to all that being a truly global citizen entails. We take a prestigious academic heritage, and we add something extra.

Situated on 28 acres of beautiful greenery, the campus is one of the finest in Thailand. It boasts individual Junior and Senior School buildings which have been specifically designed in great detail for outstanding learning. The School has numerous lawns, playgrounds and pitches where children can roam, play and compete. There are two swimming pools – one Olympic sized – and a huge Sports Hall where we host other schools in Thailand and internationally. We have a huge theatre, two beautifully designed libraries, our own lagoon and so much more. Visitors often comment that they have never seen a school quite like it.

Our students will leave our School with moral values and social conscience to serve others and to do good. Our students embody 'the five Is'. They are -

- Inspired
- Intellectual
- Independent
- Individual
- Inclusive

Wellington College Bangkok is open to students aged 2 to 18. Children are welcome to join us in Pre-Nursery and stay until Year 13 when they will take A-Levels and move on to the world's best universities. We are absolutely focused on the individual child throughout. We work with parents to share the responsibility of guiding the children to academic, social and personal success. Every child is different, and every child will follow a different path. We find what is best for each child and we develop their passions and nurture their strengths. Whether a child is starting out on their first few phrases in Mandarin or preparing for Under 13 Basketball or taking IGCSE exams, they will be doing so the Wellington Way.

Our founding school has an exceptional academic record and we follow in their footsteps along with the other Wellington Schools globally. We teach the English National Curriculum from Early Years to IGCSE and A Level exams. The programme is enhanced to reflect Thai culture, to ensure an awareness of Thailand, of South East Asia, and of the Asian continent and its place in world history and politics. Our teachers are highly qualified and very experienced both in the UK and globally. They share a passion for teaching and for continuous professional development. They believe that learning is fun and that students should love every moment that they are in the classroom and beyond!

The learning spaces extend way beyond the walls of the classroom. Classrooms are linked to each other and set around collaborative learning and play spaces. The Junior School follows a journey from Pre-Nursery to Year 6 and the progression is marked not just in the change in spaces and the quality of the work on the walls but by the development of the students. They grow in confidence and ability until they are ready to progress to our amazing state-of-the-art Senior School.

Our Early Years have developed a wonderful reputation and a huge popularity in just four years. We are determined to give our children the very best start on their journey. The teachers and leaders care enormously about the welfare and development of the children as they make those important first steps.

We reassure our parents, we keep them abreast of their children's achievements and we work together in every way.

Our Senior School has a beautiful circular atrium around which sit classrooms, shared spaces and collaborative learning areas. It will grow upwards and eventually develop a second building as our IGCSE and A-Level cohorts grow.

Students also have the chance to take part in every sport they could wish for. Our swimming squads and golf squads are very successful, boasting international level stars in the making. Our football, netball and basketball teams take on schools within Bangkok and across Asia. And children run, jump, play and experiment with each and every game, sport, pastime – because it's fun.

We run scholarship programmes in Academics, Sport and Music allowing the school to offer a first-class education to all. Our scholars inspire each and every student. They make us all proud. But every child here is a star. Every student is a champion. And every single one of us is a Wellingtonian and proud to be one.

Ploen, a Year 7 student sums it up – "*I feel proud of myself, being at Wellington and I really like it here. The teachers are really kind and take time to get to know you. The learning environment is very good and really helps me understand every topic. My school is filled with fun and laughter. I feel so lucky to be here.*"

Wellspring Learning Community

(Founded 2007)

Al Mathaf, Main Street, Near National Museum, Beirut, Lebanon
Tel: +961 1 423 444
Email: admissions@wellspring.edu.lb
Website: www.wellspring.edu.lb
Head of School: Kathleen Battah

Appointed: September 2010
School type: Co-educational Day
Age range of pupils: 3–19 years
No. of pupils enrolled as at 01/09/2022: 748
Average class size: 18-24
Teacher/pupil ratio: 1:6

Wellspring Learning Community is the only English Language IB Continuum World School in Lebanon and it is the realization of a belief that children of Lebanon deserve to study in a high quality learning environment that opens up space for developing their talents and intellectual potential, as well as their capacity for caring about the world around them. Wellspring is a non-sectarian community with no political affiliations. Depending on availability, enrollment is open throughout the year. We welcome inquiries and visits from interested families.

Authorization/Accreditations

Wellspring is authorized for the IB Diploma, Middle Years Programme, and Primary Years Programme, Council of International Schools (CIS), New England Association of Schools and Colleges(NEASC). Wellspring is an IB Continuum World School.

Vision and Mission

Wellspring is an inquiry-based learning environment where students are given every opportunity to realize their social, emotional and academic capacities. Teachers, students and parents work collaboratively in an atmosphere of mutual respect and trust by sharing a positive learning environment that builds on ongoing processes of self-reflection, evidence-based decision making, and continual improvement. Our students will become confident, resourceful, creative, caring, responsible and thinking citizens, prepared to use their education to contribute in meaningful ways to improve society; locally and internationally.

Teachers

Our 148 faculty members are highly qualified and experienced teachers; many are native English speakers. In addition to being IB trained, many teachers hold additional positions within the IB Educator Network (IBEN).

Students

Wellspring has a large international population, with 51 countries represented across our two campuses, in addition to our local students who come from diverse backgrounds within Lebanon.

Facilities

We are proud to offer two campuses in the vibrant area of Beirut. Both environments are attractive, technologically advanced, and continuously upgraded to keep pace with the demands of the educational program. Facilities include music and art rooms, science labs, computer labs, cafeteria(CCC), libraries, play areas and roof top sports spaces.

Western International School of Shanghai (WISS)

Western International School of Shanghai
上海西华外籍人员子女学校

555 Lian Min Road, Xujing Town, Qing Pu District, Shanghai, 201702 China

Tel: +86 (21) 6976 1038/1060
Email: enquiry@wiss.cn
Website: www.wiss.cn
Head of School: Mr. David Edwards
School type: Co-educational Day

Age range of pupils: 2.5–17+ years
No. of pupils enrolled as at 01/09/2022: 750
Fees as at 01/09/2022:
Day: ¥170,500–¥275,600
Early Bird Rate: ¥61,975 – ¥261,820

The Western International School of Shanghai (WISS) is a leading international school with a 15-year history of excellence in education.

WISS is unique in that it's the only international school in Mainland China that offers all four IB Programmes of education. These continuums of programmes extend across Primary Years (PYP) (which includes Early Years), Middle Years (MYP), IB Diploma Programme (IBDP), and Career-related Programme (CP). The Career-related Programme offers four pathways in Aeronautics, Art & Design, Business & Sustainability, and Sports. These continuums of programmes allow us to broaden the minds of the children in our care through innovative, high-quality, inquiry-based learning and teaching.

The WISS Education facilitates individualized pathways that empower students to become lifelong learners and develop into Global Citizens. Our school is committed to delivering an international, student-centered, and holistic learning experience. Through an inquiry and concepts-based approach to teaching and learning, students at WISS acquire the knowledge and skills for success in the 21st Century and future workplace.

WISS expertly blends academic rigor with the creative arts through our visual arts, music, performing arts programs, and athletics to create a dynamic and holistic learning environment where our students can flourish. As an international school, we believe our students' learning experience should reflect the globally-minded, diverse, and technological world we live in. We nurture our students to think independently and drive their own learning following the IB philosophy.

WISS is also home to a diverse student community of over 45 nationalities, creating a vibrant learning environment in which students explore challenging aspects of the world around them. Our school offers a truly international learning environment while still fostering an appreciation and respect for our host country through our distinguished Chinese language program and the relationships we grow with our local community through active engagement.

We are dedicated to encouraging excellence amongst our students. We, therefore, offer students in Secondary a range of scholarship opportunities that recognize and reward their unique talents, dedication to learning, and academic performance.

The Western International School of Shanghai (WISS) offers studen ts one of the largest international school campuses in Shanghai. The premium features include modern Early Years, Primary and Secondary facilities spanning over 18 acres of lush green campus grounds. The contemporary campus features open plan, bright classrooms equipped with air purification units, three well-resourced libraries, a large cafeteria, two cafes, and a multi-function community room.

In addition, students have access to state-of-the-art science and technology labs equipped with 3D printers, laser cutters, and advanced hardware and software for design. The Da Vinci Innovation Space host robotics and engineering programs for students. The creative arts program offers spacious art studios, a black box classroom theatre, the Orsini Theatre, and cutting-edge music studios. Sports facilities include grass and Astroturf football fields, a running track, basketball courts, a gymnasium equipped with a rock-climbing wall, and two swimming pools.

WISS offers a vibrant array of extra-curricular activities and is home to world-class academies, such as the ISTA Performing Arts Academy and the Stoke City FC Football Academy. The school offers unique opportunities to develop leadership through our partnerships with the Global Alliance for Innovative Learning (GAIL), the Duke of Edinburgh's International Award, and Model United Nations. Adding to the quality and experience of the WISS Education are our memberships with the China International School Sports Association (CISSA), Shanghai Schools Sports Association (SSSA), Shanghai International Schools Athletic Conference (SISAC), and the Association of China and Mongolia International Schools (ACAMIS).

Conveniently located in New Hongqiao, WISS is nestled amongst green residential spaces, with easy access to all major commercial and tourist areas.

International schools in Australasia

Schools ordered A–Z by Name

Carey Baptist Grammar School

(Founded 1923)

349 Barkers Road, Kew, VIC 3101 Australia
Tel: +61 3 9816 1222
Email: admissions@carey.com.au
Website: www.carey.com.au
Principal:
Mr Jonathan Walter BA, DipEd, MA
Appointed: January 2020

School type: Co-educational Day
Religious Denomination: Baptist
Age range of pupils: 3–18 years
No. of pupils enrolled as at 01/09/2022: 2681
Fees as at 01/09/2022:
Day (Local): $21,992 – $34,044
Day (International): $39,290 – $40,398

In our complex and ever-changing world, it's clear that today's young people will be faced with a unique set of challenges in the future. To meet these challenges, students must be able to leverage their strengths and follow their passions, whether they be academics, creators, innovators or athletes. At Carey Baptist Grammar School, we believe in adopting a broader expression of success and allowing students to fulfil their ambitions and use their strengths to contribute to the wider world.

Carey is an inclusive and diverse community. We strongly believe that co-education is a vital part of helping our students to develop who they are from an early age and are proud that our school maintains an even gender balance. By encouraging children to work effectively and respectfully with a diverse group of people, we enable them to embrace differences and to learn to understand and empathise with others.

Our award-winning wellbeing program underpins all our activities at Carey. Through nurturing student wellbeing and supporting their individual interests, we foster an environment that allows them to achieve their best while also developing individuals with integrity, resilience and a social conscience.

Recruiting and developing highly professional teaching and support staff is one of our greatest priorities. Carey is known for being innovative, progressive and leading the way in best practice teaching and learning, supporting strong academic results and personal development for each student. The Senior School offers both IB and VCE and cultivates a dynamic and stimulating environment. Our students achieve university entrance scores that place Carey among the top schools in Victoria.

Carey students are curious, aspirational and engaged global citizens. We build on their individual qualities to develop young women and men who flourish and can lead and serve with courage, compassion and intelligence.

We welcome the cultural diversity that international students bring to our community.

For more information, visit www.carey.com.au or contact our Admissions Manager on +61 3 9816 1242 or admissions@carey.com.au

St Andrew's Cathedral School

ST ANDREW'S
CATHEDRAL SCHOOL

(Founded 1885)

Sydney Square, Sydney,
NSW 2000 Australia
Tel: +61 2 9286 9500
Email: enrolments@sacs.nsw.edu.au
Website: www.sacs.nsw.edu.au
Head of School: Dr Julie McGonigle

School type: Co-educational Day
Religious Denomination: Anglican
Age range of pupils: 5–18 years
No. of pupils enrolled as at 01/09/2022: 1450
Fees as at 01/09/2022:
Day: AUS$21,264–AUS$37,278

Founded in 1885, St Andrew's Cathedral School is a coeducational, independent Anglican school, located in the heart of Sydney's CBD. Reflecting our Christian foundations, we are a strong and hopeful learning community that nurtures the individual strengths of each student in our care.

With a long history – we were originally founded as a Choral School in 1885 – we are known for our outstanding performing arts program with 25 music ensembles, including our outstanding Cathedral choristers. With extensive sporting and co-curricular opportunities – from fencing, theatre sports, debating, dance and drama – we also have an outstanding outdoor education program based at our property, Kirrikee, in the NSW Southern Highlands.

As an International Baccalaureate (IB) World School, our middle school students are taught the NSW school curriculum through the IB Middle Years framework and Senior College students can choose to study either the HSC or the International Baccalaureate (IB) Diploma.

We are the quintessential city school, located in two high-rise buildings in the centre of Sydney's CBD, enriching our curriculum with city experiences, all on our doorstep. Our buildings are purposefully designed, light filled learning spaces for Junior School, Middle School and a dedicated pre-tertiary environment for Senior College.

Our school within a school, Gawura, is a highly regarded model, noted for its innovative approach to a First Nations-led education within a mainstream system and was named 2020 Australian School of the Year.

Our teachers are experts in their chosen fields who very much enjoy the relational nature of teaching and who engage in the character development of each child, both within and outside the classroom. They are also passionate about developing their practice and benefit from a progressive professional learning program. Many of our teachers are invited to present at state and national educational conferences and professional associations, and as an educational leader, we hold conferences, host international experts and encourage thought leadership.

See how we teach character and curriculum. Visit www.sacs.nsw.edu.au

International schools in Europe

Schools ordered A–Z by Name

Academia Schools

Locations: Basel, Küsnacht, Winterthur and Zurich, Switzerland
Tel: +41 61 260 20 80
Email: info@academia-group.ch
Website: www.academia-schools.ch

Co-CEOs Academia Schools: Ludovic Allenspach, Roman Meier & Peter Petrin
School type: Co-educational Day
Age range of pupils: 3–18 years

Forever Learning

Academia Schools supports people from kindergarten through to the end of secondary school and beyond. We assist children, young people and adults with their individual learning processes and do all we can to help them achieve their goals. All of our schools foster a respectful, informal, open atmosphere, as we are convinced that this creates the best learning environment for our students.

About us

Around 600 students currently attend our six schools in ten locations in Switzerland. They are taught by over 150 members of teaching staff from different backgrounds and supported in achieving their educational goals. We are all united in our willingness to keep learning new things, to engage openly with one another and do our best to achieve the set objectives – both our own and those of our students.

Naturally bilingual.
Academia Bilingual School

We support your child to develop and achieve his or her full potential from kindergarten to the end of secondary school. Our pupils enjoy an attentive and respectful environment, small classes, bilingual teaching in German and English by mother-tongue trained teachers as well as personal support which provides the foundation for your child's further education – be it in Switzerland or abroad.

What is unique about us

Bilingual kindergarten, primary and secondary schools in Basel, Küsnacht and Winterthur.

- Strength-based lessons
- Focus on personal development of the child
- Experienced qualified native-speaking teachers
- Transparent and open communication culture

More information

www.academia-bilingual.ch

Holistic, personal, small by design.
Academia International School

We are an international school, small by design, where your child will not get lost in the crowd. We follow the British International Curriculum (Pre-IGCSE, IGCSE and A Levels) which focuses on the individual strengths of each student. We are a multi-cultural, city centre school that aims to provide academic excellence in a cosy, caring environment.

What is unique about us

Ideal preparation for studying at universities in Switzerland and around the world.

- Building on individual strengths with a broad range of subjects to choose from
- Holistic approach with innovative teaching and learning
- Outstanding team of highly qualified subject specialist teachers
- Familiar schools in the heart of Basel and Zurich.

More information

www.academia-international.ch

accadis International School Bad Homburg

accadis International School

(Founded 2004)

SÜDCAMPUS Bad Homburg, Am Weidenring 52-54, 61352 Bad Homburg, Hesse, Germany
Tel: +49 61 72 984 141
Email: info@accadis-isb.com
Website: www.accadis-isb.com
Head of School: Ms Janina Sparks

School type: Co-educational Day
Age range of pupils: 2–18 years
No. of pupils enrolled as at 01/09/2022: 600
Fees as at 01/09/2022:
Preschool: €3,360 – €4,560
Elementary School: €8,220 – €9,600
Secondary School: €11,280 – €17,280

Our mission

accadis ISB aims to develop confident, knowledgeable and caring young people prepared to create a better future. We aim to build within each child a sense of responsibility, a love for learning, self-discipline, and respect for others. Challenging programs, combined with inter-cultural understanding and respect, enable our students to reach their potential and become compassionate and lifelong learners.

Who we are

accadis ISB is situated in Bad Homburg, a leafy town in the Taunus mountains, just north of Frankfurt am Main. We are a non for profit, lively, friendly and expanding bilingual co-ed school which currently has approximately 600 students from 2-18 years of age, representing over 50 nationalities. Privately owned, it is part of a family business with links to the nearby accadis University of Applied Sciences. The school has a bilingual concept, teaching some subjects in English and some in German. accadis ISB is an official IB World School since January 2016. accadis ISB is also accredited by Cambridge Assessment International Education to teach the two year IGCSE course in Grades 9 and 10.

Our students

The school provides a supportive and challenging environment where students are encouraged to become responsible and independent learners. accadis ISB caters for a wide range of students, and is both a "local" school for families who live nearby and also an international school for students who come to us from all over the world.

Our school

accadis ISB was founded in 2004 and is situated on a state-of-the-art campus featuring its own sports hall with outdoor football pitch. Over the course of the last years, the school expanded into an adjacent building, adding an inviting library, two Art rooms, an IB Learning Suite reserved for students in Grades 11 and 12, a Drama room with stage equipment as well as further teaching rooms, providing more space for the growing Elementary and Secondary Schools. In the school year 2022-2023 accadis ISB is opening a new building exclusively for Secondary School students, catering for the ever-increasing demand. It features more than 20 new classrooms, additional specialist spaces for Science, Art, Music and Drama as well as two libraries, a Cafeteria and an auditorium for up to 250 people.

The school focuses strongly on technology. The state-of-the-art learning environment includes Smartboards in each classroom, Google Chromebook laptops, school-wide high-speed Wi-Fi and a 3D printer.

Agora Andorra International School

(Founded 1999)

Carrer del Serrat del Camp 14,
AD400 La Massana, Andorra
Tel: +376 838 366
Email: admissions@agorainternationalandorra.com
Website: www.agorainternationalandorra.com

Head of School: Mrs. Clara Pintat Rossell
School type: Co-educational Day & Boarding
No. of pupils enrolled as at 01/09/2022: 370
Average class size: 20

Agora Andorra International School is a private school located in the heart of the Pyrenees. Our principal objective is to educate our students to be multilingual, responsible, ethical and capable young people, with the motivation to succeed in all areas of their lives. Our school offers full linguistic immersion and excellent educational standards, and we are authorised to teach the prestigious International Baccalaureate (IB) Diploma Programme (DP) at Post 16 level. Moreover, we have excellent boarding facilities for international students

Agora Andorra International School is a private school member of the Globeducate group which owns and operates more than 55 schools worldwide. The school is noted for its innovative curriculum and international outlook, focussing on full immersion in various languages and achieving excellent academic standards. We have first-rate boarding facilities allowing us to welcome children from all over the world. Our three working languages are English, Spanish and French, with classes in Catalan, Andorra's official language. Our students can obtain the International Baccalaureate (IB) Diploma Programme (DP), a prestigious degree recognized by the world's leading universities.

Location

Agora Andorra International School is located in the village of l'Aldosa (La Massana) at just 10 minutes from ski slopes. The school site offers good sports facilities, social and recreational activities, swimming pool, dance study, and art and music room.

Our international boarding house enables students from all over the world to study at Agora Andorra International School and comprises a three-storey building accommodating 50 students. Boarders share rooms and the house incorporates two communal/recreational areas, a dining room, a study and all the services necessary to make our residential students' lives happy and comfortable.

Foreign languages

Spanish (ELE) English (EAL) Catalan and French

IB World School

Agora Andorra International School is authorised to teach the International Baccalaureate® (IB) Diploma Programme (DP) at Post 16 level. As an IB World School, we have created a learning environment that is pro-active, innovative and reflective and we are constantly striving to improve; our mission is to educate young people who are able to shape the world.

Agora Barcelona International School

Agora Barcelona International School
Shaping the world

(Founded 2008)

Carrer Puig de Mira, Sant Esteve Sesrovires, 08635 Barcelona, Catalonia, Spain
Tel: +34 93 779 89 28
Email: admissions@agoraisbarcelona.edu.es

Website: www.colegioagorabarcelona.com
Headmaster: Mr. Xavi Martín
School type: Co-educational Day
No. of pupils enrolled as at 01/09/2022: 470
Average class size: 18

Agora Barcelona International School stands for an innovative educational programme, excellent academic performance, and individualized attention. From Preschool onwards our students follow an enriched curriculum based on the Spanish model, with special emphasis on linguistic competence and particular attention to the arts, music, and sport.

Agora Barcelona International School is a private school, member of the Globeducate group which owns and operates more than 55 schools worldwide. The school is in Sant Esteve Sesrovires, 35 kilometers away from Barcelona city. We provide an all-round and international educational experience; a tri-lingual approach, diverse in character with a strong underlying value system catering to our students' individual needs as well as to the school community.

Our language policy involves immersion in different languages and our senior students work towards either the National Spanish Baccalaureate, the International Baccalaureate (IB) or a dual award Vocational Training with preparation to official certifications in English. Our aim is to encourage in our pupils a passion for excellence, social commitment, and critical thinking, helping them to achieve both academic and personal success.

Location

The facilities are built to suit the requirements of each stage of the curriculum. The school site accommodates classrooms, libraries, laboratories, and a fully equipped Sports Centre that incorporates two football pitches, basketball, handball, tennis and paddle tennis courts and a 25-metre indoor swimming pool. Our school is affiliated with Barcelona's renowned music centre, "Conservatori Liceu", which enables our students to experience performing in the Liceu's Concert Hall.

Foreign languages

English, German and French.

IB PROGRAM World School

Agora Barcelona International School is authorized to teach the International Baccalaureate Diploma Programme (DP) at Post 16 level. As an IB PROGRAM School, we have created a learning environment that is pro-active, innovative, and reflective and we are constantly striving to improve; our mission is to educate young people who are able to shape the world.

Agora Lledó International School

(Founded 1989)

Camino Caminàs, 175, Castelló de la Plana, 12003 Castelló, Valencia, Spain
Tel: +34 964 72 31 70
Email: admissions@lledo.edu.es
Website: www.colegioagoralledo.com

Headmaster: Mr. Luis Madrid
School type: Co-educational Day
No. of pupils enrolled as at 01/09/2022: 800
Average class size: 20

Agora Lledó International School is a private school in Castellón which places great importance on innovation, giving an all-round education and providing personalised attention for each of its pupils. The school is an official music conservatory as well as a sports centre and in 2011 it became the first school in Castellón to offer International Baccalaureate. Next year we will finalise the PYP accreditation and start the MYP accreditation to complete the IB continuum.

Agora Lledó International School is part of the Globeducate international group of schools and meets the most demanding standards of education which owns and operates more than 55 schools worldwide. We have a 100% pass rate in University Entrance Exams and we provide an international education that focuses on our globalised world, with a special emphasis on a value-based education.

In addition to a language immersion programme with a wide range of foreign languages, we offer Spanish Baccalaureate and International Baccalaureate as well as comprehensive art, music and sports programmes. The objective of our school is to awaken the students' desire to discover the world and help them to attain academic and personal success.

Location

The School is located in some wonderful natural surroundings full of orange groves and 200 metres from the neoclassical Lledó Basilica. Our wide-open spaces are one of the keys to our educational project, which gives importance to learning through living. In addition, the school is an official music conservatory as well as a sports centre with facilities that adapt to every sporting need, such as a semi-olympic swimming pool, basketball and tennis courts, two outdoor artificial turf football pitches and one indoor pitch. Thanks to these facilities Agora Lledó International School excels in sports and takes part in gymnastics, swimming and football competitions on a national level.

Foreign languages

English, German, French, Chinese

IB World School

Agora Lledó International School is authorised to teach the International Baccalaureate (IB) Diploma Programme (DP) at Post 16 level. With academic results that place it No. 1 in Spain and 5th in Europe over the last five years.

Agora Madrid International School

(Founded 1981)

Calle Duero, 35, Villaviciosa de Odón,
28670 Madrid, Spain
Tel: +34 91 616 71 25
Email: admissions@agoraism.com
Website: www.colegioagoramadrid.com

Headmaster: Mr. Luis Madrid
School type: Co-educational Day
No. of pupils enrolled as at 01/09/2022: 500
Average class size: 20

Agora Madrid International School is a private, bilingual international school in Madrid. Our curriculum is designed to facilitate an English linguistic immersion and extends from Kindergarten to Pre-University. We focus on achieving educational excellence via an enriched curriculum tailored to meet the specific needs and requirements of each of our students.

Agora Madrid International School forms part of the highly renowned education group, Globeducate that owns and operates more than 55 schools worldwide. The school has been known as a hub for the creative arts, incorporating violin and Performing Arts as curricular subjects from Primary, offering the International Baccalaureate specialized in Performing Arts, unique in Spain, and integrating an official Conservatoire.

Our senior pupils work towards the Spanish National and International Baccalaureates and we have a 100% pass rate for the Spanish University Entrance Examinations. The school offers a broad and balanced curriculum, with a particular emphasis on co-curricular subjects such as Music, Sports and Arts, designed to help each of our students achieve their full academic and personal potential.

Location

Agora Madrid International School is located in the beautiful El Bosque estate in Villaviciosa de Odón to the west of Madrid, in a quiet residential area surrounded by trees and with views towards the mountains. Our excellent facilities are purpose-built to provide for the changing needs of our students at each stage of their education and are designed to create a calm and positive environment for both study and recreation.

Agora International School Madrid has great sporting facilities, including an AstroTurf soccer pitch, a gymnasium and a fully equipped sports centre with basketball, handball, volleyball and tennis courts.

Foreign languages

English, German, French, Chinese

IB World School

Agora Madrid International School is authorized to teach the International Baccalaureate (IB) Diploma Programme (DP) at Post 16 level. As an IB World School, we have created a learning environment that is pro-active, innovative, and reflective and we are constantly striving to improve; our mission is to educate young people who are able to shape the world.

Agora Portals International School

Agora Portals International School
Shaping the world

(Founded 2008)

Carretera Vella Palma-Andratx, s/n,
Portals Nous, 07181 Mallorca, Balearic Islands, Spain
Tel: +34 964 72 31 70
Email: admissions@agoraportals.edu.es

Website: www.colegioagoraportals.com
Headmaster: Mr. Rafael Barea
School type: Co-educational Day
No. of pupils enrolled as at 01/09/2022: 1000
Average class size: 22

Agora Portals International School is a private international school in Majorca member of the Globeducate group which owns and operates more than 55 schools worldwide. We focus on achieving academic excellence, delivering a broad and balanced curriculum and meeting the individual needs of each student under our care. The school incorporates an official Music Academy and, in 2011, Agora Portals International School became the first school in the Balearic Isles to offer the International Baccalaureate to senior school students.

Agora Portals is located on the island of Majorca at Portals Nous in Calvià, and forms part of the highly respected education group, Globeducate. Our mission is to provide our students with an outstanding academic education along with a strong ethical foundation, and our curriculum is designed to facilitate linguistic immersion, particularly in English and Spanish.

Our senior students can study for both the Spanish National and the International Baccalaureates and we have a 100% pass rate for both the Spanish University Entrance Examinations and the IB Diploma. We offer full programmes in Music, Sports and the Arts and aim to equip each of our students with the academic and personal skills that they need to become confident and responsible citizens of the world.

With the aim of transmitting to students the value of preserving the seas and oceans, we have created the Aula del Mar, a project within the Agora Posidonia Experience. A unique project in the Balearic Islands and a pioneer in Spain.

Location

Agora Portals International School is situated so close to the sea and surrounded by nature, our students are lucky to be able to study in a calm, focused and positive working environment, with all the facilities and resources that they need to succeed at every stage of their education.

We have an official Music Academy on site and excellent, purpose-built sporting facilities, including outdoor courts and pitches, a fully equipped indoor sports centre and indoor swimming pool.

Foreign languages

English, German, French, Chinese

IB World School

Agora Portals International School, after 10 years of implementing the IB Diploma programme, started teaching the IB methodology from the age of 3 (the Primary Years Programme) from September 2021.

Agora Portals is listed in he top 50 schools in Spain by FORBES and the unique in the Balearic Islands.

Agora Sant Cugat International School

Agora Sant Cugat International School
Shaping the world

(Founded 1989)

Carrer Ferrer i Guàrdia, s/n, Sant Cugat del Vallés, 08174 Barcelona, Catalonia, Spain
Tel: +34 93 590 26 00
Email: ruth.sale@agorasantcugat.edu.es
Website: www.colegioagorasantcugat.es

Headmaster: Mr. Vicenç Gandol
School type: Co-educational Day
Age range of pupils: 1–18 years
No. of pupils enrolled as at 01/09/2022: 1850
Average class size: 24

Agora Sant Cugat International School is ranked among Spain's top ten schools. It is a private school and a member of the Globeducate Group which owns and operates more than 55 schools worldwide. Founded in 1989, it has become a prestigious private international school where teaching methods are innovative and every student from Infant P0 to Baccalaureate receives a personalised attention.

ASCIS is one of the few schools in Spain authorised to teach the International Baccalaureate Continuum at all levels.

The education is multilingual with English, Catalan and Spanish as the working languages and also offers Mandarin Chinese, French and German.

Teaching is mixed, plural and open and promotes respect for the beliefs of others in an atmosphere of dialogue and tolerance. ASCIS provides its students with the necessary tools for them to build their own learning by not only focusing on academic success but also on personal development and promoting healthy habits to achieve an all-round excellent physical, mental and emotional health and well-being.

This includes a very wide sporting offer, promoting arts and music, disciplines which provide them with key values such as perseverance, teamwork and self-improvement and a healthy meal programme designed by our nutrition specialists and School Chef.

Location

ASCIS Campus is located on the outskirts of Sant Cugat in natural surroundings.

Made up for several buildings, Agora Sant Cugat (Infant P1 to Baccalaureate in Can Sant Joan), Agora Patufet (Infant P0 to P5 in the centre of Sant Cugat) and Agora Pipo (Infant P0 to P2 in Volpelleres); offers a school bus service & all three buildings have train stations nearby on the FGC trainline.

ASCIS has purpose-built classrooms, science laboratories, libraries, dining rooms and kitchens and a sports area that has a full-size football pitch, two tennis padel courts and four multi-purpose courts. The School also has the latest technical equipment needed for its Vocational Training programme as well as the Josep Carreras Auditorium that seats 360 people.

Foreign Languages

English, German, French and Chinese with Spanish and Catalan taught as a foreign language for international students.

IB World School

ASCIS has implemented the International Baccalaureate Programme since 2012 and Vocational Training courses since 2016.

ASCIS is authorised to teach the International Baccalaureate (IB Continuum): Diploma Programme (DP) at Post-16 level and is one of the few schools in Spain authorised to teach the IB Primary Years Programme (PYP) and the Middle Years Programme (MYP). As an IB World School, it has created a learning environment that is pro-active, innovative and reflective and is constantly striving to improve. Its mission is to educate young people able to shape the world.

AMADEUS International School Vienna

AMADEUS
International School Vienna

(Founded 2012)

Bastiengasse 36-38, 1180 Vienna, Austria

Tel: +43 1 470 30 37 00

Email: admissions@amadeus-vienna.com

Website: www.amadeus-vienna.com

Head of School: Jeremy House

Head of Primary: Maki Nishihara

Head of Secondary: Karsten Plöger

Head of Boarding: Graham Malkin

School type:

Co-educational Day & Boarding

Age range of pupils: 3–18 years

No. of pupils enrolled as at 01/09/2022: 350

Fees as at 01/09/2022:

Day: €13,295–€29,905

Full Boarding: €46,880–€52,350

AMADEUS International School Vienna is a unique day and boarding IB World School with an integrated Music and Arts Academy. Some of the AMADEUS highlights include:

- We are in Vienna, the heart of music and culture in Europe and the 'most liveable city in the world'.
- We offer an Arts inspired curriculum, and believe that music and the arts cultivate learning.
- We are an International Baccalaureate (IB) Continuum School with Grades 1–12 (EY, PYP, MYP, DP).
- We offer the IB Career-related Programme. This is the perfect pathway for aspiring professional musicians that enables them to balance their practice and academics.
- We offer boarding in fully renovated historical buildings (since 2021).
- We are a small community based on the values happiness, kindness and imagination.

The AMADEUS experience:

We stand for 'Educational Distinction'. This is represented by seven pillars in our logo and it is through these that we accompany young people as they fulfil their highest potential.

1. Intellect:

Learning at AMADEUS is inquiry-based. It addresses real-life challenges and cultivates critical-thinking, problem-solving, and presentation skills. We provide our students with the technical scaffolding that will enable them to master fundamental knowledge and skills, whilst nurturing the confidence to have agency in one's world and put these to the test. We teach students how to think and learn, not what to think and learn.

2. Inclusivity:

The AMADEUS community is distinguished by its internationalism. We represent around 50 different nationalities and foster the development of global citizenship, cultural understanding and diplomacy.

3. Music:

We believe that education in Music and the Arts contributes to the development of well-rounded, creative and confident individuals while promoting engagement, teamwork and cultural awareness. AMADEUS Music and Arts Academy (AMAA) allows students at different levels to develop their interests and explore their talents in the areas of music, visual arts, theatre and dance.

4. Languages:

Development of language and communication skills in two or more languages is a key feature of the AMADEUS education. Our language of instruction is in English, yet we also focus on German as our host nation language. Chinese, Russian and Spanish classes are also available.

5. Vitality:

AMADEUS is a vibrant and healthy environment with fresh home-made food, lush green parks, spacious and light classrooms, and clean air. We believe that health and well being are the cornerstones for high-performance and leading a full life.

6. Virtue:

We take the approach of developing strengths rather than focusing on weaknesses. We engage students in programmes of mindfulness and emotional intelligence throughout the primary school and virtue ethics in the secondary school.

7. Aesthetic:

Students develop a quality foundation of skills in art, drama, and dance through the school's required core curriculum. This programme emphasises an exploratory learning, creativity and expression; whilst fostering students' appreciation of beauty, excellence, and wonderment.

Boarding at AMADEUS:
It is possible to become a full boarder starting in Grade 6. Boarding at AMADEUS provides students with a once in a lifetime educational experience. Together with the staff members we strive to make AMADEUS an incredible experience and major time of personal growth. The boarding experience at AMADEUS is fun and enriching. Our boarding students learn independence, leadership, and how to be part of an international community. Within the boarding programme there is something for everybody; our boarders have access to music practice rooms, academic mentoring, explorations of Vienna, sports training, and much more.

Since last year 2021 AMADEUS has a new fully renovated and exclusive Boarding House with capacity for 138 students. Currently, about 65 students (boys and girls) reside in separate sections and rooms are usually shared by two students and have a private en-suite bathroom as well as a study space.

Although boarding students live in gender-separated wings of the house, there are a number of common spaces. The cafeteria is located on the ground floor of Pfeiffer House, where students are served three warm and nutritious meals every day. On the third floor, we can find the Common Room, a comfortable and spacious social area for leisure, where students spend time relaxing and socializing. Next to the Common Room we find an audiovisual room and a music room, where students can watch films or sports on a big screen and play the piano.

About Vienna:
The AMADEUS campus is located in Vienna's 18th district, a green and distinguished residential neighborhood just a tram ride away from the city centre. Housed in a collection of fin de siècle structures, the school offers modern resources in a beautiful historic setting. Famous for its history, culture, and quality of life, the city of Vienna is both the federal capital and largest city in Austria, with a population of 1.9 million. Vienna is named "the World's Most Liveable City" by The Economist and "the World's greenest city" by Resonance, and most importantly: it is a safe city which affords our students the freedom they need to grow. With an artistic and intellectual history defined by famous residents such as Mozart, Beethoven, and Freud, Vienna lives up to its titles as the "City of Music" and "City of Dreams." The city centre is a designated UNESCO World Heritage Site, and Vienna's famed Imperial Palaces have long been a premier European tourist destination. Home to numerous high quality universities, Vienna is Austria's hub of international education and learning.

American International School Vienna

(Founded 1959)

Salmannsdorfer Strasse 47,
1190 Vienna, Austria
Tel: +43 1 401 32
Email: info@ais.at
Website: www.ais.at
Director: Kathy Miner DEd
School type: Co-educational Day
Age range of pupils: 4–18 years

No. of pupils enrolled as at 01/09/2022: 800
Fees as at 01/09/2022:
Pre-Kindergarten: €12,434
Kindergarten-Grade 5: €19,415
Grades 6-8: €21,543
Grades 9-10: €22,407
Grades 11-12: €22,739
Teacher/pupil ratio: 1:8

Set within the rich cultural context of Austria, the American International School Vienna is one of the top international schools in the country. Founded in 1959 and recently having celebrated its 60th Anniversary, AIS Vienna today serves around 800 students, representing more than 60 countries, from Pre-Kindergarten through Grade 12 (International Baccalaureate (IB) or American diploma). AIS Vienna's core values – respect, aspire, and achieve – ensure that students develop intellectually and interculturally while internalizing the commitment and leadership necessary in today's globally-minded world.

AIS Vienna provides comprehensive opportunities for learners from around the world. Our students succeed academically, as well as in athletics, music, and visual arts. A variety of activities, including class trips to mountain ranges and service-oriented community projects, allow students to practice commitment, leadership, and meaningful self-reflection. We maintain a broad set of offerings to help us serve our students and be true to our mission.

The tightly knit school community allows students to develop personal relationships with both highly qualified teachers and their peers. We maintain a culture of high expectations and close connection to the pulse of international education. Investments in the quality and skill of our staff are on-going, and recent enhancements to our facilities and technology resources are assuring our role as a vital partner and a leader in our city and region.

We welcome all to our community of learners; we work every day to assure learners understand the connections between learning and living. We make decisions based on the understanding that we are not only guiding children towards learning but building experiences and memories that will serve to inform futures not yet imagined. Our goal is to help each of our students define success in a nurturing environment that supports excellence. Ultimately, we prepare our students for the next step in their lives after AIS Vienna.

American Overseas School of Rome

(Founded 1947)

Via Cassia 811, 00189 Rome, Italy
Tel: +39 06 334 381
Email: admissions@aosr.org
Website: www.aosr.org/admissions
Head of School: Dr. Kristen DiMatteo
Appointed: July 2020

School type: Coeducational Day
Age range of pupils: 3–19
Fees as at 01/09/2022:
Pre-K3/4 – Kindergarten: €10,800 – €14,850
Grades 1 – 10: €17,680 – €23,800
Grades 11 – 13: €24,600 – €25,700

Established in 1947, the American Overseas School of Rome has a tradition of providing a rigorous and well-rounded American international education to Pre-K through Grade 12 students in a supportive environment. AOSR inspires a diverse student body to courageously meet the demands of a changing world through an engaging and creative curriculum. AOSR is committed to educating the whole child and encourages students to develop their skills as scholars, artists, and athletes.

AOSR is fully accredited by the Middle States Association of Colleges and Schools and was the first international school to be awarded MSA's prestigious International Credential, and is a member of RISA, CIS, and ECIS. AOSR is the only school in Rome to offer an extensive IB International Baccalaureate Diploma Programme and the AP Advanced Placement Program and was the first school in Italy to offer the Advanced Placement Program.

AOSR is truly an American international community and prides itself on its diverse student body that is made up of 575 students. One-third of students come from the United States, one third from Italy, and one third from 51 other countries. The perfect student-teacher ratio of approximately 12:1 allows for every AOSR student to be noticed and nurtured while engaging in a broad range of educational experiences. The global faculty is made up of 85 experienced educators who have taught at top international schools in over 50 countries. 75% of our teachers are native English speakers, and 75% hold advanced degrees.

Students benefit from a 6-acre campus with the most complete facilities of any international school in Rome. This includes a historic villa, an indoor performing arts space, outdoor tennis and basketball courts, a soccer field, an indoor gymnasium, brand new Design/Maker's Space and Technology Labs, a spacious cafeteria and outdoor covered dining space, an outdoor edible garden, and a Roman amphitheater. The AOSR campus provides the perfect space for students to engage in athletic and after-school activities programs or participate in clubs and organizations.

The diverse selection of challenging coursework, flexible academic pathways, personal attention in small classes, and commitment to athletics, technology, performing arts, and other extracurricular activities, provide a perfect platform for AOSR students to thrive now and in the future.

American School of Milan

ASM AMERICAN SCHOOL OF MILAN

(Founded 1962)

Via K. Marx, 14, 20073 Noverasco di Opera (MI), Italy
Tel: +39 02 5300 0015
Email: admissions@asmilan.org
Website: www.asmilan.org
Director: Wayne Rutherford

School type: Co-educational Day
Age range of pupils: 3–18 years
No. of pupils enrolled as at 01/09/2022: 840
Fees as at 01/09/2022:
Day: €10,800–€20,300

The American School of Milan (ASM) is an independent, co-educational college preparatory day school with a state-of-the-art campus located south of Milan.

Founded in 1962, ASM has been educating international students from more than 50 countries for more than 50 years. The school's mission is to provide a modern and rigorous education for international students to excel in the changing world of tomorrow. ASM is accredited through the Middle States Association of Colleges and Schools and is an IB World School offering the Diploma Programme since 1983.

ASM offers a student-centered, American-style education that encourages children to develop their full potential, achieve personal excellence and become global citizens committed to lifelong learning. We embrace the IB learner profile along with our school values of respect, curiosity, integrity, courage and kindness.

Technology is a key focus at ASM and an integral part of student learning. Our elementary school integrates Ipads to prepare students for the 1:1 laptop program that begins in Grade 6. The school also offers 3D design, robotics, digital art & photography and film courses in our ultramodern film studio. There is wifi, campus-wide.

Set in 9 acres of green space, our modern campus boasts many state-of-the-art science laboratories, two full-sized American gymnasia, a tennis court, a soccer field covered with grass, and a 30,000 volume library complete with e-books, not to mention a 500-seat auditorium constructed in 2019.

Currently, we have over 800 students and there are more than 100 full-time faculty employed. ASM teachers are talented, highly educated, experienced and above all, inspiring leaders. The school encourages faculty continued learning through a substantial professional growth fund.

Students are also awarded the American School High School Diploma upon graduation. ASM student IB results have consistently surpassed world averages in terms of pass rate and average points.

American School of The Hague

(Founded 1953)
Rijksstraatweg 200, 2241 BX Wassenaar, Netherlands
Tel: +31 70 512 1060
Email: admissions@ash.nl
Website: www.ash.nl

Director: J. Courtney Lowe , Ed.D.
School type: Co-educational Day
Age range of pupils: 3–18 years
No. of pupils enrolled as at 01/09/2022: 1120
Fees as at 01/09/2022:
€15,275 – €23,865

Who we are:
ASH (est.1953) is one of the most established international schools in the Netherlands. ASH families hail from more than 70 countries on 6 continents, mirroring the diversity of cultures that make The Hague, known as the City of Peace and Justice, such a rich environment. We are a private, not-for-profit institution that, at every level of organization, focuses on enhancing the student learning experience. It shows in the purpose-built ASH facilities, like our Early Childhood Center, a vibrant and joyous learning environment designed to harness inquiry and play.

From Pre-Kindergarten through High School graduation, we encourage ASH students to take control of their own learning. We know that our students will be working in jobs that may not even exist yet, so we aim to nurture confidence and agility in any stage of the learning journey here at ASH. ASH is the only school in the Netherlands offering both AP and IB, creating a pathway to graduation based on their individual passions and talents. Our students consistently outperform global averages, and supported by our dedicated College Counseling Office, they find their ways into esteemed institutions of higher education across the globe. Our graduated Class of 2021 received offers from top colleges around the world.

Only at ASH, you will find a full-inclusion program of learning support, supporting every student with great intentionality to meet their emotional, social, physical, and academic needs. American School of The Hague is accredited by the rigorous and independent New England Association of Schools and Colleges (NEASC).

What ASH students and faculty say:
"Being a critical thinker means to use your thinking process and be aware of the different aspects that make you think a certain way. And then apply that thinking process in a real-life situation, and ask yourself questions about what's happening in the world." – Lucille, student

"I chose to take the IB curriculum because it offers me many opportunities, which is important to me. I know that I want to pursue a career in Technology, but if I change my mind, I believe the curriculum will help me recognize my talents." – Vaibhav, student

"Our programs open up doors to universities around the world. Our role as counselors is to help students find the best fit and the best options for themselves. At ASH, this means in-depth course selection. We're here to guide students in making these decisions." – Ms. Elizabeth, Counselor

Follow the #ASHexperience on social media
Facebook: @AmericanSchoolTheHague
Instagram: @AmericanSchoolTheHague
LinkedIn: @AmericanSchoolTheHague
Twitter: @AmSchoolHague

Applying to ASH:
Please go to www.ash.nl/join/admissions to apply and start your ASH journey today. Here, you will find information about our curriculum, grade levels, tuition and fees, and more.

BEPS International School

(Founded 1972)

Avenue Franklin Roosevelt 21-23, Ixelles,
1050 Brussels, Belgium
Tel: +32 2 648 43 11
Email: admissions@beps.com
Website: www.beps.com
School Director: Pascale Hertay

Finance & Administration Director: Charlotte Van Brussel
School type: Co-educational Day
Age range of pupils: 2.5–18 years
No. of pupils enrolled as at 01/09/2022: 280
Fees as at 01/09/2022: Please see website

Established in 1972, BEPS International School is situated in beautiful buildings in the heart of one of Brussels' most desirable areas, close to the Bois de la Cambre and the University (UL3).

The school offers an inquiry-based learning approach through the International Early Years Curriculum, the International Primary Curriculum, the Middle Years Programme, the IB Diploma Programme and the IB Career Related Programme from the International Baccalaureate® (IB).

In 2021, BEPS International School announced its expansion by acquiring the building attached to the BEPS Primary School campus. This allows the growing BEPS Secondary School to join the Early Years & Primary School at the same location where the BEPS adventure started in 1972. The transformation of the new building gives BEPS the opportunity to design spaces for innovative, authentic, and engaging learning which matches the BEPS approach to learning in the Middle and High School.

With the growth of the Secondary school, BEPS will cater for children between 2.5 – 18 years old. The school aims to achieve its full capacity of 450 students in the coming years.

Children learning English and children with learning needs receive additional support. French is taught as a second language from the Early Years and the development of the children's Mother Tongue is encouraged.

A wide range of After school clubs are available as well as a Garderie and holiday clubs. A door-to-door bus service also runs for most areas in Brussels.

Bilingual European School

Via Val Cismon 9, 20162 Milan, Italy
Tel: +39 02 6611 7449
Email: admissions@beschool.eu
Website: www.beschool.eu
Heads of School:
Mauro Spicci & John Nicholls

School type: Co-educational Day
Age range of pupils: 2–14 years
No. of pupils enrolled as at 01/09/2022: 545
Fees as at 01/09/2022:
Day: €10,650–€12,770

The British American Pre-School and the Bilingual European School prepare children aged 2 to 14 to be the travelers of the world, providing an outstanding educational journey that successfully lays the groundwork to meet the challenges of tomorrow, developing their natural talents both in English and Italian.

BAPS, founded in 1987, offers a full immersion English programme that combines the inquiry-based and child-centered educational philosophy with the Early Years Foundation Stage curriculum (for the first three age groups) and Key Stage One (for Reception children). BAPS full immersion English approach centred on the "play based learning" and the "learning by doing" provides children with the necessary knowledge and skills for a smooth transition to the BES bilingual programme.

BES, founded in 1999, integrates the Italian Ministerial programme with the Primary Years Programme (PYP) of the International Baccalaureate, offering bilingual education of excellence with a global perspective. At BES every student is a unique and special individual engaged in hands-on, minds-on learning activities in line with the constructivist approach.

The stimulating learning landscapes, designed by the internationally renowned architect Rosan Bosch, give students the opportunity to foster a life-long love of learning. The school hosts a permanent Bruno Munari® art laboratory and an accredited LEGO® Education Innovation Studio. BES is also recognised by Avanguardie Educative as a centre of excellence for educational innovation and in collaboration with Project Zero is committed to building the learning models of the future.

BAPS and BES proudly joined Globeducate in 2021, combining the group's forward-looking project with the school's unique model of cognitive integrated bilingualism, recognized by an international team of researchers from the Goethe University Frankfurt as a role model for bilingualism in Europe and all over the world.

Bordeaux International School

(Founded 1987)

252 Rue Judaïque, 33000 Bordeaux, France

Tel: +33 5 57870211

Email: contact@bis33.com

Website: www.bordeaux-school.com

Principals: Mrs Bergey & Mme Bidalun

Appointed: September 2021

School type: Co-educational Day

Religious Denomination: Non-denominational

Age range of pupils: 3–19 years

No. of pupils enrolled as at 01/09/2022: 180

Fees as at 01/09/2022:

Day: €3,890–€14,650

Average class size: 15

Teacher/pupil ratio: 1:16 (Primary) 1:15 (Middle School) 1:8 (Upper School)

Situated in the heart of the city, BIS has over 30 years experience in helping students achieve their full potential combining a bilingual education and an international learning environment. Our students are encouraged to become confident, lifelong learners, and to make a positive influence in the world.

Our school has grown and evolved over the years whilst retaining a maximum class size of 16, ensuring an opportunity to flourish in a multicultural setting of over 25 different nationalities.

BIS has been an accredited member of the Council of International Schools (CIS) since 2001, a mark of quality assurance for all. Early Learning and Primary, under contract with the French Education Nationale, enables students to follow a fully bilingual programme. Our Middle School follows both the Education Nationale and the Cambridge International Lower Secondary programme. In Upper Secondary, we offer internationally recognised Cambridge IGCSE and A Levels.

Our mission to encourage proactive, responsible global citizens means that we pay particular attention to support in academic study. Our experienced, multi-national teaching team provides active and differentiated learning where students work in a stimulating environment, challenging themselves to develop their full potential. Qualifications are internationally recognised and over 90% of students achieved grades A*-C this year, with 100% of leavers entering a university of their choice.

We also value our school community and its qualities of understanding, tolerance and respect for others. We also organise activities such as international theme weeks, school shows, book fairs, the International award and clubs including chess, robotics and music band. Regular cultural visits are scheduled and additional sports activities take place at local sites. Boarding with a French host family extends cultural immersion.

Our online platform ensures students and parents are accompanied, informed and supported throughout the year, guaranteeing successful remote learning and a seamless transition between online and in school lessons when required.

Cambridge House Community College

(Founded 1986)

Calle Profesorado Espanol 1, Santa Barbara, 46111 Rocafort, Valencia, Spain
Tel: +34 96 390 5019
Email: info@cambridgehouse.es
Website: www.cambridgehouse.es

Executive Head: Mr. Adam Hassoun
School type: Co-educational Day
No. of pupils enrolled as at 01/09/2022: 1700
Average class size: 25

Cambridge House is a private, secular, independent school located in Valencia. We follow the English National Curriculum while meeting all Spanish schooling requirements. Cambridge House was the first school in Spain to obtain both the BSO distinction (British School Overseas) and NABBS accreditation (National Association of British Schools in Spain), seals that guarantee the educational excellence of this school founded in 1986. At present it is considered one of the best schools in Spain. We joined Globeducate in September 2021, as part of the Globeducate British International Schools cluster.

We offer our students a system of learning designed to foster curiosity and confidence along with imparting all the necessary skills and knowledge required to succeed in exams and evaluations. Our curriculum is designed to facilitate understanding of the world and the challenges we face.

English is the vehicular language of our school, and total immersion is achieved from the first day of school, in Early Years, although it is complemented with Spanish and French classes as the students progress through the school year.

Our facilities

The students have access to specialised classrooms for the development of specific activities, such as an art room, theatre workshop, laboratories, cooking classroom and an outdoor space with sports machines for the older pupils. Located on the outskirts of Valencia, in the town of Rocafort and close to a quiet residential area, the school has beautiful landscaped areas, which encourage the respect for nature that permeates the school community. The school is easily accessible by private transport, with two car parks nearby.

Students as individuals

Educational achievement is key to our philosophy, but we think beyond pure academic success. The English National Curriculum encourages students to explore the world around them, be curious about how things work, ask questions, apply critical thinking skills, and respect fellow students and teachers alike. Teamwork and communication skills form a key foundation to all our educational programmes. Additionally, all students are encouraged to become socially, ethically and environmentally aware.

We aim to prepare students for life after school, teaching them skills that will help them to succeed in secondary school, further education and the workplace. Learning experiences also take place outside the classroom; assemblies, cultural events and fun educational trips provide further opportunities to learn and develop.

More than just a school

At Cambridge House learning is not always about lessons. We offer a wide range of extra-curricular activities to choose from, exchanges and a full programme of international events with other Globeducate schools. We also encourage Outdoor Learning and rely on a House System to foster collaboration between pupils of different ages, team spirit, leadership skills and a sense of pride in belonging to a strong and committed community.

Canadian School of Florence

Senior School: Via Jacopo Nardi 18, 50132 Florence, Italy
Junior School: Via delle Fontanelle 2-4, 50014 Fiesole, Italy
Tel: +39 055 098 2744
Email: info@csflorence.it
Website: www.csflorence.it

Head of School: Gary O'Meara
School type: Co-educational Day & Boarding
Fees as at 01/09/2022:
Day: €10,750–€18,500
Full Boarding: €39,000

The Canadian School of Florence, formerly Blyth Academy of Florence, is a co-educational private international school for children aged 3 to 18 years. The school opened its first campus in Florence in 2017 with the Senior School, followed in 2021 by the Preschool and Elementary School in Fiesole. The Middle School opens in 2022.

The school follows the Canadian Ontario curriculum and hosts a unique mix of international students and local Italian students. Small class size strengthens the inclusive approach to education, allowing each student to develop their sense of excellence, trust, integrity, fairness, and compassion.

The Preschool (Pre-K to K), Elementary (Grades 1 to 5), and Middle (Grades 6 to 8) school campus is located in Fiesole, less than 2km from the Florence campus. Its experiential learning program is based on the best curriculum from Canada (Ontario), with preparation, in Italian, for the Italian programme, and the use of Jolly Phonics in the Preschool.

The Senior School is hosted in a beautiful historical building in Florence, and currently hosts more than 100 students from Grade 9 to Grade 12, preparing them for admission to prestigious universities all over the world. A boarding service is available for students who live further afield in Italy or abroad.

The Canadian School of Florence provides an inclusive learning environment, with teachers and support staff who engage with students on both academic and emotional levels. Teachers provide personalized teaching and individual care together with empathetic engagement, hands-on experiential teaching that enables curiosity, creativity, and innovative thinking.

Students enjoy engaging field trips and excursions to enhance curriculum and a broad, balanced, and relevant globally respected Ontario curriculum with an Italian bridging program.

The Canadian School of Florence belongs to Globeducate, one of the world's leading premium K12 education organisations, with more than 50 schools located in Italy, France, Spain, United Kingdom, Portugal, Canada (Blyth Academy), Andorra, and India. A fundamental aim of Globeducate is preparing each student to shape the world and to understand their place in it as a global citizen. The bespoke gold standard school quality program ensures that Globeducate's 25,000 students have the best start in life.

Colegio San Patricio El Soto

Colegio San Patricio Madrid

(Founded 1958)

Calle Jazmin 148, El Soto de la Moraleja,
28109 Alcobendas, Madrid, Spain
Tel: +34 916 500 602
Email: infosoto@colegiosanpatricio.es

Website:
www.colegiosanpatriciomadrid.com
Headmaster: Mr. Borja Díaz
School type: Co-educational Day
Age range of pupils: 12–18 years

Colegio San Patricio is a coeducational day school which provides Spanish education and IB Diploma Programme for children from 18 months to 18 years old.

Trusted generation after generation since 1958, our curriculum embeds and continually innovates with proven pedagogical methodologies, in order to offer a unique and comprehensive educational model. In our three campuses in Madrid we nurture every child's individual passions and talents in order to ensure that they flourish.

Colegio San Patricio is considered as the Best School in Spain by El Mundo "100 Best schools in Spain" guide.

Colegio San Patricio has been ranked in the Top 5 among the best 50 schools in Spain according to Forbes Magazine.

San Patricio was founded in 1958. Since then, we have had the honour of educating generations of students.

Going to school at Colegio San Patricio means that you are part of more than just a school. You become part of the SanPa Family.

IB at Colegio San Patricio:
Our El Soto campus enjoys an unbeatable location in Soto de La Moraleja. Here, secondary cycles are taught after which students can choose between National Baccalaureate or International Baccalaureate. The school offers facilities specifically designed and built for children between the ages of 12 and 18 years and has a capacity for more than 800 students.

IB at San Patricio is more than simply a qualification, the IB Diploma provides a distinctive educational experience. It allows students to study a wide range of subjects throughout their final 2 years at school, while giving them the freedom to choose which subjects to study in greater depth.

IB students follow the Creativity, Activity, Service (CAS) programme, prepare an Extended Essay and take the Theory of Knowledge course.

2021 graduates enjoyed outstanding IB results, achieving a fantastic average grade of 36, the highest in the school's history.

Our school has achieved a 100% pass rate. 26% of our IB Diploma students have achieved more than 40 points, 34% have achieved more than 38 points and 46% above 36 points. The highest grade achieved so far was a very impressive 44.

Thanks to their outstanding results our students have been accepted by some of the best Universities in the world such as Imperial, Bath, UCL in the UK, and Georgetown and University of California in the USA.

Collège du Léman

COLLÈGE DU LÉMAN
International School · Geneva

(Founded 1960)

74, route de Sauverny,
1290 Versoix GE, Switzerland
Tel: +41 22 775 56 56
Email: admissions@cdl.ch
Website: www.cdl.ch
Director General: Mrs Pauline Nord
School type:
Co-educational Day & Boarding

Age range of pupils: 2–18 years
Fees as at 01/09/2022:
Day: CHF22,900–CHF35,900
Full Boarding: CHF85,490–CHF97,200
Average class size: 18
Teacher/pupil ratio: 1:9

Collège du Léman is a prestigious Swiss international day and boarding school for boys and girls 2 to 18 years old, dedicated to inspiring individual growth, academic excellence and global citizenship.

The school's green, village campus is a welcoming and beautiful place to learn, situated on the edge of Lake Geneva, with panoramic views of the Alps and just 20 minutes from Geneva and the international airport.

Students can follow English, French or Bilingual programmes of study. The school offers International and national curricula throughout. In high school students can choose to take the IGCSE, followed by a choice of the International Baccalaureate (Diploma or Careers Programmes), our American style High School Diploma (with Advanced Placement options), the Maturité Suisse or the Baccalauréat Français. Collège du Léman has a 99% diploma pass rate and the majority of students go on to leading universities around the world.

There are more than 110 different nationalities amongst the school's 1800 students, brought together by a strong 'RISE' values system: Respect, Internationalism, Team Spirit and Excellence. This helps to shape generations that harness differences, changing our world for the better.

As part of the Nord Anglia Education family of over 70 schools around the world, Collège du Léman benefits from world-leading teacher development, and one-of-a-kind collaborations with The Juilliard School of Performing Arts, MIT and UNICEF, building the skills students need to prepare for any future.

The school's commitment to global thinking and an individual approach help each student find their place in the world, allowing them to succeed anywhere, and to discover their true potential.

Collège Français Bilingue de Londres

87 Holmes Road, Kentish Town,
London NW5 3AX UK

Tel: 020 7993 7400
Email: info@cfbl.org.uk
Website: www.cfbl.org.uk
Head of School: Mr David Gassian
School type: Co-educational Day
Age range of pupils: 3–15 years

No. of pupils enrolled as at 01/09/2022: 700
Fees as at 01/09/2022:
Nursery, Reception & Year 1: £13,670
Years 2-6: £12,010
Years 7-10: £12,260

Established in 2011, Collège Français Bilingue de Londres provides French-English bilingual education to 700 pupils aged 3 to 15 years old – from Nursery to Year 10. Tolerance and openness are central to CFBL's philosophy and permeate our community comprising some 35 different nationalities.

CFBL is rated "Outstanding" by Ofsted (Office for Standards in Education). CFBL is the first French secondary school in the UK to be rated "Outstanding", and joins the ranks of the 15% of British private schools who have obtained this rating.

Safety, well-being and eagerness to discover new things are at the heart of the philosophy of our "home of learning". Trust is the core value of our educational project. Learning to become independent and open-minded is essential to our pupils' development into well-rounded adults.

Our pupils are nurtured in a welcoming environment where they can discover the joys of learning, supported by attentive teaching staff whose approach is based on mutual trust and respect.

Our pupils are encouraged to interact, be creative and take initiatives in our multicultural environment, in which they can acquire academic knowledge and also develop the human, relational qualities which will guide them through their years at school and beyond.

Coruña British International School (A Coruña)

(Founded 2015)
Rúa Roma 1, 15008 A Coruña,
Galicia, Spain
Tel: +34 981 28 67 99
Email: admissions@biscoruna.com

Website: www.biscoruna.com
Executive Head: Mr. Dominic Abbott
School type: Co-educational Day
No. of pupils enrolled as at 01/09/2022: 360
Average class size: 20

Coruña British International School is a private, secular independent school in A Coruña. We follow the English National Curriculum while meeting all Spanish schooling requirements. We are approved and accredited by both the Galician government and the British Council. Coruña British International School belongs to Globeducate British International Schools and has been part of the Globeducate prestigious network since 2017.

The education we offer our students is high quality and individualised, with dedicated attention for each student. We aim to develop each child's full academic and personal potential and encourage our students to be curious, creative, self-disciplined and independent.

Our school currently offers classes from Early Years up to Year 8 (equivalent to the Spanish ESO 1). We are progressively adding a new cohort each year until we offer the full range of schooling, from ages 3 to 18.

Our facilities

The school is located in the beautiful city of A Coruña, 10 minutes from the city centre with easy access by car. The school buildings and facilities are modern and designed with children in mind. In September 2023, the school is moving to its new, purpose-built campus in Culleredo to enable us to continue to provide the best facilities as the school grows.

Students as individuals

Educational achievement is key to our philosophy, but we think beyond pure academic success. The English National Curriculum encourages students to explore the world around them, be curious about how things work, ask questions, apply critical thinking skills, and respect fellow students and teachers alike.

Teamwork and communication skills form a key foundation to all our educational programmes. Additionally, all students are encouraged to become socially, ethically and environmentally aware.

We aim to prepare students for life after school, teaching them skills that will help them to succeed in secondary school, further education and the workplace. Learning experiences also take place outside the classroom; assemblies, cultural events and fun educational trips provide further opportunities to learn and develop.

More than just a school

Life at Coruña British International School is not always about lessons. We have more than 30 extra-curricular activities to choose, exchanges and a full programme of international events with other Globeducate schools. We also encourage Outdoor Learning and rely on a House System to foster collaboration between pupils of different ages, team spirit, leadership skills and a sense of pride in belonging to a strong and committed community.

Ecole d'Humanité

Gmeindi 318b,
6085 Hasliberg Goldern BE, Switzerland
Tel: +41 33 972 9292
Email: admisions@ecole.ch
Website: www.ecole.ch
Head: Katja Braun

School type:
Co-educational Day & Boarding
Age range of pupils: 12–19 years
No. of pupils enrolled as at 01/09/2022: 120
Fees as at 01/09/2022:
Day: CHF28,000
Full Boarding: CHF65,000–CHF68,000

Nestled in the heart of the Swiss Alps is the Ecole d'Humanité, a school unlike any other.

The Ecole d'Humanité is a small, progressive boarding school. Through holistic education, we help young people chart their individual paths to success – as accomplished academics, creative makers, community leaders, or inventive entrepreneurs.

US High School Diploma, AP™ Program, Swiss Matura

The Ecole d'Humanité offers two educational programs: an English-language US university-prep program, including the AP™ International Diploma, and a German-language Swiss secondary program including the Swiss Matura.

A Progressive, Holistic Curriculum

An innovative and flexible teaching model sparks student curiosity and teaches 21st Century skills. In classes such as The Physics of Sports or The Mathematics of Woodworking, learners follow their interests, diving deeply into core academic subjects while developing cross-curricular skills.

Small Class Sizes

A student-teacher ratio of 4:1 and small learning groups with an average size of six allow for teachers to support each student's individual needs, interests, and talents.

An Outdoor Program Unmatched in Scope

Students venture out onto the mountain and into the forest – hiking, skiing, snowboarding, climbing, or mountain biking. There, they discover strength, resilience, grit, and teamwork – all qualities that enable students to build a life based on their personal model of success.

A Rich Education in the Arts

An arts program abundant in choice allows students to discover unknown talents, and shape their innate creative voice. Subjects offered include, theater, dance, music, fine arts, filmmaking, ceramics, experimental art, textiles, metalwork, woodshop, and much more.

Small, Family-like Boarding Houses

Ecole students live in small multi-age and gender-inclusive boarding groups in Swiss-style chalets. Our boarding program creates a welcoming, family-like atmosphere where students learn leadership, communication skills, and the importance of community.

École Jeannine Manuel – Lille

(Founded 1992)
418 bis rue Albert Bailly,
Marcq-en-Baroeul, 59700 France

Tel: +33 3 20 65 90 50
Email: admissions-lille@ejm.net
Website: www.ecolejeanninemanuel.org
Head of School: Constance Devaux
School type:
Co-educational Day & Boarding
Age range of pupils: 3–18 years

No. of pupils enrolled as at 01/09/2022: 980
Fees as at 01/09/2022:
Day: €6,225
Full Boarding: €15,985–€24,285
IB Classes: €21,495
Average class size: 25 (15 in IBDP)

École Jeannine Manuel Lille is a non-profit coeducational school founded in 1992 and welcomes students from nursery to 12th grade. As the sister campus of École Jeannine Manue Paris, the school has the same educational project and mission: promoting international understanding through bilingual education. An associated UNESCO school, École Jeannine Manuel Lille is the only non-denominational independent school in Nord-Pas-de-Calais, with over 900 pupils representing 40 nationalities and every major cultural tradition. The school's academic excellence matches it diversity: École Jeannine Manuel Lille is regularly ranked among the best French high schools (ranked first for four consecutive years). The school is accredited by the French Ministry of Education, the International Baccalaureate Organization (IBO), the Council of International Schools (CIS), and the New England Association of Schools and Colleges (NEASC).

Ecole Jeannine Manuel Lille's campus extends over 8.5 acres. It includes a boarding house, a restaurant, and state-of-the-art sports facilities including a 1600 m² gym with its own climbing wall, a 300m racing track, and two outdoor playing fields. The boarding house currently welcomes 120 pupils from 6th to 12th grade.

Each year, École Jeannine Manuel Lille welcomes non-French speaking students. These students integrate the school through the adaptation program, which provides intensive instruction in French, support in English as needed, help in understanding and adjusting to French culture, and differentiated coursework and assessment during their adaptation period. The lower and middle school follow the French national curriculum with several exceptions: English is taught every day and, in middle school, experimental sciences, history and geography are taught in English. The curriculum is enriched at all levels, not only with a more advanced English language and literature curriculum, but also, for example, with Chinese language instruction (compulsory in grades 3-4-5), an integrated science program in lower school, and independent research projects in middle school.

In upper school, tenth graders follow the French national curriculum, albeit taught 50% in French and 50% in English. In 11th grade, pupils choose between the French track (*Baccalauréat Français International*, BFI) and the International Baccalaureate Diploma Programme (IBDP). Approximately 25% of our pupils opt for the IBDP.

Admission

Although admission is competitive, the school makes every effort to reserve space for international applicants, including children of families who expect to remain in France for a limited period of time and wish to combine a cultural immersion in French education with the ability to re-enter their own school systems and excel.

École Jeannine Manuel – London

(Founded 2015)
43-45 Bedford Square,
London, WC1B 3DN UK

Tel: 020 3829 5970
Email: admissions@jmanuel.uk.net
Website:
www.ecolejeanninemanuel.org.uk
Head of School: Pauline Prévot
School type: Co-educational Day

Age range of pupils: 3–18 years
No. of pupils enrolled as at 01/09/2022: 585
Fees as at 01/09/2022:
Day: £20,760
Average class size: 16
Teacher/pupil ratio: 1:8

École Jeannine Manuel in London is a French, bilingual, international school which opened its doors in September 2015 on Bedford Square with the objective to bring a unique perspective in the landscape of international schools in London. We welcome pupils from all nationalities, cultural traditions and native languages.

Everything we do at École Jeannine Manuel is driven by our mission, which consists in *"promoting international understanding through the bilingual education of a multicultural community of students, the fostering of pedagogical innovation, and the constant exploration of best practices in the context of an ever-changing global environment."*

To achieve that, our curriculum is based on an enriched version of the international sections programs of the French Ministry of Education. The English, Science and Chinese programs were developed by our Paris sister school, a UNESCO associated school founded in 1954 and recognized as the top French Lycée for the tenth consecutive year. In History, the curriculum is complemented so pupils gain a coherent knowledge and understanding of Britain's past and that of the wider world. Co-curricular activities include sports – with various facilities at the pupil's disposal – as well as a wide range of after-school clubs.

English and French are used equally in class. We welcome non-French-speaking students at all levels and beginners in English up to Year 7. Our aim is to bring pupils to a native proficiency – oral and written – in both languages because a true bilingual education enhances pupils' capacity for abstract, conceptual thinking and develops a sense of nuance, nurtured by exposure to multiple perspectives.

The key drivers of our school's pedagogy are coherence and innovation. Inspired by current research in cognitive sciences and by best practices from around the world or designed by our school's pedagogues, our teaching methods aim to make pupils think, dare, share and care. Our international teams of teachers stimulate new ideas that lead to a creative, pioneering education: hands-on manipulations in math, inquiry-based learning in the sciences, and teamwork are among the practices that foster pupil engagement and growth.

École Jeannine Manuel welcomes pupils from Nursery to Year 13.

Sixth Formers will take either the International Option of the Baccalauréat Français International ("BFI") or the International Baccalaureate.

© Paul Riddle

École Jeannine Manuel – Paris

(Founded 1954)
70 rue du Théâtre, Paris, 75015 France

Tel: +33 1 44 37 00 80
Email: admissions@ejm.net
Website: www.ecolejeanninemanuel.org
Principal: Jérôme Giovendo
School type: Co-educational Day
Age range of pupils: 4–18 years

No. of pupils enrolled as at 01/09/2022: 2400
Fees as at 01/09/2022:
Day: €7,450–€8,215
IB Classes: €26,350
Average class size: 25

École Jeannine Manuel is a non-profit pre-K-12 coeducational school founded in 1954 with the mission to promote international understanding through bilingual (French/English) education. An associated UNESCO school, École Jeannine Manuel welcomes pupils representing 80 nationalities and every major cultural tradition. The school's academic excellence matches its diversity: École Jeannine Manuel is regularly ranked among the best French high schools (state and independent) for its overall academic performance (ranked first for ten consecutive years). The school is accredited by the French Ministry of Education, the International Baccalaureate Organization (IBO), the Council of International Schools (CIS) and the New England Association of Schools and Colleges (NEASC).

Each year, the school welcomes more than 100 new non-French speaking pupils. These students integrate the school through our adaptation program, which provides intensive instruction in French, support in English as needed, help in understanding and adjusting to French culture, and differentiated coursework and assessment during their adaptation period.

The lower and middle school follow the French national curriculum with several exceptions: English is taught every day and, in middle school, experimental sciences, history and geography are taught in English. The curriculum is enriched at all levels, not only with a more advanced English language and literature curriculum, but also, for example, with Chinese language instruction (compulsory in grades 3-4-5), an integrated science program in lower school, and independent research projects in middle school.

In upper school, tenth graders follow the French national curriculum, albeit taught 50% in French and 50% in English. In 11th grade, pupils choose between the French track (*Baccalauréat Français International*, BFI) and the International Baccalaureate Diploma Programme (IBDP). Approximately 25% of our pupils opt for the IBDP.

Over the past three years, approximately 13% of our graduating students attended US colleges or universities, 41% chose to study in the UK, and 29% entered the French higher education system. Around 7% of graduating students go on to study in countries all over the world such as the Netherlands, Switzerland, Belgium, Germany, Spain, Italy, and Australia.

Admission:

Admission is competitive and applications typically exceed available spaces by a ratio of 7:1. The school nonetheless makes every effort to reserve space for international applicants, including children of families who expect to remain in France for a limited period of time and wish to combine a cultural immersion in French education with the ability to seamlessly re-enter the school system in their home country.

Eerde International Boarding School Netherlands

(Founded 1934)
Kasteellaan 1, 7731 PJ Ommen,
Overijssel, Netherlands

Tel: +31 52 9451452
Email: admission@eerdeibs.nl
Website: www.eerde.nl
Director CEO: Niki Holterman
Appointed: January 2018
Principal: Amy Ramsey
School type:
Co-educational Day & Boarding
Age range of pupils: 4–18 years

No. of pupils enrolled as at 01/09/2022: 85
Fees as at 01/09/2022:
Primary: €9,000
Middle School Day: €19,700
High School/ IGCSE & IB Day: €22,950
Boarding: €29,100 (excl. academic fee)
Average class size: 10-15
Teacher/pupil ratio: 1:8

The learning experience at Eerde is international, intercultural and individual with personal attention for each student. Eerde is a place where your child can live, learn and develop.

Located on a tranquil estate in the forested region of Overijssel, Eerde provides a serene escape from city life and the traditional school model. Eerde is home for students from more than 20 countries, eager to embrace nature at every opportunity. While the main school building remains Eerde Castle, the classrooms and learning spaces are themselves deeply integrated into the surrounding environment. In addition, Eerde has convenient access to Amsterdam, The Hague and Rotterdam through easy rail and road links.

Eerde is an international day and boarding school that provides a learning environment where students are guided to develop their full potential. Our focus is to inspire academic excellence, stimulate inquiring minds and develop our students as active members in their community. In line with our school philosophy, our team of educational professionals are international and intercultural. Our school is consciously small-scale to ensure individual attention for all children. Our individual approach will allow your child to discover their true potential and will empower them to develop personal leadership and life skills.

Our boarders (age 12 and above) live in cozy rooms and are looked after by boarding parents, who are dedicated to creating a happy and safe home. In boarding we stimulate students to develop a sense of responsibility and care for one another. Boarders can join a variety of activities offered during the weekend. All members of our boarding community treat each other with respect, honesty and tolerance.

At Eerde there is no shortage of ways to stay active. Students can enjoy a range of team sports including basketball, volleyball and football, with the opportunity to join competitive sport clubs in the area. Aside from these, many students are involved in swimming, rowing, and most notably, equestrian activities.

Students at Eerde are encouraged to reach their full potential and become accomplished global citizens by stepping outside of the classroom walls and discovering what the world has to offer.

We believe that each students' potential lies within, we simply provide the educational tools, diverse experiences and encouraging environment, shaping their path to success.

Eerde proudly offers the IBDP and the IBCP. The school is fully accredited by CIS and MSA.

EF Academy Oxford

EF ACADEMY

International Boarding Schools

Pullens Lane, Headington,
Oxfordshire OX3 0DT UK
Tel: +41 (0) 43 430 41 00
Email: academy.admissions@ef.com
Website: www.efacademy.org
Head of School: Mr. Mark Fletcher-Single

School type:
Co-educational Day & Boarding
Age range of pupils: 16–19 years
Fees as at 01/09/2022:
Day: £29,500
Full Boarding: £44,500

At EF Academy International Boarding Schools, we empower the next generation of global changemakers. Our mission to open the world through education brings together students from all over the world to provide them with a transformational international education, thorough preparation for university and a future that knows no borders.

Our school is situated in the city of Oxford, renowned for its scholastic tradition and rich cultural and architectural heritage. EF Academy students join Oxford's vibrant academic community, which attracts leading scholars from around the world. 10 minutes from Oxford's center, the campus has spacious classrooms, modern science labs and inviting lounges. Students also benefit from access to the library and sports facilities of nearby Oxford Brookes University. In the international environment at EF Academy Oxford, students from over 60 different countries live and learn together.

Students at EF Academy Oxford follow the IB Diploma or A-Level program and they are guided through the course selection process by experienced Pathway Managers and course coordinators who help them choose classes that are in line with their university and career goals. Their studies are enhanced by a dynamic enrichment program that includes visits to the museums, theaters and galleries in Oxford, as well as Begbroke Science Park, the Culham Centre for Fusion Energy and the Mini BMW Plant in Cowley. Other academic extension opportunities to see plays and attend lectures or workshops at the University of Oxford and University College London are organized on a regular basis.

Our graduates have gone on to attend universities such as the University of Oxford, University of Cambridge and Imperial College London; all of our students receive acceptance to university degree programs, many for highly competitive courses such as economics, engineering or medicine.

Our students are supported by a team of encouraging faculty members who offer guidance on everything from homesickness to course selection. Dedicated University Advisors work together with students to help them prepare the best applications possible. Each student is supported by an academic tutor who monitors their academic progress and general well-being.

Elckerlyc International School

Klimopzoom 41, 2353 RE Leiderdorp,
South Holland, Netherlands
Tel: +31 71 5896861
Email: international@elckerlyc.net
Website: www.elckerlyc-international.nl
Headteacher: Lesley de Quartel

School type:
Co-educational Day Preparatory
Age range of pupils: 3–11 years
No. of pupils enrolled as at 01/09/2022: 128
Fees as at 01/09/2022:
Day: €3,800

Learning together, growing together

We are a small local school where our aim is to help you and your child feel at home as quickly as possible. Knowing that every child is unique, we strive to help our students develop into valuable members of a global society. It is our task to identify how best to support them on this journey. Here at Elckerlyc, we believe education is much more than numeracy and literacy. It is also about responsibility, dealing with your own and other people's emotions, respect and communication.

Elckerlyc International is a member of The Dutch International Primary Schools (DIPS). This means that our school offers international education embedded in a Dutch context; as such we operate within the framework of the Dutch educational system. As we are partly funded by the Dutch government, we can ensure that education at our school remains affordable for expat families.

ES American School

(Founded 1999)

Autovia de Castelldefels C-31 Km 191,
El Prat de Llobregat, 08820 Barcelona,
Catalonia, Spain
Tel: +34 93 479 1611
Email: admin@es-school.com
Website: www.es-school.com
Head of School: Ms. Melanie Rose

School type: Co-educational Day
Age range of pupils: 6–18 years
No. of pupils enrolled as at 01/09/2022: 115
Fees as at 01/09/2022:
Day: €10,946–€16,327
Average class size: 5-18
Teacher/pupil ratio: 1:5

ES American School offers an independent, college preparatory American curriculum for 5 to 18 year olds (1st through 12th grades) located within the campus of the Emilio Sanchez Academy, Barcelona. Our Elementary is an authorized IB PYP school, offering the International Baccalaureate Primary Years Programme, a world-renowned curricular framework, where children learn to take ownership of their own learning, increasing confidence and self-motivation. In Middle School, the enrichment program supports students to have a broad range of learning experiences. The Advanced Placement (AP) program in High School offers students the opportunity to work at a more challenging level with the potential to earn university credit. Students who elect to take the Spanish program alongside the American curriculum are eligible to homologate their diploma.

With locations in Barcelona, Spain and Naples, Florida, USA, ES American School provides students with a truly international experience enabling them to excel both academically and athletically. All students receive individual attention, close academic guidance and personal counseling. The predominant language on campus is English.

Sports are an essential part of the curriculum and students benefit from the world-class tennis program and training facilities provided by Emilio Sanchez Academy. Our students have three distinct pathways with regards to sport: high-performance tennis (offered on-site), high-performance in other sports (offered off-site), including water polo, soccer, basketball, or horse riding OR our Physical Education Program for general fitness and well-being. ES American School, Barcelona is accredited by the Middle States Association of Colleges and Schools and is authorized by the Department of Education of the Catalan Government.

Fulham School

Fulham SCHOOL

(Founded 1996)

1-3 Chesilton Road, London, SW6 5AA UK

Tel: 020 8154 6751
Email: admissions@fulham.school
Website: fulham.school
Pre-Prep & Nursery Head: Di Steven
Prep Head: Neill Lunnon
Executive Headteacher & Head of Fulham Senior School: Bex Tear
School type: Co-educational Day

Religious Denomination: Non-denominational
Age range of pupils: 3–18 years
No. of pupils enrolled as at 01/09/2022: 650
Fees as at 01/09/2022:
Day: £18,420–£21,567
Average class size: 18

About Fulham School

Fulham School is independent and co-educational, providing a rich and diverse curriculum to boys and girls from aged 3 to age 18. Founded in 1996, Fulham School believes in co-education in its broadest sense: not just girls and boys learning together, but learners of all abilities understanding that they have much to offer each other, and teachers as keen to learn and evolve as their students. Situated in the heart of Fulham, the three of the school sites, Nursery & Pre-Prep, Prep and Senior, are ideally located to take advantage of London and the endless opportunities it offers to enhance education. Specialist teachers and support staff inspire pupils to work to the limits of their potential, so they are prepared for the next steps in life while learning more about themselves and developing a broad range of interests.

Personalised Learning

Teachers work alongside pupils to support the discovery of personal interests, gifts, and talents and instil the confidence in pupils to embrace what they find most challenging and join in with everything. From the most academic to the most creative, the most driven to the most supportive, Fulham School wants each pupil to delight in what they do, not where it will get them, and to be driven on by that delight to achieve more than they ever expected.

Support

Fulham School supports the highest of academic high-flyers to achieve the scholarships and university places that will challenge them most alongside pupils whose chief passions and interests are expressed in practice and rehearsal rooms or on the sports field. All pupils are encouraged to make contributions where their strengths lie and recognise the contributions of others. *"We seek to provide life skills, the ability to make connections between and beyond subjects, the ability to work together to achieve more than any individual can alone."*

Granada College

(Founded 1999)
Educación y Formación Europea, S.A.,
Urbanización Llanos de Silva, 18230
Atarfe, Granada, Andalusia, Spain
Tel: +34 958 499 009
Website: granadacollege.es

Head of School: Mr Javier Jiménez Ortiz
School type: Co-educational Day
Age range of pupils: 0–18 years
No. of pupils enrolled as at 01/09/2022: 1000
Average class size: 22

Granada College is a private, international, bilingual and secular school that offers a personalised education from 0 to 18 years of age. Our principal objective is to provide an international education, oriented to the globalised world and with special attention to education in values. Our school offers full linguistic immersion and excellent educational standards, and we are authorised to teach the prestigious International Baccalaureate (IB) Diploma Programme (DP) a prestigious degree recognized by the world's leading universities.

Granada College is a private school, member of the Globeducate group which owns and operates more than 55 schools worldwide. We focus on achieving academic excellence, providing our students with an outstanding academic education along with a strong ethical foundation so they become global citizen who can shape the world.

Location

Granada College is located in an area surrounded by nature and tranquillity 15 minutes from Granada. Its facilities are designed to achieve the integral education of our students, with complete facilities that promote a positive environment.

Granada College has large classrooms, spacious and bright laboratory rooms, computer rooms, as well as digital classrooms with the latest advances in technology; it also has playgrounds, football pitches, basketball courts, swimming pool and a sports pavilion.

Foreign languages

English, French, Mandarin Chinese

IB World School

Granada College is the first private school to offer the International Baccalaureate® (IB) Diploma Programme in Granada.

Greene's College Oxford

GREENE'S COLLEGE OXFORD

(Founded 1967)

45 Pembroke Street, Oxford,
Oxfordshire OX1 1BP UK
Tel: 01865 664400
Email: enquiries@greenes.org.uk
Website: www.greenesoxford.com
Principal: Mrs. Carmen Dare
Appointed: September 2021

School type:
Co-educational Day & Boarding
No. of pupils enrolled as at 01/09/2022:
Sixth Form: 60
Fees as at 01/09/2022:
£21,780 (one A level starts at £8,000)
Average class size: 1-3
Teacher/pupil ratio: 1:1

What is Greene's College like?
Greene's offers a full-time, university-style sixth form education, both in Oxford, England and in Estoril, Portugal. Greene's is the oldest tutorial college in Oxford, and quite possibly in the U.K. Shortly after Greene's was established in Oxford in 1967, we moved to our present central 17th century buildings in Pembroke Street, just opposite the University of Oxford's Christ Church.

At Greene's, students are taught and supervised by our outstanding educators and academics, all trained to deliver the very best education, and to guide students towards the highest grades – while maintaining the greatest regard for student welfare and wellbeing.

Every student is allocated a Personal Tutor, who guides, mentors and encourages the student throughout his or her time at Greene's, enabling students to grow personally as well as academically. Students are also encouraged to benefit from all the numerous social, cultural and sporting activities Greene's have to offer, whether in Oxford or Estoril.

Courses are delivered to students individually or in very small groups, with some work in larger seminars. Greene's has been truly committed to the tutorial method of learning for over 50 years, and has invested much time, technology and expertise to ensure that students really benefit from a philosophy of teaching and learning that continues to be used in the most ancient of universities.

Is your child ready for a university-style setting?
Our aim is to bring all our students to the realisation that they can be independent learners, and that they have potential in areas that may surprise them. Greene's makes no selection based on academic ability, and we pride ourselves on helping a wide variety of students: for those tackling A levels for the first time, for those wanting a second chance, and for those who want a flexible timetable.

Greene's College Oxford, Estoril

GREENE'S COLLEGE OXFORD

(Founded 1967)
Rua D. Afonso Henriques no. 1614,
2765-576 Estoril, Lisbon, Portugal
Tel: +351 211 165 450
Email: enquiries@greenes.pt
Website: www.greenes.pt

Principal: Miguel Gama
School type: Co-educational Day
Age range of pupils: 14–18
No. of pupils enrolled as at 01/09/2022:
Sixth Form: 60

Greene's offers a full-time, university-style sixth form education, both in Oxford, England and in Estoril, Portugal – with academic oversight resting with the Oxford college. In Portugal, Greene's is the first tutorial college and the foremost sixth form college in the Lisbon area. Greene's is also the oldest tutorial college in Oxford, and quite possibly in the U.K. Tuition at either location can be face-to-face or online.

At Greene's, students are taught and supervised by our outstanding educators and academics, all trained to deliver the very best education, and to guide students towards the highest grades – while maintaining the greatest regard for student welfare and wellbeing. Every student is allocated a Personal Tutor, in addition to the academic specialists, who guides, mentors and encourages the student throughout his or her time at Greene's, enabling students to grow personally as well as academically. Students are also encouraged to benefit from all the numerous social, cultural and sporting activities Greene's have to offer, whether in Oxford or Estoril.

Most courses are delivered to students individually or in very small groups, with some work in larger seminars. 'Independent' and 'individual' are widely used adjectives in education, however Greene's has been truly committed to the tutorial method of learning for over 50 years, and has invested much time, technology and expertise to ensure that students really benefit from a philosophy of teaching and learning that continues to be used in the most ancient of universities.

At Greene's students are very much in control of their studies and have access to a stream of information about their progress, feedback from tutors, realistic assessments of their likely achievement, together with the reassurance of their Personal Tutor to talk through their personal academic strategy.

Is your child ready for a university-style setting?

Our aim is to bring all our students to the realisation that they can be independent learners, and that they have potential in areas that may surprise them. Greene's makes no selection based on academic ability, and we pride ourselves on helping a wide variety of students: for those tackling A levels for the first time, for those wanting a second chance, and for those who want a flexible timetable.

Haileybury

(Founded 1862)
Haileybury, Hertford,
Hertfordshire SG13 7NU UK

Tel: +44 (0)1992 706353
Email: uk.admissions@haileybury.com
Website: www.haileybury.com
The Master: Mr Martin Collier MA BA PGCE
Appointed: September 2017
School type:
Co-educational Boarding & Day
Age range of pupils: 11–18 years
(entry at 11+, 13+ and 16+)

No. of pupils enrolled as at 01/09/2022: 915
Boys: 458 ***Girls:*** 457 ***Sixth Form:*** 364
No. of boarders: 658
Fees as at 01/09/2022:
Day: £6,595–£9,920 per term
Full Boarding: £8,615–£13,580 per term
Teacher/pupil ratio: 1:7

Haileybury is an independent, co-educational boarding school, located between London and Cambridge, in 500 acres of beautiful Hertfordshire countryside. Spectacular grounds are home to outstanding facilities, excellent teaching and superb pastoral care for its community of boarding and day pupils.

Academic rigour and outstanding co-curricular provision are at the heart of the school. Pupils enjoy exceptional opportunities and a truly all-round education which enables them to discover enduring passions and talents.

Academic opportunity

The school offers a dedicated Lower School for Years 7 and 8, a wide range of GCSEs and IGCSEs and the choice of the IB Diploma Programme or A levels in the Sixth Form. Haileybury is ranked Top 10 in The Sunday Times league table for co-ed independent schools which offer the IB.

Boarding and day

More than two thirds of pupils are boarders with school life centred around 12 boarding houses and Lower School having their own house. Pupils join at 11+, 13+, 14+ or 16+ entry points. Flexi-boarding is available in Lower School, which means families do not have to commit to full boarding.

Exceptional opportunities

A key part of the school's philosophy is empowering each child to follow their passions and build self-confidence. Pupils benefit from professional sports coaching from the likes of former Wales rugby captain Michael Owen and ex-England international netballer Dani McFarlane. There is a packed co-curricular programme of more than 130 choices, from core sports to scuba diving, African drumming and beekeeping.

Haileybury offers a vast range of opportunities for pupils to immerse themselves in the Creative Arts both academically and as part of their co-curricular options. This consists of Drama, Music, Dance, LAMDA and Art partnered with excellent facilities to allow pupils to maximise their full potential in their chosen areas. The School takes pride in hosting spectacular arts productions with multiple showcases per term.

Haileybury are creative and innovative in terms of their teaching and curriculum and as such have partnered with Stanford University and the University of Oxford, to work as part of the global Stan-X study. Haileybury is the first school in Europe to participate in this pioneering study of genetics, contributing to efforts to find cures for diseases such as pancreatic cancer and diabetes.

Supportive environment

There is an emphasis on pastoral care with round-the-clock support from housemasters and housemistresses, the chaplain and tutors. The school is a home-from-home, with a warm and friendly feel. Every child is given the confidence to find their identity on a personal journey of discovery.

Haut-Lac International Bilingual School

haut lac
école internationale bilingue
international bilingual school

(Founded 1993)

Ch. de Pangires 26, St-Légier-la Chiésaz,
CH-1806 Switzerland
Tel: +41 (0)21 555 50 00
Email: admissions@haut-lac.ch
Website: www.haut-lac.ch
Infant & Primary Head: Ms Lucy Sumner
Secondary Head: Ms Rossella Cosso

School type:
Co-educational Day & Boarding
Age range of pupils: 18 months–18 years
No. of pupils enrolled as at 01/09/2022: 600
Fees as at 01/09/2022:
Day: CHF24,900–CHF36,100
Full Boarding: CHF72,000–CHF88,000
Average class size: 12
Teacher/pupil ratio: 1:6

General
Haut-Lac is:
- Your Local International School

Haut-Lac means:
- Excellence in education for 3 to 18 year olds
- 30 years' experience in bilingual education
- 100% International Baccalaureate Diploma pass rate in 2020 & 2021
- Higher education studies at top universities in Switzerland and worldwide
- Boutique boarding home for up to 30 international students and/or athletes

Haut-Lac values:
- Respect
- Resilience
- Open-mindedness
- Sense of belonging

Academics
Students develop the academic knowledge and soft skills required to succeed in the modern world.
Infant & Primary (3-11 y.o.)
- Bilingual French-English or predominantly English pathways
- Personalised programme combining Swiss, International & British curricula

Secondary
- Personalised bilingual, English-only or French-only pathways
- IB Middle Years Programme (11-16 y.o.)
- Swiss Option (11-14 y.o)
- IB Diploma Programme (16-19 y.o.)
- IB Career-Related Programme (16-19 y.o.)
- Sustainable Management
- Art & Design
- International Sports Management
- US High School Diploma (16-19 y.o.)
- Sport & Study (11-19 y.o.)
- Flexible and/or extended IBMYP, IBDP and IBCP programmes
- Ski Racing Academy

Extra-Curricular
- 151 after-school clubs
- Out-of-hours care from 7:15 to 18:00, including lunchtime supervision
- Regular student and family events
- Bilingual Winter, Spring and Summer activity camps for 4 to 15 year olds

Accreditations & Memberships
IB, CIS, WAoS Athlete-Friendly Education Centre, Eco-Schools, AVDEP, SGIS, FSEP, SEBIQ

H-FARM International School

H-FARM INTERNATIONAL SCHOOL

(Founded 1995)

Via Olivetti 1, 31056 Roncade (TV), Italy

Tel: +39 0422 789503

Email: info.tv@h-is.com

Website: www.h-is.com/it/scuole/treviso

Head of School: Mr Mauro Bordignon

Appointed: September 2011

School type:

Co-educational Day & Boarding

Age range of pupils: 3–18 years

H-FARM International School, located just outside of Venice, Italy, empowers students to be internationally-minded citizens who are able to shape their own future in a rapidly changing global community. Through innovative learning environments and the development of relationships based on compassion and respect, we enable students to become confident, creative and collaborative.

We are a community of active lifelong learners. H-FARM International School serves a diverse and growing community of students and families. We offer a broad based education which uses English as the language of instruction and learning and which aims to promote international mindedness and global citizenship. The school is authorised by the IB to offer two programmes, the Primary Years Programme (Early Years Unit (EYU) and Elementary) and Middle Years Programme. The Early Years Unit (EYU) is also inspired by Reggio Children beliefs, values and practices. The International Baccalaureate (IB) Programmes provide a challenging, internationally focused and balanced educational experience across the Primary Years (PYP) and Middle Years (MYP) Programmes.

To provide the complete IB continuum, H-FARM International School's International School of Talents sector provides the IB's Diploma Programme – an engaging curriculum entirely taught in English that prepares students to access the most prestigious universities and colleges in the world and is an unparalleled academic and life experience.

Our Campus, located just 10 minutes from Venice International Airport, boasts world class services for both boarding and day students. An unparalleled center for innovation in Europe, H-FARM students have access to a 240-bed boarding house, a sports complex with tennis & Padel courts, basketball and volleyball courts, a fully-equipped gymnasium, soccer fields, coffee shops and restaurants, innovative science and Virtual Reality laboratories.

Hochalpines Institut Ftan (HIF)

HOCHALPINES INSTITUT FTAN
SWISS INTERNATIONAL SCHOOL AND SPORTS ACADEMY

(Founded 1793)

Chalchera 154, 7551 Ftan GR, Switzerland

Tel: +41 81 861 22 11

Email: admissions@hif.ch

Website: www.hif.ch

Heads of School: Stefanie Aichholz & Dr. Christoph Hendrickx

School type: Co-educational Day & Boarding & Sports Academy

Age range of pupils: 12–18 years

No. of pupils enrolled as at 01/09/2022: 70

Fees as at 01/09/2022:

Full Boarding: CHF57,000–CHF64,000

Sports Academy: up to CHF6,000

HIF Swiss International School and Sports Academy is an open-hearted campus community where young people from around the world can thrive in the sublime, health-giving environment of the Swiss Alps. It is a co-educational secondary school offering a range of educational programmes for students in school years/grades 7 to 12. It is accredited by the Canton of Graubünden to prepare and examine students for the Swiss Matura, by Cambridge Assessment as a centre for the International General Certificate of Secondary Education (IGCSE), and proudly holds IB World School status offering the IB Diploma Programme.

Learning at HIF goes beyond the walls of the classroom. For us, education is about students discovering and developing their unique talents and individual potential – intellectual, emotional, social, artistic, sporting – which every child possesses. It is also about exploring how knowledge and skills learned in academic subjects can be applied and extended in the real world. Among the opportunities for enriched learning are excursions in Switzerland, academic clubs, hiking in the Alps, music and arts, Leadership programmes and other projects.

Whether you are an aspiring Olympic skiing champion or simply enjoy a leisurely game of tennis, sport is an essential element for us at HIF. It promotes health, well-being, resilience, self-discipline, and team spirit. What is more, sport is a source of joy, excitement, and inspiration. With its team of expert coaches and high-profile training facilities, HIF enables young talents and students interested in sports such as cross-country skiing, alpine ski, biathlon, snowboarding freestyle and ice hockey to combine competitive or leisure sports with an academic programme of their choice. Special support and mentoring programmes ensure the coordination of sport and academics. We are responsive to the needs and the development of each student, regardless of his or her performance level. Motivation and pleasure are the decisive elements in achieving the school's objectives in both athletics and academics.

Hockerill Anglo-European College

(Founded 1980)
Dunmow Road, Bishops Stortford,
Hertfordshire CM23 5HX UK

Tel: 01279 658451
Email: admissions@hockerill.com
Website: www.hockerill.com
Principal: David Woods
Appointed: September 2020
School type:
Co-educational Day & Boarding

Age range of pupils: 11–18 years
No. of pupils enrolled as at 01/09/2022: 900
Fees as at 01/09/2022:
Full Boarding: £13,599–£18,405
Average class size: 21
Teacher/pupil ratio: 1:13

Situated on a leafy campus in Bishop's Stortford, 10 minutes from London Stansted Airport, Hockerill is a leading UK school which features in the Sunday Times Guide 2022, the Good Schools Guide and the Tatler Schools Guide. It is a strong, caring community of 900 boys and girls (400 boarders and 500 day students) aged between 11 and 18. All six boarding houses are located within the campus.

Student outcomes are exceptional with results and university destinations comparing favourably to those of top independent schools. 75% of those attending UK universities go on to Russell Group destinations, with 10% taking up an Oxbridge place in 2021. The Sunday Times placed Hockerill third of all comprehensives, based on academic achievement, in its 2022 guide to the best schools in the country.

The College offers a rigorous and broad curriculum and is proud to be one of the largest state schools offering the prestigious International Baccalaureate Middle Years and Diploma programmes with consistently outstanding results. Hockerill has a special focus on languages and music with both French/English and German/English bilingual sections.

The main intake years are at ages 11 and 16. The Lower College curriculum is based on the IB Middle Years programme offering a wide range of subjects with students taking their GCSEs before moving on.

The College has a strong extra-curricular provision which includes Sports, Music Ensembles and Choirs, BMX, CCF, Young Enterprise, Duke of Edinburgh, Debating, Model United Nations, Amnesty and Charity fundraising. There are some 100 clubs on offer.

The trips and exchanges programme runs throughout the College and encompasses destinations such as Uganda, India, Japan, China, Spain, France, Croatia, Belgium, Austria, Germany and Italy.

Many events take place during the year for students including formal dinners, concerts, Speech Day, International Boarders weekend (for students and their families). As part of the regular communication, there is a termly forum for boarding parents.

ICS Côte d'Azur

ICS CÔTE D'AZUR
INTERNATIONAL SCHOOL
Shaping the world

(Founded 2006)
245 Route les Lucioles,
06560 Valbonne, France

Tel: +33 (0)4 93 64 32 84
Email: admissions@icscotedazur.com
Website: www.icscotedazur.com
Director: Ms Amanda Scott
Appointed: 2020
School type: Co-educational Day

Age range of pupils: 3–11 years
No. of pupils enrolled as at 01/09/2022: 150
Fees as at 01/09/2022:
Day: €10,645–€14,235
Average class size: 17

ICS Côte d'Azur is a bilingual, co-educational, non-sectarian, IB World Primary School serving the international and local community in the Sophia Antipolis region. The school offers Early Years and Primary Years education from KG1 (age 3) to PY6 (age 11). ICS Côte d'Azur is a member of the Globeducate network.

Formerly known as EBICA, the school's multicultural learning community enjoys a modern and secure campus in Sophia Antipolis, Valbonne, southwest of Nice. Recognised as an IB World School since 2018, ICS Côte d'Azur welcomes students from around the world, offering an international education within the inquiry-based framework of the IB Primary Years Programme, whilst also integrating the national curricula for England and France.

The school attracts internationally-minded families with aspirations for their children to learn in French and English from the early years onwards. Within the multicultural community, students are immersed in both languages with equal measure, in an environment that promotes international understanding while fostering an appreciation of French culture.

ICS Côte d'Azur offers a language support programme for French as a foreign language (FFL) learners and English as a foreign language (EFL) learners. These support lessons for beginners assist acquisition in either language, bringing them the linguistic competencies required to access the curriculum and progress with confidence.

Through learner-centred teaching, ICS Côte d'Azur empowers students, as agents in their IB journey, to develop the self-knowledge and confidence to create their successes. In an environment that fosters cross-cultural understanding, students develop the attributes of the IB learner profile, which equips them with the essential skills to be successful in a diverse and connected world.

Sophia Antipolis is a rich area for science and technology, often referred to as the 'Silicon Valley' of Europe. To reflect its location, the school offers an innovative STEAM programme (Science, Technology, Maths, Art and Engineering), with a dedicated tinkering lab called 'The Hub', LEGO® Education kits, and Apple products in the classroom. The vision behind this cutting-edge STEAM initiative is for students to acquire the critical thinking, creativity and problem-solving skills that will be essential for the future.

ICS London

ICSLONDON
INTERNATIONAL SCHOOL
Shaping the world

(Founded 1979)

Early Years and Primary School:
7B Wyndham Place, London, W1H 1PN UK
Secondary School:
21 Star Street, London, W21QB, UK
Tel: +44 (0)20 729 88800
Email: admissions@ics.uk.net
Website: www.icschool.co.uk
Head of School: David Laird

School type: Co-educational Day
Age range of pupils: 3–19 years
No. of pupils enrolled as at 01/09/2022: 175
Fees as at 01/09/2022:
Day: £19,770–£28,920
Average class size: Av 12, Max 16
Teacher/pupil ratio: 1:5

ICS London is an independent day school in the heart of central London. We are one of only two IB World Schools in the city offering the full International Baccalaureate (IB) programme for learners aged 3 to 18 years.

Providing an inclusive and international community for early years, primary, secondary and high school students, our children and young people study on two close-by locations at our primary and secondary school sites in elegant Marylebone and Paddington.

With over 40 years' experience delivering globally-recognised education, today we serve our close-knit community of students and their families with the IB Primary Years Programme (PYP), the Middle Years Programme (MYP) and the Diploma Programme (DP). With instruction in English, we are a truly international school where diversity is celebrated with around 65+ different nationalities represented each year.

Quality is assessed, recognised and assured at ICS London through accreditation with the:

- IB World School: ICS London is authorised and accredited by the International Baccalaureate. This is subject to a strict accreditation process monitored by the IB which ensures our education provision is of the highest quality.
- Independent Schools Inspectorate: This is a government approved inspectorate for independent schools which ensures quality on behalf of the UK Department for Education (DfE).

ICS London also prides itself on offering a holistic and personalised learning experience:

- Class sizes: Between 6 and 18 students
- Teacher to student ratio: 1 to 5
- In Nursery and Reception there are 2 teachers in every class
- In Secondary School each student is assigned a mentor
- Individual study plans can be tailored to meet students' needs

As a rolling admissions policy is in place, students can join anytime throughout the year. Students can also easily transfer from other curriculums, such as the UK or US and join the IB programme at ICS London.

For further information please visit www.icschool.co.uk or call +44 (0)20 7298 8800.

ICS Milan

ICS Symbiosis, Viale Ortles, 46, 20139
Milano (MI), Italy
Tel: +39 02 36592694

Email: admissions@icsmilan.com
Website: www.icsmilan.com
School type: Co-educational Day

ICS Milan International School

ICS Milan is the first school dedicated to students from 1 – 18 years that offers an international curriculum enhanced by an innovative teaching approach based on experiential learning and a STEAM agenda (Science, Technology, Engineering, Arts and Maths). With four different campuses throughout the Milan area, ICS Milan is a school of innovation that helps children grow into citizens of the world.

ICS Milan serves a diverse community of students from a range of nationalities, cultures and backgrounds. The school offers a broad-based education that uses English as the main language of learning and caters for a range of student abilities. ICS Milan's vision is to inspire, motivate, and challenge all students to achieve their personal best by providing a rich, creative, and well-balanced educational experience.

International School with Italian Roots

As Scuola Paritaria (an officially recognised school), our school also adopts the national recommendations for the curriculum issued by MIUR (the Ministry of Education). The Italian language and history programmes are designed for mother-tongue Italian speakers. A specific programme for Italian as an additional language learners is available for children of other nationalities.

ICS Values

ICS Milan teaches creativity, responsibility, respect, diversity, compassion and shared values. Students are invited to develop a sound knowledge base and to reflect on and reassess their surroundings from a variety of perspectives.

Our system fosters a balanced development of different personalities. It combines the importance of rules with a sense of expressive creativity, challenge and imagination, and it also provides the necessary tools for becoming "masters" of our own abilities.

Our teaching approach stimulates each developmental and learning phase of every child by placing respect for others and for ourselves at its centre.

Globeducate

Since 2017 ICS Milan is a proud member of the Globeducate network, which operates in more than 55 international schools in Europe, Americas and Asia, with more than 25,000 students. Globeducate's mission to prepare each student to become a global citizen that can shape the world is well-aligned to the student-centered approach at ICS Milan.

ICS Paris

23 rue de Cronstadt, 75015 Paris, France
Tel: +33 (0)1 56 56 60 70
Email: admissions@icsparis.fr
Website: www.icsparis.fr
Director: Mrs. Angela Hollington
Appointed: 2021

School type: Coeducational Day
Age range of pupils: 3–18 years
No. of pupils enrolled as at 01/09/2022: 500
Fees as at 01/09/2022:
Day: €18,651–€26,550
Average class size: 20

ICS Paris (formerly known as EIB – The Victor Hugo School) is an international day school nestled in the heart of Paris. As a member of ICS, a leading IB World School group in Europe, the school provides pathways to the world's leading universities and offers pedagogical continuity to expat families. Like its ICS sister schools in London, Milan, Rome, Nice and Valbonne, ICS Paris offers a world-class IB education.

The school welcomes students year round from Nursery to Grade 12 who wish to follow their studies in an international, Anglophone environment, obtaining the IB diploma at the end of High School. Small class sizes at all levels ensure that students remain at the centre of their learning.

Students in the Primary section follow the Primary Years Programme (PYP), allowing them to develop their critical thinking skills and thirst for knowledge. ICS Paris is a candidate school for the PYP and Middle Years Programme (MYP) and has been an IB Diploma Programme School for almost 20 years.

ICS Paris is a K-12 international school offering the real French experience. Our students benefit from regular French-language lessons from Nursery to Grade 12. As an inclusive international network encouraging cultural awareness and preparation to the world of tomorrow, the school welcomes students from over 60 different nationalities. We are able to integrate children at all phases of their language learning. Our French lessons are organised by language proficiency (beginner to advanced), and we have additional English language support classes.

Our students may also participate in a variety of activities on campus, including coding, music, theatre, and Model United Nations. As a member of Globeducate, a leading European educational group, our students have the opportunity for cultural exchange, travelling to other schools in Europe for academic, athletic and music competitions throughout the year. We nurture a deeper understanding of the world, we raise awareness, and we inspire a sense of global citizenship and responsibility.

For more information, visit our website at www.icsparis.fr or contact our admissions team directly at admissions@icsparis.fr.

Impington International College

impington international college

New Road, Impington, Cambridge, Cambridgeshire CB24 9LX UK

Tel: 01223 200402
Email: international@ivc.tmet.org.uk
Website: www.impingtoninternational.org.uk
College Principal: Ms Victoria Hearn
Appointed: 2020

School type: Co-educational Day & Boarding (in host families)
Age range of pupils: 11–19 years
No. of pupils enrolled as at 01/09/2022: 1311
Average class size: 10-15
Teacher/pupil ratio: 1:15

A World Class IB education from Impington International College – your ticket to a world of opportunity

Why choose Impington International College?

1. The quality of care is exceptional – The tutor to student ratio is approximately 1 to 15, with a dedicated Student Manager for pastoral support and guidance. In lessons, the teacher to student ratio is, on average, 1 to 10.

2. It delivers excellent outcomes – The pass rate is 100% (international average: 80%) and the average International Baccalaureate (IB) point score is 35.

3. Students go on to achieve great things – In 2020, 90% of the students went on to study at university, with 25% offered Russell Group places (including Oxbridge). In addition to this, the remaining 10% of students were successful in their job applications and seamlessly moved into the world of work.

4. Expert delivery of the International Baccalaureate – for more than 30 years, Impington International College has offered the IB and was one of the first state schools in the UK to do so. The College is consistently rated 'Outstanding' by Ofsted.

5. It is truly international – around half of students attend Impington International College from overseas, creating a culturally diverse student cohort and unique opportunities for study and trips.

Impington International College offers the following programmes to students:

- IB Diploma Programme (DP)
- IB Career-related Programme (CP)
- Extended BTECs
- The Performance School
- Sports Scholarship Programmes

Impington International College bases its teaching on the IB's mission statement and ethos, aiming to develop "inquiring, knowledgeable and caring young people who help to create a better and more peaceful world". Not only do students gain a valuable breadth of skills through either the DP or the CP but IB higher level subjects also provide the same depth of knowledge as A Levels, so students can go on to achieve excellence in whichever path they choose.

The driven cohort achieve outstanding results and have gone on to attend renowned higher education institutions around the world, including: University of Cambridge, University of Oxford, London School of Economics and Political Science, University College London, King's College London, Loughborough University, Leiden University, UCLA, The Place, Italia Conti, International University of Japan, and many more. Many students from the College's Performance School go on to join professional companies, with a number starring in the West End. Students from the sports scholarship programme often go on to study coaching and management at university, or play semi-professionally for local teams.

Institut International Saint-Dominique

Institut International Saint-Dominique

Via Igino Lega 5, 00189 Rome, Italy

Tel: +39 06 303 10817
Email: info@institutsaintdominique.it
Website: www.institutsaintdominique.it
Head of School: Bernard Lociciro
School type:
Co-educational Day & Boarding

Age range of pupils: 2–18 years
No. of pupils enrolled as at 01/09/2022: 350
Fees as at 01/09/2022:
Day: €3,900–€13,500
Weekly Boarding: €16,000
Full Boarding: €21,000

JUMP INTO A UNIQUE FRENCH INTERNATIONAL SCHOOL!
Recognized for its educational philosophy, the Saint-Dominique Institute (ISD) is one of the most prestigious French schools in Italy that combines educational excellence and well-being. The Saint-Dominique Institute is a school of the international Odyssey group and for more than 10 years a partner school of the network of the Agency for French Education Abroad (AEFE) which has more than 500 schools around the world.

All our programs from kindergarten to high school are approved by the French National Ministry of Education. Our establishment offered excellent and multilingual education (French, Italian, English) from Pre-kindergarten to High school. ISD Rome is accredited with the International Baccalaureate Organization and opens an English-speaking International Section (PRE-IB GRADE 10) from September 2022 and the Diploma Program for 2023-2024.

The learning environment plays an essential role in the development and success of each student, our spaces are designed to promote academic performance, curiosity, creativity and well-being of students through the integrated teaching of languages by teachers "mother tongue", sciences and data processing (presence of interactive screens touchscreen in the classrooms).

The boarding school: our exceptional campus on 6 hectares in a secure and green setting in the heart of a city steeped in history allows us to accommodate an increasing number of boarding students and to implement advanced teaching and learning methods. Saint-Dominique boarding school offers:

- A multilingual education
- A personalized support
- A cultural, sports and artistic program

Our boarding school is driving the development of a quality educational offer that is also rich in human experiences, acquired through a community life that requires attention and respect in the relationship with others.

- Double or single rooms
- 5/7 days possible in boarding school
- A dozen cultural and sporting activities offered

Institut Le Châtelard

Route des Narcisses 80, 1833 Les-Avants-sur-Montreux, Switzerland
Tel: +41 21 989 8000
Email: info@lechatelard.com
Website: www.ecolechatelard.ch
Head of School: Mrs Veronica Canales

School type: Girls' Boarding
Age range of girls: 13–18 years
No. of pupils enrolled as at 01/09/2022: 96
Fees as at 01/09/2022:
Full Boarding: CHF86,032–CHF102,937

Le Châtelard Academy is an international boarding school dedicated to the integral formation of young women from around the world. It is located in one of the most beautiful and peaceful areas in Switzerland, in a safe and secure environment.

Our philosophy of education is rooted in the living Catholic tradition of academic excellence, personal integrity, high moral standards and a sense of service to others. It offers every student the key to her personal happiness and fulfilment, and enables her to be successful in her personal and professional future goals. This mission is sought out through the development of talents in every aspect of the human person. Our academic program is designed so that each student can live a unique once in a lifetime educational experience.

Academic Program

Le Châtelard Academy is committed to a high quality education, with French as the language of instruction. Our curriculum focuses on individual attention of every student needs. Throughout the year our Junior High School and High School students have the advantage of learning culinary courses from the prestigious Le Cordon Bleu cooking school. They also benefit from a Savoir Vivre course every week and do social work with the elderly, the sick and the underprivileged. Le Châtelard Academy promotes Technology, Sports and the Arts.

Our team is made up of passionate educators and people with values who come from around the world, bringing with them a wealth of knowledge, experience and inspiration.

Encountering and interacting with other cultures is one of our objectives. That is why our Junior High School and High School students have the opportunity to participate in several trips during the year, such as Israel, Jordan, France, Italy, Austria, Russia, Czech Republic, Hungary among other European countries. A dynamic and professional team of helpful staff is always accompanying them on their trips.

Accreditation

Le Châtelard's academic program is designed to prepare students to take the official DELF (Diplôme Elémentaire de Langue Française) exams as well as the Cambridge English test, commonly known as "First Certificate". Cordon Bleu is honored to deliver an exclusive course covering the basic principles of traditional French cooking. Le Châtelard Institute is accredited by Cognia's Certificate of Accreditation. Meeting and exceeding those standards results in a valuable recognition of excellence.

Our school

Le Châtelard Academy was built as an elegant Belle Époque style hotel in the late 1800's. The house was equipped with modern facilities in 1992 and renovated in the past five years to offer excellent boarding facilities where tradition and innovation meet. Our bedrooms lodge 3 to 4 students and have full en-suite bathrooms and balcony. There are several living rooms, a cafeteria, a games room, dining rooms, a theatre and a chapel. We also have well-lit classrooms, a library, a computer room and a study hall. There are also painting and ceramics workshops and photography together with a Cordon Bleu kitchen classroom. Fitness, spinning and sport facilities are located in the garden flat of the building. Each student is provided with a personal iPad for their classes.

Institut Montana

INSTITUT
MONTANA – My Place to Grow®
ZUGERBERG

Schönfels 5, 6300 Zug ZG, Switzerland
Tel: +41 41 729 11 77
Email: admissions@montana-zug.ch
Website: www.montana-zug.ch
Director: Alexander Biner

School type:
Co-educational Day & Boarding
Age range of pupils: 6–19 years
No. of pupils enrolled as at 01/09/2022: 370
Average class size: 10

As a Swiss international day and boarding school, we offer the best of Swiss and International academic programmes, personalised support and a home away from home.

Students experience our international community as they become valued members of society. They learn new hobbies through our various extracurricular activities. They become well-rounded students on their path to their desired university and a successful career. All while living in a place with high security and plenty of nature.

With 370 students from over 56 countries, this is their place to grow – into a scholar, responsible young adult and a truly global citizen.

We offer a choice of academic paths, depending on whether the longer-term ambition is to graduate with the Swiss Matura or the International Baccalaureate Diploma.

- A Bilingual Elementary School for grades 1-6 where students will learn half of the subjects in German and the other half in English based on the Swiss curriculum. Boarding is only available for students who are 10 years old or older.
- A Swiss Bilingual Secondary school for grades 7-9 which is a specialised bridging programme for students who need extra help and support with German in order to transfer to the Swiss Senior HIgh school (Schweizer Gymnasium).
- A Swiss High School for grades 7-12 where students will learn in German and eventually learn English and French as well which is based on the Swiss curriculum. Successful completion guarantees a direct entry into a top Swiss university.
- An International School for grades 6-12 where students can join the Cambridge CLSP and IGCSE, the IB Diploma programme or the High School Diploma.

Our students are offered individualised academic support, college counselling and are supervised day and night on our 60-acre campus that is well-connected to major cities in Switzerland but also secluded at 1000 mt above the sea, surrounded by nature and with stunning views over the beautiful lake of Zug.

We also offer a 2- or 3-week summer session programme for students aged 10-15 in July and August where they will learn German or English alongside various academic summer classes and take field trips. As our summer motto goes, this is the place where students Learn.Grow.Move. Meet.

Inter-Community School Zurich

inter-community school zurich
EST. 1960

(Founded 1960)
Strubenacher 3, 8126 Zumikon, Switzerland
Tel: +41 44 919 8300

Email: contact@icsz.ch
Website: www.icsz.ch
Head of School: Lucy Gowdie
Secondary Principal: James Penstone
Primary Principal: Nathaniel Atherton
School type: Co-educational Day

Age range of pupils: 18 months–18 years
No. of pupils enrolled as at 01/09/2022: 840
Fees as at 01/09/2022:
Day: CHF12,220–CHF36,950
Average class size: 12-20
Teacher/pupil ratio: 1:8

School Description

The Inter-Community School Zurich (ICS) is the longest established international school in the Zurich area. A private co-educational day school, established in 1960, we provide a world-class international education for students aged 18 months to 18 years old.

Our language of instruction, in a multilingual context, is English. Our 'English as an Additional language' (EAL) programme supports students with limited English. All students learn German, the language of our host country. Students undertake the full IB Diploma. As well as offering the full IB Diploma to all students, ICS champions excellence in Sports and Arts and offers students a broad range of exciting extra – curricular opportunities alongside the academic IB programme.

Learning Beyond the Classroom

ICS believes that learning beyond the classroom, as well as within, adds value to a rigorous educational experience. We offer collaborative and innovative extra-curricular activities to inspire and engage students. Service Learning, both locally and internationally, is a key component of the ICS curriculum. Students are constantly encouraged to look beyond themselves. As a Round Square member school, ICS offers students opportunities to join Round Square Service initiatives.

Zurich, Switzerland

With vast natural and cultural resources, Switzerland is a perfect environment for "learning through doing". By deliberately structuring authentic learning experiences outside the classroom, we foster students' holistic development. Field trips are an integral part of learning at ICS, giving students the chance to apply their learning, broaden their horizons and develop leadership and independence.

Admissions

As an international school, we welcome students of all nationalities; we currently have students from 48 countries here.

We welcome applications from prospective students throughout the year. Please contact us at contact@icsz.ch if you have any questions or if you would like to arrange a visit.

Location

We are conveniently located on a single campus, situated near the Zurich city centre and easily accessed by public transportation. We also offer a school bus service.

International Bilingual School of Provence

(Founded 1984)

500 Route de Bouc-Bel-Air,
Domaine des Pins, Luynes,
Aix en Provence, 13080 France
Tel: +33 (0)4 4224 0340
Email: info@ibsofprovence.com
Website: www.ibsofprovence.com
General Director: Jean-Marc Gobbi

School type:
Co-educational Day & Boarding
Age range of pupils: 2–18 years
No. of pupils enrolled as at 01/09/2022: 850
Fees as at 01/09/2022:
Day: €12,000–€18,000
Full Boarding: €23,000–€33,000
Average class size: 16
Teacher/pupil ratio: 1:6

The International Bilingual School of Provence, an independent coeducational school located near Aix-en-Provence in the south of France, owes its international character to the diversity of its student population. The school, established since 1984, has an annual enrolment of 850 students from more than 76 different countries in its day and boarding sections. In addition to the French students who make up 50% of the student population, IBS welcomes pupils from the five continents desiring to pursue their education in English, French or both.

A particularity of the school is that the international section is not dominated by any one nationality and new students are made to feel at home immediately. Committed to French-English bilingualism, the school offers both the International Baccalaureate Diploma Programme and the French Baccalaureate. The school offers seven first languages to ensure that the student maintains his/her own language skills.

Philosophy

Small classrooms, qualified teachers, modern facilities in a tranquil, calm environment help ensure the success of each student. The campus is concentrated around the main building, a typical 'Mas' that is perfectly adapted to the daily activities of the school. IBS offers its students the most modern boarding houses and our campus includes: an audio-visual centre, fully-equipped science laboratory, newly designed dining hall, computer labs, library, swimming pool, fitness room, tennis courts, soccer field, and dance/martial arts/table tennis hall. Involvement in various extracurricular activities is expected and enhances the development of each individual's character within the spirit of the school. Politeness, respect and consideration for others are important values at IBS. Students leave IBS, the majority for university placements, as caring, responsible young citizens.

Summer school

During the spring and summer holidays, IBS offers intensive French as a Foreign Language and English immersion programmes. Over 400 students from all over the world join IBS every summer to develop their language skills while discovering the beauty of the Provence region.

Admissions

Admission applications are accepted throughout the year for interested students. For more information, contact the Admissions Department at admissions@ibsofprovence.com or consult the school website at: www.ibsofprovence.com

International College Spain

INTERNATIONAL COLLEGE SPAIN MADRID
A NORD ANGLIA EDUCATION SCHOOL

(Founded 1980)
C/Vereda Norte, 3, La Moraleja, 28109
Alcobendas, Madrid, Spain

Tel: +34 91 650 2398
Email: admissions@icsmadrid.org
Website:
www.nordangliaeducation.com/our-schools/madrid

Director: Chris Bromham
School type: Co-educational Day
Age range of pupils: 3–18 years
Fees as at 01/09/2022:
Day: €10,332–€21,735

With a vibrant community of over 70 nationalities, International College Spain is the leading international school in Madrid. ICS is the only school in Madrid to offer the International Baccalaureate Programmes throughout the whole age range (3-18). The IB diploma gives access to top universities and we are proud that 1 in 5 of our students attend the world's top 50 universities.

The school campus is situated on three hectares of land in La Moraleja, ten kilometres north of the centre of Madrid. School bus routes serve much of the city and there is excellent public transport. The facilities include separate buildings for primary and secondary schools, numerous science laboratories, an extensive arts department, music rooms, computer labs, two libraries, an interactive learning centre, extensive rooms for independent study, an auditorium, two gymnasiums, outdoor courts and running track and a cafeteria. The teaching staff is multinational, experienced and fully-qualified. The school year, from September to June with winter and spring breaks, is divided into three academic terms.

ICS has acquired a reputation for encouraging high academic achievement within a caring and stimulating environment. Central to the educational philosophy of International College Spain is the desire to promote international understanding, whilst preparing its students for the challenges of life in a multicultural global society.

ICS is part of the renowned Nord Anglia Education Group that enhances learning in 79 schools across the globe, bringing the best of the world's educational practice to the student. The school is accredited by the International Baccalaureate Organisation, The New England Association of Schools and Colleges and The Council of International Schools. ICS is approved by the Spanish Ministry of Education as a foreign school for the education of both Spanish and foreign students.

International Montessori School

Montessori

Children on the move®

(Founded 1993)

Kleinenbergstraat 97-99, 1932 St. Stevens-Woluwe, Flemish Brabant, Belgium
Tel: +32 2 767 63 60 / +32 2 721 21 11
Email: montessori-tervuren@online.be; montessori-woluwe@skynet.be
Website: www.international-montessori.org

Heads of School: Charlotte Reilly-Davidson and Nicole van Tilborg
School type: Co-educational Day
Age range of pupils: 1–18 years
No. of pupils enrolled as at 01/09/2022: 300
Fees as at 01/09/2022: €9,060 – €32,800

Multilingual Montessori Education
Montessori education offers a holistic approach helping children develop all aspects of their personality. A well-balanced child is a happy child, ready to develop to his full potential and eventually make a difference for the greater good! We take into account that different ages have the ability to reach different developmental milestones in various ways. The principle in the toddler communities and pre-schools is to offer children the opportunity to develop in harmony with their own rhythm and pace, becoming independent, with respect for all. In Primary, a vast international curriculum is offered, allowing for personal interest, decision-making, autonomous learning and related responsibilities. Thereby developing ownership, joy in learning and self-esteem in a supported and stress-free environment.

IB World School
Between our four campuses, located in Woluwe and Tervuren, we offer a bilingual curriculum to children aged 0 to 18. The International Baccalaureate Middle Years Programme and Diploma Programme allow our oldest students to benefit from low student to teacher ratios, ensuring individualised education and mentorship at all stages of their development.

Aesthetic Learning Environments
Custom-renovated historical buildings offer attractive and stimulating environments to the children, helping them to develop whilst laying the academic foundations in all subjects. Respect for learning styles is important and emphasis is placed on the development of the different intelligences.

Individualised Education
Our highly qualified teachers offer a personal and warm atmosphere. Children and older students are allowed to be whom they are meant to be and are given assistance to develop the skills to balance their opportunities.

Aside from education on the cutting edge, the school offers a bus service with door to door pick up, musical instruments for all students and an After School Hours Programme till 18.30 including outdoor play, language immersion, cooking and lots of creative projects.

International School Delft

ISD Secondary address: Colijnlaan 2, 2613 VZ Delft, Netherlands
Email: admin@internationalschooldelft.org
ISD Primary address: Jaffalaan 9, 2628 BX Delft, Netherlands
Email: admin@isdelft.nl
Tel: +31 15 8200208
Website: internationalschooldelft.com

Head of School (Secondary): Minke Veeneklaas
Head of School (Primary): Sander Raaphorst
School type: Co-educational Day
Age range of pupils: 11–16 years
No. of pupils enrolled as at 01/09/2022: 400
Fees as at 01/09/2022:
Day: €4,495–€6,055

International School Delft is located in the western part of the Netherlands, in the historical city of Delft, a centre for technical, design and artistic excellence. ISD was launched in 2014 as a small international school with less than 10 students, offering the IB Primary Years Programme. The primary school currently teaches 200 students from a diverse cultural background.

ISD's secondary campus was launched in 2019 to cater for the growing demand for international secondary education in the Delft/The Hague region. In the Secondary school we expand year-by-year- to offer all years of the Middle Years Programme by the school year 2022-23. The school currently has the candidate status for the Diploma Programme (IB DP), which will be added the year after. In the school year 2022-23, we will have around 200 students.

International School Delft strives to be a hub for the international and local communities of Delft and, as such, develops links with other schools and organisations, both international and national, in the wider region. International School Delft fosters an inclusive and friendly environment in which students are stimulated to develop into compassionate, internationally minded individuals, who strive to make a positive and peaceful change in the world. The programme aims to stimulate and builds on the natural curiosity of the student, with inspiring future oriented, inquiry-based learning.

ISD has a close relationship with the Technical University of Delft. The highly reputable TU Delft is a place of future innovation and real-world learning through its longstanding focus on design, engineering, IT and science. The partnership with the TU Delft motivates, inspires and raises the aspirations of our students. Examples of our partnership are reflected in a variety of joint projects, often focused on design thinking.

ISD, a member of Dutch International Schools, is partly state-funded and for the quality and provisions of its educational programmes accountable to the Dutch Ministry of Education.

From August 2022, we welcome students from PYP 1 to MYP 5.

International School Edward Steichen

lesc
a 21st century school

(Founded 2018)

1 Rue Edward Steichen,
9707 Clervaux, Luxembourg
Tel: +352 206 007-1
Email: info@lesc.lu
Website: www.lesc.lu
Principal: Jean Billa

School type: Co-educational Day
Age range of pupils: 4–19 years
No. of pupils enrolled as at 01/09/2022: 1000
Boys: 500 ***Girls:*** 500
Average class size: 12-25
Teacher/pupil ratio: 1:10

Lycée Edward Steichen (LESC) opened in September 2018 and as one of the new international Accredited European Schools in the Grand Duchy of Luxembourg it gives students the option to follow the European curriculum or the Luxembourg national curriculum. LESC is a co-educational non-selective day school for students aged 4-19 with currently about 1000 students on roll which will be expanding to about 1700 students in total in the next few years.

Both the secondary and the primary school are located in Clervaux in the beautiful North of the Luxembourg Ardennes. We are easily accessible via public transport. Our primary school is located on a local primary school campus that is shared with a Luxembourg primary school. At primary school level, we follow the European Schools Curriculum. We offer an anglophone, a francophone and a German-speaking European section, which caters for all students from the age of 5 to the age of 11/12. In all sections, the curriculum is taught by experienced native speaker teachers of English, French or German.

As an international school operating in the heart of one of the world's most multilingual countries, the school teaches Luxemburgish (mother tongue and beginners) as well as German, French or English as an additional language from age 4.

At secondary school level, we currently have three European school strands (anglophone, francophone and German-speaking). In the German-speaking and the francophone strand, English is taught as a first foreign language. In the anglophone strand, English is taught by experienced native speakers and French or German as a first foreign language. In addition, we also include the traditional Luxemburg school strands within our institution ('section classique' and 'section générale') in order to give students the best possible choices for their education. We offer curricula that lead either to the European baccalaureate qualification or the equivalent Luxemburg national qualifications.

As a truly international school located in a multilingual region of Europe, we welcome about 20 different nationalities at our school. In order to help students to integrate in the region, we offer Luxemburgish lessons to all our non-Luxemburg students. All teaching staff are fully qualified and must have at least 5 years professional experience. In addition, we support each student according to their individual needs via a one to one coaching program, regular Pastoral-Social-Health Education sessions and an extracurricular program of activities ranging from sports clubs, outdoor activities to the school choir, the school's own pop academy and voluntary work with local services.

As a newly opened international European school, our mission is to educate the whole child and to prepare them for the challenges of the 21st century. We aim to develop learners who become critical thinkers and well-rounded and educated students. For these reasons, in addition to offering traditional academic subjects, we also believe that the arts should play a major role in the life of the school; music, drama and dance are developed during lessons and via a range of extracurricular activities such as our pop academy and our multilingual drama group.

The school has excellent facilities including a state-of-the-art design & technology workshop, Food & Nutrition workshops, purpose designed science, music and art classrooms and networked IT suites. At primary and secondary school, all students are supported in their learning via the use of iPads. Specialist rooms and facilities include science laboratories, art studios and modern languages and humanities classrooms, two fully equipped sports halls and a swimming pool plus a self-service restaurant and cafeteria.

A wide range of sports is offered, including football, climbing, swimming, gymnastics, athletics and basketball and the school participates successfully in sporting events. Similarly, extra-curricular activities are an integral part of our school day – we offer additional activities in sport, music and drama with opportunities for overseas travel and school trips and exchanges with national and international partner schools.

As we develop as a new school, we will continue to expand our school offer, but we will remain focused on providing all children with the best possible education in an ever-changing world.

International School of Bergamo

Via Monte Gleno, 54, 24125 Bergamo, Italy
Tel: +39 035 213776
Email: info@isbergamo.com
Website: www.isbergamo.com
Heads of School: Mrs. Guia Ghidoli & Mrs. Chiara Traversi

Head of Primary: Roisin Cosgrove
Head of Secondary: Roberta Sana
School type: Co-educational Day
Age range of pupils: 2–18 years
No. of pupils enrolled as at 01/09/2022: 360

Founded in 2011 the International School of Bergamo (ISBergamo) is part of the Inspired Education Group, a leading global schools group educating over 55,000 students across a network of more than 75 schools. Committed to delivering high quality educational programmes, ISB strives to develop the intellectual, personal, emotional and social skills needed to live, learn and work in a rapidly globalising world.

The school is a friendly and innovative IB Continuum School offering the Primary, Middle Years and Diploma Programmes.

Joining the International School of Bergamo offers a fantastic opportunity to enter a safe and nurturing environment, where the Italian culture is valued alongside the recognition and appreciation of a multicultural collective diversity. Technology plays an important role in the school and is embedded in the school curriculum through a blended approach where we feel it adds value to teaching and learning.

The school is located in a modern building in the Eastern part of Bergamo, in a green and quiet environment. The area is rich in sporting facilities, including a modern football pitch situated just next to the school as well as rugby fields and an athletics track at the end of the road.

Students can benefit from a totally refurbished building with new, specialised facilities including a dedicated Early Years area, an Art & Design Lab, a school library, an innovation hub, and an outdoor multipurpose sports facility, as well as a cafeteria and playgrounds.

Recent additions to the facility include a Secondary School wing with a specialized Science Laboratory, a Music & Dance studio, and a fully equipped indoor gym.

Thanks to an efficient bus service, the school covers the city of Bergamo as well as a large number of the surrounding communities.

International School of Como

Via Adda 25,
22073 Fino Mornasco (CO), Italy
Tel: +39 031 572289
Email: info@iscomo.com
Website: www.iscomo.com

Head of School: Mr Gavin Williams
School type: Co-educational Day
Age range of pupils: 2–18 years
No. of pupils enrolled as at 01/09/2022: 400

Founded in 2002, the International School of Como (ISC) has grown to stand for excellence and has contributed to the expansion of international education in Northern Italy, as one of the almost 5,000 International Baccalaureate (IB) schools located worldwide. Today, ISC welcomes over 400 students from 2 to 18 years old of 47 nationalities and an international staff of more than 60 qualified teachers and assistants.

ISC is committed to providing children with the best educational experience possible. ISC offers the IB (International Baccalaureate) Primary Years, Middle Years and Diploma Programmes and aspires to create a community where learning is the central driving factor of a journey in which our students become ethical thinkers, creative problem-solvers, community-minded and individuals of action on the world stage.

Our state-of-the-art campus was designed and built specifically for our students and provides for every aspect of a vibrant, innovative and rigorous education. Over 10,000 square metres of internal and external spaces house our extremely large classrooms, a Robotics lab, two Art Studios, indoor gym and outdoor multipurpose sports facility, cafeteria and playgrounds. Recent additions to the facility include a Secondary School wing, 3 fully equipped Science Laboratories, a Drama Studio, and Primary and Secondary School Libraries, newly expanded and renovated.

With our efficient bus service we can cover a large number of the surrounding communities, and beyond, including: Como, Cantù/Carimate, Lecco, Varese, and Lugano (Switzerland).

At ISC we are driven by our Mission Statement which is: "*International School of Como is a student-centered community of internationally-minded learners. We offer a balanced and challenging curriculum, in a safe and nurturing environment, where we respect and value the Italian culture and our collective diversity. We empower all students to be active, reflective and responsible lifelong learners who can achieve their full potential and contribute to an ever-changing world.*"

International School of Düsseldorf e.V.

ISD
INTERNATIONAL SCHOOL OF DÜSSELDORF
SINCE 1968

(Founded 1968)

Niederrheinstrasse 323/336,
40489 Düsseldorf,
North Rhine-Westphalia, Germany
Tel: +49 (0) 211-9406 6
Email: info@isdedu.de
Website: www.isdedu.de
School Director: Frank Tschan

Appointed: 2020
School type: Co-educational Day
Age range of pupils: 3–18 years
No. of pupils enrolled as at 01/06/2022: 960
Fees as at 01/09/2022: Please enquire
Average class size: 16-18
Teacher/pupil ratio: 1:8

Welcome to ISD – where no fitting in is required!

We're proud to say that at ISD, there is no 'one size fits all'. We welcome students with different interests, talents, and abilities into our school, and support each of them to become the very best version of themselves they can be.

Flexibility is therefore a hallmark of learning at ISD: our learning environments are adaptable and dynamic; our interdisciplinary units allow students to develop creative solutions outside the bounds of a single subject; our elective courses provide opportunities for students to forge their own path; and our Additional Learning Opportunities (ALOs) allow students the freedom to discover connections between their passions and their talents.

Crucial to this flexibility, is our teaching staff. Currently representing over 28 nationalities, they bring an abundance of knowledge, experience, and diversity to our classrooms. Working collaboratively, they provide a challenging and supportive environment for all students.

Families are another key partner in the learning journey. At ISD, parents enjoy ample opportunity to participate in all aspects of school life. We believe such broad community engagement exposes our students to more varied learning opportunities, and is an important part of what makes learning at our school rich and authentic.

In fact, the idea of the "ISD family" is a defining feature of the ISD culture. Newcomers are warmly welcomed, and carefully supported to integrate quickly into the school community. For many, ISD quickly becomes a home away from home, where lifelong friendships are forged.

This, in a nutshell, is ISD: a school committed to providing an education that is relevant, today and tomorrow; an education that sees our students flourish and inspires them to make a positive difference in their world.

International School of Madrid

(Founded 1971)
Calle Rosa Jardón, 28016 Madrid, Spain

Tel: +34 91 359 21 21
Email:
info@internationalschoolofmadrid.com
Website:
www.internationalschoolofmadrid.com
Heads of School: Mr. Rich Cook & Mr. Huw Mawson

School type: Co-educational Day
Age range of pupils: 2–18 years
No. of pupils enrolled as at 01/09/2022: 820
Boys: 375 ***Girls:*** 445 ***Sixth Form:*** 100
Average class size: 20
Teacher/pupil ratio: 1:9

We are a family school in the heart of Madrid, and since 1971 have been offering a quality British education to children aged 2 to 18 from all over the world. 50 years of academic excellence. Our motto is *Respect, Loyalty and Friendship* and these words form the foundation of everything we believe in. We are known for our child-centred approach, happy atmosphere and high standards of achievement – our pupils outperform their UK and international counterparts in official examinations and also excel in sports and the arts.

We follow the English National Curriculum throughout, in parallel with 20% for Spanish studies (Spanish language & literature and humanities). This means that students can validate their studies with the Spanish system and that all of our pupils have the opportunity to learn Spanish and English to a native level.

Students complete the IGCSE programme in Years 10-11 and then undertake A-Level studies in Years 12-13. Our unique mix of advanced level British and Spanish subjects in these final years mean that our students leave prepared to enter British, US and Spanish universities, as well as those from across the world. Our students achieve highly, with 100% usually going on to attend university at 18. Our students have been awarded 73 Outstanding Cambridge Learner Awards, in recognition of their phenomenal exam results and making us one of the most successful centres in Spain.

As a British school, we employ highly qualified, native-speaking teachers who provide an education to pupils just as if they were in a school in the UK. We encourage children in active rather than passive learning. No amount of book learning can make up for an equal period of first-hand experience. Our theme is not 'I teach, you learn.' No! We prefer 'We are all here together to learn from each other'.

We recognise that each student is unique and care passionately about their social and moral development. We are committed to providing the best possible start in life for every one of our pupils. Therefore, even more important than their academic success, we are proud of how well our students behave and of the good adults that they grow up to become.

International School of Milan

Via I Maggio, 20,
20021 Baranzate (MI), Italy
Tel: +39 02 872581
Email: admissions@ism-ac.it
Website:
www.internationalschoolofmilan.it

Headmaster: Mr. Darren Nicholas
School type:
Co-educational Day & Boarding
Age range of pupils:
2–18 years (Boarding 14-18 years)
No. of pupils enrolled as at 01/09/2022: 900

Welcome to the International School of Milan. Although we are the longest established international school in the city, at our school you will find the strongest academic standards supported by the most progressive educational thinking that has served the international and Italian communities in Milan for over 60 years.

We are confident that our ethos, focused on achievement and underpinned by opportunity for all, will enable your children to develop their confidence and be ready to embrace the challenges of the future.

The IB curriculum (which runs throughout all years) is a truly international one and is a perfect fit for the needs of all our students. Our PYP, MYP and IB Diploma programmes thoroughly prepare our students for further study all around the world, including at some of the world's leading universities.

Our dedicated, international and skilled teaching body ensures that all students achieve highly at the school regardless of their ability. Their desire to challenge young minds is shaped by a growth mindset, ensuring that the focus is on every student achieving beyond what a school might 'normally expect'. In short, we believe your child can achieve more and be happier with us at IS Milan.

We opened our brand new boarding house in September 2018 and can accommodate up to approximately 45 students. With the care and attention given by our staff, boarding at IS Milan provides a truly transformative international educational experience for 14 to 18-year-olds.

The International School of Milan is proud of its position in the city as the premier international IB school in terms of its curriculum and outlook and is renowned for its high educational standards and caring learning environment. We are also an international community with over 50 nationalities and a student body that is proud to belong to our school community and enthusiastic about the learning they take part in.

We are certain that you will see the International School of Milan as a place where learning is genuinely celebrated and where each of our students are valued and challenged to succeed from the age of 2 up to 18.

International School of Modena

Piazza Montessori, 1/A,
41051 Montale Rangone (MO), Italy
Tel: +39 059 530649
Email: admissions@ismodena.it
Website:
www.internationalschoolofmodena.it

Head of School: Mrs. Caroline Troughton
School type: Co-educational Day
Age range of pupils: 3–18 years
No. of pupils enrolled as at 01/09/2022: 230

Welcome to the International School of Modena. Inaugurated in 1998 as a joint venture with Tetra Pak, whose global research and development unit is located in Modena, ISM is a proud member of Inspired which is the fastest growing premium international schools' group operating on 5 continents and educating over 50,000 students globally. Our modern, purpose-built campus, surrounded by green open spaces, is located 12km outside of the city of Modena.

We are a truly international school representing approximately 27 different nationalities and offering the full continuum of International Baccalaureate (IB) education, with the Primary Years Programme (PYP) for children ages 3 – 11, Middle Years Programme (MYP) for ages 11-16 and the Diploma Programme (DP) for 16-18 years. ISM is one of only a handful of schools in Italy currently authorised to offer this programme which will thoroughly prepare your child for study all around the world, including at some of the world's leading universities. Our innovative Early Years department features beautiful spaces and play structures specially designed to support the delivery of the IB PYP and Reggio-Inspired Early Years Curriculum.

The curriculum at ISM is carefully designed to reflect the ethos of the school and of the International Baccalaureate with a commitment to inquiry-based learning, encouraging every student to ask questions, to think for themselves and develop the skills to become confident, independent learners who will grow up to be balanced, caring and principled citizens. Our dedicated, international teaching body ensures that students achieve highly at the school. We believe in challenging young minds, ensuring that our focus is on every student achieving beyond expectations both inside and outside of the curriculum. Over the last three years we have achieved an average of 36 in the IB Diploma with a top score of 45 out of 45, allowing our students to access world class universities in numerous countries. In 2020 the school attained its highest ever average IB Diploma score of 38.3.

The International School of Modena is a small, friendly school, with just over 240 students at present but it is growing fast due to its popularity with both expat and local families. We are proud to be a premium international school offering high quality education in a caring environment with happy, contented students. We are certain that you will see that ISM is a place that celebrates learning and values each and every student, offering them a challenging, enjoyable education aimed at developing a range of skills required for future success.

International School of Monza

(Founded 1984)

Via Solferino 23, 20900 Monza (MB), Italy
Tel: +39 039 9357701
Email: admin@ismonza.it
Website: www.internationalschoolofmonza.it
Head of School: Mr. Iain Sachev

Appointed: September 2017
School type: Co-educational Day
Age range of pupils: 2.5–18 years
No. of pupils enrolled as at 01/09/2022: 280
Average class size: 17
Teacher/pupil ratio: 1:7

At International School of Monza, a full International Baccalaureate (IB) continuum school authorised to offer the Primary Years Programme (PYP), Middle Years Programme (MYP) and Diploma Programme (DP), we endeavour to deliver the International Baccalaureate programmes in the purist of forms, with the school's core values and the IB's Learner Profile embodied in everything that we do. Both the school and the group to which it belongs, have an established record of success in the IB, from age 2 1/2 all the way through to admission to the world's leading universities at age 18 and, whilst the school has a forty-year-long year history and has close ties with its sister schools around Italy and beyond, there's a fresh and unique feel to everything we do.

Perhaps most of note is the sense of collaboration that exists amongst all members of the school community. This is most evident in the way in which our highly qualified and multi-cultural teachers and inquisitive students work towards a common goal of academic success which is seamlessly balanced with an inherent commitment to active global citizenship at every level.

Although all classrooms are fitted with smart TVs and students bring Apple iPads or MacBooks to school, our teachers – who are certified Microsoft Innovative Educators – use technology in a blended approach where we feel it adds value to teaching and learning. This is done through the use of a variety of carefully selected educational technologies (including Inspired AI) and does not merely replace traditional methods (yes, we do use books and, yes, we do talk to one another). We also prepare our Italian students to sit their Quinta Elementare and Terza Media examinations with us and, year on year, they achieve truly exceptional results. Furthermore, our culminating programme, the IB Diploma, has legal equivalence to the Maturita'.

All this takes place in our city-centre campus – a stylish and colourful factory conversion – which has been specifically designed to foster collaborative approaches to teaching and learning. Our science laboratories are fitted with state-of-the-art equipment, and we also boast carefully designed on-site spaces which support the delivery of our Reggio-Inspired Early Years Curriculum, three beautiful libraries, as well as studios for visual arts, drama and music, supported by a large indoor and outdoor sports complex just a three-minute walk away. That said, living in such a culturally rich part of the world, we take many opportunities to knock down our classroom walls and learn from opportunities in the local and not-so-local area.

Our educational offering, driven by the most modern education research, truly prepares our students for the complex and interconnected world that lies ahead, whilst also ensuring that they are ever-curious and are instilled with the values will help create a more peaceful global society.

International School of Neustadt

SBW INTERNATIONAL SCHOOL NEUSTADT

(Founded 2005)

Haardterstrasse 1, 67433 Neustadt an der Weinstrasse, Germany
Tel: +49 6321 8900 960
Email: info@is-neustadt.de
Website: www.is-neustadt.de
Principal: Vjeko Kovac

School type: Co-educational Day
Age range of pupils: 4–18 years
No. of pupils enrolled as at 01/09/2022: 70
Fees as at 01/09/2022:
Day: €14,200–€16,700

The International School Neustadt (ISN) is a coeducational, full-day international school for children aged 4-18 years. ISN was founded in 2005 by the Verband der Holz- und Kunststoffverarbeitenden Industrie Rheinland-Pfalz e.V together with the financial support of the "SBW Haus des Lernens" organisation (Switzerland). With around 70 students from over 18 nations, ISN offers a caring family atmosphere both for expatriates and local families. Expatriate families enjoy the social network at ISN which eases integration into a new location, while local German parents benefit from the innovative educational program and English language instruction.

ISN offers the Cambridge Primary, IGCSE (International General Certificate of Secondary Education) and A-level programs, and is an accredited examination center for Cambridge International Examinations, offering the full range of English examinations.

ISN's campuses include a couple of adjacent vineyard villas and the school offers a full day program from 8am until 5pm. While the main language of instruction is English, German classes are also taught to all students from beginner to native-speaker level. Before- and after-school adult supervision is available each day, at no extra cost, to students from kindergarten up to grade 5. ISN also provides a wide range of after-school activities including music, chess, art and sports.

ISN is recognized by the state of Rhineland- Palatinate as an accredited supplementary school ('anerkannte Ergaenzungsschule').

The school is owned and managed by the famous Swiss education provider, SBW Haus des Lernens, which has over 40 years of experience in the field of private education, currently managing more than 10 schools throughout Switzerland and Germany. Some of the innovative approaches developed by SBW and implemented at ISN include personalized student coaching, autonomous learning and the development of learning skills.

For more information please contact the Admissions Office: info@is-neustadt.de

International School of Nice

(Founded 1977)

15 Avenue Claude Debussy,
06200 Nice, France
Tel: +33 (0)4 93 21 04 00
Email: admissions@isn-nice.com
Website: www.isn-nice.com
Director: Mrs Mel Curtis
Appointed: 2020

School type: Co-educational Day
Age range of pupils: 3–18 years
No. of pupils enrolled as at 01/09/2022: 430
Fees as at 01/09/2022:
Day: €11,400–€20,685
Average class size: 22

The International School of Nice is an accredited, co-educational, non-sectarian, IB World School, providing Anglophone education for the international community in the Cannes-Nice-Monte Carlo region. The school offers a complete international education from Young Explorers (age 3) to Grade 12 (age 18). ISN Nice is a member of the Globeducate network.

The Primary School follows the IB Primary Years Programme, a rich, inquiry-based approach to learning that focuses on the individual needs of every child. French is mandatory from age 5, and taught on a daily basis. An EAL programme parallels mainstream English in the Primary and Middle Schools.

The Middle School is a candidate for the IB Middle Years Programme, with a particular focus on the social and emotional development of students, as well as high academic standards.

The High School curriculum prepares students for the IGCSE exams, the High School Diploma and the IB Diploma. Students are guided and supported to reach their potential in a safe and caring environment. A team of highly-qualified and experienced teachers respond to students' diverse learning styles and challenges them through exciting and innovative practices. Over 95% of graduates go directly to college/university, primarily in the UK, France and North America.

The faculty represents over 30 nationalities, and the student body is truly a melting pot, representing over 65 nationalities, with students from Anglophone countries making up ca.20%. This enables cultural awareness and participation in a globalised world for all our students.

The school year is from September through June with classes meeting from 08:30 to 16:00. There are a number of extra-curricular activities, including a variety of sports, Model United Nations, Student Council and field trips. The school occupies a purpose-built facility constructed in 1987 and is located five minutes from Nice International Airport.

ISN prepares its students to excel in the world of tomorrow in an inspiring, supporting and nourishing environment.

International School of Siena

Via del Petriccio e Belriguardo, 49/1,
53100 Siena, Italy
Tel: +39 0577 328103
Email: office@issiena.it
Website:
www.internationalschoolofsiena.it

Principal: Ms. Lianne Knibb
School type: Co-educational Day
Age range of pupils: 3–18 years
No. of pupils enrolled as at 01/09/2022: 200

The International School of Siena opened in 2010 and has developed and grown considerably during the subsequent years. We are the only IB through school in Tuscany, fully authorised for the Primary Years Programme (PYP), Middle Years Programme (MYP) and Diploma Programme (DP).

Learning at IS Siena is exciting and engaging, as students strive for excellence in a climate that is caring and responsive to individual needs and goals. Our global vision is coordinated by an outstanding team of educational leaders and implemented by our highly skilled and dedicated professional staff.

In January 2019, we relocated to our stunning new school building where we enjoy a spacious, light, modern teaching spaces with a spacious indoor gym, Drama/Dance studio, 2 Libraries, Music and Art rooms and Science laboratories fitted out to the highest standards. Our Early Years spaces are specially designed to complement the Reggio Inspired teaching approach.

Learning at the International School of Siena is an international experience with students from around 20 nationalities. It leads to a perception of the world that merges understanding of our global context with the development of skills and attitudes that young people require to participate fully in the world of tomorrow, both as national and global citizens.

At the same time, we deeply appreciate the diversity of Mother tongue languages of our school community and aim to celebrate our diversity as well as supporting each student to appreciate our host country of Italy and become fully bilingual in English and Italian. We are so fortunate to be located in a beautiful area of Tuscany where we have access to a variety of cultural and educational resources in our local area which we strive to incorporate into the experience of the students, making connections between the classroom and the real world.

We are a welcoming school community in which parents, students and staff work together to provide a stimulating programme, which engages each child in an inquiry based environment.

International School of Ticino SA

Via Ponteggia, 23, Cadempino,
6814 Lugano, Switzerland
Tel: +41 919710344
Email: frontoffice@isticino.com
Website: www.isticino.com

Head of School: Mr. Andrew Ackers
School type: Co-educational Day
Age range of pupils: 3–18 years
No. of pupils enrolled as at 01/09/2022: 230

The International School of Ticino is a special and exciting place to be. We are the first and only accredited International Baccalaureate (IB), Primary Years Programme (PYP) School in Ticino, Switzerland and authorized school for the Middle Years Programme (MYP) and Diploma Programme (DP).

At the International School of Ticino we place the student at the centre of all we do to facilitate them to become lifelong learners. We achieve this through our school culture, which is rooted in the IB Mission statement, which states: The International Baccalaureate aims to develop inquiring, knowledgeable and caring young people who help to create a better and more peaceful world through intercultural understanding and respect.

The school opened as a Kindergarten in 2014. It was established to offer the local and international residents of Ticino an IB education. As of 2017 the International School of Ticino became joined by the education group Inspired, who educate over 65,000 students in 80 schools worldwide.

This grounding and combination with a leading education group has laid the foundations for the special community of learning which we see today in our new campus. The school now accommodates students from Kindergarten, 3 years old, to 18, offering the IB PYP, MYP and DP programme.

The design and build of the new campus has drawn upon our foundations, the IB mission and the vision of the school; Inspiring the Extraordinary.

We accommodate our students in a facilitated student centred learning environment, where we equip all to develop in the international sector and in line with Ticino requirements, enabling your child to study at our school from the age of 3-18/19.

The International School of Ticino is a special and exciting place to be and we look forward to welcoming you to our community for a school visit, trial day and enrolment.

International School San Patricio Toledo

International School San Patricio Toledo
An inspired school

(Founded 2006)

Juan de Vergara, 1, Urbanización La Legua, Toledo, 45005 Spain
Tel: +34 925 280 363
Email: infotoledo@colegiosanpatricio.es
Website: colegiosanpatriciotoledo.com/en

Headmaster: Mr. Simon Hatton-Burke
School type: Co-educational Day & Boarding
Age range of pupils: 3–18 years
No. of pupils enrolled as at 01/09/2022: 550
Average class size: 3-20 max

International School San Patricio Toledo Boarding School is one of the few educational institutions which offers the full continuum of the prestigious International Baccalaureate. From 1 to 18 years: PYP (Primary Years Programme), MYP (Middle Years Programme) and DP (Diploma Programme bilingual or in English).

International School San Patricio Toledo offers its students the chance to obtain the official qualification for English issued by the University of Cambridge and official qualification for French with Alliance Française and for German with the Goethe institute.

Location: Our school is located in an exclusive residential area of Toledo (less than 1 hour from Madrid by car and 30 min by high speed train). The school is located in spacious grounds of over 30,000 square meters.

The boarding school offers full and weekly boarding and is located within the school grounds, which means full access to a wealth of excellent sports and recreational facilities. This ensures that our boarding students live on a purpose designed campus with maximum security and comfort.

Furthermore, International School San Patricio Toledo Boarding School offers a complete educational experience for students between 12 years old (weekly) – 14 (full) and 18 years of age, allowing them to develop the necessary communication and social skills to thrive at university and in life.

Our school is bilingual English and Spanish throughout with additional focus on German and French language acquisition.

Accommodation: First class facilities. Lodgings are purposely designed to facilitate social cohesion and promote well being.

Life outside the classroom: all the students of the Full Boarding can access a programme of leisure and culture for the weekends throughout the school year.

International School Westpfalz

SBW INTERNATIONAL SCHOOL WESTPFALZ

(Founded 2017)

Nikolaus-von-Weis-Strasse 10,
66849 Landstuhl, Germany
Tel: +49 6371 980 930
Email: info@is-westpfalz.de
Website: www.is-westpfalz.de
Principal: Christopher Moore

School type: Co-educational Day
Age range of pupils: 4–18 years
No. of pupils enrolled as at 01/09/2022: 200
Fees as at 01/09/2022:
Day: €14,400–€16,700

The International School Westpfalz (ISW) is a coeducational, full-day international school for children aged 4-18 years. ISW was founded in 2017 by the "SBW Haus des Lernens" organisation (Switzerland). With around 200 students from over 20 nations, ISW offers a caring family atmosphere both for expatriates and local families. Expatriate families enjoy the social network at ISW which eases integration into a new location, while local German parents benefit from the innovative educational program and English language instruction.

ISW offers the Cambridge Primary, IGCSE (International General Certificate of Secondary Education) and A-level programs, and is an accredited examination center for Cambridge International Examinations, offering the full range of English examinations.

ISW is based in a beautiful former monastery in Landstuhl with the school offering a full day program from 8am until 5pm. While the main language of instruction is English, German classes are also taught daily to all students. Before- and after-school adult supervision is available each day to students from kindergarten up to grade 6. ISW also provides a wide range of after-school activities including music, drama, art and sports.

ISW is recognized by the state of Rhineland- Palatinate as an accredited supplementary school ('anerkannte Ergaenzungsschule').

The school is owned and managed by the famous Swiss education provider, SBW Haus des Lernens, which has over 40 years of experience in the field of private education, currently managing more than 10 schools throughout Switzerland and Germany. Some of the innovative approaches developed by SBW and implemented at ISW include personalized student coaching, autonomous learning and the development of learning skills. For more information please contact the Admissions Office: info@is-westpfalz.de

IPS Cascais

IPS Cascais
BRITISH INTERNATIONAL SCHOOL
PORTUGAL

(Founded 1982)
Rua da Lagoa 171, Bicesse,
2645-344 Alcabideche, Lisbon, Portugal
Tel: +351 214 570 149
Email: info@ipsschool.org
Website: www.ipsschool.org

Head of School: Neil Morris
School type: Co-educational Day
Age range of pupils:
3–12 years (up to 18 in September 2023)
No. of pupils enrolled as at 01/09/2022: 300
Average €10,733 annual fee

IPS Cascais, is a school that prides itself on the warmth of its welcome to children and parents from around the world. It is a relatively small school of around 300 children, but almost 40 different nationalities make up the close-knit community.

This multinational community helps to create a learning environment that fosters a global understanding; appreciating cultures, as well as each other. The school is proud of the high academic standards attained by the children and encourages them to achieve their best in all aspects of the curriculum.

IPS Cascais has been teaching the National Curriculum of England for 40 years, starting all the way back in 1982. In 2010, IPS Cascais moved into its sustainable, purpose-built facilities that are ideal for Primary Education. This colourful site is equipped with playing fields, a library with over 22,500 books, and plenty of accessible areas to facilitate outdoor learning.

Situated 25km to the west of Lisbon, the school attracts families living in Cascais and the surrounding localities, from Oeiras to Sintra. There are even a few families that travel in from Lisbon.

Currently at IPS Cascais, the classroom average is 18 children per class, with a 1:8 teacher-student ratio. Enabling your children to become healthy, independent, and responsible members of society is of great importance. Pupils' personal, social and emotional development is encouraged by the supportive school ethos.

IPS Cascais is proudly opening its very own Secondary school from September 2022. Year 7 will be hosted on the primary site until their brand new campus for Secondary opens in September 2023. Classes will eventually be available up until Year 13.

For further information, do not hesitate to get in touch and the team will be happy to help.

ISF Tervuren International School

Stationsstraat 3, 3080 Tervuren, Flemish Brabant, Belgium
Tel: +32 2 767 3098
Email: office@isftervuren.org
Website: www.isftervuren.org
Head of Campus: Orla McLoughlin
Deputy Head of Campus: Julie Boyd

School type: Co-educational Day
Age range of pupils: 2.5–11 years
No. of pupils enrolled as at 01/09/2022: 80
Fees as at 01/09/2022:
Please see website

The International School of Flanders – Tervuren is a small international primary school for children ages 2.5 – 11 years located approximately 15-20 minutes from Brussels. We are accredited by CIS (Council of International Schools) and COBIS (Council of British International Schools). We offer small class sizes, individual attention and differentiated learning to all of our students. We follow the UK national curriculum for Literacy and Numeracy and the IPC (International Primary Curriculum) for all other core subjects. We also offer Sport, Music, EAL, Dutch and French to our students.

Our community is truly international, and we embrace individual differences, cultures, and religions. We foster in students the values of understanding, cooperation, honesty and respect. We believe that building a child's self-esteem and confidence is paramount. Our small class sizes provide a safe, caring and secure teaching environment where children receive individual attention and enjoy learning through exploration and discovery. ISF is a Google for Education school and currently the only one in Belgium. All our students have access to Google learning resources using Chromebooks, Tablets and Interactive whiteboards. ISF is also working towards becoming a Green Flag school, and as such our students are involved in Eco-Friendly initiatives both in school and the local community.

ISF Waterloo International School

280 Chaussee de Waterloo, 1640 Rhode-St-Genese, Flemish Brabant, Belgium
Tel: +32 2 358 56 06
Email: office@isfwaterloo.org
Website: www.isfwaterloo.org
Executive Head: Belinda Yates
Deputy Executive Head: Cobus Steyn
Head of Primary School: Arancha Barrasa
Head of Secondary School: Nadim Bayeh
School type: Co-educational Day
Age range of pupils: 2.5–18 years
No. of pupils enrolled as at 01/09/2022: 225
Fees as at 01/09/2022:
Please see website

The International School of Flanders – Waterloo hosts a primary and secondary school for children between 2.5–18 years of age, located within 20 min from Brussels. We provide an international education taught in the English language. We are accredited by CIS (Council of International Schools) and COBIS (Council of British International Schools). We offer small class sizes, individual attention and differentiated learning to all of our students.

Our community is truly international, and we embrace individual differences, cultures, and religions. We foster in students the values of understanding, cooperation, honesty and respect. We believe that building a child's self-esteem and confidence is paramount. Our small class sizes provide a safe, loving and secure teaching environment where children receive individual attention and enjoy learning through exploration and discovery.

ISF is a Google for Education school and currently the only one in Belgium. All our students have access to Google learning resources using Chromebooks, Tablets and Interactive whiteboards daily. We also offer Sport, Music, EAL, and French to our students.

Primary:

In Primary School, we follow the International Primary Curriculum, which is an internationally-minded, thematic based curriculum that encourages students to develop their ability to learn and acquire the skills needed to become life-long learners. Alongside the IPC curriculum, we also run strong international literacy and numeracy programs. We also offer additional English to non-native English speakers to help them integrate faster into school life. Our curriculum includes learning about international mindedness and developing international understanding with our students working towards receiving a Global Citizenship Diploma. ISF is also working towards becoming a Green Flag school, and as such, our students are also involved in Eco-friendly initiatives both in school and the local community.

Middle & Secondary School:

Years 7-9, students follow a curriculum based on the National Curriculum of England and Wales, tailored to our student's needs in Maths, English and Science, and a modified programme in other subjects.

Years 10 – 11 students follow a two-year IGCSE year programme from Cambridge and is completed with formal examinations at the end of the 2nd year when students receive an internationally recognised set of graded certificates denoting a standardised level of formal education at secondary school.

Year 12 – 13 (A-Level) curriculum caters for students aged 17-18, preparing them for University entrance. A-Level is a two-year course in selected subjects.

Kensington School

(Founded 1968)
Avenida de Bularas No. 2, Pozuelo de Alarcón, 28224 Madrid, Spain
Tel: +34 91 7154 699
Email: kensington@kensingtonschool.net
Website: www.kensington-school.es

Headteacher: Mr Andrew de Salis
School type: Co-educational Day
Age range of pupils: 18 months–18 years
No. of pupils enrolled as at 01/09/2022: 2200
Fees as at 01/09/2022:
Day: €6,000–€7,790

Kensington, Your British School it's a co-educational school from 18 months to 18 years. Our pupils study from their first day in a British school with native teachers, following the same educational system as any child in the United Kingdom.

We aim to offer our students an excellent human and academic education, so that they leave our school as fine young men and women, fluent in English, Spanish and French with internationally-recognised qualifications and results which open the doors to any Spanish or international university. Supported in their path through the school by a personal, holistic approach to education, our children learn critical thinking, how to live and work together on their way to becoming happy, well-rounded adults.

Pupils at Kensington achieve outstanding results in external examinations [IGCSE, Cambridge, DELF and EvAU] thanks to our system of careful individual tracking of student achievement. Individual needs are met: whether they are experiencing difficulties, or whether they excel. Class teachers and tutors, the support teachers, the small groups, the concept of 'differentiation' of the British curriculum and the guidance department are key elements in a strong support system.

More than a school: Our tradition in Music, Art and Drama, our focus on languages and our love for sport are reflected in our clubs. They go beyond extra-curricular activities. The clubs are part of our DNA. Children feel responsible for getting the most out of the skill that brings them together with other pupils, they create personal bonds founded on shared interests and common projects: Music and movement, Ballet, Judo, Cookery Class, Green Activity Club, Computing Club, Creative Writing Club, Art Club, Chinese, Piano, Ukulele Club, Chess, French, Drama, Computer, Debating Club, Journalism Workshop, Public Speaking… Every pupil, regardless of their academic level, has the chance to shine in ways which will boost their self-confidence and social skills.

King William's College

KING WILLIAM'S COLLEGE

(Founded 1833)

Castletown, Isle of Man IM9 1TP UK
Tel: +44 (0)1624 820110
Email: admissions@kwc.im
Website: www.kwc.im
Principal: Mr Joss Buchanan
Appointed: January 2017
School type:
Co-educational Day & Boarding

Religious Denomination: Church of England
Age range of pupils: 11–18 years
No. of pupils enrolled as at 01/09/2022: 380
Fees as at 01/09/2022:
Day: £19,745–£26,395
Full Boarding: £32,740–£39,390
Average class size: 10-20
Teacher/pupil ratio: 1:8

We are a relatively small school, under 400 students. Approximately 25% of students board, with half of the boarders coming from the Island and the rest from a wide variety of countries around the world. We are non-selective, but through the dedication of our staff, the structure of support for each individual and the work ethic of the students, we achieve excellent results. Our students go to top universities in the UK, Europe and the USA.

The Isle of Man is a beautiful environment in which to live. It is a safe haven with a very low crime rate, giving students the freedom to explore and take advantage of the fresh air, open countryside and beaches, away from the hustle and bustle and pollution of a busy city. The Island is easy to get to with air links from the major airports in the UK.

We are one of the few UK schools where every student in the Sixth Form studies for the International Baccalaureate Diploma. The IB philosophy – particularly its emphasis on skills and its focus on internationalism – is central to our approach and we are one of the largest and most experienced IB schools in the British Isles.

Our pupils follow a broad curriculum of sporting activities, competing in the major sports against UK and Island schools. Every three years, the senior rugby and hockey teams embark on a world sports tour during the summer months. We have golf, paddle boarding and sailing on offer along with a wide variety of other extracurricular activities.

Drama and Music thrive and pupils are given the opportunity to perform at many events and productions. There are workshops throughout the year and students are also encouraged to participate in competitions.

'An Island Education for a Global Future'

King's College School, Cascais

KING'S COLLEGE SCHOOL
CASCAIS

Rua Cesário Verde 395, Pampilheira,
2750-657 Cascais, Lisbon, Portugal
Tel: +351 215 966 634
Email: cascais@kingscollegeschool.pt
Website: www.kingscollegeschool.pt
Head of School: Sarah Osborne-James

School type: Co-educational Day
Age range of pupils:
1–13 years (18 years from Sep. 2026)
No. of pupils enrolled as at 01/09/2022: 400
Fees as at 01/09/2022:
Day: €9,935–€15,800

King's College School, one of the most prestigious educational institutions in the world, is opening in Cascais, Portugal, in September 2022. The school comes with a 50-year heritage of academic excellence from King's College Schools' Group, coupled with the global experience and expertise of Inspired – the leading global education group with over 80 premium schools, across five continents.

King's College School, Cascais will offer brand new academic and sports facilities plus a boarding house in a purpose-built campus with an outstanding 40,000sqm, so that each student can benefit from a premium learning environment and thrive.

With specialised-subject teachers from Primary onwards, our premium educational programme provides students with an exclusive international curriculum, creating open-minded, creative and dynamic individuals. Students will benefit from the uniquely developed Inspired Approach to Early Years education, building up through the world-renowned Cambridge International Primary and Secondary curricula and IGCSEs. A bilingual programme is available for students up to Year 5 who are interested in following the Portuguese curriculum while also mastering the English language.

Languages and technology are also key parts of the curriculum, as are sports and performing arts. This unique learning pathway will also draw on the culture, values and heritage of Portugal. At King's College School, Cascais, we believe in creating out-of-the-box thinkers, spirited individuals; allowing our students to learn from first-hand experience, not just textbooks.

In addition, students can join an exclusive Elite Sports Programme, which offers an individualised education from Year 6 to Year 13, incorporating sports into academic progress and school life.

This curricular choice and flexibility, alongside our strong commitment to ensuring that each student achieves their personal potential to thrive in a global world, places King's College School, Cascais at the forefront of international education.

Finally, Inspired's forward-thinking approach gives our students the supportive framework they need to learn well, explore widely, develop resilience, foster curiosity and form lifelong connections.

King's College, The British School of Latvia

King's College
The British School of Latvia

(Founded 2017)

Turaidas iela 1 Pinki, Babites novads,
LV2107 Latvia
Tel: +371 257 59 043
Email: latvia@kingscollegeschools.org
Website: latvia.kingscollegeschools.org
Head of School: Ms Adele Stanford

School type: Co-educational Day
Age range of pupils: 2–18 years
No. of pupils enrolled as at 01/09/2022: 350
Fees as at 01/09/2022:
Day: €9,900–€18,428

King's College, The British School of Latvia, provides a unique educational environment that puts children and their families at the heart of all we do. Our school in Latvia is located in the municipality of Marupe in Latvia's capital city, Riga.

In school, we take pride in delivering inspirational teaching which draws on the best practices of the National Curriculum for England and Wales. This curriculum is designed to inspire children and create a desire to learn more through the linking of subjects and by providing practical learning experiences both inside and outside of the classroom.

Students gain an exemplary academic education while being equipped with the social and critical thinking skills to allow them to embrace the challenges of an ever-evolving world. We believe in values education, and therefore our values permeate all we do. Children develop a rich ethical vocabulary at King's College Latvia.

As a King's College school, we have a 50-year heritage of academic excellence. Since 1969 pupils from King's College schools have gone on to continue their studies at some of the most prestigious universities in Europe and North America. A British education gives our alumni the best opportunities to work in challenging and interesting careers all over the world. We believe that the fundamental values that they learn while at King's College will also help them to have happy and fulfilling family lives.

In choosing King's, you can be assured your child's future is in dedicated, experienced and safe hands.

King's College, The British School of Madrid

King's College
The British School of Madrid

(Founded 1969)

Paseo de los Andes 35, Soto de Viñuelas,
28760 Madrid, Spain
Tel: +34 918 034 800
Email:
kc.admissions@kingscollegeschools.org
Website:
madrid-soto.kingscollegeschools.org
Head: Matthew Taylor
Appointed: January 2017
School type:
Co-educational Day & Boarding
Age range of pupils: 20 months–18 years
No. of pupils enrolled: 1490
No. of boarders: 60
Day Fees: €2,450–€5,885 per term
Full Boarding Fees: €28,326–€34,056

King's College Madrid is a coeducational day and boarding school which provides British education for children from the age of 20 months to 18 years (Pre-pre-nursery to Year 13). It is located on an attractive 12-acre site in a leafy suburb, just 20 minutes' drive from Madrid and the main airport.

King's College is the only school in Madrid to offer both A Level & IB Diploma programmes of study in English in the Spanish capital. This allows students to choose their path of study depending on what type of learner they grow up to be, as well as their future aspirations.

This freedom of choice, coupled with the highest quality of teaching and learning allows our students to excel across the curriculum:

- Academic Results are among the best in Europe
- Year 13 Graduates go on to study at some of the best universities in the world (Russell Group, Ivy League & Oxbridge)

Since it was founded in 1969, King's College has gained a reputation for high academic standards. An experienced careers and university entrance advisory department is available to all pupils, and the Oxbridge preparatory group prepares students applying to Oxford and Cambridge universities.

Our boarding house opened in September 2011 and offers some of the best boarding accommodation in Europe. Tenbury House is home to pupils from all over the world. The new facilities offer a 'home from home' environment with shared and individual bedrooms all with en-suite bathrooms, underfloor heating and wireless internet. In addition, there is a dining room, a common room, a TV room, a study room, a kitchen that pupils can use to make light meals and a laundry. During the evenings and weekends, the students in Tenbury House have full use of these facilities and can also take advantage of many of the school's sports facilities.

King's College is the only school in Madrid accredited by the Department for Education in the UK as "Excellent" in every category that offers a British Curriculum from 20 months to 18 years.

King's InterHigh

3 Burlington Gardens, London, W1S 3EP UK

Tel: +44 (0)1873 777 444
Email: contact@kingsinterhigh.co.uk
Website: www.kingsinterhigh.co.uk
Executive Headteacher: Ashley Harrold
School type: Co-educational Day
Age range of pupils: 7–18 years

No. of pupils enrolled as at 01/09/2022: 3500
Fees as at 01/09/2022:
KS2: £2,901
KS3: £4,031
KS4: £4,838
KS5: £5,220 (A Levels)– £8,400 (IB Diploma)

King's InterHigh is the leading British international online school, catering to students aged 7-18. This independent school offers Primary, Secondary, and Sixth Form education, including International GCSEs, A Levels, and the world's first fully online IB Diploma Programme. With an immersive, personalised, and flexible approach to learning, King's InterHigh prepares students across the world for bright futures ahead.

Part of Inspired Education Group, King's InterHigh brings together over 16 years of unparalleled online education experience and 50 years of academic excellence across King's College schools. Since 2005, more than 10,000 successful alumni have graduated from King's InterHigh, progressing to fulfilling careers and top universities across the UK and internationally.

At King's InterHigh, students can learn from anywhere in the world in small, interactive classes. Fully qualified and experienced UK teachers deliver live lessons each school day, bringing learning to life with proven online education tools and cutting-edge technologies. Every lesson is also recorded to ensure every student can fit education around their lifestyle. Thanks to the school's flexibility, many students balance their learning with acting, athletics, and entrepreneurship.

Combining a stellar education with a vibrant school life, King's InterHigh also has lots happening outside the classroom. Students can participate in extra-curricular activities, socialise with their classmates online, and join in-person events (from summer camps to the Model UN) at over 70 Inspired schools around the world.

Exam results are outstanding for a non-selective online school, with 48% of university-bound students progressing to top Russell Group universities. The school also joins a legacy of IB excellence across Inspired Education, where students regularly achieve high IB results year after year. In 2021, Inspired's highest-scoring school recorded an average of 39 points.

A thriving global community where your education is built around your individual needs and interests, King's InterHigh is the school that revolves around you.

LEAF Academy (Akadémia LEAF)

Sasinkova 13, 811 08 Bratislava,
DIC: 2120216010 Slovakia
Tel: +421 949 443 573
Email: info@leafacademy.eu
Website: www.leafacademy.eu

Head of School: Mr Matej Sapak
School type: Co-educational Boarding
Age range of pupils: 14–19 years
No. of pupils enrolled as at 01/09/2022: 130
Teacher/pupil ratio: 1:3

Leaf Academy is an international boarding high school that provides world-class education for students from the central European region and beyond. The educational process is based on the American curriculum accredited by NEASC (New England Association of Schools and Colleges) with the ability to select several subjects for advanced study (Advanced Placement courses (AP)), which ensures successful admission to leading universities around the world. All the theoretical knowledge gained at Leaf Academy is constantly applied and practiced, which is an invaluable experience in choosing a future profession. The school provides an opportunity to choose a 2-year curriculum (16-19 years) or a four-year curriculum (14-15 years).

Education is conducted in four main areas:

Entrepreneurial leadership
Character development (helps young leaders identify and develop the strengths of their character, intensively work on their weaknesses to become a fully self-confident person and achieve success in the future);

Science, technology, engineering and mathematics: STEM

Central European studies (this direction combines all the humanities; literature, writing and rhetoric, history, social studies, languages, art, music).

"Extra-curricular" life is organised at an extremely high level in the school. Each of the students have the opportunity to choose what is most suitable for him: various interest clubs (languages, literature, cooking, singing, climbing, photography and much more), sports sections, volunteer activities.

All our students live in a school residence called "Astra" in twin rooms. Boys and girls live separately on different floors. The apartments are basically two-room with bathroom and toilet and 2 people live in each room. There are all the necessary amenities in the rooms. In addition to living rooms, the residence provides several common rooms for preparing homework, holding celebrations, karaoke parties and sharing movies, as well as a large conference room.

It is important to note that the school administration **is incredibly careful about security**. No one except the teachers and the students themselves has access to those floors where the students live. One of the teachers on each floor is constantly in the residence with the students, i.e. students are constantly supervised. In addition, 24 hours a day, daily by phone, you can call a medical professional and senior administrator or wellbeing assistant.

The price 21 400EUR per year includes tuition, accommodation, food, visa assistance, airport pick up and medical staff on side. The price also includes weekend activities. For a short week vacation our students can stay in the residence for additional fee or they can stay at host families. We do not charge any registration fee.

Contact details: Jana Sheppard,
International Admissions
skype jana.sheppard.marketing
phone number +421 949 443 573, WhatsApp.
WeChat: JanaShep71

L'École Trilingue

Avenida do Restelo 21,
1400-314 Lisbon, Portugal
Tel: +351 910 335 102
Email: info@lecoletrilingue.com
Website: lecoletrilingue.com
Head of School: Véronique Ferreira

School type: Co-educational Day
Age range of pupils: 2–6 years
No. of pupils enrolled as at 01/09/2022: 35
Fees as at 01/09/2022:
Day: €8,800

Based in the heart of the leafy Restelo district in Lisbon, l'École Trilingue is a small school where children can be given the individual attention they need. Pupils from 2 to 6 years old can grow, blossom and discover the world in English, French and Portuguese.

Classes are taught in English and French by highly qualified teachers who are native speakers, which ensures that pupils quickly acquire speaking and listening skills in these two languages. This approach is combined with an enhanced teaching of the Portuguese language. Our teachings are based on the French curriculum, but with an added focus on arts and culture to ensure that pupils acquire new skills and grow in confidence.

L'École Trilingue builds on the success of its sister school in London, L'école bilingue, which has been teaching children aged 3 to 11 years since 2004. It has been rated Outstanding by the English inspection board, making it one of the top-rated schools in the country. At the end of their schooling at L'école bilingue, pupils have the knowledge, confidence and flexibility to join the best secondary schools in any educational system – English, American, French or international. L'École Trilingue shares its sister school's values, and aims to provide outstanding trilingual teaching to children of all backgrounds and nationalities.

We are a small school, with a focus on providing a safe and nurturing environment so that pupils can develop their confidence and autonomy. We support each and every pupil to reach their full potential, and work closely with parents to prepare them for primary school.

Children from all educational systems are welcome from the age of 2. We do not currently host Open Days; instead families are encouraged to get in touch and visit the school at their convenience.

Please visit www.lecoletrilingue.com for more information.

Leipzig International School

(Founded 1992)
Könneritzstrasse 47, 04229 Leipzig, Saxony, Germany
Tel: +49 34 139377 500
Email: info@lis.school
Website: www.lis.school

Head of School: Mrs Brandie Smith
School type: Co-educational Day
Age range of pupils: 1–18 years
No. of pupils enrolled as at 01/09/2022: 955
Fees as at 01/09/2022:
Please refer to website

Leipzig International School (LIS) is a non-profit co-educational day school for students from age 1 to 18, who are part of Leipzig's diverse international community. Some 950 students from 70 countries attend our school and kindergarten, with the most represented nations after the host country being the United States of America, Japan, United Kingdom and the Netherlands.

The school's two sites are in residential districts in western Leipzig.

Our language of instruction is English.

The Primary School follows the International Primary Curriculum, and the Secondary School the Cambridge Secondary 1 and IGCSE Programme. The gateway to higher education is the International Baccalaureate (IB) Diploma Programme.

We create a safe and stimulating environment in which students can be happy learners, working in partnership with teachers to discover and develop their intellectual, physical, social and creative potential. All lessons are guaranteed due to qualified substitute teachers.

Hort supervision in Primary is available from 7:00 – 8:25 each day; Afternoon Hort runs from 15:00-17:00. This is covered by the school fees – no extra costs apply.

We aim to limit class size to 20 students. In many specialist and optional classes, numbers are smaller.

We welcome you to make an appointment to learn more about our school in person and take a tour around our beautiful grounds and facilities.

Loretto School

Loretto

(Founded 1827)

Pinkie House, Linkfield Road, Musselburgh, East Lothian, EH21 7RE UK

Tel: +44 (0)131 653 4455

Email: admissions@loretto.com

Website: www.loretto.com

Head of School: Dr. Graham R. W. Hawley

Appointed: 2014

School type:

Co-educational Day & Boarding

Age range of pupils: 3–18 years

No. of pupils enrolled as at 01/09/2022: 520

Fees as at 01/09/2022:

Day: £2,933–£8,385 per term

Full Boarding: £8,020–£12,315 per term

Flexi Boarding: £6,830 – £10,220 per term

Average class size:

Junior 14; Senior 17; Exam Years 15

Teacher/pupil ratio: 1:7

Loretto School, founded in 1827, is Scotland's first boarding school. Today an independent, private, boarding and day school, it welcomes girls and boys, from 3 to 18 years.

The School is set in a safe, leafy, spacious, 85 acre (34 hectare) campus in Musselburgh, East Lothian, adjacent to Edinburgh. It enjoys all the advantages of this rural setting while being globally connected, with the convenience and opportunities of being just 9 kilometres/6 miles from Scotland's capital city, its international airport, rail, and road networks.

Loretto is one of the UK's leading independent schools, with outstanding results at GCSE and A-Level. More than nine pupils out of 10 achieve places at their chosen university, including Oxford, Cambridge, St Andrews, Newcastle, and Durham. Many enter American universities – Loretto being a SAT Test Centre.

Welcoming just over 500 pupils, Loretto is a small school that strives to know every pupil personally, and offer them the opportunity to grow and develop wherever their interests lie. Loretto is also well known for its emphasis on the development of the whole person, mind, body, and spirit. The School offers a wide range of curricular and extra-curricular activities including comprehensive programmes in Sport and Creative Arts.

Loretto's campus integrates extensive playing fields, several Sports Halls, a Music School, Dance and Drama Studios as well as a dedicated Science Centre. The School also features the Loretto Golf Academy, founded in 2002 and run by PGA coaching professionals, with state-of-the-art indoor and outdoor practice Centres.

To find out more, please contact Loretto's professional, experienced and friendly Admissions team (admissions@loretto.com – 0131 653 4455). They will be pleased to provide you with all the information you need and make arrangements for your family to visit the School.

Embark on a Virtual Tour Follow Loretto pupils on a guided tour of the School and listen to what they say about life at Loretto. Find out more from the Headmaster and teaching staff about Loretto's ambition for their young people. Start your tour now at www.youtube.com/watch?v=rPEFaZPWNlw

Loughborough Grammar School

LOUGHBOROUGH
Grammar School

(Founded 1495)
Buckland House, Burton Walks,
Loughborough, Leicestershire LE11 2DU UK

Tel: 01509 233233
Email: grammar.admissions@lsf.org
Website: www.lsf.org/grammar
Headmaster: Dr Daniel Koch
Appointed: September 2022
School type: Boys' Day & Boarding
Age range of boys: 10–18 years
No. of pupils enrolled as at 01/09/2022: 880

Fees as at 01/09/2022:
Day Fees (Years 6-13):
£4,900 – £4,990 per term
Weekly boarding & tuition (Years 6-13):
£10,470 – £10,560 per term
Full boarding & tuition (no EAL) (Years 6-13): £12,030 – £12,120 per term
Full boarding with tuition & EAL (Years 6-13): £12,490 – £12,580 per term

Loughborough Grammar School is one of the oldest independent schools in the country. A top-performing, independent day and boarding school for boys aged 10-18 The Grammar School is part of the Loughborough Schools Foundation.

A passion for life & learning

This is a school where academic achievement is at the centre of everything. Dedicated staff and outstanding resources enable the boys both to fulfil their potential in examinations and to embark on intellectual adventures beyond the classroom.

However, staff understand that boys will only succeed if they feel happy and contented. Considerable focus is therefore placed on the development of a strong moral compass where kindness towards others and a commitment to fairness and equality are valued as key personal attributes.

There is an attentive system of pastoral care that ensures that each boy is supported by pastoral staff who fully know him, so that they can both monitor his progress and guide him towards areas in which he will feel challenged and fulfilled.

In the early years, boys are encouraged to try as many extra-curricular experiences as possible, gradually finding their unique niche as they progress through the School. There are over 100 clubs and societies and boys are expected to take advantage of these opportunities and to show pride in representing the School. These activities beyond the classroom play a major part in helping boys to develop into resilient young men, who are confident yet sensitive and aware of their responsibilities to others.

Boarding at the Grammar School

The success of the boarding community has been an enriching part of Loughborough Grammar School for much of its long history. With an active community of some 75 boarders, the boarding is like a concentration of the very best that the School offers, condensed into two wonderfully welcoming Houses within the campus.

Just like the Day pupils, Boarders are supported, individually known, cared for and cared about and encouraged to make the most of all the opportunities such a high achieving School provides.

Lycée français de Varsovie (French School in Warsaw)

(Founded 1919)

Ul Walecznych 4/6, 03-916 Warsaw,
Masovia, Poland
Tel: +48 22 616 54 00/01
Email: info@lfv.pl
Website: www.lfv.pl
Head of School: Anne Lesage

School type: Co-educational Day
Age range of pupils: 2–18 years
No. of pupils enrolled as at 01/09/2022: 700
Fees as at 01/09/2022:
Full Boarding: €5,300–€7,700 per term
Average class size: 20

Founded in 1919, the Lycée Français de Varsovie (French School in Warsaw – LFV) is an international school proposing the French national curriculum from Preschool to High School for children ages 2 to 18.

The school enrolls over 700 students from 45 nationalities in a true multicultural and multilingual environment. It is the only school in Poland accredited by the French Ministry of Education. The Lycée Français de Varsovie implements the same curricula as French public schools and prepares students for the same exams and diplomas. The accreditation ensures both compliance with the French model of education and high-quality teaching.

The teaching staff is composed of highly qualified, supportive and passionate teachers: all are certified by the Ministry of Education and 70% of them are native speakers.

The school is very well implemented in Warsaw (100 years of tradition and excellence) and the curricula are enhanced with Polish language classes and cultural projects. Also, the Lycée Français de Varsovie offers a large choice of over 40 extra-curricular activities for children of all ages.

Every year, the Lycée Français de Varsovie sends students to top American, British, Polish and French universities with a 100% success rate at the exam of Baccalauréat.

The school is located over two sites: Preschool and Primary school are in Sadyba/Mokotów and the Secondary and High Schools are in Saska Kepa.

The Lycée Français de Varsovie is also part of the AEFE Network (Agency For French Teaching Abroad), a global academic network which gathers more than 540 French schools around the world.

Learn more about the educational offer of LFV on our website: www.lfv.pl/en

Marymount International School Paris

Marymount Paris

(Founded 1923)

72, boulevard de la Saussaye,
92200 Neuilly-sur-Seine, France
Tel: +33 (0)1 46 24 93 25
Email: admissions@marymount.fr
Website: www.marymount.fr
Head of School: Sarah Thomas
Appointed: 2020

School type: Co-educational Day
Age range of pupils: 2–14 years
No. of pupils enrolled as at 01/09/2022: 360
Fees as at 01/09/2022:
€20,000 – €48,000
Average class size: 15
Teacher/pupil ratio: 1:4

Marymount International School Paris is an outstanding private school for children aged 2 to 14.

We are the oldest international school in France, and have a rich history of inclusion and diversity, offering a warm welcome to children from a wide range of countries, cultures and religions. Our ethos is founded on Catholic values, which underpin daily life at Marymount.

Our spacious and verdant campus is beautiful. We are fortunate to have wonderful facilities: a sports hall, three gymnasia, a library, a performing arts theatre, dedicated music rooms, a bright and spacious art room with a pottery studio, a chapel, a dining hall, excellent IT and science resources, a FabLab, and leafy gardens and spaces for outdoor learning. Our program of enriching educational visits makes best use of the cultural treasures of Paris and the rest of France.

We offer a truly international education which draws on the expert knowledge of our highly-qualified teaching team to make sure our young people thrive. We set high expectations for each child in our care and provide the extra challenge or support for those who need it. Children benefit from a dedicated French lesson every day and Francophones follow the French National Curriculum program of language study. We encourage children to speak in both languages as much as possible.

We are active members of the Global Network of RSHM Schools. Our network includes 19 schools across nine countries and three continents with shared roots all seeking to fulfill the Goals and Criteria of the RSHM. Our network includes other Marymount schools with established campuses in Los Angeles, New York, London, and Rome. We work closely on cross-curricular educational programs and exchanges for students and staff. Our fully-fledged online program includes collaborative learning with our network schools.

We offer additional student services that includes a daily hot lunch, private bus service, guidance and pastoral support as well as after-school enrichment activities.

The Parent-Teacher Organization is at the center of our family community and provides a much-appreciated support network for new parents and children. Their contributions to the life of the school through fundraising, event organizing and providing a 'soft-landing' to families who arrive during the year are the social glue that underpin our unique Marymount culture.

We are accredited by the Council of International Schools (CIS) and the Middle States Association (MSA). We welcome annual inspections from the French Académie de Versailles.

Marymount International School Rome

MARYMOUNT
INTERNATIONAL SCHOOL ROME

(Founded 1946)
Via di Villa Lauchli, 180, 00191 Rome, Italy
Tel: +39 06 3629 1012

Email: admissions@marymountrome.com
Website: www.marymountrome.com
Head of School: Ms. Sarah Gallagher
Appointed: 2016
School type: Co-educational Day
Age range of pupils: 2–18 years

No. of pupils enrolled as at 01/09/2022: 860
Fees as at 01/09/2022:
€12,200 – €24,200
Average class size: 16
Teacher/pupil ratio: 1:6

One of Italy's top schools, Marymount International School Rome offers its students a long tradition of academic excellence. Over 70 nationalities and around 20 faiths contribute to its vibrant community life, and the School has championed social justice and intercultural understanding throughout its 75 year history in the footsteps of its founders, the Religious of the Sacred Heart of Mary.

An English-language program of studies from Early Childhood through Grade 12 (ages 2-18) prepares Marymount graduates for many of the world's best universities and colleges. Marymount's International Baccalaureate Diploma Program is complemented by an American High School Diploma and Advanced Placement courses.

The curriculum, regularly revised and updated to capture emerging technologies and global concerns, is fresh and meaningful. It features a wide array of languages including Ancient Greek, Arabic, Chinese, French, German, Italian, Latin and Spanish, in keeping with Marymount's deep commitment to an international education. With over 50 electives in High School, students have every opportunity to deepen their interests and expand their horizons.

Students are encouraged to think for themselves, and are equipped to do so from the Elementary School, where they develop logical argument, rhetorical skills and philosophical vocabulary to ensure that their engagement is supported by building solid critical foundations.

Students have access to a wide variety of bespoke individual and group academic, athletic and artistic enrichment plans such as grade-level clusters, JuniOrchestra, and Model United Nations, in addition to a well-rounded extracurricular activity program and a plethora of trips at home and abroad.

Marymount's 40-acre campus features multiple outdoor spaces which include a regulation-size soccer field, multi-purpose sports fields, tennis and basketball courts. The Forest School offers a unique learning environment that encourages curiosity, observation, and exploration from Early Childhood all the way through Grade 12.

Marymount London

George Road, Kingston upon Thames,
Surrey KT2 7PE UK

Tel: +44 (0)20 8949 0571
Email: admissions@marymountlondon.com
Website: www.marymountlondon.com
Headmistress: Mrs Margaret Giblin
School type: Girls' Day & Boarding
Age range of girls: 11–18 years

No. of pupils enrolled as at 01/09/2022: 260
Fees as at 01/09/2022:
Day: £27,250
Weekly Boarding: £44,180
Full Boarding: £46,130
Average class size: 12
Teacher/pupil ratio: 1:6

Marymount London is an independent, day and boarding school for girls which nurtures the limitless potential of curious, motivated students (ages 11 to 18) of diverse faiths and backgrounds.

Founded in 1955 through the charism of the Religious of the Sacred Heart of Mary (RSHM), the School proudly stands as the first all-girls' school in the United Kingdom to adopt the International Baccalaureate curriculum (IB MYP and Diploma), where girls are inspired to learn in a creative, collaborative, interdisciplinary, and exploratory environment. Students are empowered to build their confidence, leadership skills, and sense of self on a seven-acre garden campus conveniently located just twelve miles from Central London. The campus offers outstanding facilities, including a STEAM Hub, newly refurbished sports hall, dance studio, modern dining hall, and tennis courts. The School's challenging academic program is based on the International Baccalaureate curricula:

- The Middle Years Programme (MYP), offered in Grades 6 to 10, encourages students to draw meaningful connections between eight broad and varied subject groups. With a central focus on the development of conceptual understanding and effective approaches to learning (ATL) skills, the MYP is a student-centred, inquiry based programme rooted in interdisciplinary learning.
- The International Baccalaureate Diploma Programme (DP) for Grades 11 and 12 builds on the strong foundation of the MYP, leading to independent research opportunities as well as exceptional university placement within the UK and around the world.
- Marymount is recognised around the world as a leading IB school. Its 2020 results are exceptional: 100% pass rate and an average of 38 points (vs. a global average of 29.9). The School provides a bespoke, student-centred college counselling programme which leads to successful placements in top universities in the UK and around the world.

Marymount's holistic approach to learning delivers a well-rounded education that encourages critical thinking, intercultural understanding, and participation in a wide array of interesting extracurricular offerings. Robust transport service from London/surrounding areas and boarding options (full, weekly, and flexi) are available.

Marymount offers year-round rolling admission as space allows. The admissions section of the website, featuring an online application portal, provides all of the information necessary to get started.

Applicant families are encouraged to learn more about the School's strong tradition of excellence by exploring the website and making contact with the Admissions team by phone/email.

Merchiston Castle School

MERCHISTON
EDINBURGH

A BOARDING AND DAY SCHOOL FOR BOYS AGED 7-18

(Founded 1833)

294 Colinton Road, Edinburgh, EH13 0PU UK

Tel: 0131 312 2200
Email: admissions@merchiston.co.uk
Website: www.merchiston.co.uk
Headmaster: Mr Jonathan Anderson
Appointed: August 2018
Deputy Head:
Mr Danny Rowlands (Wellbeing),
Dr Dale Cartwright (Learning and Teaching)

School type: Boys' Day & Boarding
Age range of boys: 7–18 years
No. of pupils enrolled as at 01/09/2022: 400
No. of boarders: 260
Fees as at 01/09/2022:
Day: £15,330–£26,040
Full Boarding: £22,080–£35,880
Teacher/pupil ratio: 1:9

Merchiston is one of the UK's leading boarding schools, and a member of the World Leading Schools Association (the only school in Scotland), offering the English curriculum, but with a global, outward-looking dimension. Over 65% of pupils board and a full boarding programme is provided, seven days a week. Merchiston is a remarkable school where boys make lifelong friends and community connections, whilst experiencing a world-class education and excelling far beyond their expected results.

Many schools can boast about their exceptional academic results, university success rates, extensive sporting and co-curricular programmes, welcoming atmospheres and stunning grounds and facilities. Indeed, we can do that as well.

What makes us different, however, is a combination of things: our size, a genuine focus on the needs of the individual, and the fact that we really understand boys and how to get the very best out of them.

It is a potent trio. It is what enables us to know our boys really well and to understand what makes them tick. It is why we can support them in a way that is material and motivating to them. It is the reason your son will strive for personal excellence and want to be the best version of himself. It is the secret of their, and our, success.

Our mission is to provide a caring community for every boy, which treats him as an individual, unearths and tends his talents, encourages him to pursue excellence in all he does, and enables him to really flourish.

Our community's wellbeing is central; without it no one will ever achieve their best. That's why wellbeing underpins everything we do. Our boys thrive because they are known, understood, valued, and supported in everything they do.

We would love to talk to you about your son and, more importantly, talk with him to work out what makes him tick, discuss where he wants to go next and make sure he has the toolkit to get there.

Merchiston's young men leave us as rounded individuals, not only having achieved the highest level of personal academic success, but with a sense of who they are and with respect for others, having learnt what it means to have true integrity and character.

Our success proves that what we do works.

Mirabal International School

(Founded 1982)
Calle Monte Almenara, s/n, 28660
Boadilla del Monte, Madrid, Spain
Tel: +34 916 331 711
Email: mirabal@colegiomirabal.com

Website: www.colegiomirabal.com
Director: Ms Rosario de la Cruz López
School type: Co-educational Day
Age range of pupils: 0–18 years
No. of pupils enrolled as at 01/09/2022: 1957

Mirabal International School is a school of reference in Europe. Highly regarded by its' exceptional academic standards, Mirabal has historically achieved world top positions in the annual PISAreport for Schools, an educational evaluation promoted by the Organisation for Economic Co-operation and Development (OECD).

Founded in 1982 Mirabal International School is committed to the integral education of the students, promoting values such as independence, tolerance, responsibility (diligence, generosity, honour). Located in an outstanding natural setting in the north of Madrid, Mirabal offers excellent facilities at the service of an innovative educational project based on interactive and practical learning. The school occupies a total of 45,000 m² and offers a wide range of sports and academic facilities, including tennis courts, athletics tracks, two swimming pools and several laboratories.

The constant training of teachers in active and innovative methodologies, the integration of iPads in the classroom and subjects such as robotics are some of the key tools used to bring students closer to the most advanced learning resources. Students learn to research, discriminate, contrast and select information from a very young age.

Students can choose to follow Spanish National Curriculum, the International Baccalaureate or a double-honors program. Its multilingual program is offered by native teachers and is especially designed to stimulate physical intellectual, social and artistic development.

Mirabal is a certified music school, where students can obtain an official Music Elementary Degree in the instrument of their choice. Emotional intelligence is a main focus of Mirabal's educational project. Cooperative learning, emotion management, motivation and education in values help students acquire skills such as creativity, leadership and initiative.

Montgomery International School – Brussels

Ecole Internationale Montgomery

Rue du Duc 133, 1200 Brussels, Belgium

Tel: +32 (0)2 733 63 23

Email: info@montgomery-school.be

Website: www.ecole-montgomery.be

Director: David Gerone

School type: Co-educational Day

Age range of pupils: 5–18 years

No. of pupils enrolled as at 01/09/2022: 150

Fees as at 01/09/2022:

Years 1 to 5: €9,642

Years 6 to 9: €21,953

Years 9 & 10: €23,109

Years 11 & 12: €25,412

Annual registration fee: €1,650

The **Montgomery International School Brussels** is a fully accredited IB school (PYP – MYP – DP) in the centre of Brussels, a short walk from the European Commission, NATO and various business centers.

The school offers a truly international environment, with 150 students and teachers from as many as 40 different nationalities. Class sizes are always kept small to accommodate a maximum of 16 students.

A FULLY BILINGUAL EDUCATION

We are the only school in Brussels which offers a fully bilingual IB programme in English and French from primary to secondary years. The early primary years start with 60% English and 40% French and secondary years consist of 70% English and 30% French. Moreover, we are the only school to offer the Advanced Bilingual IB Diploma. This is a differentiating factor when applying to universities.

OUR VISION

EIM caters for children between 5 – 18 years old. With highly qualified teachers and a strong, cohesive administrative team, EIM aims to help its students achieve their full potential in a supportive, inclusive and open-minded environment. From primary to the Diploma Years (11th and 12th grade) we inspire our students to become independent, critical thinkers and encourage them to develop their social and communication skills. We have a 100% success rate in the Diploma programme and pride ourselves on knowing each individual student and encouraging them to develop their strengths while following their passions.

OUR CAMPUS

Located in the centre of Brussels, the school has two nearby campuses. The Montgomery campus is for the PYP and MYP students and the new Broqueville campus is mostly dedicated to the DPs with 5 extra classrooms, a theatre and a study space. EIM has access to a wide-array of sports clubs located in the neighborhood and offers a variety of after-school activities and daycare. With the acquisition of the new campus, the school aims to reach its full capacity of 200 students in the year to come.

Mougins School

Mougins BRITISH INTERNATIONAL SCHOOL

(Founded 1964)

615 Avenue Maurice Donat, CS 12180,
06252 Mougins CEDEX, France
Tel: +33 4 93 90 15 47
Email: admissions@mougins-school.com
Website: www.mougins-school.com
Director: Mr James Wellings
Appointed: 2021

School type: Co-educational Day
Age range of pupils: 3–18
No. of pupils enrolled as at 01/09/2022: 540
Fees as at 01/09/2022:
Day: €14,175–€20,055
Average class size: 19

Located in the heart of Nice Sophia-Antipolis, Mougins School offers the excellent British school programme for students ages 3 to 18, enhanced by a pedagogy that develops methodology, collaborative learning, critical and creative thinking.

All lessons are taught in English, but the school welcomes over 500 children from 44 nationalities. Since 1987, the school boasts a state-of-the-art, green, landscaped campus with peaceful shaded spots, as well as a theatre, a synthetic football pitch, sports court for games, science laboratories, a library, a canteen with an outdoor terrace, and the Millennium Building for classrooms and administration.

Mougins School's Early Learning Centre follows the English Early Years Foundation Stage (EYFS) curriculum comprising Nursery and Reception classes, ideally preparing the children for Key Stage 1. The young learners can explore the outdoor kitchen, investigate the sensory garden, and discover the magic forest when teaching and learning is taken outside into this stimulating environment.

Following the British Curriculum, students in the Primary Section make excellent progress in oral comprehension and expression, literacy, numeracy and social skills. All subjects are taught in English and the practical methodology synonymous with the British curriculum means that different types of learners are able to progress at different rates.

Mougins School's Secondary Section provides a fantastic environment for fulfilling academic potential for students, where they are supported closely by teachers and tutors in preparation for their IGCSE and A Level examinations. They are encouraged to be keen, enthusiastic, independent learners and are given lots of opportunities to develop their interpersonal skills by working and cooperating with others. Through the curriculum they build their self-esteem and self confidence.

Mougins School has a responsibility to ensure that all of its students can enrich their lives through a wide range of activities and programmes that allow individuals to find their passions. Education is a journey and learning is a nonlinear process so through effort, perseverance and the embracing of challenges, the school's learners will go on to positively shape the lives of themselves, others and the world around them.

Munich International School e.V.

(Founded 1966)
Schloss Buchhof, Percha, 82319 Starnberg, Bavaria, Germany
Tel: +49 8151 366 0
Email: admissions@mis-munich.de
Website: www.mis-munich.de

Head of School: Mr Timothy J. Thomas
School type: Co-educational Day
Age range of pupils: 4–18 years
No. of pupils enrolled: 1200
Average class size: 18-22

Munich International School (MIS) is a community school where 1200 students from 65 nationalities learn together on a single, purpose-built campus. It was the first international school to be established in Munich (1966). MIS is officially recognised by the Bavarian ministry of education and fully accredited by the Council of International Schools (CIS) and the New England Association of Schools and Colleges (NEASC).

The School nurtures, challenges and inspires students to become academically successful, life-long learners, creative and innovative thinkers, ethical, globally-minded contributors and healthy, well-balanced individuals who will thrive and make a positive impact in a complex and changing world.

Academic Excellence

In 2021, the average diploma total was 38 points (comparable to a 1.6 Abiturnote), a leading score among international schools in Germany. All 108 candidates achieved a full IB Diploma (100 percent success rate).

Students routinely gain admission to the world's elite universities such as Stanford University, Imperial College London, Massachusetts Institute of Technology (MIT) including German universities such as the Technical University of Munich (TUM), to name just a few. Our excellent academic programmes are embedded, however, in a holistic, values-based curriculum that provides support and appropriate challenge for every child.

Unparalleled Campus

Easily accessible from Munich, the School takes full advantage of its 26-acre campus in an idyllic nature preserve near Starnberg to provide students with high-quality educational experiences both within well-equipped classrooms, laboratories and performing arts spaces and exceptional outdoor facilities.

The School offers a wide range of After School Activities and sports as well as a comprehensive competitive Athletics programme. We recruit the most caring, competent and committed teachers and staff from more than two dozen countries. These educators create a vibrant, diverse, student-centred learning programme, supported by superior facilities and resources.

Nobel Algarve British International School

Nobel Algarve BRITISH INTERNATIONAL SCHOOL

(Founded 1972)

Lagoa Campus: EN 125, Porches, 8400-400 Lagoa, Portugal
Tel: +351 282 342547
Email: info@nobelalgarve.com
Almancil Campus: Caminho das Pereiras, 8135-022 Almancil, Portugal
Tel: +351 289 246 303
Email: almancil@nobelalgarve.com

Website: www.nobelalgarve.com
Head of School: Abi Lewis
Appointed: July 2021
School type: Co-educational Day
Age range of pupils: 3–18 years
Average class size: 18-20
Teacher/pupil ratio: 1:9.5

Founded in 1972, Nobel Algarve British International School has long been regarded as Southern Portugal's premier international school. The school joined Globeducate in 2019 one of the world's leading K12 education groups with 55+ premium bilingual and international schools, and online programmes, in nine countries, educating more than 28,000 students.

Nobel Algarve British International School comprises two outstanding campuses: the flagship campus in Lagoa, and the state-of-the-art campus in Almancil. Together the campuses educate more than 1,000 students from more than 40 nationalities, aged three to 18. Students follow either a contextualised English National Curriculum, sitting IGCSEs and A-levels, or the Portuguese Curriculum in Lagoa, with the vast majority enrolling in some of the world's leading higher-education institutions.

Nobel Algarve British International School belongs to the Globeducate British International School cluster, with sister schools in Spain, France, Italy and the UK. Being part of this cluster creates opportunities for teachers and students to benefit from working on shared goals and projects such as a rich Outdoor Learning programme and on developing a British-style House System. Being a member of Globeducate brings other benefits such as projects with LEGO® Education and the Globeducate partnership with WWF (World Wildlife Fund) and Eco-Schools. Students also take part in regular global events and competitions with other schools in the group worldwide.

Both campuses have recently unveiled two ambitious expansion plans, an impressive project branded 'Nobel Algarve – Shaping the Future' to be developed in three different phases. Nobel Algarve Lagoa and Almancil will be equipped with new buildings and new classrooms with state-of-the-art features such as a next-generation Science Lab, ICT suites and multimedia centre in Almancil and a new multi-purpose gymnasium/performance space, a bespoke pre-school, and a brand-new canteen in Lagoa.

Nobel Algarve British International School believes learning goes beyond the classroom and equips pupils to face challenges confidently, building character so they manage failure with tenacity and resilience.

O Castro British International School (Vigo)

O Castro BRITISH INTERNATIONAL SCHOOL VIGO

(Founded 2008)
Camiño San Cosme 1, 36419 San Pedro de Cela (Mos), Pontevedra, Galicia, Spain
Tel: +34 986 20 00 28
Email: admissions@bisocastro.com
Website: www.bisocastro.com

Executive Head: Mr. Chistopher Long
School type: Co-educational Day
Age range of pupils: 3–18 years
No. of pupils enrolled as at 01/09/2022: 715
Average class size: 20

Located in Vigo, Galicia, O Castro British International School is a private, secular, international school for children ages 3 to 18. O Castro British International School is the only school in Vigo and Galicia to offer a full English National Curriculum from early years to sixth form. O Castro British International School belongs to Globeducate British International Schools and has been part of the Globeducate prestigious network since 2017.

With a multilingual educational programme that offers full immersion in English from day one, we aim to educate our students to become valuable and responsible members of society with the ability to understand and embrace the challenges of the world we live in today. Our curriculum is designed to bring out the best in every student.

We follow the English National Curriculum, gaining qualifications that are accepted for entry at top universities across Spain, the UK, and the rest of the world. Our school is also certified by the Galician government and regulated by the British Council and NABSS (the National Association of British Schools in Spain) who conduct regular inspections in order to ensure that we maintain the highest standards in all that we do. Likewise, from 2014 we are the only Cambridge School in Galicia.

Building confidence to last a lifetime

We are dedicated to ensuring that every student feels confident, positive and enthusiastic about learning; each student is helped to set and achieve appropriate goals. In this way they take pride in their academic and personal progress. As students move through the school they are taught how to research, study, and learn more independently, and our teachers employ a wide range of strategies to guide and direct each student's learning journey to ensure that they achieve their maximum potential.

Our campus

Founded in September 2008, it was designed to meet the high standards expected of today's international private schools. The school buildings incorporate energy-efficient facilities and classrooms, constructed with environmental conservation in mind, and the school is set in grounds of 33,000 m2. The school buildings are modern, bright and spacious, and have been carefully designed to meet each student's educational and social needs, both in terms of academic performance and extracurricular activities. Our students have access to ICT rooms, science labs, two libraries, a ballet studio, recreational and wooded areas, nature classrooms, a psychomotor skills suite, a 2,000 m2 sports centre, basketball and a multi-purpose artificial grass pitch.

Life at O Castro goes beyond the classroom. We have a full programme of extra-curricular activities, exchanges and international events with other Globeducate schools. We promote Outdoor Learning and have a traditional British House System, which encourages bonding between children of different ages, team spirit and reinforces a sense of belonging to a community.

Oporto British School

1894

OPORTO
BRITISH
SCHOOL

KNOWLEDGE · VISION · HUMANITY

(Founded 1894)

Rua da Cerca 338, Foz do Douro,
4150-201 Porto, Portugal
Tel: +351 226 166 660
Email: school@obs.edu.pt
Website: www.obs.edu.pt
Headmaster: Nick Sellers

School type: Co-educational Day
Age range of pupils: 3–18 years
No. of pupils enrolled as at 01/09/2022: 550
Fees as at 01/09/2022:
Day: €7,625–€13,040
Average class size: 15

The Oporto British School (OBS), founded in 1894, is a not-for-profit independent British school for pupils aged 3-18. The school is located in Foz do Douro, the fashionable seaside suburb of Porto. The OBS is a truly international school, with pupils from more than 30 nationalities. Today, there are around 550 pupils in the school, 50% of whom are from Portuguese families. There have been significant curriculum and campus developments over the past 5 years, with other improvements projected in the near future. The OBS embraces all that is best in a top-quality British School and has a strong commitment to international education and the nurturing of international awareness, with special recognition of the School's British roots operating in a Portuguese environment. The school articulates a clear ethos and vision for its students' experiences; this is to develop and sustain an educational environment which fosters appropriate academic and co-curricular ambition and social responsibility amongst all of its students, in line with the school's ethos of Knowledge, Vision, Humanity.

The school is the only school in Portugal that is inspected by the Independent Schools Inspectorate on behalf of COBIS, and is a fully accredited member of the Council of International Schools. The school is proud of its family-focused atmosphere and of a community determined to promote service towards the common good. The school follows its own curriculum, broadly aligned with the UK National Curriculum throughout Primary, leading to IGCSE and the International Baccalaureate in Secondary, which provides appropriate breadth and challenge to enable ingress and egress at every stage.

PaRK International School

PaRK INTERNATIONAL SCHOOL

Estrada de Alfragide 94, 2610-015
Amadora, Lisbon, Portugal
Tel: +351 215 807 000
Email: all@park-is.com
Website: www.park-is.com
Head of School: Samantha Gonçalves

School type: Co-educational Day
Age range of pupils: 1–18 years
No. of pupils enrolled as at 01/09/2022: 1950 (3 campuses)
Fees as at 01/09/2022:
Day: €6,978–€16,908

PaRK International School gives students access to an exclusive and individualised education in three different campuses in top locations in the Lisbon area.

An international school with Portuguese roots, PaRK IS welcomes students from 1 Year Old to Grade 12. Our mission is to educate and inspire students to have the skills to be happy and successful in their individually chosen path.

At PaRK IS, we teach children the skills and give them the tools to become bilingual, curious, collaborative, caring, autonomous and agile learners, to reach their full potential. Each age group is offered a demanding, dynamic, innovative and bespoke curriculum: a Bilingual Programme from Early Learning until Grade 4, Cambridge from Grade 5 (including IGCSE in Grade 9 and 10), and the internationally acclaimed IB Diploma Programme for Grades 11 and 12.

Alongside the strong academic curriculum, students receive a personalised and well-rounded education. Our Well-Being department guarantees that each student has their individual needs met, technology and innovation are fully integrated in the curriculum, and we offer exclusive Arts and Drama classes, in addition to PaRK Music Academy, where students can find a solid bridge between vocational and non-vocational music education. There is also a wide range of sporting activities, including PaRK Team, to participate in competitions with other international schools – all of these contribute to the development of students' personality, enrich their learning experience and promote academic excellence.

Finally, we offer a unique sports programme to driven students with aspirations to become accomplished athletes and players, with an individualised education for students from Grade 5 to Grade 12, which incorporates their sports' activity into academic progress and school life.

As an Inspired school, our students have access to world's best practices in education, outstanding arts and sports programmes, state of the art facilities, and chances to experience Inspired Summer Camps and Global Exchange Programmes.

With a PaRK IS education, students will be prepared for academic excellence, proficient in more than one language and equipped with key life skills to be successful in an ever-changing world.

Queen Elizabeth's School

Rua Filipe Magalhaes 1, Alvalade, 1700-194 Lisboa, Portugal
Tel: +351 21 841 0140
Email: info.qes@gmail.com
Website: qes.pt

Headmistress: Drª M Conceicao de Oliveira Martins
School type: Co-educational Day
Age range of pupils: 3–10 years

Queen Elizabeth's School (QES) is an infant and junior school with its own traditions, identity and values, aiming at providing its pupils with a solid base for acquiring the skills and aptitudes needed academically and socially in adult life. Special relevance is given to the process of learning English as a Second Language and the development of a bilingual and inter-cultural education, in an increasingly globalised society. QES was set up in 1935 by Margaret Denise Lester and is currently owned by the Fundação Denise Lester charity trust. Miss Lester built this school bearing in mind the strengthening of the ties between Portugal and England, aiming at providing Portuguese children with a good knowledge of the English language and culture. At present Queen Elizabeth's school welcomes children from different nationalities and runs the school respecting the core ideals set by the founder in accordance with the ongoing international educational policies and challenges.

Our school offers: Day Care, Nursery, Reception and Pre-primary. The methodology used is an early partial immersion and topic-based one to assure that an exciting and stimulating learning environment is delivered. The children's progress is assessed regularly whereby general objectives and specific tasks are set to ensure children become familiar with the school routines and reach their full potential in school activities. There is a strong emphasis on oral practice and production, which is developed through the learning tools of role-play, songs, storytelling and drama. At the end of the pre-primary cycle children can understand and respond to basic instructions; engage in basic daily routines in English; sing familiar English children's songs and nursery rhymes; understand familiar fairy tales and stories in English; talk about themselves, their school and household; and identify aspects of the English culture. Pre-school pupils are prepared for the Trinity Stars: Young Performers in English, by Trinity College London, confirming the focus given to the development of communication skills through drama.

The school has adopted the Cambridge Primary Curriculum, which compliments and fits in with the National Curriculum requirements in the subjects of Primary Maths, Primary Science and English as a Second Language. The children have nine hours and a half of English. In addition, 3rd grade students can still attend the English clubs two hours a week and 4th grade students can attend the English clubs three hours a week. The purpose of these clubs is to further expand our students' knowledge of the English language through extended quality exposure to English. At the end of years 2, 3, 4 the children can also take the Cambridge English Young Learners Tests (Starters, Movers and Flyers respectively). Also, 4th-grade-students are prepared for Trinity College London Language Exam in Integrated Skills in English (ISE Foundation).

The school also provides extra-curricular English classes for former students in preparation for: the Trinity College London Language Exams, namely the Integrated Skills in English (ISE I), Graded Examination in Spoken English (GESE VII) and ISE II; and the Cambridge University Examinations: First Certificate of English (FCE) and the Certificate in Advanced English (CAE).

Our pupils are also given the opportunity to prepare for the prep tests, grade 1, grade 2 and grade 3 examinations in piano and classical guitar by the internationally renowned Associated Board of the Royal Schools of Music.

80th
anniversary
Alice's adventures
Wonderland
1935
80
1965
Queen Elizabeth's School

Reddam House Berkshire

REDDAM HOUSE BERKSHIRE

(Founded 2015)

Bearwood Road, Sindlesham, Wokingham, Berkshire RG41 5BG UK
Tel: +44 (0)118 974 8300
Email: registrar@reddamhouse.org.uk
Website: www.reddamhouse.org.uk
Principal: Mr Rick Cross
School type: Co-educational Day & Boarding

Religious Denomination: Non-denominational
Age range of pupils: 3 months–18 years
No. of pupils enrolled as at 01/09/2022: 650
Fees as at 01/09/2022:
Day: £12,000–£19,248
Weekly Boarding: £27,981–£32,244
Full Boarding: £29,526–£33,789

Reddam House Berkshire is a co-educational, independent school that aspires to excellence in education for children from three months to 18 years old. This truly majestic school set in 125 acres of stunning woods and parkland is conveniently located near Wokingham in the English countryside of Berkshire, a vibrant hub with easy access to the M3, M4, Heathrow and London.

Reddam House Berkshire is renowned for its academic, cultural, and sporting excellence. It has a strong, recognisable culture that acknowledges a community of students who are nurtured as individuals, with their distinct attributes, traits and strengths celebrated.

The broad range of subjects creates a curriculum that accentuates independent inquiry. Students study up to 11 GCSEs with a free choice outside of the core subjects of Maths, English and Science. All students are encouraged to take on the Extended Project Qualification (EPQ), highly regarded by universities as demonstrating students' preparedness for undergraduate study.

Exam Results

Exam results in 2021 were outstanding with 62% of A level grades awarded being A*/A, and 63% of GCSE results being 9-7. The vast majority of students go on to higher education, with recent destinations including Cambridge, UCL and Manchester.

Boarding

Reddam House offers a range of flexible boarding options for students from the age of 8, including full and weekly boarding, extended days, and ad-hoc stays. Students who board at Reddam House can expect to be part of an inclusive, respectful, and international community where independence and self-confidence are developed and celebrated.

Beyond the Classroom

Academics is just one area in which students thrive, the extensive extracurricular activities programme provides plenty of opportunities for students to explore and develop their interests. Activities include performing and visual arts, music, photography, and computing. Regular sports fixtures include rugby, hockey, football, cricket, netball, swimming, tennis, basketball, golf, cross country, and judo.

Rome International School

RISROME
INTERNATIONAL SCHOOL

(Founded 1988)
Via Guglielmo Pecori Giraldi n.137,
00135 Rome, Italy

Tel: +39 06 8448 2651
Email: info@romeinternationalschool.it
Website: www.romeinternationalschool.it
Headteacher: Mr Scott Webber
Middle/High School Principal: Mr William Johnson
School type: Co-educational Day

Religious Denomination: Non-denominational
Age range of pupils: 2–18 years
No. of pupils enrolled as at 01/09/2022: 500
Fees as at 01/09/2022:
Day: €9,700–€24,425

Rome International School (RIS) offers an unparalleled inclusive international education that prepares students to solve problems that have not yet been imagined and to work in jobs that may not yet exist.

We continue to be the only school in Rome authorised to offer both the International Baccalaureate (IB) Primary Years Programme and IB Diploma Programme. The school is an accredited centre for the Cambridge IGCSE thereby ensuring the quality and consistency of a true international education.

Highly qualified, caring and experienced staff motivate and inspire students to achieve their potential, both academically and personally.

We teach students to think for themselves and to understand the significance of what they are learning in global and local contexts. Our inquiry-based educational approach places students at the centre of the learning process and encourages them to be active participants in their education.

Students who complete the rewarding educational journey at RIS progress to attend universities of their choice worldwide. They will have established a personal set of values that will lay the foundation for international mindedness and critical thinking to develop and flourish.

From the Duke of Edinburgh's International Award to a sustainability education partnership with WWF and Eco Schools, our community of learners can participate in enriching co-curricular and extracurricular activities that take learning beyond the classroom and make real-life connections.

The school's state-of-the-art building has been purpose-built to meet every learning and teaching requirement. Nestled in almost four hectares of natural parkland in north-west Rome, close to the city centre, our campus offers students plenty of opportunities to play, discover and experiment.

Joining RIS means joining an extended international community.

We are a member of the Globeducate ICS family of schools, united by a vision to prepare each student to become a global citizen who can shape the world.

With a student intake of over 50 different nationalities, Rome International School is the ideal context for a rewarding and progressive educational experience.

Rossall School

Rossall

INSPIRING EXCELLENCE

(Founded 1844)
Broadway, Fleetwood,
Lancashire FY7 8JW UK

Tel: +44 (0)1253 774201
Email: admissions@rossall.org.uk
Website: www.rossall.org.uk
Head: Mr Jeremy Quartermain
Appointed: August 2018
School type:
Co-educational Boarding & Day
Religious Denomination: Church of England but accept all religions

Age range of pupils: 0–18 years
No. of pupils enrolled as at 01/06/2022: 851
Fees as at 01/06/2022:
Day: £3,145–£5,050 per term
Weekly Boarding: £5,350–£8,695 per term
Full Boarding: £7,955–£12,895 per term
Average class size: 16
Teacher/pupil ratio: 1:11

The Good Schools Guide describes Rossall as 'A warm, happy and inclusive environment energised by a vision and challenge that is clearly helping all pupils to meet their potential.'

Set on an historic 160 acre campus, Rossall is one of the country's leading independent co-educational boarding and day schools, where boys and girls aged 0-18 are nurtured in a safe, secure and supportive environment.

Rossall currently provides one of the broadest curriculum programmes available in the UK independent school market. Rossall Preparatory School has a bespoke curriculum whilst the Senior School continues to follow the British National Curriculum, culminating with GCSE/iGCSE examinations at the end of Year 11. In sixth form, pupils then have the choice to study either A levels or the globally recognised IB Diploma Programme. The School boasts a current IB score average of 35 points, whilst over 60% of all grades awarded at A-Level are A*-A.

Small class sizes and a rigorous tutorial system, ensures academic excellence, with 95% of Rossall pupils entering higher education, at universities around the world.

Rossall's enviable on-campus facilities include 150 acres of outdoor grassed sports pitches, floodlit all-weather surfaces, a gymnasium, heated indoor swimming pool, Fives courts, shooting range and a multi-use-games-area (MUGA).

In September 2019, Rossall opened its brand new £4 million Sports Centre, boasting a 50m sprint track and multiple indoor courts. The School also has its very own Golf Academy (currently ranked Number 1 by the ISGA) which includes an indoor golf studio equipped with the latest video analysis equipment and GC2 launch monitor/simulator, as well as an indoor putting lab and short game facility. Rossall also boasts its own Elite Football Academy for boys and girls in partnership with the English League One football club, Fleetwood Town FC, and is home to the Lawrence House Astronomy & Space Science Centre, the only centre of its kind in Britain, specialising in astronomy education. In September 2021, Rossall became an All-Steinway School.

A huge range of extracurricular activities are offered to all pupils throughout the school. Pupils can join everything from the award-winning Chapel Choir to The Combined Cadet Force (the oldest CCF in the country!). The diverse range of clubs at Rossall ensures that there is something for everybody.

Admitting boarders as young as seven years old, Rossall's 'family structure' provides the framework for its exceptional standards of pastoral care. With major investments recently ploughed into its 10 boarding houses, each house is a well-equipped and comfortable home, which are in the process of being sensitively modernized to the highest standard.

Rossall School is a registered charity (No. 526685) that exists to provide education for children.

Royal High School Bath, GDST

(Founded 1865)

Lansdown Road, Bath, Bath & North-East Somerset BA1 5SZ UK
Tel: +44 (0)1225 313877
Email: admissions@rhsb.gdst.net
Website: www.royalhighbath.gdst.net
Head: Mrs Kate Reynolds
Head of Prep School: Ms Claire Lilley
School type: Girls' Day & Boarding
Age range of girls: 3–18 years

No. of pupils enrolled as at 01/09/2022: 580
Fees as at 01/09/2022:
Day: £5,041 (year 7)–£5,262 (Sixth Form) per term
Full Boarding: £11,234 (year 7)–£11,809 (Sixth Form) per term
Average class size: 14-18
Teacher/pupil ratio: 1:8

Royal High School Bath, GDST is a leading independent day and boarding school in the south west of England. Part of the Girls' Day School Trust family of schools, RHSB provides outstanding, contemporary, education for girls aged 3-18. The blend of academic rigour and an innovative curriculum combined with a supportive pastoral system means that students realise new talents, fulfil their potential and go on to have bright futures. Our Steinway Music School and Art School highlight our commitment to our students' creativity.

Academic

Built on the firm foundation of over 150 years of educating young women, we are an innovative, high-achieving school that provides a wonderful environment for girls to excel. From the very start of Year 7, girls are given a thorough grounding in the core subjects. This education is further enriched by Languages, PE, Arts and the Humanities, all taught by specialist teachers with a passion for their subjects. At Sixth Form, we offer a choice of A level or IB with a wide range of subjects delivered highly qualified and inspiring staff. The school's results are excellent, and consistently above the global average with students going on to study at prestigious universities in the UK and overseas, including Oxford, Cambridge, Imperial and UCL.

Community

The school is well-known for its friendliness and inclusivity. A school should be the heart of its community and we believe in organising initiatives that benefit our girls and their families as well as external charities and organisations.

Orientation

The school's expertise means the induction of students is quick and effective. A residential orientation experience helps students gain an understanding of the programme ahead and provides the space to plan their final years at school.

Boarding

With full and flexible boarding options, a diverse activities programme and excellent facilities, our girls can design their perfect home from home. Girls aged 11-16 board in School House, our stunning neo-Gothic main building while our Sixth Formers have their own dedicated house. House staff focus on creating a positive and secure atmosphere to ensure students quickly settle into a caring and supportive community. Each student is valued as an individual and their pastoral care and wellbeing are paramount.

Location

Situated in Bath, RHSB has good transport links. Just 15 minutes from M4 motorway and with easy access to London, Bristol, Cardiff and Birmingham. Mainline rail links to London Paddington. Airports in Bristol, Southampton, Heathrow and Gatwick are easy to access and a shuttle to west London for weekly boarders can be arranged as required.

Sainte Victoire International School

(Founded 2011)

Domaine de Château l'Arc, Chemin de Maurel, 13710 Fuveau, France
Tel: +33 4 42 26 51 96
Email: contact@schoolsaintevictoire.com
Website: www.schoolsaintevictoire.com
Head of School: Frederic Fabre

School type:
Co-educational Day & Boarding
Age range of pupils: 5–18 years
Fees as at 01/09/2022:
Day: €10,200–€17,900
Full Boarding: €26,800–€31,800

SVIS – Sainte Victoire International School is an IB World School located near Aix-en-Provence in the south of France. The school offers both the International Baccalaureate Diploma Programme and the Cambridge GCSE examinations. SVIS provides education for students aged 5 years to 18 years from over 40 nationalities in our Primary, Middle, and High School. From the Primary school level, teaching is bilingual, allowing students to achieve their academic potential in English and French. SVIS also offers mother-tongue classes for several additional languages.

SVIS provides an innovative and rigorous approach to teaching and learning, incorporating cross-disciplinary subjects as well as a wide range of learning opportunities that take place off-campus. These include an extensive range of local and international trips, an abundant offering of after school activities, and an ecology park. SVIS integrates sustainability goals and service-learning into the curriculum to develop students as global citizens.

The school is situated in the heart of an international 18-hole golf course, facing the Sainte Victoire mountain and offers students a healthy and peaceful school environment. SVIS is a family-friendly environment focusing on the whole child and provides opportunities for students to explore their passions in athletics and the arts. Class sizes are limited to 15 maximum allowing for individualised education programs.

School Facilities

The school facilities include an amphitheater, a library with computers, a theatre/art room, a science laboratory, an indoor gym and outstanding outdoor facilities: an 18-hole golf course, a football/rugby grass pitch, a tennis court, a basketball court and ecology park where students can grow fruit and vegetables.

Boarding Facilities

The boarding house is located 20 meters from the entrance to the school. This facility offers an exceptional living environment, where students enjoy a healthy pace of life, conducive to academic success. There is a maximum of 2 students per duplex. Each duplex is equipped with study rooms, a kitchen, 2 bathrooms, lounges, and a private terrace with outstanding views over the grounds.

Outstanding qualities of SVIS

- SVIS offers internationally renowned educational programs that are sought by leading universities.
- SVIS graduates have their first choice of leading universities.
- With more than 40 student nationalities, SVIS is a diverse and inclusive school.
- Each student receives individual support and guidance from teachers to achieve their maximum potential.
- The school provides students with opportunities to study a large variety of mother-tongue and foreign languages including English, Spanish, Russian, Chinese, Italian, German, Dutch, and Japanese.
- The school has an outstanding campus on an international 18-hole golf course in the south of France. The grounds are surrounded by pine forests.

Seaford College

(Founded 1884)
Lavington Park, Petworth,
West Sussex GU28 0NB UK

Tel: 01798 867392
Email: headmasterpa@seaford.org
Website: www.seaford.org
Headmaster: J P Green MA BA
School type:
Co-educational Day & Boarding
Age range of pupils: 5–18 years
No. of pupils enrolled as at 01/09/2022: 903

Boys: 544 ***Girls:*** 359 ***Sixth Form:*** 235
No. of boarders: 159
Fees as at 01/09/2022:
Day: £11,880–£24,630
Weekly Boarding: £24,735–£33,345
Full Boarding: £38,070
Average class size: 15-20
Teacher/pupil ratio: 1:9

Seaford is a small, friendly co-educational College, situated in an unrivalled position near Petworth, West Sussex. With its own Prep School, Senior School and Sixth Form, the College is located away from the distractions of city life, yet is still within easy reach of cultural and commercial centres. The College accepts day pupils and also offers both full and flexi-boarding for pupils aged 5-18. Seaford College is non-selective school and we are proud to offer an inclusive environment where each individual is known and valued; is given attention and respect. Our aim is to educate the whole person; to find the strengths of each boy and girl and to enable them to succeed. We are a warm, friendly school with excellent teaching and learning across all departments. In addition to this very strong academic core we offer outstanding pastoral care and an impressive programme of extra-curricular activities. With its purpose-built music school and state-of-the-art classrooms for maths and science, plus all-new boys' boarding houses. A typical Seafordian will be an articulate, confident and well-rounded young person. Seaford College offers an inspirational environment where personal bests are achieved both in and outside the classroom. Seaford College is a hidden gem, tucked away at the foot of the picturesque South Downs. Seaford College is easily accessible from London and the M25 and is only 45mins by car from Gatwick. Love to learn!

SEK Dublin International School

Belvedere Hall, Windgates, Greystones,
Co. Wicklow, A63 EY23 Ireland
Tel: +35 31 287 41 75
Email: admissions-dublin@sek.ie
Website: dublin.sek.es

Principal: Alberto Domínguez
School type:
Co-educational Day & Boarding
Age range of pupils: 11–18 years

SEK Dublin International School is a leading IB school in Ireland. Small by design, with an emphasis on personalised learning, the school's unique teaching and learning model is built on inquiry-based learning to promote critical and creative thinking.

Located in a stunning natural setting, where the landscape of the Irish countryside meets the Atlantic coast, between the towns of Bray and Greystones. The latter was named one of the best towns in the world to live as a family, and is 30 km from Dublin. SEK-Dublin combines architectural tradition with cutting-edge technology, spanning over 250,000 m2 of grounds and boasting extensive green areas where our students can enjoy a diverse range of sports and outdoor activities, while enhancing their academic development.

SEK-Dublin is the first school in Ireland authorised by the International Baccalaureate Organisation to teach the Middle Years Programme (11-16 years) and the Diploma Programme (16-19 years), taught fully in English with optional languages, including German, French and Spanish.

SEK-Dublin opened its doors in 1981. The success of the school is based on several factors including: a multicultural team of highly trained teachers; the effective use of learning technologies; an individualised programme to cover the educational needs of each student; small class sizes; and an outstanding programme guaranteed by SEK schools' standards of excellence. Aware that education does not only take place in the classroom, for our boarding students we offer residential options with carefully selected local host families or in our on-campus high quality residential facilities, and diverse extracurricular and cultural activities. These aspects combine to nurture the holistic personal and academic development of our students. This all-round education serves them well for their future, enabling them to become mature and independent individuals, and providing them with lasting memories of their experiences at school.

In all SEK International Schools we are able to offer a quality online learning model in which students are able to continue their learning if necessary, with synchronous and asynchronous classes, and with personalized monitoring by teachers and tutors, which has proved successful with students and families.

SEK International School Alborán

(Founded 1999)
C/ Barlovento 141, Urb. Almerimar, El Ejido, 04711 Almería, Andalusia, Spain
Tel: +34 900 87 87 98
Email: sek-alboran@sek.es

Website: alboran.sek.es
Principal: Luis Carlos Jiménez Gámez
School type: Co-educational Day
Age range of pupils: 4 months–18 years
No. of pupils enrolled as at 01/05/2022: 756

Located on the seashore and adjacent to the Punta Entinas Natural Park, in Almería, SEK International School Alborán is regarded as a high quality international school in Andalusia. It is the only school in Almeria that offers three IB International Baccalaureate Programmes, from 3 to 18 years of age (Primary Years Programme Middle Years Programme – MYP and the Diploma Programme, either bilingually in English and Spanish or fully in English). These programmes are coordinated closely with the Spanish education system.

For the SEK Education Group, to which SEK-Alborán belongs, physical fitness and respecting one's health are an essential element of the learning process. SEK-Alborán has extensive recreational areas, and 28,000m2 of outdoor spaces, as well as extensive sports facilities and a heated indoor pool. Its classrooms are equipped with cutting-edge technology (makerspace, video recording and editing spaces, radio, 3D printer, robotic tables, TED ED Club). It is considered a model of educational innovation in Andalusia.

Social and emotional learning programmes are of particular importance in students' curricula to foster the social and personal awareness. In the Intelligent Classroom, each student progresses according to their potential, working in teams and having individual efforts rewarded. Teachers and tutors are afforded an open space for dialogue with students and parents both in-person and online. Students can take advantage of the Flipped Classroom to work on content and tackle issues from a broad perspective, solving doubts with their teachers, and learning by doing. The HYFLEX system has been implemented due to the covid and online learning has become part of the daily life of students.

SEK-Alborán offers a bilingual Spanish-English education that is incorporated progressively over all educational stages (50% of the subjects are taught in English). It is the only school in Almeria authorized by Cambridge English Exams, Alianza Française and Goethe Institut in Almería. It also has an extensive program of exchanges and participations in United Nations Models.

In all SEK International Schools we are able to offer a quality online learning model in which students are able to continue their learning if necessary, with synchronous and asynchronous classes, and with personalized monitoring by teachers and tutors, which has proved successful with students and families.

SEK International School Atlántico

Rúa Illa de Arousa 4, Boavista. A Caeira, Poio, 36005 Pontevedra, Galicia, Spain
Tel: +34 900 87 87 98
Email: sek-atlantico@sek.es
Website: atlantico.sek.es

Principal: Jacobo Olmedo
School type: Co-educational Day
Age range of pupils: 4 months–18 years
No. of pupils enrolled as at 01/05/2022: 730

SEK International School Atlántico offers an outstanding international education to students, from 4 months to 18 years of age. SEK-Atlántico is authorised to teach the three International Baccalaureate Organisation programmes (PYP, MYP and IB). Second School in Spain with the best results in IBDP Exams in 2021 (19th in Europe).

SEK International Schools are committed to offering each student a learning experience focused on personal development and learning, preparing them for success in later life. Situated close to Pontevedra and Vigo, between the sea and the mountains, SEK-Atlántico boasts modern well-designed school spaces and buildings.

Students are afforded a bilingual education and learn to live with other cultures from an early age. The school places great importance on students' oral and written expression, fostering fluency in different languages. Considered a leader in educational innovation in Galicia, SEK-Atlántico offers learning in Galician, Spanish, English and French from year 3 of Primary.

The SEK education model allows students to play a leading role in their education. They explore and discover for themselves, and build and organise their own knowledge and skills, with expert support from teachers.

SEK-Atlántico students learn in facilities designed for their physical, social and creative development. They include: makerspaces, a psychomotor skills classroom for younger students, laboratories, music and art rooms, a library, language classrooms, a learning lab and large indoor and outdoor sports and recreational areas.

Technological spaces are integrated in the day to day lessons of the school and are designed to contribute fully to student learning. Devices have portability and compatibility enabling them to be used in any space.

From the second year of Primary to Baccalaureate, SEK-Atlántico students prepare for Cambridge University Examinations. In the Middle Years Programme and in Baccalaureate, students can also opt to take the Alliance Française Diplôme d'etude de langue française.

In all SEK International Schools we are able to offer a quality online learning model in which students are able to continue their learning if necessary, with synchronous and asynchronous classes, and with personalized monitoring by teachers and tutors, which has proved successful with students and families.

SEK International School Catalunya

(Founded 1995)

Av. del Tremolencs, 24, La Garriga,
08530 Barcelona, Catalonia, Spain
Tel: +34 900 87 87 98
Email: sek-catalunya@sek.es
Website:
catalunya.sekinternationalschools.com

Principal: Roberto Prata
School type:
Co-educational Day & Boarding
Age range of pupils: 4 months–18 years
No. of pupils enrolled as at 01/05/2022: 970

SEK International School Catalunya is located in a quiet and safe residential area spanning 100,000 m2, including a large expanse of Mediterranean forest. The school is in La Garriga, a picturesque town just 30 minutes from the centre of Barcelona, one of the most cosmopolitan cities in Europe.

SEK-Catalunya boasts modern facilities and innovative learning spaces and teaches the three International Baccalaureate Programmes. The Middle Years Programme is offered in Spanish and English and the Diploma Programme is offered entirely in English or in both languages. We are one of the leaders in the international rankings thanks to our excellent results in IB Diploma exams.

SEK-Catalunya is accredited by the New England Association of Schools and Colleges (NEASC), which is a process of external globally recognised quality assurance. NEASC accreditation allows SEK-Catalunya to offer the US High School Diploma, as a complement to the IB Diploma.

The school offers its Secondary School and Baccalaureate students the opportunity to take part in the prestigious Duke of Edinburgh's International Award, an all-round personal development scheme focused on the development and training of skills such as: leadership, autonomy, problem solving and teamwork.

The SEK-Catalunya Music School, in partnership with the Trinity College London, offers a complete curriculum for all students who wish to acquire the necessary skills to learn classical and modern music.

We also offer international boarding, housing students from Spain and abroad in modern, comfortable and functional facilities, designed for residents to live together, grow as individuals and develop their personal identity thanks to a multicultural environment and a rich offer of complementary activities.

In all SEK International Schools we are able to offer a quality online learning model in which students are able to continue their learning if necessary, with synchronous and asynchronous classes, and with personalized monitoring by teachers and tutors, which has proved successful with students and families.

SEK International School Ciudalcampo

(Founded 1975)

Urb. Ciudalcampo, Paseo de las Perdices, 2, San Sebastián de los Reyes, 28707 Madrid, Spain
Tel: +34 900 87 87 98
Email: sek-ciudalcampo@sek.es

Website: ciudalcampo.sek.es
Principal: Cecilia Villavicencio
School type: Co-educational Day
Age range of pupils: 4 months–18 years
No. of pupils enrolled as at 01/05/2022: 1400

SEK International Schools are committed to offering each student a learning experience focused on personal growth, preparing for success in later life. SEK Schools are bilingual and pioneers in offering the International Baccalaureate programmes, boasting an educational model that has made a tradition of innovation, placing them among the best schools in Spain since their foundation in 1892. SEK International School Ciudalcampo offers the IB Primary Years Programme, the IB Middle Years Programme, the IB Diploma Programme (in English and Spanish, or fully in English), and the Spanish Bachillerato LOMLOE.

SEK-Ciudalcampo offers an innovative educational model based on early stimulation, immersion in English and the development of talent and creativity in a digital environment that favours the development of emotional intelligence.

SEK Ciudalcampo boasts over 20,000m2 of grounds and buildings and a large outdoor sports complex that exceeds 10,000m2.

Through an active learning approach, SEK-Ciudalcampo turns the classrooms into a flexible learning space for all students. The student becomes an active agent, building learning for themselves. The Design Thinking methodology helps students to develop skills such as cooperation, creativity and innovation.

We believe that the way we learn has changed forever. As a result, SEK Future Learning Model is presented as a new opportunity to learn from new methodological formats, based on the Intelligent Classroom system, the use of new tools and the interaction between the different members of the educational community, offering enriched programmes such as the "Aula de Padres".

SEK-Ciudalcampo is accredited by the New England Association of Schools and Colleges (NEASC), and is the first Spanish school to be recognised as a global member of Round Square.

In all SEK International Schools we are able to offer a quality online learning model in which students are able to continue their learning if necessary, with synchronous and asynchronous classes, and with personalized monitoring by teachers and tutors, which has proved successful with students and families.

SEK International School El Castillo

(Founded 1972)

Urb. Villafranca del Castillo, Castillo de Manzanares, s/n, Villanueva de la Cañada, 28692 Madrid, Spain
Tel: +34 91 815 08 92
Email: sek-castillo@sek.es
Website:
madrid.sekinternationalschools.com

Head of School: Eloísa López
School type:
Co-educational Day & Boarding
Age range of pupils: 4 months–18 years
No. of pupils enrolled as at 01/05/2022: 1210

SEK-El Castillo School is a privileged place for coexistence and learning in the broadest sense of the word. The High Artistic Performance School (Music and Dance), the Artistic or the Research Baccalaureates, the different sports schools or the enrichment projects in collaboration with the Camilo José Cela University, are some examples.

We have been authorised as an International Baccalaureate (IB) World School for over 40 years. Currently our students can take the IB Primary Years, Middle Years and Diploma programmes either in English or following an English-Spanish bilingual syllabus, with outstanding examination results. We are also accredited by the New England Association of Schools and Colleges (NEASC) in conjunction with IB with a process of quality assurance: the Collaborative Learning protocol with a focus on impactful learning processes.

We believe that the way we learn has changed forever. As a result, SEK Future Learning Model is presented as a new opportunity to learn from new methodological formats, based on design-thinking tools, the use of new educational technology and the interaction between the different members of the educational community, offering enriched programmes such as the "Aula de Padres" and instrumental lessons for families in our Music School.

We boast first-rate sports facilities on campus and offer international boarders a professionally staffed, nurturing and safe environment. We provide linguistic immersion programmes in both our languages of instruction to ensure access to the curriculum for all our students. In addition, as part of our commitment to talent development, we offer a high-performance sports programme: SEK International Sports Academy (we are the academic partner of important clubs such as Real Madrid). This programme allows athletes to combine their academic studies with their training and competing schedules. Students can take advantage of our boarding facilities to enhance their time management. As part of our provision to develop engaged and active young adults, we offer students the opportunity to participate in the prestigious Duke of Edinburgh International Award.

In all SEK International Schools we offer a quality online learning model in which students are able to continue their learning if necessary, with synchronous and asynchronous classes, and with personalized monitoring by teachers and tutors, which has proved successful with students and families.

SEK International School Les Alpes

International School
Les Alpes · France

Saint Nicolas La Chappelle,
Flumet-Val d'Arly, 73590 Flumet, France
Tel: +34 900 87 87 98
Email: sek-lesalpes@sek.es

Website:
lesalpes.sekinternationalschools.com
Principal: Guadalupe Sánchez
School type:
Co-educational Day & Boarding
Age range of pupils: 13–15 years

SEK-Les Alpes is located in the heart of Europe, in the town of Flumet-St. Nicolas la Chapelle in the French Savoy, with school grounds spanning over 15,000 square metres. Its facilities, blending in perfectly with its Alpine surroundings, include two large buildings with dormitories and the most cutting-edge and innovative teaching resources to ensure students' all-round development.

The school was opened and founded in 1990 as a private Spanish school with recognition from the French educational authorities.

At SEK-Les Alpes we broaden the educational concept by developing learning experiences for students from 13 to 15 years of age in three languages (French, Spanish and English) in an all-round programme of formal and non formal education. The incorporation of cross-curricula aspects such as developing future entrepreneurs, leaders and young scientists affords a perspective that enriches school life.

Over 1,600 students from different nationalities have studied at the school, all sharing an interest in perfecting their French language communications skills, but also, seeking the chance to practice snow and mountain sports.

Skiing is the predominant sport at SEK-Les Alpes and is taught on the best pistes by instructors from the French Ski School.

The Megève ski resort is located close to the school with over 400 km of pistes, but Courchevel, Tignes and La Plagne, which hosted the 1992 Winter Olympics, are also easily accessible.

We have incluede the DofE, bronze category, into our academic program and in winter months, we become the headquarters of a private technical training school for high-performance ski athletes.

We also offer a wide range of sports in stunning natural settings including hiking in Col des Aravis; rafting on the Isère river; ice-skating in Megève; skiing in Tignes and Megève; orienteering, rock climbing, canyoning in La Léchère; kayaking on Anncey Lake; via ferrata.

Curricular enrichment activities are part of students' personal and academic development at SEK-Les Alpes, with visits to nearby cities such as Geneva, Chamonix, Albertville, Annecey, Grenoble, Lyon and Chambèry. Longer trips are also organised to Venice, Florence, Sienna, Milan, Verona and Paris. All these trips are coordinated by a team of teachers that take great care in supervising each programme.

In all SEK International Schools we are able to offer a quality online learning model in which students are able to continue their learning if necessary, with synchronous and asynchronous classes, and with personalized monitoring by teachers and tutors, which has proved successful with students and families.

SEK International School Santa Isabel

Calle San Ildefonso, 18,
28012 Madrid, Spain
Tel: +34 900 87 87 98
Email: sek-santaisabel@sek.es
Website: santaisabel.sek.es

Head of School: Jennifer Pro
School type: Co-educational Day
Age range of pupils: 3–12 years
No. of pupils enrolled as at 01/05/2022: 334

With more than 20 nationalities, SEK Santa Isabel offers of a dynamic multicultural environment set in the heart of Las Letras, the historic cultural district of Madrid. The only school in the center of Madrid to deliver the International Baccalaureate's Primary Years Program, students learn in real world settings where their classroom extends beyond school walls to the museums, theaters, galleries, neighborhood gardens, traditional markets and Retiro Park.

SEK-Santa Isabel offers Early Childhood and Primary Education (3-12). Our innovative educational model is based on early stimulation, immersion in English and Spanish and the development of talent, creativity, and academic achievement. We boast of a vibrant school wide community and personalized learning experiences in a safe environment that fosters emotional intelligence.

Through an active learning approach, SEK-Santa Isabel turns classrooms into flexible learning spaces. The student becomes an active agent, building learning for themselves. The Design Thinking and Design for Change methodologies helps students to discover talents and develop skills such as cooperation, creativity and innovation.

We believe that learning has changed forever. SEK-Santa Isabel provides students with the skills they need to face the challenges of the future, fostering global competencies, critical thinking, communication, public speaking and multiple intelligence.

Students take part in our renowned music school and extensive arts department, learn additional languages and can choose from a range of extracurricular activities, extended hours and sports activities. We have a spacious gym on school grounds, as well as outdoor areas for sports such as swimming, tennis and padel tennis, football and basketball. Our Stellar Programme aims to enrich personal development for high-achieving students.

SEK schools are pioneers in offering International Baccalaureate programmes, boasting an educational model that has made a tradition of innovation, placing them among the best schools in Spain since their foundation in 1892.

Sevenoaks School

(Founded 1432)
High Street, Sevenoaks, Kent TN13 1HU UK

Tel: +44 (0)1732 455133
Email: regist@sevenoaksschool.org
Website: www.sevenoaksschool.org
Head of School:
Mr Jesse R Elzinga AB MSt FCCT
Appointed: September 2020
School type:
Co-educational Day & Boarding

Age range of pupils: 11–18 years
No. of pupils enrolled as at 01/09/2022: 1164
Fees as at 01/09/2022:
Day: £25,020–£28,413
Full Boarding: £39,960–£43,353
Average class size: 8-24
Teacher/pupil ratio: 1:9

Sevenoaks is one of the leading schools in the UK, providing an outstanding modern education. All 450+ students in the sixth form study the IB Diploma Programme, which the school has taught since 1978. The leafy 100-acre campus is in the Kent countryside, just half an hour from Central London and Gatwick Airport. International students make up around 20 per cent of the student body and the school provides pupils with a balanced and intellectually stimulating education while promoting global understanding. Pastoral care is consistently excellent, enabling friendships between all members of a peer group to flourish. Sevenoaks was The Sunday Times Independent Secondary School of the Year in 2018 and 2008.

Curriculum

A wide range of subjects is offered at GCSE and IGCSE. In the sixth form all pupils study the IB Diploma Programme. Academic results are outstanding. In 2020, 18 students gained 45 points in the IB, and the average score was 40.1 points (around ten points above the world average). Virtually every student goes on to one of the world's best universities, with around 80 per cent taking places at leading UK universities, and 21 per cent accepting places at top US, Canadian, European and international universities.

A wide range of sport is offered, and pupils achieve honours in cross country, rugby, football, hockey, netball, cricket, athletics, sailing, shooting, swimming and tennis. There is a strong emphasis on music, drama and art, with chamber music a particular strength. The school is proud of its strong tradition of community service and DofE Award participation.

Facilities

Facilities are first class. Recent developments include a striking, state-of-the-art boarding house, an award-winning performing arts centre, a Science & Technology Centre uniting the four core fields of science, and an innovative Sixth Form centre. There are seven boarding houses, including five single-sex houses (13-18), and two sixth form houses (16-18). Accommodation ranges from a charming Queen Anne house to a modern building with contemporary social spaces and en-suite study bedrooms.

Entrance

Year 7 (11+): entrance examination, school reference and interview.

Year 9 (13+): pre-assessment, entrance examination or Common Entrance or scholarship examination, plus school reference and interview.

Sixth form (16+): entrance examination, personal statement and interview.

Up to 50 scholarships are awarded annually at 11, 13 and 16, for academic excellence, music, sport, art and drama, and means-tested bursaries are available.

Sevenoaks School is a registered charity for purposes of education. Charity No. 1101358.

Sotogrande International School

(Founded 1978)

Avenida La Reserva SN, Sotogrande,
Cádiz, 11310 Spain
Tel: +34 956 795 902
Email: info@sis.gl
Website: www.sis.ac
Head of School: Mr. James Kearney

School type: Co-educational Day & Boarding
Religious Denomination: Non-denominational
Age range of pupils: 4 months–18 years
No. of pupils enrolled: 1021
Fees: €8,025 – €23,100

Sotogrande International School (SIS) is one of the 75 best IB schools in the world and under the 5 best in Spain. Is a day and boarding school that follows the IB programme from 3-18 years. Home to a passionate learning community who inspire and encourage learning and intercultural understanding, promoting education as a force for good in the world.

With more than 1000 children from 54 countries, SIS is more than just a school; it's a place where individuals flourish. throughout the IB programmes, internationally qualified teachers provide a challenging, nurturing and academically-rigorous education.

Academic results are consistently excellent, with both MYP and Diploma students achieving well above world average scores year after year. As a result of the impressive average point score of 36 in 2020, 90% of students went on to be placed at their first choice of university.

Elite Sports Programme – Specialist programmes combine a world-class education with professional golf, tennis, polo, basketball, swimming and music tuition, creating opportunities for talented students to excel in their chosen field. These programmes follow a structured pathway and provide expert support and guidance, helping students work towards university scholarships in the USA and beyond.

As an Apple Distinguished School, the use of technology is creatively embedded in the curriculum for all students from the age of 3. At the same time, the F1 in Schools programme and the Hyperbaric surfboard and a hydrofoil challenge provide an exciting way for students to learn Science, Technology, Engineering and Maths (STEM) related subjects. Students are encouraged to think independently and critically, developing their unique interests, gifts and talents benefiting from opportunities to be the best they can be.

Sotogrande International Boarding House, is a warm, vibrant community with new and amazing boarding facilities, where the staff are dedicated to caring for, and getting the best out of each individual. Students are encouraged to take part in every aspect of boarding life helping them to grow into happy, motivated and morally committed citizens of the world. The academic support received by students is reflected in IB Diploma exam results where, over the past two years, the top-performing students have both been boarders, one achieving the maximum IB score of 45 points.

Boarding School Association award 2021: The International School of the Year Award was one of two new categories in the BSA Awards for 2021, Sotogrande International School, part of the Inspired Boarding Schools group, was highly commended.

Southbank International School

Southbank International School LONDON'S LEADING IB WORLD SCHOOL

(Founded 1980)

Southbank Kensington: 36-38 Kensington Park Road, London, W11 3BU UK

Southbank Hampstead:

16 Netherhall Gardens London NW3 5TH

Southbank Westminster:

63-65 Portland Place London W1B 1QR

Tel: +44 (0)20 7243 3803

Email: admissions@southbank.org

Website: www.southbank.org

Principal: Siobhan McGrath

School type: Co-educational Day

Age range of pupils: 3–18 years

Fees as at 01/09/2022:

Early Childhood EC3 (half-day programme) (3 years 2 months old): £6,410 per term

Early Childhood EC4 (4 years old): £8,885 per term

Kindergarten – Grade 5 (PYP) (5 – 11 years old): £9,700

Grades 6 – 10 (MYP) (11 – 16 years old): £10,750

Grades 11 and 12 (DP) (16 – 18 years old): £11,310

Average class size: 16

Teacher/pupil ratio: 1:10

Southbank International School is an International Baccalaureate (IB) World School for 3-18 year olds with campuses in Hampstead, Kensington and Westminster in Central London. We are the first school in the UK authorised to offer all three International Baccalaureate programmes. For over 40 years, Southbank has been at the forefront of providing internationally relevant, world class education.

We encourage our students to think critically and always challenge assumptions whilst ensuring they have an openness to the outside world and are ready to see other points of view. These qualities help our students develop to broaden their minds while excelling in their academic studies. We help them to develop as independent, confident, curious and lifelong learners who fulfil their academic potential and take the natural next step into the world's best universities.

With over seventy nationalities on our roll, we live and breathe the spirit of internationalism, as reflected in our three programmes of study and the many activities outside the classroom. Southbank uses London as our classroom, taking full advantage of the city's cultural riches, giving our students access to educational enrichment that is perhaps unparalleled anywhere else in the world.

Primary Years Programme (3-11 years old)

Based at our Hampstead and Kensington campuses, the Primary Years Programme focuses on the development of the whole child as an inquirer, both in the classroom and in the world outside. It is defined by six transdisciplinary themes of global significance, explored using knowledge and skills derived from six subject areas, with a powerful emphasis on inquiry-based learning.

Facilities at Hampstead include: A dedicated hands-on STEM lab for science, technology, engineering and maths activities; A music room with a range of percussion instruments and performance space. From the age of 5 every child learns to play the violin using the Suzuki method, learning to play through sound rather than reading music; A bespoke art room with a wide range of materials for hands-on creativity; A multi-purpose hall for lunches, sport, school 'town meetings' and concerts; A vibrant, well-stocked library, which is regularly attended by students to develop literacy and research skills; An edible courtyard that offers a quiet space for vegetable and flower growing, as well as birdhouses and a bug hotel; An attractive, bright and spacious Early Childhood suite (for students aged 3-5) with access to a dedicated outside play area with sand and climbing frame.

Facilities at Kensington include: An IT lab featuring high-performance Macs; Interactive smartboards in all classrooms; A music room with a range of instruments and digital recording equipment; Two sound-proofed rooms for music practice; A bespoke art room with a wide range of materials for hands-on creativity; A multi-purpose hall that is used for lunches, sport, school 'town meetings' and concerts; A well-stocked library, which is regularly attended by students to develop literacy and research skills; A garden featuring a climbing frame, sandpit and wide range of educational toys and equipment; An attractive, bright and spacious Early Childhood suite (for students aged 3-5) with access to a outside play area with sand and climbing frame.

Middle Years Programme (11-16 years old)

Based at our Westminster campus on Portland Place, the Middle Years Programme shares the PYP's commitment to learning through inquiry and continues to develop attributes of the IB learner profile. The MYP emphasises intellectual challenge, encouraging students to make connections between their studies in traditional subjects and the real world. At Southbank, we foster the development of skills for communication, intercultural understanding and global engagement – essential qualities for young people who are becoming global leaders.

Southbank Westminster is conveniently located near Regent's Park with good transportation links nearby. Facilities at Westminster include five science labs, a Design lab with desktop Macs to complement the 1:1 programme. Our Design labs include laser cutters, 3D printers, amongst other industry-level equipment. A hall/theatre, cafeteria, art and music rooms, and two libraries served by networked computers.

Diploma Programme (16-18 years old)

Based at Conway Street and our site open from August 2018 on the corner of Euston Road and Cleveland St, the Diploma Programme encourages students to ask challenging questions, develop a strong sense of their own identity and culture, and develop the ability to communicate with and understand people from other countries and cultures. It prepares students for the next stage in their education and the qualification is widely-recognised by the world's leading universities.

2021 saw Southbanks largest ever cohort, with 77 students entered for the IB Diploma scoring an average of 37.6 (world average 31.3). We achieved a 100% pass rate, with 33% of our students scoring 40 or more, putting them in the top 3% of students worldwide. 8 students scored a perfect score of 45 and 35% students achieved a bilingual IB Diploma. These outstanding results allowed the vast majority of students to gain admission to top universities in the UK, North America and other parts of the world.

Facilities at Conway Street include a science lab, library resource centre, art studio and language suite. Facilities at Cleveland St include a brand new art room, a large common room and a design technology lab.

Southbank also have three dedicated university counsellors specialising in North American universities, the UK and the rest of the world. All counsellors are available for individual appointments and events are organised to inform parents about university planning.

Virtual Tours

We are very proud of our school and understand that not everyone will be able to visit before they join us. We have produced virtual tours of all our campuses and we encourage you to explore these to gain an initial insight into what to expect when you arrive. View virtual tour: www.southbank.org/virtualtour

Southlands British International School

(Founded 1976)

Via Teleclide 40, Casal Palocco,
00124 Rome, Italy

Tel: +39 06 5053932
Email: info@southlands.it
Website: www.southlands.it

Principal: Mrs. Victoria Del Federico
Appointed: September 2020
School type: Co-educational Day

Age range of pupils: 3–18 years
No. of pupils enrolled as at 01/09/2022: 300
Fees as at 01/09/2022:
€7,025 – €18,450
Average class size: 16
Teacher/pupil ratio:
1:11 (Primary) & 1:8 (Senior)

Southlands British International School was founded in 1976 with a strong commitment to provide the rigour and values of a British education with a truly international outlook. We provide an immersive English education to children from the ages of three through to 18. Our students hail from all over the world and are encouraged to find their place in it through a provision grounded in global citizenship and international mindedness. Following the English National curriculum to the age of 16, followed by the IBDP, our students achieve outstanding results in a personalised and caring environment. We value Honesty, Kindness and Respect, and believe in the power of student voice, collaboration and creativity.

The school is located in the south of Rome, in a rural setting: our students truly have space to grow in every sense. We believe that learning should extend beyond the classroom: Outdoor learning features heavily in our Early Years and Primary provision, with lessons and activities happening in our dedicated learning gardens every day. A refreshed programme of co curricular activities within and outside the school day ensures that students develop new skills and build a broad range of interests, alongside supporting the community through service learning opportunities.

Our unique location means we are the only international school in the city to offer outdoor and adventure education as part of the curriculum. Trail biking, bouldering, surfing and stand up paddle are an integral part of our PE curriculum. Adventure learning in our on-campus Forest School helps students to develop essential qualities to navigate life while emphasising the importance of an ecologically sustainable future through learning grounded in nature.

Southlands is also fortunate to be part of the Globeducate group of schools: a worldwide family, which enables us to provide outstanding opportunities for students and staff to connect with partners including WWF, participate in workshops, exchanges, competitions, and build relationships to support growth and success. This is also useful for families who are moving around the world as we are increasingly able to support them with a school move when transferring to new placements.

St Edward's College, Malta

St Edward's College
Malta

(Founded 1929)

Triq San Dwardu, Birgu (Vittoriosa),
BRG 9039 Malta
Tel: +356 2788 1199
Email: admissions@stedwards.edu.mt
Website: www.stedwards.edu.mt
Headmaster: Mr Nollaig Mac an Bhaird
School type: Day & Boarding

Religious Denomination: Roman Catholic
Age range of pupils: 2–4 & 16-18 years
Age range of boys: 5–15 years
Fees as at 01/09/2022:
Day: €2,730–€7,200
Full Boarding: €15,500–€23,900

Providing a coeducational Sixth Form and Pre-School
A Top Boarding School for the IB Diploma Programme

If you are looking for a top International boarding school, then look at the Mediterranean's secret gem – The St Edward's College in Birgu, Cottonera only a few minutes from Malta's Capital, Valletta. St Edward's was established in 1929, basing itself on British Public School ideals, to fill the void left in the Maltese education system by the departure of the English Jesuits.

The College site originally served as a Military Hospital and has extensive grounds between the bastion walls and the old hospital buildings, which serve as ideal recreational areas. Throughout the years the campus has seen a number of additions, which include the Junior School building and the Kindergarten block. The College has also recently adjusted its facilities to begin accepting boarders from the ages of 11 to 18. Our boarding facilities are split over two floors where single and double rooms are available.

At St Edward's College we strive to provide students with a seamless transition from Junior school up to Sixth Form level. We prepare the boys for O'Level Matsec (local) and IGCSEs. O'Levels are available until Year 11 (age 15/16) followed by the two-year International IB Diploma programme which is recognised by both local and international universities. The College is an English speaking school so all the lessons are in conducted in English.

The College caters for boys at all stages of their studies from Nursery, through to Junior School, Secondary school and finally the International IB programme at Sixth Form level, which is the only stage besides nursery and kindergarten where girls are admitted both as day girls and as boarders. The complement of students is fairly international with local boys as well as many others who are the sons of expats working in North Africa and the Middle East besides other areas like China, Russia and Italy.

St Edward's offers a unique opportunity for parents seeking a boarding school:

- The school operates on British boarding school principles with high academic standards
- The location and environment are superb with year round sunshine on a Mediterranean island
- Malta is within three hours of any European capital city by air
- The IB Diploma is recognised by all top universities
- Our fees offer some of the best value of any European boarding schools

Come and join our students on the IB Diploma Programme!

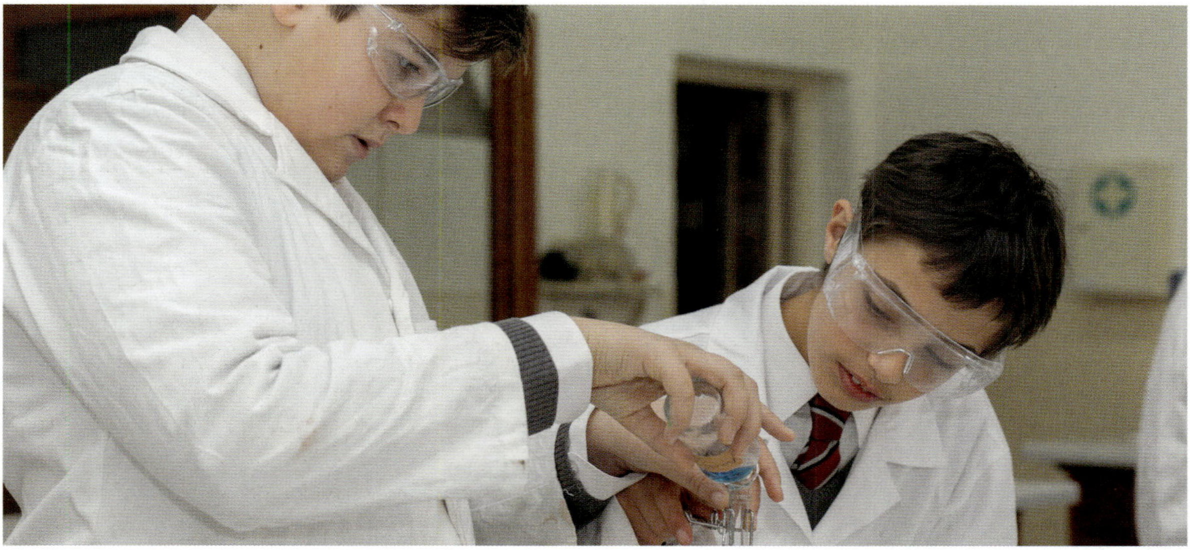

St George's British International School, Rome

(Founded 1958)
Via Cassia, km 16, La Storta,
00123 Rome, Italy

Tel: +39 06 3086001
Email: admissions@stgeorge.school.it
Website: www.stgeorge.school.it
Principal: David Tongue
Appointed: January 2019
School type: Co-educational Day

Age range of pupils: 3–18 years
No. of pupils enrolled as at 01/09/2022: 930
Fees as at 01/09/2022:
€11,100 – €21,900
Average class size: 18
Teacher/pupil ratio: 1:10

St George's British International School is a not-for-profit school, founded in 1958 to serve Rome's international community. Today St George's has grown to be one of the leading international schools of its kind in continental Europe, and educates more than 900 pupils representing nearly 100 different nationalities.

Offering an enhanced version of the UK National Curriculum through to Key Stage 4 (IGCSE), all pupils follow the International Baccalaureate Diploma Programme (IBDP) in their final two years of study. Teachers are almost exclusively UK-trained and mother-tongue English speakers.

Emphasis is on academic excellence, with recent graduating cohorts averaging a score of 37 points in the IB Diploma and securing admission to leading universities including Cambridge, Harvard, Imperial, Yale, UCL, London School of Economics and Princeton. The main campus, housing a Junior and a Senior School, is a spacious 14-acre site in the north of the city with extensive facilities: 7 fully-equipped science laboratories, specialist music, art and design technology rooms, and multiple sports amenities (including two multi-purpose Astro-turf pitches, an Olympic-size running track, rugby, tennis, basketball and volleyball courts).

St George's has a second Junior School campus in the centre of Rome, in close proximity to the Vatican. Purpose-fitted facilities include modern and bright classrooms, while the children enjoy the use of a 25m swimming pool, auditorium and gymnasium.

St George's provides extensive specialist support for pupils with additional educational needs, and the core curriculum is supplemented by a wide-range of trips organised both in Italy and beyond. New pupils can join St George's year-round, subject to availability, and early application is recommended.

St Lawrence College

ST LAWRENCE
COLLEGE

(Founded 1879)

Ramsgate, Kent CT11 7AE UK
Tel: 01843 572931
Email: admissions@slcuk.com
Website: www.slcuk.com
Head of College: Mr Barney Durrant
School type:
Co-educational Day & Boarding

Age range of pupils: 3–18 years
No. of pupils enrolled as at 01/09/2022: 585
Fees as at 01/09/2022:
Day: £8,394–£18,558
Full Boarding: £29,454–£38,952
Teacher/pupil ratio: 1:8

Founded in 1879, St Lawrence College is a thriving independent day and boarding school, providing a first class education for boys and girls from 3 to 18 years. Currently, we have approximately 585 pupils - 145 in the Junior School and 438 in the Senior School, of which 135 are boarders (boarding from 7 years of age).

Located in the Kent coastal town of Ramsgate, and within easy walking distance of the sea, the school is set in 45 acres of safe and spacious grounds, housing both beautiful historic architecture and outstanding contemporary facilities.

In the Classroom

Academic standards are high and we offer an extensive choice of GCSEs and A-levels, with an excellent success rate of pupils going on to their first choice of university.

We have continued to embed High Performance Learning and significantly developed our enrichment opportunities, through opportunities such as the London Institute of Banking and Finance Level 1 qualification in the Second Form.

Modern facilities combined with traditional values, based on our Christian roots, draw out the talents of every pupil, whilst small class sizes small ensure that our teachers can look after the individual needs of each pupil.

Outside the Classroom

We placed 2nd in the South East for both boys' and girls' indoor hockey. Outdoors, our girls made it to the semi-finals of the Tier 2 National Cup and the boys made it to the quarter-finals of the Tier 1 Championship. Our Ist VII netball team lost only one match all season, and our Rugby continues to develop. We now have 21 pupils in Kent squads and our U15's made it to the semi-final of the top-tier Kent Cup for the fourth year running. We were again recognised as a Top 100 Cricket School in the country and our 1st XI cricketers reached the South East Finals of the National T20.

Enhanced by the school's 500-seat theatre there are many opportunities for pupils to perform. All pupils benefit from an extensive activities programme which in the Senior School includes the Combined Cadet Force and a thriving Duke of Edinburgh's Award Scheme, as well as many activities including archery, golf, fencing, football, sailing, horse riding, swimming, musical theatre and more.

Boarding at St Lawrence

Strong pastoral care, high quality teaching and a great emphasis on extra-curricular activity make this a very special community in which to live and learn. Boarding is central to the school's life and is one of our great strengths. A wide range of evening and weekend activities are provided for boarders, along with additional events and fun day trips. We offer full time and weekly boarding options, and we aim to provide a 'home-from-home' for our boarding pupils.

Location

The campus is situated within walking distance of the historic seaside town of Ramsgate. It has excellent links to the continent, being near to both Dover and the Channel Tunnel. London is only 75 minutes away by high-speed rail to St Pancras International. Gatwick and Heathrow are under two hours away.

St Margaret's School, Bushey

17 49

ST MARGARET'S

SCHOOL

(Founded 1749)
Merry Hill Road, Bushey,
Hertfordshire WD23 1DT UK

Tel: +44 (0)20 8416 4400
Email:
admissions@stmargarets-school.org.uk
Website: www.stmargarets-school.org.uk
Headteacher: Lara Péchard
Appointed: January 2020
School type:
Co-educational Day & Boarding

Age range of pupils: 2–18 years
No. of pupils enrolled as at 01/09/2022: 650
Fees as at 01/09/2022:
Senior Day: £6,423 per term
Senior Full Board: £12,225 per term
Junior, Reception – Y2: £4,395 per term
Junior, Y3 – Y6: £5,367 per term
Average class size: 20

St Margaret's School in Bushey, Hertfordshire, is an independent day and boarding school for pupils aged 2 to 18. Founded in 1749, it is one of the oldest independent schools in the UK. As well as day places for all ages, there are a range of flexible boarding options for both UK and international pupils from the age of 11.

As a school with a proven record of academic success in public examinations, pupils move onto competitive courses at leading universities and institutions both in the UK and around the world. An outward looking ethos aims to encourage a genuine enthusiasm for learning and an ability to independently explore subjects beyond the classroom. The curriculum addresses a rapidly changing world filled with complex challenges as well as exciting new possibilities.

The pastoral care at St Margaret's is the central pillar upon which the success of the school is based and the quality of care and opportunity given to every one of the pupils is second to none. A rich programme of extra-curricular activities is offered and pupils are encouraged to find their talent whatever that may be. From Ballet, Chess and Lacrosse to Speech and Drama, pupils are encouraged to push their limits and discover their passions, which often become part of their adult lives.

The quality of care at St Margaret's School enables pupils to grow in an atmosphere of tolerance and understanding and leave equipped with the confidence, aptitude and skills they need for life and for work.

A beautiful 60 acre site boasts a combination of superbly resourced historic and modern buildings and is easily accessible from both London, the Home Counties and all the major London airports.

St. George's British International School (Bilbao)

St George's
BRITISH INTERNATIONAL SCHOOL
BILBAO

(Founded 1956)
Artazagane 51, 48940 Leioia, Biscay, Basque Country, Spain
Tel: +34 94 4633692
Email: admissions@bisstgeorges.com

Website: www.bisstgeorges.com
Director: Mr. Juan Martorell
School type: Co-educational Day
No. of pupils enrolled as at 01/09/2022: 300
Average class size: 20

St. George's British International School is a private school in Bilbao. St. George's British International School belongs to Globeducate British International Schools and has been part of the Globeducate prestigious network since 2017. We prepare our students for the world of tomorrow, today, throughout a multilingual education from the age of 2, combining innovative methodologies and personalised attention to ensure that every one of our students reaches their full potential. Our students develop into well-rounded, socially responsible citizens with respect for one another. Music, sport, creative arts and technology form an integral part of the curriculum.

Academic excellence since 1956

With a long heritage of education spanning more than half a century, the school has an educational philosophy based on four pillars, around which its ambitious and stimulating curriculum is structured: Enrich, Challenge, Shape and Achieve. St. George's British International has it clear: its educational project aims to enrich and challenge its students, so that each and every one of them can achieve success in their own way, and do their bit to shape the future, to change the world.

At St. George's, English is the main language for teaching and learning and we will soon offer the prestigious English National Curriculum from Early Years until graduation from secondary school. We are accredited by both the British Council and the Basque Government.

We are proud to be a part of Globeducate, which operates more than 55 schools worldwide. This international network provides our students with unique opportunities to interact with students from a wide range of cultures and nationalities.

A progressive adaptation to the English National Curriculum

At present our students follow the English National Curriculum from Pre-Nursery Class to Year 9 before switching over to the Spanish system. Since September 2021 we are gradually expanding the curriculum year by year until the entire school cohort is following the English National Curriculum, eventually studying for IGCSE and A-Level exams. This gradual transition will be completed by 2025.

Beyond the classes

We promote Outdoor Learning and the traditional House System to foster collaboration between students of different ages, team spirit, leadership skills and reinforce the sense of belonging to a community.

St. George's International School, Switzerland

(Founded 1927)

Chemin de St. Georges 19, CH-1815
Clarens/Montreux, Switzerland
Tel: +41 21 964 3411
Email: admissions@stgeorges.ch
Website: www.stgeorges.ch
Head of School: Dr. Ruth Norris

School type:
Co-educational Day & Boarding
Age range of pupils: 1.5–18 years
No. of pupils enrolled as at 01/09/2022: 400
Fees as at 01/09/2022:
Please enquire

St. George's International School is a premium day and boarding school for boys and girls from the age of 1 to 18, comprising over 60 nationalities. Situated on the banks of Lake Geneva, with magnificent views of the Alps, the school occupies 12 acres of beautiful landscape and gardens. This setting promotes intellectual calm and a deep connection to the outdoors, with incomparable opportunities for hiking, skiing, water sports and more

It was founded in 1927 by two young graduates of Oxford University and has grown to become a well-recognised international school with small teaching groups and individual attention regarding academic programmes, career advice and a structured pastoral care. Junior and Middle School pupils choose between an English-only or bilingual route through the Cambridge International Curriculum up to and including Year 9. In Senior School, pupils in Years 10 &11 choose between IGCSEs and the Pre-IB Diploma qualification, and in Years 12 & 13 between the IB Diploma and the General Diploma. Extensive English language acquisition tuition is available along with additional languages such as Spanish, German, Russian and Chinese can also be learnt and practised daily. This ensures that students not only live amidst a multicultural environment but also develop an understanding of different beliefs, religions and lifestyles.

A great deal of focus is also put on sport and performing arts at St. George's. With access to outstanding sports facilities, pupils have extensive opportunities in individual and team sports throughout the seasons. From a very young age students are encouraged to grow a mind of their own and explore their creativity through a range of performing and expressive arts in theatre, art, design and music. Collaborations with NGOs are also very frequent and allow students to develop a social conscience.

The school motto "Levavi Oculos" ensures that St. George's International School is dedicated to lifting its students' eyes to embrace the exciting challenges and opportunities that await them.

St. John's International School

ST JOHN'S INTERNATIONAL SCHOOL WATERLOO BELGIUM

(Founded 1964)
Drève Richelle 146, 1410 Waterloo,
Walloon Brabant, Belgium

Tel: +32 (0)2 352 06 10
Email: enquiries@stjohns.be
Website: www.stjohns.be
Head of School: Dr. David Brooke
School type:
Co-educational Day & Boarding

Religious Denomination:
Non-denominational
Age range of pupils: 18 months–18 years
No. of pupils enrolled as at 01/09/2022: 500
Fees as at 01/09/2022:
€7,000 – €37,600

An Internationally trusted institution with an excellent reputation

Founded in 1964 in Waterloo, Belgium, St. John's International School has established itself as one of the leading international schools in Europe. For more than 50 years, St. John's has been a trusted institution, serving the expatriate and local communities of the greater area with a vibrant, inclusive and welcoming community.

Academic excellence and so much more

With over 40 years of experience in teaching the International Baccalaureate, St. John's has a proud history of academic excellence with an experienced and dynamic teaching staff. Students are encouraged to balance high academic expectations with a fulsome commitment to unrivalled visual and performing arts and competitive sports programmes. St. John's prides itself to be able to take the individual approach with small class sizes and outstanding pastoral care.

International in more than in name only

500 students between the ages of 12 months and 18 years, representing 55 nationalities, find themselves in a truly cosmopolitan atmosphere while pursuing their curricular ambitions and extra-curricular interest. Its students are instilled with the open-mindedness to think globally and take individual responsibility for life-long learning, service, and achievement.

Learning without limits

As an International Baccalaureate (IB) World School, offering the Primary Years Programme (PYP), the Middle Years Programme (MYP) and the Diploma Programme (DP), and the only school in the Brussels area to offer the Advanced Placement (AP) programme, St. John's is the perfect springboard to top universities all over the world.

Flexible options

Fully-flexible boarding options ensure those families who travel widely can continue their professional commitments confident in the grounding of St. John's education combined with the nurturing environment of boarding at St John's Shannon house.

St. Louis School

St. Louis School
CARPE MAGNIFICENTIAM

St. Louis Colonna: Via Marco Antonio Colonna, 24, 20149 Milan – Italy
St. Louis Caviglia: Via Caviglia 1, 20139 Milan – Italy
St. Louis High School: Via Olmetto, 6, 20123 Milan – Italy
Tel: +39 02 55231235
Email: info@stlouisschool.com
Website: www.stlouisschool.com
Executive Principal High School: Mr. Gerry Rafferty
Principal Colonna School: Mrs. Kathleen Slocombe
Principal Caviglia School: Mr. Jake Burnett
School type: Co-educational Day & Boarding
Age range of pupils: 2–18 years (14-18 boarding)
No. of pupils enrolled as at 01/09/2022: 1500

Established in 1996, St. Louis is a leading co-educational Day & Boarding International School based in the Heart of Milan for 1500 students between the ages of 2 and 18.

Located across three sites, the south-east campus is comprised of an Infant, Primary and Middle School, and the High School is located in a prime position, a stone's throw from the Duomo. The Day & Boarding School, located in the Corso Sempione/Portello area, offers school opportunities for 2-14 year olds as well as full time boarding places for 14-18 year olds.

The St. Louis School's academic programme is rigorous and challenging. The Infant School programme is based on the British Early Years Foundation Stage (EYFS) Curriculum.

Primary and Middle School follow the British National Curriculum with an option for students 6 years and upwards to also follow the Italian curriculum.

The High School, which provides boarding facilities, culminates in IGCSE examinations for Years 10 -11 and the International Baccalaureate Diploma (IB) for Years 12 – 13 with over 100 students each year studying this unique course.

The approach reinforces the importance of creative and critical thinking, with the school developing independent learners well equipped to succeed in the IB and beyond. St. Louis consistently achieves outstanding academic results with the highest average IB diploma score in continental Europe seven years running (2022 average of 38/45).

The school opened its new High School in the centre of Milan (Palazzo Archinto) in September 2019. A magnificent historic building located in Via Olmetto, accomodates all senior school students from Years 10-13. Designed by architect Francesco Maria Richini in the 17th century and situated in the centre of Milan, the Palazzo provides the perfect learning environment for students of this age, blending state-of-the art educational facilities within historic surroundings.

St. Peter's International School

Quinta dos Barreleiros CCI 3952,
Volta da Pedra, 2950-201 Palmela,
Setúbal, Portugal
Tel: +351 21 233 6990
Email: geral@stpeters.pt
Website: www.st-peters-school.com
Head of School: Alex Callow

School type:
Co-educational Day & Boarding
Age range of pupils: 4 months–18 years
No. of pupils enrolled as at 01/09/2022: 1500
Fees as at 01/09/2022:
€6,303 (Nursery) – €12,804 (IBDP)

St. Peter's International school is a private school with almost three decades of experience in providing the very best in Portuguese and International Education. It provides a competitive, high-quality education from nursery to secondary school (4 months to 18 years), ensuring that students have access to the best opportunities and a high level of support to achieve their full academic and personal potential.

St. Peter's mission is to build self-reliant, critical and creative students, which prepares them for academic, personal and professional success in an ever-changing world, developing the vital skills and conceptual understandings that will help them to overcome whatever challenges they may face.

St. Peter's offers a personalised bilingual curriculum from Kindergarten and the option of the Portuguese National Curriculum or an International Curriculum from Grade 7 (delivered via the Cambridge IGCSE and IB Diploma Programmes). Academic excellence is guaranteed regardless of the pathway – St. Peter's is a well-established school with proven outstanding academic results in both the national and the international exams, ensuring that students have access to top tier universities in Portugal and abroad.

Located only 30 minutes from Lisbon, St. Peter's extensive 37,000 sqm campus has outstanding facilities for academics, arts and sports, including dedicated music and drama rooms, a modern library, 4 fully equipped laboratories, 3 football pitches, 1 rugby pitch and 2 tennis courts.

In addition, St. Peter's is home to the first on-site Boarding School in the Lisbon area, an extension of our commitment to excellence. Families living abroad can now guarantee their children have access to an international, individualised education in a safe, modern, purpose-built environment. Boarding students have access to an extensive range of extracurricular and enrichment activities both during the week and at weekends.

As part of the Inspired group of schools, our students also have access to innovative and modern practices in education, outstanding arts and sports programmes, state of the art facilities, and a range of global competitions and exchange programmes.

St. Stephen's School

(Founded 1964)
Via Aventina 3, 00153 Rome, Italy

Tel: +39 06 575 0605
Email: ststephens@sssrome.it
Website: www.sssrome.it
Head of School: Jill Muti
School type:
Co-educational Day & Boarding
Religious Denomination:
Non-denominational

Age range of pupils: 14–19 years
No. of pupils enrolled as at 01/09/2022: 300
Fees as at 01/09/2022:
Day: €26,570
Full Boarding: €41,720
Average class size: 13-18
Teacher/pupil ratio: 1:8

St. Stephen's is a coeducational, non-denominational day and boarding school, enrolling students from age 14-19 in grades 9-12 and for a postgraduate year. Founded in 1964, St. Stephen's provides a demanding classical liberal arts education taking full advantage of its location in the historic centre of Rome. Primary objectives are academic excellence, fellowship and cooperation among students and faculty, and the development of students as independent, responsible, and involved members of the larger world community. The curriculum prepares students for the American high school diploma, including a variety of Advanced Placements subjects, and the International Baccalaureate (IB), which helps students to enter universities worldwide.

The campus of St. Stephen's occupies two and one-half acres in the centre of Rome. Constructed around a central courtyard, the traditional Roman-style building contains 13 classrooms, two art studios, a music room, four science laboratories, a 14,000 volume automated library (including a collection of DVDs, videos, periodicals, and wireless internet access), two desktop computer rooms, a mobile laptop computer lab, a writing centre, a multimedia centre, photography laboratory, dining room, snack bar and student's lounge, laundry room, theatre/auditorium, dormitory rooms, resident faculty apartments, tennis, basketball and volleyball courts.

The only international school in Rome to offer a boarding programme, St. Stephen's can accommodate approximately 47 students living in single, double or triple rooms, all with internet and network access. Boarders are housed in the school building, where resident faculty supervisors provide social and academic support around the clock. Meals are served family-style in the dining hall, and boarders have access to a snack bar and lounge equipped with audio-video devices. Rome and its surroundings provide many opportunities for weekend boarding activities such as visits to historical and cultural sites, day trips to nearby beaches and ski areas, and overnight stays in scenic Tuscan or Umbrian hill towns.

Strathallan School

STRATHALLAN SCHOOL

Opportunities for *all* to excel

(Founded 1913)
Forgandenny, Perth,
Perth & Kinross PH2 9EG UK

Tel: 01738 812546
Email: admissions@strathallan.co.uk
Website: www.strathallan.co.uk
Headmaster: Mr Mark Lauder MA Hons
Appointed: 2017
School type:
Co-educational Boarding & Day
Age range of pupils: 7–18 years

No. of pupils enrolled as at 01/09/2022: 545
Fees as at 01/09/2022:
Day: £15,474–£24,474
Full Boarding: £25,140–£36,036
Average class size: 14
Teacher/pupil ratio: 1:7

Where learning comes to life

Strathallan School's mission to provide an outstanding education for all stands true to the school's original foundation over 100 years ago. Strathallan pupils excel academically, compete in sports at national and international levels and play as part of nationwide orchestras and ensembles. The school's 153 acre Perthshire campus has seen an investment of over £25m over the last fifteen years, creating exceptional facilities including a £1.2m purpose-built studio, 240-seat theatre, and extensive sports pitches and training facilities.

Where individuality is celebrated

Each individual is supported to shine during their time at school. The school's innovative teaching style and flexible curriculum – the broadest available in Scotland – are tailored to every pupil, whatever their ambitions and style of learning. In 2021, 88% of Strathallan School leavers were accepted into their first-choice of university following exceptional A Level and Higher results. Last year, 60 pupils played as part of a national sporting team and the school became British and Scottish Champions across six sports.

Where horizons expand and uncover a global outlook

Strathallan is a friendly, welcoming place with a strong sense of community. In 2019 The Care Inspectorate rated Strathallan a Grade 6 (Sector Leading) Excellent for the Quality of care and support. Despite its self-contained, rural location the school is a truly international community with pupils and alumni around the globe.

Where every pupil has the opportunity to excel

Pupils find confidence in themselves at Strathallan and each pupil is encouraged to explore their talents and to realise their potential academically, in the arts, in sport and in a host of interests and activities.

Young people leave Strathallan with the skills and knowledge to succeed in their chosen career, and the confidence to make their mark on the world.

TASIS The American School in England

THE AMERICAN SCHOOL IN ENGLAND

(Founded 1976)

Coldharbour Lane, Thorpe,
Surrey TW20 8TE UK

Tel: +44 (0)1932 582316
Email: ukadmissions@tasisengland.org
Website: www.tasisengland.org
Head of School: Mr Bryan Nixon
Appointed: July 2017
School type:
Co-educational Day & Boarding
Religious Denomination:
Non-denominational

Age range of pupils: 3–18 years
No. of pupils enrolled as at 01/09/2022: 620
Fees as at 01/09/2022:
Day: £12,770–£27,430
Full Boarding: £50,850
Average class size: 15
Teacher/pupil ratio: 1:6

TASIS The American School in England offers a challenging American curriculum with Advanced Placement (AP) courses and the International Baccalaureate (IB) Diploma Programme to students from approximately 60 nations.

Experienced and dedicated teachers provide individualised attention, nurturing each student's intellectual curiosity in small classes throughout TASIS England's three sections: Lower (ages 3-9), Middle (10-13), and Upper (14-18).

Each student is provided with multiple pathways through curricular and co-curricular programmes designed to inspire their learning, to encourage them to fulfil their potential, and to challenge them to contribute to their community.

TASIS England promotes student participation in an impressive selection of athletics, arts, and activities, nurturing the skills and attributes of life-long learning, international-mindedness, and resilience. Numerous service, travel, and leadership opportunities support and enrich each student's experience through intercultural learning and service to others.

One-to-one college counseling assists Upper School students in every step of the university selection and application process. Along with success in the IB Diploma and AP courses (similar to A-levels), accomplishments of the Class of 2020 include 61 scholarship offers, with over 85% securing places in their first-choice universities in the UK, the US, Canada, and worldwide.

The School's spacious campus, located in a quiet village 18 miles from London and 8 miles from Heathrow Airport, blends historic buildings with modern, purpose-built facilities for science, technology, theatre, visual arts, music, and sports.

Proximity to London enables the School to take full advantage of the opportunities that England and Europe offer as extensions to classroom learning, and students enjoy educational field trips, weekend activities, and travel abroad.

TASIS England's enduring goal is to provide a busy and happy environment in which each student flourishes as a principled, open-minded, compassionate member of a global community. Their confidence, resilience, and empathy as well as their academic achievements will serve as foundations for their future success in the ever-changing landscape of the world.

TASIS The American School in Switzerland

Via Collina d'Oro 15,
6926 Montagnola-Lugano, Switzerland
Tel: +41 91 960 5151
Email: admissions@tasis.ch
Website: www.tasis.ch
Head of School: Christopher Nikoloff

School type:
Co-educational Day & Boarding
Age range of pupils: 3–19 years
No. of pupils enrolled as at 01/09/2022: 700
Fees as at 01/09/2022:
Day: CHF49,500
Full Boarding: CHF91,000

Founded by M. Crist Fleming in 1956, TASIS The American School in Switzerland is an international day and boarding school committed to creating global citizens through education, travel, and service. TASIS now welcomes more than 700 students in grades Pre-Kindergarten (starting at age 3) through 12 while also offering a Postgraduate program. The student body represents 60 nationalities and speaks more than 30 different mother tongues.

High School students can choose from individual Advanced Placement courses or pursue the International Baccalaureate (IB) Diploma, helping them receive offers from more than 400 universities in 20 different nations over the past five years. The School offers an extensive Fine Arts program that includes courses in Drama, Music, and the Visual Arts, enabling aspiring artists of any ilk to find their creative voice and nurture their talent.

The campus includes more than 25 buildings dating from the 17th century Villa De Nobili to the state-of-the-art Campo Science Center, which opened in 2014. Perched on a hillside in sunny southern Switzerland with commanding views of snow-capped mountains, palm trees, and Lake Lugano, the School's enviable location makes possible an impressive Academic Travel program. Travel experiences throughout the year bring students face-to-face with the rich cultural heritage of Europe and the spectacular natural beauty of the Alps and beyond.

The School's pioneering Global Service Program transforms lives by providing every High School student with a unique opportunity to connect across borders – whether geographic, economic, or social – through comprehensive experiences that build empathy and encourage personal responsibility. The Program awakens students to humanitarian needs; inspires them to build enduring, mutually beneficial relationships; and leads them toward a life of active service and committed service.

TASIS encourages physical fitness and healthy lifestyles. Varsity sports teams compete throughout Switzerland and Europe, and a variety of other fitness activities are offered to cater to all interests. Each year also brings many opportunities to ski and explore the breathtaking Alps.

Taunton School International

206-216 Greenway Road, Taunton,
Somerset TA2 6LJ UK
Tel: 01823 703200
Email: admissions@tauntonschool.co.uk
Website: www.tauntonschool.co.uk
Principal: Adrian Hallworth

School type: Co-educational Boarding
Age range of pupils: 8–18 years
No. of pupils enrolled as at 01/09/2022: 145
Fees as at 01/09/2022:
£7,600 – £14,975

Taunton School International (TSI)

Taunton School International was established in 1996 and provides GCSE and Foundation programmes for up to 85 boys and girls aged 14-18. Our GCSE/Pre-IB programmes offer over 23 examinable subjects and are the ideal preparation for students wishing to go on to the Sixth Form to study A-levels, IB, BTECs or the Foundation programme. Our Foundation programmes are designed for those students with a keen interest in the world of business and who are looking for an alternative and more focused route to university. At Taunton School, we encourage all of our students to fully involve themselves in the school community and beyond. There are more than 100 clubs and societies on offer which provide many opportunities for our International students to integrate with the British students, including sports teams, orchestras, performing arts, after-school clubs, weekend trips and numerous inter-house competitions which run throughout the school year.

Taunton School International Middle School (TSIMS)

TSIMS is the newest addition to the Taunton School family and was established in 2012 to provide the crucial stepping stone into the British education system for younger international students aged 8–14 years old. TSIMS students are provided with an intensive education designed to meet all their educational needs and is the perfect choice for students whose level of English is not yet good enough to access the Prep School, Senior School, TSI or indeed, any other British boarding school.

Summer School

Taunton School has been running its own summer schools for more than 20 years.

All our summer programmes have 3 hours of English lessons and 2 hours of further tuition each day, taught by experienced and well-qualified teachers in groups of no more than 12 students (average class size is 8). Students can attend for between 2 and 6 weeks.

Our prices are genuinely all-inclusive with all courses offering a wide range of sports, activities, trips, excursions and cultural experiences.

The British School of Amsterdam

THE BRITISH SCHOOL OF AMSTERDAM

(Founded 1978)

Havenstraat 6, 1075 PR Amsterdam,
North Holland, Netherlands
Tel: +31 (0)20 679 7840
Email: info@britams.nl
Website: www.britishschool.amsterdam
Principal: Ruth Sanderson
Appointed: August 2022

School type: Co-educational Day
Age range of pupils: 3–18 years
No. of pupils enrolled as at 01/09/2022: 1020
Fees as at 01/09/2022:
Day: €8,265–€18,252
Average class size: 20

The British School of Amsterdam (BSA) is the very best that British international education offers. An accredited provider of the National Curriculum used in England leading to the highly regarded GCSE and A Level qualifications to the international community in Amsterdam. In 2021, BSA students at A Level achieved 51% A*/A grades and 87% A/C, and for GCSE achieved 59% A*/A and 92% A*/C.

We have three school sections, the Early Years School for children aged 3 to 6 years old, the Junior School for 6 to 11 year olds and the Senior School for 11 to 18 year olds. Each has their own distinctive character that offers a stimulating environment where pupils benefit from small class sizes and truly talented teaching staff. Classes for the Early Years and Junior Schools do not exceed 24 and for the Senior School, we do not exceed 22 in a class. A high proportion of our teachers have experience in the UK and we can proudly say have been with the BSA for a long time, some exceeding over 20 years with the school. As well as an academic focus, our teachers recognise your child as an individual and know not just their names but their hopes, anxieties, their quirks and enthusiasms.

Our school building has some of the finest educational facilities in the city of Amsterdam including a magnificent sports hall, beautiful playgrounds, a large theatre, fully equipped science laboratories and music rooms. The school is located in Amsterdam Oud-Zuid near several green spaces, and is easily accessible for families commuting from different parts of the city and surrounding areas.

The British School of Brussels (BSB)

(Founded 1969)

Pater Dupierreuxlaan 1,
3080 Tervuren, Belgium
Tel: +32 (0)2 766 04 30
Email: admissions@britishschool.be
Website: www.britishschool.be
Principal: Melanie Warnes MA
Co-Heads of Post 16: Sue Munday & James Willis

School type: Co-educational Day
Age range of pupils: 1–18 years
No. of pupils enrolled as at 01/09/2022: 1350
Fees as at 01/09/2022:
Day: €30,235–€38,685
Average class size: 16-25
Teacher/pupil ratio: 1:9

The British School of Brussels (BSB) was founded in 1969 and officially opened in 1970. Set in a beautiful site of ten hectares, surrounded by woodlands and lakes near the Africa Museum in Tervuren, it is 20 minutes drive from central Brussels. The School is a co-educational, non-selective day school for children aged 1 to 18 years, with 1,300 currently on roll. There is an Early Childhood Centre for children aged 1-3 years. 30% of the students are British with approximately 70 other nationalities represented.

The British-based curriculum is offered within an international context with courses leading to GCSE and IGCSE examinations 16 years old and GCE A Levels, as well as Vocational Courses (BTEC in Business, Hospitality and Sport. The International Baccalaureate (IB) Diploma Programme is offered (bilingual French & Dutch options) in addition to A Levels. Our Primary school offers a bespoke curriculum with Integrated Learning Themes that are inquiry based and skills driven, with plenty of outdoor learning.

As an international school operating in the heart of one of the world's most multilingual countries, the school offers a bilingual French/English programme for students age 4 to 14 to complement the English-medium teaching. French is compulsory for all students from the age of 4 and Dutch is introduced at age 7. German, Dutch and Spanish are offered as an additional language from age 11. There is an English Language Immersion Programme for non-native English speakers and an Additional Educational Needs Department.

The school has excellent facilities including a state-of-the-art design and technology workshop, food technology rooms, drama studios, nine science laboratories, four art studios and networked IT suites. Primary School provides 1:1 I-pads and laptops are provided for Secondary students in selected year groups.

In 2016 BSB opened its new Sports Centre with a Swimming Pool, Sports Hall, international competition standard Gymnasium, Fitness Suite and Dance Studio. In 2020 the school renewed is outdoor sports pitches for football, rugby, tennis, running, long-jump and even has a climbing/bouldering wall. BSB is the only international school in Belgium to have its own 25m indoor swimming pool.

The arts play a major role in the life of the school; music, drama and dance thrive and a wide range of performances are held regularly in the 240-seat theatre. The music department has a music technology suite, full scale recording studio and a rehearsal studio.

There is a wide range of enrichment activities in sports, music and drama with frequent opportunities for overseas travel and school journeys.

Advise on further education and on a choice of career is available to all students. Throughout the year multinational career counsellors run events and host guest speakers to guide students in making their post-graduate plans.

In 2020, BSB students achieved a 100% pass rate in A Level, BTEC and IB Diploma. At A Level, our students excelled with an impressive 43% of grades at A*/A (27.6% national average 2020) and 98% achieving A*/C. The results in the BTEC courses continue to be outstanding, with 56% of the grades achieved at Distinction level.

Our IB Diploma students again produced some remarkable results with a 38 point average (IB 2020 world average of 29.9 points).

BSB does not select students for ability. For many, English is not the native language. This makes successes even more tremendous. The programmes are led by a highly committed and well-qualified team of teachers and our academic, university and pastoral support is organised throughout the two years to help individual students to be the best they can be and aim high.

From Harvard to Cambridge, from medicine to architecture, our students head for top universities worldwide. There is a long list of famous BSB Alumni including authors, TV producers, actresses and Olympic medalists.

The British School of Milan (Sir James Henderson)

(Founded 1969)

Via Carlo Alberto Pisani Dossi, 16,
20134 Milan, Italy
Tel: +39 02 210941
Email: info@bsm.school
Website: www.britishschoolmilan.com
Principal: Dr Chris Greenhalgh

School type: Co-educational Day
Age range of pupils: 3–18 years
No. of pupils enrolled as at 01/09/2022: 720
Fees as at 01/09/2022:
€12,140 – €19,580
Teacher/pupil ratio: 1:10

BSM Mission Statement

To inspire learning within a caring, creative and international community, to pursue excellence, and to challenge students to think critically as they prepare for the world beyond.

The British School of Milan, founded in 1969, is rated among the top 5 IB schools in Europe, No.1 in Italy, and top 50 in the world. The BSM is the only school in Milan passing all the standards set by UK Government Inspectors (ISI).

The BSM is a not-for-profit school which provides a world-class education to 720 students aged 3 to 18 from over 40 different nationalities. The school values cultural diversity and offers a rich international experience while rigorously following the UK National Curriculum from Nursery to Year 11 with the IB pursued in Years 12 an 13.

Academic results are outstanding and students progress to top universities around the globe. In the last few years they have gained places at Oxford, Cambridge, Yale, LSE, Imperial, University College London, The University of Edinburgh, Trinity College Dublin, Università Bocconi, University of British Colombia, Sciences-Po and many other leading universities.

There is a strong emphasis on co-curricular activities with over 100 options available. The school is particularly proud of its exceptional music, art and drama departments. In addition, BSM acts as the Italian centre for the exam board of the Royal School of Music. The school nourishes a strong tradition of community service, with a scholarship and bursary fund recently inaugurated and its involvement in the International Duke of Edinburgh's Award Scheme.

The BSM is situated just outside the centre of Milan, close to the metro and on several bus routes. Linate airport and the popular Milano 2 residences are just minutes from the school.

Admission applications are accepted throughout the year.

The British School Warsaw

THE BRITISH SCHOOL WARSAW
A NORD ANGLIA EDUCATION SCHOOL

(Founded 1992)

Primary, Secondary School & IB College: Limanowskiego 15, 02-943 Warsaw, Masovia, Poland
Early Years Centre: Jaroslawa Dabrowskiego 84, 02-571 Warsaw, Masovia, Poland
Tel: +48 22 842 32 81
Email: admissions@thebritishschool.pl

Website: www.thebritishschool.pl
Principal: Ms Sue Hill
Appointed: 2020
Deputy Principal: Dr Jacek Latkowski
School type: Co-educational Day
Age range of pupils: 2.5–18 years
Average class size: 20
Teacher/pupil ratio: 1:11

The British School Warsaw was established in 1992 by Iwona Thomas in partnership with Nord Anglia Education. It opened its doors with a total of 35 students wishing to follow an English curriculum. At present, we are proud to be educating over 1000 students from the international community in Warsaw.

At The British School Warsaw, your child will receive the very best of British academics, delivered by outstanding teachers in an international environment that promotes respect, discipline and hard work. Your child will leave our school with everything they need for success – whatever they choose to be or do in life. Your family will be part of a vibrant, international community that promotes well-being and social responsibilty, whilst developing cultural awareness.

Our students learn using the the world's most respected curricula, enabling a life-long love of learning and academic results that opens pathways to the world's best universities.

For Primary students, we offer a perfect blend of English National Curriculum and International Primary Curriculum (IPC) which provides young, globally minded students with a skillset enabling them to smoothly transition to the next stages of international education through iGCSE and IBDP. For our Senior students, we offer the internationally-recognised and highly regarded IB Diploma Programme. The skills and attributes developed through this programme provide outstanding preparation for higher education giving our students the best opportunity to access the world's top universities.

We are unique in Warsaw in that we are part of a family of over 73 schools with Nord Anglia Education (NAE) which allows us to leverage international collaborations. Our students have the opportunity to travel to our expedition based snow-sports centre in Switzerland; renovate schools in Tanzania; perform with over 500 talented musicians at the Juilliard School, New York; attend Space camp and STEAM festival at MIT University and take over UNICEF Headquarters in NY.

Our teacher standards are second to none, partly thanks to a global Education Team that drives success in academics, quality assurance, accreditation and safeguarding across our schools.

The International School of Monaco

THE INTERNATIONAL SCHOOL OF MONACO

(Founded 1994)

10-12 Quai Antoine Premier,
Monte Carlo, 98000 Monaco
Tel: +377 9325 6820
Email: admissions@ismonaco.com
Website: ismonaco.com
Director:
Mr. Stuart Bryan MA Hons, PGCE, ACE, NPQEL

School type: Co-educational Day
Age range of pupils: 3–18 years
No. of pupils enrolled as at 01/09/2022: 740
Fees as at 01/09/2022:
Day: €23,100 – €29,400

Founded in 1994, the International School of Monaco (ISM) is an independent, co-educational, not-for-profit day school situated on Port Hercule in Monaco. ISM is the only fully accredited international private school in the Principality of Monaco and today caters to 740 pupils aged from 3-18, drawn from over fifty nationalities.

In August 2020 the school signed a historic collaboration agreement with King's College School, Wimbledon, as part of the school's aim to be among the best in Europe.

Driven by its vision of international education with distinction, ISM's mission is to provide an outstanding education for students so that they are happy, confident, independent, multilingual and responsible global citizens. The school's values emphasise integrity, learning, caring and respect, with strong emphasis placed on excellence, wellbeing and multilingualism as well as international mindedness and digital citizenship.

ISM offers a distinctive bilingual education in English and French for students in the Early Years and Primary Schools (Kindergarten to Year 6), and from Year 7 onwards, the Secondary School offers a broad and balanced curriculum in English, leading to Cambridge IGCSE and the IB Diploma qualifications. The school offers both the IB Diploma Programme (IBDP) and the IB Career-related Programme (IBCP). Languages are an important part of the curriculum, with Spanish, Italian, Russian and German, in addition to French, on offer. Highly qualified teachers and support staff are recruited from around the world.

There is an extensive programme of enrichment including sports, Model United Nations, an annual Arts Festival, the Duke of Edinburgh's International Award plus ABRSM and LAMDA music and drama qualifications. The school's unique location on the Côte d'Azur enables access to world-class museums and places of interest.

Outreach is an important element of school life, and students participate in a wide range of giving projects throughout the year via the school's philanthropy clubs, Student Council initiatives, and the PTA, in partnership with local charities and environmental associations.

Pastoral care is a major priority for the school; an extensive PSHE (Personal, Social and Health Education) programme is delivered by teachers who receive regular training in child protection and welfare, and a full-time Head of Wellbeing is supported by a wellbeing team including a school counsellor.

ISM students are well-rounded, academically successful individuals who are admitted to top universities in Europe, the UK and North America. ISM graduates go on to pursue exciting careers in many diverse fields.

Thornton College

THORNTON

(Founded 1917)

College Lane, Thornton, Milton Keynes,
Buckinghamshire MK17 0HJ UK

Tel: 01280 812610

Email: admissions@thorntoncollege.com

Website: www.thorntoncollege.com

Headteacher: Dr Louise Shaw

Appointed: November 2021

School type: Girls' Day & Boarding

Age range of girls:

3–18 years (Boarding from age 8)

No. of pupils enrolled as at 01/09/2022: 402

No. of boarders: 60

Fees as at 01/09/2022:

Prep Termly Boarder (Years 3-6):

£8,220 (per term) – £24,660 (per annum)

Senior Termly Boarder:

£10,195 (per term)– £30,585 (per annum)

Sixth Form Termly Boarder:

£10,195 per term– £30,585 (per annum)

Average class size: 14

Teacher/pupil ratio: 1:20

Thornton is a leading independent day and boarding school for girls. It is one of the most successful non-selective schools in the UK with an enviable reputation for academic success. Thornton offers a warm and nurturing educational environment alongside a rigorous and exciting curriculum.

Students receive an outstanding education and make excellent progress at Thornton. Our academic results are testament to the way the girls are challenged and motivated to give their best in all they do. We offer the girls the opportunity to thrive and achieve in a caring environment. Staff support and encourage each individual on their educational journey, celebrating their talents and nurturing their character so that they are able to be the very best version of themselves.

We are a Catholic school with a strong Christian ethos. Children of all Christian denominations, of other faiths and of no faith are welcome in our school. All are equally valued and all are equally important.

Boarding is 'upstairs' in our main Manor House offering a home from home experience. The boarding bedrooms and living room areas are bright and spacious. Thornton offers flexi, weekly and termly boarding for UK and international students with a full programme of exciting evening and weekend activities.

The school is set in 25 acres of beautiful parkland just outside Milton Keynes on the Buckinghamshire/Northamptonshire border. It is within easy reach of Buckingham, Milton Keynes and London. Thornton College is part of an international family of schools in twenty eight countries around the world giving students a unique global outlook and understanding.

Thornton College offers exceptional teaching and excellent pastoral care where each girl is known and encouraged to develop her strengths to pursue, with confidence, the next stage of life.

United Lisbon International School

Avenida Marechal Gomes da Costa 9,
1800-255 Lisbon, Portugal
Tel: +351 218 370 973
Email: info@unitedlisbon.school
Website: www.unitedlisbon.school

Head of School: Dr. José Azcue
School type: Co-educational Day
Age range of pupils: 3–18 years
No. of pupils enrolled as at 01/09/2022: 300+
Fees as at 01/09/2022: Please see website

United Lisbon International School (ULIS) is a world-class international English-language school in the center of Lisbon. ULIS is one of the select few prestigious Microsoft Showcase schools in Portugal.

It is a modern and innovative international school, offering English-language academic programs from Early Childhood (from 3 years) to grade 12, with a challenging curriculum based on US standards (NEASC) and leading to internationally acknowledged university-preparatory program the International Baccalaureate (IB) Diploma.

The school offers an education inspired by and fit for the 21st century; an international education founded on rigorous standards of excellence, seamlessly integrating technology into the learning environment.

The School's Mission

United Lisbon's philosophy is to nurture the individual learner: by providing a rich environment of opportunities to grow academically as well as personally. With the vision "to empower and inspire the younger generation for a sustainable world", United Lisbon provides rigorous academic programs, a strong focus on the skills and values children will need to be successful in tomorrow's world. The School's modern pedagogy creates a student-centered learning ecosystem that instills relevant skills through guided inquiry, collaborative learning, and seamless integration of technology, to strengthen and further personalize the learning experience of each individual student.

Curriculum

United Lisbon offers a quality academic program that follows the American Common Core standards. By partnering with Common Ground Collaborative, the school has created a dynamic learning culture where learners become experts who have deep conceptual understandings, high-level competencies, and a strong positive moral character. The learning pathway culminates with the International Baccalaureate program in Grades 11 and 12 in which the students will graduate with the IB Diploma. The first graduating class will complete their IB in 2023.

United Lisbon Academy

With over 6,500 sqm of its own outdoor play and sports facilities, United Lisbon enjoys an impressive extracurricular program. With a diverse set of activities on offer, the school partners with leading institutions to create experiences unique to students, including Sporting FC, Clube de Rugby do Técnico and Lisboa Racket Centre.

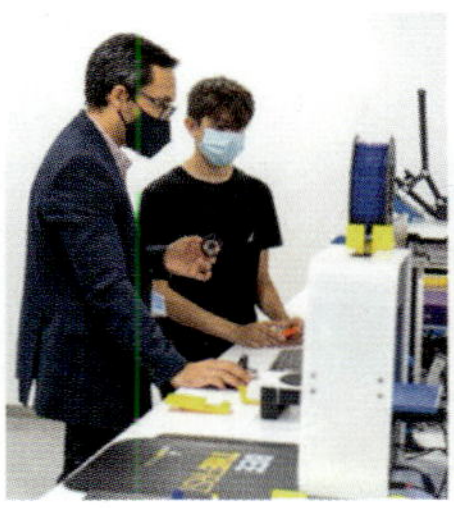

UWC Adriatic

COLLEGIO DEL MONDO UNITO DELL'ADRIATICO O.N.L.U.S.

(Founded 1982)
Località Duino 29,
34011 Duino-Aurisina TS, Italy
Tel: +39 040 3739111

Email: uwcad@uwcad.it
Website: www.uwcad.it
Head of College: William Turner
Appointed: August 2019
School type: Co-educational Boarding
Religious Denomination:
Non-denominational

Age range of pupils: 16–19 years
No. of pupils enrolled as at 01/09/2022: 168
Fees as at 01/09/2022:
Two-year Fee:
€46,000 (scholarships available)
Average class size: 14
Teacher/pupil ratio: 1:7

UWC Adriatic is set in the seaside village of Duino, near Trieste, in an area strongly influenced by political and ethnic divisions during the two World Wars and just a few kilometers away from where the Iron Curtain once divided Western Europe from the communist bloc during the Cold War. By entering this arena of ethnic and historical complexity, UWC Adriatic has embraced an educational role of highly-charged political meaning and stepped into a world of extraordinary cultural diversity.

Since 1982 UWC Adriatic offers the IB Diploma standard courses, to which the College adds Arabic, several central European languages, Environmental Systems and Societies, Music and World Arts and Cultures. All students take Italian, though not necessarily as an IBDP exam subject. A particular emphasis is placed on the "service" component of its Creativity, Activity, Services (CAS) programme, with music also playing a significant role thanks to the presence of the International Community Music Academy (ICMA).

UWC Adriatic is one of the oldest-standing United World Colleges and has collaborative relations with many associations that lead volunteering activities in a wide range of areas. UWC Adriatic also capitalises its seaside setting on Trieste's karst highlands nearby the Alps to offer its students a host of related outdoor activities: sailing, kayaking, climbing, hiking and cross-country skiing opportunities provide invigorating and highly enjoyable breaks from academic endeavors during students' two years in Duino. The UWC educational model prioritises student initiative, so new student-led CAS activities are also encouraged.

The College has seven student residences, an academic building, a science laboratory and an Art Centre scattered around the village of Duino. Every residence is manned by one or more residence tutors. A fully equipped music centre is available, as well as sports facilities shared with local associations. Purnama House (a new residence currently being refurbished and used as a teacher residence and for isolation purposes), has formed part of the COVID-19 medical provisions since the 2020-21 academic year. The College also ensures that the medical staff are available 24 hours a day.

Admissions

Students can apply through their UWC national committee or through the UWC Global Selection Programme.

UWC Maastricht

(Founded 2009)
Discuswrorp 65, 6225 XP Maastricht,
Limburg, Netherlands

Tel: +31 432 410 410
Email: admissions@uwcmaastricht.nl
Website: www.uwcmaastricht.nl
Head of College: Lodewijk van Oord
School type:
Co-educational Day & Boarding

Age range of pupils: 4–19 years
No. of pupils enrolled as at 01/09/2022: 900
Fees as at 01/09/2022:
Ranging from: €6,330 in primary school – €30,000 in the residential programme (scholarships available)

UWC Maastricht (UWCM) in the Netherlands is part of UWC, a worldwide family of 18 international schools and colleges working towards global peace and sustainability (information on all UWC schools is available at www.uwc.org/schools). The School operates within the Dutch public educational system and is subsidized by the Dutch government.

Outside the Classroom

UWC Maastricht focuses a lot on social impact and therefore has a program which includes action-oriented courses, social entrepreneurship and community service projects. The students develop the skills and attitudes needed to be active participants in our society, and to identify problems and injustices. They design a local Project Week themselves, providing service to the local community; they also organise and lead conferences and learn to engage critically with the world around them. With students from more than 100 nationalities and many different backgrounds, there are always unique insights and interesting discussions.

Inside the Classroom

UWC Maastricht consists of a primary and a secondary school. The Primary Curriculum (4-11 years-old) is composed of different subjects at various levels of English language proficiency. Students then continue with the International Baccalaureate Middle Years Program (11-16 year-olds), which encourages them to become critical and reflective thinkers. The last two years at UWC Maastricht students follow the International Baccalaureate Diploma Programme or Career-related Programme (16-19 years-old). This includes Dutch, Spanish, German, Italian, Arabic, World Arts and Cultures, Global Politics, Visual Arts, Film and Music, alongside other courses.

Campus and Facilities

UWCM campus is close to the city centre and is surrounded by sports fields, a nature reserve and modern housing. Students live on residences across three buildings consisting of three floors, each comprised of six rooms. Every room hosts four students of different nationalities. Each floor has a common room, study room, laundry room and kitchenette and is supported by a Residence Mentor who lives in an adjacent apartment.

Admission

We look forward to your application via uwcmaastricht.nl

Vittoria International School

(Founded 2008)
Via delle Rosine 14, 10123 Turin, Italy

Tel: +39 011 889870
Email: infovis@vittoriaweb.it
Website: www.vittoriaweb.it
Head of School: Marcella Margaria Bodo
School type: Co-educational Day
Age range of pupils: 3–19 years

Fees as at 01/09/2022:
Nursery School: €5,000
Cambridge Primary: €5,500
Cambridge Lower Secondary: €6,100
Cambridge IGCSE: €10,100
IBDP: €10,950

Founded in 1975 as one of the first linguistic high schools in Italy, the Vittoria International School Torino offers bilingual education from elementary school through to the IB diploma. Located in the heart of Turin's city centre, the school provides a modern and innovative learning environment for students of all ages and nationalities.

From the school's inception, we have leveraged the best of tradition and innovation both in the choice of educational pathways and teaching methods. Fully certified by the Italian Ministry of Education, the school offers bilingual Primary and Lower Secondary programs, in addition to two separate high school courses: the traditional Italian program, and an international curriculum in English. An authorized IB World School since 2008, we have offered the IBDP (grades 11–12) and a Cambridge Upper Secondary School IGCSE (grades 9–10) since 2010. In September 2018 we began welcoming students in the Primary (grades 1-5) and Lower Secondary (grades 6-8) years as well.

Our range of study pathways and programs is constantly expanding and is progressively adapted to the individual needs of our students. The final scores and completion rates of our students are consistently above the international average. We provide professional, personalized career and university guidance, and our students go on to study at world-class universities around the globe. We support our student's pursuit of excellence in extracurricular activities, and many have excelled nationally and internationally in sports and the arts.

A low student-teacher classroom ratio allows for individual attention as part of a socially and academically rich formative experience.

Our teachers are all graduates – IB and Cambridge trained. They are passionate about their subjects and dedicated to their students.

A vibrant discussion of global issues begins in our classrooms and extends into CAS projects. Students experience world issues as they play out in our local community and abroad. We also have an ongoing relationship with important international organizations located in Turin.

World International School of Torino

WINS
WORLD INTERNATIONAL SCHOOL
TORINO

The Key to a Global Future

Via Traves 28, 10151 Torino, Italy
Tel: +39 0111972111
Email:
info@worldinternationalschool.com
Website: worldinternationalschool.com

School Manager: Ms Giulia Mazzocchi
School type:
Co-educational Day & Boarding

Who we are

World International School of Torino is an International Baccalaureate® World School for the PYP (Primary Years Programme), the MYP (Middle Years Programme) and the DP (Diploma Programme).

WINS was founded in 2017 by the Formiga Family, with their 60 years of experience in international education.

Teachers and students from all over the world, programs of excellence and integrated use of technology are joined by numerous creative, artistic and sporting activities.

Campus and facilities

Our 16,000 square meters Campus is equipped with a swimming pool, indoor and outdoor sports fields, libraries, music, science and art labs, spacious classrooms and a boarding house for students living far from Turin.

The high-quality internal canteen, a rich program of extra-curricular activities and the shuttle bus are only some of the services you can find at WINS, offered to ensure a welcoming, safe and comfortable environment for the students and their families.

Boarding House

Our Boarding House is the first one in Piedmont. It is designed for WINS students aged 13 and above who want to live an amazing international learning experience. Starting from the school year 2022-2023 it will be open 7 days a week.

Our Community

Our community is made up of more than 60% international families and our teachers come from many different nations.

The truly multicultural context of our school and the high standards of its academic programs nurture the intellectual growth of our students, helping them become open-minded, principled, and inquiring citizens of the world.

Our values and mission

WINS core values are to be found in the daily commitment of teachers and each faculty member, who work together with families and students to ensure the proper differentiation and the fulfillment of students' potential.

Our mission is to create a safe and respectful learning environment to support children in the development of their individual talents by fostering critical thinking from an early age.

WINS Foundation

WINS Foundation pursues educational and cultural projects to lay the foundations for a better and sustainable society, made up of responsible, knowledgeable and international-minded citizens.

The Foundation has several courses of action: it provides money, goods or services to support people in need; it carries out projects in the fields of education, professional development and acts against educational poverty; it organizes cultural, artistic or recreational activities of social interest; it disseminates the culture of volunteering and organizes activities of educational guidance and prevention of early school leaving.

Accreditations

- AFEC: WINS is the first Athlete Friendly Education School in Italy, to support athletes in achieving their educational and athletic goals.
- CAMBRIDGE: WINS is a Cambridge English Exams Preparation Center and the only authorized Cambridge Assessment Admissions Testing Center within the Piedmont region.
- TRINITY: WINS is a registered Trinity College London® Examination Centre.
- KiVa: WINS implements the KiVa anti-bullying international program aimed at preventing bullying within the school.

Zurich International School

Zurich International School

Steinacherstrasse 140,
8820 Wädenswil ZH, Switzerland
Tel: +41 58 750 2500
Email: admissions@zis.ch
Website: www.zis.ch
Director: Ms Lisa Lyle

School type: Co-educational Day
Age range of pupils: 3–18 years
No. of pupils enrolled as at 01/09/2022: 1200
Fees as at 01/09/2022:
Day: CHF25,900–CHF36,600

Zurich International School is a leading, non-profit day school offering a comprehensive education program in English for students, both local and expat, aged 3 to 18, with an additional bilingual pathway (English/German) for children aged 3 to 8.

ZIS understands that education is about finding the right balance. Our goal is to ensure that children develop a love of learning, so we give them a safe environment to explore without fear of failure. Our rigorous curriculum – including the International Baccalaureate Diploma Programme (IB) and Advanced Placement courses (AP) – provides a foundation that helps students go on to the most prestigious universities. It also prepares them for a future that requires compassion, leadership, adaptability, resilience and original thinking. What they learn is transferable and transformative.

We encourage students to discover new ideas and possibilities, learning by trying and doing. Each child is inspired to take their own path and challenged to excel, but also to protect their mental health and look out for others.

Every student explores a wide range of extracurricular activities and we encourage them to try new things by creating an environment in which they can be adventurous because they feel supported.

ZIS is truly international with our 1,200 students representing over 70 nationalities and speaking 40 mother-tongue languages. With the opening of a new state-of-the-art Middle School in August 2022, ZIS is made up of a Secondary Campus for ages 11 to 18 in Adliswil and a Lower School for ages 3 to 11 in Waedenswil.

The longest accredited international school in Switzerland, ZIS is an International Baccalaureate Organisation World School, accredited by the New England Association of Schools and Colleges Commission on International Education and approved by Zurich's Department of Education.

Learn, Care, Challenge, Lead are the cornerstones of our mission.

International schools in North America

Schools ordered A–Z by Name

British International School of Chicago, Lincoln Park

BRITISH INTERNATIONAL SCHOOL OF CHICAGO, LINCOLN PARK
A NORD ANGLIA EDUCATION SCHOOL

(Founded 2001)

814 & 821 W Eastman Street,
Chicago, IL 60642 USA
Tel: +1 773 907 5000
Email: admissions@bischicagolp.org
Website: www.bischicagolp.org
Principal: Mr. Mike Henderson
School type: Co-educational Day

Age range of pupils: 15 months–11 years
No. of pupils enrolled as at 01/09/2022: 575
Fees as at 01/09/2022:
Day: $8,900–$32,950
Average class size: 20
Teacher/pupil ratio: 1:10

British International School of Chicago, Lincoln Park is a private international school for student's ages 15 months to 11 years old offering individualized, global and innovative hands-on learning experiences through the English National Curriculum and the International Primary Curriculum. Every student in our school reaches their potential through differentiated instruction delivered by highly trained faculty. Our high number of specialist teachers and specialist classrooms provide even our youngest students, a breadth of environments and experiences.

Located in the attractive Lincoln Park neighborhood of Chicago, we offer our students a more than 74,000 square foot urban campus with state of the art facilities and learning extending beyond the classrooms in Chicago's leading academic, cultural and arts institutions. Our students also benefit from collaborations with world renowned institutions through our Julliard-Nord Anglia Performing Arts Programme, which prepares them for the world's stage and our MIT STEAM curriculum which focuses on transferrable skills in an evolving world. Additionally, our students are gaining global perspective on sustainability through work with UNICEF and the 17 sustainable development goals.

We connect our students, representing over 40 nationalities, with their peers in our network of Nord Anglia schools worldwide, and these meaningful interactions and collaborations provide a truly international education. Our online Global Campus provides learning opportunities and challenges for the students which gives direct links to other Nord Anglia students around the world. Our extensive enrichment programs give our students opportunities to build on their passions and strengths in over 30 after school clubs and sports.

We have a vibrant school life with an actively engaged parent community, social interactions, house system and many cultural celebrations. Our values curriculum focuses on the personal, social and emotional development of our students, preparing them not only academically but developing their character and moral compass. Our students continue their secondary education at our second campus located in the South Loop.

Dwight School

(Founded 1872)
291 Central Park West,
New York, NY 10024 USA

Tel: +1 212 724 6360
Email: admissions@dwight.edu
Website: www.dwight.edu
Chancellor: Stephen H. Spahn
Vice Chancellor: Blake Spahn
Head of School: Dianne Drew

School type: Co-educational Day
Age range of pupils: 2–18 years
No. of pupils enrolled as at 01/09/2022: 920
Fees as at 01/09/2022:
Day: US$56,250

Celebrating 150 years, Dwight is a leading private international school committed to educating the next generation of innovative global leaders – one student at a time. We're dedicated to crafting a personalized journey for every student based on individual interests and passions. We call this igniting the "spark of genius" in every child. Personalized learning, together with community and global vision, are the three pillars upon which a Dwight world-class education rests.

Innovation is an integral part of daily life on campus and takes many forms, from being the first school in the Americas to offer all four International Baccalaureate (IB) programs, to empowering student entrepreneurs to translate their novel ideas into reality through our unique Spark Tank incubator program, supported by The Dwight School Foundation.

Dwight's inspiring faculty – master teachers from all corners of the globe – encourage students to believe in their own talents, follow their hearts, and take intellectual risks through the International Baccalaureate. No two student journeys are the same. Offering one of the lowest student-faculty ratios among independent schools in New York City, Dwight provides one-on-one attention and ample opportunities for students to excel within and beyond the classroom through extensive language, design, and technology instruction; rich visual and performing arts programs; championship-winning athletic teams; and global leadership training.

Dwight has been an accredited IB World School since 1980, and no other curriculum fits better with Dwight's vision of educating innovative global leaders poised to succeed in today's global marketplace. The academic breadth and depth of the IB are unparalleled; it is the "gold standard" worldwide in pre-university preparation.

With a global network of Dwight Schools in New York, London, Seoul, Shanghai, and Dubai, students have numerous opportunities to travel and participate in cross-campus cultural and curricular exchange programs beginning in grade 5. These shared, enriching experiences prepare them for a future as leaders on the global stage, and the connections they forge will last a lifetime.

Dwight Global Online School, our campus in the cloud, ranked the #2 best online high school in the U.S. by *Newsweek*, offers students in grades 6-12 the flexibility to pursue their passions beyond the classroom. Students can take IB or AP online classes from anywhere, and come to Dwight's campus in New York for in-person experiences a few times a year.

Dwight's college counseling team provides expertise and guidance for students beginning early in grade 9. Our graduates attend top colleges and universities, including Harvard, Yale, Princeton, MIT, Stanford, Columbia, Dartmouth, Cornell, McGill, Oxford, and the University of Edinburgh, among others. Upon graduation, they join a vibrant Dwight alumni network that stretches across the globe.

EF Academy New York

EF ACADEMY

International
Boarding Schools

582 Columbus Avenue,
Thornwood, NY 10594 USA
Tel: +1 914 495 6056
Email: academy.admissions@ef.com
Website: www.efacademy.org
Head of School: Dr. Vladimir D. Kuskovski

School type:
Co-educational Day & Boarding
Age range of pupils: 14–19 years
Fees as at 01/09/2022:
Day: US$42,000
Full Boarding: US$65,500

At EF Academy International Boarding Schools, we empower the next generation of global changemakers. Our mission to open the world through education brings together students from all over the world to provide them with a transformational international education, thorough preparation for university and a future that knows no borders.

Our New York campus, which attracts bright students from around the world, is located in upper New York State, approximately 45 minutes away from Manhattan. EF Academy's secure campus offers 97 acres of wooded grounds, running trails and playing fields in the quiet suburban town of Thornwood. Our facilities include a premier science center, fully-equipped gym, auditorium, spacious classrooms and comfortable on-campus residences.

Instruction and guidance at EF Academy New York is highly personal. Students engage in interactive lessons led by experienced teachers and they benefit from the individualized support they receive from dedicated University and Academic Advisors who help them achieve their goals.

At EF Academy New York, students follow the US High School Diploma program from Grades 9-12, a typical qualification for students applying to North American universities. In this program, students can also take IB classes from Grade 11 or enroll in the full IB Diploma. Built into every course is an emphasis on multilingualism and intercultural exchange, which allows students to expand their worldviews as they progress through the rigorous and rewarding curricula. To ensure our students enjoy a well-rounded experience, we offer more than 75 clubs and activities, and have a range of varsity sports teams.

Our graduates have been accepted to top-ranked universities such as Harvard University, Cornell University, New York University, Johns Hopkins University and the University of Pennsylvania, as well as international universities ranked highly for the fields of business, engineering, art and other subjects.

EF Academy Pasadena

EF ACADEMY

International Boarding Schools

1539 E Howard St.,
Pasadena, CA 91104 USA
Tel: +1 626 507 9223
Email: academy.admissions@ef.com
Website: www.efacademy.org
Head of School: Dr. Sally Mingarelli

School type:
Co-educational Day & Boarding
Age range of pupils: 14–19 years
Fees as at 01/09/2022:
Day: US$42,000
Full Boarding: US$68,500

At EF Academy International Boarding Schools, we empower the next generation of global changemakers. Our mission to open the world through education brings together students from all over the world to provide them with a transformational international education, thorough preparation for university and a future that knows no borders.

EF Academy Pasadena's 16-acre campus offers students a perfect preview into a university-like lifestyle in southern California. Classes take place in bright, modern classrooms primed for debate and discussion. Science and tech labs are equipped to bring experiments and designs to life. Artists create and exhibit their work in our studios and gallery space. The student center, cafeteria and sports facilities – including outdoor basketball and beach volleyball courts, a soccer field, recreational swimming pool, fitness center, dance studio and competition hall – all encourage students to live a balanced, healthy lifestyle.

Our curriculum follows the US High School Diploma, with Advanced Placement (AP) courses giving students the chance to take university-level classes and demonstrate skills in their strongest subjects. Throughout their studies, students benefit from the individualized support of dedicated University and Academic Advisors who help them define and achieve their goals.

Our bespoke Global Leadership Program develops students' global competencies as they collaborate with peers to present solutions to real-world challenges and gives them the opportunity to present a portfolio of work on a pathway that interests them most: Global Entrepreneurs, Global Citizens or Global Innovators.

Built into every course at EF Academy is an emphasis on multilingualism and intercultural exchange, which allows students to expand their worldviews as they progress through the rigorous and rewarding curricula. To ensure our students enjoy a well-rounded experience, we offer a variety of clubs, activities and sports.

EF Academy graduates have been accepted to top-ranked universities including Cornell University, New York University, UC Berkeley, University of Oxford, University of Cambridge and many international universities ranked highly for the fields of business, engineering and art among others.

Greengates School

(Founded 1951)

Av. Circunvalación Pte. 102,
Balcones de San Mateo, Naucalpan,
Estado de México, C.P. 53200 México
Tel: +52 55 5373 0088
Email: kuroda@greengates.edu.mx
Website: www.greengates.edu.mx
General Director: Clarisa Desouches Ph.D.
Headmaster: Rupert Cox
Head of the Secondary School:
Christopher Woodall
School type: Co-educational Day
Age range of pupils: 3–18 years
No. of pupils enrolled as at 01/09/2022: 1100
Fees as at 01/09/2022:
Please contact the school

Greengates School, founded in 1951, is an independent, selective K-12 coeducational British international school of approximately 1100 students. At Greengates School we encourage our students to develop character, self-discipline, respect and reflection in a challenging learning environment.

Greengates School has been held in high esteem for over 70 years. It is recognized in Mexico and the world for its high academic standards, respectful treatment of all and for being a truly international and multi-cultural community. It is a self-sustained day school set in the municipality of Naucalpan de Juárez, just northwest of Mexico City. Our campus covers an area of over 20,000 square meters, with purpose-built facilities that include two libraries, nine science laboratories, six computer media centres, four art studios, a theatre, an auditorium, a large gymnasium, basketball courts, an indoor swimming pool, an organic learning garden, a cafeteria, an all-weather field and an adventure playground; Moctezuma's Lion, designed by the renowned architect Javier Senosiain.

At Greengates School we act with integrity and seek to motivate our students to become socially responsible citizens while achieving academic excellence. The majority of our students come from the diplomatic and business communities in Mexico City. Greengates' mission to educate internationally minded students occurs within the context of a track record of academic excellence. Over 50 different nationalities are represented and while there is a significant population of long-term locally based students, annual turnover averages 20%, so newcomers are ever present and warmly embraced.

The teaching body at Greengates is comprised of almost 140 teachers from a wide variety of backgrounds. Alongside the many British teachers, highly qualified and experienced educators come from around the world; Australia, Canada, Ireland, France, Mexico, and the USA, with all religions represented. Teachers bring a selection of different skills and modern method to the classroom and beyond. Approaches to teaching and learning are central to students' success.

As a British international school, the language of instruction is English, though all students from the age of six study Spanish at the appropriate level,

and some 55% of students who require Mexican educational qualifications take a limited number of courses in Spanish. Support in both languages is given as required. Furthermore, French is taught in the Secondary School and can be taken at IGCSE and IB Diploma. Korean and Japanese are also available as options of the diploma.

The Primary School is a fully accredited International Early Years Curriculum (IEYC) and International Primary Curriculum (IPC) School with aspects of mastering in its practice. Learning with the IEYC and IPC means that children focus on a combination of academic, personal and international learning that is exciting, engaging and challenging. The aim of the IEYC and IPC is to help every child enjoy the learning of a wide range of subjects, including science, history, geography and art. It also focuses on developing an enquiring mind, the personal goals that will help throughout teenage and adult years, to develop a sense of his or her own nationality and culture, while at the same time developing a profound respect for the nationalities and cultures of others.

The Secondary School prepares students for the International General Certificate of Secondary Education (IGCSE Cambridge, UK). We offer a wide range of IGCSE subjects. Our IGCSE results are always above the world average. The IGCSE two-year course is studied prior to embarking on the IB Diploma Programme.

In the Lower and Upper Sixth Forms, all students follow the International Baccalaureate Diploma Programme (IB). The Secondary School has been authorised to offer the Diploma Programme since 1986, obtaining a pass rate of 98-100% during each of the last five years, with overall points scores consistently well above the world average. Each year Greengates sends students to top colleges and universities which include: Boston University, Brown University, Stanford University, Syracuse University, University of California Berkeley, University of California San Diego, University of Oregon and University of Wisconsin Madison in the US; Durham University, Imperial College London, King's College London, London School of Economics and Political Science, University of Edinburgh and University of Manchester in the UK; McGill University, University of British Columbia, University of Toronto and University of Waterloo in Canada; Okayama University in Japan; University of Sydney in Australia and Erasmus University Rotterdam, Tilburg University and University of Amsterdam in the Netherlands, just to mention a few. Greengates students have received over 4.5M US Dollars in financial aid and scholarships over the past five years.

International School of Los Angeles

International School Los Angeles Lycée International

(Founded 1978)
1105 W. Riverside Drive,
Burbank, CA 91506 USA
Tel: +1 626 695 5159
Email: admissions@lilaschool.com
Website: www.internationalschool.la

Head of School: Mr Michael Maniska
School type: Co-educational Day
Age range of pupils: 3–18 years
No. of pupils enrolled as at 01/09/2022: 1040
Fees as at 01/09/2022:
Day: $19,895–$25,725

The International School of Los Angeles is a non-profit, independent, international preschool through 12th grade school committed to bilingual education and academic excellence in a nurturing environment. The School's mission is to develop bilingual critical thinkers who are open-minded, confident and caring, and equipped to thrive in a diverse, competitive world.

Recognized as one of the most academically challenging private high schools in the United States, the International School of Los Angeles has been leading the way in bilingual education for more than 40 years.

Students study a common bilingual program from preschool through 8th grade, after which they choose one of two rigorous programs that culminates in the International Baccalaureate® Diploma or the French baccalauréat. After 10th grade, students formally apply to, and enroll in, the International Baccalaureate® Diploma Programme or the French baccalauréat program. All choices provide academically demanding and well-balanced courses of study that meet the needs of highly motivated students and empower them to be successful citizens of the world.

With multiple Los Angeles-area campuses, the School holds accreditation from the French Ministry of Education, the Western Association of Schools and Colleges (WASC), the California Association of Independent Schools (CAIS), and the International Baccalaureate® (IB). The School is also a member of the National Association of Independent Schools (NAIS) and the National Honor Society (NHS) networks.

The International School of Los Angeles is committed to the values of respect, excellence, and diversity, and to preparing students of all backgrounds to excel in and contribute to a global world. Since 1978, the School has been instilling the love of learning in all its students through small classes and low student-to-teacher ratios. With over 65 nationalities and 40 spoken languages represented on the campuses, students study and live in a diverse global community every day.

La Citadelle International Academy of Arts & Science

La Citadelle

International Academy of Arts & Science

(Founded 2000)

36 Scarsdale Road, North York,
Toronto ON, M3B 2R7 Canada
Tel: +1 416 385 9685
Email:
headmaster@lacitadelleacademy.com
Website: www.lacitadelleacademy.com
Head of School: Alfred Abouchar B.Sc., M.Sc, B.Ed., M.Ed., PhD (ABD)

Appointed: 2000
School type: Co-educational Day
Age range of pupils: 2–18 years
No. of pupils enrolled as at 01/09/2022: 180
Fees as at 01/09/2022:
Day: CAD$13,875–CAD$28,800
Average class size: Max 16
Teacher/pupil ratio: 1:8

Established in 2000 with only 5 students in Richmond Hill, La Citadelle relocated to North York in 2001 and then to its present larger facility in the heart of the city in 2015. La Citadelle has since seen its enrolment and reputation grow exponentially. Spanning all grade levels, from Prep-K to Grade 12, La Citadelle offers a comprehensive and academically advanced curriculum in Languages (French, English, Mandarin, Spanish), Mathematics, Sciences, Technology, Humanities and Arts, along with its Reach Ahead and enriched IB and AP programs, providing both its national and international student population with the highest caliber of education and instruction needed to successfully pursue higher education with scholarships in the most prominent universities in Canada and around the world.

An established and highly reputable private school, La Citadelle's dedicated team of educators believe that all students are special, that they all have hidden talents, along with an enormous potential to achieve and that it is their duty and responsibility as educators to tap into students' capabilities and talents while providing them with a substantially structured program and discipline model in a warm, safe and inviting environment where students can learn and succeed with joy, enthusiasm, and determination.

La Citadelle's holistic learning environment extends traditionally beyond the classroom with a variety of activities, field trips, and both national and international travels, which are complemented by intramural / extracurricular sports, academic competitions and clubs, musical performances, social activities, and more. With a solid level of individual student support and a low student/teacher ratio, La Citadelle's multicultural environment additionally provides its student population an unparalleled support system and a rich social setting that fosters lifelong friendships.

Le Lycée Français de Los Angeles

Le Lycée Français
de Los Angeles

3261 Overland Avenue,
Los Angeles, CA 90034 USA

Tel: +1 310 836 3464
Email: generalinfo@LyceeLA.org
Website: www.lyceela.org
President: Mrs. Clara-Lisa Kabbaz
Admissions Director: Mrs. Sophie Darmon
School type: Co-educational Day
Age range of pupils:
3 years 9 months–18 years

No. of pupils enrolled as at 01/09/2022: 740
Boys: 320 ***Girls:*** 420
Fees as at 01/09/2022:
Day: $23,000–$34,900
Average class size: 1:15
Teacher/pupil ratio: 1:8

We Teach the World.
Founded in 1964 Le Lycée Français de Los Angeles is an international, independent, coed school providing a global education with dual curriculums to students from preschool to 12th grade. It is located on 6 unique and age-appropriate campuses in the West Los Angeles area. The school offers the choice of an English-language college prep program and another entirely taught in French, both of which nurture the mind, body and character of every student.

In addition to strong academics, athletics, arts, and music, many clubs/extracurricular activities ensure a balanced education and encourage every child to develop his full potential. Le Lycée Français de Los Angeles' student body is made up of more than 700 pupils from over 45 countries, 70 percent of whom are U.S. citizens. The diverse and engaging community of students, parents and teachers fosters a caring and nurturing environment, creating globally-minded world citizens.

Over the last five decades Le Lycée Français de Los Angeles graduates have enrolled in the most prestigious colleges and universities in the world, and proceeded to distinguish themselves in the arts, humanities and sciences.

Le Lycée Français de Los Angeles is accredited by the Western Association of Schools and Colleges, as well as being fully recognized by the French Ministry of Education.

Diplomas:
College Board AP Capstone
Classic Baccalaureate (BAC)
Baccalauréat Français International (BFI)
U.S. High School Diploma

Tradition – Innovation – Excellence
No French knowledge required to enroll

Meadowridge School

(Founded 1985)

12224 240th Street, Maple Ridge BC,
V4R 1N1 Canada
Tel: +1 604 467 4444
Email: admissions@meadowridge.bc.ca
Website: www.meadowridge.bc.ca
Head of School: Mr. Scott Banack
Deputy Head of School: Mr. Terry Donaldson

School type: Co-educational Day
Age range of pupils: 4–18 years
No. of pupils enrolled as at 01/09/2022: 650
Fees as at 01/09/2022:
Domestic Fees: C$25,925
International Fees: C$35,925

Meadowridge School exists as a point of departure for parents and students who are seeking more meaning from education; an unfettered education that has greater impact on the whole individual and more relevance to the realities of the world.

As an International Baccalaureate (IB) Continuum World School, we offer the academically-rigorous Primary Years Programme (PYP), Middle Years Programme (MYP) and Diploma Programme (DP) to students from Junior Kindergarten to Grade 12. This continuum of learning supports the growth and development of the whole child in a safe, supportive, and challenging environment. Through inquiry-based instruction, students learn to engage with challenging and complex questions effectively and creatively.

Our school, from classroom to natural woodland, is the setting for our program that challenges students to find out more about their own beliefs and society through striving for excellence in academics, arts, and service to the community.

Just 45 minutes east of Vancouver, British Columbia, Meadowridge is located in beautiful Maple Ridge on a unique, pastoral 27-acre campus complete with a regenerative farm, campground, gardens, greenhouses, a discovery forest, and stream for students across the continuum to engage and explore. Our 152,000 square foot facility includes state-of-the-art science labs, a theatre, a design lab, and an international-sized soccer pitch.

As an International Baccalaureate World School, Meadowridge is committed to providing our students the highest quality of education and the knowledge to become engaged participants in the global community.

Through our outstanding teaching, programs, and facilities, Meadowridge develops the confidence in students to not only meet the future, but also to create it.

Mulgrave, The International School of Vancouver

(Founded 1993)

2330 Cypress Bowl Lane,
West Vancouver BC, V7S 3H9 Canada
Tel: +1 604 922 3223
Email: admissions@mulgrave.com
Website: www.mulgrave.com
Head of School: John Wray
Appointed: 2010

School type: Co-educational Day
Age range of pupils: 3–18 years
No. of pupils enrolled as at 01/09/2022: 1025
Fees as at 01/09/2022:
Day: CND$25,000
Average class size: PYP: 20, MYP: 18, DP:13

Mulgrave, The International School of Vancouver is a multicultural, gender-inclusive International Baccalaureate World School (pre-school to Grade 12). Nestled on the slopes of Cypress Mountain, overlooking the Pacific Ocean and downtown Vancouver, our stunning campus provides students and faculty custom-built spaces where they can inspire each other as they are all inspired by the views. Our diverse community is united in its commitment to develop the interpersonal and intercultural skills, attitudes, and values that will allow our students to thrive and be happy no matter where in the world they find themselves. Our graduates go on to post-secondary institutions across the globe; this year, they have accepted offers spanning from UBC and McGill in Canada, to UPenn and USC in the United States, and to UCL in and Hong Kong University abroad.

Our Mission: Inspiring Excellence in Education and Life

Through the continuous pursuit of personal best, Mulgrave strives to equip lifelong learners to thrive in a culturally diverse and interdependent world. Our goal is for students to embrace, with passion and confidence, their responsibility to make a difference by serving their communities, both locally and in the world at large.

Our Culture: A warm, vibrant, supportive community

Developing a strong aptitude for learning, service, and leadership is inherent to our school's ethos, as is a strong culture of caring and support. Mulgrave is highly valued for our positive community spirit, enriched by the diversity of families from more than 42 countries, and its vibrant learning atmosphere. Experienced teachers from around the world provide a comprehensive, appropriately challenging, and personalised IB curriculum to an equally ambitious and capable student body.

Our Strategic Plan 2021-2024: Weaving Our Future, Common Threads

Over this three year period, it is our intention, while being true to our school's guiding statements, to build on our success from our previous strategic plan and to ensure that we continue to provide an outstanding future-oriented education for the students in our care. We will engage student agency and technology to continue to support increased personalisation of learning, curriculum and support. We will focus on student health and wellbeing with more emphasis on social and emotional learning and the use of outdoor education experiences. And we will focus on students' skill development with special emphasis on creativity, global citizenship, and social entrepreneurship.

Accreditations

Mulgrave is proud to be an accredited member of the Council of International Schools (CIS), the Independent Schools Association of British Columbia (ISABC), and Canadian Accredited Independent Schools (CAIS), and is also authorised by the International Baccalaureate Organization as an IB Continuum School.

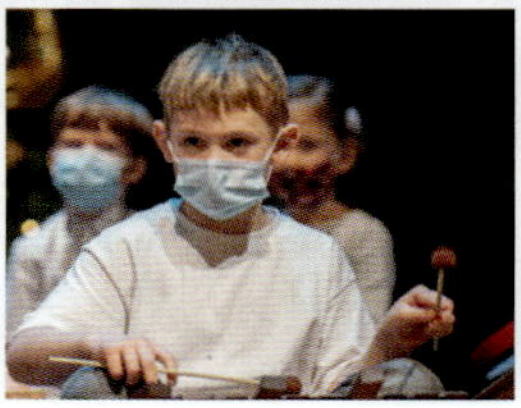

Pan-American School

(Founded 1971)

632-4005 San Antonio de Belen,
Heredia, Costa Rica
Tel: +506 2298 5700
Email: info@panam.ed.cr
Website: www.panam.ed.cr
Head of School: Alan Wrafter
Appointed: July 2019

School type: Co-educational Day
Age range of pupils: 18 months–18 years
No. of pupils enrolled as at 01/09/2022: 540
Fees as at 01/09/2022:
Day: US$6,870–US$13,445
Teacher/pupil ratio: 1:6

Pan-American School was founded in 1971 and offers an inclusive education to students from 1.5 to 18 years. Our 35,000m2 purpose-built campus is designed for learning in harmony with nature and is strategically located in the western suburbs of San José close to multiple residential areas, multinational business parks and free zones.

We offer the PYP, MYP and DP, grounded in the unique context and values of Costa Rica, and students can graduate with the IB Diploma, US High School Diploma, and the Costa Rican Bachillerato.

We pride ourselves on developing English-Spanish bilingual learners, equipped for success in an ever-changing world. Our broad and rigorous curriculum includes: skills for life; social and emotional development; arts, design, and physical education programs; and a unique focus on service and global sustainability.

Sports and wellbeing form an essential part of life at Pan-American School; we offer: afternoon sports programmes for all students from PreKinder to Grade 5; competitive sports training for Secondary School students; and a Morning Fitness programme for all Secondary School students which facilitates a developmentally-appropriate start to the day's learning. Our students compete nationally and internationally, and in 2022 our female Basketball and Volleyball teams were crowned AASCA champions of Central America, and PAS students won placements in AASCA swimming, tennis and mathematics competitions.

We prepare students to respond to challenges with optimism and an open mind, who are confident in their own identities, make ethical decisions, join with others in celebrating our common humanity and are prepared to apply what they learn in real-world, complex and unpredictable situations.

Our diversity is our greatest strength, and we welcome students from all backgrounds, ensuring that we provide for their individual needs via our caring and dedicated team of educators, learning and emotional support, and language acquisition specialists.

Rochambeau, The French International School

ROCHAMBEAU
THE FRENCH INTERNATIONAL SCHOOL

9600 Forest Rd, Bethesda, MD 20814 USA

Tel: +1 301 530 8260
Email: admissions@rochambeau.org
Website: www.rochambeau.org
Head of School: Mr Xavier Jacquenet
Appointed: September 2020
School type: Co-educational Day
Age range of pupils: 2–18 years

No. of pupils enrolled as at 01/09/2022: 1150
Fees as at 01/09/2022:
Grade 5: US$23,640
Grades 6-9: US$24,410
Grades 10-12: US$28,580
Average class size: 18
Teacher/pupil ratio: 1:13

Are you looking for an exceptional multicultural learning experience for your child? Perhaps you want to increase his or her cognitive development and linguistic ability with a bilingual education. If so, look no further than Rochambeau, The French International School of Washington DC. The school has been in existence since 1955. It started with 11 students and has grown to 1150 students in 2022, representing over 80 nationalities. As part of the French Network of School Abroad (AEFE) students can seamlessly move to and from other schools within the network around the world.

Rochambeau has two campuses all located in Bethesda and welcomes students from age 2 through 12th grade. The maternelle (preschool) program, noted as the "crown jewel of the French school system," emphasise play, written and oral skills, and learning to live in a community. Students appreciate the holistic approach implemented in this well-balanced comprehensive program. Motor skills, expression, and movement are also taught to these young minds.

Children can enroll in the school without any knowledge of French until the third grade. In addition to French, students have the option of learning a number of languages, including Arabic, German, Latin, and Spanish. Students at Rochambeau participate in a number of extracurricular activities, including soccer, theater, basketball, swimming, tennis, and rock climbing. Students receive their US high school diploma at the end of 11th grade and the French Baccalaureate at the end of 12th grade. Rochambeau also offers the IB program as of 9th grade. Graduates of Rochambeau go on to study in both the US and internationally, attending some of the top universities around the world.

For more information, please see Rochambeau's website: www.rochambeau.org. Explore everything the school has to offer to broaden your child's horizons and increase his or her linguistic ability. Check it out today!

Stratford Hall

STRATFORD HALL
IB WORLD SCHOOL

(Founded 2000)
3000 Commercial Drive, Vancouver BC, V5N 4E2 Canada
Tel: +1 604 436 0608

Email: info@stratfordhall.ca
Website: www.stratfordhall.ca
Head of School: Richard Kassissieh
Junior School Principal: Dr. Michael Palmer
Senior School Principal: Meg Chamberlin

School type: Co-educational Day
Age range of pupils: 5–18 years
No. of pupils enrolled as at 01/09/2022: 540
Fees as at 01/09/2022:
Annual Tuition: CAD$24,540 – CAD$28,670
Average class size: 20-22

Stratford Hall is an independent, gender-inclusive, nondenominational, university preparatory day school with a student population of 540 ranging from Kindergarten to Grade 12. Our location in a vibrant, urban setting in East Vancouver, British Columbia reflects our diverse community of students. Through the continuum of International Baccalaureate (IB) programmes, the Primary Years Programme (Kindergarten – Grade 5), Middle Years Programme (Grades 6 -10) and Diploma Programme (Grades 11 & 12) the School provides a level of individual challenge and academic rigour beyond the norm. Equally important is our commitment to the IB Learner Profile as a guide fostering international-mindedness in students and adults alike.

At Stratford Hall, your child will be given the opportunity to learn and to thrive; to discover their unique strengths, and to explore the diverse opportunities our rapidly changing world offers. Under the care and guidance of Stratford Hall staff, they will grow and mature, while equipping themselves with intellectual tools, strength of character, and a global perspective.

Stratford Hall is a not-for-profit school operating under the authority of the Ministry of Education of British Columbia.

Our Mission

Stratford Hall educates students to the highest global standards through the programmes of the International Baccalaureate. Excellence and confidence are developed through a challenging academic curriculum with further emphasis on creativity, action and service. We foster a strong pluralistic community built on integrity and respect.

Our Vision

Stratford Hall strives to be a global leader in the International Baccalaureate community. Our students will gain a deep understanding of the world around them, and they will act on their connections to the outside community. They will excel to the best of their abilities, and graduates will be equipped to achieve their chosen goals. This is accomplished by acquiring and retaining the best teachers, and by a commitment to a balanced and enriched curriculum. The success of Stratford Hall is deeply rooted in the establishment of a supportive, knowledgeable and committed community.

Stratford Hall is proud to be an accredited member of the Independent Schools Association of British Columbia (ISABC), Canadian Accredited Independent Schools (CAIS), National Association of Independent Schools (NAIS), and is authorized by the International Baccalaureate Organization as an IB Continuum School.

TFS – Canada's International School

(Founded 1962)
306 Lawrence Avenue East,
Toronto ON, M4N 1T7 Canada
Tel: +1 416 484 6533

Email: admissions@tfs.ca
Website: www.tfs.ca
Head of School: Norman Gaudet
Appointed: 2021
School type: Co-educational Day
Religious Denomination: Non-denominational

Age range of pupils: 2–18 years
No. of pupils enrolled as at 01/09/2022: 1500
Fees as at 01/09/2022:
Day: CAD$22,180–CAD$37,630
Average class size: Max 22
Teacher/pupil ratio: Varies

TFS' mission is to develop multilingual critical thinkers who celebrate difference, transcend borders and strive for the betterment of humankind. As the pioneer of French immersion in Canada, the TFS education is unparalleled in its excellence, preparing students for success in today's global world.

Bilingual and coed since 1962, TFS teaches the curricula of France and Ontario through the framework established by the IB programs (PYP, MYP and bilingual IB Diploma Program). We want our students to exude academic ambition, benefit from an all-round development as individuals and citizens, and view the world from an international perspective. TFS students master French and English, while balancing rigorous science, arts and humanities programs.

No prior knowledge of French is necessary, but all students are bilingual when they graduate due to our successful Intro program, offered until Grade 7. TFS students are well-rounded, inquisitive learners, forming friendships for life within our supportive community. Co-curricular programs include competitive sports, robotics, and music, visual and dramatic arts. Students benefit from exceptional facilities, a 26-acre ravine, and a diverse, non-denominational environment. TFS has campuses in Toronto and Mississauga.

In addition to being authorized by the IB, TFS is accredited by the Ministry of Education of Ontario, the French Ministry of Education, and Canadian Accredited Independent Schools (CAIS). TFS is also a member of the Conference of Independent Schools of Ontario (CIS), the Council of International Schools, and Agence pour l'enseignement français à l'étranger (aefe).

Please visit us at www.tfs.ca.

The Biltmore School

THE BILTMORE SCHOOL

Established 1926

(Founded 1926)
1600 S. Red Road, Miami, FL 33155 USA
Tel: +1 305 266 4666
Email: info@biltmoreschool.com
Website: www.biltmoreschool.com
Principal: Gina C. Duarte-Romero M.Ed.

Assistant Principal: Ana V. Seoane
School type: Co-educational Day
Age range of pupils: 1–14 years
No. of pupils enrolled as at 01/09/2022: 200
Fees as at 01/09/2022:
US$9,800 – US$20,800

Originally founded in Coral Gables in 1926, The Biltmore School is one of the oldest operating schools in Miami Dade County. Our school boasts a tradition of educational excellence that has provided guidance to children for over 90 years.

Our Director, Gina Romero and our Biltmore Faculty members are actively involved in the Project Zero research initiative sponsored by Harvard University that promotes creative thinking, encourages children to be self-reliant, and empowers them to think "outside the box" through a challenging curriculum that incorporates instruction maximizing multiple intelligences, individual learning styles and modalities. Through participation in ongoing professional development workshops in partnership with Florida International University, our staff under the guidance of our director actively explore Visible Thinking strategies that promote the highest levels of intelligences, abstract, and critical thinking in children of all ages.

During the 2007-2008 school year our school was awarded accreditation by AISF (Association of Independent Schools of Florida), SACS (Southern Association of Colleges and Schools) and CASI (Council on Accreditation and School Improvement). The Biltmore School is also accredited by the Middle States Association of Colleges and Schools Commissions on Elementary and Secondary Schools and the National Council for Private School Accreditation. The Biltmore School has also been an IB World School since March 2012 and offers the IB Primary Years Programme.

The Biltmore School believes that students are capable and knowledgeable agents of their learning. We feel that it is the responsibility of the educator to be both the partner and guide in the growth and development of the child. It is through much research and collaboration that our school has embraced and synthesized diverse educational views and practices to best benefit our students.

The Biltmore School offers a comprehensive program for students from age one through eighth grade.

THINK Global School

1460 Broadway #4027, New York,
NY 10036 USA
Tel: +1 347 281 6855
Email: info@thinkglobalschool.org
Website: www.thinkglobalschool.com
Headteachers:
Adnan Mackovic & Chelle Marshall

School type: Co-educational Boarding
Age range of pupils: 15–18 years
No. of pupils enrolled as at 01/09/2022: 60
Fees as at 01/09/2022:
Sliding-scale, maximum: $94,050
Teacher/pupil ratio: 1:4

At THINK Global School (TGS), the world is its students' classroom. Learning takes place in a different country every three months, spanning ten extraordinary locations over three years. During their time abroad, students come face-to-face with global issues, visionary speakers, and international communities as they work towards an accredited high school diploma.

Through place-based learning, students at THINK Global School experience real-world issues firsthand and interact closely with the communities they immerse themselves within. Each eight-week term is held in a different country, so students regularly learn in the world rather than just about it: the community becomes their classroom, and its denizens their teachers.

These firsthand experiences are integral to the THINK Global School educational experience, as they breed empathy and cultivate a deep understanding of peoples, cultures, and surroundings. Better yet, they help develop the skills, knowledge, and experiences necessary to become the changemakers of tomorrow.

During their time abroad, students also build lifelong bonds with their classmates, who hail from over thirty countries and inform discussions just as much as the locations THINK Global School inhabits. By reaching across cultural and geographical divides, students at THINK Global School overcome biases while developing a deeper understanding of their shared humanity.

Academics

THINK Global School believes that the key to student engagement and success is a focus on three core aspects: mastery, autonomy, and purpose. Its Changemaker Curriculum was constructed around these three cornerstones alongside using place- and project-based learning as a medium for deep learning. The Changemaker Curriculum draws from this century's most innovative and effective educational models, combining high academic standards with interdisciplinary, project- and problem-based learning.

Teacher-led Modules

THINK Global School does not employ a traditional classroom dynamic; rather, learning is student-centered and focused on projects that explore real-world challenges. Students select from one of three country-specific projects at the start of each term, each designed to build their knowledge in a specific subject area. The following eight weeks are then spent interacting firsthand with local communities, cultures, and environments as they work in teams towards a solution to their project's driving question. Learning cultivates each term with a project-based showcase, where students have the opportunity to share their takeaways with both the TGS and local community.

Each project is built around learning targets, which serve as the backbone of the Changemaker Curriculum. By constructing projects around learning targets, THINK Global School ensures that each student receives a comprehensive education, as satisfying each learning target at least once is a condition for graduation.

Personal Projects

Students also engage in at least one personal project each term. Through personal projects, students formulate their own driving questions and select the learning targets and 21st-century skills they'd like to focus on. It's an opportunity to pursue passions or tackle a subject they'd like to become more knowledgeable in.

Personal projects can take many forms, including completing an additional AP course, conducting scientific research and presenting findings, crafting an original piece of art, or creating a paper or presentation to document new understanding of an element of local culture or history.

Focus on Social-Emotional Learning

Due to its small class sizes, students at THINK Global School also receive a lot of individualized attention. They work one-on-one with advisors and counselors to ensure they have balance in their lives when it comes to academics, mental health, and physical fitness. By emphasizing a whole-child approach, students at THINK Global School are more engaged in their studies and more comfortable in their community and surroundings.

University Preparation

The Changemaker Curriculum goes above and beyond to prepare students for the academic and social rigors of university. By letting students guide their own learning and imbuing every aspect of their education with compassion and service, they're empowered to become leaders in their university communities and beyond.

An education at THINK Global School includes regular one-on-one sessions with a college and career counselor, designed to give all of the tools students need to navigate the university admissions process.

While over 90% of THINK Global School students go on to university, our faculty and counselors provide full support to students who envision a different route to success. Gap years have become an increasingly popular choice for students who aren't quite ready to leave the travel and experiential learning behind, and they provide an excellent way to continue building upon the skills they mastered at THINK Global School.

Many in-demand jobs also no longer require a college degree. Due to this, our faculty and counselors help students who demonstrate a natural ability in skills like coding or graphic design to navigate their goals and jumpstart their careers.

The Village School

THE VILLAGE SCHOOL
A NORD ANGLIA EDUCATION SCHOOL

(Founded 1966)
13051 Whittington Drive,
Houston, TX 77077 USA

Tel: +1 281 496 7900
Email: admissions@thevillageschool.com
Website: www.thevillageschool.com
Head of School: Mr. Bill Delbrugge
Appointed: July 2021
School type:
Co-educational Day & Boarding

Age range of pupils: 2–18 years
No. of pupils enrolled as at 01/09/2022: 1500
Fees as at 01/09/2022:
Day: US$19,425–US$32,675
Full Boarding: US$57,850–US$76,850
Average class size: 18
Teacher/pupil ratio: 1:9

The Village School is a premier Preschool through 12th grade private day and boarding school in Houston, Texas USA. Village has a tradition of accelerated learning paired with hands-on innovative methods of teaching. Village offers an American educational experience to its global student body who represent six continents and more than 80 countries. The Village School is a member of the Nord Anglia Education Network of Schools.

Dedicated to STEAM Education

The Village School's long-standing excellence in STEAM education and project-based learning offer our students the opportunity to explore solutions for real world problems. Village secures summer internships within the Houston community for its high school students in the fields of medicine, energy, technology and more.

Four Diploma Options

Village is proud to offer four rigorous diploma options: the International Baccalaureate Diploma Program, the Entrepreneurship Diploma, the Pre-Medical Science Diploma and The Village School U.S. Diploma.

Elite College Counseling

Our college counseling team begins working with students as early as 9th grade on the thoughtful selection, application, and admission to their top-choice college or university. The team also helped the graduating class of 2022 earn over $18M in scholarships and admissions into several of the world's top colleges and universities.

Competitive Athletics

Village offers a full range of competitive sports such as basketball, cross country, football, golf, lacrosse, soccer, swimming, tennis, track, and volleyball. Village is an annual contender in district, regional, and state championships.

Boarding Program

Houston is the number one most diverse city in America and The Village School was ranked #1 most diverse school in Texas. We mirror the city of Houston with our diverse community of students and faculty who hail from all over the world. We offer both 5- and 7-day boarding options for students from grades 7th and above. Last school year, our Boarding Program was home to more than 150 students from over 20 countries.

Premier Collaborations

Village students benefit from our collaborations with esteemed institutions such as Massachusetts Institute of Technology (MIT), The Juilliard School and UNICEF.

International schools in South America

Schools ordered A–Z by Name

Escola do Futuro – São Paulo

R. Dr. Francisco Pati 40, Cidade São Francisco, São Paulo, SP 05352-120 Brazil
Tel: +55 (11) 2168 4100
Av. Corifeu de Azevedo Marques 5240, Butantã, São Paulo, SP 05340-002
Tel: +55 (11) 3198 9295

Email: visitas@escoladofuturo.com.br
Website: www.escoladofuturo.com.br
Headmaster: Ivonne Betsabé Muniz
School type: Co-educational Day
Age range of pupils: 2–18 years
No. of pupils enrolled as at 01/09/2022: 600

Bringing World Leaders Together

Escola do Futuro does not have this name by chance. The institution offers a bilingual curriculum developed on the basis of multicultural and Christian values from Preschool to Grade 12. The students experience a learning environment of total immersion in English where they acquire the cultural knowledge needed to gain proficiency in the target language, as well as preparing to face future challenges as leaders who can change the world into a better place. Escola do Futuro's goal is to bring together world citizens. The students acquire full proficiency in additional languages, such as English and Spanish and also build the necessary cultural references and values which will allow them to interact naturally and consciously wherever they are. The students learn to accept and welcome diversity. The educational philosophy is based on a skill-driven curriculum focused on the development of autonomy and critical thinking; so students become aware of their transforming role in making a better world. The School's vision is clearly reflected in its environment, where the purpose built facilities integrate the learning process. The classrooms, common areas, such as the cafeteria, patio, and courts, invite the students to interact socially, while allowing them to respect each other's individuality. The international program provides students with the opportunity to pursue higher education abroad; anchored in the education of professionals that face the challenges of tomorrow, as citizens of the world.

St. Paul's School

St. Paul's School

MANIBUS POTENTIA STUDIUM ANIMIS

(Founded 1926)

Rua Juquiá 166, Jardim Paulistano,
São Paulo, SP 01440-903 Brazil
Tel: +55 11 3087 3399
Email: head@stpauls.br
Website: www.stpauls.br
Head Teacher: Mr Titus Edge

School type: Co-educational Day
Religious Denomination: Non-denominational
Age range of pupils: 3–18 years
Average class size: 6-19
Teacher/pupil ratio: 1:14

St. Paul's School was the first British School to be established in São Paulo (Brazil) and continues to offer an Anglo-Brazilian curriculum, embracing the best of both cultures. As an all-through (ages 3-18) co-educational school, offering the IGCSE and IB courses to pupils, we are affiliated to a global network of top UK Schools through our membership of HMC (Headmaster's Conference) and COBIS (Council of British International Schools). Almost 100 years old, we draw on our proud heritage as the first British school in Latin America to be recognised as a British School Overseas (BSO) by the UK government. Yet, we look forward with creativity and confidence.

At St. Paul's we always strive to be our better selves. We have the courage of our convictions, essential values, freedom to imagine and create. This is achieved through our high quality British and Brazilian holistic education which drives the personal and academic development of pupils, within a framework of a caring, inclusive and united community.

It is our aim to discover the passion and talents of every pupil, and create the right environment to develop these. The school prides itself on an excellent enrichment programme ranging from MUN to Duke of Edinburgh, from knitting classes to a robotics programme, from mathematical Olympiads to outstanding drama and music. We have been awarded as a Microsoft Showcase School and an Apple Distinguished School in recognition for our excellence in transforming and enhancing our physical and online learning environment to deliver more personalised education to our pupils.

The school is a positive agent of change, helping its pupils to be caring individuals ready to inspire and mobilise those around them to impact the world for the best. Our commitment to broad educational experiences opens many opportunities for pupils who go on to leading universities in the United Kingdom, America and Brazil.

Metropolitan School of Panama

METROPOLITAN SCHOOL OF PANAMA
A NORD ANGLIA EDUCATION SCHOOL
(Founded 2011)

Green Valley, Panama Norte,
Panama City, Panama
Tel: +507 317 1130
Email:
admissions@themetropolitanschool.com
Website:
www.themetropolitanschool.com

Headteacher: Mr. Daniel McKee
School type: Co-educational Day
Age range of pupils: 3–18 years
No. of pupils enrolled as at 01/09/2022: 755
Fees as at 01/09/2022:
Day: $10,149–$20,169
Teacher/pupil ratio: 1:7

The Metropolitan School of Panama, is an International Baccalaureate (IB) World School for students aged 3-18. It is the only IB continuum school in Panama authorized to offer the PYP, MYP and DP programmes in the country.

Founded in 2011 to offer a world-class academic Preschool through 12th grade program, the school has more than 775 students hailing from 45 nationalities and 125 faculty members with extensive international experience. Our school is committed to each child reaching their personal level of excellence through a balanced academic program that nurtures their self-esteem and potential and engages them in the world that surrounds them.

The MET is proud to form part of Nord Anglia Education, the world's leading premium schools organization, uniting with 73 other outstanding schools in 30 countries worldwide. NAE's global family of schools share a common philosophy that there is no limit to what its students can achieve. Our students also benefit from collaborations with world renowned institutions through our Juilliard-Nord Anglia Performing Arts Programme, which prepares them for the world's stage and our MIT STEAM curriculum which focuses on transferable skills in an evolving world. Additionally, students gain a global perspective on sustainability through work with UNICEF and the 17 sustainable development goals. Our global scale enables us to recruit and retain the best teachers in the world, offering a quality education to your child here in Panama.

New Campus. New Opportunities.

The MET recently moved to a new 5 hectare campus offering unparalleled educational facilities not just in Panama but in Central America.

MET students discover a world beyond the traditional classroom with 89 modern learning spaces designed for collaborative learning; including 7 fully-equipped science labs, a STEAM lab, black box theater, FIFA sized soccer field, a 25 meter pool and specialized areas for design, technology and music.

We are a school committed to the education of the future and we are proud to offer a 1-to-1 technology program for all students, implementing Apple technology throughout the school.

Our goal is to educate your child for the future, enhancing learning through collaborations with the world's best organizations. Individually tailoring our approach to your child enabling them to achieve outstanding academic results while developing the skills and mind-set to thrive in a changing world.

Children as young as three can join us and build the foundation they need to open up new possibilities and eventually secure a place at the

college of their choice. The excellent results and acceptances at the world's leading universities are a testament to our excellent execution of the IB Program and our dedicated, experienced and highly qualified teachers. The 2020 MET class achieved an excellent 96% IB pass rate, significantly higher than the international average of 80%. Graduates from the MET attend some of the most prestigious colleges and universities worldwide. Our 2021 graduating class received scholarship offers totalling over $3M USD.

Come and learn about life as a student at the Metropolitan School of Panama. You want the best for your child. So do we. We promise to support your child to love learning and achieve more than they ever thought possible.

You won't find an international school in Panama better equipped to prepare your child for a successful future. Our new facilities will provide a unique place where there is no limit to what your child can accomplish. Enrolment is open throughout the year.

We always welcome enquiries and visits from prospective families. To explore the MET difference please contact: admissions@themetropolitanschool.com

The British College of Brazil

THE BRITISH COLLEGE OF BRAZIL
A NORD ANGLIA EDUCATION SCHOOL

Chácara Flora Campus (2-18 years old): Rua Álvares de Azevedo, 50, Chácara Flora, São Paulo, SP 04671-040 Brazil
Cidade Jardim Campus (2-10 years old): Avenida Engenheiro Oscar Americano, 630, Cidade Jardim, São Paulo, SP 05673-050 Brazil
Tel: +55 11 5547 3030

Email: info@britishcollegebrazil.org
Website: www.britishcollegebrazil.org
Headteacher: Mr. Nick West
School type: Co-educational Day
Age range of pupils: 2–18 years
No. of pupils enrolled as at 01/09/2022: 520
Average class size: 16
Teacher/pupil ratio: 1:10

The British College of Brazil (BCB), a Nord Anglia Education school, is São Paulo's school of choice for expatriate families looking to provide their children with an international education. We offer engaging learning environments to students in Early Years, Primary and Secondary school in a warm and supportive atmosphere where they can thrive. Our schools and the one-of-a-kind opportunities we create inside and outside the classroom enrich learning, instill lifelong memories and a deep sense of achievement. We welcome your family to become a valued member of our community.

At the British College of Brazil we teach the English National Curriculum adapted to an international environment, the IGCSE in Year 10 and 11 followed by the IB Diploma Programme in Years 12 and 13. Throughout our core curricula and programs we help your child to develop a global mindset and nurture essential skills such as creativity, collaboration and resilience. We want every student to become lifelong learners, to try something new and, above all, to be ambitious.

We are part of the Nord Anglia Education family of 77 international schools, boarding schools and private schools located in 31 countries around the world. Together we are able to enrich your child's learning experience with opportunities beyond the ordinary.

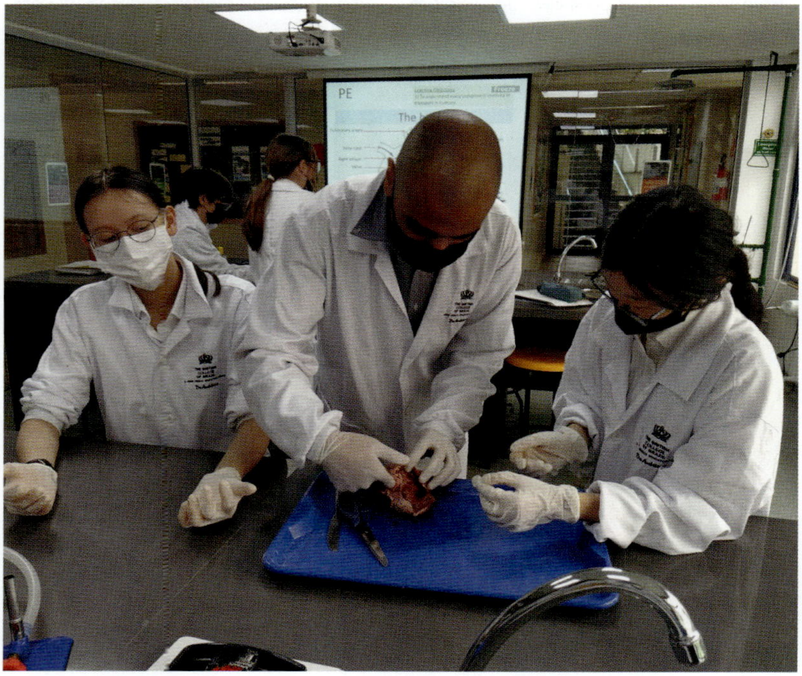

From online debates and challenges, Global Campus connects our students around the world to learn together every day. Our unique international programs provide our students a great opportunity to broaden their horizons, expand cultural knowledge and foster connections. They can either opt for summer camps in exciting locations from Oxford to Florida, to Switzerland, or choose spending a year in one of our boarding schools – Windermere Preparatory School, The Village School or North Broward Preparatory School, through our Study Abroad Program. Through our Global expeditions in Tanzania or Switzerland or participating in our Performing Arts Festival in Miami or in The Global Games in Orlando, Nord Anglia's students grow up with a well-rounded view of the world, a passion for learning and discovery, and life-long memories of achievement and leadership.

Additionally, our collaborations with world leading institutions such as The Julliard School, The Massachusetts Institute of Technology (MIT), and UNICEF enhance the curriculum and offer exceptional professional development for teachers. This approach results in high academic outcomes, and equips students with the skills that are essential to thrive in the 21st century.

We believe that there is no limit to what our students, our people, and our communities can achieve. We encourage your child to set their sights higher by fostering a global perspective together with our school's personalised approach to learning – helping every child to succeed, thrive and love learning.

The British School, Rio de Janeiro

The British School Rio de Janeiro

A caring community, striving for excellence, where every individual matters.

(Founded 1924)

Rua Real Grandeza 99, Botafogo, Rio de Janeiro, RJ 22281-030 Brazil

Tel: +55 21 2539 2717

Email: edu@britishschool.g12.br

Website: www.britishschool.g12.br

Directors: Jeremy Wong/Mark Waldron/ Fernanda Reis

School type: Co-educational Day

Age range of pupils: 2–18 years

No. of pupils enrolled as at 01/09/2022: 2234

Boys: 1037 ***Girls:*** 1197

Fees as at 01/09/2022:

Day: R80,000 approx

Average class size: 12-24

Teacher/pupil ratio: 1:7.3

Founded in 1924, we are a non-profit, independent and coeducational day school offering a complete and coherent curriculum for students of all nationalities from ages 2-18. Our school aims to give students a broad, balanced and relevant educational experience. The educational Philosophy and practice are primarily British in nature with international and Brazilian elements incorporated, where appropriate. The programmes of study are: Early Years Foundation Stage (EYFS) and International Primary Curriculum (IPC) for 2 to 11 year olds; Key Stage 3 (Middle Years) of the UK National Curriculum for 11 to 14 year olds; Cambridge IGCSE for 14 to 16 year olds; and the International Baccalaureate (IB) Diploma for 16 to 18 year olds.

Over 80% of our students are from Brazilian families and the remainder are from over 40 different countries, with British and American students being the biggest proportion. English is the main language of instruction with Portuguese, French and Spanish also being taught.

The school is an IB World School accredited by the Council of International Schools (CIS). The director is a member of the Latin American Heads Conference (LAHC). It has approximately 2200 students located on three sites. The Zona Sul Unit – Botafogo Site houses a primary school and the first year of secondary school. The secondary school is based at the Zona Sul Unit – Urca Site, close to the Sugar Loaf. The Barra Unit is a full unit located in the Barra suburb. It houses a full school with students from age 2 (Pre-Nursery) to age 18 (Class 11 / Year 13).

Classes are generally small and school environment is pleasant, well-resourced and stimulating, with a strong focus on health, safety and security. Performing arts, sports, Model United Nations, Duke of Edinburgh's Award Scheme and work experience provide a wide range of co-curricular opportunities. Experiences beyond the school include numerous local day visits and national or international residential trips for most year groups from primary Class 3 / Year 5 upwards.

Our teachers are well-qualified (some 30% being recruited from overseas) and supported by a robust and effective programme of continuing professional development.

Our school provides a caring and friendly, yet demanding, learning environment and makes every effort to ensure that each individual has the opportunity to develop their particular abilities and talents to the full. The emphasis on academic achievement is also balanced by our concern to meet our students' physical, emotional and social needs. Personal development and social responsibility are an integral part of our educational programme. We place a high value on good social behavior and ethical standards, with respect for the individual and the environment. We want our students to be happy in school and we hope that their school experience will be fondly and warmly remembered for life. We believe that this can be achieved through high expectations; clear guidelines and limits; constant encouragement; and addressing individual needs.

Extracurricular Activities

Football, capoeira, volleyball, basketball, ballet, artistic gymnastics, judo, choir, music (instruments and singing), cooking, drama and arts are available.

Facilities

Air-conditioned classrooms, interactive Whiteboards, computers, laptops, tablets, science and computer & technology & robotics labs, libraries, gymnasiums and open spaces for sports and games, playgrounds with a variety of toys, auditoriums for Drama classes, presentations and art exhibitions, sickbays (first-aid – nurses), and dining halls.

Directory of international schools

International schools in Africa

Schools ordered A–Z by Country

Key to directory

Country	**Whereford**
Name of school or college	**College Academy**
Indicates that this school has a profile	***For further details see p***
Address and contact number	Which Street, Whosville, Wherefordshire AB12 3CD **Tel:** 01000 000000
Head's name	**Head Master:** Dr A Person
Age range	**Age range:** 11–18
Number of pupils. B = boys G = girls VIth = sixth form	**No. of pupils:** 660 B330 G330 VIth 200
Fees per annum. Day = fees for day pupils. WB = fees for weekly boarders. FB = fees for full boarders.	**Fees:** Day £11,000 WB £16,000 FB £20,000
Curriculum	**Curriculum:** National, IBDP, ALevs
Language of instruction	**Language instr:** English, French
Memberships/Accreditation	(AISA) (COB) (EAR)

Key to icons

Key to symbols:

- Boys' school
- Girls' school
- Boarding accommodation

Member of:

- (AISA) Association of International Schools in Africa
- (CEE) Central and Eastern European Schools Association
- (EAR) East Asia Regional Council of Overseas Schools
- (ECIS) European Council of International Schools
- (RS) Round Square

Accreditation:

- (CIS) Council of International Schools
- (COB) Council of British International Schools

Please note: Schools are coeducational day schools unless otherwise indicated

ANGOLA

Luanda International School
Via S6, Bairro de Talatona, Município de Belas, Luanda
Tel: +244 932 337 056
Age range: 3–18
No. of pupils: 416
Curriculum: IBDP, IBMYP, IBPYP
Language instr: English

Lycée Français Alioune Blondin Beye
Zona escolar 1° de Maio (Baïrro), Luanda 5332
Tel: +244 924 946 151

BENIN

EFE Montaigne
Cotonou
Tel: +229 21 30 17 28

English International School
Haie Vive, Cotonou 08 BP 0430
Tel: +229 21 30 92 87
Language instr: English

New Covenant American School International
Lot 1283, Rue 517, Cotonou 08 BP 909
Tel: +229 9764 0832

QSI International School of Benin
Lot #126 & #127, Zone Residentielle de la Radio, Camp Guezo, Cotonou 02 BP 1087
Tel: +229 66 62 12 46

BOTSWANA

Broadhurst Primary School
Private Bag Br 114, 8578 Lenyaphiri Rd, Gaborone
Tel: +267 3971221

Daystar Primary School
Mahalapye
Tel: +267 4711801

Delta Waters International School
Private Bag 0153, Boseja, Maun
Tel: + 267 66 60 560

Enko Botho International School
Plot 60114, Block 7, near Botswana Qualifications Authority and HRDC, Gaborone
Tel: +267 363 54 19
Curriculum: IBDP
Language instr: English

Gaborone International School
P.O. Box AD 590 ADD, Post Net Kgale View, Gaborone
Tel: +267 316 2230
Curriculum: IGCSE

Kgaswe International School
Extension Four, (Next to Magistrates Court), Palapye
Tel: +267 492 0441

Kopano Primary School
PO Box 206, Selebi Phikwe
Tel: +267 2610552

Legae Academy
PO Box 750, Mogoditshane, Kweneng District, Gaborone
Tel: +267 3924 313
Curriculum: UK, IGCSE, ALevs
Language instr: English

Maru-a-Pula School
Plot 4725, Maruapula Way, Gaborone
Tel: +267 391 2953
Curriculum: ALevs

Northside Primary School
PO Box 897, Plot 2786, Tshekedi Crescent Ext 9, Gaborone
Tel: +267 395 2440
Curriculum: IBPYP
Language instr: English

Rainbow Schools
Plot 24436, G-West, Gaborone
Tel: +267 393 6932
Age range: 3–18
Curriculum: ALevs

Thornhill Primary School
PO Box 163, Gaborone
Tel: +267 395 2490

Westwood International School
Phase 4, Plot 22978, Mmankgwedi Road, Gaborone
Tel: +267 390 6736
Age range: 4–19
Curriculum: IBDP, IBMYP, IBPYP, IGCSE
Language instr: English

BURKINA FASO

Enko Ouaga International School
Zogona, venant du Boulevard Charles de Gaulle, premier six-mètres après la mosquée de Zogona à gauche, Ouagadougou
Tel: +226 25 36 01 77
Age range: 11–20 years
Curriculum: IBDP
Language instr: French, English

International School of Ouagadougou
Ouagadougou 01 BP 1142
Tel: +226 50 36 21 43
Age range: 3–19 years
Curriculum: IBDP, SAT
Language instr: English

CAMEROON

Academic School of Excellence
Bastos, Yaoundé
Tel: +237 222 20 03 23
Curriculum: IBDP
Language instr: English, French

African American Academy
53 West Road, President Park, PO Box 6972
Tel: +237 11 310 3040
Curriculum: IGCSE

American School of Douala
BP 1909, Douala
Tel: +237 3342 1437
Age range: 3–16
No. of pupils: 110 *B50 G60*
Curriculum: USA

American School of Yaounde
BP 7475, Yaounde
Tel: +237 2223 0421
Age range: 3–18
No. of pupils: 170 *B85 G85 VIth20*
Curriculum: IBDP, IBMYP, IBPYP
Language instr: English

Enko Bonanjo International School
Rue 1.171, no. 414, in front of Camwater, Bonanjo, Douala
Tel: +237 655 397 144
Age range: 11–19 years
Curriculum: IBDP, IGCSE

Enko La Gaiete International School
P.O. Box 784728, Nouvelle Route Bastos (échangeur simplifié), Yaoundé 14853
Tel: +237 653 23 56 52
Age range: 11–19 years
Curriculum: IBDP, IGCSE
Language instr: English

Rain Forest International School
S I L BP 1299, Yaounde
Tel: +237 677 937 162
Age range: 12–19
No. of pupils: 105
Curriculum: ACT, AP, SAT, TOEFL, USA
Language instr: English

The Bridge International School
Po.Box.: 4157, Douala Bonamoussadi
Tel: +237 698 87 60 19
Curriculum: IPC, UK, IGCSE

COTE D'IVOIRE

Enko Riviera International School
Riviera Golf, Carrefour M'Pouto, Sol Beni, next to the Embassy of Lebanon, Abidjan
Tel: +225 22 54 10 98
Age range: 11–16 years
Curriculum: IBDP, IBMYP
Language instr: English, French

International Community School of Abidjan
Boulevard Arsène Usher Assouan, Riveria III, Abidjan
Tel: +225 22 47 11 52
Age range: 4–18
Curriculum: AP, IBDP, SAT, USA

International University Demonstration School (IUDS)
Cocody, Riviera-Bonoumin, Abidjan 06 06 BP 2556
Tel: +225 22 49 70 90
Age range: 1–19
Curriculum: USA
Language instr: English

DEMOCRATIC REPUBLIC OF THE CONGO

Ecole Internationale Bilingue Le Cartésien (EIBC)
34, 7ème Rue, Q. Industriel, Limete, Kinshasa
Tel: +243 812621704
Age range: 3–19
No. of pupils: 500
Curriculum: IBDP
Language instr: French, English

English-Speaking School of Lubumbashi
1 Route Kipopo (Quartier Golf), Lubumbashi
Tel: +243 81 19 87 013
Language instr: English

Institut Aurora
8 Avenue Kalemie, Commune de la Gombe, Kinshasa
Tel: +243 971 744 509
Curriculum: IBMYP
Language instr: English, French

Jewels International School of Kinshasa
O.U.A., Commune of Ngaliemc, Kinshasa
Tel: +243 99 99 09 163
Curriculum: IBPYP
Language instr: English
AISA

The American School of Kinshasa
Rte de Matadi, Ngaliema Kinshasa I, Kinshasha
Tel: +243 818846619
No. of pupils: 163
Curriculum: AP, IBDP, IBMYP, IBFYP, SAT
AISA

EGYPT

AIA School
Plots 2 & 3 Section 1, Abis, Alexandria
Tel: +20 12 8621 5550
Curriculum: IBDP
Language instr: English, Arabic

Al Afak Al Gadeda International School
1st compound, Behind Police Academy, Infront of Gehaz A Tagamoa Al Awal, New Cairo City, Cairo
Tel: +20 2 2246 4608
Curriculum: USA

Al Bashaer School
Lot 3, Al Shatr District 13, Zahraa El Maadi, Cairo
Tel: +20 2 2517 8305
Curriculum: UK, USA

Al Manar Language School
School's Zone behind the court building, Ismailia
Tel: +20 6 4320 3125

Alexandria House of English
KM 8 Alexandria-Cairo Agriculture Rd, Alexandria
Tel: +20 3 500 3007
Curriculum: National, UK, USA, IGCSE, ALevs

AlWaha Language Schools-American School
Mariotic, Behind Cataract Hotel, Giza
Tel: +20 2 3382 1900
Curriculum: USA

Amal Language School
18 ST 105 Maadi Al Khabiri Al Wasti Al Maadi, Cairo
Tel: +20 1 1411 43111
Curriculum: National, UK, USA

American International School in Egypt – West Campus
Sheikh Zayed City, Entrance 2, Greens Compound, Giza 12588
Tel: +20 2 3854 0600
Curriculum: IBDP
ECIS

American International School in Egypt, Main Campus
PO Box 8090, Masaken, Nasr City, Cairo 11371
Tel: +20 2 2618 8400
Age range: 4–18
No. of pupils: 1408 *B829 G579*
Curriculum: AP, IBDP, SAT, USA
Language instr: English
CIS ECIS

American School Beverly Hills Cairo
El-Sheikh zayed city, 6th of October City, Cairo
Tel: +20 2 3857 0510
Curriculum: USA

American School of Alexandria
Off Gamila Abu Hreid Street, Seouff Shaman, Alexandria
Tel: +20 3 330 7555
Age range: 4–18
No. of pupils: 217
Curriculum: AP, USA

Amgad International School – Maadi
Taqseem Lasilky, New Maadi Behind Caltex Gaz station, ELnasr Street
Tel: +20 2 25166619
Age range: 4–19
Curriculum: USA, IGCSE

Bedayia International School
1st Urban Distrcit, El Banafseg Zone, New Cairo City, Cairo 11865
Curriculum: IBDP
Language instr: English

British Columbia Canadian International School
5th Settlement Section, 34 Suez Road Entrance, P.O Box 98, El Sherouk City, Cairo
Tel: +20 1 0021 28112

Cairo American College
PO Box 39, Maadi, Cairo 11431
Tel: +20 2 2755 5555
Age range: 4–18
No. of pupils: 850 *B446 G404*
Curriculum: ACT, AP, IBDP, IBPYP, SAT, USA
Language instr: English
ECIS

Cairo British School
39 El Kods El Sharif Street, Lebanon Square, Mohandeseen, Cairo 12411
Tel: +20 23 346 0109
Age range: 2–11
No. of pupils: 99 *B50 G49*
Curriculum: SAT, UK
Language instr: English

Cairo Covenant School
27 Mohammed Sabri Ali, Almazah, Heliopolis, Cairo
Curriculum: USA

Cairo English School
PO Box 8020, Masaken, Nasr City, Cairo 11371
Tel: +20 22 249 0200
Age range: 3–15
No. of pupils: 457 *B297 G160*
Curriculum: IBDP, UK
Language instr: English
CIS ECIS

Cairo Modern International School
1st compound, Al Rehab City main road, Cairo
Tel: +20 23442859
Curriculum: USA

Carleton College
Greenland Compound, Al-Shorouk City, Cairo

City International School – American City College
16 Shagaret El Dor St, Zamalek, Cairo
Tel: +20 2 2736 0285
Curriculum: USA, IGCSE

Collège Saint-Marc
El Shatby, Alexandria 21526
Tel: +20 3 597 2709
Age range: 4–18
No. of pupils: 2700

Creative International School
Korneish El Nil, Imababa, Qanater Road, Giza, Cairo
Tel: +20 2 3891 1037
Curriculum: USA

Dar El Tarbiah School
(IGCSE School Zamalek Campus), 24 Ismail Mohamed Street, Zamalek, Cairo
Tel: +20 2 7360472
Curriculum: USA, IGCSE

Delta American School
8 Talkha, Damietta Highway, Mansoura, Dakahlia
Tel: +20 1 0907 00727
Age range: 5–18
Curriculum: USA

Deutsche Evangelische Oberschule Kairo
P.O. Box 131, Orman, Cairo
Tel: +20 2 3748 1475

Deutsche Schule Beverly Hills Kairo
Beverly Hills, 16th District, Beverly Hills Rd, Giza, Cairo
Tel: +20 38578070
Curriculum: IBDP
Language instr: English

Deutsche Schule der Borromäerinnen Alexandria
32, Rue Salah-El-Dine, Alexandria 21131
Tel: +20 3 398 0145

Deutsche Schule der Borromäerinnen Kairo
8, Mohamed Mahmoud Str., Bab El Louk, Cairo 11111
Tel: +20 2 27900088

Deutsche Schule Hurghada
Post Box 99, Hurghada, Red Sea
Tel: +20 100 4612747
Curriculum: IBDP
Language instr: English

Dover American International School
Street 10, Hamza Ibn Abdel-Motaleb, Zone (9) El- Shorouk City, Cairo
Tel: +20 2 2479 6120
Curriculum: USA

Dr Nermien Ismail Language School NIS
Tagamoa El-Awaal, End of Zakor Hussein, Cairo
Tel: +20 114 5599992
Curriculum: IBDP, UK, USA, IGCSE
Language instr: English

Dream International School
Champs Elysee, St. Dream Land, 6th October City, Giza
Tel: +20 2 38580661
Curriculum: National, USA

Ecole Oasis Internationale
Zahraa El Maadi, Quarter no 3 and no 7 Part A & B, Cairo
Tel: +20 2 2516 2608
Age range: 3–18 years
No. of pupils: 1445
Curriculum: IBDP, IBMYP, IBPYP, IBCP
Language instr: French
CIS

Egypt British International School
5th Urban District, El Banafseg Zone, Area 1, New Cairo City, Cairo
Tel: +20 2 2920 010
Age range: 3–18
No. of pupils: 1000
Curriculum: UK
COB

Egypt Modern School
1 km after Abis Gate, Cairo-Alexandria Agricultural Road, Alexandria 21529
Tel: +20 1 2277 86406
Age range: 4–19
No. of pupils: 75
Curriculum: USA

Egyptian English Language School
Moustafa Kamel St behind Fire Station, Mandara, Alexandria
Tel: +20 5321040
Curriculum: National, UK, USA, IGCSE

Egyptian Language School (Katameya Campus)
5th Compound, Katameya, Cairo
Tel: +20 2 759 2270
Curriculum: National, UK, USA, IGCSE

El Alsson British and American International Schools – New Giza
PO Box 16, KM 22 Cairo-Alex Road, Smart Village, Cairo 12577
Tel: +202 38270800
Age range: 3–18 years
No. of pupils: 2500
Curriculum: UK, USA
Language instr: English

El Fouad International School
El-Ahrar Rd, Kafr Mohammed Hussein, El-Shaheed Ahmed Fouar Bakr St, Zagazig, Sharqia
Tel: +55 2375551
No. of pupils: 2000
Curriculum: USA, IGCSE

El Gouna International School
Downtown El Gouna, Near Hurghada, Red Sea 84513
Tel: +20 65 3580080
Age range: 3.5–18 years
No. of pupils: 251
Curriculum: National, UK, IGCSE, ALevs

El Massira Integrated School
10th of Ramadan City, N.B 7, Sharqia
Tel: +20 2 15 383 501
No. of pupils: 4000
Curriculum: USA

Elite International School
Behind El-Nozha airport, Abesten ring road, Alexandria
Tel: +20 109 330 7078
Age range: 3–16 years
No. of pupils: 350
Curriculum: IBDP, IBMYP, IBPYP
Language instr: English, Arcbic

El-Quds Language Schools
American Division – Moustafa kamel St., Off 45 St Miami, Alexandria
Tel: +20 3 962 5553
Curriculum: National, UK, USA, IGCSE

El-Rowad School
8 Mostafa El Nahhas St.8th District, Nasr City, Cairo
Tel: +20 24723685

Europa-Schule Kairo
Abdel Malik Ben Marwan Street, Tagamoa El Khames, New Cairo City, Cairo
Tel: +20 2 25373301

Evolution International School
New Giza Campus, Km 22, Cairo/Alex desert Road, 6th October City, Giza 12588
Tel: +20 1 0036 66223
Curriculum: IBDP
Language instr: English

FES Futures International School
Behind Shooting Club, Investors Land, Kattemeya, Cairo
Tel: +20 1 275793041
Curriculum: FrenchBacc, UK, USA

GEMS Academy Alexandria
Kilo 13 Alexandria-Cairo Agricultural Road, Alexandria
Tel: +2 03 5190 800
Curriculum: IBPYP, FrenchBacc, UK
Language instr: English, French

Global Paradigm International School
First Settlement, Block K1, Sector 8, New Cairo City, Cairo 16834
Tel: +20 222 461 809/10/12
Curriculum: IBDP
Language instr: English

Green Heights International School
First District, Alamn Alaam Compound, Behind Mirage City, New Cairo City, Cairo
Tel: +20 2 2328 5079
Curriculum: UK, USA, IGCSE

Green Land – Pré Vert International Schools – GPIS-Egypt
405, Geziret Mohamed Road, Giza
Tel: +20 2 01002226053/50/54
Age range: 3–18
No. of pupils: 1123
Curriculum: IBDP, IBMYP, IBPYP
Language instr: French, English, Arabic

Hayah International Academy
South of Police Academy, 5th District, New Cairo
Tel: +202 25373000/3333
No. of pupils: 1467
Curriculum: IBDP, IBPYP
Language instr: English

Heritage International School
P.O. Box 38, 12568 6th of October City, Giza
Tel: +20 2 3825 3688/9
Curriculum: USA

IBCA International School
Qetaa an Nahdah, Amreya 1, Alexandria
Tel: +20 3 955 6000
Curriculum: IBDP, IBMYP, IBPYP
Language instr: English

Integrated Thebes American College in Cairo
Box 3021 Madinat Alsalam, Cairo
Tel: +20 22 4772317
Age range: 3–18
No. of pupils: 500
Curriculum: USA

International American School of Alexandria
Agriculture Road, 2k pass abees Gate, Alexandria
Tel: +20 3 955 4334
Curriculum: USA

International Arab Egyptian School
Kilo 4.5, Ezz El Din, Ismailia
Tel: +20 264 3312327
Age range: 3–18
No. of pupils: 145 B40 G105
Curriculum: National

International New Future School (Neue Deutsche Schule Alexandria)
El Prince Street, off Moustafa Kamel Street, Mandara Kebly, Alexandria
Tel: +203 958 64 81
Curriculum: IBDP
Language instr: English

International School of Elite Education
Road 90- Behind El Masraweya Compound, Cairo 11835
Tel: :+20 111 114 3225
Age range: 4–18
Curriculum: IBDP, UK, USA

International Schools of Egypt – Alexandria
PO Box 402, Sidi Gaber, Alexandria
Tel: +20 3 54 4498
Age range: 3–18
No. of pupils: 210 B120 G90
Curriculum: National, UK, IGCSE
ECIS

International Schools of Kenana – American Division
30th KM Cairo Ismalia Road, Cairo
Tel: + 20 12 279 400 75
Curriculum: USA

Irish School Cairo – Dokki Primary & Nursery
33 Hussein street, Dokki, Cairo
Tel: +20 2 3337 2044
Curriculum: UK

Jana Dan International School
Al Gamea Al Haditha St, Al Abageyah, Qism El-Khalifa, Cairo
Tel: +20 111 330 1111
Curriculum: USA

Leaders International College
21 El Narges Service Area, 5th Settlement, New Cairo City, Cairo
Tel: +20 127 292 4777
Curriculum: IBDP, IBMYP, IBPYP
Language instr: English

Lycée Français du Caire
Terrain no. 5, Division Cité El Meerag, 2ème Megawara, Cairo
Tel: +20 2 2726 0900
Curriculum: FrenchBacc

Lycée International Balzac
Le Nouveau Caire, 5ème Arrondissement, Rue 90 El Shamaly, Cairo
Tel: +20 2 253 793 58/61
Curriculum: FrenchBacc

Maadi British International School
4th District next to Wadi Degla Club, Zahraa El Maadi, Cairo
Tel: +20 22 7058671/2/3/4/5
Age range: 3–11
No. of pupils: 370 B180 G190
Curriculum: SAT, UK
Language instr: English
COB ECIS

Maadi Community School
Building 10, Road 77, Maadi, Cairo 11431
Tel: +20 2 2358 5911
Age range: 3–14
No. of pupils: 81
Curriculum: USA, IGCSE

Majesty International Schools
Plot (1-2), AlKhamayel Phase III, El Shiekh Zayed City, Giza
Tel: +20 10 305 03000
Age range: 3–16 years
No. of pupils: 350
Curriculum: UK, USA
Language instr: English

MALVERN COLLEGE EGYPT
For further details see p. 52
B2-B3 South Ring Road, Investment Zone Kattameya, Cairo
Tel: +202 26144400
Email: info@malverncollege.edu.eg
Website: malverncollege.edu.eg
Headmaster & Head of Secondary School: Richard Moore
Age range: 2.6–18 years
No. of pupils: 920
Fees: *Day* E£130,000–E£277,000
Curriculum: IBDP, IGCSE, ALevs
Language instr: English

Manarat El Mostaqbal American School
Opposite Carrefour, City Center, off the Qattamiya Ring Road, Mokattam, Cairo
Tel: +20 2 7296788
Curriculum: USA

Manaret Heliopolis International School
Hazem Salah Street, Ext. Mostafa El Nahas, Nasr City, Cairo 11351
Tel: +20 224 71 33 32
Age range: 3–13 years
No. of pupils: 600
Curriculum: IBDP, IBMYP, IBPYP
Language instr: English

Manor House American School – Middle & High School
59 El Hussein Street, Dokki, Cairo
Tel: +20 33371067
Age range: 10–18
Curriculum: USA, IGCSE

Mansoura College
Mansoura-Demietta Road, Mansoura, Dakahlia
Tel: +20 50 258 8888
Age range: 4–18
Curriculum: USA, IGCSE
Language instr: English

Memphis International School
K 36 Misr Ismailia Road, Infront of El Sherouk City Gate 1, Cairo
Tel: +20 102 538 9021
Curriculum: USA

Menese International School
29Km. Misr Ismailia Road, Cairo
Tel: +202 24772241/2
Curriculum: USA

Misr Language School – American Section
Beginning Of Cairo-Fayoum Highway, Remayah Sq, Giza
Tel: +20 2 3376 0170
Age range: 3–18
No. of pupils: 2655
Curriculum: USA, ALevs

Modern Education Schools
Street 2, 1st District, Area No 4, 5th Settlement, New Cairo City, Cairo 11835
Tel: +20 2 2758 3307
Age range: 4–19
Curriculum: SAT, UK, USA, IGCSE

Modern English School Cairo
South of Police Academy, PO Box 5, New Cairo City, Cairo 11835
Tel: +202 2618 9600
Age range: 3.5–18
No. of pupils: 2136
Curriculum: ACT, AP, IBDP, SAT, UK, USA, IGCSE, ALevs
Language instr: English
ECIS

Mokatam Language and International School
Land piece 7377 area F, PO Box 116, Cairo
Tel: +20 2 2507 9167
Age range: 4–18
Curriculum: IGCSE
Language instr: English, Arabic

Narmer American College
20 El-Narguis Service Area, New Cairo City, Cairo 11477
Tel: +202 29201200
Age range: 3–18
Curriculum: AP, IBDP, SAT, USA, IGCSE
Language instr: English

Nefertari International School
Km 22 Cairo-Ismailia Desert Road, Nefertari Street, Cairo 11341
Tel: +20 1026604040
Age range: 3–18
No. of pupils: 4542
Curriculum: IBDP, FrenchBacc, SAT, IGCSE
Language instr: English, Arabic

New Cairo British International School
Road 17, 1st Zone, 3rd Settlement, 5th District, New Cairo City, Cairo
Tel: +20 2 2565 7115
Age range: 3–18
No. of pupils: 710
Curriculum: IBDP, IBPYP, National, UK, GCSE, IGCSE, ALevs
Language instr: English
CIS COB ECIS

New Castle International School
Al Bashair District, in Al Bashair Service Center, 6th of October City, Giza
Tel: +20 1 023680517
Curriculum: IBDP
Language instr: English, Arabic

New Generation International Schools
27th KM Cairo-Ismailia Rd, Cairo
Tel: +20 2 24772258
Curriculum: USA

New Horizon International School
PO Box 1079, Maadi, Cairo
Tel: +20 2 2733 2058
Age range: 4–16
Curriculum: National, UK, IGCSE
CIS ECIS

New Horizon Junior & High School
PO Box 1079, Zahraa Al Maadi City, Sector #3, Maadi, Cairo
Tel: +20 22 516 2685
Age range: 4–17
No. of pupils: 539 *B*277 *G*262
Curriculum: GCSE
ECIS

New Ramses College
PO Box 2035, 14 Lofty El Saied St Ghamra, Cairo Box 2035
Tel: +20 2 26 824 008

New Vision International Schools
S1-14 Beverly Hills, Sheikh Zayed, Giza 12588
Tel: 0020 120 4265778
Curriculum: IBDP, IBMYP, IBPYP
Language instr: Arabic, English

Notion International School
Metwaly el Sharawy street (Lebeny), Maryotyah, Giza
Tel: +20 1120004926
Curriculum: IBDP, IBMYP, IBPYP
Language instr: English

October Manor House International School
5th District, First Suburb, New Cairo City, Cairo
Tel: +20 2 26 17 21 33
Curriculum: SAT, UK, IGCSE

Orouba Language School – Dokki
8 Hussein Wassef Street, Dokki, Giza, Cairo
Tel: +20 3 748 4496

Orouba Language School – Maadi
1 Amr Street, District 6, New Maadi, Cairo
Tel: +20 2 516 8091

Own Heliopolis Language School
The Mosque Street, Fifth Area, Misr Construction Buildings, Heliopolis, Cairo
Tel: +20 106 407 0705

Pakistan International School
12 Midan Tehran, Dokki, Cairo
Tel: +2 (0)2 2737 2417
Age range: 3–18
No. of pupils: 300

Pioneers International School
Moustafa Kamel Street, Behind El Malaha fire station, Mandara, Alexandria
Tel: +20 35 371 820
Age range: 5–18
Curriculum: ALevs

Port Said International Schools
Mohamed Aly Street (In front of Golf), Port Said
Tel: +20 66 372 9644 / 374 3724 / 374 3728

Princeton International School
Zizinia, 5th Settlement, Close to AUC Gate 4, New Cairo City, Cairo
Tel: +20 10 9149 7999
Curriculum: IBDP, IBPYP
Language instr: English, French

Rahn Schulen Kairo
Extension of Hassan Ma'moun Str., Zaher Buildings, Nasr City, Cairo 11371
Tel: +20 10 27933321
Curriculum: IBDP
Language instr: German

Rajac Language School
Km 30 Cairo-Ismailia Desert Road, Ismailia, Cairo
Tel: +20 2 24772201
Age range: 4–19
No. of pupils: 2700
Curriculum: USA, IGCSE

Saint Fatima School
66 Ismael El Kabbany Street, First District, Nasr City, Cairo
Tel: +20 2 22600961
Age range: 4–19
No. of pupils: 300
Curriculum: USA

Saint Peter's School
3 Abdel Rahman El Rafei Street, Hegaz Square, Heliopolis, Cairo
Tel: +2 (0)2 26235797
Curriculum: USA

Salahaldin International School
Yasmeen Service Court, Land No 90, 5th Compound, New Cairo City, Cairo
Tel: +20 2 26133473
Age range: 4–18 years
Curriculum: IBDP
Language instr: English, Arabic

Sama American School
Maadi, Kattameya ring road, Opposite Carrefour, Cairo
Tel: +20 2 27304101
Curriculum: USA

Schutz American School
Post Box 1000, Alexandria
Tel: +20 3 576 2205
Age range: 3–18 years
Curriculum: IBPYP
Language instr: English, Arabic

Sharm International British School
PO Box 56, Halomy Street, Sharm El Sheikh, South Sinai
Tel: +20 10 0046 4175
Age range: 2–16
Curriculum: UK, IGCSE
Language instr: English

Sheraton Heliopolis Language Schools
2 Khaled Ibn El Walid st., Sheraton District, Cairo
Tel: +20 2 22662090
Curriculum: USA

SKILLS – Suad Kafafi International Language Learning Schools
Manasourriah 2 Km from Ring Road, By Saqqara Pyramid, Giza
Tel: +20 2 33624788
Age range: 2–18
Curriculum: USA

Smart International Schools
Abeess 4th, School Complex, Alexandria
Tel: +20 1 2700 39367
Age range: 2–16 years
Curriculum: IGCSE
Language instr: English

St. John American School
KM 30 Cairo – Suez Road, Patmos, Cairo
Tel: +20 2 29228114
Curriculum: USA

St. Joseph American School
PO Box 82, Banks Street, Um el Sid, Hadaba, Sharm El Sheikh, South Sinai 46619
Tel: +20 100 210 8164
Curriculum: USA

Sunrise International School
Mubarak 1, Behind Nile Hospital, Hurghada, Red Sea
Tel: +20 65 3554660

Taymour English School – Roushdy Branch
14 Roushdy Street, Roushdy, Alexandria
Tel: +20 3 522 3021
Age range: 3–18
No. of pupils: 400

The British International School, Cairo
PO Box 137, Gezira, Cairo
Tel: +202 3827 0444
Age range: 3–18 years
Curriculum: IBDP, UK, GCSE, IGCSE
Language instr: English
COB

The British School Al Rehab
Al Rehab City, Suez Road, New Cairo City, Cairo
Tel: +202 2 607 0292
Age range: 3–18
No. of pupils: 940 *B*516 *G*424
Curriculum: UK, IGCSE, ALevs
Language instr: English
COB

The British School in Cairo
D3 Ring Road Maadi, Cairo
Tel: +20 100 250 67 08
Age range: 3–18
No. of pupils: 400
Curriculum: National, UK

The British School Madinaty
Talaat Mostafa Road, Madinaty City, Suez Road, Cairo 19511
Tel: +20 221 109 874/5/6
Age range: 4–11
Curriculum: IPC, UK
Language instr: English
COB

The British School of Egypt
9th Zone Service Centre, Sheikh Zayed City, Giza
Tel: +20 120 8787 015
Age range: 4–18
No. of pupils: 300
Curriculum: UK, IGCSE
COB

The British School, Alexandria
Mahmoud Aboul Ela Street, Kafr Abdou, Roushd, Alexandria
Tel: +2 03 544 5426
Age range: 3–18
No. of pupils: 530 *B*270 *G*260 *VIth*25
Curriculum: UK, GCSE, IGCSE, ALevs
Language instr: English
COB

The International School of Choueifat – Cairo
Fifth Urban Community, New Cairo City, Cairo
Tel: +20 2 2542 8777
ECIS

The International School of Choueifat – City of 6 October
Dreamland, City of 6 October, Cairo 12582
Tel: +20 100 606 9001
Age range: 3–15
No. of pupils: 102 *B*58 *G*44
ECIS

The International School of Egypt
El Tessen Road, 5th Settlement, District 6, Zone 2, New Cairo City, Cairo
Tel: +20 2 2564 7038
Curriculum: IBDP
Language instr: English

Uptown International School
Al Abageyah, El Mukkatam, Cairo 11571
Tel: +20 12 2584 7419
Curriculum: IBPYP
Language instr: English, Arabic

Windrose Academy
Plot 1 B Investment Land, Maadi, Cairo
Tel: +20122 4777177
Age range: 3–13
Curriculum: UK
Language instr: English

ERITREA

Asmara International Community School (AICS)
Asmara
Tel: +291 1 161705
Age range: 2–19
Curriculum: IBDP, IPC, TOEFL, USA
Language instr: English
AISA

ESWATINI

Sifundzani School
Fonteyn Road, Mbabane
Tel: +268 404 1157
Age range: 5–17
No. of pupils: 623 *B*279 *G*344
AISA

UFS International
Jabula Crescent, Mhlambanyatsi
Tel: +268 2467 4134
Age range: 5–13
Curriculum: National, UK
Language instr: English

Waterford Kamhlaba UWC of Southern Africa
Waterford Park, Mbabane H100
Tel: +268 24220867
Age range: 11–20 years
No. of pupils: 600
Curriculum: IBDP, IGCSE
Language instr: English

ETHIOPIA

Andinet International School
P.O. Box 1289, Addis Ababa
Tel: +251 11 6479986/9
Curriculum: AICE, UK, IGCSE, ALevs

Bingham Academy
PO Box 4937, Addis Ababa
Tel: +251 11 27 91 791
Age range: 4–18
No. of pupils: 330 *B*170 *G*160 *VIth*23
Curriculum: SAT, GCSE, IGCSE, ALevs
Language instr: English
AISA

British International School, Addis Ababa
Ring Road, Bole, Addis Ababa
Tel: +251 11 663 07 07
Curriculum: UK
Language instr: English
AISA

German Embassy School Addis Ababa
PO Box 1372, Addis Abeba
Tel: +251 11 553 4465
Age range: 1–18
No. of pupils: 300
Curriculum: IBDP
Language instr: English, German

International Community School of Addis Ababa
Mauritania Road, Old Airport, Addis Ababa
Tel: +251 11 317 1544
Age range: 3–18
No. of pupils: *B*405 *G*394
Curriculum: ACT, IBDP, IBPYP, SAT, USA
Language instr: English
AISA

Lycée Franco-Éthiopien Guébré-Mariam
Churchill Road, BP 1496, Addis Ababa
Tel: +251 11 155 16 03
Curriculum: FrenchBacc

One Planet International School
P.O. Box 3115 Code 1250, Addis Ababa
Tel: +251 116 18 10 10
Curriculum: USA

Sandford International School
PO Box 30056 MA, Addis Ababa
Tel: +251 111 233726
Age range: 3–18
Curriculum: IBDP
Language instr: English
AISA

GABON

American International School Libreville
BP 4000, Quartier Glass, Libreville
Tel: +241 0174 3332
Language instr: English
AISA

Lycée Franco-Britannique Ecole Internationale
Batterie V, B.P. 159, Libreville
Tel: +241 01 17 37 117
Age range: 3–18 years
No. of pupils: 200
Curriculum: IBDP, IBMYP, IBPYP
Language instr: French, English

The International School of Gabon Ruban Vert
Batterie IV, Libreville, Gabon 2144
Tel: +241 11 44 26 70
Age range: 2–19 years
Curriculum: IBDP, IBPYP
Language instr: English, French
AISA

GHANA

Accra Grammar School (AGS)
P.O. Box VV54, Accra-Dodowa Road, Oyibi
Tel: +233 (0)27 700 0034
Curriculum: USA

Akosombo International School
PO Box 77, Akosombo
Tel: +233 034 2290032
Age range: 4–18
No. of pupils: 2049

Alpha Beta Education Centres – Primary, JHS & Christian College
3 High Street, Dansoman opp. Total Filling Station, Sahara
Tel: +233 (0)302 308 002
Curriculum: IGCSE, ALevs

Al-Rayan International School
Boundry Road, East Legon, Accra
Tel: +233 (0)541 897254
Age range: 2–19
No. of pupils: 550 *B287 G253*
Curriculum: IBDP, IBMYP, IBPYP, IBCP, SAT, UK, IGCSE
Language instr: English, French
AISA

Association International School
6 Patrice Lumumba Road, Airport Residential Area, Accra
Tel: +233 0302 777735
Age range: 2–18
No. of pupils: 400
Curriculum: AP, IBDP, IBMYP, UK, USA, IGCSE
Language instr: English

Aves International Academy
VRA Road Community 25, Tema
Tel: +233 266 153097
Curriculum: IBDP
Language instr: English

Cornerstone International Academy
No.2. Harare Street, Off Mensah Wood Avenue, East Legon, Accra
Tel: +233 265 055439
Curriculum: IBPYP
Language instr: English, French

Datus International School
Fraiser Road, P.O.Box cs 8001, Tema Community 7, Tema
Tel: +233 55 738 7463
Curriculum: IBPYP
Language instr: English

Dayspring International Academy
PO Box AF 1814, Adenta
Tel: +233 242511271

Delhi Private School (DPS) International Ghana
Community 25, Tema
Tel: +233 55 662 0540
Curriculum: IBDP
Language instr: English

DPS International Ghana
Community 25, Tema
Tel: +233 556620540
Curriculum: IGCSE, ALevs

Galaxy International School
3rd Osu Badu Link Airport, West Residential Area, Accra
Tel: +233 302 911 646
Curriculum: IGCSE, ALevs
Language instr: English
AISA COB

German Swiss International School
P.O. Box 30526, Ring Road Central, Accra
Tel: +233 (0)302 22 35 22

Ghana Christian International High School
Box DD 66, Dodowa
Tel: +233 0307079798
Curriculum: UK

Ghana International School
PO Box 2856, Accra
Tel: +233 21 777163/773299/775143
Age range: 3–18
No. of pupils: 1174 *B624 G550*
Curriculum: UK, USA, ALevs
Language instr: English
AISA CIS

Healthy-Mind International School
Boundary Road, Madina, Accra
Tel: +233 (0)55 139 9944
Curriculum: IBPYP
Language instr: English, French

International Community College
No. BAE 29, Baatsona Community 16, Tema
Tel: +233 302 969 529
Age range: 11–18
No. of pupils: 300
Curriculum: IGCSE

International Community School Ghana (ICS Ghana) – Accra Campus
Opposite Mensvic Hotel, East Legon, Accra
Tel: +233 (0) 302 541652
Curriculum: UK, IGCSE, ALevs
RS

International Community School Ghana (ICS Ghana) – Kumasi Campus
Pakyi No. 1, P.O Box KS 10631, Kumasi
Tel: +233 (0) 322091443
Curriculum: UK, IGCSE, ALevs
Language instr: English
RS

International School of Ahafo
c/o Newmont Ghana Gold Limited, 40/41 Senchi Street, Airport Residential Area, PMB, Airport Post Office, Accra
Tel: +233 503 017 826
Age range: 4–14
No. of pupils: 35
Curriculum: IPC
AISA

LAS Liberty School
43 Kinshasa Avenue, East Legon, PO Box CT 8373, Accra
Tel: +233 (0)501 454 292
Age range: 3 months–18 years
No. of pupils: 100
Curriculum: SAT, USA
Language instr: English
AISA

Le Lycée Français d'Accra – J Prévert
6 Tanbu Street, East Legon, PO Box CT 1813, Cantonments
Tel: +233 302 50 71 71
Curriculum: FrenchBacc

Learning Skills International School
Adjiringanor, Near Buildaf Estates, Accra
Tel: +233 546 88 4146
Curriculum: IBPYP
Language instr: English

Lincoln Community School
#126/21 Reindolf Road, Abelemkpe, Accra
Tel: +233 302 21 8100
Age range: 4–18 years
No. of pupils: 560
Curriculum: IBDP, IBMYP, IBPYP, SAT
Language instr: English
AISA CIS

Merton International School
PO Box OS 1740, Osu, Accra
Tel: +233 302 220174
Age range: 4–16
No. of pupils: 100
Curriculum: UK, IGCSE

Morgan International Community School
PO Box SW 63, Gomoa-Manso, Swedru
Tel: +233 205 560 199
Curriculum: IBDP, SAT, IGCSE
Language instr: English

SOS-Hermann Gmeiner International College
Private Mail Bag, Community 6, Tema
Tel: +233 303 202907
Age range: 14–18
No. of pupils: 319 *B157 G162*
Curriculum: IBDP, IBMYP, ALevs
Language instr: English
AISA ISA

Takoradi International School
PO Box 453, Takoradi
Tel: +233 31 20 25 681
AISA

Tema International School
PO Box CO 864, Tema International Close, Tema
Tel: +233 24 9637 762; +233 30 3305134
Age range: 11–19
No. of pupils: 320 *B160 G160*
Curriculum: IBDP, IBMYP, IBPYP, IGCSE
Language instr: English
ISA

The Hilltop School
University P. O. Box. 212, Kumasi
Tel: +233 (0)322 299 229
Age range: 5–18
No. of pupils: 900
Curriculum: IGCSE, ALevs

The Owl's Nest International School
4, Shippi Close, Cantonments, Accra
Tel: +233 245 113 227
Age range: 18 months–7
Curriculum: UK

The Roman Ridge School
PO Box GP 21057, 8 Onyasia Crescent, Roman Ridge, Accra
Tel: +233 302 780456 / 7
Age range: 4–18
No. of pupils: 434 *B226 G208 VIth30*
Curriculum: National, ALevs
Language instr: English

Vilac International School
Adjacent Redeemed Baptist Church, Off ARS-IPS PO Box Ms444,Mile 7,Achimota
Tel: +233 302 410516

GUINEA

American International School of Conakry
Nongo Stadium, Conakry
Tel: +224 654 28 4530
Age range: 2–18
Curriculum: USA
Language instr: English

KENYA

Aga Khan Academy Mombasa
PO Box 80100-90066 Mbuyuni Road, Kizingo, Mombasa
Tel: +254 (0)735 931 144
Age range: 6–18 years
No. of pupils: 673
Curriculum: IBDP, IBMYP, IBPYP
Language instr: English, Swahili

Braeburn Garden Estate School
PO Box 16944, 00620 Mobil Plaza, Nairobi
Tel: +254 720 667 622
Age range: 2–20
No. of pupils: 754
Curriculum: IBDP, IBCP, UK, IGCSE, ALevs
Language instr: English

Braeburn Imani International School
PO Box 750, 00100 Thika
Tel: +254 (0)20 2029322/44
Age range: 2–18
No. of pupils: 230
Curriculum: UK, IGCSE, ALevs
Language instr: English

Braeburn Kisumu International School
PO Box 1276, 40100 Kisumu
Tel: +254 (057) 202 3471
Age range: 18 months–16 years
No. of pupils: 110
Curriculum: UK, IGCSE

Braeburn Mombasa International School
PO Box 83009, 80100 Mombasa
Tel: +254 20 202 6156
Age range: 2–18
No. of pupils: 185
Curriculum: UK, IGCSE, ALevs
Language instr: English

Braeburn Nanyuki International School
PO Box 1537, 10400 Nanyuki
Tel: +254 (0)20 211 3624
Age range: 2–13
No. of pupils: 140
Curriculum: UK

Braeburn School
PO Box 45112, 00100 Nairobi
Tel: +254 20 5018000
Age range: 3–18
No. of pupils: 900
Curriculum: IGCSE, ALevs
Language instr: English

Braeside School
PO Box 25578, 00603 Nairobi
Tel: +254 20 501 8000
Age range: 2–18
No. of pupils: 960
Curriculum: UK, IGCSE, ALevs

Brookhouse School, Karen
Magadi Road, Nairobi
Tel: +254 (0)722 204 413
Curriculum: UK
Language instr: English

Brookhouse School, Runda
Off Kiambu Road, Nairobi
Tel: +254 (0)704 392 000
Curriculum: UK
Language instr: English

Cavina School
PO Box 43090, Nairobi
Tel: +254 20 2573630 / +254 706232334
Age range: 3–13
No. of pupils: 200 *B100 G100*
Curriculum: UK
Language instr: English

Coast Academy
PO Box 82988, Mombasa
Tel: +254 202107788
Curriculum: UK, IGCSE, ALevs

German School Nairobi (Michael Grzimek Schule)
Limuru Road, opposite Village Market, P.O. Box 978, 00621 Nairobi
Tel: + 254 0721 258417

Greensteds International School
Private Bag, Nakuru
Tel: +254 50 50770
Age range: 6–18
No. of pupils: 280
Curriculum: UK

HILLCREST PREPARATORY SCHOOL
For further details see p. 49
Langata Road, Karen, Nairobi
Tel: +254 724 256173
Age range: 18 months–13 years
No. of pupils: 270
Curriculum: UK

HILLCREST SECONDARY SCHOOL
For further details see p. 49
PO Box 24819 -00502 Karen, Langata Rd, Nairobi
Tel: +254 733 255442
Email: admin@hillcrest.ac.ke
Website: www.hillcrest.ac.ke
Head of Secondary: John Eveson
Age range: 13–18 years
No. of pupils: 570
Curriculum: UK, IGCSE, ALevs
Language instr: English

International School of Kenya
End of Peponi Road/Kirawa Road, PO Box 14103, Nairobi 00800
Tel: +254 20 209 1308/9
Age range: 4–18 *B4–18 G4–18*
No. of pupils: 874
Curriculum: IBDP, SAT, USA
Language instr: English

Kenton College Preparatory School
PO Box 25406 – 00603, Lavington, Nairobi
Tel: +254 020 3541 513
Age range: 6–13+
No. of pupils: 362 *B176 G186*
Curriculum: UK
Language instr: English

Light Academy Schools
PO BOX 13413, Nairobi 00100
Tel: +254 724 10 00 00

Light International School (LIS) Mombasa
Off Greenwood Drive, Nyali, PO Box 1835 80100
Tel: 00254733968605
Age range: 14–19
Curriculum: UK, IGCSE

Lycee Denis Diderot
PO Box 47525, Nairobi 100
Tel: +254 20 2437 714
Age range: 3–19
Curriculum: FrenchBacc

Mombasa Academy
Sea-view Road – Nyali, P.O. Box 86487-80100, Mombasa
Tel: +254 41 4471629; +254 41 4473246
Age range: 3–18
Curriculum: UK, IGCSE, ALevs

M-PESA Foundation Academy
P.O. Box 7954, 01000 Thika
Tel: +254 703 200 000
Age range: 13–18 years
No. of pupils: 610
Curriculum: IBDP, IBMYP, IBCP
Language instr: English

Mustard Seed Schools
PO Box 16105-20100, Nakuru
Tel: +254 51 20 2130541
Age range: 14–19
No. of pupils: 600
Curriculum: IGCSE

Nairobi Academy Secondary School
PO Box 24817-00502, Nairobi
Tel: +254 722 208365
Age range: 12–18
Curriculum: UK, IGCSE, ALevs
Language instr: English

Nairobi Jaffery Academy
Jaffery Islamic Centre, El Molo Drive, off James Gichuru Road, Opposite Shell Petrol Station 603
Tel: +254 4349208
Curriculum: UK, IGCSE, ALevs

Naisula School
P O Box 41, Nairobi-Namanga Road, 01100 Kajiado
Tel: +254 712245702
Curriculum: IBDP
Language instr: English, Swahili

Oshwal Academy Nairobi Junior High
1st Parklands Avenue, Nairobi
Tel: +254 20 3745 544
Age range: 12–16
No. of pupils: 836
Curriculum: IGCSE

Oshwal Academy Nairobi Senior High
PO Box 1130 00606, Sarit Centre, Nairobi
Tel: +254 20 268 0530
Language instr: English
AISA

Pembroke House School
PO Box 31, 20116 Gilgil
Tel: +254 708 143 600
Age range: 6–13
No. of pupils: 190 *B*101 *G*89
Curriculum: UK

Peponi House Preparatory School
PO Box 23203, Lower Kabete, Nairobi 00604
Tel: +254 (0)20 2585710
Age range: 6–13
No. of pupils: 387 *B*193 *G*194
Language instr: English

Peponi School
Box 236, Ruiru
Tel: +254 020 3546456
Age range: 12–19
No. of pupils: 92 *B*64 *G*58
Curriculum: UK, ALevs

Premier Academy
PO Box 39513, Nairobi 623
Tel: +254 722 205 855
Age range: 14–19
No. of pupils: 500
Curriculum: UK, ALevs

Rift Valley Academy
PO Box 80, Kijabe 220
Tel: +254 713000700
Age range: 4–18
No. of pupils: 500
Curriculum: USA

Rosslyn Academy
PO Box 14146, Nairobi 00800
Tel: +254 20 263 5294
Age range: 4–18
No. of pupils: 650
Curriculum: ACT, SAT, USA
Language instr: English
AISA

Rusinga Schools
PO Box 25088-00603, Lavington, Nairobi
Tel: +254 722 205 341
Age range: 4–19
Curriculum: UK

SABIS International School – Runda
Situated off Kiambu Road, after the Northern Bypass Underpass, Runda
Tel: +254 743 162 670

Sandpiper International School
Off Lamu Road, Along Golf Course Drive, Opposite Africa Pearl Hotel, Malindi
Tel: +254 788 062 618
Age range: 2–10
No. of pupils: 60 *B*30 *G*30
Curriculum: UK
Language instr: English

St Andrew's Prep School
Private Bag, Molo 20106
Tel: +254 (0)20 202 57 09; +254 (0)722 209750
Age range: 5–13
No. of pupils: 230
Curriculum: UK
Language instr: English
AISA

St Andrew's Senior School
Private Bag, Molo 20106
Tel: +254 (0)20 202 57 08; +254 (0)735 337736
No. of pupils: 320
Curriculum: UK, IGCSE
Language instr: English
AISA COB RS

St Austin's Academy
PO Box 25138, James Gichuru Road, Lavington
Tel: +254 20 216 56 53
Age range: 14–19
No. of pupils: 460
Curriculum: IGCSE

St Christopher's Secondary School
PO Box 21378, Nairobi 505
Tel: +254 20 208 4267
Age range: 11–19
No. of pupils: 200
Curriculum: IGCSE

St Mary's School
PO Box 40580, Rhapta Road, Nairobi 00100
Tel: +254 20 4444 569
Age range: 8–19 years
No. of pupils: 758
Curriculum: IBDP, National, IGCSE
Language instr: English

The Aga Khan Academy, Nairobi
1st Parklands Avenue, off Limuru Road, PO Box 44424-00100, Nairobi
Tel: Junior: +254 0733 758 510, Senior: +254 736 380 101
Age range: 3–19 years
No. of pupils: 1020
Curriculum: IBDP, IBMYP, IBPYP
Language instr: English
AISA

The Aga Khan Nursery School, Nairobi
PO Box 14998, Nairobi 00800
Tel: +254 020 374 2114
Curriculum: IBPYP

The Banda School
PO Box 24722, Nairobi 00502
Tel: +254205131100
Age range: 2–13
No. of pupils: 400 *B*185 *G*215
Curriculum: UK
Language instr: English

The Vale School Muthaiga
No. 73 Muthaiga Road, Nairobi
Tel: +254 708 191397
Curriculum: IBPYP
Language instr: English

West Nairobi School
P.O. Box 1333, Karen 00502
Tel: + 254 0709 331 000

LESOTHO

American International School of Lesotho
14 United Nations Road, Maseru
Tel: +266 2232 2987
Language instr: English
AISA

Machabeng College, International School of Lesotho
PO Box 1570, Tona Kholo Rd, Maseru
Tel: +266 2231 3224
Age range: 11–23
Curriculum: IBDP, National, SAT, ALevs
Language instr: English
AISA CIS

Maseru Preparatory School
PO Box 34, Maseru 100
Tel: +266 22 312276
Age range: 3–12
Curriculum: IBPYP, UK

LIBERIA

American International School of Monrovia
Old Road, Congo Town, Monrovia
Tel: +231 777 818 775
Age range: 4–12
Curriculum: USA
AISA

LIBYA

Benghazi European School
PO Box 300, Benghazi
Tel: +218 61 223 3188
Age range: 14–19
Curriculum: IGCSE

Canadian International School Libya
Al Serraj, Tripoli
Tel: +218 94 411 7101
Age range: 2.5–11

International School Benghazi
Al Hawaree, Benghazi
Tel: +218 61 470 0005
Age range: 4–18
Language instr: English

ISM International School
Hai Andalus, Tripoli
Tel: +218 91 668 7834

The British School of Benghazi
PO Box 536, Benghazi
Tel: +218 61 2225822
Age range: 3–18
Curriculum: UK, IGCSE

MADAGASCAR

Ambatovy International School
Management Housing Village, Takapala, Toamasina
Tel: +261 32 44 668 67
AISA

The American School of Antananarivo
Lotissement Le Park Alarobia, Antananarivo 101
Tel: +261 20 22 420 39
Age range: 2–18
Curriculum: IBDP, IBPYP, USA
Language instr: English
AISA

MALAWI

Bambino Schools
P.O. Box 1614, Lilongwe
Tel: +265 111 761 372
Curriculum: IGCSE

Bishop Mackenzie International School
PO Box 102, Lilongwe
Tel: +265 1 756 631
Age range: 5–18
No. of pupils: 660 *B*330 *G*330 *VIth*60
Curriculum: IBDP, IBMYP, IBPYP, UK
Language instr: English
AISA CIS

Hillview International Primary School
PO Box 5809, Limbe
Tel: +265 1 843540
Age range: 4–11
No. of pupils: 175
Curriculum: National, SAT, UK, IGCSE

Kamuzu Academy
Private Bag 1, Mtunthama
Tel: +265 1 259 288
Age range: 10–18
No. of pupils: 521 *B*266 *G*255 *VIth*92
Curriculum: UK, IGCSE, ALevs
Language instr: English

Mzuzu Academy
PO Box 20165, Mzuzu
Tel: +265 1 931 714
Age range: 4–16
No. of pupils: 247 *B*131 *G*116
Curriculum: UK, IGCSE
Language instr: English

Sir Harry Johnston International Primary School
Box 52, Kalimbuka Road, Zomba
Tel: +265 1525280
Age range: 2–16
No. of pupils: 180
Curriculum: UK

Southend Secondary School
Chikawa Road, PO Box 2764, Blantyre
Tel: +265 1 638 058
Age range: 14–19

St Andrew's International High School
Private Bag 211, Brereton Drive, Nyambadwe, Blantyre
Tel: +265 310 000 437
Age range: 11–18
No. of pupils: *B*327 *G*283
Curriculum: IGCSE, ALevs
Language instr: English

St Andrew's International Primary School
PO Box 593, Blantyre
Tel: +265 1833 4281
Age range: 4–11
No. of pupils: 402 *B*210 *G*192
Curriculum: UK

MALI

American International School of Bamako
Bougouba, Rue 90, Bamako
Tel: +223 2022 4738
Age range: 3–18
No. of pupils: 160 *B*80 *G*80
Curriculum: ACT, AP, SAT, USA
Language instr: English

Ecole Maternelle Les Lutins
BP 326, Bamako
Tel: +223 20 74 42 99

Enko Bamako International School
Quartier du Fleuve, rue 310, porte 510, Ancien CompuMali, En face de l'industrie Boissons et G+, Bamako
Tel: +223 63 21 24 26
Age range: 11–19 years
Curriculum: IBDP
Language instr: English, French

Lycèe Français Libertè De Bamako
Boulevard du Peuple, 910 Bamako
Tel: +223 44980180
Curriculum: FrenchBacc

MAURITANIA

American International School of Nouakchott
PO Box 3107, Nouakchott
Tel: +222 45252967
Age range: 3–20
Curriculum: USA
Language instr: English

Lycee Francais Theodore Monod
BP 4911, Nouakchott
Tel: +222 45 25 18 50
Curriculum: FrenchBacc

TLC International School
55 E. Nord, Nouakchott
Tel: +222 46041532
Curriculum: USA

MAURITIUS

Alexandra House School
King George V Avenue, Floreal
Tel: +230 696 4108
Age range: 4–11
No. of pupils: 100 *B*55 *G*45 *VIth*15
Curriculum: UK
Language instr: English

Clavis International Primary School
Montagne Ory, Moka
Tel: +230 433 4439/4337708
Age range: 3–11
No. of pupils: 540 *B*290 *G*250
Curriculum: IBPYP
Language instr: English, French

Ecole Du Centre – College Pierre Poivre
Helvetia, Saint Pierre,
Tel: 00 230 433 2475
Curriculum: FrenchBacc

Ecole du Nord
Village Labourdonnais, Mapou, 31803 Ile Maurice
Tel: +230 266 3009
Curriculum: FrenchBacc

International Preparatory School
Village Labourdonnais, Mapou 31803
Tel: +230 266 1973
Age range: 3–11
No. of pupils: 384 *B*200 *G*184
Curriculum: IBPYP
Language instr: English, French

Le Bocage International School (Progos)
Mount Ory, Moka 80803
Tel: +230 433 9900
Age range: 11–19
No. of pupils: 600
Curriculum: IBDP, IBMYP, IBCP, IGCSE
Language instr: English

Lycee La Bourdonnais
Rochecouste street, Forest Side, Curepipe
Tel: +230 6706 097
Curriculum: FrenchBacc

Northfields International High School
Labourdonnais Village, Mapou
Tel: +230 266 9448/9
Curriculum: IBDP, IBMYP
Language instr: English

Westcoast International Primary School
Flic en Flac Road, Cascavelle
Tel: +230 452 9193
Age range: 4–11
Curriculum: IPC

Westcoast International Secondary School
Flic en Flac Road, Cascavelle
Tel: +230 489 2034
Curriculum: IBDP
Language instr: English

MOROCCO

Al Akhawayn School of Ifrane (ASI)
Al Akhawayn University, BP 104, Ifrane 53000
Tel: +212 535 86 21 99
Curriculum: USA
Language instr: English

American Academy Casablanca
RN 3020 Ville Verte, Casa Green Town, Bouskoura 27182
Tel: +212 529 039112
Curriculum: IBDP
Language instr: English, French

American School of Marrakesh
Route de Ouarzazate, BP 6195, Marrakech
Tel: +212 (0)24 32 98 60/61
Age range: 4–18
Curriculum: IBDP, USA
Language instr: English

American School of Tangier
149 Rue Christophe Colomb, Tangier 90 000
Tel: +212 539 93 98 28/27
Age range: 2–19
No. of pupils: 340 *B*178 *G*162
Curriculum: SAT, TOEFL, USA
Language instr: English, French, Arabic

British International School of Casablanca
P3020 Route Sidi Messoud, 20000
Tel: (+212) 520 500 200
Curriculum: UK, IGCSE, ALevs

Casablanca American School
Route de la Mecque, Lotissement Ougoug, Quartier Californie, Casablanca 20150
Tel: +212 522 79 39 39
Age range: 3–18
No. of pupils: 693
Curriculum: AP, IBDP, SAT
Language instr: English

Ecole Andre Chenier
32 Avenue Mohamed Lyazidi, Rabat 10020
Tel: +212 5 37 72 45 21
No. of pupils: 700

Ecole Paul Cézanne de Rabat
Place Jean Courtin, Agdal, Rabat BP 768 10000
Tel: +212 5 37 67 26 37
No. of pupils: 720

Écoles Al Madina, Site Ain Sebaa
Km 9, route de Rabat, Hay Chabab, Ain sébàa, Casablanca 20250
Tel: +212 0522 75 69 69
Curriculum: IBMYP
Language instr: French, Arabic

Écoles Al Madina, Site Californie
Lotissement Bellevue 2, Rue 3 Californie, Casablanca
Tel: +212 522 5050 9 7/8/9
Age range: 2–18
No. of pupils: 3575 *B*1866 *G*1709
Curriculum: IBMYP, National
Language instr: French, Arabic

Écoles Al Madina, Site Polo
52 Bd Nador, Casablanca 20420
Tel: +21 20 22 210 505
Curriculum: IBMYP
Language instr: French, Arabic

GDGSR – Khouribga
Bld 2 Mars, Khouribga
Tel: +212 (0)6 00 03 40 11
Curriculum: IBMYP
Language instr: Arabic, French

GDGSR – Youssoufia
Rue Allal Ben Abdellan, Youssoufia
Tel: +212 (0)6 00 03 77 53
Curriculum: IBMYP
Language instr: Arabic, French

George Washington Academy
Km 5.6 Rte d\'Azemour, Dar Bouazza, Casablanca 20220
Tel: +212 522 953 000
Curriculum: IBDP, USA
Language instr: English, French, Arabic

Groupe scolaire Alkaraouiyine
350 Boulevard Sebta, Lotisement Anfa, Mohammedia 28000
Tel: +212 23 30 13 57
Age range: 11–16
Curriculum: IBMYP, National
Language instr: Arabic, French

Groupe Scolaire La Résidence
87-89 Avenue 2 mars. Casablanca
Tel: +212 522 809050/51
Age range: 2–20
No. of pupils: 3611
Curriculum: IBMYP
Language instr: French

Institut Scolaire les Palmiers
76 Rue Abdelhamid Bnou Badis, Casablanca Ain sebâa 20250
Tel: +212 522343757
Language instr: Arabic, English, French

Institution El Yakada
Lotissement Koutoubia, Route de Kenitra, Salé 11160
Tel: +212 (0)5 37 84 48 44
Curriculum: IBMYP
Language instr: English

International School of Morocco
3 Impasse Jules Gros, Quartier Oasis, Casablanca 20150
Tel: +212 0 552 993 987
Curriculum: IBPYP, UK
Language instr: English
COB ECIS

Khalil Gibran School
4 Avenue Bir Kacem,, Souissi
Tel: 212 (0) 537 75 29 48
Curriculum: UK, IGCSE, ALevs
COB

Lycee Lyautey
260 Boulevard Ziraoui, Casablanca 20040
Tel: +212 5 22 43 69 00
Age range: 14–19
No. of pupils: 3500

Newton International School
Rue Ibn Khafaja, Anfa, Mohammedia 208000
Tel: +212 5 23 31 65 52
Curriculum: IBMYP
Language instr: French

Planete Montessori International School
Lotissement Palm Tree Paradise No. 5, Mechouar Essaid, Marrakech
Tel: +212 6 23 86 14 29
Curriculum: IBPYP
Language instr: English, French

Rabat American School
c/o US Embassy, BP 120 Rabat
Tel: +212 537 75 85 90
Age range: 4–18
No. of pupils: 422 *B*230 *G*192
Curriculum: IBDP, SAT, USA
Language instr: English
ECIS

Saudi School in Rabat
Ecole Saoudienne a Rabat quartier Bir Kacem, lotiss. Larouikane no 65, Rabat
Tel: +212 5 37659481
Language instr: English

MOZAMBIQUE

Aga Khan Academy Maputo
Av. Zimbabwe, 212 Matola, Maputo
Tel: +258 21 720963
Age range: 3–13 years
No. of pupils: 100
Curriculum: IBDP, IBMYP, IBPYP
Language instr: English, Portuguese

American International School of Mozambique
Caixa Postal 2026, Maputo
Tel: +258 21 49 1994
Curriculum: IBDP, IBMYP, IBPYP
Language instr: English

École Française de Maputo
Rua 3 853 no. 203, Bairro Polana, Caniço B
Tel: +258 21 48 59 27
Curriculum: FrenchBacc

Enko Benga International School
Moatize, Tete
Tel: +258 84 717 5447
Curriculum: IBPYP
Language instr: English

Enko Riverside International School
Rua José Macamo 175, Polana, Maputo
Tel: +258 845 40 91 51
Age range: 11–19 years
Curriculum: IBDP, IGCSE
Language instr: English

Enko Sekeleka International School
Complexo Residencial de Nhamacunda, Vilankulo
Tel: +258 82 992 2112
Age range: 2–19 years

Maputo International School
C.P. 4152 Maputo, 389 Rua da Nachingwea, Maputo
Tel: +258 21 492131/195
Age range: 3–18
No. of pupils: 436 *B*220 *G*216
Curriculum: National, UK, IGCSE
AISA

NAMIBIA

Deutsche Hohere Privatschule Windhoek
Postfach 78, Church Strasse 11-15, Windhoek
Tel: +264 61 373 100
Age range: 4–19
No. of pupils: 943

St George's Diocesan School
PO Box 68, Windhoek
Tel: +264 61234133
Age range: 4–18
No. of pupils: 761 *B*400 *G*361
Curriculum: IGCSE, ALevs
Language instr: English
RS

St Paul's College
PO Box 11736, Windhoek 9000
Tel: +264 61 227783
Age range: 6–18
No. of pupils: 574 *B*274 *G*300
Curriculum: National
Language instr: English

Windhoek International School
P/Bag 16007, Scheppmann Street, Pioneerspark, Windhoek
Tel: +264 61 241 783
Age range: 2–18
No. of pupils: 503 *B*229 *G*274
Curriculum: IBDP, IBPYP, IGCSE
Language instr: English
AISA CIS

NIGER

American International School of Niamey
BP 11201, Niamey
Tel: +227 20 72 39 42
Age range: 3–18
No. of pupils: 84
Curriculum: USA
AISA

Lycée Enoch Olinga
B.P. 366, Quartier Daresalam (face marché Daresalam), Niamey 8001
Tel: +227 94 54 60 75
Curriculum: IBDP
Language instr: French

NIGERIA

Access High Schools
PO Box 388, State Housing Estate Pos, Calabar 540001
Curriculum: SAT, TOEFL, UK, GCSE

Acorns and Oaks Academy
11 Ambrose Ogbonna Avenue, Off Stadium Road, Port Harcourt, Rivers State
Tel: +234 (0)704 489 3886
Curriculum: UK
Language instr: English
COB

Aduvie International School
Plot 273 BO8, Cadastral Zone, Jahi District
Tel: +234 0808 939 4474
Age range: 4–18
Curriculum: IGCSE
AISA

American Christian Academy
PO Box 19629, 2,4,6 Shell Close, Onireke, Ibadan
Tel: +234 22 41 3240

American International School of Abuja
Plot 346, Cadastral Zone B 02, Durumi District, Abuja
P.M.B. 5080 Wuse
Tel: +234 703 215 3798
Age range: 2–14
No. of pupils: 185 *B*90 *G*95
AISA

American International School of Lagos
Behind 1004 Federal Estates, Lagos
Tel: +234 11 77 64 535
Curriculum: IBDP
Language instr: English

Attwool Sunflower School – Pre-school & Primary
Plot 24 C, Adwwunmi Adebimpe Drive, By Mobolasji Johnson Place, Lekki Phase 1, Lagos
Tel: +234 1 2952 234

AUN Academy
99 Lamido Zubairu Way, Yola By Pass, PMB 2255
Tel: + 234 706 778 9426
Curriculum: National, UK, USA

Avi-Cenna International School
6 Harold Shodipo Crescent, GRA Ikeja, Lagos
Tel: +234 1 3426273
Age range: 2 –16
No. of pupils: 550 *B*290 *G*260
Curriculum: UK, IGCSE
Language instr: English

Bridge House College
8 Royal Palm Drive, Osborne Foreshore Estate, Phase II, Ikoyi, Lagos
Tel: +234 802 842 7208
Age range: 16–18
Curriculum: UK, ALevs
COB

British International School Nigeria
1 Landbridge Avenue, Oniru Private Estate, Victoria Island
Tel: (234) 01-2915022
Age range: 11–18
No. of pupils: 360 *B*200 *G*160
Curriculum: UK, ALevs
Language instr: English
AISA COB

British Nigerian Academy
Drive 6, Prince and Princess, Duboyi District, P.M.B 5285, Wuse, Abuja
Tel: +234 8144084741
Age range: 10–18
Curriculum: IBDP
Language instr: English

Brookstone School
Off Sani Abacha Road, GRA Phase 3, Port Harcourt Rivers State
Tel: +234 084 789584
Age range: 3–17
No. of pupils: 525
Curriculum: National, UK
Language instr: English
COB ECIS

Brookstone School Secondary
International Airport Road, Igwruta 234
Tel: +234 8089791810
Curriculum: National, SAT, TOEFL, IGCSE

Buckswood School Nigeria
Lords Estate,, Ago-Oko Titun,, Sagamu/Abeokuta Express Way
Tel: +2348090851745
Curriculum: UK, IGCSE, ALevs

Cedar Court British International School
10 Imgbi Road, by Intercontinental Hotel, Amarata Yenagoa
Tel: +234 7063430738

Cedec International Secondary School
41 Alhaji Yusuf Adebayo Street, Olodi Apapa, Lagos State
Tel: +234 01 4709106; 08033063540
COB

Children's International School
Funke Zainab Usman Street (End of Admiralty Road), Lekki Phase 1, Lagos
Tel: +234 9038 485 768
Language instr: English
AISA

Chrisland School, Opebi
26 Opebi Road, Ikeja, Lagos PMB 21612
Tel: + 234 1 8191827015
AISA

City of Knowledge Academy
Itanrin Ososa Junction, Benin-Sagamu Expressway, Ijebu Ode
Tel: +234 1 8987 373
Age range: 11–18

Corona Schools Trust Council
72 Raymond Njoku, SW Ikoyi, Lagos
Tel: +234-7027999797
Curriculum: UK, IGCSE
AISA COB

Cradle to Crayon/ Springhall British School
37 Lake Chad Crescent, Maitama, Abuja
Tel: +234 703 595 4101
Language instr: English
COB

CTC International Schools
Presidential Boulevard, Sagamu, Ogun State 100001
Tel: +234 8104 6010 94
Curriculum: UK

Day Waterman College
Lagos Liaison Office 18B, Thompson Avenue, Iyoki, Lagos
Tel: +234 (1) 279 3836; (0)705 678 0016
Age range: 11–16
No. of pupils: 458 *B*234 *G*224
Curriculum: National, UK, IGCSE
COB

Delightsome Land School
229A & 229B Muri Okunola Street Victoria Island, Lagos
Tel: +234 1270 1223
Curriculum: UK
COB

Divine Royal International School
Along Nkpor-Umuoji Road, Nkpor Anambra State
Tel: +234 (0)7038638417
Curriculum: National, UK, IGCSE
COB

D-Ivy College
32 Allen Avenue, Ikeja, Lagos
Tel: +234 8033 568 390
No. of pupils: 80
Language instr: English

Dowen College
18 Adebayo Dohery Road, Lekki Phase 1, Lagos
Tel: +234 12 706 010
Language instr: English
AISA

Ebenezery Heights International Schools
007-013 Soji Olagunju Street, Off Alpha Beach Road, Lekki
Tel: +234 702 819 4549
Curriculum: UK

École Française de Kano
4 Hospital Road, Kano
Tel: +234 64972779
Curriculum: UK

Edgewood College
Plot 3, Block 14, Kayode Otitoju Street (Road 38), Off Admiralty Way (By Tantalizers), Lekki Phase 1
Tel: +234 803 534 4633
Age range: 11–18
Curriculum: IGCSE

Emerald Schools
c/o 8/10 Olawale Daodu Street, Ifako Gbagada, Lagos
Tel: +234 18 54 57 78
Language instr: English
AISA

FAMAKS International Schools
Plot 8 Fajuyi Adekunle Crescent, Off Ajayi Crowther Street, Asokoro, Abuja
Tel: +234 808 305 1079 / +234 929 104 56
Age range: 2–10
Curriculum: IPC
Language instr: English
AISA COB

Funtaj International School
Plot 474, Nelson Mandela Street, Asokoro, Abuja
Tel: +234 7026 349 286
Age range: 5–18
No. of pupils: 300

Gapbridge Private School
Plot 688G Somide Odujinrin Street, Omole Phase 11, Lagos
Tel: +234 8124402070
Curriculum: National, UK, IGCSE, ALevs

GLISTEN INTERNATIONAL ACADEMY
For further details see p. 48
Plot 1457 Cadastrial Zone B8, Jahi District, Abuja
Tel: +234 90 3888 2824
Email: info@glisteninternationalacademy.com
Website: www.glisteninternationalacademy.com
Head of School: Eneh Charles Chibuzor
Age range: 3–17 years
Language instr: English

Grange School
6 Harold Shodipo Crescent, PO Box 22, Ikeja, Lagos
Tel: +234 1 2957630
Age range: 4–16
No. of pupils: 720
Curriculum: UK
Language instr: English
AISA COB ECIS

Greenoak International School, Nigeria (Primary)
99 Tombia Street Extension, Gra Phase 3, Port Harcourt
Tel: +234 80 86 73 74 01
Curriculum: IPC
Language instr: English
AISA COB

Greensprings School, Lagos
P.O. Box 4801K Ikeja Headquarters, Ikeja, 32 Olatunde Ayoola Avenue, Anthony, Lagos
Tel: +234 8776874
Age range: 3 months–18 years
Curriculum: IBDP
Language instr: English
AISA

Grenville Primary School
18 Ladoke Akintola Street, Ikeja
Tel: +234 8035 726 614
Age range: 4–11
Curriculum: UK

Grenville Secondary School
15 Joel Ogunnaike Street, Ikeja
Tel: +234 8035 726 614
Age range: 11–16
Curriculum: IGCSE

Halifield School
2 Oki Lane, Maryland
Tel: +234 8150 904 604
Age range: 4–18
Curriculum: UK

Hillcrest School (Jos)
13 Old Bukuru Road, Jos
Tel: +234 803 7190351
Language instr: English
AISA

Ibadan International School
24 Jibowu Crescent, Iyaganku, Ibadan
Tel: +234 2 291 8483
Age range: 2–18 years
No. of pupils: 465
Curriculum: IBPYP
Language instr: English
AISA

Inspire Academy
Plot 7, Abdulhahab Folawiyo Ave, Former First Ave, Gwarinpa Housing Estate, Abuja
Tel: +234 802 5068312
Curriculum: UK
Language instr: English
COB

International Community School, Abuja
PO Box 3972, Abuja
Tel: +234 9 523 3520
Age range: 2–18
No. of pupils: 500 B220 G280
Curriculum: ACT, AP, SAT, USA, IGCSE
Language instr: English
AISA CIS

James Hope College
Obi Ikechukwu Road (Formerly Old Lagos-Asaba Road), Agbor Obi, Agbor
Tel: +234 704 597 7883
Curriculum: UK
Language instr: English
COB

KAD Academy
No. 5 Rock Close,, Malali,, Kaduna
Tel: +234706 258 1020
Curriculum: UK

Kaduna International School
PO Box 2947, 1 Wurno Road, Kaduna
Tel: 002348166481918
Age range: 3–12
No. of pupils: 154 B79 G75
Curriculum: National, UK
AISA COB

Lagos Preparatory School, Ikoyi
36-40 Glover Road, Ikoyi, Lagos
Tel: +234 903 378 0406
Age range: 18 Months–14 Years
Curriculum: UK
Language instr: English
AISA COB

Lekki British School
Victoria Arobieke Street, Off Admiralty Way, Lekki Peninsular Phase 1, Lagos
Tel: +234 12 708 300
Curriculum: UK
Language instr: English
AISA COB

Lifeforte International School
Lifeforte Boulevard, Awotan Gra, Ibadan
Tel: +234 28 103 832
Language instr: English
AISA

Lifespring Montessori School
Plot 1, Block B4, CMD/ Jubilee Road, Magodo
Tel: +234 803 3673 067
Curriculum: National, UK

Lycée Français Louis-Pasteur
16 Younis Bashorun Street, Victoria Island Annex, PO Box 72172
Tel: +234 1 270 05 45
Curriculum: FrenchBacc

Meadow Hall School
Meadow Hall Way, Alma Beach Estate, Lekki-Epe Expressway, Lekki, Lagos
Tel: +234 9053816215
COB

Netherlands International School Lagos (NISL)
13 A/B Walter Carrington Crescent, Victoria Island, Lagos
Tel: +234 808 221 1745
Age range: 2–12
No. of pupils: 150
Curriculum: IPC, National, UK

Nigeria LNG School
Nigeria LNG Residential Area, Bonny Island
Tel: +234 80390 52602
Language instr: English
AISA

Nigerian Turkish International College – Abuja
Ahmadu Bello Way, by Kashim Ibrahim Way, Wuse 2
Tel: +234 806 061 27 89
Age range: 4–18

Nigerian Turkish International College – Kaduna
Rigachukun, 9km Along Kaduna-Zaria Road, Kaduna
Tel: +234 803 768 78 60
Age range: 4–18

Nigerian Turkish International College – Kano
Hadeja Road by Pass by Ring Road, Yankaba
Tel: +234 703 498 85 05
Age range: 4–18

Nigerian Turkish International College – Lagos
4A Agbaoku Street, Off Odepi Road, Ikeja
Tel: +234 814 686 26 41
Age range: 4–18

Nigerian Turkish International College – Ogun
Ogd Drive, Ibadan, Lagos
Tel: +234 704 536 07 94
Age range: 4–18

Nigerian Turkish International College – Yobe
Mamudoo, Potiskum
Tel: +234 803 597 08 90
Age range: 4–18

Noble Hall Leadership Academy for Girls
Plot 273, Institutes and Research District, Abuja
Tel: +234 8032 032291
Curriculum: UK, IGCSE
Language instr: English
COB

Norwegian International School
GPA Phase 111, Port Harcourt
Tel: +234 (0)84300501
Language instr: English
AISA

Oakland International British School
Tennesse Crescent, Off Panama Street, Ministers Hill, Maitama, Abuja
Tel: +234 905 623 8659
Curriculum: UK
Language instr: English
COB

Ocean Crest School
TF Kuboye Street, Lekki – Epe Express Way, Lagos
Tel: +234 816 0000 580
Age range: 1.5–11

Olashore International School
Oba Oladele Olashore Way, Iloko-Ijesa P.M.B.5059
Tel: +234 (0)813 609 7630; +234 (0)807 450 3993
Curriculum: UK, IGCSE
Language instr: English
AISA COB

Oxbridge Tutorial College
49 Sobo Arobiodu Street, GRA, Ikeja, Lagos
Tel: +234 12955473
Age range: 16–18 years
No. of pupils: 150 B70 G80
Curriculum: SAT, TOEFL, UK, USA, ALevs
Language instr: English
COB

Pampers Private School Alaka
99 Owukori Crescent, Alaka Estate, Surulere, Lagos
Tel: +234 (0)813 002 7220
Language instr: English

Pampers Private School Lekki
Plot 12, Block 88, Otunba Adedoyin Ogungbe Crescent, off Admiralty Road, Lekki Phase 1, Lekki
Tel: +234 (0)816 152 0932
Language instr: English
AISA

Pegasus Schools, Eket
North End of St. Gregory Street, Eket, Akwa Ibom
Tel: +234 802 499 7603
No. of pupils: 622
Language instr: English

Pinefield School
Christ Avenue, Off Admiralty Road, Lekki Phase 1, Victoria Island, Lagos
Tel: +234 (0)802 315 8055

Premiere Academy
Federal Housing Estate, Phase 2, 23409 Lugbe, Abuja
Tel: +234 706 979 7855
Curriculum: SAT, IGCSE

Rainbow College
51 Johnson Street, Off Bode Thomas Street, Surulere
Tel: +234 818 049 2228
Age range: 11–18
No. of pupils: 600
Curriculum: USA

Redeemer's International School
Apapa Road, Ebute Metta, Lagos
Tel: +234 817 070 2111
Language instr: English

Regent Secondary School
Plot 858 Mabushi District, FCT, Abuja
Tel: +234 80784 879[illegible]6
Curriculum: UK, IGCSE
(AISA) (COB)

Sacred Heart Primary School
Independence Way, PO Box 620, Kaduna
Tel: +234 803 701 7438
Age range: 5–12
No. of pupils: 296 B159 G137

St Saviour's School
54 Alexander Avenue, Ikoyi, Lagos
Tel: +234 1 342 6946
Age range: 4–11
No. of pupils: 320
Curriculum: IPC, UK
(COB)

Start-Rite Schools
Plot 1036, Adesoji Aderemi Street,, Off Samuel Jereton Mariere Road,, After Zone E, National Assembly
Tel: +234 8106334006
Curriculum: UK
(COB)

Surefoot International School
Plot 5 Port Managers Quarters, Zone 6 Murtalla Mohammed Highway, Calabar
Tel: +234 816 461 8596
(AISA)

Temple Preparatory and Secondary School
Temple drive off Olusoji Idowu Street, Ilupeju, Lagos
Tel: +234 18 940 981
Curriculum: UK, IGCSE
Language instr: English
(AISA)

Temple School
1 Temple Drive, Off Olusoji Idowu Street, Ilupeju, Lagos
Tel: +234 809 854 7988
Age range: 1–16
Curriculum: UK, IGCSE
Language instr: English
(AISA) (COB)

Temple School (Early Years)
213 Ikorodu Road, Ilupeju, Lagos
Tel: +234 1 733 9369
Curriculum: UK, IGCSE

The Centagon International School
29/31 Mississippi Street, Maitama
Tel: +234 805 728 0323
Age range: 4–18
Curriculum: USA

The International School of IITA
PMB 5320, Ibadan, Oyo State
Tel: +234 (0)700 800 4482 (Ext:2593)
Age range: 3–12
No. of pupils: 58 *B27 G31*
Curriculum: IBPYP, UK, USA
Language instr: English
(AISA)

The Primegate School
Primegate Avenue, off G.U.Ake road, Eligbolo, Port Harcourt
Tel: +234 705 808 2630
No. of pupils: 550
Curriculum: National, UK
Language instr: English
(COB)

The Priory Preparatory School
1 Sikiru Alade Oloko Crescent, off Admiralty Way, Lekki Peninsula Phase 1
Tel: +234 7036875744
Age range: 4–13
Curriculum: IPC

The Regent School
1 Euphrates Street, Federal Capital Territory, Abuja
Tel: +234 703 779 3322
Age range: 2–11
No. of pupils: 249 *B142 G107*
Curriculum: National, UK
Language instr: English
(AISA) (COB)

THE RIVERBANK SCHOOL
For further details see p. 50
RCCG City of David, Dideolu Estate, Victoria Island
Tel: +234 (0) 909 859 872
Email: info@riverbankschools.org
Website: www.riverbankschools.org
Principal: Regina Jemide
Age range: 2–13 years
Curriculum: SAT, UK
(COB)

Thomas Adewumi International College (TAICO)
Adewumi Drive, Oko, Omu Aran, Kwara State
Tel: +234 (0)803 563 8036/+234 (0)803 824 5006
Age range: 11–16
No. of pupils: 365
Curriculum: SAT, UK, GCSE

Vivian Fowler Memorial College for Girls
Plot 5 Balogun Street, Chief T A Doherty Layout, Oregun, Ikeja, Lagos
Tel: +234 1 806 155 0543
(AISA) (COB)

Whiteplains British School
Plot 528 Cadastral Zone B4, Opposite National War College Site, Jabi
Tel: +234 8033 453 457
Curriculum: ALevs

REPUBLIC OF THE CONGO

American International School of Brazzaville
PO Box 1780, Bacongo, Brazzaville
Tel: +242 06 868 0804
Curriculum: USA
(AISA)

International School Pointe Noire
Lotissement Tchikobo, Pointe-Noire
Tel: +234 748 7700
Language instr: English
(AISA)

RWANDA

Green Hills Academy
PO Box 6419, Nyarutarama, Kigali
Tel: +250 735 832 348
Age range: 3–19
No. of pupils: 1550
Curriculum: IBDP, SAT, IGCSE
Language instr: English, French
(RS)

International School Kigali
PO Box 6217, Kigali
Tel: +250 78 83 02 899
Age range: 3–18
Curriculum: USA
(AISA) (CIS)

Kigali International Community School
Caisse Sociale Estates, Gaculiro, Kigali BP 6558
Tel: +25 783307282
Age range: 4–18
No. of pupils: 230
Curriculum: ACT, AP, SAT, USA
Language instr: English
(AISA)

SENEGAL

Cours Sainte Marie de Hann
Route Des Peres Maristes, BP 98, Dakar
Tel: +221 33 832 08 29
Curriculum: IBDP
Language instr: English, French

Dakar Academy
BP 3189, Dakar
Tel: +221 33 832 0682
Age range: 5–20
No. of pupils: 236 *B117 G119*
Curriculum: ACT, AP, SAT, USA
Language instr: English

Enko Keur Gorgui International School
Cité Keur Gorgui, Mermoz-Sacré-Cœur, Dakar
Tel: +221 33 821 30 64
Age range: 11–19 years
Curriculum: IBDP, IBMYP

Enko Waca International School
BP 24340, Ouakam, Dakar
Tel: +221 33 820 49 29
Age range: 11–19 years
Curriculum: IBDP
Language instr: French, English

International School of Dakar
BP 5136 Fann, Dakar
Tel: +221 33 860 2332
Age range: 3–18
Curriculum: IBDP, IBMYP, IBPYP, USA
Language instr: English
(AISA) (CIS) (ECIS)

Le Collège Bilingue de Dakar
Sacré Coeur 3, Cité Keur Gorgui No.53, Dakar 00221
Tel: +221 33 860 60 10
Curriculum: IBDP
Language instr: English, French

Lycée Billes
Commune de Plan Jaxaay-Cité, Gendarmerie Rufisquel, Dakar
Tel: +221 77 413 73 55
Curriculum: IBDP
Language instr: English, French

SEYCHELLES

Independent School Seychelles
Union Vale, Ile Du Port, Mahe
Tel: +248 432 2337
Age range: 3–18 years
No. of pupils: 1017
Curriculum: SAT, UK, IGCSE, ALevs
Language instr: English

International School, Seychelles
PO Box 315, Mont Fleuri, Victoria Mahe
Tel: +248 4610444
Age range: 3–18
No. of pupils: 650 *VIth35*
Curriculum: SAT, UK, IGCSE, ALevs
Language instr: English

Vijay International School
Baie St Anne, Praslin
Tel: +248 4236116
Age range: 3–18

SIERRA LEONE

American International School of Freetown (Sierra Leone)
24 Hillcot Brow Hill Station, Freetown
Tel: +232 22 232 480 / +232 76 622 453
Age range: 3–14
(AISA)

British International School and Montessori Education Freetown
No.1 Samsumana Drive, Off Leicester Peak Road, Immat Area, Freetown
Tel: +232 76 567509
Curriculum: UK, IGCSE
(COB)

SOUTH AFRICA

Academia Private School
24 Ludorf Street, Bela-Bela 480
Tel: +27 14 736 5881
Curriculum: UK, IGCSE, ALevs

Alma Mater International School
PO Box 2980, Krugersdorp 1740
Tel: + 27 11 660 7567
Curriculum: UK, ALevs

Amazing Grace Private School
359 Pretoria Avenue, Ferndale, Randburg, Johannesburg 2194
Tel: +27 732127905
Age range: 5–19 years

American International School of Cape Town
42 Soetvlei Avenue, Constantia 7806, Cape Town
Tel: 27 21 713 2220
Age range: 4–18
No. of pupils: 302
Curriculum: AP, SAT, USA
Language instr: English
(AISA)

American International School of Johannesburg
Midrand, Johannesburg
Tel: +27 11 464 1505
Age range: 4–18
No. of pupils: 1150
Curriculum: IBDP, SAT, USA
Language instr: English
(AISA)

Bishops Diocesan College
Camp Ground Road, Rondebosch, Cape Town 7700
Tel: +27 21 659 1000
Age range: B5–18
No. of pupils: 1350
Curriculum: National
Language instr: English

Blouberg International School
74 Ringwood Drive, Parklands, Cape Town 7441
Tel: +27 21 557 9071
Curriculum: UK, IGCSE

Bridge House School
PO Box 444, Franschhoek 7690
Tel: +27 021 874 8100
Age range: 2–18 years
Language instr: English
(RS)

British International College – Bryanston
130 Bryanston Drive, Bryanston
Tel: +27 11 706 7775
Age range: 13–19
No. of pupils: 160
Curriculum: IGCSE

Charter College
2 Johan Road, Honeydew, 1746
Tel: +27 11 794 7132
Age range: 14–19
No. of pupils: 200
Curriculum: IGCSE

Charterhouse Preparatory School
10 Erasmus Road, Radiokop, cnr Christiaan De Wet & Erasmus Rds 2040
Tel: +27 11 475 6809
Curriculum: UK

Cornwall Hill College
PO Box 621, Nellmapius Drive, Irene 0062
Tel: +27 12 667 1360
Language instr: English
(RS)

Courtney House International School
100 Florence Ribeiro Avenue,, Bailey's Muckleneuk,, Pretoria 181
Tel: +27 082 305 0165
Age range: 3–18
Curriculum: UK, IGCSE, ALevs

Crawford International Bedfordview
7 Marais Road, Bedfordview, 2008 Johannesburg, Gauteng
Tel: +27 87 350 4633
Curriculum: IBPYP
Language instr: English, Afrikaans

Crawford International Bryanston
6 Hobart Road, Bryanston, Sandton, 2191 Johannesburg, Gauteng
Tel: +27 11 706 6609
Language instr: English, Afrikaans

Crawford International Fourways
16 Campbell Road, Craigavon, Fourways, Sandton, 2191 Johannesburg, Gauteng
Tel: +27 11 465 4418
Curriculum: IBPYP
Language instr: English

Crawford International La Lucia
79 Armstrong Avenue, La Lucia, 4001 Durban, KwaZulu-Natal
Tel: +27 31 562 9444
Curriculum: IBPYP
Language instr: English, Afrikaans

Crawford International Lonehill
17 Lonehill Boulevard, Lonehill, 2062 Johannesburg, Gauteng
Tel: +27 11 467 0936/5
Curriculum: IBPYP
Language instr: English, Afrikaans

Crawford International North Coast
Watson Highway, 4399 Tongaat, KwaZulu-Natal
Tel: +27 32 943 3240
Curriculum: IBPYP
Language instr: English, Afrikaans

Crawford International Pretoria
555 Sibelius Street, Lukasrand, 0181 Pretoria, Gauteng
Tel: +27 12 343 5903
Curriculum: IBPYP
Language instr: English, Afrikaans

Crawford International Ruimsig
Cnr Peter and Kuilstock Roads, Ruimsig, 1724 Roodepoort, Gauteng
Tel: +27 11 958 0707
Curriculum: IBPYP
Language instr: English, Afrikaans

Crawford International Sandton
Crawford Estate Waterstone Drive (off Benmore Road), Benmore, Sandton, 2196 Johannesburg, Gauteng
Tel: +27 11 784 3447
Curriculum: IBPYP
Language instr: English, Zulu

Dainfern College
96 Broadacres Drive, Dainfern, Johannesburg
Tel: +27 011 469 0635
Age range: 5–18 years
No. of pupils: 1000
Curriculum: ALevs

Greenwich College
PO Box 69075, Bryanston 2021
Tel: +27 11 463 9779
Age range: 14–19
No. of pupils: 120
Curriculum: GCSE, IGCSE, ALevs

Hilton College
Private Bag 6001, Hilton 3245 Kwazulu Natal
Tel: +27 33 383 0100
Age range: B11–18

Hout Bay International School
61 Main Road, Hout Bay, Cape Town 7806
Tel: +27 21 791 7900
Age range: 2–18 years
No. of pupils: 400
Curriculum: IBDP, IBMYP, IBPYP, IGCSE
Language instr: English

International School of Cape Town
Woodland Heights, Edinburgh Close, Wynberg, 7800 Cape Town
Tel: +27 21 761 6202
Age range: 3.5–18
No. of pupils: 450
Curriculum: National, SAT, UK, IGCSE, ALevs
Language instr: English

International School of Helderberg
Postnet Suite 214, Private Bag X29, Somerset West, Cape Town 7310
Tel: +27 21 851 6290
(ISA)

International School of South Africa
Nelson Mandela Drive, Libertas, Mahikeng 2745
Tel: +27 18 381 1102
Age range: 4–18
No. of pupils: 720
Curriculum: SAT, UK, IGCSE, ALevs
Language instr: English
(ECIS)

Jacaranda Academy
37 Van Tonder Avenue, Edenglen, Edenvale
Tel: +27 011 609 6218
Age range: 5–14 years

Lycée Français Jules Verne
PO Box 556, Morningside, Johannesburg 2057
Tel: +27 11 884 89 36
No. of pupils: 1200
Curriculum: FrenchBacc

Michaelhouse
R103, Balgowan 3275
Tel: +27 33 234 1000
Age range: B13–18
No. of pupils: 567
Language instr: English

Mokopane Destiny Academy
c/o Geyser and Fourie, RET Centre, 0601 Mokopane, Limpopo
Tel: +27 15 491 2049
Curriculum: IBMYP, IBPYP
Language instr: English

North American International School
PO Box 14582, Hatfield, Pretoria
Tel: +27 124 601 1544
Language instr: English
AISA

Penryn College
PO Box 2835, Nelspruit 1200
Tel: +27 13 758 9000
Language instr: English
RS

Reddam House Atlantic Seaboard
20 Cavalcade Road, Green Point, Cape Town 8051
Tel: +27 (0) 21 433 0105
Age range: 3–18 years
Language instr: English

Reddam House Ballito
Ballito Drive, Dolphin Coast, KwaZulu-Natal
Tel: +27 31 140 8808
Age range: 1–18 years
Language instr: English

Reddam House Bedfordview
28 Smith Road, Bedfordview, Johannesburg 2007
Tel: +27 (0) 11 615 6710
Age range: 1–18 years
Language instr: English

Reddam House Constantia
Reddam Avenue, Steenberg Boulevard, Constantia
Tel: +27 (0) 21 702 2322
Age range: 3–18 years
Language instr: English

Reddam House Durbanville
Mosselbank River Avenue, Durbanville, Cape Town
Tel: +27 (0) 21 975 6650
Age range: 1–18 years
Language instr: English

Reddam House Helderfontein
1 Chattan Road, Glenferness, Fourways, Johannesburg, Midrand
Tel: +27 (0) 10 060 4232
Age range: 1–18 years
Language instr: English

Reddam House Somerset
Reunion Drive, Somerset West, Cape Town 7130
Tel: +27 (0) 100 604 230
Age range: 1–18
Curriculum: National

Reddam House Umhlanga
21 Preston Drive, Prestondale, Umhlanga 4021
Tel: +27 (0) 31 566 5736
Age range: 1–18 years
Language instr: English

Reddam House Waterfall
Country Estate Road, Midrand, Johannesburg
Tel: +27 (0) 10 060 0107
Age range: 1–18 years
Language instr: English

Reddford House Blue Hills
Blue Hills Estate, 5 Mopani Road, Blue Hills, Midrand 1685
Tel: +27 (0) 10 060 0761
Age range: 1–18 years
Language instr: English

Reddford House Northcliff
14th Avenue, Fairlands, Randburg, Johannesburg
Tel: +27 (0) 10 060 4234
Age range: 1–18 years
Language instr: English

Reddford House The Hills
Garsfontein Road, Pretoria East 0057
Tel: +27 (0) 10 060 0757
Age range: 1–18 years
Language instr: English

Redhill School
20 Summit Road, Morningside, Sandton, Johannesburg 2057
Tel: +27 11 783 4707
Curriculum: IBDP

Roedean School
Princess of Wales Terrace, Parktown 2193
Tel: +27 11 647 3200
Language instr: English
RS

Silver Oaks International
40 Pinaster Avenue, Hazelwood, Pretoria
Tel: +27 12 346 4770
Curriculum: ALevs

St Andrew's College
PO Box 182, Makhanda (Grahamstown) 6140
Tel: +27 (0) 46 603 2300
Age range: B13–18 years
Language instr: English

St Cyprian's School
Gorge Road, Oranjezicht 8001
Tel: +27 21 461 1090
Language instr: English
RS

St John's College
St David Road, Houghton, Johannesburg 2198
Tel: +27 104 920 300
Curriculum: UK, ALevs

St Stithian's College
Private Bag 2, Randburg 2125 Gauteng
Tel: +27 11 577 6000
Age range: 4–18

Stanford Lake College
PO Box 271, Haenertsburg, Magoebaskloof 0730
Tel: +27 15 276 6103
Age range: 12–19
Language instr: English
RS

Star College Boys High Durban
20 Kinloch Avenue, Westville North, Durban 3630
Tel: +27 31 262 71 91
Language instr: English

Star College Capetown
22 Elgin Road, Sybrand Park, Cape Town 7700
Tel: +27 21 6970194
Language instr: English

Star College Girls High Durban
20 Kinloch Avenue, Westville North, Durban 3630
Tel: +27 31 2627190
Age range: 5–18
No. of pupils: 215
Curriculum: National
Language instr: English

Star College Johannesburg
C/o Eastwood & Peter Wessels St., Turffontein, Johannesburg
Tel: +27 11 4345234
Language instr: English

Star College Pretoria
25 Meadow Ave, Pretoria 0041
Tel: +27 12 8072346
Language instr: English

Star College Primary Durban
20 Kinloch Avenue, Westville North, Durban 3630
Tel: +27 31 2627190
No. of pupils: 389
Language instr: English

SUDAN

Cambridge International School – Bahry
Ahmed Gasim Street, Bahri
Tel: 00 249 85 235799
Age range: 5–18
No. of pupils: 218
Curriculum: IGCSE

Cambridge International School – Khartoum
Taief- Nakheel Street, Khartoum
Tel: +249 83 253669
Age range: 6–18
No. of pupils: 500
Curriculum: IGCSE

Cambridge International School – Omdurman
Almulazmeen/ Nile Street, Omdurman
Tel: +249 87 563499
Age range: 6–18
No. of pupils: 482
Curriculum: IGCSE

Confluence International School of Khartoum
Building No.5, Gamhouria Avenue, Khartoum 11111
Tel: +249 960099970
Curriculum: IBDP, IBMYP, IBPYP
Language instr: English, Arabic

Khartoum American School
c/o US Embassy, P.O. Box 699, Khartoum
Tel: +249 15 577 0105 / +249 15 577 0107
Age range: 3–18
No. of pupils: 222 B132 G90
Curriculum: SAT, USA
AISA CIS

Khartoum International Community School
PO Box 1840, Khartoum
Tel: +249 183 215 000
Age range: 3–18
No. of pupils: 400 B222 G178
Curriculum: ACT, IBDP, IBPYP
Language instr: English
AISA CIS ECIS

Unity High School
Al Qasr Street, Khartoum
Tel: +249 844 663 6692
Age range: 5–18
Curriculum: UK

TANZANIA

Academic International School
PO Box 63333, Dar es Salaam
Tel: +255 222780444 / +255 222781346
Language instr: English

Al Muntazir School
PO Box 21735, Dar es Salaam
Tel: +255 22 215 0161
Age range: 3–18
No. of pupils: 3173 *B*1501 *G*1672
Curriculum: National, UK

Braeburn Dar es Salaam International School
PO Box 31158, Dar es Salaam
Tel: +255 (0)763 086 646
Age range: 2–16
No. of pupils: 216
Curriculum: SAT, UK, IGCSE
Language instr: English

Braeburn International School Arusha
PO Box 14268, Arusha
Tel: +255 (0)250 5716
Age range: 2–19
No. of pupils: 424
Curriculum: UK, IGCSE, ALevs
AISA COBIS ECIS

Canon Andrea Mwaka School
PO Box 228, Dodoma
Tel: +255 26 2323220
Age range: 3–15
No. of pupils: 280 *B*130 *G*150
Curriculum: UK, IGCSE
Language instr: English

Dar Es Salaam Independent School
PB 32391, Plot 92, Mikocheni, Dar es Salaam
Tel: 002 278 1515
Curriculum: UK

Dar es Salaam International Academy
PO Box 23282, Dar es Salaam
Tel: +255 22 2600 202
Age range: 5–16
No. of pupils: 254 *B*131 *G*123
Curriculum: IBDP, IBMYP, IBPYP
Language instr: English
AISA

Ecole française Arthur Rimbaud de Dar es Salaam
PO Box 2183, Plot 282, Msasani Road, Masaki, Dar es Salaam
Tel: +255 765 562 235
Curriculum: FrenchBacc

Feza Schools
PO Box 77965, Dar Es Salaam
Tel: +255 712 339 239

Geita Gold International School
PO Box 532, Geita
Tel: +255 28 252 05000
AISA CIS

Genesis Schools
1408 Itagi Street, Dar es Salaam
Tel: +255 222 666 147
AISA

Haven of Peace Academy
PO Box 70020, Dar es Salaam
Tel: +255 22 2650604
Age range: 5–18
No. of pupils: 300 *B*145 *G*155
Curriculum: UK
AISA

Hope International School
PO Box 7640, Moshi
Tel: +255 763 270 467
Age range: 3–16
No. of pupils: 115
Language instr: English

International School of Tanganyika Ltd
United Nations Road, PO Box 2651, Dar es Salaam
Tel: +255 22 2151817
Age range: 4–19
No. of pupils: 1020 *B*515 *G*505
Curriculum: IBDP, IBMYP, IBPYP, SAT, TOEFL
Language instr: English
AISA CIS ECIS

International School of Zanzibar
PO Box 1787, Zanzibar
Tel: +255 777 477 053
Age range: 2–18 years
No. of pupils: 175
Curriculum: IPC, IGCSE, ALevs
Language instr: English

Iringa International School
PO Box 912, Lumumba Street, Gangilonga, Iringa
Tel: +255 26 2702018
Age range: 3–17
No. of pupils: 123 *B*60 *G*63 *VIth*2
Curriculum: IBPYP, IGCSE, ALevs
Language instr: English
AISA

Isamilo International School Mwanza
Box 42, Mwanza
Tel: +255 28 2500497
Curriculum: UK, IGCSE, ALevs
Language instr: English
AISA

Kennedy House International School
Nelson Mandela Road, PO Box 350, Usa River
Tel: +255 (0)689 119 788
Age range: 2–14
No. of pupils: 100
Curriculum: UK
Language instr: English

Kwanza International School
Bagamoyo Road, Dar es Salaam
Tel: +225 222 771 961
AISA

Laureate International School – DSM Secondary
Bagamoyo Road, Behind Shamo Industries, Dar Es Salaam
Tel: +255 222 627 729
Age range: 11–20
No. of pupils: 300
Curriculum: IGCSE

Morogoro International School
PO Box 1015, Morogoro
Tel: +255 (0)23 260 4864
Age range: 2.5–18
No. of pupils: 300
Curriculum: UK, IGCSE
Language instr: English

St. Constantine's International School
PO Box 221, Arusha
Tel: +255 753 871 855
Language instr: English
AISA

The Aga Khan Mzizima Secondary School
P.O. Box 21563, Fire Road, Upanga, Dar es Salaam
Tel: +255 22 215 1253
Age range: 11–18
No. of pupils: 722 *B*393 *G*329
Curriculum: IBDP, IBPYP, National, ALevs
Language instr: English

The Aga Khan Primary School, Dar es Salaam
PO Box 10263, Dar es Salaam
Tel: +255 22 2152484
Age range: 3–12
No. of pupils: 920

The Latham School
Bahari Beach, P.O. Box 23119, Dar es Salaam
Tel: +255 767 528 426

UWC East Africa, Arusha Campus
PO Box 2691, Arusha
Tel: +255 78 449 0133
Age range: 3–19
Curriculum: IBDP, IBMYP, IBPYP
Language instr: English
AISA CIS

UWC East Africa, Moshi Campus
PO Box 733. Lema Road, Moshi
Tel: +255 27 2755004
Age range: 3–19
Curriculum: ACT, IBDP, IBMYP, IBPYP, SAT, TOEFL
Language instr: English
AISA CIS

THE GAMBIA

Banjul American Embassy School
P.O. Box 2596, Serrekunda
Tel: +220 4495920
Age range: 3–12
Curriculum: USA
Language instr: English
AISA

Banjul American International School
Atlantic Road, Fajara, Serrekunda
Tel: +220 4495920
Curriculum: USA
AISA

Ecole Française de Banjul
Atlantic Road – Fajara, PO Box 4682, Bakau
Tel: +220 4495487
No. of pupils: 80

Marina International School
P.O.Box 717, Banjul
Tel: +220 449 4374
Language instr: English
AISA

Shiloh Bilingual Education Centre International School
Bijilo, Serreku
Tel: +220 996 1756
Curriculum: UK
Language instr: English, French
AISA

TOGO

American International School of Lome
35 Kayigan Lawson, Lome
Tel: +228 22 61 1896
Age range: 3–18
No. of pupils: 73
Curriculum: USA
AISA

Arc-en-Ciel International School
Nyekonakpoe, Lomé BP: 2985
Tel: +228 2222 0329
Age range: 1–18
No. of pupils: 567
Curriculum: IBDP, IBMYP, IBPYP
Language instr: French, English
ECIS

International Christian School of Lomé
PO Box 582, Lomé
Tel: +228 222 1404
Language instr: English
AISA

The British School of Lomé
Residence du Benin, Lomé 20050
Tel: +228 2226 46 06
Age range: 18 months–18 years
No. of pupils: 300
Curriculum: IBDP, SAT, UK, IGCSE
Language instr: English

TUNISIA

American Cooperative School of Tunis
ACST BP150, Cite Taieb
M' Hiri, Laouina 2045
Tel: +216 71 760 905
Age range: 4–18
No. of pupils: 450 *B225 G225*
Curriculum: AP, IBDP, SAT, TOEFL
Language instr: English
CIS ECIS

British International School of Tunis
49 Rue du Parc, La
Soukra, Tunis 2036
Tel: +216 71 865 682
Age range: 3–16
Curriculum: UK
Language instr: English
COB

École Canadienne de Tunis
Rue des Minéraux
Charguia 1, Tunis 2035
Tel: +216 71 206 035
Curriculum: IBDP, IBMYP, IBPYP
Language instr: French

École Robert Desnos
92 bis route de l'hôpital militaire,
El Omrane, 1005 Tunis
Tel: +216 71 957 526
Age range: 4–11
No. of pupils: 1150

Groupe Scolaire International Les Nouvelles Générations
km5 Route Ajim-Houmt Souk,
Bousmayel, Ajim, 4135 Djerba
Tel: +216 36 015 861
Curriculum: IBDP, IBMYP, IBPYP
Language instr: French, Arabic

International School of Carthage
Les Jardins de Carthage,
2046 Ain Zaghouan
Tel: +216 29 517 777

John Dewey School de Sousse
Sahloul, Sousse 4054
Tel: +216 73 823 401
Curriculum: IBPYP
Language instr: Arabic, French

Lycée Pierre Mendès France
B.P. 125, 9 rue Pierre Mendès
France, El Mahrajène 1082
Tel: +216 70 014 900
Curriculum: FrenchBacc

UGANDA

ACORNS INTERNATIONAL SCHOOL (AIS)
For further details see p. 46
Plot 328, Kisota Road, (Along)
Northern Bypass, Kisaasi
Roundabout, Kampala
Tel: +256 393 202 665
Age range: 18 months–18 years
No. of pupils: 500
Curriculum: IBDP, IBMYP, IBPYP
Language instr: English

Aga Khan High School, Kampala
PO Box 6837, Kampala
Tel: +256 414 308 245
No. of pupils: 1680
Curriculum: IBDP, IGCSE
Language instr: English

AMBROSOLI INTERNATIONAL SCHOOL
For further details see p. 47
Plot 10-12 Binayomba Street,
Bugolobi, Kampala
Tel: +256 414 220416
Email: admissions@ambrosolischool.com
Website: www.ambrosolischool.com
Head of School: Emma Norris
Age range: 3–11 years
Fees: $150
Curriculum: IPC, UK
Language instr: English
AISA CIS

Ecole Française Les Grands Lacs
PO Box 7212, Kampala
Tel: +256 414 341 660
Curriculum: FrenchBacc

Galaxy International School Uganda
Plot 1077 Lubowa Estate, Entebbe
Road, P.O. Box 11119, Kampala
Tel: +256 781 468 000
AISA

GEMS Cambridge International School – Kampala
Plot 102/104 Butabika Road, Before
Royal Palms Estate, Luzira, Kampala
Tel: +256 755 177 982
Age range: 2.5–18
(boarding from 7)
Curriculum: UK, IGCSE
Language instr: English
COB

International School of Uganda
272 Lubowa Estate,
Lubowa, Kampala
Tel: +256 41 4200374
Age range: 2.5–19 years
No. of pupils: 556
Curriculum: IBDP, IBMYP, IBPYP
Language instr: English
AISA CIS

Kampala International School Uganda (KISU)
P.O.Box 34249, Bukoto, Kampala
Tel: +256 752 711 882;
+256 752 711 909
Age range: 2–18 years
No. of pupils: 450
Curriculum: IBDP, IGCSE
Language instr: English
CIS

Rainbow International School Uganda
P.O. Box 7632, Kampala
Tel: +256 312 266696/7
Age range: 2–18
No. of pupils: 850
Curriculum: UK, IGCSE, ALevs
Language instr: English
COB EAR

ZAMBIA

Acacia International School
Plot 5379/M, Nakatindi
Road, Livingstone
Tel: +260 950318656
Curriculum: UK

American International School of Lusaka
PO Box 320176, Lusaka
Tel: +260 211 260509
Age range: 2–18
No. of pupils: 580 *B301 G279*
Curriculum: IBDP, IBMYP, IBPYP
Language instr: English
AISA CIS

Banani International School
Private Bag RW 199X, Lusaka
Tel: +260 211 214785
Curriculum: UK, IGCSE

Baobab College
Kafue Road, Lilayi Lusaka,
P.O Box 350099, Chilanga
Tel: +260966876804
Curriculum: UK, IGCSE, ALevs

Ecole Française Champollion
Plot 22725, Alick Nkhata
Avenue, Longacres, Lusaka
Tel: +260 21 12547122
Age range: 2–18
No. of pupils: 100

International School of Lusaka
PO Box 50121, Ridgeway, Lusaka
Tel: +260 211 252291
Age range: 2–18
No. of pupils: 676 *B348 G328 VIth56*
Curriculum: IBDP, IBPYP, IGCSE
Language instr: English
AISA CIS

Kabitaka School
Kabitaka Hills Estate, PO
Box 110506, Solwezi
COB

Lechwe School
PO Box 20830, Kitwe
Tel: +260 21 2 222530/227040
Age range: 2–18
No. of pupils: 390
Curriculum: SAT, UK, IGCSE, ALevs
Language instr: English

Lusaka International Community School
PO Box 30528, Lusaka
Tel: +260 211 290 626
Age range: 2–17
No. of pupils: 242
Curriculum: UK
AISA CIS

Martin House Trust School
Kalundu Farm, Chisamba
Road, Chisamba
Tel: +260 96 2143920
Age range: 2–11

Musikili Primary School
PO Box 670370, Mazabuka
Tel: +260 213 235779
Age range: 5–13

Pestalozzi Education Centre
Box 194 Postbag E835, Lusaka
Tel: +260 978 950 599
Age range: 7–19 years
Curriculum: IBDP
Language instr: English

Simba International School
PO Box 240216, Ndola 10101
Tel: +260 21 2 613674
Age range: 4–19
No. of pupils: 600
Curriculum: IGCSE

The Italian School of Lusaka
Private Bag E675, Lusaka 675
Tel: +260 211 256 306
Age range: 5–12
No. of pupils: 150
Curriculum: IGCSE

Trident Preparatory School
Educore Services Ltd,
PO Box 110506,
Tel: +260 962 422 210
Curriculum: UK
(COB)

ZIMBABWE

Divaris Makaharis School
Lot 13Cnr Lavenham/Northolt Rd, Bluffhill, Harare
Tel: +263 4 310085
Curriculum: UK

Falcon College
PO Esigodini, Esigodini
Tel: +263 086 770 04566
Age range: 13–18 years
No. of pupils: 450
Curriculum: UK, IGCSE, ALevs
Language instr: English

Harare International School
66 Pendennis Road, Mount Pleasant, Harare
Tel: +263 4 870 514
Age range: 3–19
No. of pupils: 430
Curriculum: IBDP, IBMYP, IBPYP, USA
Language instr: English
(AISA) (CIS)

Peterhouse Boys School
P Bag 3741, Marondera
Tel: +263 (0)279 22200/4

Peterhouse Girls School
Private Bag 3774, Marondera
Tel: +263 279 23599
Age range: G12–19
Curriculum: UK, IGCSE, ALevs

Peterhouse Group of Schools
Private Bag 3741, Marondera
Tel: +263 (0)279 22200/4
Age range: 12–18
No. of pupils: 915 *B*515 *G*400
Curriculum: UK, IGCSE, ALevs
Language instr: English

Ruzawi School
Private Bag 3713, Marondera
Tel: +263 65 232 4104/5
Age range: 5–18
No. of pupils: 390

Springvale House Preparatory School
Springvale House, P Bag 3741, Marondera
Tel: +263 (0)279 23598

St George's College
Private Bag 7727, Causeway, Harare
Tel: +263 4 792 709
Age range: *B*13–18
No. of pupils: 750
Curriculum: UK, IGCSE, ALevs
Language instr: English

St Johns College
179 Fisher Avenue, Rolf Valley, Borrowdale, Harare
Tel: +263 24 870 942/285 0626
Age range: 12–18
No. of pupils: 570
Language instr: English

St John's Preparatory School for Boys
PO Box BW300, Fisher Avenue, Borrowdale, Harare
Tel: +263 4885128/121
Age range: *B*6–12
No. of pupils: *B*545
Curriculum: National, UK
Language instr: English

The Heritage School
P.O.Box BW1220, Borrowdale, Harare
Tel: +263 242 862 285
Age range: 1–18 years
No. of pupils: 900
Curriculum: UK, IGCSE, ALevs

International schools in Asia

Schools ordered A–Z by Country

Key to directory

Country	**Whereford**
Name of school or college	**College Academy**
Indicates that this school has a profile	***For further details see p***
Address and contact number	Which Street, Whosville, Wherefordshire AB12 3CD **Tel:** 01000 000000
Head's name	**Head Master:** Dr A Person
Age range	**Age range:** 11–18
Number of pupils. B = boys G = girls VIth = sixth form	**No. of pupils:** 660 B330 G330 VIth 200
Fees per annum. Day = fees for day pupils. WB = fees for weekly boarders. FB = fees for full boarders.	**Fees:** Day £11,000 WB £16,000 FB £20,000
Curriculum	**Curriculum:** National, IBDP, ALevs
Language of instruction	**Language instr:** English, French
Memberships/Accreditation	(AISA) (COB) (EAR)

Key to icons

Key to symbols:

- Boys' school
- Girls' school
- Boarding accommodation

Member of:

- (AISA) Association of International Schools in Africa
- (CEE) Central and Eastern European Schools Association
- (EAR) East Asia Regional Council of Overseas Schools
- (ECIS) European Council of International Schools
- (RS) Round Square

Accreditation:

- (CIS) Council of International Schools
- (COB) Council of British International Schools

Please note: Schools are coeducational day schools unless otherwise indicated

BAHRAIN

Abdul Rahman Kanoo International School
P.O. Box 2512, Manama
Tel: +973 1787 5055
Age range: 3–18
No. of pupils: 2194
Curriculum: IBDP, IPC, National, UK, IGCSE
Language instr: English, Arabic
CIS

Al Ahlia School
Building 166, Street. 45, Block 545, Al Qurayya
Tel: +973 77476666
Curriculum: IBDP
Language instr: English, Arabic

Al Hekma International School
Building No 1962, Road 4363, Sanad 743, PO Box 26489 Adliya
Tel: +973 17 620 820/17 623 999
Age range: 3–18
Curriculum: USA

Al Mahd Day Boarding School – Saar Campus
PO Box 30331, Manama
Tel: +973 17 792 422
Age range: 4–16
No. of pupils: 4000
Curriculum: IGCSE

Al Noor International School
PO Box 85, Manama
Tel: + 973 1 773 6773
Age range: 4–19
Curriculum: National, UK, IGCSE, ALevs

Al Raja School
PO Box 1, Manama
Tel: +973 1725 4414
Age range: 5–18
Curriculum: USA
Language instr: English, Arabic

American School of Bahrain
Building 1528, Road 3429, Block 934, North Riffa (Riffa Alshamali), Riffa
Tel: +973 17 211 800
Curriculum: IBDP
Language instr: English, Arabic

Arabian Pearl Gulf (APG) School
PO Box 26299, Adliya, Manama
Tel: +973 17 403 666
Age range: 4–18
No. of pupils: 1452
Curriculum: IBDP, IGCSE
Language instr: English, French, Arabic

Bahrain Bayan School
Building No. 230, Road 4112, Block 841, Isa Town
Tel: +973 7712 2244
No. of pupils: 1147
Curriculum: IBDP, National, USA
Language instr: English, Arabic

Bahrain School
PO Box 934, Manama
Tel: +973 17727 828
Age range: 5–19
No. of pupils: 450
Curriculum: IBDP
Language instr: English

Beacon Private School
Building 101, Avenue 14, Block 109, PO Box 52030, Al Hidd
Tel: +973 66 00 00 88
Curriculum: IBDP
Language instr: English, Arabic

Britus International School
PO Box 18041, Building 208, Road 408, Block 704, Salmabad
Tel: +973 1759 8440
Age range: 3–18
No. of pupils: 2000
Curriculum: IBDP, SAT, USA, IGCSE
Language instr: English

Capital School
PO.Box: 54420, Al Ahli Club, Mahooz Zinj
Tel: +973 1700 8880
Age range: 3–11
Curriculum: UK

Creativity Private School
PO Box 24176, Muharraq
Tel: +973 1724 3855
Age range: 4–14
Curriculum: USA, IGCSE

Hawar International School
P.O. Box 38338, West Riffa
Tel: +973 13 666 555
Curriculum: IBDP
Language instr: English

IBN KHULDOON NATIONAL SCHOOL
For further details see p. 77
Building 161, Road 4111, Area 841, P.O. Box 20511, Isa Town
Tel: +973 17780661
Email: k.algosaibi@ikns.edu.bh
Website: www.ikns.edu.bh
President: Kamal Abdel-Nour
Age range: 4–18 years
No. of pupils: 1700
Curriculum: IBDP, IBMYP, IBPYP, National, SAT, TOEFL, USA
Language instr: English, Arabic

Lycée Français MLF de Bahreïn
PO Box 24447, Muharraq
Tel: +973 1732 3770
Age range: 6–17
No. of pupils: 430
Language instr: French

Modern Knowledge Schools
PO Box 15826, Bldg 515, Manama
Tel: +973 17727838
Age range: 3–18
Curriculum: IBDP, USA
Language instr: English

Nadeen School
PO Box 26367, Adliya
Tel: +973 1772 8886
Age range: 2–12
No. of pupils: 370
Curriculum: UK
Language instr: English

Naseem International School
PO Box 28503, Riffa
Tel: +973 17 782 000
Age range: 3–18
No. of pupils: 1014 *B603 G411*
Curriculum: IBDP, IBMYP, IBPYP, IBCP, National, SAT, IGCSE
Language instr: English, Arabic
CIS ECIS

Quality Education School – Al Zamil Garden Budaiya Campus
Behind Fire Station, Budaiya
Tel: +973 17 692 917
Age range: 3–16
Curriculum: UK, IGCSE

Quality Education School – Khalil Kanoo Gardens Campus
Near Salmaniya, Manama
Tel: +973 17 277 984
Age range: 5–18
Curriculum: IGCSE

Riffa Views International School
PO Box 3050, Manama 934
Tel: +973 1656 5000
Age range: 4–18
Curriculum: IBDP, USA
Language instr: English
CIS

Sacred Heart School
PO Box 388, Isa Town, Manama
Tel: +973 17684367
Age range: 4–19
No. of pupils: 60
Curriculum: IGCSE
Language instr: English

Shaikha Hessa Girls' School
PO Box 37799, Riffa
Tel: +973 17 756 111
Curriculum: IBDP
Language instr: English
CIS

St Christopher's School
PO Box 32052, Isa Town
Tel: +973 1760 5000
Age range: 3–18
No. of pupils: 2253 *B1140 G1113 VIth283*
Curriculum: IBDP, SAT, UK, GCSE, IGCSE, ALevs
Language instr: English

Talent International & The Infant School (Manama Branch)
Rd No 5641, Salihiya, Manama
Tel: +973 17 252346
Age range: 3 months–18 years
Curriculum: UK, GCSE
Language instr: English

Talent International & The Infant School (Riffa Branch)
Rd No 2506, Riffa
Tel: +973 17 770078
Age range: 3 months–18
Curriculum: UK, GCSE
Language instr: English

The Asian School
PO Box 1143, Manama
Tel: + 973 17722886
Age range: 4–19
Curriculum: National

The British Preparatory School
Rahim Villas, Entrance 300, Saar Avenue
Tel: +973 17792010
Age range: 18 months–6
Curriculum: UK
Language instr: English

The British School of Bahrain
PO Box 30733 – Budaiya, Building 1080, Road 1425, Block 1014, Hamala
Tel: +973 1 761 0920
Age range: 3–18 years
Curriculum: UK, GCSE, ALevs
Language instr: English

The Children's Academy, Bahrain
Northern Governorate, off Janabiya Highway,
Tel: +973 17613234
Curriculum: UK

The Indian School
PO Box 558, Isa Town
Tel: +973 17684166
Age range: 4–19
No. of pupils: 8650

The International School of Choueifat – Manama
Bldg. 110, Area 257, Road 59, Choueifat Avenue, Manama, Amwaj Islands
Tel: +973 160 33 333
Age range: 4–19
No. of pupils: 600
Curriculum: USA

BANGLADESH

Abdul Kadir Molla International School
16/8 Baghdi (Dhaka-Sylhet Highway), Narsingdi Sadar, Narsingdi 1600, Dhaka
Curriculum: IBPYP
Language instr: English, Bengali

American International School, Dhaka
PO Box 6106, Gulshan, 1212 Dhaka
Tel: +880 2 984 2452
Age range: 3–18
No. of pupils: 730
Curriculum: ACT, AP, IBDP, IBPYP, SAT, USA
Language instr: English

American Standard International School
Plot 20B Road No. 79/82, Gulshan, 1212 Dhaka
Language instr: English

Australian International School, Dhaka
Joarshchara, Khilkhet, 1229 Dhaka
Tel: +880 17 11567236
Curriculum: IBDP, IBMYP, IBPYP
Language instr: English

Chittagong Grammar School (CGS)
321/11 Sarson Road, Chittagong
Tel: +880 3 162 2472
Curriculum: UK, GCSE, ALevs

Chittagong Grammar School (CGS) Dhaka
Block-B, House No. 83, Road No. 4, Banani, 1213 Dhaka
Curriculum: UK, GCSE, ALevs

Crans-Montana International School
1492, C D A Avenue, East Nasirabad, Panchlaish, Chittagong
Tel: +880 3 165 7126
Curriculum: IBPYP
Language instr: English, Bengali

East West International School & College
265/1 West Shewrapara, Mirpur 1216 Dhaka
Curriculum: UK, IGCSE
Language instr: English

Ecole Française Internationale de Dhaka
Plot 13, Embassy Road, Baridhara, Dhaka
Tel: +880 2 882 40 56
No. of pupils: 110
Curriculum: National

Grace International School
63 Gulshan North Ave, 1212 Dhaka
Tel: +880 171 330 3468
Age range: 3–16
No. of pupils: 230
Curriculum: UK, IGCSE

Hurdco International School
Bashundhora Main Gate, 1229 Dhaka
Tel: +880 2 841 5034
Age range: 3–18
Curriculum: UK, ALevs

International School Dhaka (ISD)
Plot 80, Block E, Bashundhara R/A, (Opposite Apollo Hospitals Dhaka), 1229 Dhaka
Tel: +880 2 843 1101
Age range: 2–19
No. of pupils: 535
Curriculum: IBDP, IBMYP, IBPYP
Language instr: English

Oxford International School – Main Campus
House # 34, Road # 27 (old), New 16, Dhanmondi R/A, 1209 Dhaka
Tel: +880 2 911 5392
No. of pupils: 2500
Curriculum: UK, GCSE, ALevs

Pledge Harbor International School
Singer Dighi, Maona, Gazipur 1741, Dhaka
Tel: +880 961 443 3444
Curriculum: IBDP, IBMYP, IBPYP, IBCP
Language instr: English

Royal Institute of Smart Education RISE
Subidbazar, Sylhet
Tel: +880 173 070 0877
Curriculum: USA, IGCSE, ALevs

Scholastica High School (Senior Campus, Uttara)
Plot 2, Road 8 and 9, Sector 1, Uttara Model Town, 1230 Dhaka
Tel: +880 2 589 56053
Age range: 14–19
Curriculum: UK, ALevs

Sunnydale School
House #2/A, Road #8, Dhanmondi R/A, 1205 Dhaka
Tel: +880 171 338 9795
Curriculum: UK, GCSE, ALevs

Sunshine Grammar School and College
House 11, Road 1, Nasirabad H/S, 4000 Chittagong
Tel: +880 3 165 5319
Age range: 3–18
Curriculum: UK, GCSE, ALevs
Language instr: English

Sylhet Khananchibari International School and College
Nayasarak Road, 3100 Sylhet
Tel: +880 8 217 18011
No. of pupils: 1500
Curriculum: UK

The Aga Khan School, Dhaka
Road 9, Sector 4, Uttara Model Town, 1230 Dhaka
Tel: +880 2 589 54042
No. of pupils: 1216
Curriculum: IBDP, IBPYP

William Carey Academy
G.P.O. Box 96, 1986/A Zakir Hossain By-Lane, East Nasirabad, 4000 Chittagong
Tel: +880 3 165 2034
Curriculum: USA
Language instr: English

BRUNEI DARUSSALAM

Bright Jigsaw International School
No. 675, Kampong Salambigar, Jalan Muara, Bandar Seri Begawan BC 1515
Tel: +673 2341035
Age range: 4–11

INTERNATIONAL SCHOOL BRUNEI
For further details see p. 79
Jalan Utama Salambigar, Kampong Sungai Hanching, Berakas 'B' BC2115
Tel: +673 233 0608
Email: admissionmgr@ac.isb.edu.bn
Website: www.isb.edu.bn
Headteacher: Tony Macfadyen
Age range: 2–18 years
No. of pupils: 1200
Fees: $6,840–$11,700
Curriculum: IBDP, National, SAT, UK, GCSE, IGCSE
Language instr: English

JERUDONG INTERNATIONAL SCHOOL
For further details see p. 82
Jalan Universiti, Kampong Tungku, Bandar Seri Begawan BE2119
Tel: +673 241 1000 (Ext: 1206/7100/1214)
Email: admissions@jis.edu.bn
Website: www.jerudong internationalschool.com
Principal: Nicholas Sheehan
Age range: 2–18 years (Boarding from 8 years)
No. of pupils: 1652 *VIth*366
Fees: *Day* B$18,108–B$26,952 *WB* B$17,688–B$23,500 *FB* B$23,688–B$29,500
Curriculum: IBDP, SAT, UK, GCSE, IGCSE, ALevs
Language instr: English

Seri Mulia Sarjana International School
Spg. 340 Kg. Mata-Mata, Jalan Gadong, BE 1718, Bandar Seri Begawan, Negara
Tel: +673 2421311
Curriculum: UK

CAMBODIA

Abundant Life International School
House 94, ST 315, Tuol Kouk, Phnom Penh
Tel: +855 88 690 1111
Curriculum: USA

Asian Hope International School
168 Chres Village Road, Sen Sok Khan, Phnom Penh Thmey, Phnom Penh
Tel: +855 23 885 170
Age range: 3–18
No. of pupils: 391
Curriculum: National, UK, IGCSE, ALevs
Language instr: English

Australian International School Phnom Penh
76 Angkor Boulevard, Sangkat Toul Sangke, Khan Russey Keo, Phnom Penh
Tel: +855 (0)92 111 136
Curriculum: IBDP, IBMYP, IBPYP, IBCP
Language instr: English, Khmer

Canadian International School of Phnom Penh
Koh Pich (Diamond Island), Elite Town Street, Phnom Penh
Tel: +855 23 900 399
Curriculum: IBDP
Language instr: English, French

CIA FIRST International School
No. 9/107, Street 2004, Phnom Penh
Tel: +855 (0)12 2000 11
Curriculum: USA

East-West International School
#131 Street 143, Boeung Keng Kang 3, Phnom Penh
Tel: +855 (0)23 998 244
Age range: 2–18 years
No. of pupils: 500
Curriculum: IPC, IGCSE, ALevs
Language instr: English, Khmer

Footprints International School
Street 135, No. 84, Phnom Penh
Tel: +855 (0)17 222 054
Age range: 2–17
Curriculum: IGCSE, ALevs
Language instr: English

HOPE International School – Phnom Penh Campus
PO Box 2521, Phnom Penh 3 12000
Tel: +855 12 550 522
No. of pupils: 400
Curriculum: IBDP, IGCSE
Language instr: English

HOPE International School – Siem Reap Campus
Phum Bos Kralanh, Sangkat Chreav, Krong Siem Reap, Siem Reap Province
Tel: +855 78 210 320

iCAN British International School
85 Sothearos Blvd, Sangkat Tonle Bassac, Phnom Penh
Tel: +855 23 222 416 8
Age range: 5–19
No. of pupils: 340
Curriculum: IPC

International School of Phnom Penh
PO Box 138, Hun Neang Boulevard, Phnom Penh
Tel: +855 23 425 088
Age range: 3–18
No. of pupils: 900
Curriculum: IBDP, IBMYP, IBPYP
Language instr: English
CIS EAR ECIS

International School of Siem Reap
0404 Wat Damnak Village, Salakamreuk Commune, PO Box 93035
Tel: +855 63 964 983
Age range: 2.5–18
Curriculum: UK, IGCSE, ALevs

Jay Pritzker Academy
PO Box 93298, Siem Reap
Tel: +855 (0)92 655 322
Age range: 4–12

Lycée Français René-Descartes
Rue Christopher Howes (rue 96), Wat Phnom BP 1132, Phnom Penh
Tel: +855 (0)23 722 044
Curriculum: FrenchBacc

Northbridge International School Cambodia
PO Box 2042, Phnom Penh 3
Tel: +855 23 900 749
Age range: 2–18
No. of pupils: 700
Curriculum: IBDP, IBMYP, IBPYP
Language instr: English

Paragon International School Cambodia – Primary Campus
No: 39, St: 315, Boeng Kok 1 Toul Kork, Phnom Penh
Tel: +855 (23) 88 40 40
Age range: 4–11
Curriculum: UK

Paragon International School Cambodia – Secondary Campus
No: 2843, St: 3, Sangkat Tonle Basak Khan Chamkar Morn, Phnom Penh
Tel: +855 (23) 21 40 40
Age range: 5–19
No. of pupils: 765 *B401 G364*
Curriculum: National, SAT, UK
Language instr: English

St. George's International School
P.O. Box 93236, #93, Thmor Meas Road, Salakamreuk Commune, Siem Reap
Tel: +855 (0)63 96 90 36
Curriculum: UK, IGCSE

The Giving Tree School
761 Preah Monivong Blvd, Phnom Penh
Tel: +855 17 997 112
Curriculum: IBPYP
Language instr: English, French

Western International School (WIS)
#46, St. 337 Boeung Kok II, Toul Kork, Phnom Penh
Tel: +855 23 990 699
Curriculum: USA

CHINA

Access International Academy Ningbo
No1 Ai Xue Road, Beilun District, Ningbo, Zhejiang 315800
Tel: +86 574 8686 9999
Age range: 4–18
Curriculum: USA
Language instr: English
EAR

AISB-Hope International
Building 5, Dayu, Yard 4, Chaoyang Farm, Chaoyang District, Beijing 100018
Tel: +86 10 8431 2141
Age range: 5–18 years
Curriculum: AP
Language instr: English

Alcanta International College
14 Guang Sheng Road, Nansha District, Guangzhou City, Guangdong 511458
Tel: +86 20 8618 3999/3666
Age range: 12–19
Curriculum: IBDP
Language instr: English, Mandarin

American International School of Guangzhou
No 3 Yan Yu Street South, Ersha Island, Yuexiu District, Guangzhou, Guangdong 510105
Tel: +86 20 8735 3392
Age range: 3–18 years
No. of pupils: 1000
Curriculum: IBDP, IBPYP
Language instr: English
EAR

Bade Intercultural Academy, Chengdu
168 Zhongli Road, Banzhuyuan Town, Xindu District, Chengdu, Sichuan
Tel: +86 130 7600 8225
Curriculum: IBMYP, IBPYP
Language instr: English, Chinese

Baowei Kindergarten
No.4 Baiyun Road, Xicheng District, Beijing 100045
Tel: +86 13716522908
Curriculum: IBPYP
Language instr: Chinese, English

Beanstalk International Bilingual School BIBS – Chaoyang Changying Campus
No. 1 Yaojia Street, Chaoyang District
Tel: +8610 8456 6019
Curriculum: IBDP, IBMYP, IBPYP

Beanstalk International Bilingual School BIBS – Chengdu Campus
No. 351 Honghe Street, Longquanyi district, Chengdu, Sichuan
Tel: +86 28 8481 0088
Curriculum: IBDP, IBPYP

Beanstalk International Bilingual School BIBS – Haidian Sijiqing Campus
Yanxitai, Jushan Village, Sijiqing, Haidian District, Beijing
Curriculum: IBDP, IBMYP, IBPYP

Beanstalk International Bilingual School BIBS – Kunming Campus
No. 986 Yongzheng Street, Chenggong District, Kunming, Yunnan
Tel: +86871 6747 8668
Curriculum: IBDP, IBPYP
Language instr: English, Chinese

Beanstalk International Bilingual School BIBS – Shunyi Campus
No. 15 Liyuan Jie, TianZhu County, Shunyi District, Beijing 100000
Tel: +86 10 6456 0618
Curriculum: IBDP, IBMYP, IBPYP
Language instr: English

Beanstalk International Bilingual School BIBS – Upper East Side Campus
No.6 North East 4th Ring Rd, Chaoyang District, Beijing 100016
Tel: +86 10 5130 7951
Curriculum: IBPYP
Language instr: English

Beijing Bacui Bilingual School
No 1 Bacui Road, Chaoyang District, Beijing 100025
Tel: +86 10 6549 8092

Beijing BISS International School
No 17, Area 4, An Zhen Xi Li, Chaoyang District, Beijing 100029
Tel: +86 10 64 433151
Age range: 2–19 years
Curriculum: IBDP, IBMYP, IBPYP
Language instr: English

Beijing Chaoyang KaiWen Academy
No.46 Baoquansan Street, Chaoyang District, Beijing
Tel: +86 108 302 8199
Curriculum: IBDP
Language instr: English, Chinese

Beijing City International School
77 Baiziwan Nan Er Road, Chaoyang District, Beijing 100022
Tel: +86 10 8771 7171
Age range: 3–18
No. of pupils: 1029 *B428 G601*
Curriculum: IBDP, IBMYP, IBPYP, SAT
Language instr: English
CIS EAR

Beijing Concord College of Sino-Canada
Conglin, Zhuangyuan, Tongzhou District, Beijing 101118
Tel: +86 108 959 1234
Language instr: English

Beijing Enlighten School
No. 300 Shunbai Road, Chaoyang District, Beijing
Tel: +86 10 6431 9970
Curriculum: IBPYP
Language instr: English, Chinese

Beijing Haidian International School
No.368-2 Hanhe Road, Haidian District, Beijing 100195
Tel: +86 10 8843 8003
Curriculum: IBDP
Language instr: English

Beijing Huijia Kindergarten, Beiou Campus
No.80 Maliandao Road, Xicheng District, Beijing 100085
Tel: +86 10 63354580
Curriculum: IBPYP
Language instr: Chinese, English

Beijing Huijia Kindergarten, Changhewan Campus
No.59 Gaoliangqiao Xiejie Road, Changhewan Community, Haidian District, Beijing 100044
Tel: +86 10 82149978
Curriculum: IBPYP
Language instr: Chinese, English

Beijing Huijia Kindergarten, Shijixin Campus
No. 3 Landianchang West Road, Haidian District, Beijing 100097
Tel: +86 10 88874145
Curriculum: IBPYP
Language instr: Chinese, English

Beijing Huijia Kindergarten, Wanquan Campus
No. 35 Bagou South Road, Wanquan Xinxin Jiayuan Building 14, Haidian District, Beijing 100089
Tel: +86 10 8255 1751
Age range: 2–6
No. of pupils: 110
Curriculum: IBPYP
Language instr: Chinese

Beijing Huijia Kindergarten, Xibahe Dongli Campus
No.103 Xibahe Dongli, Chaoyang District, Beijing 100028
Tel: +86 (10) 64655212
Age range: 2–6
No. of pupils: 120
Curriculum: IBPYP
Language instr: Chinese

Beijing Huijia Private School
157 Changhuai Road, Changping District, Beijing 102200
Tel: +86 (10) 608 49399
Age range: 3–19
No. of pupils: 2100
Curriculum: IBDP, IBMYP, IBPYP
Language instr: Chinese, English

Beijing International Bilingual Academy
Monet Garden, No 5 Yumin Road, Houshayu, Shunyi, Beijing 101300
Tel: +86 10 80410390
Curriculum: IBDP, IBMYP
Language instr: English
EAR

Beijing Royal Foreign Language School
No. 11, Wangfu Street, Changping District, Beijing 102209
Tel: +86 10 81 785 511
Curriculum: IBMYP, IBPYP
Language instr: Chinese, English

Beijing Royal Kindergarten
No. 11, Wangfu Street, Changping District, Beijing 102209
Curriculum: IBPYP
Language instr: English, Chinese

Beijing Royal School
No. 11, Wangfu Street, Changping District, Beijing 102209
Tel: +86 10 81 785 511
Age range: 14–19
No. of pupils: 200
Curriculum: IBDP, USA
Language instr: English, Chinese

Beijing Shuren-Ribet Private School
Beijing Tongzhou District, Songzhuang Xiaopu South # 1, Beijing 101118
Tel: +86 10 80856787
Age range: 4–18
Curriculum: ACT, SAT, USA

Beijing World Youth Academy
18 Hua Jia Di Bei Li, Chao Yang District, Beijing 100102
Tel: +86 10 6470 6336
Age range: 11–18
No. of pupils: 685
Curriculum: IBDP, IBMYP
Language instr: English

Beijing Xin Fuxue International Academy
No. 99 Jingshun Road, Shunyi District, Beijing
Tel: +86 10 8942 0199
Curriculum: IBMYP
Language instr: English, Chinese

Boren Sino Canadian School
No. 20, Shuanglong Avenue, Jiangmen City, Guangdong
Tel: +86 750 3218848
Curriculum: National

Boston International School
9 Jinghui West Road, New District, Wuxi, Jiangsu 214000
Tel: +86 400 032 8000
Age range: 2–18
No. of pupils: 133 B65 G68
Curriculum: IBDP, IBMYP, IBPYP
Language instr: English
CIS

Bright Academy
Building 39#, ShiFoYing XiLi, Chaoyang District, Beijing 100025
Curriculum: IBPYP
Language instr: English, Chinese

BRITISH SCHOOL OF BEIJING, SHUNYI
For further details see p. 59
South Side, No. 9 An Hua Street, Shunyi District, Beijing 101318
Tel: +8610 8047 3558
Email: admissions@bsbshunyi.com
Website: www.bsbshunyi.com
Principal: Jayne Needham
Age range: 2–18 years
No. of pupils: 1100
Fees: Day RMB141,940–RMB318,790
Curriculum: IBDP, UK, IGCSE
Language instr: English, German
CIS

Bubble Kingdom International Kindergarten
No. 431, Linjiang Avenue, Zhujiang New Town, Tianhe District, Guangzhou, Guangdong 510620
Tel: +86 20 6622 2520
Curriculum: IBPYP
Language instr: English, Chinese

Buena Vista Concordia International School
BaoAn exit, GuangShen HighWay, XiCheng (Buena Vista) BaoAn, Shenzhen, Guangdong
Tel: +86 755 2823 8166
Curriculum: National, USA

Canada British Columbia International Schools – Hefei
5th Floor, International Department, Hefei No.1 High School, 2356 Xizang Road, Binhu New District, Hefei, Anhui
Tel: +86 199 5605 8176
Curriculum: IBDP
Language instr: English, Chinese

Canadian Foreign Language School-Cambridgeshire
Inside Agile Cambridgeshire, Nancun Town, Panyu District, Guangzhou, Guangdong 511442
Tel: +86 186 2078 9095
Curriculum: IBPYP
Language instr: English, Chinese

Canadian International School of Beijing
38 Liangmaqiao Lu, Chaoyang District, Beijing 100125
Tel: +86 10 64657788
Age range: 18 months–18 years
No. of pupils: 1093 B547 G546
Curriculum: IBDP, IBMYP, IBPYP, SAT
Language instr: English

Canadian International School of Beijing – Jianguomen DRC Campus
No.1 Xiushui Street, Chaoyang District, Beijing 100600
Tel: +86 10 85315312
Language instr: Chinese, English

Canadian International School of Guangzhou
122 Dongyi Road, Panyu District, Guangzhou, Guangdong
Tel: +86 020 3993 9920
Age range: 2–18

Canadian International School of Hefei
Fuxing Rd., High-Tech Zone, Hefei, Anhui 230088
Tel: +86 551 6267 6776
Curriculum: IBDP, IBMYP, IBPYP
Language instr: English

Canadian International School of Shenyang
No.301 Hui Shan Road, Hunnan District, Shenyang, Liaoning 110167
Tel: +86 24 66675379
Curriculum: IBDP, IBMYP, IBPYP
Language instr: Spanish, Chinese

Changchun American International School
2899 Dong Nan Hu Road, Changchun, Jilin 130033
Tel: +86 431 8458 1234
Age range: 3–18
No. of pupils: 400
Curriculum: IBDP, IBMYP, IBPYP
Language instr: English

Changping Huijia Kindergarten of Beijing
Building No.25, Zone 1, Yunqu Garden, Huilongguan Cultural Community, Changping District, Beijing 102208
Tel: +86 10 81715252
Curriculum: IBPYP
Language instr: Chinese, English

Changsha Huijia Kindergarten, Jujiangyuan Campus
Jintai Road, Xiangjiangshijicheng Community, Kaifu District, Changsha, Hunan 410000
Tel: +86 (0)731 85798618
Curriculum: IBPYP
Language instr: English, Chinese

Changsha Huijia Kindergarten, Yongjiangyuan Campus
Jiangwan Road, Kaifu District, Changsha, Hunan 415000
Tel: +86 731 85185289
Curriculum: IBPYP
Language instr: Chinese, English

Changsha WES Academy
8 Dongyi Road, Xingsha, Changsha National Economic & Technical Development Zone, Changsha, Hunan 410100
Tel: +86 731 82758900
Curriculum: IBDP, IBPYP
Language instr: English

Changwai Bilingual School
No.66 Hengshan Road, Changzhou, Jiangsu 213022
Tel: +86 519 86921160
Age range: 4–14
No. of pupils: 2100
Curriculum: IBDP, IBMYP, IBPYP, IPC

Chengdu International School
68 Tong Gui Road, Jin Jiang District, Chengdu, Sichuan 61066
Tel: +86 28 6517 5228/9

Chengdu Meishi International School
1340 Middle Section of Tianfu Avenue, Chengdu, Sichuan 610042
Tel: +86 028 8533 0653
Age range: 6–18
Curriculum: IBDP, IBMYP, IBPYP
Language instr: English, Chinese

Chenshan School
QiYunXiDaDao, XiuNing District, Huangshan, Anhui 245400
Tel: +86 559 7511878
Curriculum: IBDP
Language instr: English, Chinese

China World Academy Changshu
No.8 Yijia Road, Changshu, Jiangsu 215500
Tel: +86 185 0152 9096
Curriculum: IBDP
Language instr: English, Chinese

Chongqing Bachuan International High School
666 Tashan East Street, Tongliang District, Chongqing 402560
Curriculum: USA

Citic Lake Bilingual International School
Citic Lake Community, Lishui Town, Nanhai District, Foshan, Guangdong
Tel: +86 (0)757 81008639
Curriculum: IBDP, IBPYP
Language instr: English

Clifford School
Panyu, Guangzhou, Guangdong 511495
Tel: +86 20 8471 1441

Cogdel Cranleigh School, Changsha
117 Lixin Street, Changsha Economy and Technology Zone, Changsha, Hunan
Tel: +86 731 8406 1777
Age range: 7–18 years
Curriculum: IBDP, IBPYP, UK
Language instr: English, Chinese

CONCORDIA INTERNATIONAL SCHOOL SHANGHAI
For further details see p. 62
999 Ming Yue Road, JinQiao, Pudong, Shanghai 201206
Tel: +862 1 5899 0380
Email: admissions@concordiashanghai.org
Website: www.concordiashanghai.org
Head of School: Steve Winkelman
Age range: 3–18 years
No. of pupils: 1200
Fees: RMB201,000
Curriculum: USA
Language instr: English

Confucius International School
No.232, Songling Road, Laoshan District, Qingdao, Shandong 266100
Tel: +86 532 6889 8000
Curriculum: IGCSE, ALevs

Country Garden Silver Beach School
Country Garden Silver Beach, Renshan Town, Huidong County, Huizhou, Guangdong 516347
Tel: +86 139 2910 2096
Curriculum: IBDP, IBPYP
Language instr: English, Chinese

DALIAN AMERICAN INTERNATIONAL SCHOOL
For further details see p. 63
No. 2 Dianchi Road, Golden Pebble Beach National Resort, Dalian Development Area, Jinzhou District, Dalian, Liaoning 116650
Tel: +86 411 8757 2000
Email: admissions@daischina.org
Website: www.daischina.org
Head of School: Richard Swann
Age range: 4–18 years
Language instr: English

DALIAN MAPLE LEAF FOREIGN NATIONALS SCHOOL
For further details see p. 64
78 Caiyun Road, Xigang, Dalian, Liaoning
Tel: +86 411 6760187
Email: admin.mlfns@mapleleaf.net.cn
Website: www.mapleleafschools.com
Principal: Jade Kersey
Age range: 3–15 years
No. of pupils: 200
Fees: *Day* US$9,700–US$20,500

Dalian Maple Leaf International High School
Fushun Street, Jinzhou, Dalian, Liaoning
Tel: +86 400 655 6877
Age range: 14–19

Daystar Academy
No. 2, Shunbai Road, Chaoyang District, Beijing
Tel: +86 (0)10 64337366
Curriculum: IBDP, IBMYP, IBPYP
Language instr: English

Dehong Beijing International Chinese School
Block #1, Luneng Grassetown, Bifu Road, Tongzhou District, Beijing 101100
Tel: +86 10 8083 6983
Curriculum: IBDP
Language instr: English, Chinese

Dehong Shanghai International Chinese School
1935 Shuguang Road, Maqiao, Minhang District, Shanghai 201111
Tel: +86 21 3329 9458
Curriculum: IBDP
Language instr: English, Chinese

Deutsche Botschaftsschule Peking
Liangmaqiao Lu 49 A, Chaoyang District, Beijing 100125
Tel: +86 10 6532 2535

Deutsche Schule Shanghai Pudong
1100 Jufeng Lu, Shanghai 201206
Tel: +86 (21) 68 97 55 08

Dongguan Hanlin Experimental School
Chuangye Road No.5, Wanjiang District, Dongguan, Guangdong 523000
Tel: +86 769 22783301
Curriculum: IBPYP
Language instr: Chinese

DULWICH COLLEGE BEIJING
For further details see p. 66
89 Capital Airport Road, Shunyi District, Beijing 101300
Tel: +86 10 6454 9000
Email: admissions.beijing@dulwich.org
Website: beijing.dulwich.org
Head of College: Anthony Coles
Age range: 3–18 years
No. of pupils: 1570
Fees: *Day* RMB221,000–RMB332,000
Curriculum: IBDP, IGCSE
Language instr: English

Dulwich College Kindergarten, Shanghai
425 LanAn Road, JinQiao, Pudong, Shanghai 201206
Tel: +86 21 5899 9910
Age range: 2–7
Curriculum: UK

DULWICH COLLEGE SHANGHAI PUDONG
For further details see p. 68
266 Lan An Road, Jinqiao, Pudong, Shanghai 201206
Tel: +8621 3896 1200
Email: admissions.shanghaipudong@dulwich.org
Website: shanghai-pudong.dulwich.org
Head of School: Garry Russell
Age range: 2–18 years
No. of pupils: 1600
Fees: *Day* RMB243,500–RMB357,100
Curriculum: IBDP, UK, IGCSE
Language instr: English

DULWICH COLLEGE SHANGHAI PUXI
For further details see p. 69
2000 Qianpujing Road, Maqiao, Minhang District, Shanghai 201111
Tel: +86 21 3329 9310
Email: admissions.shanghaipuxi@dulwich.org
Website: shanghai-puxi.dulwich.org
Head of College: David Ingram
Age range: 2–18 years
No. of pupils: 500
Fees: *Day* ¥126,200–¥357,100
Curriculum: IBDP, UK, IGCSE
Language instr: English, Mandarin, Spanish

DULWICH COLLEGE SUZHOU
For further details see p. 70
360 Gang Tian Road, Suzhou Industrial Park, Suzhou, Jiangsu 215021
Tel: +86 512 6295 9500
Email: admissions.suzhou@dulwich.org
Website: suzhou.dulwich.org
Head of School: David Massiah
Age range: 2–18 years
No. of pupils: 900
Fees: RMB250,000
Curriculum: IBDP, IGCSE
Language instr: English

DULWICH INTERNATIONAL HIGH SCHOOL SUZHOU
For further details see p. 71
Fangzhong Street, Near East Zhong Xin Avenue, Suzhou, Jiangsu 215021
Tel: +86 512 6787 5003
Email: admissions.dhsz@dulwich.org
Website: suzhou-high-school.dulwich.org
Head of School: Sarah Tielman
Age range: 14–19 years
No. of pupils: 750
Fees: *Day* RMB206,000 *WB* RMB25,900 *FB* RMB39,300
Curriculum: IGCSE, ALevs
Language instr: English

DULWICH INTERNATIONAL HIGH SCHOOL ZHUHAI
For further details see p. 72
No. 29 Hongjing Road, Guangdong-Macao in-depth cooperation zone in Hengqin, Zhuhai, Guangdong 519060
Tel: +86 756 8693133
Email: admissions.dhzh@dulwich.org
Website: zhuhai-high-school.dulwich.org
Head of School: Matthew Conn
Age range: 14–18 years
No. of pupils: 300
Fees: *Day* RMB180,000–RMB200,000 RMB210,000–RMB230,000
Curriculum: IGCSE, ALevs
Language instr: English

Eaglebridge International School
9 Guoqiang Road, Zhengxing New District, Dandong, Liaoning
Tel: +86 415 228 3333
Curriculum: USA

ECNU Affiliated Bilingual
569 Anchi Road, Jiading District, Shanghai 201805
Tel: +86 400 920 6698
Curriculum: IBDP
Language instr: English

ECNU Affiliated Bilingual Kindergarten
221 Rong Ze Road, Shanghai 201805
Tel: +86 13 5246 94182
Curriculum: IBPYP
Language instr: English, Chinese

Ecole Francaise Internationale de Canton
Caibin Middle Road, Shangshui Street 62-70, Jinshazhou, Baiyun District, Guangzhou, Guangdong
Tel: +86 20 3879 7324
Curriculum: FrenchBacc
Language instr: French, English, Chinese

École francaise internationale de Wuhan
Campus international 10-1 Bo Xue Lu, Wuhan, Hubei 430056
Tel: +86 27 8473 9018

EtonHouse International School Times Residence, Chengdu
180 Zhiquan Section, East Avenue, Times Residence, Chengdu, Sichuan 610061
Tel: +86 28 8477 7977
Curriculum: IBPYP
Language instr: English

EtonHouse International School, Dongguan
19 Guangchang North Road, Gaobu, Dongguan, Guangdong 523270
Tel: +86 769 8878 5333
Curriculum: IBPYP
Language instr: English

EtonHouse International School, Foshan
32 Fufeng Square, 1st Foping No.4 Road, Guicheng, Nanhai, Foshan, Guangdong
Tel: +86 757 6668 8333
Curriculum: IBPYP
Language instr: English, Chinese

EtonHouse International School, Nanjing
10 South Qing'ao Rd, Jianye District, Nanjing, Jiangsu 210019
Tel: +86 25 8669 6778
Curriculum: IBPYP

EtonHouse International School, Riverside
AddressSouth Pudong Road 1570, Pudong, Shanghai
Tel: +86 21 5068 9695
Curriculum: IBPYP
Language instr: English, Chinese

EtonHouse International School, Suzhou
102 Kefa Road, Suzhou Science & Technology Town, Suzhou, Jiangsu 215163
Tel: +86 512 6825 5666
Age range: 2–18 years
No. of pupils: 134
Curriculum: IBDP, IBMYP, IBPYP
Language instr: English

Etu King's Kindergarten of Wuhan
Building 1, Phase 5, Tongan Home, Houhu Avenue, Houhu Street, Wuhan, Hubei
Tel: +86 27 8228 6677
Curriculum: IBPYP
Language instr: English, Chinese

Exploratory Model Primary School
Chongqing BI Academy, No. 766 Konggang East Road, Yubei District, Chongqing, Sichuan 401120
Tel: +86 186 2076 5920
Curriculum: IBPYP
Language instr: English, Chinese

Fuzhou International Preschool @ 1 Park Avenue
1 Park Avenue, Jinju Road 826, Jinshan District, Fuzhou, Fujian 350000
Tel: +86 0591 83505222
Curriculum: IBPYP
Language instr: English, Chinese

Golden Apple International Preschool and Kindergarten
No. 7 Chuangrui Road, Hi-tech District, Chengdu, Sichuan 610041
Tel: +86 28 8523 7403
Curriculum: IBPYP
Language instr: Chinese, English

Golden Apple Jincheng No. 1 Secondary School
No. 99 Xianglong 3rd Street, High-tech Zone, Chengdu, Sichuan 610041
Tel: +86 28 6010 9299
Curriculum: IBDP
Language instr: English, Chinese

Golden Apple New Montessori Kindergarten (Jincheng Lake)
No. 900 Jincheng Avenue, High Tech Zone, Chengdu, Sichuan 610041
Tel: +86 28 8523 1763
Curriculum: IBPYP
Language instr: Chinese

Golden Apple Tianfu International Preschool and Kindergarten
No. 187 Shengxing Street, Jiannan Street North, Hi-tech District, Chengdu, Sichuan 610041
Tel: +86 28 8517 1648
Curriculum: IBPYP
Language instr: English

Grand Canadian Academy (GCA Jiaxing)
288 Zhenxing Donglu, Tongxiang, Zhejiang 314500
Tel: +86 573 8810 7576

Green Oasis School
No.4030, Shennan Middle Road, Tianmian, Futian District, Shenzhen, Guangdong 518026
Tel: +86 755 8395 9000
Age range: 5–16
Curriculum: IGCSE

Guangdong Country Garden School
Beijiao Town, Shunde District, Foshan City, Guangdong
Tel: +86 757 2667 7888
Curriculum: IBDP, IBMYP, IBPYP
Language instr: Chinese, English

Guangdong Shunde Desheng School
Minxing Road, New District, Daliang, Shunde, Guangdong 528300
Tel: +86 0757 22325121
Age range: 12–18 years
No. of pupils: 300
Curriculum: IBDP
Language instr: English

Guangzhou Huamei International School
No. 23 Huamei Road, Tianhe District, Guangzhou, Guangdong 510520
Tel: +86 20 8721 0178
Curriculum: IBPYP, USA
Language instr: English

Guangzhou International Kindergarten Huangpu ZWIE
No. 438 Fengle South Road, Huangpu District, Guangzhou, Guangdong 510700
Tel: +86 20 6298 6871
Curriculum: IBPYP
Language instr: Chinese

Guangzhou International Middle School Huangpu ZWIE
No. 438 Fengle South Road, Huangpu District, Guangzhou, Guangdong 510700
Tel: +86 40 0780 2003
Curriculum: IBMYP
Language instr: English, Chinese

Guangzhou International Primary School Baiyun ZWIE
No. 998 Tonghe Road, Baiyun District, Guangzhou City, Guangdong 510515
Tel: +86 20 3724 8715
Curriculum: IBPYP
Language instr: English, Chinese

Guangzhou International Primary School Huangpu ZWIE
No. 188 Huangpu East Road, Huangpu District, Guangzhou, Guangdong 510700
Tel: +86 40 0780 2003
Curriculum: IBPYP
Language instr: English, Chinese

Guangzhou Nanfang International School
No.1 Yu Cui Yuan North, Yinglong Road, Longdong, Tianhe District, Guangzhou, Guangdong
Tel: +86 20 8708 5090
Age range: 2.5–19
No. of pupils: 200
Curriculum: IBDP, IBMYP, IBPYP, UK, IGCSE, ALevs
Language instr: English

Guiyang Huaxi Country Garden International School
Country Garden Community, Mengguan Town, Huaxi District, Guiyang, Guizhou 550026
Tel: +86 (0)851 8365 885
Curriculum: IBPYP
Language instr: English, Chinese

Hailiang Foreign Language School
No. 199 West 3rd Ring Road, Taozhu Street, Zhuji, Zhejiang
Tel: +86 575 8900 3608
Curriculum: IBDP, IBPYP
Language instr: English, Chinese

Hangzhou Binjiang Wickham Kindergarten
No.525 Weiye Road Binjiang District, Hangzhou, Zhejiang 31500
Curriculum: IBPYP
Language instr: English, Chinese

Hangzhou Future Sci-Tech City Wickham Kindergarten
No. 968-8, Gaojiao, Road, Yuhang District, Hangzhou, Zhejiang 311100
Tel: +86 571 8866599
Curriculum: IBPYP
Language instr: English, Chinese

Hangzhou Greentown Yuhua Qinqin School
2 Zhujia Road, Yuhang District, Hangzhou, Zhejiang 311112
Curriculum: IBPYP
Language instr: English, Chinese

Hangzhou Greentown Yuhua School
No. 532 Wenyi West Road, Hangzhou, Zhejiang 310012
Tel: +86 571 88477561
Curriculum: IBMYP
Language instr: Chinese, English

Hangzhou International School
78 Dongxin Street, Bin Jiang District, Hangzhou, Zhejiang 310053
Tel: +86 571 8669 0045
Age range: 2–18
No. of pupils: 670
Curriculum: IBDP, IBMYP, IBPYP
Language instr: English
EAR ECIS

Hangzhou Shanghai World Foreign Language School
167 Li Shui Road, Hangzhou, Zhejiang 310015
Tel: +86 571 8998 1588
Curriculum: IBPYP
Language instr: English

Hangzhou Victoria Kindergarten (Jiarun)
4th Tower, Jiarun Mansion, Jinji Road, Xiaoshan District, Hangzhou, Zhejiang
Tel: +86 571 8380 3939
Curriculum: IBPYP
Language instr: English, Chinese

Hangzhou Victoria Kindergarten (Landscape Bay)
Hongyi Road, Jinghai Bay Community, Xiaoshan District, Hangzhou, Zhejiang
Tel: +86 571 8351 5277
Language instr: English, Chinese

Hangzhou Wesley School (Binjiang Campus)
1426 Wentao Road, Binjiang District, Hangzhou, Zhejiang 310000
Tel: +86 571 8791 6660
Curriculum: IBPYP
Language instr: English, Chinese

Hangzhou Wesley School (Blue Peacock Campus)
Chunque Road, Gongshu District, Hangzhou, Zhejiang 311231
Tel: +86 571 8882 6660
Curriculum: IBPYP
Language instr: English, Chinese

Hangzhou Wesley School (Gongshu Campus)
269 Gongfa Road, Gongshu District, Hangzhou, Zhejiang 311231
Tel: +86 571 8882 8880
Curriculum: IBPYP
Language instr: English, Chinese

Hangzhou Wickham International School
533 Jingchang Road, Yuhang District, Hangzhou, Zhejiang
Tel: +86 0571 88665901
Curriculum: IBPYP
Language instr: Chinese

Hangzhou World Foreign Language School
66 Muge Road, Banshan Street, Gongshu District, Hangzhou, Zhejiang 310000
Tel: +86 189 5814 3128
Age range: 13–18 years
No. of pupils: 42
Curriculum: IBDP
Language instr: English, Chinese

Harrow Beijing
No. 287 Hegezhuang Village, Cuigezhuang County, Chaoyang District, Beijing 100102
Tel: +86 10 6444 8900
Age range: 2–18 years
Curriculum: UK, IGCSE, ALevs
CIS

Harrow International School Shanghai
School Campus, No.588 Gaoxi Road, Pudong, Shanghai 200131
Tel: +86 21 6881 8282
Age range: 2–18
Curriculum: UK, IGCSE, ALevs

Hefei Run'an Boarding School
292 Fanhua West Road, Economic & Technology Development Zone, Hefei, Anhui 230601
Tel: +86 551 6982 1861
Age range: 6–12
No. of pupils: 150
Curriculum: IBMYP, IBPYP
Language instr: Chinese, English

Hefei Xinhua Academy
No.7888 Changjiang West Road, Hefei, Anhui 230088
Tel: +86 551 6558 6888
Curriculum: IBPYP
Language instr: English, Chinese

Henan Jianye Little Harvard Bilingual School
No.31, East Section of Weisi Road, Jinshui District, Zhengzhou, Henan
Tel: +86 371 8655 0161
Age range: 6–12
No. of pupils: 780
Curriculum: IBPYP
Language instr: English, Chinese

Hengyang Royal Kindergarten
No. 8 Changfeng Avenue, Huaxin, Hengyang, Hunan
Tel: +86 73 4841 7888
Curriculum: IBPYP
Language instr: English, Chinese

Hong Qiao International School
218 South Yi Li Road, Shanghai 201103
Tel: +86 21 62682074
No. of pupils: 460
Curriculum: IBPYP

Huaer Zizhu Lemania College Shanghai
A9, No. 155 Tan Jiatang Road, Min Hang District, Shanghai 200241
Curriculum: IBDP
Language instr: English, Chinese

Huanan Country Garden International Kindergarten
Huanan Country Garden, Nancun Town, Panyu District, Guangzhou, Guangdong 511442
Curriculum: IBPYP
Language instr: English, Chinese

Hübschmann Zhan International School
No. 2-1 Hun He Shi Street, Economic & Technological Development Area, Shenyang, Liaoning 110027
Tel: +86 24 3120 0049
Age range: 6–18 years
No. of pupils: 90
Curriculum: IBDP
Language instr: English, German

Innova Early Years Center, Yizhuang Campus
Floor 1, Building B, Zhaolin Plaza, Yizhuang, Beijing 100026
Curriculum: IBPYP
Language instr: English, Chinese

International Montessori School of Beijing
Building 8, 2A, Xiang Jiang Bei Lu, Chao Yang District, Beijing 100103
Tel: +86 (10) 6432 8228
Age range: *Co-ed* 18 months–12 years
Language instr: English, Chinese

International School of Beijing-Shunyi
No 10 An Hua Street, Shunyi District, Beijing 101318
Tel: +86 10 8149 2345 ext 1001
Age range: 3–18 years
No. of pupils: 1750
Curriculum: IBDP
Language instr: English

International School of Dongguan
#11 Jin Feng Nan Road, Dongguan, Guangdong 523000
Tel: +86 769 2882 5882
Age range: 3–18
No. of pupils: 361
Curriculum: IBDP
Language instr: English

International School of Nanshan Shenzhen
11 Longyuan Road, Taoyuan Sub-District, Nanshan District, Shenzhen, Guangdong 518052
Tel: +86 755 2666 1000
Age range: 3–19
Curriculum: IBDP, IBMYP, IBPYP
Language instr: English

International School of Qingdao (MTI)
Baishan Campus, Shazikou, Dongjiang, Laoshan District, Qingdao, Shandong 266102
Tel: +86 532 8881 5668
Age range: 5–18
Curriculum: National, USA
Language instr: English

International School of Tianjin
Weishan Road, Shuanggang, Jinnan District, Tianjin 300350
Tel: +86 22 2859 2001
Age range: 3–18
No. of pupils: 470
Curriculum: ACT, IBDP, IBMYP, IBPYP, SAT
Language instr: English

International School of Wuxi
300 Xing Chuang Si Lu, New District, Wuxi, Jiangsu 214028
Tel: +86 0510 8101 9012
Curriculum: USA

ISA Science City International School
66 Yushu South Road, Science City, Huangpu District, Guangzhou, Guangdong
Tel: +86 20 3736 2580
Curriculum: IBDP, IBMYP, IBPYP
Language instr: English, Chinese

ISA Tianhe International School
Block C2-2 Redtory, No.128 Siheng Road, Yuan Village, Tianhe District, Guangzhou, Guangdong 510655
Tel: +86 20 8890 0909
Age range: 2–11 years
No. of pupils: 350
Curriculum: IBMYP, IBPYP
Language instr: English

Ivy Academy
East Lake Villas, No 35 Dongzhimenwai Street, Suite D-102, Beijing 100027
Tel: +86 10 8451 1380
Age range: 2–6
Language instr: English, Chinese

IVY Kindergarten of Tongzhou District, Beijing
Hebin Road No.1, Yongshun Town, Tongzhou District, Beijing 101100
Tel: +86 10 8969 6628
Curriculum: IBPYP
Language instr: English, Chinese

Jianye Xie He Cheng Bang Kindergarten
Minhang Road, Zhongzhou Avenue, Zhengzhou, Henan 450003
Curriculum: IBPYP
Language instr: English, Chinese

Jiaxiang International High School
No. 6, Chenhui North Road, Jinjiang District, Chengdu, Sichuan
Tel: +86 (0)28 69919908
Curriculum: IBDP
Language instr: English

Jurong Country Garden School
No.2 Oiuzhi Road, Jurong Economic Development Zone, Zhengjiang City, Jiangsu 212400
Tel: +86 511 8078 0326
Curriculum: IBDP, IBMYP, IBPYP
Language instr: English

Kang Chiao International School (East China Campus)
No.500, Xihuan Rd., Huaqiao Economic Development Zone, Kunshan City, Jiangsu 215332
Tel: +86 512 3686 9833
Curriculum: IBDP, IBMYP
Language instr: English, Chinese

Keystone Academy
11 Anfu Street, Houshayu, Hou Sha Yu Town, Shunyi District, Beijing 101318
Tel: +86 10 8049 6008
Curriculum: IBDP, IBMYP
Language instr: English, Chinese

Kunming International Academy
Yan Jia Di Xiao Qu, Kunming, Yunnan 650034
Tel: +86 871 412 6887
Age range: 4–16
No. of pupils: 200
Curriculum: USA
Language instr: English

Kunming World Youth Academy
Building 2, No.3 High School Dianchixingcheng Campus, Chenggong District, Kunming, Yunnan 650500
Tel: +86 871 6745 1511
Curriculum: IBDP
Language instr: English, Chinese

Lady Eleanor Holles International School Foshan (LEH Foshan)
26 Jingping Road, Chancheng District, Foshan City, Guangdong 528000
Tel: +86 (0)757 8262 6121
Age range: 10–18
Curriculum: UK, IGCSE, ALevs
Language instr: English

Lanzhou Country Garden School
Qingbaishi Street, Chengguan District, Lanzhou, Gansu 730000
Tel: +86 931 8790000
Curriculum: IBDP, IBPYP
Language instr: English, Chinese

Le Petit Lotus Bleu
Shanghai Aiju Primary School, No. 247 Anfu Lu, Xuhui District, Shanghai 200031
Tel: +86 21 54043697 (Ext:636)

LÉMAN INTERNATIONAL SCHOOL CHENGDU
For further details see p. 85
No.1080 Da'an Road, Zheng Xing County, Tianfu New Area, Chengdu, Sichuan 610218
Tel: +86 28 6703 8650
Email: admissions@lis-chengdu.com
Website: www.lis-chengdu.com
Principal: Tom Ferguson
Age range: 2–18 years
No. of pupils: 450
Fees: *Day* RMB142,500–RMB249,000
Curriculum: IBDP, IBMYP, IPC
Language instr: English

Lycee Francais de Shanghai-Qingpu Campus
350 Gao Guang Lu, Qingpu District, Shanghai 201702
Tel: +86 21 3976 0555
Curriculum: FrenchBacc

Lycée Français International Charles de Gaulle de Pekin
3 Xinjin Lu, Beijing 100015
Tel: +86 10 8474 7088
Curriculum: FrenchBacc

Macau Anglican College
109-117 Avenida Padre Tomas Pereira, Taipa, Macau SAR
Tel: +853 2885 0000
Curriculum: UK, IGCSE

Malvern College Chengdu
Zhi Wu Yuan South Gate, Tianhui Town, Jinniu District, Chengdu, Sichuan 610083
Tel: +86 28 68937366
Curriculum: UK, IGCSE, ALevs
Language instr: English

Malvern College Qingdao
No. 77 Xifu Cavalry Mountain Town, Cheng Yang District, Qingdao, Shandong
Tel: +86 532 5865 9999
Age range: 11–18
Curriculum: UK, IGCSE, ALevs
Language instr: English

Manila Xiamen International School
No 735 Long Hu Shan Lu, Zeng Cuo An, Si Ming District, Xiamen, Fujian 361005
Tel: +86 592 2516373
Curriculum: IBDP, IBMYP
Language instr: English

MOK Kindergarten
Huatang Golf Villa comprehensive Business Building, Yanjiao, Sanhe, Langfang, Hebei 065201
Curriculum: IBPYP
Language instr: English, Chinese

Morgan Henry Bilingual Kindergarten
567 Jinfeng Road, Huacao Town, Minhang District, Shanghai 201107
Tel: +86 21 6091 3366
Curriculum: IBPYP
Language instr: English, Chinese

Nanchang International School
1122 Phoenix Centre Road, Hong Gu Tan District, Nanchang, Jiangxi 330038
Tel: +86 791 83855352
Curriculum: IBPYP
Language instr: English

Nanjing Eternal Sea Kindergarten
No. 8 Huitong Road, Qixia District, Nanjing, Jiangsu 210000
Tel: +852 25 5870 6268
Curriculum: IBPYP
Language instr: English

Nanjing International School
No. 8 Xueheng Road, Nanjing, Jiangsu 210023
Tel: +86 25 85899111
Age range: 3–18
No. of pupils: 670
Curriculum: IBDP, IBMYP, IBPYP
Language instr: English

Nansha College Preparatory Academy
180 Gang Qian Boulevard, Nansha, Guangzhou, Guangdong 511458
Tel: +86 20 3468 3339
Curriculum: USA

Nanshan Chinese International College Immersion
33 Shizhou Zhong Road, Nanshan District, Shenzhen, Guangdong 518053
Tel: +86 755 3320 9038

Nantong Stalford International School
No. 46 Hongxing Road, NETDA, Nantong, Jiangsu 226015
Tel: +86 4008 4008 [illegible]3
Curriculum: IBDP, IBPYP
Language instr: English, Chinese

Nanwai King's College School
188 Qingyuan Road, Jingkai District, Wuxi, Jiangsu
Tel: +86 0510 6851 6[illegible]72
Curriculum: IBDP
Language instr: English, Chinese

New Oriental Academy
101 Manbai Road, Machikou Town, Changping District, Beijing 102206
Tel: +86 40 0688 1000
Curriculum: IBDP, IBMYP
Language instr: English, Chinese

New Oriental Stars Kindergarten
Room 506, 5th Floor, Building F, Phoenix Plaza, No. A5, Shuguangxili, Chaoyang District, Beijing 100028
Tel: +86 40 0066 5030
Curriculum: IBPYP
Language instr: English

Ningbo Huamao International School
No 2 Yinxian dadao (Middle), Ningbo, Zhejiang 315[illegible]9
Tel: +86 574 8821 1160
Age range: 2–18
No. of pupils: *730 B44[illegible] G300 VIth16*
Curriculum: IBDP, IBMYP, IBPYP
Language instr: English

Ningbo Huijia Kindergarten, Tingxiangyuan Campus
Tingxiangyuan of Century City, Hangzhouwan New District, Ningbo, Zhejiang 315[illegible]36
Tel: +86 (0)574 589758[illegible]9
Curriculum: IBPYP
Language instr: English, Chinese

Ningbo Zhicheng School
No 377 Jiangbei Road, Jiangbei District, Ningbo, Zhejiang 315033
Tel: +86 574 8756 4017

Nord Anglia Chinese International School, Shanghai
1399 Jinhui Road, Minhang, Shanghai 201107
Tel: +86 (021) 2403 8800
Curriculum: IBDP
Language instr: Chinese, English

NORD ANGLIA INTERNATIONAL SCHOOL SHANGHAI, PUDONG
For further details see p. 89
2888 Junmin Road, Pudong New District, Shanghai 201315
Tel: +86 (0)21 5812 7455
Email: admissions@naispudong.com
Website: naispudong.com
Principal: Lesley-Ann Wallace
Age range: 2–18 years
Fees: RMB117,370–RMB333,680
Curriculum: IBDP, National, SAT, UK, IGCSE
Language instr: English

Nord Anglia School Beijing, Fangshan
No. 236 Beiliuzhuang Village, Qinglonghu Town, Fangshan District, Beijing
Tel: +86 10 8865 8000
Curriculum: IBDP
Language instr: English, Chinese

Nord Anglia School Foshan
No. 55 Dongxi Avenue, West Bank, Xiqiao Town, Nanhai District, Foshan, Guangdong
Tel: +86 757 8121 7688
Curriculum: IBDP
Language instr: English

Nord Anglia School Jiaxing
No. 353 Qingze Road, Economic Development Zone, Jiaxing, Zhejiang 314000
Tel: +86 189 6734 1988
Curriculum: IBDP
Language instr: English, Chinese

Nord Anglia School Nantong
No. 99, Jiangcheng Road, Sutong Park, Nantong, Jiangsu 226000
Tel: +86 513 8918 3800
Curriculum: IBDP
Language instr: English, Chinese

Nord Anglia School Ningbo, Fenghua
No. 88 Wenbo Road, Xiaowangmiao Street, Fenghua District, Ningbo, Zhejiang 315500
Tel: +86 574 8720 3280
Curriculum: IBDP
Language instr: English, Chinese

Olive Tree International Academy, BFSU
No.136 Xincheng Road, Nanyuan Street, Yuhang District, Hangzhou, Zhejiang
Tel: +86 571 8610 0011
Curriculum: IBMYP, IBPYP
Language instr: English, Chinese

Oriental Cambridge International School (Shenyang/Benxi Campus)
No 23, Mulan Road, Xihu District, Benxi, Liaoning 117000
Curriculum: IBDP
Language instr: English, Chinese

Oriental English College, Shenzhen
No 10 Xuezi Road, Education Town, Bao'an, Shenzhen, Guangdong 518128
Tel: +86 755 2751 2624
Age range: 6–18 years
Curriculum: IBDP, IBPYP
Language instr: Chinese, English

Oujing International Kindergarten
Beicun Road, Yiwu, Zhejiang 322000
Tel: +86 159 8561 7777
Curriculum: IBPYP
Language instr: English

Overseas Chinese Academy Suzhou
208 Zhong Nan Street, Suzhou Industrial Park, Jiangsu 215021
Tel: +86 (512) 65001600
Curriculum: IBDP, IBPYP
Language instr: Chinese, English

Oxford International College, Chengdu
185 Taoqi Road, Bali District, Chengdu, Sichuan 610051
Tel: +86 28 8351 7000
Curriculum: UK, IGCSE, ALevs

Oxstand International School, Shenzhen
No.2040, BuXin Road, Luohu District, Shenzhen, Guangdong
Tel: +86 755 2580 5707
Curriculum: IBDP
Language instr: English

Peking University Experimental School (Jiaxing)
No.2339, Huayuan Road, Jiaxing, Zhejiang
Tel: +86 573 8280 8280
Curriculum: IBDP, IBPYP
Language instr: English, Chinese

Phoenix City International Kindergarten
No. 1 Yaxi Road, Phoenix City, Yongnin Street, Zengcheng District, Guangzhou, Guangdong 511340
Tel: +86 20 3298 8186
Curriculum: IBPYP
Language instr: English, Chinese

Phoenix City International School
Xintang Town, Zengcheng City, Guangzhou, Guangdong 511340
Tel: +86 20 6228 6902
Curriculum: IBMYP, IBPYP
Language instr: Chinese, English

Qingdao Academy
No 111 Huazhong Road, Gaoxin District, Qingdao, Shandong 266111
Tel: +86 532 5875 3788
Curriculum: IBDP
Language instr: English, Chinese

Qingdao Amerasia International School
68 Shandongtou Lu, Qingdao, Shandong 266061
Tel: +86 532 8388 9900
Curriculum: IBDP, IBMYP, IBPYP
Language instr: English

Qingdao No.1 International School of Shangdong Province (QISS)
232 Songling Road, Qingdao, Shandong 266061
Tel: +86 532 6889 8888
Age range: 3–17
Curriculum: UK
Language instr: English

QSI International School of Chengdu
American Garden, 188 South 3rd Ring Road, Chengdu, Sichuan 610041
Tel: +86 28 8511 3853
Age range: 3–18 years
No. of pupils: 350
Curriculum: ACT, AP, IBDP, SAT, USA
Language instr: English

QSI International School of Dongguan
2nd Floor, Block A2, Dong Cheng Center, Dongguan City, Guangdong 523000
Tel: +86 769 2230 0131
Age range: 2–17
No. of pupils: 117
Curriculum: USA
Language instr: English

QSI International School of Shenyang
Fuli Segovia, The Phoenix Street 77, 8-1, Dongling District, Shenyang, Liaoning
Tel: +86 024 2379 7530

QSI International School of Shenzhen
5th Floor, Bitao Building, 8 Tai Zi Road, Shekou, Shenzhen, Guangdong 518067
Tel: +86 755 2667 6031
Age range: 2–18 years
No. of pupils: 1000
Curriculum: AP, IBDP, SAT, USA
Language instr: English
EAR

QSI International School of Zhuhai
No. 168 Anning Road, Xianzhou District, Zhuhai, Guangdong 519000
Tel: +86 756 815 6134
Age range: 2–18
No. of pupils: 39 *B21 G18*
Curriculum: USA
Language instr: English

RDFZ King's College School Hangzhou
No. 1 Guowen Road, Hangzhou, Zhejiang 310000
Tel: +86 571 5639 5678
Curriculum: IBDP
Language instr: English, Chinese

Saint Paul American School
18 Guan Ao Yuan, Qinghe, Haidian District 100192
Tel: 86-10-80703429
Curriculum: USA

Sanya Foreign Language School Kindergarten
No. 84,Hedong Road, Jiyang District, Sanya, Hainan
Tel: +86 898 8869 1631
Curriculum: IBPYP
Language instr: English, Chinese

Sanya Overseas Chinese School – Nanxin Campus
Shang Bao Po Road, Lizhi District, Sanya, Hainan
Tel: +86 89 8886 9023
Curriculum: IBDP
Language instr: English, Chinese

School of the Nations
Rua de Minho, Taipa, Macau SAR
Tel: +853 2870 1759
Age range: 3–18
Curriculum: IBDP, IGCSE
Language instr: English

Seven Star Kindergarten Xiamen
No. 146 Qixing West Road, Siming District, Xiamen, Fujian
Tel: +86 59 2766 6678
Curriculum: IBPYP
Language instr: English, Chinese

Shanghai American School (Pudong Campus)
Shanghai Links Executive Community, 1600 Lingbai Road, Sanjiagang, Pudong, Shanghai 201201
Tel: +86 21 6221 1445 (Ext:2000)
Age range: 4–18
No. of pupils: 2950
Curriculum: AP, IBDP, SAT
Language instr: English
EAR ECIS

Shanghai American School (Puxi Campus)
26 Jinfeng Road, Huacao Town, Minhang District, Shanghai 201107
Tel: +86 21 6221 1445
Age range: 3–18
No. of pupils: 2853
Curriculum: AP, IBDP, SAT
Language instr: English
EAR ECIS

Shanghai Baoshan Happykids Kindergarten
No. 218, Lane 2488, Wenchuan Road, Baoshan District, Shanghai
Tel: +86 21 5678 7887
Curriculum: IBPYP
Language instr: English, Chinese

Shanghai BeiBeiJia Olion Kindergarten
No. 377 Baoju Road, Shanghai
Tel: +86 137 6467 7623
Curriculum: IBPYP
Language instr: English, Chinese

Shanghai Changning International School
No 79, Lane 261, Jiangsu Lu, Shanghai 200050
Tel: +86 21 6252 3688
Age range: 3–15
No. of pupils: 510 *B260 G250*

SHANGHAI COMMUNITY INTERNATIONAL SCHOOL
For further details see p. 98
1161 Hongqiao Road, Shanghai 200051
Tel: +86 21 6261 4338
Email: admissions@scis-china.org
Website: www.scis-china.org
Director of Schools: Daniel Eschtruth
Age range: 2–18 years
No. of pupils: 1550
Fees: *Day* RMB126,500–RMB285,000
Curriculum: AP, IBDP, IBMYP, IBPYP, USA
Language instr: English
EAR

SHANGHAI COMMUNITY INTERNATIONAL SCHOOL – PUDONG CAMPUS
For further details see p. 98
800 Xiuyan Road, Kangqiao, Pudong, Shanghai 201315
Tel: +86 21 5812 9888
Age range: 2–18
No. of pupils: 650
Curriculum: IBDP, IBMYP, IBPYP
Language instr: English
EAR

Shanghai Hongwen School
No 318 Chuanda Road, Pudong, Shanghai
Tel: +86 189 1784 6368
Curriculum: IBDP
Language instr: English, Chinese

Shanghai Ivy School
No. 816 Xiuyan Road, Pudong New Area, Shanghai 200000
Tel: +86 40 0050 5553
Curriculum: IBPYP
Language instr: English, Chinese

Shanghai Liaoyuan Bilingual School
No. 150 Pingyang Road, Minhang District, Shanghai
Tel: +86 21 6480 6128
Curriculum: IBDP, IBMYP, IBPYP
Language instr: English, Chinese

Shanghai Livingston American School
No. 580 Gan Xi Road, Changning District, Shanghai 200335
Tel: +86 21 62383511

Shanghai Pinghe School
261 Huang Yang Road, Pudong, Shanghai
Tel: +86 21 5031 0791
Age range: 5–18
No. of pupils: 1550
Curriculum: IBDP
Language instr: English, Chinese

Shanghai Qibao Dwight High School
Physical Campus, 3233 Hongxin Road, Minhang District, Shanghai 201101
Tel: +86 21 6461 0367
Curriculum: IBDP
Language instr: English

Shanghai Qingpu World Foreign Language Kindergarten
639 Panwen Road, Qingpu District, Shanghai 201702
Tel: +86 21 3988 6958
Curriculum: IBPYP
Language instr: English, Chinese

Shanghai Qingpu World Foreign Language School
Longlian Road 915, Qingpu District, Shanghai 201700
Tel: +86 21 6928 0977
Curriculum: IBPYP
Language instr: English, Chinese

Shanghai Shangde Experimental School
No 1688 Xiu Yan Road, Pudong New District, Shanghai 201315
Tel: +86 21 6818 0001 or +86 21 6818 0191
Curriculum: IBDP, IBMYP, IBPYP
Language instr: English

Shanghai Singapore International School
301 Zhujian Road, Minhang District, Shanghai 201106
Tel: +86 21 62219288
Age range: 2–18
No. of pupils: 1400
Curriculum: IBDP, IBCP, IGCSE
Language instr: English
CIS

Shanghai United International School
248 Hong Song Road (E), Gubei, Minhang District, Shanghai 201103
Tel: +8621 51753030
No. of pupils: 1985
Curriculum: IBDP, IBPYP
Language instr: English

Shanghai United International School, Jiaoke
No. 55, Wan Yuan Road, Minhang District, Shanghai
Tel: +86 21 64807218

Shanghai United International School, Pudong
48 Xueye Road, Pudong District, Shanghai
Tel: +86 21 58869990

Shanghai United International School, Shangyin
No. 185, Long Ming Road, Minhang District, Shanghai
Tel: +86 21 54178143

Shanghai United International School, Wanyuan
No. 509 Pingji Road, Minhang District, Shanghai
Tel: +86 21 64980188

Shanghai United International School, Wenzhou
No.1, Chuitai Road Louqiao Industrial Park, Ouhai District, Wenzhou, Zhejiang
Tel: +86 577 8629 9077

Shanghai United International School, Xiamen
No. 850 Honglianbeier Road, Siming District, Xiamen, Fujian
Tel: +86 592 52058500

Shanghai Victoria Kindergarten (Gumei)
No. 300 Gumei Road, Minhang District, Shanghai
Tel: +86 21 6401 1084
Curriculum: IBPYP
Language instr: English, Chinese

Shanghai Victoria Kindergarten (Pudong)
38-39 Yinxiao Road, Pudong District, Shanghai
Tel: +86 21 5045 9084
Curriculum: IBPYP
Language instr: English, Chinese

Shanghai Victoria Kindergarten (Qibao)
No. 1225 Xinzhen Road, Minhang District, Shanghai
Tel: +86 21 5415 0469
Curriculum: IBPYP
Language instr: English, Chinese

Shanghai Victoria Kindergarten (Xuhui)
71-1 Huating Road, Xuhui District, Shanghai
Tel: +86 21 5403 6901
Curriculum: IBPYP
Language instr: English, Chinese

Shanghai World Foreign Language Middle School
380 Pu Bei Road, Xu Hui District, Shanghai 200233
Tel: +8621 6436 3556
Curriculum: IBDP, IBMYP
Language instr: Chinese

Shanghai World Foreign Language Primary School
No 380 Pubei Road, Xu Hui District, Shanghai 200233
Tel: +86 21 5419 2245
Curriculum: IBPYP
Language instr: English, Chinese

Shekou International School
Jingshan Villas, Nanhai Boulevard, Shekou, Nanshan, Shenzhen, Guangdong
Tel: +86 755 2669 3669
Age range: 2–18 years
No. of pupils: 1000
Curriculum: IBDP, IBPYP, SAT
Language instr: English
EAR

Shen Wai International School
29 Baishi 3rd Road, Nanshan District, Shenzhen, Guangdong 518053
Tel: +86 755 8654 1200
Age range: 4–19
No. of pupils: 1040
Curriculum: IBDP, IBMYP, IBPYP
Language instr: English
CIS EAR

Sheng Kung Hui Choikou School
Avenida Dr Franscisco V Machado S/N, Macau SAR
Tel: +853 2834 1791

Shenyang No.2 Sino-Canadian High School
198 Shenbei Road, Shenbei New District, Shenyang, Liaoning 110164
Tel: +86 024 88043958
Curriculum: National

Shenyang Transformation International School
160 Quan Yun San Road, Hunnan District, Shenyang, Liaoning 110167
Tel: +86 024 3126 2277
Age range: 3–18
No. of pupils: 125
Curriculum: USA
Language instr: English
EAR

Shenzhen American International School
No. 82, Gongyuan Rd, Shekou, Nanshan, Shenzhen, Guangdong 518067
Tel: +86 755 8619 4800
Curriculum: USA

SHENZHEN COLLEGE OF INTERNATIONAL EDUCATION
For further details see p. 99
No. 3, Sixth Antuoshan Road, Futian District, Shenzhen, Guangdong
Tel: +86 755 8349 5025
Email: info@scie.com.cn
Website: www.scie.com.cn
Headteacher: Neil Mobsby
Age range: 14–18 years
No. of pupils: 1800
Fees: RMB248,000–RMB278,000
Curriculum: AP, UK, USA, IGCSE, ALevs
Language instr: English
CIS EAR

Shenzhen Concord College of Sino-Canada
166 Nanguang Road, Nanshan District, Shenzhen, Guangdong
Tel: +86 755 2656 8886
Language instr: Chinese
RS

Shenzhen Futian Funful Bilingual School
Goldfield Seaview Gardens, South Xinzhou Road, Futian District, Shenzhen, Guangdong
Tel: +86 755 2381 0830
Age range: 3–12
Language instr: English, Putonghua

Shenzhen Longgang Bantian Walton International Kindergarten
No.7-99 Yayuan Road, Bantian Street, Longgang District, Shenzhen, Guangdong 518000
Curriculum: IBPYP
Language instr: English, Chinese

SMIC Private School
No. 169, Qing-Tong Road, Pudong New Area, Shanghai 201203
Tel: +86 21 2033 2515
Curriculum: USA

SNU-K International Department
Yidu Road Longchengyihao, Chengdu, Sichuan 610101
Tel: +86 18428393839
Curriculum: IBPYP
Language instr: Chinese, English

Soochow Foreign Language School
No. 188, Yucheng Road, Xiangcheng District, Suzhou, Jiangsu
Tel: +86 512 8918 0556
Curriculum: IBDP, IBPYP
Language instr: English, Chinese

Soong Ching Ling School
No 2 Ye Hui Road, Zhao Xiang, Qing Pu District, Shanghai 201703
Tel: +86 21 6975 6670
No. of pupils: 900

Springboard International Bilingual School
Gucheng Village, 15 Huosha Road, Houshayu Town, Shunyi District, Beijing 101318
Tel: +86 10 80490307
Age range: 3–18 years
Curriculum: IBDP
Language instr: English, Chinese

Suzhou Foreign Language School
No.201, Zhuyuan Road, Suzhou, Jiangsu
Tel: +86 512 8718 8009
Curriculum: IGCSE, ALevs

Suzhou Industrial Park Foreign Language School
No.89, Suzhou Industrial Park, Suzhou, Jiangsu 215021
Tel: +86 512 6289 7710
Curriculum: IBDP
Language instr: English

Suzhou Innovation Academy
100 Xiangcheng Ave, Xiangcheng District, Suzhou, Jiangsu
Tel: +86 (0)512 65490211
Curriculum: IBDP
Language instr: English

Suzhou North America High School
268 Tian E Dang Road, Wuzhong District, Suzhou, Jiangsu 215000
Tel: +86 512 6625 8897
Curriculum: IBDP
Language instr: English, Chinese

Suzhou Science and Technology Town Foreign Language School
No. 180 Jia Ling Jiang Road, Suzhou New District, Suzhou, Jiangsu 215163
Tel: +86 512 69370111
Curriculum: IBPYP
Language instr: English, Chinese

Suzhou Singapore International School
208 Zhong Nan Street, Suzhou Industrial Park, Jiangsu 215021
Tel: +86 512 6258 0388
Age range: 2–18 years
No. of pupils: 1000
Curriculum: IBDP, IBMYP, IBPYP, SAT
Language instr: English
CIS EAR

Suzhou Victoria Kindergarten
Bay Garden Community, Phase 3, 1 Linglong Street, Suzhou Industrial Park, Suzhou, Jiangsu
Tel: +86 512 8081 1610
Curriculum: IBPYP
Language instr: English, Chinese

Taicang Walton Foreign Language School
No. 200 Middle Suzhou Road, Taicang, Jiangsu 215400
Tel: +86 (0)512 33062226
Curriculum: IBDP, IBPYP
Language instr: English, Chinese

Teda International School
72 Third Avenue, Teda, Tianjin 300457
Tel: +86 22 6622 6158
Age range: 3–18
No. of pupils: 326 B166 G160
Curriculum: AP, SAT, USA
Language instr: English
CIS EAR

The Affiliated Foreign Language School of SCNU
No. 2, Science Avenue, Science City, Huangpu District, Guangzhou, Guangdong 510633
Tel: +86 20 3205 1890
Curriculum: IBMYP, IBPYP
Language instr: English, Chinese

The Affiliated International School of Shenzhen University
A105, No.101, Qianhai Rd, Nanshan District, Shenzhen, Guangdong 518054
Tel: +86 755 2606 0520
Curriculum: IGCSE, ALevs

The British International School Shanghai, Puxi
111 Jinguang Road, Huacao Town, Minhang District, Puxi, Shanghai 201107
Tel: +86 (0)21 62217542
Age range: 2–18
Curriculum: IBDP, UK, IGCSE
Language instr: English
COB

The British School of Beijing, Sanlitun
5 Xiliujie, Sanlitun Road, Chaoyang District, Beijing 100027
Tel: +8610 8532 3088
Age range: 1–11
No. of pupils: 700
Curriculum: UK
COB

The British School of Guangzhou
983-3 Tonghe Road, Baiyun District, Guangzhou, Guangdong 510515
Tel: +86 20 8709 4788
Age range: 1–18
No. of pupils: 1450
Curriculum: UK, IGCSE, ALevs
Language instr: English
COB

The British School of Nanjing
No.16 Hanfu Road, Jiangning District, Nanjing, Jiangsu
Tel: +86 25 5210 8987
Age range: 2–18 years
No. of pupils: 400
Curriculum: UK, IGCSE, ALevs
COB

The Garden International School
Agile Cambridgeshire, Panyu District, Guangzhou, Guangdong 511400
Tel: +86 (0)20 3482 3833
Curriculum: IBPYP
Language instr: English

The International School of Macao
Macau University of Science and Technology (Block K), Avenida Wai Long, Taipa, Macau SAR
Tel: +853 2853 3700
Age range: 3–17
No. of pupils: 840 B420 G420
Curriculum: IBDP
Language instr: English

The Kindergarten of Hefei Run'an Boarding School
No. 268 Cui Wei Road, Economic and Technological Development Zone, Hefei, Anhui 230601
Tel: +86 (0)551 63821888
Curriculum: IBPYP
Language instr: English

The MacDuffie School, Shanghai
No. 799 North Hui Feng Road, Fengxian District, Shanghai 201403
Tel: +86 21 400 600 2260
Curriculum: IBDP
Language instr: English

Tianjin International School
1 Sishui Dao, Hexi District, Tianjin 300222
Tel: +86 22 8371 0900
Curriculum: USA
Language instr: English
EAR

Tianjin Yinghua International School
Yongyang West Road, Wuqing District, Tianjin
Tel: +86 22 5961 1161

Times College
18 Shennong Road, Qixia District, Nanjing, Jiangsu
Tel: +86 25 85539090
Curriculum: IBDP, IBMYP, IBPYP
Language instr: English, Chinese

Tsinghua International School
Campus of Tsinghua High School, Zhongguancun North Street, Haidian District, Beijing 100084
Tel: +86 10 62797000
Curriculum: UK

Tungwah Wenzel International School
No. 17 Keyuan Road, Songshan Lake High-Tech Industrial Zone, Dongguan, Guangdong
Tel: +86 769 2289 0858
Curriculum: IBDP, IBMYP, IBPYP
Language instr: English

Ulink College
180 Gang Qian Boulevard, Nansha, Guangzhou, Guangdong 511458
Tel: +86 20 3909 0100
Curriculum: IGCSE, ALevs

ULink College of Shanghai
No.559,Laiting South Road, Jiuting, Songjiang District, Shanghai 201615
Tel: +86 (0)21 67663819
Curriculum: IBDP
Language instr: Chinese, English

Utahloy International School Guangzhou (UISG)
800 Sha Tai Bei Road, Bai Yun District, Guangzhou, Guangdong 510515
Tel: +8620 8720 2019
Age range: 2–18
No. of pupils: 900
Curriculum: IBDP, IBMYP, IBPYP, TOEFL
Language instr: English
CIS EAR

Utahloy International School Zengcheng (UISZ)
San Jiang Town, Zeng Cheng City, Guangdong 511325
Tel: +86 20 8291 3201
Age range: 2–18
No. of pupils: 200
Curriculum: IBDP, IBMYP, IBPYP
Language instr: English
CIS

UWC Changshu China
No. 88 Kunchenghuxi Road, Changshu, Jiangsu 215500
Tel: +86 512 5298 2602
Age range: 15–19 years
No. of pupils: 580
Curriculum: IBDP
Language instr: English

Vanke School Pudong
No 1700-2-4 Kangqiao Road, Pudong, Shanghai
Tel: +86 21 3463 3623
Curriculum: IBDP
Language instr: English, Chinese

Victoria Kindergarten Shenzhen (Futian)
No.2135 Fuqiang Road, Futian District, Shenzhen, Guangdong
Tel: +86 755 8296 1010
Curriculum: IBPYP
Language instr: English, Chinese

Victoria Kindergarten Shenzhen (Le Parc)
317 Fuzhong Road, Futian District, Shenzhen, Guangdong
Tel: +86 755 8328 2004
Curriculum: IBPYP
Language instr: English, Chinese

Victoria Kindergarten Shenzhen (Lilin)
7 LongChuanTang Street, DongBin Road, Nanshan District, Shenzhen, Guangdong
Tel: +86 130 5815 8907
Curriculum: IBPYP
Language instr: English, Chinese

Victoria Kindergarten Shenzhen (Shenzhen Bay)
Shenzhen Bay Science & Technology Ecological Park, Building 5, Floor 3, Nanshan District, Shenzhen, Guangdong
Tel: +86 755 8653 7070
Curriculum: IBPYP
Language instr: English, Chinese

Wahaha International School
5 Yaojiang Road, Shangcheng District, Hangzhou, Zhejiang 310008
Tel: +86 571 8780 1933
Curriculum: IBMYP, IBPYP
Language instr: English, Chinese

Weihai IVY International School
Jingzi Scenic Area, Huancui District, Weihai, Shandong
Tel: +86 400 886 1771
Curriculum: IGCSE, ALevs

Weihai Zhongshi International School (WZIS)
42 East Jiang Su Road, New Industrial District, Weihai, Shandong 264211
Tel: +86 63 1599 6381
Age range: 5–18
No. of pupils: 340
Curriculum: UK

WELLINGTON COLLEGE INTERNATIONAL HANGZHOU
For further details see p. 109
2399 Xue Zhi Road, Xiaoshan District, Hangzhou, Zhejiang 311231
Tel: +86 (571) 823[illegible] 6366
Email: admissions.wcih@wellingtoncollege.cn
Website: hangzhou.wellingtoncollege.cn
Master: Kathryn Richardson
Age range: 2–18 years
Curriculum: UK, IGCSE, ALevs
Language instr: English, Mandarin

Wellington College International Shanghai
No.1500 Yao Long Road, Pudong, Shanghai 200124
Tel: +86 21 5185 3866
Age range: 3–18 years
No. of pupils: 1100
Curriculum: IBDP, IFC, UK, IGCSE
Language instr: English

Wellington College International Tianjin
No 1 Yide Dao, Hong Qiao District, Tianjin 300120
Tel: +86 22 8758 719[illegible]
Age range: 2–18
Curriculum: UK, IGCSE, ALevs

Western Academy Of Beijing
PO Box 8547, 10 Lai Guang Ying Dong Lu, Chao Yang District, Beijing 100102
Tel: +86 10 5986 5588
Age range: 3–18
No. of pupils: 1362
Curriculum: IBDP, IBMYP, IBPYP
Language instr: English

WESTERN INTERNATIONAL SCHOOL OF SHANGHAI (WISS)
For further details see p. 113
555 Lian Min Road, Xujing Town, Qing Pu District, Shanghai 201702
Tel: +86 (21) 6976 1038/1060
Email: enquiry@wiss.cn
Website: www.wiss.cn
Head of School: David Edwards
Age range: 2.5–17+ years
No. of pupils: 750
Fees: *Day* ¥170,500–¥275,600 ¥61,975–¥261,820
Curriculum: IBDP, IBMYP, IBPYP
Language instr: English

WHBC of Wuhan Foreign Languages School
7th Floor Administration Building, 48 Wan Song Yuan Road, Wuhan, Hubei 430022
Tel: +86 27 8555 7389
Curriculum: IBDP, IBMYP, IBPYP
Language instr: English

Whittle School & Studios – Shenzhen Campus
8 Hai Cheng Road, Nanshan District, Shenzhen, Guangdong 518067
Tel: +86 755 8785 1818

Wuhan Australian International School
No.322 Luoshi Road, Hongshan District, Wuhan, Hubei
Tel: +86 27 8710 5088
Curriculum: IBPYP
Language instr: Chinese

Wuhan Yangtze International School
Wuhan International Educational Center, Bo Xue Road, Wuhan Economic & Technology Development Zone, Wuhan, Hubei 430056
Tel: +86 27 8423 8713
Curriculum: USA
Language instr: English

Wuxi Foreign Language School
1 Xifeng Road, Taihuxincheng, Wuxi, Jiangsu 214131
Curriculum: IBPYP
Language instr: Chinese

Wuxi United International School
No. 8, Wenjing Road, Xishan District, Xidong New Town, Wuxi, Jiangsu 214104
Tel: +86 510 8853 7700
Curriculum: IBDP
Language instr: English

Wycombe Abbey International School
No.9 Huanhu North Road, Wujin Economic Zone, Changzhou, Jiangsu 213149
Tel: +86 0519 8888 0686
Age range: 3–18
Curriculum: UK

X.L.X. Kindergarten (Qingcheng Campus)
No.5, Building 7, Lane 2501, Guyang North Road, Songjiang District, Shanghai
Tel: +86 21 6029 1140
Curriculum: IBPYP
Language instr: English, Chinese

X.L.X. Kindergarten (Tangzhen Campus)
No. 58 Hongya Road, Pudong New District, Shanghai
Tel: +86 21 6070 2623
Curriculum: IBPYP
Language instr: English, Chinese

Xiamen International School
262 Xing Bei San Lu, Xinglin, Jimei District, Xiamen, Fujian 361022
Tel: +86 592 625 6581
Age range: 3–18
No. of pupils: 450 B250 G220
Curriculum: ACT, IBDP, IBMYP, IBPYP, SAT
Language instr: English

Xi'an Hanova International School
188 Yudou Road, Yanta District, Xian, Shaanxi 710077
Tel: +86 29 88693780
Curriculum: IBDP, IBMYP, IBPYP
Language instr: English

Xi'an Liangjiatan International School (XLIS)
International Community, Xi'an, Shaanxi 710100
Tel: +86 29 85915100-8000
Age range: 3–18 years
Curriculum: IBDP, IBMYP, IBPYP
Language instr: English

Xiaomiao Kindergarten (Luoxiu Campus)
No. 1977 Luoxiu Road, Minghang District, Shanghai 201104
Tel: +86 21 5481 6417
Curriculum: IBPYP
Language instr: English, Chinese

Xiaomiao Kindergarten (Xinsong Campus)
No.47, Lane 499, Xinli Road, Minhang District, Shanghai
Tel: +86 21 6492 0495
Curriculum: IBPYP
Language instr: English, Chinese

Xining International Academy
Tianjin Lu, Xining, Qinghai 810003
Tel: +86 97 1630 7721
Curriculum: USA

Yang Guang Qing School of Beijing
2 Tianbao North Street, Daxing District, Beijing
Tel: +86 10 6787 1129
Curriculum: National

Yantai American School
No. 8 San Lei Lu, Laishan District, Yantai, Shandong 264003
Tel: +86 535 214 3762
Curriculum: USA

Yantai Huasheng International School
100 Jinshajiang Lu, Development Area, (Intersection of Jinshajiang Lu and Tianshan Lu), Yantai, Shandong 264000
Tel: +86 53 5610 1166
Curriculum: USA

Yew Chung International School of Beijing
Honglingjin Park, 5 Houbalizhuang, Chaoyang District, Beijing 100025
Tel: +86 10 8585 1836
Age range: 2–18 years
No. of pupils: 750
Curriculum: IBDP, UK, IGCSE
Language instr: Chinese, English

Yew Chung International School of Chongqing
No 2 Huxia Street, Yuan Yang Town, New Northern Zone, Chongqing 401122
Tel: +86 23 8879 1600
Age range: 3–18 years
Curriculum: IBDP, SAT, UK, IGCSE, ALevs
Language instr: English, Chinese

Yew Chung International School of Qingdao
72 Tai Hang Shan Lu, Qingdao West Coast New Area, Huangdao, Shandong 266555
Tel: +86 532 8699 5551
Age range: 2–18 years
No. of pupils: 331
Curriculum: IBDP, UK, ALevs
Language instr: English

Yew Chung International School of Shanghai – Century Park Campus
1433 Dong Xui Road, Pudong, Shanghai 200127
Tel: +86 21 2226 7666
Age range: 10–18 years
Curriculum: IBDP, National, UK, IGCSE
Language instr: English, Chinese

Yew Chung International School of Shanghai – Gubei Campus
18 West Rong Hua Road, Gubei New Area, Puxi, Shanghai 201103
Tel: +86 21 2226 7666
Age range: 2–18 years
No. of pupils: 2500
Curriculum: UK, IGCSE
Language instr: English, Chinese

Yew Chung International School of Shanghai – Hongqiao Campus
11 Shui Cheng Road, Puxi, Shanghai 200336
Tel: +86 21 2226 7666
Age range: 2–18 years
No. of pupils: 2500
Curriculum: IBDP, National, UK
Language instr: English, Chinese (Mandarin)
CIS

Yew Chung International School of Shanghai – Regency Park Campus
1817 Hua Mu Road, Pudong, Shanghai 201204
Tel: +86 21 2226 7666
Age range: 2–9 years
Curriculum: National, UK
Language instr: English, Chinese
CIS

YK Pao School
1800, Lane 900, North Sanxin Road, Songjiang District, Shanghai 201602
Tel: +86 21 61671999
Curriculum: IBDP
Language instr: English

Yuwen Princeton Kindergarten
Qingshan Distict, Qingdongdonglu, Baotou, Inner Mongolia AR 014030
Curriculum: IBPYP
Language instr: English, Chinese

Zhongshan Academy
No.9, Area 4, Tiantongyuan, Changping District, Beijing
Tel: +86 10 8482 9307
Curriculum: IBPYP
Language instr: English, Chinese

Zhuhai International School
Qi ' Ao Island, Tang Jia Wan, Zhuhai, Guangdong 519080
Tel: +86 756 331 5580
Curriculum: IBDP, IBMYP, IBPYP
Language instr: English

EAST TIMOR

Dili International School
14 Rue Avenue de Portugal, Pantai Kelapa, Dili
Tel: +670 77316065
Curriculum: IBMYP, IBPYP

QSI International School of Dili
Marconi, Aldea 4, Fatuhada, Dili
Tel: +670 332 2389
Age range: 5–13
No. of pupils: 31
Curriculum: USA
Language instr: English

HONG KONG, CHINA

American International School Hong Kong
125 Waterloo Road, Kowloon Tong, Kowloon, Hong Kong, SAR
Tel: +852 2336 3812
Age range: 3–18
No. of pupils: 840
Curriculum: AP, SAT, USA
Language instr: English
EAR

American School Hong Kong
6 Ma Chung Road, Tai Po, New Territories, Hong Kong, SAR
Tel: +852 3919 4100
Curriculum: IBDP
Language instr: English

Anfield School
No. 1, Lung Pak Street, Tai Wai, Shatin, Hong Kong, SAR
Tel: +852 2692 8823
Curriculum: UK
CIS

Australian International School Hong Kong
3A Norfolk Road, Kowloon Tong, Hong Kong, SAR
Tel: +852 2304 6078
Age range: 4–18
No. of pupils: 1125 B564 G561
Curriculum: IBDP
Language instr: English

California School
3/F, Front Block, 550 Nathan Road, Lung Ma Building, Yau Ma Tei, Kowloon, Hong Kong SAR
Tel: +852 2388 9844
Curriculum: UK, IGCSE, ALevs

Canadian International School of Hong Kong
36 Nam Long Shan Road, Aberdeen, Hong Kong, SAR
Tel: +852 2525 7088
Age range: 3–18
No. of pupils: 1835
Curriculum: IBDP, IBMYP, IBPYP
Language instr: English
CIS EAR

Carmel School
460 Shau Kei Wan Road, Shau Kei Wan, Hong Kong, SAR
Tel: +852 3665 5388
Age range: 1–18
No. of pupils: 398 B187 G211
Curriculum: IBDP, IBMYP, IBPYP
Language instr: English
EAR

Causeway Bay Victoria International Kindergarten
32 Hing Fat Street, Causeway Bay, Hong Kong, SAR
Tel: +852 2578 9998
Curriculum: IBPYP

Chinese International School
1 Hau Yuen Path, Braemar Hill, Hong Kong, SAR
Tel: +852 2 510 7288
Age range: 4–18
No. of pupils: 1479
Curriculum: ACT, IBDP, IBMYP, SAT
Language instr: English
CIS EAR ECIS

Christian Alliance International School
33 King Lam Street, Lai Chi Kok, Kowloon, Hong Kong, SAR
Tel: +852 3699 3899
Curriculum: IBDP

Concordia International School
68 Begonia Road, Yau Yat Chuen, Kowloon, Hong Kong, SAR
Tel: +852 2789 9890
Age range: 12–19
No. of pupils: 100
Curriculum: AP, SAT, USA

Creative Primary School
2A Oxford Street, Kowloon Tong, Kowloon, Hong Kong, SAR
Tel: +852 2336 0266
No. of pupils: 660
Curriculum: IBPYP

Delia School Of Canada
Tai Fung Avenue, Taikoo Shing, Hong Kong, SAR
Tel: +852 3658 0338
Age range: 4–20
No. of pupils: 897

Diocesan Boys' School
131 Argyle Street, Mong Kok, Kowloon, Hong Kong, SAR
Tel: +852 2711 5911
Age range: B12–18
No. of pupils: 1420
Curriculum: IBDP
Language instr: English

Discovery Bay International School
Discovery Bay, Lantau Island, Hong Kong, SAR
Tel: +852 2987 7331
Age range: 3–18 years
No. of pupils: 1000
Curriculum: UK, IGCSE, ALevs
Language instr: English

Discovery Mind Primary School – Discovery Bay Campus
1/F, Shop 102, 92 Siena Avenue, Discovery Bay North Plaza, Lantau Island, Hong Kong, SAR
Tel: +852 2914 2202
Age range: 2–11
No. of pupils: 78
Curriculum: IPC

Discovery Mind Primary School – Tung Chung Campus
G/F, Shop A-D, Seaview Crescent, 8 Tung Chung Waterfront Road, Tung Chung, Hong Kong, SAR
Tel: +852 2915 0666
Age range: 2–11
No. of pupils: 100
Curriculum: IPC

Discovery Montessori Academy
Block1, Discovery Bay North, Lantau Island, Hong Kong SAR
Tel: +852 2812 9668
Curriculum: IBPYP
Language instr: English, Chinese

ESF Abacus International Kindergarten
Mang Kung Uk Village, Clearwater Bay Road, Hong Kong SAR
Tel: +852 27195712
Age range: 3–5 years
No. of pupils: 190
Curriculum: IBPYP
Language instr: English, Mandarin

ESF Beacon Hill School
23 Ede Road, Kowloon Tong, Hong Kong SAR
Tel: +852 2336 5221
Age range: 5–11 years
No. of pupils: 540
Curriculum: IBPYP, UK
Language instr: English
CIS

ESF Bradbury School
43C Stubbs Road, Hong Kong SAR
Tel: +852 2574 8249
Age range: 5–11 years
No. of pupils: 720
Curriculum: IBPYP
Language instr: English
CIS

ESF Clearwater Bay School
DD229, Lot 235, Clearwater Bay Road, New Territories, Hong Kong SAR
Tel: +852 2358 3221
Age range: 5–11 years
No. of pupils: 720
Curriculum: IBPYP, UK
Language instr: English
CIS

ESF Discovery College
38 Siena Avenue, Discovery Bay, Lantau Island, Hong Kong SAR
Tel: +852 3969 1000
Age range: 5–18 years
No. of pupils: 1400
Curriculum: IBDP, IBMYP, IBPYP, IBCP
Language instr: English
CIS

ESF Glenealy School
7 Hornsey Road, Mid Levels, Hong Kong SAR
Tel: +852 2522 1919
Age range: 5–11 years
No. of pupils: 360
Curriculum: IBPYP
Language instr: English

ESF Hillside International Kindergarten
43B Stubbs Road, Hong Kong SAR
Tel: +852 2540 0066
Age range: 3–5 years
No. of pupils: 366
Curriculum: IBPYP
Language instr: English

ESF Island School
20 Borrett Road, Hong Kong SAR
Tel: +852 2524 7135
Age range: 11–18 years
No. of pupils: 1200
Curriculum: IBDP, IBMYP, IBCP, UK, IGCSE
Language instr: English

ESF Jockey Club Sarah Roe School
2B Tin Kwong Road, Homantin, Kowloon, Hong Kong SAR
Tel: +852 2761 9893
Age range: 5–19
No. of pupils: 70
Curriculum: UK
Language instr: English

ESF Kennedy School
19 Sha Wan Drive, Pokfulam, Hong Kong SAR
Tel: +852 2579 5600
Age range: 5–11 years
No. of pupils: 900
Curriculum: IBPYP, UK
Language instr: English

ESF King George V School
2 Tin Kwong Road, Homantin, Kowloon, Hong Kong SAR
Tel: +852 2711 3029
Age range: 11–18 years
No. of pupils: 1846
Curriculum: IBDP, IBMYP, IGCSE
Language instr: English

ESF Kowloon Junior School
20 Perth Street, Homantin, Kowloon, Hong Kong SAR
Tel: +852 3765 8700
Age range: 5–11 years
No. of pupils: 900
Curriculum: IBPYP, UK
Language instr: English

ESF Peak School
20 Plunkett's Road, The Peak, Hong Kong SAR
Tel: +852 2849 7211
Age range: 4–11 years
No. of pupils: 360
Curriculum: IBPYP
Language instr: English

ESF Quarry Bay School
6 Hau Yuen Path, Braemar Hill, North Point, Hong Kong SAR
Tel: +852 2566 4242
Age range: 5–11 years
No. of pupils: 720
Curriculum: IBPYP
Language instr: English

ESF Renaissance College
5 Hang Ming Street, Ma On Shan, New Territories, Hong Kong SAR
Tel: +852 3556 3556
Age range: 5–18 years
No. of pupils: 2100
Curriculum: IBDP, IBMYP, IBPYP, IBCP
Language instr: English

ESF Sha Tin College
3 Lai Wo Lane, Fo Tan, Sha Tin, New Territories, Hong Kong SAR
Tel: +852 2699 1811
Age range: 11–18 years
No. of pupils: 1200
Curriculum: IBDP, IBMYP, IBCP, IGCSE
Language instr: English

ESF Sha Tin Junior School
3A Lai Wo Lane, Fo Tan, Sha Tin, New Territories, Hong Kong SAR
Tel: +852 2692 2721
Age range: 5–11 years
No. of pupils: 900
Curriculum: IBPYP, UK
Language instr: English

ESF South Island School
50 Nam Fung Road, Hong Kong SAR
Tel: +852 2555 9313
Age range: 11–18 years
No. of pupils: 1430
Curriculum: IBDP, IBMYP, IBCP, IGCSE
Language instr: English

ESF Tsing Yi International Kindergarten
Maritime Square, 33 Tsing King Road, Tsing Yi, New Territories, Hong Kong SAR
Tel: +852 2436 3355
Age range: 3–5 years
No. of pupils: 352
Curriculum: IBPYP
Language instr: English

ESF Tung Chung International Kindergarten
1/F, Commercial Accommodation, The Visionary, 1 Ying Hong Street, Tung Chung, Lantau, New Territories, Hong Kong SAR
Tel: +852 3742 3500
Age range: 3–5 years
No. of pupils: 312
Curriculum: IBPYP
Language instr: English

ESF West Island School
250 Victoria Road, Pokfulam, Hong Kong SAR
Tel: +852 2819 1962
Age range: 11–18 years
No. of pupils: 1220
Curriculum: IBDP, IBMYP, IBCP, UK, IGCSE
Language instr: English

ESF Wu Kai Sha International Kindergarten
599 Sai Sha Road, Ma On Shan, Sha Tin, Hong Kong SAR
Tel: +852 2435 5291
Age range: 3–5 years
No. of pupils: 343
Curriculum: IBPYP
Language instr: English

French International School
165 Blue Pool Road, Happy Valley, Hong Kong, SAR
Tel: +852 25776217
Age range: 3–18 years
No. of pupils: 2700
Curriculum: IBDP, FrenchBacc, IGCSE
Language instr: English

Funful Sear Rogers International School
1 Cumberland Road, Kowloon Tong, Hong Kong, SAR
Tel: +852 2408 6683
Age range: 5–11
Language instr: English

G. T. (Ellen Yeung) College
10, Ling Kong Street, Tiu Keng Leng, Tseung Kwan O, Hong Kong, SAR
Tel: +852 2535 6867
Curriculum: IBDP
Language instr: English, Chinese

Galilee International School
G/F & 1/F, Peace Garden, 2 Peace Avenue, Ho Man Tin, Kowloon, Hong Kong, SAR
Tel: +852 2390 3000
Age range: 2–6 years
No. of pupils: 80
Curriculum: IBPYP
Language instr: English, Mandarin, Cantonese

German Swiss International School
11 Guildford Road, The Peak, Hong Kong, SAR
Tel: +852 2849 6216
Age range: 3–18 years
No. of pupils: 1300
Curriculum: IBDP, IGCSE
Language instr: English, German

Hamilton Hill International Kindergarten
2/F Tang Kung Mansion, 31 Tai Koo Shing Road, Tai Koo, Hong Kong SAR
Tel: +852 2567 5454
Language instr: English, Chinese

Han Academy
G/F – 2/F, 33-35 Wong Chuk Hang Road, Aberdeen, Hong Kong, SAR
Tel: +852 3998 6300
Curriculum: IBDP
Language instr: English, Chinese

Harrow International School Hong Kong
38 Tsing Ying Road, Tuen Mun, Hong Kong, SAR
Tel: +852 2824 9099
Age range: 3–18 years

HKCA Po Leung Kuk School
62 Tin Hau Temple Road, Hong Kong, SAR
Tel: +852 3465 8400
Age range: 3–12 years
Curriculum: IBPYP
Language instr: English, Putonghua

HKMA David Li Kwok Po College
8 Hoi Wang Road, Mongkok West, Kowloon, Hong Kong, SAR
Tel: +852 2626 9100
Age range: 12–20
No. of pupils: 850
Curriculum: National
Language instr: English, Cantonese, Putonghua

HONG KONG ACADEMY
For further details see p. 76
33 Wai Man Road, Sai Kung, Hong Kong, SAR
Tel: +852 2655 1111
Email: admissions@hkacademy.edu.hk
Website: www.hkacademy.edu.hk
Head of School: Stephen Dare
Age range: 3–18 years
No. of pupils: 500
Fees: HK$149,800
Curriculum: ACT, IBDP, IBMYP, IBPYP
Language instr: English

Hong Kong International School
1 Red Hill Road, Tai Tam, Hong Kong, SAR
Tel: +852 3149 7001
Age range: 4–18
No. of pupils: 2700
Curriculum: AP, USA
Language instr: English
EAR

International Christian School
1 On Muk Lane, Shek Mun, Sha Tin, Hong Kong, SAR
Tel: +852 3920 0000
EAR

International College Hong Kong
60 Sha Tau Kok Road, Shek Chung Au, Sha Tau Kok, New Territories, Hong Kong, SAR
Tel: +852 2655 9018
Age range: 11–18
Curriculum: IBDP, UK, IGCSE
Language instr: English

International College Hong Kong – Hong Lok Yuen
20th Street, Hong Lok Yuen, Tai Po, New Territories, Hong Kong, SAR
Tel: +852 26586935
Age range: 3–11
No. of pupils: 427 *B*229 *G*198
Curriculum: IBPYP
Language instr: English
CIS

Island Christian Academy
70 Bridges Street, Sheung Wan, Hong Kong, SAR
Tel: +852 2537 2552
Curriculum: IPC

Japanese International School
4663 Tai Po Road, Tai Po, New Territories, Hong Kong, SAR
Tel: +852 2834 3531
Age range: 4–11
No. of pupils: *B*85 *G*84
Curriculum: IBPYP
Language instr: English

Kellett School
7 Lam Hing Street, Kowloon Bay, Hong Kong, SAR
Tel: +852 3120 0700
Age range: 4–18
No. of pupils: 1300
Curriculum: UK, IGCSE, ALevs
Language instr: English

Kiangsu & Chekiang Primary School
30 Ching Wah Street, North Point, Hong Kong, SAR
Tel: +852 2570 4594
Age range: 3–12
No. of pupils: 290
Curriculum: UK

Kiangsu-Chekiang College, International Section
20 Braemar Hill Road, North Point, Hong Kong, SAR
Tel: +852 2570 1281
Age range: 3–18
Curriculum: IBDP, UK, IGCSE
Language instr: English, Mandarin

Kingston International Kindergarten
12-14 Cumberland Road, Kowloon Tong, Hong Kong, SAR
Tel: +852 2337 9049
Curriculum: IBPYP
Language instr: English, Putonghua

Kingston International School
113 Waterloo Road, Kowloon Tong, Hong Kong, SAR
Tel: +852 2337 9031
Age range: 1–11 years
No. of pupils: 420
Curriculum: IBPYP
Language instr: English, Mandarin

Lantau International School – Pui O Campus
House 19, South Lantau Road, Lo Wai Village, Lantau Island, Hong Kong, SAR
Tel: +852 2984 0302
Curriculum: UK

Logos Academy
1 Kan Hok Lane, Tseung Kwan, Hong Kong, SAR
Tel: +852-23372123
Age range: 6–18
No. of pupils: 2100
Curriculum: IBDP
Language instr: English

MALVERN COLLEGE HONG KONG
For further details see p. 86
3 Fo Chun Road, Pak Shek Kok, Hong Kong, SAR
Tel: +852 3898 4688
Email: admissions@malverncollege.org.hk
Website: www.malverncollege.org.hk
Headmaster: Robin A. Lister
Age range: 5–18 years
No. of pupils: 1000
Fees: HK$178,010
Curriculum: IBDP, IBMYP, IBPYP
Language instr: English

NORD ANGLIA INTERNATIONAL SCHOOL, HONG KONG
For further details see p. 90
11 On Tin Street, Lam Tin, Kowloon, Hong Kong, SAR
Tel: +852 3958 1428
Email: admissions@nais.hk
Website: www.nais.hk
Principal: Kenny Duncan
Age range: 3–18 years
Fees: HK$83,430–HK$175,100
Curriculum: IBDP, UK, IGCSE
Language instr: English
COB

Norwegian International School Hong Kong
170 Kam Shan Road, Kam Shan Village, Tai Po, Hong Kong, SAR
Tel: +852 2658 0341
Curriculum: IPC

Parkview International Pre-school
Tower 18 Parkview, 88 Tai Tam Reservoir Road, Hong Kong, SAR
Tel: +852 2812 6023
Age range: 1–5
Curriculum: IBPYP
Language instr: English, Putonghua

Parkview International Pre-School (Kowloon)
Podium Level, Kowloon Station, 1 Austin Road West, Kowloon, Hong Kong, SAR
Tel: +852 2812 6801
Age range: 1–6
No. of pupils: 450
Curriculum: IBPYP
Language instr: English

Po Leung Kuk Choi Kai Yau School
6 Caldecott Road, Piper's Hill, Kowloon, Hong Kong, SAR
Tel: +852 2148 2052
Curriculum: IBDP

Shrewsbury International School Hong Kong
10 Shek Kok Road, Tseung Kwan O, Hong Kong, SAR
Tel: +852 2480 1500
Age range: 3–11
Curriculum: UK
Language instr: English

Singapore International School (Hong Kong) – Preparatory Years & Primary Section
23 Nam Long Shan Road, Aberdeen, Hong Kong, SAR
Tel: +852 2872 0266
Age range: 4–12

Singapore International School (Hong Kong) – Secondary Section
2 Police School Road, Wong Chuk Hang, Hong Kong, SAR
Tel: +852 2919 6966
Age range: 3 years 8 months–18 years
No. of pupils: 1400
Curriculum: IBDP, IGCSE
Language instr: English

St. Paul's Co-educational College
33 MacDonnell Road, Central, Hong Kong, SAR
Tel: +852 2523 1187
Age range: 11–18
No. of pupils: 1300
Curriculum: IBDP

Stamford American School Hong Kong
25 Man Fuk Road, Ho Man Tin, Kowloon, Hong Kong, SAR
Tel: +852 3467 4500
Age range: 5–18
Curriculum: IBDP
Language instr: English

The Harbour School
332 Ap Lei Chau Bridge Road, Ap Lei Chau, Hong Kong, SAR
Tel: +852 3905 0180
Curriculum: USA
Language instr: English
EAR

The Independent Schools Foundation Academy
1 Kong Sin Wan Road, Pokfulam, Hong Kong, SAR
Tel: +852 2202 2000
Age range: 5–18
No. of pupils: 1650 *B*830 *G*820 *VIth*80
Curriculum: ACT, IBDP, IBMYP, SAT
Language instr: English, Chinese
CIS

Think International School
117 Boundary Street, Kowloon Tong, Hong Kong, SAR
Tel: +852 2338 3949
Curriculum: IBPYP, IGCSE

Victoria (Belcher) International Kindergarten
Portion of Level 3 (Kindergarten Area), The Westwood, 8 Belchers Street, Hong Kong, SAR
Tel: +852 2542 7001
Age range: 2–6
Curriculum: IBPYP
Language instr: English, Mandarin, Cantonese

Victoria (Harbour Green) International Kindergarten
8 Sham Mong Road, G/F., Harbour Green, Kowloon, Hong Kong SAR
Tel: +852 2885 1928
Curriculum: IBPYP
Language instr: English

Victoria (Homantin) International Nursery
1/F., Carmel-on-the-Hill, 9 Carmel Village Street, Homantin, Kowloon, Hong Kong, SAR
Tel: +852 2762 9130
Curriculum: IBPYP
Language instr: English

Victoria (South Horizons) International Kindergarten
Podium Level 2, Phase 2, South Horizons, Ap Lei Chau, Hong Kong, SAR
Tel: +852 2580 8633
Curriculum: IBPYP
Language instr: Cantonese, English, Mandarin

Victoria Kindergarten
G/F., 2-8 Hong On Street, Kornhill, Hong Kong, SAR
Tel: +852 2885 3331
Curriculum: IBPYP
Language instr: English

Victoria Nursery
Ko Fung Court, Harbour Heights, 5 Fook Yum Road, North Point, Hong Kong, SAR
Tel: +852 2571 7888
Age range: 2–6
Curriculum: IBPYP
Language instr: Cantonese, English, Mandarin

Victoria Shanghai Academy (VSA)
19 Shum Wan Road, Aberdeen, Hong Kong, SAR
Tel: +852 3402 1000
Age range: 5 yrs 8 mths–18 yrs
No. of pupils: 1800
Curriculum: IBDP, IBMYP, IBPYP
Language instr: English, Putonghua
(CIS)

Yew Chung International School of Hong Kong
3 To Fuk Road, Kowloon, Hong Kong, SAR
Tel: +852 2338 7106
Age range: 6 months–18 years
Curriculum: IBDP, UK, GCSE
Language instr: English, Chinese

Yew Chung International School of Hong Kong – Early Childhood Education
3 Somerset Road, Kowloon Tong, Hong Kong, SAR
Tel: +852 2336 3443
Age range: 6 months–5 years
Curriculum: UK
Language instr: English, Chinese

Yew Chung International School of Hong Kong – Primary Section
2 Kent Road, Kowloon Tong, Hong Kong SAR
Tel: +852 2336 7292
Age range: 5–11 years
Curriculum: UK
Language instr: English, Chinese

YMCA of Hong Kong Christian College
2 Chung Yat Street, Tung Chung, Lantau Island, Hong Kong, SAR
Tel: +852 2988 8123
Age range: 11–21
Curriculum: National, UK, IGCSE, ALevs

INDIA

Aditya Birla World Academy
Vastushilp Annexe, Gamadia Colony, J D Road, Tardeo, Mumbai, Maharashtra 400034
Tel: +91 22 2352 8400
Curriculum: IBDP
Language instr: English

Aga Khan Academy Hyderabad
Survey No 1/1 Hardware Park, Maheshwaram Mandal, Rangareddy District, Hyderabad, Telangana 501510
Tel: +91 40 66291313
Age range: 6–18 years
No. of pupils: 630
Curriculum: IBDP, IBMYP, IBPYP
Language instr: English

Ahmedabad International School
Opp Rajpath Row Houses, Behind Kiran Motors, Judges Bungalow Road, Bodakdev, Ahmedabad 380015
Tel: +91 79 2687 2459
Age range: 3–17
No. of pupils: 1200
Curriculum: IBDP, IBPYP, IGCSE, ALevs
Language instr: English

Ajmera Global School
Yogi Nagar, Eksar Road, Borivali West, Mumbai, Maharashtra 400092
Tel: +91 22 32401053
Curriculum: IBPYP
Language instr: English

Akal Academy Baru Sahib
Via Rajgarh, Teh. Pachhad, Distt. Sirmore, Himachal Pradesh 173101
Tel: +91 9816400538
Curriculum: IBPYP
Language instr: English

Akshar Árbol International School – ECR Campus
Bethel Nagar, North 9th Street, Injambakkam, Chennai, Tamil Nadu 600115
Tel: +91 94449 73275
Curriculum: IBPYP
Language instr: English

Al Fajr International School
No. 7 & 8, II Main Road, Nehru Nagar, Perungudi, Chennai 600 096
Tel: +91 044 455 72228
Curriculum: UK, IGCSE

Al Qamar Academy
14 Kalyani Nagar, Opp Journalist's Colony, Kottivakkam, Chennai, Tamil Nadu 600041
Tel: +91 44 2451 1226
Age range: 12–16
No. of pupils: 300
Curriculum: IGCSE

All Saints' College
Nainital, Uttarakhand 263002
Tel: +91 5942 235121
Age range: G5–18
No. of pupils: 800
Curriculum: National
(RS)

Alliance World School
C-54/A, Sector-56, Noida, Uttar Pradesh 201301
Tel: +91 12 0258 9073
Age range: 4–19
No. of pupils: 100
Curriculum: IGCSE

aLphabet School
178 St. Mary's Road, Alwarpet, Chennai, Tamil Nadu 600018
Tel: +91 44 4211 2025
Curriculum: IBMYP, IBPYP
Language instr: English

American Embassy School
Chandragupta Marg, Chanakyapuri, New Delhi, Delhi 110021
Tel: +91 11 2688 8854
No. of pupils: 1200
Curriculum: ACT, AP, IBDP, SAT
Language instr: English

American International School – Chennai
100 Feet Road, Taramani, Chennai 600113
Tel: +91 44 2254 9000
Age range: 3–18
No. of pupils: 226 B116 G110
Curriculum: IBDP
Language instr: English
(CIS) (ECIS)

AMERICAN SCHOOL OF BOMBAY
For further details see p. 54
SF 2, G-Block, Bandra Kurla Complex Road, Bandra East, Mumbai, Maharashtra 400051
Tel: SS: +91 22 6772 7272
ES: +91 22 6131 3600
Email: inquiry@asbindia.org
Website: www.asbindia.org
Head of School: Paul Richards
Age range: 3–18 years
No. of pupils: 576
Fees: Day US$20,000–US$35,020
Curriculum: AP, IBDP, IBPYP, SAT, USA
Language instr: English

Amity Global School, Gurgaon
Main Sector Road 4, Sector 46, Gurgaon, Harayana 122002
Tel: +91 84 4848 1410
No. of pupils: 60
Curriculum: IBDP, IBPYP
Language instr: English

Amity Global School, Noida
A Block, C Block, Sector 44, Noida, Uttar Pradesh 201301
Tel: +91 12 0243 2959
Curriculum: IBPYP
Language instr: English

Amity International School Saket
M Block, Saket, New Delhi, Delhi 110017
Tel: +91 11 29561606
Age range: 4–12

Amrita International Vidyalayam
Choodasandra, Huskur P.O., Bengaluru, Karnataka 560099
Tel: +91 90 1920 2583
Curriculum: IBPYP
Language instr: English

Apeejay School International, South Delhi
Sheikh Sarai-Phase I, Panchsheel Park, New Delhi, Delhi 110017
Tel: +91 11 26016935
Curriculum: IBDP, IBMYP, IBPYP
Language instr: English

APL Global School
Survey No 104/8C3, Foundry Road, Okiiam Thoraiopakkam, Chennai, Tamil Nadu 600097
Tel: +91 44 4282 3272
Curriculum: UK, IGCSE, ALevs

Ascend International School
5 'F' Block, Opp. Govt. Colony, Bandra Kurla Complex (Bandra E), Mumbai, Maharashtra 400051
Tel: +91 22 7122 2000
Age range: 3–13
No. of pupils: 280
Curriculum: IBDP, IBMYP, IBPYP
Language instr: English

ASIS Chennai
Parvathi Avenue Madanandapuram, Udhaya Nagar Main Road, Porur, Chennai, Tamil Nadu 600116
Tel: +91 80 1213 7777
Age range: 2–19 years

Bangalore International School
Geddalahalli, Hennur Bagalur Road, Kothanur Post, Bengaluru, Karnataka 560077
Tel: +91 80 2846 5060/2844 5852
Age range: 3–18
No. of pupils: 502
Curriculum: AP, IBDP, UK, USA, IGCSE, ALevs
Language instr: English
CIS EAR ECIS RS

BD Somani International School
625 GD Somani Marg, Cuffe Parade, Mumbai, Maharashtra 400005
Tel: +91 22 2216 1355
Age range: 13–17
No. of pupils: 190
Curriculum: IBDP, IGCSE
Language instr: English

Billabong High International (Santa Cruz)
Ajivasan, Off. Juhu Tara Road, Opp. Lido Cinema, Next to SNDT College, Santa Cruz West, Mumbai, Maharashtra 400049
Tel: +91 22 26613389
Curriculum: UK, IGCSE

Billabong High International School (Thane)
Road no. 27, Shreenagar, Wagle Estate, Thane West, Thane, Maharashtra 400604
Tel: +91 84960 60000
Curriculum: IBDP
Language instr: English, Hindi

Bishop Cotton School
Shimla, Himachal Pradesh 171002
Tel: +91 17 7262 0880
Age range: B7–18

BLiSS Edify International School, Pune
38 Phase 1, Rajiv Gandhi Infotech Park, Hinjawadi, Pune, Maharashtra 411057
Tel: +91 77 4185 0000
Curriculum: IBMYP
Language instr: English

Bloomingdale International School
Municipal Employee Colony, Main Road, Vijayawada, Andhra Pradesh 520010
Tel: +91 7799787827
Curriculum: IBMYP, IBPYP
Language instr: English

Bluebells School International
Kailash (Opp) Lady Shriram College, New Delhi, Delhi 110048
Tel: +91 011 29232963
Age range: 4–18
No. of pupils: B976 G893
Curriculum: National
Language instr: English

Bodhi International School
Shikargarh Enclave, Near Mini Market, Jodhpur, Rajasthan 342015
Tel: +91 291 2970100-1
Curriculum: IBPYP
Language instr: English

Bombay International School
Gilbert Building, 2nd Cross Lane, Babulnath, Mumbai, Maharashtra 400007
Tel: +91 22 2364 8206
Curriculum: IBDP, IBPYP

Bright Start Fellowship International School
Fellowship Society Campus, Near August Kranti Maidan, Gowalia Tank, 400036
Tel: +91 22 23803388
Curriculum: UK, IGCSE, ALevs

British Oak Tree Nursery
Site No-4 Mayfield Garden Sector 57, Opp Orchid Islands, Gurgaon, Haryana
Tel: +91 95 8294 8440
Curriculum: UK
COB

Buddhi School
1&2 Dasarahalli Extension, HA Farm Post, (Next to Legacy Apartments), Opposite to Shoba Moonsto+, Bengaluru, Karnataka 560024
Tel: +91 92420 20302
Curriculum: UK, IGCSE, ALevs

Bunts Sangha's S.M. Shetty International School & Jr. College
Hiranandani Gardens, Powai, Mumbai, Maharashtra 400076
Tel: +91 22 61327346
Curriculum: IBDP
Language instr: English

Calcutta International School
724 Anandapur, E M Bypass, Kolkata, West Bengal 700107
Tel: +91 33 2443 2054
Age range: 3–18
No. of pupils: 642 B360 G282
Curriculum: IBDP, UK, IGCSE, ALevs
Language instr: English

Caledonian International School
Near Power Gym, Saili Road, Pathankot, Punjab 145001
Tel: +91 98880 00189
Curriculum: IBMYP
Language instr: English

Calorx Olive International School
Besides Ahmedabad Dental College, Near Arjun Farm, Ranchodpura – Bhadaj Road, Ahmedabad, Gujarat 380058
Tel: +91 90 9993 3804
Curriculum: IBDP, IBMYP, IBPYP
Language instr: English

Cambridge International School
Choti Baradari, Phase II, Jalandhar, Punjab 144001
Tel: +91 181 462 3955
Curriculum: IBDP, IBPYP

Cambridge International School – Dasuya
Hazipur Road, Dasuya, Hoshiarpur, Punjab 144205
Tel: +91 1883 502108
Age range: 3–18
No. of pupils: 300

Campion International School
River Side Avenue, Shalbari, West Bengal
Tel: +91 99335 39999
Age range: 4–19
Curriculum: UK, IGCSE, ALevs

Canadian International School
Survey No 4 & 20, Manchenahalli, Yelahanka, Bengaluru, Karnataka 560064
Tel: +91 80 4249 4444
Age range: 3–19+
No. of pupils: 420 B220 G200
Curriculum: IBDP, SAT
Language instr: English
CIS

Candor International School
Koppa-harapanhalli Road, Hullahalli, Off, Bannerghatta Main Rd, near Electronic City, Bengaluru, Karnataka 560105
Tel: +91 77 6029 9992
Age range: 3–17
No. of pupils: 600
Curriculum: IBDP, IBPYP
Language instr: English

Chatrabhuj Narsee School
Valley of Flower, Next to Gundecha Premiere Tower, off. Western Express Highway, Kandivali East, Mumbai, Maharashtra 400101
Tel: +91 22 2886 6677
Curriculum: IBDP
Language instr: English

Chinmaya International Residential School
Nallur Vayal Post, Siruvani Road, Coimbatore, Tamil Nadu 641114
Tel: +91 422 261 3300/3303
Age range: 10–19
No. of pupils: 500 B320 G180
Curriculum: IBDP, National
Language instr: English

Chinmaya International Vidyalaya
P-125, Warangade, Maan, Taluka and Dist: Palghar, Boisar, Maharashtra 401501
Tel: +91 73 7848 9121
Curriculum: IBPYP
Language instr: English, Hindi

CHIREC International
1-55/12C, CHIREC Avenue, Kothaguda, Kondapur, Hyderabad, Telangana 500084
Tel: 91 40 44760999
Age range: 2.5–18
No. of pupils: 1298
Curriculum: IBDP, IGCSE, ALevs

Choithram International
Choithram Hospital Campus, 5 Manik Bagh Road, Indore, Madhya Pradesh 452014
Tel: +91 731 2360345/6
Age range: 3–19
No. of pupils: 500
Curriculum: IBDP, IBMYP, IBPYP
Language instr: English

Christ Church School
Clare Road, Byculla, Mumbai, Maharashtra 400008
Tel: +91 22 2309 9892
Curriculum: IBDP
Language instr: English

Christ Junior College
29 Hosur Road, Suddagunte Palya, Bengaluru, Karnataka 560029
Tel: +91 80 40129292
Curriculum: IBDP
Language instr: English

Christ Junior College – Residential
Mysore Road, Kanmanike, Kumbalgodu, Bengaluru, Karnataka 560074
Tel: + 91 80 28437915
Age range: B16–19
No. of pupils: 40 B40
Curriculum: IBDP
Language instr: English

CP Goenka International School – Juhu
Plot No 44, Gulmohar Cross Road No 1, JVPD, Vile Parle (West), Mumbai, Maharashtra 400049
Tel: +91 93 2259 1709
Curriculum: IBDP, IGCSE
Language instr: English

CPS Global School – Anna Nagar Campus
A 80, IIIrd Avenue, Annanagar, Chennai, Tamil Nadu 600102
Tel: +91 44 4351 5121
Curriculum: IBDP
Language instr: English

CPS Global School – Thirumazhisai Campus
SH 50, Thiruvallur High Road, Thirumazhisai, Chennai, Tamil Nadu 600124
Tel: +91 44 3500 3800
Curriculum: IBDP
Language instr: English

Crossroads International School
11-12 Modern Complex, Devendra Dham Ki Gali, Opposite Celebration Mall, Udaipur, Rajasthan 313001
Tel: +91 29 4298 0215
Curriculum: IBPYP
Language instr: English, Hindi

Cygnus World School
Besides Motnath Mahadev Temple, Harni, Vadodara, Gujarat 390022
Tel: +91 90 9913 0334
Curriculum: IBDP
Language instr: English, Hindi

D Y Patil International College
DY Patil Knowledge City, Charholi(BK), Via. Lohegaon, Pune, Maharashtra 412105
Tel: +91 20 30612700/752/753
Age range: 3–17
Curriculum: IBDP, IGCSE
Language instr: English

D Y Patil International School, Lohagaon
Charoli Bd., Lohagaon, Pune, Maharashtra 412105
Tel: +91 020 30612 714

D Y Patil International School, Nagpur
MIHAN Project Area, Village Khapri (Railway), Nagpur, Maharashtra 441108
Tel: +91 22 3928 5999
Language instr: English

D Y Patil International School, Nerul
Dr D Y Patil Vidhyanagar, Sector 7, Nerul, Navi Mumbai, Maharashtra 400706
Tel: +91 22 47700840
Curriculum: IBDP

D Y Patil International School, Worli
Opp MIG Colony A, Worli, Mumbai, Maharashtra 400025
Tel: +91-22 69047999
Curriculum: IBDP, IBPYP, IGCSE
Language instr: English

Daly College
Residency Area, Indore, Madhya Pradesh 452001
Tel: +91 7312 719000
Language instr: English
RS

De Paul International Residential School
Belagola, Srirangapatna, Taluk, Avverahalli, Karnataka 571606
Tel: +91 9535187506
Age range: 4–18
Curriculum: IGCSE

Delhi Public School Ghaziabad
Site #3, Industrial Area, Meerut Road, Ghaziabad, Uttar Pradesh 201002
Tel: +91 120 2712236
No. of pupils: 5500
Curriculum: IBDP, IBPYP
Language instr: English

Deutsche Schule New Delhi
EP16/17 Chandragupta Marg, Chanakyapuri, New Delhi, Delhi 110021
Tel: +91 11 2611 2193

Dhirubhai Ambani International School
Bandra-Kurla Complex, Bandra (East), Mumbai, Maharashtra 400098
Tel: +91 22 40617000
Age range: 4–18
No. of pupils: 1026
Curriculum: IBDP, National
Language instr: English
RS

Diamond Stone International School
Nallur Road, Madivallam Cross, Hosur, Tamil Nadu 635109
Tel: +91 766 731 2999
Language instr: English, Hindi, Tamil

Don Bosco International School
Nathalal Parekh Marg, Matunga (E), Mumbai, Maharashtra 400019
Tel: +91 22 2412 7474
Curriculum: IBDP, IBPYP
Language instr: English

DPS International, Gurgaon
HS-01, Block W, South City II, Gurgaon, Haryana 122001
Tel: +91 8377000164
Curriculum: IBDP, IBMYP, IBPYP
Language instr: English

DPS International, Saket
P-37 MB Road, Sector VI, Pusph Vihar, Saket, New Delhi, Delhi 110057
Tel: +91 11 2956 1187
Age range: 11–18
Curriculum: National, IGCSE, ALevs
Language instr: English

DPSG Palam Vihar
951 Major Sushil Aima Marg, Sector 1, Palam Vihar, Gurugram, Haryana 122017
Tel: +91 85 9502 0202
Curriculum: IBPYP
Language instr: English, Hindi

Dr Pillai Global Academy
Plot No 1, RSC 48, Gorai – II, Borivali (W), Mumbai, Maharashtra 400092
Tel: +91 22 2868 4467/87
Age range: 3–18
Curriculum: IBDP, IGCSE, ALevs
Language instr: English

Dr Pillai Global Academy, New Panvel
Sector-7, Khanda Colony, New Panvel, Navi Mumbai, Maharashtra 410206
Tel: +91 22 2748 1737
Age range: 3–17 years
No. of pupils: 508
Curriculum: IBDP
Language instr: English

DRS International School
Survey No. 523 Opp.Apparel Park, Gundla Pochampally, Medchal Mandal, Telangana, Hyderabad 500100
Tel: +91 40 237 92123/4/5
Curriculum: IBDP, IBPYP
Language instr: English

DSB International School
Urmi Estate 95, Ganpatrao Kadam Marg, Opposite Peninsula Business Park, Mumbai, Maharashtra 400013
Tel: +91 73 0459 7529
Age range: 3–18 years
No. of pupils: 210
Curriculum: IBDP, UK, IGCSE
Language instr: English, German
COB

Dwarkibai Gangadhar Khetan International School
Krishna Realties, Behind Sunder Nagar, Off. S.V. Road & Link Road, Malad (West), Mumbai, Maharashtra 400064
Tel: +91 22 28785360
Curriculum: UK, ALevs

Eastern Public School
Ward 1, Abbas Nagar, Bhopal, Madhya Pradesh 462036
Tel: +91 755 2805695
Curriculum: IBDP, IBPYP

Ecole Mondiale World School
Gulmohar Cross Road No. 9, J.V.P.D. Scheme, Juhu, Mumbai, Maharashtra 400049
Tel: +91 22 26237265/66
Age range: 1–18
No. of pupils: 550
Curriculum: IBDP, IBMYP, IBPYP
Language instr: English
ECIS

Edubridge International School
Wadilal A. Patel Marg, Grant Road (East), Mumbai, Maharashtra 400007
Tel: +91 22 238 999 11
Curriculum: IBDP, IBMYP, IBPYP
Language instr: English

Ela Green School
No.1 Karambur Village, Chengalpattu Taluk, Kandchipuram District, Urapakkam, Maraimalai Nagar, Chennai, Tamil Nadu 603209
Tel: +91 89 3995 8989
Curriculum: IBMYP, IBPYP
Language instr: English

Elpro International School
Elpro compound, Entrance from Shridhar Nagar road, Pimpri-Chinchwad Link Road, Pune, Maharashtra 411033
Tel: +91 20 6733 3500
Curriculum: IBDP
Language instr: English

European International School
7A, Wisecy House, 14/15 Nanchundaroa Road, Injambakkam, Chennai, Tamil Nadu 600115
Tel: +91 44 24492562

Excelsior American School
Sector 43 behind Dell Building, C-2 Block, Sushant Lok, Phase 1, Gurugram, Haryana 122001
Tel: +91 1 124 4049342
Curriculum: IBDP, UK, IGCSE, ALevs
Language instr: English

Fazlani L'Académie Globale
Shiv das Chapsi Marg, Opp. Wallace Flour Mills, Mazagaon, Mumbai, Maharashtra 400009
Tel: +91 222 373 2730
Curriculum: IBPYP
Language instr: English

FirstSteps School
Opp. Blind Girls Hostel, Sector 26, Chandigarh, Punjab 160019
Tel: +91 172 2793992
Age range: 2–15
No. of pupils: 265 B151 G114
Curriculum: IBPYP, IGCSE
Language instr: English

Fountainhead School
Opp Ambetha Water Tank, Kunkni, Rander-Dandi Road, Surat, Gujarat 395005
Tel: +91 800 0130 031
Age range: 3–17 years
No. of pupils: 1900
Curriculum: IBDP, IBMYP, IBPYP
Language instr: English

Fravashi International Academy
Adjacent to Gangapur Dam Rest House, Gangapur – Dugaon Road, Dugaon Village, Nashik, Maharashtra 422203
Tel: +912532215000
Curriculum: UK, IGCSE, ALevs

G D Goenka Global School
S-3130, DLF 3, Near Neelkanth Hospital, Gurugram, Haryana 122010
Curriculum: IBPYP
Language instr: English, Hindi

G D Goenka World School
G D Goenka Education City, Sohna-Gurgaon Road, Sohna, Haryana 122103
Tel: +91 95 1363 1471
Curriculum: IBDP, IBPYP
Language instr: English

G Global School
29A, Rajagoundampalayam 2nd Street, Pallipalayam Road, Tiruchengodu, Tamil Nadu 637211
Tel: +91 42 8825 0999
Curriculum: IBPYP
Language instr: English, Tamil

Garodia International Centre for Learning
153, Garodia Nagar, Ghatkopar East, Mumbai, Maharashtra 400077
Tel: +91 22 25061133/3157
No. of pupils: 365
Curriculum: IBDP
Language instr: English

Gateway International School
TOD Ashram, Jabakadal Street, Padur, Kazhipattur Post, Kelambakkam, Chennai, Tamil Nadu 603103
Tel: + 91 860 811 7700
Curriculum: IBDP, IBMYP, IBPYP
Language instr: English

GEMS Akademia International School
Bakrahat Road, Thakurpukur, P.O. Rasapunja, Kolkata, West Bengal 700104
Tel: +91 (033) 249 80671
Age range: 2–17
Curriculum: National, IGCSE, ALevs
Language instr: English

GEMS Cambridge International School – Batala
Amritsar Road, Batala, Punjab 143505
Tel: +91 9257292300
Age range: 3–13
No. of pupils: 200

GEMS Cambridge International School – Hoshiarpur
Jalandhar – Phagwara, ByPass Road, Hoshiarpur, Punjab 146111
Tel: +91 97798 89306
Age range: 3–16
No. of pupils: 1100

GEMS Genesis International School
Near Viashnovedi Circle, SP Ring Road, Ahmedabad, Gujarat 382421
Tel: +91 927 4 022333
Curriculum: UK, IGCSE, ALevs

GEMS International School – Palam Vihar Gurgaon
Block C-2, Palam Vihar, Gurgaon, Haryana 122015
Tel: +91 124 463 6900
Age range: 4–17
No. of pupils: 1032
Curriculum: National
Language instr: English

GEMS Modern Academy – Gurgaon
Block E, South City II, Gurgaon, Haryana 122018
Tel: +91 124 652 1700
Age range: 1–17
Curriculum: National
Language instr: English

GEMS Modern Academy – Kochi
Plot B1-4, Smart City Kochi, Opp. Infopark Phase II, Brahmapuram, Kochi, Kerala 682303
Tel: +91 48 4258 7800
Curriculum: IBPYP
Language instr: English

Genesis Global School
A-12, Sector 132, Noida Expressway, Uttar Pradesh 201304
Tel: +91 9711 000626
Age range: 2.5–18 years
Curriculum: IBDP, IBMYP, IBPYP
Language instr: English

German International School Chennai
4/391 Ram Garden Anna Salai, Palavakkam, Chennai, Tamil Nadu 600041
Tel: +91 44 2451 2504
Age range: 5–18
No. of pupils: 300

GJR International School
1/1 & 1/2 Chinnappanahalli, Bangalore, Karnataka 560037
Tel: +91 96 0648 9500
Age range: 3–11 years
No. of pupils: 360
Curriculum: IBPYP
Language instr: English

Glendale Academy
Beside Sun City, Artillery Centre Gate, Hyderabad, Telangana 500086
Tel: +91 7416 7419 36
Curriculum: UK, IGCSE

Glendale International School
Plot A, Road No. 20, HMDA Layout, Tellapur, Hyderabad, Telangana 502032
Tel: +91 90 3000 1128
Age range: 1.5–11 years
No. of pupils: 250
Curriculum: IBPYP
Language instr: English

Global City International School
135, 5th Main, 6th Cross, Malleshpalya, New Thippasandra Post, Near CV Raman Nag+, Bengaluru, Karnataka 560075
Tel: +91 80 25349199
Age range: 4–16
Curriculum: IGCSE

Global English School – Calicut
Kaimpalam, Pantheerankavu-Mankavu Road, Pantheerankavu, Calicut, Kerala
Tel: +91 495 243 5511
Age range: 5–16
No. of pupils: 300
Curriculum: IGCSE

Global Indian International School (GIIS) Uppal Campus
Survey No. 8 & 9, Peerjadiguda, Uppal Mandal, Hyderabad, Telangana

Global Indian International School (GIIS) Ahmedabad Campus
Godrej Garden City, Jagatpur, Ahmedabad, Gujarat 382470
Tel: +91 80 0572 2810

Global Indian International School (GIIS) Balewadi Campus
Kul Echoloch', Near Balewadi Sports Complex, Nande-Balewadi Road, Mahalunge, Pune, Maharashtra 411045
Tel: +91 80 0572 2810

Global Indian International School (GIIS) Bannerghatta Campus
Bannerghatta Main Road, Gollahalli, Bannerghatta, Bangalore, Karnataka 560083
Tel: +91 80 0572 2810

Global Indian International School (GIIS) Hadapsar Campus
Leisure Town, Behind Amanora Fire Station, Malwadi, Hadapsar, Pune, Maharashtra 411028
Tel: +91 80 0572 2810

Global Indian International School (GIIS) Noida Campus
D-5, Sector 71, (2 Km from Noida City Centre Metro Station), Noida, Uttar Pradesh 201301
Tel: +91 80 0572 2810

Global Indian International School (GIIS) Surat Campus
Chalthan (Next to Chokhi Dhani), Kadodara–Palsana Highway, Surat, Gujarat 394305
Tel: +91 80 0572 2810

Global Indian International School (GIIS) Whitefield Campus
No-5, 6, 8 Heggondahalli Village, Whitefield Sarjapur Main Road, Gunjur Post, Bangalore, Karnataka 560087
Tel: +91 80 0572 2810

Goldcrest International
Sector 29, Plot No: 59, Near Rajiv Gandhi Park, Navi Mumbai, Maharashtra 400703
Tel: +91 22 2789 2261
Curriculum: IBDP

Good Shepherd International School
Good Shepherd Knowledge Village, M Palada PO, Ootacamund, Tamil Nadu 643 004
Tel: +91 423 2550371
Age range: 8–17
No. of pupils: 1000
Curriculum: IBDP, IGCSE
Language instr: English

GPS Brookes Kochi
P.O, Thiruvaniyoor,
Thiruvankulam – Chottanikkara
Rd, Kochi, Kerala 682308
Tel: +91 484 271 3745
Curriculum: IBDP
Language instr: English

Grassroots Global School
7/4, Lynwood Avenue,
Mahalingpuram, Chennai,
Tamil Nadu 600034
Tel: +91 44 2825 5969
Curriculum: IBPYP

Greenwood High International School
No.8-14, Chickkawadayara
Pura, Near Heggondahalli,
Gunjur Post, Varthur via,
Bengaluru, Karnataka 560087
Tel: +91 80 22010500
Age range: 6–19 years
Curriculum: IBDP

Harvest International School
Jassowal-Kular, Tehsil Jagraon,
Ludihana, Punjab 141023
Tel: +91 98 76500635
Age range: 11–18
No. of pupils: 190
Curriculum: IGCSE, ALevs

Harvest International School
Carmalaram post silk farm,
Kodathi village, Off sarjapur
road, near Kodathi village,
Bangalore, Karnataka 560035
Tel: +91 80 6733 1884
Curriculum: IBPYP
Language instr: English, Hindi

Hebron School
Lushington Hall, Ootacamund,
Tamil Nadu 643001
Tel: 0091 423 2225820
Age range: 5–19
No. of pupils: 373 *B194 G179*
Curriculum: UK, IGCSE, ALevs
Language instr: English

Heritage Xperiential Learning School Gurgaon
Sector 62, Gurgaon,
Haryana 122011
Tel: +91 124 2855124
Curriculum: IBDP, IBPYP
Language instr: English, Hindi

HFS International Powai
Richmond Street, Hiranandani
Gardens, Powai, Mumbai,
Maharashtra 400076
Tel: +91 22 2576 3001
Curriculum: IBDP
Language instr: English

Hill Spring International School
C Wing, NSS Educational Complex,
MP Mill Compound, Tardeo,
Mumbai, Maharashtra 400034
Tel: +91 22 2355 6201
No. of pupils: 600
Curriculum: IBDP, IBPYP
Language instr: English

Hillside Academy
Road No 46, Jubilee Hills,
Hyderabad, Telangana 500033
Tel: +91 40 2354 6113

Himalayan International Residential School
P. O. Rajganj, Dist Jalpaiguri,
West Bengal 735134
Tel: +91 98008 72984
Curriculum: National,
UK, IGCSE, ALevs

Himali Boarding School
Doomaram, P.O. Kurseong, Dist
Darjeeling, West Bengal 734203
Tel: +913542332529
Curriculum: UK, IGCSE, ALevs

Hindustan International School
40 GST Road, St Thomas Mount,
Guindy, Chennai, Tamil Nadu
Tel: +91 44 2234 2020
Age range: 4–18
Curriculum: IGCSE

HLC International – Chennai
Wing Haven Gardens, Karanai,
Chennai, Tamil Nadu 603103
Tel: +91 99628 05259
Age range: 5–18
No. of pupils: 300
Curriculum: IGCSE

HUS International School
5/63 Old Mahabalipuram
Ro, Egattur Village, Padur
PO, Kelambakkam, Chennai,
Tamil Nadu 600130
Tel: +91 9500 118651
Curriculum: IBDP, IBMYP, IBPYP
Language instr: English

HVB Global Academy
79 Marine Drive, Mumbai,
Maharashtra 400020
Tel: +91 22 6143 6000/71
Curriculum: IGCSE, ALevs

India International School
Kshipra Path, Opp VT
Road, Mansarovar, Jaipur,
Rajasthan 302020
Tel: +91 141 2786401
Age range: 6–18
No. of pupils: 2182 *B1330 G852*
Curriculum: IBDP,
National, UK, ALevs

India International School
26/1, Sarjapur Road,
Chikkabellandur, Bengaluru,
Karnataka 560035
Tel: +91 080 2843 9001

Indus International School (Bangalore)
Billapura Cross, Sarjapur,
Bengaluru, Karnataka 562125
Tel: +91 80 2289 5900
Age range: 8–18
No. of pupils: 600
Curriculum: IBDP, IBMYP, IBPYP
Language instr: English

Indus International School, Hyderabad
Survey No 424 & 425, Kondakal
Village, Near Mokila (M),
Shankarpally, Hyderabad,
Telangana 501203
Tel: +91 8417 302100
Age range: 5–18 years
No. of pupils: 350
Curriculum: IBDP, IBMYP, IBPYP
Language instr: English

Indus International School, Pune
576 Bhukum, Near Manas Resort, Tal
Mulshi, Pune, Maharashtra 411042
Tel: +91 80 2289 5900
Curriculum: IBDP, IBMYP, IBPYP

International Fateh Academy
Academy Road, Jandiala Guru,
Amritsar, Punjab 143001
Tel: +91 18 3243 0205
Curriculum: IBPYP
Language instr: English, Punjabi

International School Aamby
Aamby Valley City, Ambavene,
Pune, Maharashtra 410401
Tel: +91 20 3910 2500
Age range: 8–18
No. of pupils: 100
Curriculum: IPC, IGCSE
Language instr: English

International School Kashmir (ISK)
Baghat Chowk, Srinagar,
Jammu & Kashmir
Tel: +91 9419038733
Language instr: English

International School of Hyderabad
c/o ICRISAT, Patancheru,
Hyderabad, Telangana 502324
Tel: +91 4030713865
Age range: 3–18 years
No. of pupils: 400
Curriculum: IBDP, USA, IGCSE
Language instr: English

International Village School Chennai
33A, Clasic Farms Road,
Sholinganallur, Chennai,
Tamil Nadu 600119
Tel: +91 44 4860 3757
Age range: 2–11
No. of pupils: 40
Curriculum: IBPYP
Language instr: English

Inventure Academy
Whitefield – Sarjapur Road,
Chikkavaderapura, Near
Dommasandra Circle,
Bengaluru, Karnataka 562125
Tel: +91 80 27822101
Curriculum: National,
UK, IGCSE, ALevs

Ithaka International School
Near Kanuparthipadu,
Golagamudi Road, Nellore,
Andhra Pradesh
Tel: +91 861 6521 111
Age range: 5–18
No. of pupils: 300

Jain International Residential School
Jakkasandra Post, Kanakpura
Road, Ramanagara District,
Bengaluru, Karnataka 562112
Tel: +91 80 2757 7750
Age range: 9–18
No. of pupils: *B500 G250*
Curriculum: IBDP, National,
SAT, TOEFL, IGCSE, ALevs
Language instr: English

Jamnabai Narsee International School
Narsee Monjee Bhavan, N.S.
Road No.7, J.V.P.D Scheme,
Vile Parle (West), Mumbai,
Maharashtra 400049
Tel: +91 (0)22 26187575/ 7676
Age range: 3–19
No. of pupils: 660
Curriculum: ACT, AP, IBDP, IBMYP,
IBPYP, National, SAT, TOEFL, IGCSE
Language instr: English

Jayshree Periwal High School
3, Adjoining Stadium, Ajmer
Road, Chitrakoot, Jaipur,
Rajasthan 302021
Tel: +91 141 4132222

Jayshree Periwal International School
Mahapura, SEZ Road, Ajmer Road, Jaipur, Rajasthan 302026
Tel: +91 97827 44444/44445
Age range: 12–18
No. of pupils: 800 B500 G300
Curriculum: IBDP, IBPYP
Language instr: English

JBCN International School – Oshiwara
Survey No. 41, CTS No. 1, Off Andheri Link Road, Behind Tarapore Towers, Mhada Colony, Oshiwara, Andher+, Mumbai, Maharashtra 400058
Tel: +91 22 2630 2398
Curriculum: IBDP, IBPYP
Language instr: English

JBCN International School – Parel
Yogi Mansion, CTS No. 244, Dr Vinay Walimbe Road, Off Dr S.S. Rao Marg, Parel East, Mumbai, Maharashtra 400012
Tel: +91 22 2411 4627
Age range: 3–18 years
Curriculum: IBDP, IBPYP, UK, IGCSE
Language instr: English

JG International School
JG Campus of Excellence, JG Campus Road, Ahmedabad, Gujarat 380061
Tel: +91 79 65411315
Age range: 3–18
No. of pupils: 1000
Curriculum: IBDP
Language instr: English

Johnson Grammar School ICSE&IBDP
Street No 3, Kakatiya Nagar, Habsiguda, Hyderabad, Andhra Pradesh 500007
Tel: +91 81064 72685
No. of pupils: 5500
Curriculum: IBDP
Language instr: English

Jyotirmay International School
Opp Wageshwar Temple, Gat No 2188 A, Pl No. 8 & 9 A, Bhd. Rambhau Moze Engineering College, BAIF Rd, Wagholi, Pune, Maharashtra 412207
Tel: +91 20 65100784
Curriculum: UK, IGCSE

K.R. Mangalam Global School
N-Block, Nandi Vithi Road, Greater Kailash-1, New Delhi, Delhi 110048
Tel: +91 97 1885 8181
Curriculum: IBDP, IBMYP, IBPYP
Language instr: English, Hindi

K.R. Mangalam Global School, Gurugram
D-23, South City 1, Near Patio Club, Gurugram, Haryana 122001
Tel: +91 87 5004 5132
Curriculum: IBPYP
Language instr: English, Hindi

Kai Early Years
66/2, 2nd Main Road, Nallurhalli, Whitefield, Bangalore, Karnataka 560066
Tel: +91 97 4048 0123
Age range: 2–6 years
Curriculum: IBPYP
Language instr: English, Hindi

KC High
12/4, Arunachalam Road, Kotturupuram, Chennai, Tamil Nadu 600085
Tel: +91 (44) 2447 3551
Curriculum: IBDP
Language instr: English

Kennedy High – The Global School
Bachupally, Miyapur-Medchal Highway, Hyderabad, Telangana 500090
Tel: +91 40 64646477
Age range: 5–18
No. of pupils: 300

KiiT International School
KiiT Campus 9, Patia, Bhubaneswar, Odisha 751024
Tel: +91 674 2725805
Age range: 3.5–18 years
No. of pupils: 1650
Curriculum: IBDP, National, IGCSE
Language instr: English

King's College India
A1 Sector 5, Rohtak, Haryana 124001
Tel: +91 708 200 5414
Age range: 3–18
Curriculum: UK, IGCSE
Language instr: English

Knowledgeum Academy
44/4 District Fund Road, Jayanagar 9th Block, Bangalore, Karnataka 560069
Tel: +91 73 5301 2391
Curriculum: IBDP
Language instr: English

Kodaikanal International School
PO Box 25, Seven Roads Junction, Kodaikanal, Tamil Nadu 624101
Tel: +91 4542 247500
Age range: 3–18
No. of pupils: 393
Curriculum: ACT, IBDP, IBMYP, IBPYP, SAT, USA
Language instr: English

Kohinoor American School
Old Mumbai – Pune Highway, Near to The Dukes Retreat, Khandala, Maharashtra 410301
Tel: +91 9324323003
Age range: 12–18
No. of pupils: 120
Curriculum: IBDP, IBMYP
Language instr: English

L'Ecole Française Internationale de Bombay
Ashishwang Bungalow, Plot No.72, Pochkhanwala Road, Worli, Mumbai, Maharashtra 400030
Tel: + 91 (0)22249 08801
Curriculum: FrenchBacc

Lady Andal Venkatasubba Rao Matriculation School
Shenstone Park, No.7 Harrington Road, Chennai, Tamil Nadu 600031
Tel: +91 44 2836 3404
Curriculum: IBPYP
Language instr: English

Lakshmipat Singhania Academy
12B Alipore Road, Kolkata, West Bengal 700027
Tel: +91 33 2479 3600

Lalaji Memorial Omega International School
79, Omega School Road (Pallavaram Road), Kolapakkam, Kovur Post, Chennai, Tamil Nadu 600128
Tel: +91 44 66241127
Age range: 3–18
No. of pupils: 4252
Curriculum: IBDP, GCSE, IGCSE, ALevs
Language instr: English

Lancers International School
DLF Phase V, Sector 53, Gurgaon, Haryana 122001
Tel: +91 124 423 8753
Age range: 18 months–18 years
No. of pupils: 900
Curriculum: IBDP, IBMYP, IBPYP
Language instr: English

Learning Panorama School
Plot no 25c, Old MHB Colony, OPP Vaidya Kumar Gdn, Nr Don Bosco School, Gorai Link Road, Borivali(W), Mumbai, Maharashtra 400092
Tel: +91 22 6553 9224

Legacy School, Bangalore
6/1 A, 6/2 Byrathi Village, Bidarahalli Hobli, East Taluk, Bengaluru, Karnataka 560077
Tel: +91 70222 92405
Age range: 2.5–18 years
No. of pupils: 766
Curriculum: IBDP, UK, IGCSE, ALevs
Language instr: English

Lycée français de Pondichéry
12 rue Victor Simonel, Pondicherry, Tamil Nadu 605001
Tel: +91 413 233 58 31

M Ct M Chidambaram Chettyar International School
179, Luz Church Road, Mylapore, Chennai, Tamil Nadu 600004
Tel: +91 44 2467 0120
Age range: 11–19
No. of pupils: 39 B21 G18
Curriculum: IBDP, IGCSE
Language instr: English

Mahatma Gandhi International School
Sheth Motilal Hirabhai Bhavan, Opp. Induben Khakhrawala, Mithakali, Navrangpura, Ahmedabad, Gujarat 380006
Tel: +91 79 2 646 3888
No. of pupils: 180
Curriculum: IBDP, IBMYP, IBCP
Language instr: English

Mahindra International School
P26, Rajeev Gandhi Infotech park, Phase 1, Hinjewadi, Pune, Maharashtra 411057
Tel: +91 2042954444
Age range: 3–18
No. of pupils: 342
Curriculum: IBDP, IBMYP, IBPYP
Language instr: English

Mainadevi Bajaj International School
Plot No: 23-A, 24-28 Swami Vivekanand Road, Malad (West), Mumbai, Maharashtra 400064
Tel: +91 22 28733807
Curriculum: IBDP

Mallya Aditi International School
Yelahanka New Town, Bengaluru, Karnataka 560106
Tel: +91 80 40447000
Age range: 5–18
No. of pupils: 592
Curriculum: National

Manchester International School
SF 29/3A, Hudco Colony, Vellakinar, Coimbatore, Tamil Nadu 641029
Tel: +91 422 655 5551
Curriculum: IBDP, IBMYP, IBPYP
Language instr: English

Manthan International School Kompally
1150 Ayyappa Society Main Road, Madhapur, Hyderabad, Telangana 500081
Tel: +91 4220 6060
Curriculum: IBCP, UK, IGCSE

Maple Bear Canadian School
4-7 C DDA Shopping Centre, New Friends Colony, New Delhi, Delhi 110025
Tel: +91 9711165900

Mayo College
Sri Nagar Road, Ajmer, Rajasthan 305007
Tel: +91 145 266 1697
Age range: B9–17 years
No. of pupils: 731
Language instr: English

Mayo College Girls' School
Mayo Link Road, Ajmer, Rajasthan 305001
Tel: +91 145 266 128
Language instr: English

Meridian School, Banjara Hills
#8-2-541, Road No.7, Banjara Hills, Hyderabad, Telangana 500034
Tel: +91 80 9691 8857
Curriculum: IBPYP
Language instr: English, Hindi

Meridian School, Madhapur
#11/4 & 11/5, Opp: Hitech City, Kukatpally Bypass Road, Khanamet Village, Sherlingampally Mandal, Hyderabad, Telangana 500081
Tel: +91 99 4804 3440
Curriculum: IBPYP
Language instr: English, Hindi

MET Rishikul Vidyalaya – Bhujbal Knowledge Centre, Mumbai
Bandra Reclamation, Bandra (West), Mumbai, Maharashtra 400050
Tel: +91 22 2644 0446
Age range: 5–18
No. of pupils: 2200
Curriculum: IGCSE

Metro Delhi International School
AIPF Campus, Mission Hospital Road, Sat Bari, Chattarpur, New Delhi, Delhi 110074
Tel: +91 8860150178
Curriculum: USA

MGD Girls' School
Tonk Rd, Ashok Nagar, Jaipur, Rajasthan 302001
Tel: +91 1412 364478
Language instr: English

Miri Piri Academy
Guru Ki Wadali, Chheharta, Amritsar, Punjab 143105
Tel: +91 805 401 8906
Curriculum: UK, IGCSE, ALevs

MM International School
MM Educational Complex, Mullana, Ambala, Haryana 133003
Tel: +91 1731 275400
Age range: 2–19

MM International School
Patan By Pass Road, Behind Global College,, Jabalpur, Madhya Pradesh 482004
Tel: +91 8109000157

Modern High School for Girls
78, Syed Amir Ali Avenue, Kolkata, West Bengal 700019
Tel: +913322875326
Age range: 3–18
No. of pupils: 3000
Curriculum: IBDP
Language instr: English

Modern School
Sector E, Aliganj, Lucknow, Uttar Pradesh 226024
Tel: +91 955 493 3337
Curriculum: IBPYP

Mody School
Mody Institute of Education & Research, Lakshmangarh, Rajasthan 332311
Tel: +91 91 16637196
Language instr: English

Motilal Nehru School of Sports
Grand Trunk Road, Rajiv Gandhi Education City, Rai, Sonipat, Haryana 131029
Tel: +91 1302 366201
Language instr: English

Mount Litera School International
GN Block, Behind Asian Heart Hospital, Near UTI Building, Bandra Kurla Complex, Bandra- East, Mumbai, Maharashtra 400051
Tel: +91 22 6229 6000
Curriculum: IBDP, IBMYP, IBPYP

Mussoorie International School
Srinagar Estate, Polo Ground, Mussoorie, Uttarakhand 248179
Tel: +91 135 2630250
Age range: G6–19 years
Curriculum: IBDP, IGCSE, ALevs
Language instr: English

Nahar International School
Nahar's Amrit Shakti, Chandivali Farm Road, Off Saki Vihar Road, Andheri East, Mumbai, Maharashtra 400072
Tel: +91 (0)22 6838 5500
No. of pupils: 1200
Curriculum: IBDP
Language instr: English

Navrachana International School
Vasna Bhayali Road, Bhayali, Vadodara, Gujarat 391410
Tel: +91 265 225 3851/2/3/4
Curriculum: IBDP, IBMYP, IBPYP
Language instr: English

Neerja Modi School
Shipra Path, Near Building Technology Park, Mansarovar, Jaipur, Rajasthan 302020
Tel: +91 141 2785 484
Curriculum: IBDP

Neev Academy – North Campus
No. 14, Park Road, Tasker Town, Bengaluru, Karnataka 560001
Tel: +91 80 41144285
Curriculum: IBPYP
Language instr: English

Neev Academy – Yemalur Campus
No. 16, Yemalur-Kempapura Main Road, Opp. Sai Garden Apartments, Yemalur, Bengaluru, Karnataka 560037
Tel: +91 80 71101700
No. of pupils: 350
Curriculum: IBDP, IBMYP, IBPYP
Language instr: English

NES International School Dombivli
Sankara Nagar, Kalyan-Shil Road Opp. DNS Bank, Sonarpada, Dombivli (E), Thane, Mumbai, Maharashtra 421203
Tel: +91 84 22994436
Curriculum: IBPYP
Language instr: English, Hindi

NES International School Mumbai
Malabar Hill Road, Vasant Garden, Mulund(W), Mumbai, Maharashtra 400082
Tel: +91 22 25911478
Curriculum: IBDP, IBMYP, IBPYP
Language instr: English

NEXT School
Park Road, Off Devi Dayal Road, Mulund W, Mumbai, Maharashtra 400080
Tel: +91 22 25600036
Curriculum: IBDP, IBMYP, IBPYP
Language instr: English

Niraj International School
Kandlakoya, 5 km from Dhola-ri-Dhani, Hyderabad, Telangana 132133
Tel: +91 84 18200476
Curriculum: IBPYP
Language instr: English

Oakridge International School, Bachupally
Survey No 166/6, Bowrampet Village, Near Bachupally, Hyderabad, Telangana 500043
Tel: +91 720 764 8111
Curriculum: IBDP, IBPYP, IGCSE

Oakridge International School, Bengaluru
Varthur Road, Near Dommassandra Circle, Sarjapur Hobli, Bengaluru, Karnataka 562125
Tel: +91 0802 254 3600
Age range: 3–18
No. of pupils: 891
Curriculum: IBDP, IBMYP, IBPYP
Language instr: English

Oakridge International School, Gachibowli
Khajaguda, Nanakramguda Road, Cyberabad, Hyderabad, Telangana 500008
Tel: +91 7207 648 111
Age range: 2–18
Curriculum: IBDP, IBMYP, IBPYP
Language instr: English

Oakridge International School, Mohali
Next to Thunderzone Amusement Park, Mohali, Punjab 140307
Tel: +91 752 701 3370
Curriculum: IBPYP, IGCSE
Language instr: English

Oakridge International School, Visakhapatnam
NH 5 Road, Behind HP Petrol Bunk, Maharajpeta Junction, Tagarapuvalasa, Visakhapatnam, Andhra Pradesh 531162
Tel: +91 773 081 6999
Curriculum: IBDP, UK, IGCSE
Language instr: English

Oasis International School
No. 29, 1st Stage, 1st Block, HBR Layout, Bengaluru, Karnataka 560043
Tel: +91 8025433053
Curriculum: IBPYP, UK, IGCSE

Oberoi International School
Oberoi Garden City, Off Western Express Highway, Goregaon (E), Mumbai, Maharashtra 400063
Tel: +91 22 4236 3131
Age range: 3–18 years
No. of pupils: 1616 B816 G800
Curriculum: IBDP, IBMYP, IBPYP, IGCSE
Language instr: English

Oberoi International School – JVLR Campus
Jogeshwari Vikroli Link Road, Jogeshwari East, Mumbai, Maharashtra 400060
Curriculum: IBDP, IBMYP, IBPYP
Language instr: English

P P Savani Cambridge International School
Mota varaccha, Abrama Road, At & Po Abrama Tah-Kamrej, Surat, Gujarat 394150
Tel: +912616503388
Curriculum: UK, IGCSE

Panbai International School
Guru Narayan Rd, Sen Nagar, Near.B.M.C office, Santacruz (East), Mumbai, Maharashtra 400055
Tel: +91 22 2617 7771
Curriculum: UK, IGCSE

Pathways School (Gurgaon NCR South)
Baliawas, Off Gurgaon Faridabad Road, Gurgaon, Haryana 122003
Tel: +91 124 487 2000
Curriculum: IBDP, IBMYP, IBPYP, IBCP
Language instr: English

Pathways School Noida
Sector 100, Noida NCR East, New Delhi, Delhi 110062
Tel: +91 120 461 7000
Curriculum: IBDP, IBMYP, IBPYP
Language instr: English

Pathways World School
Aravali Retreat, Off Gurgaon Sohna Road, Gurgaon, Haryana 122102
Tel: +91 124 451 3000
Age range: 2–19
No. of pupils: 748 *B*483 *G*265
Curriculum: IBDP, IBMYP, IBPYP
Language instr: English

Pinnacle High International School
Sunder lane, Orlem, Malad (w), Mumbai, Maharashtra 400064
Tel: +91 22 2844 9155
Curriculum: UK, IGCSE, ALevs

Podar International School
Ramee Emerald Building, Near Shamrao Vithal Bank, S.V.Road, Khar (West), Mumbai, Maharashtra 400052
Tel: +91 22 2648 7321
Age range: 3–18
No. of pupils: 1013 *B*500 *G*513
Curriculum: IBDP, IBPYP
Language instr: English

Podar International School (Kalyan)
H/N 9, Next to Union Cricket Ground, Gandhari Village, Khadakpada, Kalyan, Maharashtra 421301
Tel: +91 251 2203028
Curriculum: IBCP, UK, IGCSE

Podar O.R.T International School, Worli
PODAR-ORT School Building, 68, Worli Hill Estate, Worli, Mumbai, Maharashtra 400018
Tel: +91 7506112200
Curriculum: IBDP, IBMYP, IBPYP
Language instr: English

Primus Public School
Post Box 21, Chikanayakanahalli Village, Off. Sarjapur Road, Bengaluru, Karnataka 560035
Tel: +91 80 2574 1450
Curriculum: UK, IGCSE, ALevs

Prometheus School
I-7, Jaypee Wishtown, Sector 131, Noida, Uttar Pradesh 201304
Tel: +91 99 9987 6583
Curriculum: IBDP, IBMYP, IBPYP
Language instr: English, Hindi

Punjab Public School
Nabha, Punjab 147201
Tel: +91 9316 780250

Queen Mira International School
Melakkal Road, Kochadai, Madurai, Tamil Nadu 625016
Tel: +91 96557 77000
Curriculum: National

Rasbihari International School
Vrindavan, Nashik-Ozar Road, Nashik, Maharashtra 422003
Tel: +91 253 230 4622
Age range: 3–14
Curriculum: IBPYP, IGCSE
Language instr: English

RBK International Academy
Opp. Indian Oil Nagar, Near Shankara Colony, Ghatkopar-Mankhurd Link Road, Mumbai, Maharashtra 400088
Tel: +91 7400091646/7/8/9
Curriculum: IBDP, IBMYP, IBPYP
Language instr: English

Redbridge International Academy
#114, S Bingipura Village, Hulimangala Post, Begur-Koppa Road, Bangalore, Karnataka 560105
Tel: +91 9620863456
Curriculum: IBDP
Language instr: English

RIMS International School and Junior College
New Link Road, Near Fun Republic, Andheri West, Mumbai, Maharashtra 400049
Tel: +91 22 6699 4333
Age range: 11–19
No. of pupils: 200
Curriculum: IGCSE

Riverside International School
c/o Project India, Project India Educational Center, Mori, Godavari 533250
Tel: +91 8862226492
Age range: 5–18
No. of pupils: 418
Curriculum: USA

Rockwell International School
Sy No.160(p), Gandipet Main Rd, Kokapet, Hyderabad, Telangana 500075
Tel: +91 9618662201
Curriculum: IBDP
Language instr: English

Rungta International School
Near Nandan Van, Veer Savarkar Nagar, Raipur, Chhattisgarh 492099
Tel: +91 98261 45333
Curriculum: IBDP, IBMYP, IBPYP
Language instr: English

Ryan Global School
Yamuna Nagar, Lokhandwala, Andheri (west), Mumbai, Maharashtra 400058
Tel: +91 22 2632 0203/05
Curriculum: IBPYP, IGCSE

Sancta Maria International School – Faridabad
Sector 93, Faridabad, Haryana 121002
Tel: +91 99991 16900
Age range: 5–18 years
Curriculum: IBDP
Language instr: English

Sancta Maria International School – Hyderbad
Survey No 106/107, Serilingampally, Hyderbad, Telangana 500019
Tel: +91 40 2301 1222
Age range: 3–19 years
Curriculum: IGCSE, ALevs

Sangam School of Excellence
N.H. 79, Atun, Bhilwara By Pass, Chittorgarh Highway, Bhilwara, Rajasthan 311001
Tel: +91 1482 249 700
Age range: 4–19
No. of pupils: 1200
Curriculum: IBDP
Language instr: English

Sanjay Ghodawat International School
Gat No. 555, Kolhapur – Sangli Highway, Atigre, Maharashtra
Tel: +91 231 2689700
Curriculum: IBDP
Language instr: English

Sanskar School
117-121, Vishwamitra Marg, Hanuman Nagar Ext., Sirsi Road, Jaipur, Rajasthan 302012
Tel: +91 0141 2246189
Age range: 4–17
No. of pupils: 2302 *B*1502 *G*800
Curriculum: IBDP, IBPYP
Language instr: English

Sarala Birla Academy
Bannerghatta PO, Jigni Road, Bengaluru, Karnataka 560083
Tel: +91 80 41348200/03
Age range: 10–18
No. of pupils: 426
Curriculum: IBDP
Language instr: English

SCAD World School
SCAD Knowledge City, Palladam – Pollachi Highway, Palladam, Tamil Nadu 641664
Tel: +91 8012551468
Curriculum: UK, IGCSE, ALevs

Scindia Kanya Vidyalya
Moti Mahal Road, Gwalior, Madhya Pradesh 474009
Tel: +91 751 232 2137

Scottish High International School
G-Block, Sector 57, Sushant Lok-II, Gurugram, Haryana 122011
Tel: +91 124 4112781-90
Age range: 3–17 years
Curriculum: IBDP, IBPYP, National, IGCSE
Language instr: English

Seedling International Academy
Sector-4, Park Lane, Jawahar Nagar, Jaipur, Rajasthan 302004
Tel: +91 141 2653377
Curriculum: IBDP
Language instr: English

SelaQui International School
PO Sela Kui, Chakrata Road, Dehradun, Uttarakhand 248197
Tel: +91 7669 04 04 04
Language instr: English

Shantiniketan International School
35-25, GKColony, Ramakrishnapuram, Secunderabad, Telangana 500056
Tel: +91 73311 95555
Curriculum: IBPYP
Language instr: English

Sharanya Narayani International School
#232/1, Thoranahalli, Byranahalli post, Near Hoskote, Bengaluru, Karnataka 563130
Tel: +91 80 46629500
Age range: 2.8–18
Curriculum: IBDP, IBPYP
Language instr: English

Shigally Hill International Academy
P.O.Box No. 239, Doon Valley, Shigally Estate, Mussoorie Road, Via Malsi Deer Park, Guniyal Gaon, Dehradun, Uttarakhand 248001
Tel: +91 98370 98368
No. of pupils: 200

Shiv Nadar School Gurugram
DLF City, Phase -1 Block -E, Pahari Road, Gurugram, Haryana
Tel: +91 124 4549200
Curriculum: IBDP
Language instr: English

Shiv Nadar School Noida
Plot No -SS -1, Expressway Sector 168, Noida, Uttar Pradesh 201305
Tel: +91 8130200199
Curriculum: IBDP
Language instr: English

Shree Swaminarayan Gurukul Vishwavidya Pratishthanam SGVP
Nr. SGVP Circle, SG Highway, Chharodi, Ahmedabad, Gujarat 382481
Tel: +91 2717 242138/9
Curriculum: National, UK, IGCSE

Silver Oaks International School, Bangalore
Sy No:188/3 & 188/4, Sarjapur Road, Dommasandra village, Bengaluru, Karnataka 562125
Tel: +91 97394 75900
Curriculum: IBDP, IBMYP, IBPYP
Language instr: English

Silver Oaks International School, Hyderabad
Miyapur-Dindigal Road, Bachupally, Hyderabad, Telangana 500090
Tel: +91 40 23047777
Curriculum: IBPYP

Silver Oaks International School, Visakhapatnam
Adj Gitam Medical College, Yendada Road, Rushikonda, Visakhapatnam, Andhra Pradesh 530045
Curriculum: IBPYP

Singapore International School, Mumbai
On National Highway No. 8, Post Mira Road, Dahisar, Mumbai, Maharashtra 401104
Tel: +91 222 828 5200
Age range: 4–18
No. of pupils: 501
Curriculum: IBDP, IBPYP, UK
Language instr: English

Smt. Sulochanadevi Singhania School
Pokharan Road No.1, J K Gram, Thane (West), Maharashtra 400606
Tel: +91 22 4036 8410/1
Curriculum: IBDP
Language instr: English

South City International School
375 Prince Anwar Shah Road, Kolkata, West Bengal 700068
Tel: +91 33 4007 2000
Age range: 5–19
No. of pupils: 300

Sreenidhi International School
Near Appa Junction, Moinabad, Hyderabad, Telangana 500075
Tel: +91 9912244409
Age range: 3–18 years
No. of pupils: 900
Curriculum: IBDP, IBMYP, IBPYP, SAT
Language instr: English

SRV International School
Marappan Thottam, 4/3 Gandhi Salai, Pattanam Road, Rasipuram, Namakkal, Tamil Nadu 637408
Tel: +91 96 5562 4458
Curriculum: IBPYP
Language instr: English

Step by Step School
Plot A 10, Sector 132 Taj Expressway, Noida, Uttar Pradesh 201303
Tel: +91 12 0508 7300
Curriculum: IBDP
Language instr: English

STONEHILL INTERNATIONAL SCHOOL
For further details see p. 102
Near the International Airport, No.259/333/334/335, Tarahunise Post, Jala Hobli, Bengaluru, Karnataka 562157
Tel: +91 70 2666 6911
Email: admissions@stonehill.in
Website: www.stonehill.in
Head of School: Brian D. Brumsickle
Age range: 3–18 years
No. of pupils: 600
Curriculum: IBDP, IBMYP, IBPYP
Language instr: English

Strawberry Fields High School
Sector 26, Chandigarh, Punjab 160019
Tel: +91 172 279 5903/5904
Age range: 5–18
No. of pupils: 1722 *B955 G767 VIth135*
Curriculum: IBDP
Language instr: English

Suncity School
Suncity Township, Sector 54, Gurgaon, Haryana 122002
Tel: +91 (0)124 4845300 (Ext:302)
Curriculum: IBDP
Language instr: English

Sunflower English School
Sunflower House, 80 Feet Road, Near Bhaktinagar Circle, Rajkot, Gujarat 360002
Tel: +91 93772 12341
Language instr: English

Sunshine Worldwide Secondary School
20/1-B, Bainguinim, Off NH-748 By-pass Kadamba Road, Old Goa, Goa 403402
Tel: +91 98 5032 3818
Curriculum: IBPYP
Language instr: English, Hindi

SVKM JV Parekh International School
CNM School Campus, Dadabhai Road, Off. S.V. Road, Vile Parle (West), Mumbai, Maharashtra 400056
Tel: +91 22 4233 3030
Curriculum: IBDP

Symbiosis International School
Symbiosis Viman nagar Campus, Off. New AirPort road, Viman Nagar, Pune, Maharashtra 411014
Tel: +91 20 2655 7300
Curriculum: IBDP, IBPYP
Language instr: English

Taktse International School
PO Box 90, Gangtok, Sikkim 737101
Tel: +91 3592 237081
Age range: 4–19

TCIS
Survey no. 215/3, Varthur Sharjapur, Whitefield Main Road, Bangalore, Karnataka
Tel: +91 78 9902 5222
Curriculum: IBPYP
Language instr: English, Hindi

Thakur International School
C.T.S. No. 1299 Shivaji Road, Off M.G. Road, Kandivali (W), Mumbai, Maharashtra 400067
Tel: +91 22 2802 1333
Age range: 2–19
Curriculum: IGCSE, ALevs

The Assam Valley School
P.O. Balipara, Dist. Sonitpur, Balipara, Assam 784101
Tel: +91 9678074320

The British School
Dr Jose P Rizal Marg, Chanakyapuri, New Delhi, Delhi 110021
Tel: +91 11 4066 4166
Age range: 3–18
No. of pupils: 1134 *B555 G579 VIth148*
Curriculum: IBDP, IGCSE
Language instr: English

The British School, Chandigarh
Sector 44 B, Chandigarh, Punjab 160044
Tel: +91 172 4605000

The British School, Sector 8, Panchkula
Panchkula, Haryana 134109
Tel: +91 172 4646246
Age range: 2–11
No. of pupils: 300
Curriculum: IGCSE

The Cambridge School
7& 7/1 Satyendra Nath, Majumder Sarani, Kolkata, West Bengal 700026
Tel: +91 33 82320 42019
Curriculum: UK

The Cathedral & John Connon School
6 Purshottamdas Thakurdas Marg, Mumbai, Maharashtra 400001
Tel: +91 22 2200 1282
Age range: 3–18 years
No. of pupils: 2072
Curriculum: IBDP, National, UK, USA, IGCSE
Language instr: English

The Cathedral Vidya School, Lonavala
Village Shilatne, Taluk Maval,
Post Office Karla, Pune,
Lonavala, Maharashtra 410405
Tel: +91 2114 282693
Curriculum: IBDP, IGCSE
Language instr: English

The Doon School
Mall Road, Dehradun,
Uttarakhand 248001
Tel: +91-135 2526 400
Age range: B12–18
Curriculum: IBDP, National, IGCSE
Language instr: English
(RS)

The DPSG International (Delhi Public School Ghaziabad International)
P.O. Dasna, Hindon Nagar,
Dasna, Kallu Garhi, Ghaziabad,
Uttar Pradesh 201303
Tel: +91 858 795 1424
Curriculum: IBPYP
Language instr: English

The Emerald Heights International School
Opposite Akashwani,
A. B. Road, Rau, Indore,
Madhya Pradesh 453331
Tel: +91 872 000 9992/3
Age range: 4–19
Curriculum: IGCSE
Language instr: English
(RS)

The Galaxy School
SNK Main Building, University
Road, Rajkot, Gujarat 360005
Tel: +91 281 2588391/2588392
Curriculum: IBDP

The Gaudium School
Survey No. 148, Nanakramguda
Village, Serilingampally,
Nanakramguda, Hyderabad,
Telangana 500008
Tel: +91 73370 00200
Curriculum: IBDP, IBPYP
Language instr: English, Hindi

The Heritage School, Kolkata
994 Maduraha, Chowbaga
Road, Anandpur, PO East
Kolkata Township, Kolkata,
West Bengal 700107
Tel: +91 33 2443 0448
Curriculum: IBDP

The International School Bangalore
Whitefield-Sarjapur Road,
Near Dommasandra Circle,
Bengaluru, Karnataka 562125
Tel: +91 80 6723 5900
Age range: 3–18
No. of pupils: 1100
Curriculum: IBDP, IGCSE
Language instr: English

The Lawrence School
Sanawar, MDR 10, Solan,
Himachal Pradesh 173202
Tel: +91 1792 261208
Language instr: English
(RS)

The New Tulip International School
Sterling City, Bopal,
Ahmedabad, Gujarat 380058
Tel: +91 27 17 329210
Age range: 5–18

The Pupil, Saveetha Eco School
4/68, Thiruverkkadu Road,
Behind Saveetha Dental
College, Poonamallee,
Chennai, Tamil Nadu 600056
Tel: +91 44 2680 2013
Curriculum: IBPYP
Language instr: English, Tamil

The Rajkumar College
Dr Radha Krishnan Road,
Gavliwad, Rajkot, Gujarat 360001
Tel: +91 281 246 6064
Language instr: English
(RS)

The Riverside School
307 Behind C.S.D Depot, Off
Airport Road, Cantonment,
Ahmedabad, Gujarat 380004
Tel: +91 79 22861321
Age range: 4–16

The Sanskaar Valley School
Chandanpura, Bhopal,
Madhya Pradesh 462016
Tel: +91 755 325 5346
Language instr: English
(RS)

The Scindia School
The Fort, Gwalior, Madhya
Pradesh 474008
Tel: +91 751 2480750
Language instr: English
(RS)

The Shri Ram School
Moulsari Avenue DLF Phase-3,
Gurgaon, Haryana 122002
No. of pupils: 227
Curriculum: IBDP
Language instr: English

The Universal School
Plot No. 17, Near Lion's Garden,
Tilak Road, Ghatkopar (E),
Mumbai, Maharashtra 400077
Tel: +91 773 8146 123
Age range: 4–19
Curriculum: IBDP, IGCSE
Language instr: English, Hindi

The White School International
HiLITE Knowledge Village,
Parammal, Perumanna,
Kozhikode, Kerala 673019
Tel: +91 95260 777 78
Curriculum: IBDP, IBMYP, IBPYP
Language instr: English, Malayalam

TIPS Bengaluru
HBR Layout, Nagawara,
Bangalore, Karnataka 560045
Tel: +91 77 082 95959

TIPS Chennai
No. 50/51, First Main Road,
Perungudi Industrial Estate,
Perungudi, Chennai,
Tamil Nadu 600069
Tel: +91 44 7118 8011
Curriculum: IBDP, IBPYP
Language instr: English

TIPS COIMBATORE
For further details see p. 108
193 Sathy Road, S.S.Kulam P.O.,
Coimbatore, Tamil Nadu 641107
Tel: +91 42 2236 6666
Email:
askcbemain@tipsglobal.net
Website: www.tipsglobal.org
Founder: Ashok Kumar
Age range: 2.6–17 years
Curriculum: IBDP, IBPYP, IGCSE
Language instr: English

TIPS Erode
Chennimalai Road,
Senapathipalayam,
Goundachi palayam post,
Erode, Tamil Nadu 638112
Tel: +91 967745 8888
Curriculum: IBPYP, IGCSE, ALevs
Language instr: English

TIPS Karur
S.F.No. 371 & 379/1,
Pazhamapuram, Poolampalayam
(Post), Punnam Village,
Karur, Tamil Nadu 639163
Tel: +91 75 5815 9111

TIPS Kochi
Edachira, Thengode(Post),
Kakkanad, Kochi, Kerala 682030
Tel: +91 48 4485 4850
Curriculum: IBPYP
Language instr: English

TIPS Madurai
No.3, VP Rathnasamy Nadar
Street, BB Kulam, Madurai,
Tamil Nadu 625002
Tel: +91 97 8944 1188

TIPS Salem
No 2, Mangayarkarasi Street, Off
Advitha Ashram Road, Fairlands,
Salem, Tamil Nadu 636016
Tel: +91 92 8258 8888
Curriculum: IBPYP
Language instr: English, Tamil

TIPS Tirupur
No.10/720, Arulpuram, Arulpuram
(P.O.), Palladam Road,
Tirupur, Tamil Nadu 641605
Tel: +91 75 5817 9111

TIPS Trichy
49/3, K.Kallikudi (North), Dindigul
Main Road, Ramji Nagar, Srirangam
Tk, Trichy, Tamil Nadu 620009
Tel: +91 73 3911 1777

Treamis
Hulimangala Post, near Electronics
City, Bengaluru, Karnataka 560105
Tel: +91 99723 99046
Age range: 4–19
Curriculum: IBDP, IBPYP,
IGCSE, ALevs
Language instr: English, Kannada

Trinity International School
Plot No 247-248, Near Gokul
Hall, Sion (E), Mumbai,
Maharashtra 400022
Tel: +91 22 24094344
Age range: 14–19
Curriculum: IGCSE

Trio World Academy
3/5 Kodigehalli Main Road,
Sahakar Nagar, Bengaluru,
Karnataka 560092
Tel: +91 80 40611222
Curriculum: IBDP, IBPYP

Trivandrum International School
Edackcode, PO Korani,
Trivandrum, Kerala 695104
Tel: +91 471 2619051
Curriculum: IBDP, IBPYP
(RS)

Unison World School
Mussoorie Diversion Road,
Dehradun, Uttarakhand 248009
Tel: +91 135 7113000
Age range: G9–16
No. of pupils: 450
Curriculum: UK, IGCSE, ALevs
Language instr: English

United World Academy (UWA)
Sy No. 1/1 and 62, Chikkawadayerapura, Sarjapur Hobali, Anekal Taluk, Bengaluru, Karnataka 560087
Tel: +91 7624981601

Uttpal Shanghvi School
East West Road No 3, J.V.P.D. Scheme, Juhu, Mumbai, Maharashtra 400049
Tel: +91 22 2620 7413
Age range: 4–19
No. of pupils: 300

UWC Mahindra College
Village Khubavali, PO Paud, Taluka Mulshi, Pune, Maharashtra 412108
Tel: +91 97644 42751 54
Age range: 15–19 years
No. of pupils: 240
Curriculum: IBDP
Language instr: English

Vaels International School
Pon Vidhyashram Gardens, Off East Coast Road, Injambakkam, Chennai, Tamil Nadu 600115
Tel: +91 44 6565 2992
Curriculum: National, UK, IGCSE, ALevs

Vibgyor High School, Pune (NIBM Road)
Dorabjee Paradise, Near Palace Orchard, Off. Corinthian Club Road, Extn NIBM Road, Mohammedwadi, Hadapsar, Pune, Maharashtra 411060
Tel: +91 20 3044 6000
Age range: 14–19
Curriculum: National, IGCSE

Vibgyor High, Mumbai (Goregagon)
Motilal Nagar – 1, Srirang Sabde Marg, Off. Link Road Goregaon, Mumbai, Maharashtra 400104
Tel: +91 22 3957 7070
Age range: 14–19
Curriculum: National, IGCSE

Vibgyor High, Vadodara
Opp Banco Product, Padra Road, B/H Bhayali Railway Station, Vadodara, Gujurat 391410
Tel: +91 265 3076 101
Age range: 14–19
Curriculum: IGCSE, ALevs

Victorious Kidss Educares
Survey No. 53, 54 & 58, Hissa No. 2/1A, Off. Shreeram Society, Nagar Road Kharadi, Pune, Maharashtra 4 1014
Tel: +91 20-67116300/ /2
Age range: 6 weeks– 9 years
No. of pupils: 906
Curriculum: IBDP, IBMYP, IBPYP
Language instr: English

Vidhyashram International School
Ahead of Shikargarh Mini Market, Defence Lab Road, Jodhpur, Rajasthan 342015
Tel: +91 291 222 7976
Age range: 4–19
No. of pupils: 300
Curriculum: UK, IGCSE

Vidya Global School
Vidya Knowledge Park, Baghpat Road, Meerut, Uttar Pradesh 250002
Tel: +91 121 2439188/89/92
Age range: 4–16
Curriculum: IBPYP, National, IGCSE

Vidyanjali International School
20/1, Ram Mohon Dutta Road, Kolkata, West Bengal 700020
Tel: +91-33-2486 1771
Curriculum: UK

Vikaasa World School
Ponnagaram Compound, New Jail Road, Madurai, Tamil Nadu 625014
Tel: +91 9597607888
Curriculum: IGCSE, ALevs

Vishwashanti Gurukul
Rajbaug, off Pune-Solapur Highway, Loni, Pune, Maharashtra 412201
Tel: +91 20 39210000
Age range: 5–18
No. of pupils: 350 *B*200 *G*150
Curriculum: IBDP, IBMYP, IBPYP, UK, IGCSE
Language instr: English

VIVA The School
Beside VVIT college campus, NAMBUR village, Pedakakani Mandal, Nambur, Guntur, Andhra Pradesh 522508
Tel: +91 73 3114 2336
Curriculum: IBPYP
Language instr: English, Telugu

Vivek High School
Vidya Path, Sector 38-B, Chandigarh, Punjab 160036
Tel: +91 172 269 8988
Language instr: English

Welham Boys' School
5 Circular Rd, Dalanwala, Dehradun, Uttarakhand 248001
Tel: +91 135 265 7120

Wisdom High International School
Rameshwar Nagar, Anandwali, Gangapur Road, Nashik, Maharashtra 422007
Tel: +91 253 2338795
Age range: 11–19
Curriculum: IGCSE

Witty International School Bhilwara
7 D 8, Ahead Shreenath Circle, RC Vyas Colony, Bhilwara, Rajasthan 311001
Tel: +91 1482 239153
Age range: 5–18

Witty International School Malad
Ramchandra Lane, Malad (W), Mumbai, Maharashtra 400064
Tel: +91 22 28882310
Age range: 5–18
No. of pupils: 300
Curriculum: IGCSE

Witty International School Udaipur
1 Witty Lane, Gaurav Path, Nathdwara Road, Opp Sukher Thana, Udaipur, Rajasthan 313004
Tel: +91 92142 55667
Age range: 5–18

Witty World Goregaon
Plot No 165, Near Ayappa Temple, Bangur Nagar, Goregaon, Mumbai, Maharashtra 400062
Tel: +91 92230 11704
Age range: 5–11

Wockhardt Global School
Dr Habil Khorakiwala Education and Health Foundation, E-1/ NP-1, SEZ, Five Star Industrial Estate, MIDC, Shen+, Aurangabad, Maharashtra 431154
Tel: +91 240 6662888
Curriculum: IBDP, IBMYP, IBPYP
Language instr: English

Woodstock School
Mussoorie, Uttarakhand 248179
Tel: +91 135 263 9000
Age range: 11–18 years
No. of pupils: 435
Curriculum: ACT, AP, IBDP, IBMYP, SAT, UK, USA
Language instr: English

Yadavindra Public School
New Lal Bagh, Patiala, Punjab
Tel: +91 1752 215634
Language instr: English

INDONESIA

ACG School Jakarta
Jl Warung Jati Barat No.19, RW.5, Jati Padang, Kec. Ps. Minggu, Kota Jakarta Selatan, Daerah Khusus I, Jakarta, DKI 12540
Tel: +62 21 2978 0200 / +62 816 297800
Age range: 3–17 years
No. of pupils: 230
Curriculum: IBDP, IBPYP
Language instr: English

ACS Jakarta
Jl Bantar Jati, Kelurahan Setu, Jakarta Timur, DKI 13880
Tel: +62 21 8459 7175
Age range: 4–18
No. of pupils: 830 *B*460 *G*370 *VIth*54
Curriculum: IBDP, IGCSE
Language instr: English

Al Firdaus
Jl. Dr. Soepomo No 6A, Surakarta, Jateng 57131
Curriculum: IBMYP, IBPYP
Language instr: English, Indonesian

Al Jabr Islamic School
Jl Bango II No 38, Pondok Labu, Jakarta, DKI 12450
Tel: +62 21 75913675
Curriculum: IBMYP, IBPYP, IBCP
Language instr: English

Australian Independent School (AIS) Indonesia
Jalan Imam Bonjol No.458a, Pemecutan, Denpasar Barat, Denpasar, Bali 80119
Tel: +62 361 845 20000
Age range: 3–18
No. of pupils: 220
Curriculum: IBDP
Language instr: English

Australian Independent School, Jakarta – Kemang Campus
Jl. Kemang Timur No. 81, Bangka, Mampang Prapatan, Jakarta Selatan, DKI 12730
Tel: +62 21 7179 2949
Age range: 4–11
No. of pupils: 100

Australian Independent School, Jakarta – Pejaten Campus
Jl. Pejaten Barat No. 69, Pejaten Barat, Pasar Minggu, Jakarta Selatan, DKI 12510
Tel: +62 21 7884 8285
Age range: 12–19
No. of pupils: 180
Curriculum: IBDP
Language instr: English

Bali Island School
Jalan Danau Buyan IV No. 15, Sanur, Denpasar, Bali 80228
Tel: +62 361 288 770
Age range: 3–18
No. of pupils: 290 *B*141 *G*149
Curriculum: IBDP, IBMYP, IBPYP
Language instr: English
CIS EAR

Bandung Alliance Intercultural School
Jalan Bukanggamanik Kav 2, Kota Baru Parahyangan, Bandung, Jabar 40553
Tel: +62 22 8681 3949
Age range: 4–18
No. of pupils: 200
Curriculum: AP, USA
EAR

Bandung Independent School
Jl. Surya Sumantri No. 61, Bandung, Jabar 40164
Tel: +62 22 201 4995
Age range: 3–18
No. of pupils: *B*107 *G*119
Curriculum: ACT, AP, IBDP, IBMYP, IEPYP, SAT, USA
Language instr: English
CIS EAR

Batam Island International Student Learning Center
Batu Ampar, Batam, Riau
Tel: +62 778 414 272
Age range: 4–11
No. of pupils: 111
Curriculum: USA

Beacon Academy
Jalan Pegangsaan Dua. No 66, Kelapa Gading, Jakarta Utara, DKI 14250
Tel: +62 21 460 3480
Curriculum: IBDP, IBPYP
Language instr: English

Bina Bangsa School, Kebon Jeruk (Secondary and Junior College Campus)
Jl Arjuna Selatan Kav 87, Kebon Jeruk, Jakarta Barat, DKI 11530
Tel: +62 21 532 8833
Age range: 11–19
No. of pupils: 200
Curriculum: IGCSE

Binus School Simprug
Jl Sultan Iskandar, Muda Kav G-8, Simprug, Jakarta Selatan, DKI 12220
Tel: +62 21 724 3663
No. of pupils: 1300
Curriculum: IBDP, IBMYP, IBPYP
Language instr: English

British School Jakarta
Bintaro Jaya Sector IX, Jl. Raya Jombang, Ciledug, Pondok Aren, Tangerang, Banten 15227
Tel: +62 21 745 1670
Age range: 3–18
No. of pupils: 1370
Curriculum: IBDP, IBMYP, IBCP, IGCSE
Language instr: English
CIS EAR ECIS

BTB School (Sekolah Bina Tunas Bangsa)
Jl. Pluit Tumur Blok MM, Jakarta Utara, DKI 14450
Tel: +62 21 30031300
Age range: 2–18
Curriculum: IBDP
Language instr: English

Bunda Mulia School
Jl. Lodan Raya No. 2, Jakarta Utara, DKI 14430
Tel: +62 21 690 9742
Age range: 4–19
No. of pupils: 300
Curriculum: IGCSE

Canggu Community School
Jalan Subak Sari, Banjar Tegal Gundul, Canggu, Bali 80361
Tel: +62 361 8446391
Age range: 3–18
Curriculum: IBDP, UK, IGCSE
CIS EAR

Cita Hati Christian Senior School – East Campus
JL Kejawan Putih Barat 28-30, Pakuwon City, Surabaya, Jatim 60112
Tel: +62 31 591 5773
Age range: 12–18
Curriculum: IBDP
Language instr: English

Cita Hati Christian Senior School – West Campus
Jl. Bukit Golf L2 No. 1, Citraland, Surabaya, Jatim 60211
Tel: +62 31 7404959
Curriculum: IBDP, IGCSE
Language instr: English

Deutsche Schule Jakarta
Jl. Puspa Widya No 8, Bumi Serpong Damai, Tangerang, Banten 15322
Tel: +62 (0)21 5378080

Elyon Christian School
Raya Sukomanunggal Jaya 33A, Surabaya, Jatim 60187
Tel: +62 31 7325 999
Curriculum: National, IGCSE

Equal Bright School
Jl Setiabudi 20, Bandung, Jabar 40141
Tel: +62 22 70900038
Age range: 5–11
No. of pupils: 100
Curriculum: IPC

Gandhi Memorial Intercontinental School, Jakarta
Jl HBR Motik Block-6D Kav-1 Kemayoran, Jakarta Pusat DKI 14410
Tel: +62 21 65865671
Age range: 3–19
Curriculum: IBDP, IBMYP, IBPYP, IBCP
Language instr: English

Global Jaya School
Emerald Boulevard, Bintaro Jaya Sektor IX, Pondok Aren, Tangerang, Banten 15224
Tel: +62 21 745 7562
Age range: 4–18
No. of pupils: 921
Curriculum: IBDP, IBMYP, IBPYP
Language instr: English, Indonesian

Global Sevilla International School
Jl. Pulo Mas Jaya, Pacuan Kuda Pulo Mas., Jakarta Timur, DKI 13210
Tel: +62 21 4788 2288
Age range: 1–19
No. of pupils: 300
Curriculum: IGCSE

Global Sevilla Puri Indah Campus
Jl Kembangan Raya Blok JJ No. 1, Puri Indah, Jakarta Barat, DKI 11610
Tel: +66 21 580 6699
Age range: 4–19
Curriculum: IGCSE

GMIS – Bali
Jl Tukad Yeh Penet No 8A Renon, Denpasar, Bali 80235
Tel: +62 361 239744
Age range: 3–17
No. of pupils: 550
Curriculum: IBDP, IBMYP, IBPYP, IBCP, TOEFL, IGCSE
Language instr: English

GREEN SCHOOL BALI
For further details see p. 74
Jalan Raya Sibang Kaja, Abiansemal, Badung, Bali 80352
Email: mads.hedegaard@greenschool.org
Website: www.greenschool.org/bali
Head of School: Sal Gordon
Age range: 3–18 years
No. of pupils: 375
Fees: *Day* US$7,800–US$19,992
Language instr: English, Bahasa

Hillcrest School
Jalan HIS, No. 1, Sentani, Papua 99352
Tel: +62 967 591460
Age range: 5–18
No. of pupils: 160 *B*77 *G*83
Curriculum: ACT, AP, SAT, USA
Language instr: English
EAR

Hope Academy
Puri Indah CBD, Jl. Puri Indah Raya Blok U 1, Kembangan Selatan, Jakarta Barat, DKI 11610
Tel: +62 895 4262 88800
Curriculum: IBPYP
Language instr: English

Ichthus School – West Campus
Jl Surya Mandala 3 Blok N2 No 11, Sunrise Garden, Jakarta Barat, DKI 11520
Tel: +62 21 581 2228
Age range: 5–18
No. of pupils: 300
Curriculum: IGCSE

IPEKA Integrated Christian School
Komplek Taman Meruya Ilir, Jalan Batu Mulia Blok K, RT.11/RW.7, Meruya Utara, Kembangan, RT.11/RW.7, Meruya Utara, Kem+, Jakarta Barat, DKI 11620
Tel: +62 21 58905890
Curriculum: IBDP
Language instr: English, Indonesian

Islamic Village School
Jl. Islamic Raya No.1, Komplek Islamic Village, Kelapa Dua, Tangerang, Banten 15810
Tel: +62 21 547 0787
Curriculum: IBPYP
Language instr: English, Indonesian

JAKARTA INTERCULTURAL SCHOOL
For further details see p. 84
Jalan Terogong Raya No. 33, Cilandak, Jakarta Selatan, DKI 12430
Tel: +62 21 50989555
Email: admissions@jisedu.or.id
Website: www.jisedu.or.id
Interim Head: Maya Nelson
Age range: 3–18 years
Curriculum: IBDP
Language instr: English
CIS

Jakarta Multicultural School
Jl. Pisangan Raya No. 99 (Taman Wisata Situ Gintung), Cirendeu, Ciputat Timur, Banten 15419
Tel: +62 21 744 4864
Age range: 1.5–18
Curriculum: IBDP

Jakarta Nanyang School
Jl. Sekolah Foresta No. 1, Foresta, BSD City, Tangerang, Banten 15331
Tel: +62 21 50 555 999
Curriculum: UK, IGCSE, ALevs

Kanaan Global School
Taman Surya, Jl. Boulevard blok L2, Perumahan Taman Surya 3, Jakarta Barat, DKI 11830
Tel: +62 21 6197205
Curriculum: National, UK

Kinderstation Primary
Jl. Adisucipto Km 9 No 9B, Maguwo, Yogyakarta, DIY 55282
Tel: +62 274 489671
Age range: 2–11

Kingston School
Kompleks Graha Metropolitan, Jln. Kapten Sumarsono Blok E 25/26, Medan, Sumut 20124
Tel: +62 61 8458555
No. of pupils: 450
Curriculum: IPC, National, UK, IGCSE

Lycée Français de Bali
76 Jalan Umalas Kauh, Kerobokan, Bali 80117
Tel: +62 361 4732 314
Curriculum: FrenchBacc

Lycée Français Louis-Charles Damais
Jl. Cipete Dalam No. 32, Jakarta Selatan, DKI 12410
Tel: +62 21 750 30 62
Curriculum: FrenchBacc

Madania
Telaga Kahuripan, Parung, Bogor, Jabar 16330
Tel: +62 251 602777
Curriculum: IBPYP
Language instr: English

Makassar Independent School
Botolempangan 17/19, Makassar, Sulsel 90125
Tel: +62 411 315 889
Age range: 5–13
No. of pupils: 26
Curriculum: UK

Manado Independent School
Jl. Walanda Maramis, North Minahasa, Sulut 95371
Tel: +62 431 893300
Curriculum: UK

Medan Independent School
Jl. Jamin Ginting Km. 10 / Jl. Tali Air No.5, Medan, North Sumatra 20141
Tel: +62 61 836 1816
Age range: 3–18 years
No. of pupils: 80
Curriculum: IBDP, IBMYP, IBPYP
Language instr: English

Mentari Intercultural School Bintaro
Jalan Perigi Baru No.7A, Tangerang, Pd. Aren, Tangerang Selatan, Banten 15228
Tel: +62 21 745 8418
Curriculum: IBDP
Language instr: English

Mentari Intercultural School Jakarta
Jl. H. Jian No.2, RT.4/RW.3, North Cipete, Kby. Baru, Jakarta Selatan, DKI 12150
Tel: 21 727 94 870
Age range: 5–17
Curriculum: IBDP, IBMYP, IBPYP, National, UK
Language instr: English

Mountainview Christian School
Jl. Nakula Sadewa Raya No 55, Salatiga, Jateng 50711
Tel: +62 298 311673
Age range: 5–19
No. of pupils: 230
Curriculum: ACT, AP, SAT, USA
Language instr: English

Mt Zaagkam School
Tembagapura Raya Street No. 605, Tembagapura, Papua 99967
Tel: +62 901 408 767
Age range: 3–12
Curriculum: IBPYP
Language instr: English

Mutiara Harapan Islamic School
Jl. Pondok Kacang Raya No. 2, Pondok Kacang Timur, Pondok Aren, Tangerang, Banten 15426
Tel: +62 (0)21 74860451
Curriculum: IBPYP
Language instr: English

New Zealand Independent School
Jl Kemang Selatan I no 1A, Kemang, Jakarta Selatan, DKI 12730
Tel: +62 21 7183222
Curriculum: IGCSE, ALevs
Language instr: English

Nord Anglia School Jakarta
Jalan NIS 1, Kenanga Terusan, Ampera Raya-Cilandak, Jakarta Selatan, DKI 12560
Tel: +62 811 9727 979
Age range: 18 months–12 years
No. of pupils: 300
Curriculum: IPC, UK

North Jakarta Intercultural School
PO Box 6759/JKUKP, Jalan Raya Kelapa Nias, Kelapa Gading Permai, Jakarta Utara, DKI 14250
Tel: +62 21 4586 5222; +62 21 36 700 770
Age range: 4–16
Curriculum: IBDP, IBMYP, IBPYP, SAT, USA
Language instr: English, Indonesian

Pelangi School (Yayasan Cahaya Pelangi Bali)
Br. Kumbuh, Mas, Bali
Tel: +62 821 4524 7146
Curriculum: IPC

Penabur Secondary Tanjung Duren (PSTD)
Jl. Tanjung Duren Raya no.4, building D, Grogol, Jakarta Barat, DKI 11470
Tel: +62 21 560 2042
Age range: 11–18

PSKD Mandiri
PO Box 6013, Menteng, Jakarta Pusat, DKI 10310
Tel: +62 21 392 4384

Raffles Christian School
Jl Gedung Hijau Raya 1 No 1, Pondok Indah, Jakarta Selatan, DKI 12310
Tel: +62 21 7590 3342
Curriculum: UK, ALevs

Rama School
Kemban Kuning, Ubrug, Jatiluhur, PO Box 60, Purwakarta, Jabar 41011
Tel: +62 264 207052
Age range: 3–15
No. of pupils: 240
Curriculum: National

Saint Peter's School
Boulevard Timur Raya No. 8, Kelapa Gading, Jakarta Utara, DKI 14240
Tel: +62 21 452 4246
Age range: 4–19
No. of pupils: 300
Curriculum: GCSE

Sampoerna Academy, Jakarta Campus
L'Avenue Campus, Jln. Raya Pasar Minggu, Kav. 16 Pancoran, Jakarta 12780
Tel: +62 (0)21 5022 22 34
Curriculum: IBDP
Language instr: English, Indonesian

Sampoerna Academy, Medan Campus
Jln. Jamin Ginting, Kompleks Citra Garden, Medan
Tel: +62 (0)61 821 27 15
Curriculum: IBDP
Language instr: English, Indonesian

SDK BPK Penabur Banda
Jl Bahureksa No 26, Bandung, Jabar 40115
Tel: +62 22 4210787
Curriculum: IBPYP
Language instr: English

Sekolah Bogor Raya
Perumahan Danau Bogor Raya, Bogor, Jabar 16143
Tel: +62 251 837 8873
No. of pupils: 500
Curriculum: IBDP, IBPYP
Language instr: English

Sekolah Buin Batu
Jl Kayu Besi No 400, Townsite PTAMNT, Buin Batu, West Sumbawa, NTB
Tel: +62372 635318 Ext:48443
Curriculum: IBPYP

Sekolah Cikal Amri-Setu
Jl. Setu Raya No. 3, Cipayung, Jakarta Timur, DKI
Tel: +62 811 1156 599
Curriculum: IBDP, IBMYP
Language instr: English, Indonesian

Sekolah Cikal Cilandak
Jl. Letjen. TB. Simatupang Kav. 18, Cilandak, Jakarta Timur, DKI
Tel: +62 21 7590 2580
Curriculum: IBPYP
Language instr: English

Sekolah Cikal Surabaya
Jl. Raya Lontar No. 103, Kelurahan Lontar, Kecamatan Sambikerep, Surabaya, Jatim
Tel: +62 815 1550 1010
Curriculum: IBPYP
Language instr: English

Sekolah Ciputra, Surabaya
Puri Widya Kencana, Citraland, Surabaya, Jatim 60213
Tel: +62 31 741 5018
Age range: 1–18
No. of pupils: 1300
Curriculum: IBDP, IBMYP, IBPYP
Language instr: English

Sekolah Cita Buana
Jl Paso No 84, Jagakarsa, Jakarta Selatan, DKI 12620
Tel: +62 21 7820088
Age range: 3–13
No. of pupils: 270

Sekolah Djuwita Batam
Komplek Anggrek Mas 1 Batam Center, Batam, Kepri 29432
Tel: +62 778 464 005
Curriculum: UK, IGCSE

Sekolah Global Indo-Asia
Jalan Raya Batam Centre Kav SGIA, Batam Centre, Batam Island, Kepri
Tel: +62 778 467333
Age range: 2.5 Yrs–17 Yrs
Curriculum: IBDP, IBPYP
Language instr: English

Sekolah Mutiara Nusantara
Jl. Sersan Bajuri – Setiabudi, Km 1.5, RT 3 RW 1, Bandung, Jabar 40559
Tel: +62 22 201 7773
Age range: 3–18 years
Curriculum: IBDP
Language instr: English

Sekolah Paradisa Cendekia
Jalan Pulo, Leuwinanggung, Kalimanggis, Cibubur, DKI
Tel: +62 21 28671700
Curriculum: IBPYP
Language instr: English, Indonesian

Sekolah Pelita Harapan, Kemang Village
Jl. Pangeran Antasari 36, Kemang Village, Jakarta Selatan, DKI 12150
Tel: +62 21 290 56 789
Curriculum: IBDP

Sekolah Pelita Harapan, Lippo Cikarang
Jl. Dago Permai No.1 Komp. Dago Villas, Lippo Cikarang, Bekasi, Jabar 17550
Tel: +62 21 897 2786 87
Age range: 3–18
Curriculum: IBDP
Language instr: English

Sekolah Pelita Harapan, Lippo Village
2500 Boulevard Palem Raya, Lippo Village, Tangerang, Banten 15810
Tel: +62 21 546 0234
Age range: 1–18
No. of pupils: 2145
Curriculum: IBDP, IBMYP, IBPYP, SAT
Language instr: English

Sekolah Pelita Harapan, Sentul City
Jl. Babakan Madang, Sentul City, Bogor, Jabar 16810
Tel: +62 21 8796 0234
Age range: 4–20
No. of pupils: 380 *B*190 *G*190
Curriculum: IBDP, IBMYP, IBPYP, National
Language instr: English
CIS

Sekolah Pilar Indonesia
Jl Dewa 9, Ciangsana, Kawasan Cibubur, Bogor, Jabar 16968
Tel: +62 21 84936222
Age range: 3–17
No. of pupils: 320
Curriculum: IBPYP

Sekolah Tunas Bangsa
Jalan Arteri Supadio, (Achmad Yani II) Km 2, Pontianak, Kalbar 78391
Tel: +62 561 725555
No. of pupils: 377
Curriculum: IBPYP
Language instr: English

Sekolah Victory Plus
Jl Kemang Pratama Raya, AN 2-3 Kemang Pratama, Bekasi, Jabar 17116
Tel: +62 21 8240 3878
Curriculum: IBDP, IBMYP, IBPYP, National, UK
Language instr: English

Semarang Multinational School
Jalan Jangli Raya 37, Candisari, Semarang, Jateng 50254
Tel: +62 24 8311424
Age range: 1–11
No. of pupils: 72 *B*32 *G*40
Language instr: English

Sinarmas World Academy
Jl TM Pahlawan Seribu, CBD Lot XV, BSD City, Tangerang, Banten 15322
Tel: +62 21 5316 1400
Age range: 3–18
No. of pupils: *B*261 *G*239
Curriculum: IBDP, IBMYP
Language instr: English, Chinese
CIS EAR

Sinarmas World Academy Thamrin
Gedung CHUBB Square, Thamrin Nine Podium, 8th Floor, Jl. MH. Thamrin No. 10, Jakarta Pusat, DKI 10230
Tel: +62 21 29937234 (Ext:300)
Curriculum: UK

SIS Cilegon
Jl. Raya Merak No. 49, Bonakarta, Cilegon, Banten 42414
Tel: +62 254 394 460
Age range: 2–12 years

SIS Kelapa Gading
Jl. Pegangsaan Dua No. 83, Kelapa Gading, Jakarta Utara, DKI 14250
Tel: +62 21 460 8888
Age range: 2–19 years
Curriculum: IBDP
Language instr: English

SIS Medan
Royal Sumatra Complex, Jl. Letjen Jamin Ginting Km. 8,5, Medan, Sumut
Tel: +62 61 836 2880
Age range: 2–19 years
Curriculum: IBDP

SIS Palembang
199 Kelurahan Duku Kecamatan Ilir Timur III, Palembang, Sumsel 30114
Tel: +62 711 562 6778
Age range: 2–16 years

SIS Pantai Indah Kapuk
Jl. Mandara Indah 4, Pantai Indah Kapuk, Jakarta Utara, DKI 14460
Tel: +62 21 588 3835
Age range: 2–19 years
Curriculum: IBDP

SIS Semarang
Jl. Bukit Candi Golf No. 20, Graha Candi Golf Residence, Semarang, Jateng 50274
Tel: +62 24 850 9108
Age range: 2–19 years

SIS South Jakarta
Jl. Bona Vista Raya, Lebak Bulus, Jakarta Selatan, DKI 12440
Tel: +62 21 759 14414
Age range: 2–18 years
Curriculum: IBDP
Language instr: English

SMA Pradita Dirgantara
Jl. Cendrawasih No.4. Adi Sumarmo Airport Complex, Surakarta, Jateng 57375
Tel: +62 71 7467 569
Curriculum: IBDP
Language instr: English

Springfield School – Permata Buana 1 Campus
Pulau Sebaru Blok L4/1, Taman Permata Buana, Jakarta Barat, DKI 11610
Tel: +62 21 58357830
Age range: 2–18
Curriculum: USA

Stamford School, Bandung
Allegro Altura Complex, Jalan Citra Green, Dago, Bandung, Jabar 40142
Tel: +62 22 251 5255
Curriculum: IBDP
Language instr: English, Indonesian

Stella Maris School
Sektor 8A, Vatican Cluster, Gading Serpong, Tangerang, Banten 15310
Tel: +62 21 54 212 999
Curriculum: IBDP
Language instr: English

Surabaya European School
At Pakuwon Golf & Family Club, Villa Bukit Regensi, Pakuwon Indah, Surabaya, Jatim 60123
Tel: +62 31 739 17 51
Age range: 3–16
Curriculum: IPC, UK, IGCSE

Surabaya Intercultural School
Citra Raya, Lakarsantri, Tromol Pos 2/SBDK, Surabaya, Jatim 60225
Tel: +62 31 741 4300
Age range: 3–18 years
Curriculum: ACT, IBPYP, SAT

Taman Rama School
Jl. Cokroaminoto No. 382 Ubung Kaja, Denpasar Utara, Bali 80116
Tel: +62 361 414849
Curriculum: National, UK, IGCSE, ALevs

The Independent School Batam
Complex Rosedale Blok E 123-124, Batam, Kepri 24893
Tel: +62 778 461696
Age range: 4–19
No. of pupils: 70
Curriculum: UK
ISA

The Intercultural School of Bogor
Jalan Papandayan No 7, Bogor, Jabar 16151
Tel: +62 251 8324 360
Age range: 2–13
Language instr: English
EAR

Tunas Muda School Kedoya
Jl Angsana Raya D8/2, Taman Kedoya Baru, Jakarta Barat, DKI 11520
Tel: +62 21 581 8766
No. of pupils: 274
Curriculum: IBPYP
Language instr: English, Indonesian

Tunas Muda School Meruya
Jl. Meruya Utara No. 71, Kembangan, Jakarta Barat, DKI 11620
Tel: +62 (0)21 587 0329
Age range: 1–18
No. of pupils: 1130
Curriculum: IBDP, IBMYP, IBPYP
Language instr: English, Bahasa Indonesia

Tzu Chi School, Pantai Indah Kapuk
Jl. Pantai Indah Kapuk Boulevard, Tzu Chi Centre, Kelurahan Kamal Muara, Kecamatan Penjaringan, Jakarta Utara, DKI 14470
Tel: +62 21 5055 6668
Curriculum: IBDP, IBMYP
Language instr: English

Wesley School
Kotak Pos 275, Malang, Jatim 65101
Tel: +62 341 586410
Age range: 5–18
No. of pupils: 110 *B*55 *G*55
Curriculum: AP, SAT, USA
Language instr: English

Yogyakarta Independent School
Jl. Tegal Mlati No. 1, Jombor Lor, Sinduadi, Mlati, Sleman, Yogyakarta, DIY 55284
Tel: +62 274 530 5147
Age range: 3–16
No. of pupils: 97 *B*56 *G*41
Curriculum: IBDP, IBMYP, IBPYP, IPC, IGCSE, ALevs
Language instr: English
EAR

YPJ School Kuala Kencana
Jalan Irian Jaya Barat No.1, Kuala Kencana, Timika, Papua 99910
Curriculum: IBPYP
Language instr: English

YPJ School Tembagapura
Jalan Raya Tembagapura No. 605, PO Box 14, Tembagapura, Papua 99910
Curriculum: IBPYP
Language instr: Indonesian

IRAN

École Française de Téhéran
1623 Shariati Avenue, Tehran
Tel: +98 21 2264 1703
Age range: 5–18
No. of pupils: 238

German Embassy School Tehran (DBST)
Shariati, under the Sadr Bridge, Shahid Keshani St. (Mahale Darbdowom), Tehran
Tel: +98 21 22 60 49 02
Curriculum: IBPYP
Language instr: English

Mehr-e-Taban International School
Ghasrodasht st, corner of Shahed st, Shiraz, Fars
Tel: +98 713 6359983
Age range: 6–18
Curriculum: IBDP, IBMYP, IBPYP
Language instr: English

Shahid Mahdavi Educational Complex
Kouh-Daman, Minai, Zanbagh, Ejazi, Zafaranie St., Tehran 19888-7536
Tel: +98 21 22435550 (Ext:190)
Curriculum: IBDP, IBMYP, IBPYP
Language instr: English, Persian

Soodeh Educational Complex
End of Arabshahi Avenue, Ashrafi Isfahani Highway, Tehran 1461988511
Tel: +98 21 44 24 97 03
Curriculum: IBMYP
Language instr: English

IRAQ

British International Schools in Kurdistan
Mosul Road, Erbil
Tel: +964 750 251 9141

Canadian International School – Erbil
Permam Street, Near Kurdistan TV, Erbil, Kurdistan
Tel: +964 750 568 1313
Age range: 3–18 years

Da Vinci World School
Amed Street, Malta QR, Duhok, Kurdistan Region
Tel: +964 750 757 4333
Curriculum: IBDP, IBMYP, IBPYP
Language instr: English

Deutsche Schule Erbil
Postfach 67, Post Office Newroz, 100-Meter-Street, Erbil, Kurdistan
Tel: +964 770 3016 560
Curriculum: IBDP
Language instr: German

Global United School
Iraq-Baghdad-Palestine Street, Residential Quarter 510-lane 16-building 20, Baghdad
Tel: +964 782 714 9199
Curriculum: IBPYP
Language instr: English

International College University School (ICUS) Baghdad
Zayouna, Baghdad
Tel: +964 7828867431
Curriculum: IBPYP
Language instr: English

International Maarif Schools Erbil
P.O. Box No. 43/0383, Mardin District, 120m Street, Opposite to Toreq Village, Erbil
Tel: +964 (66) 264 49 17/18
Curriculum: IBDP, IBMYP, IBPYP
Language instr: Arabic, English, Kurdish,Turkish

The International School of Choueifat – Dream City
100 Meter Street, Dream City, Erbil, Kurdistan
Tel: +964 750 373 9444

The International School of Choueifat – Erbil
Massif Road, Khanzad Area, Erbil, Kurdistan
Tel: +964 750 813 9853
Age range: 4–18
No. of pupils: 670

The International School of Choueifat – Sulaimani
Qasimlu Street, Sulaimani, Kurdistan
Tel: +964 053 328 5412

ISRAEL

Anglican International School Jerusalem
PO Box 191, 82 Rechov Haneviim, Jerusalem 91001
Tel: +972 2 567 7200
Age range: 3–18
No. of pupils: 310
Curriculum: IBDP, IBMYP, SAT
Language instr: English

Collège français Marc Chagall
Aharon Chelouche 24 St, Tel Aviv
Tel: +972 3 517 2429
Curriculum: FrenchBacc

Eastern Mediterranean International School
Hakfar Hayarok school, Ramat Hasharon 4870000
Tel: +972 3 6730232
Curriculum: IBDP
Language instr: English

Jerusalem American International School
Goldstein Youth Village, P.O. Box 117, Jerusalem
Tel: +972 2 679 9611
Curriculum: USA

Lycée Français de Jérusalem
66, Haneviim Street 9514117, B.P. 37001, Jérusalem
Tel: +972 2 538 41 02
Curriculum: FrenchBacc

Tabeetha School
PO Box 8710, 21 Yefet Street, Jaffa
Tel: +972 3 6821581/19357
Age range: 3–18
No. of pupils: 330
Curriculum: UK, ALevs

Talitha Kumi School
PO Box 7, Beit Jala
Tel: +972 2 2741247
Age range: 3–18
No. of pupils: 830

TreeHouse International School (TH3)
Ramot Yam 55, Herzliya
Tel: +972 9 955 3336
Age range: 6–9
Curriculum: UK

Walworth Barbour American International School
P.O. Box 484, 65 Hashomron Street, Even Yehuda, Netanya 40500
Tel: +972 9 890 1000
Age range: 5–19

JAPAN

ABC International School
2-11-8 Moto-Azabu, Minato-ku, Tokyo, Kanto 106-0046
Tel: +813 6812 6737

Abroad International School – Okayama
Yanagimachi 1-10-9, Kitaku, Okayama, Chugoku 700-0904
Tel: +81 86 221 0144
Curriculum: IBPYP
Language instr: English, Japanese

Abroad International School – Osaka
Being Yotsubashi Bldg 6F, 1-3-2 Kitahorie, Nishi-ku, Osaka, Kansai 550-0014
Tel: +81 66 535 0500
Curriculum: IBPYP
Language instr: English

Aichi International School
Nijigaoka3-4, Meito-ku, Nagoya, Aichi, Chubu 465-0078
Tel: +81 52 788 2255
Curriculum: USA

AICJ Junior & Senior High School
2-33-16 Gion, Asaminami-ku, Hiroshima, Chugoku 731-0138
Tel: +81 82 832 5037
Curriculum: IBDP
Language instr: English

AIE International High School
1-48 Hama, Awaji, Hyogo, Kansai 656-2304
Tel: +81 799 74 0020
Curriculum: IBDP
Language instr: English

Angel Kindergarten
80-6 Ojiri Shimonagakubo, Nagaizumi, Shizuoka, Chubu 411-0934
Tel: +81 55 987 5323
Curriculum: IBPYP
Language instr: English, Japanese

Aoba-Japan Bilingual Preschool – Mitaka Campus
4-15-41 Shimorenjaku, Mitaka, Tokyo, Kanto 181-0013
Tel: +81 42 229 8977
Curriculum: IBPYP
Language instr: English, Japanese

Aoba-Japan Bilingual Preschool – Nakano Campus
3-6-17-2F Minamidai, Nakano-ku, Tokyo, Kanto 164-0014
Tel: +81 36 380 3218
Curriculum: IBPYP
Language instr: English, Japanese

Aoba-Japan Bilingual Preschool – Waseda Campus
1-14-8 Takadano-baba, Shinjuku-ku, Tokyo, Kanto 169-0075
Tel: +81 3 6385 2818
Curriculum: IBPYP
Language instr: English, Japanese

Aoba-Japan International School
7-5-1 Hikarigaoka, Nerima-ku, Tokyo 179-0072
Tel: +81 3 4578 8832
Age range: 2–18 years
No. of pupils: 600
Curriculum: IBDP, IBMYP, IBPYP
Language instr: English
(CIS) (EAR) (ECIS)

Asahijuku Secondary School
2590 Mitsushitori, Kita-ku, Okayama, Chugoku 709-2136
Tel: +81 86 726 0111
Curriculum: IBDP, IBMYP
Language instr: English, Japanese

Canadian Academy
4-1 Koyo-Cho Naka, Higashinada-ku, Kobe, Hyogo, Kansai 658-0032
Tel: +81 78 857 0100
Age range: 3–18
No. of pupils: 603 *B*306 *G*297
Curriculum: ACT, AP, IBDP, IBMYP, IBPYP, SAT, USA
Language instr: English
(CIS) (EAR)

Canadian International School Tokyo
5-8-20 Kitashinagawa, Shinagawa-ku, Tokyo, Kanto 141-0001
Tel: +81 3 5793 1392
Age range: 5–18
No. of pupils: 250 *B*150 *G*100
Curriculum: AP, IBPYP
Language instr: English
(EAR)

Chiyoda Jogakuen Senior High School
Chiyoda-ku, Tokyo, Kanto 102-0081
Tel: +81 3 3263 6551
Curriculum: IBDP
Language instr: English, Japanese

Christian Academy in Japan
1-2-14 Shinkawacho, Higashikurume, Tokyo, Kanto 203-0013
Tel: +81 424 710 022
Language instr: Japanese
(EAR)

Columbia International School
153 Matsugo, Tokorozawa, Saitama, Kanto 359-0027
Tel: +81 4 2946 1911
Age range: 4–18
No. of pupils: 233
Curriculum: USA

Deutsche Schule Kobe International (DSKI)
3-2-8 Koyochonaka, Higashinada-ku, Kobe, Hyogo, Kansai 658-0032
Tel: +81 78 857 9777
Age range: 2–12
No. of pupils: 100
Curriculum: IBPYP
Language instr: English, German, Japanese

Deutsche Schule Tokyo Yokohama
2-4-1 Chigasaki Minami, Tsuzuki-ku, Yokohama, Kanagawa, Kanto 224-0037
Tel: +81 45 941 4841

Doshisha International Academy Elementary School
7-31-1 Kizugawa-dai, Kizugawa, Kyoto, Kansai 619-0225
Tel: +81 774 71 0810
Curriculum: IBPYP
Language instr: English

Doshisha International School, Kyoto
7-31-1 Kizugawa-dai, Kizugawa, Kyoto, Kansai 619-0225
Tel: +81 774 71 0810
Age range: 10–18 years
No. of pupils: 37
Curriculum: IBDP, IBPYP
Language instr: English

Eisugakkan School
980-1, Hikino-cho, Fukuyama, Hiroshima, Chugoku 721-8502
Tel: +81 84 941 4115
Age range: 12–18
Curriculum: IBDP, IBPYP
Language instr: Japanese

Enishi International School
2-12-32 Kikui Nishi Ward, Nagoya, Aichi 451-0044
Tel: +81(0)52 581 0700
Curriculum: IBMYP, IBPYP
Language instr: English, Japanese

Everest International School, Japan
Ikegawa Building, Aasagaya Minami 3-34-16, Suginami- Ku, Tokyo, Kanto 166-0004
Tel: +81 3 5335 7379
Age range: 5–11

Fukuoka Daiichi High School
22-1 Tamagawa cho, Minami-ku, Fukuoka, Kyushu 815-0037
Tel: +81 9 2541 0165
Curriculum: IBDP
Language instr: English, Japanese

Fukuoka International School
3-18-50 Momochi, Sawara-ku, Fukuoka, Kyushu 814-0006
Tel: +81 92 841 7601
Age range: 3–19
No. of pupils: 282
Curriculum: IBDP, IBMYP, IBPYP, SAT
Language instr: English
(EAR)

Global Indian International School (GIIS) Higashi Kasai Campus
9-3-6 Higashikasai, Edogawa-Ku, Tokyo, Kanto 134-0084
Tel: +81 35 676 5081
Curriculum: IBDP, IBPYP
Language instr: English, Japanese

Global Indian International School (GIIS) Nishi Kasai Campus
8-3-13 Nishikasai, Edogawa Ku, Tokyo, Kanto 134-0088
Tel: +81 35 696 7141
Curriculum: National, UK, IGCSE

Global Indian International School (GIIS) Seishincho Campus
2-10-1 Seishincho, Edogawa Ku, Tokyo, Kanto 134-0087
Tel: +81 33 686 3055

Gregg International School
1-14-6 Jiyugaoka, Meguro-Ku, Tokyo, Kanto 152-0035
Tel: +81 3 3725 8000
Age range: 2–12

Hiroshima International School
3-49-1 Kurakake, Asakita-Ku, Hiroshima, Chugoku 739-1743
Tel: +81 82 843 4111
Age range: 3–18
No. of pupils: 120 *B*60 *G*60
Curriculum: IBDP, IBMYP, IBPYP, IGCSE
Language instr: English
(CIS)

Hokkaido International School
1-55 5-jo, 19-chome, Hiragishi, Toyohira-ku, Sapporo, Hokkaido 062-0935
Tel: +81 11 816 5000
Age range: 3–20
No. of pupils: 190 *B*95 *G*95
Curriculum: AP, IPC, SAT
(EAR)

Hokkaido International School – Niseko Branch
12 Aza Fujimi, Niseko-Cho, Abuta Gun, Hokkaido 048-1501
Tel: +81 136 55 5252
Age range: 3–11
No. of pupils: 21 *B*10 *G*11
Curriculum: IPC, UK, USA

Horizon Japan International School
1-24 Onocho, Kanagawa-ku, Yokohama, Kanagawa, Kanto 221-0055
Tel: +81 45 624 8717
Age range: 3–18 years
Curriculum: IBDP, IBMYP, IBPYP, UK
(CIS) (ECIS)

Horizon Sendai Primary School
4-2-540 Takamori, Izumi-ku, Sendai, Miyagi, Tohoku 981-3203
Tel: +81 22 739 9622
Curriculum: IBPYP
Language instr: English, Japanese

Ikuei Nishi Jr. & Sr. High School
637-1 4 chome Mimatsu, Nara 631-0074
Tel: +81 74 247 0688
Curriculum: IBMYP
Language instr: English, Japanese

India International School in Japan
1-20-20, Ojima, Koto-Ku -135-0004, Tokyo, Kanto 136-0072
Tel: +81 03 3635 7850
Curriculum: IBDP
Language instr: English

International School Kitakyushu
Yahata Higashi-ku, Takami 2-chome, Shinnittetsu, Shijo Kaikan, Kitakyushu, Fukuoka, Kyushu
Tel: +81 (0)93 882 0020
Age range: 3–19

International School of Nagano
1-2-2 Minami-Matsumoto, Matsumoto, Nagano, Chubu 390-0832
Tel: +81 26 387 5971
Curriculum: IBPYP
Language instr: English

International School of the Sacred Heart
4-3-1 Hiroo, Shibuya-ku, Tokyo, Kanto 150-0012
Tel: +81 3 3400 3951
Age range: *B*3–5 *G*3–18
No. of pupils: 542 *B*16 *G*526
Curriculum: AP, SAT
Language instr: English
(CIS) (EAR)

Inter-Pacific High School Japan
Tokyo Tanashi Nishitokyo Town 2-16-10, Tokyo, Kanto 188-0011
Tel: +81 42 467 4777
Age range: 14–19
No. of pupils: 100
Curriculum: AP, USA

Joy to the World
American International School, 112-0002
Tel: 0081 3-5684-0247
Curriculum: USA

K. International School Tokyo
1-5-15 Shirakawa, Koto-ku, Tokyo, Kanto 135-0021
Tel: +81 3 3642 9993
Age range: 3–18
No. of pupils: 650
Curriculum: IBDP, IBMYP, IBPYP, IGCSE
Language instr: English
(CIS) (EAR)

Kaichi Nihonbashi Gakuen
7-6 Nihonbashi Bakurocho 2-chome, Chuo-ku, Tokyo, Kanto 103-8384
Tel: +81 3 3662 2507
Curriculum: IBDP, IBMYP
Language instr: English, Japanese

Kaichi-Nozomi Elementary School
3400 Tutudo Aza Suwa, Tsukubamirai, Ibaraki, Kanto 300-2435
Tel: +81 0297 38 6000
Curriculum: IBPYP
Language instr: English, Japanese

KAIS International School
3-10-60 Kami-Osaki, Shinagawa-ku 141-0021
Tel: 011-81-354-21-0127
Curriculum: USA

Kansai Christian School
282-2 Oaza Misato, Heguri-cho, Ikoma-gun, Nara, Kansai 636-0904
Tel: +81 745 45 6422
Age range: 6–18
No. of pupils: 51 *B*21 *G*30
Curriculum: USA

Kansai International Academy
4-1-31 Shinzaike-Minamimachi, Nada-ku, Kobe, Hyogo, Kansai 657-0864
Tel: +81 78 882 6680
Curriculum: IBDP, IBPYP
Language instr: English, Japanese

Katoh Gakuen Gyoshu Junior & Senior High School
1361-1 Nakamiyo Okanomiya, Numazu, Shizuoka, Chubu 410-0011
Tel: +81 55 924 3322
Age range: 3–18
No. of pupils: 590 *B*280 *G*310
Curriculum: IBDP, IBMYP
Language instr: English, Japanese

Kids Tairiku Yokohama Nakagawa
1-19-23 Nakagawa, Tsuzuki-Ku, Yokohama, Kanagawa, Kanto 224-0001
Tel: +81 45 914 3770
Curriculum: IBPYP
Language instr: English, Japanese

Kindai University High School
5-3-1 Wakaenishishinmachi, Higashiosaka, Osaka, Kansai 578-0944
Tel: +81 66 722 1261
Curriculum: IBDP
Language instr: English, Japanese

Kobe Bilingual School
7-1-25 Momoyamadai, Kobe, Hyogo 655-0854
Tel: +81 78 742-7101
Age range: 6 months–12
No. of pupils: 120
Curriculum: UK
Language instr: English, Japanese

Korea International School
2-13-35 Toyokawa, Ibaraki, Osaka, Kansai 567-0057
Tel: +81 72 643 4200
Curriculum: IBDP
Language instr: English

Kumamoto International School
2-18-8 Nishibaru, Higashi-ku, Kumamoto, Kyushu 861-8029
Tel: +81 96 285 3938
Curriculum: IBPYP
Language instr: English, Japanese

Kyoto International School
252 Shinhigashidoin-cho, Sakyo-ku, Kyoto, Kansai 606-8355
Tel: +81 75 451 1022
Age range: 3–14
No. of pupils: 79
Curriculum: IBPYP
Language instr: English
(EAR)

Liberty International School
342-16 Shimohiratsuka, Tsukuba, Ibaraki, Kanto 305-0813
Tel: +81 29 855 0177
Age range: 3–14
No. of pupils: 200
Curriculum: USA

Linden Hall High School
3-10-1 Futsukaichikita, Chikushino, Fukuoka, Kyushu 818-0056
Tel: +81 92 929 4558
Age range: 12–18 years
No. of pupils: 86
Curriculum: IBDP
Language instr: English, Japanese

Lycée français international de Kyoto
411 Motoshinmeicho, Tominokojidori Gojo agaru, Shimogyo-ku, Kyoto, Kansai 600-8065
Tel: +81 75 354 5240
Age range: 3–18
No. of pupils: 160
Curriculum: FrenchBacc
Language instr: French, Japanese

Lycée français international de Tokyo
5-57-37 Takinogawa Kita-ku, 114-0023
Tel: +81 (0)3 6823 6580
Curriculum: FrenchBacc

Makuhari International School
3-2-9 Wakaba, Mihama-ku, Chiba, Kanto 261-0014
Tel: +81 43 296 0277
Age range: 4–11
No. of pupils: 300
(CIS) (EAR)

Marist Brothers International School
1-2-1 Chimori-Cho, Suma-Ku, Kobe, Hyogo, Kansai 654-0072
Tel: +81 78 732 6266
Age range: 3–19
No. of pupils: 336 *B*164 *G*172
Curriculum: AP, IBDP, USA
Language instr: English
(EAR)

Matsumoto Kokusai High School
3-6-25 Muraimachi minami, Matsumoto, Nagano, Chubu 399-0036
Tel: +81 263 88 0033
Age range: 15–18
Curriculum: IBDP
Language instr: English, Japanese

Meikei High School
1-1 Inarimae, Tsukuba, Ibaraki, Kanto 305-8502
Tel: +81 29 851 6611
Age range: 12–18
No. of pupils: 1518 *B*752 *G*766
Curriculum: AP, IBDP, SAT
Language instr: English, Japanese

Miura Gakuen High School
3-80 Kinugasa-sakae, Yokosuka, Kanagawa 238-0031
Tel: +81 46 852 0284
Curriculum: IBDP
Language instr: English, Japanese

Mizuho School
3-2-25, Shakujiidai, Nerima-ku, Tokyo, Kanto 177-0045
Tel: +81 3 5372 1525
Curriculum: IBPYP
Language instr: English

Nagoya International Junior and Senior High School
1-16, Hiroji-Honmachi, Showa-Ku, Nagoya, Aichi, Chubu 466-0841
Tel: +81 52 858 2200
Curriculum: IBDP
Language instr: English

Nagoya International School
2686 Minamihara, Nakashidami, Moriyama-ku, Nagoya, Aichi, Chubu 463-0002
Tel: +81 52 736 2025
Age range: 3–18
No. of pupils: *B*147 *G*171
Curriculum: IBDP, IBMYP, IBPYP
(CIS) (EAR)

New International School of Japan
3-18-32 Minami-Ikebukuro, Toshima-ku, Tokyo, Kanto 171-0022
Tel: +81 3 3980 1057
Age range: 3–18
No. of pupils: 255
Language instr: English, Japanese

Nishimachi International School
2-14-7 Moto Azabu, Minato-ku, Tokyo, Kanto 106-0046
Tel: +81 3 3451 5520
Age range: 5–15
No. of pupils: 410
Language instr: English
(CIS) (EAR) (ECIS)

NUCB International College
4-4 Sagamine Komenoki, Nisshin, Aichi, Chubu 470-0193
Tel: +81 56 173 8181
Age range: 15–18 years
No. of pupils: 225
Language instr: English

Okayama University of Science High School
Daiomachi No. 1, Kita-ku, Okayama, Chugoku 700-0005
Tel: +81 (0)86 256 8511
Curriculum: IBDP
Language instr: English, Japanese

Okinawa Christian School International
1835 Zakimi, Yomitan, Nakagami-cho, Okinawa, Kyushu 904-0301
Tel: +81 98 958 3000
Age range: 3–18
No. of pupils: 500
Curriculum: USA

Okinawa International School
143 Tamagusuku Fusato, Nanjo City, Okinawa, Kyushu 901-0611
Tel: +81 (0)98 948 7711
Curriculum: IBDP, IBMYP, IBPYP

Osaka International High School
1-28 Matsushita-cho, Moriguchi-shi, Osaka, Kansai 570-8787
Tel: +81 6 6992 5931
Curriculum: IBDP
Language instr: English, Japanese

Osaka International School of Kwansei Gakuin
4-4-16 Onohara-nishi, Minoh, Osaka, Kansai 562-0032
Tel: +81 72 727 5050
Age range: 4–18 years
Curriculum: IBDP, IBMYP, IBPYP
Language instr: English
CIS EAR

Osaka Jogakuin Senior High School
2-26-54 Tamatsukuri, Chuo-ku, Osaka, Kansai 540-0004
Tel: +81 6 6761 4113
Curriculum: IBDP
Language instr: English, Japanese

Osaka YMCA International School
6-7-34 Nakatsu, Kita-ku, Osaka, Kansai 531-0071
Tel: +81 6 6345 1661
Age range: 3–14
Curriculum: IBDP, IBMYP, IBPYP
Language instr: English

Phoenix House International School
11 Yonban-cho, Chiyoda-ku, Tokyo, Kanto 102-0081
Age range: 5–11 years
Curriculum: UK

Ritsumeikan Uji Junior and Senior High School
33-1 Hachikenyadani, Hirono-cho, Uj , Kyoto, Kansai 611-0031
Tel: +81 774 41 3000
Age range: 12–17 years
No. of pupils: 1702
Curriculum: IBDP
Language instr: English, Japanese

Sai Sishya International School
6-18-2 Higashi Kasai, Edogawa Ku, Tokyo, Kanto 134-0084
Tel: +8 70 1393 5515
Curriculum: IBPYP
Language instr: English, Japanese

Saint Maur International School
83 Yamate-cho, Naka-ku, Yokohama, Kanagawa, Kanto 231-8654
Tel: +81 45 641 5751
Age range: 2–18
No. of pupils: 490
Curriculum: AP, IBDP, IPC, SAT, UK, USA, IGCSE
Language instr: English, French
CIS EAR

Sapporo Nihon University High School
5-7-1 Nijigaoka, Kitahiroshima, Hokkaido 061-1103
Tel: +81 11 375 2611
Curriculum: IBDP
Language instr: English, Japanese

Seisen International School
1-12-15 Yoga, Setagaya-ku, Tokyo, Kanto 158-0097
Tel: +81 3 3704 2661
Age range: B2–5 G2–18
No. of pupils: 635
Curriculum: IBDP, IBMYP, IBPYP, SAT, USA, IGCSE
Language instr: English
CIS EAR

Sendai Ikuei Gakuen
2-4-1 Miyagino, Miyagino-ku, Sendai, Miyagi, Tohoku 983-0045
Tel: +81 22 256 4141
Age range: 12–18 years
No. of pupils: 3150
Curriculum: IBDP, IBMYP
Language instr: English, Japanese

Seta International School
27-12, Seta 1-chome, Setagaya-ku, Tokyo, Kanto 158-0095
Tel: +81 3 5717 6769

Shinagawa International School
4-8-8 Higashishinagawa, Shinagawa, Tokyo, Kanto 140-0002
Tel: +81 3 6433 1531
Curriculum: IBPYP
Language instr: English

Shizuoka Salesio School
3 Chome-2-1 Nakanogo, Shimizu Ward, Shizuoka, Chubu 424-8624
Tel: +81 54 345 2296
Curriculum: IBDP, IBMYP, IBPYP
Language instr: English, Japanese

Shogaku Gakuen Educational Foundation
747 Kokuba, Naha, Okinawa, Kyushu 902-0075
Tel: +81 98 832 1767
Curriculum: IBDP
Language instr: English

Shohei Junior and Senior High School
851 Shimono, Sugito, Saitama, Kanto 345-0044
Tel: +81 48 034 3381
Curriculum: IBDP, IBMYP
Language instr: English

Shukoh Middle School
Sendai Ikuei Gakuen, 241 Miyagino, Miyagino-ku, Sendai, Miyagi, Tohoku 985-0853
Tel: +81 22 256 4141
Curriculum: IBMYP
Language instr: English, Japanese

St Michael's International School
3-17-2 Nakayamate-Dori, Chuo-ku, Kobe, Hyogo, Kansai 650-0004
Tel: +81 78 231 8885
Age range: 3–11
No. of pupils: 172 B85 G87
Curriculum: SAT, UK
Language instr: English
CIS COB EAR

St. Joseph's Primary School
11-1 HigashiTerao-Kitadai, Tsurumi-ku, Yokohama, Kanagawa, Kanto 230-0016
Tel: +81 45 581 8808
Curriculum: IBPYP
Language instr: English, Japanese

St. Mary's International School
1-6-19 Seta, Setagaya Ku, Tokyo, Kanto 158-8668
Tel: +81 3 3709 3411
Age range: B5–18
No. of pupils: 920
Curriculum: IBDP, SAT
Language instr: English
CIS EAR

Summerhill International School
2-13-8 Moto-Azabu, Minato-ku, Tokyo, Kanto 106-0046
Tel: +81 3 3453 0811
Curriculum: IBPYP
Language instr: English, Japanese

Sunnyside International School
Iwai 4-10-25, Gifu, Chubu 501-3101
Tel: +81 58 241 1000
Curriculum: IBPYP
Language instr: English, Japanese

Tamagawa Academy K-12 & University
6-1-1 Tamagawa Gakuen, Machida, Tokyo, Kanto 194-8610
Tel: +81 42 739 8111
Age range: 12–19
No. of pupils: 2300
Curriculum: IBDP, IBMYP
Language instr: English, Japanese

Tathva International School
Edogawa-ku4-1-1 Higashi komatsugawa, 132-0033
Curriculum: UK, IGCSE, ALevs

Teikyo University Kani Junior & Senior High School
1-1-1 Katsuragaoka, Kani, Gifu, Chubu 509-0237
Tel: +81 57 464 3211
Curriculum: IBDP
Language instr: English, Japanese

The American School in Japan
1-1-1 Nomizu, Chofu, Tokyo, Kanto 182-0031
Tel: +81 42 234 5300
Age range: 3–19
No. of pupils: 1540
Curriculum: ACT, AP, SAT, TOEFL, USA
EAR

The British School in Tokyo
1-21-18 Shibuya, Shibuya-ku, Tokyo, Kanto 150-0002
Tel: +81 3 5467 4321
Age range: 3–18
No. of pupils: 1000
Curriculum: UK
Language instr: English
COB

The Montessori School of Tokyo
3-5-13 Minami Azabu Minato-ku,, 106-0047
Tel: 0081 3 5449 7067

Tohoku International School
7-101-1 Yakata, Izumi-ku, Sendai, Miyagi, Tohoku 981-3214
Tel: +81 22 348 2468
Age range: 4–18
No. of pupils: 92 B45 G47
Curriculum: AP, IBDP, IBPYP, SAT
EAR

Tokai Gakuen High School
2-901 Nakahira Tenpaku-ku, Nagoya, Aichi, Chubu 468-0014
Tel: +81 52 801 6222
Curriculum: IBDP
Language instr: English, Japanese

Tokyo International School
3-4-22 Mita, Minato-Ku, Tokyo, Kanto 108-0073
Tel: +81 3 5484 1160
Age range: 3–12
No. of pupils: 340
Curriculum: IBMYP, IBPYP
Language instr: English
CIS EAR

Tokyo West International School
185 Umetsubo-machi, Hachioji, Tokyo, Kanto 192-0013
Tel: +81 42 691 1441
Curriculum: IBPYP
Language instr: English

Tsukuba International School
Kamigo 7846-1, Tsukuba, Ibaraki, Kanto 300-2645
Tel: +81 29 886 5447
Age range: 3–16
Curriculum: IBDP, IBMYP, IBPYP
Language instr: English
EAR

UPBEAT International School – Atsuta Campus
2-3-18, Hachiban, Atasuta, Nagoya, Aichi, Chubu
Tel: +81 (0)52 661 3155
Curriculum: IBPYP
Language instr: English, Japanese

UPBEAT International School – Nakagawa Campus
2-13, Juichibancho, Nakagawa, Nagoya, Aichi, Chubu
Tel: +81 (0)52 661 3155
Language instr: English, Japanese

UPBEAT International School – Tempaku Campus
201, Shimadagaoka, Tempaku, Nagoya, Aichi, Chubu
Tel: +81 (0)12 080 3763
Language instr: English, Japanese

UWC ISAK Japan
5827-136 Nagakura, Karuizawa-machi, Kitasaku-gun, Nagano, Chubu 389-0111
Tel: +81 26 746 8623
Age range: 15–19
No. of pupils: 190
Curriculum: IBDP
Language instr: English

Wakakusa Kindergarten
3-15-4 Yoshida, Nagano, Chubu 381-0043
Tel: +81 26 241 4151
Curriculum: IBPYP
Language instr: English, Japanese

Willowbrook International School
2-14-28 Moto-azabu, Minato-ku, Tokyo, Kanto 106-0046
Tel: +81 3 3449 9030
Curriculum: IBPYP
Language instr: English

Yamata Kindergarten
351-1 Higashiyamatacho, Tsuzuki Ward, Yokohama, Kanagawa, Kanto 224-0024
Tel: +81 45 592 4850
Curriculum: IBPYP
Language instr: Japanese

Yokohama International School
258 Yamate-cho, Naka-ku, Yokohama, Kanagawa, Kanto 231-0862
Tel: +81 45 622 0084
Age range: 3–18
Curriculum: IBDP, IBMYP, IBPYP, SAT
Language instr: English
(CIS) (EAR) (ECIS)

Yoyogi International School
5-67-5 Yoyogi, Shibuya-ku, Tokyo, Kanto 151-0053
Tel: +81 3 5478 6714
Curriculum: IBPYP
Language instr: English

JORDAN

Abdul Hamid Sharaf School
PO Box 6008, Amman 11118
Tel: +962 6 592 4188
Age range: 3–18
No. of pupils: 570 *B300 G270*
Curriculum: National, SAT, UK, USA, IGCSE, ALevs
Language instr: English, Arabic

Ahliyyah School for Girls
PO Box 2035, Jabal Amman, Amman 11181
Tel: +962 6 4649861
Age range: G6–18
Curriculum: IBDP, IBMYP, IBPYP, IBCP, National, ALevs
Language instr: English

Al Asriyya Modern School
PO Box 1002, Amman 11821
Tel: +962 6 533 7267

Al Ittihad School for Girls
Almadinai Alriadiah, PO Box 6804, Amman 11118
Tel: +962 6 5107990
Age range: G12–16
No. of pupils: 1000
Curriculum: UK

Al Ra'ed Al Arabi School
PO Box 9071, Amman 11191
Tel: +962 6 5659816
Age range: 4–18

American Community School Amman
PO BOX 310, Amman 11831
Tel: +962 6 581 3944
Age range: 3–18
Curriculum: USA
Language instr: English

Amman Academy
PO Box 840, Khalda 11821
Tel: +962 6 535 4118
Curriculum: IBDP, IBMYP, IBPYP
Language instr: English

Amman Baccalaureate School
Al Hijaz Street, Dabouq, PO Box 441 Sweileh 11910, Amman
Tel: +962 6 5411191
Age range: 4–18
No. of pupils: 1180
Curriculum: IBDP, IBMYP, IBPYP, IBCP
Language instr: English, Arabic
(CIS) (ECIS) (RS)

Amman Baptist School
P.O.Box 17033, Alrabieh – Abdallah Bin Rawaha St. 300 m off Mecca str+, Amman 11195
Tel: +962 6 551 6907
Curriculum: IBDP
Language instr: English, Arabic

Amman National School
PO Box 140565, Amman 11814
Tel: +962 654 11067/8
Curriculum: IBDP, IBMYP
Language instr: English

Aqaba International School
PO Box 529, 77110 Aqaba
Tel: +962 3 203 9933
Age range: 4–16
Curriculum: IBDP, National, UK
Language instr: English, Arabic

Asamiah International School
Khalda, Taqi al-Din al-Subki, Amman
Tel: +962 6 5335 301
Age range: 3–18 years
No. of pupils: 725
Curriculum: IBDP, IBMYP, IBPYP
Language instr: English, Arabic

Bishop's School for Boys
PO Box 2001, Amman 11181
Tel: +962 6 4653668
Language instr: English

British International Academy (BIA)
P.O.Box 829, Amman 11831
Tel: +962 6 5508200
Curriculum: IBDP, IBMYP, IBPYP
Language instr: English, Arabic

Cambridge High School
Al Rabia, Abdel Kareem Al Dabbas Street, PO Box 851771, Amman 11185
Tel: +962 6 5512556
Age range: 4–18
No. of pupils: 1018 *B549 G469 VIth94*
Curriculum: IBDP, IBMYP
Language instr: English

Canadian International School – Amman
20 Al Mikyal Street, Deir Ghbar, Amman
Tel: +962 6 593 9370
Curriculum: IBDP, IBMYP, IBPYP
Language instr: English

Collège De La Salle – Frères
P.O.Box 926126, Ar-Razi St., Jabal Al-Hussien, Amman 11110
Tel: +962 6 5666428
Curriculum: IBDP, IBMYP
Language instr: English, Arabic

English Talents School
P.O.Box 18082, Amman 11195
Tel: +962 65370201
Curriculum: IBDP, IBMYP
Language instr: English

IBN Rushd National Academy
PO Box 940397, Amman 11194
Tel: +962 6 5377601
Curriculum: IBDP, IBMYP, IBPYP
Language instr: English, Arabic

International Community School
PO Box 2002, Amman 11181
Tel: +962 6 4790666
Age range: 3–18
No. of pupils: 800
Curriculum: SAT, UK, GCSE, IGCSE, ALevs
Language instr: English
(CIS) (COB) (ECIS)

International French School of Amman
PO Box 830059, Abdoun, Amman 11183
Tel: +962 6 430 06 00
Curriculum: FrenchBacc

International Independent Schools IIS
3348 Tlaa Al-Ali, 11953
Tel: +962-6-5733377
Curriculum: National, UK, USA, IGCSE, ALevs

Islamic Educational College – Al Jubeiha
P.O Box 373, Amman 11941
Tel: +962 6516 0121
Age range: 16–18
Curriculum: IBDP
Language instr: English, Arabic

Islamic Educational College – Jabal Amman
P.O Box 385, Amman 11118
Tel: +962 6464 1331
(ECIS)

Jordanian International Schools
PO Box 188, Amman 11821
Tel: +962 6 5623777
Age range: 3–18
No. of pupils: 529
Curriculum: IGCSE

Jubilee School
P.O.Box: 830578, Amman 11183
Tel: +962 6 5238216
Curriculum: IBDP
Language instr: English

King's Academy
PO Box 9 Madaba, Manja 16188
Tel: +962 6 4300230
Age range: 12–18
No. of pupils: 660
Curriculum: AP, USA
Language instr: English
CIS RS

Mashrek International School
PO Box 1412, Amman 11118
Tel: +962 79 9577771
Age range: 3–18 years
No. of pupils: 1668
Curriculum: IBDP, IBMYP, IBPYP, National
Language instr: Arabic, English
CIS ECIS

Modern American School
P.O. Box 950553 – Sweifieh, Amman 11195
Tel: +962 6 5862779
Age range: 3–18
Curriculum: IBDP, National, UK, USA
Language instr: English, Arabic

Modern Montessori School
PO Box 1941, Khilda, Amman 11821
Tel: +9626 5535190
Age range: 3–18 years
No. of pupils: 1808
Curriculum: IBDP, IBMYP, IBPYP
Language instr: English, Arabic
ECIS

National Orthodox School
P.O.Box 941502, Amman 11194
Tel: +962 6 5674418
Curriculum: IBDP, IGCSE
Language instr: Arabic, English
CIS

New English School
PO Box 154, Khalda, Amman 11821
Tel: +962 (0)6 5517111
Age range: 4–19
No. of pupils: 2050
Curriculum: National, SAT, UK, ALevs
ECIS

Oxford Schools
PO Box 960628, Amman 11196
Tel: +962 6516 0961
Age range: 4–19
No. of pupils: 500

Pearl International Academy
Affash Aalawi Shudayfat St., Al-Rawnaq, Bayader Wadi Al-Seer, Amman
Tel: +962 770777705

RAMS (Rawdat Al-Maaref Schools and College)
PO Box 676, Khalda, Amman 11821
Tel: +962 6552 8599
Age range: 4–19
No. of pupils: 300

Rosary Sisters School – Aqaba
PO Box 1367, Aqaba 77110
Tel: +962 3 201 42 62

THE INTERNATIONAL ACADEMY – AMMAN
For further details see p. 106
PO Box 144255, King Hussein Parks, Sa'eed Khair Street, Amman 11814
Tel: +962 6550 2055
Email: info@iaa.edu.jo
Website: www.iaa.edu.jo
Director: Hana Kanan
Age range: 3–18 years
No. of pupils: 1181 *B626 G555*
Curriculum: IBDP, IBMYP, IPC, National
Language instr: English
CIS ECIS

The International School of Choueifat – Amman
Wadi Essir, Amman 11810
Tel: +962 6 429 1133
Age range: 3–18
No. of pupils: 1274 *B742 G532*
Curriculum: AP, SAT
Language instr: English

The Little Academy
PO Box 143771, Amman 11844
Tel: +962 65858282
Curriculum: IBPYP
Language instr: English

Whitman Academy
PO BOX 142011, 11814
Tel: +962 (06) 552 5094
Curriculum: USA

KAZAKHSTAN

Dostyk American International School
TCO, Dostyk Village, 37 Vladimirskaya Street, Atyrau 060011
Tel: +7 712 220 92 03
Age range: 4–11 years
No. of pupils: 125
Curriculum: USA
Language instr: English

Galaxy International School
4th Microdistrict 9, Almaty A10A5M5
Tel: +7 727 243 77 80
Age range: 6–18 years
No. of pupils: 420
Curriculum: UK, IGCSE, ALevs
Language instr: English

Haileybury Almaty
112 Al-Farabi Avenue, Almaty 050040
Tel: +7 727 355 01 00
Age range: 4–18 years
Curriculum: UK, GCSE, IGCSE, ALevs
Language instr: English

Haileybury Astana
Ivan Panfilov bldg. 4, Nur-Sultan 010000
Tel: +7 717 255 98 55
Age range: 2–18 years
No. of pupils: 600
Curriculum: IBDP, UK, GCSE, IGCSE, ALevs
Language instr: English

International College of Continuous Education, Almaty
69A Zheltoksan Street, Almaty 480004
Tel: +7 727 279 97 36
Age range: 3–18
No. of pupils: 324 *B175 G149*
Curriculum: IBMYP, IBPYP
Language instr: English

International College of Continuous Education, Astana
8/4 Tashenov Street, Nur-Sultan 010000
Tel: +7 717 242 55 54
Age range: 3–17
No. of pupils: 140 *B70 G70*
Curriculum: IBMYP, IBPYP
Language instr: English, Russian

International School of Almaty
40b Satpayev Street, Almaty 050057
Tel: +7 727 274 48 08
Age range: 7–18
No. of pupils: 350
Curriculum: IBMYP, IBPYP
Language instr: Russian, English

Kazakhstan International School
Al-Farabi Avenue 118/15, Almaty 050062
Tel: +7 727 356 50 00
Age range: 2–19 years
Curriculum: IBDP, IBMYP, IBPYP
Language instr: English

Lyceum School Nurorda
Kassym Amanzholov Street 34, Nur-Sultan 020000
Tel: +8 717 242 78 29
CIS

Miras International School, Almaty
190 Al-Farabi Avenue, Almaty 050043
Tel: +7 727 227 69 42
Age range: 3–18 years
Curriculum: IBDP, IBMYP, IBPYP
Language instr: English
CIS ECIS

Miras International School, Astana
Kuishi Dina Street 34, Nur-Sultan 010009
Tel: +7 717 236 98 67
Age range: 5–18 years
Curriculum: IBDP, IBMYP, IBPYP
Language instr: English, Russian, Kazakh
CIS ECIS

QSI Almaty International School
185 Baiken Ashimov Street, Kalkaman 2 Micro-District, Nauryzbay District, Almaty 050006
Tel: +7 727 381 87 10
Age range: 3–18 years
Curriculum: AP, USA
Language instr: English

QSI International School of Astana
17 Bayan-Sulu Street, Komsomolskiy Village, Nur-Sultan 010000
Tel: +7 717 227 77 60
Age range: 3–18 years
Curriculum: USA
Language instr: English

QSI International School of Atyrau
473 Sultan Beibarys Prospect, Atyrau 060011
Tel: +7 712 251 83 97
Age range: 3–18 years
Language instr: English

Spectrum International School
Kasym Amanzholov Street 34, South-East (right side) m-n, Nur-Sultan
Tel: +7 707 926 36 46

Tien Shan International School
Karasai District Raimbek Rural District, South of the village Dolan, Almaty 040922
Tel: +7 727 344 12 66

KUWAIT

A'Takamul International School
PO Box 2975,, 32030
Tel: +965 25522204
Curriculum: USA

Al Amal Indian School, Salmiya
PO Box 5213, AlKhansa Street, 22062 Salmiya, Hawalli
Tel: +965 2571 2971

Al Ghanim Bilingual School
PO Box 3014, Safat, 31013
Kuwait City, Al-Asimah
Tel: +965 2564 4953
Age range: 4–15
No. of pupils: 1000
Curriculum: National, USA
ECIS

Al Ru'ya Bilingual School
Block 2, Street 3, Parcel
94, 44230 Sabah Al Salem,
Mubarak Al-Kabeer
Age range: 2–18
No. of pupils: 1547 *B920* G627
CIS ECIS

Al-Bayan Bilingual School
PO Box 24472, Safat 13105
Tel: +965 222 75 000
Age range: 3–18
No. of pupils: 1850 *B995* G855
Curriculum: AP, National,
SAT, TOEFL, USA
CIS

American Arab Bilingual Academy
PO Box 237, Safat, 13098
Kuwait City, Al-Asimah
Tel: +965 2263 9681
Age range: 3–18
No. of pupils: 644 *B447* G197
Curriculum: National, USA

American Creativity Academy
PO Box 1740, Hawally 32018
Tel: +965 2267 3333
Age range: 3–18 years
No. of pupils: 5500
Curriculum: IBDP, USA
Language instr: English

American International School of Kuwait
PO Box 3267, Salmiya 22033
Tel: +965 1 843 247
Age range: 4–18 years
No. of pupils: 2324
Curriculum: IBDP, IBMYP,
IBPYP, SAT, USA
Language instr: English
ECIS

DANAH Universal School of Kuwait
Block 1, Salem Bin Towaim,
Al-Daway Street (Street 100)
Tel: +965 2566 2546
Curriculum: USA

Dasman Model Bilingual School
PO Box 426, Dasman 15455
Tel: +965 22277377
Age range: 2–18
No. of pupils: 1500
Curriculum: AP, USA

Dasman Model School
PO Box 3366, Salmiya 22034
Tel: +965 2243 0704/6
Age range: 3–19
No. of pupils: 1488 *B925* G563
Curriculum: National,
SAT, TOEFL, USA
CIS

Fahaheel Al Watanieh Indian Private School
49, South St., P.O.Box:
9951, Ahmadi 61010
Tel: +965 23983595

Fawzia Sultan International School
PO Box 719, Safat 13008
Tel: +965 220 52 822
Curriculum: USA

Future Bilingual School (Boys Campus)
Block 9 Street 16, Off Makkah Street,
Behind Ahmadi Educational Area
Tel: +965 23924243
Curriculum: USA

Gulf English School
P O Box 33106, Al Dimanah
Street, Block 5, Salmiya
Tel: +965 2575 7952
Curriculum: IGCSE, ALevs
ECIS

Ideal Education School, Kuwait
PO Box 27557, Safat 13136
Tel: +965 240 3668
Age range: 3–21
No. of pupils: 186 *B110* G76
CIS

Indian Central School
Jaleeb Al Shoyoukh, Block 1 St 100
Opp NBK, PO Box 6391 32038
Tel: +965 4330244
Age range: 4–18
No. of pupils: 300

Indian Educational School
Jleeb Al Shyoukh-School Street,,
Tel: +965 2434 0882

International Academy of Kuwait
Haroon Al Rashid Street,
Salmiya 22053
Tel: +965 25632370
Age range: 3–16
No. of pupils: 650
Curriculum: IPC

International British School, Kuwait
PO Box 47401, Kuwait
City, Al-Asimah
Tel: +965 2392 2430
Curriculum: UK
Language instr: English
COB

Iqra'a Bilingual School
Block 4, Street 25, Jleeb Al Shuyoukh
Tel: +965 22219900
Language instr: English
AISA

Khalifa School
PO Box 58, Safat 13001
Tel: +965 2574 4105
Age range: 3–21+
No. of pupils: 197 B125 G72
Curriculum: UK, USA
Language instr: English, Arabic
CIS

Kuwait American School
PO Box 5150, Salmiya – 22062
Tel: +965 2572 0920
Age range: 2–16
Curriculum: USA

Kuwait Bilingual School
PO Box 3125, Al Jahra City 01033
Tel: +965 2458 1118; +965 1877 881
Age range: 3–18
No. of pupils: 1850
Curriculum: IBMYP, IBPYP,
National, SAT, TOEFL
Language instr: English, Arabic

Kuwait English School
PO Box 8640, Salmiya, 22057
Kuwait City, Al-Asimah
Tel: +965 2565 5216
Age range: 3–18
No. of pupils: 2480
Curriculum: UK, ALevs
Language instr: English
ECIS

Kuwait International English School
PO Box 93, Dasman 15451
Tel: +965 2262 8447; +965 22642047
Age range: 3–18
No. of pupils: 327
Curriculum: IGCSE

Kuwait National English School
PO Box 44273, Hawally, 32057
Kuwait City, Al-Asimah
Tel: +965 2265 6905
Age range: 3–16
No. of pupils: 600
Curriculum: UK
CIS ECIS

Little Land Nursery & Montessori Centre
House 7, Street 40, Block 4,
Faiha, Kuwait City, Al Asimah
Tel: +965 225 55433
Curriculum: IBPYP
Language instr: English, Arabic

Lycee Francais De Koweit
PO Box 9450, Hamad Al-
Mubarak Street, Salmiya 22095
Tel: +965 257 300 24
Age range: 4–18
No. of pupils: 1160

Manarat School
PO Box 27557, Safat 13136
Tel: +965 257 22 083
Language instr: English
CIS

New English School
PO Box 6156, 32036 Hawelli
Tel: +965 25318060
Age range: 3.5–18 years
No. of pupils: 2404
Curriculum: UK, IGCSE, ALevs
Language instr: English
ECIS

New Pakistan International School
Block-9, Surraqa Bin Malik Street,
(Near Doctor's Complex), Hawally
Tel: +965 22213153
No. of pupils: 2345
Curriculum: IGCSE, ALevs

Oxford Academy
Salwa, Block 7, Street 1,
Rumaithiya 25510
Tel: +965 22980598
Age range: 3–16
No. of pupils: 1200
Curriculum: UK

Reborn Kids Education Academy (RKEA)
Block 5, St. 507, Al-Siddiq
Tel: +965 2208 6688
Curriculum: IBPYP
Language instr: English

Salwa Infant School
Block 7, Street 2, Salwa
Tel: +965 65553702
COB

The American Academy for Girls
PO Box 22156, Safat, 13082
Kuwait City, Al-Asimah
Tel: +965 2563 9612
Age range: 3–18
No. of pupils: 830
Curriculum: USA

The American Baccalaureate School
Abraq Khaitan, Block 6,, Street
#59,, Ibn Zuhair Street,
Tel: (+965) 24 791 791
Curriculum: USA

The American School of Kuwait
Hawalli-Al-Muthanna st,
Block 7, Bldg 90017, PO Box
6735 Hawalli 32042
Tel: +965 2 266 4341
Age range: 3–18
No. of pupils: 1325
Curriculum: AP, SAT, TOEFL

The American United School of Kuwait
Sabah Al Salem Area, Block 1, 101 street Intersection of 6th Ring, Road & Fahaheel E+, Sabah Al Salem 13034
Tel: +965 25530150
Curriculum: USA
(CIS)

The British School of Kuwait
Safat 13130, Kuwait 26922
Tel: +965 2562 1701
Age range: 3–19
No. of pupils: 1700 *B*925 *G*775 *VIth*85
Curriculum: National, UK, GCSE, IGCSE, ALevs
Language instr: English
(COB)

The English Academy
PO Box 1081, Surra 45701
Tel: +965 2265 1062/63
Age range: 3–18
No. of pupils: 1000 *B*700 *G*300
Curriculum: UK, ALevs
Language instr: English, Arabic

The English Playgroup
Street 2, Block 7, Salwa
Tel: +965 25627192
Age range: 4–11
Curriculum: UK
Language instr: English, Arabic
(COB)

The English School Fahaheel
PO Box 7209, Fahaheel, 64003 Kuwait City, Al-Asimah
Tel: +965 2371 1070
Age range: 3–18
No. of pupils: 1050 *VIth*37
Curriculum: UK, IGCSE, ALevs
Language instr: English

The English School for Girls
Salwa Block 7, Street 1, Opposite Yarmouk Club, Kuwait City, Al-Asimah
Tel: +965 2202 1260
Age range: 3–16
Curriculum: UK

The English School, Kuwait
PO Box 379, Safat 13004
Tel: +965 2227 1385
Age range: 2–13
No. of pupils: 630 *B*315 *G*315
Curriculum: National, UK
Language instr: English
(COB) (ECIS)

The Indian Community School
Essa Al Qatami Street, Jiddha 8, Block 10, Salmiya
Tel: 00965 25629583

Universal American School
PO Box 17035, Khaldiya 72451
Tel: +965 1822827
Age range: 3–18
No. of pupils: 1600 *B*900 *G*700
Language instr: English
(CIS) (ECIS)

KYRGYZSTAN

ESCA Bishkek International School
67a Bronirovannaya Street, Chui Oblast, Bishkek 720044
Tel: +996 312 21 44 06
Age range: 2–17 years
No. of pupils: 240
Curriculum: IBDP, IBMYP, IBPYP, IGCSE
Language instr: English

Hope Academy of Bishkek
Gogolya 127 b, Bishkek 720011
Tel: +996 312 681 079
No. of pupils: 150
Curriculum: UK

Oxford International School
Mira Avenue 153/1, Bishkek
Tel: +996 700 55 11 55
Curriculum: IBDP
Language instr: English, Russian

QSI International School of Bishkek
14A Tynystanova Street, Bishkek 720055
Tel: +996 312 563139
Age range: 4–15
No. of pupils: 103
Curriculum: USA
Language instr: English

Silk Road International School
Mikroregion 11, Aytieva 7a, Bishkek 720049
Tel: +996 312 520290/520390
Age range: 5–17
No. of pupils: 460 *B*230 *G*230
Curriculum: IGCSE, ALevs
(ECIS)

LAOS

French International High School Vientiane
BP 2526, route de Thadeua, Vientiane
Tel: +856 21 260 926
Age range: 2–16
No. of pupils: 616
Language instr: French

Kiettisack International School
Lao-Thai Friendship Road – PO Box 4348, Sokpaluang Village, Sisattanak District
Tel: +856 21 314979
Curriculum: National, UK, IGCSE

Panyathip International School
Saphanthong Neua Village, Sisattanak District, Vientiane
Tel: +856 21 412 825
Age range: 5–19
Curriculum: UK, IGCSE

The Australian International School
Nongdoung Village, Sikkhotabong District, Vientiane
Tel: +856 20 2222 0528
Curriculum: National, IGCSE

Vientiane International School
PO Box 3180, Phonesavanh Road, Saphanthong Tai Village, Sisattanak District, Vientiane
Tel: +856 21 31 8100
Age range: 4–18 years
No. of pupils: 455
Curriculum: IBDP, IBMYP, IBPYP
Language instr: English
(CIS) (EAR)

LEBANON

Ahliah School
Wadi Abou Jmil Downtown, Beirut
Tel: +961 1 372 960
Curriculum: USA
(CIS)

Al-Hayat International School
Aramoun
Tel: +961 5 806 306
Curriculum: IBDP, IBMYP, IBPYP
Language instr: Arabic, English

American Community School at Beirut
PO Box 8129, Riad Solh, Beirut 11072260
Tel: +961 1 374 370
Age range: 3–18
No. of pupils: 1023
Curriculum: IBDP, SAT, TOEFL
Language instr: English
(ECIS)

Antonine International School
PO Box 55035, Ajaltoun, Dekwaneh
Tel: +961 9 230969
No. of pupils: 1300
Curriculum: IBDP
Language instr: English

Brummana High School
PO Box 36, Brummana BT
Tel: +961 4 960 430
Age range: 3–18
No. of pupils: 1215
Curriculum: IBDP, UK, IGCSE
Language instr: English

Cadmous College
Tyre, Jwar Al Nakhel
Tel: +9617380391/2
Curriculum: IBDP
Language instr: English

Christian Teaching Institute
Mar Maroun Street, Horsh Tabet, Sin el Fil, Beirut
Tel: +961 1 497974
Curriculum: IBDP
Language instr: English, Arabic

City International School
P.O.Box 11-472 Riad El Solh, Beirut
Tel: +961 137 5410
Language instr: English
(ECIS)

Collège Mariste de Champville
Dik El-Mehdi
Tel: +961 4 913 327
Age range: 3–18
No. of pupils: 3140
Curriculum: FrenchBacc

College Notre Dame De Jamhour
PO Box 45-151, Hazmieh
Tel: +961 5 924151
Age range: 4–19
No. of pupils: 2811
Curriculum: FrenchBacc

College Notre Dame de Nazareth
Achrafieh, Nasra Street, PO Box 165108, Beirut
Tel: +961 1 327 150
Age range: 5–18
No. of pupils: 1547

Collège Protestant Français
Rue Madame Curie, BP 13-6283, Chouran, Beirut 1102-2110
Tel: +961 1 811 892

Collège Protestant Français Montana
Rue 4, Dik El Mehdi
Tel: +961 4 914 006
Curriculum: IBDP
Language instr: English, Arabic

Eastwood College – Kafarshima
P.O. Box 46, Kafarshima
Tel: +961 5 431525
Curriculum: IBDP
Language instr: English, Arabic

Eastwood International School
Sami Solh St, Mansourieh El Metn
Tel: +961 4 409307
Age range: 3–18
No. of pupils: 410 *B*203 *G*207
Curriculum: AP, IBDP, IBMYP, IBPYP, National, SAT, USA
Language instr: English

German International School Beirut
PO Box 11-3888, Bliss Street, Ras Beirut, Beirut
Tel: +961 1 740523
Age range: 3–18
No. of pupils: 1050
Curriculum: IBDP
Language instr: English

Grand Lycee Franco – Libanais
Rue Beni Assaf, BP 155-636, Beirut 1100 2060
Tel: +961 1 420700
Age range: 3–18
No. of pupils: 3000

Greenfield College
Al Mourouj Street – Eir Hassan, Beirut
Tel: +961 1 834 838
Curriculum: IBDP, National, FrenchBacc, USA
Language instr: English

Hariri High School II
Rue Abdul Kader, Batrakiyyeh, Beirut
Tel: +961 1 373 310
Curriculum: IBDP
Language instr: English, Arabic

Institut Moderne Du Liban
Rue 51 n.19 Metn nord, Fanar, Région Jaber 90593
Tel: +961 1680160/1/2
Age range: 3–18
No. of pupils: 380
Curriculum: IBDP, IBMYP
Language instr: French

International College Beirut
P.O. Box 113-5373, Hamra, Bliss Street, Beirut
Tel: +961 1 374980
Age range: 3–18
No. of pupils: 3650
Curriculum: IBDP, IBPYP
Language instr: Arabic, English, French
CIS

International College, Ain Aar
Bliss Street, PO Box 113-5373, Beirut
Tel: +96 149 28468
Curriculum: IBPYP
Language instr: Arabic, English, French

Jesus & Mary School
Rabweh, Cornet Chahwan
Tel: +961 4910531/2/3/4/5
Curriculum: IBDP
Language instr: English, Arabic

Leila C. Saad SABIS School El-Metn
Dhour El Choueir, El-Metn
Tel: +961 4 297 666
Age range: 4–11

LWIS Hazmieh
Hazmieh – 503A str., Near City Center, Beirut
Tel: +961 5 453 241
Age range: 3–18
No. of pupils: 110
Curriculum: IBPYP
Language instr: English, Arabic

LWIS Keserwan-Adma International School
Mar Nohra, Fatqa, Keserwan
Tel: +961 9 740 226
Age range: 3–18
No. of pupils: 400
Curriculum: IBDP, USA
Language instr: English

LWIS Universal School of Lebanon
Bterram Al-Koura,
Tel: +961 (6) 930 964
Curriculum: IBDP, National, USA
Language instr: English, Arabic

LWIS-City International School
Hussein Beyhum Street, Zkak El-Blat, Down Town, Beirut
Tel: +961 (1) 369 500
Curriculum: IBDP
Language instr: English, Arabic

Lycee Abdallah Rassi
Halba, Akkar
Tel: +961 6 690 642
Age range: 4–11
No. of pupils: 303

Lycee Abdel Kader
BP 11-8464 Riad El Solh, 110 722 270 LIBAN
Tel: +961 (01) 365 429
Curriculum: FrenchBacc

Lycée Franco-Libanais Nahr Ibrahim
Al Maayssra Nahr,
Tel: +961 9 446457/8/9
Curriculum: FrenchBacc

Makassed Houssam Eddine Hariri High School
PO Box 67, Saida
Tel: +961 7 739898
Age range: 3–18
No. of pupils: 1520 B835 G685
Curriculum: IBDP, IBPYP, National, FrenchBacc, SAT, TOEFL
Language instr: Arabic, English, French

Monsif National School
Monsif Main Road, Monsif
Tel: +961 9 790170
Curriculum: IBDP
Language instr: English, Arabic

Montana International College
Street 4, Dik El Mehdi, P.O.Box: 11 Mazraat Yachouh,
Tel: +961 4 914 006
Curriculum: National, USA

Rafic Hariri High School – Saida
P.O.Box 384, Saidon
Tel: +961 7 723 551
Curriculum: IBPYP
Language instr: English

SABIS International School – Adma
Orange Zone, Adma
Tel: +961 9 854 154
Age range: 3–18
No. of pupils: 420

Sagesse High School
Aïn Saadeh, Metn
Tel: +961 1 872 145
Age range: 3–18
No. of pupils: 1525
Curriculum: IBDP, National
Language instr: English

Saint Joseph School
Cornet Chahwan
Tel: +961 4925005
Curriculum: IBDP
Language instr: English, Arabic

The International School of Choueifat – Choueifat
Charles Saad Street, Amrosioeh, Choueifat
Tel: +961 5 431600
Age range: 3–18
No. of pupils: 1421
Curriculum: USA, ALevs

The International School of Choueifat – Koura
Fih Village, Koura
Tel: +961 6 930 740
Age range: 3–18
No. of pupils: 819 B462 G357
Curriculum: UK, IGCSE, ALevs

Universal College-Aley
P.O. Box 284, Aley
Tel: +961 5 556665
Language instr: English

WELLSPRING LEARNING COMMUNITY
For further details see p. 112
Al Mathaf, Main Street, Near National Museum, Beirut
Tel: +961 1 423 444
Email: admissions@wellspring.edu.lb
Website: www.wellspring.edu.lb
Head of School: Kathleen Battah
Age range: 3–19 years
No. of pupils: 748
Curriculum: IBDP, IBMYP, IBPYP, National
Language instr: English

MALAYSIA

Alice Smith School
2 Jalan Bellamy, 50460 Kuala Lumpur
Tel: +60 3 2148 3674
Age range: 3–18 years
No. of pupils: 1550
Curriculum: GCSE, ALevs
Language instr: English
CIS COB EAR

Asia Pacific International School
No. 1, Persiaran A, Off Jalan Lapangan, Terbang Subang, 47200 Subang, Selangor
Tel: +60 3 7847 1000
Age range: 4–18
No. of pupils: 342

Australian International School Malaysia
22 Jalan Anggerik, The Mines Resort City, 43300 Seri Kembangan, Selangor
Tel: +60 3 8949 5000
Age range: 3–18
Language instr: English
CIS

Beaconhouse-Newlands, Kuala Lumpur International School
823 & 984 Batu 9, Jalan Cheras, 43200 Kuala Lumpur
Tel: +60 3 9075 1662/63

Cempaka International Ladies' College
Persiaran Timur Kampong L.B. Johnson, 71760 Seremban, Negeri Sembilan
Age range: G11–18
Language instr: English

Cempaka International School
No 19, Jalan Setiabakti 1, Damansara Heights, Kuala Lumpur
Tel: +60 3 2094 0623
Curriculum: IBDP
ISA

Dalat International School
Jalan Tanjung Bungah, 11200 Tanjung Bungah, Penang
Tel: +60 4 899 2105
Age range: 3–18
No. of pupils: 400 B200 G200
Curriculum: ACT, SAT, USA
Language instr: English
EAR

Destiny Academy
No. 4 Taman Mas Ria, Jalan Junid Dalam, 84000 Muar, Johor
Tel: +60 6 959 2059
Curriculum: USA

Deutsche Schule Kuala Lumpur
Lot 5, Lorong Utara B,,
Off Jalan Utara, 46200
Petaling Jaya, Selangor
Tel: +60 3 7956 6557

DISTED College
340 Macalister Road, 10350
George Town, Penang
Tel: +60 4 2296579
Curriculum: UK, ALevs

Eaton International School
Persiaran Puncak Utama, Jade
Hills, 43000 Kajang, Selangor
Tel: +60 3 87414965
Curriculum: UK, IGCSE

elc International School
3664, Jalan Sierramas
Barat, Sierramas, 47000
Sungai Buloh, Selangor
Tel: +60 3 6156 5001/2
Age range: 3–16
No. of pupils: 650
Curriculum: UK
Language instr: English

ELC International School Cyberjaya
Lingkaran Cyber Point Barat,
63000 Cyberjaya, Selangor
Tel: +60 3 8319 1641
Age range: 4–16 years
No. of pupils: 350
Curriculum: UK, IGCSE

Epsom College in Malaysia
Persiaran Kolej, 71760 Bandar
Enstek, Negeri Sembilan
Tel: +60 6 2404 188
Age range: 3–18 years
No. of pupils: 400
Curriculum: UK
Language instr: English

Fairview International School Ipoh (FISI)
Hala Lapangan Suria, Medan
Lapangan, Suria, 31350 Ipoh, Perak
Tel: +60 5 313 6888
Age range: 3–16 years
Curriculum: IBMYP, IBPYP
Language instr: English

Fairview International School Johor Bahru (FISJB)
Lot PTD 168450, Jalan Dato' Onn
Utama, Bandar Dato' Onn, Mukim
Tebrau, 81100 Johor Bahru, Johor
Tel: +60 7 364 3378
Age range: 3–16 years
Curriculum: IBMYP, IBPYP

Fairview International School Kuala Lumpur (FISKL)
Lot 4178, Jalan 1/27D, Section 6,
Wangsa Maju, 53300 Kuala Lumpur
Tel: +60 3 4142 0888
Age range: 3–19 years
Curriculum: IBDP, IBMYP, IBPYP
Language instr: English, Mandarin

Fairview International School Penang (FISP)
Tingkat Bukit Jambul 1, Bukit Jambul
Indah, 11900 Bayan Lepas, Penang
Tel: +60 4 640 6633
Age range: 3–16 years
Curriculum: IBMYP, IBPYP

Fairview International School Subang Jaya (FISJ)
2A, Jalan TP 2, Sime UEP Industrial
Park, 47600 Subang Jaya, Selangor
Tel: +60 3 8023 7777
Age range: 3–16 years
Curriculum: IBMYP, IBPYP

Garden International School
16 Jalan Kiara 3, Off Jln Bukit
Kiara, 50480 Kuala Lumpur
Tel: +60 3 6209 6888
Age range: 3–18
No. of pupils: 2000
Curriculum: UK, IGCSE, ALevs
Language instr: English

Garden International School Kuantan
A6230 Jalan Tengku Muhamad,
Taman Pantai Chempedak,
25050 Kuantan, Pahang
Tel: +60 3 6209 6888
Curriculum: UK, IGCSE

GEMS International School – Pearl City
No. 2, Persiaran Mutiara 5, Pusat
Komersial Bandar Tasek Mutiara,
14120 Simpang Ampat, Penang
Tel: +60 4 509 7000
Age range: 3–18
Curriculum: UK, IGCSE
Language instr: English

Global Indian International School (GIIS) Kuala Lumpur Campus
242 Lorong Abdul Samad, off
Jalan Sultan Abdul Samad,
Brickfields, 50470 Kuala Lumpur
Tel: +60 1 9616 0075
Curriculum: UK, IGCSE

HELP International School HIS
No 2 Persiaran Cakerawala,
Subang Bestari, Seksyen U4,
40150 Shah Alam, Selangor
Tel: +60 3 7809 7000
Curriculum: IPC, UK, IGCSE, ALevs

HIBISCUS International School
No 2 Jalan Udang Harimau
3, Taman Sri Segambut,
52000 Kuala Lumpur
Tel: +60 3 6242 5544
Age range: 4–18
No. of pupils: 139
Curriculum: IGCSE

IGB International School
Jalan Sierramas Utama,
Sungai Buloh, Kuala Lumpur,
Selangor 47000
Tel: +60 3 6145 4688
Age range: 3–19
Curriculum: IBDP, IBMYP, IBPYP, IBCP
Language instr: English

International Islamic School
Batu 8, Jalan Sungai Pusu,
Gomback, 53100 Kuala Lumpur
Tel: +60 3 6188 4400
Age range: 4–11
No. of pupils: 800

International School of Kuantan
Jalan IM 7/9, Bandar Indera
Mahkota, 25200 Kuantan, Pahang
Tel: +60 9573 6010
Curriculum: AP, USA
Language instr: English

Kelantan International School
5376B, Jalan Telipot, 15150
Kota Bharu, Kelantan
Tel: +60 9 744 6991

Kinabalu International School
PO Box 12080, 88822 Kota
Kinabalu, Sabah
Tel: +60 88 224526
Age range: 3–18
No. of pupils: 460

King Henry VIII College – Malaysia
Persiaran Bestari, Cyber 11,
63000 Cyberjaya, Selangor
Tel: +60 (03) 8800 9888
Age range: 3–18

Kingsley International School
Persiaran Kingsley, Kingsley
Hills, Putra Heights, 47650
Subang Jaya, Selangor
Tel: +60 3 5481 6090
Curriculum: UK, IGCSE, ALevs

Kolej Tuanku Ja'afar
71700 Mantin, Negeri Sembilan
Tel: +60 6 7582561
Age range: 3–19 years
No. of pupils: 800
Curriculum: IPC, National,
UK, IGCSE, ALevs
Language instr: English

Kolej Yayasan UEM
Lembah Beringin, PO Box 62,
35900 Tanjung Malim, Perak
Tel: +60 3 6460 1234
Curriculum: UK, ALevs

Labuan International School
Lot 11334, Kampung Tanjung Aru,
Jalan Tanjung Aru, 87008 Labuan
Tel: +6 087 597300
Curriculum: National, UK

Lodge Group of Schools
Lorong Keranji 4E, Jalan
Keranji 4, Tabuan Desa,
93350 Kuching, Sarawak
Tel: +60 8 2363554

Lycée Français de Kuala Lumpur
34, Jalan Dutamas Raya,
51200 Kuala Lumpur
Tel: +60 (03) 6250 4415
Curriculum: FrenchBacc

Malacca Expatriate School
No 2-12, Jalan Siakap 1A,
Taman Permatang Pasir
Perdana, 75460 Malacca
Tel: +60 6 269 3300
Age range: 4–16
No. of pupils: 200
Curriculum: SAT, UK, IGCSE

Marlborough College Malaysia
Jalan Marlborough, 79200
Iskandar Puteri, Johor
Tel: +60 7 560 2200
Age range: 3–18 years
No. of pupils: 780
Curriculum: IBDP, UK, IGCSE
Language instr: English

Matrix Global Schools
PT 12652, Sendayan, Merchant
Square, Persiaran 1, Sendayan
Utama, Pusat Dagangan
Sendayan, 71950 Bandar Sri
Sendayan, Negeri Sembilan
Tel: +60 6 781 9888
Age range: 3–17
No. of pupils: 730
Curriculum: National, IGCSE
Language instr: English,
Bahasa Melayu

MAZ International School
No. 1 MAZ House, Jalan 20/19, Paramount Gardens, 46300 Petaling Jaya, Selangor
Tel: +60 3 78742930
Curriculum: UK, IGCSE, ALevs

Methodist College
Off Jalan Tun Sambanthan 4, Brickfields, 50470 Kuala Lumpur
Tel: +60 3 2274 1851
Age range: 16–19

Mont'Kiara International School
22 Jalan Kiara, Mont'Kiara, 50480 Kuala Lumpur
Tel: +60 3 2093 8604
Age range: 3–18
No. of pupils: 600
Curriculum: IBDP, IBMYP, IBPYP, SAT, USA
Language instr: English

Mutiara International Grammar School
Lot 707, Jalan Kerja Ayer Lama, Ampang Jaya, 68000 Ampang, Selangor
Tel: +60 3 4257 5036
Age range: 3–17 years
Curriculum: UK, IGCSE
Language instr: English

Nexus International School Malaysia
No 1 Jalan Diplomatik 3/6, Presint 15, 62050 Putrajaya
Tel: +60 3 8889 3868
Age range: 3–18 years
Curriculum: IBDP, IPC, UK, GCSE, IGCSE
Language instr: English

Prince of Wales Island International Primary School (POWIIS Primary)
Sunrise Tower, Mezzanine Floor, 190-192 Persiaran Gurney, 10250 Penang
Tel: +60 4 828 9999
Age range: 3–11

Prince of Wales Island International School (POWIIS)
1 Jalan Sungai Air Putih 6, Bandar Baru Air Putih, 11000 Balik Pulau, Penang
Tel: +60 4 8689999
Curriculum: UK
Language instr: English

R.E.A.L Schools, Cheras Campus
Lot 217, Batu 13, Jalan Hulu Langat, 43100 Hulu Langat, Selangor
Tel: +60 3 9021 3601

R.E.A.L Schools, Johor Bahru Campus
Lot 2361, Jalan Persiaran Sri Plentong, Bandar Baru Permas Jaya, 81750 Masai, Johor
Tel: +60 7 3864468

R.E.A.L Schools, Shah Alam Campus
Lot No. 5, Jalan Merah Saga U9/5, 40250 Shah Alam, Selangor
Tel: +60 3 7842 3228

Raffles American School
Raffles K12 Sdn Bhd, Jalan Raffles, 79050 Iskandar Puteri, Johor
Tel: +60 7 509 8750
Age range: 3–18 years
Curriculum: AP, IBDP, SAT
Language instr: English

Rafflesia International School Kajang Campus
Jalan Kajang 2 Utama, Seksyen 2,, 43000 Kajang, Selangor
Tel: +603 8741 7099
Curriculum: IPC, UK, IGCSE

Rafflesia International School Puchong Campus
Persiaran Sierra 2, Bandar 16 Sierra, 47100 Puchong, Selangor
Tel: +60 3 8953 9088
Curriculum: IPC, UK, IGCSE

Repton International School Malaysia
No. 8, Jalan Purnama, Bandar Seri Alam, 81750 Johor Bahru, Johor
Tel: +60 7 888 999
Curriculum: IBDP
Language instr: English

Sayfol International School
No. 261 Jalan Ampang, 50450 Kuala Lumpur
Tel: +60 3 4256 8791
Age range: 4–18
No. of pupils: 1000
Curriculum: UK

Sekolah Sri KDU (Kota Damansara)
No. 5 & 7, Jalan Teknologi 2/1, Kota Damansara, 47810 Daerah Petaling, Selangor
Tel: +60 3 6145 3888
Age range: 4–16 years
Language instr: English

Sri Ara International School
23 Jalan Straits View, 80200 Johor Bahru, Johor
Tel: +60 7 222 2089
Age range: 4–19
No. of pupils: 110
Curriculum: IGCSE

Sri Emas International School
Lot 1214, Seksyen 40, Batu 10, Lebuhraya Persekutuan, Off Jalan SS 7/2, 47300 Petaling Jaya, Selangor
Tel: +60 3 7865 5787
Age range: 11–16
No. of pupils: 700
Curriculum: GCSE

Sri KDU International School (Klang)
PT 4194, Jalan Tampin 1/KU1, Off Jalan Goh Hock Huat, Sungai Pinang, 41050 Klang, Selangor
Tel: +60 3 3082 6888
Age range: 3–18 years
Language instr: English

Sri KDU International School (Kota Damansara)
No. 3, Jalan Teknologi 2/1, Kota Damansara, 47810 Daerah Petaling, Selangor
Tel: +60 3 6145 3888
Age range: 6–17 years
Curriculum: IBDP
Language instr: English

Sri KDU International School (Subang Jaya)
Jalan MP2, Tropicana Metropark, 47500 Subang Jaya, Selangor
Tel: +60 3 5036 8900
Age range: 3–18 years
Curriculum: UK, IGCSE, ALevs
Language instr: English

Sri Kuala Lumpur School
No 1 Jalan SS 15/7A, 47500 Subang Jaya, Selangor
Tel: +60 3 56343491
Age range: 6–17
Curriculum: UK, IGCSE

St Christopher's International Primary School
10 Nunn Road, 10350 George Town, Penang
Tel: +60 4 226 3589
Age range: 3–11
No. of pupils: 580 B291 G289
Curriculum: IPC, UK
Language instr: English

St. Joseph's Institution International School Malaysia (Tropicana PJ Campus)
No. 1, Jalan PJU 3/13, 47410 Petaling Jaya, Selangor
Tel: +60 3 8605 3605
Curriculum: IBDP
Language instr: English

Stella Maris Medan Damansara
7, Lorong Setiabistari 2, Bukit Damansara, 50490 Kuala Lumpur
Tel: +60 3 20830025
Age range: 5–19
No. of pupils: 822
Curriculum: IBDP, IGCSE, ALevs
Language instr: English

Straits International School
No.2, Lilitan Sungai Tiram, 11900 Bayan Lepas, Penang
Tel: +60 4 643 1815
Curriculum: UK, IGCSE

Sunway International School, Bandar Sunway
No. 3, Jalan Universiti, Bandar Sunway, 47500 Selangor
Tel: +60 3 7491 8070
Curriculum: IBDP

Sunway International School, Sunway Iskandar
Jalan Persiaran Medini 3, Sunway Iskandar, 79250 Johor
Tel: +60 7 533 8070
Age range: 4–18
No. of pupils: 244
Curriculum: IBDP, IBMYP, IBCP
Language instr: English

Tanarata International Schools
Kajang-Serdang Road, 43000 Selangor
Tel: +60 3 8737 7366
Curriculum: UK, IGCSE, ALevs

Taylor's College Sri Hartamas
No.1, Jalan Taylor's, 47500 Subang Jaya, Selangor
Tel: +60 3 5629 5000
Curriculum: ALevs
Language instr: English

Taylor's College Subang Jaya
No 1 Jalan SS15/8, 47500 Subang Jaya, Selangor
Tel: +60 3 5636 2641
Age range: 16–19
No. of pupils: 100
Curriculum: ALevs

Taylor's International School, Kuala Lumpur
No 9 Jalan 1/75C, Off Jalan Pria Taman Maluri, 55100 Kuala Lumpur
Tel: +60 3 9200 9898
Age range: 4–16
No. of pupils: 1550
Curriculum: UK, IGCSE

Tenby Schools Ipoh
16 Persiaran Meru Utama, Bandar Meru Raya, 30020 Ipoh, Perak
Tel: +60 5 5252628
Language instr: English
COB EAR

Tenby Schools Miri
Lot 1070C, Block 5, Jalan Desa Senadin, Kuala Baram District, Miri, Sarawak
Tel: +60 8 5491526
Language instr: English
COB

Tenby Schools Penang
No. 2, Lintang Lembah Permai 1, 11200 Tanjung Bungah, Penang
Tel: +60 4 892 7777
Language instr: English
COB

Tenby Schools Setia Eco Gardens
7, Jalan Laman Setia Utama, Taman Setia Utama, 81550 Johor Bahru, Johor
Tel: +60 7 5588812
Age range: 3–16
No. of pupils: 344 B172 G172
Curriculum: IPC, UK, IGCSE
Language instr: English
COB

Tenby Schools Setia Eco Hill
No. 6, Jalan Ecohill 1, Setia Ecohill, 43500 Semenyih, Selangor
Tel: +60 3 8725 5625

Tenby Schools Setia Eco Park
No.1, Jalan Setia Tropika U13/18T, Seksyen U13, 40170 Shah Alam, Selangor
Tel: +60 3 3342 1535
Language instr: English
COB

THE BRITISH INTERNATIONAL SCHOOL OF KUALA LUMPUR
For further details see p. 105
No 1 Changkat Bukit Utama, Bandar Utama, 47800 Petaling Jaya, Selangor
Tel: +60 3 7727 7775
Email: admissions@britishschool.edu.my
Website: www.britishschool.edu.my
Principal: Mike O'Connor
Age range: 2–18 years
No. of pupils: 1200
Fees: RM44,270–RM99,970
Curriculum: UK, IGCSE, ALevs
COB EAR

The International School @ Park City Kuala Lumpur
No 1 Jalan Intisari, Desa Park City, 52200 Kuala Lumpur
Tel: +60 3 6280 8880
Age range: 3–18
No. of pupils: 1100
Curriculum: UK, IGCSE, ALevs
Language instr: English

THE INTERNATIONAL SCHOOL OF KUALA LUMPUR (ISKL)
For further details see p. 107
2, Lorong Kelab Polo Di Raja, Ampang Hilir, 55000 Kuala Lumpur
Tel: +60 3 4813 5000
Email: admissions@iskl.edu.my
Website: www.iskl.edu.my
Head of School: Rami Madani
Age range: 3–18 years
No. of pupils: 1500
Fees: *Day* RM59,000–RM120,400
Curriculum: AP, IBDP, SAT
Language instr: English
CIS EAR

The International School of Penang (Uplands)
Jalan Sungai Satu, Batu Feringgi, 11100 Penang
Tel: +604 8819 777
Age range: 4–18 years
No. of pupils: 650
Curriculum: IBDP, IBPYP, GCSE, IGCSE
Language instr: English

TIPS Kuala Lumpur
TIPS Valley International School, 55 Jalan Thamby Abdullah, 50470 Kuala Lumpur
Tel: +60 3 2859 2522

Tunka Putra School
Jalan Stadium, Petra Jaya, 93050 Kuching, Sarawak
Tel: +60 82 539 800
Curriculum: IPC, National, UK, IGCSE

UCSI International School
1 Persiaran UCSI International School, 71010 Port Dickson, Negeri Sembalan
Tel: +60 6653 6888
Curriculum: IBDP, IBMYP, IBPYP
Language instr: English

Wadi Sofia College
Binjai, Kubang Kerian, 16150 Kota Bharu, Kelantan
Tel: +60 9 764 1724
Age range: 14–19
No. of pupils: 300
Curriculum: UK

Westlake International School
Lot 18662, Jalan Universiti, Taman Bandar Barat, 31900 Kampar, Perak
Tel: +60 5 467 2222
Curriculum: UK, IGCSE, ALevs

Woodlands International School
No.1 Jalan Teku, 96000 Sibu, Sarawak
Tel: +60 84 239761
Curriculum: IPC, UK, IGCSE, ALevs

Zenith International School
126, Jalan S2 B4, Uptown Avenue, 70300 Seremban, Negeri Sembilan
Tel: +60 1300 222 188
Curriculum: IPC, UK, IGCSE

MONGOLIA

American School of Ulaanbaatar
Khan Uul District, Post Office Box 2365, Central Post Office, Ulananbaatar 15160
Tel: +976 11 348888
No. of pupils: 623
Curriculum: AP, USA

British School of Ulaanbaatar
4nd Khoroo, Khan-Uul District, Ulaanbaatar 17043
Tel: +976 11 347788
Age range: 3–19
No. of pupils: 352
Curriculum: UK, IGCSE
Language instr: English
COB

International School of Ulaanbaatar
PO Box 36/10, Khan-Uul District 15th Horoo, 4 Seasons Garden, Ulaanbaatar-36 17032
Tel: +976 70160010
Age range: 3–18
Curriculum: IBDP, IBMYP, IBPYP
Language instr: English
CIS EAR

Shine Ue School
UNESCO St 12, Sukhbaatar District, Ulaanbaatar 14220
Tel: +976 7012 8044
Curriculum: IBDP
Language instr: English

The English School of Mongolia
Bayanzurkh District, 1 Khoroo, Ulaanbaatar 13380
Tel: +976 70 15 40 15
Age range: 3–17
No. of pupils: 800
Curriculum: IBDP, IBPYP
Language instr: English

Ulaanbaatar Elite International School
Seoul Street, 2nd Khoroo, Sukhbaatar District, Ulaanbaatar 14523
Tel: +976 70105010
Age range: 6–17
Curriculum: UK, IGCSE, ALevs
Language instr: English
COB ECIS

MYANMAR

Ayeyarwaddy International School
No.25(B), 52nd St, Between 33rd and 34th St, Chan Aye Tharzan Township, Mandalay
Tel: +959 265459667
Curriculum: USA
EAR

Bahan International Science Academy
No.25, Po Sein Road, Bahan Township, Yangon
Tel: +95 1 548452
Curriculum: IBDP
Language instr: English

Dulwich College Yangon – Pun Hlaing Campus
Pun Hlaing Estate Avenue, Hlaing Tharyar Township, Yangon 11401
Tel: +95 (0)9 409 607 479
Age range: 2–17
No. of pupils: 200
Curriculum: UK
Language instr: English

Dulwich College Yangon – Star City Campus
Kyaik Khauk Pagoda Road, Thanlyin Township, Yangon 11291
Tel: +95 (0)9 409 607 479
Age range: 2–15
No. of pupils: 330
Curriculum: UK
Language instr: English

International School of Myanmar
No W-22, Mya Kan Thar Main Road, Mya Kan Thar Housing, 5th Quarter, Hlaing Township, Yangon
Tel: +95 1 530060
Age range: 2–17
No. of pupils: 1076
Curriculum: AP, SAT, USA
Language instr: English
EAR

Mandalay International Science Academy
No.118 (A,B,D), Block 51 4/3, 58 street, Bet 27 & 28 str), Kan Kauk Qtr, Chan Aye Thar Zan Township, Mandalay
Tel: +95 2 72753

Myanmar International School
No. 20 Pyin Nya Waddy Street, Yankin Township, Yangon
Tel: +95 1 558115
Age range: 5–16
No. of pupils: 329
Curriculum: IGCSE

Myanmar International School Yangon (MISY) Mandalay
No. 23 48th Street, between Manawhari and Aung Yadanar Roads, Chan Mya Thar Si Township, Mandalay
Tel: +95 2 80926
Age range: 3–17 years
Curriculum: UK, IGCSE, ALevs

Myanmar International School Yangon (MISY) Yangon
No. 24 Sae Myaung Street, 11th Quarter, Yankin Township, Yangon
Tel: +95 1 657885
Age range: 3–17 years
No. of pupils: 600
Curriculum: UK, IGCSE, ALevs
Language instr: English

Nay Pyi Taw International Science Academy
No.14, Oattara Thiri Myo Thit, (Near Sinma Living Mall), Nay Pyi Taw
Tel: +95 067 8433134

Royal British International School Yangon
15 Thukhitar Street, Moe Kaung Road, Yankin Township, Yangon
Tel: +95 15 794 92
Curriculum: IPC, UK, IGCSE, ALevs

Shu Khinn Thar International College
No.235, Shu Khinn Thar Myo Pat Road, Thaketa Township, Yangon
Tel: +95 1 450396

SIS Yangon
29 Quarter Thuwunna Villa, Previous(1)/Present (6A) Paw San Hmwe Road, Thingangyun Township, Yangon
Tel: +95 9 426 888 100
Age range: 2–16 years

Thalun International School
108 Hnin Si St, Yangon
Tel: +95 979 389 9809

The British School Yangon
Taw Win Street, Mayangone, Yangon
Tel: +95 9795541805
Curriculum: UK, IGCSE

The International School Yangon
20 Shwe Taungyar Street, Bahan Township, Yangon 11181
Tel: +95 1 512793/94/95
Age range: 4–18
No. of pupils: 740
Curriculum: IBDP, SAT, TOEFL, USA
Language instr: English

Yangon American International School
No. 2A, Yangon-Insein Road, Building (2), No. 9 Ward, Hlaing Township, Yangon
Tel: +95 997 701 2100
Curriculum: IBPYP
Language instr: English, Burmese

Yangon International School
No. 117 Thumingalar Housing, Thingangyun Township, Yangon
Tel: +95 1 578171
Curriculum: IBDP, USA
Language instr: English

NEPAL

Andrew J Wild College
140 Rup Bahadur Gali, Pani Pokhari, Maharajgunj, Kathmandu
Tel: +977-014428197, 9801100501
Curriculum: UK, ALevs

Cosmos International College
Palikhe Chowk, Pokhara
Tel: +977 61 541324
Curriculum: UK, GCSE, ALevs

Delhi Public School – BPKIHS
Ghopa, Dharan, Sunsari 56700
Tel: +977 25 523 308
Age range: 5–18
No. of pupils: 300

Gandaki Higher Secondary Boarding School
PO Box 9, Lamachaur, Pokhara
Tel: +977 61 440 414
No. of pupils: 1072
Curriculum: ALevs

Genius School Lalitpur
Ringroad, Mahalaxmisthan, Lalitpur
Tel: +977 1 5170746
Curriculum: IBPYP
Language instr: English

International French School of Kathmandu
Po Box 452, Lazimpat, Kathmandu
Tel: +977 1 400 16 73
Curriculum: National

Kathmandu International Study Centre
PO Box 2714, Jawalakhel, Kathmandu
Tel: +977 1 5538720
Age range: 4–18
No. of pupils: 170 *B*101 *G*84
Curriculum: National, UK, IGCSE, ALevs
Language instr: English

Lincoln School
PO Box 2673, Rabi Bhawan, Kathmandu
Tel: +977 14 270482
Age range: 3–19
No. of pupils: 340 *B*175 *G*165
Curriculum: AP, SAT, USA
Language instr: English

Lumbini International College
Mahalakshmisthan, Lagankhel, G.P.O. Box No: 8975, Lalitpur EPC 5666
Tel: +977 552 7054
Age range: 16–19
No. of pupils: 200
Curriculum: ALevs

Malpi International College (MIC)
GPO Box No 8975, EPC 4073, Subarna Shamsher Marg, Baluwatar
Tel: +977 1 444 2066
Curriculum: National, UK, ALevs

Modern Indian School
GPO Box No 1497, Chobar
Tel: +977 1 433 0163
Age range: 5–18
No. of pupils: 2000

Novel Academy
PO Box 38, New Road, Pokhara
Tel: +977 61 535629
Curriculum: UK, ALevs

Orient College
Narayan Gopal Chowk, Maharajgunj, Kathmandu
Tel: +977 1 4017813
Curriculum: ALevs

Premier International School
Khumaltar Height, Satdobato, Lalitpur
Tel: +977 1 552 8032
Age range: 3–12
No. of pupils: 314
Curriculum: IBDP, IBMYP, IBPYP
Language instr: English, Nepali

Rato Bangala School
PO Box 202, PatanDhoka, Lalitpur
Tel: +977 1 5534318
Curriculum: UK, ALevs

Swostishree Gurukul
Kathmandu 44600
Tel: +977 1 4890316
Curriculum: IBPYP
Language instr: English, Nepali

The British School Kathmandu
PO Box 566, Jhamsikhel, Lalitpur, Kathmandu
Tel: +977 1 5521794
Age range: 3–18
No. of pupils: 519 *B*254 *G*265 *VIth*40
Curriculum: UK, IGCSE, ALevs
Language instr: English

Ullens School
Khumaltar-5, Lalipur, Post Box Number 8975, EPC 1477, Kathmandu
Tel: +977 1 5230824
Curriculum: IBDP
Language instr: English

OMAN

ABA – An IB World School
PO Box 372, Medinat Al Sultan Qaboos, Post Code 115, Muscat 115
Tel: +968 24955800
Age range: 3–18
No. of pupils: 1020 *B*540 *G*480 *VIth*140
Curriculum: IBDP, IBMYP, IBPYP, SAT
Language instr: English

Al Batinah International School
PO Box 193, Postal Code 321, Sohar
Tel: +968 26850001
Curriculum: IBDP, IBMYP, IBPYP

Al Injaz Private School
P.O. Box 2111, P.C. 133, Al Khuwair, Muscat
Tel: +968 2458 5299
Age range: 5–18
Curriculum: IGCSE

Al Sahwa Schools
House No: 592, Way No: 3052, Shatti Al Qurum, Muscat
Tel: + 968 2460 7620 / 7621 / 2469 3887
Age range: 3 –17
No. of pupils: 1191 *B*595 *G*620
Curriculum: IBMYP, IBPYP, National, UK, IGCSE
Language instr: English, Arabic

Al Shomoukh International School
Sheikh Salim Al Hashimy Al Seeb Al Khoud Street Building, Number 381, Muscat
Tel: +96 89 29 62 715
Language instr: English

Alruwad International School
Al Salam Street, Opposite Al Khoudh Police Station, Seeb
Tel: +968 2455 4711
Curriculum: IBDP, IBMYP, IBPYP
Language instr: English, Arabic

American British Academy
PO Box 372, PC 115, Madinat Qaboos, Muscat
Tel: +968 24955800
Curriculum: IBDP, IBMYP

Assafwah Private Schools
PO Box 27, Al Khoudh, Muscat 132
Tel: +968 24546929
Curriculum: UK, IGCSE, ALevs

Azzan Bin Qais International School – Bawsher
PO Box 32, Bareeq Al Shatti Mall, Muscat 103
Tel: +968 24210200
Age range: 3–18 years
No. of pupils: 1300
Curriculum: IGCSE, ALevs

Bangladesh School Muscat
Building No 305, Way No 3605, 18 November Street, Al Ghubrah (North)
Tel: +968 2449 7127
Age range: 5–18
No. of pupils: 2200

British School Salalah
PO Box 71, A'Daharez, Salalah 214
Tel: +968 2323 5242
Age range: 4–12
No. of pupils: 40
Curriculum: UK

Hay Al Sharooq International School
PO Box 888, Sur 411
Tel: +968 252 40 100
Age range: 3–12
Curriculum: IPC, UK

Hay Al Sharooq International School
Oman PO BOX 888, PC 411 Sur
Tel: +968 252 40 100
Curriculum: National, UK

Indian School – Buraimi
PO Box 388, Buraimi 512
Tel: +968 2564 3220
Age range: 5–18
No. of pupils: 300

Indian School – Rustaq
PO Box 475, Rustaq 318
Tel: +968 2687 6833
Age range: 5–18
No. of pupils: 200

Indian School – Thumrait
PO Box 105, Thumrait 222
Tel: +968 924 646 70
Age range: 5–18
No. of pupils: 100

Indian School Muscat
PO Box 2470, Ruwi PC 112
Tel: 00968 24702567
Age range: 4–18
No. of pupils: 2500

Knowledge Gate International School
Way 2947, Al Marafah Street, Al Hail, Musca
Tel: +968 24 07 35 00
Age range: 3–18 years
Curriculum: GCSE, ALevs

Madinat Al Sultan Qaboos Private School
PO Box 412, Muscat 116
Tel: +968 246699739
Age range: 4–19

Muscat International School
PO Box 1031, Postal Code 112, Ruwi
Tel: +968 24565550
Age range: 3–18
No. of pupils: 1086 *B637 G449*
Curriculum: National, SAT, TOEFL, UK, IGCSE, ALevs
Language instr: English

MySchool Oman
Al Hail South, Al Seeb, Al Huda Street, Way # 2933, Building # 3344, Muscat
Tel: +968 24555171
Age range: 3–17
No. of pupils: 315
Curriculum: IBMYP, IBPYP
Language instr: English, Arabic

OURPLANET International School Muscat
Al-Inshirah Street, Building No. 205, Plot No. 95, Block No. 221, Muscat, 111
Tel: +968 2200 5642
Curriculum: IBPYP

Pakistan School Muscat
PO Box 987, Ruwi, Muscat 112
Tel: +968 24 702 489

PDO School
Kauther St, PO Box 81 Muscat, Postal Code 100
Tel: +968 246 77279
Curriculum: UK

Royal Flight School
PO Box 301, Muscat 111
Tel: +968 24516444
Age range: 3–11
No. of pupils: 330
Curriculum: UK

The American International School of Muscat (TAISM)
PO Box 584, Azaiba Postal Code 130
Tel: +968 2459 5180
Age range: 3–19
No. of pupils: 800
Curriculum: AP, USA

The British School – Muscat
PO Box 1907 Ruwi, Postal Code 112
Tel: +96 82 4600 842
Age range: 3–18
No. of pupils: 900 *B450 G450*
Curriculum: UK, ALevs
Language instr: English

The Indian School
PO Box 1887, CPO Seeb, Postal Code 111, Muscat 111
Tel: +968 24491587
Age range: 3–18
No. of pupils: 3125 *B1596 G1529*
Curriculum: TOEFL
Language instr: English

The International School of Choueifat – Muscat
Postal Code 111 C.P.O., Muscat
Tel: +968 2453 4000

The Sri Lankan School Muskat
PO Box 2433, Ruwi 112
Tel: +968 24811005
Age range: 3–18
No. of pupils: 580
Curriculum: UK

The Sultan's School
PO Box 665, Seeb 121
Tel: +968 24536 777
Age range: 4–18
No. of pupils: 1119
Curriculum: IBDP, IGCSE
Language instr: Arabic, English

PAKISTAN

Aitchison College
The Mall, Lahore 54000
Tel: +92 42 6363063
Age range: *B*4–18
Curriculum: ALevs

Angels International College
Faisal Town, Near Faisal Valley, West Canal Road, Faisalabad, Punjab 38000
Tel: +92 41 8850012
Curriculum: IBDP, IBMYP, IBPYP
Language instr: English

Beaconhouse College Campus Gulberg
3-C, Zafar Ali Road, Lahore 54000
Tel: +92 42 3588 6239
Curriculum: IBDP
Language instr: English

Beaconhouse Newlands Islamabad
Hill View Road, Mohra Noor, Islamabad 44000
Tel: +92 51 261 3935/6/7
Curriculum: IBDP, IBPYP
Language instr: English

Beaconhouse Newlands Lahore
632/1 Street 10, Phase VI DHA, Lahore 54000
Tel: +92 (42) 111 111 020
Curriculum: IBPYP
Language instr: English

Beaconhouse Newlands Multan
4A, Officers Colony, Khanewal Road, Multan, Punjab 60000
Tel: +92 61 111 111 020
Curriculum: IBPYP
Language instr: English, Urdu

Beaconhouse School System, Clifton Campus
Frere Town, 2/3 McNeil Road, Clifton, Karachi 75600
Tel: +92 21 35659190
Curriculum: IBPYP
Language instr: English

Beaconhouse School System, Defence Campus
207 A, Saba Avenue, Phase VIII, DHA, Karachi, Sindh 75500
Tel: +92 2135847083 84
Curriculum: IBDP
Language instr: English

Beaconhouse School System, Margalla Campus
Pitras Bukhari Rd, H-8/4, Islamabad 44000
Tel: +92 3345501113
Curriculum: IBDP
Language instr: English

Beaconhouse School System, PECHS Campus
35P/1, Block 6 Extension, PECHS, Karachi 75100
Tel: +92 21 34380045
Curriculum: IBDP
Language instr: English

Bloomfield Hall Schools
Head Office, 13 – A, Block S., Gulberg II,, Lahore
Tel: +92 42 35764687
Curriculum: UK, ALevs

British Overseas School
AL 7/8, 14th/15th Lane, Off Khayaban-e-Hilal, DHA Phase VII, Karachi
Tel: +922 13 584 2307
Age range: 3–18

EMS High School
House # 33, Street #60, F 11/4, Islamabad 44000
Tel: +92 51 346 5286344
Curriculum: UK, IGCSE

Foundation Public School
A Level Campus, 42B, Block 6, PECHS, Dr Mahmood Hussain Road, Karachi
Tel: +92 3452 5413
Age range: 16–18
Curriculum: UK, ALevs

Foundation Public School – O Level Defence Campus
PN Shifa Road, Behind Tooba Masjid,, Defence Phase II, Karachi
Tel: +92 3539 0634
Age range: 14–16
No. of pupils: 550

Froebel's International School
Street 13, Sector F 7/2, Islamabad 44000
Tel: +92 51 265 2164
Curriculum: UK, IGCSE, ALevs

Happy Home School- O Level Maryam Faruqi Campus
5/3 Modern Housing Society, Shaheed-e-Millat Road, Karachi
Tel: +92 4557603
Age range: 2.5–18
Curriculum: National, UK, ALevs

Headstart School, Kuri Campus
Kuri Road, Off Park Rd, Near CDA/ Park Enclave, Islamabad 44000
Tel: +92 51 8435 473
Age range: 2–19 years
No. of pupils: 2500
Curriculum: IBDP, IBMYP, IBPYP, IGCSE, ALevs
Language instr: English

Ilmesters Academy
B-31, PECHS, Block-6, Near Progressive Center, Karachi 75400
Tel: +92 21 34524423
Age range: 2.5–19 years
No. of pupils: 250
Curriculum: IBDP, IBMYP, IBPYP
Language instr: English, Urdu

International School of Islamabad
Sector H-9/1, Johar Road, P.O. Box 1124, Islamabad 44000
Tel: +92 51 443 4950
Age range: 2–19 years
No. of pupils: 270
Curriculum: IBDP, IBPYP, SAT, USA
Language instr: English

Karachi American School
Amir Khusro Road, Karachi 75350
Tel: +92 21 3453 9096
Age range: 3–18
No. of pupils: 336 B189 G147
Curriculum: USA
Language instr: English

Kingston College
1 Canal Road, Khaira, Lahore, Punjab
Tel: +92 42 3652 6047
Curriculum: IBPYP
Language instr: English

LACAS School – Gujranwala Campus
Their Sansi, Near Judicial Colony, Canal Bank Road, Gurjanwala
Tel: +92 55 4001 591
Age range: 5–18
No. of pupils: 300

Lahore American School
15 Upper Mall Canal Bank, Lahore 54000
Tel: +92 42 576 2406
Age range: 4–18
No. of pupils: 410 B310 G100

Lahore Grammar School Defence (Phase 1)
136 – E, Phase 1 Defence Housing Authority (DHA), Lahore Cantt, Punjab, Lahore 54810
Tel: +92 (42) 358 94306
Curriculum: IBPYP
Language instr: English

Lahore Grammar School Defence (Phase V)
#483/4, Block G, Education City, Phase V, Defence Housing Authority (DHA), Lahore Cantt, Lahore, Punjab 54810
Tel: +92 42 37176005/6/7
Curriculum: IBPYP
Language instr: English

Lahore Grammar School International
32/3, Sector J, DHA Phase VIII, Lahore 54972
Tel: +92 42 37175751
Curriculum: IBDP, IBMYP, IBPYP
Language instr: English

Lahore Grammar School Islamabad
Plot # 86, Faiz Ahmad Faiz Road, Sector H-8/1, Islamabad 44000
Tel: +92 51 4922092
Curriculum: IBPYP
Language instr: English

Lawrence College
Ghora Gali, Murree
Tel: +92 51 3751004
Curriculum: UK

Learning Alliance
32/1 J block, DHA Phase VIII, Lahore 54000
Tel: +92 42 111 66 66 33
Curriculum: IBDP, IBMYP, IBPYP, ALevs
Language instr: English

Links School
D-101/1, Block 4, Clifton, Karachi
Tel: +92 215874322
Age range: 3–11
COB

Pak Turk International School – Islamabad Girls Campus
Plot # 87 and 88, Sector H-8/1, Islamabad 44000
Tel: +92 51 4442713

Roots International Schools Islamabad Pakistan
Campus # 66, Street 7, Wellington Campus H-8/4, Islamabad
Tel: +92 51 8439001-7
Curriculum: IBDP, SAT, IGCSE, ALevs
Language instr: English

Roots IVY International School – Chaklala Campus
Walayat Homes, Chakalala Scheme 3, Rawalpindi
Tel: +92 51 578 8380
Curriculum: IBPYP
Language instr: English

Roots Ivy International School – DHA Phase V Lahore
Plot #550/1, Sector G, DHA, Phase V (6,192.65 km), Lahore 54000
Tel: +92 302 6274309
Curriculum: IBPYP
Language instr: English, Urdu

Roots IVY International School – Faisalabad Campus
Opposite Guttwala Park, Faisalabad
Tel: +92 321 8912555
Curriculum: IBPYP
Language instr: English

Roots IVY International School – Riverview Campus
Main GT Road, Rawalpindi
Tel: +92 (0)51 4917302/3
Language instr: English

Roots Millennium Schools, Flagship Campus
No. 308, Street No. 3, Sector I-9/3, Islamabad 44000
Tel: +92 51 8439981-6
Language instr: English

Roots Millennium Schools, One World Campus
Head Office, No.80, Street 1, Sector E-11/4, Islamabad 44000
Tel: +92 51 111 111 193
Curriculum: IBMYP
Language instr: English

Sadiq Public School
Ahmedpur Road, Bahawalpur 63100
Tel: +92 621 2877692
No. of pupils: 2045
Curriculum: UK, ALevs

Schole International Academy
273/1/1A, Adjacent Ilma University, Near Suzuki Showroom, Korangi Creek, Karachi, Sindh
Tel: +92 (21) 350 93330
Curriculum: IBPYP
Language instr: English, Urdu

Sheikh Zayed International Academy
Street 8, Sector H-8/4, Islamabad
Tel: +92 51 4939298
Age range: 2–18 years
Curriculum: IBDP, IBMYP, IBPYP, UK, GCSE, IGCSE, ALevs
Language instr: English

SICAS DHA Phase VI
310/2F DHA, Phase 6, Lahore, Punjab 54770
Tel: +92 4237338361-3
Curriculum: IBPYP
Language instr: English

Southshore School for A Level Studies
SL-10, 14th Street off Khayaban-e-Shaheen, D.H.A Phase VIII
Tel: +92 21 3525 0071

Springfield Public School & College
15-C Main Harley Street, Rawalpindi, Punjab 46000
Tel: +92 51 111 777 464
Age range: 11–19

St Mary's Academy
Tulsa Road, Lalazar, Rawalpindi 46000
Tel: +92 51 5178321
Curriculum: UK, GCSE

The Avicenna School – Tipu Sultan Road (Girls Campus)
17 Al-Hamra CHS, Block 7/8, Main Tipu Sultan Road, Karachi
Tel: +92 34537414
Curriculum: ALevs

The Avicenna School – Tipu Sultan Road Campus (Boys and Girls)
36 Modern Housing Society, Main Tipu Sultan Road, Karachi
Tel: +92 21 3453 3760
Age range: 16–19
Curriculum: ALevs

The City School – A Level Campus
30-E, Industrial Area, Gurumangat Road, Gulberg-III, Lahore
Tel: +92 42 35773321
Age range: 16–19
Curriculum: ALevs

The City School, Capital Campus Islamabad
Pitras Bokhari Road, Sector H-8/1, Islamabad
Tel: +92 051 4939280
Age range: 5–19
Curriculum: IGCSE
Language instr: English

The City School, Kohat Campus
Near OTS Bypass, Bowana Road, Kohat
Tel: +92 922 861105 7
Age range: 6–16
No. of pupils: 100

The Democratic School
Masjid Ismail Road, Sitara Sapna City, Faisalabad, Punjab 38900
Tel: +92 33 030 00275
Curriculum: IBPYP
Language instr: English, Urdu

The Educational World (FB Area Senior Chapter)
D 16, Block 4, FB Area, Karachi 75950
Tel: +92 3636 2879
Age range: 8–16
No. of pupils: 200
Curriculum: UK

The International School (TIS)
Executive, 51-C Old Clifton, Near Mohatta Palace, Karachi 75600
Tel: +92 21 35835805-6
Age range: 3–18
No. of pupils: 250 *B*130 *G*120 *VIth*50
Curriculum: IBDP, IBMYP, IBPYP, UK, IGCSE
Language instr: English

The International School of Choueifat – Lahore
662-G/1, Abdul Haque Road, Johar Town, Lahore 54700
Tel: +92 423 530 0028/9
Age range: 3–19
No. of pupils: 1459
Curriculum: AP, USA

The Learning Tree
F-8, Khayaban-e-Saadi, Block 5, Clifton, Karachi, Sindh 75600
Tel: +92 213 587 0001
Curriculum: IBPYP
Language instr: English

The Lyceum School
78 Clifton, Karachi 75600
Tel: +92 213 582 1741
Curriculum: ALevs
Language instr: English
(RS)

TNS Beaconhouse Defence
483/3 Sector G, Phase 5, DHA, Lahore, Punjab
Tel: +92 42 371 762 41 – 43
Age range: 3–19 years
Curriculum: IBDP, IBMYP, IGCSE
Language instr: English

TNS Beaconhouse Gulberg
1-H Jail Road, Gulberg II, Lahore, Punjab
Tel: +92 42 111 867 867
Curriculum: IBMYP
Language instr: English, Urdu

PALESTINE

Al Mustaqbal Schools
P.O. Box 2422, Al Tireh, Ramallah
Tel: +970 02 296 1583
Age range: 2 –18
No. of pupils: 630 *B*384 *G*246
Curriculum: IGCSE

Ramallah Friends School (Lower School)
Ramallah
Tel: +970 2 295 6240
Curriculum: IBPYP
Language instr: English

Ramallah Friends School (Upper School)
P.O Box 66, Ramallah
Tel: +970 2 295 2286
Age range: 4–18
No. of pupils: 1040
Curriculum: IBDP, IBMYP
Language instr: English

The American International School in Gaza
Nazareth Street, Rinal, Gaza
Tel: +972 8 288 0441
Age range: 2–18 years
No. of pupils: 230
Curriculum: USA

PHILIPPINES

Assumption College San Lorenzo
San Lorenzo Drive, San Lorenzo Village, 1223 Makati City, Metro Manila
Tel: +63 2 8817 0757
Curriculum: IBDP
Language instr: English, Filipino

Australian International School, Manila
8428 Dr. A. Santos Avenue (Sucat Road), Brgy. BF Homes 1, 1720 Paranaque City, Metro Manila
Tel: +63 91 7525 8109
Age range: 3–16
No. of pupils: 147 *B*75 *G*72
Language instr: English

Bannister Academy
Circulo Verde, Calle Industria, Bagumbayan, Quezon City, Metro Manila
Tel: +63 0998 575 7448
Curriculum: IBDP
Language instr: English, Pilipino

Benedictine International School
Capitol Hills Drive, Matandang Balara, Quezon City, Metro Manila
Tel: +63 917 193 2363
Age range: 4–16
Language instr: English

Brent International School Baguio
Brent Road, 2600 Baguio City, Cordillera
Tel: +63 74 442 4050
Curriculum: IBDP
Language instr: English

Brent International School Manila
Brentville Subdivision, Mamplasan, 4024 Biñan, Calabarzon
Tel: +63 2 8779 5140
Curriculum: IBDP
Language instr: English

Brent International School Subic
Building 6601 Binictican Drive, Subic Bay Freeport Zone, Zambales, 2222 Subic, Central Luzon
Tel: +63 47 252 6871/72
Curriculum: IBDP
Language instr: English

Brentwood College of Asia International School
Naga City, Bicol
Tel: +63 54 472 6345
Language instr: English
(ISA)

Britesparks International School
#15 Metropoli Drive, C5-Bagumbayan, 1110 Quezon City, Metro Manila
Tel: +63 917 324 1706
Age range: 2–15

British School Manila
36th Street, University Park, Bonifacio Global City, 1634 Taguig City, Metro Manila
Tel: +63 2 8860 4800
Age range: 3–18 years
Curriculum: IBDP, UK
Language instr: English

Cebu International School
Pit-os, 6000 Cebu City, Central Visayas
Tel: +63 32 342 7788
Age range: 3–18 years
Curriculum: IBDP, IBMYP, IBPYP
Language instr: English

Chiang Kai Shek College
1274 Padre Algue Street, Tondo, 1012 Manila, Metro Manila
Tel: +63 2 252 6161
Curriculum: IBDP
Language instr: English, Pilipino

Chinese International School Manila
Upper McKinley Road, McKinley Hill, Fort Bonifacio, 1634 Taguig City, Metro Manila
Tel: +63 2 8743 8134
Curriculum: IBDP
Language instr: English

CIE British School
168 President Magsaysay Street, Kasambagan, 6000 Cebu City, Central Visayas
Tel: +63 917 322 5444

Domuschola International School
#13 J. Cruz Street, Ugong, 1609 Pasig City, Metro Manila
Tel: +63 2 8635 2002
Curriculum: IBDP, IBPYP
Language instr: English, Filipino

Eton International School
CCP Complex, Roxas Boulevard, Pasay, Metro Manila
Tel: +63 917 631 4547
Language instr: English

Faith Academy
Penny Lane Street, Valley Golf Subdivision, San Juan, 1900 Cainta, Calabarzon
Tel: +63 2 8651 7100
Age range: 3–18 years

Fountain International School
#1 Goverment Center Cor
Col. Bonny Serrano, 1500
San Juan, Metro Manila
Tel: +63 2 8723 7307
Age range: 4–18 years
Curriculum: IGCSE, ALevs
Language instr: English

German European School Manila
75 Swaziland Street, Better Living
Subdivision, 1711 Paranaque
City, Metro Manila
Tel: +63 2 8776 1000
Age range: 3–18 years
Curriculum: IBDP, IBPYP, IBCP
Language instr: English

Hope Christian High School
1242 Benavidez Street, Santa
Cruz, 1003 Manila, Metro Manila
Tel: +63 2 5310 8071
Curriculum: IBPYP
Language instr: English, Chinese

Immaculate Conception Academy
10 Grant Street, Greenhills,
San Juan, Metro Manila
Tel: +63 2 8723 7041
Curriculum: IBDP
Language instr: English, Tagalog

International British Academy
KM25 General Aguinaldo
Highway, Anabu 2D, 4103
Imus City, Calabarzon
Tel: +63 46 471 5922
Age range: 3–17 years
Curriculum: UK, IGCSE
Language instr: English

International School Manila
University Parkway, Fort
Bonifacio Global City, 1634
Taguig City, Metro Manila
Tel: +63 2 8840 8400
Age range: 3–18 years
Curriculum: IBDP
Language instr: English

Keys School Manila
951 Luna Mencias Street, corner
Araullo Street, Addition Hills, 1550
Mandaluyong City, Metro Manila
Tel: +63 2 8727 9357
Age range: 2–18 years
Curriculum: IBDP
Language instr: English

Kids International Learning Academy
#4 Cobra Street Village East,
1900 Cainta, Calabarzon
Tel: +63 2 8655 9841
Language instr: English

Learning Links Academy
Alcalde Street, Tibig, Silang,
4118 Cavite, Calabarzon
Tel: +63 917 305 8574
Language instr: English

MIT International School
Alabang-Zapote Road, corner Don
Manolo Boulevard, Alabang, 1770
Muntinlupa City, Metro Manila
Tel: +63 2 8809 1616
Language instr: English

Mother Goose Lipa
City Park Avenue, corner of
Gladiola Street, City Park Subd.,
Sabang, 4217 Lipa City, Calabarzon
Tel: +63 43 702 9630
Curriculum: IBPYP
Language instr: English, Pilipino

Multiple Intelligence International School
4 Escaler Street, Loyola Heights,
1108 Quezon City, Metro Manila
Tel: +63 920 927 3664
Age range: 3–18 years

Noblesse International School
Circumferential Road, Friendship
Highway, Cutcut, Santo Domingo,
2009 Angeles City, Central Luzon
Tel: +63 45 459 9000
Age range: 3–18 years
Curriculum: IBDP, IBPYP
Language instr: English

NORD ANGLIA INTERNATIONAL SCHOOL MANILA
For further details see p. 88
Bradco Avenue, Aseana,
Paranaque City, Metro
Manila 1701
Tel: +63 2 7987 7878
Email: admissions@naismanila.edu.ph
Website: naismanila.edu.ph
Head of School: Chris Pooley
Age range: 2–18 years
No. of pupils: 200
Fees: Day Php427,919–Php1,475,588
Curriculum: UK, IGCSE, ALevs
Language instr: English

ONE International School Philippines
Atmosphere Resorts & Spa, 6217
Maayong Tubig, Central Visayas
Tel: +63 917 312 0517
Curriculum: UK

Reedley International School
J. Cruz Street, Ugong, 1604
Pasig City, Metro Manila
Tel: +63 917 507 9306
Language instr: English

Saint Jude Catholic School
327 Ycaza Street, San Miguel,
1005 Manila, Metro Manila
Tel: +63 2 8735 6386
Curriculum: IBDP
Language instr: English

Singapore School Cebu
Zuellig Avenue, North Reclamation
Area, Mandaue City, 6014
Cebu, Central Visayas
Tel: +63 32 236 5772
Curriculum: IBDP
Language instr: Chinese, English

Singapore School Manila
Lots 1 & 40, Block 2 East Street,
East District, Asena City,
Paranaque City, Metro Manila
Tel: +63 2 7500 4672
Curriculum: IBDP
Language instr: English

Southville International School & Colleges (SISC)
1281 Luxembourg Street,
corner Tropical Avenue, B.F.
Homes International, 1740 Las
Pinas City, Metro Manila
Tel: +63 2 8825 6374
Age range: 3–18 years
Curriculum: IBDP
Language instr: English

Stonyhurst Southville International School – Batangas City Campus
Gov. Antonio Carpio Road, Gulod
Itaas, Batangas City, Calabarzon
Tel: +63 43 723 3595

Stonyhurst Southville International School – Malarayat Campus
Mahogany Avenue, Dagatan,
4217 Lipa City, Calabarzon
Tel: +63 43 757 4878

The Beacon Academy
Cecilia Araneta Parkway,
4024 Binan, Calabarzon
Tel: +63 2 425 1326
Curriculum: IBDP, IBMYP
Language instr: English

The Beacon School
PCPD Building, 2332 Chino Roces
Avenue Extension, Taguig City 1630
Tel: +632 840 5040 loc 105
Age range: 5–14
No. of pupils: 269 B144 G125
Curriculum: IBMYP, IBPYP
Language instr: English

Victory Christian International School
339 Robinson Circle, Capt.
Henry Javier Drive, Oranbo,
1600 Pasig City, Metro Manila
Tel: +63 2 8671 8505
Curriculum: IBDP
Language instr: English

Westfields International School
21-2 Friendship Highway, Cutcut,
2009 Angeles City, Central Luzon
Tel: +63 917 510 0002
Age range: 2–18 years
Language instr: English

Xavier School
64 Xavier Street, Greenhills West,
1500 San Juan, Metro Manila
Tel: +63 2 8723 0481
Age range: B3–18 years
Curriculum: IBDP
Language instr: English

QATAR

ACS Doha International School
Building No. 10, Street No. 161, Area
number/Zone 70, Al Kheesa, Doha
Tel: +974 4474 9000
Age range: 3–18 years
Curriculum: IBDP, IBMYP, IBPYP, IBCP

Al Bayan Educational Complex for Girls
PO Box 23533, Doha
Tel: +974 44591791
Age range: G3–18
Language instr: English

Al Hekma International School
PO Box 11157, Dafna Doha
Tel: +974 4493 5522
Age range: 3–11

Al Jazeera Academy
PO Box 22250, Mesaimeer, Doha
Tel: +974 4469 3777
Age range: 3–19
No. of pupils: 1340
Curriculum: UK
Language instr: English

Al Khor International School
Al Khor Community, PO
Box 22166, Doha
Tel: +974 4473 4666
Age range: 4–18
No. of pupils: 1650 B950 G700
Curriculum: SAT, UK
Language instr: English

Alpha Cambridge School
P.O. Box 8055, Street 300 Zone
91, Al Mashaf, Al Wukhair
Tel: +974 4463 7494

American School of Doha
PO Box 22090, Doha
Tel: +974 4459 1500
Age range: 4–18
No. of pupils: 2250 B1275 G1275
Curriculum: ACT, AP, IBDP, SAT, USA
Language instr: English

Arab International Academy
Al Sadd Area, Sports Roundabout, Doha 15810
Tel: +974 40414999
Curriculum: IBDP, IBMYP, IBPYP
Language instr: Arabic, English

Awfaz Global School
PO Box 6303, Doha
Tel: 974 44814331
Age range: 2–12
No. of pupils: 405

AWSAJ Academy
PO Box 6639, Doha
Tel: +974 4454 2111
Age range: 7–16
No. of pupils: 181
Curriculum: USA
CIS

Beta Cambridge School
P.O. Box 300, Al Wakra
Tel: +974 4463 7494

Cambridge International School for Girls
PO Box 23018, Al Nuaija East, Doha
Tel: +974 446 59106
Age range: 4–18
No. of pupils: 300
Curriculum: UK

Cardiff International School
No 40 University Road, Near Qatar University, Dafna, Doha
Tel: +974 4411 4683
Age range: 5–9
No. of pupils: 100
Curriculum: UK

Compass International School Doha, Gharaffa
P.O. Box 23479, Plot 13, Al Waab Al Abareeq Street, Gharaffa Area No. 31, Doha
Tel: +974 4034 9666
Curriculum: IBDP, UK, IGCSE
COB

Compass International School Doha, Madinat Khalifa
P.O. Box 22463, Al Baihaqi Street, Building 34, Zone 32, Street 926, Madinat Khalifa
Tel: +974 4034 9888
Age range: 3–19
No. of pupils: 1600
Curriculum: IBDP, IPC, UK, IGCSE
Language instr: English, French
COB ECIS

Compass International School Doha, Rayyan
Wadi Al Ghusm Street, Al Rayyan, Doha
Tel: +974 4034 9777
Curriculum: IBDP, UK
COB

Deutsche Internationale Schule Doha
Ibn Seena School Street No. 30, Doha
Tel: +974 4451 6836
Age range: 3–18
No. of pupils: 320
Curriculum: IBDP
Language instr: English, German

Doha British School
PO Box 6142, Doha
Tel: +974 4019 8000
Age range: 3–18
No. of pupils: 2100
Curriculum: IBDP, National, SAT, UK, IGCSE
Language instr: English
CIS

Doha College
PO Box 7506, Doha
Tel: +974 4407 6777
Age range: 3–18
No. of pupils: 1890 *B*937 *G*953
Curriculum: UK
Language instr: English
CIS COB

Doha English Speaking School
PO Box 7660, Doha
Tel: +974 4459 2750
Age range: 3–11
No. of pupils: 708 *B*364 *G*344
Curriculum: UK
Language instr: English
COB

Doha Modern Indian School
P.O. Box 47391, Abu Hamour, Doha
Tel: +974 4458 3121

Dukhan English Speaking School
PO Box 100,001, Dukhan
Tel: +974 4471 6231/147
Age range: 4–16
No. of pupils: 602 *B*296 *G*306
Curriculum: SAT, UK

Etqan Global Academy
Zone 70, Street 120, Property #345, Umsuwiya street, Al Khisa
Tel: +974 4435 0475
Curriculum: IBPYP
Language instr: English, Arabic

GEMS American Academy Qatar (GAAQ)
Mian Street, Al Wukair, Al Wakra
Tel: +974 4 032 9000
Age range: 3–18 years
Curriculum: USA
Language instr: English

GEMS Wellington School (WSQ)
Mian Street, Al Wukair, Al Wakra
Tel: +974 4041 7445
Age range: 3–18 years
Curriculum: UK
Language instr: English

Global Academy International
PO Box 23161, Doha
Tel: 00 974 4465 5001
Age range: 4–18
No. of pupils: 1460

Hayat Universal School (HUBS)
PO Box: 6124, Doha
Tel: +974 4468 7171
Curriculum: UK
CIS

International School of London (ISL) Qatar
PO Box 18511, North Duhail, Doha
Tel: +974 4433 8600
Age range: 3–18 years
No. of pupils: 1161
Curriculum: IBDP, IBMYP, IBPYP, USA
Language instr: English
ECIS

Iqra English Girls School
PO Box 22786, Doha
Tel: +974 4451 0053
Age range: 5–11
No. of pupils: 100
Curriculum: UK

King's College, Doha
Al Thumama, Doha
Tel: +974 3145 8794/5/6

Loydence Academy
PO Box 4524, Doha
Tel: 00974 44918111
Age range: 4–11
Curriculum: UK

Loyola International School
Al Andalus Street, Al Nasr, Doha
Tel: 00974 44311390
Age range: 4–11

Lycée Bonaparte
Al Intisar Street, PO Box 6110, Doha
Tel: +974 44 96 03 00
Age range: 4–18
Curriculum: National
Language instr: French

Lycee Franco-Qatarien Voltaire
PO Box 12634, Campus West Bay, Zone 66 Al Dafna (Legtaifeya) rue no 973, Doha
Tel: +974 40354040
Curriculum: IBDP

Middle East International School
PO Box 269, Doha
Tel: +974 4444 9892
Age range: 4–18
No. of pupils: 500
Curriculum: USA

Newton British Academy AlDafna
Al Dafna, Doha
Tel: +974 441 422 94
Age range: 3–12
No. of pupils: 540
Curriculum: UK, IGCSE
Language instr: English

Newton British Academy Barwa City
Barwa City, Doha
Tel: +974 400 615 01
Age range: 2–14
No. of pupils: 300

Newton British School Al Waab
Al Waab, Doha
Tel: +974 444 724 27
Age range: 3–12 years
No. of pupils: 700
Curriculum: UK
Language instr: English

Newton International School
D-Ring Road, Doha
Tel: +974 446 662 46
Age range: 3–13
Curriculum: UK

Newton International School Lagoon
PO Box 8449, Doha
Tel: +974 441 222 54
Age range: 4–19
Curriculum: IGCSE
Language instr: English

Newton International School West Bay, Doha
West Bay, Doha
Tel: +974 449 355 07
Age range: 3–11
Curriculum: UK

Noor Al Khaleej International School
PO Box 24550, Doha
Tel: +974 4 466 6110
Age range: 3–19
Curriculum: UK, IGCSE

Nord Anglia International School, Al Khor
Building 3, Taimiyah Street, Zone 74, Al Khor
Tel: +974 44379600

Olive International School – Doha
Nuaija, Doha
Tel: +974 4417 1734
Age range: 5–10

Oryx International School
Mesaimeer Campus, Barwa City Street, Mesaimeer, Doha
Tel: +974 403 600 63
Curriculum: UK, GCSE, IGCSE
CIS

Pak Shamaa School and College
PO Box 22579, Doha
Tel: +974 4416 3712
Age range: 2–18
No. of pupils: 803

Park House English School
PO Box 23512, Doha
Tel: +974 4468 3800
Age range: 3–18
No. of pupils: 973 *B474 G499*
Curriculum: SAT, UK

Pearling Season International School of Doha
P.O Box 47021, 46, Al Khudari street (810), Bin Dirham (25), Al Manso+, Doha
Tel: +974 4032 2422
Curriculum: IPC, UK, IGCSE

Philippine School Doha
Saad Bin Surara Old Murror, Al Messilah Area, PO Box 19664, Doha
Tel: +974 4440 9888
Age range: 4–18
No. of pupils: 3000

Qatar Academy Al Khor
P.O.Box: 60774, Mowasalat Street, Al Khor
Tel: +974 44546775
Age range: 3–18 years
No. of pupils: 1243
Curriculum: IBDP, IBMYP, IBPYP
Language instr: Arabic, English

Qatar Academy Al Wakra
P.O. Box: 2589, Al Farazdaq Street, street No.: 1034, Zone 90, Doha
Tel: +974 44547418
Age range: 3–17 years
No. of pupils: 1186
Curriculum: IBDP, IBMYP, IBPYP
Language instr: Arabic, English
(ECIS)

Qatar Academy Doha
P.O. Box: 1129, Luqta Street, Doha
Tel: +974 44542000
Age range: 3–18 years
No. of pupils: 1884
Curriculum: IBDP, IBMYP, IBPYP
Language instr: Arabic, English
(CIS) (ECIS)

Qatar Academy Msheireb
Msheireb Downtown Doha
Tel: +974 44542116
Age range: 3–10 years
No. of pupils: 400
Curriculum: IBPYP
Language instr: English, Arabic

Qatar Academy Sidra
P.O. Box: 34077, Doha
Tel: +974 44542322
Age range: 3–18 years
No. of pupils: 680
Curriculum: IBDP, IBMYP, IBPYP
Language instr: English

Qatar International School
PO Box 5697, Doha
Tel: +974 4483 3456
Age range: 3–18
Curriculum: UK
Language instr: English

Qatar Leadership Academy
PO Box 24421, Al Khor Street, Al Khor
Tel: +974 445422222
Age range: B11–18
No. of pupils: 111
Curriculum: SAT, TOEFL
Language instr: English
(ECIS)

SEK INTERNATIONAL SCHOOL QATAR
For further details see p. 95
Onaiza 65, Doha
Tel: +974 4012 7633
Email: info@sek.qa
Website: www.sek.qa
Head of School: Verónica Sánchez
Age range: 3–18 years
Curriculum: IBDP, IBMYP, IBPYP
Language instr: Arabic, English, Spanish

Sherborne Qatar
PO Box 1108, Doha
Tel: +974 4459 6400
Age range: 3–18
No. of pupils: *B400 G400 VIth80*
Curriculum: UK, IGCSE, ALevs
Language instr: English
(COB)

Stafford Sri Lankan School Doha
PO Box 30220, Doha
Tel: +974 44694869
Age range: 4–19
Curriculum: IGCSE
Language instr: English

Step One International School
Musa Bin Omair St, Doha
Tel: +974 44772228
Curriculum: UK
(CIS)

Sunbeam Kindergarten
Al Bayyan Gardens Compound, (Near Al Saad Sports Stadium), PO Box 19612
Tel: +974 4444 0108
Age range: –12
Curriculum: UK

Swiss International School Qatar
Al Hashimaya Street, Al Luqta, Doha
Tel: +974 40363131
Curriculum: IBDP, IBMYP, IBPYP
Language instr: English

Tariq Bin Ziad School
Al Dafaf Street, Street 893, Al Sadd Area, Doha
Tel: +974 44542005
Curriculum: IBPYP
Language instr: English, Arabic

The Cambridge School
PO Box 22580, Al Madeed Street, Mamoura Area
Tel: +974 4469 6590
Age range: 14–19
No. of pupils: 1500
Curriculum: UK, ALevs

The English Modern School
PO Box 875, Doha
Tel: +974 44883806/07
Age range: 3–18
No. of pupils: 2300 *B1212 G1088 VIth105*
Curriculum: IGCSE, ALevs
Language instr: English

The Gulf English School
PO Box 2440, Doha
Tel: +974 4457 8777
Age range: 3–18
No. of pupils: 1535
Curriculum: IBDP, UK
Language instr: English
(CIS)

The International School of Choueifat – Doha
Al Onaizah Street no. 825, West Bay Area no. 66, Doha
Tel: +974 4 495 9595
Age range: 3–19
No. of pupils: 800
Curriculum: IGCSE

The Pearl School
Al Hadara Street, Al Rowdah, Doha
Tel: +974 44442555
Age range: 5–18
No. of pupils: 40

The Royal Grammar School Guildford in Qatar
Um Salal Mohamed, Street No. 631, Building No. 17, Zone No. 71, P.O. Box 75465
Tel: + 974 40360450
Curriculum: UK, IGCSE, ALevs
(COB)

The Scholars' International School
PO Box 201308, Doha
Tel: +974 44336336
Age range: 3–14

Vision International School – Qatar
Majilis Al Taawon Street, Almuftah Village, Al Wakra
Tel: +974 4487 0995
Age range: 3–18

REPUBLIC OF KOREA

Asia Pacific International School
820 wolgye 2-dong Nowon-gu, Seoul 139-724
Tel: +82 (0)2 907 2747
Age range: 4–18
Curriculum: AP, National, USA
Language instr: English
(EAR)

Branksome Hall Asia
234 Global edu-ro, Daejeong-eup, Seogwipo-si, Jeju-do 63644
Tel: +82 64 902 5000
Age range: 3–19 years
Curriculum: IBDP, IBMYP, IBPYP

British Education Korea
The British Prep, 244 Yeoksam-ro,, Gangnam-gu, South Korea 06226
Tel: 82-2-6203-9500
Curriculum: UK
(COB)

British International Academy
24, Deokpo 3-gil, Geoje 53213
Tel: +82 055 688 5154
Curriculum: IBDP, IBMYP, IBPYP

BUSAN FOREIGN SCHOOL
For further details see p. 60
45, Daecheon-ro 67 beon-gil, Haeundae-gu, Busan 48084
Tel: +82 (0)51 747 7199
Email: bfs@busanforeignschool.org
Website: www.busanforeignschool.org
Upper School Principal: Carl Brenneman
Age range: 3–18 years
No. of pupils: 250
Curriculum: AP, SAT, USA
(EAR)

CHADWICK INTERNATIONAL
For further details see p. 61
45, Art center-daero 97 beon-gil, Yeonsu-gu, Incheon 22002
Tel: +82 32 250 5000
Email: songdo-admissions@chadwickschool.org
Website: www.chadwickinternational.org
Head of School: Frederick T. Ted Hill
Age range: 4–18 years
No. of pupils: 1378
Curriculum: IBDP, IBMYP, IBPYP
Language instr: English
(CIS) (EAR)

Chung Nam Samsung Academy
77 Samseong-ro, Tangjeong-myeon, Asan-si, Chungcheongnam-do
Tel: +82 41 339 3000
Curriculum: IBDP
Language instr: English, Korean

Daegu International School (DIS)
22, Palgong-ro 50-gil, Dong-gu, Daegu, North Gyeongsang 41021
Tel: +82 53 980 2100
Age range: 4–18 years
No. of pupils: 320

DULWICH COLLEGE SEOUL
For further details see p. 67
6 Sinbanpo-ro 15-gil, Seocho-gu, Seoul 06504
Tel: +82 2 3015 8500
Email: admissions@dulwich-seoul.kr
Website: seoul.dulwich.org
Head of School: Gudmundur Hegner Jonsson
Age range: 3–18 years
No. of pupils: 700
Fees: 34,500,000–37,000,000
Curriculum: IBDP, UK, IGCSE
Language instr: English

Dwight School Seoul
21 World Cup Buk-ro 62-gil, Mapo-gu, Seoul 03919
Tel: +82 2 6920 8600
Age range: 3–18
Curriculum: IBDP, IBMYP, IBPYP, SAT
Language instr: English
CIS EAR

Gyeonggi Academy of Foreign Languages
30, Gosan-ro 105 Beon-gil, Uiwang-si, Gyeonggi-do 16075
Tel: +82 (0)31 361 0500
Age range: 15–18
Curriculum: IBDP
Language instr: English

Gyeonggi Suwon International School
451 YeongTong-Ro, YeongTong-Gu, Suwon City, Gyeonggi-Do 16706
Tel: +82 31 695 2800
Curriculum: IBDP, IBMYP, IBPYP
Language instr: English
EAR

Gyeongnam International Foreign School
49-22, Jodong-gil, Sanam-myeon, Sacheon-si, Gyeongnam 52533
Tel: +82 (0)55 853 5125
No. of pupils: 115
Curriculum: IBDP, IBMYP, IBPYP
Language instr: English

Hyundai Foreign School
3rd Floor, Hanmaeum Community Center, 30 Badeurae 1-gil, Dong-Gu, Ulsan 44033
Tel: +82 52 252 2851
Age range: 3–14 years
No. of pupils: 50
Language instr: English

International Christian School Pyongtaek
367-3 Shindae dong, Pyongtaek 450-820
Tel: +82 316 511 376
Language instr: English
EAR

International Christian School Uijeongbu
Jindeung-ro 28, Uijongbu 11608
Tel: +82 31 855 1276
Language instr: English
EAR

International School of Busan
50 Gijang-daero, Gijang-eup, Gijang-gun, Busan 46081
Tel: +82 51 742 3332
Age range: 2–18
No. of pupils: 310
Curriculum: IBDP, IBMYP, IBPYP, IGCSE
Language instr: English

International School of Koje
302 Okpo 1 Dong, Geoje-Si, Gyeongnam 656 904
Tel: +82 55 687 3283
Age range: 2–18 years
No. of pupils: 150 *B80 G70*
Curriculum: IPC, IGCSE, ALevs
Language instr: English

Korea Foreign School
7-16, Nambusunhwan-ro 364-gil, Seocho-gu, Seoul 06739
Tel: +82 2 571 2917/18
Curriculum: IBMYP, IBPYP
Language instr: English
CIS EAR

Korea International School
373-6 Baekhyun-dong, Bundang-gu, Seonhnam-si, Gyeonggi-do 463-420
Tel: +82 31 789 0505
Age range: 4–18
EAR

Korea Kent Foreign School
13 Jayang-Ro 35-Gil, Gwangjin-Gu, Seoul, 04993
Tel: +82 2 2201 7091
Curriculum: USA
EAR

NORTH LONDON COLLEGIATE SCHOOL JEJU
For further details see p. 92
33, Global edu-ro 145beon-gil, Daejeong-eup, Seogwipo-si, Jeju-do 63644
Tel: +82 64 793 8001
Email: admissions@nlcsjeju.kr
Website: www.nlcsjeju.co.kr
Principal: Lynne Oldfield
Age range: 4–18 years
No. of pupils: 1476
Fees: 31,808,331–44,584,739
Curriculum: IBDP, IGCSE
Language instr: English

Seoul Foreign British School
39 Yeonhui-ro 22 gil, Seodaemun-gu, Seoul 120-823
Tel: +82 2 330 3100
Age range: 3–14
No. of pupils: 300
Curriculum: SAT, UK
Language instr: English

SEOUL FOREIGN SCHOOL
For further details see p. 97
39 Yeonhui-ro 22-gil, Seodaemun-gu, Seoul 03723
Tel: +82 2 330 3100
Email: admissions@seoulforeign.org
Website: www.seoulforeign.org
Head of School: Colm Flanagan
Age range: 2–18 years
No. of pupils: 1500
Curriculum: ACT, IBDP, IBMYP, IBPYP, SAT, UK, USA, IGCSE
Language instr: English
EAR

Seoul International School
388-14 Bokjeong-dong, Sujeong-gu, Seongnam, Gyeonggi-do, Seoul 461-200
Tel: +82 31 750 1200
Age range: 4–19
No. of pupils: 999 *B490 G509*
Curriculum: USA
EAR

SIS Gwangju
2~6F, SIS Bldg, 17 Obang-ro, Nam-gu, Gwangju
Tel: +62 21 759 14414

Taejon Christian International School
77 Yongsan 2 Ro, Yuseong Gu, Daejeon 305-500
Tel: +82 42 620 9000
No. of pupils: 600
Curriculum: IBDP, IBMYP, IBPYP
Language instr: English
EAR

Westminster Canadian Academy
36 Dolmugae-Gil,, Gwacheon-City, Gyeonggi-Do
Tel: +82 (0) 2 504 7200
Curriculum: National

Yongsan International School of Seoul
285 Itaewon-ro, Yongsan-gu, Seoul 04347
Tel: +82 2 797 5104
Age range: 5–18
Curriculum: AP, SAT, USA
Language instr: English
EAR

REPUBLIC OF MALDIVES

Billabong High EPS International School
EPSS Building, Ameenee Magu, Male 20371
Tel: +960 330 9005
Age range: 5–14
No. of pupils: 600

Lale Youth International School
Reethigas Hingun, Hulhumale 23000
Tel: +960 335 0029
Age range: 14–19
Curriculum: IGCSE, ALevs

SAUDI ARABIA

Abdulaziz International School – Al Sulaimaniah
Prince Turki Bin Abdullah Al Saud Street, PO Box 68629, Riyadh 11537
Tel: +966 011 473 8555

Abdulaziz International School – Al Wadi
Al Wadi, Area Exit 6, Riyadh
Tel: +966 55 584 6789

Advanced Generations School – Elementary Boys
Al Nahdah District, Jeddah 23437
Tel: +966 420 2432
Age range: 4–12

Advanced Generations School – Elementary Girls
Al Nahdah District, Jeddah 23437
Tel: +966 420 2283
Age range: 4–12

Advanced Learning Schools
PO Box 221985, Riyadh 11311
Tel: +966 1 207 0926
Age range: 4–18
No. of pupils: 465
Curriculum: IBDP, IBMYP, IBPYP
Language instr: English
CIS

Ajial Aseer International School
PO Box 43, Khamis Mushayt
Tel: +966 7 223 1967
Age range: 4–15
No. of pupils: 180 *B*100 *G*80
Language instr: English

Al Alia International Indian School
PO Box 281025, Riyadh 11392
Tel: +966 4128884
Age range: 5–18
No. of pupils: 300

Al Andalus Private Schools
Batarji Street, Azzahra Dist, Jeddah 21443
Tel: +966 556 645 532
Curriculum: IBPYP
Language instr: English, Arabic

Al Anjal Private School
PO Box 849, Hofuf 31982
Tel: +966 2 683 0551
Age range: 5–18
No. of pupils: 1628
Curriculum: USA

Al Bayan Model School Girls
PO Box 13949, Jeddah 21414
Tel: +966 6611004
Curriculum: USA

Al Faris International School
Tawaan Area, Imam Saud Road, Khan Younes Street, Riyadh 9483
Tel: +966 011 454 9358
Age range: 3–18
No. of pupils: 2439
Curriculum: IBDP, IBMYP, IBPYP
Language instr: English

Al Hussan International Grammar School
16th Street, Madinat Al Umal, Al Khobar 34442
Tel: +966 882 1845

Al Hussan International School Jubail
P.O. Box 10957, Jubail 31961
Tel: +966 13 341 5561

Al Hussan International School Khobar
PO Box 297, Dammam 31411
Tel: +966 13 858 7566
Age range: 3–18 years
Curriculum: IBDP, IGCSE, ALevs

Al Hussan International School Riyadh
P.O. Box 259777, Riyadh 11351
Tel: +966 011 248 9338

Al Hussan International School Yanbu
Prince Sultan Road, Radwa 3, Yanbu 46452
Tel: +966 14 392 1121

Al Isra International School
P.O Box 145333, Yanbu
Tel: +04 3908412
Curriculum: UK, IGCSE

Al Majd International School
PO Box 76240, Al Khobar 31952
Tel: +966 13 858 0383/0380/0377
Age range: 5–18
No. of pupils: 500

Al Omam International School
4283 Tal Al Asfar, Al Rihab District, Jeddah
Tel: +966 2 6746557
Age range: 5–18
No. of pupils: 300
Curriculum: USA

Al Reeyada International School
PO Box 5282, Al Hasa 31982
Tel: +966 1 3599 3961
Curriculum: UK, IGCSE, ALevs

Al Rissalah International School
Sulemaniah Street, East of Jazirah Supermarket, PO Box 250905, Riyadh 11391
Tel: +966 1 465 79 90
Age range: 4–18
Curriculum: USA, IGCSE

Al Rowad International School
P.O. Box 93354, Al-Nuzha, Riyadh 11673
Tel: +966 11 281 3003
Curriculum: UK, USA, IGCSE, ALevs

Al Waha International School
PO Box 12491, Jeddah 21473
Tel: +966 2 672 9660
Age range: 3–16
No. of pupils: 668 *B*388 *G*280

Al-Afaq International School
Hail Street, Al Hamra District, PO Box 9717, Jeddah 21423
Tel: +966 12 665 2423
Age range: 4–19
Curriculum: USA

Al-Bassam International School
Dammam
Tel: +966 013 843 4999
Curriculum: IBPYP
Language instr: English, Arabic

Al-Bassam School – Girls Section
PO Box 945, Dammam 31421
Tel: +966 3 8094040
Age range: 4–18
No. of pupils: 300

Aldenham Prep Riyadh
Al Noura, As Sahafah, Riyadh 13321
Age range: 3–11 years

Al-Faisal International School
Al-Moalifeen Street, Jeddah
Tel: +966 2 6761955
Age range: 3–15
No. of pupils: 100
Curriculum: UK

Al-Oruba International School
Ahmed Bin Roshed Street, Fasil Bin Fahd Road, Al Rafeeah Zone Riyadh 23661, Riyadh 11553
Tel: +4153264
Age range: 4–19
No. of pupils: 3020
Curriculum: SAT, USA

American International School – Riyadh
PO Box 990, Riyadh 11421
Tel: +966 11 491 4270
Age range: 4–18
No. of pupils: 1355
Curriculum: IBDP, USA
Language instr: English
CIS ECIS

American International School of Jeddah
P.O. Box 127328, Jeddah 21352
Tel: +966 12 232 8668
Age range: 3–18 years
Curriculum: IBDP
Language instr: English

American School Dhahran
PO Box 31677, Al-Khobar 31952
Tel: +966 (0)13 330 0555
Curriculum: IBDP

Aqeeq International Academy
2644 Abi Al Hasan Al Husari, Al Aqeeq Dist. Unit No 1, Riyadh 13511-6812
Tel: +966 920 00 304
Age range: 3–18
Language instr: English, Arabic

Bangladesh International School, Jeddah (Bangla Section)
Nuzlah Sharqia, Kilo-3, Post Box 31598, Jeddah 21418
Tel: +966 02 6800520

Bangladesh International School, Jeddah (Bangla Section) Riyadh
Office No. 107 & 116, First Floor Babtain building, Olayah Street 11351
Tel: +966 05 46888648

Banoo IQRA International School
PO Box 27523, Riyadh 11427
Tel: +966 1 471 4162
Age range: 5–18
No. of pupils: 300

Baraem RAIS – Dhahran – Al-Dana
Afif St, Dana Al Janubiyah, Dhahran 34453
Tel: +966 581865531

Baraem RAIS – Riyadh – Al-Sahafa
6965 Prince Abdullah Bin Saud Bin Abdullah Snatan Al Saud, Al Yasmin, Riyadh 13325 3800
Tel: +966 2145475

Bayan Gardens School
PO Box 180, Al Khobar 31952
Tel: +966 3 882 2645
Age range: 3–13
No. of pupils: 350
Curriculum: USA
Language instr: Arabic, English

Bright Minds International School
Pr. Sultan Street, Behind Haram Center, An Naim District, Jeddah
Tel: +966 (0)12 654 2505
Curriculum: IBPYP
Language instr: English, Arabic

British International School of Al Khobar
PO Box 4359, Al Khobar 31952
Tel: +966 13 882 5425
Age range: 3–18
No. of pupils: 750 *B*400 *G*300 *VIth*50
Curriculum: UK, GCSE, IGCSE, ALevs
Language instr: English
CIS

British International School Riyadh
PO Box 85769, Al Hamra, Riyadh 11612
Tel: +966 11 248 2387/0386
Age range: 3–18
No. of pupils: 1400 *B*850 *G*550 *VIth*70
Curriculum: UK
Language instr: English
CIS COB

Coral International School
Alrawdah District, PO Box 9864, Jeddah 21423
Tel: +966 2 683 2002
Age range: 4–18
No. of pupils: 783
Curriculum: USA

Dar Al Fikr Schools
PO Box 14279, Jeddah 21424
Tel: +966 2 631 1118
Age range: 3–19
No. of pupils: 643
Curriculum: AP, USA

Dar Jana International School-Rawda Campus
PO Box 118149, Jeddah 21312
Tel: +966 2 664 8310
Curriculum: USA

Deutsche Internationale Schule Jeddah
P.O. Box 7510, Jeddah 21472
Tel: +966 12 691 3584
Curriculum: IBDP
Language instr: English

Dhahran Ahliyya Schools
P.O.Box 39333, Dhahran 31942
Tel: +966 138919222
Age range: *B*3–18
Curriculum: IBMYP, IBPYP, SAT, USA
Language instr: English, Arabic

Dhahran British Grammar School
PO Box 31677, Al-Khobar 31952
Tel: +966 13 330 0555
Age range: 4–18
No. of pupils: 700 *B*350 *G*350 *VIth*37
Curriculum: UK, GCSE, IGCSE, ALevs
Language instr: English
CIS

Dhahran Elementary/ Middle School
PO Box 31677, Al-Khobar 31952
Tel: +966 13 330 0555 (Ext:2353)

Dunes International School
King Saud Road (Al-Qashla Road), PO Box 8627, Al-Andalus 34437
Tel: +966 3 8145850
Age range: 3–14

Ecole Internationale Arc de Triomphe
PO Box 32546, Jeddah 21438
Tel: + 966 12 6065 421
Curriculum: FrenchBacc

Green Hills International School
PO Box 118707, Jeddah 21312
Tel: +966 12 6063959
Age range: 4–19
No. of pupils: 800

Hala International School
Al Khwarazmi Street, Al Aziziya District, Jeddah, KSA
Tel: +966 12 6715543
Curriculum: IGCSE, ALevs

Horizon International School
Abdullah Alanqari Street, Al Wurud, Riyadh
Tel: +966 11 460 4646
Age range: 5–18
Curriculum: USA

International Indian School – Jeddah
PO Box 14861, Jeddah 21434
Tel: + 966 6751536
Age range: 4–19

International Programs School
Prince Sultan Road, Qurtoba, Al Khobar 34236
Tel: +966 13 857 5603
Age range: 4–17 years
No. of pupils: 1370
Curriculum: IBDP, IBPYP, SAT, USA
Language instr: English

International Schools Group (ISG) Dammam
PO Box 31677, Al-Khobar 31952
Tel: +966 13 808 4676

International Schools Group (ISG) Jubail
PO Box 10059, Jubail 31961
Tel: +966 13 341 7550
Age range: Pre-K–Grade 12
No. of pupils: 410 *B*210 *G*200
Curriculum: IBDP, USA
Language instr: English

Italian School
North Cornich Road, Jeddah 21434
Tel: +966 2 606 4335
Age range: 14–19

Jeddah Knowledge International School
Al Salamah District, Mohammed Mosaud St. (Behind Iceland), PO Box 7180, 21462 Jeddah
Tel: +966 2 691 7367
Age range: 3–18
No. of pupils: 2014
Curriculum: IBDP, IBMYP, IBPYP, National, USA
Language instr: English, Arabic
CIS ECIS

Jeddah Prep and Grammar School
PO Box 6316, Jeddah 21442
Tel: +966 2 654 2354
Age range: 3–18 *B*3–18 *G*3–18
No. of pupils: 593 *B*450 *G*450 *VIth*83
Curriculum: UK, IGCSE, ALevs
Language instr: English
COB

Jeddah Private International School
Jeddah
Tel: +966 126 064 309
Age range: 4–11

Jubail International School
PO Box 10957, Jubail 31961
Tel: +966 3 341 8710
Age range: 3–18
No. of pupils: 357 *B*181 *G*176
Curriculum: UK, USA
CIS

King Abdulaziz School
Ali Ibn Abi Taleb Road, P.O. Box 43111, Medina 41561
Tel: +966 553 039 300/+966 503 454 420
No. of pupils: 149
Curriculum: IBDP, IBMYP, IBPYP
Language instr: English

King Faisal Pre-School
PO Box 94558, Riyadh 11614
Tel: +966 1 482 0802
Curriculum: IBPYP
Language instr: English, Arabic

King Faisal School
PO Box 94558, Riyadh 11614
Tel: +966 1 482 0802
No. of pupils: 1230
Curriculum: IBDP, IBMYP, IBPYP, National, SAT, TOEFL
Language instr: English, Arabic

Learning Caravan International School
PO Box 295160, Riyadh 11351
Tel: +966 1 463 45 73
Age range: 3–11
Curriculum: UK

Les Écoles Internationales Al-Kawthar
PO Box 52280, Jeddah 21563
Tel: +966506561717; +966506359280
Age range: 3–11
Curriculum: IBPYP
Language instr: French

MADAC Schools
P.O.Box 444, Jabla bin Thour Street, Abu Kubir District, Medina
Tel: +966 555261230
Curriculum: IBPYP
Language instr: English, Arabic

Manarat Jeddah International School – Boys
PO Box 40513, Jeddah 21511
Tel: +966 12 2678 3215
Age range: 11–19

Manarat Jeddah International School – Girls
PO Box 40513, Jeddah 21511
Tel: +966 12 6730 225
Age range: 11–19

Multinational School – Riyadh
Al Barkah x7, Al Falah District, Othman Bin Affah Main Road
Tel: +966 1 2751751
No. of pupils: 1600
Curriculum: IGCSE, ALevs

Nada International School
PO Box 1065, Al-Ahsa 30150
Tel: +966 1 3532 3338
Language instr: English
ECIS

Najd International School
Intersection of Imam Road, with Eastern Ring Road, Riyadh
Tel: +96614563922
Age range: 4–18
No. of pupils: 3800

New Middle East International School
PO Box 250377, Riyadh 11391
Tel: +966 1 4161201
Age range: 3–16
No. of pupils: 3500

New World International School
PO Box 3682, Dammam 31481
Tel: +966 13 814 4801
Age range: 4–19
No. of pupils: 300
Curriculum: IGCSE, ALevs

Nobels International School
PO Box 51868, Al Rawdah District, Jeddah
Tel: +966 02 664 3288
Age range: 3–18
No. of pupils: 800

Nün Academy
7639 Omair Ibn Abi Waqqas, Al Murjan District, Al Murjan District, Jeddah 23715
Tel: +966 509 939 702
Curriculum: UK
CIS

Orbit International School Khobar
P.O. Box 31153, Al-Khobar 31952
Tel: +966 13 847 5555

Pakistan International School (English Section) Jeddah
PO Box 4690, Al-Rehab District, Jeddah 21412
Tel: +966 12 673 8670
Age range: 3–18
Curriculum: UK, IGCSE, ALevs

Pakistan International School (English Section) Riyadh
PO Box 6891, Riyadh 11452
Tel: +966 11 8805327
Age range: 3–18
No. of pupils: 300
Curriculum: IGCSE

Qodrat Alajyal
Medina
Curriculum: IBPYP
Language instr: Arabic, French

Qurtubah Private Schools
Prince Sultan Street, North-West Al-Tareekh Square, Jeddah 21581
Tel: +966 551757472
Curriculum: IBPYP
Language instr: Arabic

Radhwa International School Yanbu
P.B.No. 32006, Yanbu 41912
Curriculum: IBPYP
Language instr: English

RAIS – Dammam – AlZahour for Boys
Anas Ibn Malik St, Az Zuhur, Dammam 32423
Tel: +966 138307890

RAIS – Dammam – AlZahour for Girls
Anas Ibn Malik St, Az Zuhur, Dammam 32423

RAIS – Dammam – Hamra International for Girls
6350 Anas Ibn Malik St, Al Hamra, Dammam 32422 3411
Tel: +966 591415477

RAIS – Jeddah – Abhor for Girls
Jeddah

RAIS – Riyadh – Mogharazat for Boys
Prince Muqrin Ibn Abdulaziz St, Al Mughrizat, Riyadh 12481
Tel: +966 920033433

RAIS – Riyadh – Mogharazat for Girls
Prince Muqrin Ibn Abdulaziz St, Al Mughrizat, Riyadh 12481

RAIS – Riyadh – Qurtoba for Girls
2590 Al Bayt Al Atiq, Qurtubah, Riyadh 13245 6874
Tel: +966 920033099

Rand International School
PO.box 9712, Dammam 31423
Tel: +966 13 8504488
Curriculum: IBPYP
Language instr: Arabic, English

Riyadh Schools
An Namudhajiyah, Prince Fahd bin Salman Road, Riyadh
Tel: +966 11 402 8411
Language instr: English, Arabic

Saad National School
PO Box 30531, Al Khobar 31952
Tel: +966 13 858 0055
Age range: 4–19
Curriculum: National

Sands International School
Shuraih Ibn Al Arith, Sulaimaniyah, Riyadh 12223
Tel: +966 11 4634124
Age range: 1–16
No. of pupils: 800

Saud International School
Hamdan Street, Sulaimaniyah, Riyadh
Tel: +966 920002877
Age range: 2–18
No. of pupils: 844
Curriculum: USA

SEK INTERNATIONAL SCHOOL RIYADH
For further details see p. 96
Al Toq Street, Ar Rabi, Riyadh 13315
Tel: +966 53 063 3295
Email: admissions@sek.sa
Website: www.sek.sa
Principal: Ivan Martinez Pastor
Age range: 3–12 years

Thamer International School
PO Box 52799, Jeddah
Tel: +966 12 6977033
Age range: 5–18
Curriculum: IGCSE

The British International School of Jeddah
PO Box 6453, Jeddah 21442
Tel: +966 1 2 699 0019
Age range: 3–18
No. of pupils: 1531 *B*843 *G*688 *VIth*140
Curriculum: IBDP, IGCSE
Language instr: English

The KAUST School
Safaa Gardens School, Office 1132, 4700 KAUST, Thuwal 23955-6900
Tel: +966 12 808 6803
Curriculum: IBDP, IBMYP, IBPYP
Language instr: English

The Kingdom Schools
P.O. Box. 484, Riyadh 11321
Tel: +966 11 275 5555
Age range: 4–18
Curriculum: USA
Language instr: English

The World Academy – King Abdullah Economic City
P.O. Box 8299, Jeddah 21482
Tel: +966 (0)554712325
Age range: 3–17
Curriculum: USA
Language instr: English

Waad Academy
Obhur, Jeddah 23828
Tel: +966 1223 99710

Yusr International School
King Abdulaziz Road, Opp Red Sea Mall, An Nahdah, Jeddah 23614
Tel: +966 55 506 3771
Curriculum: IBMYP, IBPYP
Language instr: English, Arabic

Yusr International School, Makkah Branch
Al Hamra Umm Al Jud, Al-takhasosy, Mecca
Tel: +966 55 539 8976
Curriculum: IBPYP
Language instr: English, Arabic

Zahrat Al Sahraa International School
Hassan Basalma Street, PO Box 13259, Jeddah 21493
Tel: +966 12 6671199
Age range: 3–18
No. of pupils: 1050
Curriculum: USA

SINGAPORE

ACS (International), Singapore
61 Jalan Hitam Manis, Singapore 278475
Tel: +658 6472 1477
Age range: 11–19
No. of pupils: 960
Curriculum: IBDP, IGCSE
Language instr: English

Anglo-Chinese School (Independent)
121 Dover Road, Singapore 139650
Tel: +65 6773 1633
Age range: *B*13–18 *G*17–18
No. of pupils: 2898 *B*2664 *G*234
Curriculum: IBDP, UK
Language instr: English

Ascensia International School
Blk 106A Henderson Crescent, #01-01 Henderson Area Office, Singapore 151106
Tel: +65 6466 5505
Curriculum: IBDP, IBPYP
Language instr: English

Australian International School, Singapore
1 Lorong Chuan, 556818
Tel: +65 6653 7906
Age range: 2 months–18 years
No. of pupils: 2700
Curriculum: IBDP, IBPYP, National
Language instr: English

Canadian International School, Lakeside Campus
7 Jurong West Street 41, Singapore 659414
Tel: +65 6743 8088
Age range: 2–18
No. of pupils: 3000
Curriculum: IBDP, IBMYP, IBPYP
Language instr: English

Canadian International School, Tanjong Katong Campus
371 Tanjong Katong Road, Singapore 437128
Tel: +65 6345 1573
Curriculum: IBPYP

Chatsworth International School
72 Bukit Tinggi Road, Singapore 289760
Tel: +65 6463 3201
Age range: 3–18 years
No. of pupils: 600
Curriculum: IBDP, IBMYP, IBPYP, USA
Language instr: English

Chatsworth International School – Orchard Campus
37 Emerald Hill, Singapore 229313
Tel: +65 6737 5955
Age range: 2–11
Language instr: English

Dover Court International School Singapore
301 Dover Road, Singapore 139644
Tel: +65 6775 7664
Age range: 3–18 years
No. of pupils: 1800
Curriculum: IBDP, UK
Language instr: English

DPS International School
36 Aroozoo Avenue, Singapore 539842
Tel: +65 6285 6300
Age range: 2–18
Curriculum: UK, IGCSE, ALevs

DULWICH COLLEGE (SINGAPORE)
For further details see p. 65
71 Bukit Batok West Avenue 8, Singapore 658966
Tel: +65 6890 1003
Email: admissions.singapore@dulwich.org
Website: singapore.dulwich.org
Headmaster: Nick Magnus
Age range: 2–18 years
No. of pupils: 2730
Fees: Day S$17,780–S$49,310 FB S$35,300
Curriculum: IBDP, IGCSE
Language instr: English, Mandarin

EtonHouse International School, Broadrick
51 Broadrick Road, Singapore 439501
Tel: +65 6346 6922
Age range: 3–11 years
No. of pupils: 375
Curriculum: IBPYP
Language instr: English

EtonHouse International School, Claymore
15 Claymore Road, Singapore 229542
Tel: +65 6737 3322

EtonHouse International School, Islander
35 Allanbrooke Road, Singapore 099982
Tel: +65 6274 2211

EtonHouse International School, Mountbatten 223
223 Mountbatten Road, #01-18, Singapore 398008
Tel: +65 6440 5100

EtonHouse International School, Mountbatten 717
717 Mountbatten Road, Singapore 437737
Tel: +65 6440 0777

EtonHouse International School, Mountbatten 718
718 Mountbatten Road, Singapore 437738
Tel: +65 6846 3322
Curriculum: IBPYP
Language instr: English

EtonHouse International School, Newton
39 Newton Road, Singapore 307966
Tel: +65 6352 3322
Curriculum: IBPYP
Language instr: English

EtonHouse International School, Orchard
10 Tanglin Road, Singapore 247908
Tel: +65 6513 1155
Curriculum: IBDP, IBPYP
Language instr: English, Spanish

EtonHouse International School, Robertson Walk
Robertson Walk, 11 Unity Street, #02-20, Singapore 237995
Tel: +65 6221 1050

EtonHouse International School, Sentosa
33 Allanbrooke Road, Sentosa, (5 mins from Sentosa Cove and Harbourfront), Singapore 099981
Tel: +65 6377 3322

Etonhouse International School, Thomson
8 Thomson Lane, (5 mins from Newton/Novena & 10 mins from Orchard), Singapore 297743
Tel: +65 6252 3322
Curriculum: IBPYP
Language instr: English, Mandarin

EtonHouse International School, Upper Bukit Timah
215 Upper Bukit Timah Road, Singapore 588184
Tel: +65 6762 3322

EtonHouse International School, Vanda
1 Vanda Road, Singapore 287771
Tel: +65 6468 7880

EtonHouse International School, Zhong Hua
681 Bukit Timah Road #01-03, Singapore 269782
Tel: +65 6467 3322

GESS International School
2 Dairy Farm Lane, Singapore 677621
Tel: +65 6461 0881
Age range: 2–18 years
No. of pupils: 1800
Curriculum: Abitur, IBDP, IBMYP, IBPYP, National
Language instr: English, German

Global Indian International School (GIIS) East Coast Campus
82 Cheviot Hill, Singapore 459663
Tel: +65 6914 7100
Age range: 2 1/2–17 years
Curriculum: IBPYP, UK, IGCSE
Language instr: English

Global Indian International School (GIIS) SMART Campus
27 Punggol Field Walk, Singapore 828649
Tel: +65 6914 7100
Age range: 2 1/2–18 years
No. of pupils: 2850
Curriculum: IBDP, IBPYP, IGCSE
Language instr: English

Hillside World Academy
11 Hillside Drive, 548926
Tel: +65 6254 0200
Age range: 3–19
No. of pupils: 250
Curriculum: IBDP, IBMYP, IBPYP
Language instr: English, Chinese

Hollandse School Singapore
65 Bukit Tinggi Road, Singapore 289757
Tel: +65 64 66 0662
Age range: 2–12
No. of pupils: 410
Curriculum: IPC
Language instr: Dutch, English

Hwa Chong International School
663 Bukit Timah Road, Singapore 269783
Tel: +65 6464 7077
Age range: 12–18 years
No. of pupils: 1008
Curriculum: IBDP
Language instr: English

Insworld Institute
100 Victoria Street, #08-02 National Library Building, Singapore 188064
Tel: +65 6732 1728
Age range: 12–21 years
No. of pupils: 100
Curriculum: UK, IGCSE, ALevs
Language instr: English

International Community School
27A Jubilee Road, Singapore 128575
Tel: +65 6776 7435
EAR

ISS International School
21 Preston Road, 109355
Tel: +65 6475 4188
Age range: 4–19
No. of pupils: 310
Curriculum: IBDP, IBMYP, IBPYP
Language instr: English
CIS EAR

Madrasah Aljunied Al-Islamiah
30 Victoric Lane, Singapore 198424
Tel: +65 6391 5970/1
Curriculum: IBDP
Language instr: English, Malay

Nexus International School (Singapore)
1 Aljunied Walk, Singapore 387293
Tel: +65 6536 6566
Age range: 3–18 years
No. of pupils: 1050
Curriculum: IBDP, IBPYP, UK, IGCSE, ALevs
Language instr: English

North London Collegiate School Singapore
130 Depot Road, Singapore 109708
Tel: +65 6989 3000
Curriculum: IBDP, IBMYP
Language instr: English

NPS International School
10-12 Chai Chee Lane, Singapore 469021
Tel: +65 62942400
Age range: 3–18 years
No. of pupils: 1750
Curriculum: IBDP, SAT, IGCSE
Language instr: English

Odyssey The Global Preschool – Fourth Avenue
20 Fourth Avenue, 268669
Tel: +65 6781 8800
Curriculum: IBPYP
Language instr: English, Chinese

Odyssey The Global Preschool – Wilkinson
101 Wilkinson Road, 436559
Tel: +65 6781 8800
Age range: 8 months–6 years
No. of pupils: 220
Curriculum: IBPYP
Language instr: English, Chinese

One World International School
21 Jurong West Street 81, Singapore 649075
Tel: +65 69146700
Age range: 3–18 years
No. of pupils: 1450
Curriculum: IBDP, IBPYP

Overseas Family School
25F Paterson Road, Singapore 238515
Tel: +65 6 738 0211
Age range: 3–18
No. of pupils: 3670 B1893 G1782
Curriculum: IBDP, IBMYP, IGCSE
Language instr: English

Pegasus International College (Singapore)
331 North Bridge Road, #11-01 Odeon Towers, Singapore 188720
Tel: +65 6392 3850

Rosemount International School
25 Ettrick Terrace, Siglap 458588
Tel: +65 6446 4636

Singapore American School
40 Woodlands Street 41, Singapore 738547
Tel: +65 6363 3403
Age range: 3–21
No. of pupils: 2196
Curriculum: ACT, AP, SAT, TOEFL, USA
EAR

Singapore Chinese Girls School
190 Dunearn Road, 309437
Tel: +65 6252 7966
Age range: 6–16
Curriculum: National

Singapore Korean School
71 Bukit Tinggi Road
Singapore 289759
Tel: +65 6741 0778
Age range: 4–19

Sir Manasseh Meyer International School
3 Jalan Ulu Sembawang,
Singapore 758932
Tel: +65 6331 4633

St Francis Methodist School
492 Upper Bukit Timah Road, 678095
Tel: +65 6760 0889
Age range: 12–20
Curriculum: IBDP
Language instr: English

ST. JOSEPH'S INSTITUTION INTERNATIONAL
For further details see p. 101
490 Thomson Road
Singapore 298191
Tel: +65 6353 9383
Email: admissions.hs@sji-international.com.sg
Website: www.sji-international.com.sg
HS Principal: Roisin Paul
Age range: 4–18 years
No. of pupils: 2000
Fees: S$32,978
Curriculum: IBDP, IPC, IGCSE
Language instr: English

Stamford American International School
1 Woodleigh Lane, 357684
Tel: +65 6653 7907
Age range: 2 months–18 years
No. of pupils: 2972
Curriculum: IBDP, IBMYP, IBPYP, USA
Language instr: English

Swiss School in Singapore
38 Swiss Club Road,
Singapore 288140
Tel: +65 64 68 21 17
Age range: 2–12
No. of pupils: 250
Language instr: French/German, English

TANGLIN TRUST SCHOOL, SINGAPORE
For further details see p. 104
95 Portsdown Road, 139299
Tel: +65 67780771
Email: admissions@tts.edu.sg
Website: www.tts.edu.sg
CEO: Craig Considine
Age range: 3–18 years
No. of pupils: 2800
Fees: S$29,916–S$36,696
Curriculum: IBDP, UK, IGCSE, ALevs
Language instr: English

The Little Skool-House International (By-the-Vista)
170 Ghim Moh Road, Ulu Pandan Community Club,
#03-01, Singapore 279621
Tel: +65 6468 3725
Curriculum: IBPYP
Language instr: English

UWC South East Asia, Dover Campus
1207 Dover Road, 139654
Tel: +65 6775 5344
Age range: 4–18 years (Boarding from 13)
No. of pupils: 3008
Curriculum: IBDP, IGCSE
Language instr: English

UWC South East Asia, East Campus
1 Tampines Street 73, 528704
Tel: +65 6305 5344
Age range: 4–18 years (Boarding from 13)
No. of pupils: 2608
Curriculum: IBDP, IGCSE
Language instr: English

XCL World Academy
2 Yishun Street 42, Singapore 768039
Tel: +65 6871 8835
Age range: 2–18 years
No. of pupils: 700
Curriculum: IBDP, IBMYP, IBPYP, IBCP
Language instr: English

SRI LANKA

Adventist International School
103/A Jude Mawatha,
Negombo 11500
Tel: +94 312 237 181
Curriculum: UK, ALevs

British School in Colombo
63 Elvitigala Mawatha,
Mawatha, Colombo 8
Tel: +94 11 5329 329
Age range: 2–18
Curriculum: UK, IGCSE, ALevs
Language instr: English

Cambridge International School
148 Aluthmawatha Road, Colombo 15
Tel: +94 11 4618705
Age range: 4–18
No. of pupils: 700
Curriculum: UK

Colombo International School
28 Gregory's Road, Colombo 7
Tel: +94 11 2697 587
Age range: 2–18
No. of pupils: 1650 *B900 G750 VIth290*
Curriculum: SAT, UK, IGCSE, ALevs
Language instr: English

Colombo International School – Kandy Branch
175 Paranagantota Road,
Mawilmada, Kandy
Tel: +94 81 2234298
Age range: 3–19
No. of pupils: 700
Curriculum: UK, ALevs

Elizabeth Moir School
4/20 Thalakotuwa Gardens, Colombo 5
Tel: +94 11 2512275
Age range: 2.5–18 years
No. of pupils: 520
Curriculum: UK, IGCSE, ALevs
Language instr: English

Gateway College Colombo
185, Koswatta Road, (Via Parliment Road, Off Royal Gardens), Rajagiriya
Tel: +94 11 2888288
Age range: 2.5–18 years

Gateway College Dehiwala
285/1 Galwihara Road, Dehiwala
Tel: +94 11 5757234
Age range: 2.5–18 years

Gateway College Kandy
80 Wariyapola Sri Sumangala Mawatha, Asgiriya, Kandy
Tel: +94 81 2200300
Age range: 2.5–18 years

Gateway College Negombo
No 62, Negombo Road, Kurana
Tel: +94 31 2227772
Age range: 2.5–18 years

Ilma International Girl's School
4/100, Thalakotuwa Gardens, Colombo 5
Tel: + 94 11 4362212
Curriculum: National, UK

Jennings International College
Nainamadama, Wennappuwa
Tel: +94 31 2254187
Age range: 4–19
No. of pupils: 1000

NICE International School
222/6 Kimbulapitiya Road, Kadirana North, PO Box 51, Negombo 11500
Tel: +94 31 2234512
Age range: 2–18
No. of pupils: 150

Royal Institute International School
191 Havelock Road,
Colombo 10250
Tel: + 94 11 259 2747
Age range: 3–18
No. of pupils: 1900
Curriculum: IGCSE

Stafford International School
37 Guildford Crescent, Colombo
Tel: +94 11 269 4592
Age range: 3–17
No. of pupils: 800
Curriculum: IGCSE, ALevs

The Overseas School of Colombo
PO Box 9, Pelawatte,
Battaramulla 10120
Tel: +94 11 2784 920-2
Age range: 3–18 years
Curriculum: IBDP, IBMYP, IBPYP
Language instr: English

Wycherley International School Gampaha
No. 05 Mudungoda,
Miriswatta, Gampaha
Tel: +94 77 003 7037
Curriculum: UK

SYRIAN ARAB REPUBLIC

Pakistan International School of Damascus
PO Box 9787, Yaa'four, Damascus
Tel: +963 11 3921479
Age range: 14–18 years
Curriculum: IGCSE

The International School of Choueifat – Damascus
PO Box 302, Achrafieh Sahnaya, Amman Road,
Daraa Highway, Damascus
Tel: +963 99 300 635
Age range: 3–18
No. of pupils: 1000

TAIWAN

American School in Taichung
21-1 Chu Yuan Lane, Beitun, Taichung City 406051
Tel: +886 4 2239 7532
Language instr: English

Dah Yung Kao Mei Preschool
No. 267 Cuihua Road, Gushan District, Kaohsiung City 80449
Tel: +886 7 533 6746
Curriculum: IBPYP
Language instr: English, Chinese

Dominican International School
76 Tah Chih Street, Taipei 10464
Tel: +886 2 2533 8451
Age range: 4–17
No. of pupils: 465
EAR

Hsinchu International
Niu Pu East Road, #290, Hsinchu 30091
Tel: +886 3 538 8113
Age range: 4–18
No. of pupils: 315 *B*153 *G*162 *VIth*21
Curriculum: ACT, AP, SAT, USA
Language instr: English
EAR

I-Shou International School
No 6, Sec 1, Xuecheng Rd., Dashu Dist., Kaohsiung City 84048
Tel: +886 7 657 7115
Age range: 2–18
No. of pupils: 700
Curriculum: IBDP, IBMYP, IBPYP, SAT, TOEFL
Language instr: Chinese, English
CIS

Ivy Collegiate Academy
320, Lane 165, Section 1, Tan-Hsing Rd, Tan-Tzu Shiang/Taichung
Tel: +886 4 25395011
Age range: 12–17

Kang Chiao International School (Taipei Campus)
No. 800, Huacheng Road, Xindian District, New Taipei City 23153
Tel: +886 2 8665 2070
Curriculum: ACT, AP, IBDP, IBMYP, SAT
Language instr: Chinese, English

Kaohsiung American School
889 Cueihua Road, Zuoying District, Kaohsiung City 81354
Tel: +886 7 586 3300
Age range: 4–18
No. of pupils: 800
Curriculum: IBDP, IBMYP, USA
Language instr: English
EAR

Mingdao High School
497, Sec. 1, Zhongshan Rd., Wuri Dist., Taichung City 41401
Tel: +886 4 23372101
Curriculum: IBDP, IBMYP
Language instr: English

Morrison Academy
System Services, 136-1 Shui Nan Road, Taichung 40679
Tel: +886 4 2297 3927
Age range: 5–18
No. of pupils: 800 *B*400 *G*400
Curriculum: AP, SAT, USA
Language instr: English
EAR

Morrison Academy Bethany Campus
97 Ting Chou Road, Section 3, #97, Taipei 10090
Tel: +886 2 236 59691
No. of pupils: 900
Curriculum: USA

Pacific American School
No. 307, Sec 1, Xing Long Road, Zhubei City, Hsinchu County
Tel: +886 3 5586688

Starlight International Kindergarten – Feng Yuan Campus
No. 569 Sec. 7, Fengyuan Blvd., Shengang District, Taichung City
Tel: +886 4 2520 8466
Curriculum: IBPYP
Language instr: English, Chinese

Starlight International Kindergarten – Hui Wen Campus
No. 8 Sec. 1 Huilai Road, Nantun District, Taichung City
Tel: +886 4 2251 4007
Curriculum: IBPYP
Language instr: English, Chinese

Taichung City Starlight Experimental Education
No. 23 Daguan Road, Nantun District, Taichung City 408
Tel: +886 4 2389 1626
Curriculum: IBPYP
Language instr: English, Chinese

Taipei Adventist American School
No. 64 Lane 80 Zhuang Ding Rd., Shihlin 111, Taipei
Tel: +886 02 2861 6400
Age range: 6–14
No. of pupils: 120
Curriculum: USA
Language instr: English

Taipei American School
800 Chung Shan North Road, Sec 6, Taipei
Tel: +886 22 873 9900
Age range: 4–17
No. of pupils: 2235 *B*1115 *G*1120
Curriculum: AP, IBDP, SAT, USA
Language instr: English
EAR ECIS

Taipei European School
Swire European Campus, 31 Jian Ye Road, Yang Ming Shan, Shihlin, Taipei 11193
Tel: +886 2 8145 9007
Age range: 3–18 years
Curriculum: IBDP, SAT, UK
Language instr: English, French, German

Taipei Kuei Shan School
200 Mingde Road, Taipei 11280
Tel: +886 2 2821 2009
Age range: 4–18 years
No. of pupils: 700
Curriculum: IBDP, IBMYP, IBPYP
Language instr: Chinese, English

Victoria Academy
1110 Jhen-Nan Rd., Douliu, Yun-Lin 640
Tel: +886 5 5378899 (Ext:22)
Curriculum: IBDP
Language instr: Chinese, English

TAJIKISTAN

Dushanbe International School
Bofande Ulitsa 9, Dushanbe
Tel: +992 372 214947
Age range: 5–18
No. of pupils: 135 *B*84 *G*51
ECIS

QSI International School of Dushanbe
Sovetskaya 85, Dushanbe 734001
Tel: +992 37 224 8737
Age range: 3–13
No. of pupils: 30
Curriculum: USA
Language instr: English

THAILAND

Adventist International Mission School
195 Moo 3, Muaklek, Saraburi 18180
Tel: +66 (0)36 720 675

AIT International School
Km. 42, Phaholyothin Highway, Klong Luang, Patumthani 12120
Tel: +66 (C)2 524 5984
Age range: 3–12
No. of pupils: 285
Curriculum: National

American Pacific International School
158/1 Moo 3, Hangdong-Samoeng Road, Banpong, Hangdong, Chiang Mai 50230
Tel: +66 53 365 303/5
Age range: 2–18
No. of pupils: 380
Curriculum: AP, IBDP, IBMYP, IBPYP, USA
Language instr: English
EAR

Amnuay Silpa School
304/1 Sri Ayutthaya Road, Ratchathewee, Bangkok 10400
Tel: +66 2 354 5267
Age range: 3–18
No. of pupils: 920
Curriculum: GCSE

Anglo Singapore International School
341 Sukhumvit 31 (Soi Si Yak Sawatdee), Klongtan, Wattana, Bangkok 10110
Tel: +66 02 662 3105 6
Age range: 3–12
No. of pupils: 211 *B*107 *G*104
Curriculum: National, UK
Language instr: English, Thai, Chinese
CIS

Ascot International School
80/82 Ramkhamhaeng Soi 118, Sapansung, Bangkok 10240
Tel: +66 2 373 4400
Age range: 2–18 years
No. of pupils: 400
Curriculum: IBDP, IBPYP, UK, IGCSE
Language instr: English
CIS

Assumption Commercial College
141 Soi Sathorn 13, Sathorn Rd Sathorn, Bangkok 1012
Tel: +662 2113744
Curriculum: National

Bangkok Adventist International School
P.O. Box 234 Prakhanong, Klongtan Nua, Wattana, Bangkok 10110
Tel: +66 2 381 9406
Age range: 4–17
No. of pupils: *B*54 *G*46
Curriculum: USA
Language instr: English

Bangkok Christian College
35 Pramoan Road, Silom Bangrak, Bangkok 10500
Tel: +66 2 637 1852
Curriculum: USA

Bangkok Christian International School
53 Soi 44 Pattanakarn Road, Suan Luang, Bangkok 10250
Tel: +662 322 1979
Age range: 4–18
No. of pupils: 300
Curriculum: AP, USA

Bangkok Grace International School
79/3-12 Latphrao Soi 112, Wangthonglang, Bangkok 10310
Tel: +66 2 539 4516/7/8
Age range: 2–18
No. of pupils: 42 *B23 G19*
Curriculum: USA
Language instr: English
EAR

BANGKOK PATANA SCHOOL
For further details see p. 56
643 Lasalle Road (Sukhumvit 105), Bangna Tai, Bangna, Bangkok 10260
Tel: +66 2 785 2200
Email: admissions@patana.ac.th
Website: www.patana.ac.th
Age range: 2–18 years
Curriculum: IBDP, IGCSE
Language instr: English
CIS EAR

Bangkok Prep International School
23 Sukhumvit 53, Vadhana District, Bangkok 101 0
Tel: +66 2 700 5858
Age range: 3–18 years
No. of pupils: 1300
Curriculum: UK, ALevs
Language instr: English

Beaconhouse Yamssard International School – Pattankarn
166/1 Pattanakarn Soi 78, Prawet, Bangkok 10250
Tel: +66 2 722 2571
Age range: 2–11

Berkeley International School
123 Bangna-Trad Road, Bangna, Bangkok 10260
Tel: +662(0)2 747 4788
EAR

Bloomsbury International School Hatyai
2119 Moo 6, Airport-Lopburirames Road, Kuanlung, Hatyai, Songkhla 90110
Tel: +66 74 251 255/6
Curriculum: UK
CIS

Brighton College International School Bangkok
8/8 Krungthep Kreetha Soi 15 Yaek 4 (Surao Yai), Hua Mak, Bang Kapi, Bangkok 10240
Tel: +66 (0)2 136 7898
Age range: 2–18
Curriculum: UK, GCSE, ALevs
Language instr: English

British Columbia International School
608/1 Kalaprapruk Road, Bangwar, Phasichareon, Bangkok 10160
Tel: +66 2 802 1188
Age range: 12–18
Curriculum: National

British International School, Phuket
59 Moo 2, Thepkrasattri Road, T. Koh Kaew, A. Muang, Phuket 83000
Tel: +66 (0) 76 335 555
Age range: 1–18
No. of pupils: 900 *B450 G450*
Curriculum: IBDP, SAT, UK, IGCSE
Language instr: English
CIS

British School Bangkok Ltd
36 Sukhumvit Soi 4, Soi Nana, Bangkok 10110
Tel: +66 2 656 7734
Age range: 2–11
No. of pupils: 178 *B102 G76*
Curriculum: SAT, UK
Language instr: English
CIS

Bromsgrove International School Early Years Campus
344 Mu 12, Ramkamhaeng 164 Road, Minburi, Bangkok 10510
Tel: +66 2540 7122 3
Age range: 2–7
No. of pupils: 40

Bromsgrove International School Primary and Secondary Campus
555 Mu 9, Windsor Park and Golf Club,, Suwinthawong Road, Minburi, Bangkok 10510
Tel: +66 2989 4873
Age range: 2–18
No. of pupils: 400 *B200 G200*
Curriculum: UK, IGCSE, ALevs
Language instr: English
CIS

California Prep International School (CPIS)
9 Moo 11, A Banpa, Kaeng Khoi, Saraburi
Tel: +66 (0)36 358714
Curriculum: USA

Canadian International School of Thailand
1001 Charan Sanitwong 46, Bangyeekhan, Bang Phlat, Bangkok 10700
Tel: +66 02 886 9464
Curriculum: IBMYP, IBPYP
Language instr: English, Thai

Charter International School
36 Chalermprakiat Ror 9 Road, Pravate, Bangkok 10250
Tel: +66 2 7268283/4
Age range: 3–18
No. of pupils: 345 *B175 G170*
Curriculum: IGCSE, ALevs
Language instr: English
CIS

Chiang Mai International School
PO Box 38, 13 Chetupon Road, Chiang Mai 50000
Tel: +66 (53) 306152-3
Age range: 4–18
Curriculum: AP, USA
EAR

Christian German School Chiangmai
PO Box 12, Chiangmai 50140
Tel: +66 53 816 624

Concordian International School
918 Moo 8, Bangna-Trad Highway Km 7, Bangkaew, Bangplee Samutprakarn 10540
Tel: +66 2 706 9000
Age range: 2–18
No. of pupils: *B361 G309*
Curriculum: IBDP, IBMYP, IBPYP
Language instr: English, Chinese
CIS EAR

Crescent International School
72 Soi Sribumphen, Rama 4 Road, Tungmahamek, Sathon 1 10120
Tel: +66 2679 8777
Curriculum: National, UK, IGCSE

D-PREP International School
38, 38/1-3, 39, Moo 6, Bangna Trad Rd., Km. 8, Bang Kaeo, Bang Phli District, Samut Prakan 10540
Tel: +66 95 879 4944
Age range: 4–18 years
Curriculum: IBPYP
Language instr: English, Thai

Ekamai International School
57 Ekamai 12 (Soi Charoenjai), Sukhumvit 63 Road, Klongtan Neua, Wattana, Bangkok 10110
Tel: +66 023 913 593
Language instr: English
EAR

Garden International School (Bangkok campus)
2/1 Yen Akart Soi 2, Yen Akart Road, Sathorn, Bangkok 10120
Tel: +66 2249 1880
Age range: 2–18 years
No. of pupils: 236 *B118 G118*
Curriculum: UK, IGCSE
Language instr: English

Garden International School (Rayong Campus)
188/24 Moo 4, Pala-Ban Chang Road, Tambol Pala, Ban Chang, Rayong 21130
Tel: +66 3803 0808
Age range: 3–18 years
No. of pupils: 475
Curriculum: IBDP, UK, IGCSE
Language instr: English
CIS

Global English School
24/29-32 Pracha Raj Rd, Muang Nonthaburi, Nonthaburi 11000
Tel: +66 (0)2 968 4870
Age range: 3–16
No. of pupils: 300
Curriculum: USA

Global Indian International School (GIIS) Bangkok Campus

Grace International School
88 Muu 3 T.Harn Kaew A. Hang Dong, Chiang Mai 50230
Tel: +66 53 131 175
Age range: 5–19
No. of pupils: 558
Curriculum: USA
EAR

Harrow International School Bangkok
45 Soi Kosumruamchai 14, Kosumruamchai Road, Don Mueang Subdistrict, Don Mueang District, Bangkok 10210
Tel: +66 02 503 7222
Age range: 18 months–18 years
No. of pupils: 1640
Curriculum: UK, IGCSE, ALevs
CIS

Heathfield International School
10/22 Moo 4, Sukhapiban 3 (Rakhambaeng Road), Saphansung, Bangkok
Tel: +662 372 2678
Age range: 2–15
No. of pupils: 154 *B74 G80*
Curriculum: UK
CIS

Hua Hin International School
549 Moo 7, Hin Lek Fai, Hua Hin, Prachuap Khiri Khan 77110
Tel: +66 32 900 632
Curriculum: IBDP
Language instr: English, Thai

International Community School
1225 The Parkland Road, Bangna, Bangkok 10260
Tel: +66 2 338 0777
(EAR)

International Pioneers School
20 Radruam Charoen, Charoen Nakorn Soi 14, Charoen Nakorn Road,, Klongsan 10600
Tel: +66 2 862 3030
Age range: 3–18
Curriculum: UK, IGCSE, ALevs

INTERNATIONAL SCHOOL BANGKOK
For further details see p. 78
39/7 Soi Nichada Thani, Samakee Road, Pakkret, Nonthaburi 11120
Tel: +66 2 963 5800
Email: admissions@isb.ac.th
Website: www.isb.ac.th
Head of School: Andrew Davies
Age range: 3–18 years
No. of pupils: 1700
Fees: US$16,751–US$30,441
Curriculum: IBDP, USA
Language instr: English
(EAR)

International School Eastern Seaboard
282 Moo 5 T. Bowin, SriRacha, Chonburi 20230
Tel: +66 38 372 591
Age range: 3–18
No. of pupils: 260
Curriculum: IBDP
Language instr: English
(EAR)

International School of Chonburi
315 Moo 1 Banglamung Soi 39, Nongprue Banglamung, Chonburi 20150
Tel: +66 38 241 085
Age range: 2–11
No. of pupils: 50
Curriculum: UK

Kevalee International School
90 Hathairaj 37 Road, Klongsamwa District, Bangkok 10510
Tel: +66 2 9066427
Age range: 2.5–17 years
No. of pupils: 105
Curriculum: USA
Language instr: English

Kiddykare International Kindergarten
59/34 Sukhumvit 26, Klongton, Bangkok 10110
Tel: +66 2665 6777
Age range: 18 months–6 years
No. of pupils: B11 G29
Curriculum: UK
Language instr: English

Kids Academy International Pre-School
52/1-2 Sukhumvit 63, Soi 2, Bangkok 10110
Tel: +66 2 714 3636
Age range: 18 months–6 years
No. of pupils: 181
Curriculum: UK
Language instr: English

Kincaid International School of Bangkok
205/73-74, Pasooksanti3, Pattanakarn 69, Pravej, Bangkok 10250
Tel: +66 2 321 7010
Age range: 4–17

KIS International School
999/123-124 Pracha Utit Road, Samsennok, Huay Kwang, Bangkok 10310
Tel: +66 (0)2 2743444
Age range: 3–19 years
No. of pupils: 750
Curriculum: IBDP, IBMYP, IBPYP, IBCP
Language instr: English
(CIS) (EAR)

Krabi International School
188 Moo 6, Nong Thale, Muang, Krabi 81180
Tel: +66 (0)75 656 900
Age range: 5–18 years
No. of pupils: 150
Curriculum: UK, IGCSE, ALevs
Language instr: English

Ladybird International Kindergarten
21 Soi Promsri 2, Sukhumvit 39, Bangkok 10110
Tel: +66 2382 3338
Age range: 18 months–5
Curriculum: UK, USA
Language instr: English

Lanna International School Thailand
300 Grandview, Moo 10, Chiang Mai – Hang Dong Road, Chiang Mai 5010
Tel: +66 53 806230/1
Age range: 3–19
No. of pupils: 490
Curriculum: SAT, UK, IGCSE, ALevs
Language instr: English
(EAR)

Lertlah School, Phetkasem Road
45 Petkasem Road, Soi Phetkasem 77, Nongkhaem District, Bangkok 10160
Tel: +66 2 809 9081 5
Age range: 2–12
No. of pupils: 1300

Lycee Francais International de Bangkok
498, soi Rhamkhamhaeng 39 (Thep Leela 1), Wangthonglang, Bangkok 10310
Tel: +66 2 934 8008
Language instr: French

Magic Years International School
22/122, Moo 3, Soi Prasoet Islam, Bang Talat, Pakkret, Nonthaburri 11120
Tel: +66 2156 6222
Age range: 1–12 years
No. of pupils: 150
Curriculum: IBPYP
Language instr: English

Modern International School Bangkok
125-135 Soi Phobmitr, Sukhumvit 39 Road, Wattana 10110
Tel: +66 2258 8222
Curriculum: UK, IGCSE, ALevs

Montfort International College
19/1 Montfort Rd, T.Tasala A.Muang, Chiang Mai 50000
Tel: +66 5324 5570-5
Age range: 4–19

Mulberry House International Pre-school
7 Soi Tonson, Ploenchit Road, Lumpini Sub-district, Pathumwan District, Bangkok 10330
Tel: +66 2010 5620
Age range: 2–6
Curriculum: UK
Language instr: English

Nakornpayap International School
240 Moo 6 Sanphisua, Muang Chiang Mai 50300
Tel: +66 (0) 53 110 680
Age range: 3–18 years
No. of pupils: 500
Curriculum: AP, USA
Language instr: English
(EAR)

New Sathorn International School
289/2, 289/5 Soi Naradhiwas Rajanakharindra 24, Naradhiwas Rajanakarindra Rd, Chongnonsri, Yannawa, Bangkok 10120
Tel: +66 26 722 100-1
Age range: 2–17
Curriculum: UK, USA
Language instr: English

NIST INTERNATIONAL SCHOOL
For further details see p. 87
36 Sukhumvit Soi 15, Wattana, Bangkok 10110
Tel: +66 2 017 5888
Email: admissions@nist.ac.th
Website: www.nist.ac.th
Head of School: James Dalziel
Age range: 3–18 years
No. of pupils: 1720
Fees: THB541,700–THB975,800
Curriculum: IBDP, IBMYP, IBPYP
Language instr: English
(CIS) (EAR) (ISA)

Niva International School
18 Soi Phokaew 3 Yeak 9, Ladprao 101, Bangkapi, Bangkok 10240
Tel: +66 2 948 4605 7
Age range: 3–18
No. of pupils: 327

Pan-Asia International School
100 Moo 3, Charaemprakiat, Rama 9 St, Soi 67, Kwang Dokmai Prawet District, Bangkok 10250
Tel: +66 2 726 6273-4
Curriculum: IBDP, IBMYP
Language instr: English

Panyaden International School
218 Moo 2, T.Namprae, A.Hang Dong, Chiang Mai 50230
Tel: +66 80 078 5115
Curriculum: IBDP, UK
Language instr: English

Patanadek School
144/1 Sri Chan Rd, T Naimueang, A Mueang 40000
Tel: +66 43 222 869
Age range: 4–19

Prem Tinsulanonda International School
234 Moo 3, Huay Sai, Mae Rim, Chiang Mai 50180
Tel: +66 53 301 500
Age range: 3–19
No. of pupils: 500
Curriculum: IBDP, IBMYP, IBPYP, IBCP
Language instr: English
(CIS) (EAR) (RS)

QSI International School of Phuket
81/4 Mool, Chalermprakiat r.9 Road, T. Kathu, A. Kathu, Phuket 83120
Tel: +66 76 304 312
Age range: 3–16
No. of pupils: 126
Curriculum: USA
Language instr: English

Ramkhamhaeng Advent International School
1 Soi Ramkhamhaeng 119, Sukhapibal 3, Huamark, Bangkapi, Bangkok 10240
Tel: +66 2 370 0316
Age range: 3–18
No. of pupils: 700
Curriculum: USA

Rasami British International School
48/2 Soi Rajavithi 2, Rajavithi Road, Samsennai, Phayathai 10400
Tel: +66 2644 5291
Age range: 2–17
No. of pupils: 200
Curriculum: UK

RC International School
25/3-4 Ruamrudee Soi 1, Ploenchit Road, Bangkok 10330
Tel: +66 2 254 4380
Age range: 18 months–13
No. of pupils: 150
Curriculum: UK

REGENTS INTERNATIONAL SCHOOL PATTAYA
For further details see p. 94
33/3 Moo 1, Pong, Banglamung, Chonburi 20150
Tel: +66 (0)93 135 7736
Email: admissions@regents-pattaya.co.th
Website: www.nordangliaeducation.com/our-schools/pattaya
Principal: Sarah Osborne-James
Age range: 2–18 years
No. of pupils: 800
Fees: THB316,350
Curriculum: IBDP, UK, ALevs
Language instr: English

RIS Swiss Section-Deutschsprachige Schule Bangkok
6/1 Ramkamhaeng Road, Minburi 10510
Tel: +66 2 5180 340
Age range: 2–18
No. of pupils: 310
Curriculum: National

Roong Aroon International School
391/5 Soi 33 Rama 2 Road (Soi Wat Yai Rom), Bang Khunthien, Bangkok 10150
Tel: +66 (0)2 870 7512 3
Curriculum: IBMYP
Language instr: English, Thai

Ruamrudee International School
6 Ramkhamhaeng 184, Minburi, Bangkok 10510
Tel: +66 (0)2 791 8900
Age range: 3–18 years
No. of pupils: 900
Curriculum: AP, IBDP, SAT, TOEFL, USA
Language instr: English
EAR

Sarasas Extra School
336/7 Soi Satupradit 20 Rd, Bangkok 10120
Tel: +66 2212 0157
Age range: 3–17
No. of pupils: 2500

Satit Bilingual School of Rangsit University
52/347 Muang Ake, Phahonyothin Road., Lak Hok, Mueang, Pathum Thani 12000
Tel: +66 2 792 7500 4
Curriculum: IBPYP, IGCSE
Language instr: English

Shrewsbury International School
1922 Charoen Krung Road, Wat Phrayakrai, Bang Kholame, Bangkok 10120
Tel: +66 2 675 1888
Age range: 3–18
No. of pupils: 1600
Curriculum: UK, GCSE, IGCSE, ALevs
CIS

Siam International School
55/5 Moo 1, Klong 3, Rangsit-Nakhonnayok Road, T.Bungyeetho, Thanyaburi Pathumthani, Bangkok 12130
Tel: +66 85 009 9059
Age range: 4–19
No. of pupils: 250

Silver Fern International School
16 Moo 21 Airport Road, Tambon Neua Muang, Amphoe Muang, Roi-Et 45000
Tel: +66 994 671 222
Curriculum: IBPYP
Language instr: English

Singapore International School of Bangkok
Pracha Utit Campus, 498/11 Soi Ramkhamhaeng 39 (Tepleela 1), Wangthonglang, Bangkok 10310
Tel: +66 2 158 9191
Age range: 2–18
Curriculum: IBDP, IGCSE, ALevs
Language instr: English, Chinese, Thai
EAR

Srithammarat Suksa School
1 Rajadamnurn Road, Nakon Sri Thammarat 80000
Tel: +66 75 313 717
Age range: 4–19

ST ANDREWS INTERNATIONAL SCHOOL BANGKOK
For further details see p. 100
1020 Sukhumvit Road, Phra Khanong, Khlong Toei, Bangkok 10110
Tel: +662 056 9555
Email: admissions@standrews.ac.th
Website: www.standrews.ac.th
Head of School: Paul Schofield
Age range: 2–18 years
No. of pupils: 2000
Fees: *Day* THB331,000–THB702,000
Curriculum: IBDP, IGCSE
Language instr: English
CIS

St Andrews International School, Dusit Campus
253/1 Sawankhaloke Road, Dusit, Bangkok 10300
Tel: +66 (0)2668 6231
Age range: 2–11
Curriculum: UK

St Andrews International School, Green Valley Campus
Moo 7, Ban Chang-Makham Koo Road, Ban Chang, Rayong 21130
Tel: +66 38 030611
Age range: 2–18
No. of pupils: 450
Curriculum: IBDP, IBPYP, UK, IGCSE
Language instr: English

St Andrews International School, Sathorn Campus
9 Sathorn Soi 4, North Sathorn Road, Bangrak 10500
Tel: +66 (0)2632 1995
Age range: 2–11

St Andrews International School, Sukhumvit Campus
7 Sukhumvit 107 Road, Bangna, Bangkok 10260
Tel: +66 (0)2393 3883
Age range: 2–18
No. of pupils: 500
Curriculum: IBDP, IBPYP, IBCP
Language instr: English

St Andrews Samakee International School
43 Soi Tiwanond 48, Nonthaburi 11000
Tel: +66 2952 4003
Age range: 1–14

St Mark's International School
900 New Rama 9 Road, Suanluang, Bangkok 10250
Tel: +662 300 5463 4
Age range: 4–16
No. of pupils: 60

St Stephen's International School
998 Viphavadi-Rangsit Road, Lad Yao, Chatuchak, Bangkok 10900
Tel: +66 (0)2 513 0270
Age range: 3–18
No. of pupils: 457 *B227 G230 VIth30*
Curriculum: IPC, UK, IGCSE, ALevs
Language instr: English
CIS

St Stephen's International School, Khao Yai
49/1-3 Moo 4, Thanarat Road, Nongnamdaeng, Pak Chong, Nakhon Ratchasima 30130
Tel: +66 (0)864688040
Age range: 3–16
No. of pupils: 140 *B70 G70*
Curriculum: IPC, UK, IGCSE
Language instr: English

Thai Sikh International School
1799 Rim Thang Rod Fai Kao, Moo 1 Samrong Nua, Samut Prakarn 10270
Tel: +66 2 743 5049 – 52
Age range: 5–16
No. of pupils: 342
CIS

Thai-Chinese International School
101/177 Moo 7 Soi Mooban Bangpleenives, Prasertsin Road, Bangplee Yai, Samutprakarn 10540
Tel: +66 2 751 1201
Curriculum: USA
Language instr: English
EAR

The American School of Bangkok – Green Valley Campus
900 Moo 3 Bangna-Trad Road Km. 15 Bangplee, Samutprakarn, Bangkok 10540
Tel: +66 (0)2026 3518
Age range: 4–18 years
Curriculum: IBDP, USA

The American School of Bangkok – Sukhumvit Campus
59-59/1 Sukhumvit Road Soi 49/3 Wattana, Bangkok 10110
Tel: +66 (0)2620 8600
Age range: 4–18 years
Curriculum: USA

The British International School of Northern Thailand
Located Near Wat Baan Ta Tempel, Municipal Bridge, Baan Ta Mor Som, A.Maung 52000
Tel: +66 54 324596
Age range: 2–18
No. of pupils: 300
Curriculum: UK

The City School
18 Soi Sukhumvit 49/4, Khlong Tan Nuea, Watthana, Bangkok 10110
Tel: +66 2 381 2919
No. of pupils: 200
CIS

The International School of Samui
141/21 Moo 6, Bophut, Koh Samui, Surat Thani 84320
Tel: +66 (0)77 48 45 48
Age range: 2–16
No. of pupils: 250 *B121 G114*
Curriculum: UK, IGCSE
Language instr: English
COB

The Regent's School, Bangkok
601/99 Pracha-Uthit Road, Wangthonglang, Bangkok 10310
Tel: +66 (0)2 957 5777
Curriculum: IBDP
Language instr: English
CIS

Traill International School
36 Soi 18, Ramkangheng
Road, Huamark, Bangkok
Tel: +66 2718 8779
Age range: 5–16
No. of pupils: 160
Curriculum: UK

Udon Thani International School (UDIS)
222/2 Moo. 2 Mittrapab Road,
Tumbonkudsra, Aumpearmuang,
Udon Thani 41000
Tel: +66 (0)42 110 379
Curriculum: IBPYP
Language instr: English

UWC Thailand International School
115/15 Moo 7 Thepkasattri Road,
Thepkasattri, Thalang, Phuket 83110
Tel: +66 76 336 076
Age range: 2–18 years
Curriculum: IBDP, IBMYP, IBPYP

Varee Chiangmai International School
59 Moo 6 Mahidol Rd, Nonghoi,
Muang, Chiang Mai 50000
Tel: +66 5314 0233
Age range: 4–19
No. of pupils: 200
Curriculum: UK

WELLINGTON COLLEGE INTERNATIONAL SCHOOL BANGKOK
For further details see p. 110
18 Krungthep Kreetha
Road, Saphan Sung
District, Bangkok 10250
Tel: +66 2 087 8888
Email: admissions@wellingtoncollege.ac.th
Website: www.wellingtoncollege.ac.th
Master: Christopher Nicholls
Age range: 2–18 years
No. of pupils: 640
Curriculum: UK, IGCSE, ALevs
Language instr: English

Wells International School – Bang Na Campus
10 Srinakarin Soi 62, Nong Bon,
Prawet, Bangkok 10250
Tel: +66 02 746 6060 1
Curriculum: IBPYP
Language instr: English, Thai

Wells International School – On Nut Campus
2209 Sukhumvit Road, Bangchak,
Prakanong, Bangkok 10260
Tel: +66 097 920 8511
Age range: 5–19
No. of pupils: 520
Curriculum: AP, IBDP, SAT, USA
Language instr: English

TURKMENISTAN

QSI Ashgabat International School
Berzengi, Ataturk St, Ashgabat
Tel: +993 12 489 027
Age range: 3–18
No. of pupils: 250
Curriculum: USA
Language instr: English

UNITED ARAB EMIRATES

Abu Dhabi International (Pvt) School
Karamah Street, PO Box
25898, Abu Dhabi
Tel: +971 2 443 4433
Age range: 3–18
No. of pupils: 3225
Curriculum: IBDP
Language instr: English

Abu Dhabi Junior Academy
PO Box 43286, Abu Dhabi
Tel: +971 58 151 2655
Curriculum: UK

Ajman Academy
Sheikh Ammar Road,
Mowaihat 2, Ajman
Tel: +971 6 731 4444
No. of pupils: 990
Curriculum: IBMYP, IBPYP, IGCSE
Language instr: English

Ajman Modern School
PO Box 1778, Ajman
Tel: +971 6 7431 168
Age range: 3–15
No. of pupils: 800

Ajyal International School
Behind Sheukha Fatma Mosque,
10 Minutes from Mazyad Mall,
Mohammad Bin Zayed City
Tel: +971 2552 2668
Age range: 4–18
Curriculum: UK

Al Adab Iranian Private School for Boys
Behind Al Bustan Center, Al
Nahda 1, Qusais, Dubai
Tel: +971 42633405
Age range: 5–19
No. of pupils: 600
Curriculum: IBDP
Language instr: English

Al Adhwa Private School
PO Box 64997, Falai Hazza'a, Al Ain
Tel: +971 3 7828870
Age range: 4–18
No. of pupils: 536
Curriculum: USA

Al Ain Academy
PO Box 88228, Al Ain
Tel: +971 3 715 1000
Curriculum: UK

Al Ain American School
PO Box 100774, Al Ain
Tel: +971 3 7675030
Age range: 3–14 years
Curriculum: USA

Al Ain English Speaking School
PO Box 17939, Al – Ain
Tel: +971 3 7678636
Age range: 3–18
No. of pupils: 440

Al Ain International School
PO Box 88228,, Salam Street, Al Ain
Tel: +971 3 7151000
Curriculum: UK

Al Amana Private School
PO Box 27194, Sharjah
Tel: +971 6 5676783
Age range: 3–18
No. of pupils: 800
Curriculum: IGCSE

Al Ansar International School
PO Box 43114, Sharjah
Tel: +971 6 545 9441
Curriculum: IGCSE, ALevs

Al Basma British School
PO Box No 45994, Behind
Deerfields Mall, Abu Dhabi
Tel: +971 2 562 3454

Al Bateen Academy
PO Box 128484, Abu Dhabi
Tel: +971 2 813 2000
Curriculum: IBDP, IBPYP

Al Bustan Private School
PO Box 7443, Opp Madinat
Zayed Market, Abu Dhabi
Tel: + 971 2 6330036
Curriculum: USA

Al Dhafra Private School
PO Box 25801, Abu Dhabi
Tel: +971 2 610 8400/1
Age range: 3–18
Curriculum: National, UK, USA

Al Diyafah High School
PO Box 24023, Dubai
Tel: + 971 4 2671115
Curriculum: UK, IGCSE, ALevs

Al Ittihad Private School Jumeirah
PO Box 37090, Jumeirah-Dubai
Tel: +971 43 945 111
Curriculum: USA
Language instr: English

Al Ittihad Private School Mamzar
Cairo Road, Mamzar-Dubai
Tel: +971 42 966 314
Curriculum: USA
Language instr: English

Al Khaleej National School
PO Box 26780, Dubai
Tel: + 971 4 2173 900
Age range: 3–18
Curriculum: SAT, TOEFL, USA
Language instr: English

Al Maali International School
PO Box 42007, Abu Dhabi
Tel: +971 2 559 1000
Curriculum: USA

Al Maaref Private School
PO Box 87823, Dubai
Tel: +971 4 2988881
Age range: 4–18 years

Al Ma'Arifa Private School
Box 7190, Al Yarmook, Sharjah
Tel: +971 6 5014444
Curriculum: UK, USA, IGCSE

Al Mamoura Academy
Abu Dhabi
Tel: +971 2 885 7100
Curriculum: IBCP, USA

Al Manhal International School
P.O.Box:3110,
Tel: 00971 2-4998777
Curriculum: UK, USA

Al Mawakeb School – Al Barsha
PO Box 35001, Dubai
Tel: +971 4 3478288

Al Mawakeb School – Al Garhoud
PO Box 10799, Dubai
Tel: +971 4 2851415
Age range: 3–18
Curriculum: National,
SAT, TOEFL, USA

Al Muna Academy
PO Box 12848, Abu Dhabi
Tel: +971 2 501 4777
Curriculum: UK

Al Murooj English School
Al Azra Area, Sharjah
Tel: 00 971 6 527 3720
Age range: 4–11
Curriculum: UK

Al Murooj Scientific Private School
Kalidiyah Khalifa Bin Shakhbun
St, PO Box 42275, Abu Dhabi
Tel: +971 2 6669229

Al Nahda International Schools
PO Box 815, Abu Dhabi
Tel: +971 2 445 4200/2984
Age range: 4–18
No. of pupils: 3500 *B*1200 *G*3300
Curriculum: SAT, TOEFL, ALevs

Al Nahda National Schools
PO Box 815, Abu Dhabi
Tel: +971 2 4477600
Curriculum: SAT, TOEFL, UK, USA, IGCSE

Al Najah Private School
PO Box 284, Abu Dhabi
Tel: +971 2 553 0935
Curriculum: IBDP

Al Rabeeh School
PO Box 41807, Abu Dhabi
Tel: +971 2 4482856
Age range: 3–12
No. of pupils: 798 *B*425 *G*373
Curriculum: National, UK
Language instr: English, Arabic

Al Resalah School of Science
PO Box 1250, Sharjah
Tel: +971 6 522 1222
Curriculum: USA

Al Salam Private School and Nursery
Al Nahda 2, Al Ghusais, PO Box 5251, Dubai
Tel: +971 4 267 9594
Age range: 4–18
No. of pupils: 600

Al Sanawbar School
PO Box 1781, Al Ain
Tel: + 971 3 7679 889
Curriculum: USA

Al Shohub School
PO Box 31515, Abu Dhabi
Tel: +971 2 5559995
Age range: *B*3–9 *G*3–18
No. of pupils: 913 *B*19[illegible] *G*716 *VIth*11
Curriculum: UK, IGCSE, ALevs
Language instr: English

Al Yasat Private School
Abu Dhabi 25586
Tel: +971 2 641 2300
Age range: 3–8
No. of pupils: 500
Curriculum: USA

Al Yasmina Academy
PO Box 128484, Abu Dhabi
Tel: +971 2 501 4888
Age range: 3–18
Curriculum: UK

Al-Mizhar American Academy for Girls
PO Box 78484, Dubai
Tel: +971 4 288 7250
Age range: *G*4–19
No. of pupils: 650
Curriculum: USA

Ambassador International Academy
Al Khail Gate, Al Quoz, Plot No. 3653942, Dubai
Tel: +971 4 580 6999
Curriculum: IBMYP, IBPYP
Language instr: English

Ambassador School
PO Box 126924, Plot No 317-278, 41 A Street, Mankhool, Bur Dubai, Dubai
Tel: +971 4 379 9333
Age range: 6–18
No. of pupils: 602

American Community School Sharjah
PO Box 31809, Maliha Road, Sharjah
Tel: +971 6 5227583
Age range: 5–18
No. of pupils: 100
Curriculum: USA

American Community School, Abu Dhabi
PO Box 42114, Abu Dhabi
Tel: +971 2 681 5115
Age range: 4–18
Curriculum: IBDP, USA
Language instr: English

American International School Dubai
PO Box 87727, Dubai
Tel: +971 4 2988666

American International School in Abu Dhabi
PO Box 5992, Abu Dhabi
Tel: +971 2 4444 333
Age range: 4–18
No. of pupils: 1400 *B*682 *G*718 *VIth*180
Curriculum: IBDP, IBPYP, SAT, USA
Language instr: English

American School of Dubai
PO Box 7118, Dubai
Tel: +971 4 395 0005
Age range: 4–18
No. of pupils: 1850
Curriculum: AP, SAT, USA

Apple International School
PO Box 33963, Dubai
Tel: +971 4 263 8989
Age range: 4–14
No. of pupils: 2020

Arab Unity School
PO Box 10563, Rashidiya, Dubai
Tel: +971 4 2886226/7
Age range: 3–18
No. of pupils: 3321 *B*1742 *G*1579
Curriculum: UK, IGCSE, ALevs

Arcadia School
District 9, Orchid Street, Jumeirah Village Triangle, Dubai
Tel: +971 4 552 2600

Asian International Private School – Madinat Zayed (Western Zone)
PO Box 50251, Zayed City, Abu Dhabi
Tel: +971 2 88 47470
Age range: 4–19
No. of pupils: 300

Asian International Private School – Ruwais (Western Zone)
ADNOC Building, PO Box 12000, Ruwais, Abu Dhabi
Tel: +971 2 8778789

Australian International School
PO Box 43364, Sharjah
Tel: +971 6 558 9967
No. of pupils: 1200
Curriculum: IBDP
Language instr: English

Australian School of Abu Dhabi
Khalifa City B, PO Box 36044, Abu Dhabi
Tel: +971 2 5866980
Curriculum: IBDP, IBMYP, IBPYP
Language instr: English

Bradenton Preparatory Academy
PO Box 111123, Dubai Sports City, Dubai
Tel: +971 4 818 3600
Age range: 5–18
No. of pupils: 206

Brighton College Abu Dhabi
PO Box 129444, Abu Dhabi
Tel: +971 2 815 6500
Curriculum: UK
Language instr: English

Brighton College Al Ain
PO Box 14000, Al Ain
Tel: +971 (0)3 7133 999
Curriculum: UK
Language instr: English

Cambridge International School – Dubai
PO Box 60835, Dubai
Tel: +971 4 282 4646
Age range: 3–18
No. of pupils: 2009 *B*1200 *G*809
Curriculum: UK, ALevs
Language instr: English

Canadian International School Abu Dhabi
PO Box 3976, Khalifa A City, Abu Dhabi
Tel: +971 2 556 4206
Age range: 4–19
No. of pupils: 300

Capital School
PO Box 236498, Baghdad Street, Al Qusais
Tel: +971 4 2381 888
Age range: 4–11

Central School Dubai
PO Box 90697, Dubai
Tel: +971 4 2674433
Age range: 3–18
No. of pupils: 2789

Clarion School
P.O. Box 2819, Dubai
Tel: +971 04 457 4321

Collegiate International School
50 Al Maydar Street, Umm Suqeim 2, P.O. Box: 121306, Dubai
Tel: +971 4 427 1400
Curriculum: IBDP, IBCP

Cranleigh Abu Dhabi
PO BOX 51072, Abu Dhabi
Tel: +971 (0)2 497 0000
Age range: 3–18
Curriculum: UK, GCSE, IGCSE, ALevs
Language instr: English

Crescent English High School Dubai
PO Box 923, Al Qusais, Dubai
Tel: +971 4 29 888 66
Age range: 3–18
No. of pupils: 1432

Dar Al Marefa Private School
P.O.Box: 112602, Dubai 112602
Tel: +971 42885782
Curriculum: IBDP, IBMYP, IBPYP

Dawha High School
PO Box 5914, Orouba Street Khalidiya, Sharjah
Tel: +971 6 522 6500
No. of pupils: 2000
Curriculum: USA

Deira International School
PO Box 79043, Dubai
Tel: +9714 2325552
Age range: 3–18
No. of pupils: 1750
Curriculum: IBDP, IBCP, UK, IGCSE
Language instr: English
(CIS)

Deira Private School
Al Twar 3, PO Box 231959, Dubai
Tel: +971 4 2641595
Age range: 4–11
No. of pupils: 111
Curriculum: National
Language instr: English

Delhi Private School Dubai
PO Box 33321, The Gardens, Jebel Ali Dubai
Tel: +971 4 882 1848
Age range: 3–18
No. of pupils: 3274

Delhi Private School Sharjah
PO Box 26005, Sharjah
Tel: +971 6 5345352
Curriculum: National

Delta English School
PO Box 20121, Sharjah
Tel: 00 971 6 5359244
Age range: 3–16

Dubai American Academy
PO Box 32762, Al Barsha, Dubai
Tel: +971 4 347 9222
Age range: 3–18
No. of pupils: 2500 B1255 G1245
Curriculum: IBDP, USA
Language instr: English
(CIS) (ECIS)

Dubai British Foundation
Jumeirah Islands,
Tel: +971 (0)4 558 7308
Curriculum: UK

Dubai British School
Springs 3, Emirates Hills,
PO Box 37828, Dubai
Tel: +971 4361 9361
Age range: 3–18
No. of pupils: 1039 B531 G508
Curriculum: GCSE, IGCSE, ALevs
Language instr: English
(CIS) (COB)

Dubai British School Jumeirah Park
Al Warood St 1, Jumeirah Park Dubai,
Tel: +971 (0)4 552 0247
Age range: 3–18
Curriculum: UK, IGCSE, ALevs

Dubai Carmel School
PO Box 51977, Dubai
Tel: + 971 4 267 5424
Age range: 4–11
No. of pupils: 830
Curriculum: IGCSE

Dubai College
PO Box 837, Al Sufouh, Dubai
Tel: +971 4 399 9111
Age range: 11–18
No. of pupils: 885
Curriculum: UK, GCSE, IGCSE, ALevs
Language instr: English
(COB)

Dubai English Speaking College
PO Box 125814, Dubai
Tel: +971 (0) 4360 4866
Age range: 11–18
No. of pupils: 350

Dubai English Speaking School
PO Box 2002, Dubai
Tel: +971 4 3371457
Age range: 3–11
No. of pupils: 875 B450 G425
Curriculum: UK
Language instr: English
(COB)

Dubai International Academy, Al Barsha
P.O. Box: 118111, Al Barsha, Dubai
Tel: +971 4 524 4800
Curriculum: IBDP, IBMYP, IBPYP
Language instr: English

Dubai International Academy, Emirates Hills
P.O. Box: 118111, First Al Khail Street, Emirates Hills, Dubai
Tel: +971 4 368 4111
Age range: 3–18
No. of pupils: 1660 B830 G830
Curriculum: IBDP, IBMYP, IBPYP, IBCP
Language instr: English, Arabic

Dubai International School – Al Garhoud
PO Box 15495, Dubai 16029
Tel: +971 4 282 3513
Age range: 3–19

Dubai International School – Al Qouz Branch
PO Box 125676, Dubai
Tel: +971 4 3385530
Age range: 3–18
No. of pupils: 2010

Dubai Modern Education School
PO Box 61720, Dubai
Tel: +971 4 2885115
Age range: 4–18
No. of pupils: 2470

Dubai National School – Al Barsha Branch
PO Box 24060, Al Barsha, Dubai
Tel: + 971 4 3474 555
Age range: 4–18
No. of pupils: 2579
Curriculum: SAT

Dubai Scholars Private School
PO Box 2819, Dubai
Tel: + 971 4 2988892

Dunecrest American School
P.O. Box 624265, Wadi Al Safa 3 (next to Al Barari), Dubai
Tel: +971 4 508 7444
Curriculum: IBDP
Language instr: English

Dwight School Dubai
Umm Sequim Street, Al Barsha South 2, Dubai
Tel: +971 800 394448
Age range: 3–18
Curriculum: IBDP, IBMYP, IBPYP, USA
Language instr: English

Elite English School
PO Box 51212, Near Century Mall, Al Wuheida Road, Deira
Tel: +971 4 2688244
Curriculum: National

Elite Private School
Mohammed Bin Zayed City, P.O.Box 41231, Opposite of Al Ain University,, ME9 P14, Abu Dhabi
Tel: + 971 2 4475800
Curriculum: USA

Emirates Future International Academy
PO Box 128576, Abu Dhabi
Tel: +971 2 5525 188
Age range: 4–19
No. of pupils: 2700
Curriculum: USA

Emirates International School – Jumeirah
PO Box 6446, Dubai
Tel: +971 4 3489804
Age range: 3–18
No. of pupils: 2013
Curriculum: IBDP, IBMYP, IBPYP, IBCP
Language instr: English

Emirates International School – Meadows
PO Box 120118, Dubai
Tel: +971 4 362 9009
Age range: 3–18
No. of pupils: 1500 B800 G700
Curriculum: IBDP, IBMYP, IBPYP, IGCSE
Language instr: English
(CIS)

Emirates National School – Abu Dhabi City Campus
P.O. Box 44759, Abu Dhabi
Tel: +971 2 642 5993
No. of pupils: 2050
Curriculum: IBDP, IBMYP, IBPYP
Language instr: English

Emirates National School – Al Ain City Campus
PO Box 69392, Al Ain
Tel: +971 3 761 6888
No. of pupils: 2149
Curriculum: IBDP, IBMYP, IBPYP
Language instr: English, Arabic

Emirates National School – Branch 3
P.O. Box 44759, Khalifa Bin Shakhbout Street, Abu Dhabi
Curriculum: IBPYP
Language instr: English

Emirates National School – Mohammed Bin Zayed Campus
PO Box 44321, Mussafah, Abu Dhabi
Tel: +971 2 559 00 00
Age range: 3.8–17
No. of pupils: 3544
Curriculum: IBDP, IBMYP, IBPYP, National
Language instr: Arabic, English

Emirates National School – Ras Al Khaimah Campus
Ras Al-Khaimah
Tel: +971 7 203 3333
Curriculum: IBDP, IBMYP, IBPYP
Language instr: English

Emirates National School – Sharjah Campus
Al Rahmaniya, Sharjah
Tel: +971 6 599 0999
Curriculum: IBDP, IBMYP, IBPYP
Language instr: English

Emirates Private School Abu Dhabi
PO Box 2564, Abu Dhabi 2564
Tel: +971 2444 8863
Age range: 3–18
No. of pupils: 1150
Curriculum: USA

Emirates Private School Al Ain
PO Box 17549, Al Ain
Tel: + 971 3 7679322
Age range: 4–18
Curriculum: ACT, UK, USA, ALevs

English School in Kalba
PO Box 17555, Sharjah
Tel: +971 9 2778199
Age range: 4–11
No. of pupils: 100
Curriculum: GCSE

Fairgreen International School
PO Box 392024, The Sustainable City, Dubai
Tel: +971 4 875 4999
Age range: 3–16
No. of pupils: 470
Curriculum: IBDP, IBMYP, IBPYP, IBCP, UK, GCSE, ALevs
Language instr: English

Far Eastern Private School
PO Box 29047, Sharjah
Tel: +971 6 568 0888
Curriculum: National

First Steps School and Nursery
PO Box 32283, Abu Dhabi
Tel: +971 2 4454920
Age range: 18 months–4 years
Curriculum: National, UK

Foremarke School Dubai
P.O. Box 391984, Al Barsha South, Dubai
Tel: +971 4 818 8600
Curriculum: UK

Fujairah Private Academy
PO Box 797, Fujairah
Tel: +971 9 2224001
Age range: 3 –18

GEMS American Academy Abu Dhabi
16th Street, Khalifa City A, Abu Dhabi
Tel: +971 2 557 4880
Age range: 4–18 years
No. of pupils: 1800
Curriculum: IBDP, IBPYP, USA
Language instr: English

GEMS Cambridge International School – Abu Dhabi
Bani Yas East, Next to Bawabat Al Sharq Mall, Abu Dhabi
Tel: +971 2510 4343
Age range: 3.8–17
No. of pupils: 3500
Curriculum: UK, IGCSE
Language instr: English

GEMS Dubai American Academy
Suite 4503, Fraser Suites Dubai, Sidra Tower, Sheikh Zayed Road, P.O.Box 502305, Dubai
Tel: 00971 4704 9777
Age range: 4–17
No. of pupils: 2700
Curriculum: USA
Language instr: English

GEMS FirstPoint School
PO Box 48684, Dubai
Tel: +971 4 2789700
Age range: 3–19
No. of pupils: 840
Curriculum: UK, GCSE, IGCSE, ALevs
Language instr: English
(COB)

GEMS Founders School, Dubai
Al Barsha South, Dubai
Tel: +971 4519 5222
Age range: 4–13
Curriculum: UK
Language instr: English

GEMS Heritage Indian School – Dubai
Phase 2 Bldg., GEMS New Millennium School, Al Khail Road, Dubai
Tel: +971 4 445 2960
Age range: 4–15
Language instr: English

GEMS International School – Al Khail
Al Khail Road, Dubai
Tel: +971 4 339 6200
Age range: 4–17
No. of pupils: 693
Curriculum: IBDP, IBMYP, IBPYP, IBCP
Language instr: English

GEMS Jumeirah Primary School
PO Box 29093, Al Safa 1, Dubai
Tel: +971 4 3943500
Age range: 3–18
No. of pupils: 1150 *B560 G590*
Curriculum: UK
Language instr: English
(COB)

GEMS Metropole School
Honsho Road, P.O. BOX 392980, Dubai
Tel: +971 4 550 7200
Age range: 3–14
No. of pupils: 2001
Curriculum: UK, IGCSE
Language instr: English

GEMS Millennium School – Sharjah
Sharjah School Zone Area, PO Box – 31910, Sharjah
Tel: +971 6 5358176
Age range: 5–18

GEMS Modern Academy – Dubai
PO Box 53663, Nad al Sheeba 3,4, Dubai
Tel: +971 4 326 3339
Age range: 16–18 years
No. of pupils: 217
Curriculum: IBDP, IBPYP
Language instr: English

GEMS New Millennium School – Al Khail
Al Khail Road, Dubai
Tel: +971 4 4452900
Age range: 4–17
No. of pupils: 783
Language instr: English

GEMS Our Own Indian School – Al Quoz
PO Box 26845, Dubai
Tel: +971 4 3391188
Age range: 4–17
No. of pupils: 3646
Language instr: English

GEMS Royal Dubai School
PO Box 121310, Dubai
Tel: +971 4 288 6499
Age range: 3–11
No. of pupils: 1150
Curriculum: UK
Language instr: English
(COB)

GEMS United Indian School
42nd St., Baniyas West, Abu Dhabi
Tel: +971 2 2059777
Age range: 5–17
Language instr: English

GEMS Wellington Academy – Al Khail
Al Khail Road, Dubai
Tel: 00971 4512 9100
Age range: 4–13
No. of pupils: 830
Curriculum: UK, IGCSE
Language instr: English
(COB)

GEMS Wellington Academy – Silicon Oasis
Dubai Silicon Oasis, Dubai
Tel: +971 4 342 4040
Age range: 3–18
Curriculum: IBDP, IBCP, UK
(COB)

GEMS Wellington International School
PO Box 37486, Al Sufouh 1, Sheikh Zayed Road, Dubai
Tel: +971 (4) 348 4999
Age range: 3–18
No. of pupils: 2500
Curriculum: IBDP, IBCP, UK
Language instr: English
(COB)

GEMS Wellington Primary School
PO Box 114652, Dubai
Tel: +971 4 343 3266
Age range: 5–11
Curriculum: UK
Language instr: English
(COB)

GEMS Westminster School – Ras Al Khaimah
P.O Box: 12975, Ras Al Khaimah
Tel: +971 7 2035999
Age range: 4–11
No. of pupils: 1069
Curriculum: UK
Language instr: English

GEMS Westminster School – Sharjah
Sharjah
Tel: +971 6 542 6323
Age range: 4–13
No. of pupils: 2518
Curriculum: UK, IGCSE
Language instr: English

GEMS Winchester School – Abu Dhabi
Al Markaziyah, Abu Dhabi
Tel: +971 2 403 5499
Age range: 4–14
No. of pupils: 902
Curriculum: UK, IGCSE
Language instr: English

GEMS Winchester School – Dubai
Oud Metha Road, Next to American hospital, Dubai
Tel: +971 4 337 4112
Age range: 4–14
Curriculum: UK, ALevs
Language instr: English
(AISA)

GEMS World Academy – Abu Dhabi
Fatima Bint Mubarak Street, PO Box 110273, Abu Dhabi
Tel: +971 2 641 6333
Age range: 4–11
No. of pupils: 530
Curriculum: IBPYP, USA
Language instr: English
(CIS)

GEMS World Academy – Dubai
Al Khail Road, Al Barsha South, Dubai
Tel: +971 4 373 6373
Age range: 3–18
No. of pupils: 1500
Curriculum: IBDP, IBMYP, IBPYP, IBCP
Language instr: English
(CIS)

German International School Dubai
PO Box 391162, DIAC, Dubai
Tel: +971 4 456 2718
Age range: 3–19
No. of pupils: 506

German International School Sharjah
Al Abar, Sharjah
Tel: +971 6 5676014
Age range: 3–19
No. of pupils: 200
Curriculum: IBDP
Language instr: English

German School Abu Dhabi
PO Box 4150, Abu Dhabi
Tel: +971 2 6668668

Global Indian International School (GIIS) Abu Dhabi Campus
Street 12, Plot 17, Behind Lulu Hypermarket, Baniyas East, Abu Dhabi
Tel: +971 02 5079555

Global Indian International School (GIIS) Dubai Campus
Near Al Manar Islamic Center, Al Meydan Road, Dubai
Tel: +971 300 444 7392

Global Indian School, Ajman
P.O. Box: 1382, Al Jurf 2, Ajman
Tel: +971 6 743 7477
Age range: 4–19

Goodwill Children Private School
ME-10, Muhammad Bin Zayed City, Mussafah
Tel: +971 2 553 4277
Age range: 4–11
No. of pupils: 200

Greenfield International School
Dubai Investments Park, Dubai
Tel: +971 (0)4 885 6600
Age range: 3–18 years
No. of pupils: 1211
Curriculum: IBDP, IBMYP, IBPYP, IBCP
Language instr: English

Greenwood International School
PO Box 79595, Dubai
Tel: +971 4 2888 000
Age range: 3–18
No. of pupils: 836

Gulf Asian English School
PO Box 3406, Sharjah
Tel: +971 6 5340000
Age range: 4–18
No. of pupils: 273

Gulf Model School
PO Box 13683, Dubai
Tel: +971 4 2544222
Curriculum: National, UK

Hartland International School
Sobha Hartland,, Nad Al Sheba Mohammed Bin Rashid Al Maktoum City,,
Tel: +971 4 407 9444
Curriculum: UK, IGCSE, ALevs
(COB)

HH Shaikh Rashid Al Maktoum Pakistan School, Dubai
Baghdad Street, Dubai
Tel: +971 4298 8303
Age range: 3–18
No. of pupils: 1348

Horizon School
Al Wasl Road, Jumeirah, Dubai
Tel: +9714 3422891
Age range: 3–11
No. of pupils: 415
Curriculum: UK
Language instr: English

iCademy Middle East
PO Box: 502981, Block 12, Floor 1, Unit F12, Dubai, Knowledge Village
Tel: +971 444 01212
Age range: 5–12
(CEE)

Indian High School
Oud Metha Rd, Dubai
Tel: +971 4 337 7475
Language instr: English
(RS)

Indian School Ras Al Khaimah
PO Box 4943, Ras Al Khaimah
Tel: +971 7 2288346
Age range: 4–11

Institute of Applied Technology
Abu Dhabi
Tel: +971 2 8131 555

International Academic School
P.O Box: 300165, Al Warqa 1, Dubai
Tel: +971 4 2800 993
No. of pupils: VIth1200
Curriculum: National, USA

International Community School (ICS) Mushrif
24th Street, Al Mushrif Area, Abu Dhabi 55022
Tel: +971 2 633 0444
Age range: 3–18 years
No. of pupils: 1500
Curriculum: IBDP, USA
Language instr: English, Arabic

International Concept for Education (ICE Dubai)
Al meydan Rd, Nad al Shebal, Near Meydan Hotel, Meydan, Dubai
Tel: +971 4 3377818
Curriculum: IBPYP
Language instr: English, French

International School of Arts and Sciences Dubai
PO Box 35901, Al Warqaa, Dubai
Tel: +971 4 280 0459
Age range: 5–18
No. of pupils: 463
Curriculum: AP, SAT, USA

International School of Creative Science
PO Box 25779, Sharjah
Tel: +971 6 534 4444
Age range: 5–18
No. of pupils: 1200
Curriculum: GCSE, IGCSE

Iqraa International School
PO Box 3598, Sharjah
Tel: +971 6 535 1166
Age range: 4–18
Curriculum: USA

Japanese School
PO Box 8120, Abu Dhabi
Tel: +971 2 446104
Age range: 4–19
No. of pupils: 78

Japanese School in Dubai
PO Box 7149, Dubai
Tel: +971 4 3449119
Age range: 4–16
No. of pupils: 148

Jebel Ali School
PO Box 17111, Dubai
Tel: +971 4 884 6485
Age range: 4–16
No. of pupils: 650
Curriculum: UK
(COB)

JSS International School
671-1431 Al Barsha South, PO Box 37232, Dubai
Tel: +971 4 325 6886
Age range: 4–15
No. of pupils: 1380

Jumeira Baccalaureate School
53 B Street, off Al Wasl Road, Jumeira 1, Dubai
Tel: +971 (0)4 344 6931
Age range: 3–19 years
No. of pupils: 1098
Curriculum: IBDP, IBMYP, IBPYP, IBCP
Language instr: English

Jumeirah College
Street 19, Safa 1, PO Box 74856, Dubai
Tel: +971 4 395 5524
Age range: 11–18
No. of pupils: 1100
Curriculum: UK, ALevs
Language instr: English
(COB)

Jumeirah English Speaking School (JESS), Arabian Ranches
Main entrance of Arabian Ranches community, PO Box 24942, Dubai
Tel: +971 4 3619019
Age range: 3–18
No. of pupils: 1378
Curriculum: IBDP, UK, IGCSE
Language instr: English
(COB) (ECIS)

Jumeirah English Speaking School (JESS), Jumeirah
PO Box 24942, Dubai
Tel: +971 4 3619019
Age range: 3–11
Curriculum: UK

Kent College Dubai
PO Box 334022, Dubai
Tel: +971 4343 0987
Age range: 3–18
Curriculum: IBDP, IBCP, UK, GCSE, ALevs
Language instr: English
(COB)

Kings' School Al Barsha
PO Box 38199, Dubai
Tel: +971 4 356 6900
No. of pupils: 1700
Curriculum: UK, GCSE, ALevs
(COB)

Kings' School Dubai
PO Box 38199, Dubai
Tel: +971 4 348 3939
Age range: 3–11 years
No. of pupils: 940
Curriculum: National, UK

Kings' School Nad Al Sheba
PO Box 38199, Dubai
Tel: +971 4 237 5555
No. of pupils: 550
Curriculum: UK

Latifa School for Girls
PO Box 11533, Dubai
Tel: +971 4 3361065
Age range: G3–18
Curriculum: UK, GCSE, IGCSE, ALevs
Language instr: English

Leaders Private School
PO Box 45094, Sharjah
Tel: +971 6 522 55 60
Age range: 3–16
No. of pupils: 1700

Liwa International School
PO Box 81685, Al Ain
Tel: +971 3 7810444
Age range: 4–18
No. of pupils: 1404
Curriculum: USA

Lycee Francais International
PO Box 2226, Dubai
Tel: +971 4 336 8552
Age range: 3–16
No. of pupils: 1428

Lycée Français International Georges Pompidou – École de Sharjah
PO Box 294471, Dubai
Tel: +971 65673430
Curriculum: FrenchBacc

Lycee Libanais Francophone Prive
PO Box 28759, Dubai
Tel: +971 4 264 0800
Age range: 3–15
No. of pupils: 783

Lycee Louis Massignon
PO Box 2314, Abu Dhabi
Tel: +971 2 444 80 85
Age range: 4–18
No. of pupils: 1470
Curriculum: National

MADAR International School
PO Box 15658, Al Ain
Tel: +971 3 76 11 330
Age range: 4–17
No. of pupils: 2012
Curriculum: USA

Mirdif American School
P.O. Box 79195, Algeria Street -11A- Mizhar 1, Dubai
Tel: +971 4 288 3303
No. of pupils: 895
Curriculum: USA

MSB Private School
PO Box 94550, Dubai
Tel: +971 4 2677100
Age range: 3–16
No. of pupils: 496

New Academy School
PO Box 11439, Dubai
Tel: +971 4 398 8873
Age range: 3–18
No. of pupils: 710

New Indian Model School
PO Box 3780, Sharjah
Tel: +971 6 5228035
Age range: 4–19
No. of pupils: 300

New Indian Model School (Dubai)
PO Box 3100, Dubai
Tel: +971 4 2824313
Age range: 3–19

New World Private School
PO Box 56988, Dubai
Tel: +971 42610033
Age range: 3–18

Nord Anglia International School, Dubai
off Hessa Street, Dubai
Tel: +971 (0)4 2199 999
Curriculum: IBDP
COB

North London Collegiate School Dubai
Nad Al Sheba, Mohammed Bin Rashid Al Maktoum City, Dubai
Tel: +971 (0)4319 0888
Age range: 2–18
Curriculum: IBDP, IBMYP, IBPYP
Language instr: Arabic, English

Our Own English High School (OOB)
PO Box 150807, Sharjah
Tel: +971 6 5355227
Age range: 6–17
No. of pupils: 3481
Language instr: English

Our Own English High School (OOD)
PO Box 3004, Dubai
Tel: +971 4 236 1335
Age range: 3–18
No. of pupils: 9344

Our Own English High School (OOF)
PO Box 967, Fujairah
Tel: +971 9 222 7127
Age range: 4–19
No. of pupils: 3100

Our Own English High School (OOL)
PO Box 80369, Al Ain
Tel: +971 3 767 9747
Age range: 3–18
No. of pupils: 1865

Our Own English High School (OOS)
PO Box 2676, Sharjah
Tel: + 971 6 5386486
Age range: 4–17
No. of pupils: 7522
Language instr: English

Our Own High School (OOW)
PO Box 35519, Dubai
Tel: +971 4 2800077
Age range: 6–17
No. of pupils: 4723
Language instr: English

Our Own High School Al Warqa'a
PO Box 35519, Dubai
Tel: +971 4 2800077
Age range: 4–19
No. of pupils: 4734

Pakistan Education Academy
PO Box 621, Dubai
Tel: +971 4 3370126
Age range: 4–8
No. of pupils: 1682

Pakistan Islamia Higher Secondary School
Post Box No 1493, Sharjah
Tel: +971 (0)6 5670700
Age range: 14–19
No. of pupils: 2200

Philadelphia Private School Dubai
PO Box 185020, Dubai
Tel: +971 4 26 46 202
Age range: 4–19
No. of pupils: 792

Pristine Private School
PO Box 60830, Dubai
Tel: +971 4 2674299
Age range: 3–18
No. of pupils: 600

Providence English Private School
PO Box 25532, Sharjah
Tel: +971 6 5340443
Age range: 3–18
Curriculum: National, UK, IGCSE

Raffles International School
Al Baghla Street, Umm Suqeim 3, PO Box 122900, Dubai
Tel: +971 4 4271200
Curriculum: UK
CIS

Raffles World Academy
Al Marcup Street, Umm Suqeim 3, P.O. Box 122900, Dubai
Tel: +971 4 4271351/2
Age range: 3–18+
Curriculum: IBDP, IBMYP, IBPYP, IBCP, SAT, IGCSE
Language instr: English

Raha International School
Khalifa City 'A', Al Raha Gardens, Abu Dhabi
Tel: +971 (0)2 556 1567
Age range: 4–18 years
No. of pupils: 2833
Curriculum: IBDP, IBMYP, IBPYP
Language instr: English
ECIS

Rajagiri International School
PO Box 62012, Al Warqaa 1, Dubai
Tel: +971 4 2800691
Age range: 3–12
No. of pupils: 1163

Ras Al Khaimah Academy
PO Box 975, Ras Al Khiamah
Tel: +971 7 236 2441
Age range: 2.5–18
No. of pupils: 1300 *B700 G600*
Curriculum: IBDP, IBPYP, SAT, UK
Language instr: English

Ras Al Khaimah American Academy for Girls
Sultan Al Kabeer Road, Ras Al Khaimah
Tel: +971 7 2211462
Age range: 4–11
No. of pupils: 420

Rashid School for Boys
PO Box 2861, Dubai
Tel: +971 4 3361300
Age range: B3–18
No. of pupils: 650
Curriculum: SAT, TOEFL, UK, ALevs
Language instr: English, Arabic

Regent International School
The Greens, Emirates Living Community, PO Box 2487, Dubai
Tel: +971 4 360 8830
Age range: 3–18
Curriculum: UK, ALevs

Repton School Abu Dhabi
PO Box 45016, Al Reem Island, Abu Dhabi
Tel: +971 2 508 1900
Curriculum: UK

Repton School, Dubai
PO Box 300331, Nad Al Sheba 3, Dubai
Tel: +971 4 426 9300
Age range: 3–18
No. of pupils: 2123
Curriculum: IBDP, IBCP, UK, IGCSE
Language instr: English
COB

Ryan International School, Sharjah
P.O. Box 2913, Sharjah
Tel: +971 6 534 1119
Age range: 4–16
No. of pupils: 100

SABIS International School – Yas Island
Yas East, Yas Island, Abu Dhabi
Tel: +971 2 565 0065

Safa British School
PO Box 71091, Dubai
Tel: +971 4 388 4300
Age range: 3–11

Safa Community School
PO Box 71091, Dubai
Tel: +971 4 385 1810
Age range: 3–14
No. of pupils: 750

Scholars Indian School RAK
PO Box 3659, Ras Al Khaimah
Tel: +971 7 222 7600
Age range: 14–19
No. of pupils: 1000

Scholars International Academy
PO Box 47425, Sharjah
Tel: +971 6 5355033
Age range: 4–11
No. of pupils: 800
Curriculum: UK

School of Modern Skills
PO Box: 57475, Dubai
Tel: +971 42887765
Language instr: English
ISA

Sharjah American International School
PO Box 5201, Sharjah
Tel: +971 6 5380000
Age range: 4–18
No. of pupils: 1600 *B900 G700*
Curriculum: AP, SAT, USA
Language instr: English

Sharjah British International School
PO Box 631, Sharjah
Tel: +971 6 5347722
Age range: 4–18
No. of pupils: 400
Curriculum: ALevs

Sharjah English School
PO Box 1600, Sharjah
Tel: +971 (6) 558 9304
Age range: 3–11
No. of pupils: 320 B165 G155
Curriculum: UK

Sharjah Public School
PO Box 20268, Sharjah 20268
Tel: +971 6 5221244
Age range: 3–17
No. of pupils: 800

SKBZ Bangladesh Islamia Pvt. School
PO Box 3174, Abu Dhabi
Tel: +971 2 4446904
Age range: 4–19
No. of pupils: 440

Springdale Indian School
Al Azra Area, PO Box 27060, Sharjah
Tel: +971 6 524 3335
Curriculum: National

St Mary's Catholic High School
PO Box 52232, Dubai
Tel: +971 4 3370252
Age range: 5–19
No. of pupils: 1966
Curriculum: IGCSE

St Mary's Catholic High School
PO Box 1665, Fujairah
Tel: +971 70 9 2282828
Curriculum: GCSE, ALevs

Star International School
PO Box 51008, Dubai
Tel: +971 4288 4644
Age range: 3–13

Star International School, Mirdif
24B Street, Mirdif, Dubai
Tel: +971 4 288 4644
Age range: 3–12
No. of pupils: 304

Sunmarke School
District 5 (Behind Limitless Building on Al Khail Road), Jumeirah Village Triangle, Dubai
Tel: +971 4 423 8900
Curriculum: IBDP, IBCP
Language instr: English

Sunrise English Private School
PO Box 71356, Mussafah, Abu Dhabi
Tel: +971 2 5529989
Age range: 14–19
No. of pupils: 1240

Swiss International Scientific School in Dubai
Dubai Healthcare City, Phase 2, Al Jaddaf, PO Box 505002, Dubai
Tel: +971 4 375 0600
Age range: 3–18
No. of pupils: 1200
Curriculum: IBDP, IBMYP, IBPYP, IBCP
Language instr: English, French, German

Taaleem
PO Box 76691, 1st Floor Century Plaza, Jumeira Road
Tel: +971 4 349 8806
Age range: 3–19
No. of pupils: 4280 B1828 G2452
Curriculum: IBDP, IBMYP, IBPYP, National, UK, USA, IGCSE, ALevs
Language instr: English

The Arbor School
Al Furjan, PO Box 413898, Dubai
Tel: +971 (0) 4 581 4100
Age range: 3–11
Curriculum: UK

The British International School, Abu Dhabi
PO Box 60968, Abu Dhabi
Tel: +971 2 510 0176
Age range: 3–18
No. of pupils: 1800
Curriculum: IBDP, UK, IGCSE
Language instr: English
(RS)

The British School – Al Khubairat
PO Box 4001, Abu Dhabi
Tel: +971 2 4462280
Age range: 3–18
No. of pupils: 1284 B673 G611
Curriculum: UK
(COB)

The Cambridge High School – Abu Dhabi
PO Box 27602, Abu Dhabi
Tel: +971 2 552 1621
Age range: 3–19
No. of pupils: 1600 B866 G734
Curriculum: UK, ALevs
Language instr: English

The Children's Garden
Green Community, Dubai Investments Park,
Tel: +971 (0)4 885 3484
Age range: 2–6

The English College
Safa 1, off Sheikh Zayed Road (opposite Oasis Centre), PO Box 11812, Dubai
Tel: +971 4 394 3465
Age range: 3–18
No. of pupils: 960
Curriculum: UK, GCSE, ALevs
Language instr: English

The Indian Academy, Dubai
Behind Madina Mall, Al Muhaisnah – 4, P.O: 55510, Plot No: 245-703, Dubai
Tel: +971 4264 6733
Age range: 3–18
Curriculum: National

The Indian Academy, Sharjah
Next to Sharjah Transport Authority Al Azrah, PO Box 60709, Sharjah
Tel: +971 06 577 0949
Curriculum: National

The International School of Choueifat – Abu Dhabi
PO Box 7212, Mushrif Area, Abu Dhabi
Tel: +971 2 446 1444
Age range: 3–18
No. of pupils: 2876 B1639 G1237

The International School of Choueifat – Abu Dhabi Khalifa City
PO Box 502, Abu Dhabi Khalifa City, Abu Dhabi
Tel: +971 2 556 2555

The International School of Choueifat – Ajman
Al Tallah 2, South Sector, Ajman
Tel: +971 6 742 1111

The International School of Choueifat – Al Ain
Bldg. #103, Saeed Ibn Shakhboot St., Ugdat Al Mutawaa, Al Muwaiji, Al Ain
Tel: +971 3 767 8444
Age range: 3–18
No. of pupils: 618 B387 G231

The International School of Choueifat – Dubai
Hessa Street, Al Sufouh 2 area, Jumeirah, Dubai
Tel: +971 4 399 9444
Age range: 3–19
No. of pupils: 3210 B1745 G1465
Curriculum: AP, SAT, ALevs

The International School of Choueifat – Dubai
Al Sufouh Road, near Dubai College, Dubai 2077
Tel: +971 4 399 9444

The International School of Choueifat – Dubai Investments Park
Dubai Investments Park 1, Dubai
Tel: +971 4 884 7884
Age range: 4–18
No. of pupils: 1648

The International School of Choueifat – Ras Al Khaimah
PO Box 1644, Ras Al Khaimah
Tel: +971 7 235 3446
Age range: 3–18
No. of pupils: 200
Curriculum: AP, USA

The International School of Choueifat – Ruwais
Bldg. # GB115 2nd Street East, Adjacent to Emirates General Market, Ruwais Housing Division
Tel: +971 2 876 2525
Age range: 4–19
No. of pupils: 1800

The International School of Choueifat – Sharjah
University Road, Industrial Area 6, Sharjah
Tel: +971 6 558 2211
Age range: 3–18
No. of pupils: 3338 B1935 G1403
Curriculum: AP, UK, ALevs
Language instr: English

The International School of Choueifat – Umm Al Quwain
Al Hamra, Clock Roundabout, Umm Al Quwain
Tel: +971 6 766 5888
Age range: 4–11
No. of pupils: 620

The Kindergarten Starters
PO Box 4973, Dubai
Tel: +971 4 2824090
Age range: 3–11

The Millennium School
P.O. Box 32446, Dubai
Tel: +971 4 298 8567
Language instr: English
(RS)

The Model School
PO Box 25723, Abu Dhabi
Tel: +971 2 5527200
Age range: 4–19
No. of pupils: 300

The Oxford School Dubai
PO Box 50091, Dubai
Tel: +971 4 2543666
Age range: 3–18
No. of pupils: 1828
Curriculum: ALevs

The Pearl Academy
PO Box 128484, Abu Dhabi
Tel: +971 2 641 8887
Age range: 3–11
Curriculum: National, UK

The School of Research Science
44 Baghdad Street, Dubai
Tel: +971 4 6011011
Age range: 3–18
Language instr: English, Arabic

The Sheffield Private School
PO Box 92665, Dubai
Tel: +971 4 2678444
Age range: 4–18
No. of pupils: 740 *B*408 *G*332
Curriculum: UK
Language instr: English

The Sheikh Zayed Private Academy
PO Box 42989, Abu Dhabi
Tel: +971 2 619 5555
Age range: G3–18
No. of pupils: 305
Curriculum: USA
(CIS)

The WellSpring School
34B St, Ras Al-Khaimah,
Tel: +971-07-2362446
Curriculum: USA

The Westminster School
Al Ghusais School Zone,
PO Box 27016, Dubai
Tel: +971 4 2988333
Age range: 3–17
No. of pupils: 5100 *B*2800 *G*2300
Curriculum: UK
Language instr: English

The Winchester School
PO Box 38058, The Gardens,
Jebel Ali, Dubai
Tel: +9714 8820444
Age range: 3–18
Curriculum: UK

United International Private School
PO Box 60817, Dubai
Tel: +971 4 2543888
Age range: 5–16
No. of pupils: 1000

Universal American School, Dubai
PO Box 79133, Al Rashidiya, Dubai
Tel: +971 4 232 5222
Age range: 3–18
No. of pupils: 1100 *B*616 *G*484
Curriculum: IBDP, IBPYP, SAT, USA
Language instr: English, Arabic
(CIS)

Uptown International School
Corner of Algeria Road & Tripoli Street, Mirdif, PO Box 73181, Dubai
Tel: +971 (0)4 2515001
Age range: 2–17 years
No. of pupils: 1230
Curriculum: IBDP, IBMYP, IBPYP
Language instr: English
(ECIS)

Victoria English School
PO Box 25549, Sharjah
Tel: +971 6 5227770
Age range: 2–18
No. of pupils: 582 *B*309 *G*273
Curriculum: UK
Language instr: English

Victoria International School of Sharjah
PO Box 68600, Al Mamzar, Sharjah
Tel: +971 6 577 1999
Curriculum: IBDP

Victory Heights Primary School
PO Box 454959 Dubai,
Tel: (+971) 4 423 1100
Curriculum: UK
(COB)

Wesgreen International School
PO Box 40658, Sharjah
Tel: +971 6 534 6333
Age range: 1–17
No. of pupils: 1388 *B*720 *G*668
Curriculum: UK
Language instr: English
(CIS)

West Yas Academy
Zone K – Yas Island – Abu Dhabi,
Opp. West Yas Plaza, Abu Dhabi
Tel: +971 2 885 7001
Curriculum: USA

UZBEKISTAN

Oxbridge International School
Oymarik Street 10, Mirzo Ulug'bek District, Tashkent 100124
Curriculum: IBDP, IBMYP, IBPYP
Language instr: English, Russian

Smart School
Amir Temur Avenue 33,
Mirabad District, Tashkent
Tel: +998 71 2319955
Curriculum: IBDP
Language instr: English, Russian

Tashkent International School
38 Sarikulskaya Street,
Tashkent 100005
Tel: +998 71 291 9670
Age range: 3–19
No. of pupils: 457 *B*232 *G*225
Curriculum: ACT, IBDP, IBMYP, IBPYP, SAT, TOEFL, USA
Language instr: English
(CEE) (CIS) (ECIS)

Tashkent Ulugbek International School
Jamshid Shoshoy street
5-A, 100100 Tashkent
Tel: +998 71 255 17 24
Age range: 6–16
No. of pupils: 200 *B*118 *G*82
Curriculum: ALevs
(ECIS)

The British School of Tashkent
Yassi Street Bld 15-a Mirzo-Ulugbeck District, Tashkent
Tel: +998 712 626 020
No. of pupils: 422
Curriculum: UK, IGCSE
Language instr: English
(COB)

VIETNAM

American International School of Vietnam
220 Nguyen Van Tao, Nha Be District, Ho Chi Minh City
Tel: +84 28378 00808
Curriculum: IBDP, IBMYP, IBPYP, SAT, USA
Language instr: English, Vietnamese
(CIS) (EAR)

Asian International School Primary School
(Caothang Campus 1),
177 bis Caothang Street,
Ward 12, District 10 848
Tel: +84 8 38680259
Curriculum: USA

AUSTRALIAN INTERNATIONAL SCHOOL (AIS)
For further details see p. 55
264 Mai Chi Tho Street,
An Phu ward, Thu Duc City, Ho Chi Minh City
Tel: +84 28 3742 4040
Email: info@aisvietnam.com
Website: www.aisvietnam.com
Executive Principal: Davina McCarthy
Age range: 18 months–18 years
No. of pupils: 1200
Fees: 257,000,000–734,000,000
Curriculum: IBDP, IBPYP, IGCSE

British International School, Hanoi
Hoa Lan Road, Vinhomes Riverside,
Long Bien District, Hanoi 100000
Tel: +84 24 3946 0435
Age range: 2–18 years
No. of pupils: 1100
Curriculum: IBDP, IPC, UK, IGCSE
(CIS)

BRITISH INTERNATIONAL SCHOOL, HO CHI MINH CITY
For further details see p. 58
246 Nguyen Van Huong Street, Thao Dien, Thu Duc City, Ho Chi Minh City
Tel: +84 (0)28 3744 2335
Email: bis.admissions@bisvietnam.com
Website: www.bisvietnam.com
Principal: Anthony Rowlands
Age range: 2–18 years
No. of pupils: 2300
Fees: US$12,300–US$34,800
Curriculum: IBDP, IGCSE
Language instr: English
(CIS)

British Vietnamese International School, Hanoi
72A Nguyen Trai Street, Thanh Xuan District, Hanoi
Tel: +84 24 6266 8800

British Vietnamese International School, Ho Chi Minh City
44-46 Street 1, Binh Hung, Binh Chanh, Ho Chi Minh City
Tel: +84 83 758 0717 Ext:211

Canadian International School – Vietnam
No. 86, Road 23, Phu My Hung, Tan Phu Ward, District 7, Binh Chanh District, Ho Chi Minh City
Tel: +84 94 295 8557
Curriculum: IBDP
Language instr: English

Concordia International School Hanoi
Van Tri Golf Compound, Kim No, Dong Anh, Hanoi
Tel: +84 (0) 24 3795 8878
Age range: 3–18 years
No. of pupils: 380
Curriculum: AP
Language instr: English

English French School (EFS)
So 3 Duong 46, Thao Dien,
Quan 2, Ho Chi Minh City
Age range: 5–11 years
No. of pupils: 20
Curriculum: FrenchBacc, UK
Language instr: English, French

EUROPEAN INTERNATIONAL SCHOOL HCMC
For further details see p. 73
730 Le Van Mien Street, Thao Dien Ward, Thu Duc City,
Ho Chi Minh City 70000
Tel: +8428 7300 7257
Email: info@eishcmc.com
Website: www.eishcmc.com
Head of School: John Veitch
Age range: 2–18 years
No. of pupils: 600
Fees: 241,000,000–664,000,000
Curriculum: IBDP, IBMYP, IBPYP
Language instr: English

Fosco International School (FIS)
40 Ba Huyen Thanh Quan, Ward 6, District 3,, Ho Chi Minh City
Tel: +84 28 3930 5930
Age range: 18 months–11 years
Curriculum: USA

Global Indian International School (GIIS) Vietnam Campus
Ho Chi Minh City

Green Shoots International School
414/7 Cua Dai, Cam Chau, Hoi An, Quang Nam Province 560000
Tel: 0084 235 392 4954
Age range: 2–16
Curriculum: UK, IGCSE
Language instr: English, French
COB

Hanoi Academy
D45 – D46, Ciputra International City, Hanoi
Tel: +84 43 7430135
Age range: 2–18
Curriculum: National

Hanoi International School
48 Lieu Giai Street, Ba Dinh District, Hanoi
Tel: +84 4 3832 8140
Age range: 4–18
No. of pupils: 270 *B*130 *G*140
Curriculum: IBDP, IBMYP, IBPYP
Language instr: English
CIS

HOI AN INTERNATIONAL SCHOOL
For further details see p. 75
24 Phan Ba Phien, Hoi An
Tel: +84 (0)235 651 8518
Email: admissions@hais.edu.vn
Website: www.hais.edu.vn
CEO & Founder: Tran Hanh An
Age range: 2–18 years

Horizon International Bilingual School – Hanoi Campus
98 To Ngoc Van St, Villa 1, 2,, District Tay Ho, Hanoi
Tel: +84 3719 49 53
Age range: 14–17
No. of pupils: 207 *B*135 *G*72
Curriculum: National
Language instr: English, Vietnamese

Horizon International Bilingual School – HCMC Campus
6-6A-8, Duong 44, Thao Dien Ward, District 2
Tel: +84 8 5402 2482
Age range: 5–18
No. of pupils: 286
Curriculum: SAT, UK, IGCSE, ALevs

International German School HCMC
12 Vo Truong Toan, An Phu Ward, District 2, Ho Chi Minh City
Tel: +84 (0)28 37 44 63 44
Curriculum: IBDP
Language instr: English, German

INTERNATIONAL SCHOOL HO CHI MINH CITY (ISHCMC)
For further details see p. 80
28 Vo Truong Toan St., An Phu ward, Thu Duc City, Ho Chi Minh City
Tel: +84 28 3898 9100
Email: admissions@ishcmc.edu.vn
Website: www.ishcmc.com
Head of School: Kim Green
Age range: 2–18 years
Curriculum: IBDP, IBMYP, IBPYP
Language instr: English
CIS EAR ECIS

International School of Vietnam
No. 6-7 Nguyen Cong Thai Street, Dai Kim Urban area, Hoang Mai, Hanoi
Tel: +84 (0)435 409 183
Curriculum: IBDP, IBPYP
Language instr: English

International School Saigon Pearl
92 Nguyen Huu Canh Street, Ward 22, Binh Thanh District, Ho Chi Minh City
Tel: +84 8 2222 7788/99
Language instr: English

International Schools of North America
Street 20, Him Lam Residential Area, Binh Chanh District, Ho Chi Minh City
Tel: +84 28 730 97 99
Age range: 5–19
No. of pupils: 425
Curriculum: IBDP, IBMYP, IBPYP
Language instr: English

KinderWorld International Kindergarten (KIK) @ Hanoi Towers
3rd Floor, 49 Hai Ba Trung Street, Hoan Kiem District, Hanoi
Tel: +84 4 3934 7243

KinderWorld International Kindergarten (KIK) @ The Manor (Hanoi)
C5-C11, 1st Floor, The Manor Building, My Dinh, Me Tri New Urban, Tu Liem District, Hanoi
Tel: +84 4 3794 0209

KinderWorld International Kindergarten (KIK) @ The Manor (HCMC)
The Manor Building, 91 Nguyen Huu Canh Street, Binh Thanh District, Ho Chi Minh City
Tel: +84 8 3514 3036

Lycée Français Alexandre Yersin
12 Nui Truc, Ba Dinh, Hanoi
Tel: +844 3843 67 79
Curriculum: FrenchBacc

Pegasus International College – Da Nang
Vung Trung 3, Phu My An New Urban Area, Hoa Hai Ward, Ngu Hanh Son District, Da Nang City
Tel: +84 023 6730 1555

Pegasus International College – Hanoi
No. 2/2C, Doan Van Phuc Diplomatic Area, Kim Ma Street, Ba Dinh District, Hanoi
Tel: +84 024 7304 1555

QSI International School of Haiphong
Lot CC2, Me Linh Village, Anh Dung Ward, Duong Kinh District, Haiphong
Tel: +84 31 381 4258
Age range: 2–18 years
Curriculum: IBDP, USA
Language instr: English

Renaissance International School Saigon
74 Nguyen Thi Thap Street, Binh Thuan Ward, District 7, Ho Chi Minh City
Tel: +84 283 7733 171
Age range: 2–18
No. of pupils: 560
Curriculum: IBDP, UK, IGCSE
Language instr: English
RS

Saigon South International School
78 Nguyen Duc Canh, Tan Phong Ward, District 7, Ho Chi Minh City 70000
Tel: +84 28 5413 0901
Age range: 3–18
No. of pupils: 1005 *B*486 *G*519 *VIth*74
Curriculum: AP, IBDP, SAT, USA
Language instr: English
EAR

Singapore International School (SIS) @ BDNC
Lot F7, Le Loi Street, Binh Duong New City, Hoa Phu Ward, Thu Dau Mot City, Binh Duong Province
Tel: +84 27 4730 0777
Age range: 3–17 years

Singapore International School (SIS) @ Can Tho
Nguyen Van Cu Street, An Binh Ward, Ninh Kieu District, Can Tho City
Tel: +84 29 2730 1777
Age range: 3–17 years

Singapore International School (SIS) @ Ciputra
Block C3 (NT III B) Ciputra Hanoi International City, Phu Thuong Ward, Tay Ho District, Hanoi
Tel: +84 24 7304 3777
Age range: 3–11 years

Singapore International School (SIS) @ Da Nang
SIS Building, Vung Trung 3 Street, Phu My An New Urban Area, Hoa Hai Ward, Ngu Hanh Son District, Da Nang City
Tel: +84 23 6730 1777
Age range: 3–17 years

Singapore International School (SIS) @ Gamuda Gardens
Gamuda Gardens 2 Road, Gamuda Gardens, Km 4.4 Phap Van, Hoang Mai District, Hanoi
Tel: +84 24 7304 1777
Age range: 3–16 years

Singapore International School (SIS) @ Ha Long
Hung Thang Urban and Service Area, Hung Thang Ward, Halong City, Quang Ninh Province
Tel: +84 20 3655 8811
Age range: 3–17 years

Singapore International School (SIS) @ Saigon South
No. 29, Road No. 3, Trung Son Residential Area, Hamlet 4, Binh Hung Ward, Binh Chanh District, Ho Chi Minh City
Tel: +84 28 7301 3777
Age range: 4–17 years

Singapore International School (SIS) @ Van Phuc
2D Van Phuc Diplomatic Compound, 46 Van Bao Street, Ba Dinh District, Hanoi
Tel: +84 24 7304 2777
Age range: 3–11 years

Singapore International School (SIS) @ Vung Tau
Dai An Residential, Ward 9, Vung Tau City
Tel: +84 25 4730 1777
Age range: 3–17 years

Singapore Vietnam International School (SVIS) @ Nha Trang
Vinh Diem Trung Residential Area, Nha Trang City
Tel: +84 25 8730 1777

St. Paul American School Hanoi
Splendora New Urban, Km 10 + 600 Thang Long Highway, Hoai Duc Hanoi
Tel: +84 24 3399 6464
Curriculum: AP, USA
EAR

TH School
6 Chua Boc, Quang Trung, Dong Da, Hanoi
Tel: +84 24 7309 2253
Age range: 2–18
No. of pupils: 170 B90 G80
Curriculum: ACT, IPC, SAT, IGCSE, ALevs
Language instr: English

The ABC International School
#2 1E Street, Khu Dan Cu, Trung Son, Binh Hung, Binh Chanh, Ho Chi Minh City
Tel: +84 28 5431 1833
Age range: 2–18
No. of pupils: 750
Curriculum: AP, UK, IGCSE, ALevs
Language instr: English
COB

The Asian International School
177 Bis 2 Cao Thang, Phuong 12, Quan 10 (6,272.60 mi), Ho Chi Minh City 72510
Tel: +84 28 3868 0270
Curriculum: USA
CIS

The International School @ Park City Hanoi
Le Trong Tan Road, Ha Dong District, Hanoi
Tel: +84 93 44 55 228
Age range: 3–18 years

United Nations International School of Hanoi
G9 Ciputra, Tay Ho, Hanoi
Tel: +84 24 7300 4500
Age range: 3–18
No. of pupils: 1130
Curriculum: IBDP, IBMYP, IBPYP
Language instr: English
CIS EAR ECIS

Vietnam-Finland International School
01, D1 Street, Tan Phong Ward, District 7, Ho Chi Minh City
Tel: +84 28 37 755 110
Curriculum: IBDP
Language instr: English, Vietnamese

Wellspring International Bilingual School – Hanoi
No. 95, Ai Mo Town, Bo De ward, Long Bien District, Hanoi
Tel: +84 24 3766 3838
Age range: 5–18
Curriculum: IGCSE
Language instr: English, Vietnamese

Wellspring Saigon International Bilingual School
92 Nguyen Huu Canh Street, Ward 22, Binh Thanh District, Ho Chi Minh City
Tel: +84 28 3840 9292
Age range: 5–18
Curriculum: IGCSE
Language instr: English, Vietnamese

Western Australian Primary and High School
43 Nguyen Thong Street, Ward 7, District 3, Ho Chi Minh City
Tel: +84 28 7109 5077
Age range: 2–18 years
No. of pupils: 2500
Curriculum: IBDP
Language instr: English

YEMEN

Mohammed Ali Othman School
PO Box 5713, Taiz
Tel: +967 (4)223671
Age range: 3–18
No. of pupils: 1000
Curriculum: UK, IGCSE, ALevs
COB

Sana'a British School
PO Box 15546, Sana'a
Tel: +967 1 203950
Age range: 2–18
No. of pupils: 201 B91 G110
Curriculum: National, UK, IGCSE, ALevs
Language instr: English

International schools in Australasia

Schools ordered A–Z by Country

Key to directory

Country	**Whereford**
Name of school or college	**College Academy**
Indicates that this school has a profile	***For further details see p***
Address and contact number	Which Street, Whosville, Wherefordshire AB12 3CD **Tel:** 01000 000000
Head's name	**Head Master:** Dr A Person
Age range	**Age range:** 11–18
Number of pupils. B = boys G = girls VIth = sixth form	**No. of pupils:** 660 B330 G330 VIth 200
Fees per annum. Day = fees for day pupils. WB = fees for weekly boarders. FB = fees for full boarders.	**Fees:** Day £11,000 WB £16,000 FB £20,000
Curriculum	**Curriculum:** National, IBDP, ALevs
Language of instruction	**Language instr:** English, French
Memberships/Accreditation	(AISA) (COB) (EAR)

Key to icons

Key to symbols:

- Boys' school
- Girls' school
- Boarding accommodation

Member of:

- (AISA) Association of International Schools in Africa
- (CEE) Central and Eastern European Schools Association
- (EAR) East Asia Regional Council of Overseas Schools
- (ECIS) European Council of International Schools
- (RS) Round Square

Accreditation:

- (CIS) Council of International Schools
- (COB) Council of British International Schools

Please note: Schools are coeducational day schools unless otherwise indicated

AUSTRALIA

Adelaide High School
West Terrace, Adelaide SA 5000
Tel: +61 8 8231 9373
Age range: 12–18
No. of pupils: 1400 *E*700 *G*700
Curriculum: National
Language instr: English
CIS

Adelaide Secondary School of English
253 Torrens Road, West Croydon SA 5008
Tel: +61 8 8340 3733
Age range: 12–18
No. of pupils: 447 *B*220 *G*227
Language instr: English
CIS

Al Zahra College
3-5Wollongong Road, Arncliffe NSW 2205
Tel: +061(002)9599-0 61
Curriculum: IBDP, IBMYP, IBPYP

All Saints College
PO Box 165, Ewing Avenue, Bull Creek, Willetton WA 6151
Tel: +61 8 9313 9333
Age range: 3–18

Anglican Church Grammar School
Oaklands Parade, East Brisbane QLD 4169
Tel: +61 7 3896 2200
Curriculum: IBDP, IBPYP
Language instr: English

Ascham School
188 New South Head Road, Edgecliff NSW 2027
Tel: +61 2 8356 7000
Age range: *G*3–18
No. of pupils: 1000
Curriculum: National

Australian International Academy
Melbourne Senior Campus, 56 Bakers Road, North Coburg VIC 3058
Tel: +61 3 9350 4533
Age range: 5–18 years
No. of pupils: 1700
Curriculum: IBDP, IBMYP, IBPYP
Language instr: English

Australian International Academy – Caroline Springs Campus
183-191 Caroline Springs Boulevard, Caroline Springs, Melbourne VIC 3023
Tel: +61 3 8372 5446
Curriculum: IBDP, IBPYP
Language instr: English

Australian International Academy – Kellyville Campus
57-69 Samantha Riley Drive, Kellyville, Sydney NSW 2155
Tel: +61 02 8801 3100
Age range: 5–16
Curriculum: IBDP, IBMYP, IBPYP, National
Language instr: English

Australian International Academy – Sydney Campus
420 Liverpool Road, Strathfield, Sydney NSW 2135
Tel: +61 2 9642 0104
Age range: 5–18
No. of pupils: 433 *B*241 *G*192
Curriculum: IBDP, IBMYP, IBPYP, National
Language instr: English

Ballarat Grammar
201 Forest Street, Wendouree VIC 3355
Tel: + 61 3 5338 0700
Curriculum: IBPYP
Language instr: English
RS

Banksia Park International High School
610 Milne Road, Banksia Park SA 5091
Tel: +61 8 8264 8122
Age range: 13–18
No. of pupils: *B*300 *G*300
Language instr: English
CIS

Barker College
91 Pacific Highway, Hornsby NSW 2077
Tel: +61 2 8438 7999
Curriculum: IBPYP
Language instr: English

Bendigo Senior Secondary College
PO Box 545, Bendigo VIC 3550
Tel: +61 03 5443 1222
Age range: 16–21
No. of pupils: 1800
Language instr: English
CIS

Bendigo South East College
Ellis St, Flora Hill VIC 3550
Tel: +61 354 434 522
Language instr: English
CIS

Berwick Grammar School
80 Tivendale Rd Officer, Officer, Melbourne VIC 3809
Tel: +61 3 9703 8111
Age range: *B*3–18
Curriculum: National
Language instr: English

Billanook College
197-199 Cardigan Road, Mooroolbark VIC 3138
Tel: +61 397 255 388
Language instr: English
RS

Brighton Grammar School
90 Outer Crescent, Brighton VIC 3186
Tel: +61 3 8591 2200
Age range: *B*3–18
No. of pupils: 1300
Language instr: English

Brighton Primary School
59 Wilson Street, Brighton, Melbourne VIC 3186
Tel: +61 39592 0177
Age range: 5–12
No. of pupils: 800
Curriculum: IBPYP
Language instr: English
CIS

Brisbane Grammar School
Gregory Terrace, Brisbane QLD 4000
Tel: +617 3834 5200
Age range: *B*10–18
Language instr: English

Camberwell Grammar School
PO Box 151, Balwyn, Victoria VIC 3186
Tel: +61 3 9835 1777
Age range: *B*4–18
No. of pupils: *B*1300
Language instr: English

Cambridge Primary School
Carruthers Drive, Hoppers Crossing VIC 3029
Tel: +61 (03) 9748 9011
Age range: 5–12
Language instr: English

Canberra Girls Grammar School
Melbourne Avenue, Deakin ACT 2600
Tel: +61 2 6202 6400
Age range: *B*3–8 *G*3–17
No. of pupils: 1600
Curriculum: IBDP, IBPYP
Language instr: English

Canberra Grammar School
40 Monaro Crescent, Red Hill, Canberra ACT 2603
Tel: + 61 2 6260 9700
Age range: *B*4–18 *G*4–7
No. of pupils: 1647 *B*1547 *G*100 *VIth*149
Curriculum: IBDP, IBPYP
Language instr: English

CAREY BAPTIST GRAMMAR SCHOOL
For further details see p. 116
349 Barkers Road, Kew VIC 3101
Tel: +61 3 9816 1222
Email: admissions@carey.com.au
Website: www.carey.com.au
Principal: Jonathan Walter
Age range: 3–18 years
No. of pupils: 2681
Fees: $21,992–$34,044
Curriculum: IBDP, National
Language instr: English

Caulfield Grammar School – Caulfield Campus
PO Box 610, 217 Glen Eira Road East, St Kilda VIC 3185
Tel: +61 3 9524 6300
Age range: 3–18
Curriculum: IBPYP
Language instr: English

Caulfield Grammar School – Malvern Campus
5 Willoby Avenue, Glen Iris VIC 3146
Tel: +61 3 9885 5995

Caulfield Grammar School – Wheelers Hill Campus
74-82 Jells Road, Wheelers Hill VIC 3150
Tel: +61 3 8562 5300
Curriculum: IBMYP, IBPYP
Language instr: English

Caulfield Junior College
186 Balaclava Rd, Caulfield North VIC 3161
Tel: +61 395 096 872
Language instr: English
CIS

Charles Campbell College
3 Campbell Rd, Paradise SA 5075
Tel: +61 881 654 700
Language instr: English
CIS

Christ Church Grammar School
PO Box 399, Claremont WA 6010
Tel: +61 8 9442 1555
Age range: *B*5–18
No. of pupils: 1610
Curriculum: National
Language instr: English

Concordia College
24 Winchester St, Highgate SA 5063
Tel: +61 8 8272 0444
Curriculum: IBDP, IBMYP, IBPYP
Language instr: English

Cranbrook School
5 Victoria Road, Bellevue Hill NSW 2023
Tel: +61 2 9327 9000
Age range: B3–18 years
No. of pupils: 1500
Curriculum: IBDP, IBMYP, IBPYP, National
Language instr: English

Creek Street Christian College
91 Creek Street, Bendigo VIC 3550
Tel: +61 3 5442 1722
Curriculum: IBDP
Language instr: English

Elonera Montessori School
21 Mount Ousley Road, Wollongong NSW 2519
Tel: +61 2 4225 1000
Curriculum: IBDP

Encounter Lutheran College
64 Adelaide Road, Victor Harbor SA 5211
Tel: +61 8 8552 8880
Curriculum: IBMYP, IBPYP
Language instr: English

Faith Lutheran College
130 Magnolia Road, Tanunda SA 5352
Tel: +61 8 8561 4200
Curriculum: IBMYP
Language instr: English

Fintona Girls' School
79 Balwyn Road, Balwyn VIC 3103
Tel: +61 3 9830 1388
Curriculum: IBPYP

Firbank Grammar Junior School – Brighton Campus
51 Outer Crescent, Brighton, Melbourne VIC 3186
Tel: +61 3 9591 5141
No. of pupils: 290
Curriculum: IBPYP
Language instr: English

Firbank Grammar Junior School – Sandringham Campus
45 Royal Avenue, Sandringham VIC 3191
Tel: +61 3 9533 5711
Curriculum: IBPYP
Language instr: English

Geelong Grammar School
50 Biddlecombe Avenue, Corio VIC 3214
Tel: +61 3 5273 9200
Age range: 3–18
Curriculum: IBDP, IBPYP, National, SAT
Language instr: English

Geraldton Grammar School
134 George Road, Geraldton WA 6530
Tel: +61 899 657 800
Age range: 3–18
No. of pupils: 550 *VIth*40
Curriculum: National
Language instr: English

German International School Sydney
33 Myoora Road, Terrey Hills NSW 2084
Tel: +61 2 9485 1900
Age range: 3–19 years
No. of pupils: 380
Curriculum: IBDP, National
Language instr: English, German

Glenunga International High School
L'Estrange Street, Glenunga SA 5064
Tel: +61 88 379 5629
Age range: 11–18
No. of pupils: 1540
Curriculum: IBDP
Language instr: English

Golden Grove Lutheran Primary School
21-23 Richardson Drive, Wynn Vale SA 5127
Tel: +61 8 8282 6000
Curriculum: IBPYP
Language instr: English

Good News Lutheran College
580 Tarneit Road, Tarneit VIC 3029
Tel: +61 3 8742 9000
Curriculum: IBMYP, IBPYP
Language instr: English

Good Shepherd Lutheran College – Howard Springs Campus
Corner of Whitewood Road & Kundook Place, Howard Springs NT 0835
Tel: +61 8 89830300
Age range: 3–18
No. of pupils: 1120
Curriculum: IBMYP, IBPYP
Language instr: English

Good Shepherd Lutheran College – Noosa
115 Eumundi Road, Noosaville QLD 4566
Tel: +61 7 5455 8600

Good Shepherd Lutheran College – St Andrew Leanyer Campus
95 Leanyer Drive, Leanyer NT 0812
Tel: +61 8 8983 0300
Curriculum: IBPYP
Language instr: English

Grace Christian College
20 Kinchington Road, Leneva, Mellboune V C 3691
Tel: +61 02 6056 2299
Age range: 5–18
No. of pupils: 117
Curriculum: IBDP
Language instr: English

Grimwade House
67 Balaclava Road, Caulfield VIC 3161
Tel: +61 3 9865 7800
Age range: 5–11
No. of pupils: 680

Haileybury
855-891 Springvale Road, Keysborough VIC 3173
Tel: +61 3 9904 6000
Age range: 3–18
No. of pupils: 3662 *B*2131 *G*1531
Curriculum: National
Language instr: English

Haileybury Rendall School
6057 Berrimah Road, Berrimah NT 0828
Tel: +61 8 7913 0084
Age range: 12–18
No. of pupils: 650 *B*325 *G*325
Language instr: English

Hills Grammar
43 Kenthurst Road, Kenthurst NSW 2156
Tel: +61 2 9654 2111
Age range: 3–18 years
No. of pupils: 1000
Language instr: English

Hills International College
105-111 Johanna Street, Jimboomba QLD 4280
Tel: +61 7 5546 0667
Age range: 4–18
No. of pupils: 500
Curriculum: IBPYP, National, SAT, TOEFL
Language instr: English

Holy Trinity Primary School
18-20 Theodore Street, Curtin ACT 2605
Tel: +61 26281 4811
Age range: 4–12 years
No. of pupils: 390
Curriculum: IBPYP
Language instr: English

Hunter Valley Grammar School
42 Norfolk Street, Ashtonfield NSW 2323
Tel: +61 2 4934 2444
Age range: 3–18 years
No. of pupils: 1150
Curriculum: IBMYP, IBPYP, IBCP
Language instr: English

IES College
495 Boundary Street, Spring Hill QLD 4004
Tel: +61 7 3832 7699
Curriculum: IBDP
Language instr: English

Immanuel College
32 Morphett Road, Novar Gardens SA 5040
Tel: +61 08 8294 3588
Curriculum: IBMYP, National
Language instr: English

Immanuel Gawler
11 Lyndoch Road, Gawler East SA 5118
Tel: +61 8 8522 5740
Age range: 5–13 years
No. of pupils: 334
Curriculum: IBPYP

Immanuel Primary School
Saratoga Drive, Novar Gardens SA 5040
Tel: +61 8 8294 8422
Age range: 3–12
No. of pupils: 670
Curriculum: IBPYP
Language instr: English

International School of Western Australia
193 St Brigids Terrace, Doubleview, Perth WA 6018
Tel: +61 8 9285 1144
Age range: 4–18
No. of pupils: 350
Curriculum: ACT, AP, IBDP, IBMYP, IBPYP, National, SAT
Language instr: English

Islamic College of Melbourne (ICOM)
83 Wootten Road, Tarneit VIC 3029
Tel: +61 3 8742 1739
Curriculum: IBDP
Language instr: English

Ivanhoe Grammar School
PO Box 91, The Ridgeway, Ivanhoe VIC 3079
Tel: +61 3 9490 3501
Age range: 3–18
No. of pupils: 2220
Curriculum: IBDP, National
Language instr: English

John Paul College
John Paul Drive, Daisy Hill QLD 4127
Tel: +61 7 3826 3333
Age range: 6 weeks–18 years
No. of pupils: 1950
Curriculum: IBPYP
Language instr: English

John Wollaston Anglican Community School
Centre Road, Camillo WA 6111
Tel: +61 (08) 9495 8100
Age range: 3–18
No. of pupils: 1000
Curriculum: IBPYP
Language instr: English

Kambala
794 New South Head Road, Rose Bay, Sydney NSW 2029
Tel: +612 93886777
No. of pupils: 1000
Curriculum: IBDP
Language instr: English

Kardinia International College
29-31 Kardinia Drive, Bell Post Hill, Geelong VIC 3215
Tel: +61 3 5278 9999
Age range: 3–18 years
Curriculum: IBDP, IBPYP
Language instr: English

Kingswood College
355 Station Street, Box Hill, Melbourne VIC 3128
Tel: +61 3 9896 1700
Curriculum: IBPYP
Language instr: English

Launceston Church Grammar School
10 Lyttleton Street, East Launceston TAS 7250
Tel: +61 3 6336 5900
Curriculum: IBPYP
Language instr: English

Lauriston Girls' School
38 Huntingtower Road, Armadale VIC 3143
Tel: +61 3 9864 7555
Age range: *G*3–18
No. of pupils: 920
Curriculum: IBDP
Language instr: English

Loreto College
316 Portrush Road, Marryatville SA 5068
Tel: +61 8 8334 4200
Language instr: English

Lycée Condorcet – The International French School of Sydney
758 Anzac Parade, Maroubra, Sydney NSW 2035
Tel: +61 2 9344 8692
Age range: 3–18 years
No. of pupils: 1089
Curriculum: IBDP
Language instr: English

Mansfield Steiner School
91 Highett Street, Mansfield VIC 3722
Tel: +61 3 57791445
Curriculum: IBDP
Language instr: English

Mater Christi College
28 Bayview Road, Belgrave, Melbourne VIC 3160
Tel: +61 3 9754 6611
Age range: 12–18
No. of pupils: 720
Curriculum: IBMYP
Language instr: English

Melbourne Grammar School
355 St Kilda Road, Melbourne VIC 3004
Tel: +61 3 9865 7555

Melbourne Montessori School
741 Hawthorn Road, Brighton East VIC 3187
Tel: +61 3 9131 5200
Age range: 2–12 years
No. of pupils: 450
Curriculum: IBDP
Language instr: English

Mentone Girls' Grammar School
11 Mentone Parade, Mentone VIC 3194
Tel: +61 3 9581 1200
Age range: *G*3–18
No. of pupils: 800
Curriculum: IBPYP, National
Language instr: English
CIS

Mercedes College
540 Fullarton Road, Springfield SA 5062
Tel: +61 8 8372 3200
Age range: 5–18 years
Curriculum: IBDP, IBMYP, IBPYP
Language instr: English
CIS

Merici College
Wise Street, Braddon ACT 2612
Tel: +61 2 6243 4100
Age range: 11–18 years
No. of pupils: 780
Curriculum: IBDP, IBMYP
Language instr: English

Methodist Ladies' College
207 Barkers Road, Kew VIC 3101
Tel: +61 3 9274 6316
Age range: *B*6 weeks–4 years *G*6 weeks–18 years
Curriculum: IBDP, National
Language instr: English
CIS

MLC School
Rowley Street, Burwood, Sydney NSW 2134
Tel: +61 2 9747 1266
Age range: *G*4–18 years
No. of pupils: 1297
Curriculum: IBDP
Language instr: English
RS

Monte Sant' Angelo Mercy College
PO Box 1064, 128 Miller Street, North Sydney NSW 2059
Tel: +61 2 9409 6200
Age range: *G*12–18
No. of pupils: 1170
Curriculum: IBDP, IBMYP
Language instr: English

Montessori International College
880-932 Maroochydore Road, Forest Glen QLD 4556
Tel: +61 7 5442 3807
Language instr: English

Moreton Bay Boys' College
302 Manly Road, Manly West QLD 4179
Tel: +61 07 3906 9444
No. of pupils: 530
Curriculum: IBPYP

Moreton Bay College
450 Wondall Rd, Manly West QLD 4179
Tel: +61 7 3390 8555
No. of pupils: 1200 *G*1200
Curriculum: IBPYP
Language instr: English, French, Japanese

Mosman Church of England Preparatory School
PO Box 950, Spit Junction NSW 2088
Tel: +61 2 9968 4044
Age range: *B*4–11
No. of pupils: 290
Curriculum: National

Mount Scopus Memorial College
245 Burwood Highway, Burwood VIC 3125
Tel: +61 3 9834 0000
No. of pupils: 1503
Curriculum: IBMYP, IBPYP
Language instr: English

Navigator College
PO Box 3199, Port Lincoln SA 5606
Tel: +61 8 86825099
Age range: 4–18
Curriculum: IBMYP, IBPYP

New England Girls' School
Uralla Road, Armidale NSW 2350
Tel: +61 2 6774 8700
Age range: *G*4–18
No. of pupils: 400 *B*40 *G*360

Newington College – Lindfield
26 Northcote Road, Lindfield, New South Wales NSW 2070
Tel: +61 2 9416 4280
Age range: 5–12 years
Curriculum: IBPYP
Language instr: English

Newington College – Stanmore
200 Stanmore Road, Stanmore NSW 2048
Tel: +61 2 9568 9333
Age range: *B*3–18 years
No. of pupils: 2088
Curriculum: IBDP, TOEFL
Language instr: English

Oakleigh Grammar
77-81 Willesden Road, Oakleigh VIC 3166
Tel: +61 3 9569 6128
Age range: 2–18
No. of pupils: 904
Curriculum: IBMYP
Language instr: English

Our Lady of the Nativity
29 Fawkner Street, Aberfeldie VIC 3040
Tel: +61 3 9337 4204
Curriculum: IBPYP
Language instr: English

Our Saviour Lutheran School
28 Taylors Road West, Aberfoyle Park SA 5159
Tel: +61 8 8270 5488
Curriculum: IBPYP
Language instr: English

Pembroke School
342 The Parade, Kensington Park SA 5068
Tel: +61 8 8366 6200
Age range: 4–18
No. of pupils: 1550 *B*800 *G*750
Curriculum: IBDP, IBPYP, National
Language instr: English

Penrith Anglican College
PO Box 636, Kingswood NSW 2747
Tel: +61 247 36 8100
Age range: 5–18
No. of pupils: 1300 *B*650 *G*650
Curriculum: National
Language instr: English

Plenty Valley Christian College
840 Yan Yean Road, Doreen VIC 3754
Tel: +61 3 9717 7400
Age range: 5–12
Language instr: English

Presbyterian Ladies' College – Perth
14 McNeil Street, Peppermint Grove, Perth WA 6011
Tel: +61 8 9424 6444
Age range: G3–18 years
Curriculum: IBDP, IBPYP
Language instr: English

Presbyterian Ladies' College Melbourne
141 Burwood Highway, Burwood VIC 3125
Tel: +61 3 9808 5811
Age range: G6 months–18 years
No. of pupils: 1500
Curriculum: IBDP
Language instr: English

Preshil – The Margaret Lyttle Memorial School
395 Barkers Road, Kew, Melbourne VIC 3101
Tel: +613 9817 6135
Age range: 3–18
No. of pupils: 275
Curriculum: IBDP, IBMYP, IBPYP

Prince Alfred College
PO Box 571, Kent Town SA 5071
Tel: +61 8 8334 1200
Age range: B2–18
Curriculum: IBDP, IBPYP
Language instr: English

Queenwood
Locked bag 1, Mosman NSW 2088
Tel: +61 2 89687777
Age range: G5–18 years
No. of pupils: 900
Curriculum: IBDP, National
Language instr: English

Radford College
College Street, Bruce, Canberra ACT 2617
Tel: +61 2 6162 5332
Curriculum: IBDP, IBPYP

Ravenswood
10 Henry Street, Gordon, Sydney NSW 2072
Tel: +612 9498 9898
Age range: G5–18 years
Curriculum: IBDP, IBPYP
Language instr: English

Reddam ELS Lindfield
15a Treatts Road, Lindfield NSW 2070
Tel: +61 2 9415 8099
Age range: 1–5 years

Reddam ELS St Leonards
80 Christie Street, St Leonards NSW 2065
Tel: +61 2 9439 8434
Age range: 1–5 years

Reddam ELS Woollahra
70 Edgecliff Road, Woollahra NSW 2025
Tel: +61 2 9369 4096
Age range: 1–5 years

Reddam House Sydney
56 Mitchell Street, Bondi NSW 2026
Tel: +61 2 9300 8200
Age range: 1–18 years
Language instr: English

Redeemer Lutheran School, Nuriootpa
Box 397, Nuriootpa SA 5355
Tel: +61 885 621655
No. of pupils: B197 G202
Curriculum: IBPYP
Language instr: English

Redlands
272 Military Road, Cremorne NSW 2090
Tel: +61 2 9908 6479
Age range: 3–19 years
Curriculum: IBDP, National
Language instr: English

Rivercrest Christian College
Gate 6, 500 Soldiers Road, Clyde North VIC 3978
Tel: +61 3 9703 9777
Age range: 3–18 years
No. of pupils: 673
Curriculum: IBPYP
Language instr: English

Roseville College
Locked Bag 34, 27 Bancroft Avenue, Roseville NSW 2069
Tel: +61 2 9884 1100
Curriculum: IBPYP
Language instr: English

Sacred Heart College Geelong
Retreat Road, Newtown VIC 3220
Tel: +61 3 52214211
Age range: G11–16
Curriculum: IBMYP
Language instr: English

Santa Maria College
50 Separation Street, Northcote, Melbourne VIC 3070
Tel: +61 3 9488 1600
Curriculum: IBMYP

Santa Sabina College
90 The Boulevarde, Strathfield, Sydney NSW 2135
Tel: +61 2 9745 7000
Age range: B4–10 G4–19
No. of pupils: 1210
Curriculum: IBDP, IBPYP
Language instr: English

Scotch College
76 Shenton Road, Swanbourne, Perth WA 6010
Tel: +61 8 9383 6800
Age range: B3–18
No. of pupils: 1450
Curriculum: IBDP, IBMYP, IBPYP
Language instr: English

Scotch Oakburn College
85 Penquite Road, Newstead TAS 7250
Tel: +61 363 363 300
Language instr: English

Serpell Primary School
Tuckers Rd, Templestowe VIC 3106
Tel: +61 398 428 182

Seymour College
546 Portrush Road, Glen Osmond, Adelaide SA 5064
Tel: +61 8 8303 9000
Curriculum: IBDP
Language instr: English

Somerset College
Somerset Drive, Mudgeeraba QLD 4213
Tel: +61 (0)7 5559 7100
Curriculum: IBDP, IBMYP, IBPYP
Language instr: English

Sophia Mundi Steiner School
St. Mary's Abbotsford Convent, 1 St Heller's Street, Abbotsford, Melbourne VIC 3067
Tel: +61 3 9419 9229
Age range: 5–18
No. of pupils: 200
Curriculum: IBDP, National
Language instr: English

Southern Christian College
150 Redwood Road, Kingston, Tasmania TAS 7050
Tel: +613 6229 5744
Curriculum: IBDP, IBMYP, IBPYP
Language instr: English

ST ANDREW'S CATHEDRAL SCHOOL
For further details see p. 117
Sydney Square, Sydney NSW 2000
Tel: +61 2 9286 9500
Email: enrolments@sacs.nsw.edu.au
Website: www.sacs.nsw.edu.au
Head of School: Julie McGonigle
Age range: 5–18 years
No. of pupils: 1450
Fees: *Day* AUS$21,264–AUS$37,278
Curriculum: IBDP, IBMYP
Language instr: English

St Andrews Lutheran College
PO Box 2142, Burleigh BC QLD 4220
Tel: +61 7 5568 5900
Age range: 5–18 years
Curriculum: IBPYP
Language instr: English

St Andrew's School
22 Smith Street, Walkerville SA 5081
Tel: +61 8 81685537
Curriculum: IBPYP

St Brigid's College
200 Lesmurdie Road, Lesmurdie, Perth WA 6076
Tel: +61 8 9290 4200
Age range: B3–12 G3–17
No. of pupils: 1300
Language instr: English

St Dominic's Priory College
139 Molesworth Street, North Adelaide SA 5006
Tel: +61 8 8267 3818
Language instr: English

St Gregory's College Campbelltown
100 Badgally Road, Gregory Hills NSW 2557
Tel: +61 2 4629 4222
Curriculum: IBPYP
Language instr: English, Spanish

St John's Anglican College
College Avenue, Forest Lake QLD 4078
Tel: +61 (0)7 3372 0111
Curriculum: IBPYP
Language instr: English

St John's Lutheran School, Eudunda, Inc.
8 Ward Street, Eudunda SA 5374
Tel: +61 8 8581 1282
Age range: 5–13
No. of pupils: 107
Curriculum: IBPYP
Language instr: English, Japanese

St Leonard's College
163 South Road, Brighton East, Melbourne VIC 3187
Tel: +61 3 9909 9300
Age range: 3–18
No. of pupils: B750 G750
Curriculum: IBDP, IBPYP, National
Language instr: English

St Margaret's School
27-47 Gloucester Avenue, Berwick, Melbourne VIC 3806
Tel: +61 3 9703 8111
Age range: B3–11 years G3–18
No. of pupils: 950
Curriculum: IBPYP, National
Language instr: English

St Mary Star of the Sea College
15 Harbour St, Wollongong NSW 2500
Tel: +61 (0)2 4228 60[illegible]1
Curriculum: IBMYP
Language instr: English

St Michael's Lutheran School
6 Balhannah Rd, Hahndorf SA 5250
Tel: +61 8 8388 7228
No. of pupils: 290
Curriculum: IBPYP
Language instr: English

St Paul's Grammar School
Locked Bag 8016, Penrith NSW 2751
Tel: +61 2 4777 4888
Age range: 4–18
No. of pupils: 840 *B*420 *G*420 *VIth*100
Curriculum: IBDP, IBMYP, IBPYP
Language instr: English

St Paul's School Brisbane
34 Strathpine Rd, Bald Hills QLD 4036
Tel: +61 732 611 388
Language instr: English
RS

St Peter's Anglican Primary School
Howe Street, Campbelltown NSW 2560
Tel: +61 (2) 4627 2990
Curriculum: IBPYP
Language instr: English

St Peter's College
Hackney Road, Hackney, Adelaide SA 5069
Tel: +61 8 8404 0400
Age range: *B*3–18
Curriculum: IBDP
Language instr: English

St Peter's Girls' School
Stonyfell Road, Stonyfell SA 5066
Tel: +61 88 334 2200
Curriculum: IBDP, IBPYP

St Peters Lutheran College
66 Harts Road, Indooroopilly QLD 4068
Tel: +61 7 3377 6222
Age range: 5–18
No. of pupils: 2038 *B*1045 *G*993 *VIth*188
Curriculum: IBDP, IBPYP
Language instr: English

St Peters Lutheran School
71 Cumming Street, Blackwood SA 5051
Tel: +61 8 8278 0800
Age range: 4–12
No. of pupils: 244
Curriculum: IBPYP
Language instr: English

St Philips College, Australia
Schwarz Crescent, Alice Springs NT 0870
Tel: +61 889 504 511
Language instr: English

Tara Anglican School for Girls
Masons Drive, North Parramatta, Sydney NSW 2151
Tel: +61 2 9630 6655
Curriculum: IBMYP, IBPYP
Language instr: English

The Armidale School
Locked Bag 3003, 87 Douglas Street, Armidale NSW 2350
Tel: +61 2 6776 5800
Age range: *B*4–18 *G*4–11
Curriculum: IBMYP, IBPYP, National

The Essington School
PO Box 42321, Casuarina NT 0811
Tel: +61 8 8985 0100
Age range: 3–16
No. of pupils: 3087 *B*2811 *G*276
Curriculum: National
Language instr: English

The Friends' School
23 Commercial Road, North Hobart TAS 7002
Tel: +61 3 6210 2200
Age range: 4–18 years
No. of pupils: 1250
Curriculum: IBDP, IBPYP
Language instr: English

The Hutchins School
71 Nelson Road, Sandy Bay, Tasmania TAS 7005
Tel: +61 3 6221 4200
CIS

The Illawarra Grammar School
10-12 Western Ave, Wollongong NSW 2500
Tel: +61 2 4220 0200
Age range: 3–18
No. of pupils: 900
Curriculum: IBPYP
Language instr: English

The Kilmore International School
40 White Street, Kilmore VIC 3764
Tel: +61 3 5782 2211
Age range: 8–18 years
No. of pupils: 400
Curriculum: IBDP
Language instr: English

The King's School
PO Box 1, Parramatta NSW 2124
Tel: +612 9683 8555
No. of pupils: 365
Curriculum: IBPYP, National
Language instr: English

The King's School, Tudor House
6480 Illawarra Highway, Moss Vale NSW 2577
Tel: +61 2 4868 0000
Age range: *B*4–12
Curriculum: IBPYP

The Montessori School
PO Box 194, Landsdale WA 6065
Tel: +61 89 409 9151
Curriculum: IBDP
Language instr: English

The Norwood Morialta High School
Morialta Road West, Rostrevor SA 5073
Tel: +61 8 83650455
Age range: 12–19
No. of pupils: 1532 *B*870 *G*662
Curriculum: IBMYP
Language instr: English
CIS

The Riverina Anglican College
127 Farrer Road, Wagga Wagga NSW 2650
Tel: +61 (0)2 6933 1811
Curriculum: IBDP
Language instr: English

The Scots College
Locked Bag 5001, Bellevue Hill, Sydney NSW 2023
Tel: +61 2 9391 7600
Age range: *B*3–18
Language instr: English

The Scots School Albury
393 Perry Street, Albury NSW 2640
Tel: +61 (0)2 6022 0000
No. of pupils: 491 *B*244 *G*247
Curriculum: IBPYP
Language instr: English

The Southport School
2 Winchester Street, Southport QLD 4125
Tel: +61 755 319 911
Language instr: English
RS

Thomas Mitchell Primary School
Thomas Mitchell Drive, Endeavour Hills VIC 3802
Tel: +61 397 062 254
CIS

Tintern Grammar
90 Alexandra Road, PO Box 26, Ringwood East VIC 3135
Tel: +61 3 9845 7777
Age range: 4–18
No. of pupils: 1000
Curriculum: IBDP
Language instr: English

Toorak College
PO Box 150, Mount Eliza VIC 3930
Tel: +61 3 9788 7200
Age range: 3–18
Curriculum: IBPYP
Language instr: English
ECIS

Townsville Grammar School
45 Paxton Street, North Ward QLD 4810
Tel: +61 7 4722 4900
Age range: 4–18
No. of pupils: 1400 *B*700 *G*700 *VIth*160
Curriculum: IBDP
Language instr: English

Treetops Montessori School
PO Box 59, Darlington WA 6076
Tel: +61 8 9299 6725
No. of pupils: 130
Curriculum: IBDP, IBCP
Language instr: English

Trinity Anglican School
200-212 Progress Rd, White Rock, Queensland QLD 4868
Tel: +61 7 4036 8111
No. of pupils: 850
Language instr: English
RS

Trinity Grammar School Preparatory School
115-125 The Boulevarde, Strathfield NSW 2135
Tel: +61 2 8732 4600
Curriculum: IBPYP

Trinity Grammar School, Kew
40 Charles Street, Kew VIC 3101
Tel: +61 3 9854 3600
Curriculum: IBPYP
Language instr: English

Trinity Grammar School, Sydney
119 Prospect Road, Summer Hill NSW 2130
Tel: +61 2 9581 6000
No. of pupils: 2071
Curriculum: IBDP, IBPYP
Language instr: English

Trinity Lutheran College
920 Fifteenth Street, Mildura VIC 3500
Tel: +61 3 5023 7013
Curriculum: IBPYP
Language instr: English

Trinity Lutheran College
PO Box 322, Ashmore City QLD 4214
Tel: +61 7 5556 8200
Age range: 4–18
Curriculum: IBPYP, National
Language instr: English

Waikerie Lutheran Primary School
16 McCutcheon Street,
Waikerie SA 5330
Tel: +61 8 8541 2344
Age range: 5–13
No. of pupils: 100
Curriculum: IBPYP
Language instr: English

Walford Anglican School for Girls
316 Unley Road, Hyde Park SA 5061
Tel: +61 8 8272 6555
Age range: *G*1–18
No. of pupils: *G*720
Curriculum: IBDP, IBMYP, IBPYP
Language instr: English

Wenona School
176 Walker Street, North
Sydney NSW 2060
Tel: +61 2 9409 4400
Curriculum: IBPYP
Language instr: English

Wesley College Melbourne – Elsternwick Campus
5 Gladstone Parade,
Elsternwick VIC 3185
Tel: +61 3 8102 6808
Age range: 3–15
No. of pupils: 402
Curriculum: IBMYP, IBPYP
Language instr: English

Wesley College Melbourne – Glen Waverley Campus
620 High Street Road, Glen
Waverley VIC 3150
Tel: +61 3 8102 6508
Age range: 3–18
No. of pupils: 1230
Curriculum: IBMYP, IBPYP
Language instr: English

Wesley College Melbourne – St Kilda Road Campus
577 St Kilda Road,
Melbourne VIC 3004
Tel: +613 8102 6508
Age range: 3–18
No. of pupils: 3300
Curriculum: IBDP, IBMYP, IBPYP, National
Language instr: English

Westminster School, Adelaide
1/23 Alison Avenue, Marion SA 5043
Tel: +61 882 760 276
Language instr: English
(RS)

Woodcroft College
Bains Road, Morphett Vale SA 5162
Tel: +61 8 8322 2333
Age range: 4–18
No. of pupils: 1300
Curriculum: IBDP, IBMYP, IBPYP
Language instr: English
(CIS)

Woodleigh School
485 Golf Links Road,
Langwarrin South VIC 3911
Tel: +61 3 5971 6100
Curriculum: IBPYP
Language instr: English

Xavier College, Kostka Hall Campus
47 South Road, Brighton,
Melbourne VIC 3186
Tel: +61 3 9519 0600
Curriculum: IBPYP

Xavier College, Senior Campus
135 Barkers Road, Kew VIC 3101
Tel: +61 3 9854 5411

FIJI

International School Nadi
Box 9686 Nadi Airport, Nadi
Tel: +679 6702 060
Curriculum: IBDP, IBMYP, IBPYP
Language instr: English

International School Suva
Lot 59, Siga Road, Laucala
Beach Estate, Suva
Tel: +679 339 3300
Age range: 3–18 years
No. of pupils: 550
Curriculum: IBDP, IBMYP, IBPYP
Language instr: English

Pacific Harbour International School
PO Box 50, Pacific Harbour, Deuba
Tel: +679 3450005
Age range: 5–16
No. of pupils: 130 *B*70 *G*60
Curriculum: National
Language instr: English

Port Vila International School
PO Box 302, Port Vila, Vanuatu
Tel: +678 23837

GUAM

St John's School
911 Marine Drive, Tumon Bay 96913
Tel: +1 (671) 646 8080
Age range: 3–18
No. of pupils: 525 *B*253 *G*272 *VIth*42
Curriculum: ACT, IBDP, SAT
Language instr: English
(EAR)

NEW ZEALAND

ACG Parnell College
2 Titoki Street, Parnell,
Auckland 1052
Tel: +64 9 308 1666
Age range: 4–18 years
Curriculum: IBDP
Language instr: English

ACG Remuera ELS
27 Ohinerau Street, Remuera,
Auckland 1050
Tel: +64 9 523 0177
Age range: 1–5 years

ACG Strathallan
50 Hayfield Way, RD1
Papakura, Auckland 2580
Tel: +64 9 295 0830
Age range: 3–17 years
Language instr: English

ACG Sunderland
6 Waipareira Avenue,
Henderson, Auckland 0610
Tel: +64 9 838 7070
Age range: 3–17 years
Language instr: English

ACG Tauranga
6 Keenan Road, (off Pyes Pa
Road), Tauranga 3173
Tel: +64 7 213 0100
Age range: 3–17 years
Language instr: English

ATEA College
21 Domain Road, Panmure,
Auckland 1072
Age range: 4–18
No. of pupils: 14 *VIth*4
Curriculum: IGCSE, ALevs

Auckland International College
37 Heaphy Street, Blockhouse
Bay, Auckland 0600
Tel: +64 9 309 4480
Age range: 15–18
No. of pupils: 371
Curriculum: IBDP
Language instr: English

Chilton Saint James School
PO Box 30090, Lower Hutt 5040
Tel: +64 4 566 4089
Age range: *B*2–5 *G*2–18
No. of pupils: 405 *B*15 *G*390
Curriculum: IGCSE
Language instr: English

City Impact Church School
PO Box 35 211, North Shore
City, Albany 0753
Tel: +64 9 477 0302
Age range: 5–18
No. of pupils: 300
Curriculum: IGCSE

Destiny School New Zealand
PO Box 76201, Manukau 2241
Tel: +64 9 5277 312
Age range: 5–18
No. of pupils: 200
Curriculum: IGCSE

Diocesan School for Girls
Clyde Street, Epsom, Auckland 1051
Tel: +64 9 520 0221
Age range: *G*3–18
Curriculum: IBDP, IBPYP
Language instr: English

Eden Christian Academy
PO Box 134, Tuakau 2342
Tel: +64 9 237 8228
Age range: 4–18
No. of pupils: 300
Curriculum: IGCSE

Huanui College
328 Ngunguru Road, Glenbervie
RD 3, Whangarei 0173
Tel: +64 9 459 1930
Age range: 10–18 years
No. of pupils: 330
Language instr: English

John McGlashan College
2 Pilkington Street, Maori
Hill, Dunedin 9010
Tel: +64 3 467 6620
Age range: *B*11–18 years
Curriculum: IBDP
Language instr: English

King's College, Auckland
Golf Ave, Otahuhu, Auckland 1062
Tel: +64 9276 0600
Language instr: English

Kristin School
360 Albany Highway,
Albany, Auckland 0632
Tel: +64 9 415 9566
Age range: 6 months–18 years
No. of pupils: 1750
Curriculum: IBDP, IBMYP, IBPYP, National
Language instr: English

Manukau Christian School
77 Rogers Road,
Manurewa, Auckland
Tel: +64 9 269 1050
Curriculum: UK, IGCSE, ALevs

Penguins School of Early Learning
197 Whitford Road, Howick,
Auckland 2016
Tel: +64 9 537 4970
Age range: 1–5 years

Pinehurst School
PO Box 302-308, North Harbour,
North Shore City 0751
Tel: +64 9 414 0960
Age range: 5–18
Curriculum: National, IGCSE

Queen Margaret College
53 Hobson Street, PO Box 12274, Thorndon, Wellington 6011
Tel: +64 4 473 7160
Age range: G3–18
No. of pupils: 700
Curriculum: IBDP, IBMYP, IBPYP
Language instr: English

Saint Kentigern Boys' School
PO Box 28790, Remuera, Auckland 1541
Tel: +64 9 520 7682
No. of pupils: 530

Saint Kentigern College
130 Pakuranga Road, Pakuranga, Auckland 1021
Tel: +64 9 577 0749
Age range: 11–18 years
No. of pupils: 2250
Curriculum: IBDP
Language instr: English

Saint Kentigern Girls' School
PO Box 28399, Remuera, Auckland 1541
Tel: +64 9 520 1400
No. of pupils: 200

Scots College
PO Box 15064, Strathmore, Wellington 6243
Tel: +64 4 388 0850
Age range: 5–18 years
No. of pupils: 960
Curriculum: IBDP, IBMYP, IBPYP
Language instr: English

Selwyn House School
PO Box 25049, 122 Merivale Lane, Christchurch 8014
Tel: +64 3 3557299
No. of pupils: G220
Curriculum: IBPYP
Language instr: English

Shirley Boys' High School
PO Box 27 025, Christchurch 8640
Tel: +64 3 375 7057
Age range: 14–18
No. of pupils: 1250
Curriculum: IGCSE

Springbank School
PO Box 404, Kerikeri 0293
Tel: +64 9 4075236
Curriculum: UK, IGCSE, ALevs

St Cuthbert's College
122 Market Road, Epsom, Auckland 1051
Tel: +64 9 520 4159
Age range: G5–18
No. of pupils: 1420
Curriculum: IBDP
Language instr: English

St Margaret's College
12 Winchester Street, Merivale, Christchurch 8014
Tel: +64 3 379 2000
Age range: G5–18 years (boarding 11-18)
No. of pupils: 830
Curriculum: IBDP
Language instr: English

St Mark's Church School
13 Dufferin Street, PO Box 7445, Wellington 6021
Tel: +64 4 385 9489
Age range: 3–13
No. of pupils: 300
Curriculum: IBPYP

St Peter's College
23 Mountain Road, Grafton, Auckland 1023
Tel: +64 9 524 8108
Age range: 11–18
No. of pupils: 1200
Curriculum: UK

St Peter's School, Cambridge
1716 Hamilton Road, Private Bag 884, Cambridge 3450
Tel: +64 7 827 9899
Age range: 11–18
No. of pupils: 1077 B496 G581
Curriculum: IBDP, National, IGCSE
Language instr: English

Wentworth College
PO Box 650, Whangaparoa
Tel: +64 9 424 3273
Age range: 11–18
Curriculum: IGCSE

Zig Zag Zoo ELS
7 Henry Street, Queenstown 9300
Tel: +64 3 409 0441
Age range: 1–5 years

PAPUA NEW GUINEA

Alotau International School
PO Box 154, Alotau, Milne Bay Province
Tel: +675 641 1078
No. of pupils: 100

Boroko East International School
PO Box 1319, Boroko NCD
Tel: +675 325 5037
No. of pupils: 650

Ela Murray International School
PO Box 1137, Boroko NCD
Tel: +675 325 2833
No. of pupils: 550
Language instr: English

Gordon International School
PO Box 1825, Boroko
Tel: +675 325 4088
No. of pupils: 580

Goroka International School
PO Box 845, Goroka EHP
Tel: +675 732 1452
No. of pupils: 75

Kamarau International School
PO Box 224, Buka
Tel: +675 973 9033
No. of pupils: 100

Kimbe International School
PO Box 307, Kimbe
Tel: +675 983 5078
No. of pupils: 300

Kiunga International School
PO Box 109, Kiunga
Tel: +675 548 1110
No. of pupils: 75

Korobosea International School
PO Box 1319, Boroko
Tel: +675 325 5358
No. of pupils: 680

Kundiawa International School
PO Box 165, Kundiawa
Tel: +675 535 1263
No. of pupils: 60

Lae International School
PO Box 2130, Lae
Tel: +675 472 1011
No. of pupils: 550

Madang International School
PO Box 306, Madang
Tel: +675 422 2472
No. of pupils: 110

Mount Hagen International School
PO Box 945, Mt Hagen
Tel: +675 542 1964
No. of pupils: 110

Popondetta International School
PO Box 10, Popondetta
Tel: +675 629 7180
No. of pupils: 60

Port Moresby Grammar School
PO Box 1149, Port Moresby 121
Tel: +675 323 6577
Age range: 6–20
No. of pupils: 1050

Port Moresby International School
PO Box 276, Boroko
Tel: +675 325 6690
No. of pupils: 960
Curriculum: ACT, IBDP
Language instr: English

Rabaul International School
PO Box 855, Kokopo
Tel: +675 982 8770
No. of pupils: 140

Tabubil International School
PO Box 408, Tabubil
Tel: +675 649 9233
No. of pupils: 400

Wewak International School
PO Box 354, Wewak
Tel: +675 456 3576
No. of pupils: 70

SOLOMON ISLANDS

Woodford International School
Prince Philip Highway, P.O. Box R44, Kukum, Honiara
Tel: +677 30186
Age range: 3–12
Curriculum: IBPYP, SAT
Language instr: English

TONGA

Ocean of Light International School
Kolomotu'a / Hofoa, PO Box 2878, Nuku'alofa
Tel: +676 25 332
Age range: 4–19
No. of pupils: 340
Curriculum: IGCSE

International schools in Europe

Schools ordered A–Z by Country

Key to directory

Country	**Whereford**
Name of school or college	**College Academy**
Indicates that this school has a profile	***For further details see p***
Address and contact number	Which Street, Whosville, Wherefordshire AB12 3CD **Tel:** 01000 000000
Head's name	**Head Master:** Dr A Person
Age range	**Age range:** 11–18
Number of pupils. B = boys G = girls VIth = sixth form	**No. of pupils:** 660 B330 G330 VIth 200
Fees per annum. Day = fees for day pupils. WB = fees for weekly boarders. FB = fees for full boarders.	**Fees:** Day £11,000 WB £16,000 FB £20,000
Curriculum	**Curriculum:** National, IBDP, ALevs
Language of instruction	**Language instr:** English, French
Memberships/Accreditation	(AISA) (COB) (EAR)

Key to icons

Key to symbols:

- Boys' school
- Girls' school
- Boarding accommodation

Member of:

- (AISA) Association of International Schools in Africa
- (CEE) Central and Eastern European Schools Association
- (EAR) East Asia Regional Council of Overseas Schools
- (ECIS) European Council of International Schools
- (RS) Round Square

Accreditation:

- (CIS) Council of International Schools
- (COB) Council of British International Schools

Please note: Schools are coeducational day schools unless otherwise indicated

ALBANIA

Albanian College Durres
Lagjia Nr. 1, Rruga Anastas Durrsaku, Durres 2001
Tel: +355 44 513 471
Language instr: English

GDQ International Christian School
c/o AEP (Box 89), K.F. 119, Tirana
Tel: +355 (0)4 244 8173
Age range: 5–19
Curriculum: UK, USA, IGCSE

Memorial International School of Tirana
Rruga Dritan Hoxha Nr.1, Tirana
Tel: +355 4 223 7375
Age range: 6–17
No. of pupils: 161 *B7 G90*
Curriculum: National, UK
Language instr: English

QSI Tirana International School
Rruga Vilat Gjermane, Kutia Postare 1527, Tirana
Tel: +355 4 236 5239
Age range: 2–18 years
No. of pupils: 352
Curriculum: IBDP
Language instr: English

Shkolla Udha e Shkronjave
rr. Qemal Stafa, nr.226, (pranë shkollës, Tirana
Tel: +355 4 226 7048

World Academy of Tirana
Rruga e Rezervave, Lunder, Tirane
Tel: +355 69 6056 123
Age range: 3–18 years
Curriculum: IBDP, IBMYP, IBPYP
Language instr: English

ANDORRA

AGORA ANDORRA INTERNATIONAL SCHOOL
For further details see p. 122
Carrer del Serrat del Camp 14, AD400 La Massana
Tel: +376 838 366
Email: admissions@agorainternationalandorra.com
Website: www.agorainternationalandorra.com
Head of School: Clara Pintat Rossell
No. of pupils: 370
Curriculum: IBDP
Language instr: English, Spanish, French, Catalan

ARMENIA

QSI International School of Yerevan
PO Box 82, Astarak Highway 49/15, Yerevan 0088
Tel: +374 10 349130
Age range: 3–13
No. of pupils: 61
Curriculum: USA
Language instr: English

Quantum College
Bagratuniats 23/2, Shengavit, Yerevan 0046
Tel: +374 10 422217
Curriculum: IBDP
Language instr: English

Shirakatsy Lyceum International Scientific-Educational Complex
35 Artem Mikoyan Street, Yerevan 0079
Tel: +374 10 680 102
Age range: 2–18
No. of pupils: 1010
Curriculum: IBDP, IBMYP, IBPYP
Language instr: Armenian

UWC Dilijan
7 Getapnya Street, Dilijan 3903
Tel: +44 (0)1446 799000
Age range: 16–18
No. of pupils: 219
Curriculum: IBDP
Language instr: English

AUSTRIA

AMADEUS INTERNATIONAL SCHOOL VIENNA
For further details see p. 128
Bastiengasse 36-38, 1180 Vienna
Tel: +43 1 470 30 37 00
Email: admissions@amadeus-vienna.com
Website: www.amadeus-vienna.com
Head of School: Jeremy House
Age range: 3–18 years
No. of pupils: 350
Fees: *Day* €13,295–€29,905 *FB* €46,880–€52,350
Curriculum: IBDP, IBMYP, IBPYP
Language instr: English

American International School – Salzburg
Moosstrasse 106, 5020 Salzburg
Tel: +43 662 824617
Age range: 13–19
No. of pupils: 84
Curriculum: AP, SAT, USA

AMERICAN INTERNATIONAL SCHOOL VIENNA
For further details see p. 130
Salmannsdorfer Strasse 47, 1190 Vienna
Tel: +43 1 401 32
Email: info@ais.at
Website: www.ais.at
Director: Kathy Miner
Age range: 4–18 years
No. of pupils: 800
Fees: €12,434
Curriculum: AP, IBDP, National, SAT, USA
Language instr: English
CEE CIS ECIS

Anton Bruckner International School (ABIS)
Bruckner Tower, Wildbergstrasse 18, 4040 Linz, Upper Austria
Tel: +43 7327 11691
Curriculum: IBMYP, IBPYP
Language instr: English, German

Campus Wien West
Seuttergasse 29, 1130 Vienna
Tel: +43 680 5577 573
Curriculum: IBDP
Language instr: English

Danube International School Vienna
Josef-Gall Gasse 2, 1020 Vienna
Tel: +43 1 7203110
Age range: 3–18
No. of pupils: 500
Curriculum: IBDP, IBMYP, IBPYP
Language instr: English
CIS ECIS

European High School BRG 15
Henriettenplatz 6, 1150 Vienna
Tel: +43 1 8936743
Age range: 14–19

European Middle School
Neustiftgasse 100, 1070 Vienna
Tel: +43 1 526 19 78
Age range: 10–14

International Christian School of Vienna
Panethgasse 6a, (right by Wagramer Strasse), 1220 Vienna
Tel: +43 1 25122 0
Age range: 5–20 years
No. of pupils: 300
Curriculum: ACT, IBDP, SAT, USA
Language instr: English
ECIS

International Highschool Herzogberg
Herzogbergstraße 230, 2380 Perchtoldsdorf, Lower Austria
Tel: +43 6991 7750 055
Curriculum: IBDP
Language instr: English, German

International School Carinthia
Rosentaler Straße 15, 9220 Velden Am Worthersee, Carinthia
Tel: +43 4274 52471 10
Age range: 6–15 years
Curriculum: IBDP, IBMYP, IBPYP
Language instr: English, German

International School Kufstein Tirol
Andreas-Hofer-Straße 7, 6330 Kufstein, Tyrol
Tel: +43 5372 21990
Curriculum: IBDP
Language instr: English

Junior High School Neue Mittelschule
Carlbergerstrasse 72, 1230 Vienna
Tel: +43 1 869 76 23
Age range: 14–19

Lycée Français de Vienne
Liechtensteinstrasse 37 A, 1090 Vienna
Tel: +43 1 317 22 41
Age range: 4–18
No. of pupils: 1950
Language instr: French

Marie Jahoda School Vienna
Herbstsraße 86, 1160 Vienna
Tel: +43 1 492 43 23
Age range: 4–11
No. of pupils: 380

Schloss Krumbach International School GmbH
Schloss 1, 2851 Krumbach, Lower Austria
Tel: +43 6765 409630
Age range: 12–19 years
No. of pupils: 30
Curriculum: IBDP, ALevs
Language instr: English, German

St. Gilgen International School
Ischlerstrasse 13, 5340 St. Gilgen, Salzburg
Tel: +43 62 272 0259
Age range: 9–18 years
No. of pupils: 220
Curriculum: IBDP, IBMYP, IGCSE
Language instr: English
CIS ECIS

Theresianische Foundation Academy
Favoritenstraße 15, 1040 Vienna
Tel: +43 1 505 15 71 0

VBS Vienna Bilingual School
Scheibenbergstrasse 63, 1180 Vienna
Tel: +43 1 470 63 69
Age range: 4–11
No. of pupils: 250
Language instr: English, German

Vienna International School
Strasse der Menschenrechte 1, 1220 Vienna
Tel: +43 1 203 5595
Age range: 3–18
No. of pupils: *B*743 *G*657
Curriculum: IBDP, IBMYP, IBPYP
Language instr: English
CEE CIS ECIS

AZERBAIJAN

Azerbaijan British College
20/41 Mikayil Aliyev str., Baku
Tel: +994 50 844 85 67
Curriculum: UK, IGCSE, ALevs
CIS

Baku International Education Complex
Metbuat pr 54, Yasamal, Baku 1001
Tel: +994 50 423 49 10
Curriculum: IBPYP
Language instr: English, Russian

Baku Talents Education Complex
Sabail District, Salyan Highway (New Bibiheybet mosque), Baku 1023
Tel: +994 50 292 22 95
Language instr: English, Azeri

British School in Baku
13 Koroglu Ragimov Str, Baku AZ1072
Tel: +99412 465 80 86
Age range: 4–18
No. of pupils: 500 *B*250 *G*250
Curriculum: UK
Language instr: English
COB ECIS

CET Gunar – Baku Oxford School
8 A Abbaszadeh Str., AZ 1073, Baku
Tel: +994 12 510 80 01
Age range: 4–18
Curriculum: National, UK, IGCSE, ALevs

Dunya School
9 Ajami Nakhchivani street, Baku AZ1130
Tel: +994 12 563 59 40/47/48
Curriculum: IBDP, IBPYP
Language instr: English

European Azerbaijan School
7 Basti Bagirova, Yasamal District, Baku City
Tel: +994 12 539 89 35/36/37/38
Curriculum: IBDP, IBMYP, IBPYP
Language instr: English
ECIS

Idrak Lyceum
2 Samad Vurghun, Sumqayit 5001
Tel: +994 18 655 59 73
Curriculum: IBDP
Language instr: English

Istak Lyceum
Fatalikhan khoyski 109, Baku AZ1052
Tel: +994 12 4658410
Curriculum: AP, SAT, IGCSE
Language instr: English, Azerbaijani

QSI Baku International School
Darnagul Qasabasi, Str Ajami Nakchivani, Block 3097, Baku 1108
Tel: +994 12 440 66 16
Age range: 2–18
No. of pupils: 151
Curriculum: AP, SAT, USA
Language instr: English

SABIS Sun International School – Baku
Zigh Highway, 22km towards H. Aliyev Int. Airport, Dreamland, Baku
Tel: +994 12 404 74 41

The International School of Azerbaijan, Baku
Yeni Yasamal, Stonepay, Royal Park, Baku AZ1070
Tel: +994 12 404 01 12
Age range: 2–17
No. of pupils: 630 *B*335 *G*295
Curriculum: IBDP, IBMYP, IBPYP
Language instr: English
CEE CIS

XXI Century International Education and Innovation Center
30 Inshaatchilar Avenue, Baku 1065
Tel: +994 12 510 0205

BELARUS

QSI International School of Minsk
Perioluk Bogdanovicha, 15, 220040 Minsk
Tel: +375 17 280 66 00
Age range: 3–18
No. of pupils: 154
Curriculum: USA
Language instr: English

Stembridge Private School
31 Nekrasova Street, Minsk
Tel: +375 296 67 61 21
Curriculum: IBDP
Language instr: English, Russian

BELGIUM

Antwerp International School
Veltwijcklaan 180, Ekeren, 2180 Antwerp
Tel: +32 (0)3 543 93 00
Age range: 2–18
No. of pupils: 392 *B*188 *G*192
Curriculum: IBDP, IBMYP, IBPYP
CIS ECIS

BEPS INTERNATIONAL SCHOOL
For further details see p. 134
Avenue Franklin Roosevelt 21-23, Ixelles, 1050 Brussels
Tel: +32 2 648 43 11
Email: admissions@beps.com
Website: www.beps.com
School Director: Pascale Hertay
Age range: 2.5–18 years
No. of pupils: 280
Curriculum: IBMYP, IPC
Language instr: English

Bogaerts International School
555 Rue Engeland, 1180 Brussels
Tel: +32 2 230 03 39
Curriculum: IBDP, IBMYP, IBPYP
Language instr: English, French

Brussels International Catholic School
Rue Général Leman 86, 1040 Brussels
Tel: +32 223 302 18
Age range: 2–18
No. of pupils: 625
Curriculum: IGCSE, ALevs
Language instr: English, French
ECIS

Da Vinci International School
Verbondstraat 67, 2000 Antwerp
Tel: +32 3216 12 32
Age range: 2.5–18 years
Curriculum: IBDP
Language instr: English

European School Brussels I
Avenue du Vert Chasseur 46, 1180 Bruxelles
Tel: +32 2 373 8611
Age range: 4–18
No. of pupils: 3100

European School Brussels II
Avenue Oscar Jespers 75, 1200 Brussels
Tel: +32 2 774 22 24
Age range: 6–18
No. of pupils: 2900

European School Brussels III
Boulevard du Triomphe 135, 1050 Brussels
Tel: +32 2 629 4700
Curriculum: IBCP

European School of Bruxelles-Argenteuil
Square d'Argenteuil 5, 1410 Waterloo, Brussels
Tel: +32 2357 06 70
Curriculum: IBDP
Language instr: English, French

European School of Mol
Europawijk 100, 2400 Mol, Antwerp
Tel: +32 14 563 111
Age range: 3–18
No. of pupils: 750
Language instr: English, French, German, Dutch

INTERNATIONAL MONTESSORI SCHOOL
For further details see p. 171
Kleinenbergstraat 97-99, 1932 St. Stevens-Woluwe, Flemish Brabant
Tel: +32 2 767 63 60 / +32 2 721 21 11
Email: montessori-tervuren@online.be; montessori-woluwe@skynet.be
Website: www.international-montessori.org
Heads of School: Charlotte Reilly–Davidson & Nicole van Tilborg
Age range: 1–18 years
No. of pupils: 300
Fees: €9,060–€32,800
Curriculum: IBDP, IBMYP
Language instr: English, French

International School Ghent
De Pintelaan 258, 9000 Ghent, East Flanders
Tel: +32 9 221 23 00
Age range: 2.5–12
No. of pupils: 93
Curriculum: IPC, UK
Language instr: English

International School of Belgium
Kontichsesteenweg 40, 2630 Aartselaar, Antwerp
Tel: +32 3 271 0943
Age range: 3–18 years
No. of pupils: 200
Curriculum: IBDP, IPC, IGCSE
Language instr: English

International School of Leuven
Geldenaaksebaan 335, 3001 Heverlee, Flemish Brabant
Tel: +32 16 375 790
Age range: 2–11
Curriculum: IPC

Internationale Deutsche Schule Brüssel
Lange Eikstraat 71, Wezembeek-Oppem, 1970 Brussels
Tel: +32 2 785 01 30
Age range: 2–19
No. of pupils: 600
Curriculum: Abitur, GCSE, ALevs
Language instr: German, English

ISF TERVUREN INTERNATIONAL SCHOOL
For further details see p. 188
Stationsstraat 3, 3080
Tervuren, Flemish Brabant
Tel: +32 2 767 3098
Email: office@isftervuren.org
Website: www.isftervuren.org
Head of Campus: Orla McLoughlin
Age range: 2.5–11 years
No. of pupils: 80
Language instr: English
CIS COB

ISF WATERLOO INTERNATIONAL SCHOOL
For further details see p. 189
280 Chaussee de Waterloo,
1640 Rhode-St-Genese,
Flemish Brabant
Tel: +32 2 358 56 06
Email: office@isfwaterloo.org
Website: www.isfwaterloo.org
Executive Head: Belinda Yates
Age range: 2.5–18 years
No. of pupils: 225
Language instr: English
CIS COB

Le Verseau International School
Rue De Wavre 60, 1301
Wavre, Walloon Brabant
Tel: +32 10 23 17 17
Curriculum: IGCSE
Language instr: French

Lycée Français International Anvers
Lamorinièrestraat 168A,
2018 Antwerp
Tel: +32 3 239 18 89
Age range: 2.5–19
No. of pupils: 175
Curriculum: FrenchBacc

Lycee Francais Jean Monnet
9 Avenue Lycee Francais,
1180 Brussels
Tel: +32 2 374 58 78
Curriculum: FrenchBacc

MONTGOMERY INTERNATIONAL SCHOOL – BRUSSELS
For further details see p. 207
Rue du Duc 133, 1200 Brussels
Tel: +32 (0)2 733 63 23
Email: info@montgomery-school.be
Website: www.ecole-montgomery.be
Director: David Gerone
Age range: 5–18 years
No. of pupils: 150
Fees: €9,642
Curriculum: IBDP, IBMYP, IBPYP
Language instr: English, French

Scandinavian School of Brussels
Square d'Argenteuil 5, 1410
Waterloo, Walloon Brabant
Tel: +32 2 357 06 70
Age range: 15–20
No. of pupils: 150 *B75 G75*
Curriculum: National
Language instr: English

Shape International School
SHAPE, Rue Grande,
7010 Mons, Hainaut
ECIS

ST. JOHN'S INTERNATIONAL SCHOOL
For further details see p. 241
Drève Richelle 146, 1410
Waterloo, Walloon Brabant
Tel: +32 (0)2 352 06 10
Email: enquiries@stjohns.be
Website: www.stjohns.be
Head of School: David Brooke
Age range: 18 months–18 years
No. of pupils: 500
Fees: €7,000–€37,600
Curriculum: AP, IBDP, IBMYP, IBPYP
Language instr: English
CIS ECIS

The British International School of Brussels
163 Av Emile Max, 1030 Brussels
Tel: +32 2 736 8981
Age range: 3–11
No. of pupils: 121 *B63 G58*
Curriculum: UK
Language instr: English
COB ECIS

The British Junior Academy of Brussels
83 Boulevard St Michel,
Etterbeek, 1040 Brussels
Tel: +32 2 732 5376
Age range: 3–13 years
Curriculum: UK

THE BRITISH SCHOOL OF BRUSSELS (BSB)
For further details see p. 250
Pater Dupierreuxlaan
1, 3080 Tervuren
Tel: +32 (0)2 766 04 30
Email: admissions@britishschool.be
Website: www.britishschool.be
Principal: Melanie Warnes
Age range: 1–18 years
No. of pupils: 1350
Fees: *Day* €30,235–€38,685
Curriculum: IBDP, UK, GCSE, IGCSE, ALevs, CSFS
Language instr: English, French (bilingual programme ages 4-14)
CIS COB ECIS

The Courtyard International School of Tervuren
Stationsstraat 49a, 3080 Tervuren
Curriculum: IBMYP, IBPYP
Language instr: English, French

The International School of Brussels (ISB)
Kattenberg 19, 1170 Brussels
Tel: +32 2 661 4211
Age range: 3–18
No. of pupils: 1500
Curriculum: AP, IBDP, IBCP, SAT, USA
Language instr: English
CIS

BOSNIA & HERZEGOVINA

Maarif Schools of Sarajevo
Ul. Hasiba Brankovica
2A, 71000 Sarajevo
Tel: +387 33 257 260
Curriculum: IBDP
Language instr: English, Bosnian

QSI International School of Sarajevo
Omladinska #16, 71320,
Vogosca-Sarajevo
Tel: +387 33 424450
Age range: 3–17
No. of pupils: 136
Curriculum: USA
Language instr: English

Richmond Park International School, Bihac
Dacka 42, 77000 Bihac
Tel: +387 37 941 170
Age range: 3–18
Language instr: English

Richmond Park International School, Sarajevo
Francuske revolucije bb,
71000 Ilid a – Sarajevo
Tel: +387 33 944 130
Age range: 3–19
Language instr: English

Richmond Park International School, Tuzla
Slavinovickog odreda
bb, 75000 Tuzla
Tel: +387 35 951 315
Age range: 3–19
Language instr: English

UWC Mostar
Spanski trg 1, Mostar 88000
Tel: +387 36 320 601
Age range: 16–19
No. of pupils: 200
Curriculum: IBDP
Language instr: English

BULGARIA

American College Arcus
16 Dragoman Str., 5000
Veliko Tarnovo
Tel: +359 62 619959
Age range: 14–19
No. of pupils: 189 *B82 G107*
Curriculum: IBDP, IBMYP, National
Language instr: English
ECIS

American College of Sofia
P.O. Box 873, 1000 Sofia
Tel: +359 2 434 10 08
Age range: 13–19
No. of pupils: 800
Curriculum: AP, IBDP, SAT, USA
Language instr: English

American English Academy Sofia
1 Orlova Krusha Str., Lozen
Area, 1151 Sofia
Tel: +359 2 973 12 22
Curriculum: USA
Language instr: English

Anglo American School of Sofia
1 Siyanie St., 1137 Sofia
Tel: +359 2 923 88 10
Age range: 4–18
No. of pupils: 580
Curriculum: IBDP
Language instr: English
CEE CIS COB ECIS

BRITANICA Park School
27 Momino Venche Street,
Dragalevtsi Quarter, Sofia
Tel: +359 2 4887877
Curriculum: IBDP
Language instr: English, Bulgarian

British International School Classic
7 Lady Strangford Street,
4000 Plovdiv
Tel: +359 886 902 295
Age range: 6–19
Curriculum: IBDP, National, UK, IGCSE
Language instr: English, Bulgarian
COB

British School of Sofia
18, Radi Radev Street,
Lozenets, 1700 Sofia
Tel: +359 886 510 510
Curriculum: IBDP, IBCP, UK
Language instr: English, Bulgarian
CIS COB

Lycée Français de Sofia Victor Hugo
complexe MAXI, 110
Simeonovsko chaussée,
quartier Vitosha, 1700 Sofia
Tel: +359 2 9632964
Age range: 4–18
No. of pupils: 625

Meridian 22 Private High School
Mladost 2 bl.227, 1799 Sofia
Tel: +359 2 8876 423; +359 2 8840 238
Curriculum: IBDP
Language instr: English

Private Primary School 'Progressive Education'-Sofia
107 Nishava Str., Sofia 1408
Tel: +359 882 741 944
Curriculum: IBPYP
Language instr: English

Simeon Radev School
Blagoy Gebrev 17, 25/11A, 2304 Pernik
Tel: +359 76670140
Age range: 14–19

St. George International School and Preschool
47 Nikola Vaptsarov blvd., Lozenetz, 1407 Sofia
Tel: +359 2 414 44 14
Curriculum: National, UK, IGCSE, ALevs
COB

Uwekind International School
136 Voivodina Mogila Street, Knyajevo, 1619 Sofia
Tel: +359 2 8572000
Age range: 4–19
No. of pupils: 370
Curriculum: IBDP, IBMYP
Language instr: English, Bulgarian

Zlatarski International School
49 Kliment Ohridski Boulevard, 1756 Sofia
Tel: +359 2 876 67 67
Age range: 13–19
No. of pupils: 300 *B*150 *G*150
Curriculum: IBDP, National
Language instr: English

CROATIA

American International School of Zagreb
Damira Tomljanovica Gravrana 3, 10020 Zagreb
Tel: +385 1 7999 300
Age range: 3–18
No. of pupils: 211 *B*108 *G*103
Curriculum: AP, IBDP, SAT, USA
Language instr: English
CEE ECIS

Bright Horizons – International School of Zagreb
Sveti Duh 122, 10000 Zagreb
Tel: +385 1 37 45 146
No. of pupils: 105
Curriculum: UK
Language instr: English
COB

British International School of Zagreb
Dedici 102, 10000 Zagreb
Tel: +385 1 4611 007
Curriculum: IPC, UK
COB

École Française Internationale de Zagreb
Fratrovac ulica 36, 10000 Zagreb
Tel: +385 1 234 7710

Split International School
Bihacka ul. 2, 21000 Split
Tel: +385 91 6182877

CYPRUS

American Academy Larnaca
PO Box 40112, Gregoris Afxentiou Avenue, Larnaca 6301
Tel: +357 24 815400
Age range: 4–19
No. of pupils: 937 *B*470 *G*467 *VIth*116
Curriculum: GCSE, ALevs

American Academy Primary School
7 Lefkas Street, 3070, Limassol
Tel: +357 25 382782
Age range: 4–11
No. of pupils: 390
Curriculum: UK

American Academy Secondary School
24 Despinas Pattichi Str, 3071, Limassol
Tel: +357 2533 7054
Age range: 2–19
No. of pupils: 750
Curriculum: UK, GCSE, IGCSE, ALevs
Language instr: English

American International School in Cyprus
PO Box 23847, 11 Kassos Str, Nicosia 1686
Tel: +357 22 316345
Age range: 3–19
No. of pupils: 315
Curriculum: IBDP, SAT, USA
Language instr: English
ECIS

école Franco-Chypriote
P.O. Box 22091, Nicosia 1517
Tel: +357 22 66 53 18
Curriculum: FrenchBacc

Foley's Grammar and Junior School
40 Homer Street, Limassol 3095
Tel: +357 25 582191
Age range: 4–18
No. of pupils: 530 *B*255 *G*275 *VIth*55
Curriculum: UK, GCSE, IGCSE, ALevs
Language instr: English

Forum Private Institute and Language Centre
PO Box 25567, Nicosia 1310
Tel: 00 357 22 446 344
Age range: 11–17

Girne American University
University Drive, PO Box 5, 99428 Karmi Campus, Karaoglanoglu, Kyrenia, TRNC
Tel: +90 850 650 20 00
Age range: 2–18
No. of pupils: 854 *B*447 *G*407
Curriculum: National, UK, IGCSE, ALevs
Language instr: English
ECIS

Highgate Private School
5 Irinikou, Agioi Trimithias, PO Box 20748, Nicosia 2670
Tel: +357 22 780527
Age range: 2–18
No. of pupils: 300
Curriculum: UK

International School of Paphos
100 Aristotelous Savva Ave, Anavargos, PO Box 62018, 8060 Paphos
Tel: +357 26 821700
Age range: 3–18
No. of pupils: 643 *B*314 *G*329 *VIth*31
Curriculum: UK, IGCSE, ALevs
Language instr: English

KES School of Languages
5, Kallipolis Avenue, 1055 Nicosia
Tel: +357 22 875737

Logos School of English Education
33-35 Agialousa Street, PO Box 51075, Limassol 3501
Tel: +357 253 36061
Age range: 3 –18
No. of pupils: 290
Curriculum: UK, IGCSE, ALevs
Language instr: English

PASCAL Private English School – Larnaka
2, Polytechniou Street, Larnaka, 7103 Aradippou
Tel: +357 22509300
Age range: 12–18
No. of pupils: 620
Curriculum: IBDP, UK, IGCSE, ALevs
Language instr: English

PASCAL Private English School – Lefkosia
177, Kopegchagis Street, Lefkosia, 2306 Lakatamia
Tel: +357 22509000
Age range: 12–18
No. of pupils: 300
Curriculum: IBDP, National, IGCSE, ALevs
Language instr: English

The American Academy Nicosia
PO Box 21967, Nicosia 1515
Tel: +357 22 664 266
Curriculum: USA

The English Learning Centre
138 Vasileos Constantinou, Limassol 3080
Tel: + 357 2538 7674
Age range: 7–18
No. of pupils: 500
Curriculum: IGCSE

The English School of Kyrenia
Bilim Sokak, Bellapais, Kyrenia, North Cyprus
Tel: +90 392 444 0375
Age range: 2–18 years
No. of pupils: 900
Curriculum: IBDP, GCSE, ALevs
Language instr: English
COB

The English School, Cyprus
P O Box 23575, 1684 Nicosia
Tel: +357 22 799 300
Age range: 11–19
No. of pupils: 1150 *B*500 *G*650 *VIth*300
Curriculum: UK, IGCSE, ALevs
Language instr: English

The Falcon School
P O Box 23640, Nicosia 1685
Tel: +357 22 424 781
Age range: 4–18
No. of pupils: 360 *B*170 *G*190 *VIth*60
Curriculum: GCSE, IGCSE, ALevs
Language instr: English

The G C School of Careers
96 Steliou Hadjipetri Street, Nicosia 2057
Tel: +357 224 64400

The Grammar School Limassol
Katinas Paxinou Panthea Hill, PO Box 51340, Limassol 3504
Tel: +357 25727933
Age range: 11–19
No. of pupils: 682

The Grammar School Limassol – Junior School
Manoli Kalomiri & Theklas street, PO Box 51340, Limassol 3504
Tel: +357 25352141

The Grammar School, Nicosia
PO Box 22262, Anthoupolis Highway, Pano Deftera 1519
Tel: + 357 22 695 695

The Heritage Private School
Palodina, Limassol CY-4549
Tel: +357 25 367 018
Age range: 2–18

The Junior & Senior School
P O Box 23903, Kyriakou
Matsi Avenue, Ayioi
Omoloyites, 1687 Nicosia
Tel: +357 22664855
Age range: 3–18
Curriculum: SAT, UK
Language instr: English

The Senior School
PO Box 25445, 2237 Nicosia
Tel: +357 22660156
Age range: 14–19
No. of pupils: 583
Curriculum: UK, IGCSE

Xenion Education
55, 1st April Avenue, PO Box
33900, 5281 Paralimni
Tel: +357 23811080
Age range: 4–19
No. of pupils: 560
Curriculum: UK, IGCSE, ALevs

CZECH REPUBLIC

1st International School of Ostrava
Gregorova 3, 702 00 Ostrava
Tel: +420 723 332 653
Curriculum: IBDP
Language instr: English

Carlsbad International School
Slovenska 477/5, 360 01 Karlovy Vary
Tel: +420 353 227 387
Age range: 14–18
No. of pupils: 75
Curriculum: IBDP
Language instr: English

Christian International School of Prague (CISP)
Legerova 5, 120 00 Prague 2
Tel: +420 272 730 091
Age range: 6–18
No. of pupils: 160
Curriculum: AP, USA
Language instr: English

Deutsche Schule Prag
Schwarzenberská 1/700,
158 00 Prague 5
Tel: +420 235 311 725

Dino High School s.r.o.
Bellova 352, 109 00 Prague 10
Tel: +420 240 200 082
Curriculum: IBDP
Language instr: Czech, English

Gymnasium Evolution
Jizni Mesto, Tererova 2135
/ 17, 149 00 Prague 4
Tel: +420 267 914 553
Curriculum: IBDP
Language instr: English, Czech

Gymnázium Duhovka
Ortenovo námestí 34, Hole
ovice, 170 00 Prague 7
Tel: +420 241 404 217
Curriculum: IBDP
Language instr: English, Czech

International Montessori School of Prague
Hrudickova 2107/16,
148 00 Prague 4
Tel: +420 272 937 758
Age range: 1.5–12

International School of Brno
Cejkovicka 10, 628 00
Brno-Vinohrady
Tel: +420 544 212 313
Age range: 3–19 years
No. of pupils: 160
Curriculum: IBDP, IBPYP, National
Language instr: English

International School of Prague
Nebusicka 700, 164 00 Prague 6
Tel: +420 220 384 111
Age range: 3–19
No. of pupils: 851 *B*432 *G*419
Curriculum: AP, IBDP, SAT
Language instr: English

International School Olomouc
Rooseveltova 101, 779 00 Olomouc
Tel: +420 585 754 880
Curriculum: UK
Language instr: English

Lycee Francais De Prague
Drtinova 7, 150 00 Prague 5
Tel: +420 222 550 000
Age range: 4–19
No. of pupils: 680

Meridian International School
Frydlantska 1350/1, 182 00 Prague 8
Tel: +420 286 581 805
Curriculum: UK
Language instr: English

Open Gate School
Babice 5, 251 01 Rícany
Tel: +420 724 730 512
Curriculum: IBDP
Language instr: English

Ostrcilova International School
Ostrcilova 1/2557, 702 00 Ostrava
Tel: +420 596 113 411
Age range: 3–11
No. of pupils: 200

Park Lane International School – Prague 1
Vald tejnská 151/6a, 118 01 Prague 1
Tel: +420 257 316 182
Age range: 10–18
Curriculum: IBDP, UK, IGCSE
Language instr: Czech, English

Park Lane International School – Prague 6
Norbertov 3, 162 00 Prague 6
Tel: +420 220 512 653
Age range: 3–10
Curriculum: UK, IGCSE

PORG International School – Ostrava
Rostislavova 7, 703 00 Ostrava
Tel: +420 597 071 020
Curriculum: IBDP
Language instr: English

PORG International School – Prague
Pod Krcskym lesem 1300/25,
142 00 Prague 4
Tel: +420 244 403 650
Curriculum: IBDP

Prague British International School
Brunelova 960/12, 142 00 Prague 4
Tel: +420 272 181 911
Age range: 2–18
No. of pupils: 350
Curriculum: SAT, UK
Language instr: English

PRIGO Language and Humanities Grammar School
Mojmirovcu 1002/42, Mariánské
Hory, 709 00 Ostrava
Curriculum: IBDP
Language instr: English

Riverside International School
Roztocka 9/43, Sedlec,
160 00 Prague 6
Tel: +420 2 24315336
Age range: 3–18
No. of pupils: 290
Curriculum: AP, IBDP,
National, IGCSE, ALevs
Language instr: English

Sunny Canadian International School
Straková 522, 252 42
Jesenice, Osnice
Tel: +420 734 827 106

The Ostrava International School
Gregorova 2582/3, 702 00 Ostrava
Tel: +420 724 142 287
Age range: 3–18
No. of pupils: 250
Curriculum: IBDP, IBMYP, IBPYP, UK
Language instr: English

The Prague British School – Kamyk Site
K Lesu 558/2, 142 00 Prague 4
Tel: +420 226 096 200
Age range: 1–18
No. of pupils: 650 *B*320 *G*330
Curriculum: IBDP, IBCP, SAT
Language instr: English

The Prague British School – Vlastina Site
Vlastina 19, 161 00 Prague 6
Tel: +420 22 609 6200

Townshend International School
Hradcany 1070, 373 41 Hluboka
Tel: +420 387 688 113
Age range: 3–18
Curriculum: UK, IGCSE, ALevs
Language instr: English

Zakladni Skola a Materska Skola Klas s.r.o
kolní námestí 37, 533 51
Rosice nad Labem
Tel: +420 774 305 011
Language instr: Czech, English

Zakladni Skola Buresova
Zernosecká 3/1597, 182 00 Prague 8
Age range: 6–15

DENMARK

Aarhus International School
Dalgas Avenue 12, 8000
Aarhus, Midtjylland
Tel: +45 2030 2079
Curriculum: IBMYP, IBPYP
Language instr: English

Bernadotte Skolen
Hellerupvej 11, Hellerup, 2900
Copenhagen, Hovedstaden
Tel: +45 3962 1215
Age range: 6–16
No. of pupils: 560 *B*270 *G*290

Bjorn's International School
Gartnerivej 5, 2100
Copenhagen, Hovedstaden
Tel: +45 3929 2937
Age range: 6–16
No. of pupils: 165
Curriculum: National, IGCSE
Language instr: English, Danish

Copenhagen International School
Levantkaj 4-14, 2150
Copenhagen, Hovedstaden
Tel: +45 3946 3300
Age range: 3–19
No. of pupils: 950
Curriculum: IBDP, IBMYP, IBPYP, SAT, USA
Language instr: English
CIS ECIS

Esbjerg International School
Guldager Skolevej 4, 6710
Esbjerg, Syddanmark
Tel: +45 7610 5399
Age range: 3–17
No. of pupils: 185
Curriculum: IBMYP, IBPYP
Language instr: English, Danish

Herlufsholm Skole
Herlufsholm Allé 170, 4700
Naestved, Sjaelland
Tel: +45 5575 3500
Age range: 15–20
No. of pupils: 643
Curriculum: IBDP, National
Language instr: English
RS

Institut Sankt Joseph
Dag Hammarskjölds Allé 17, 2100
Copenhagen, Hovedstaden
Tel: +45 3538 4735

International School Ikast-Brande
Bøgildvej 2, 7430 Ikast, Midtjylland
Tel: +45 9715 6465
Curriculum: National, UK, IGCSE

International School of Aarhus
Engtoften 22, 8260
Aarhus, Midtjylland
Tel: +45 8611 4560
Age range: 5–16
Curriculum: UK
COB

International School of Billund
Skolevej 24, 7190 Billund,
Syddanmark
Tel: +45 2632 7800
Age range: 3–14 years
No. of pupils: 450
Curriculum: IBMYP, IBPYP
Language instr: English

International School of Hellerup
Rygårds Allé 131, 2900
Hellerup, Hovedstaden
Tel: +45 7020 6368
Age range: 3–19 years
No. of pupils: 600
Curriculum: IBDP, IBMYP, IBPYP
Language instr: English

Lycée Français Prins Henrik
Frederiksberg Allé 22A, 1820
Frederiksberg, Hovedstaden
Tel: +45 3355 0064

North Zealand International School
Christianshusvej 16, 2970
Hørsholm, Hovedstaden
Tel: +45 4557 2616
Age range: 4–16
No. of pupils: 220
Curriculum: IBDP, IGCSE
Language instr: English
ECIS

Ranum Efterskole College
Kaervej 6/8, 9681 Ranum,
Nordjylland
Tel: +45 9666 4400
Age range: 5–12
No. of pupils: 121

Rygaards School
Bernstorffsvej 54, 2900
Hellerup, Hovedstaden
Tel: +45 3962 1053
Age range: 4–16
No. of pupils: 460
Curriculum: UK, IGCSE
Language instr: English
COB ECIS

Sankt Petri Skole
Larslejsstraede 5, 1451
Copenhagen, Hovedstaden
Tel: +45 3313 0462
Age range: 4–18
No. of pupils: 600

Skt. Josef's International School
Frederiksborgvej 10, 4000
Roskilde, Sjaelland
Tel: +45 4635 2526
Age range: 5–16
Curriculum: UK
Language instr: English

Sønderborg International School
Agervang 14, 6400
Sønderborg, Syddanmark
Tel: +45 7443 0110
Age range: 6–16 years
Curriculum: UK, IGCSE

VpR International
Trekronervej 10-14, 8800
Viborg, Midtjylland
Tel: +45 4085 3949
Curriculum: UK, IGCSE

ESTONIA

Audentes School
Tondi str 84, 11316 Tallinn, Harju
Tel: +372 699 6591
Age range: 2–18
No. of pupils: 520
Curriculum: IBDP

International School of Estonia
Juhkentali 18, 10132 Tallinn, Harju
Tel: +372 666 4380
Age range: 3–19
No. of pupils: 130 B62 G68
Curriculum: IBDP, IBMYP, IBPYP
Language instr: English
CEE CIS

International School of Tallinn
Keevise 2, 11415 Tallinn, Harju
Tel: +372 5066 080
Curriculum: IBDP, IBMYP, IBPYP
Language instr: English, Estonian

Tallinn European School
Tehnika 18, 10149 Tallinn, Harju
Tel: +372 735 0550
Age range: 4–18
Language instr: English, French

Tallinna Saksa Gümnasium
J. Sütiste tee 20, 13411 Tallinn, Harju
Tel: +372 6 522 240
Age range: 11–18
No. of pupils: 1280

Tartu International School
J. Liivi 2d, 50409 Tartu
Tel: +372 742 4241
Curriculum: IBPYP
Language instr: English

FINLAND

Aalto University School of Business
Mikkeli Campus, Lönnrotinkatu
5, 50100 Mikkeli, South Savo
Tel: +358 (0)50 4389837
Age range: 16–19
No. of pupils: 4000

Deutsche Schule Helsinki
Malminkatu 14, 00100
Helsinki, Uusimaa
Tel: +358 9 685065-0
Language instr: German, Finnish

Ecole Français Jules Verne
Ratakatu 6A, 00120
Helsinki, Uusimaa
Tel: +358 9 565 19 26

European School of Helsinki
Bulevardi 18, 00120
Helsinki, Uusimaa
Tel: +358 295 332 451

Helsingin Suomalainen Yhteiskoulu
Isonnevantie 8, 00320
Helsinki, Uusimaa
Tel: +358 9 4774 1814
Age range: 9–19
No. of pupils: 1200 B600 G600
Curriculum: IBDP, National

International School Cygnaeus
Tasavallankatu 1, 28100
Pori, Satakunta
Tel: +358 2 621 5227
Age range: 4–11
No. of pupils: 50

International School of Helsinki
Selkämerenkatu 11, 00180
Helsinki, Uusimaa
Tel: +358 9 686 6160
Age range: 4–18
No. of pupils: 320
Curriculum: IBDP, IBMYP, IBPYP, SAT
Language instr: English
CEE CIS ECIS

International School of Vantaa
Hagelstamintie 1, 01520
Vantaa, Uusimaa
Tel: +358 9 8392 4810
Age range: 6–16
No. of pupils: 350
Language instr: English

Kotkansaari School
The Central Street, 28 Centre
Street, 48100 Kotka, Kymenlaakso
Tel: +358 234 4531
Age range: 13–15
No. of pupils: 411

Maunula Primary School
Maunulanmaki 5, 00630
Helsinki, Uusimaa
Tel: +358 9 310 82484
Age range: 6–12
No. of pupils: 340

Mussalon ala-asta
Rajakalliontie 10, 48310
Kotka, Kymenlaakso
Tel: +358 234 5802
Age range: 4–19

Myllytullin Koulu
Kirkkokatu 1, 90100 Oulu,
North Ostrobothnia
Tel: +358 8 44 703 9633
Age range: 5–13
No. of pupils: 70

Oulu International School
Kasarmintie 4, 90130 Oulu,
North Ostrobothnia
Tel: +358 50 371 6977
No. of pupils: 280
Curriculum: IBMYP, IBPYP
Language instr: English

Rajala School
Sammakkolammentie 14,
70200 Kuopio, North Savo
Tel: +358 44 718 4356

The English School
Mäntytie 14, 00270
Helsinki, Uusimaa
Tel: +358 10 321 7920

FRANCE

American School of Paris
41 rue Pasteur, 92210 Saint-Cloud
Tel: +33 01 41 12 86 55
Age range: 3–18 years
No. of pupils: 800
Curriculum: ACT, AP, IBDP, SAT, USA
Language instr: English
(CIS) (ECIS)

Apex2100 Academy
Le Rosset, 73320 Tignes
Curriculum: IBDP, IBCP
Language instr: English, French

BORDEAUX INTERNATIONAL SCHOOL
For further details see p. 136
252 Rue Judaïque,
33000 Bordeaux
Tel: +33 5 57870211
Email: contact@bis33.com
Website:
www.bordeaux-school.com
Principals: Mrs Bergey
& Mme Bidalun
Age range: 3–19 years
No. of pupils: 180
Fees: *Day* €3,890–€14,650
Curriculum: National,
UK, IGCSE, ALevs
Language instr: English,
French, Spanish
(CIS) (ECIS)

Chavagnes International College
96 Rue du Calvaire, 85250
Chavagnes-en-Paillers
Tel: +33 2 51 42 39 82
Age range: 11–18
No. of pupils: 200

Cite Scolaire Internationale de Lyon
Section Anglophone, 2 Place
de Montreal, 69361 Lyon
Tel: +33 4 7869 6006
Age range: 6–18
No. of pupils: 1600
Curriculum: SAT
(ECIS)

Collège de Niki de St Phalle – Anglophone Section
Chemin du Darbousson, Sophia
Antipolis, 06905 Valbonne
Tel: +33 4 92915130
Age range: 11–15
No. of pupils: 200
Curriculum: National

Collège EIB Monceau
16, rue Margueritte, 75017 Paris
Tel: +33 (0)1 46 22 40 20
Age range: 3–10

College Hauts Grillets
10 Bd Hector Berlioz, 78100
Saint-Germain-en-Laye
Tel: +33 1 30 87 46 20
Age range: 11–18

College International de Fontainebleau
Anglophone Section, 48 Rue
Geurin, 77300 Fontainbleau
Tel: +33 1 6422 1177
Age range: 6–18
No. of pupils: 450 *VIth*44
Curriculum: FrenchBacc, UK, IGCSE
(ECIS)

College Marcel Roby (American Section)
2 bis rue du Fer a Cheval, 78100
Saint Germain en Laye
Tel: +33 1 34 51 74 85
Age range: 11–15
Curriculum: USA

College Sainte Clotilde
9 rue de Bel Orme, 33000 Bordeaux
Tel: +33 5 56 48 29 06
Age range: 14–19

Collège-Lycée Saint François-Xavier
3 rue Thiers, 56000 Vannes
Tel: +33 (0)2 97 47 12 80
Curriculum: IBDP
Language instr: English, French

Cours Moliere
2-4 Boulevard Soult, 75012 Paris
Tel: +33 1 43 43 44 96
Age range: 5–18
No. of pupils: 300
Curriculum: FrenchBacc, IGCSE

Deutsche Schule Toulouse
Eurocampus 2, 2 Allée de
l'Herbaudiére, Colomiers,
31770 Toulouse
Tel: +33 5 67 73 29 20
Age range: 4–18
No. of pupils: 210

Don Bosco Landser
1 Rue Don Bosco, 68440 Landser
Tel: +33 3 89 81 31 03
Age range: 4–19

Ecole Active Bilingue
Administration, 117 Boulevard
Malesherbes, 75008 Paris
Tel: +33 1 45 63 62 22
Age range: 3–18
No. of pupils: 3000
Curriculum: AP, IBDP, SAT, ALevs
(ECIS)

Ecole des Francs Bourgeois
21 rue St Antoine, 75004 Paris
Tel: +33 1 44 59 20 90
Age range: 11–19
Language instr: French

Ecole Des Roches
295 avenue Edmond Demolins,
27130 Verneuil d'Avre et d'Iton
Tel: +33 (0) 232 6040 00
Age range: 11–18 years
No. of pupils: 320
Curriculum: IBDP
Language instr: English, French

Ecole Européenne de Strasbourg
2 Rue Peter Schwarber, CS
60014, 67015 Strasbourg
Tel: +33 (0)3 88 34 82 20

ÉCOLE JEANNINE MANUEL – LILLE
For further details see p. 144
418 bis rue Albert Bailly,
Marcq-en-Baroeul 59700
Tel: +33 3 20 65 90 50
Email: admissions-lille@ejm.net
Website:
www.ecolejeanninemanuel.org
Head of School: Constance
Devaux
Age range: 3–18 years
No. of pupils: 980
Fees: *Day* €6,225 *FB* €15,985–
€24,285 €21,495
Curriculum: IBDP,
National, FrenchBacc
Language instr: French, English
(CIS)

ÉCOLE JEANNINE MANUEL – PARIS
For further details see p. 146
70 rue du Théâtre, Paris 75015
Tel: +33 1 44 37 00 80
Email: admissions@ejm.net
Website:
www.ecolejeanninemanuel.org
Principal: Jérôme Giovendo
Age range: 4–18 years
No. of pupils: 2400
Fees: *Day* €7,450–€8,215 €26,350
Curriculum: IBDP, IGCSE
Language instr: English, French
(CIS) (ECIS)

Ecole Privée Bilingue Internationale
Domaine de massane,
34670 Baillargues
Tel: +33 4677 07844
Curriculum: IBDP, IBMYP
Language instr: English, French

Ecole Privée Val Saint André
19, Av Henri Malacrida,
13100 Aix-en-Provence
Tel: +33 442 271 447
Curriculum: FrenchBacc, UK, IGCSE

EIB Grenelle
176 rue de Grenelle, 75007 Paris
Tel: +33 (0)6 49 85 21 49

EIB Lamartine School
123 Rue de la Pompe, 75116 Paris
Tel: +33 1 45 53 89 36
Age range: 3–10

EIB Monceau School
6 Avenue Van Dyck, 75008 Paris
Tel: +33 1 46 22 14 24
Age range: 3–11
No. of pupils: 1000

Ermitage International School
46 Avenue Eglé, 78600
Maisons-Laffitte
Tel: +33 139 62 81 75
Age range: 3–18 years
No. of pupils: 1470
Curriculum: IBDP, IBMYP
Language instr: English, French
(RS)

Eurecole
5 rue de Lubeck, 75116 Paris
Tel: +33 1 40 70 12 81
Age range: 2–15
No. of pupils: 190
Curriculum: National
(ECIS)

Forest International School
28 Chemin du Tour d'Echelle
du Mur, de Cloture de la Foret
de Marly, 78750 Mareil Marly
Tel: +33 1 39 16 87 35
Language instr: English
(ECIS)

Franklin St Louis De Gonzague
12 Rue Benjamin Franklin, 75116 Paris
Tel: +33 1 44 30 45 50
Age range: 6–18
No. of pupils: 1500
Curriculum: GCSE

Hattemer
52 rue de Londres, 75008 Paris
Tel: +33 1 43 87 59 14
Age range: 4–18 years
No. of pupils: 350
Curriculum: IBDP
Language instr: English, French

ICS CÔTE D'AZUR
For further details see p. 160
245 Route les Lucioles,
06560 Valbonne
Tel: +33 (0)4 93 64 32 84
Email:
admissions@icscotedazur.com
Website:
www.icscotedazur.com
Director: Amanda Scott
Age range: 3–11 years
No. of pupils: 150
Fees: *Day* €10,645–€14,235
Curriculum: IBPYP, IGCSE
Language instr: English, French

ICS PARIS
For further details see p. 163
23 rue de Cronstadt, 75015 Paris
Tel: +33 (0)1 56 56 60 70
Email: admissions@icsparis.fr
Website: www.icsparis.fr
Director: Angela Hollington
Age range: 3–18 years
No. of pupils: 500
Fees: *Day* €18,651–€26,550
Curriculum: IBDP, IPC, IGCSE
Language instr: English, French

INTERNATIONAL BILINGUAL SCHOOL OF PROVENCE
For further details see p. 169
500 Route de Bouc-Bel-Air, Domaine des Pins, Luynes, Aix en Provence 13080
Tel: +33 (0)4 4224 0340
Email: info@ibsofprovence.com
Website: www.ibsofprovence.com
General Director: Jean-Marc Gobbi
Age range: 2–18 years
No. of pupils: 850
Fees: *Day* €12,000–€18,000 *FB* €23,000–€33,000
Curriculum: AP, IBDP, National, FrenchBacc, SAT, TOEFL, UK, USA, GCSE, IGCSE, ALevs
Language instr: English, French
ECIS

International School of Béarn
200 Boulevard du Cami Salié, 64000 Pau
Tel: +33 559 09 94 74
Age range: 2–18
No. of pupils: 265
Curriculum: SAT, UK
Language instr: English, French, Spanish
ECIS

International School of Lyon
80 Chemin du Grand Roule, 69110 Sainte Foy Lès Lyon
Tel: +33 (0) 478 866 190
Age range: 3–18
No. of pupils: 252
Curriculum: IBDP, IBPYP, IGCSE
Language instr: English
ECIS

International School of Marseille
27 Boulevard de la Corderie, 13007 Marseille
Tel: +33 491 53 00 00
Age range: 2–11
No. of pupils: 65
Curriculum: National
ECIS

INTERNATIONAL SCHOOL OF NICE
For further details see p. 182
15 Avenue Claude Debussy, 06200 Nice
Tel: +33 (0)4 93 21 04 00
Email: admissions@isn-nice.com
Website: www.isn-nice.com
Director: Mel Curtis
Age range: 3–18 years
No. of pupils: 430
Fees: *Day* €11,400–€20,685
Curriculum: ACT, AP, IBDP, IBPYP, SAT, UK, USA, IGCSE, ALevs
Language instr: English, French
CIS ECIS

International School of Paris
6 rue Beethoven, 75016 Paris
Tel: +33 1 42 24 09 54
Age range: 3–18
No. of pupils: 700
Curriculum: IBDP, IBMYP, IBPYP
Language instr: English
CIS ECIS

International School of Toulouse
2 Allee De L'Herbaudiere, Route de Pibrac, 31770 Colomiers
Tel: +33 5 62 74 26 74
Age range: 3–18
No. of pupils: B237 G238
Curriculum: IBDP, IBPYP, IPC, UK, IGCSE
Language instr: English
CIS ECIS

Internationale Deutsche Schule Paris (iDSP)
18 Rue Pasteur, 92210 Saint-Cloud
Tel: +33 (0)146028568
Age range: 3–18
No. of pupils: 360
Curriculum: Abitur
Language instr: German, French

La Villa Blanche – Notre Dame du Sacre Coeur
3 rue Pasteur, 6500 Menton
Tel: +33 4 92 10 56 10
Age range: 14–19

Lennen Bilingual School – Primary Campus
176 rue de Grenelle, 75007 Paris
Tel: +33 1 44 42 99 00

Lindenwood International School
Centre Ville, 78124 Mareil-sur-Mauldre
Tel: +33 6 13 47 77 89
Age range: 3–16 years
Language instr: English, French

Lycee de Sevres, International Sections
Rue Lecocq, 92310 Sevres
Tel: +33 1 46 23 9635
Age range: 11–18
No. of pupils: 620

Lycée EIB Etoile School
9 rue Villaret de Joyeuse, 75017 Paris
Tel: +33 1 45 63 30 73
Age range: 15–20
No. of pupils: 400
Curriculum: National

Lycée International de Saint Germain-en-Laye, American Section
2 bis rue du Fer à Cheval, 78100 Saint-Germain-en-Laye
Tel: +33 1 34 51 74 85
Age range: 4–18 years
No. of pupils: 700
Curriculum: National, FrenchBacc, USA
Language instr: French, English

Lycee International Des Pontonniers
1 Rue des Pontonniers, 67081 Strasbourg
Tel: +33 3 88 37 15 25
Age range: 5–18
No. of pupils: 870
Curriculum: IGCSE

Lycée International François 1ER
11 rue Victor Hugo, 77300 Fontainebleau
Tel: +33 1 60 74 58 30
Age range: 14–19

Lycee Internationale de Saint Germain-en-Leye – British Section
BP 70107, 78101 Saint Germain En Laye
Tel: +33 1 34516264
Age range: 5–18
No. of pupils: 680
Curriculum: UK, IGCSE

Lycee Louis de Foix
4 Avenue Jean Rostand, BP 331, 64103 Bayonne
Tel: +33 5 59 63 31 10
Age range: 14–19

Lycee Notre Dame
Rue Principale, 49310 La Salle de Vihiers
Tel: +33 2 41 49 02 50
Age range: 11–19
No. of pupils: 300

Lycee Notre Dame du Grandchamp
97 rue Royale, RP 934, 78000 Versailles
Tel: +33 1 39 24 12 80
Age range: 14–19
No. of pupils: 200

Lycee Pierre de Coubertin
320 Boulevard du 8 Mai, 62225 Calais
Tel: +33 3 21 46 88 00
Age range: 14–19

Malherbe International School
19 Rue Du 11 Novembre, 78110 Le Vesinet
Tel: +33 1 39 76 47 37
Age range: 2–15
No. of pupils: 150
Curriculum: UK
Language instr: English, French

MARYMOUNT INTERNATIONAL SCHOOL PARIS
For further details see p. 202
72, boulevard de la Saussaye, 92200 Neuilly-sur-Seine
Tel: +33 (0)1 46 24 93 25
Email: admissions@marymount.fr
Website: www.marymount.fr
Head of School: Sarah Thomas
Age range: 2–14 years
No. of pupils: 360
Fees: €20,000–€48,000
Curriculum: USA
Language instr: English
CIS ECIS

Massillon – Ecole Bilingue Internationale
5 Rue Bansac, 63000 Clermont-Ferrand
Tel: +33 4 73 98 09 73
Age range: 3–18 years
No. of pupils: 1500
Curriculum: FrenchBacc, SAT, IGCSE
Language instr: English, French

Montessori International Bordeaux
47 Avenue de la Poterie, 33170 Gradignan
Tel: +33 6 51 27 98 19
Curriculum: IBDP, IBMYP, IBPYP
Language instr: English, French

MOUGINS SCHOOL
For further details see p. 208
615 Avenue Maurice Donat, CS 12180, 06252 Mougins CEDEX
Tel: +33 4 93 90 15 47
Email: admissions@mougins-school.com
Website: www.mougins-school.com
Director: James Wellings
Age range: 3–18
No. of pupils: 540
Fees: *Day* €14,175–€20,055
Curriculum: UK, GCSE, IGCSE, ALevs
COBIS

Notre Dame International High School
106 Grande-Rue, 78480 Verneuil-sur-Seine
Tel: +33 9 70 40 79 22
Age range: 15–18 years
No. of pupils: 40
Curriculum: IBDP, USA
Language instr: English, French

Ombrosa, Lycée Multilingue de Lyon
95 Quai Clemenceau,
69300 Caluire
Tel: +33 4 78 23 22 63
Age range: 2–18
No. of pupils: 1007 *B*528 *G*479
Curriculum: AP, IBDP, National
Language instr: English, Spanish

SAINTE VICTOIRE INTERNATIONAL SCHOOL
For further details see p. 220
Domaine de Château
l'Arc, Chemin de Maurel,
13710 Fuveau
Tel: +33 4 42 26 51 56
Email: contact@schoolsaintevictoire.com
Website: www.schoolsaintevictoire.com
Head of School: Frederic Fabre
Age range: 5–18 years
Fees: *Day* €10,200–€17,900 *FB* €26,800–€31,800
Curriculum: IBDP, IGCSE
Language instr: English, French

Saudi School in Paris
60 bis avenue d'Iéna, 75016 Paris
Tel: +33 1 40 73 80 40
Language instr: English

Sections Internationales de Sèvres
1 Parvis Charles De Gaulle, 92310 Sevres
Tel: +33 1 72 77 70 43
Age range: 3–19
No. of pupils: 262
Curriculum: FrenchBacc

SEK INTERNATIONAL SCHOOL LES ALPES
For further details see p. 228
Saint Nicolas La Chappelle,
Flumet-Val d'Arly, 73590 Flumet
Tel: +34 900 87 87 98
Email: sek-lesalpes@sek.es
Website: lesalpes.sekinternationalschools.com
Principal: Guadalupe Sánchez
Age range: 13–15 years

The American School of Grenoble
Cité Scolaire Internationale, 4 Place de Sfax BP 1570, 38000 Grenoble
Tel: +33 4 38 12 25 47
Age range: 10–18
No. of pupils: 33 *B*18 *G*15
Curriculum: AP, SAT, USA
Language instr: English
CIS ECIS

The British School of Paris
38 Quai De L'Ecluse, 78290
Croissy-sur-Seine
Tel: +33 1 34 80 45 96
Age range: 3–18
No. of pupils: 800 *B*400 *G*400 *VIth*100
Curriculum: GCSE, ALevs
Language instr: English
COB

Trillium International School
9 rue de la sabotte,
78160 Marly-le-Roi
Tel: +33 1 78 64 88 15
Curriculum: National, UK

GEORGIA

British International School of Tbilisi
Leo Kvachadze 17 (Lisi Lake Area), Tbilisi 0186 0186
Tel: +995 322 251 253
Age range: 3–16 years
Curriculum: IPC, SAT, UK, GCSE, IGCSE, ALevs

Buckswood International School Tbilisi
52 Rustaveli Street,
Tskneti, Tbilisi 0189
Tel: +995 877 992 993
Language instr: English, Russian
ECIS

Chaglar International School
Shuamta Street No:21 3.,
Varketilli, Tbilisi
Tel: +995 32 276 2662
Age range: 4–19
No. of pupils: 110
Curriculum: UK, IGCSE

European School
#2 I. Skhirtladze Str., Tbilisi 0177
Tel: +995 32 239 59 64
Age range: 3–18
No. of pupils: 806
Curriculum: AP, IBDP, IBMYP, IBPYP, IBCP, National, USA
Language instr: English
CIS

New School, International School of Georgia
35 Tskneti Highway,
0179 Bagebi, Tbilisi
Tel: +995 32 223 1728
Age range: 3–19
No. of pupils: 600
Curriculum: IBDP, IBMYP, IBPYP
Language instr: English, Georgian

QSI International school of Tbilisi
Village Zurgovani, Tbilisi
Tel: +995 32 253 7672
Age range: 4–18
No. of pupils: 146
Curriculum: SAT, USA
Language instr: English

St George's British Georgian School
M. Aleksidze II Lane 6 (By Sports Palace), Tbilisi
Tel: +995 32 260 99 89
Curriculum: National, UK, IGCSE, ALevs
Language instr: English

GERMANY

ACCADIS INTERNATIONAL SCHOOL BAD HOMBURG
For further details see p. 121
SÜDCAMPUS Bad Homburg,
Am Weidenring 52-54, 61352
Bad Homburg, Hesse
Tel: +49 61 72 984 141
Email: info@accadis-isb.com
Website: www.accadis-isb.com
Head of School: Janina Sparks
Age range: 2–18 years
No. of pupils: 600
Fees: €3,360–€4,560
Curriculum: IBDP
Language instr: English, German

Aloisiuskolleg
Elisabethstraße 18, 53177 Bonn,
North Rhine-Westphalia
Tel: +49 228 82003 (101)
Curriculum: IBDP
Language instr: English, German

Bavarian International School gAG (BIS) – City Campus
Leopoldstrasse 208, 80804
Munich, Bavaria
Tel: +49 89 89655 203
Curriculum: IBPYP
Language instr: English

Bavarian International School gAG (BIS) – Haimhausen Campus
Hauptstrasse 1, 85778
Haimhausen, Bavaria
Tel: +49 (0)81 33 917 203
Age range: 3–18 years
No. of pupils: 1150
Curriculum: IBDP, IBMYP, IBPYP, IBCP
Language instr: English
CIS ECIS

Berlin Brandenburg International School
Schopfheimer Allee 10, 14532
Kleinmachnow, Brandenburg
Tel: +49 33 203 8036 0
Age range: 3–19
No. of pupils: 700
Curriculum: IBDP, IBMYP, IBPYP, IBCP
Language instr: English
CIS ECIS

Berlin British School
Dickensweg 17-19, 14055 Berlin
Tel: +49 (0)30 35109 180
Age range: 2–18
No. of pupils: 480
Curriculum: IBDP, IBPYP, UK, IGCSE
Language instr: English
COB ECIS

Berlin Cosmopolitan School
Rückerstrasse 9, 10119 Berlin
Tel: +49 30 688 33 23 0
Curriculum: IBDP, IBPYP

Berlin International School
Lentzeallee 8/14, 14195 Berlin
Tel: +49 (0) 30 8200 7790
Age range: 6–18
No. of pupils: 825 *B*410 *G*415
Curriculum: IBDP, IBPYP, SAT, IGCSE
Language instr: English, German
CIS ECIS

Berlin Metropolitan School
Linienstrasse 122, 10115 Berlin
Tel: +49 30 8872 7390
Age range: 5–11
No. of pupils: 424 *B*192 *G*232
Curriculum: IBDP, IBPYP, National
Language instr: English, German
ECIS

Bertolt-Brecht-Gymnasium Dresden
Lortzingstrasse 01, 01307
Dresden, Saxony
Tel: +49 351 449040
Curriculum: IBDP
Language instr: English

Black Forest Academy
Postfach 1109, 79396 Kandern,
Baden-Württemberg
Tel: +49 7626 91610
Age range: 10–19
No. of pupils: *B*160 *G*164
Curriculum: ACT, AP, SAT, USA
Language instr: English
CIS

Bonn International School e.V.
Martin-Luther-King Strasse 14, 53175
Bonn, North Rhine-Westphalia
Tel: +49 228 30854 0
Age range: 3–19
No. of pupils: 730
Curriculum: IBDP, IBMYP, IBPYP, SAT
Language instr: English
CIS ECIS

Ceclilien Gymnasium
Schorlemerstrasse 99, 40547
Düsseldorf, North Rhine-Westphalia
Tel: +49 211 892 33 11

Dresden International School e.V
Annenstrasse 9, 01067
Dresden, Saxony
Tel: +49 351 440070
Age range: 1–19
No. of pupils: 497 *B*257 *G*240
Curriculum: ACT, IBDP, IBMYP, IBPYP, USA
Language instr: English
CIS ECIS

Ecole Élémentaire Franco-Allemande de Stuttgart – Sillenburch
Silberwaldstrasse 22, 70619
Stuttgart, Baden-Württemberg
Tel: +49 711 216 20 860
Age range: 6–11
No. of pupils: 500

École française de Sarrebruck et Dilling
Halbergstrasse 112, 66121
Saarbrücken, Saarland
Tel: +49 68 162 624

École française Pierre et Marie Curie
Wieblinger Weg 9, 69123
Heidelberg, Baden-Württemberg
Tel: +49 62 21840 983

École Grundschule Voltaire
Kurfürstenstrasse 53, 10785 Berlin
Tel: +49 30 4110015

Erasmus International School
Flotowstrasse 10, 14480
Potsdam, Brandenburg
Tel: +49 331 237 2790
Age range: 4–18
No. of pupils: 80 *B*37 *G*43
Curriculum: UK, IGCSE
Language instr: English

European School Karlsruhe
Aldert Schweitzerstrasse 1, 76139
Karlsruhe, ?Baden-Württemberg
Tel: +49 7 21 6 80 09 0
Age range: 3–19
No. of pupils: 950

European School Munich
Elise-Aulinger Strasse 21,
81739 Munich, Bavaria
Tel: +49 89 62 8160
Age range: 3–19
No. of pupils: 1345

European School of Frankfurt
Praunheimer Road 126,
60439 Frankfurt, Hesse
Tel: +49 69 92 88 74 0
Age range: 4–19
No. of pupils: 1080

Franconian International School
Marie-Curie-Strasse 2, 91052
Erlangen, Bavaria
Tel: +49 9131 940390
Age range: 3–18 years
No. of pupils: 650
Curriculum: IBDP, IBMYP, IPC
Language instr: English
CIS ECIS

Frankfurt International School
An der Waldlust 15, 61440
Oberursel, Hesse
Tel: +49 6171 2024 0
Age range: 3–18 years
No. of pupils: 1800
Curriculum: IBDP, IBPYP, IBCP
Language instr: English

Frankfurt International School (Wiesbaden Campus)
Rudolf-Dietz-Strasse 14, Naurod,
65207 Wiesbaden, Hesse
Tel: +49 6127 99400
Age range: 3–14
No. of pupils: 220 *B*110 *G*110
Curriculum: IBPYP
Language instr: English, German

Groupe Scolaire Jean de la Fontaine
Meckenheimer Strasse
45, Mehelm, 53179 Bonn,
North Rhine-Westphalia
Tel: +49 228 9538031
Age range: 4–18
No. of pupils: 190

Gymnasium im Stift Neuzelle
Stiftsplatz 7, 15898 Neuzelle,
Brandenburg
Tel: +49 341 3939 2810
Curriculum: IBDP
Language instr: English, German

Hansa-Gymnasium, Hamburg-Bergedorf
Hermann-Distel-Strasse
25, 21029 Hamburg
Tel: +49 (0)40 724 18 60
Age range: B10–19 G10–19
No. of pupils: *VIth*185
Curriculum: Abitur, IBDP, TOEFL
Language instr: German, English

Heidelberg International School
Wieblinger Weg 7, 68782
Heidelberg, Baden-Württemberg
Tel: +49 6221 75 90 600
Age range: 4–18 years
No. of pupils: 258
Curriculum: IBDP, IBMYP, IBPYP
Language instr: English
ECIS

Heidelberg Private School Centre (Heidelberger Privatschulcentrum)
Kurfürsten-Anlage 64-68, 69115
Heidelberg, Baden-Württemberg
Tel: +49 62 21 70504 038
Curriculum: IBDP, IBPYP

IBSM – International Bilingual School Munich gGmbH
Lerchenauerstrasse 197,
80935 Munich, Bavaria
Tel: +49 89 41 11 49 550
Age range: 6–10 years
No. of pupils: 87
Curriculum: IBPYP
Language instr: English, German

Independent Bonn International School
Tulpenbaumweg 42, 53177
Bonn, North Rhine-Westphalia
Tel: +49 228 323 166
Age range: 3–13
No. of pupils: 225 *B*110 *G*115
Curriculum: UK
Language instr: English
CIS COB ECIS

International Kids Campus GmbH
Lerchenauerstrasse 197,
80935 Munich, Bavaria
Tel: +49 89 411149 550
Age range: 2.5–6 years
No. of pupils: 48
Curriculum: IBPYP
Language instr: English, German

International School Augsburg (ISA)
Wernher-von-Braun-Strasse 1a,
86368 Gersthofen, Bavaria
Tel: +49 821 45 55 60 0
Age range: 3–18
No. of pupils: 350
Curriculum: IBDP, IBPYP
Language instr: English
CIS

International School Braunschweig-Wolfsburg
Helmstedter Strasse 37, 38126
Braunschweig, Lower Saxony
Tel: +49 531 889210 0
Age range: 4–19
No. of pupils: 256
Curriculum: IBDP, IGCSE
Language instr: English

International School Hannover Region
Bruchmeisterallee 6, 30169
Hannover, Lower Saxony
Tel: +49 511 270 416 50
Age range: 3–18 years
No. of pupils: 591 *B*287 *G*304
Curriculum: IBDP, IBMYP, IBPYP
Language instr: English
CIS ECIS

International School Mainfranken e.V.
Kalifornienstrasse 1, 97424
Schweinfurt, Bavaria
Tel: +49 9721 53861-80
Age range: 6–18
No. of pupils: 105
Curriculum: IBDP, IBMYP, IBPYP
Language instr: English

International School of Bremen
Badgasteiner Strasse
11, 28359 Bremen
Tel: +49 421 5157790
Age range: 3–18
No. of pupils: 345
Curriculum: ACT, IBDP, IPC, SAT, IGCSE
Language instr: English
ECIS

INTERNATIONAL SCHOOL OF DÜSSELDORF E.V.
For further details see p. 176
Niederrheinstrasse 323/336,
40489 Düsseldorf, North
Rhine-Westphalia
Tel: +49 (0) 211-9406 6
Email: info@isdedu.de
Website: www.isdedu.de
School Director: Frank Tschan
Age range: 3–18 years
No. of pupils: 960
Curriculum: IBDP, IBMYP, IBPYP, USA
Language instr: English

International School of Hamburg
Hemmingstedter Weg
130, 22609 Hamburg
Tel: +49 (0)40 8000 500
Age range: 3–18
No. of pupils: 770
Curriculum: IBDP, IBMYP, IBCP, IPC, SAT
Language instr: English
CIS ECIS

INTERNATIONAL SCHOOL OF NEUSTADT
For further details see p. 181
Haardterstrasse 1, 67433
Neustadt an der Weinstrasse
Tel: +49 6321 8900 960
Email: info@is-neustadt.de
Website: www.is-neustadt.de
Principal: Vjeko Kovac
Age range: 4–18 years
No. of pupils: 70
Fees: *Day* €14,200–€16,700
Curriculum: IBDP, IGCSE
Language instr: English

International School of Stuttgart, Degerloch Campus
Sigmaringestrasse 257, 70597 Stuttgart, Baden-Württemberg
Tel: +49 71 17696 000
Age range: 3–18 years
No. of pupils: 820
Curriculum: IBDP, IBMYP, IBPYP
Language instr: English

International School of Stuttgart, Sindelfingen Campus
Hallenserstrasse 2, 71065 Sindelfingen, Baden-Württemberg
Tel: +49 70 316859 780
Age range: 3–18 years
No. of pupils: 820
Curriculum: IBMYP, IBPYP
Language instr: English

International School of Ulm/Neu Ulm
Schwabenstraße 25, 89231 Neu-Ulm, Bavaria
Tel: +49 731 379 353-0
Age range: 3–18
No. of pupils: 290
Curriculum: IBDP, IBPYP, IGCSE
Language instr: English
ECIS

International School Ruhr
Moltkeplatz 1 + 61, 45138 Essen, North Rhine-Westphalia
Tel: +49 (0)201 479 104 09
Age range: 3–19
No. of pupils: 153
Curriculum: IBDP, IBPYP, IGCSE
Language instr: English

INTERNATIONAL SCHOOL WESTPFALZ
For further details see p. 186
Nikolaus-von-Weis-Strasse 10, 66849 Landstuhl
Tel: +49 6371 980 930
Email: info@is-westpfalz.de
Website: www.is-westpfalz.de
Principal: Christopher Moore
Age range: 4–18 years
No. of pupils: 200
Fees: *Day* €14,400–€16,700
Curriculum: IGCSE, ALevs
Language instr: English

Internationale Friedensschule Köln
Neue Sandkaul 29, 50859 Cologne, North Rhine-Westphalia
Tel: +49 221 310 6340
Age range: 6–19
No. of pupils: 530
Curriculum: IBDP, IBPYP, IGCSE
Language instr: English, German
ECIS

Internationales Gymnasium Geithain
Friedrich-Fröbel-Strasse 1, 04643 Geithain, Saxony
Tel: +49 34 34146 012
Age range: 17–19
No. of pupils: 5
Curriculum: IBDP
Language instr: German

Internationales Gymnasium Reinsdorf
Mittlerer Schulweg 13, 08141 Reinsdorf, Saxony
Tel: +49 37 634082 300
Curriculum: IBDP
Language instr: English, Spanish

ISF International School Frankfurt Rhein-Main
Strasse zur Internationalen Schule 33, 65931 Frankfurt, Hesse
Tel: +49 69 954319 710
Age range: 3–18
No. of pupils: 850 *B*425 *G*425 *VIth*160
Curriculum: Abitur, AP, IBDP, SAT, IGCSE
Language instr: English
ECIS

ISR International School on the Rhine – NRW
Konrad-Adenauer-Ring 2, 41464 Neuss, North Rhine-Westphalia
Tel: +49 2131 40388-0, -11
Age range: 3 (Kindergarten)/5-6 (Primary)–18 years (Middle and Upper School)
No. of pupils: 700
Curriculum: AP, IBDP, SAT, IGCSE
Language instr: English
ECIS

Josef-Schwarz-Schule (JSS)
Georg-Ohm-Strasse 15, 74235 Erlenbach, Baden-Württemberg
Tel: +49 71 324884 980
Age range: 5–11
Curriculum: National
Language instr: English, German

Kämmer International Bilingual School
Paderbornerstrasse 1, 30539 Hannover, Lower Saxony
Tel: +49 51 12200 890
Age range: 1–18
No. of pupils: 400
Language instr: German, English
ECIS

Leibniz Privatschule Elmshorn
Ramskamp 64B, 25337 Elmshorn, Schleswig-Holstein
Tel: +49 41 212610 40
Age range: 6–19
No. of pupils: 1000
Curriculum: IBDP
Language instr: English, German

LEIPZIG INTERNATIONAL SCHOOL
For further details see p. 198
Könneritzstrasse 47, 04229 Leipzig, Saxony
Tel: +49 34 139377 500
Email: info@lis.school
Website: www.lis.school
Head of School: Brandie Smith
Age range: 1–18 years
No. of pupils: 955
Curriculum: IBDP, IPC, IGCSE
Language instr: English
CIS ECIS

Leonardo Da Vinci Campus
Zu den Luchbergen 13, 14641 Nauen, Brandenburg
Tel: +49 33 217487 820
Curriculum: IBDP
Language instr: English, Spanish

Lycée Antoine-de-Saint-Exupéry de Hambourg
Antoine de Saint Exupéry, Hartsprung 23, 22529 Hamburg
Tel: +49 (0)40 790147 0
Curriculum: FrenchBacc

Lycée Français
Derfflingerstrasse 7, 10785 Berlin
Tel: +49 30 257589 51
Age range: 12–18
No. of pupils: 558

Lycée français de Düsseldorf
Graf-Recke-Straße 220, 40237 Düsseldorf, North Rhine-Westphalia
Tel: +49 21 16107 950
Age range: 3–18
No. of pupils: 570
Curriculum: National, FrenchBacc
Language instr: French, German, English

Lycée Français Jean Renoir
Berlepschstrasse 3, 81373 Munich, Bavaria
Tel: +49 89 72100 70
Curriculum: FrenchBacc

Lycée Français Victor Hugo
Gontardstrasse 11, 60488 Frankfurt am Main
Tel: +49 (0)69 74 74 98 149

Lycée français Victor-Hugo
Gontardstrasse 11, 60488 Frankfurt, Hesse
Tel: +49 69 74 74 98 0
Curriculum: National, FrenchBacc
Language instr: French, German

Main Taunus International School
Hugenottenstrasse 119, 61381 Friedrichsdorf, Hesse
Tel: +49 (0)6172 76465-0
Language instr: English, German

Metropolitan International School (MIS Heidelberg)
Mozartstrasse 4, 69120 Heidelberg, Baden-Württemberg
Tel: +49 6221 726 7900
Age range: 10 months–6 years

Metropolitan International School (MIS Mannheim)
SoHo TURLEY, Turley-Strasse 12, 68167 Mannheim, Baden-Württemberg
Tel: +49 6214 458 8282
Age range: 10 months–6 years

Metropolitan International School (MIS Viernheim)
Walter-Gropius-Allee 3, 68519 Viernheim, Hesse
Tel: +49 6204 7087 796
Age range: 4–18 years
Curriculum: IBDP
Language instr: English, German

Metropolitan School Frankfurt
Eschborner Landstrasse 134-142, 60489 Frankfurt, Hesse
Tel: +49 69 96 86 405-0
Age range: 3–18 years
No. of pupils: 620
Curriculum: IBDP, IBPYP
Language instr: English
CIS

MUNICH INTERNATIONAL SCHOOL E.V.
For further details see p. 209
Schloss Buchhof, Percha, 82319 Starnberg, Bavaria
Tel: +49 8151 366 0
Email: admissions@mis-munich.de
Website: www.mis-munich.de
Head of School: Timothy J. Thomas
Age range: 4–18 years
No. of pupils: 1200
Curriculum: IBDP, IBMYP, IBPYP
Language instr: English
CIS ECIS

Netzaberg Middle School
Unit 28130, 09144 Munich, Bavaria
Tel: +49 96 459179 229

Nymphenburger Schulen
Sadelerstrasse 10, 80638 Munich, Bavaria
Tel: +49 89 159 120
Age range: 10–18
Curriculum: IBDP, National
Language instr: German, English

Phorms Campus Berlin Mitte
Ackerstrasse 76, 13355 Berlin
Tel: +49 30 467 986 303/0/9
Age range: 3–19
No. of pupils: 570 *B*280 *G*290
Curriculum: Abitur, National, UK
Language instr: English, German
ECIS

Phorms Campus Berlin Süd
Harry-S.-Truman-Allee 3, 14167 Berlin
Tel: +49 30 916 849 90
Age range: 1–18
No. of pupils: 500
Curriculum: AP, UK, ALevs

Phorms Campus Hamburg
Wendenstrasse 35-43,
20097 Hamburg
Tel: +49 40 325 370 50

Phorms Campus Munich
Maria-Theresia-Straße 35,
81675 Munich, Bavaria
Tel: +49 89 324 9337 00
Curriculum: IBDP
Language instr: English

Phorms Frankfurt City
Fürstenbergerstraße 3-9,
60322 Frankfurt, Hesse
Tel: +49 69 173 92 550

Phorms Taunus Campus
Waldstrasse 91, 61449
Steinbach, Hesse
Tel: +49 6171 206 02 70

Prälat-Diehl-Schule Oberstufe
Darmstädter Strasse 90A,
64521 Gross Gerau, Hesse
Tel: +49 6152 93350
No. of pupils: 1400
Curriculum: UK

Private Herder-Schule
Luisenstrasse 134-135, 42103
Wuppertal, North Rhine-Westphalia
Tel: +49 202 313170
Age range: 10–20
No. of pupils: 150
Curriculum: Abitur, National, TOEFL
Language instr: German
(ISA)

QSI International School of Münster
Lettisches Centrum Münster
e.V., Salzmannstrasse 152, 48159
Münster North Rhine-Westphalia
Tel: +49 251 38349446

Schule Birklehof
Birklehof 1, 79856 Hinterzarten,
Baden-Württemberg
Tel: +49 7652 1220
Language instr: German
(RS)

Schule Schloss Salem
Schlossbezirk 1, 88682 Salem,
Baden-Württemberg
Tel: +49 7553 919 352
Age range: 10–19
No. of pupils: 600
Curriculum: Abitur, IBDP, National
Language instr: English, German
(RS)

SIS Swiss International School Berlin
Heerstrasse 465, (school entrance
at Reimerweg 11), 13593 Berlin
Tel: +49 30 36 43 98 20
Age range: 3–16 years
Curriculum: IBDP, ALevs
Language instr: English, German

SIS Swiss International School Frankfurt
An den drei Hasen 34-36,
61440 Oberursel, Hesse
Tel: +49 61 71 88 75 80 11
Age range: 4–12 years
Language instr: English, German

SIS Swiss International School Friedrichshafen
Fallenbrunnen 1, 88045
Friedrichshafen, Baden-Württemberg
Tel: +49 7541 954 37 0
Age range: 3–16 years
Curriculum: IBDP
Language instr: English, German

SIS Swiss International School Ingolstadt
Stinnesstrasse 1, 85057
Ingolstadt, Bavaria
Tel: +49 841 981 446 0
Age range: 3–16 years
Curriculum: IBDP
Language instr: English, German

SIS Swiss International School Kassel
Johanna-Waescher-Strasse
15, 34131 Kassel, Hesse
Tel: +49 561 316 68 30
Age range: 4–16 years
Language instr: English, German

SIS Swiss International School Regensburg
Klosterackerweg 1, 93049
Regensburg, Bavaria
Tel: +49 941 9925 930 0
Age range: 3–16 years
Curriculum: IBDP
Language instr: English, German

SIS Swiss International School Stuttgart-Fellbach
Schmidener Weg 7/1,
70736 Stuttgart-Fellbach,
Baden-Württemberg
Tel: +49 711 469 194 10
Age range: 3–16 years
Curriculum: IBDP
Language instr: English, German

St. George's School Cologne
Husarenstrasse 20, 50997 Cologne,
North Rhine-Westphalia
Tel: +49 2233 808 870
Age range: 2–18
No. of pupils: 830 *B*430 *G*400 *VIth*150
Curriculum: IBDP, IBCP, GCSE, IGCSE
Language instr: English
(COB)

St. George's School Duisburg-Düsseldorf
Am Neuen Angerbach 90, 47259
Duisburg, North Rhine-Westphalia
Tel: +49 203 456 860
Age range: 3–18
No. of pupils: 376 *B*196 *G*180
Curriculum: IBDP, IBCP, UK, ALevs
(COB)

St. George's School Munich
Heidemannstrasse 182,
80939 Munich, Bavaria
Tel: +49 89 72469 330
Curriculum: IBDP, IBCP
Language instr: English, German

Stiftung Landheim Schondorf am Ammersee
Country Home 1-14, 86938
Schondorf am Ammersee, Bavaria
Tel: +49 8192 8090
Language instr: German
(RS)

Stiftung Louisenlund
Louisenlund 9, 24357 Güby,
Schleswig-Holstein
Tel: +49 (0)4354 999 0
No. of pupils: 440
Curriculum: IBDP
(RS)

Strothoff International School Rhein-Main Campus Dreieich
Frankfurterstrasse 160-166,
63303 Dreieich, Hesse
Tel: +49 6103 8022 500
Age range: 3–18
Curriculum: ACT, IBDP,
IBMYP, IBPYP, SAT
Language instr: English
(ECIS)

Taunus International Montessori School
Zimmersmuehtenweg 77,
61440 Oberursel, Hesse
Tel: +49 6171 913310
Age range: 1–6
No. of pupils: 60

UWC Robert Bosch College
Kartäuserstrasse 119, 79104
Freiburg, Baden-Württemberg
Tel: +49 761 708 395 00
Age range: 16–19
No. of pupils: 200
Curriculum: IBDP
Language instr: English

GIBRALTAR

Loreto Convent School
13 Europa Road, GX11 1AA
Tel: +350 200 75781
Age range: 1–12 years
No. of pupils: 422 *B*193 *G*229
Curriculum: UK
Language instr: English

Prior Park School
Sacred Heart Terrace,
Tel: 00350 200 62006
Curriculum: UK
(COB)

St Anne's Middle School
St Anne's Road,
Tel: +350 20077161
Age range: 8–12
No. of pupils: 450

GREECE

American Community Schools of Athens
129 Aghias Paraskevis Str.,
Halandri, 152 34 Athens
Tel: +30 210 639 3200
Age range: 3–18 years
No. of pupils: 1100
Curriculum: IBDP
Language instr: English
(ECIS)

American Farm School
Marinou Antipa 54, PO Box
23, Thessaloniki 551 02
Tel: +30 23104 92700
Curriculum: USA

Anatolia High School
PO Box 21021, 60 John Kennedy
Avenue, 555 35 Pylea
Tel: +30 2310 398 200
Curriculum: IBDP, IBMYP
Language instr: English
(IBDP), Greek (MYP)

Byron College
7 Filolaou Street, 15344 Gerakas
Tel: +30 210 60 47 722 – 5
Age range: 3–18
Curriculum: UK, GCSE, IGCSE, ALevs
Language instr: English
(COB)

Campion School Athens
PO Box 674 84, Pallini 153 02
Tel: +30 210 607 1700
Age range: 3–18
No. of pupils: 510
Curriculum: IBDP
Language instr: English
(COB) (ECIS)

Costeas-Geitonas School
Pallini – Attikis, Athens 15351
Tel: +30 210 6030 411
Curriculum: IBDP, IBMYP, IBPYP
Language instr: English

Deutsche Schule Athen
Dimokritou 6 & Germanikis Scholis
Athinon, GR 151 23 Maroussi
Tel: +30 210 6199260-5

Deutsche Schule Thessaloniki – DST
PO Box 51, Thessaloniki-Thermi km 9, GR-55102 Thessaloniki-Fin
Tel: +30 2310 475 900

European Interactive School (DES)
Barakos Hill, Ribas 19400
Tel: +30 210 8974143
Curriculum: IBPYP
Language instr: English, Greek

Geitonas School
International Baccalaureate Diploma Programme, PO Box 74128, Sternizes, Koropi, Attiki 166 02
Tel: +30 210 9656200-10
Age range: 4–19
No. of pupils: 2147 *B*1100 *G*1047
Curriculum: IBDP
Language instr: English

HAEF, Athens College
15 Stephanou Delta Street, Psychico, Athens 15452
Tel: +30 2106798100
Curriculum: IBMYP
Language instr: English, Greek

HAEF, Athens College Elementary
Paleopanagias Avenue, Kantza 15351
Tel: +30 2106798100
Curriculum: IBPYP
Language instr: English, Greek

HAEF, John M. Carras Kindergarten
15 Stephanou Delta Street, Psychico, Athens 15452
Tel: +30 2106798100
Curriculum: IBPYP
Language instr: English, Greek

HAEF, Psychico College
15 Stephanou Delta Street, Psychico, Athens 15452
Tel: +30 2106798100
Curriculum: IBDP, IBMYP
Language instr: English, Greek

HAEF, Psychico College Elementary
Paleopanagias Avenue, Kantza 15351
Tel: +30 2106798100
Curriculum: IBPYP
Language instr: English, Greek

I.M. Panagiotopoulos School
Milisi 3, Pallini, Athens 153 51
Tel: +30 21 0666 6117
Age range: 3–18
Curriculum: National
Language instr: English

Institut Français de Thessalonique
Leoforos Stratou 2A, Thessaloniki
Tel: +30 23 10 821 231
Age range: 4–18
No. of pupils: 70

International School of Athens
PO Box 51051, Kifissia, Athens 14510
Tel: +30 210 6233 888
Age range: 3–18
No. of pupils: 324 *B*189 *G*135 *VIth*25
Curriculum: AP, IBDP, IBMYP, IBPYP, SAT
Language instr: English

International School of Larissa
Tyrnavos 40100, Larissa 40100
Tel: +30 24920 22233
Age range: 4–18
No. of pupils: 300
Curriculum: USA

International School of Piraeus
66-70 Praxitelous street, Piraeus 18532
Tel: +30 210 417 5580
Curriculum: IBPYP
Language instr: English

Ionios School
PO Box 13622, Filothei 15202
Tel: +30 210 6857130
Curriculum: IBDP

Lampiri Schools
Metamorphosis 155 and Ilissou, Moschato, Athens
Tel: +30 210 9480530
Curriculum: IBDP
Language instr: English

Lycée Franco-Hellénique Eugène Delacroix
B.P. 60050, Rues Chlois & Trikalon, 153 54 Aghia Paraskevi-Athènes
Tel: +30 211 300 91 00
Curriculum: FrenchBacc, IGCSE

Mary N. Raptou School SA
Karditsis 21, Larissa 41335
Tel: +30 2410 625724
Language instr: English

Moraitis School
A Papanastasiou & Ag Dimitriou, Paleo Psychico, Athens 15452
Tel: +30 210 679 5000
Age range: 4–18
No. of pupils: 1800
Curriculum: IBDP, National, SAT, TOEFL
Language instr: English

Pierce – The American College of Greece
6 Gravias Street, Aghia Paraskevi, Athens 153 42
Tel: +30 210 600 9800 (Ext:1060)
Curriculum: IBDP
Language instr: English, Greek

Pinewood – American International School of Thessaloniki, Greece
14th km Thessalonikis – N. Moudanion, P.O. Box 60606, Thermi – Thessaloniki GR-57001
Tel: +30 2310 301 221
Age range: 3–18
No. of pupils: 330 *B*165 *G*165
Curriculum: IBDP, SAT, USA
Language instr: English

Platon School
Eleytheriou Venizelou Street, Glyka Nera, Attika 15354
Tel: +30 210 6611 793
Curriculum: IBDP, IBMYP, IBPYP

St Catherine's British School
Leoforos Venizelou 77, Lykovrissi, Athens 141 23
Tel: +30 210 2829 750
Age range: 3–18
No. of pupils: 1060
Curriculum: IBDP, UK
Language instr: English
(COB)

St Lawrence College
PO Box 7422, 16602 Varkiza Attiki, Athens
Tel: +30 21 0891 7000
Age range: 3–19
No. of pupils: 755 *B*372 *G*383
Curriculum: UK, IGCSE, ALevs
Language instr: English
(COB)

Ziridis Bilingual School
Christoupoli, Athens 19004
Tel: +30 210 6685600
Age range: 3–17
No. of pupils: 1600

HUNGARY

American International School of Budapest
Nagykovácsi út 12, Nagykovácsi 2094
Tel: +36 26 556 000
Age range: 3–20
No. of pupils: *B*434 *G*429
Curriculum: IBDP, SAT, USA
Language instr: English
(CEE) (CIS) (ECIS)

BME International Secondary School
Egry Jozsef utca 3-11, Budapest 1111
Tel: +36 12094983
Curriculum: IBDP
Language instr: English

Britannica International School
Kakukk Way 1-3, 1121 Budapest
Tel: +36 1 466 9794
Age range: 5–18
No. of pupils: *B*150 *G*140
Curriculum: National, UK, IGCSE, ALevs
Language instr: English
(COB)

Budapest British International Academy
1025 Budapest,, Berkenye utca 13-15,
Tel: +36 30 563 55 28
Curriculum: UK
(COB)

Budapest British International School
4 Zsolna utca, Budapest 1125
Tel: +36 70 425 5225
Curriculum: IBMYP, UK
Language instr: English

Deutsche Schule Budapest Thomas Mann Gymnasium
Cinege út 8/C, Budapest CH-1121
Tel: +36 1 39191 00

Greater Grace International School of Budapest
Szilagyi Erzsebet Fasor 22/B, Budapest 1125
Tel: + 36 1 275 4795

International Christian School of Budapest
H-2049 Diosd, Ifjusag 11
Tel: +36 23 381 986
Age range: 5–18
No. of pupils: 225
Curriculum: USA
Language instr: English
(CEE)

International School of Budapest
Konkoly Thege M u 21, Budapest 1121
Tel: +36 1 395 6543
Age range: 5–18 years
No. of pupils: 400
Curriculum: IBDP, National
Language instr: English

International School of Debrecen (ISD)
Heltai Gáspár Street 1, 4002 Debrecen
Tel: +36 20 404 4822
Curriculum: IBPYP
Language instr: English, Hungarian

QSI International School of Pápa
Komáromi út 12, 8500 Pápa
Tel: +36 89 777 999

SEK Budapest International School
Hüvösvölgyi út 131, Budapest 1021
Tel: +36 1 394 2968
Curriculum: IBDP
Language instr: English
ISA

The British International School
Kiscelli Köz 17, Budapest 1037
Tel: +36 1 200 9971
Age range: 3–18
No. of pupils: 800
Curriculum: IBDP, UK, GCSE
Language instr: English
COB ECIS

ICELAND

International School of Iceland
Löngulínu 8, 210 Gar abær
Tel: +354 590 3106
Age range: 5–15
No. of pupils: 90 *B*48 *G*42
Curriculum: IPC, National
Language instr: English, Icelandic
ECIS

IRELAND

Castle Park School
Castle Park Road, Dalkey, Co Dublin
Tel: +353 1 280 3037
Age range: 3–12
No. of pupils: 286 *B*162 *G*124
Language instr: English

Cistercian College
Mount St. Joseph Abbey, Roscrea
Tel: + 353 505 23344
Age range: *B*12–19
Curriculum: National
Language instr: English

Headfort School
Kells, Co Meath
Tel: +353 4692 40065
Age range: 7–13
No. of pupils: 105 *B*65 *G*40

International School of Dublin
Synge Street, Dublin D08 PW64
Tel: +353 087 329 1417
Age range: 3.5–12 years
No. of pupils: 50
Curriculum: IBPYP
Language instr: English, Spanish

John Scottus School
Old Conna, Ferndale Road, Rathmichael, Co. Dublin
Tel: +353 (1) 668 0828

Lycée Français d'Irlande – Collège et Lycée
Eurocampus Dublin, Roebuck Road, Clonskeagh, Dublin 14
Tel: +353 1 288 4834
Age range: 11–18
No. of pupils: 490
Curriculum: FrenchBacc

Nord Anglia International School Dublin
South County Business Park, Leopardstown, Dublin 18
Tel: +353 1 5442323
Age range: 3–18 years
Curriculum: IBDP, IBMYP, IBPYP
Language instr: English

Sandford Park School
Ranelagh, Dublin 6
Tel: +353 1 4971417
Age range: 12–18
No. of pupils: 350
Language instr: English

SEK DUBLIN INTERNATIONAL SCHOOL
For further details see p. 222
Belvedere Hall, Windgates, Greystones, Co. Wicklow A63 EY23
Tel: +35 31 287 41 75
Email: admissions-dublin@sek.ie
Website: dublin.sek.es
Principal: Alberto Domínguez
Age range: 11–18 years
Curriculum: IBDP, IBMYP
Language instr: English

St Andrew's College
Booterstown Avenue, Blackrock, County Dublin
Tel: +353 1 288 2785
Age range: 4–18 years
No. of pupils: 1250
Curriculum: ACT, IBDP, National, SAT
Language instr: English
AISA CIS ECIS

St Columba's College
Kilmashogue Lane, Whitechurch, Dublin 16
Tel: +353 1 4906791
Age range: 11–18
No. of pupils: 295 *B*159 *G*136 *VIth*137
Curriculum: National
Language instr: English

Sutton Park School
St Fintan's Road, Sutton, Dublin 13
Tel: +353 1 8322940
Age range: 4–18
No. of pupils: 278 *B*167 *G*111
Curriculum: SAT
CIS

The King's Hospital
Palmerstown, Dublin 20
Tel: +353 1 643 6564
Age range: 12–18 years
No. of pupils: 740 *B*400 *G*340
Curriculum: National

Villiers School
North Circular Road, Limerick V94 F983
Tel: +353 61 451447
No. of pupils: 600
Curriculum: IBDP
Language instr: English

ITALY

Ambrit International School
Via F Tajani 50, 00149 Rome
Tel: +39 06 5595 305/301
Age range: 3–14
No. of pupils: 450 *B*225 *G*225
Curriculum: IBMYP, IBPYP, National
Language instr: English

AMERICAN OVERSEAS SCHOOL OF ROME
For further details see p. 131
Via Cassia 811, 00189 Rome
Tel: +39 06 334 381
Email: admissions@aosr.org
Website: www.aosr.org/admissions
Head of School: Kristen DiMatteo
Age range: 3–19
Fees: €10,800–€14,850
Curriculum: AP, IBDP, National, SAT, USA
Language instr: English
ECIS

AMERICAN SCHOOL OF MILAN
For further details see p. 132
Via K. Marx, 14, 20073 Noverasco di Opera (MI)
Tel: +39 02 5300 0015
Email: admissions@asmilan.org
Website: www.asmilan.org
Director: Wayne Rutherford
Age range: 3–18 years
No. of pupils: 840
Fees: *Day* €10,800–€20,300
Curriculum: IBDP, SAT
Language instr: English

Andersen International School
Via Don Carlo, San Martino 8, 20133 Milan
Tel: +39 02 70 00 65 80
Age range: 18 months–14 years
No. of pupils: 500
Curriculum: UK
Language instr: English
COB

BILINGUAL EUROPEAN SCHOOL
For further details see p. 135
Via Val Cismon 9, 20162 Milan
Tel: +39 02 6611 7449
Email: admissions@beschool.eu
Website: www.beschool.eu
Heads of School: Mauro Spicci & John Nicholls
Age range: 2–14 years
No. of pupils: 545
Fees: *Day* €10,650–€12,770
Curriculum: IBPYP
Language instr: English, Italian

Britannia International School of Rome
Via Ernesto Parisi 11, 00134 Rome
Tel: +39 06 713 54252
Age range: 2–11
No. of pupils: 135
Curriculum: UK

British School Genova
Piazzale dei Traghetti, Iqbal 5, 16123 Genoa
Tel: +39 010 540903
Age range: 4–19

Cabella International Sahaja School CISS
Via Martiri della Libertà 11, Cabella Ligure, 15060 Alessandria
Tel: +39 0143 919805
Curriculum: IPC, UK

Canadian College Italy (CCI – The Renaissance School)
Via Cavour 13, Lanciano, 66034 Chieti
Tel: +39 872 714969
Age range: 15–19
ECIS

CANADIAN SCHOOL OF FLORENCE
For further details see p. 138
Via Jacopo Nardi 18, 50132 Florence
Tel: +39 055 098 2744
Email: info@csflorence.it
Website: www.csflorence.it
Head of School: Gary O'Meara
Fees: *Day* €10,750–€18,500 *FB* €39,000

Canadian School of Milan
Via M. Gioia 42, 20124 Milano
Tel: +39 02 67074775
Curriculum: IBDP, IBMYP
Language instr: English

Castelli International School
Via Degli Scozzesi 13, Grottaferrata, 00046 Rome
Tel: +39 06 94315779
Age range: 5–14 years
No. of pupils: 125
Curriculum: National, UK, IGCSE

Collegio San Carlo
Corso Magenta, 71, 20123 Milan
Tel: +39 02 43 06 31
Curriculum: IBDP
Language instr: English

Core International School
Via Crati 19, 00199 Rome
Tel: +39 068411137
Curriculum: UK

Deledda International School
Corso Mentana 27, 16128 Genoa
Tel: +39 010 5536268
No. of pupils: 770
Curriculum: IBDP, IBMYP
Language instr: English

Deutsche Schule Genua
Scuola Germanica di Genova, Via Mylius 1, 16128 Genoa
Tel: +39 010 564 334

Deutsche Schule Mailand
Scuola Germanica di Milano, Via Legnano 24, 20121 Milan
Tel: +39 (0)2 6597614

Ecole Française de Naples Alexandre Dumas
Via Francesco Crispi no 86, 80121 Naples
Tel: +39 (0)81 66 89 36

European School of Varese
Via Montello 118, 21100 Varese
Tel: +39 332 806 111
Age range: 4–18
No. of pupils: 1350

German School of Rome
Via Aurelia Antica 397-403, 00165 Rome
Tel: +39 06 663 8776
Age range: 4–18
No. of pupils: 700

GIS The International School of Monza srl
Via Federico Confalonieri 18, 20900 Monza (MB)
Tel: +39 039 2287034
Curriculum: IBPYP
Language instr: English, Italian

Gonzaga International School
Via Piersanti Mattarella 38/42, 90141 Palermo
Tel: +39 91 302093
Age range: 18 months–18 years
No. of pupils: 190
Curriculum: IBDP, IBMYP, IBPYP
Language instr: English

Greenwood Garden School
Via Vito Sinisi 5, 00189 Rome
Tel: +39 06 3326 6703
Age range: 2–6
No. of pupils: 44 *B*22 *G*22
Curriculum: USA
Language instr: English

H-FARM INTERNATIONAL SCHOOL
For further details see p. 157
Via Olivetti 1, 31056 Roncade (TV)
Tel: +39 0422 789503
Email: info.tv@h-is.com
Website: www.h-is.com/it/scuole/treviso
Head of School: Mauro Bordignon
Age range: 3–18 years
Curriculum: IBMYP, IBPYP
Language instr: English, Italian

H-International School Rosà
Via Segafredo 50, 36027 Rosà
Tel: +39 0424 582191
Age range: 4–14
No. of pupils: 276 *B*137 *G*139
Curriculum: National, TOEFL
Language instr: English, Italian

H-International School Vicenza
Borgo Santa Lucia, 51 Vicenza, 36100 Vicenza
Tel: +39 444 54 50 07
Age range: 18 months–16 years
No. of pupils: 213
Curriculum: IBDP, IBMYP, IBPYP, National, UK
Language instr: English

ICS MILAN
For further details see p. 162
ICS Symbiosis, Viale Ortles, 46, 20139 Milano (MI)
Tel: +39 02 36592694
Email: admissions@icsmilan.com
Website: www.icsmilan.com
Curriculum: IBMYP
Language instr: English, Italian

INSTITUT INTERNATIONAL SAINT-DOMINIQUE
For further details see p. 165
Via Igino Lega 5, 00189 Rome
Tel: +39 06 303 10817
Email: info@institutsaintdominique.it
Website: www.institutsaintdominique.it
Head of School: Bernard Lociciro
Age range: 2–18 years
No. of pupils: 350
Fees: *Day* €3,900–€13,500 *WB* €16,000 *FB* €21,000
Curriculum: IBDP, FrenchBacc
Language instr: English, French

International School Brescia
Via Benaco 34/B, Bedizzole, 25080 Brescia
Tel: +39 030 2191182
Age range: 3–19 years
No. of pupils: 150
Curriculum: IBDP, IBMYP, IBPYP

INTERNATIONAL SCHOOL OF BERGAMO
For further details see p. 174
Via Monte Gleno, 54, 24125 Bergamo
Tel: +39 035 213776
Email: info@isbergamo.com
Website: www.isbergamo.com
Heads of School: Mrs. Guia Ghidoli & Mrs. Chiara Traversi
Age range: 2–18 years
No. of pupils: 360
Curriculum: IBDP, IBMYP, IBPYP
Language instr: English, Italian

International School of Bologna
Via della Libertà 2, 40123 Bologna
Tel: +39 051 6449954
Age range: 3–18
No. of pupils: 270
Curriculum: IBDP, IBMYP, IBPYP
Language instr: English

INTERNATIONAL SCHOOL OF COMO
For further details see p. 175
Via Adda 25, 22073 Fino Mornasco (CO)
Tel: +39 031 572289
Email: info@iscomo.com
Website: www.iscomo.com
Head of School: Gavin Williams
Age range: 2–18 years
No. of pupils: 400
Curriculum: IBDP, IBMYP, IBPYP
Language instr: English, Italian

International School of Florence
Via del Carota 23/25, Bagno a Ripoli, 50012 Florence
Tel: +39 055 6461 007
Age range: 3–18
No. of pupils: 439 *B*216 *G*223 *VIth*28
Curriculum: IBDP, IBPYP, National, SAT, USA
Language instr: English, Italian

International School of Lago Patria
Via 1a Marenola, 17, 80014 Giugliano in Campania
Tel: +39 081 5096452
Language instr: English

INTERNATIONAL SCHOOL OF MILAN
For further details see p. 178
Via I Maggio, 20, 20021 Baranzate (MI)
Tel: +39 02 872581
Email: admissions@ism-ac.it
Website: www.internationalschoolofmilan.it
Headmaster: Darren Nicholas
Age range: 2–18 years (Boarding 14-18 years)
No. of pupils: 900
Curriculum: IBDP, IBMYP, IBPYP
Language instr: English

INTERNATIONAL SCHOOL OF MODENA
For further details see p. 179
Piazza Montessori, 1/A, 41051 Montale Rangone (MO)
Tel: +39 059 530649
Email: admissions@ismodena.it
Website: www.internationalschoolofmodena.it
Head of School: Caroline Troughton
Age range: 3–18 years
No. of pupils: 230
Curriculum: IBDP, IBMYP, IBPYP
Language instr: English

INTERNATIONAL SCHOOL OF MONZA
For further details see p. 180
Via Solferino 23, 20900 Monza (MB)
Tel: +39 039 9357701
Email: admin@ismonza.it
Website: www.internationalschoolofmonza.it
Head of School: Iain Sachev
Age range: 2.5–18 years
No. of pupils: 280
Curriculum: IBDP, IBMYP, IBPYP
Language instr: English, Italian

INTERNATIONAL SCHOOL OF SIENA
For further details see p. 183
Via del Petriccio e Belriguardo, 49/1, 53100 Siena
Tel: +39 0577 328103
Email: office@issiena.it
Website: www.internationalschoolofsiena.it
Principal: Lianne Knibb
Age range: 3–18 years
No. of pupils: 200
Curriculum: IBDP, IBMYP, IBPYP
Language instr: English, Italian

International School of Talents – Multicampus (IST)
Via degli Alpini, 28/5, 31046 Oderzo, Treviso
Tel: +39 0422 789 503
Curriculum: IBDP

International School of Trieste
Via Conconello 16, 34151 Trieste
Tel: +39 040 211 452
Age range: 2–18
No. of pupils: 335 *B*165 *G*170
Curriculum: AP, USA
Language instr: English
ECIS

International School of Turin
Strada Pecetto 34, 10023 Chieri, Turin
Tel: +39 011 645 967
Age range: 3–18 years
Curriculum: IBDP, IBMYP, IBPYP
Language instr: English
CIS ECIS

International School of Venice
Via Bissagola 25, 30173 Mestre, Venezia
Tel: +39 041 983 711
Language instr: English, Italian
ECIS

International School of Verona
Aleardo Aleardi, Via Segantini 20, 37138 Verona
Tel: +39 04557 8200
Age range: 3–18
No. of pupils: 730
Curriculum: IBDP, National, IGCSE
Language instr: English
ECIS

ISE Kiddy English
Via Antonio Bordoni 2, 20124 Milan
Tel: +39 02 87258880
Age range: 2–6 years
Language instr: English

Kendale International Primary School
86 Via Gradoli, Tombe di Nerone, 00189 Rome
Tel: +39 06 3326 7608
Age range: 3–11
No. of pupils: 100 *B*48 *G*52
Curriculum: UK
Language instr: English

Little Genius International
Via di Grotte Portella 28, 00044 Frascati, Rome
Tel: +39 06 97245148

Livorno Elementary/ Middle School
Unit 31301, Box 66, 09613-0005 Livorno
Tel: +39 050 54 7573
Age range: 4–14
No. of pupils: 150
Curriculum: USA

Lonati Anglo American School
Via Bormioli 60, 25135 Brescia
Tel: +39 03 02 35 73 60
Age range: 5–12
No. of pupils: 121
Curriculum: IBPYP
Language instr: English

Lycée Chateaubriand de Rome
PATRIZI/Malpighi, Via di Villa Patrizi 9, 00161 Rome
Tel: +39 06 441 604 1
Curriculum: FrenchBacc

Lycée français Jean Giono de Turin
Corso Casale 324, 10132 Torino
Tel: +39 011660 29 55
Curriculum: FrenchBacc

Lycée Victor Hugo
Palazzo Venturi Ginori, Via della Scala 85, 50123 Florence
Tel: +39 055 266 991
Curriculum: FrenchBacc

MARYMOUNT INTERNATIONAL SCHOOL ROME
For further details see p. 203
Via di Villa Lauchli, 180, 00191 Rome
Tel: +39 06 3629 1012
Email: admissions@marymountrome.com
Website: www.marymountrome.com
Head of School: Sarah Gallagher
Age range: 2–18 years
No. of pupils: 860
Fees: €12,200–€24,200
Curriculum: AP, IBDP
Language instr: English
CIS ECIS

O.M.C. – Collegio Vescovile Pio X
Borgo Cavour 40, 31100 Treviso
Tel: +39 0422 411725
Curriculum: IBDP
Language instr: English

QSI International School of Brindisi
Via Benvenuto Cellini 25, 72100 Brindisi
Tel: +39 0831 518764
Age range: 3–13
No. of pupils: 34
Curriculum: USA
Language instr: English

ROME INTERNATIONAL SCHOOL
For further details see p. 217
Via Guglielmo Pecori Giraldi n.137, 00135 Rome
Tel: +39 06 8448 2651
Email: info@romeinternationalschool.it
Website: www.romeinternationalschool.it
Headteacher: Scott Webber
Age range: 2–18 years
No. of pupils: 500
Fees: *Day* €9,700–€24,425
Curriculum: IBDP, IBPYP, UK, GCSE, IGCSE
Language instr: English
ECIS

Scuola Svizzera di Catania
Via M.R Imbriani 32, 95128 Catania
Tel: +39 095 447116
Age range: 3–15
No. of pupils: 70

Scuola Svizzera di Milano
Via Appiani 21, 20121 Milan
Tel: +39 02 655 57 23
Age range: 2–18
No. of pupils: 360

Smiling International School
Via Roversella 2, 44121 Ferrara
Tel: +39 05 32209416
Age range: 2–18 years
Curriculum: IBDP
Language instr: English, Italian

SOUTHLANDS BRITISH INTERNATIONAL SCHOOL
For further details see p. 234
Via Teleclide 40, Casal Palocco, 00124 Rome
Tel: +39 06 5053932
Email: info@southlands.it
Website: www.southlands.it
Principal: Victoria Del Federico
Age range: 3–18 years
No. of pupils: 300
Fees: €7,025–€18,450
Curriculum: IBDP, UK, IGCSE
Language instr: English

ST GEORGE'S BRITISH INTERNATIONAL SCHOOL, ROME
For further details see p. 236
Via Cassia, km 16, La Storta, 00123 Rome
Tel: +39 06 3086001
Email: admissions@stgeorge.school.it
Website: www.stgeorge.school.it
Principal: David Tongue
Age range: 3–18 years
No. of pupils: 930
Fees: €11,100–€21,900
Curriculum: IBDP, UK, GCSE, IGCSE
Language instr: English
CIS COB ECIS

St. Francis International School
Via delle Benedettine, 50/b, 00135 Rome
Tel: +39 (0)6 35 5110 23
Curriculum: UK, USA

St. Louis Archinto
Via Olmetto 6, 20123 Milan
Tel: +39 02 36723970
Age range: 13–18 years

St. Louis Colonna
Via Marco Antonio Colonna 24, 20149 Milan
Tel: +39 02 33007523
Age range: 2–13 years

ST. LOUIS SCHOOL
For further details see p. 242
SLS S.P.A., Via E. Caviglia, 1, 20139 Milan
Tel: +39 02 55231235
Email: info@stlouisschool.com
Website: www.stlouisschool.com
Executive Principal High School: Gerry Rafferty
Age range: 2–18 years (14-18 boarding)
No. of pupils: 1500
Curriculum: IBDP, UK, IGCSE
Language instr: English, Italian

ST. STEPHEN'S SCHOOL
For further details see p. 244
Via Aventina 3, 00153 Rome
Tel: +39 06 575 0605
Email: ststephens@sssrome.it
Website: www.sssrome.it
Head of School: Jill Muti
Age range: 14–19 years
No. of pupils: 300
Fees: *Day* €26,570 *FB* €41,720
Curriculum: ACT, AP, IBDP, SAT, USA
Language instr: English
CIS ECIS

The Anglo-Italian School, Montessori Division
Ex NATO Base, Building H
Viale della Liberazione, 1, 80124 Bagnoli, Naples
Tel: +39 081 570 6587
Age range: 2 –15
No. of pupils: 346 *B*180 *G*166
Curriculum: National, USA
ECIS

THE BRITISH SCHOOL OF MILAN (SIR JAMES HENDERSON)
For further details see p. 251
Via Carlo Alberto Pisani Dossi, 16, 20134 Milan
Tel: +39 02 210941
Email: info@bsm.school
Website: www.britishschoolmilan.com
Principal: Chris Greenhalgh
Age range: 3–18 years
No. of pupils: 720
Fees: €12,140–€19,580
Curriculum: IBDP, UK, IGCSE
Language instr: English
COB

The English International School of Padua
Via Forcellini 168, 35128 Padova
Tel: +39 049 80 22 503
Age range: 2–18
No. of pupils: 759 *B398 G361*
Curriculum: IBDP, National, SAT, UK, IGCSE, ALevs
Language instr: English
ECIS

The International School in Genoa
Via Romana Della Castagna 11A, 16148 Genova
Tel: +39 010 386528
Age range: 3–18 years
No. of pupils: 363
Curriculum: IBDP, IPC, National, SAT
Language instr: English
CIS ECIS

The International School of Naples
Viale della Liberazione, 1, 80125 Bagnoli, Naples
Tel: +39 081 762 8429
Age range: 4–18
No. of pupils: 242 *B120 G122*
Curriculum: National, SAT, USA
CIS ECIS

The New School Rome
via della camilluccia 669, 00135 Rome
Tel: +39 06 329 4269
Age range: 3–18 years
No. of pupils: 225
Curriculum: UK, GCSE, ALevs
COB

The Udine International School
Via Martignacco 187, 33100 Udine
Tel: +39 0432 541119
Age range: 2–13
Language instr: English
CIS

UWC ADRIATIC
For further details see p. 256
Località Duino 29, 34011 Duino-Aurisina TS
Tel: +39 040 3739111
Email: uwcad@uwcad.it
Website: www.uwcad.it
Head of College: William Turner
Age range: 16–19 years
No. of pupils: 168
Fees: €46,000
Curriculum: IBDP
Language instr: English

Villa Grimani International School
Via Leonardo da Vinci 4, 35027 Noventa Padovana
Tel: +39 049 8933833
Age range: 3–13
ECIS

VITTORIA INTERNATIONAL SCHOOL
For further details see p. 258
Via delle Rosine 14, 10123 Turin
Tel: +39 011 889870
Email: infovis@vittoriaweb.it
Website: www.vittoriaweb.it
Head of School: Marcella Margaria Bodo
Age range: 3–19 years
Fees: €5,000
Curriculum: IBDP, IGCSE
Language instr: English

WORLD INTERNATIONAL SCHOOL OF TORINO
For further details see p. 259
Via Traves 28, 10151 Torino
Tel: +39 0111972111
Email: info@worldinternationalschool.com
Website: worldinternationalschool.com
School Manager: Giulia Mazzocchi
Curriculum: IBDP, IBMYP, IBPYP
Language instr: English

KOSOVO

Finnish Schools International
Magjistralja Prishtine, Ferizaj, Tek rrethi i QMI-së,
Tel: 00381 45 235650
Age range: 3–18

International Learning Group School – ILG School
Veternik 1, 10000 Prishtina
Tel: +386 38 722 893
Curriculum: IBDP, IBMYP, IBPYP
Language instr: English

International School of Prishtina
Preoc, Marigona Residence, Gracanica 10000
Tel: +386 49 770513 / +386 49 425216
Age range: 6–18
No. of pupils: 425
Curriculum: National
ECIS

Kindergarten & Primary School 'Yllka'
Rr. Fan Noli Nr: 1, Prizren
Tel: +377 44 669665 / +381 29 233237

Mehmet Akif College – Gjakova
Rr. Zidi Sadikagas, ish TMK, Gjakovë
Tel: +386 49 773 775

Mehmet Akif College – Lipjan
Banullë, Lipjan
Tel: +38138581999 / +38649770514
No. of pupils: 563
ECIS

Mehmet Akif College – Prizren
Korishë, Prizren
Tel: +38129233441 / +37744140900

QSI International School of Kosovo
24 Maji-ARBERIA Street #15, 10000 Pristina
Tel: +386 49 775 731

LATVIA

Exupery International School
Jauna iela 8, Pinki, Babites pagasts LV-2107
Tel: +371 26 62 23 33
Age range: 2.5–18 years
No. of pupils: 234
Curriculum: IBDP, IBPYP, IGCSE, ALevs
Language instr: English
CIS

International School of Latvia
Meistaru 2, Pinki, Babites pag., Babites nov., LV-2107
Tel: +371 6775 5146
Age range: 3–18
No. of pupils: 363
Curriculum: IBDP, IBMYP, IBPYP, SAT
Language instr: English
CEE CIS

International School of Riga
Zvejnieku iela 12, Riga 1048
Tel: +371 6762 4622
Age range: 2–14
Curriculum: IBDP, IBPYP
Language instr: English
CIS

International School Premjers
1 Lomonosova Str., Bld. 7, Riga 1019
Tel: +371 67218501
Curriculum: IBDP, IBMYP
Language instr: English, Russian

KING'S COLLEGE, THE BRITISH SCHOOL OF LATVIA
For further details see p. 193
Turaidas iela 1 Pinki, Babites novads LV2107
Tel: +371 257 59 043
Email: latvia@kingscollegeschools.org
Website: latvia.kingscollegeschools.org
Head of School: Adele Stanford
Age range: 2–18 years
No. of pupils: 350
Fees: *Day* €9,900–€18,428
Curriculum: UK, IGCSE, ALevs
Language instr: English

LITHUANIA

Erudito Licejus, Kaunas
J. Gruodzio g. 9, 44293 Kaunas
Tel: +370 65 788 820
Curriculum: IBDP
Language instr: English, Lithuanian

Erudito Licejus, Vilnius
Aludariu g. 3, 01113 Vilnius
Tel: +370 66 719 972
Curriculum: IBDP
Language instr: English, Lithuanian

Kaunas Jesuit High School
Rotuses a. 9, 44280 Kaunas
Tel: +370 8 37 28 05 25
Age range: 11–19
No. of pupils: 780 *B322 G358*
Curriculum: IBDP
Language instr: Lithuanian, English

Klaipeda Universa Via International School
Baltikalnio street 11, Klaipeda
Tel: +370 8 46 38 34 65
Curriculum: IBPYP
Language instr: English, Lithuanian

The American International School of Vilnius
Subaciaus 41, 11350 Vilnius
Tel: +370 5 212 1031
Age range: 3–16
No. of pupils: 171 *B25 G34*
Curriculum: IBDP
CEE CIS ECIS

Vilniaus Karalienes Mortos mokykla
Luksines g. 29, 11332 Vilnius
Tel: +370 63 007 474
Curriculum: IBDP
Language instr: English, Lithuanian

Vilnius International Meridian School (VIMS)
M.Dauk os g. 7, 02101 Vilnius
Tel: +370 5 2 728 725
Curriculum: UK, IGCSE, ALevs

Vilnius International School
Turniskiu Str 21, Rusu Str
3, 01125 Vilnius
Tel: +370 5 276 1564
Curriculum: IBMYP, IBPYP

Vilnius Private Gymnasium
V. Grybo street 7, 10313 Vilnius
Tel: +370 69 854 808
Curriculum: IBDP
Language instr: English, Lithuanian

LUXEMBOURG

Ecole Privee Over the Rainbow
5, rue d'Orval, Luxembourg L 2270
Tel: +352 26 09 45 42
Age range: 4–11
Curriculum: IPC

European School of Luxembourg
Boulevard Konrad Adenauer 23, Kirchberg, Luxembourg L-1115
Tel: +352 43 20 82 1
Age range: 4–18
No. of pupils: 3008

Fräi-Ëffentlech Waldorfschoul Lëtzebuerg
45 rue de l'Avenir, Luxembourg 1147
Tel: +352 466932
No. of pupils: 349
Curriculum: IBDP
Language instr: French

INTERNATIONAL SCHOOL EDWARD STEICHEN
For further details see p. 173
1 Rue Edward Steichen, 9707 Clervaux
Tel: +352 206 007-1
Email: info@lesc.lu
Website: www.lesc.lu
Principal: Jean Billa
Age range: 4–19 years
No. of pupils: 1000 *B*500 *G*500
Language instr: English, French, German

International School of Luxembourg
36 Boulevard Pierre Dupong, 1430 Luxembourg
Tel: +352 26 04 40
Age range: 3–18
No. of pupils: 1357 *B*727 *G*630
Curriculum: ACT, IBDP, SAT, IGCSE
Language instr: English
(CIS) (ECIS)

OTR International School Luxembourg
7 Rue Val Ste Croix, 1371 Luxembourg
Tel: +352 2609 45 42
Curriculum: IBMYP
Language instr: English, French

St George's International School Luxembourg A.S.B.L.
11 Rue des Peupliers, L-2328 Luxembourg
Tel: +352 423224
Age range: 3–18+
No. of pupils: 800 *B*400 *G*400 *VIth*70
Curriculum: IPC, UK, IGCSE, ALevs
Language instr: English
(CIS) (COB) (ECIS)

VAUBAN, Ecole et Lycée Français de Luxembourg
1-3 rue Albert Einstein, 1484 Luxembourg
Tel: +352 28 10 14 00
Curriculum: FrenchBacc

MACEDONIA

IPS Macedonia
st. Dragisha Mishovic building 2, Detska gradinka Orce Nikolov, 1000 Skopje
Tel: +389 (0)2 3073 700
Curriculum: IBMYP, IBPYP
Language instr: English

NOVA International Schools
Praska 27, 1000 Skopje
Tel: +389 2 3061 907
Age range: 16–18
No. of pupils: 606 *B*306 *G*300
Curriculum: IBDP, IBMYP
Language instr: English

QSI International School of Skopje
Zenevska #51, 1000 Skopje
Tel: +389 2 305 1844
Age range: 5–13
No. of pupils: 103
Curriculum: USA
Language instr: English

MALTA

QSI International School of Malta
Triq Durumblat, Mosta 4815
Tel: +356 21 423067
Age range: 5–18
Curriculum: USA
Language instr: English

San Andrea School
L-Imselliet, Zebbiegh MST 11
Tel: +356 21 43 88 00
Age range: 4–16
No. of pupils: 800
Curriculum: IGCSE

San Anton School
L-Imselliet, Zebbiegh MGR2850
Tel: +356 2158 1907
Age range: 3–16
No. of pupils: 1000
Curriculum: UK, GCSE

ST EDWARD'S COLLEGE, MALTA
For further details see p. 235
Triq San Dwardu, Birgu (Vittoriosa) BRG 9039
Tel: +356 2788 1199
Email: admissions@stedwards.edu.mt
Website: www.stedwards.edu.mt
Headmaster: Nollaig Mac an Bhaird
Age range: 2–4 & 16-18 years *B*5–15 years
Fees: *Day* €2,730–€7,200 *FB* €15,500–€23,900
Curriculum: IBDP, National, IGCSE
Language instr: English

Theresa Nuzzo (Marsa) School
Balbi Street, Marsa HMR 14
Tel: +356 7924 0391
Age range: 5–10
No. of pupils: 320

Verdala International School
Fort Pembroke, Pembroke PBK 1641
Tel: +356 21375133
Age range: 3–18
No. of pupils: 520
Curriculum: IBDP, IBCP, IPC, SAT, IGCSE
Language instr: English
(ECIS)

MOLDOVA

QSI International School of Chisinau
48/2 Nicolae Costin Street, Chisinau MD 2051
Tel: +373 22 588 346
Age range: 3–13
No. of pupils: 47
Curriculum: USA
Language instr: English

MONACO

Lycée Albert 1er
4 Place de la Visitation, Monaco 98000
Tel: +377 98 98 80 54
Age range: 15–18
No. of pupils: 825

THE INTERNATIONAL SCHOOL OF MONACO
For further details see p. 253
10-12 Quai Antoine Premier, Monte Carlo 98000
Tel: +377 9325 6820
Email: admissions@ismonaco.com
Website: ismonaco.com
Director: Stuart Bryan
Age range: 3–18 years
No. of pupils: 740
Fees: €23,100–€29,400
Curriculum: IBDP, IPC, IGCSE
Language instr: English, French
(CIS) (ECIS)

MONTENEGRO

Adriatic College
13. Jula, Budva 85312
Tel: +382 69 324 101
Curriculum: IBDP
Language instr: English

Arcadia Academy
Donja Lastva, Jadranska magistrala, Tivat 85332
Tel: +382 32 662 662
Language instr: English

KSI Montenegro
Seljanovo bb, Porto Montenegro, Tivat
Tel: +382 32 672 655
Age range: 3–18
No. of pupils: 120
Curriculum: IBDP, IBMYP, IBPYP
Language instr: English

QSI International School of Montenegro
Ul. Romanovih 33, Zabjelo, 81000 Podgorica
Tel: +382 20 641 734
Age range: 5–13
No. of pupils: 42 *B*20 *G*22
Language instr: English

NETHERLANDS

AFNORTH International School
Ferdindand Bolstraat 1, 6445
EE Brunssum, Limburg
Tel: +31 45 5278221
Age range: 4–19
No. of pupils: 1000
Curriculum: ACT, AP, SAT, UK, USA
Language instr: English, German, French
(ECIS)

AMERICAN SCHOOL OF THE HAGUE
For further details see p. 133
Rijksstraatweg 200,
2241 BX Wassenaar
Tel: +31 70 512 1060
Email: admissions@ash.nl
Website: www.ash.nl
Director: J. Courtney Lowe
Age range: 3–18 years
No. of pupils: 1120
Fees: €15,275–€23,865
Curriculum: ACT, AP, IBDP, SAT, TOEFL, USA
Language instr: English
(CIS) (ECIS)

Amity International School Amsterdam
Amsterdamseweg 204, 1182 HL
Amsterdam, North Holland
Tel: +31 20 3454481
Curriculum: IBDP, IBMYP, IBPYP
Language instr: English

Amsterdam International Community School
Prinses Irenestraat 59, 1077 WV
Amsterdam, North Holland
Tel: +31 20 5771240
Age range: 4–19
Curriculum: IBDP, IBMYP, IBPYP, IBCP, IPC
Language instr: English
(CIS) (ECIS)

Amsterdam Liberal Arts & Sciences Academy (ALASCA)
Geertje Wielemaplein 1, 1095
MM Amsterdam, North Holland
Tel: +31 20 2623240
Curriculum: IBDP
Language instr: English, Dutch

College Den Hulster
PO Box 60, 5900 AB Venlo, Limburg
Tel: +31 77 3590300
Age range: 12–18
No. of pupils: 1500

Deutsche Internationale Schule Den Haag
van Bleiswijkstraat 125, 2582 LB
The Hague, ?South Holland
Tel: +31 70 3549454
Age range: 3–18
No. of pupils: 220

EERDE INTERNATIONAL BOARDING SCHOOL NETHERLANDS
For further details see p. 147
Kasteellaan 1, 7731 PJ
Ommen, Overijssel
Tel: +31 52 9451452
Email: admission@eerdeibs.nl
Website: www.eerde.nl
Director CEO: Niki Holterman
Age range: 4–18 years
No. of pupils: 85
Fees: €9,000
Curriculum: IBDP, IGCSE
Language instr: English
(CIS) (ECIS)

ELCKERLYC INTERNATIONAL SCHOOL
For further details see p. 149
Klimopzoom 41, 2353 RE
Leiderdorp, South Holland
Tel: +31 71 5896861
Email: international@elckerlyc.net
Website: www.elckerlyc-international.nl
Headteacher: Lesley de Quartel
Age range: 3–11 years
No. of pupils: 128
Fees: *Day* €3,800
Curriculum: IPC, National
Language instr: English

European School Bergen
Molenweidtje 5, 1862 BC
Bergen, North Holland
Tel: +31 72 5890109
Age range: 4–18
No. of pupils: 600 *B*300 *G*300
Language instr: French, Dutch, English, German

Gifted Minds International School
c/o Corporate Office, Landtong 18,
1186 GP Amstelveen, North Holland
Tel: +31 23 888 8874
Curriculum: IBPYP, USA
Language instr: English

HSV International Primary School – KSS Location
Koningin Sophiestraat 24a, 2595
TG The Hague, South Holland
Tel: +31 70 3243453
Age range: 4–11
No. of pupils: 540
Curriculum: IPC
Language instr: English
(ECIS)

HSV International Primary School – NSL Location
Nassaulaan 26, 2514 JT The
Hague, South Holland
Tel: +31 70 3184950
Age range: 4–11
Curriculum: IPC
Language instr: English
(ECIS)

HSV International Primary School – VNS Location
Van Nijenrodestraat 16, 2597
RM The Hague, South Holland
Tel: +31 70 3281441
Age range: 4–11
No. of pupils: 100
Curriculum: IPC
Language instr: English

International Primary School GSV
Rijksstraatweg 24, 9752 AE Haren
Tel: +31 50 5270818
Age range: 4–12
No. of pupils: 100
Curriculum: IPC

INTERNATIONAL SCHOOL DELFT (PRIMARY)
For further details see p. 172
Jaffalaan 9, 2628 BX Delft
Tel: +31 15 2850038
Age range: 4–11 years
No. of pupils: 400
Curriculum: IBMYP, IBPYP
Language instr: English

INTERNATIONAL SCHOOL DELFT (SECONDARY)
For further details see p. 172
Colijnlaan 2, 2613 VZ Delft
Tel: +31 15 8200208
Email: admin@internationalschooldelft.org
Website: internationalschooldelft.com
Head of School (Secondary): Minke Veeneklaas
Age range: 11–16 years
No. of pupils: 400
Fees: *Day* €4,495–€6,055
Language instr: English

International School Eindhoven
Oirschotsedijk 14b, 5651 GC
Eindhoven, North Brabant
Tel: +31 40 2519437
Age range: 4–18
No. of pupils: 1200
Curriculum: IBDP, IBMYP, IPC
Language instr: English
(CIS) (ECIS)

International School of Amsterdam
PO Box 920, Sportlaan 45, 1180
AX Amstelveen, North Holland
Tel: +31 20 347 1111
Age range: 2–18
No. of pupils: 1366
Curriculum: IBDP, IBMYP, IBPYP
Language instr: English
(CIS) (ECIS)

International School The Rijnlands Lyceum Oegstgeest
Apollolaan 1, BA 2341
Oegstgeest, South Holland
Tel: +31 71 5193555
Age range: 11–18
No. of pupils: 1200
Curriculum: IBDP, IBMYP
Language instr: English
(ECIS)

International School Twente
Tiemeister 20, 7541 WG
Enschede, Overijssel
Tel: +31 53 482 11 30
Curriculum: IBDP
Language instr: English

International School Utrecht
Van Bijnkershoeklaan 8, 3527 XL Utrecht
Tel: +31 30 8700400
Age range: 4–18 years
No. of pupils: 900
Curriculum: IBDP, IBMYP, IBPYP
Language instr: English

Laar & Berg
Langsakker 4, 1251 GB
Laren, North Holland
Tel: +31 35 5395422
Age range: 11–18
No. of pupils: 800 *B*406 *G*394
Curriculum: IBDP, IBMYP, National
Language instr: English, Dutch
(CIS)

Lycee Francais Vincent Van Gogh
Scheveningseweg 237, 2584 AA
The Hague, ?South Holland
Tel: +31 70 3066920
Curriculum: FrenchBacc

Maartenscollege & International School Groningen
Hemmenlaan 2, 9751 NS
Haren, Groningen
Tel: +31 50 5340084
Age range: 11–18
No. of pupils: 200
Curriculum: IBDP, IBMYP
Language instr: English
(ECIS)

Marcanti College
Jan van Galenstraat 31, 1051 KM
Amsterdam, North Holland
Tel: +31 20 6069000

Marnix College Ede
Prins Bernhardlaan 30, 6713
MC Ede, Gelderland
Tel: +31 31 8650035
Age range: 12–19
No. of pupils: 1376

Montessori Lyceum Amsterdam
Pieter de Hoochstraat 59, 1071 ED Amsterdam, North Holland
Tel: +31 20 6767855
Age range: 11–18
No. of pupils: 1600

Nord Anglia International School Rotterdam
Verhulstlaan 21, 3055 WJ Rotterdam, South Holland
Tel: +31 10 4225351
Age range: 3–18 years
No. of pupils: 250
Curriculum: IBDP, IPC
Language instr: English
CIS ECIS

OBS Dubbeldam
Eikenlaan 25, 3319 SC Dordrecht, South Holland
Tel: +31 78 6160151
Age range: 4–11

Rivers International School Arnhem
Groningensingel 1245, 6835 HZ Arnhem, Gelderland
Tel: +31 26 3202840
Age range: 12–18
No. of pupils: 155 *B80 G75*
Curriculum: IBDP, IBMYP
Language instr: English
ECIS

Rotterdam International Secondary School
Bentincklaan 294, 3039 KK Rotterdam, South Holland
Tel: +31 (0)10 890 77 44
Age range: 12–18 years
No. of pupils: 380
Curriculum: IBDP, IBCP, IGCSE
Language instr: English
CIS ECIS

Stedelijk Gymnasium Nijmegen
Kronenburgersingel 269, 6511 AS Nijmegen, Gelderland
Tel: +31 24 3220606
Age range: 14–19
No. of pupils: 1320

The British School in The Netherlands
Jan van Hooflaan 3, 2252 BG Voorschoten, South Holland
Tel: +31 (0)70 315 4077
Age range: 3–18
Curriculum: IBDP, IBCP, GCSE, ALevs
Language instr: English
COB

THE BRITISH SCHOOL OF AMSTERDAM
For further details see p. 249
Havenstraat 6, 1075 PR Amsterdam, North Holland
Tel: +31 (0)20 679 7840
Email: info@britams.nl
Website: www.britishschool.amsterdam
Principal: Ruth Sanderson
Age range: 3–18 years
No. of pupils: 1020
Fees: *Day* €8,265–€18,252
Curriculum: UK, GCSE, IGCSE, ALevs
Language instr: English
COB

The International School of The Hague
Wijndaelerweg 11, 2554 BZ The Hague, South Holland
Tel: +31 70 328 1450
Age range: 4–18 years
No. of pupils: 1500
Curriculum: IBDP, IBMYP, IBCP
Language instr: English
CIS ECIS

UWC MAASTRICHT
For further details see p. 257
Discuswerp 65, 6225 XP Maastricht, Limburg
Tel: +31 432 410 410
Email: admissions@uwcmaastricht.nl
Website: www.uwcmaastricht.nl
Head of College: Lodewijk van Oord
Age range: 4–19 years
No. of pupils: 900
Fees: €6,330–€30,000
Curriculum: IBDP, IBMYP, IGCSE
Language instr: English
ECIS

Violenschool International Primary School – Frans Hals Location
Frans Halslaan 57, 1213 BK Hilversum, North Holland
Tel: +31 35 6930641
Age range: 4–8
No. of pupils: 135

NORWAY

Aalesund International School
Borgundvegen 418, 6015 Aalesund, Møre og Romsdal
Tel: +47 908 69 948
Age range: 5–15
Curriculum: IBMYP, IBPYP
Language instr: English

Arendal International School
Julius Smiths vei 40, 4817 His, Aust-Agder
Tel: +47 37 055 100
Curriculum: IBMYP, IBPYP
Language instr: English

Birralee International School
Bispegata 9c, 7012 Trondheim, Trøndelag
Tel: +47 73 87 02 60
Age range: 4–16
No. of pupils: 250 *B121 G129*
Curriculum: UK, IGCSE
Language instr: English
ECIS

British International School of Stavanger (BISS) Gausel
Gauselbakken 107, Gausel, 4032 Stavanger, Rogaland
Tel: +47 519 50 250
Age range: 2–19
No. of pupils: 530
Curriculum: IBDP, IBMYP, IBPYP, IBCP
Language instr: English
COB

Children's International School Fredrikstad
Torsnesveien 5-7, 1630 Gamle Fredrikstad, Østfold
Tel: +47 690 02 500
Age range: 6–16
No. of pupils: 231
Curriculum: IBMYP, IBPYP
Language instr: English

Children's International School Moss
Moss Verk 1, 1534 Moss, Østfold
Tel: +47 400 01 128
Age range: 6–16
No. of pupils: 268
Curriculum: IBMYP, IBPYP
Language instr: English

Children's International School Sarpsborg
Tuneveien 20, 1710 Sarpsborg, Østfold
Tel: +47 400 02 607
Curriculum: IBMYP, IBPYP
Language instr: English, Norwegian

Deutsche Schule Oslo – Max Tau
Sporveisgata 20, 0354 Oslo
Tel: +47 22 93 12 20

Gjøvikregionen International School
Studieveien 17, 2815 Gjøvik, Oppland
Tel: +47 240 76 141
Curriculum: IBMYP, IBPYP
Language instr: English, Norwegian

International School of Bergen
Sandslihaugen 30, 5254 Bergen, Hordaland
Tel: +47 55 30 63 30
Age range: 3–16
No. of pupils: 180
Curriculum: IBMYP, IBPYP, National
Language instr: English
CIS ECIS

International School of Stavanger
Treskeveien 3, 4043 Hafrsfjord, Rogaland
Tel: +47 51 55 43 00
Age range: 3–18
No. of pupils: 630
Curriculum: ACT, IBDP, SAT, UK, USA, IGCSE
Language instr: English, Dutch French, German, Norwegian, Spanish
CIS COB ECIS

International School Telemark
Hovet Ring 7, 3931 Porsgrunn, Telemark
Tel: +47 35291400
Age range: 6–16
No. of pupils: 133 *B73 G60*
Curriculum: IBMYP, IBPYP
Language instr: English

Kristiansand International School
Kongsgård alle 20, 4631 Kristiansand, Vest-Agder
Tel: +47 95826601
Age range: 6–16 years
No. of pupils: 194
Curriculum: IBMYP, IBPYP
Language instr: English

Lycée Français René Cassin
Skovveien 9, 0257 Oslo
Tel: +47 22 92 51 20
Curriculum: FrenchBacc

Norlights International School
Skådalsveien 33, 0781 Oslo
Tel: +47 40 07 35 50
Curriculum: IBDP, IBMYP, IBPYP
Language instr: English

Oslo International School
PO Box 53, 1318 Bekkestua, Akershus
Tel: +47 67 8182 90
Age range: 3–18
No. of pupils: 600 *B320 G280*
Curriculum: IBDP, IPC, SAT
Language instr: English
CIS ECIS

Skagerak International School
Framnesveien 7, 3222 Sandefjord, Vestfold
Tel: +47 33456500
Age range: 4–19
No. of pupils: 360 *B180 G180*
Curriculum: IBDP, IBMYP, IBPYP
Language instr: English
ECIS

The Children's House
Åsenvegen 100, 4055 Sola, Rogaland
Tel: +47 47 48 22 92
Age range: 2–7
No. of pupils: 158 *B86 G72*
ECIS

Tromsø International School
4 Breiviklia, 9019 Tromsø, Troms
Tel: +47 99200780
Curriculum: IBMYP, IBPYP
Language instr: English

UWC Red Cross Nordic
Hauglandsvegen 304, 6968 Flekke, Sogn og Fjordane
Tel: +47 5773 7000
Age range: 16–19
No. of pupils: 200
Curriculum: IBDP, SAT
Language instr: English

POLAND

2 Spoleczne Liceum Ogolnoksztalcace STO im. Pawla Jasienicy (2SLO)
ul. Nowowiejska 5, 00-643 Warsaw, Masovia
Tel: +48 22 825 11 99
Curriculum: IBDP
Language instr: English

Akademeia High School in Warsaw
ul. Ledóchowskiej 2, 02-972 Warsaw, Masovia
Tel: +48 22 299 8787
Curriculum: UK, IGCSE, ALevs
Language instr: English

American Elementary School
ul Lowicka 41, 81-504 Gdyina, Pomerania
Tel: +48 58 664 69 71

American School of Warsaw
Bielawa, ul Warszawska 202, 05-520 Konstancin-Jeziorna, Masovia
Tel: +48 22 702 8500
Age range: 3–18
Curriculum: ACT, AP, IBDP, IBMYP, IBPYP, SAT
Language instr: English
(CEE) (CIS) (ECIS)

ATUT Bilingual Primary School
ul. Raclawicka 101, 53-149 Wroclaw, Lower Silesia
Tel: +48 71 782 26 25
Curriculum: IBMYP
Language instr: English

British International School of Cracow
ul.Smolensk 25, 31-108 Kraków, Lesser Poland
Tel: +48 1229 264 78
Age range: 3–19
No. of pupils: 230
Curriculum: IBDP
Language instr: English
(COB) (ECIS)

British International School of the University of Lodz
ul Matejki 34a, 90-237 Lodz
Tel: +48 42 635 60 06
Age range: 5–19
Curriculum: IBDP, UK, IGCSE, ALevs
Language instr: English
(COB)

British International School Wroclaw
Al Akacjowa 10/12, 53-134 Wroclaw, Lower Silesia
Tel: +48 71 7966861
Age range: 3–18
No. of pupils: *B*55 *G*54
Curriculum: National, UK, IGCSE, ALevs
Language instr: English
(COB) (ECIS)

British Primary School of Wilanow
ul. Hlonda 12, 02-972 Warsaw, Masovia
Tel: +48 22 111 0062
Curriculum: UK
Language instr: English
(COB)

Da Vinci's International Schools
Pilotów 4c Street, 31-362 Kraków, Lesser Poland
Tel: +48 608 322 388
Curriculum: IBDP
Language instr: English

Edison Primary School
ul. Królewicza Jakuba 69, 02-956 Warsaw, Masovia
Tel: +48 22 858 81 60
Curriculum: UK
(COB)

International American School
Ul Dembego 18, 02-796 Warsaw, Masovia
Tel: +48 22 649 1442
Curriculum: IBDP
Language instr: English

International British School Vocandus
ul. Woronicza 16, 91-030 Lodz
Tel: +48 696 050 078
Age range: 5–18
No. of pupils: 24 *B*14 *G*10
Curriculum: National, UK, IGCSE
(ECIS)

International European School Warsaw
ul. Wiertnicza 140, 02-952 Warsaw, Masovia
Tel: +48 22 842 44 48
Curriculum: IBDP
Language instr: English

International High School of Wroclaw
ul. Raclawicka 101, 53-149 Wroclaw, Lower Silesia
Tel: +48 71 782 26 26
Curriculum: IBDP, IBMYP
Language instr: English

International Primary School
52 Drukarska St, 53-312 Wroclaw, Lower Silesia
Tel: +48 503 188 843
Curriculum: IBPYP
Language instr: English

International School of Gdansk
ul. Sucha 29, 80-531 Gdansk, Pomerania
Tel: +48 58 342 31 00
Age range: 5–18
No. of pupils: 300
Curriculum: IBPYP, USA
Language instr: English, Polish

International School of Krakow
ul Sw Floriana 57, Lusina, 30-698 Krakow, Lesser Poland
Tel: +48 12 270 1409
Age range: 3–18
No. of pupils: 160 *B*76 *G*84
Curriculum: AP, IBDP, SAT
Language instr: English
(CEE) (CIS)

International School of Poznan
Ul Taczanowskiego 18, 60-147 Poznan, Greater Poland
Tel: +48 61 646 37 60
Curriculum: IBDP, IBPYP
Language instr: English

Kolegium Europejskie
ul. Metalowców 6, 31-537 Kraków, Lesser Poland
Tel: +48 12 632 46 29
Age range: 12–18
No. of pupils: 130 *B*50 *G*80
Curriculum: IBDP, National
Language instr: English

LYCÉE FRANÇAIS DE VARSOVIE (FRENCH SCHOOL IN WARSAW)
For further details see p. 201
Ul Walecznych 4/6, 03-916 Warsaw, Masovia
Tel: +48 22 616 54 00/01
Email: info@lfv.pl
Website: www.lfv.pl
Head of School: Anne Lesage
Age range: 2–18 years
No. of pupils: 700
Fees: *FB* €5,300–€7,700
Curriculum: FrenchBacc
Language instr: French

Monnet International School
ul. Abramowskiego 4, 02-659 Warsaw, Masovia
Tel: +48 22 852 31 10
No. of pupils: 67
Curriculum: IBDP, IBMYP, IBPYP
Language instr: English

Open Future International School
ul. Kwiecista 25, 30-389 Kraków, Lesser Poland
Tel: +48 123 524 525
Curriculum: IBPYP
Language instr: English, Polish

Paderewski Private Grammar School
ul Symfoniczna 1, 20-853 Lublin
Tel: +48 81 740 7543
Age range: 13–19
No. of pupils: 220
Curriculum: IBDP, IBMYP, IBPYP, ALevs
Language instr: English

Polish British Academy of Warsaw
ul. Wiertnicza 75, ul. Wiertnicza 43, 02-952 Warsaw, Masovia
Tel: +48 501 115 114
Curriculum: UK
(COB)

Poznan British International School
ul Darzyborska 1a, 61-303 Poznan, Greater Poland
Tel: +48 61 870 97 30
Age range: 2 –15
Curriculum: IPC, National
(COB)

Private High School Gaudium et Studium
ul. st. Michala 50 M, 61-118 Poznan
Tel: +48 60 892 1887
Curriculum: IBDP
Language instr: English, Polish

Private Primary School 97
Abramowskiego Street 4, 02-659 Warsaw, Masovia
Tel: +48 22 853 36 60
Curriculum: IBPYP
Language instr: English

Prywatne Liceum Ogolnoksztalcace im.M.Wankowicza
ul. Witosa 18, 40-832 Katowice, Silesia
Tel: +48 32 254 9194
Age range: 15–19
Curriculum: IBDP, National
Language instr: Polish, English

Szczecin International School
ul Starzynskiego 3-4, 70-506
Szczecin, West Pomerania
Tel: +48 91 4240 300
Curriculum: IBDP, IBMYP, IBPYP
Language instr: English

Szczecinska Szkola Witruwianska SVS
Wojska Polskiego, 164, 71-335
Szczecin, West Pomerania
Tel: +48 512 868 176
Curriculum: IBPYP
Language instr: English, Polish

Szkola Europejska – Gimnazjum / Liceum
ul Tuszynska 31, 93-020 Lódz
Tel: +48 42 682 3696
Language instr: English

Thames British School Mokotów Campus
ul. Józefa i Jana Rostafinskich
1, 02-593 Warsaw, Masovia
Tel: +48 53 091 7566
Age range: 2.5–12 years
Language instr: English, Polish

Thames British School Ochota (Wawelska) Campus
66/74 Wawelska Str., 02-
034 Warsaw, Masovia
Tel: +48 22 822 15 75
Age range: 6–14
Language instr: English, Polish

Thames British School Park Szczesliwice Campus
Usypiskowa 5, 02-386
Warsaw, Masovia
Tel: +48 666 924 205
Age range: 2.5–7

Thames British School Piaseczno
Mazowiecka 43, 05-502
Bobrowiec, Masovia
Tel: +48 508 399 732
Age range: 2.5–11

Thames British School Wlochy Campus
ul. Gladka 31, 02-172
Warsaw, Masovia
Tel: +48 510 161 597
Age range: 14–18
Curriculum: IBDP, IGCSE
Language instr: English

THE BRITISH SCHOOL WARSAW
For further details see p. 252
Limanowskiego 15, 02-
943 Warsaw, Masovia
Tel: +48 22 842 32 81
Email: admissions@thebritishschool.pl
Website: www.thebritishschool.pl
Principal: Sue Hill
Age range: 2.5–18 years
Curriculum: IBDP, IPC, UK, IGCSE
Language instr: English
COB ECIS

The Canadian School of Warsaw
Kanadyjska Szkola Podstawowa, Ul.
Belska 7, 02-638 Warsaw, Masovia
Tel: +48 22 646 92 89
Curriculum: IBPYP
Language instr: English

The Nazareth Middle and High School in Warsaw
ul. Czerniakowska 137, 00-
720 Warsaw, Masovia
Tel: +48 22 841 3854/+48 601 644 102
Age range: G13–19
Curriculum: IBDP
Language instr: English, Polish

Towarzystwo Edukacyjne Vizja
Okopowa 59, 01-043
Warsaw, Masovia
Tel: +48 57 775 5001
Curriculum: IBDP
Language instr: English, Polish

VIII Prywatne Akademickie Liceum Ogólnokształcace
ul Karmelicka 45, 31-128 Krakow
Tel: +48 12 632 93 13
Age range: 6–18 years
No. of pupils: 830
Curriculum: IBDP, National
Language instr: English

Warsaw Montessori High School
ul. Pytlasinskiego 13a, 00-
777 Warsaw, Masovia
Tel: +48 787 095 835
Curriculum: IBDP
Language instr: English, Polish

Wroclaw International School
ul. Raclawicka 101, 53-149
Wroclaw, Lower Silesia
Tel: +48 71 782 26 24
Curriculum: IBMYP, IBPYP
Language instr: English

Zespól Szkól Ogólnokształcacych im. Pawla z Tarsu
ul Poezji 19, 04-994 Warsaw, Masovia
Tel: +48 22 789 14 02
No. of pupils: 75
Curriculum: IBDP
Language instr: English

PORTUGAL

Carlucci American International School of Lisbon
Rua Antonio dos Reis, 95,
2710-301 Linhó, Lisbon
Tel: +351 219 239 800
Age range: 3–18
No. of pupils: 600
Curriculum: IBDP, SAT, USA
Language instr: English

CLIB – The Braga International School
Rua da Igreja Velha –
Gualtar, 4710-069 Braga
Tel: +351 253 679 860
Age range: 3–18
No. of pupils: 249 *B*124 *G*125
ECIS

CLIP – Oporto International School
Rua de Vila Nova 1071,
4100-506 Porto
Tel: +351 226 199 160
Age range: 5–18
No. of pupils: 497 *B*282 *G*215
CIS ECIS

Colégio Atlântico
Av. da Ponte It 356/A, Pinhal de
Frades, 2840-167 Seixal, Lisbon
Tel: +351 212 247 828
Curriculum: IBDP
Language instr: English, Portuguese

Colégio Luso-Internacional do Centro
Rua D João Pereira Venâncio,
2430-291 Marinha Grande, Leiria
Tel: +351 244 503 710
Age range: 3–18
Curriculum: UK
Language instr: English, Portuguese

Colégio Mira Rio
Estrada de Telheiras 113,
1600-768 Lisbon
Tel: +351 213 030 480
Curriculum: IBDP
Language instr: English, Portuguese

Colegio Planalto
Rua Armindo Rodrigues
28, 1600-414 Lisbon
Tel: +351 217 541 530
No. of pupils: 550
Curriculum: IBDP, National
Language instr: English

Colégio Santiago Internacional
Praça Zacarias Guerreiro
29, 8800-391 Tavira, Faro
Tel: +351 281 328 677
Age range: 4–18
Curriculum: IGCSE

Escola da APEL
Caminho dos Saltos 6 ou Rua do
Til 69, 9050-219 Funchal, Madeira
Tel: +351 291 740 470
Curriculum: IBDP
Language instr: English

GREENE'S COLLEGE OXFORD, ESTORIL
For further details see p. 154
Rua D. Afonso Henriques no.
1614, 2765-576 Estoril, Lisbon
Tel: +351 211 165 450
Email: enquiries@greenes.pt
Website: www.greenes.pt
Principal: Miguel Gama
Age range: 14–18
No. of pupils: *VIth*60
Curriculum: IGCSE, ALevs
Language instr: English

International Christian School of Cascais
Av. de Sintra 1154, 2755-
322 Cascais, Lisbon
Tel: +351 214 842 279
Age range: 4–18
No. of pupils: *B*23 *G*22
Curriculum: SAT, USA
Language instr: English

International School of Palmela
Av. Vila Amélia, Lote 171-
172, Cabanas, 2950-805
Quinta do Anjo, Setúbal
Tel: +351 966 216 593
Language instr: English, Portuguese
ECIS

International Sharing School – Madeira
Caminho dos Saltos 6, 9050-
219 Funchal, Madeira
Tel: +351 291 773 218
Age range: 3–16 years
No. of pupils: 160
Curriculum: IBMYP, IBPYP, National, UK
Language instr: English

International Sharing School – Taguspark
Avenida Dr. Mário Soares 14,
2740-119 Oeiras, Lisbon
Tel: +351 214 876 140
Age range: 1–18 years
No. of pupils: 400
Curriculum: IBDP, IBMYP, IBPYP
Language instr: English

IPS CASCAIS
For further details see p. 187
Rua da Lagoa 171, Bicesse, 2645-344 Alcabideche, Lisbon
Tel: +351 214 570 149
Email: info@ipsschool.org
Website: www.ipsschool.org
Head of School: Neil Morris
Age range: 3–12 years (up to 18 in September 2023)
No. of pupils: 300
Fees: €10,733
Curriculum: UK
Language instr: English

KING'S COLLEGE SCHOOL, CASCAIS
For further details see p. 192
Rua Cesário Verde 395, Pampilheira, 2750-557 Cascais, Lisbon
Tel: +351 215 966 634
Email: cascais@kingscollegeschool.pt
Website: www.kingscollegeschool.pt
Head of School: Sarah Osborne-James
Age range: 1–13 years (18 years from Sep. 2026)
No. of pupils: 400
Fees: *Day* €9,935–€15,800

L'ÉCOLE TRILINGUE
For further details see p. 197
Avenida do Restelo 21, 1400-314 Lisbon
Tel: +351 910 335 102
Email: info@lecoletrilingue.com
Website: lecoletrilingue.com
Head of School: Véronique Ferreira
Age range: 2–6 years
No. of pupils: 35
Fees: *Day* €8,800
Curriculum: FrenchBacc
Language instr: English, French

Lisbon Montessori School
Rua de Santana 169c, Alto do Cobre, 2750-833 Cascais, Lisbon
Tel: +351 939 016 234
Age range: 2.5–12
Language instr: English

Lycée Français International de Porto
R. Gil Eanes 27, 4150-348 Porto
Tel: +351 226 153 030
Age range: 4–18
No. of pupils: 921
Curriculum: FrenchBacc

NOBEL ALGARVE BRITISH INTERNATIONAL SCHOOL
For further details see p. 210
EN 125, Porches, 8400-400 Lagoa
Tel: +351 282 342547
Email: info@nobelalgarve.com
Website: www.nobelalgarve.com
Head of School: Abi Lewis
Age range: 3–18 years
Curriculum: AP, UK, GCSE, IGCSE, ALevs
Language instr: English

Oeiras International School
Quinta Nossa Senhora da Conceicao, Rua Antero de Quental no 7, 2730-013 Barcarena, Oeiras, Lisbon
Tel: +351 211 935 330
Age range: 6–18
No. of pupils: 420
Curriculum: IBDP, IBMYP, IBPYP
Language instr: English

OPORTO BRITISH SCHOOL
For further details see p. 212
Rua da Cerca 338, Foz do Douro, 4150-201 Porto
Tel: +351 226 166 660
Email: school@obs.edu.pt
Website: www.obs.edu.pt
Headmaster: Nick Sellers
Age range: 3–18 years
No. of pupils: 550
Fees: *Day* €7,625–€13,040
Curriculum: IBDP, UK, IGCSE
Language instr: English
CIS COB ECIS

PARK INTERNATIONAL SCHOOL
For further details see p. 213
Estrada de Alfragide 94, 2610-015 Amadora, Lisbon
Tel: +351 215 807 000
Email: all@park-is.com
Website: www.park-is.com
Head of School: Samantha Gonçalves
Age range: 1–18 years
No. of pupils: 1950
Fees: *Day* €6,978–€16,908
Curriculum: IBDP

PaRK International School – Cascais
Rua Cesário Verde 395, Pampilheira, 2750-657 Cascais, Lisbon
Tel: +351 214 831 211

PaRK International School – Praça de Espanha
Av. Columbano Bordalo Pinheiro 52, 1070-064 Lisbon
Tel: +351 215 855 000

PaRK International School – Restelo
Av. das Descobertas 21, 1400-091 Lisbon
Tel: +351 213 026 316
Curriculum: UK, IGCSE

Prime School Estoril
Rua Antoine de Saint-Exupéry, 2765-043 Estoril, Lisbon
Tel: +351 966 155 909
Age range: 11–18
Curriculum: IGCSE

Prime School Lisbon
19, R. Calçada Ribeiro Santos, 1200-769 Lisbon
Tel: +351 965 002 675

Prime School São Pedro do Estoril
Av. Marginal 435, 02765-315 Estoril, Lisbon
Tel: +351 966 155 909

Prime School Sintra
R. Mestre Neves 20, 2710-422 Sintra, Lisbon
Tel: +351 966 155 909
Age range: 2–18
Curriculum: IGCSE

QUEEN ELIZABETH'S SCHOOL
For further details see p. 214
Rua Filipe Magalhaes 1, Alvalade, 1700-194 Lisboa
Tel: +351 21 841 0140
Email: info.qes@gmail.com
Website: qes.pt
Headmistress: M Conceicao de Oliveira Martins
Age range: 3–10 years
Curriculum: UK

Saint Dominic's International School, Portugal
Rua Maria Brown, Outeiro de Polima, 2785-816 S Domingos de Rana, Lisbon
Tel: +351 21 444 0434
Age range: 3–18 years
No. of pupils: 800
Curriculum: IBDP, IBMYP, IBPYP
Language instr: English
CIS ECIS

St James' Primary School
Rua dos Depósitos de Água 339, 2750-561 Cascais, Lisbon
Tel: +351 214 864 754
Age range: 6–10

St Julian's School
Quinta Nova, 2775-588 Carcavelos e Parede, Lisbon
Tel: +351 214 585 300
Age range: 3–18
No. of pupils: 1070 *B*553 *G*517 *VIth*122
Curriculum: IBDP, National, SAT, UK
Language instr: English
CIS COB ECIS

ST. PETER'S INTERNATIONAL SCHOOL
For further details see p. 243
Quinta dos Barreleiros CCI 3952, Volta da Pedra, 2950-201 Palmela, Setúbal
Tel: +351 21 233 6990
Email: geral@stpeters.pt
Website: www.st-peters-school.com
Head of School: Alex Callow
Age range: 4 months–18 years
No. of pupils: 1500
Fees: €6,303–€12,804
Curriculum: IBDP
Language instr: English, Portuguese

TASIS Portugal
Estrada Nacional No 9, Quinta da Beloura II, 2710-697 Sintra, Lisbon
Tel: +351 219 241 004
Age range: 3–14 years

The British School of Lisbon
Rua de S. Paulo 89, 1200-427 Lisbon
Tel: +351 211 511 942
Age range: 3–11 years

UNITED LISBON INTERNATIONAL SCHOOL
For further details see p. 255
Avenida Marechal Gomes da Costa 9, 1800-255 Lisbon
Tel: +351 218 370 973
Email: info@unitedlisbon.school
Website: www.unitedlisbon.school
Head of School: José Azcue
Age range: 3–18 years
No. of pupils: 300

Vale Verde International School
Apartado 125, 8601-927 Luz, Lagos, Faro
Tel: +351 282 697 205
Age range: 11–18
Curriculum: UK, IGCSE, ALevs
ECIS

Vilamoura International School
Apartado 856, 8125-911 Vilamoura, Faro
Tel: +351 289 303 280
Age range: 2–18
No. of pupils: 500 *B*267 *G*233
Curriculum: National, UK, IGCSE
Language instr: English, Portuguese
ECIS

ROMANIA

Acorns British Style Nursery
63 Popa Soare Street, Sector 2, 031122 Bucharest
Tel: +40 788 418 186
COB

American International School of Bucharest
Sos Pipera-Tunari 196, Voluntari, Jud Ilfov 077190 Bucharest
Tel: +40 (21) 204 4300
Age range: 2–19
No. of pupils: 830 *B*448 *G*382
Curriculum: IBDP, IBMYP, IBPYP, SAT
Language instr: English
(CEE) (CIS) (ECIS)

British International School of Timisoara
8 Aurora Street, 300291 Timisoara
Tel: +40 726 707 446
Curriculum: IBDP
Language instr: English

British School of Bucharest
42 Erou Iancu Nicolae Street, 077190 Bucharest
Tel: +40 21 267 89 19
Age range: 2–18
No. of pupils: 500 *B*250 *G*250 *VIth*38
Curriculum: UK, GCSE, IGCSE, ALevs
Language instr: English
(COB) (ECIS)

Bucharest – Beirut International School
Sos.Vergului, nr.14, District 2, 022448 Bucharest
Tel: +40 (0)744 309 199
Curriculum: IBDP, IBPYP
Language instr: English

Cambridge School of Bucharest
Strada Erou Iancu Nicolae Nr. 126 C, 077190 Voluntari, Ilfov
Tel: +40 21 210 2131
Age range: 2–19 years
No. of pupils: 700
Curriculum: IGCSE
Language instr: English

Cambridge School of Constanta
No. 3 Capidava Street, Constanta
Tel: +40 241 647745
Age range: 4–18
No. of pupils: 250
Language instr: English

Centrul Gifted Education
Strada Berzei 22, Bucharest

Colegiul German Goethe
Strada Cihoschi nr. 17, Sector 1, Bucharest
Tel: +40 21 211 34 25
Age range: 11–18
No. of pupils: 1450

Genesis College
Straulesti Street, 89A District 1, Bucharest
Tel: +40 73 310 7914
Curriculum: IBDP, IBMYP, IBPYP
Language instr: English, Romanian

Gradinita BritAcademy Sector 2
Olimpiadei, nr.36, sect.2, Bucharest
Tel: +40 740329105
Curriculum: UK
(COB)

Hermann Oberth International German School
34E Pipera Blvd, Voluntari, Ilfov
Tel: +4 021 231 20 45
Age range: 2–18 years
No. of pupils: 250
Curriculum: IBDP
Language instr: English, German

International British School of Bucharest
21-25 Agricultori St. District 2, 021481 Bucharest
Tel: +40 21 253 1698
Age range: 3–18
No. of pupils: 340 *VIth*45
Curriculum: UK, GCSE, IGCSE, ALevs
Language instr: English
(CEE) (COB) (ECIS)

International School of Bucharest
1R Gara Catelu Str., Sector 3, Bucharest 032991
Tel: +40 21 3069530
Age range: 2–18 years
No. of pupils: 710
Curriculum: IBDP, SAT, UK, IGCSE, ALevs
Language instr: English
(CIS) (COB)

King's Oak British International School
72 Petre Aurelian, Greenlake Residences, Bucharest Sector 1
Tel: +40 21 380 3535
Age range: 1–13
No. of pupils: 139 *B*70 *G*69
Curriculum: National, UK
Language instr: English
(CIS) (COB) (ECIS)

Lauder Reut Education Complex
15 Iuliu Barasch st, District 3, 030791 Bucharest
Tel: +40 31 805 57 72
Age range: 4–18

Liceul Teoretic Scoala Europeana Bucuresti
33 Baiculesti st., 013913 Bucharest
Tel: +40 21 3117 770
Curriculum: IBDP
Language instr: English

Little London International Academy
Strada Erou Iancu Nicolae 65, Pipera, 077190 Voluntari, Ilfov
Tel: +40 721 689 762
Curriculum: IBPYP
Language instr: English

Lycée Français Anna de Noailles
160A, Soseaua Bucuresti-Ploiesti, Sector 1, 015016 Bucharest
Tel: +40 212 125 893
Age range: 4–18
No. of pupils: 934

Mark Twain International School
25 Erou Iancu Nicolae Street, Voluntari, Ilfov 077190
Tel: +40 735 000 160
Age range: 2–19 years
No. of pupils: 500
Curriculum: IBDP, IBMYP, IBPYP, National
Language instr: English, Romanian
(CIS) (ECIS)

Nikolaus-Lenau-Lyzeum Timisoara
Strada Gheorge Lazar nr. 2, 300078 Timisoara
Tel: +40 256 290987
Age range: 11–18
No. of pupils: 1300

Olga Gudynn International School
5 Erou Iancu Nicolae Street, Voluntari, Ilfov, Bucharest
Tel: +4 0734411365; +4 0317172722
Age range: 3–15
Curriculum: National
(CEE) (COB) (ECIS)

Paradis International School
Str. Iancu Flondor, Nr. 2 M, Lasi
Tel: +40 722133091
Curriculum: UK

Pick Me Academy
Nr. 9, Dragos Voda Street district 2,
Tel: +40 726 000 640
Curriculum: UK
(COB)

Royal School in Transylvania
44-46 Henri Barbusse Street, Cluj-Napoca
Tel: +40 770 103 108
Curriculum: IGCSE, ALevs
(COB)

Seven Hills International School
Str. Palas nr 5B, United Business Centre 2, Etaj 3, 700051 Iasi
Tel: +40 770 687 719
(COB)

Transylvania College
Aleea Baisoara 2A, 400445 Cluj-Napoca
Tel: +40 (0) 264 418 990
Age range: 2–18
Curriculum: UK, IGCSE, ALevs
Language instr: English, Romanian

Verita International School
Soldat Gheorghe Pripu Street 22A, 1st District, Bucharest
Tel: +40 21 311 8811
Curriculum: IBDP
Language instr: English

RUSSIAN FEDERATION

Alabuga International School
Nord Drive, Building 1, Yelabuga, Tatarstan 423600
Tel: +7 855 575 3405
Curriculum: IBMYP, IBPYP
Language instr: English, Russian

British School St Petersburg
Zhdanovskaya Ulitsa, 45, St. Petersburg 197110
Tel: +7 812 46 777 46
Curriculum: UK

Brookes Moscow
Lazorevyy Proezd, 7, Moscow 129323
Tel: +7 (499) 110 70 01
Age range: 2–18 years
No. of pupils: 550
Curriculum: IBDP, IBMYP, IBPYP
Language instr: English

Brookes Saint Petersburg
Tatarskiy Pereulok, 3-5, Saint Petersburg 197198
Tel: +7 (812) 320 89 25
Age range: 3–18 years
No. of pupils: 120
Curriculum: IBDP, IBMYP, IBPYP

CET International Primary School
Vodoprovodnaya 2, Tyumen 625002
Tel: +7 3452 63 10 55
Age range: 3–11
Curriculum: IPC, UK
Language instr: English

CIS Russia – Festivalnaya Campus
Festivalnaya Street, 7A, 125565
Tel: +7 (903) 281 2720
Age range: 3–13
Curriculum: UK
Language instr: English

CIS Russia – Skolkovo Senior Campus
Odintsovo District, Zarechye,, Berezovaya Str., 1A, Moscow 143085
Tel: +7 903 726 2811
Curriculum: IGCSE, ALevs
Language instr: English, Russian
(ECIS)

CIS Russia – St Petersburg Campus
Ulitsa Mebelnaya 11A, St. Petersburg 197345
Tel: +7 812 604 33 22
Age range: 3–18
No. of pupils: 175
Language instr: English

Deutsche Schule Moskau
Prospekt Wernadskogo 103/5, Moscow 119526
Tel: +7 495 434 31 25

'Education through Dialogue' School
Nekrasova Street, 19 St. Petersburg 191014
Tel: +7 812 272 0360
Language instr: English

European Gymnasium
Sokolnichesky Val., d.28, Sokolniki, Moscow 107113
Tel: +7 985 795 4273
Age range: 4–18
Curriculum: IBDP, IBMYP, IBPYP
Language instr: Russian, English

International School in Novie Veshki
p. Veshki, residential complex Novie Veshki, Green Boulevard, VL.86, Mytishchi district, Moscow 141031
Tel: +7 499 707 8899
Curriculum: IBPYP
Language instr: English

International School of Herzen University
Vosstania str., 8 B, St. Petersburg
Tel: +7 812 275 7684
Age range: 6–18
No. of pupils: 115
Curriculum: IBDP, IBMYP
Language instr: English, Russian

International School of Kazan
5 Mavlyutova St., Kazan
Tel: +7 843 204 12 82
Curriculum: IBDP, IBMYP, IBPYP
Language instr: English, Russian
(CIS)

International School of Samara
ul. Kyibysheva, Building 32, Samara 443099
Tel: +7 846 332 2880
Curriculum: IBPYP
Language instr: English, French, Russian

Istochnik International School
62 Tsentralnaya St., Leninsky Village of Ulyanovsk 432067
Tel: +7 8422 260417

Kaluga International School
Lunacharskogo 16, Kaluga
Tel: +7 4843 400444
Age range: 3–15
No. of pupils: 50
Curriculum: IBPYP
Language instr: English

Khoroshevskaya Shkola
45 Marshala Tukhachevskogo St., appt. 2, Moscow 123154
Tel: +7 (499) 401 02 71
Curriculum: IBDP
Language instr: English, Russian

Letovo School
35 Valovaya str., Moscow
Tel: +7 8 800 100 51 15
Curriculum: IBDP, IBMYP
Language instr: English, Russian

Lycée Français de Moscou Alexandre-Dumas
7A Milioutinsky per, Moscow 101000
Tel: +7 495 514 15 46
Curriculum: FrenchBacc

Lyceum-Boarding School No. 2 – Municipal Autonomous Educational Institution
11 Shamil Usmanov Street, Kazan 420095
Tel: +7 8435 543234
Language instr: English, Russian
(ECIS)

Moscow Economic School, Odintsovo Branch
1-A, Zaitsevo Village, Odintsovo Region, Moscow Oblast 143020
Tel: +7 495 780 5230
Age range: 3–16 years
No. of pupils: 620
Curriculum: IBDP, IBMYP, IBPYP
Language instr: Russian, English
(ECIS)

Moscow Economic School, Presnya Campus
29 Zamorenova Street, Moscow 123022
Tel: +7 499 255 55 66
Age range: 3–18
No. of pupils: *B*324 *G*293 *VIth*29
Curriculum: IBDP, IBMYP, IBPYP
Language instr: English, Russian
(CEE) (CIS) (ECIS)

Moscow International Gymnasia
111123 3rd Vladimirskaya Str, House 5, Moscow
Tel: +7 (095) 304 3794
Age range: 6–10
No. of pupils: 65 *B*30 *G*35

President School
Ilyinsky Pod, 2, bld. 1 (in the village of ParkVille Zhukovka), Zhukovka village, Odintsovo district, Moscow Region 143082
Tel: +7 495 955 0000
Age range: 4–18
No. of pupils: 442
Curriculum: IBDP
Language instr: Russian, English

Private Lomonosov School Nizhny Novgorod
Gogol Street, 62, Nizhny Novgorod 603109
Tel: +7 831 430 08 63
Curriculum: IBDP, IBMYP, IBPYP
Language instr: Russian

Russian International School
Domodedevo, Moscow Oblast, Moscow
Tel: +7 (495) 974 04 55
Age range: 5–18
No. of pupils: 300
Curriculum: National

The Anglo-American School of Moscow
1 Beregovaya Street, Moscow 125367
Tel: +7 (495) 231 44 88
Age range: 5–18
No. of pupils: 1111 *B*595 *G*580
Curriculum: ACT, AP, IBDP, IBPYP, SAT
Language instr: English
(CEE) (CIS) (ECIS)

The British International School, Moscow
Novoyasenevsky prospekt 19/5, Moscow 117593
Tel: +7 495 426 0311; +7 495 987 4486
Age range: 3–18
No. of pupils: 1200 *B*650 *G*550
Curriculum: IBDP, National, UK, ALevs
Language instr: English
(CIS) (COB) (ECIS)

The English International School Moscow
Zeleny prospect 66-a, Moscow 111396
Tel: +7 495 301 2104
Age range: 3–18
Curriculum: UK, IGCSE, ALevs
(COB)

The International Gymnasium of the Skolkovo Innovation Center
Skolkovo Innovation Center, Zvorykin Street 7, Moscow 143026
Tel: +7 (495) 956 00 33
Curriculum: IBDP, IBMYP, IBPYP
Language instr: English

The International School of Moscow
Buildings 5 & 6, Krylatskaya Street 12, Krylatskoe, Moscow 121552
Tel: +7 499 922 4400
Age range: 2–13
No. of pupils: 890 *B*437 *G*453
Curriculum: UK, IGCSE, ALevs
Language instr: English
(COB)

Vnukovo International School
Pervomaiskoe, Rogozinino Lugovaya Street 20b, Moscow 108808
Tel: +7 (495) 431 70 70
Curriculum: IBDP
Language instr: Russian

XXI Century Integration International Secondary School
16 Marshala Katukova St., Building 3, Moscow 123592
Tel: +7 495 750 3102
Age range: 5–18 years
No. of pupils: 180
Curriculum: IBDP, IBMYP, IBPYP
Language instr: English, Russian

SERBIA

British International School Belgrade
Radoja Dakica 44, 11000 Belgrade
Tel: +381 113 066 096
Age range: 4–18
No. of pupils: 230
(COB) (ECIS)

Chartwell International School
Teodora Drajzera 38, 11000 Belgrade
Tel: +381 113 675 340
Age range: 2–14
(COB)

Crnjanski High School
Djordja Ognjanovica 2, 11030 Belgrade
Tel: +381 112 398 388
Age range: 14–19
Curriculum: IBDP, IGCSE
Language instr: English

International School
45 Sumatovacka Street, Belgrade
Tel: +381 (0)11 4011 220
Age range: 11–19 years
No. of pupils: 250
Curriculum: IBDP
Language instr: English

International School of Belgrade
Temisvarska 19, 11040 Belgrade
Tel: +381 112 069 999
Age range: 4–18
No. of pupils: 364
Curriculum: IBDP, IBMYP, IBPYP, SAT
Language instr: English
(CEE) (CIS) (ECIS)

PRIMA International School
Dragana Mancea Street,
Senjak, Belgrade
Tel: +381 113 690 825
Curriculum: UK, IGCSE, ALevs
(COB)

Ruder Bo kovic
Kneza Vi eslava 17, 11000 Belgrade
Tel: +381 113 540 786
Curriculum: IBDP, IBMYP, IBPYP, IGCSE
Language instr: English

SLOVAKIA

Cambridge International School Bratislava
Úprkova 3, Bratislava 81104
Tel: +421 2 207 206 79
Age range: 2–18
No. of pupils: 450
Curriculum: UK, IGCSE, ALevs
Language instr: English

English International School of Bratislava
Kalinciakova 12, Bratislava 83101
Tel: +421 907 462 297
Curriculum: IBDP, IBMYP
Language instr: English

LEAF ACADEMY (AKADÉMIA LEAF)
For further details see p. 196
Sasinkova 13, 811 08
Bratislava DIC: 2120216010
Tel: +421 949 443 573
Email: info@leafacademy.eu
Website: www.leafacademy.eu
Head of School: Matej Sapak
Age range: 14–19 years
No. of pupils: 130
Language instr: English

QSI International School of Bratislava
Záhradnicka 1006/2, Samorin 93101
Tel: +421 903 704 436
Age range: 3–18 years
No. of pupils: 288
Curriculum: AP, IBDP, SAT, USA
Language instr: English

Súkromná spojená skola
Starozagorská 8, 040 23 Ko ice
Curriculum: IBPYP
Language instr: English, Slovak

The British International School, Bratislava
J. Vala tana Dolinského 1
(Pekníkova 6), Bratislava 841 02
Tel: +421 2 6930 7081
Age range: 2 –18
Curriculum: IBDP, UK, ALevs
Language instr: English
(COB)

SLOVENIA

British International School of Ljubljana
Podmilscakova ulica
18, 1000 Ljubljana
Tel: +386 40 486 548
Age range: 3–18
No. of pupils: 70 *B*36 *G*34
Curriculum: IPC, SAT, UK, IGCSE, ALevs
Language instr: English
(COB)

Gimnazija Bezigrad
Periceva 4, 1000 Ljubljana
Tel: +386 13 000 400
Age range: 14–19
No. of pupils: 74
Curriculum: IBDP, IBMYP, National
Language instr: English
(ECIS)

IES Ljubljana International School
Zlatek 15, 1000 Ljubljana
Tel: +386 51 662 042
Language instr: English

QSI International School of Ljubljana
Dolgi most 6A, 1000 Ljubljana
Tel: +386 1 244 1750
Age range: 3–17
No. of pupils: 108
Curriculum: AP, SAT, USA

Vector International Academy
Stula 23, 1000 Ljubljana
Tel: +386 40 862 445
Curriculum: IBDP
Language instr: English, French

SPAIN

AGORA BARCELONA INTERNATIONAL SCHOOL
For further details see p. 123
Carrer Puig de Mira, Sant Esteve Sesrovires, 08635
Barcelona, Catalonia
Tel: +34 93 779 89 28
Email: admissions@agoraisbarcelona.edu.es
Website: www.colegioagorabarcelona.com
Headmaster: Xavi Martín
No. of pupils: 470
Curriculum: IBDP
Language instr: English, Spanish, Catalan, French/German
(ISA)

AGORA LLEDÓ INTERNATIONAL SCHOOL
For further details see p. 124
Camino Caminàs, 175,
Castelló de la Plana, 12003
Castelló, Valencia
Tel: +34 964 72 31 70
Email: admissions@lledo.edu.es
Website: www.colegioagoralledo.com
Headmaster: Luis Madrid
No. of pupils: 800
Curriculum: IBDP
Language instr: English, Spanish
(ISA)

AGORA MADRID INTERNATIONAL SCHOOL
For further details see p. 125
Calle Duero, 35, Villaviciosa
de Odón, 28670 Madrid
Tel: +34 91 616 71 25
Email: admissions@agoraism.com
Website: www.colegioagoramadrid.com
Headmaster: Luis Madrid
No. of pupils: 500
Curriculum: IBDP
Language instr: English, Spanish

Agora Patufet Infant School
C/ Sant Jordi 22, Sant Cugat del Vallés, 08172 Barcelona, Catalonia
Tel: +34 93 674 12 39
Age range: 0–6 years

AGORA PORTALS INTERNATIONAL SCHOOL
For further details see p. 126
Carretera Vella Palma-Andratx,
s/n, Portals Nous, 07181
Mallorca, Balearic Islands
Tel: +34 964 72 31 70
Email: admissions@agoraportals.edu.es
Website: www.colegioagoraportals.com
Headmaster: Rafael Barea
No. of pupils: 1000
Curriculum: IBDP
Language instr: English, Spanish

AGORA SANT CUGAT INTERNATIONAL SCHOOL
For further details see p. 127
Carrer Ferrer i Guàrdia, s/n,
Sant Cugat del Vallés, 08174
Barcelona, Catalonia
Tel: +34 93 590 26 00
Email: ruth.sale@agorasantcugat.edu.es
Website: www.colegioagorasantcugat.es
Headmaster: Vicenç Gandol
Age range: 1–18 years
No. of pupils: 1850
Curriculum: IBDP, IBMYP, IBPYP, National
Language instr: English, Spanish, Catalan
(ISA)

Almunecar International School
Calle Pinariego, Los Pinos, 18690
Almuñecar, Granada, Andalusia
Tel: +34 9586 35911
Age range: 3–18
No. of pupils: 280
Curriculum: UK, IGCSE

Aloha College Marbella
Urbanización el Angel, 29660
Marbella, Málaga, Andalusia
Tel: +34 95 281 41 33
Age range: 3–18
No. of pupils: 800
Curriculum: IBDP, SAT, UK, IGCSE, ALevs
Language instr: English, Spanish
(COB) (ECIS)

American School of Barcelona
Calle Balmes 7, Esplugues
de Llobregat, 08950
Barcelona, Catalonia
Tel: +34 93 371 4016
Age range: 3–18
No. of pupils: 850
Curriculum: IBDP, National, SAT
Language instr: English
(ECIS)

American School of Bilbao
Soparda Bidea 10, 48640 Berango,
Biscay, Basque Country
Tel: +34 94 668 0860
Age range: 2–18
No. of pupils: 375 *B*185 *G*190 *VIth*35
Curriculum: IBDP, IBMYP, IBPYP, IGCSE
Language instr: English
(CIS) (ECIS)

American School of Las Palmas
Carretera de los Hoyos, Km
1.7, 35017 Las Palmas de Gran
Canaria, Las Palmas, Can+
Tel: +34 928 430 023
Age range: 3–18
Curriculum: AP, USA

American School of Madrid
Apartado 80, 28080 Madrid
Tel: +34 91 740 19 00
Age range: 3–18
No. of pupils: 900
Curriculum: IBDP, SAT, USA
Language instr: English
(ECIS)

American School of Valencia
Urbanización Los Monasterios,
Apartado de Correos 9,
46530 Puzol, Valencia
Tel: +34 96 140 5412
Age range: 2–18
No. of pupils: 792 *VIth*104
Curriculum: ACT, IBDP, National, SAT, USA
Language instr: English, Spanish, Valencia
(ECIS)

Angel de la Guarda
Calle Andalucía 17-20,
03016 Alicante, Valencia
Tel: +34 9652 61899
Curriculum: IBDP
Language instr: English, Spanish

Aquinas American School
Calle Transversal Cuatro, 4,
Urbanización Monte Alina, Pozuelo
de Alarcon, 28223 Madrid
Tel: +34 91 352 31 20
Age range: 3–18
No. of pupils: 650
Curriculum: AP, IBDP, SAT, USA
Language instr: English

Areteia School
C/ Salvia 24 Urb. La Moraleja,
28109 Alcobendas, Madrid
Tel: +34 91 650 74 08
Age range: 3–20

Aula Escola Europea
Avinguda Mare de, Déu de Lorda,
34-36, 08034 Barcelona, Catalonia
Tel: +34 93 203 03 54
No. of pupils: 1250
Curriculum: IBDP
Language instr: Catalan

Baleares International College, Mallorca, Sa Porrassa
Crta. Cala Figuera, 3A, Sa Porassa,
07181 Calvia, Balearic Islands
Tel: +34 971 133167
Age range: 3–18
No. of pupils: 230
Curriculum: AP, SAT, TOEFL, ALevs
(COB)

Baleares International College, Mallorca, San Augustin Campus
Calle de Marià Villangómez,
17, Palma De Mallorca, 07015
Sant Agusti, Balearic Islands
Tel: +34 9 7140 3161
Curriculum: UK
(COB)

Bell-lloc Del Pla
Carrer de Can Pau Birol, 2,
17005 Girona, Catalonia
Tel: +34 972 232 111
Curriculum: IBDP
Language instr: Spanish

Bellver International College
Calle Jose Costa Ferrer No
5, Palma de Mallorca, 07015
Marivent, Balearic Islands
Tel: +34 971 401679
Age range: 3–18
No. of pupils: 300 *B153 G147*
Curriculum: UK, IGCSE, ALevs
Language instr: English

Benjamin Franklin International School
Martorell i Pena 9, 08017
Barcelona, Catalonia
Tel: +34 93 434 2380
Age range: 3–18
Curriculum: ACT, IBDP,
National, SAT, TOEFL, USA
Language instr: English
(ECIS)

Brains International School, Conde de Orgaz
Calle Frascuelo 2, 28043 Madrid
Tel: +34 913 889 355
Curriculum: IBPYP
Language instr: English, Spanish

Brains International School, La Moraleja
Calle Salvia No. 48, 28109
Alcobendas, Madrid
Tel: +34 916 504 300
Curriculum: IBDP
Language instr: English

British College La Cañada
Calle 299, No 25, La Canada,
Paterna, 46182 Valencia
Tel: +34 96 132 40 40
Age range: 3–18
No. of pupils: 50

British College of Gava
Carrer de Josep Lluís Sert 32, 08850
Gavà, Barcelona, Catalonia
Tel: +34 932 777 899
Curriculum: IBDP
Language instr: English, Spanish

British Council School
Calle Solano,5-7, Pozuelo de
Alarcón, 28223 Madrid
Tel: +34 91 337 3612
Age range: 2–18
No. of pupils: 1955 *B969 G986 VIth225*
Curriculum: National,
SAT, UK, IGCSE
Language instr: English, Spanish
(ECIS)

British School Alzira
Ctra. Alzira a Tavernes km.
11, La Barraca de Aguas
Vivas, 46792 Valencia
Tel: +34 902 123 883
Age range: 1–18
Curriculum: UK

British School of Córdoba
Calle México 4, 14012
Córdoba, Andalusia
Tel: +34 957 767 048
Age range: 3–18
Curriculum: UK

British School of Gran Canaria
Apartado 11, Tafira Alta,
35017 Las Palmas de Gran
Canaria, Las Palmas, Can+
Tel: +34 9 28 351167
Age range: 3–18
No. of pupils: 569
Curriculum: UK, ALevs
Language instr: English
(COB)

British School of Lanzarote
Calle, 1 Juan Echevarria 10, 35509
Tahiche, Lanzarote, Canary Islands
Tel: +34 928 810085
Age range: 4–16
No. of pupils: 200 *B100 G100*

British School of Tenerife
Ctra. de La Luz, s/n, 38300 La
Orotava, Tenerife, Canary Islands
Tel: +34 922 33 69 29

British School of Valencia
Avda Peris y Valero 53, 55,
57, 46006 Valencia
Tel: +34 96 374 29 30
Age range: 2–18
Curriculum: UK, ALevs

C.E. Punta Galea
Urbanización Punta Galea
Playa del Sardinero, 1,
28290 Las Rozas, Madrid
Tel: +34 91 630 26 41
Curriculum: IBDP
Language instr: Spanish

Calpe School
Los Eucaliptos 60, Urbanazacion
Linda Vista Baja, San
Pedro de Alcantara, 29670
Málaga, Andalusia
Tel: +34 952 786 029
Age range: 2–11
No. of pupils: 100
Curriculum: SAT, UK

CAMBRIDGE HOUSE COMMUNITY COLLEGE
For further details see p. 137
Calle Profesorado Espanol
1, Santa Barbara, 46111
Rocafort, Valencia
Tel: +34 96 390 5019
Email: info@cambridgehouse.es
Website:
www.cambridgehouse.es
Executive Head: Adam Hassoun
No. of pupils: 1700
Curriculum: National, UK
Language instr: English, Spanish

Canterbury School
San Lorenzo Campus, 35018 San
Lorenzo, Las Palmas, Canary Islands
Tel: +34 828 11 34 00
Curriculum: UK

Casvi International American School
C/ Gavilán, 2, Tres Cantos,
28760 Madrid
Tel: +34 91 804 02 12
Age range: 3–18 years
No. of pupils: 300
Curriculum: IBDP, IBMYP, IBPYP
Language instr: English, Spanish

Caxton College
C/ Mas de León, 5, 46530
Puzol, Valencia
Tel: +34 96 142 4500
Age range: 1–18 years
No. of pupils: 1595
Curriculum: UK, IGCSE, ALevs
Language instr: English

Centre Cultural I Esportiu Xaloc
Can Tries, 4-6, L'Hospitalet
de Llobregat, 08902
Barcelona, Catalonia
Tel: +34 93 335 1600
Curriculum: IBDP, IBPYP
Language instr: Spanish

Centro de Estudios Ibn Gabirol Colegio Estrella Toledano
Paseo de Alcobendas
7 (La Moraleja), 28109
Alcobendas, Madrid
Tel: +34 916 50 12 29
Curriculum: IBDP
Language instr: English

Centro Educativo Agave
Camino de la Gloria no 17,
04230 Huercal de Almería,
Almería, Andalusia
Tel: +34 9503 01026
Curriculum: IBDP
Language instr: English

Chester College International School
Travesía de Montouto 2, 15894
Santiago de Compostela,
A Coruña, Galicia
Tel: +34 981 819 160
Curriculum: USA
Language instr: English, Spanish

Colegio Adharaz
Urb. La Vina. C/ Garnacha 1, 41807
Espartinas, Seville, Andalusia
Tel: +34 955 713 820
Curriculum: IBPYP
Language instr: English, Spanish

Colegio Alameda de Osuna
Paseo de la Alameda de
Osuna, 60, 28042 Madrid
Tel: +34 91 742 70 11
Curriculum: IBDP, IBMYP, IBPYP
Language instr: English, Spanish

Colegio Alauda
Cerillo 6, 14014 Córdoba, Andalusia
Tel: +34 957 40 55 07
Curriculum: IBDP
Language instr: English

Colegio Alegra
Calle de Sorolla 4, 28222
Majadahonda, Madrid
Tel: +34 916 39 79 03
Curriculum: IBDP, IBMYP
Language instr: English, Spanish

Colegio Alemán Alberto Durero de Sevilla
Avda. Cueva de Altamira s/n,
41020 Seville, Andalusia
Tel: +34 954 999 509
Curriculum: UK

Colegio Altaduna
Ctra. de Alicún KM. 8,
04740 Roquetas de Mar,
Almería, Andalusia
Tel: +34 950 559 500

Colegio Altasierra
Urb. La Viña. C/ Garnacha 2., 41807
Espartinas, Seville, Andalusia
Tel: +34 954 614 760
Curriculum: IBPYP
Language instr: English, Spanish

Colegio Altocastillo
Ctra. de Córdoba s/n,
23005 Jaén, Andalusia
Tel: +34 953 296 910

Colegio Arcangel Rafael
Calle Maqueda no.
4, 28024 Madrid
Tel: +34 91 711 93 00
Curriculum: IBDP, IBMYP, IBPYP
Language instr: English, Spanish

Colegio Arenas
Llano de Los Tarahales, 76,
35013 Las Palmas de Gran
Canaria, Las Palmas, Can+
Tel: +34 928 41 59 96
Language instr: Spanish

Colegio Arenas Atlántico
Paseo San Patricio, No 20,
35413 Trasmontaña, Las
Palmas, Canary Islands
Tel: +34 928 629 140
Age range: 3–18
No. of pupils: 306 *B*179 *G*127
Curriculum: IBDP, IBMYP, National
Language instr: Spanish

Colegio Arenas Internacional
Avenida del Mar 37, Lanzarote,
35509 Costa Teguise, Las
Palmas, Canary Islands
Tel: +34 928 590 835
Curriculum: IBDP, IBMYP, IBPYP
Language instr: Spanish

Colegio Arenas Sur
Las Margaritas s/n, 35290 San
Agustín, Las Palmas, Canary Islands
Tel: +34 928 765 934
No. of pupils: 620
Curriculum: IBDP
Language instr: Spanish

Colegio Atalaya
Calle Pico Alcazaba 24-28,
Urbanización El Marqués,
29680 Estepona, Málaga
Tel: +34 952 003 171
Curriculum: IBDP
Language instr: English, Spanish

Colegio Brains Maria Lombillo
Calle Maria Lombillo
5, 28027 Madrid
Tel: +34 917 421 060
Age range: 6–18 years
Curriculum: IBDP, IBPYP
Language instr: English, Spanish

Colegio Camarena Canet
C/ De la Rosa s/n, 46529 Canet
d'en Berenguer, Valencia
Tel: +34 960 609 036
Curriculum: IBMYP, IBPYP
Language instr: English, Spanish

Colegio Camarena Valterna
Calle Carlina s/n 46980,
Valterna, Urb. Lloma Llarga,
Paterna, Valencia
Tel: +34 961 381 898
Curriculum: IBPYP
Language instr: English, Spanish

Colegio Cervantes
Avda. de la Fuensanta, 37,
14010 Córdoba, Andalusia
Tel: +34 957 255150
Curriculum: IBDP
Language instr: Spanish

Colegio CEU San Pablo Montepríncipe
Avda. Montepríncipe, s/n, 28668
Boadilla del Monte, Madrid
Tel: +34 91 352 05 23
No. of pupils: 1200
Curriculum: IBDP, IBPYP
Language instr: Spanish, English

Colegio CEU San Pablo Sanchinarro
Niceto Alcalá Zamora,
43, 28050 Madrid
Tel: +34 91 392 34 40/41
Curriculum: IBDP
Language instr: English

Colegio CEU San Pablo Valencia
Edificio Seminario Metropolitano,
46113 Moncada, Valencia
Tel: +34 961 36 90 14
Curriculum: IBDP, IBPYP
Language instr: Spanish

Colegio de San Francisco de Paula
C/ Santa Angela de la Cruz,
11, 41003 Seville, Andalusia
Tel: +34 95 422 4382
Age range: 3–18
Curriculum: IBDP, IBMYP,
IBPYP, National
Language instr: Spanish, English

Colegio Ecos
C/ Velázquez, 7. Urb. Elvira,
La Mairena, Ojén, 29612
Marbella, Málaga, Andalusia
Tel: +34 952 831 027
Curriculum: IBPYP
Language instr: English, Spanish

Colegio El Planet
Partida Planet 71, 03590
Altea, Alicante, Valencia
Tel: +34 965 844 224
Language instr: English

Colegio El Romeral
Calle De Eolo 2, 29010
Málaga, Andalusia
Tel: +34 952 070 370
Curriculum: IBPYP
Language instr: English, Spanish

Colegio El Tomillar
C/ Pantano de la Serena,
48. Las Vaguadas, 06010
Badajoz, Extremadura
Tel: +34 924 268 807

Colegio El Valle Alicante
Avda. Condomina 65, 03540
Alicante, Valencia
Tel: +34 965 155 619
Curriculum: IBDP, IBMYP, IBPYP
Language instr: English, Spanish

Colegio El Valle II – Sanchinarro
Calle Ana De Austria,
60, 28050 Madrid
Tel: +34 91 7188426
Curriculum: IBDP

Colegio Entrepinos
C/ Escultor León Ortega s/n,
Bellavista, 21110 Aljaraque,
Huelva, Andalusia
Tel: +34 959 319 125

Colegio Grazalema
C/ Caracola, 2. Urb. Valdelagrana,
11500 El Puerto de Santa
María, Cádiz, Andalusia
Tel: +34 956 561 542
Curriculum: IBPYP
Language instr: English, Spanish

Colegio Guadalete
C/ Ubrique, 36. Urb. Valdelagrana,
11500 El Puerto de Santa
María, Cádiz, Andalusia
Tel: +34 956 561 646
Curriculum: IBPYP
Language instr: English, Spanish

Colegio Guadalimar
Ctra. de Córdoba s/n,
23005 Jaén, Andalusia
Tel: +34 953 295 083

Colegio Heidelberg
Apartado de Correos 248,
Barranco Seco 15, 35090 Las
Palmas de Gran Canaria,
Las Palmas, Can+
Tel: +34 928 350 462
Age range: 3–18
Curriculum: IBDP, IBMYP
Language instr: Spanish

Colegio HH. Maristas Sagrado Corazón Alicante
Calle de la Isla de Corfú, 5,
03005 Alicante, Valencia
Tel: +34 965 130 941
Curriculum: IBDP
Language instr: Spanish

Colegio Hispano Inglés de Las Palmas
(Secondary & Bachillerato),
Bandama Country, Finca
Los Fierros, Tafira Alta, Las
Palmas, Canary Islands
Tel: +34 928 25 16 16
Curriculum: UK, IGCSE

Colegio Inglés English School of Asturias
Finca La Llosona s/n,
33192 Pruvia, Asturias
Tel: +34 985 237 171
Age range: 3–18 years
Curriculum: IBDP
Language instr: English, Spanish

Colegio Internacional de Levante
Río Jalón 25 Urbanización
Calicanto, 46370 Valencia
Tel: +34 961980650
Curriculum: IBDP, IBMYP
Language instr: Spanish
ISA

Colegio Internacional Meres
Carretera Meres, s/n,
33199 Meres, Asturias
Tel: +34 985 792 427
Curriculum: IBDP, IBMYP, IBPYP

Colegio Internacional Peñacorada
Calle Bandonilla 32, CP Armunia,
24009 León, Castile & León
Tel: +34 987 202352
Language instr: Spanish

Colegio Internacional SEK Eirís
C Castaño de Eiris, 1, 15009
A Coruña, Galicia
Tel: +34 981 28 44 00
Age range: 3–18 years
No. of pupils: 720 *B*360 *G*360 *VIth*30
Curriculum: IBDP, National
Language instr: Spanish, English
ISA

Colegio Internacional Torrequebrada
C/ Ronda del Golf Este, 7-11,
Urbanización Torrequebrada,
29639 Benalmádena,
Málaga, Andalusia
Tel: +34 952 57 60 65
Age range: 2–18
Curriculum: IBDP, IBMYP, IBPYP
Language instr: English, Spanish

Colegio Juan de Lanuza
Crta Areopuerto 275, 50011
Zaragoza, Aragon
Tel: +34 976 300 336
Age range: 2–18
No. of pupils: 630
Language instr: Spanish, English

Colegio Las Chapas
Urb. Las Chapas s/n. 29604
Marbella, Málaga, Andalusia
Tel: +34 952 831 616
Curriculum: IBPYP
Language instr: English, Spanish

Colegio Legamar
Ctra. Leganés-Fuenlabrada Km.
1.5, 28914 Leganés, Madrid
Tel: +34 916 933 812
Curriculum: IBDP
Language instr: English, Spanish

Colegio Liceo Europeo
C/ Camino Sur 10, 28100
Alcobendas, Madrid
Tel: +34 91 650 00 00
Curriculum: IBDP, IBMYP, IBPYP, IBCP
Language instr: English, Spanish

Colegio Logos
Urbanización Molino de la Hoz c/,
Sacre 2, 28232 Las Rozas, Madrid
Tel: +34 91 630 34 94
Curriculum: IBDP
Language instr: English

Colegio Madrid
Avda. del Comandante
Franco 8, 28016 Madrid
Tel: +34 910 572 501
Curriculum: IBDP
Language instr: Spanish

Colegio Manuel Peleteiro
Monte Redondo – Castiñeiriño,
15702 Santiago de Compostela,
A Coruña, Galicia
Tel: +34 98 1591475
Curriculum: IBDP

Colegio Marcote
Avda del Puente, 80 (Cabral),
36318 Vigo, Pontevedra, Galicia
Tel: +34 986 251 511
No. of pupils: 350
Language instr: Spanish

Colegio Mater Salvatoris
Calle Valdesquí no. 4,
28023 Madrid
Tel: +34 91 307 1243
Curriculum: IBDP
Language instr: Spanish

Colegio Monaita
C/ Acequia de la Madraza s/n,
18015 Granada, Andalusia
Tel: +34 958 806 940
Curriculum: IBPYP
Language instr: English, Spanish

Colegio Montecalpe
Urb. San García, C/ La Carpa s/n,
11207 Algeciras, Cádiz, Andalusia
Tel: +34 956 605 888

Colegio Montserrat
Av Vallvidrera, 68, 08017
Barcelona, Catalonia
Tel: +34 932 038 800
Curriculum: IBDP, IBMYP
Language instr: English, Spanish

Colegio Mulhacén
Ctra. Pinos Puente 10, 18015
Granada, Andalusia
Tel: +34 958 806 800
Curriculum: IBPYP
Language instr: English, Spanish

Colegio Nuestra Señora de Europa
C/ Estrada de Goñi, 3, 48993
Getxo, Biscay, Basque Country
Tel: +34 94 491 03 92
Age range: 3–18
No. of pupils: 750
Language instr: Spanish

Colegio Nuestra Señora del Recuerdo
Plaza Duque de Pastrana
5, 28036 Madrid
Tel: +34 91 3022640
Age range: 3–18
Curriculum: IBDP
Language instr: Spanish, English

Colegio Obradoiro
Rua Obradoiro 49, 15190
A Coruña, Galicia
Tel: +34 981 281 888
Curriculum: IBDP, IBMYP, IBPYP
Language instr: English, Spanish

Colegio Parque
Calle Piamonte, 19 Urbanización
Parquelagos, La Navata,
28420 Galapagar, Madrid
Tel: +34 918 590 630
Curriculum: IBDP
Language instr: English, Spanish

Colegio Puertapalma
Avda. de las Vaguadas 44,
06010 Badajoz, Extremadura
Tel: +34 924 267 763

Colegio Puertoblanco
Calle Goleta 2, 11207
Algeciras, Cádiz, Andalusia
Tel: +34 956 604 422

Colegio Retamar
Madrid España, c/ Pajares
22, 28223 Madrid
Tel: +34 91 714 10 22
Age range: B6–18
No. of pupils: 2100
Curriculum: IBDP
Language instr: Spanish

Colegio Saladares
Ctra. de Alicún. KM. 10300,
04721 El Parador de las
Hortichuelas, Almería, An+
Tel: +34 950 559 644

Colegio San Cayetano
Av. Picasso 21, 07014 Palma De
Mallorca, Balearic Islands
Tel: +34 971 220 575
Curriculum: IBDP
Language instr: English, Spanish

Colegio San Fernando
Avenida San Agustín, s/n,
33400 Avilés, Asturias
Tel: +34 985 565 745
Curriculum: IBDP, IBMYP, IBPYP

Colegio San Jorge
Soc. Coop. Enseñanza la
Alcayna. CIF: F30410328, Avda.
Picos de Europa s/n, 30507
Molina de Segura, Murcia
Tel: +34 968 430 711
Curriculum: IBDP
Language instr: English, Spanish

COLEGIO SAN PATRICIO EL SOTO
For further details see p. 139
Calle Jazmin 148, El Soto
de la Moraleja, 28109
Alcobendas, Madrid
Tel: +34 916 500 602
Email:
infosoto@colegiosanpatricio.es
Website: www.
colegiosanpatriciomadrid.com
Headmaster: Borja Díaz
Age range: 12–18 years
Curriculum: IBDP
Language instr: English, Spanish

Colegio San Patricio La Moraleja
Paseo de Alcobendas
9, La Moraleja, 28109
Alcobendas, Madrid
Tel: +34 916 500 791
Age range: 2–11 years

Colegio San Patricio Serrano
Calle Serrano 200, 28002 Madrid
Tel: +34 915 638 420
Age range: 2–11 years

Colegio Sierra Blanca
Avenida de Plutarco 34,
29010 Málaga, Andalusia
Tel: +34 952 070 650
Curriculum: IBPYP
Language instr: English, Spanish

Colegio Suizo de Madrid
Carretera de Burgos km 14,
28108 Alcobendas, Madrid
Tel: +34 91 650 58 18
Age range: 3–18
No. of pupils: 600

Colegio Tierrallana
C/ Abeto, s/n. Urb.Dehesa Golf,
21110 Aljaraque, Huelva, Andalusia
Tel: +34 959 522 810

Colegio Timon
Rusia 11, 28022 Madrid
Tel: +34 91 5346935
Age range: 2–15
No. of pupils: 150

Colegio Valdefuentes
Ana de Austria 6, Sanchinarro,
28050 Madrid
Tel: +34 917 188 229
Curriculum: IBDP
Language instr: English, Spanish

Colegio Virgen de Europa
C/ Valle de Santa Ana No.
1, Las Lomas, 28669 Boadilla
del Monte, Madrid
Tel: +34 91 633 0155
Curriculum: IBDP, IBMYP, IBPYP
Language instr: English, Spanish

Colegios Ramón Y Cajal
C/ Arturo Soria, 206, 28043 Madrid
Tel: +34 91 413 56 31
Curriculum: IBMYP, IBPYP
Language instr: English

College Saint-Exupery
Camino Ancho 85, 28109
Alcobendas, Madrid
Tel: +34 91 650 70 19

Complejo Educativo Mas Camarena
C/ 1 Urbanización, Mas Camarena,
46117 Bétera, Valencia
Tel: +34 961687535
Age range: 6–18
No. of pupils: 2500
Curriculum: IBDP, IBMYP,
IBPYP, IBCP, USA
Language instr: English, Spanish

Cooperativa de Enseñanza San Cernin
Avda. Baranain 3, 31007
Pamplona, Navarre
Tel: +34 948176288
Curriculum: IBDP
Language instr: English

CORUÑA BRITISH INTERNATIONAL SCHOOL (A CORUÑA)
For further details see p. 142
Rúa Roma 1, 15008 A Coruña, Galicia
Tel: +34 981 28 67 99
Email: admissions@biscoruna.com
Website: www.biscoruna.com
Executive Head: Dominic Abbott
No. of pupils: 360
Curriculum: National, UK
Language instr: English, Spanish, French, Galician

Costa Blanca International College
Av. Del Albir s/n, (partida Sanz), 03503 Benidorm, Alicante, Valencia
Tel: +34 96 680 34 11
Age range: 3–18
No. of pupils: 300
Curriculum: UK
Language instr: Spanish, English

Deutsche Schule in der provinz Malaga – Coleg
Apartado de Correos 318, 29600 Marbella, Málaga, Andalusia
Tel: +34 952 831 417

Deutsche Schule Madrid
Colegio Alemán de Madrid, Calle Monasterio de Guadalupe 7, 28049 Madrid
Tel: +34 91 558 02 00

Deutsche Schule Valencia – Colegio Alemán Valencia
Jaime Roig 14-16, 46010 Valencia
Tel: +34 96 3690100

École Française Bel Air
Caretera C-246 KM 42, 8810 Saint Pere de Ribes, Barcelona, Catalonia
Tel: +34 938 962267
Age range: 4–16
No. of pupils: 740

Ecole Saint-Louis des Français
Calle Portugalete 1, Pozuelo de Alarcón, 28223 Madrid
Tel: +34 91 352 05 17
Age range: 4–18
No. of pupils: 100
Curriculum: National

El Centro Ingles
Apartado Correos 85, Carretera Fuentebravia KM1.2, 11500 Puerto de Santa Maria, Cádiz, Andalusia
Tel: +34 956 850560
Age range: 2–18
No. of pupils: 805 *B*404 *G*401 *VIth*77

El Limonar International School (ELIS) Murcia
Colonia Buenavista s/n, 30120 El Palmar, Cádiz, Andalusia
Tel: +34 968 882 818
Age range: 3–18
No. of pupils: 780
Curriculum: IGCSE, ALevs
Language instr: English, Spanish

El Limonar International School (ELIS) Villamartin
c/ Filipinas, 15 – Urb. Blue Lagoon, 03193 San Miguel de Salinas, Alicante, Valencia
Tel: +34 966 722 821
Age range: 3–18
No. of pupils: 510
Curriculum: UK, IGCSE, ALevs
Language instr: English, Spanish

El Plantío International School of Valencia
Calle 233 No36 Urb El Plantío, La Cañada, 46182 Paterna, Valencia
Tel: +34 96 132 14 10
Age range: 2–18
No. of pupils: 650
Curriculum: IBDP, National, UK, IGCSE
Language instr: English, Spanish

Elian's British School of La Nucía
Av. El Copet 5, 03530 La Nucía, Alicante, Valencia
Tel: +34 966 877 055

English Academy Santa Claus
Carrer Lleó XIII, No 12, 08022 Barcelona, Catalonia
Tel: +34 93 417 18 47
Age range: 3–12
No. of pupils: 100
Curriculum: USA

English School Los Olivos
Avda Los Almendros 13, Valencia
Tel: +34 963 631 409
Age range: 3–18
Curriculum: National, UK, IGCSE, ALevs

ES AMERICAN SCHOOL
For further details see p. 150
Autovia de Castelldefels C-31 Km 191, El Prat de Llobregat, 08820 Barcelona, Catalonia
Tel: +34 93 479 1611
Email: admin@es-school.com
Website: www.es-school.com
Head of School: Melanie Rose
Age range: 6–18 years
No. of pupils: 115
Fees: *Day* €10,946–€16,327
Curriculum: AP, IBPYP, SAT, USA
Language instr: English

Escola Internacional del Camp
Salvador Espiriu s/n, 43840 Salou, Tarragona, Catalonia
Tel: +34 977325620
Age range: 1–19
No. of pupils: 560 *B*280 *G*280 *VIth*45
Curriculum: IBDP, National
Language instr: English, Spanish, Catalan

Escola Pia Sabadell
Carrer Escola Pia 92, 08201 Sabadell, Barcelona, Catalonia
Tel: +34 93 748 44 30
Curriculum: USA

Escuela Ideo
Carretera de Colmenar a Alcobendas, Km. 0,500, 28049 Madrid
Tel: +34 917 523 343
Curriculum: IBDP
Language instr: English, Spanish

Escuela Suiza de Barcelona
Alfonso XII 95-105, 08006 Barcelona, Catalonia
Tel: +34 932 096544
Age range: 3–18
No. of pupils: 640

Eurocolegio Casvi Boadilla
C/ Miguel Ángel Cantero Oliva, 13, Boadilla del Monte, Madrid
Tel: +34 91 632 96 53
Curriculum: IBMYP, IBPYP
Language instr: Spanish

Eurocolegio Casvi Villaviciosa
Avenida de Castilla, 27, Villaviciosa de Odón, 28670 Madrid
Tel: +34 91 616 22 18
Age range: 3–18 years
No. of pupils: 1060
Curriculum: IBDP, IBMYP, IBPYP
Language instr: English, Spanish

Europa International School
Av Pla del Vinyet 110, 08172 Sant Cugat del Vallés, Barcelona, Catalonia
Tel: +34 93 589 8420
Age range: 1–18
No. of pupils: 1315 *B*625 *G*690 *VIth*80

Everest School Monteclaro
C/Rosas s/n, Urb Monteclaro, Urb Monteclaro, 28223 Madrid
Tel: +34 91 799 48 88
Age range: 3–18
No. of pupils: 1000
Curriculum: IGCSE

Fundacion Privada Oak House School
Sant Pere Claver 12-18, 08017 Barcelona, Catalonia
Tel: +34 932 524 020
Age range: 3–17
Curriculum: IBDP, UK
Language instr: English

GRANADA COLLEGE
For further details see p. 152
Educación y Formación Europea, S.A., Urbanización Llanos de Silva, 18230 Atarfe, Granada, Andalusia
Tel: +34 958 499 009
Website: granadacollege.es
Head of School: Javier Jiménez Ortiz
Age range: 0–18 years
No. of pupils: 1000
Curriculum: IBDP
Language instr: English, Spanish

Gredos San Diego (GSD) Las Rozas
C/ Clara Campoamor, 1, 28232 Las Rozas, Madrid
Tel: +34 91 640 89 23
Curriculum: IBDP
Language instr: English

Green Valley School
Cami de la Vileta 210, Son Puig, 07011 Palma De Mallorca, Balearic Islands
Tel: +34 971 160 817
Curriculum: IBDP
Language instr: English

GRESOL International-American School
Ctra. Sabadell a Matadepera, (BV-1248) km. 6, 08227 Terrassa, Barcelona, Catalonia
Tel: +34 937 870 158
Curriculum: IBDP
Language instr: English, Spanish

Hamelin-Laie International School
Ronda 8 de Marc 178-180, 08390 Montgat, Barcelona, Catalonia
Tel: +34 93 5556717
Age range: 18 months–18 years
Curriculum: IBDP
Language instr: English, Spanish, Catalan

Hastings School
Calle Manuel Maranon 8, 28043 Madrid
Tel: +34 918 33 77 90
Age range: 2–18 years
No. of pupils: 1247
Curriculum: IBDP, UK
Language instr: English, Spanish

Holy Mary British Catholic School
Calle Cinca 20, 28002 Madrid
Tel: +34 91 287 2752
Age range: 2–18
No. of pupils: 575
Curriculum: UK, GCSE, ALevs
Language instr: English

I.E.S. Clot de la Illot
Avinguda els Furs 4, Campello, 3560 Alicante, Valencia
Tel: +34 965 632 854
Age range: 4–19

Iale International School, L'Eliana
Calle Campoamor 24,
46183 L'Eliana, Valencia
Tel: +34 962 740 272
Age range: 4–19

Institucion Educativa SEK (San Estenislao de Kostka)
Ciudalcampo Urb. San Sebastian de los Reyes, 28707 Madrid
Tel: +34 91 659 63 00
Language instr: Spanish

Instituto Saudi de Madrid
Avenida de Ahones,11,
28043 Madrid
Tel: +34 9138 84406
Language instr: English

Internacional Aravaca
Calle Santa Bernarcita
3, 28023 Madrid
Tel: +34 913 571 256
Curriculum: IBPYP
Language instr: English, Spanish

INTERNATIONAL COLLEGE SPAIN
For further details see p. 170
C/Vereda Norte, 3 La Moraleja,
28109 Alcobendas Madrid
Tel: +34 91 650 2398
Email: admissions@icsmadrid.org
Website: www.nordangliaeducation.com/our-schools/madrid
Director: Chris Bromham
Age range: 3–18 years
Fees: *Day* €10,332–€21,735
Curriculum: IBDP, IBMYP, IBPYP
Language instr: English

International English School of Castellón
Ronda Circunvalación 346-348, 12004 Castellón de la Plana, Castellón, Valencia
Tel: +34 964 261 241

International School of Barcelona
Passeig Isaac Albeniz s/n, Vallpineda, 08870 Sitges, Barcelona, Catalonia
Tel: +34 93 894 20 40
Age range: 2–18
Curriculum: IBDP, National, SAT, UK
Language instr: English

International School of Catalunya (ISCAT)
Manuel Raspall 8, 08530 La Garriga, Barcelona, Catalonia
Tel: +34 93 841 4077
Age range: 3–18
Curriculum: UK
Language instr: English

INTERNATIONAL SCHOOL OF MADRID
For further details see p. 177
Calle Rosa Jardón, 28016 Madrid
Tel: +34 91 359 21 21
Email: info@internationalschoolofmadrid.com
Website: www.internationalschoolofmadrid.com
Heads of School: Mr. Rich Cook & Mr. Huw Mawson
Age range: 2–18 years
No. of pupils: 820 *B*375 *G*445 *VIth*100
Curriculum: UK, IGCSE, ALevs
Language instr: English, Spanish

INTERNATIONAL SCHOOL SAN PATRICIO TOLEDO
For further details see p. 185
Juan de Vergara, 1, Urbanización La Legua, Toledo 45005
Tel: +34 925 280 363
Email: infotoledo@colegiosanpatricio.es
Website: colegiosanpatriciotoledo.com/en
Headmaster: Simon Hatton-Burke
Age range: 3–18 years
No. of pupils: 550
Curriculum: IBDP, IBMYP, IBPYP
Language instr: English, Spanish

Irabia-Izaga Colegio
Calle Cintruénigo, 31015 Pamplona, Navarre
Tel: +34 948 12 62 22
Curriculum: IBDP
Language instr: English, Spanish

Jesuitinas Donostia, Nuestra Señora de Aranzazu
Paseo de Errondo 121, Aiete, 20009 Donostia-San Sebastian, Gipuzkoa, Basque Co+
Tel: +34 943 212 307
Curriculum: IBDP
Language instr: English, Spanish

KENSINGTON SCHOOL
For further details see p. 190
Avenida de Bularas No. 2, Pozuelo de Alarcón, 28224 Madrid
Tel: +34 91 7154 699
Email: kensington@kensingtonschool.net
Website: www.kensington-school.es
Headteacher: Andrew de Salis
Age range: 18 months–18 years
No. of pupils: 2200
Fees: *Day* €6,000–€7,790
Curriculum: UK
Language instr: English

Kensington School Barcelona
Carrer Dels Cavaller 31-33, 08034 Barcelona, Catalonia
Tel: +34 93 203 5457
Age range: 3–18
No. of pupils: 240
Curriculum: UK, IGCSE, ALevs
Language instr: English

King Richard III College
Calle Oratorio 4, Portals Nous, 07181 Calvià, Mallorca, Balearic Islands
Tel: +34 971 675 850/1
Age range: 2–18
No. of pupils: 350 *B*190 *G*160
Curriculum: National, UK, IGCSE, ALevs
Language instr: English

King's College School, The British School of Madrid (La Moraleja)
Paseo de Alcobendas 5, La Moraleja, 28109 Alcobendas, Madrid
Tel: +34 916 585 540
Age range: 2–16 years
Curriculum: UK, IGCSE, ALevs
Language instr: English

King's College, The British School of Alicante
Glorieta del Reino Unido No. 5, 03008 Alicante, Valencia
Tel: +34 96 510 6351
Age range: 2–18 years
Curriculum: UK, IGCSE, ALevs
Language instr: English

KING'S COLLEGE, THE BRITISH SCHOOL OF MADRID (SOTO DE VIÑUELAS)
For further details see p. 194
Paseo de los Andes 35, Soto de Viñuelas, 28760 Madrid
Tel: +34 918 034 800
Email: kc.admissions@kingscollegeschools.org
Website: madrid-soto.kingscollegeschools.org
Head: Matthew Taylor
Age range: 20 months–18 years
No. of pupils: 1490
Fees: *Day* €2,450–€5,885 *FB* €28,326–€34,056
Curriculum: IBDP, UK, GCSE, IGCSE, ALevs
Language instr: English

King's College, The British School of Murcia
Calle Pez Volador s/n, Urbanización La Torre Golf Resort, 30709 Roldán, Murcia
Tel: +34 968 032 500
Age range: 18 months–18 years
Curriculum: UK, GCSE, ALevs
Language instr: English

King's Infant School, The British School of Madrid (Chamartín)
Prieto Urena 9E, 28016 Chamartín, Madrid
Tel: +34 913 505 843
Age range: 18 months–7 years
Language instr: English

La Miranda the Global Quality School
Carrer del Canigó 15, 08960 Sant Just Desvern, Barcelona, Catalonia
Curriculum: IBDP, IBMYP
Language instr: English, Spanish

Laude Colegio Palacio de Granda
C/ El Llugarín, 4, 33199 Granda, Siero, Asturias
Tel: +34 985 792 031
Age range: 1–18 years
No. of pupils: 530
Language instr: English, Spanish

Laude El Altillo School
C/ Santiago de Chile, s/n, 11407 Jerez de la Frontera, Cádiz, Andalusia
Tel: +34 956 302 400
Age range: 2–18 years
No. of pupils: 1120
Curriculum: IBDP, IBMYP, National
Language instr: English, Spanish, French

Laude Fontenebro School
C/ Colonia del Redondillo, 8 Moralzarzal, 28411 Madrid
Tel: +34 91 857 89 42
Age range: 1–18 years
No. of pupils: 500
Language instr: English, Spanish

Laude Lady Elizabeth School
Entrada Norte de la Cumbre del Sol, 03726 Benitachell, Alicante, Valencia
Tel: +34 965 731 960
Age range: 2–18 years
No. of pupils: 960
Curriculum: UK, GCSE, ALevs

Laude Newton College
Camino Viejo de Elche-Alicante Km, 3, Alicante, Valencia
Tel: +34 96 545 14 28
Age range: 1–18 years
No. of pupils: 1306
Curriculum: IBDP, IBMYP
Language instr: Spanish, English

Laude San Pedro International College
Urb.Nueva Alcántara, Avda. La Coruña, 2, 29670 San Pedro de Alcántara, Málaga, Andalusia
Tel: +34 952 799 900
Age range: 3–18 years
No. of pupils: 850
Language instr: English, Spanish

Laude The British School of Vila-real
Ctra. Vila-real a Burriana 3o Sedeny, 12540 Vila-real, Castellón, Valencia
Tel: +34 964 500 155
Age range: 2–18 years
No. of pupils: 610
Curriculum: IPC, UK, GCSE, IGCSE, ALevs
Language instr: English, Spanish

Les Alzines
La Creu de Palau 2, 17003 Girona, Catalonia
Tel: +34 972 212162
Age range: G0–18
Curriculum: IBDP
Language instr: Spanish

Lestonnac L'Ensenyança
Carrer Arc de Sant Llorenç, 2, 43003 Tarragona, Catalonia
Tel: +34 977 23 25 19
Curriculum: IBDP
Language instr: English

Liceo Sorolla c
Avda. Bularas 4, 28224 Pozuelo de Alarcón, Madrid
Tel: +34 91 715 04 99
Curriculum: IBDP
Language instr: English

Lycée Français de Palma
Calle Salud 4, 7014 Palma De Mallorca, Balearic Islands
Tel: +34 971 739260
Age range: 4–18
No. of pupils: 550

Lycée Français Molière
Calle Cristo 27, 28691 Villanueva de la Canada, Madrid
Tel: +34 91 815 50 00
Curriculum: FrenchBacc

Lycée Français Murcie
Avenida del Golf, 107 Urbanización Altorreal, Apartado de correos 133, 30506 Molina de Segura, Murcia
Tel: +34 968 64 80 65
No. of pupils: 650
Curriculum: FrenchBacc

Lycée Français Renée-Verneau de Gran Canaria
Carretera de Taliarte s/n, 35214 Telde, Gran Canaria, Canary Islands
Tel: +34 928 576 091
No. of pupils: 388

Lycée International Barcelona – Bon Soleil
Camí de la Pava, no. 15, Gavà, 08850 Barcelona, Catalonia
Tel: +34 93 633 13 58
Age range: 3–18 years
No. of pupils: 1412
Curriculum: IBDP
Language instr: English, French, Spanish

Maristes Sants Les Corts
C/Vallespir 160, 08014 Barcelona, Catalonia
Tel: +34 934 908 625
Age range: 16–18 years
No. of pupils: 45
Curriculum: IBDP
Language instr: Catalan, Valencian, Spanish

Mayfair International Academy
Avda. De Las Golondrinas, Atalaya Park, Estepona, 29680 Málaga, Andalusia
Tel: +34 952 78 49 23
Age range: 14–19
Curriculum: UK, ALevs

MIRABAL INTERNATIONAL SCHOOL
For further details see p. 206
Calle Monte Almenara, s/n, 28660 Boadilla del Monte, Madrid
Tel: +34 916 331 711
Email: mirabal@colegiomirabal.com
Website: www.colegiomirabal.com
Director: Rosario de la Cruz López
Age range: 0–18 years
No. of pupils: 1957
Curriculum: IBDP, IBMYP
Language instr: English, Spanish

Montessori British School, Murcia
c/ Ermita Vieja, 26B, 30006 Murcia
Tel: +34 868 86 34 16
Age range: 1–12 years
Curriculum: SAT

Montessori School Los Fresnos Mataespesa
Calle Navacerrada 13, 28430 Alpedrete, Madrid
Tel: +34 91 857 1743
Age range: 11–18
No. of pupils: 200

Montjuïc Girona International School
C/ Bellpuig, Nº 8-10, 17007 Girona, Catalonia
Tel: +34 972 212 838
Age range: 0 years–18 years
No. of pupils: 250
Language instr: Spanish, Catalan, English, French

Morna International College
Apartado 333, Santa Gertrudis, 07814 Ibiza, Balearic Islands
Tel: +34 971 19 76 72
Age range: 3–18
Curriculum: UK, IGCSE, ALevs
Language instr: English

New Castelar College
Las Palmas S/N 30740, San Pedro del Pinatar, Murcia
Tel: +34 968 178 276
Language instr: English, Spanish
ECIS

Novaschool Sunland International
Cartera Cartama-Pizarra, Nueva Aljaima, Cartama Estacion, Málaga, Andalusia
Tel: +34 952 42 4253
Age range: 3–18
No. of pupils: 180 *B*90 *G*90
Curriculum: National, UK

Numont School
C/ Parma, 16, 28043 Madrid
Tel: +34 913 002 431
Age range: 3–11
No. of pupils: 320

O CASTRO BRITISH INTERNATIONAL SCHOOL (VIGO)
For further details see p. 211
Camiño San Cosme 1, 36419 San Pedro de Cela (Mos), Pontevedra, Galicia
Tel: +34 986 20 00 28
Email: admissions@bisocastro.com
Website: www.bisocastro.com
Executive Head: Chistopher Long
Age range: 3–18 years
No. of pupils: 715
Curriculum: National, UK
Language instr: English, Spanish, French, Galician

Oakley College
Calle Zuloaga, 17, Tafira Alta, 35017 Las Palmas de Gran Canaria, Las Palmas, Can+
Tel: +34 928 354247
Age range: 2–18
No. of pupils: 610 *B*310 *G*300 *VIth*40
Curriculum: UK, GCSE, IGCSE, ALevs

Phoenix International School
Calle Albacete, Urb Las Comunicaciones, 03193 San Miguel de Salinas, Valencia
Tel: +34 965 720 785
Age range: 1–18
No. of pupils: 130

Princess Margaret School
Passeig de la Fond d'en Fargas 15-17, 8032 Barcelona, Catalonia
Tel: +34 934 290 313
Age range: 3–16
Curriculum: IBMYP, IBPYP
Language instr: English, Spanish

Queen's College, The English School
Juan de Saridakis 64, 07015 Palma de Mallorca, Balearic Islands
Tel: +34 971 401011
Age range: 3–18
No. of pupils: 423 *B*185 *G*223 *VIth*50
Curriculum: National, UK, GCSE, IGCSE, ALevs
Language instr: English

Richmond International School
Rambla del Garraf 14-16, 08810 Sant Pere de Ribes, Barcelona, Catalonia
Tel: +34 93 893 67 12
Age range: 3–18
Curriculum: UK, IGCSE
Language instr: English

Runnymede College
c/Salvia 30, La Moraleja, 28109 Alcobendas, Madrid
Tel: +34 916 508 302
Age range: 3–18
No. of pupils: 702 *B*361 *G*341
Curriculum: UK, IGCSE, ALevs
Language instr: English

Santa Clara International School
Carrer de Pomaret 17-19, 08017 Barcelona, Catalonia
Tel: +34 93 212 35 93

Scandinavian School of Madrid
Camino Ancho 14, La Moraleja, 28109 Alcobendas, Madrid
Tel: +34 91 650 01 27
Age range: 2–18
Curriculum: National
CIS

Schellhammer International School
Calle Flaminio 2, Urb. Valle Romano, 29680 Estepona, Málaga, Andalusia
Tel: +34 952 907 892
Age range: 16–18
Curriculum: ALevs

SEK INTERNATIONAL SCHOOL ALBORÁN
For further details see p. 223
C/ Barlovento 141, Urb. Almerimar, El Ejido, 04711 Almeria, Andalusia
Tel: +34 900 87 87 98
Email: sek-alboran@sek.es
Website: alboran.sek.es
Principal: Luis Carlos Jiménez Gómez
Age range: 4 months–18 years
No. of pupils: 756
Curriculum: IBDP, IBMYP, IBPYP
Language instr: English, Spanish

SEK INTERNATIONAL SCHOOL ATLÁNTICO
For further details see p. 224
Rúa Illa de Arousa 4, Boavista. A Caeira, Poio, 36005 Pontevedra, Galicia
Tel: +34 900 87 87 98
Email: sek-atlantico@sek.es
Website: atlantico.sek.es
Principal: Jacobo Olmedo
Age range: 4 months–18 years
No. of pupils: 730
Curriculum: IBDP, IBMYP, IBPYP
Language instr: Spanish, English

SEK INTERNATIONAL SCHOOL CATALUNYA
For further details see p. 225
Av. del Tremolencs, 24, La Garriga, 08530 Barcelona, Catalonia
Tel: +34 900 87 87 98
Email: sek-catalunya@sek.es
Website: catalunya.sekinternationalschools.com
Principal: Roberto Prata
Age range: 4 months–18 years
No. of pupils: 970
Curriculum: IBDP, IBMYP, IBPYP
Language instr: English, Spanish, Catalan

SEK INTERNATIONAL SCHOOL CIUDALCAMPO
For further details see p. 226
Urb. Ciudalcampo, Paseo de las Perdices, 2, San Sebastián de los Reyes, 28707 Madrid
Tel: +34 900 87 87 98
Email: sek-ciudalcampo@sek.es
Website: ciudalcampo.sek.es
Principal: Cecilia Villavicencio
Age range: 4 months–18 years
No. of pupils: 1400
Curriculum: IBDP, IBMYP, IBPYP
Language instr: English, Spanish

SEK INTERNATIONAL SCHOOL EL CASTILLO
For further details see p. 227
Urb. Villafranca del Castillo, Castillo de Manzanares, s/n, Villanueva de la Cañada, 28692 Madrid
Tel: +34 91 815 08 92
Email: sek-castillo@sek.es
Website: madrid.sekinternationalschools.com
Head of School: Eloísa López
Age range: 4 months–18 years
No. of pupils: 1210
Curriculum: IBDP, IBMYP, IBPYP, National
Language instr: English, Spanish

SEK INTERNATIONAL SCHOOL SANTA ISABEL
For further details see p. 229
Calle San Ildefonso, 18, 28012 Madrid
Tel: +34 900 87 87 98
Email: sek-santaisabel@sek.es
Website: santaisabel.sek.es
Head of School: Jennifer Pro
Age range: 3–12 years
No. of pupils: 334
Curriculum: IBPYP
Language instr: English, Spanish

Shoreless Lake School
Apdo 239, 30850 Totana, Murcia
Tel: +34 968 424 386
Age range: 14–18
No. of pupils: 200
Curriculum: AP, USA

Sierra Bernia School
San Rafael S/N, Alfaz del Pi, 03580 Alicante, Valencia
Tel: +34 96 687 5149
Age range: 3–18
No. of pupils: 100 *B50 G50*
Curriculum: UK, GCSE, IGCSE, ALevs
Language instr: English

SOTOGRANDE INTERNATIONAL SCHOOL
For further details see p. 231
Avenida La Reserva SN, Sotogrande, Cádiz, 11310
Tel: +34 956 795 902
Email: info@sis.gl
Website: www.sis.ac
Head of School: James Kearney
Age range: 4 months–18 years
No. of pupils: 1021
Fees: €8,025–€23,100
Curriculum: IBDP, IBMYP, IBPYP, National
Language instr: English

St George's English Academy Bilbao
Alameda Urquijo 100, 48013 Bilbao, Biscay, Basque Country
Tel: +34 944 772 989

St Paul's School
Avenida Pearson 39-45, C/ Joan d'Alòs 19 · 21, 08034 Barcelona, Catalonia
Tel: +34 932 030 500
Age range: 3–18
No. of pupils: 670
Curriculum: UK

St Peter's School Barcelona
C/Eduard Toldrà, 18, 08034 Barcelona, Catalonia
Tel: +34 93 204 36 12
Age range: 1–18
Curriculum: IBDP, IBMYP, IBPYP
Language instr: English, Spanish

St. Anthony's College
Camino de Coin KM 5,25, Mijas Costa, 29649 Málaga, Andalusia
Tel: +34 952 47 31 66
Age range: 3–18
No. of pupils: 400
Curriculum: IGCSE

St. George, The British School Madrid
Calle Padres Dominicos 1, 28050 Madrid
Tel: +34 916 508 440
Age range: 2–18 years
Curriculum: IBDP, UK, IGCSE
Language instr: English, Spanish

St. George, The British School of Catalunya
Paseo de la Reina Elisenda de Montcada 18, 08034 Barcelona, Catalonia
Tel: +34 931 293 024
Age range: 2–18 years
Curriculum: IBDP, UK, IGCSE
Language instr: English, Spanish

ST. GEORGE'S BRITISH INTERNATIONAL SCHOOL (BILBAO)
For further details see p. 239
Artazagane 51, 48940 Leioia, Biscay, Basque Country
Tel: +34 94 4633692
Email: admissions@bisstgeorges.com
Website: www.bisstgeorges.com
Director: Juan Martorell
No. of pupils: 300
Curriculum: National, UK, IGCSE
Language instr: English, Spanish, French, Basque

St. Michael's – El Parque
C/ Río Guadiana 2, 28669 Boadilla del Monte, Madrid
Tel: +34 91 633 00 78

St. Michael's – Escorial
C/Udala 13, Urb la Pizarra,, San Lorenzo de El Escorial, 28200 Madrid
Tel: +34 91 896 21 69
Age range: 6–18
No. of pupils: 300
Curriculum: UK

St. Michael's – Las Lomas
C/Valle de Bielsa 4, 28669 Boadilla del Monte, Madrid
Tel: +34 91 307 71 74
Age range: 6–18
No. of pupils: 300
Curriculum: UK

Sunny View School
c/ Tereul No 32, Cerro de Toril, 29620 Torremolinos, Málaga, Andalusia
Tel: +34 952 383164
Age range: 4–18
No. of pupils: 300
Curriculum: ALevs

Swans International Primary School
Urbanizacion El Capricho s/n, 29602 Marbella, Málaga, Andalusia
Tel: +34 952 773 248
Age range: 3–11
No. of pupils: 250
Curriculum: IPC

Swans International Secondary School
C/Lago de los Cisnes, s/n, Urb. Sierra Blanca, 29602 Marbella, Málaga, Andalusia
Tel: +34 952 902 755
Age range: 3–18
No. of pupils: *B340 G340 VIth55*
Curriculum: IBDP, IGCSE
Language instr: English

The Academy International School
Camí de Son Ametler Vell, 250, 07141 Marratxí, Balearic Islands
Tel: +34 971 605008
Age range: 2–19 years
Curriculum: IBDP, UK, IGCSE
Language instr: English

The Benalmádena International College
Clle Catamaran s/n, Nueva Torrequebrada, 29630 Benalmádena, Málaga, Andalusia
Tel: +34 952 561 666
Age range: 4–19
No. of pupils: 300
Curriculum: UK

The British College
Urbanización Torremuelle, C/ Paseo del Genil s/n, 29630 Benalmádena Costa, Málaga, Andalusia
Tel: +34 952 44 22 15
Age range: 1–18
Curriculum: National, UK, IGCSE, ALevs

The British International School of Marbella
Calle Jacinto Benavente S/N, 29601 Marbella, Málaga, Andalusia
Tel: +34 952 779 264
Age range: 2–12
Curriculum: UK
Language instr: English

The British School of Almeria
Calle de Alemania 28, Roquetas De Mar 04740, Almeria, Andalusia
Tel: +34 950 338 860
Age range: 3–18
Curriculum: UK, IGCSE
Language instr: English

The British School of Aragon
Calle Valencia, KM 8,500, 50410 Cuarte de Huerva, Zaragoza
Tel: +34 976 50 52 23
Curriculum: IBDP
Language instr: English, Spanish

The British School of Barcelona
Calle Ginesta 26, Castelldefels, 08860 Barcelona, Catalonia
Tel: +34 93 665 1584
Age range: 3–18
No. of pupils: *B489 G481*
Curriculum: IBCP, UK, IGCSE, ALevs
Language instr: English

The British School of Málaga
Avenida Centaurea 8, Cerrado de Calderón 29018, Málaga, Andalusia
Tel: +34 952 290 149
Age range: 3–18
No. of pupils: 675
Curriculum: National, IGCSE, ALevs
Language instr: English

The British School of Navarra
Avenida Juan Pablo II, 31004 Pamplona, Navarre
Tel: +34 948 242 826
Curriculum: UK
Language instr: English

The British School of Seville
Urbanizacion Pinar de la Juliana, Bollullos de la Mitacion, Seville
Tel: +34 902 024 890
Age range: 5–16
Curriculum: UK, IGCSE
Language instr: English, Spanish

The English International College
Urb Ricmar, Crtr de Cádiz Km 189.5, 29600 Marbella, Málaga, Andalusia
Tel: +34 952 83 1058/9
Age range: 3–18
No. of pupils: 500
Curriculum: SAT, UK, GCSE, IGCSE, ALevs
Language instr: English
COB

The English School
Calle Pintor Gisbert, 3, Mutxamel, 3110 Alicante, Valencia
Tel: +34 965 95 10 17
Curriculum: UK
Language instr: English, Spanish

The Global College
C. de Castellón de la Plana 8, 28006 Madrid
Tel: +34 915 689 937
Curriculum: IBDP
Language instr: English, Spanish

The International School Estepona
Centro Commercial La Zarza Calle Azahar, Urbanisation El Paraiso, 29688 Estepona, Málaga, Andalusia
Tel: +34 952 88 47 89
Age range: 2–12
Curriculum: SAT, UK

Willow International School
Pueblo Bravo, Av. del Mar, 2b, 03170 Ciudad Quesada, Alicante, Valencia
Tel: +34 602 490 917
Age range: 6–18
Curriculum: UK
Language instr: English

Wingate School
Mirador de la Cumbrita, 10, Cabo Blanco, Arona, Tenerife, Canary Islands
Tel: +34 922 720 102
Curriculum: UK, IGCSE, ALevs

Xàbia International School (Primary)
Ctra Partitxol 70, Alicante, Valencia
Tel: +34 96 647 21 21
Age range: 2–11
No. of pupils: 160
Curriculum: UK

Xàbia International School (Secondary)
Apartado de Correos 311, 03730 Jávea, Alicante, Valencia
Tel: +34 96 647 1785
Age range: 12–18
No. of pupils: 130
Curriculum: UK, ALevs
Language instr: English, Spanish, German, French

Yago School
Avda. Antonio Mairena, 54, 41950 Castilleja de la Cuesta, Seville, Andalusia
Tel: +34 955 51 1234
Age range: 0–18 years
No. of pupils: 800
Curriculum: IBDP
Language instr: English, Spanish

Zürich Schule Barcelona
73 Pearson Avenue, 08034 Barcelona, Catalonia
Tel: +34 932 037 606
Curriculum: IBPYP
Language instr: German, Spanish

SWEDEN

Aranäsgymnasiet
Gymnasiegatan 44, 434 42 Kungsbacka, Halland
Tel: +46 300 83 40 00
No. of pupils: 1400
Curriculum: IBDP
Language instr: English

Bladins International School of Malmö
Box 20093, Själlandstorget 1, 200 74 Malmö, Skåne
Tel: +46 40 987970
Age range: 3–16
No. of pupils: 371
Curriculum: IBDP, IBMYP, IBPYP
Language instr: English
ECIS

British International School of Stockholm
Östrka Valhallavagen 17, 182 68 Djursholm, Stockholm
Tel: +46 8 755 2375
Age range: 3–16
No. of pupils: 334 *B*183 *G*151
Curriculum: IBDP, SAT, UK
Language instr: English
COB ECIS

Engelska Skolan Norr
Roslagstullsbacken 4, Stockholm
Curriculum: UK

Europaskolan in Södermalm
Gotlandsgatan 43, 116 65 Stockholm
Tel: +46 8 335054
Curriculum: IBMYP, IBPYP

Futuraskolan International School of Stockholm
Erik Dahlbergsgatan 58, 115 57 Stockholm
Tel: +46 736 001 314
Language instr: English, Swedish
ECIS

International IT College of Sweden
Halsobrunnsgatan 6, 104 30 Stockholm
Tel: +46 8 704 22 15
Age range: 16–19

International Pre School of Lund
Warholmsvag 2, 224 65 Lund, Skåne
Tel: +46 46140767
Age range: 3–6
No. of pupils: 30

International School of Helsingborg
Östra Vallgatan 9, 254 37 Helsingborg, Skåne
Tel: +46 42 105 705
Age range: 3–20
No. of pupils: 450
Curriculum: IBDP, IBMYP, IBPYP, SAT
Language instr: English
ECIS

International School of the Gothenburg Region (ISGR)
Molinsgatan 6, 411 33 Göteborg, Västra Götaland
Tel: +46 31 708 92 00
Age range: 5–18
No. of pupils: 831
Curriculum: IBMYP, IBPYP
Language instr: English
CIS ECIS

Internationella Engelska Skolan
Ostgotagatan 12, 582 32 Linköping, Östergötland
Tel: +46 13 35 5680
Age range: 4–19
No. of pupils: 800

Internationella Engelska Skolan Orebro
Hagmarksgatan 39, Örebro
Tel: +46 19 2652240
Age range: 6–9
No. of pupils: 480

Internationella Engelska Skolan Taby (Junior School)
Nytorpsvägen 36, 183 53 Taby, Stockholm
Tel: +46 8 120 457 66
No. of pupils: 1120
Curriculum: National

Kungsholmen's Gymnasium, International Section
Hantverkargatan 67-69, PO Box 12601, 112 92 Stockholm
Tel: +46 8 508 38 006
Age range: 16–20
No. of pupils: 450 *B*175 *G*275
Language instr: English
ECIS

Lund International School
Warholmsväg 3, 224 65 Lund, Skåne
Tel: +46737087926
Age range: 3–13
No. of pupils: 170 *B*85 *G*85
Curriculum: IBMYP, IBPYP
Language instr: English

Lycée Français Saint Louis de Stockholm
Essingestråket 24, 112 66 Stockholm
Tel: +46 8 4413030
Age range: 6–18
No. of pupils: 600

Malmö Borgarskola
Box 17029, 200 10 Malmö, Skåne
Tel: +46 4034 1000
Age range: 16–19
No. of pupils: 240 *B*90 *G*150
Curriculum: IBDP, IBCP
Language instr: English
ECIS

Malmö International School
Packhusgatan 2, 205 80 Malmö, Skåne
Tel: +46 (0)733 23 70 37
Age range: 6–16
No. of pupils: 360
Curriculum: IBMYP, IBPYP
Language instr: English
ECIS

Sigtunaskolan Humanistiska Läroverket
Box 508, 193 28 Sigtunase, Stockholm
Tel: +46 8 592 571 00
Age range: 13–19
Curriculum: IBDP, IBMYP, IBCP
Language instr: English, Swedish

Stockholm International School
Johannesgatan 18, 111 38 Stockholm
Tel: +46 (0)8 412 40 00
Age range: 3–18
No. of pupils: 600
Curriculum: IBDP, IBMYP, SAT
Language instr: English
CIS ECIS

Uppsala International School – Kvarngärdesskolan
Thunmansgatan 47, 754 21 Uppsala
Tel: +46 18 727 5900
Age range: 6–16
No. of pupils: 104 *B*52 *G*52
ECIS

SWITZERLAND

academia College
Lagerstrasse 1, 8004 Zürich ZH
Tel: +41 58 440 90 2[illegible]

ACADEMIA SCHOOLS
For further details see p. 120
Steinentorstrasse 30,
4051 Basel BS
Tel: +41 61 260 20 [illegible]0
Email:
info@academia-group.ch
Website:
www.academia-schools.ch
Co-CEOs Academia Schools: Ludovic Allenspach, Roman Meier & Peter Petrin
Age range: 3–18 years
Curriculum: National, IGCSE, ALevs
Language instr: English, German

Aiglon College
Avenue Centrale 61, 1885 Chesières
Tel: +41 (0)24 496 61[illegible]7
Age range: 9–18 years
No. of pupils: 420
Curriculum: IBDP, SAT, UK, IGCSE
Language instr: English
CIS COB ECIS RS

Bilingual School Terra Nova
Florastr 19, 8700 Küsnacht ZH
Tel: +41 44 910 43 00
Age range: 4–14
No. of pupils: 200 *B*102 *G*98
Curriculum: National
Language instr: German, English
ECIS

BKA International School
Gellertstrasse 25, 4052 Basel BS
Tel: +41 61 311 76 62
Curriculum: IBPYP
Language instr: English, German

Brillantmont International School
Avenue Secrétan 16
1005 Lausanne VD
Tel: +41 21 310 04 00
Age range: 11–18
No. of pupils: 140
Curriculum: AP, SAT, UK, USA, IGCSE, ALevs
Language instr: English
CIS ECIS

British School of Geneva
Avenue de Châtelaine 95A, Châtelaine, 1219 Geneva GE
Tel: +41 22 795 75 10
Age range: 4–18
Curriculum: UK, IGCSE, ALevs
Language instr: English
COB

Buissonnets Montani
Rue Saint-Guérin 26, 1950 Sion VS
Tel: +41 27 322 00 80

Campus Muristalden Gymnasium
Muristrasse 8, 3000 Bern BE
Tel: +41 31 350 42 50

Collège Alpin Beau Soleil
Route du Village 1, 1884 Villars-sur-Ollon
Tel: +41 24 496 26 26
Age range: 11–18 years
Curriculum: IBDP, National, FrenchBacc, SAT, TOEFL, UK, IGCSE
Language instr: English, French

Collège Champittet, Nyon
Chemin du Joran 11a, 1260 Nyon VD
Tel: +41 22 364 52 50
Age range: 3–10
Curriculum: National

Collège Champittet, Pully
Chemin de Champittet 1, 1009 Pully VD
Tel: +41 21 721 05 05
Age range: 3–18 years
No. of pupils: 600
Curriculum: IBDP, National, FrenchBacc
Language instr: French, English

COLLÈGE DU LÉMAN
For further details see p. 140
74, route de Sauverny, 1290 Versoix GE
Tel: +41 22 775 56 56
Email: admissions@cdl.ch
Website: www.cdl.ch
Director General: Pauline Nord
Age range: 2–18 years
Fees: *Day* CHF22,900–CHF35,900 *FB* CHF85,490–CHF97,200
Curriculum: AP, IBDP, IPC, National, FrenchBacc, SAT, IGCSE, ALevs
Language instr: English, French
CIS ECIS

Collège et Lycée St-Charles
Route de Belfort 10, 2900 Porrentruy JU
Tel: +41 32 466 11 57
Curriculum: IBDP, IBMYP
Language instr: English

Ecole des Arches
Chemin de Mornex 2-4, PO Box 566, 1001 Lausanne VD
Tel: +41 21 311 09 69
Age range: 16–21
No. of pupils: *B*120 *G*80
Curriculum: IBDP
Language instr: French

ECOLE D'HUMANITÉ
For further details see p. 143
Gmeindi 318b, 6085 Hasliberg Goldern BE
Tel: +41 33 972 9292
Email: admisions@ecole.ch
Website: www.ecole.ch
Head: Katja Braun
Age range: 12–19 years
No. of pupils: 120
Fees: *Day* CHF28,000 *FB* CHF65,000–CHF68,000
Curriculum: AP, USA
Language instr: German, English

Ecole française de Bâle – Section Elémentaire
Engelgasse 103, 4052 Basel BS
Tel: +41 61 311 07 30
Age range: 6–11
No. of pupils: 100

Ecole Francaise de Berne
Sulgenrain 11, 3007 Bern BE
Tel: +41 31 376 17 57
No. of pupils: 150
Curriculum: National

Ecole française de Lausanne Valmont
Route d'Oron 47, 1010 Lausanne VD
Tel: 41 (0)21 652 37 33
Curriculum: FrenchBacc

Ecole Mosaic
23, avenue Dumas, 1206 Geneva GE
Tel: +41 22 346 21 69
Age range: 3–12
No. of pupils: 250
Curriculum: UK
Language instr: English, French
COB

Ecole Moser Genève
81 Chemin De-La-Montagne, 1224 Chêne-Bougeries GE
Tel: +41 (0)22 860 80 80
Curriculum: IBDP
Language instr: English, French

Ecole Moser Nyon
4-6 Avenue Reverdil, 1260 Nyon VD
Tel: +41 (0)22 593 88 88
Curriculum: IBDP
Language instr: English, French

Ecole Nouvelle de la Suisse Romande – Chailly
Chemin de Rovéréaz 20, CP 161, 1012 Lausanne
Tel: +41 21 654 65 00
Age range: 3–18
No. of pupils: 600
Curriculum: IBDP
Language instr: French, English
CIS

École Primaire Française de Genève
3 Chemin des Vergers, 1208 Geneva GE
Tel: +41 22 735 60 20
Age range: 5–11

Ecole Riviera
Avenue des Planches 25, Case Postale 1347, 1820 Montreux VD
Tel: +41 21 961 18 72
Age range: 3 months–12 years

ELA Basel
Gartenstrasse 93, 4052 Basel BS
Tel: +41 61 313 05 80
Curriculum: UK
Language instr: English
COB

Freies Gymnasium Zürich
Arbenzstrasse 19, 8034 Zürich ZH
Tel: +41 43 456 77 77
Age range: 11–14
Language instr: English, German

Geneva English School
36 Route de Malagny, 1294 Genthod GE
Tel: +41 22 775 0440
Age range: 3–14
No. of pupils: 286
Curriculum: UK, IGCSE, ALevs
Language instr: English
COB

Gymnasium, Wirtschafts- und Fachmittelschule Thun
Seestrasse 66, 3604 Thun BE
Tel: +41 (0)33 359 58 58
Age range: 14–19
Curriculum: National

HAUT-LAC INTERNATIONAL BILINGUAL SCHOOL
For further details see p. 156
Ch. de Pangires 26, St-Légier-la Chiésaz CH-1806
Tel: +41 (0)21 555 50 00
Email: admissions@haut-lac.ch
Website: www.haut-lac.ch
Infant & Primary Head: Lucy Sumner
Age range: 18 months–18 years
No. of pupils: 600
Fees: *Day* CHF24,900–CHF36,100 *FB* CHF72,000–CHF88,000
Curriculum: IBDP, IBMYP, USA

HOCHALPINES INSTITUT FTAN (HIF)
For further details see p. 158
Chalchera 154, 7551 Ftan GR
Tel: +41 81 861 22 11
Email: admissions@hif.ch
Website: www.hif.ch
Heads of School: Stefanie Aichholz & Dr. Christoph Hendrickx
Age range: 12–18 years
No. of pupils: 70
Fees: *FB* CHF57,000–CHF64,000 CHF6,000
Curriculum: IBDP, IGCSE
Language instr: English, German

Hull's School
Falkenstrasse 28a, 8008 Zürich ZH
Tel: +41 44 254 30 40
Age range: 16–19
Curriculum: GCSE, ALevs

Institut auf dem Rosenberg
Hohenweg 60, 9000 St Gallen SG
Tel: +41 71 277 77 77
Age range: 7–19
No. of pupils: 150 *B*90 *G*60
Curriculum: IBDP
Language instr: English, German
ECIS

Institut Florimont
37 Avenue du Petit-Lancy, 1213 Petit-Lancy GE
Tel: +41 2287 90000
Age range: 3–18 years
No. of pupils: 1625
Curriculum: IBDP, FrenchBacc, SAT, IGCSE
Language instr: English, French

Institut International de Lancy
24, avenue Eugène-Lance, Grand-Lancy CH-1212
Tel: +41 22 794 2620
Age range: 3–19 years
No. of pupils: 1420
Curriculum: IBDP, FrenchBacc, IGCSE
Language instr: English, French

INSTITUT LE CHÂTELARD
For further details see p. 166
Route des Narcisses 80, 1833 Les-Avants-sur-Montreux
Tel: +41 21 989 8000
Email: info@lechatelard.com
Website: www.ecolechatelard.ch
Head of School: Veronica Canales
Age range: *G*13–18 years
No. of pupils: 96
Fees: *FB* CHF86,032–CHF102,937
Language instr: French

Institut Le Rosey
Château du Rosey, 1180 Rolle VD
Tel: +41 21 822 5500
Age range: 8–18
No. of pupils: 420 *B*210 *G*210 *VIth*160
Curriculum: ACT, IBDP, IPC, FrenchBacc, SAT, TOEFL
Language instr: English, French
CIS ECIS

INSTITUT MONTANA
For further details see p. 167
Schönfels 5, 6300 Zug ZG
Tel: +41 41 729 11 77
Email: admissions@montana-zug.ch
Website: www.montana-zug.ch
Director: Alexander Biner
Age range: 6–19 years
No. of pupils: 370
Curriculum: IBDP, USA
Language instr: English, German
CIS ECIS

Institut Monte Rosa
Avenue de Chillon 57, 1820 Montreux VD
Tel: +41 21 965 4545
Age range: 8–20
No. of pupils: 70 *B*45 *G*25
Curriculum: AP, SAT, TOEFL, USA
Language instr: English
ECIS

Institut Villa Pierrefeu
Route de Caux 28, 1823 Glion Sur Montreux VD
Tel: +41 21 963 73 11
Age range: *G*15–30+
No. of pupils: 30

INTER-COMMUNITY SCHOOL ZURICH
For further details see p. 168
Strubenacher 3, 8126 Zumikon
Tel: +41 44 919 8300
Email: contact@icsz.ch
Website: www.icsz.ch
Head of School: Lucy Gowdie
Age range: 18 months–18 years
No. of pupils: 840
Fees: *Day* CHF12,220–CHF36,950
Curriculum: IBDP, IBMYP, IBPYP
Language instr: English
CIS ECIS RS

International School Altdorf
St. Josefsweg 15, 6460 Altdorf UR
Tel: +41 41 874 0000
Age range: 13–19 years
No. of pupils: 100
Curriculum: IBDP, IBCP, IGCSE
Language instr: English

International School Basel
Fleischbachstrasse 2, 4153 Reinach
Tel: +41 61 715 33 33
Age range: 3–19 years
No. of pupils: 1248
Curriculum: IBDP, IBMYP, IBPYP, SAT
Language instr: English
ECIS

International School of Berne
Allmendingenweg 9, 3073 Gümligen, Bern
Tel: +41 (0)31 959 10 00
Age range: 3–19 years
No. of pupils: 276
Curriculum: IBDP, IBMYP, IBPYP
Language instr: English
CIS ECIS

International School of Central Switzerland
Lorzenparkstrasse 8, 6330 Cham ZG
Tel: +41 41 781 44 44
Age range: 3–18 years
Curriculum: IBDP, IBPYP
Language instr: English

International School of Geneva (Campus des Nations)
11 route des Morillons, 1218 Grand Saconnex GE
Tel: +41 22 770 4700
Age range: 3–11
No. of pupils: 963
Curriculum: IBDP, IBMYP, IBPYP, IBCP
Language instr: English, French

International School of Geneva (La Châtaigneraie Campus)
2 chemin de la Ferme, 1297 Founex VD
Tel: +41 22 960 9111
Age range: 3–19
No. of pupils: 1538
Curriculum: IBDP, IBPYP, IGCSE
Language instr: English, French

International School of Geneva (La Grande Boissière Campus)
62, route de Chêne, 1208 Geneva GE
Tel: +41 22 787 2400
Age range: 3–19
No. of pupils: 4438 *B*2326 *G*2112 *VIth*320
Curriculum: IBDP
Language instr: English, French

International School of Kreuzlingen Konstanz
Hauptstrasse 27, 8280 Kreuzlingen TG
Tel: +41 71 672 2727
Age range: 3–18 years
Language instr: English, German, French

International School of Lausanne
Chemin de la Grangette 2, 1052 Le Mont-sur-Lausanne VD
Tel: +41 21 560 02 02
Age range: 3–18
No. of pupils: 880
Curriculum: IBDP, IBMYP, IBPYP, SAT
Language instr: English
CIS ECIS

International School of Rheinfelden
Zürcherstrasse 9, Drei Könige, 4310 Rheinfelden AG
Tel: +41 61 831 06 06
Age range: 2–14
No. of pupils: 80
Curriculum: IBPYP
Language instr: English, German

International School of Schaffhausen
Mühlentalstrasse 280, 8200 Schaffhausen SH
Tel: +41 52 624 1707
Age range: 1–18
No. of pupils: *B*125 *G*98 *VIth*10
Curriculum: IBDP, IBMYP, IBPYP
Language instr: English

INTERNATIONAL SCHOOL OF TICINO SA
For further details see p. 184
Via Ponteggia, 23, Cadempino, 6814 Lugano
Tel: +41 919710344
Email: frontoffice@isticino.com
Website: www.isticino.com
Head of School: Andrew Ackers
Age range: 3–18 years
No. of pupils: 230
Curriculum: IBDP, IBMYP, IBPYP
Language instr: English, Italian

International School of Zug & Luzern, Riverside Campus
Rothustrasse 4b, 6331 Hünenberg ZG
Tel: +41 41 768 2950
Age range: 12–18
Curriculum: AP, IBDP, IBMYP, IBCP, SAT, TOEFL
Language instr: English
ECIS

International School of Zug & Luzern, Zug Campus
Walterswil, 6340 Baar ZG
Tel: +41 41 768 29 00
Age range: 3–18
No. of pupils: 1250
Curriculum: UK, USA
Language instr: English
ECIS

International School Rheintal
Aeulistrasse 10, 9470 Buchs SG
Tel: +41 81 750 6300
Age range: 3–18
No. of pupils: 142
Curriculum: IBDP, IBMYP, IBPYP
Language instr: English

International School Zurich North
Industriestrasse 50, 8304 Wallisellen ZH
Tel: +41 44 830 7000
Age range: 2–18
No. of pupils: 200 B100 G100
Curriculum: IBPYP, IGCSE
Language instr: English

International School Zurich West
Unterrohrstrasse 3, 8952 Schlieren ZH
Tel: +41 44 433 3000
Age range: 3–11

John F. Kennedy International School
8 Chilchgasse, 3792 Saanen BE
Tel: +41 (0) 33 755 15 74
Age range: 2.5–14 years
No. of pupils: 100
Curriculum: IPC
Language instr: English, French

Juventus Schule Zürich
Lagerstrasse 45, Postfach 3021, Zürich 8021
Tel: +41 43 268 25 11
Age range: 16–21
No. of pupils: 1000 B500 G500
Language instr: English, German, French, Italian

Kantonsschule Baden
Seminarstrasse 3, 5400 Baden AG
Tel: +41 056 200 04 44

Kantonsschule Kusnacht
village Strasse 30, 8700 Kusnacht ZH
Tel: +41 44 913 1717

Kumon Leysin Academy of Switzerland
1854 Leysin VD
Tel: +41 24 4935 335
Age range: 16–19
No. of pupils: 182 B85 G97
Curriculum: AP, SAT, TOEFL

La Côte International School Aubonne
Chemin de Clamogne 8, 1170 Aubonne VD
Tel: +41 (0)22 823 26 26
Age range: 2–18 years
No. of pupils: 420
Curriculum: IBDP, IBMYP, IPC, National, UK, IGCSE
Language instr: English French

La Garenne International School
Chemin des Chavasses 23, 1885 Chesières-Villars VD
Tel: +41 24 495 29 38
Age range: 5–19 years
No. of pupils: 150
Curriculum: IBDP, IBMYP, UK
Language instr: English, French

Lakeside School Horgen
Alte Landstrasse 33-35, 8810 Horgen ZH
Tel: +41 43 244 00 70
Curriculum: National
Language instr: English, German

Lakeside School Küsnacht
Seestrasse 5, 8700 Kusnacht ZH
Tel: +41 44 914 2050
Age range: 3–12
Curriculum: National
Language instr: English, German

Le Régent International School
Rue du Zier 4, CH-3963 Crans-Montana
Tel: +41 (0)27 480 3201
Age range: 3–18 years
Curriculum: IBDP
Language instr: English, French

Lemania – Verbier International School
Chalet Mascotte, Route de Verbier Station 88, 1936 Verbier VS
Tel: +41 27 565 26 56
Age range: 3–16
No. of pupils: 80
Curriculum: UK, IGCSE
Language instr: English, French

Lemania College Lausanne
Chemin de Préville 3, 1003 Lausanne VD
Tel: +41 21 320 15 01
Age range: 15–20 years
No. of pupils: 30
Curriculum: IBDP
Language instr: English

Leysin American School in Switzerland
3 Chemin de la Source, 1854 Leysin VD
Tel: +41 24 493 4878
Age range: 12–18 years
No. of pupils: 300
Curriculum: AP, IBDP, USA
Language instr: English

Lyceum Alpinum Zuoz
Aguêl 185, 7524 Zuoz GR
Tel: +41 81 851 30 00
Age range: 12–19 years
No. of pupils: 315
Curriculum: IBDP, IBCP
Language instr: English, German

Montreux International School
Avenue de Chillon 60, 1820 Montreux VD
Tel: +41 79 596 29 06
Curriculum: IBCP
Language instr: English

Mutuelle d'études secondaires
7 bis Boulevard Carl Vogt, 1205 Geneva GE
Tel: +41 (0)22 741 00 01
Age range: 15–22
No. of pupils: 60
Curriculum: IBDP
Language instr: French

Neuchâtel Junior College
Cret Taconnet 4, 2002 Neuchatel NE
Tel: +41 (0)32 722 1860
Age range: 16–18 years
No. of pupils: 75
Curriculum: AP, SAT
Language instr: English

Obersee Bilingual School
Eichenstrasse 4C, 8808 Pfaeffikon ZH
Tel: +41 55 511 38 00
Curriculum: IBDP
Language instr: English, German

Rudolf Steiner Schule Oberaargau
Ringstrasse 30, 4900 Langenthal BE
Tel: +41 (0)62 922 69 05
Curriculum: IBDP
Language instr: English, German

Scuola Rudolf Steiner ii Lugano Origlio
via ai Magi 4, 6945 Origlio TI
Tel: +41 (0)91 966 29 62
Curriculum: IBDP
Language instr: English, Italian

SIS Swiss International School Basel
Erlenstrasse 15, 4058 Basel BS
Tel: +41 61 683 71 40
Age range: 3–18 years
Curriculum: IBDP, IGCSE
Language instr: English, German

SIS Swiss International School Männedorf-Zürich
Seestrasse 57, 8708 Männedorf ZH
Tel: +41 44 921 50 50
Age range: 3–12 years
Language instr: English, German

SIS Swiss International School Päffikon-Schwyz
Eichenstrasse 5, 8808 Pfäffikon SZ
Tel: +41 55 415 44 00
Age range: 3–16 years
Language instr: English, German

SIS Swiss International School Rotkreuz-Zug
Suurstoffi 41c, 6343 Rotkreuz ZG
Tel: +41 41 757 57 11
Age range: 3–16 years
Language instr: English, German

SIS Swiss International School Schönenwerd
Schachenstrasse 24, 5012 Schönenwerd SO
Tel: +41 62 312 30 30
Age range: 3–12 years
Language instr: English, German

SIS Swiss International School Winterthur
Technoparkstrasse 1, 8406 Winterthur ZH
Tel: +41 52 202 82 11
Age range: 3–12 years
Language instr: English, German

SIS Swiss International School Zürich
Seidenstrasse 2, 8304 Wallisellen ZH
Tel: +41 44 388 99 44
Age range: 3–18 years
Curriculum: IBDP
Language instr: English, German

SIS Swiss International School Zürich-Wollishofen
Seestrasse 271, 8038 Zürich ZH
Tel: +41 43 399 88 44
Age range: 3–12 years
Language instr: English, German

ST. GEORGE'S INTERNATIONAL SCHOOL, SWITZERLAND
For further details see p. 240
Chemin de St. Georges 19, CH-1815 Clarens/Montreux
Tel: +41 21 964 3411
Email: admissions@stgeorges.ch
Website: www.stgeorges.ch
Head of School: Ruth Norris
Age range: 1.5–18 years
No. of pupils: 400
Curriculum: IBDP, SAT, TOEFL, USA, IGCSE
Language instr: English

Stiftsschule Engelberg
Benediktinerkloster 5,
Engelberg 6390
Tel: +41 41 639 61 00
Age range: 12–19 years
No. of pupils: 120
Curriculum: IBDP, National
Language instr: German, English

Surval Montreux
Route de Glion 56, 1820
Montreux VD
Tel: +41 21 966 16 16
Language instr: English
(COB)

Tandem IMS (International Multilingual School)
Zurich Campus, Seefeldstrasse
111, 8008 Zürich ZH
Tel: +41 43 500 10 30
Curriculum: UK

TASIS THE AMERICAN SCHOOL IN SWITZERLAND
For further details see p. 247
Via Collina d'Oro 15, 6926
Montagnola-Lugano
Tel: +41 91 960 5151
Email: admissions@tasis.ch
Website: www.tasis.ch
Head of School: Christopher Nikoloff
Age range: 3–19 years
No. of pupils: 700
Fees: *Day* CHF49,500
FB CHF91,000
Curriculum: ACT, AP, IBDP, SAT, USA
Language instr: English
(CIS) (ECIS)

The Bell Language School
12 Chemin des Colombettes,
1202 Geneva GE
Tel: +41 22 749 16 00
Age range: 2–17
No. of pupils: 345

The British School, Bern
Sperlisacher 2, 3075 Rüfenacht BE
Tel: +41 31 952 7555
Age range: 3–12
No. of pupils: 100 *B*50 *G*50
Curriculum: UK
Language instr: English
(ECIS)

ZURICH INTERNATIONAL SCHOOL
For further details see p. 260
Steinacherstrasse 140,
8820 Wädenswil ZH
Tel: +41 58 750 2500
Email: admissions@zis.ch
Website: www.zis.ch
Director: Lisa Lyle
Age range: 3–18 years
No. of pupils: 1200
Fees: *Day* CHF25,900–CHF36,600
Curriculum: AP, IBDP, SAT
Language instr: English

TURKEY

ABC Okullari
Yenibati Mahallesi 2398, Sok. No. 15,
Batikent, Ankara, Central Anatolia
Tel: +90 312 256 12 22
Curriculum: IBPYP
Language instr: English, Turkish

ABC Okullari Goksu Kampüsü
Göksu Mahallesi 93, Cadde
No. 6/1A, Eryaman, Ankara,
Central Anatolia
Tel: +90 312 444 2221
Curriculum: IBDP, IBPYP
Language instr: English, Turkish

Açi Schools
Bahçeköy Valide Sultan Cad
Su Kemeri Mevkii No:2, Sariyer,
34473 Istanbul, Marmara
Tel: +90 212 349 07 00
Age range: 3–17
Curriculum: National, IGCSE, ALevs
(CIS)

Acibadem Schools – Acibadem Campus
Acibadem Mah. Cecen Sok.
No:48 Ic Kapi No:1, Üsküdar,
34730 Istanbul, Marmara
Tel: +90 216 510 52 32
Curriculum: IBPYP
Language instr: Turkey

Ahmet Ulusoy College
Menderes Cad, Anda Sok
No 16, Incek, 06000 Ankara,
Central Anatolia
Tel: +90 312 460 20 20
Age range: 14–18
Curriculum: National, SAT, TOEFL, IGCSE
Language instr: English

Aka School
Radyum Sok No 21 Basin Sitesi,
Bahcelievler, Istanbul, Marmara
Tel: +90 212 557 27 72
Age range: 5–18
No. of pupils: 503 *B*238 *G*265
Curriculum: IBDP, National
Language instr: Turkish, English

ALKEV Schools
Alkent 2000 Mah. Mehmet
Yesilgül Cd. No: 7, Büyükcekmece,
34535 Istanbul, Marmara
Tel: +90 212 886 88 40
Curriculum: IBDP
Language instr: English, German

Antalya College
Bayindir Mah 333 Sok, PK 545,
Antalya, Mediterranean
Tel: +90 242 238 23 00
Age range: 5–17
No. of pupils: 1600
Curriculum: IGCSE

AREL Schools (Kindergarten/Primary/Middle/High)
Merkez Mah, Selahattin Pinar Sok,
No:3 Yenibosna, Bahcelievler,
34197 Istanbul, Marmara
Tel: +90 212 550 49 30
Age range: 3–18
No. of pupils: 1030 *B*520 *G*510
Curriculum: IBMYP, IBPYP
Language instr: Turkish, English

Avrupa Koleji
Prof Muammer Ahsoy Cad No 10,
Zeytinburnu, Istanbul, Marmara
Tel: +90 212 547 80 10
Age range: 5–19
No. of pupils: 508
(ECIS)

Balikesir Aci College
Cayirhisar Mah. Yeni Izmir yolu
Cad. 3B, 10185 Balikesir, Marmara
Tel: +90 266 239 85 85
Curriculum: IBDP
Language instr: English, Turkish

Beykoz Doga Campus
Fener Yolu Cad. No:6
Dereseki, Akbaba, Beykoz,
81650 Istanbul, Marmara
Tel: +90 216 320 52 00
Curriculum: IBPYP
Language instr: English

Bilkent Laboratory & International School
East Campus, 06800 Ankara,
Central Anatolia
Tel: +90 312 290 53 61
Age range: 4–18
No. of pupils: 575 *B*264 *G*311
Curriculum: IBDP, IBMYP, IBPYP, National, SAT, UK
Language instr: English, Turkish
(CIS) (ECIS)

Bodrum Marmara Elementary School
Cumhuriyet Avenue No. 2,
48420 Bodrum, Aegean
Tel: +90 252 358 61 13
Curriculum: IBPYP
Language instr: English, Turkish

Bodrum Marmara Private College
Cumhuriyet Avenue No. 2,
48420 Bodrum, Aegean
Tel: +90 252 358 61 13
Curriculum: IBDP
Language instr: English, Turkish

British Embassy School Ankara
Sehit Ersan Caddesi 46/A, Cankaya,
06680 Ankara, Central Anatolia
Tel: +90 312 468 65 63
Age range: 3–13
No. of pupils: 200
Curriculum: IPC, SAT, UK
Language instr: English
(COB)

British International School Istanbul – Etiler
Etiler Mahallesi Cengiz Topel
Caddesi Tugcular Sokak No. 27,
Besiktas, 34337 Istanbul, Marmara
Tel: +90 212 257 51 36
Age range: 2.5–11 years

British International School Istanbul – Zekeriyaköy
Zekeriyaköy Mahallesi, Kilyos
Caddesi No. 227/12, Sariyer,
Istanbul, Marmara
Tel: +90 212 202 70 27
Age range: 2.5–18 years
Curriculum: IBDP
Language instr: English

Cakir Schools
Orhaneli Yolu, Egitimciler Cd
15, Nilüfer, Bursa, Marmara
Tel: +90 224 451 93 30
Curriculum: IBDP, IBMYP, IBPYP
Language instr: Turkish

Çanakkale Özel ilkokulu
Izmir Yolu 12. Km
Güzelyali, Güzelyali, 17100
Canakkale, Marmara
Tel: +90 286 232 86 86
Curriculum: IBPYP
Language instr: English, Turkish

Darussafaka Schools
B.dere cad. Derbent Mevkii,
Sariyer, 34457 Istanbul, Marmara
Tel: +90 212 286 22 00

Deutsche Schule Istanbul – Özel Alman Lisesi
Sahkulu Bostani Sokak No. 10,
Beyoglu, 34420 Istanbul, Marmara
Tel: +90 212 245 13 90

Deutsche Schule Izmir
Kuscular Cad. No. 82, Kuscular
Köyü, Urla, 35430 Izmir, Aegean
Tel: +90 232 234 75 07
Age range: 2–19
No. of pupils: 157
Curriculum: IBDP
Language instr: German, English

Edirne Beykent Schools
Ayse Kadin Tren Gari Yani,
22100 Edirne, Marmara
Tel: +90 506 301 70 73

Egitmen Koleji
Istasyon Mah. Fevzi Çakmak
Cad. No: 123, Tuzla, 34940
Istanbul, Marmara
Tel: +90 216 446 48 46
Curriculum: IBPYP
Language instr: Turkish

Emine Ornek Schools
Bademli Mah, Egitim Cad 12 Sokak
No 2, 16940 Bursa, Marmara
Tel: +90 224 549 16 00
Language instr: English, Turkish
(CIS) (ECIS)

Enka Schools – Adapazari Campus
Dagdibi Mahallesi, Enka Yolu Caddesi, No. 60/A, Adapazari, Marmara
Tel: +90 264 323 37 74
Curriculum: IBMYP, IBPYP
Language instr: English, Turkish

Enka Schools – Istanbul Campus
Sadi Gülcelik Spor Sitesi, Istinye, 34460 Istanbul, Marmara
Tel: +90 212 705 65 00
Curriculum: IBDP, IBMYP, IBPYP, National, IGCSE
Language instr: English, Turkish
CIS ECIS RS

Ernst-Reuter-Schule
Tunus Cad 56, Kavaklidere, 06680 Ankara, Central Anatolia
Tel: +90 312 426 63 82
No. of pupils: 184
Curriculum: IBDP
Language instr: English, German

Eskisehir Gelisim Okullari
Asagi Sögütönü Mah. 993, Sokak No. 14, Tepebasi, 26200 Eskisehir, Central Anatolia
Tel: +90 222 313 01 01
Curriculum: IBDP
Language instr: English, Turkish

Eyüboglu Atasehir Primary School
2 Cadde 59 Ada Manolya 4, Bloklari yani No 6, Atasehir, 34758 Istanbul, Marmara
Tel: +90 216 522 12 22
Curriculum: IBPYP

Eyüboglu Kemerburgaz Middle School
Mithatpasa Mah. Pirinccikoy Yolu, 34075 Istanbul, Marmara
Tel: +90 216 522 12 72
Curriculum: IBMYP
Language instr: English, Turkish

Eyüboglu Kemerburgaz Preschool & Primary School
Mithatpasa Mah. Pirinccikoy Yolu, 34075 Istanbul, Marmara
Tel: +90 216 522 12 72
Language instr: English

Eyüboglu Schools
Esenevler Mah, Dr Rüstem Eyüboglu sok 3, Ümraniye, 34762 Istanbul, Marmara
Tel: +90 216 522 12 12
Age range: 3–18 years
No. of pupils: 2953
Curriculum: IBDP, IBMYP, IBPYP, National
Language instr: Turkish, English
CIS

Ezgililer Private Primary School
Kusculu Mah. 1728 Sok. No.6, Ilkadim, Samsun, Black Sea
Tel: +90 362 233 21 22
Curriculum: IBPYP
Language instr: English

Feyziye Mektepleri Vakfi Isik Okullari
Tesvikiye Cad. No:06, Nisantasi, 34365 Istanbul, Marmara
Tel: +90 212 233 12 03
Age range: 3–18
No. of pupils: 3947
CIS

FMV Ayazaga Isik High School
Maslak Mah. Büyükdere Cad. No:106, Sisli, Sariyer, 34460 Istanbul, Marmara
Tel: +90 212 286 11 30
Curriculum: IBDP
Language instr: English, Turkish

FMV Ayazaga Isik Primary & Middle School
Maslak Mah. Büyükdere Cad. No:106, Sisli, Sariyer, 34460 Istanbul, Marmara
Tel: +90 212 286 11 30
Curriculum: IBPYP
Language instr: English, Turkish

FMV Erenköy Isik High School
Sinan Ercan Cad. No:19, Erenköy, 34736 Istanbul, Marmara
Tel: +90 216 385 31 47
Curriculum: IBDP
Language instr: English, Turkish

FMV Erenköy Isik Primary & Middle School
Sinan Ercan Cad. No:19, Erenköy, 34736 Istanbul, Marmara
Tel: +90 216 385 31 47
Curriculum: IBPYP
Language instr: English, Turkish

FMV Isik High School
Tesvikiye Cad. No:6 Nisantasi, 34365 Istanbul, Marmara
Tel: +90 212 233 12 03
Curriculum: IBDP
Language instr: English, Turkish

FMV Isik Primary & Middle School
Tesvikiye Cad. No:06, Nisantasi, 34365 Istanbul, Marmara
Tel: +90 212 233 12 03
Curriculum: IBPYP
Language instr: English, Turkish

FMV Ispartakule Isik High School
Tahtakale Mah. Gaffar Okkan Cad. No: 5/7 Blok No: 1, Avcilar, 34325 Istanbul, Marmara
Tel: +90 212 648 09 75
Curriculum: IBDP
Language instr: English, Turkish

FMV Ispartakule Isik Primary & Middle School
Tahtakale Mah. Gaffar Okkan Cad. No: 5/7 Blok No: 1, Avcilar, 34325 Istanbul, Marmara
Tel: +90 212 648 09 75
Curriculum: IBPYP
Language instr: English, Turkish

Gazi University Foundation Private High School
Ali Suavi Street, Eti Quarter No 15, Maltepe, 06570 Ankara, Central Anatolia
Tel: +90 312 232 28 12
Curriculum: IBDP

Gaziantep Kolej Vakfi Cemil Alevli College
Guvenevler Mah., Hoca Ahmet Yesevi Caddesi, No. 2, Sehitkamil, 27060 Gaziantep, Southeastern Anatolia
Tel: +90 342 321 01 00
Age range: 4–17 years
No. of pupils: 1350
Curriculum: IBDP
Language instr: English

Gökkusagi Koleji – Bahçelievler
Eski Londra Asfalti No: 15 Haznedar, Bahcelievler, 34180 Istanbul, Marmara
Tel: +90 212 644 59 00
No. of pupils: 200
Curriculum: IBDP
Language instr: English, Turkish

Gökkusagi Koleji – Bahçesehir
Orhan Gazi Mah, 1654 sk. No. 40, Esenyurt, Istanbul, Marmara
Tel: +90 212 672 84 26
Curriculum: IBPYP
Language instr: English, Turkish

Gökkusagi Koleji – Beylikdüzü
Adnankahveci Mh. Fabrikalar Cd. No. 4, Beylikdüzü, Istanbul, Marmara
Tel: +90 212 855 89 04 07

Gökkusagi Koleji – Ümraniye
Inkilap Mh. Alemdag Cd. Üntel Sk. No. 30, Ümraniye, Istanbul, Marmara
Tel: +90 216 634 60 60
Curriculum: IBPYP
Language instr: English

Hisar School
Göktürk Merkez Mahallesi Istanbul Caddesi No. 3, Eyüp, Kemerburgaz, 34077 Istanbul, Marmara
Tel: +90 212 364 00 00
Age range: 4–17
No. of pupils: 1248 *B661 G587*
Curriculum: AP, National, SAT
Language instr: Turkish
CIS ECIS

IDV Özel Bilkent High School
IDV Özel Bilkent Ilkokulu, Ortaokulu ve Lisesi Universiteler Mah 1600, Cad. No. 6, Dogu Kampus, 06800 Ankara, Central Anatolia
Tel: +90 312 290 89 39
Age range: 4–18
No. of pupils: 325
Curriculum: IBDP, National
Language instr: English, Turkish
ECIS

IDV Özel Bilkent Middle School
IDV Özel Bilkent Ilkokulu, Ortaokulu ve Lisesi, Universiteler Mah 1600, Cad. No. 6, Dogu Kampus, 06800 Ankara, Central Anatolia
Tel: +90 312 290 54 40
No. of pupils: 325
Curriculum: IBMYP, IBPYP

IDV Özel Bilkent Primary School
IDV Özel Bilkent Ilkokulu, Ortaokulu ve Lisesi, Universiteler Mah 1600, Cad. No. 6, Dogu Kampus, 06800 Ankara, Central Anatolia
Tel: +90 312 290 54 40
No. of pupils: 400

IELEV Private High School
Ensar Cad. No:4/3 Nisantepe Mah. B Blok, Çekmeköy, 34794 Istanbul, Marmara
Tel: +90 216 304 30 92
Age range: 14–19
No. of pupils: 381
Curriculum: IBDP
Language instr: English, German, Turkish

International Pre-School PLUS
Bagdat Cad. Kadiköy., Istanbul, Marmara
Tel: +90 216 350 06 06
Language instr: English, German, French
ISA

Irmak School
Cemil Topuzlu Caddesi No. 100, Caddebostan P.K. 34728, Kadiköy, Istanbul, Marmara
Tel: +90 216 411 39 23
Age range: 5–18
No. of pupils: 620 *B310 G310*
Curriculum: IBPYP, National, SAT
Language instr: Turkish, English
ECIS

Isikkent Egitim Kampusu
6240/5 Sokak No. 3, Karacaoglan Mah., Yesilova, Bornova, 35070 Izmir, Aegean
Tel: +90 232 462 71 00
Age range: 3–18
No. of pupils: 745 *B400 G345*
Curriculum: IBDP, IBMYP, IBPYP, National
Language instr: Turkish, English
CIS

Istanbul Beykent Schools
Gurpinar E-5 Yol Ayrimi, Beykent Büyükçekmece, 34500 Istanbul, Marmara
Tel: +90 212 872 64 32

Istanbul Coskun College
Sema Egitim Hiz. A.S, Zümrütevler Mah. Emek Cad. Maltepe, 34852 Istanbul, Marmara
Tel: +90 216 370 55 55
Language instr: English

Istanbul International Community School
Karaagac Koyu Mahallesi, Kahraman Caddesi, 27/1, Buyukcekmece, 34500 Istanbul, Marmara
Tel: +90 212 857 82 64
Age range: 3–18 B3–18 G3–18
No. of pupils: 600
Curriculum: IBDP, IBMYP, IBPYP
Language instr: English
CEE CIS ECIS

Istanbul International School
Turistik Camilica Cad. No. 12 Büyük Camilica, Istanbul, Marmara
Tel: +90 216 335 00 55
Age range: 3–18
Curriculum: IGCSE
Language instr: English, Turkish
ISA

Istanbul Marmara Private College
Marmara Egitim Köyü, Maltepe, 34857 Istanbul, Marmara
Tel: +90 216 626 10 00
Curriculum: IBDP, IBPYP
Language instr: English, Turkish

ISTEK 1915 Canakkale Schools
Ismetpasa Mah. 55 Sok. No 2/1, Canakkale, Marmara
Tel: +90 286 501 18 81

ISTEK Acibadem Schools
Acibadem Mah. Bag Sok. No 6, Kadiköy, 34718 Istanbul, Marmara
Tel: +90 216 325 30 75
Curriculum: IBDP, IBPYP
Language instr: English

ISTEK Afyon Schools
Selcuklu Mah. 1523. Sokak Uydukent, Afyonkarahisar, Aegean
Tel: +90 272 214 51 51

ISTEK Antalya Konyaalti Schools
Uncali Mah. 1257 Sk. No 3, Konyaalti, Antalya, Mediterranean
Tel: +90 242 229 30 80
Curriculum: IBPYP
Language instr: English, Turkish

ISTEK Antalya Lara Schools
2421 Sok. No 1 Güzeloba Mah., Muratpasa, Antalya, Mediterranean
Tel: +90 242 502 36 46
Curriculum: IBDP, IBPYP
Language instr: English, Turkish

ISTEK Atanur Oguz Schools
Balmumcu Mah. Gazi Umurpasa Sk. No 26, Balmumcu, 34349 Istanbul, Marmara
Tel: +90 212 211 34 60
Curriculum: IBDP, IBPYP
Language instr: English

ISTEK Bandirma Schools
600 Evler Mah. Atatürk Cad. No 157, 10200 Bandirma, Marmara
Tel: +90 266 714 36 42

ISTEK Baris Schools
Bagdat Cad. No. 238/1, Ciftehavuzlar, Kadiköy, 34730 Istanbul, Marmara
Tel: +90 216 360 12 18
Age range: 3–11 years
No. of pupils: 625
Curriculum: IBPYP
Language instr: Turkish, English

ISTEK Belde Schools
Kuzguncuk Mah. Rasimaga Sok. No 7/4, Üsküdar, 34664 Istanbul, Marmara
Tel: +90 216 495 96 23
Curriculum: IBPYP
Language instr: English

ISTEK Bilge Kagan Schools
Senlikköy Mah. Florya Cad. No 2 Florya, Bakirköy, 34153 Istanbul, Marmara
Tel: +90 212 663 29 71
Curriculum: IBPYP
Language instr: English

ISTEK Denizli Schools
Selcukbey Mah. 737 Sok. No 13, Merkezefendi, 20030 Denizli, Aegean
Tel: +90 258 257 19 19

ISTEK Izmir Schools
Mavisehir Mah. 2040 Sok. No 13, Karsiyaka, Izmir, Aegean
Tel: +90 232 324 05 05

ISTEK Kasgarli Mahmut Schools
Eski Edirne Asfalti No 512, Sultangazi, 34110 Istanbul, Marmara
Tel: +90 212 594 26 11/12
Age range: 3–11 years
No. of pupils: 300
Curriculum: IBPYP
Language instr: English, Turkish

ISTEK Kemal Atatürk Schools (Kindergarten & Primary School)
Tarabya Bayiri Cad. No 60, Tarabya/Sariyer, 34457 Istanbul, Marmara
Tel: +90 212 262 75 75
Age range: 3–10 years
Curriculum: IBPYP
Language instr: Turkish, English

ISTEK Kocaeli Schools
Barbaros Mah. Yunus Emre Cad. No 12. Basiskele, Izmit/Kocaeli, Marmara
Tel: +90 262 335 43 55

ISTEK Kusadasi Schools
Degirmendere, Ahmet Pinari Cad. No 8, Kusadasi, 09400 Aydin, Aegean
Tel: +90 256 988 02 56

ISTEK Kütahya Schools
Osmangazi Mah. Tavsanli Karayolu Bulvari üzeri No 33, Kütahya, Aegean
Tel: 0274 666 0 777

ISTEK Lüleburgaz Schools
Atatürk Mah. Istanbul Asfalti Yolu No 11, Lüleburgaz, Kirklareli, Marmara
Tel: +90 288 412 12 00

ISTEK Mersin Schools
Gökcebelen Mah. 33195, Sk. No 2, Yenisehir, 33115 Mersin, Mediterranean
Tel: +90 324 473 24 21

ISTEK Osmaniye Schools
Fakiusagi Mah. 54005 sok. No14, Osmaniye, Mediterranean
Tel: +90 328 888 00 33

ISTEK Semiha Sakir Schools
Caddebostan Mah. Bagdat Cad. No 238/1, Kadiköy, 34730 Istanbul, Marmara
Tel: +90 216 360 12 18

ISTEK Ulugbey Schools
Atalar Mah. Akgün Sok. No 23, Kartal, 34862 Istanbul, Marmara
Tel: +90 216 488 13 08
Curriculum: IBPYP
Language instr: English, Turkish

ISTEK Yalova Schools
Liman Sok. No 4, Dereagzo Mevkii, Yalova, Marmara
Tel: +90 226 811 58 28

ITÜ ETA Vakfi Doga Koleji
Barbaros Mah. Halk Cad. Kardelen Sok. N.:2 Incity C Blok, Atasehir, Istanbul, Marmara
Tel: +90 216 4853580
Curriculum: IBDP
Language instr: English

ITU Gelistirme Vakfi Özel Ekrem Elginkan Lisesi
ITU Ayazaga Kampusu, Maslak, 34469 Istanbul, Marmara
Tel: +90 212 367 1300
Curriculum: IBDP
Language instr: English

Izmir SEV Schools
77 Sokak No. 45, Göztepe, 35290 Izmir, Aegean
Tel: +90 232 355 04 44
Curriculum: USA
CIS

Jale Tezer Educational Institutions
Jale Tezer Primary & Secondary Schools (Gazi Osman Pasa Campus), Bagcilar Mahallesi Acin Caddesi No:7, Cankaya, 06670 Ankara, Central Anatolia
Tel: +90 312 447 49 49
Age range: 3–18
No. of pupils: 3000
Curriculum: IBDP, IGCSE, ALevs
Language instr: English, Turkish

Keystone International Schools
Küçük Çamlica Mahallesi Gülhan Sk. No.1/1-2 PK, Üsküdar, 34660 Istanbul, Marmara
Tel: +90 216 370 49 51

Kirmizi Cizgi Schools
Fener Mah.1964 Sok. Yaliyar Si?t. No : 30/C-D, 07060 Antalya, Mediterranean
Tel: +90 242 242 99 98
Curriculum: IBDP
Language instr: English, Turkish

Kocaeli Marmara Private College
Dumlupinar Mah. Sehit Turgut Cicek Cad. No. 47, 41250 Kartepe, Marmara
Tel: +90 262 373 1313
Curriculum: IBDP
Language instr: English, Turkish

Kultar Koleji
Atakoy 9-10, Ataköy, 34156 Istanbul, Marmara
Tel: +90 212 559 04 88
No. of pupils: 332
Language instr: English

Kültür2000 College
Karaagac Mah., Sirtköy Bulvari No. 2, Büyükcekmece, 34500 Istanbul, Marmara
Tel: +90 212 850 81 81
Age range: 11–18
No. of pupils: 148
Curriculum: IBDP, IBMYP
Language instr: English, Turkish

Maya Schools Antalya
Demircikara Mah. 1436. Sk. No:6 Muratpasa, Antalya, Mediterranean 07100
Tel: +90 (242) 242 62 22
Curriculum: IBDP, IBFYP
Language instr: English, Turkish

MEF International Schools, Istanbul – Ulus High
Ulus Mah. Leylak Sok. No. 22, Ulus, Besiktas, 34340 Istanbul, Marmara
Tel: +90 212 362 26 33 (Ext:1360/1332)
Age range: 11–18 years
No. of pupils: 192
Curriculum: IBDP, IGCSE
Language instr: English

MEF International Schools, Istanbul – Ulus Primary
Ulus Mah. Leylak Sok. No. 22, Ulus, Besiktas, 34340 Istanbul, Marmara
Tel: +90 212 362 26 33 (Ext:1341/1344)
Age range: 3–11 years
No. of pupils: 157
Curriculum: IBPYP
Language instr: English

MEF International Schools, Izmir
Dokuz Eylül Mah. 699. Sokak No. 2, Gaziemir, Izmir, Aegean
Tel: +90 232 274 74 74
Curriculum: IBDP
Language instr: English

Minecan Okullari
Karsli mah 82064 sok. No. 12-14, Cukurova, 010101 Adana, Mediterranean
Tel: +90 322 233 30 45
Curriculum: IBPYP
Language instr: English, Turkish

Muruvvet Evyap Schools
Maden District Bakir Street, No. 2A/2B/2C, Sariyer, 34450 Istanbul, Marmara
Tel: +90 212 342 43 33
Age range: 4–18
No. of pupils: 900
Curriculum: IBPYP
Language instr: Turkish

Nesibe AYDIN Educational Institutions (Konya)
Beyhekim Mh. Darülhilafet Sk. No:1 Selcuklu, 42130 Konya, Central Anatolia
Tel: +90 332 320 85 11
Curriculum: IBPYP
Language instr: Turkish

Nesibe Aydin Okullari
Haymana Yolu 5. Km, Karsiyaka Mahallesi 577. Sokak No. 1, Gölbasi, 06830 Ankara, Central Anatolia
Tel: +90 312 498 25 25
Curriculum: IBDP, IBPYP
Language instr: English

NUN Middle & High School
Elmali Mahallesi, Beykoz Elmali Yolu Sokak No. 5/1, Beykoz, Istanbul, Marmara
Tel: +90 216 686 16 86
Curriculum: IBDP, IBMYP
Language instr: English, Turkish

NUN Primary School
Burhaniye Mahallesi Haci Resit Pasa Sk. No. 18, Üsküdar, Istanbul, Marmara
Tel: +90 216 686 16 86
Curriculum: IBPYP
Language instr: English

Özel Antalya Toplum Koleji Anadolu Lisesi
Altinkale, Palmiye Cd. No 10/A, 07192 Dösemealti, Antalya, Mediterranean
Tel: +90 242 443 30 80
Curriculum: IBDP
Language instr: English, Turkish

Özel Ari Anadolu Lisesi
Ögretmenler cad. No. 16/ C 100, Yil Cukurambar, Çankaya, 06530 Ankara, Central Anatolia
Tel: +90 312 286 85 85
Curriculum: IBDP
Language instr: English

Özel Atayurt Ilkokulu
Yukari Sögütönü Mah., Bursa Yolu 10.km. 951 sokak No. 146, 26563 Eskisehir, Central Anatolia
Tel: +90 222 315 03 60
Curriculum: IBPYP
Language instr: Turkish

Özel Büyük Kolej
Baglar Caddesi No 184, Hulya Sokak No. 7, Gaziosmanpasa, 06700 Ankara, Central Anatolia
Tel: +90 312 446 66 76
Age range: 5–17
No. of pupils: 1859 *B947 G912*

Özel Çag Lisesi
Yasar Baybogan Kampüsü, Adana-Mersin Karayolu Üzeri, Yenice, Tarsus, 33800 Mersin, Mediterranean
Tel: +90 324 651 33 86
Age range: 6–17
No. of pupils: 510 *B270 G240*
Curriculum: National

Özel Egeberk Anaokulu
Özlüce Mah. Hazal Sk. No:3 Nilüfer, 16010 Bursa, Marmara
Tel: +90 533 593 92 90
Curriculum: IBPYP
Language instr: English

Ozel Ilk Cizgi Kindergarten
Nilüfer Hatun Caddesi, ilk Cizgi Sokak, No:5, Osmangazi, 16265 Bursa, Marmara
Tel: +90 224 244 91 91
Curriculum: IBPYP
Language instr: English, Turkish

Ozel Istanbul Akademik Sistem Okullari
Basaksehir Mah. Yücelen Sok. No. 5, Basaksehir, Istanbul, Marmara
Curriculum: IBDP
Language instr: English, Turkish

Özel Kariyer Ilkokulu
Turgut Özal Mh. 2212.Sk No:4, Cakirlarciftligi/Batikent, 06370 Ankara, Central Anatolia
Tel: +90 312 566 22 32
Curriculum: IBPYP
Language instr: Turkish

Özel Yönder Ilkokulu
Atatürk mah. Girne cad. 6-6/1, Atasehir, 34758 Istanbul, Marmara
Tel: +90 216 455 07 07
Language instr: Turkish

Pakistan Embassy International Study Group
2119 Sok, No. 11, Musafa Kemal Mah, Cankaya, Ankara, Central Anatolia
Tel: +90 312 219 43 56
Age range: 4–18
No. of pupils: 280
Curriculum: IGCSE

Private ALEV Schools
Kadirova Cad. 52/3, Ömerli Mah. Cekmeköy, 34797 Istanbul, Marmara
Tel: +90 216 435 83 50
Age range: 3–19
No. of pupils: 910
Curriculum: IBDP
Language instr: Turkish, German, English

Private Kocaeli Bahcesehir Anatolian High School
Fatih Mah, Demokrasi Cad No.8 B.K.3, Köseköy, 41135 Kartepe, Marmara
Tel: +90 262 373 69 69
Curriculum: IBDP
Language instr: English, Turkish

Private Sahin Schools
Prof. Dr. Sabahattin Zaim Bulvari Karaman Yolu 4., Km Karakamis Mah., 54100 Adapazari, Marmara
Tel: +90 264 777 17 00
Curriculum: IBPYP
Language instr: Turkish

Private Sanko Schools
Pancarli District Kültür Street No. 10, 27060 Sehitkamil, Southeastern Anatolia
Tel: +90 342 211 55 00
Curriculum: IBPYP
Language instr: English, Turkish

Robert College of Istanbul
Kurucesme Cad No 87, Arnavutkoy, 34345 Istanbul, Marmara
Tel: +90 212 359 22 22
Age range: 14–19
No. of pupils: 997 *B499 G498*
Curriculum: AP, National, SAT, USA
Language instr: English, Turkish

SEV American College
Nisantepe Mah. Kerem Sok. 76, No. 5-9, Cekmeköy, 34794 Istanbul, Marmara
Tel: +90 216 625 27 22
Curriculum: IBDP
Language instr: English

Tarabya British Schools
Salcikir Caddesi No. 44, Tarabya, 34457 Istanbul, Marmara
Tel: +90 212 223 86 46
Curriculum: IGCSE, ALevs
Language instr: English, Turkish

Tarsus American School
Cengiz Topel Caddesi, Caminur Mahallesi No. 66, Tarsus, 33440 Mersin, Mediterranean
Tel: +90 324 241 81 81
Age range: 5–18
No. of pupils: 551 *B287 G264*
Curriculum: IBDP, SAT, TOEFL
Language instr: English

Tas Private Elementary School
Cevizlik Mah. Hallac Hüseyin, Sk. No. 11, Bakirköy, 34142 Istanbul, Marmara
Tel: +90 212 543 60 00
Curriculum: IBPYP
Language instr: Turkish, English

TED Ankara College Foundation High School
Golbasi Taspinar Koyu Yumrubel, Mevkii No. 310, 06830 Ankara, Central Anatolia
Tel: +90 312 586 90 00
Age range: 5–18
No. of pupils: 1499
Curriculum: IBDP, National
Language instr: English

TED Bursa College
21 Yüzyil Cad Mürsel, Köyü Mevkii, Bademli, Bursa, Marmara
Tel: +90 224 549 21 00
Curriculum: IBDP
Language instr: English

TED Istanbul College Foundation
Cavusbasi Acarkent D Girisi, 81686 Istanbul, Marmara
Tel: +90 216 485 03 33
Age range: 4–18
No. of pupils: 1311 *B671 G640*

Terakki Foundation – Levent Campus
Ebulula Mardin Cad. Öztürk Sok No. 2, Levent, 34335 Istanbul, Marmara
Tel: +90 212 351 00 60
Curriculum: IBDP, IBPYP
Language instr: English, Turkish

Terakki Foundation – Tepeoren High School
Medeniyet Blv. No. 55L, Tuzla, 34959 Istanbul, Marmara
Tel: +90 216 709 18 77
Curriculum: IBDP
Language instr: English, Turkish

Terakki Foundation – Tepeoren Kindergarten & Primary School
Medeniyet Blv. No. 55L, Tuzla, 34959 Istanbul, Marmara
Tel: +90 216 709 18 77
Curriculum: IBPYP
Language instr: English, Turkish

Tev Inanc Turkes High School For Gifted Students
Muallimköy Mah. 4126, Sok. No. 25/A, 41490 Gebze, Marmara
Tel: +90 262 679 36 36
Curriculum: IBDP
Language instr: English

The Koç School
Tepeören Mahallesi, Eski Ankara Asfalti Caddesi No. 60, 34941 Istanbul, Marmara
Tel: +90 216 585 62 00
Age range: 5–18
No. of pupils: 2197
Curriculum: IBDP, National, SAT
Language instr: Turkish, English
(ECIS)

The Sezin School
Ulubatli Hasan Caddesi No:18, Cekmeköy, 34782 Istanbul, Marmara
Tel: +90 216 642 00 10
Curriculum: IBDP
Language instr: English, Turkish

Üsküdar American Academy
Vakif Sk., No. 1 Baglarbasi, Uskudar, 33664 Istanbul, Marmara
Tel: +90 216 333 11 00
Curriculum: IBDP
Language instr: English

Yeni Yol Schools
Yeniakcayir Mahallesi No. 551, Tepebasi, Eskisehir, Central Anatolia
Tel: +90 222 230 39 00
Curriculum: IBDP, IBPYP
Language instr: English, Turkish

YUCE Schools
Ozel YUCE Okullari, Zuhtu Tigrel Caddesi, Ismet Eker Sokak No 5, Oran, 06450 Ankara, Central Anatolia
Tel: +90 312 490 02 02
Curriculum: IBDP, IBMYP, IBPYP
Language instr: English

Zafer Koleji
Eskisehir Yolu, Baglica Kavsagi No. 461, Cayyolu, 06790 Ankara, Central Anatolia
Tel: +90 312 444 55 12
Curriculum: IBDP
Language instr: English

UK

St Peter's 13-18
Clifton, York, North Yorkshire YO30 6AB
Tel: 01904 527300
Age range: 13–18 years
Curriculum: National, UK
Language instr: English

Abbotsholme School
Rocester, Uttoxeter, Staffordshire ST14 5BS
Tel: 01889 590217
Age range: 2–18 years
No. of pupils: 285
Curriculum: GCSE, IGCSE, ALevs
Language instr: English
(RS)

Abingdon School
Park Road, Abingdon, Oxfordshire OX14 1DE
Tel: +44 (0)1235 849029
Age range: *B*11–18 years
Language instr: English

Ackworth School
Pontefract Road, Ackworth, Pontefract, West Yorkshire WF7 7LT
Tel: 01977 233 600
Age range: 2.5–18 years
No. of pupils: 510
Curriculum: GCSE, ALevs
Language instr: English

ACS Cobham International School
Heywood, Portsmouth Road, Cobham, Surrey KT11 1BL
Tel: +44 (0) 1932 867251
Age range: 2–18 years
Curriculum: IBDP
Language instr: English

ACS Egham International School
London Road, Egham, Surrey TW20 0HS
Tel: +44 (0) 1784 430800
Age range: 4–18 years
Curriculum: IBDP, IBMYP, IBPYP, IBCP
Language instr: English

ACS Hillingdon International School
108 Vine Lane, Hillingdon, Uxbridge, Middlesex UB10 0BE
Tel: +44 (0) 1895 259771
Age range: 4–18 years
Curriculum: IBDP, IBCP
Language instr: English

Adcote School for Girls
Little Ness, Shrewsbury, Shropshire SY4 2JY
Tel: 01939 260202
Age range: *G*7–18 years

Aldenham School
Elstree, Hertfordshire WD6 3AJ
Tel: 01923 858122
Age range: 3–18 years
Language instr: English

Ampleforth College
York, North Yorkshire YO62 4ER
Tel: 01439 766000
Age range: 11–18 years

Ardingly College
College Road, Ardingly, Haywards Heath, West Sussex RH17 6SQ
Tel: +44 (0)1444 893320
Age range: 13–18
No. of pupils: 559
Curriculum: IBDP, National, UK, GCSE, IGCSE, ALevs
Language instr: English

Ashford School
East Hill, Ashford, Kent TN24 8PB
Tel: +44 (0)1233 625171
Age range: 3 months–18 years
No. of pupils: 916 *B*471 *G*445 *VIth*127
Curriculum: GCSE, ALevs
Language instr: English

Ashgrove School
116 Widmore Road, Bromley, Kent BR1 3BE
Tel: 020 8460 4143
Age range: 3–11 years

Ashville College
Green Lane, Harrogate, North Yorkshire HG2 9JP
Tel: +44 (0)1423 566358
Age range: 2–18 years
Language instr: English

Badminton School
Westbury Road, Westbury-on-Trym, Bristol, Bristol BS9 3BA
Tel: 0117 905 5200
Age range: *G*3–18 years
Curriculum: GCSE, IGCSE, ALevs

Bales College
742 Harrow Road, Kensal Town, London, London W10 4AA
Tel: 020 8960 5899
Age range: 11–19
No. of pupils: 90 *B*60 *G*30
Curriculum: GCSE, IGCSE, ALevs

Bangor Independent School
The Old Canonry, 39 Ffordd Gwynedd, Bangor, Gwynedd LL57 1DT
Tel: 01248 354635
Age range: 3–11 years
Curriculum: UK

Barnard Castle Senior School
Barnard Castle, Durham DL12 8UN
Tel: +44 (0)1833 696030
Age range: 11–18 years
No. of pupils: 715
Curriculum: GCSE, IGCSE, ALevs
Language instr: English

Bath Academy
27 Queen Square, Bath, Bath & North-East Somerset BA1 2HX
Tel: 01225 334577
Age range: 14–19+
Curriculum: IGCSE, ALevs

Battle Abbey School
High Street, Battle, East Sussex TN33 0AD
Tel: 01424 772385
Age range: 3 months–18 years
Curriculum: GCSE, ALevs

Bedales School
Church Road, Steep, Petersfield, Hampshire GU32 2DG
Tel: 01730 300100
Age range: 13–18 years

Bede's Senior School
Upper Dicker, Hailsham, East Sussex BN27 3QH
Tel: +44 (0)1323 843252
Age range: 13–18 years
Curriculum: GCSE, IGCSE, ALevs

Bedford Girls' School
Cardington Road, Bedford, Bedfordshire MK42 0BX
Tel: 01234 361900
Age range: *G*7–18 years
Curriculum: IBDP, GCSE, ALevs
Language instr: English

Bedford School
De Parys Avenue, Bedford, Bedfordshire MK40 2TU
Tel: 01234 362200
Age range: *B*7–18 years
Curriculum: IBDP, GCSE, IGCSE, ALevs
Language instr: English

Bedstone College
Bedstone, Bucknell, Shropshire SY7 0BG
Tel: 01547 530303
Age range: 4–18 years
Language instr: English

Bellerbys College Brighton
1 Billinton Way, Brighton, East Sussex BN1 4LF
Tel: +44 (0)1273 339333
Age range: 14–19 years
Curriculum: GCSE, ALevs

Bellerbys College London
Bounty House, Stowage, Greenwich, London, London SE8 3DE
Tel: +44 (0)208 694 7000
Age range: 14–19 years
Curriculum: GCSE, ALevs

Benenden School
Cranbrook, Kent TN17 4AA
Tel: 01580 240592
Age range: *G*11–18 years
Language instr: English

Berkhamsted School
Overton House, 131 High Street, Berkhamsted, Hertfordshire HP4 2DJ
Tel: 01442 358001
Age range: 3–18 years
No. of pupils: 1883 *VIth*422
Curriculum: GCSE, ALevs

Bethany School
Curtisden Green, Goudhurst, Cranbrook, Kent TN17 1LB
Tel: 01580 211273
Age range: 11–18 years
No. of pupils: 356 *B*246 *G*110 *VIth*73
Curriculum: GCSE, ALevs
Language instr: English

Bishop's Stortford College
School House, Maze Green Road, Bishop's Stortford, Hertfordshire CM23 2PQ
Tel: +44 (0)1279 838575
Age range: 13–18 years
Language instr: English

Bishop's Stortford College Prep School
School House, Maze Green Road, Bishop's Stortford, Hertfordshire CM23 2PQ
Tel: +44 (0)1279 838583
Age range: 4–13 years
Language instr: English

Bloxham School
Bloxham, Banbury, Oxfordshire OX15 4PE
Tel: 01295 720222
Age range: 11–18 years

Blundell's School
Tiverton, Devon EX16 4DN
Tel: 01884 252543
Age range: 11–18 years

Bootham School
York, North Yorkshire YO30 7BU
Tel: 01904 623261
Age range: 11–18 years

Box Hill School
London Road, Mickleham, Dorking, Surrey RH5 6EA
Tel: 01372 373382
Age range: 11–18 years
No. of pupils: 425
Curriculum: IBDP, GCSE, IGCSE
Language instr: English

Bradfield College
Bradfield, Berkshire RG7 6AU
Tel: 0118 964 4516
Age range: 13–18 years
No. of pupils: 820
Curriculum: IBDP, UK, GCSE, IGCSE, ALevs
Language instr: English

Brentwood School
Middleton Hall Lane, Brentwood, Essex CM15 8EE
Tel: 01277 243243
Age range: 3–18 years
No. of pupils: 1850
Curriculum: IBDP, GCSE, IGCSE, ALevs
Language instr: English

Brighton College
Eastern Road, Brighton, East Sussex BN2 0AL
Tel: 01273 704200
Age range: 3–18 years
Curriculum: GCSE, IGCSE, ALevs

Bristol Grammar School
University Road, Bristol, Bristol BS8 1SR
Tel: 0117 973 6006
Age range: 4–18 years
Curriculum: IBDP, GCSE, IGCSE, ALevs
Language instr: English

Brockwood Park School
Brockwood Park, Bramdean, Alresford, Hampshire SO24 0LQ
Tel: +44 (0)1962 771744
Age range: 14–19 years
Language instr: English

Bromsgrove School
Worcester Road, Bromsgrove, Worcestershire B61 7DU
Tel: +44 (0)1527 579679
Age range: 13–18 years
No. of pupils: 1300
Curriculum: IBDP, ALevs
Language instr: English

Brooke House College
12 Leicester Road, Market Harborough, Leicestershire LE16 7AU
Tel: 01858 462452
Age range: 11–19 years

Bryanston School
Blandford Forum, Dorset DT11 0PX
Tel: 01258 484633
Age range: 3–18 years
No. of pupils: 806
Curriculum: IBDP, IBCP, GCSE, ALevs
Language instr: English

Buckswood School
Broomham Hall, Rye Road, Guestling, Hastings, East Sussex TN35 4LT
Tel: 01424 813 813
Age range: 10–19 years
Curriculum: IBDP, UK, GCSE, IGCSE, ALevs

Burgess Hill Girls
Keymer Road, Burgess Hill, West Sussex RH15 0EG
Tel: 01444 241050
Age range: *B*2.5–4 years *G*2.5–18 years
No. of pupils: 505 *B*29 *G*476 *VIth*70
Curriculum: UK, GCSE, ALevs
Language instr: English

Campbell College
Belmont Road, Belfast, County Antrim BT4 2ND
Tel: 028 9076 3076
Age range: *B*11–18 years
Curriculum: GCSE, ALevs

Canford School
Canford Magna, Wimborne, Dorset BH21 3AD
Tel: 01202 841254
Age range: 13–18 years
Curriculum: GCSE, IGCSE, ALevs
Language instr: English

Cardiff Academy
Harlech Court, Bute Terrace, Cardiff, Glamorgan CF10 2FE
Tel: 02920 318 318
Curriculum: ALevs

Cardiff Sixth Form College
1-3 Trinity Court, 21-27 Newport Road,, Cardiff CF24 0AA
Tel: +44 (0)29 2049 3121
Age range: 15–18 years

Carfax College
39-42 Hythe Bridge Street, Oxford, Oxfordshire OX1 2EP
Tel: +44 (0)1865 200676
Age range: 11–21 years
No. of pupils: 24
Curriculum: GCSE, ALevs

Caterham School
Harestone Valley, Caterham, Surrey CR3 6YA
Tel: 01883 343028
Age range: 11–18
No. of pupils: *B*478 *G*422 *VIth*321
Curriculum: UK, GCSE, IGCSE, ALevs
Language instr: English

CATS Canterbury
68 New Dover Road, Canterbury, Kent CT1 3LQ
Tel: +44 (0)1227866540
Age range: 14–21 years
No. of pupils: 450
Curriculum: IBDP, UK, IGCSE, ALevs
Language instr: English

CATS College Cambridge
Elizabeth House, 1 High Street, Chesterton, Cambridge, Cambridgeshire CB4 1NQ
Tel: +44 (0)1223 314431
Age range: 14–19+ years
Curriculum: GCSE, ALevs

CATS London
43-45 Bloomsbury Square, London, London WC1A 2RA
Tel: 02078 411580
Age range: 15–24
Curriculum: National, UK, IGCSE, ALevs
Language instr: English

Centre Academy London
92 St John's Hill, Battersea, London, London SW11 1SH
Tel: 020 7738 2344
Age range: 9–19 years
Language instr: English

Charterhouse
Godalming, Surrey GU7 2DX
Tel: +44 (0)1483 291501
Age range: B13–18 years G16–18 years
No. of pupils: 895
Curriculum: IBDP, National, UK, GCSE, IGCSE, ALevs
Language instr: English

Chase Grammar School International Study Centre
Convent Close, Cannock, Staffordshire WS11 0UR
Tel: +44 (0)1543 501800
Age range: 9–19 years

Cheltenham College
Bath Road, Cheltenham, Gloucestershire GL53 7LD
Tel: 01242 265600
Age range: 13–18 years
Curriculum: GCSE, IGCSE, ALevs

Cheltenham Ladies' College
Bayshill Road, Cheltenham, Gloucestershire GL50 3EP
Tel: +44 (0)1242 520691
Age range: G11–18 years
No. of pupils: 876
Curriculum: IBDP, GCSE, IGCSE, ALevs
Language instr: English

Chetham's School of Music
Long Millgate, Manchester, Greater Manchester M3 1SB
Tel: 0161 834 9644
Age range: 8–18 years
No. of pupils: 300
Curriculum: GCSE, IGCSE, ALevs

Chigwell School
High Road, Chigwell, Essex IG7 6QF
Tel: 020 8501 5700
Age range: 4–18 years
Curriculum: GCSE, ALevs

Christ College
Brecon, Powys LD3 8AF
Tel: 01874 615440
Age range: 7–18 years
No. of pupils: 370
Curriculum: GCSE, ALevs
Language instr: English

Christ's Hospital
Horsham, West Sussex RH13 0LJ
Tel: 01403 211293
Age range: 11–18
No. of pupils: 900
Curriculum: IBDP, National, GCSE, IGCSE, ALevs

City of London Freemen's School
Ashtead Park, Ashtead, Surrey KT21 1ET
Tel: 01372 277933
Age range: 7–18
No. of pupils: 877 *VIth*213
Curriculum: GCSE, ALevs

Clayesmore School
Blandford Road, Iwerne Minster, Dorset DT11 8LL
Tel: 01747 813111
Age range: 3–18 years
Curriculum: GCSE, IGCSE, ALevs
Language instr: English

Clifton College
32 College Road, Clifton, Bristol, Bristol BS8 3JH
Tel: 0117 315 7000
Age range: 13–18 years
Curriculum: ALevs

Clifton College Preparatory School
The Avenue, Clifton, Bristol, Bristol BS8 3HE
Tel: +44 (0)117 315 7502
Age range: 2–13 years

Cobham Hall School
Brewers Road, Cobham, Kent DA12 3BL
Tel: 01474 823371
Age range: G11–18 years
No. of pupils: 150
Curriculum: UK, GCSE, IGCSE
Language instr: English

COLLÈGE FRANÇAIS BILINGUE DE LONDRES
For further details see p. 141
87 Holmes Road, Kentish Town,, London NW5 3AX
Tel: 020 7993 7400
Email: info@cfbl.org.uk
Website: www.cfbl.org.uk
Head of School: David Gassian
Age range: 3–15 years
No. of pupils: 700
Fees: £13,670
Curriculum: FrenchBacc
Language instr: French, English

Colston's School
Stapleton, Bristol, Bristol BS16 1BJ
Tel: 0117 965 5207
Age range: 3–18 years
No. of pupils: 816
Curriculum: ALevs

Concord College
Acton Burnell Hall, Acton Burnell, Shrewsbury, Shropshire SY5 7PF
Tel: +44 (0)1694 731631
Age range: 13–18 years
No. of pupils: 600
Curriculum: UK, GCSE, ALevs

Cranleigh School
Horseshoe Lane, Cranleigh, Surrey GU6 8QQ
Tel: +44 (0) 1483 273666
Age range: 7–18 years (including Prep School)
No. of pupils: 683 *B*397 *G*286 *VIth*256
Curriculum: GCSE, IGCSE, ALevs

Culford School
Culford, Bury St Edmunds, Suffolk IP28 6TX
Tel: 01284 728615
Age range: 1–18
No. of pupils: 750
Curriculum: GCSE, IGCSE, ALevs
Language instr: English

Dauntsey's
High Street, West Lavington, Devizes, Wiltshire SN10 4HE
Tel: 01380 814500
Age range: 11–18
No. of pupils: 820 *B*407 *G*413 *VIth*270
Curriculum: GCSE, ALevs

Dean Close School
Shelburne Road, Cheltenham, Gloucestershire GL51 6HE
Tel: +44 (0)1242 258000
Age range: 13–18 years
No. of pupils: 490
Curriculum: GCSE, IGCSE, ALevs
Language instr: English

Deenway Montessori School & Unicity College
3-5 Sidmouth Street, Reading, Berkshire RG1 4QX
Tel: 0118 9574737
Age range: 3–18+ years

Denstone College
Uttoxeter, Staffordshire ST14 5HN
Tel: 01889 590484
Age range: 4–18 years
No. of pupils: 735
Curriculum: GCSE, IGCSE, ALevs

Deutsche Schule London
Douglas House, Petersham Road, Richmond, Surrey TW10 7AH
Tel: +44 (0)20 8940 2510
Age range: 3–18 years
Curriculum: Abitur, IBDP, National
Language instr: English, German

Didac School
16 Trinity Trees, Eastbourne, East Sussex BN21 3LE
Tel: +44 1323 417276
Age range: 16–18 years

DLD College London
199 Westminster Bridge Road, London, London SE1 7FX
Tel: +44 (0)20 7935 8411
Age range: 14–19 years
No. of pupils: 375
Curriculum: GCSE, IGCSE, ALevs
Language instr: English

Dover College
Effingham Crescent, Dover, Kent CT17 9RH
Tel: 01304 205969
Age range: 3–18 years
Language instr: English

d'Overbroeck's
333 Banbury Road, Oxford, Oxfordshire OX2 7PL
Tel: 01865 688 600
Age range: 11–18 years
Curriculum: GCSE, IGCSE, ALevs
Language instr: English

Downe House School
Downe House, Cold Ash, Thatcham, West Berkshire RG18 9JJ
Tel: +44 (0)1635 200286
Age range: G11–18 years
No. of pupils: 590
Curriculum: GCSE, IGCSE, ALevs
Language instr: English

Downside School
Stratton-on-the-Fosse, Radstock, Bath, Bath & North-East Somerset BA3 4RJ
Tel: 01761 235100
Age range: 11–18 years
No. of pupils: 360
Curriculum: GCSE, IGCSE, ALevs
Language instr: English

Duke of Kent School
Peaslake Road, Ewhurst, Surrey GU6 7NS
Tel: 01483 277313
Age range: 3–16 years
No. of pupils: 316
Curriculum: GCSE

Dulwich College
Dulwich Common,
London SE21 7LD
Tel: 020 8693 3601
Age range: B0–18 years
Curriculum: National, GCSE, IGCSE, ALevs
Language instr: English

Durham School
Quarryheads Lane, Durham,
Durham DH1 4SZ
Tel: +44 (0)191 731 9270
Age range: 11–18 years

Dwight School London
6 Friern Barnet Lane,
London, London N 1 3LX
Tel: 020 8920 0600
Age range: 2–18 years
Curriculum: IBDP, IBMYP, IBPYP, GCSE
Language instr: English

Earlscliffe
29 Shorncliffe Road,
Folkestone, Kent CT20 2NB
Tel: +44 (0)1303 253951
Age range: 15–19 years
Curriculum: ALevs

Eastbourne College
Old Wish Road, Eastbourne,
East Sussex BN21 4JX
Tel: 01323 452323 (Admissions)
Age range: 13–18 years
Curriculum: GCSE, IGCSE, ALevs

Ecole Charles De Gaulle – Wix
Clapham Common North Side,
London, London SW4 0AJ
Tel: +44 20 7738 0287
Age range: 5–11
No. of pupils: 100
Curriculum: National

Ecole Française de Bristol
Stanton Road, Southmead,
Bristol, Bristol BS10 5SJ
Tel: +44 (0)117 9692490
Age range: 3–11 years

Ecole Francaise Jacques Prevert
59 Brook Green, London,
London W6 7BE
Tel: 020 7602 6871
Age range: 4–11
No. of pupils: *B*139 *G* 24

ÉCOLE JEANNINE MANUEL – LONDON
For further details see p. 145
43-45 Bedford Square,
London, London WC1B 3DN
Tel: 020 3829 5970
Email: admissions@jmanuel.uk.net
Website: www.ecolejeanninemanuel.org.uk
Head of School: Pauline Prévot
Age range: 3–18 years
No. of pupils: 585
Fees: *Day* £20,760
Curriculum: IBDP, FrenchBacc, IGCSE
Language instr: English, French
COB ECIS

École Primaire Marie D'Orliac
60 Clancarty Road, London,
London SW6 3AA
Tel: +44 (0)20 7736 5863
Age range: 4–11
Curriculum: National

EF ACADEMY OXFORD
For further details see p. 148
Pullens Lane, Headington,
Oxfordshire OX3 0DT
Tel: +41 (0) 43 430 41 00
Email: academy.admissions@ef.com
Website: www.efacademy.org
Head of School: Mark Fletcher-Single
Age range: 16–19 years
Fees: *Day* £29,500 *FB* £44,500
Curriculum: IBDP, ALevs
Language instr: English

EIFA International School
36 Portland Place, London,
London W1B 1LS
Tel: +44 (0)20 7637 5351
Age range: 21 months–18 years
No. of pupils: 310
Curriculum: IBDP, National, IGCSE
Language instr: English, French

Ellesmere College
Ellesmere, Shropshire SY12 9AB
Tel: 01691 622321
Age range: 7–18 years
No. of pupils: 550
Curriculum: IBDP, UK, GCSE, ALevs
Language instr: English

Elmhurst Ballet School
249 Bristol Road, Edgbaston,
Birmingham, West Midlands B5 7UH
Tel: 0121 472 6655
Age range: 11–19
No. of pupils: *B*64 *G*125 *VIth*69
Curriculum: National, UK, GCSE, ALevs
Language instr: English

Embley
Embley Park, Romsey,
Hampshire SO51 6ZE
Tel: 01794 512206
Age range: 2–18 years
No. of pupils: 600
Language instr: English

Epsom College
Epsom, Surrey KT17 4JQ
Tel: 01372 821000
Age range: 11–18
No. of pupils: 884
Curriculum: GCSE, IGCSE, ALevs

Eton College
Windsor, Berkshire SL4 6DW
Tel: +44 (0)1753 370 611
Age range: *B*13–18 years
No. of pupils: 1342
Curriculum: GCSE, IGCSE, ALevs
Language instr: English

Fairview International School, Bridge of Allan
52 Kenilworth Road, Bridge
of Allan, Stirling FK9 4RY
Tel: +44 (0)1786 231952
Age range: 5–18 years
Curriculum: IBMYP
Language instr: English

Farlington School
Strood Park, Horsham,
West Sussex RH12 3PN
Tel: 01403 282573
Age range: 4–18
No. of pupils: 311
Curriculum: SAT, GCSE, IGCSE, ALevs
Language instr: English

Farringtons School
Perry Street, Chislehurst,
Kent BR7 6LR
Tel: 020 8467 0256
Age range: 3–18 years
No. of pupils: 700 *B*366 *G*334 *VIth*100
Curriculum: National, GCSE, IGCSE, ALevs
Language instr: English

Felsted School
Felsted, Great Dunmow,
Essex CM6 3LL
Tel: +44 (0)1371 822600
Age range: 4–18 years
Curriculum: IBDP, UK, GCSE, IGCSE, ALevs
Language instr: English
RS

Fettes College
Carrington Road, Edinburgh,
Edinburgh EH4 1QX
Tel: +44 (0)131 332 2281
Age range: 13–18 years
Curriculum: IBDP, UK, GCSE, IGCSE, ALevs, Scot Nat
Language instr: English

Finborough School
The Hall, Great Finborough,
Stowmarket, Suffolk IP14 3EF
Tel: 01449 773600
Age range: 2–18 years
Curriculum: GCSE, ALevs

Framlingham College
College Road, Framlingham,
Suffolk IP13 9EY
Tel: 01728 723789
Age range: 2–18
No. of pupils: 700
Curriculum: GCSE, IGCSE, ALevs
Language instr: English

Frensham Heights
Rowledge, Farnham,
Surrey GU10 4EA
Tel: 01252 792561
Age range: 3–18
No. of pupils: 497 *B*267 *G*230 *VIth*105
Curriculum: GCSE, ALevs

FULHAM SCHOOL
For further details see p. 151
1-3 Chesilton Road, London,
London SW6 5AA
Tel: 020 8154 6751
Email: admissions@fulham.school
Website: fulham.school
Pre-Prep & Nursery Head: Di Steven
Age range: 3–18 years
No. of pupils: 650
Fees: *Day* £18,420–£21,567
Curriculum: IBDP, GCSE, ALevs
Language instr: English

Fulneck School
Fulneck, Pudsey, Leeds,
West Yorkshire LS28 8DS
Tel: 0113 257 0235
Age range: 3–18
No. of pupils: 350
Curriculum: National, UK, GCSE, ALevs

Fyling Hall School
Robin Hood's Bay, Whitby,
North Yorkshire YO22 4QD
Tel: 01947 880353
Age range: 4–18 years

George Watson's College
69-71 Colinton Road, Edinburgh, Edinburgh EH10 5EG
Tel: 0131 446 6000
Age range: 3–18 years
Curriculum: ALevs, Scot Nat, SVQ, CSFS
Language instr: English

Giggleswick School
Settle, North Yorkshire BD24 0DE
Tel: 01729 893000
Age range: 11–18 years

Glenalmond College, Perth
Glenalmond, Perth, Perth & Kinross PH1 3RY
Tel: 01738 842000
Age range: 12–18 years
Curriculum: GCSE, IGCSE, ALevs

Godolphin and Latymer School
Iffley Road, Hammersmith, London, London W6 0PG
Tel: +44 (0)20 8741 1936
Age range: G11–18 years
No. of pupils: 800
Curriculum: IBDP, GCSE, IGCSE, ALevs
Language instr: English

Godolphin School
Milford Hill, Salisbury, Wiltshire SP1 2RA
Tel: 01722 430509
Age range: G11–18
No. of pupils: 380 *VIth*100
Curriculum: GCSE, IGCSE, ALevs

Gordonstoun
Elgin, Moray IV30 5RF
Tel: 01343 837829
Age range: 4.5–18 years
Curriculum: SAT, GCSE, IGCSE, ALevs

Gosfield School
Cut Hedge Park, Halstead Road, Gosfield, Halstead, Essex CO9 1PF
Tel: 01787 474040
Age range: 2–18 years

Grantham Preparatory International School
Gorse Lane, Grantham, Lincolnshire NG31 7UF
Tel: +44 (0)1476 593293
Age range: 3–11 years
Language instr: English

GREENE'S COLLEGE OXFORD
For further details see p. 153
45 Pembroke Street, Oxford, Oxfordshire OX1 1BP
Tel: 01865 664400
Email: enquiries@greenes.org.uk
Website: www.greenesoxford.com
Principal: Carmen Dare
No. of pupils: *VIth*60
Fees: £21,780
Curriculum: GCSE, ALevs

Greenfields Independent Day & Boarding School
Priory Road, Forest Row, East Sussex RH18 5JD
Tel: +44 (0)1342 822189
Age range: 2–18 years
Curriculum: GCSE, ALevs

Gresham's Nursery and Pre-Prep School
Market Place, Holt, Norfolk NR25 6BB
Tel: 01263 714575
Age range: 2–7 years

Gresham's Prep School
Holt, Norfolk NR25 6EY
Tel: 01263 714600
Age range: 7–13 years
Language instr: English

Gresham's Senior School
Cromer Road, Holt, Norfolk NR25 6EA
Tel: 01263 714500
Age range: 13–18 years
No. of pupils: 540
Curriculum: IBDP, UK, GCSE, IGCSE, ALevs
Language instr: English

HAILEYBURY
For further details see p. 155
Haileybury, Hertford, Hertfordshire SG13 7NU
Tel: +44 (0)1992 706353
Email: uk.admissions@haileybury.com
Website: www.haileybury.com
The Master: Martin Collier
Age range: 11–18 years *AGE1 *** DESCRIPTION REQUIRED* (entry at 11+, 13+ and 16+)
No. of pupils: 915 *B*458 *G*457 *VIth*364
Fees: *Day* £6,595–£9,920 *FB* £8,615–£13,580
Curriculum: IBDP, GCSE, IGCSE, ALevs
Language instr: English

Halcyon London International School
33 Seymour Place,, London W1H 5AU
Tel: +44 (0)20 7258 1169
Age range: 11–18
No. of pupils: 195
Curriculum: IBDP, IBMYP, UK
Language instr: English

Harrogate Ladies' College
Clarence Drive, Harrogate, North Yorkshire HG1 2QG
Tel: 01423 504543
Age range: G11–18 years

Headington School Oxford
London Road, Oxford, Oxfordshire OX3 7TD
Tel: +44 (0)1865 759100
Age range: G11–18 years
Curriculum: IBDP, GCSE, ALevs
Language instr: English

Heathfield School
London Road, Ascot, Berkshire SL5 8BQ
Tel: 01344 898343
Age range: G11–18 years
Curriculum: GCSE, IGCSE, ALevs
Language instr: English

Hill House
17 Hans Place, Chelsea, London, London SW1X 0EP
Tel: 020 7584 1331
Age range: 4–13
No. of pupils: 600 *B*350 *G*250

HOCKERILL ANGLO-EUROPEAN COLLEGE
For further details see p. 159
Dunmow Road, Bishops Stortford, Hertfordshire CM23 5HX
Tel: 01279 658451
Email: admissions@hockerill.com
Website: www.hockerill.com
Principal: David Woods
Age range: 11–18 years
No. of pupils: 900
Fees: *FB* £13,599–£18,405
Curriculum: IBDP, IBMYP, GCSE
Language instr: English

Holy Trinity School
Birmingham Road, Kidderminster, Worcestershire DY10 2BY
Tel: +44 (0)1562 822929
Age range: 4–18 years
Language instr: English

Hurstpierpoint College
College Lane, Hurstpierpoint, West Sussex BN6 9JS
Tel: 01273 833636
Age range: 4–18
No. of pupils: 1156
Curriculum: GCSE, ALevs

ICS LONDON
For further details see p. 161
7B Wyndham Place, London, London W1H 1PN
Tel: +44 (0)20 729 88800
Email: admissions@ics.uk.net
Website: www.icschool.co.uk
Head of School: David Laird
Age range: 3–19 years
No. of pupils: 175
Fees: *Day* £19,770–£28,920
Curriculum: IBDP, IBMYP, IBPYP, TOEFL
Language instr: English

IMPINGTON INTERNATIONAL COLLEGE
For further details see p. 164
New Road, Impington, Cambridge, Cambridgeshire CB24 9LX
Tel: 01223 200402
Email: international@ivc.tmet.org.uk
www.impingtoninternational.org.uk
College Principal: Victoria Hearn
Age range: 11–19 years
No. of pupils: 1311
Curriculum: IBDP
Language instr: English

Instituto Español Vicente Cañada Blanch
317 Portobello Road, London, London W10 5SZ
Tel: +44 (0) 20 8969 2664
Age range: 4–19
No. of pupils: 405

International School of Aberdeen
Pitfodels House, North Deeside Road, Pitfodels, Cults, Aberdeen, Aberdeen AB15 9PN
Tel: 01224 730300
Age range: 3–18 years
Curriculum: ACT, IBDP, SAT, IGCSE
Language instr: English

International School of Creative Arts (ISCA)
Framewood Road, Wexham, Buckinghamshire SL2 4QS
Tel: +44 (0)1753 208820
Age range: 15–19 years
No. of pupils: 85
Language instr: English

International School of London (ISL)
139 Gunnersbury Avenue, London, London W3 8LG
Tel: +44 (0)20 8992 5823
Age range: 3–18 years
No. of pupils: 500
Curriculum: IBDP, IBMYP, IBPYP
Language instr: English & Mother-tongue

Ipswich School
Henley Road, Ipswich, Suffolk IP1 3SG
Tel: 01473 408300
Age range: 2–18 years
No. of pupils: 893
Curriculum: GCSE, IGCSE, ALevs
Language instr: English

Kent College Pembury
Old Church Road, Pembury, Tunbridge Wells, Kent TN2 4AX
Tel: +44 (0)1892 822006
Age range: G3–18 years
No. of pupils: 500
Curriculum: GCSE, ALevs
Language instr: English

Kent College, Canterbury
Whitstable Road, Canterbury, Kent CT2 9DT
Tel: +44 (0)1227 763 231
Age range: 0–18 years (Boarding from 8) *Garden Cottage Nursery* 0–3 years
No. of pupils: 800
Curriculum: IBDP, UK, GCSE, IGCSE, ALevs
Language instr: English

Kilgraston School
Bridge of Earn, Perth, Perth & Kinross PH2 9BQ
Tel: 01738 812257
Age range: *G*5–18 years
Curriculum: National, UK, GCSE, ALevs, Scot Nat
Language instr: English

Kimbolton School
Kimbolton, Huntingdon, Cambridgeshire PE28 0EA
Tel: 01480 860505
Age range: 4–18 years
Curriculum: GCSE, ALevs
Language instr: English

King Edward's School
Edgbaston Park Road, Birmingham, West Midlands B15 2UA
Tel: 0121 472 1672
Age range: *B*11–18 years
No. of pupils: 885 *VIth*221
Curriculum: IBDP, GCSE, IGCSE
Language instr: English

King Edward's Witley
Petworth Road, Godalming, Surrey GU8 5SG
Tel: 01428 686735
Age range: 11–18 years
No. of pupils: 420
Curriculum: IBDP, UK, GCSE, IGCSE, ALevs
Language instr: English

King Fahad Academy
Bromyard Avenue, Acton, London, London W3 7HD
Tel: 020 8743 0131
Age range: 3–19
Curriculum: IBDP, IBMYP, USA, ALevs
Language instr: English

KING WILLIAM'S COLLEGE
For further details see p. 191
Castletown, Isle of Man IM9 1TP
Tel: +44 (0)1624 820110
Email: admissions@kwc.im
Website: www.kwc.im
Principal: Joss Buchanan
Age range: 11–18 years
No. of pupils: 380
Fees: *Day* £19,745–£26,395 *FB* £32,740–£39,390
Curriculum: IBDP, GCSE, IGCSE
Language instr: English

Kingham Hill School
Kingham, Chipping Norton, Oxfordshire OX7 6TH
Tel: 01608 658999
Age range: 11–18 years
Language instr: English

King's Bruton
The Plox, Bruton, Somerset BA10 0ED
Tel: 01749 814200
Age range: 13–18 years
No. of pupils: 360
Curriculum: GCSE, IGCSE, ALevs

King's College
South Road, Taunton, Somerset TA1 3LA
Tel: 01823 328200
Age range: 13–18 years

King's College School
Southside, Wimbledon Common, London, London SW19 4TT
Tel: 020 8255 5300
Age range: *B*7–18 years *G*16–18 years
No. of pupils: 1477 *VIth*419
Curriculum: IBDP, GCSE, ALevs
Language instr: English

King's Ely
Ely, Cambridgeshire CB7 4EW
Tel: 01353 660707
Age range: 2–18
No. of pupils: 1023
Curriculum: GCSE, IGCSE, ALevs
Language instr: English

KING'S INTERHIGH
For further details see p. 195
3 Burlington Gardens, London, London W1S 3EP
Tel: +44 (0)1873 777 444
Email: contact@kingsinterhigh.co.uk
Website: www.kingsinterhigh.co.uk
Executive Headteacher: Ashley Harrold
Age range: 7–18 years
No. of pupils: 3500
Fees: £2,901
Curriculum: National, UK, IGCSE, ALevs

King's Rochester
Satis House, Boley Hill, Rochester, Kent ME1 1TE
Tel: 01634 888555
Age range: 13–18 years
No. of pupils: 600 *VIth*95
Curriculum: GCSE, IGCSE, ALevs

Kingsley School
Northdown Road, Bideford, Devon EX39 3LY
Tel: 01237 426200
Age range: 0–18 years
No. of pupils: 395
Curriculum: GCSE, ALevs

Kingswood School
Lansdown Road, Bath, Bath & North-East Somerset BA1 5RG
Tel: 01225 734200
Age range: 9 months–18 years
Curriculum: GCSE, ALevs
Language instr: English

Kirkham Grammar School
Ribby Road, Kirkham, Preston, Lancashire PR4 2BH
Tel: 01772 684264
Age range: 3–18 years
No. of pupils: 870 *B*455 *G*415 *VIth*180
Curriculum: GCSE, ALevs
Language instr: English

La Petite Ecole Bilingue – Stewart
90 Oxford Gardens, London, London W10 5UW
Tel: +44 208 964 43 56
Age range: 3–10
Curriculum: National, UK

La Scuola Italiana a Londra
154-156 Holland Park Avenue, London, London W11 4UH
Tel: +44 (0)20 7603 5353

Lancing College
Lancing, West Sussex BN15 0RW
Tel: 01273 452213
Age range: 13–18
No. of pupils: 550 *B*342 *G*208 *VIth*255
Curriculum: GCSE, IGCSE, ALevs
Language instr: English

Landmark International School
The Old Rectory, 9 Church Lane, Fulbourn, Cambridge, Cambridgeshire CB21 5EP
Tel: 01223 755100
Age range: 4–16 years
No. of pupils: 100
Curriculum: IGCSE
Language instr: English

Langley Senior School & Sixth Form
Langley Park, Loddon, Norwich, Norfolk NR14 6BJ
Tel: 01508 520210
Age range: 10–18 years

Leighton Park School
Shinfield Road, Reading, Berkshire RG2 7ED
Tel: 0118 987 9600
Age range: 11–18 years
No. of pupils: 520
Curriculum: IBDP, UK, GCSE, IGCSE, ALevs
Language instr: English

Leweston Senior School
Sherborne, Dorset DT9 6EN
Tel: 01963 210691
Age range: 11–18 years
Curriculum: GCSE, ALevs

Lichfield Cathedral School
The Palace, The Close, Lichfield, Staffordshire WS13 7LH
Tel: 01543 306170
Age range: 2.5–18 years

Lime House School
Holm Hill, Dalston, Carlisle, Cumbria CA5 7BX
Tel: 01228 710225
Age range: 7–18 years
No. of pupils: 182
Curriculum: GCSE, IGCSE, ALevs

Lincoln Minster School
The Prior Building, Upper Lindum Street, Lincoln, Lincolnshire LN2 5RW
Tel: 01522 551300
Age range: 4–18 years
No. of pupils: 500

Llandovery College
Queensway, Llandovery, Carmarthenshire SA20 0EE
Tel: +44(0)1550 723000
Age range: 4–18 years
Curriculum: GCSE, IGCSE, ALevs

Lomond School
10 Stafford Street, Helensburgh, Argyll & Bute G84 9JX
Tel: +44 (0)1436 672476
Age range: 3–18 years
No. of pupils: 320
Curriculum: IBDP, IBCP
Language instr: English

Longridge Towers School
Longridge Towers, Berwick-upon-Tweed, Northumberland TD15 2XQ
Tel: 01289 307584
Age range: 3–19 years
No. of pupils: 313

Lord Wandsworth College
Long Sutton, Hook, Hampshire RG29 1TA
Tel: 01256 862201
Age range: 11–18 years
Curriculum: GCSE, IGCSE, ALevs
Language instr: English

LORETTO SCHOOL
For further details see p. 199
Pinkie House, Linkfield Road, Musselburgh, East Lothian EH21 7RE
Tel: +44 (0)131 653 4455
Email: admissions@loretto.com
Website: www.loretto.com
Head of School: Graham R. W. Hawley
Age range: 3–18 years
No. of pupils: 520
Fees: *Day* £2,933–£8,385 *FB* £8,020–£12,315 £6,830–£10,220
Curriculum: SAT, GCSE, IGCSE, ALevs, Scot Nat

LOUGHBOROUGH GRAMMAR SCHOOL
For further details see p. 200
Buckland House, Burton Walks, Loughborough, Leicestershire LE11 2DU
Tel: 01509 233233
Email: grammar.admissions@lsf.org
Website: www.lsf.org/grammar
Headmaster: Daniel Koch
Age range: *B*10–18 years
No. of pupils: 890
Fees: £4,900
Curriculum: GCSE, IGCSE, ALevs
Language instr: English

Luckley House School
Luckley Road, Wokingham, Berkshire RG40 3EU
Tel: 0118 978 4175
Age range: 11–18 years
Curriculum: GCSE, ALevs

Lucton School
Lucton, Herefordshire HR6 9PN
Tel: 01568 782000
Age range: 1–18 years (Boarding from 7)
No. of pupils: 300
Curriculum: National, IGCSE, ALevs
Language instr: English

LVS Ascot
London Road, Ascot, Berkshire SL5 8DR
Tel: 01344 882770
Age range: 4–18 years
No. of pupils: 800
Curriculum: GCSE, ALevs

Lycée Français Charles de Gaulle de Londres
35 Cromwell Road, London, London SW7 2DG
Tel: 020 7584 6322
Age range: 3–18 years
No. of pupils: 3450
Language instr: French, English

Lycée International de Londres Winston Churchill
54 Forty Lane, London, London HA9 9LY
Tel: +44 (0)203 824 4900
Age range: 3–18 years
Curriculum: IBDP, FrenchBacc, UK, IGCSE
Language instr: English, French

Malvern College
College Road, Malvern, Worcestershire WR14 3DF
Tel: +44 (0)1684 581515
Age range: 13–18 years
No. of pupils: 660
Curriculum: IBDP, GCSE, IGCSE, ALevs
Language instr: English

Malvern St James Girls' School
15 Avenue Road, Great Malvern, Worcestershire WR14 3BA
Tel: 01684 892288
Age range: *G*4–18
No. of pupils: 410
Curriculum: GCSE, IGCSE, ALevs

Manchester High School for Girls
Grangethorpe Road, Manchester, Greater Manchester M14 6HS
Tel: 0161 224 0447
Age range: *G*4–18 years
No. of pupils: 1000
Curriculum: GCSE, ALevs
Language instr: English

Marlborough College
Bath Road, Marlborough, Wiltshire SN8 1PA
Tel: 01672 892200
Age range: 13–18
No. of pupils: 960
Curriculum: ALevs
Language instr: English

MARYMOUNT LONDON
For further details see p. 204
George Road, Kingston upon Thames, Surrey KT2 7PE
Tel: +44 (0)20 8949 0571
Email: admissions@marymountlondon.com
Website: www.marymountlondon.com
Headmistress: Margaret Giblin
Age range: *G*11–18 years
No. of pupils: 260
Fees: *Day* £27,250 *WB* £44,180 *FB* £46,130
Curriculum: IBDP, IBMYP
Language instr: English

Mayfield School
The Old Palace, Mayfield, East Sussex TN20 6PH
Tel: 01435 874642
Age range: G11–18 years
No. of pupils: 405
Curriculum: GCSE, IGCSE, ALevs

MERCHISTON CASTLE SCHOOL
For further details see p. 205
294 Colinton Road, Edinburgh, Edinburgh EH13 0PU
Tel: 0131 312 2200
Email: admissions@merchiston.co.uk
Website: www.merchiston.co.uk
Headmaster: Jonathan Anderson
Age range: *B*7–18 years
No. of pupils: 400
Fees: *Day* £15,330–£26,040 *FB* £22,080–£35,880
Curriculum: GCSE, IGCSE, ALevs, Scot Nat
Language instr: English

Methodist College
1 Malone Road, Belfast, County Antrim BT9 6BY
Tel: 028 9020 5205
Age range: 4–18 years

Michael Hall School
Kidbrooke Park, Priory Road, Forest Row, East Sussex RH18 5JA
Tel: 01342 822275
Age range: 0–19 years
Language instr: English

Mill Hill School
The Ridgeway, Mill Hill Village, London, London NW7 1QS
Tel: 020 8959 1176
Age range: 13–18 years
No. of pupils: 876 *VIth*312
Curriculum: TOEFL, UK, GCSE, ALevs

Millfield School
Butleigh Road, Street, Somerset BA16 0YD
Tel: 01458 442291
Age range: 13–18 years
No. of pupils: 1301
Curriculum: GCSE, IGCSE, ALevs

Milton Abbey School
Blandford Forum, Dorset DT11 0BZ
Tel: 01258 880484
Age range: 13–18 years
Curriculum: GCSE, ALevs
Language instr: English

Monkton Senior School
Monkton Combe, Bath, Bath & North-East Somerset BA2 7HG
Tel: 01225 721133
Age range: 13–18 years
No. of pupils: 372 *B*215 *G*157 *VIth*140
Curriculum: GCSE, IGCSE, ALevs

Monmouth School for Boys
Almshouse Street, Monmouth, Monmouthshire NP25 3XP
Tel: 01600 713143
Age range: *B*11–18 years

Monmouth School for Girls
Hereford Road, Monmouth, Monmouthshire NP25 5XT
Tel: 01600 711100
Age range: *G*11–18 years

Moreton Hall
Weston Rhyn, Oswestry, Shropshire SY11 3EW
Tel: +44 (0)1691 773671
Age range: 11–18 years

Mount Kelly
Parkwood Road, Tavistock, Devon PL19 0HZ
Tel: +44 (0)1822 813100
Age range: 3–18 years
Curriculum: UK, GCSE, IGCSE, ALevs

Mount St Mary's College
College Road, Spinkhill, Near Sheffield, Derbyshire S21 3YL
Tel: 01246 433388
Age range: 11–18 years
No. of pupils: 350
Curriculum: GCSE, IGCSE, ALevs
Language instr: English

Moyles Court School
Moyles Court, Ringwood, Hampshire BH24 3NF
Tel: 01425 472856
Age range: 2–16 years

New Hall School
The Avenue, Boreham, Chelmsford, Essex CM3 3HS
Tel: 01245 467588
Age range: 1–18 years
No. of pupils: 1400
Curriculum: UK, IGCSE
Language instr: English

North London Collegiate School
Canons, Canons Drive, Edgware, Middlesex HA8 7RJ
Tel: +44 (0)20 8952 0912
Age range: G4–18 years
No. of pupils: 1080
Curriculum: IBDP, GCSE, IGCSE, ALevs
Language instr: English

Oakham School
Chapel Close, Oakham, Rutland LE15 6DT
Tel: 01572 758758
Age range: 10–18 years
No. of pupils: 1040 *B*537 *G*503 *VIth*376
Curriculum: IBDP, IBMYP, GCSE, IGCSE, ALevs
Language instr: English

Oaks International School
Cherry Hinton Road Cambridge, Cambridgeshire CE1 8DW
Tel: +44 (0) 1223 416938
Age range: 2–11 years
Curriculum: IPC, UK

Oswestry School
Upper Brook Street, Oswestry, Shropshire SY11 2TL
Tel: +44 (0)1691 6557 1
Age range: 4–18 years
Language instr: English

Oundle School
The Great Hall, New Street, Oundle, Northamptonshire PE8 4GH
Tel: +44 (0)1832 277122
Age range: 11–18 years
Language instr: English

Oxford International College
1 London Place, Oxford, Oxfordshire OX4 1BD
Tel: +44 (0)1865 203988
Age range: 14–19 years

Padworth College
Sopers Lane, Reading, Berkshire RG7 4NR
Tel: 0118 983 2644
Age range: 14–19 years
Curriculum: GCSE, IGCSE, ALevs

Pangbourne College
Pangbourne, Reading, Berkshire RG8 8LA
Tel: 0118 984 2101
Age range: 11–18 years
No. of pupils: 458
Curriculum: ALevs
Language instr: English

Plymouth College
Ford Park, Plymouth, Devon PL4 6RN
Tel: 01752 505100
Age range: 3–18 years
No. of pupils: 569 *B*329 *G*240
Curriculum: UK, GCSE, IGCSE, ALevs
Language instr: English

Pocklington School
West Green, Pocklington, York, North Yorkshire YO42 2NJ
Tel: 01759 321200
Age range: 3–18 years
No. of pupils: 730 *B*376 *G*354 *VIth*150
Curriculum: GCSE, IGCSE, ALevs
Language instr: English

Prior Park College
Ralph Allen Drive, Bath, Bath & North-East Somerset BA2 5AH
Tel: +44 (0)1225 835353
Age range: 11–18 years
Curriculum: GCSE, ALevs

Prior's Field
Priorsfield Road, Godalming, Surrey GU7 2RH
Tel: 01483 810551
Age range: G11–18
No. of pupils: 450
Curriculum: GCSE, IGCSE, ALevs

Queen Anne's School
6 Henley Road, Caversham, Reading, Berkshire RG4 6DX
Tel: 0118 918 7300
Age range: G11–18 years
Curriculum: GCSE, IGCSE, ALevs

Queen Ethelburga's Collegiate
Thorpe Underwood Hall, Ouseburn, York, North Yorkshire YO26 9SS
Tel: 01423 33 33 30
Age range: 3–19 years
No. of pupils: 1400
Curriculum: National, UK, GCSE, IGCSE, ALevs
Language instr: English

Queen Margaret's School
Escrick Park, York, North Yorkshire YO19 6EU
Tel: 01904 727600
Age range: G11–18 years

Queen Mary's School
Baldersby Park, Topcliffe, Thirsk, North Yorkshire YO7 3BZ
Tel: 01845 575000
Age range: *B*4–7 years *G*4–16 years

Queen Victoria School
Dunblane, Perthshire FK15 0JY
Tel: 01786 822288
Age range: 11–18 years
Curriculum: Scot Nat, SVQ, CSFS

Queen's College
Trull Road, Taunton, Somerset TA1 4QS
Tel: +44 (0)1823 272559
Age range: 3 months–18 years

Radley College
Radley, Abingdon, Oxfordshire OX14 2HR
Tel: 01235 543000
Age range: *B*13–18 years

Ratcliffe College
Fosse Way, Ratcliffe on the Wreake, Leicester, Leicestershire LE7 4SG
Tel: +44 (0)1509 817000
Age range: 3–18 years (Boarding from 11)
Language instr: English

REDDAM HOUSE BERKSHIRE
For further details see p. 216
Bearwood Road, Sindlesham, Wokingham, Berkshire RG41 5BG
Tel: +44 (0)118 974 8300
Email: registrar@reddamhouse.org.uk
Website: www.reddamhouse.org.uk
Principal: Rick Cross
Age range: 3 months–18 years
No. of pupils: 650
Fees: *Day* £12,000–£19,248 *WB* £27,981–£32,244 *FB* £29,526–£33,789
Curriculum: UK, GCSE, ALevs
Language instr: English

Redmaids' High School Senior & Sixth Form
Westbury Road, Westbury-on-Trym, Bristol, Bristol BS9 3AW
Tel: 0117 962 2641
Age range: G11–18 years
Curriculum: IBDP, GCSE, IGCSE, ALevs
Language instr: English

Reed's School
Sandy Lane, Cobham, Surrey KT11 2ES
Tel: 01932 869001
Age range: *B*11–18 *G*16–18
No. of pupils: 650 *B*590 *G*60 *VIth*230
Curriculum: GCSE, IGCSE, ALevs
Language instr: English

Rendcomb College
Rendcomb, Cirencester, Gloucestershire GL7 7HA
Tel: 01285 831213
Age range: 3–18 years

Repton School
The Hall, Repton, Derbyshire DE65 6FH
Tel: 01283 559200
Age range: 13–18 years
Curriculum: GCSE, IGCSE, ALevs

Rikkyo School in England
Guildford Road, Rudgwick, Horsham, West Sussex RH12 3BE
Tel: 01403 822107
Age range: 10–18
No. of pupils: 116 *B*65 *G*51
Curriculum: GCSE

Rishworth School
Rishworth, Halifax, West Yorkshire HX6 4QA
Tel: 01422 822217
Age range: 3–18
No. of pupils: 600 *B*331 *G*269 *VIth*90
Curriculum: GCSE, ALevs

Rochester Independent College
254 St Margaret's Banks, Rochester, Kent ME1 1HY
Tel: +44 (0)163 482 8115
Age range: 11–18 years

Rockport School
15 Rockport Road, Craigavad, Holywood, County Down BT18 0DD
Tel: 028 9042 8372
Age range: 3–18 years
Curriculum: GCSE, ALevs

Roedean School
Roedean Way, Brighton,
East Sussex BN2 5RQ
Tel: 01273 667500
Age range: G11–18 years
No. of pupils: 675 *VIth*155
Curriculum: GCSE, IGCSE, ALevs
Language instr: English

Rookwood School
Weyhill Road, Andover,
Hampshire SP10 3AL
Tel: 01264 325900
Age range: 2–18 years

ROSSALL SCHOOL
For further details see p. 218
Broadway, Fleetwood,
Lancashire FY7 8JW
Tel: +44 (0)1253 774201
Email: admissions@rossall.org.uk
Website: www.rossall.org.uk
Head: Jeremy Quartermain
Age range: 0–18 years
No. of pupils: 851
Fees: *Day* £3,145–£5,050
WB £5,350–£8,695
FB £7,955–£12,895
Curriculum: IBDP, National,
GCSE, IGCSE, ALevs
Language instr: English

ROYAL HIGH SCHOOL BATH, GDST
For further details see p. 219
Lansdown Road, Bath, Bath &
North-East Somerset BA1 5SZ
Tel: +44 (0)1225 313877
Email: admissions@rhsb.gdst.net
Website:
www.royalhighbath.gdst.net
Head: Kate Reynolds
Age range: G3–18 years
No. of pupils: 580
Fees: *Day* £5,041–£5,262
FB £11,234–£11,809
Curriculum: IBDP,
National, GCSE, ALevs
Language instr: English

Royal Russell School
Coombe Lane, Croydon,
Surrey CR9 5BX
Tel: 020 3657 3669
Age range: 11–18
No. of pupils: 590 *B*310 *G*280 *VIth*180
Curriculum: GCSE, ALevs

Rugby School
Lawrence Sheriff Street, Rugby,
Warwickshire CV22 5EH
Tel: +44 (0)1788 556274
Age range: 11–18
Curriculum: IBDP, National,
GCSE, IGCSE, ALevs

Ruthin School
Mold Road, Ruthin,
Denbighshire LL15 1EE
Tel: 01824 702543
Age range: 11–18 years
Curriculum: GCSE, ALevs

Rydal Penrhos Senior School
Pwllycrochan Avenue, Colwyn
Bay, Clwyd LL29 7BT
Tel: +44 (0)1492 530155
Age range: 11–18 years
Curriculum: IGCSE, ALevs
Language instr: English

Ryde School with Upper Chine
Queen's Road, Ryde, Isle
of Wight PO33 3BE
Tel: 01983 562229
Age range: 2 1/2–18 years
No. of pupils: 800
Curriculum: IBDP, IBCP,
National, GCSE, ALevs
Language instr: English

Rye St Antony
Pullen's Lane, Oxford,
Oxfordshire OX3 0BY
Tel: 01865 762802
Age range: *B*3–11 years *G*3–18 years
Language instr: English

Saint Felix School
Halesworth Road, Southwold,
Suffolk IP18 6SD
Tel: 01502 722175
Age range: 2–18
No. of pupils: 312 *B*167 *G*145 *VIth*65
Curriculum: GCSE, ALevs
Language instr: English

Scarborough College
Filey Road, Scarborough,
North Yorkshire YO11 3BA
Tel: +44 (0)1723 360620
Age range: 3–18 years
No. of pupils: 484
Curriculum: IBDP, GCSE, IGCSE
Language instr: English

SEAFORD COLLEGE
For further details see p. 221
Lavington Park, Petworth,
West Sussex GU28 0NB
Tel: 01798 867392
Email:
headmasterpa@seaford.org
Website: www.seaford.org
Headmaster: J P Green
Age range: 5–18 years
No. of pupils: 903 *B*544
*G*359 *VIth*235
Fees: *Day* £11,880–£24,630
WB £24,735–£33,345 *FB* £38,070
Curriculum: National,
GCSE, IGCSE, ALevs
Language instr: English

Sedbergh School
Station Road, Sedbergh,
Cumbria LA10 5HG
Tel: 015396 20535
Age range: 3–19 years
Curriculum: GCSE, IGCSE, ALevs

SEVENOAKS SCHOOL
For further details see p. 230
High Street, Sevenoaks,
Kent TN13 1HU
Tel: +44 (0)1732 455133
Email:
regist@sevenoaksschool.org
Website:
www.sevenoaksschool.org
Head of School: Jesse R Elzinga
Age range: 11–18 years
No. of pupils: 1164
Fees: *Day* £25,020–£28,413
FB £39,960–£43,353
Curriculum: IBDP, National,
GCSE, IGCSE
Language instr: English

Shebbear College
Shebbear, Beaworthy,
Devon EX21 5HJ
Tel: 01409 282000
Age range: 4–18 years
Curriculum: GCSE, ALevs
Language instr: English

Sherborne Girls
Bradford Road, Sherborne,
Dorset DT9 3QN
Tel: 01935 812245
Age range: G11–18 years
Curriculum: GCSE, IGCSE, ALevs
Language instr: English

Sherborne International
Newell Grange, Newell,
Sherborne, Dorset DT9 4EZ
Tel: +44 (0)1935 814743
Age range: 8–17 years
Curriculum: National, GCSE, IGCSE
Language instr: English

Sherborne School
Abbey Road, Sherborne,
Dorset DT9 3LF
Tel: +44 (0)1935 812249
Age range: *B*13–18 years
Curriculum: GCSE, IGCSE, ALevs
Language instr: English

Sherfield School
South Drive, Sherfield-on-Loddon,
Hook, Hampshire RG27 0HU
Tel: 01256 884800
Age range: 3 months–18 years
Curriculum: GCSE, IGCSE, ALevs
Language instr: English

Shiplake College
Henley-on-Thames,
Oxfordshire RG9 4BW
Tel: +44 (0)1189 402455
Age range: *B*11–18 years
*G*16–18 years
No. of pupils: 480 *B*420 *G*60 *VIth*200
Curriculum: GCSE, IGCSE, ALevs
Language instr: English

Shrewsbury School
The Schools, Shrewsbury,
Shropshire SY3 7BA
Tel: 01743 280552
Age range: 13–18 years
No. of pupils: 820 *B*535 *G*285
Curriculum: GCSE, IGCSE, ALevs
Language instr: English

Sibford School
Sibford Ferris, Banbury,
Oxfordshire OX15 5QL
Tel: 01295 781200
Age range: 3–18 years
Language instr: English

Sidcot School
Oakridge Lane, Winscombe,
Somerset BS25 1PD
Tel: 01934 843102
Age range: 3–18 years
No. of pupils: 603
Curriculum: IBDP, GCSE, ALevs
Language instr: English

Slindon College
Slindon House, Slindon, Arundel,
West Sussex BN18 0RH
Tel: 01243 814320
Age range: *B*8–18 years
Curriculum: UK, GCSE, IGCSE, ALevs
Language instr: English

SOUTHBANK INTERNATIONAL SCHOOL – HAMPSTEAD
For further details see p. 232
16 Netherhall Gardens,
London, London NW3 5TH
Tel: 020 7243 3803
Age range: 3–11 years
No. of pupils: 210
Curriculum: IBPYP
Language instr: English
ECIS

SOUTHBANK INTERNATIONAL SCHOOL – KENSINGTON
For further details see p. 232
36-38 Kensington Park Road,
London, London W11 3BU
Tel: +44 (0)20 7243 3803
Email:
admissions@southbank.org
Website: www.southbank.org
Principal: Siobhan McGrath
Age range: 3–18 years
Fees: £6,410
Curriculum: IBPYP
Language instr: English

SOUTHBANK INTERNATIONAL SCHOOL – WESTMINSTER
For further details see p. 232
63-65 Portland Place, London, London W1B 1QR
Tel: 020 7243 3803
Age range: 11–19
Curriculum: IBDP, IBMYP
Language instr: English

St Andrew's College Cambridge
13 Station Road, Cambridge, Cambridgeshire CB1 2JB
Tel: +44 (0)1223 903048
Age range: 15–18 years

St Catherine's, Bramley
Station Road, Bramley, Guildford, Surrey GU5 0DF
Tel: 01483 899609
Age range: *G*4–18
Curriculum: UK, GCSE, IGCSE, ALevs

St Christopher School
Barrington Road, Letchworth Garden City, Hertfordshire SG6 3JZ
Tel: 01462 650 850
Age range: 3–18 years

St Clare's, Oxford
139 Banbury Road, Oxford, Oxfordshire OX2 7AL
Tel: +44 (0)1865 552031
Age range: 14–18 years
No. of pupils: 280
Curriculum: IBDP
Language instr: English

St David's College
Gloddaeth Hall, Llandudno, Clwyd LL30 1RD
Tel: 01492 875974
Age range: 9–19 years
Curriculum: GCSE, ALevs

St Dunstan's College
Stanstead Road, London, London SE6 4TY
Tel: 020 8516 7200
Age range: 3–18
No. of pupils: 870
Curriculum: National, UK, ALevs
Language instr: English

St Edmund's College & Prep School
Old Hall Green, Nr Ware, Hertfordshire SG11 1DS
Tel: 01920 824247
Age range: 3–18 years

St Edmund's School
St Thomas Hill, Canterbury, Kent CT2 8HU
Tel: 01227 475601
Age range: 2–18 years
No. of pupils: 602
Curriculum: National, GCSE, ALevs

St Edward's, Oxford
Woodstock Road, Oxford, Oxfordshire OX2 7NN
Tel: +44 (0)1865 319200
Age range: 13–18 years
No. of pupils: 775
Curriculum: IBDP, GCSE, IGCSE, ALevs
Language instr: English

St Francis' College
Broadway, Letchworth Garden City, Hertfordshire SG6 3PJ
Tel: 01462 670511
Age range: *G*3–18 years
Language instr: English

St George's Ascot
Wells Lane, Ascot, Berkshire SL5 7DZ
Tel: 01344 629900
Age range: *G*11–18 years
Curriculum: GCSE, ALevs
Language instr: English

St George's School for Girls
Garscube Terrace, Edinburgh, Edinburgh EH12 6BG
Tel: 0131 311 8000
Age range: *B*2–5 years *G*2–18 years
Curriculum: UK, GCSE, IGCSE, ALevs, Scot Nat, CSFS
Language instr: English

St Helen's School
Eastbury Road, Northwood, Middlesex HA6 3AS
Tel: +44 (0)1923 843210
Age range: *G*3–18 years
No. of pupils: 1150
Language instr: English

St James Senior Boys School
Church Road, Ashford, Surrey TW15 3DZ
Tel: 01784 266930
Age range: *B*11–18
No. of pupils: 403 *VIth*65
Curriculum: GCSE, IGCSE, ALevs

St John's College
Grove Road South, Southsea, Portsmouth, Hampshire PO5 3QW
Tel: 023 9281 5118
Age range: 4–18 years
Language instr: English

St John's School
Epsom Road, Leatherhead, Surrey KT22 8SP
Tel: 01372 373000
Age range: 11–18
No. of pupils: 840
Curriculum: National, GCSE, ALevs
Language instr: English

St John's School
Broadway, Sidmouth, Devon EX10 8RG
Tel: 01395 513984
Age range: 2–18 years
Curriculum: GCSE, IGCSE

St Joseph's College
Belstead Road, Ipswich, Suffolk IP2 9DR
Tel: 01473 690281
Age range: 3–18
Curriculum: GCSE, IGCSE, ALevs

ST LAWRENCE COLLEGE
For further details see p. 237
Ramsgate, Kent CT11 7AE
Tel: 01843 572931
Email: admissions@slcuk.com
Website: www.slcuk.com
Head of College: Barney Durrant
Age range: 3–18 years
No. of pupils: 585
Fees: *Day* £8,394–£18,558 *FB* £29,454–£38,952
Curriculum: GCSE, ALevs
Language instr: English

St Leonards School
The Pends, St Andrews, Fife KY16 9QJ
Tel: 01334 472126
Age range: 5–18 years
No. of pupils: 590
Curriculum: IBDP, IBMYP, IBPYP, IBCP, GCSE, IGCSE
Language instr: English

ST MARGARET'S SCHOOL, BUSHEY
For further details see p. 238
Merry Hill Road, Bushey, Hertfordshire WD23 1DT
Tel: +44 (0)20 8416 4400
Email: admissions@stmargarets-school.org.uk
Website: www.stmargarets-school.org.uk
Headteacher: Lara Péchard
Age range: 2–18 years
No. of pupils: 650
Fees: £6,423
Curriculum: GCSE, IGCSE, ALevs

St Mary's Calne
Curzon Street, Calne, Wiltshire SN11 0DF
Tel: 01249 857200
Age range: *G*11–18 years
No. of pupils: 360 *VIth*115
Curriculum: GCSE, IGCSE, ALevs
Language instr: English

St Mary's Music School
Coates Hall, 25 Grosvenor Crescent, Edinburgh, Edinburgh EH12 5EL
Tel: 0131 538 7766
Age range: 9–19 years
Curriculum: IGCSE, ALevs, Scot Nat, CSFS

St Mary's School
Bateman Street, Cambridge, Cambridgeshire CB2 1LY
Tel: 01223 353253
Age range: *G*4–18 years
Curriculum: GCSE, ALevs

St Mary's School Ascot
St Mary's Road, Ascot, Berkshire SL5 9JF
Tel: 01344 296614
Age range: *G*11–18 years
Curriculum: GCSE, IGCSE, ALevs
Language instr: English

St Paul's School
Lonsdale Road, Barnes, London, London SW13 9JT
Tel: 020 8748 9162
Age range: *B*13–18 years
Curriculum: UK, IGCSE, ALevs

St Swithun's School
Alresford Road, Winchester, Hampshire SO21 1HA
Tel: 01962 835700
Age range: *G*11–18 years
No. of pupils: 510
Curriculum: GCSE, ALevs

St Teresa's Effingham (Senior School)
Beech Avenue, Effingham, Surrey RH5 6ST
Tel: 01372 452037
Age range: *G*11–18
No. of pupils: 640 *VIth*90
Curriculum: GCSE, ALevs

St. James School
22 Bargate, Grimsby, North-East Lincolnshire DN34 4SY
Tel: 01472 503260
Age range: 11–18 years
Language instr: English

St. Michael's School
Bryn, Llanelli, Carmarthenshire SA14 9TU
Tel: 01554 820325
Age range: 3–18 years

Stamford High School
St. Martin's Street, Stamford, Lincolnshire PE9 2LL
Tel: 01780 484200
Age range: G11–18 years
Curriculum: GCSE, ALevs

Stamford School
Southfields House, Stamford, Lincolnshire PE9 2BQ
Tel: 01780 750300
Age range: B11–18 years
Curriculum: GCSE, IGCSE, ALevs

Stanborough Secondary School
Stanborough Park, Garston, Watford, Hertfordshire WD25 9JT
Tel: 01923 673268
Age range: 11–18 years
Language instr: English

Stephen Perse Sixth Form
Bateman Street, Cambridge, Cambridgeshire CB2 1NA
Tel: 01223 454700 (Ext: 3000)
Age range: 16–18 years
Curriculum: IBDP, GCSE, IGCSE, ALevs
Language instr: English

Stewart's Melville College
Queensferry Road, Edinburgh, Edinburgh EH4 3EZ
Tel: +44 (0)131 311 1000
Age range: B12–18 years
Curriculum: National, Scot Nat, CSFS

Steyning Grammar School
Shooting Field, Steyning, West Sussex BN44 3RX
Tel: +44 (0)1903 814555
Age range: 11–18
No. of pupils: 1975
Curriculum: GCSE, ALevs
Language instr: English

Stoke College
Stoke-by-Clare, Sudbury, Suffolk CO10 8JE
Tel: 01787 278141
Age range: 3–18
No. of pupils: B143 G98
Curriculum: GCSE

Stonar School
Cottles Park, Atworth, Melksham, Wiltshire SN12 8NT
Tel: 01225 701740
Age range: 2–18 years
No. of pupils: 370
Curriculum: GCSE, IGCSE, ALevs

Stonyhurst College
Stonyhurst, Clitheroe, Lancashire BB7 9PZ
Tel: 01254 827073
Age range: 3–18 years
No. of pupils: 801
Curriculum: IBDP, IBCP, GCSE, ALevs

Stover School
Stover, Newton Abbot, Devon TQ12 6QG
Tel: +44 (0)1626 354505
Age range: 3–18 years

Stowe School
Buckingham, Buckinghamshire MK18 5EH
Tel: 01280 818000
Age range: 13–18 years
Curriculum: UK, GCSE, IGCSE, ALevs
Language instr: English

STRATHALLAN SCHOOL
For further details see p. 245
Forgandenny, Perth, Perth & Kinross PH2 9EG
Tel: 01738 812546
Email: admissions@strathallan.co.uk
Website: www.strathallan.co.uk
Headmaster: Mark Lauder
Age range: 7–18 years
No. of pupils: 545
Fees: *Day* £15,474–£24,474 *FB* £25,140–£36,036
Curriculum: GCSE, ALevs, Scot Nat

Sutton Valence School
North Street, Sutton Valence, Kent ME17 3HL
Tel: 01622 845200
Age range: 11–18 years
No. of pupils: 557
Curriculum: UK, GCSE, IGCSE, ALevs
Language instr: English

Talbot Heath
Rothesay Road, Talbot Woods, Bournemouth, Dorset BH4 9NJ
Tel: 01202 761881
Age range: G3–18 years
Curriculum: GCSE, ALevs

TASIS THE AMERICAN SCHOOL IN ENGLAND
For further details see p. 246
Coldharbour Lane, Thorpe, Surrey TW20 8TE
Tel: +44 (0)1932 582316
Email: ukadmissions@tasisengland.org
Website: www.tasisengland.org
Head of School: Bryan Nixon
Age range: 3–18 years
No. of pupils: 620
Fees: *Day* £12,770–£27,430 *FB* £50,850
Curriculum: ACT, AP, IBDP, SAT, TOEFL, USA
Language instr: English
(CIS) (ECIS)

Taunton School
Staplegrove Road, Taunton, Somerset TA2 6AD
Tel: +44 (0)1823 703703
Age range: 0–18 years
No. of pupils: 1000
Curriculum: IBDP, UK, GCSE, IGCSE, ALevs
Language instr: English

TAUNTON SCHOOL INTERNATIONAL
For further details see p. 248
206-216 Greenway Road, Taunton, Somerset TA2 6LJ
Tel: 01823 703200
Email: admissions@tauntonschool.co.uk
Website: www.tauntonschool.co.uk
Principal: Adrian Hallworth
Age range: 8–18 years
No. of pupils: 145
Fees: £7,600–£14,975

Teikyo School UK
Framewood Road, Wexham, Buckinghamshire SL2 4QS
Tel: 01753 663711
Age range: 15–18 years

Tettenhall College
Wood Road, Tettenhall, Wolverhampton, West Midlands WV6 8QX
Tel: 01902 751119
Age range: 2–18 years
No. of pupils: 410
Curriculum: National, UK, GCSE, IGCSE, ALevs

The Abbey School
Kendrick Road, Reading, Berkshire RG1 5DZ
Tel: 0118 987 2256
Age range: G3–18 years
No. of pupils: 1000
Curriculum: IBDP, GCSE, IGCSE, ALevs
Language instr: English

The American School in London
One Waverley Place, London, London NW8 0NP
Tel: 020 7449 1221
Age range: 4–18
No. of pupils: 1350 *B696 G654*
Language instr: English
(CIS) (ECIS)

The Chalfonts Independent Grammar School
19 London Road, High Wycombe, Buckinghamshire HP11 1BJ
Tel: +44 (0)1494 875502
Age range: 11–18 years
Curriculum: IBDP, IBMYP, UK

The Hammond School
Mannings Lane, Chester, Cheshire CH2 4ES
Tel: 01244 305350
Age range: 11–19+ years

The King's School, Canterbury
Lattergate Office, 25 The Precincts, Canterbury, Kent CT1 2ES
Tel: 01227 595501
Age range: 13–18 years
Curriculum: GCSE, IGCSE, ALevs
Language instr: English

The Leys School
Trumpington Road, Cambridge, Cambridgeshire CB2 7AD
Tel: 01223 508900
Age range: 11–18 years
No. of pupils: 567
Curriculum: GCSE, ALevs, CSFS

The Manchester Grammar School
Old Hall Lane, Fallowfield, Manchester, Greater Manchester M13 0XT
Tel: 0161 224 7201
Age range: B7–18 years
Language instr: English

The Mary Erskine School
Ravelston, Edinburgh, Edinburgh EH4 3NT
Tel: +44 (0)131 347 5700
Age range: G12–18 years
Curriculum: Scot Nat, CSFS

The Mount School York
Dalton Terrace, York, North Yorkshire YO24 4DD
Tel: 01904 667500
Age range: G3–18 years

The Mount, Mill Hill International
Milespit Hill, London
London NW7 2RX
Tel: +44 (0)20 3826 33
Age range: 13–17 years
No. of pupils: 80
Curriculum: UK, GCSE, IGCSE

The Oratory School
Woodcote, Reading,
Berkshire RG8 0PJ
Tel: 01491 683500
Age range: 11–18 years
Curriculum: UK, GCSE, ALevs
Language instr: English

The Peterborough School
Thorpe Road, Peterborough,
Cambridgeshire PE3 6AP
Tel: 01733 343357
Age range: 6 weeks–18 years
No. of pupils: 440
Curriculum: GCSE, ALevs

The Portsmouth Grammar School
High Street, Portsmouth,
Hampshire PO1 2LN
Tel: +44 (0)23 9236 0036
Age range: 2.5–18 years
Curriculum: IBDP
Language instr: English

The Purcell School, London
Aldenham Road, Bushey,
Hertfordshire WD23 2TS
Tel: 01923 331100
Age range: 10–18 years

The Read School
Drax, Selby, North Yorkshire YO8 8NL
Tel: 01757 618248
Age range: 4–18 years
Language instr: English

The Royal Hospital School
Holbrook, Ipswich, Suffolk IP9 2RX
Tel: 01473 326136
Age range: 11–18 years
No. of pupils: 720
Curriculum: GCSE, ALevs
Language instr: English

The Royal Junior School
Portsmouth Road, Hindhead,
Surrey GU26 6BW
Tel: 01428 607977
Age range: 6 weeks–11 years

The Royal Masonic School for Girls
Rickmansworth Park,
Rickmansworth,
Hertfordshire WD3 4HF
Tel: 01923 773168
Age range: *B*2–4 years *G*2–18 years
Language instr: English

The Royal School
Farnham Lane, Haslemere,
Surrey GU27 1HQ
Tel: 01428 605805
Age range: 11–18 years
Curriculum: National,
UK, GCSE, ALevs
Language instr: English

The Royal School Dungannon
2 Ranfurly Road, Dungannon,
County Tyrone BT71 6EG
Tel: 028 8772 2710
Age range: 11–18 years
Curriculum: GCSE, ALevs
Language instr: English

THORNTON COLLEGE
For further details see p. 254
College Lane, Thornton,
Milton Keynes,
Buckinghamshire MK17 0HJ
Tel: 01280 812610
Email: admissions@thorntoncollege.com
Website: www.thorntoncollege.com
Headteacher: Louise Shaw
Age range: G3–18 years
(Boarding from age 8)
No. of pupils: 402
Fees: £8,220–£24,660
Curriculum: GCSE, ALevs

Tonbridge School
High Street, Tonbridge, Kent TN9 1JP
Tel: 01732 304297
Age range: *B*13–18 years
No. of pupils: 798
Curriculum: GCSE, IGCSE, ALevs

Total French School, Aberdeen
c/o Albyn School, 17-23
Queen's Road, Aberdeen,
Aberdeenshire AB15 4PB
Tel: +44 (0)1224 329884

Trent College and The Elms
Derby Road, Long
Eaton, Nottingham,
Nottinghamshire NG10 4AD
Tel: 0115 8494949
Age range: 0–18 years
No. of pupils: 1121
Curriculum: GCSE, IGCSE, ALevs

Tring Park School for the Performing Arts
Mansion Drive, Tring,
Hertfordshire HP23 5LX
Tel: 01442 824255
Age range: 8–19 years
No. of pupils: 370 *B*112 *G*258 *VIth*171
Curriculum: National,
GCSE, IGCSE, ALevs
Language instr: English

Trinity School
Buckeridge Road, Teignmouth,
Devon TQ14 8LY
Tel: 01626 774138
Age range: 3–18 years
Language instr: English

Truro School
Trennick Lane, Truro,
Cornwall TR1 1TH
Tel: 01872 272763
Age range: 3–18 years
Curriculum: National,
GCSE, IGCSE, ALevs
Language instr: English

Tudor Hall School
Wykham Park, Banbury,
Oxfordshire OX16 9UR
Tel: 01295 263434
Age range: G11–18 years
Language instr: English

Uppingham School
Uppingham, Rutland LE15 9QE
Tel: +44 (0)1572 822216
Age range: 13–18 years

UWC Atlantic
St Donat's Castle, St Donat's,
Llantwit Major, Vale of
Glamorgan CF61 1WF
Tel: +44 (0)1446 799000
Age range: 16–19 years
No. of pupils: 350
Curriculum: IBDP
Language instr: English

Warminster School
Church Street, Warminster,
Wiltshire BA12 8PJ
Tel: +44 (0)1985 210100
Age range: 2–18 years
No. of pupils: 550
Curriculum: IBDP, IBCP, GCSE, ALevs
Language instr: English

Warwick School
Myton Road, Warwick,
Warwickshire CV34 6PP
Tel: 01926 776400
Age range: *B*7–18
No. of pupils: 1214 *VIth*249
Curriculum: GCSE, IGCSE, ALevs

Wellington College
Duke's Ride, Crowthorne,
Berkshire RG45 7PU
Tel: +44 (0)1344 444000
Age range: 13–18 years
No. of pupils: 1090 *B*610
*G*480 *VIth*475
Curriculum: IBDP, UK,
GCSE, IGCSE, ALevs
Language instr: English

Wellington School
South Street, Wellington,
Somerset TA21 8NT
Tel: 01823 668800
Age range: 3–18 years
Language instr: English

Wells Cathedral School
The Liberty, Wells, Somerset BA5 2ST
Tel: +44 (0)1749 834200
Age range: 2–18 years

West Buckland School
Barnstaple, Devon EX32 0SX
Tel: 01598 760000
Age range: 3–18 years

Westbourne School
Hickman Road, Penarth,
Glamorgan CF64 2AJ
Tel: 029 2070 5705
Age range: 2–18 years
No. of pupils: 351
Curriculum: IBDP, GCSE, IGCSE
Language instr: English

Westfield School
Oakfield Road, Gosforth,
Newcastle upon Tyne,
Tyne & Wear NE3 4HS
Tel: 0191 255 3980
Age range: G3–18
No. of pupils: 315 *VIth*50
Curriculum: ALevs
RS

Westminster School
Little Dean's Yard, Westminster,
London, London SW1P 3PB
Tel: 020 7963 1000
Age range: *B*13–18 years
*G*16–18 years
Curriculum: GCSE, IGCSE, ALevs

Westonbirt School
Westonbirt, Tetbury,
Gloucestershire GL8 8QG
Tel: 01666 880333
Age range: 11–18 years
Language instr: English

Whitgift School
Haling Park, South Croydon,
Surrey CR2 6YT
Tel: +44 20 8633 9935
Age range: *B*10–18 years
No. of pupils: 1550
Curriculum: IBDP, UK, GCSE, IGCSE, ALevs
Language instr: English

Winchester College
College Street, Winchester,
Hampshire SO23 9NA
Tel: 01962 621100
Age range: *B*13–18 years
Language instr: English

Windermere School
Patterdale Road, Windermere,
Cumbria LA23 1NW
Tel: 015394 46164
Age range: 3–18 years
No. of pupils: 350
Curriculum: IBDP, IBCP, GCSE, IGCSE
Language instr: English

Woldingham School
Marden Park, Woldingham,
Surrey CR3 7YA
Tel: 01883 349431
Age range: *G*11–18
No. of pupils: 611
Curriculum: GCSE, ALevs

Woodbridge School
Burkitt Road, Woodbridge,
Suffolk IP12 4JH
Tel: +44 (0)1394 615000
Age range: 4–18
No. of pupils: 901
Curriculum: GCSE, IGCSE, ALevs
Language instr: English

Woodhouse Grove School
Apperley Bridge, Bradford,
West Yorkshire BD10 0NR
Tel: 0113 250 2477
Age range: 11–18 years
No. of pupils: 751 *B*408 *G*343 *VIth*200
Curriculum: GCSE, IGCSE, ALevs

Worksop College
Cuthbert's Avenue, Worksop,
Nottinghamshire S80 3AP
Tel: 01909 537100
Age range: 11–18 years
Language instr: English

Worth School
Paddockhurst Road, Turners Hill,
Crawley, West Sussex RH10 4SD
Tel: +44 (0)1342 710200
Age range: 11–18
No. of pupils: 580 *VIth*222
Curriculum: IBDP, National, GCSE, IGCSE, ALevs
Language instr: English

Wotton House International School
Wotton House, Horton
Road, Gloucester,
Gloucestershire GL1 3PR
Tel: +44 (0)1452 764248
Age range: 7–16 years
Curriculum: IBMYP
Language instr: English

Wrekin College
Wellington, Shropshire TF1 3BH
Tel: +44 (0)1952 265600
Age range: 11–18 years
Language instr: English

Wychwood School
74 Banbury Road, Oxford,
Oxfordshire OX2 6JR
Tel: +44 (0)18655 57976
Age range: *G*11–18 years
Language instr: English

Wycliffe College
Bristol Road, Stonehouse,
Gloucestershire GL10 2AF
Tel: 01453 822432
Age range: 3–19 years
No. of pupils: 696
Curriculum: GCSE, IGCSE, ALevs

Wycombe Abbey
Frances Dove Way, High Wycombe,
Buckinghamshire HP11 1PE
Tel: +44 (0)1494 520381
Age range: *G*11–18 years
No. of pupils: 663
Curriculum: GCSE, IGCSE, ALevs

Yehudi Menuhin School
Stoke Road, Stoke d'Abernon,
Cobham, Surrey KT11 3QQ
Tel: 01932 864739
Age range: 7–19
No. of pupils: 80 *B*42 *G*38 *VIth*36
Curriculum: GCSE, IGCSE, ALevs
Language instr: English

UKRAINE

Brookes CIL International School
Parus Business Center, 2
Mechnikov Street, Kyiv 01023
Tel: +380 443337773
Curriculum: AP

Gymnasium A+
Berezneva Str. 14, 02160 Kyiv
Tel: +38 44 363 14 03
Curriculum: IBDP
Language instr: English, Ukrainian

Meridian International School
Provulok 5A, Kvitnevy, Kiev 04108
Tel: +380 44 433 9748
Age range: 3–18
No. of pupils: 315

Pechersk School International Kyiv
7a Victora Zabily, Kyiv 03039
Tel: +380 44 377 5292
Age range: 3–18
No. of pupils: 450
Curriculum: IBDP, IBMYP, IBPYP, SAT
Language instr: English

QSI Kyiv International School
3A Svyatoshinsky
Provuluk, Kyiv 03115
Tel: +38 (044) 452 27 92
Age range: 3–18 years
No. of pupils: 780
Curriculum: AP, IBDP, USA
Language instr: English

Simferopol International School
Barrikadnaya 59A, Simferopol,
Crimea 95000
Tel: +7 3652 54 06 06
Age range: 2–17
No. of pupils: 185 *B*125 *G*60
Curriculum: National, UK
Language instr: Russian, Ukrainian, English

The British International School Ukraine (Nivki Primary Campus)
36a Scherbakivskogo Str., Kyiv 03190
Tel: +38 (044) 239 21 21
Language instr: English

The British International School Ukraine (Pechersk Campus)
1 Dragomirova Street, Kiev 01103
Tel: +38 (044) 596 18 28
Curriculum: IBDP
Language instr: English

International schools in North America

Schools ordered A–Z by Country

Key to directory

Country	**Whereford**
Name of school or college	**College Academy**
Indicates that this school has a profile	***For further details see p***
Address and contact number	Which Street, Whosville, Wherefordshire AB12 3CD **Tel:** 01000 000000
Head's name	**Head Master:** Dr A Person
Age range	**Age range:** 11–18
Number of pupils. B = boys G = girls VIth = sixth form	**No. of pupils:** 660 B330 G330 VIth 200
Fees per annum. Day = fees for day pupils. WB = fees for weekly boarders. FB = fees for full boarders.	**Fees:** Day £11,000 WB £16,000 FB £20,000
Curriculum	**Curriculum:** National, IBDP, ALevs
Language of instruction	**Language instr:** English, French
Memberships/Accreditation	(AISA) (COB) (EAR)

Key to icons

Key to symbols:

- Boys' school
- Girls' school
- Boarding accommodation

Member of:

- (AISA) Association of International Schools in Africa
- (CEE) Central and Eastern European Schools Association
- (EAR) East Asia Regional Council of Overseas Schools
- (ECIS) European Council of International Schools
- (RS) Round Square

Accreditation:

- (CIS) Council of International Schools
- (COB) Council of British International Schools

Please note: Schools are coeducational day schools unless otherwise indicated

ANGUILLA

Omololu International School
P.O Box 703, The Valley BWI, AI2640
Tel: +1 264 497 5430
Curriculum: IBPYP
Language instr: English

ANTIGUA

Island Academy International School
Oliver's Estate, PO Box W1884, St John's
Tel: +1 268 460 1094
Age range: 3–18
No. of pupils: 270
Curriculum: IBDP, National
Language instr: English

Soufriere Primary
St Mark
Tel: +1 767 448 0373

ARUBA

International School of Aruba
Wayaca 238A, Oranjestad
Tel: +297 583 5040
Age range: 3–19
No. of pupils: 190
Curriculum: AP, SAT, TOEFL, USA
Language instr: English

BAHAMAS

Aquinas College
PO Box N-7540, Nassau 7540
Tel: + 1 242 361 5534

Bishop Michael Eldon School
East Sunrise Highway, PO Box 40667, Freeport
Tel: +1 242 373 3579
Age range: 4–18
Curriculum: ACT, AP, SAT, GCSE

King's College School, The Bahamas
Western Road, Nassau, New Providence
Tel: +1 242 820 0976
Age range: 4–12 years

Kingsway Academy
PO Box N 4378, Bernard Road, Nassau
Tel: +1 242 324 5049
Age range: 4–18
No. of pupils: 1005
Curriculum: AP, USA

Lucaya International School
Chesapeake Drive, Freeport
Tel: +1 242 373 4004
Age range: 3–18
No. of pupils: 240
Curriculum: ACT, IBDP, IBPYP, IGCSE
Language instr: English
CIS

Lyford Cay International School
Lyford Cay Drive, PO Box N-7776, Nassau NB
Tel: +1 242 362 4774
Age range: 3–18
No. of pupils: 273 *B*133 *G*140
Curriculum: IBDP, IBMYP, IBPYP, IBCP, National, SAT, UK, USA
Language instr: English
CIS ECIS

St Andrew's International School
PO Box EE 17340, Yamacraw Hill Road, Nassau, NP
Tel: +1 242 677 7800
Age range: 4–18
Curriculum: AP, IBDP, IBPYP, SAT, UK, USA
Language instr: English
CIS ECIS

St Johns College
PO Box N 4858, Nassau NP
Tel: +1 242 322 3249
Age range: 4–17
No. of pupils: 1015
Curriculum: SAT

St. Andrews Anglican School
P.O. Box EX-29093, Georgetown, Exuma
Tel: +1 242 336 4130

St. Anne's School
P.O. Box SS-6256, Nassau
Tel: +1 242 324 1203

Summit Academy
PO Box EE-17972, Nassau
Tel: +1 242 394 4781
Curriculum: IPC

Tambearly School
P.O. Box N-4284, Nassau
Tel: +1 242 327 5965
Curriculum: USA

Temple Christian School
4th Terrace Collins Avenue, Nassau N-1566
Tel: +1 242 325 1119
Age range: 3–18
No. of pupils: 1240
Curriculum: USA

BERMUDA

Bermuda High School
19 Richmond Road, Pembroke HM08
Tel: +441 295 6153
Age range: *B*16–18 *G*4–18
No. of pupils: 640
Curriculum: IBDP, SAT, GCSE, IGCSE
Language instr: English

Bermuda Institute
234 Middle Road (P. O. Box SN 114), Southampton SN BX
Tel: +1 441 238 1566
Age range: 4–18
No. of pupils: 241 *B*120 *G*121
Curriculum: USA
Language instr: English

Chatmore British International School
Rockmore Estate, 9 St Marks Road, Smiths FL06
Tel: +1 441 236 3339
Curriculum: IPC, UK, IGCSE
Language instr: English
COB

Saltus Grammar School
PO Box HM 2224, Hamilton HM JX
Tel: +1 441 292 6177
Age range: 5–18
No. of pupils: 1022 *B*613 *G*409
Curriculum: AP, SAT

Somersfield Academy
107 Middle Road, Devonshire DV 06
Tel: +1 441 236 9797
Age range: 3–18 years
No. of pupils: 529
Curriculum: IBDP, IBMYP
Language instr: English

Warwick Academy
117 Middle Road, Warwick PG01
Tel: +1 441 236 1917/239 9452
Age range: 4–18
No. of pupils: 830
Curriculum: IBDP, IBCP, UK, IGCSE
Language instr: English

BRITISH VIRGIN ISLANDS

Cedar International School
Waterfront Drive, Kingston
Tel: +1 284 494 5262
Age range: 3–18
No. of pupils: 240 *B*120 *G*120
Curriculum: IBDP, IBMYP, IBPYP
Language instr: English
CIS

CANADA

Alberta

Calgary French and International School
700-77th Street SW, Calgary AB, Alberta T3H 5R1
Tel: +1 403 240 1500
Curriculum: IBDP
Language instr: English, French

Lycee Louis Pasteur The International French School
4099 Garrison Boulevard SW, Calgary AB, Alberta T2T 6G2
Tel: +1 403 243 5420
Age range: 3–17
No. of pupils: 380
Curriculum: FrenchBacc
Language instr: French, English

Strathcona-Tweedsmuir School
RR 2, Okotoks AB, Alberta T1S 1A2
Tel: +1 403 938 4431
Age range: 5–18
No. of pupils: 700
Curriculum: IBDP, IBMYP, IBPYP, FrenchBacc
Language instr: English

British Columbia

Alexander Academy
200-688 West Hastings Street, Vancouver BC, British Columbia V6B 1P1
Tel: +1 604 687 8832
Curriculum: IBDP
Language instr: English, French

Aspengrove School
7660 Clark Drive, Nanaimo BC, British Columbia V0R 2H0
Tel: +1 250 390 2201
Age range: 3–18
No. of pupils: 310
Curriculum: IBDP, IBMYP, IBPYP
Language instr: English

Brentwood College School
2735 Mount Baker Road, Mill Bay BC, British Columbia V0R 2P1
Tel: +1 250 743 5521
Age range: 14–18
No. of pupils: 435 *B*226 *G*109
Curriculum: AP, National

Brockton School
3467 Duval Road, North Vancouver BC, British Columbia V7J 3E8
Tel: +1 604 929 9201
Age range: 5–18
Curriculum: IBDP, IBMYP, IBPYP, IBCP, National
Language instr: English

Brookes Westshore
1939 Sooke Road, Victoria BC, British Columbia V9B 1W2
Age range: 11–18
Curriculum: IBDP, IBMYP
Language instr: English

Fraser Valley School
19533 64th Avenue, Surrey BC, British Columbia V3S 4J3
Tel: +1 604 427 2282
Age range: 5–13
No. of pupils: 129
Curriculum: IBPYP
Language instr: English

Glenlyon Norfolk School
801 Bank Street, Victoria BC, British Columbia V8S 4A8
Tel: +1 250 370 6801
Age range: 4–18 years
No. of pupils: 690
Curriculum: IBDP, IBMYP, IBPYP
Language instr: English

Island Pacific School
671 Carter Road, Box 128, Bowen Island BC, British Columbia V0N 1G0
Tel: +1 604 947 9311
Age range: 11–14
Curriculum: IBMYP
Language instr: English

Lowell High School
750 Hamilton Street, Suite 210, Vancouver BC, British Columbia V6B 2R5
Tel: +1 604 336 0456
Curriculum: IBDP
Language instr: English, Chinese

MEADOWRIDGE SCHOOL
For further details see p. 271
12224 240th Street, Maple Ridge BC, British Columbia V4R 1N1
Tel: +1 604 467 4444
Email: admissions@meadowridge.bc.ca
Website: www.meadowridge.bc.ca
Head of School: Scott Banack
Age range: 4–18 years
No. of pupils: 650
Fees: C$25,925
Curriculum: IBDP, IBMYP, IBPYP
Language instr: English

MULGRAVE, THE INTERNATIONAL SCHOOL OF VANCOUVER
For further details see p. 272
2330 Cypress Bowl Lane, West Vancouver BC, British Columbia V7S 3H9
Tel: +1 604 922 3223
Email: admissions@mulgrave.com
Website: www.mulgrave.com
Head of School: John Wray
Age range: 3–18 years
No. of pupils: 1025
Fees: *Day* CND$25,000
Curriculum: ACT, IBDP, IBMYP, IBPYP
Language instr: English

Pacific Academy
10238 168th Street, Surrey BC, British Columbia V4N 1Z4
Tel: +1 604 581 5353
Age range: 5–18
No. of pupils: 1400
Curriculum: IBDP
Language instr: English

Pearson College UWC
650 Pearson College Drive, Victoria BC, British Columbia V9C 4H7
Tel: +1 250 391 2411
Age range: 16–19
No. of pupils: 200
Curriculum: IBDP, SAT
Language instr: English

SenPokChin School
1156 SenPokChin Blvd, Oliver BC, British Columbia V0H 1T8
Tel: +1 250 498 2019
Age range: 4–12
No. of pupils: 96
Curriculum: IBPYP
Language instr: English, nsyilxcen

Shawnigan Lake School
1975 Renfrew Road, Postal Bag 2000, Shawnigan Lake BC, British Columbia V0R 2W1
Tel: +1 250 743 5516
Age range: 13–18
No. of pupils: 493
Language instr: English

Southpointe Academy
1900 56th Street, Tsawwassen BC, British Columbia V4L 2B1
Tel: +1 604 948 8826
Curriculum: AP, IBMYP, IBPYP
Language instr: English

Southridge School
2656 160th Street, Surrey BC, British Columbia V3S 0B7
Tel: +1 604 535 5056
Age range: 4–17
No. of pupils: 667
Curriculum: AP, IBMYP, IBPYP
Language instr: English

St. John's Academy Shawnigan Lake
2371 Shawnigan Lake Road, Shawnigan Lake BC, British Columbia V0R 2W5
Tel: +1 250 220 4888
Curriculum: IBMYP
Language instr: English

STRATFORD HALL
For further details see p. 275
3000 Commercial Drive, Vancouver BC, British Columbia V5N 4E2
Tel: +1 604 436 0608
Email: info@stratfordhall.ca
Website: www.stratfordhall.ca
Head of School: Richard Kassissieh
Age range: 5–18 years
No. of pupils: 540
Fees: CAD$24,540–CAD$28,670
Curriculum: IBDP, IBMYP, IBPYP
Language instr: English

Unisus Junior School
7808 Pierre Dr, Summerland BC, British Columbia V0H 1Z2
Tel: +1 250 404 3232
Curriculum: IBPYP
Language instr: English, Spanish

Unisus School
7808 Pierre Dr, Summerland BC, British Columbia V0H 1Z2
Tel: +1 250 404 3232
Curriculum: IBDP
Language instr: English

White Rock Christian Academy
2265 -152nd Street, Surrey BC, British Columbia V4A 4P1
Tel: +1 604 531 9186
Curriculum: IBDP, IBMYP, IBPYP
Language instr: English

New Brunswick

Rothesay Netherwood School
40 College Hill Road, Rothesay NB, New Brunswick E2E 5H1
Tel: +1 506 847 8224
Age range: 11–18
Curriculum: IBDP
Language instr: English

Newfoundland and Labrador

Lakecrest Independent School
58 Patrick Street, St. John's NL, Newfoundland and Labrador A1E 2S7
Tel: +1 709 738 1212
Curriculum: IBPYP
Language instr: English

Nova Scotia

Halifax Grammar School
945 Tower Road, Halifax NS, Nova Scotia B3H 2Y2
Tel: +1 902 423 9312
Age range: 3–18
No. of pupils: 500 *B*283 *G*242
Curriculum: IBDP
Language instr: English

King's-Edgehill School
11 King's-Edgehill Lane, Windsor NS, Nova Scotia B0N 2T0
Tel: +1 902 798 2278
Age range: 11–19
No. of pupils: 350
Curriculum: IBDP
Language instr: English

Sacred Heart School of Halifax
5820 Spring Garden Rd, Halifax NS, Nova Scotia B3H 1X8
Tel: +1 902 422 4459

Ontario

Académie de la Capitale
1010 Morrison Dr Suite 200, Ottawa ON, Ontario K2H 8K7
Tel: +1 613 721 3872
Curriculum: IBPYP
Language instr: French, English

Académie Ste Cécile International School
925 Cousineau Road, Windsor ON, Ontario N9G 1V8
Tel: +1 519 969 1291
Age range: 5–19
No. of pupils: 260
Curriculum: AP, IBDP, IBMYP, National, SAT
Language instr: English

Albert College
160 Dundas Street West, Belleville ON, Ontario K8P 1A6
Tel: +1 613 968 5726
Age range: 2.5–18

Appleby College
540 Lakeshore Road West, Oakville ON, Ontario L6K 3P1
Tel: +1 905 845 4681 ext. 200
Age range: 12–18

Ashbury College
362 Mariposa Avenue, Ottawa ON, Ontario K1M 0T3
Tel: +1 613 749 5954
Age range: 9–18
No. of pupils: 700
Curriculum: IBDP
Language instr: English

Bayview Glen
275 Duncan Mill Road, Toronto
ON, Ontario M3B 3H9
Tel: +1 416 443 1030

Branksome Hall
10 Elm Avenue, Toronto
ON, Ontario M4W 1N4
Tel: +1 416 920 9741
Age range: *AGE1 *** DESCRIPTION REQUIRED* 4–17 (Residence from Grade 7+)
No. of pupils: 900
Curriculum: IBDP, IBMYP, IBPYP
Language instr: English

Bronte College
88 Bronte College Court, 1444 Dundas Cres, Mississauga
ON, Ontario L5C 1E9
Tel: +1 905 270 7788
Curriculum: IBDP
Language instr: English

Crescent School for Boys
2365 Bayview Avenue, Toronto
ON, Ontario M2L 1A2
Tel: +1 416 449 2556
Age range: B8–18
No. of pupils: 725
Language instr: English

Elmwood School
261 Buena Vista Road, Ottawa
ON, Ontario K1M 0V9
Tel: +1 613 749 6761
Age range: G3–18
No. of pupils: 360
Curriculum: IBDP, IBMYP, IBPYP
Language instr: English

Fern Hill School
801 North Service Road, Burlington ON, Ontario L7P 5B6
Tel: +1 905 634 8652
Language instr: English

Kempenfelt Bay School
576 Bryne Drive, Barrie
ON, Ontario L4N 9P6
Tel: +1 705 739 4731
Language instr: English

Khalsa School Malton
7280 Airport Rd., Mississauga
ON, Ontario L4T 2H3
Tel: +1 905 671 2010
Curriculum: IBMYP
Language instr: English

King Heights Academy
28 Roytec Road, Woodbridge
ON, Ontario L4L 8E4
Tel: +1 905 652 1234
Curriculum: IBPYP
Language instr: English

LA CITADELLE INTERNATIONAL ACADEMY OF ARTS & SCIENCE
For further details see p. 269
36 Scarsdale Road, North York, Toronto ON, Ontario M3B 2R7
Tel: +1 416 385 9685
Email: headmaster@lacitadelleacademy.com
Website: www.lacitadelleacademy.com
Head of School: Alfred Abouchar
Age range: 2–18 years
No. of pupils: 180
Fees: *Day* CAD$13,875–CAD$28,800
Curriculum: AP, IBMYP
Language instr: English, French

Lakefield College School
4391 County Road 29, Lakefield
ON, Ontario K0L 2H0
Tel: +1 705 652 3324
Language instr: English

London International Academy
365 Richmond Street, London, ON, Ontario N6A 3C2
Tel: +1 519 433 3388
Age range: 13–18 years
No. of pupils: 150
Curriculum: IBDP
Language instr: English, Spanish

Lynn-Rose Heights Private School
7215 Millcreek Drive, Mississauga
ON, Ontario L5N 3R3
Tel: +1 905 567 3553
Curriculum: IBDP, IBMYP, IBPYP
Language instr: English

MacLachlan College
337 Trafalgar Road, Oakville
ON, Ontario L6J 3H3
Tel: +1 905 844 0372
Age range: 3–11
No. of pupils: 200
Curriculum: AP, IBPYP
Language instr: English

Matthews Hall
1370 Oxford Street West, London
ON, Ontario N6H 1W2
Tel: +1 519 471 1506
Age range: 4–14
No. of pupils: B126 G111
Curriculum: National
Language instr: English

NOIC Academy
50 Featherstone Avenue, Markham ON, Ontario L3S 2H4
Tel: +1 905 472 2002
Age range: 15–19
No. of pupils: 250
Curriculum: IBDP
Language instr: English

Richland Academy
11570 Yonge Street, Richmond Hill, ON, Ontario L4E 3N7
Tel: +1 905 224 5600
Curriculum: IBPYP
Language instr: English, French

Ridley College
PO Box 3013, 2 Ridley Road, St Catharines ON, Ontario L2R 7C3
Tel: +1 905 684 1889
Age range: 4–18 years
No. of pupils: 711
Curriculum: IBDP, IBMYP, IBPYP, National
Language instr: English

Southern Ontario Collegiate
28 Rebecca Street, Hamilton
ON, Ontario L8R 1B4
Tel: +1 905 546 1500

St Andrew's College
15800 Yonge Street, Aurora
ON, Ontario L4G 3H7
Tel: +1 905 727 3178
Age range: B10–18
No. of pupils: 650

St Clement's School
21 St. Clements Avenue, Toronto
ON, Ontario M4R 1G8
Tel: +1 416 483 4835
Language instr: English

St John's – Kilmarnock School
2201 Shantz Station Road, Box 179, Breslau (Waterloo Region)
ON, Ontario N0B 1M0
Tel: +1 519 648 2183
Age range: 4–18
No. of pupils: 400
Curriculum: IBDP, IBMYP, IBPYP
Language instr: English

St Jude's Academy
2150 Torquay Mews, Mississauga
ON, Ontario L5N 2M6
Tel: +1 905 814 0202
Curriculum: IBDP, IBMYP, IBPYP

St Mildred's Lightbourn School
1080 Linbrook Road, Oakville
ON, Ontario L6J 2L1
Tel: +1 905 845 2386
Language instr: English

Sunnybrook School
469 Merton Street, Toronto
ON, Ontario M4S 1B4
Tel: +1 416 487 5308
Curriculum: IBPYP

TFS – CANADA'S INTERNATIONAL SCHOOL
For further details see p. 276
306 Lawrence Avenue East, Toronto ON, Ontario M4N 1T7
Tel: +1 416 484 6533
Email: admissions@tfs.ca
Website: www.tfs.ca
Head of School: Norman Gaudet
Age range: 2–18 years
No. of pupils: 1500
Fees: *Day* CAD$22,180–CAD$37,630
Curriculum: IBDP, IBMYP, IBPYP
Language instr: French, English

The Leo Baeck Day School
36 Atkinson Avenue, Thornhill
ON, Ontario L4J 8C9
Tel: +1 905 709 3636
Curriculum: IBMYP, IBPYP

The York School
1320 Yonge Street, Toronto
ON, Ontario M4T 1X2
Tel: Admissions: +1 416 646 5275 Switchboard: +1 416 926 1325
Age range: 4–18
No. of pupils: 700
Curriculum: IBDP, IBMYP, IBPYP
Language instr: English

TMS School
500 Elgin Mills Road East, Richmond Hill ON, Ontario L4C 5G1
Tel: +1 905 889 6882
Curriculum: IBDP, IBMYP
Language instr: English

Town Centre Montessori Private Schools
155 Clayton Drive, Markham
ON, Ontario L3R 7P3
Tel: +1 905 470 1200
Curriculum: IBDP, IBMYP, IBPYP
Language instr: English

Upper Canada College
200 Lonsdale Road, Toronto
ON, Ontario M4V 1W6
Tel: +1 416 488 1125
Curriculum: IBDP, IBMYP, IBPYP
Language instr: English

Walden International School
1030 Queen Street West, Brampton ON, Ontario L6X 0B2
Tel: +1 905 338 6236
Curriculum: IBPYP
Language instr: English, French

Wheatley School
497 Scott Street, St Catharines
ON, Ontario L2M 3X3
Tel: +1 905 641 3012
No. of pupils: 180
Curriculum: IBMYP
Language instr: English

Quebec

Académie Antoine-Manseau
20 rue St Charles Borromée Sud, CP 410, Joliette QC, Quebec J6E 3Z9
Tel: +1 450 753 4271
No. of pupils: 612
Language instr: French

Académie François-Labelle
1227 rue Notre Dame, Repentigny QC, Quebec J5Y 3H2
Tel: +1 450 582 2020
Curriculum: IBPYP

Académie Lafontaine
2171 boulevard Maurice, Saint-Jérôme, Québec QC, Quebec J7Z 4M7
Tel: +1 450 431 3733
No. of pupils: 1293
Language instr: French

Alexander von Humboldt Schule
216, rue Victoria, Baie d'Urfé QC, Quebec H9X 2H9
Tel: +1 514 457 2886

Bishop's College School
80 Moulton Hill Road, PO Box 5001, Station Lennoxville, Sherbrooke QC, Quebec J1M 1Z8
Tel: +1 819 566 0227
Age range: 13–18
No. of pupils: 246 *B*148 *G*98 *VIth*68
Curriculum: IBDP
Language instr: English, French

Campus Notre-Dame-de-Foy
5000 rue Clement-Lockquell, St-Augustin-de Desmaures QC, Quebec G3A 1B3
Tel: +1 418 872 8041

Centennial Academy
3641 Prud'homme Avenue, Montréal QC, Quebec H4A 3H6
Tel: +1 514 486 5533
No. of pupils: 225
Language instr: English

Collège Charlemagne
5000 rue Pilon, Pierrefonds, Montréal QC, Quebec H9K 1G4
Tel: +1 514 626 7060
No. of pupils: 1235
Curriculum: IBMYP
Language instr: French

Collège Charles-Lemoyne – Campus Longueuil
901, chemin Tiffin, Longueuil QC, Quebec J4P 3G6
Tel: +1 514 875 0505
Curriculum: IBMYP, IBPYP
Language instr: English, French

Collège de l'Assomption
270 boulevard de l'Ange-Gardien, L'Assomption, Montréal QC, Quebec J5Y 3R7
Tel: +1 450 589 5621
No. of pupils: 1336
Curriculum: IBMYP
Language instr: French

Collège de Lévis
9 rue Mgr Gosselin, Levis QC, Quebec G6V 5K1
Tel: +1 418 833 1249
Language instr: French

Collège du Mont-Sainte-Anne
2100 Chemin de Sainte-Catherine, Sherbrooke QC, Quebec J1N 3V5
Tel: +1 819 823 3003
Age range: *B*12–17
No. of pupils: 260
Language instr: French

Collège Esther-Blondin
101 rue Sainte-Anne, Saint-Jacques QC, Quebec J0K 2R0
Tel: +1 450 839 3672
Age range: 12–17
Curriculum: IBMYP
Language instr: French

Collège François-de-Laval
6 rue de la Vieille-Université, Québec QC, Quebec G1R 5X8
Tel: +1 418 694 1020
Age range: 12–18
No. of pupils: 810
Language instr: French

Collège Jean-de-Brebeuf
3200, chemin de la Côte-Sainte-Catherine, Montréal QC, Quebec H3T 1C1
Tel: +1 514 342 9342
Curriculum: IBDP, IBMYP
Language instr: French

Collège Jésus-Marie de Sillery
2047 chemin Saint-Louis, Québec City QC, Quebec G1T 1P3
Tel: +1 418 687 9250
Age range: B5,6,7 & 12+G5–17
No. of pupils: 1000
Curriculum: IBMYP
Language instr: French

Collège Laflèche
1687 boulevard du Carmel, Trois-Rivières QC, Quebec G8Z 3R8
Tel: +1 819 375 7346
Age range: 18–20
No. of pupils: 1300 *B*400 *G*900
Language instr: French

Collège Laurentien
1200, 14th Avenue, Val-Morin QC, Quebec J0T 2R0
Tel: +1 819 322 2913
Age range: 12–16
No. of pupils: 10 *B*5 *G*5 *VIth*12
Curriculum: UK, IGCSE, ALevs
Language instr: French

Collège Marie-de-l'Incarnation
725 rue Hart, Trois-Rivières QC, Quebec G9A 4R9
Tel: +1 819 379 3223

Collège Mont Notre-Dame de Sherbrooke
114 rue Cathédrale, Sherbrooke QC, Quebec J1H 4MI
Tel: +1 819 563 4104
No. of pupils: 573
Curriculum: IBMYP
Language instr: French

Collège Notre-Dame-de-Lourdes
845 chemin Tiffin, Longueuil QC, Quebec J4P 3G5
Tel: +1 450 670 4740
Age range: 12–17
No. of pupils: 960
Curriculum: IBMYP
Language instr: French

Collège Saint-Joseph de Hull
174 rue Notre-Dame-de-l'île, Gatineau QC, Quebec J8X 3T4
Tel: +1 819 776 3123
Language instr: French

Collège Saint-Maurice
630 rue Girouard Ouest, Saint-Hyacinthe QC, Quebec J2S 2Y3
Tel: +1 450 773 7478 Ext:222
Age range: G12–17
No. of pupils: 700
Curriculum: IBMYP, National
Language instr: French

Collège Saint-Paul
235 rue Ste-Anne, Varennes QC, Quebec J3X 1P9
Tel: +1 450 652 2941
No. of pupils: 786
Language instr: French

Collège Ville-Marie
2850 rue Sherbrooke Est, Montréal QC, Quebec H2K 1H3
Tel: +1 514 525 2516
No. of pupils: 550
Curriculum: IBMYP
Language instr: French

Ecole Internationale de Montreal Primaire
5010 Avenue Coolbrook, Montreal QC, Quebec H3X 2K9
Tel: +1 514 596 5721
Age range: 4–11

École Internationale des Apprenants
4505 Boul Henri-Bourassa O, Saint-Laurent QC, Quebec H4L 1A5
Tel: +1 514 334 4153
Curriculum: IBPYP
Language instr: French

École Les Mélèzes
393 de Lanaudière, Joliette QC, Quebec J6E3L9
Tel: +1 450 752 4433
Curriculum: IBPYP
Language instr: French

École Marie-Clarac
3530 Boul Gouin Est, Montréal-Nord QC, Quebec H1H 1B7
Tel: +1 514 322 1160
Curriculum: IBMYP
Language instr: French

École Plein Soleil (Association Coopérative)
300, rue de Montréal, Sherbrooke QC, Quebec J1H 1E5
Tel: +1 819 569 8359
Age range: 4–12
No. of pupils: 205
Curriculum: IBPYP, National
Language instr: French

École secondaire Saint-Joseph de Saint-Hyacinthe
2875 avenue Bourdages Nord, Saint-Hyacinthe QC, Quebec J2S 5S3
Tel: +1 450 774 3775
Curriculum: IBMYP
Language instr: French

Le Collège Saint-Bernard
25 avenue des Frères, Drummondville QC, Quebec J2B 6A2
Tel: +1 819 478 3330
Curriculum: IBMYP
Language instr: French

L'École des Ursulines de Québec
4 rue du Parloir, CP 820, Haute – Ville, Québec QC, Quebec G1R 4S7
Tel: +1 418 692 2612
Curriculum: IBPYP

Lower Canada College
4090, avenue Royal, Montréal QC, Quebec H4A 2M5
Tel: +1 514 482 9916
Age range: 5–18 years
No. of pupils: 850
Curriculum: IBDP, IBMYP, SAT
Language instr: English, French

Miss Edgar's & Miss Cramp's School
525 Mount Pleasant Road, Westmount QC, Quebec H3Y 3H6
Tel: +1 514 935 6357
Age range: G5–18
No. of pupils: G300
Language instr: English, French

Pensionnat du Saint-Nom-de-Marie
628 chemin de la Côte, St Catherine, Outremont QC, Quebec H2V 2C5
Tel: +1 514 735 5261
No. of pupils: 1030
Curriculum: IBMYP
Language instr: French

Selwyn House School
95, chemin Côte St-Antoine, Westmount QC, Quebec H3Y 2H8
Tel: +1 514 931 9481
Age range: 5–17
No. of pupils: 540
Language instr: English, French

Stanstead College
450 Duferin Street, Stanstead QC, Quebec J0B 3E0
Tel: +1 819 876 2702
Age range: 11–18
No. of pupils: 200

The Sacred Heart School of Montreal
3635 Atwater Ave., Montreal QC, Quebec H3H 1E4
Tel: +1 514 937 2845
Age range: G12–17 years
No. of pupils: 250

Saskatchewan

Athol Murray College of Notre Dame
PO Box 100, Wilcox SK, Saskatchewan S0G 5E0
Tel: +1 306 732 1203
Age range: 14–18 years

LCBI High School
700 Ash Street, Box 459, Outlook SK, Saskatchewan S0L 2N0
Tel: +1 306 867 8971
Age range: 14–18
No. of pupils: 80
Language instr: English

Luther College High School
1500 Royal Street, Regina SK, Saskatchewan S4T 5A5
Tel: +1 306 791 9150
Age range: 16–18
No. of pupils: 450
Curriculum: IBDP
Language instr: English

CAYMAN ISLANDS

Cayman International School
P.O. Box 31364, 95 Minerva Drive, Camana Bay, Grand Cayman KY1-1206
Tel: +1 345 945 4664
Age range: 3–18
Curriculum: IBDP
Language instr: English

Cayman Prep & High School
PO Box 10013, Grand Cayman KY1-1001
Tel: +1 345 949 9115
Curriculum: UK, IGCSE, ALevs

Grace Christian Academy
21 Crescent Close, Grand Cayman
Tel: +1 345 945 0899
Curriculum: USA

St Ignatius Catholic School
PO Box 2638, 597 Walkers Road, Grand Cayman KY1-1102
Tel: +1345 949 9250
Curriculum: UK, IGCSE, ALevs

Triple C School
P.O. Box 10498, 74 Fairbanks Road, George Town, Grand Cayman KY1-1005
Tel: + 1 345 949 6022
Curriculum: USA

COSTA RICA

American International School of Costa Rica
Ciudad Cariari, La Asuncion, Belen, Heredia
Tel: +506 2293 2567
Age range: 4–18
No. of pupils: 170 *B*90 *G*80
Curriculum: AP, SAT

Anglo American School
La Unión, 1 Km al norte de Sub Estación Electríca del ICE, Provincia de Cartago, Tres Rios, San Jose
Tel: +506 2279 2626
Age range: 3–11
Curriculum: IBDP, USA

Centro Educativo Futuro Verde
1 km este del Banco Nacional, Cóbano, Puntarenas 60111
Tel: +506 2642 0291
Curriculum: IBDP
Language instr: English, Spanish

Centro Educativo Nueva Generacion
Sn Rafael de Heredia Del parqu 1 km al norte, Heredia 24-3015
Tel: +506 2237 8927
Curriculum: IBDP
Language instr: English

Colegio del Valle S.A.(Blue Valley School)
From Multiplaza, 1.2 Km. northwest, right hand side of the road, Guachipelín, Escazú, San José
Tel: +50 6 2215 2204
Age range: 3.5–18 years
No. of pupils: 857
Curriculum: IBDP
Language instr: English, Spanish

Colegio Humboldt
Contiguo a la Iglesia Nuestra Señora de Loreto, Pavas, San José
Tel: +506 2 232 1455

Colegio Internacional SEK Costa Rica
Cipreses de Curridabat, San José 963 2050
Tel: +506 2 272 5464
Curriculum: IBDP
Language instr: Spanish, English

Colegio Los Ángeles
Calle Luisa, San José
Tel: +506 2232 0122
Curriculum: IBDP
Language instr: English

Colegio Miravalle
800m al sur de la esquina sureste de los Tribunales de Justicia, Cartago
Tel: +506 2552 7378
Curriculum: IBDP
Language instr: English, Spanish

Colegio Saint Francis
San Vicente, Moravia, San José
Tel: +506 2430 7639
Curriculum: IBDP
Language instr: English, Spanish

Costa Rica International Academy
500 mts sur del Hotel Westin Conchal, Brasilito, Guanacaste
Tel: +506 2654 5042
Age range: 2–19
No. of pupils: 320 *B*160 *G*160
Curriculum: ACT, AP, SAT, USA
Language instr: English

Country Day School
Apartado 1139-1250, Escazú, San José
Tel: +506 2289 0919
Age range: 2–19
No. of pupils: 844 *B*424 *G*420
Curriculum: AP, SAT

Del Mar Academy
P.O. Box: 130, Nosara, Nicoya, Guanacaste 5233
Tel: +506 2682 1211
Curriculum: IBDP
Language instr: English

European School
Heredia, San Pablo, P.O. Box: 177, Heredia
Tel: +506 2261 0717
Age range: 4–18
No. of pupils: 518
Curriculum: IBDP
Language instr: English

Falcon International School
Herradura Beach, Puntarenas
Tel: +506 2637 7400
Curriculum: USA

Franz Liszt Schule
800 metros al sur de la gasolinera, Hermanos Montes a mano izq, Santa Ana, San José 10901
Tel: +506 2203 8128
Curriculum: IBDP
Language instr: English, German

Golden Valley School
Del Lubricentro San Francisco 800 mts. Suroeste, Portones azules grandes a mano derecha, San Isidro, Heredia 40604
Tel: +506 2268 9114
Curriculum: IBDP
Language instr: English, Spanish

Instituto Dr. Jaim Weizman
100 norte, 100 oeste Compañía Nacional de Fuerza y Luz, Carretera Anonos, Mata Redonda, San José 4114-100
Tel: +506 2220 1050
No. of pupils: 300
Curriculum: IBDP, IBMYP, IBPYP
Language instr: English, Spanish

International Christian School
San Miguel de Santo Domingo, Heredia
Tel: +506 22411445
Curriculum: IBDP, National, USA
Language instr: English, Spanish

Iribó School
Del restaurante la casa de Doña, Lela 800 metros al sur, Curridabat, San José 662-2050 S
Tel: +506 4000 8989
Curriculum: IBDP
Language instr: Spanish

La Paz Community School
500 metros sur de la ferreteria, Buenaventura, Flamingo, Guanacaste 50309
Tel: +506 2654 4532
Curriculum: IBDP
Language instr: English

Lighthouse International School
1 km north of the Guachipelin Tunnel, Escazú, San José 29028
Tel: +506 2215 2390
Age range: 3–18 years
No. of pupils: 210
Curriculum: IBDP, USA
Language instr: English, Spanish

Lincoln School
Barrio Socorro, Santo Domingo de Heredia
Tel: +506 2247 6600
Age range: 4–19
No. of pupils: 632 *VIth632*
Curriculum: ACT, IBDP, National, SAT, USA
Language instr: English

Marian Baker School
PO Box 4269-1000, San José 1000
Tel: +506 2273 0024
Age range: 3–18
No. of pupils: 199
Curriculum: AP, IBDP, USA
Language instr: English, Spanish

Methodist School of Costa Rica
Sabanilla, Montes de Oca, San José 11502
Tel: +506 2280 1230
Curriculum: IBDP
Language instr: English, Spanish

PAN-AMERICAN SCHOOL
For further details see p. 273
632-4035 San Antonio de Belen, Heredia
Tel: +506 2298 5700
Email: info@panam.ed.cr
Website: www.panam.ed.cr
Head of School: Alan Wrafter
Age range: 18 months–18 years
No. of pupils: 540
Fees: Day US$6,870–US$13,445
Curriculum: IBDP, IBMYP, IBPYP
Language instr: English, Spanish

Saint Gregory School
San Juan de La Unión, Cartago
Tel: +1 506 2279 4444
Curriculum: IBDP
Language instr: English, Spanish

Saint Mary School
Apartado 1471, Escazu 1250, San Jose Escazú 1250
Tel: +506 2215 2133
Curriculum: IBDP
Language instr: Spanish

Saint Paul College
San Rafael, Alajuela
Tel: +506 2438 0824 (Ext:108)
Curriculum: IBDP
Language instr: English, Spanish

St. Jude School
1.5 Kilometros al Oeste de Davivienda, Santa Ana, San José 488-6150
Tel: +506 2203 6474
Curriculum: IBDP
Language instr: Spanish

The British School of Costa Rica
PO Box 8184, San José 1000
Tel: +506 2220 0131
Age range: 4–18
Curriculum: IBDP, National, UK
Language instr: English, Spanish

UWC Costa Rica
De la esquina sureste de la Iglesia Católica, 400m al norte, Santa Ana, San José 10901
Tel: +506 22825609
Age range: 16–19
No. of pupils: 204
Curriculum: IBDP
Language instr: English, Spanish

Yorkín School
800 metros sur y 200 metros este de la casa de Doña Lela, Lomas de Ayarco Sur, Curridabat, San José 11801
Tel: +506 4000 8900
Curriculum: IBDP

CUBA

Ecole Française de la Havane
Calle 15 N° 18004 entre 180 y 182, Siboney, Havana
Tel: +53 7 273 62 64
Age range: 4–18
No. of pupils: 184
Curriculum: FrenchBacc

International School of Havana
115 Calle 22 entre, Avenida 1ra y 3ra, Miramar, Havana
Tel: +53 7214 0773
Age range: 2 1/2–17 years
No. of pupils: 330
Curriculum: IBDP, IPC, IGCSE
Language instr: English

DOMINICA

Dominica Seventh-Day Adventist Secondary School
Chambers Street, Glanvillia, Portsmouth
Tel: +1 767 445 5152

Newtown Primary School
Victoria Street, Newtown, Roseau
Tel: +1 767 448 0287
Age range: 4–11

DOMINICAN REPUBLIC

Abraham Lincoln School
Central Romana Corporation Ltd, La Romana 22000
Tel: +1 809 723 2055
Age range: 4–18
No. of pupils: 450
Curriculum: UK, IGCSE, ALevs
Language instr: English

American School of Santo Domingo
Calle C #7, Cuesta Hermosa III, Arroyo Hondo, Santo Domingo
Tel: +001 809 567 6824
Age range: 5–18
Curriculum: AP, National, USA
Language instr: English, Spanish

Ashton School
Jacinto Mañón #16, Ensanche Paraíso, Santo Domingo 11105
Tel: +1 809 562 0891
Curriculum: USA

Babeque Secundaria
Roberto Pastoriza #329, Ens. Naco, Distrito Nacional, Santo Domingo 10124
Tel: +1 809 567 9647
Curriculum: IBDP
Language instr: Spanish

Cap Cana Heritage School
Ciudad Las Canas, Cap Cana,
Tel: +1 809 695 5519
Curriculum: USA

Carol Morgan School
Avenida Sarasota, Apartado 1169, Santo Domingo
Tel: +1 809 947 1005/6
Age range: 4–18
No. of pupils: 1100 *B506 G594*
Language instr: English

Cathedral International School
Juan Goico Alix #1, Ensanche Ozama, Santo Domingo
Tel: +1 809 592 9997

Colegio Bilingue New Horizons Santo Domingo
Ave. Sarasota 51, Bella Vista, Santo Domingo
Tel: +1 809 5334915

Colegio Internacional SEK Las Américas
C/ El Altar y Rep. de Colombia, Arroyo Hondo II, Santo Domingo
Tel: +1 809 2380737
Language instr: Spanish

Comunidad Educativa Conexus
Máximo Avilés Blonda 34, Evaristo, Santo Domingo
Tel: +1 809 334 5634
Curriculum: IBDP
Language instr: English, Spanish

Garden Kids School
Calle Los Pinos, No 4 La Mulata, Sosua
Tel: +1809 571 2857
Curriculum: National, USA

Instituto Cultural Domínico-Americano
Ave. Abraham Lincoln 21, Santo Domingo,
Tel: +1 809 535 0665
Curriculum: IBCP, USA

Instituto Iberia
José Giménez Miralles 12, Santiago De Los Caballeros 51054
Tel: +1 809 736 9111
Curriculum: IBDP
Language instr: English, Spanish

Instituto Leonardo Da Vinci
Carretera Don Pedro Km 1, Esq. Calle El Guano, Santiago de los Caballeros
Tel: +1 809 734 1535
Curriculum: IBDP
Language instr: English, Spanish

Lycée Alexandre Dumas
Rue Marcadieu Bourdon, BP 2213, Port Au Prince
Tel: +509 29 40 61 42
Curriculum: FrenchBacc

Lycée Français de Saint Domingue
Rafael Damirón Esq. Jimenez Moya, Centro de los Heroes, Saint Domingue
Tel: +1 809 638 7021

Notre Dame School
Manuel de Jesus Troncoso 52, Ensanche Paraiso Z-7, Santo Domingo
Tel: +1 809 565 2511
Age range: 4–18
No. of pupils: 441 *B223 G218*
Curriculum: National, USA
Language instr: English

Puntacana International School
Punta Cana Village, Across from Puntacana Int'l Airport, Punta Cana
Tel: +1 809 959 3382
Age range: 2–18
CIS

Saint George School
C/ Porfirio Herrera #6, Ens. Piantini, Santo Domingo
Tel: +1 809 562 5262
Age range: 2–18
Curriculum: IBDP
Language instr: English, Spanish
CIS

Saint Joseph School
Ave. Pedro H. Ureña No. 95, Ens. La Esperilla, Santo Domingo
Tel: +1 809 540 8992
Curriculum: USA

Saint Thomas School
Juan Tomas Mejia y Cotes #43, Arroyo Hondo Viejo, Santo Domingo
Tel: +1 809.732.5870
Curriculum: USA

Santiago Christian School
Autopista Duarte Km 5 1/2, Sabaneta La Palomas, Santiago
Tel: +1 809 570 6140
Age range: 3–18
No. of pupils: 470
Curriculum: AP, USA

St. Michael's School
Héctor Inchaustegui #8, Piantini, Santo Domingo
Tel: +1 809 563 1707
Curriculum: USA

St. Patrick School
Calle Jose A. Aybar Castellanos No.163, La Esperilla, Santo Domingo
Tel: +1 809 338 5995
Curriculum: USA

The Americas Bicultural School
Calle Fernando Valerio No. 2, Ensanche La Julia, Santo Domingo
Tel: +1 809 535 3371
Language instr: English, French, Spanish, Mandarin
ISA

The Community for Learning
Carretera La Isabela No. 101 La Meseta Arroyo Hondo, Santo Domingo
Tel: +1 809 563 2708

The International School of Sosua
La Mulata 1, El Batey, Puerto Plata
Tel: +1 809 571 3271
Age range: 3–16
No. of pupils: 125
Curriculum: USA

DUTCH CARIBBEAN

Caribbean International Academy
#4 Tigris Road, Cupecoy, St Maarten
Tel: +1 721 545 3871
Age range: 3–18 years

ECUADOR

Academia Cotopaxi American International School
PO Box 17-11-6510, Quito, Pichincha
Tel: +593 (0)2 382 3270
Age range: 3–17
No. of pupils: *B*348 *G*293
Curriculum: IBDP, IBPYP
Language instr: English

Academia Naval Almirante Illingworth
Ave José Gómez Gault KM 8 1/2, Vía Daule, Guayaquil, Guayas
Tel: +593 (0)4 3703300
Curriculum: IBDP

Alliance Academy International
Juan José Villalengua 789 & 10 de Agosto Ave., Quito, Pichincha
Tel: +593 2 393 3800
Age range: 3–18 years
Curriculum: USA
Language instr: English

Atenas Unidad Educativa
Calle Gabriel Roman y Av. Pedro Vasconez, Yacupamba, Izamba, Ambato, Tungurahua EC 180156
Tel: +593 3 285 4297
Curriculum: IBDP
Language instr: English

Centro Educativo La Moderna
Km 2,5 Vía a Samborondón, Guayaquil, Guayas
Tel: +593 42830581
Curriculum: IBDP
Language instr: English

Centro Educativo Naciones Unidas
Samborondón Km. 1 detrás del C.C. La Piazza, Samborondón, Guayas EC 092301
Tel: +593 (0)4 6018560
Curriculum: IBDP, IBMYP, IBPYP
Language instr: English, Spanish

Colegio Alemán Humboldt – DS Samborondón
Av. Ing. León Febres-Cordero #4571, Ciudad Celeste, Samborondón, Guayas EC 090902
Tel: +593 (4) 259 7800
Curriculum: IBDP
Language instr: Spanish, German

Colegio Alemán Humboldt de Guayaquil
Ciudadela Los Ceibos, Dr. Héctor Romero 216 y Av. Dr. José M. García Moreno, Guayaquil, Guayas EC 090904
Tel: +593 (0)4 2850260
Curriculum: IBDP
Language instr: Spanish, German, English

Colegio Alemán Quito – Deutsche Schule Quito
Calle Alfonso Lamiña S6-120, vía a Lumbisí – Cumbayá, Quito, Pichincha
Tel: +593 (0)2 3560124

Colegio Alemán Stiehle Cuenca Ecuador
Autopista Cuenca – Azogues, Km 11,5, Sector Challuabamba, Cuenca, Azuay
Tel: +593 (0)7 4075646
Curriculum: IBDP
Language instr: Spanish

Colegio Americano De Guayaquil
Direccion General, Casilla 3304, Guayaquil, Guayas
Tel: +593 (0)4 3082 020
Curriculum: IBDP
Language instr: English, Spanish

Colegio Americano de Quito
Casilla 17-01-157, Quito, Pichincha
Tel: +593 (0)2 3976 300
Age range: 4–18
No. of pupils: 2806
Curriculum: AP, IBDP, IBMYP, IBPYP, SAT, TOEFL
Language instr: English

Colegio Balandra Cruz del Sur
Perimeter Road, The Prosperina, Guayaquil, Guayas
Tel: +593 (0)4 285 0020
Curriculum: IBDP
Language instr: Spanish

Colegio Becquerel
Tulipanes E12-50 y Los Rosales, Quito, Pichincha
Tel: +593 (0)2 2257896
Curriculum: IBDP

Colegio Católico José Engling
Calle Juan Montalvo s/n, Barrio La Dolorosa, Tumbaco, Quito, Pichincha EC 17172010
Tel: +593 (0)2 237 4329
Curriculum: IBDP
Language instr: English, Spanish

Colegio Experimental Británico Internacional
Amagasí del Inca, Calle de las Nueces E18-21, y Las Camelias, Quito, Pichincha
Tel: +593 (0)2 3261254
Age range: 2–18
Curriculum: IBDP, IBMYP, IBPYP
Language instr: Spanish, English

Colegio Internacional Rudolf Steiner
Calle Francisco Montalvo Nro 212, y Av Mariscal Sucre, (Av Occidental), Sector Cochabampa, Quito, Pichincha
Tel: +593 2244 3315
Age range: 3–18 years
No. of pupils: 475
Curriculum: IBDP, IBMYP, IBPYP
Language instr: Spanish

Colegio Internacional SEK Ecuador
De los Guayacanes N51-69 y Carmen Olmo Mancebo, San Isidro de El Inca, Quito, Pichincha
Tel: +593 2 2401 896
Age range: 3–18
No. of pupils: 1630 *B*831 *G*799 *VIth*95
Curriculum: IBDP, IBMYP, IBPYP
Language instr: English, Spanish
ISA

Colegio Internacional SEK Guayaquil
Vía Salinas Km. 20.5, Guayaquil, Guayas EC 11373
Tel: +593 4 3904794
Age range: 2–18
No. of pupils: 299 *B*152 *G*147
Curriculum: IBDP, IBPYP
Language instr: Spanish, English

Colegio Internacional SEK Los Valles
Eloy Alfaro S8-48 y De los Rosales, San Juan de Cumbayá, Quito, Pichincha EC 1717933
Tel: +593 2 3566220
Curriculum: IBDP, IBPYP

Colegio Intisana
Avenida Occidental 5329, y Marcos Joffre, Quito, Pichincha
Tel: +593 2 2440 128
Curriculum: IBDP
Language instr: Spanish

Colegio Letort
Los Guayabos Nro E 13-05 y Farsalias, San Isidro del Inca, Quito, Pichincha
Tel: +593 2 326 0202
No. of pupils: 572
Curriculum: IBDP, IBMYP, IBPYP
Language instr: Spanish

Colegio Los Pinos
Calle Agustín Zambrano entre Vicente Pajuelo y Tomás Chariove, Quito, Pichincha EC 170104
Tel: +593 2 246 3189
Age range: G4–18
No. of pupils: 987
Curriculum: IBDP, TOEFL
Language instr: Spanish, English, French

Colegio Menor Campus Samborondon
Km. 8 Vía Samborondón, Guayaquil, Guayas
Tel: +59 34 5000250
Age range: 5–18
Curriculum: USA

Colegio Menor San Francisco de Quito
Juan Montalvo N2-168 y Manuela Sáenz, Cumbayá, Quito, Pichincha
Tel: +59 32 4008100
Curriculum: National, USA

Colegio Séneca
Calle Juan Díaz y Paseo de la Universidad # 20, Urb. Iñaquito Alto, Quito, Pichincha EC 170523
Tel: +593 22 922 544
Curriculum: IBDP

Colegio Stella Maris
Avenida 6 y Calle 14, Manta, Manabí
Tel: +593 5 2611352
Curriculum: IBDP
Language instr: Spanish

EducaMundo
Km 12 Av. León Febres-Cordero, Urb. Villa Club, entre las etapas Aura y Doral, Guayaquil, Guayas
Tel: +593 4372 5860
Curriculum: IBDP
Language instr: English, Spanish

EMDI School
EMDI sector B, Parroquia Alangasi, Valle de los Chilos, Quito, Pichincha
Tel: +593 2278 8652
Curriculum: IBDP
Language instr: English, Spanish

Escuela Particular Liceo Panamericano – Sede Centenario
Dolores Sucre 302 y Nicolás Augusto González, Guayaquil
Tel: +593 (0)4 3707888
Curriculum: IBPYP
Language instr: English, Spanish

Inter-American Academy Guayaquil
Puerto Azul, 10.5 via a la costa, Guayaquil, Guayas
Tel: +593 4 3713360
Age range: 2–18
No. of pupils: 260 B130 G130
Curriculum: ACT, AP, SAT, USA

ISM Academy Quito
San Miguel de Anagaes, Quito, Pichincha EC 170124
Tel: +593 2 2414 198
Curriculum: IBDP, IBMYP
Language instr: Spanish

ISM International Academy
Calle Unión 886 y Ave Geovanny Calle, Sector Calderon, Quito, Pichincha
Tel: +593 2 282 0549
Curriculum: IBDP, IBMYP
Language instr: English, Spanish

JESSS – International Christian Academy
Pasaje E18 No 52-120 y, De los Nogales, Quito, Pichincha EC 170124
Tel: +593 9 9901 9696
Curriculum: IBPYP
Language instr: English, Spanish

La Salle Conocoto
Av. Abdón Calderón S18 – 104, Conocoto, Quito, Pichincha EC 170156
Tel: +593 2 234 2115
Curriculum: IBDP
Language instr: English, Spanish

La Salle Latacunga
Calle Quijano y Ordoñez 532, Y Av. General Maldonado, Latacunga, Cotopaxi EC 050104
Tel: +593 32 807 884 / +593 32 801 333
Curriculum: IBDP
Language instr: English

Liceo del Valle
km 1 vía a Pintag, Valle de los Chillos, Quito, Pichincha
Tel: +593 2 2330703
Age range: 3–18
Curriculum: IBDP, IBMYP, IBPYP
Language instr: Spanish

Liceo José Ortega y Gasset
Calle de los Cipreses N64-332 y Manuel Ambrosi, Quito, Pichincha EC 170309
Tel: +593 22482976
Curriculum: IBDP
Language instr: Spanish

Liceo Panamericano Internacional
Km 3.5 vía Samborondón, Samborondon, Guayas
Tel: +593 04 3707888
Curriculum: IBDP, IBPYP
Language instr: English

Logos Academy
Km 14.5 Via a la Costa, Guayaquil, Guayas
Tel: +59 34 390 0125
Curriculum: IBDP, National
Language instr: Spanish, English

Ludoteca Elementary & High School, Padre Victor Grados
Av Simón Bolívar y Camino de los Incas # 5-6, Nueva Vía Oriental, Quito, Pichincha
Tel: +593 2 268 8142
Curriculum: IBDP, IBMYP, IBPYP
Language instr: English, Spanish

Lycée La Condamine
Calle Japón Y Naciones Unidas, Quito, Pichincha
Tel: +593 2 292 10 90
Age range: 4–18
No. of pupils: 1255
Curriculum: FrenchBacc

Martim Cererê Unidad Educativa Particular Bilingüe
De Los Guayacanes N51-01, y Los Álamos, Quito, Pichincha EC 170150
Tel: +593 2 380 2980
Curriculum: IBDP
Language instr: English, Spanish

The British School Quito
Via Cununyacu, Km 2.5 Tumbaco, PO Box 17-21-52, Quito, Pichincha
Tel: +593 2 2 374 649
Age range: 3–19
No. of pupils: 218 B132 G86
Curriculum: IBDP, SAT, UK, USA
Language instr: English
CIS COB

Unidad Educativa Alberto Einstein
Av Diego Vásquez de Cepeda N77-157 y Alberto Einstein, Casilla Postal 17-11-5018, Quito, Pichincha
Tel: +593 2 393 2570
Age range: 3–18
No. of pupils: 700 B350 G350 VIth90
Curriculum: IBDP, IBMYP, IBPYP
Language instr: Spanish, English

Unidad Educativa Bilingüe Delta
Kilómetro 12.5 Vía Puntilla-Samborondón, Guayaquil, Guayas
Tel: +593 4 251 1266
Curriculum: IBDP
Language instr: English

Unidad Educativa Bilingüe Hontanar
Calle El Canelo E17-121 y Las Nueces, Sector Amagasí del Inca., Quito
Tel: +593 2 3261 264
Curriculum: IBDP
Language instr: English, Spanish

Unidad Educativa Bilingüe Mixta Sagrados Corazones
El Oro 1219 y Avenida Quito, Guayaquil, Guayas
Tel: +593 04 2440087
Curriculum: IBDP, IBMYP

Unidad Educativa Bilingüe Nueva Semilla
Barrio Centenario Calle D and Argüelles, Guayaquil, Guayas
Tel: +593 4 2441174
Curriculum: IBDP
Language instr: English

Unidad Educativa Bilingüe Nuevo Mundo
Calle Celeste Blacio de Rendón #112, y Km. 2,5 Vía Samborondón, Guayaquil, Guayas
Tel: +593 4 2 830 095
Curriculum: IBDP, IBMYP
Language instr: English

Unidad Educativa Bilingüe Torremar
Km 14.5 via La Puntilla, La Aurotra (Perimetral), Al lado de Parques de la Paz, Guayaquil, Guayas
Tel: +59 34 251 2512
Language instr: Spanish

Unidad Educativa Bilingüe William Caxton College
Moises Luna Andrade y Calle 6, Quito, Pichincha EC 170144
Tel: +593 2 340 6309
Curriculum: IBDP
Language instr: English, Spanish

Unidad Educativa 'Cap. Edmundo Chiriboga G.'
Av 9 de Octubre y Garcia Moreno, Riobamba, Chimborazo
Tel: +593 (0)3 294 0845
Language instr: Spanish

Unidad Educativa Cristo Rey
Calle Cristo Rey entre Sucre y Baquerizo Moreno, Portoviejo, Manabí EC 13010014
Tel: +593 052632558
Curriculum: IBDP
Language instr: Spanish

Unidad Educativa 'Émile Jaques-Dalcroze'
Av. Ilaló y Río Pastaza No. 777, Valle de Los Chillos, Quito, Pichincha
Tel: +593 2 2861 500
Curriculum: IBDP, IBMYP

Unidad Educativa Isaac Newton
Guayabos N50-120 y Los Álamos, Quito, Pichincha EC 170149
Tel: +593 22405001
Curriculum: IBDP
Language instr: Spanish

Unidad Educativa 'Julio Verne'
De Los Nopales #58 Y De Los Helechos, Quito, Pichincha EC 170150
Tel: +593 2280 7117
Curriculum: IBDP
Language instr: English, Spanish

Unidad Educativa Maurice Ravel
Av. Cantabria OE2- 8 y Av. Cacha (Sector San José de Morán), Quito, Pichincha EC 170155
Tel: +593 2 202 3508
Curriculum: IBDP
Language instr: Spanish

Unidad Educativa Monte Tabor Nazaret
Km 13.5 Via Samborondón, Guayaquil, Guayas
Tel: +593 4 259 0370
Curriculum: IBDP, IBPYP
Language instr: Spanish, English, German

Unidad Educativa Particular Bilingüe Ecomundo
Av. Juan Tanca Marengo Km 2, Guayaquil, Guayas EC 90112
Tel: +593 4 3703700 (Ext:115-118)
Curriculum: IBDP, IBMYP

Unidad Educativa Particular Bilingüe Leonardo da Vinci
Vía a San Mateo Km. 2.4, a 100 metros de la Urbanización Ciudad del Mar, Manta, Manabí EC 130802
Tel: +593 5 3 700 865
Curriculum: IBDP
Language instr: Spanish

Unidad Educativa Particular Bilingüe Principito y Marcel Laniado de Wind
Avenida Luis Ángel León Roman y 1era Avenida 5ta, Machala, El Oro EC 0701835
Tel: +593 72981881
Curriculum: IBDP
Language instr: English

Unidad Educativa Particular Bilingüe Santo Domingo de Guzmán
Calle 5ta # 608 y Las Monjas (URDESA), Guayaquil, Guayas
Tel: +593 2 882 561
Curriculum: IBDP
Language instr: Spanish

Unidad Educativa Particular Hermano Miguel De La Salle
Av. Solano 7-01 y Luis Moreno Mora, Cuenca, Azuay
Tel: +593 7 281 0349
Curriculum: IBDP
Language instr: English, Spanish

Unidad Educativa Particular Javier
Km 5.5 vía a la Costa, Guayaquil, Guayas
Tel: +593 4 2001590/3520/0724
Age range: 2–18
No. of pupils: 1500
Curriculum: IBDP
Language instr: Spanish

Unidad Educativa Particular Politécnico
Campus Politécnico 'Gustavo Galindo Velasco', Km. 30.5 vía Perimetral, contiguo a Ceibos Norte, Guayaquil, Guayas
Tel: +593 4 226 9654
Age range: 3–18
Curriculum: IBDP, IBMYP, IBPYP
Language instr: Spanish

Unidad Educativa Particular Redemptio
10 de Agosto 701 entre Colón y Juan Montalvo, Jipijapa, Manabí
Tel: +593 5 2 600 475
Curriculum: IBDP
Language instr: English, Spanish

Unidad Educativa Particular 'Rosa de Jesús Cordero'
Parroquia Ricaurte, Sector el Tablón, Cuenca, Azuay EC 010162
Tel: +593 7 2890503
Curriculum: IBDP
Language instr: Spanish

Unidad Educativa Paul Dirac
Av. Pedro Vicente Maldonado y la Cocha, Quito, Pichincha EC 170146
Tel: +593 2 691 241 (Ext:1)
Curriculum: IBDP
Language instr: English, Spanish

Unidad Educativa Saint Dominic School
César Davila N10-222 y Charles Darwin, Quito, Pichincha
Tel: +593 (0)2 3959960
Curriculum: IBDP
Language instr: Spanish

Unidad Educativa Salesiana Cardenal Spellman
Mercadillo OE340 y Ulloa, Quito, Pichincha EC 1703125
Tel: +593 2 3560 001/2/3
Curriculum: IBDP
Language instr: Spanish

Unidad Educativa Salinas Innova
Av. Carlos Espinoza Larrea, via a salinas, Junto al centro de atención ciudadana, Salinas, Santa Elena EC 241550
Tel: +593 4 277 5954
Language instr: Spanish

Unidad Educativa San Francisco de Sales
Av. Cristobal Colón E10-07 y Tamayo, Quito, Pichincha
Tel: +593 2903 861
Curriculum: IBDP
Language instr: English, Spanish

Unidad Educativa San Jose La Salle
Tomás Martínez 501 y Baquerizo Moreno, Guayaquil, Guayas EC 090150
Tel: +593 4 25 631 37
Curriculum: IBDP
Language instr: Spanish

Unidad Educativa Santana
Av. los Cerezos S/N y vía a Racar, Cuenca, Azuay
Tel: +593 7 4121879
Age range: 3–18
No. of pupils: 800
Curriculum: IBDP
Language instr: Spanish

Unidad Educativa Terranova
Calle De Los Rieles 507, y Ave Simón Bolívar, San Juan Alto de Cumbayá, Quito, Pichincha
Tel: +593 2 356 4000
Curriculum: IBDP, IBMYP, IBPYP
Language instr: English, Spanish, French

Unidad Educativa Theodore W. Anderson
Av. Gaspar de Villarroel E5-35 e Isla Isabela, Quito, Pichincha EC 170104
Tel: +593 2 2604 4738
Language instr: Spanish

Unidad Educativa Tomás Moro
Av De Las Orquideas E13-120, y De Los Guayacanes, Quito, Pichincha
Tel: +593 2 2405357
Curriculum: IBDP, IBMYP, IBPYP
Language instr: Spanish

Unidad Educativo Bilingüe CEBI
Calle Modesto Chacón y Av. Pedro Vásconez Sevilla, Parroquia Izamba, Ambato, Tungurahua
Tel: +593 3 373 0370
Curriculum: IBDP, IBMYP, IBPYP
Language instr: Spanish

Victoria Bilingual Christian Academy
Melchor de Valdez Oe-9240, Pbx: 253-6116, Quito, Pichincha EC 170528
Tel: +593 (0)2 2536116
Curriculum: IBDP
Language instr: Spanish

Young Living Academy
Km. 24 vía a la Costa, Chongoncito, Guayaquil, Guayas
Tel: +593 9965 4897
Curriculum: IBDP
Language instr: English, Spanish

EL SALVADOR

Academia Britanica Cuscatleca
Apartado Postal 121, Santa Tecla, La Libertad
Tel: +503 2201 6222/6252/6261
Age range: 3–18
No. of pupils: 1500
Curriculum: IBDP, IPC, National, UK, IGCSE
Language instr: English (PE, Art in Spanish)

Colegio Internacional de San Salvador
Apartado 05-15, San Salvador
Tel: +503 2224 1330
Age range: 4–19
No. of pupils: 318 B154 G164
Curriculum: ACT, AP, National, SAT, USA

Colegio La Floresta
Estamos en el Km. 13 1/2, Carretera al Puerto de La Libertad,
Tel: +503 2534 8800
Age range: G6–17
No. of pupils: 642
Curriculum: IBDP
Language instr: Spanish

Colegio Lamatepec
Carretera al Puerto de La Libertad Km 12.5, Calle Nueva a Comasauga Santa Tecla, La Libertad, San Salvador
Tel: +503 2534 8900
Age range: B6–18
No. of pupils: 655
Curriculum: IBDP
Language instr: Spanish, English

Colegio Maya
7a calle poniente Bis #4925, Colonia Escalón, San Salvador
Tel: +503 2263 2358
Age range: 4–19
Curriculum: National, USA

Colegio Salvadoreño Inglés
No 113, 85 Avenida Norte, Colonia Escalón, San Salvador
Tel: +503 2263 7586
Curriculum: UK

Deutsche Schule – Escuela Alemana San Salvador
Calle del Mediterráneo, Jardines de Guadalupe, Antiguo Cuscatlán, San Salvador CA
Tel: +503 2243 4898
No. of pupils: 588
Curriculum: IBDP
Language instr: Spanish

Escuela Americana
VIPSAL #1352, PO Box 025364, Miami FL 33102-5364, USA
Tel: +503 2528 8300
Age range: 4–18
Curriculum: USA
Language instr: English

Escuela Panamericana
Final Pje Union, Calle El Carmen #1348, Colonia Esculon, San Salvador
Tel: +503 2505 7558
Age range: 4–19
No. of pupils: 435 *B*220 *G*215
Curriculum: National, SAT, USA
Language instr: English, Spanish

Lycée Français de San Salvador Antoine et Consuelo de Saint-Exupéry
km 10 1/2 carretera a Santa Tecla, La Libertad, San Salvador
Tel: +503 22 280615
Curriculum: FrenchBacc

GUATEMALA

American School of Guatemala
11 Calle 15-79 Zona 15 Vista Hermosa III, Guatemala
Tel: +502 2500 9595
Age range: 4–18
Curriculum: National, USA
Language instr: Spanish, English

Antigua Green School
Calle del Portal No. 11, Finca Azotea, Antigua
Tel: +502 4060 0023

Antigua International School
Km 74.8, Ruta Nacional 14, Ciudad Vieja, Sacatepequez
Tel: +502 4138 3110
Age range: 4–18
No. of pupils: 300
Curriculum: AP, SAT, USA
Language instr: English, Spanish

Centro Escolar Campoalegre
35 Calle and 12 Av Final, Zona 11, Código 01011
Tel: +502 2380 3900
Age range: *G*7–18
Curriculum: IBDP
Language instr: Spanish

Centro Escolar 'El Roble'
11 Avenida Sur Final Zona 11, Guatemala City 01011
Tel: +502 2387 7000
Curriculum: IBDP
Language instr: Spanish

Centro Escolar Entrevalles
Km. 16.8 Antigua Carretera a El Salvador, Santa Catarina Pinula
Tel: +502 6685 4700
Curriculum: IBDP
Language instr: Spanish, English

Centro Escolar Solalto
Km. 22.5 Carretera a Fraijanes, Fraijanes,
Tel: +502 6686 0500
Age range: *B*7–18
No. of pupils: 369 *B*369
Curriculum: IBDP
Language instr: English, Spanish

Christian American School
8va. Avenida 9-41, zona 8 de Mixco, Sector A-10 Finca Santa Barbará, San Cristóbal
Tel: +502 2218 1100
Curriculum: USA

Colegio Decroly Americano
11 Calle 6-47, Finca El Naranjo, Zona 4 de Mixco, Guatemala City
Tel: +502 23802380 (Ext:4014/4020)
Age range: 15 months–18
No. of pupils: 994 *B*491 *G*503
Curriculum: AP, SAT, USA
Language instr: English, Spanish

Colegio Interamericano
Boulevard La Montana, Finca El Socorro, Zona 16 1016
Tel: +502 2200 2990
No. of pupils: 1200
Curriculum: USA

Colegio Internacional SEK Guatemala
Km.20.5 carretera Brisas Pavón, carretera a Lo de Diéguez, Fraijanes
Tel: +502 66 70 26 00

Colegio Julio Verne
1a Avenida 2-62 Zona1, Aldea Don Justo Km. 18.5 a San Jose Pinula, 01062 Fraijanes
Tel: +502 6661 1800/4
Curriculum: National, FrenchBacc

Colegio Maya – The American International School of Guatemala
Km 12.5 Carretera a El Salvador, Santa Catarina Pinula 1051
Tel: +502 6644 1200
Age range: 3–18
No. of pupils: 372
Curriculum: AP, USA

Equity American School
15 Avenida A 21-00, Zona 13, Guatemala City 01013
Tel: +502 2390 6800
Curriculum: USA

Inter-American School
0 Avenida 1-43 Zona 6, Quetzaltenango
Tel: +502 7761 4080
Curriculum: USA

QSI International School of Belize
11/13 Dean Crescent, University Heights, University Heights, Cayo District Belize
Tel: +501 832 2666
Age range: 4–12
Curriculum: USA

Village School
Km 25.5 Carretera a El Salvador, Finca Labor El Rosario, Villa Canales
Tel: +502 6643 6300
Age range: 4–18
No. of pupils: 680
Curriculum: USA

HAITI

Union School Haiti
Route du Canape-Vert, Petion Ville
Tel: +509 2943 4923
Curriculum: USA
Language instr: English, French

JAMAICA

American International School of Kingston
2 College Green Avenue, Kingston
Tel: +1 876 702 2070
Age range: 3–18
No. of pupils: 277 *B*147 *G*130
Curriculum: IBDP
Language instr: English

Hillel Academy
PO Box 2687, 51 Upper Mark Way, Kingston 8
Tel: +1 876 925 1980
Age range: 3–19 years
No. of pupils: 702
Curriculum: IBDP, IGCSE
Language instr: English

MÉXICO

Alexander Bain Colegio
Barranca de Pilares 29, Colonia Tlacopac, San Angel, México D.F. C.P. 01040
Tel: +52 55 5595 0493
Age range: 3–12
Curriculum: IBPYP
Language instr: Spanish

American Institute of Monterrey – APS Campus
La República No. 300, Col. La Aurora, Santa Catarina, Nuevo León C.P. 66378
Tel: +52 81 8048 3700
Age range: 11–18 years
Language instr: English, Spanish

American Institute of Monterrey – San Pedro Campus
Perseverancia 100, Col. Balcones del Valle, San Pedro Garza García, Nuevo León C.P. 66220
Tel: +52 81 8174 3700
Age range: 2–11 years
Language instr: English, Spanish

American Institute of Monterrey – Valle Oriente Campus
Ave. Humberto Junco Voigt No. 2305, Col. Valle Oriente, San Pedro Garza García, Nuevo León C.P. 66260
Tel: +52 81 1958 9800
Age range: 2–16 years
Language instr: English, Spanish

American School Foundation of Chiapas
Blvd. Belisario Dominguez 5588-F, Fraccion Las Cinco Plumas, Terán, Tuxtla Gutierrez, Chiapas C.P. 29052
Tel: +52 961 346 4840
Curriculum: IBPYP
Language instr: English, Spanish

American School Foundation of Guadalajara
Colomos 2100, Col. Providencia, Guadalajara, Jalisco C.P. 44630
Tel: +52 33 3648 0299
Age range: 3–18
No. of pupils: 1400 *B*700 *G*700
Curriculum: AP, National, SAT, TOEFL, USA
Language instr: English, Spanish

American School Foundation of Monterrey
Ave. Ignacio Morones Prieto No. 1500, Col. San Isidro, Santa Catarina, Nuevo León C.P. 66190
Tel: +52 81 5000 4400
Age range: 3–18
No. of pupils: 561

American School of Pachuca
Blvd Valle de Anáhuac s/n, Col San Javier, Pachuca, Hidalgo C.P. 42086
Tel: +52 771 713 1058
Age range: 4–14
No. of pupils: 830
Curriculum: USA

American School of Puerto Vallarta
Albatros 129, Col. Marina Vallarta, Puerto Vallarta, Jalisco C.P. 48335
Tel: +52 322 226 7670
Age range: 3–18
No. of pupils: 348
Curriculum: AP, SAT

Avalon International School
Av. San Jerónimo 1135, San Jerónimo de Lídice La Magdalena Contreras, Mexico D.F. C.P. 10200
Tel: +52 555 595 5582
Curriculum: IBPYP
Language instr: English, Spanish

Bachillerato Alexander Bain, SC
Las Flores 497, Tlacopac, San Ángel, Ciudad de México C.P. 01049
Tel: +52 (55) 5683 2971
Age range: 12–18
No. of pupils: 610
Curriculum: IBDP, IBMYP
Language instr: Spanish, English

Bachillerato UPAEP Atlixco
Camino a la Uvera #2004, Ex-Hacienda La Blanca, 74365 Atlixco, Puebla
Tel: +52 244 445 1991
Curriculum: IBCP
Language instr: English, Spanish

Bachillerato UPAEP San Martín
C/ Lardizabal s/n Col. La Purisima, San Martín Texmelucan, Puebla C.P. 74030
Curriculum: IBCP
Language instr: English, Spanish

Bachillerato UPAEP Santa Ana
Avenida Tecpanxochitl 52 A, San Pedro Tlalcuapan, Chiautempan, Tlaxcala C.P. 90845
Tel: +52 246 46 496 33
Curriculum: IBCP
Language instr: English, Spanish

British American School S.C.
Fuente del Niño #16 Col. Tecamachalco, Naucalpan de Juárez, Estado de México C.P. 53950
Tel: +55 52 94 37 21
Curriculum: IBPYP
Language instr: English

Centro de Enseñanza Técnica y Superior – Campus Mexicali
Calzada del Cetys S/N, Colonia Rivera, Mexicali, Baja California C.P. 21259
Tel: +52 686 567 3704
Curriculum: IBDP

Centro de Ensenanza Tecnica y Superior – Campus Tijuana
Av. CETYS Universidad, No. 4 Fracc. El Lago, Tijuana, Baja California C.P. 22210
Tel: +52 664 903 1800
No. of pupils: 608
Curriculum: IBDP
Language instr: Spanish

Centro Educativo Alexander Bain Irapuato
Enrique del Moral Domínguez 335, Ejido Lo de Juárez, 36630, Irapuato, Guanajuato
Tel: +52 462 114 2246
Age range: 3–19
No. of pupils: 391
Curriculum: IBDP, IBPYP
Language instr: Spanish, English

Centro Educativo CRECER AC
Calle del Vecino No 3, Atlihuetzia, Yahuquehmecan, Tlaxcala C.P. 90459
Tel: +52 24 646 13 148
Curriculum: IBMYP, IBPYP

Centro Escolar Instituto La Paz, SC
Av Plan de San Luis 445, Col Nueva Santa María, Ciudad de México C.P. 02800
Tel: +52 55 55 56 66 46
Age range: 3–15
No. of pupils: 1200
Curriculum: IBMYP, IBPYP, National
Language instr: Spanish, English

Churchill College
Moctezuma 125, Colonia San Pablo Tepetlapa, Ciudad de México C.P. 04620
Tel: +52 55 56 19 82 43
Curriculum: IBDP, National, UK, IGCSE
Language instr: Spanish, English

Colegio Álamos
Acceso al Aeropuerto 1000, Colonia Arboledas, Santiago de Querétaro, Querétaro C.P. 76940
Tel: +52 442 182 0222
Curriculum: IBDP
Language instr: Spanish

Colegio Alemán de Guadalajara
Av Bosques de los Cedros No. 32, Las Cañadas, Zapopan, Jalisco C.P. 45132
Tel: +52 33 3685 0136
Age range: 16–19 years
Curriculum: IBDP
Language instr: Spanish, German

Colegio Alfonsino de San Pedro AC
Galeana 257 Pte, San Pedro, Garza Garcia, Nuevo León C.P. 68230
Tel: +52 81 8338 3818
Age range: 1–16

Colegio Americano de Durango
Francisco Sarabia 416 Pte, Apartado Postal 495, Durango C.P. 34000
Tel: +52 618 811 5098
Age range: 2–18
No. of pupils: 475 *B*240 *G*235
Curriculum: National, SAT, USA
Language instr: English, Spanish

Colegio Americano de San Carlos
Blvd. Luis Encinas S/N, esquina Faustino Félix, Colonia Miramar, Guaymas, Sonora C.P. 85450
Tel: +52 622 221 2551
Curriculum: IBPYP
Language instr: English, Spanish

Colegio Americano de Torreón
Paso del Algodón #500, Fraccionamiento Los Viñedos, Torreón, Coahuila C.P. 27019
Tel: +871 222 51 00
Age range: 3–18
Curriculum: ACT, AP, National, SAT, TOEFL, USA, ALevs
Language instr: English

Colegio Anglo Mexicano de Chiapas
Av Pmarrosa No 239, Colonia Pomarosa, Tuxtla Gutiérrez, Chiapas
Tel: +52 961 60 232274
Language instr: English

Colegio Arji
Avenida México # 2, esquina Periférico, Colonia del Bosque, Villahermosa, Tabasco C.P. 86160
Tel: +52 993 3 510 250
Age range: 3–18
No. of pupils: 1200
*B*600 *G*600 *VIth*80
Curriculum: IBDP, IBMYP, IBPYP
Language instr: English, Spanish

Colegio Atid AC
Av. Carlos Echanove #224, Col. Vista Hermosa Cuajimalpa, Ciudad de México C.P. 05100
Tel: +52 55 5814 0800
Age range: 4–18
Curriculum: IBDP, IBMYP, IBPYP, IBCP
Language instr: English, Spanish

Colegio Bilingüe Carson de Ciudad Delicias
Ave 50 Aniversario 1709, Delicias, Chihuahua C.P. 33058
Tel: +52 (639) 472 9340
Curriculum: IBPYP

Colegio Bosques
Prol. Zaragoza No. 701, Fracc. Valle de las Trojes, Aguascalientes C.P. 20115
Tel: +52 449 162 04 05
Curriculum: IBMYP, IBPYP

Colegio Británico
Calle Pargo # 24, S.M. 3, Cancun, Quintana Roo C.P. 77500
Tel: +52 (998) 884 1295
No. of pupils: 370 *B*120 *G*250
Curriculum: IBDP, IBPYP
Language instr: English, Spanish

Colegio Buena Tierra SC
Camino Viejo a San Mateo 273, San Salvador Tizatlalli, Metepec, Estado de México C.P. 52172
Tel: +52 722 271 2500
Language instr: English, Spanish

Colegio Celta Internacional
Libramiento Sur-Poniente Km 4+200, Colonia Los Olvera, Villa Corregidora, Querétaro C.P. 76902
Tel: +52 442 227 36 00
No. of pupils: 840
Curriculum: IBMYP, IBPYP, IBCP
Language instr: English, Spanish

Colegio Ciudad de México
Campos Elíseos # 139, Col Polanco, Ciudad de México C.P. 11560
Tel: +52 55 5254 4053
Age range: 2–18
No. of pupils: 1400
Curriculum: IBDP, IBMYP, IBPYP
Language instr: Spanish, English

Colegio Ciudad de Mexico – Plantel Contadero
Calle de la Bolsa 456, El Contadero, Cuajimalpa, Ciudad de México C.P. 05500
Tel: +52 58 12 06 10
No. of pupils: 450
Curriculum: IBPYP

Colegio Columbia
Poza Rica #507, Col Petrolera, Tampico, Tamaulipas C.P. 89110
Tel: +52 833 213 0054/1045
Age range: 2–15
No. of pupils: 820 *B*429 *G*391
Curriculum: National

Colegio Discovery
Circuito Interior Norte Socorro Romero, Sánchez, No. 3525, Col. San Lorenzo, Tehuacán, Puebla
Tel: +52 238 3820005
Curriculum: IBDP, IBMYP, IBPYP
Language instr: Spanish

Colegio El Camino
Callejon del Jornongo #210, Colonia El Pedregal, Cabo San Lucas, B.C.S. C.P. 23453
Tel: +52 624 143 2100 (Ext:112)
Age range: 3–18 years
Curriculum: IBDP, IBPYP
Language instr: English, Spanish

Colegio Euroamericano de Monterrey
Blvd Diaz Ordaz 250 Ote, Colonia Santa Maria, Monterrey, Nuevo León C.P. 64650
Tel: +52 81 8248 8400
Age range: 2–15
No. of pupils: 1321 *B*691 *G*630
Curriculum: National, USA
Language instr: English, Spanish German

Colegio Fontanar
Camino al Fraccionamiento, Vista Real 119, Corregidora, Querétaro C.P. 76900
Tel: +52 442 228 13 65
No. of pupils: 630
Curriculum: IBDP
Language instr: Spanish

Colegio Hebreo Maguen David
Antiguo Camino a Tecamachalco #370, Lomas de Vista Hermosa, Ciudad de México
Tel: +52 (55) 52 46 26 00
Age range: 2–18 years
No. of pupils: 1194
Curriculum: IBDP, IBMYP, IBPYP, National, TOEFL
Language instr: Spanish, Hebrew, English

Colegio Hebreo Monte Sinai AC
Av Loma de la Palma 133, Col Vista Hermosa, Cuajimalpa, Ciudad de México C.P. 05109
Tel: +52 55 52 53 01 68
Curriculum: IBDP, IBMYP, IBPYP
Language instr: Spanish, English

Colegio Hebreo Tarbut
Av. Loma del Parque 216, Colonia Lomas de Vista Hermosa, Ciudad de México C.P. 05100
Tel: +52 55 5814 0500
Language instr: Spanish, English Hebrew

Colegio Inglés
Real San Agustin #100, Col San Agustin Campestre, Garza Garcia, Nuevo León C.P. 66270
Tel: +52 81 8133 1700
Age range: 4–16
Curriculum: National

Colegio Internacional de México
Río Magdalena 263, Colonia Tizapan San Ángel, Álvaro Obregón, Ciudad de México D.P. 01090
Tel: +52 55 55 50 01 01
Age range: 3–18
Curriculum: IBMYP, IBPYP
Language instr: English, Spanish

Colegio Internacional SEK Guadalajara
Daniel Comboni #850, Colonia Jardines de Guadalupe, Zapopan Jalisco C.P 45030
Tel: +52 33 36202423
Curriculum: IBDP
Language instr: English, Spanish

Colegio Internacional Terranova
Av Palmira No. 705, Privadas del Pedregal, San Luis Potosí C.P. 78295
Tel: +52 444 8 41 64 22
Curriculum: IBDP, IBMYP, IBPYP

Colegio La Paz de Chiapas
Carretera Tuxtla, Villaflores N° 1170, Tuxtla Gutiérrez, Chiapas C.P. 29089
Tel: +52 961 663 7000
Curriculum: IBDP, IBMYP
Language instr: Spanish

Colegio Laureles IAP
Inzancanac s/n esq Jugueteros y Canteros, Barrio Tlatel Xochitenco, Chimalhuacan, Estado de México C.P. 56330
Tel: +52 5 55852 9002
Language instr: English, Spanish

Colegio Linares AC
Marina Silva de Rodriguez 1301 Pte, Colonia centro Linares, Nuevo León C.P. 67700
Tel: +52 821 212 0269
Curriculum: IBDP

Colegio Madison Chihuahua
Fuente Trevi #7001, Fracc. Puerta de Hierro, Chihuahua C.P. 31205
Tel: +52 614 430 1464
Age range: 3–15
No. of pupils: 475
Curriculum: IBPYP
Language instr: English, Spanish

Colegio Madison Torreón
Blvd. De la Senda #321, Fracc. Residencial Senderos, Torreón, Coahuila C.P. 27018
Tel: +52 87 1193 4400

Colegio Maria Montessori de Monclova
Blvd Harold R Pape Nro 2002, Col Jardines del Valle, Monclova, Coahuila C.P. 25730
Tel: +52 866 633 2993
Curriculum: IBDP

Colegio Merici
Granjas 45, Col Palo Alto, Cuajimalpa, Ciudad de México C.P. 05110
Tel: +52 55 55703183

Colegio Montessori Sierra Madre
Avenida Licenciado Benito Juárez Sur 250, Centro de San Pedro Garza García, San Pedro Garza García, Nuevo León C.P. 66200
Tel: +52 81 8124 6400
Age range: 3–15

Colegio Monteverde
Av Santa Lucia No 260, Col Prados de la Montaña, Cualjimalpa, Ciudad de México C.P. 05610
Tel: +52 55 50819700
Age range: *B*2–6 *G*2–19
No. of pupils: 686
Curriculum: IBDP, UK
Language instr: Spanish, English

Colegio Nuevo Continente
Nicolás San Juan 1141, Colonia Del Valle, Ciudad de México C.P. 03100
Tel: +52 55 5575 4066
Curriculum: IBDP
Language instr: English, Spanish

Colegio Olinca Altavista
Av Altavista No 130, Colonia San Angel, Delegación Álvaro Obregón, Ciudad de México C.P. 01060
Tel: +52 55 56160216
Language instr: Spanish

Colegio Simón Bolivar
Av. Río Mixcoac No.125, Col. Insurgentes, Mixcoac, Ciudad de México C.P. 03920
Tel: +52 55 55 63 6300
No. of pupils: 626

Colegio Springfield, SC
Isidro Fabela Nte 1061, Col Tres Caminos, Toluca, Estado de México C.P. 50020
Tel: +52 722 272 0586
Language instr: Spanish

Colegio Suizo de México – Campus Cuernavaca
Calle Amates s/n, Col. Lomas de Ahuatlán, Cuernavaca, Morelos C.P. 62130
Tel: +52 777 323 5252
Curriculum: IBDP
Language instr: English

Colegio Suizo de México – Campus México DF
Nicolás San Juan 917, Col del Valle, Ciudad de México C.P. 03100
Tel: +52 55 55 43 78 62
Age range: 3–19
No. of pupils: 726
Curriculum: IBDP
Language instr: English

Colegio Suizo de México – Campus Querétaro
Circ. La Cima 901, Fracc. La Cima, Santiago de Querétaro, Querétaro C.P. 76146
Tel: +52 442 254 3390
Age range: 3–19
No. of pupils: 305
Curriculum: IBDP
Language instr: Spanish, German, English

Colegio Vista Hermosa
Bachillerato, Av Loma de Vista Hermosa 221, Cuajimalpa, Ciudad de México C.P. 05100
Tel: +52 55 50914630
Age range: 13–18
No. of pupils: 900 *B*400 *G*500
Curriculum: IBDP, IBMYP, TOEFL
Language instr: Spanish

Colegio Williams
Mixcoac Campus, Empresa 8, Col Mixcoac, Alcaldía Benito Juárez, Ciudad de México C.P. 03910
Tel: +52 55 1087 9797
Curriculum: IBDP, IBMYP, IBPYP
Language instr: Spanish

Colegio Williams de Cuernavaca
Luna #32, Jardines de Cuernavaca, Cuernavaca, Morelos C.P. 62360
Tel: +52 (777) 3223640
Age range: 1–19
No. of pupils: 850 *B*460 *G*390
Curriculum: IBDP, IBMYP, IBPYP, National, TOEFL
Language instr: English, Spanish

Colegio Williams Unidad San Jerónimo
Presa Reventada No 53, Col San Jerónimo Lídice, Del. Magdalena Contreras, Ciudad de México C.P. 10400
Tel: +52 55 1087 9797
Curriculum: IBPYP
Language instr: Spanish, English

Colegio Xail
Calle Xail No 10, Col. Lázaro Cárdenas, San Francisco de Campeche, Campeche C.P. 24520
Tel: +52 981 813 0322
Curriculum: IBMYP, IBPYP

Discovery School
Chilpancingo No 102, Colonia Vista Hermosa, Cuernavaca, Morelos C.P. 62290
Tel: +52 777 318 5721
Curriculum: IBPYP
Language instr: English

Educare Centro de Servicios Educativos S.C.
Norte 26 #498, Orizaba, Veracruz C.P. 94300
Tel: +52 272 7241194
Language instr: Spanish

Escuela Alexander Bain SC
Barranca de Pilares 4, Tlacopac, San Ángel, Ciudad de México C.P. 01049
Tel: +52 56 833 255
Age range: 3–12
Language instr: Spanish

Escuela Ameyalli SC
Calzada de las Águilas 1972, Axomiatla, Ciudad de México C.P. 01820
Tel: +52 55 12 85 70 20
Age range: 2–18
Curriculum: IBMYP, IBPYP
Language instr: Spanish, English

Escuela Bancaria y Comercial, SC
Paseo de la Reforma No 202 Edif E 3er piso, Col Juárez, Del Cuauhtemoc, Ciudad de México C.P. 06600
Tel: +52 (55) 91 49 20 79
Language instr: Spanish

Escuela John F. Kennedy
Av Sabinos 272, Jurica, Querétaro C.P. 76100
Tel: +52 442 218 0075
Age range: 3–19
No. of pupils: 1444 *B751 G693*
Curriculum: IBDP, IBMYP, IBPYP
Language instr: English, Spanish

Escuela Lomas Altas S.C.
Montañas Calizas #305, Lomas de Chapultepec, Ciudad de México C.P. 11000
Tel: +52 55 55 20 53 75/20 37 25
Age range: 1 –13
No. of pupils: 260 *B124 G136*
Curriculum: IBPYP
Language instr: English, Spanish

Escuela Mexicana Americana, A. C.
Gabriel Mancera 1671, Col. Del Valle, Ciudad de México C.P. 03100
Tel: +52 55 240214
Curriculum: IBDP
Language instr: English, Spanish

Escuela Secundaria y Preparatoria de la Ciudad de Mexico
Campos Eliseos # 139, Col Polanco, Ciudad de México C.P. 11560
Tel: +52 5545 5761
Curriculum: IBCP

Eton, SC
Domingo García Ramos s/n, Col. Prados de la Montaña, Santa Fe, Cuajimalpa, Ciudad de México C.P. 05619
Tel: +52 5 261 5800
Age range: 2–18
Curriculum: IBDP, IBMYP
Language instr: Spanish, English

Formus
Cañón de la Mesa 6745, Monterrey, Nuevo León C.P. 64898
Tel: +52 8317 8560
Curriculum: IBMYP
Language instr: Spanish

Fundación Colegio Americano de Puebla
Av 9 Pte 2709, La Paz, Puebla C.P. 72160
Tel: +52 22 2303 0400
Age range: 6 months–19 years
Curriculum: IBDP, IBMYP, IBPYP, IBCP
Language instr: Spanish, English

GREENGATES SCHOOL
For further details see p. 266
Av. Circunvalación Pte. 102, Balcones de San Mateo, Naucalpan, Estado de México C.P. 53200
Tel: +52 55 5373 0088
Email: kuroda@greengates.edu.mx
Website: www.greengates.edu.mx
General Director: Clarisa Desouches
Age range: 3–18 years
No. of pupils: 1100
Curriculum: IBDP, IPC, UK, IGCSE
Language instr: English

Greenville International School
Prolongación Arco Noroeste s/n, Colonia González 1ra Sección, Villahermosa, Tabasco C.P. 86039
Tel: +52 993 310 8060
Curriculum: IBDP, IBMYP, IBPYP
Language instr: English

Harmony School
Mariano Narváez 414, Col. Los Alpes Norte, Saltillo, Coahuila C.P 25253
Tel: +52 84 4485 5598
Curriculum: IBPYP
Language instr: English, Spanish

Humanitree
725 Sierra Madre, Lomas de Chapultepec, Miguel Hidalgo, Ciudad de México C.P. 11000
Tel: +52 55 8620 7301
Curriculum: IBDP
Language instr: English, Spanish

Instituto Alexander Bain SC
Cascada 320, Jardines del Pedregal, Ciudad de México
Tel: +52 55 5595 6579
Age range: 2–13
No. of pupils: *B381 G382*
Curriculum: IBMYP, IBPYP, National
Language instr: Spanish, English

Instituto Anglo Británico Campus Cumbres
Paseo de los leones 7001, Avenida Bosque de las Lomas, Valle de Cumbres, García, Nuevo León C.P. 66035
Tel: +52 81 8526 2222
Age range: 1–15
No. of pupils: 428
Curriculum: IBMYP, IBPYP
Language instr: English, Spanish

Instituto Anglo Británico Campus La Fe
Av. Isidoro Sepúlveda #555, Col. La Encarnación, Apodaca, Nuevo León C.P. 66633
Tel: +52 8183 21 5000
Age range: 1–15
Curriculum: IBMYP, IBPYP
Language instr: English, Spanish

Instituto Bilingüe Rudyard Kipling
Cruz de Valle Verde No 25, Santa Cruz del Monte, Naucalpan, Estado de México C.P. 53110
Tel: +52 55 5572 6282
Age range: 3–18
Curriculum: IBDP, IBMYP, IBPYP
Language instr: Spanish, English

Instituto Bilingüe Victoria A.C.
Vicente Suárez No. 9, Barrio de la Magdalena, Tequisquiapan, Querétaro C.P. 76750
Tel: +52 414 273 3739
Age range: 3–18
No. of pupils: 528
Curriculum: IGCSE

Instituto Cervantes, A.C.
Prol. León García # 2355, Col. General I. Martínez, San Luis Potosí C.P. 78360
Tel: +52 444 815 91 50
Age range: 2 1/2–15 years
No. of pupils: 1370
Curriculum: IBMYP, IBPYP
Language instr: Spanish

Instituto D'Amicis, AC
Camino a Morillotla s/n, Colonia Bello Horizonte, Puebla C.P. 72170
Tel: +52 222 303 2618
Curriculum: AP, IBDP, IBMYP, IBPYP, IBCP
Language instr: Spanish

Instituto Educativo Olinca
Periférico Sur 5170, Col Pedregal de Carrasco, Delegación Coyoacán, Ciudad de México C.P. 04700
Tel: +52 55 5606 3113/4197
Age range: 1.5–18 years
No. of pupils: 1600
Curriculum: IBDP, IBMYP, IBPYP
Language instr: Spanish, English, French

Instituto Educativo Olinca Plantel Cuernavaca
Paseo de Atzingo No 515, Colonia Lomas de Atzingo, Cuernavaca, Morelos C.P. 62180
Tel: +52 777 313 1232

Instituto Internacional Octavio Paz
Calle Internacional 63 Fracc. Las Brisas el Jaguey, Col. Las Redes, Chapala, Jalisco C.P. 45903
Tel: +52 376 766 0903
Curriculum: IBDP

Instituto Jefferson Internacional
Boulevard Jefferson No 666, Morelia, Michoacán C.P. 58080
Tel: +52 443 3237967
Age range: 1–19
No. of pupils: 600
Curriculum: IBDP, IBMYP, IBPYP
Language instr: Spanish

Instituto Kipling de Irapuato
Villa Mirador 5724, Villas de Irapuato, Irapuato, Guanajuato C.P. 36670
Tel: +52 462 6230165
Age range: 2–18
No. of pupils: *B611 G687*
Curriculum: IBMYP, IBPYP
Language instr: Spanish, English

Instituto Ovalle Monday – Plantel Secundaria
Guillermo Massieu Helguera 265, Col. Residencial La Escalera, Del. Gustavo A. Madero, Ciudad de México C.P. 07320
Tel: +52 5586 0316 (Ext:101)
Curriculum: IBMYP
Language instr: Spanish

Instituto para la Educación Integral del Bachiller (INEDIB)
Calle 20 de Noviembre No. 310, San Mateo Oxtotitlán, Toluca, Estado de México C.P. 50100
Tel: +52 722 278 10 40
Language instr: Spanish

Instituto Piaget
Nubes 413, Col Jardines del Pedregal, Ciudad de México C.P. 01900
Tel: +52 555568 8881
Age range: 2–18
No. of pupils: 550
Curriculum: IBPYP
Language instr: English, Spanish

Instituto Sanmiguelense
Escuadrón 201, No. 10 Palmita de Landeta Km. 0.5, San Miguel de Allende, Guanajuato C.P. 37748
Tel: +52 415 154 8484
Age range: 16–18 years
No. of pupils: 130
Curriculum: IBDP
Language instr: Spanish

Kinder Kri-Kri
Circuito Puericultores No 6, Ciudad Satélite, Naucalpan, Estado de México C.P. 53100

Kipling Esmeralda
Av. Parque de los Ciervos No.1, Hacienda de Valle Escondido, Zona Esmeralda, Atizapan de Zaragoza, EEstado de México C.P. 52937
Tel: +52 55 55726282
Curriculum: IBDP, IBMYP, IBPYP
Language instr: Spanish

Kipling Satélite
Cruz de Valle Verde No 25, Sta. Cruz del Monte, Naucalpan, Estado de México C.P. 53110

La Escuela de Lancaster A.C.
Av Insurgentes sur 3838, Tlalpan, Ciudad de México C.P. 14000
Tel: +52 5556 6697 96
Curriculum: IBDP, IBPYP
Language instr: English, Spanish

Liceo de Apodaca Centro Educativo
Ave. Virrey de Velazco No. 500, Apodaca, Nuevo León C.P. 66606
Tel: +52 81 83862089
Curriculum: IBMYP, IBPYP
Language instr: English

Liceo de Monterrey
Humberto Junco Voigt #400, Col. Valle Oriente, San Pedro Garza García, Nuevo León C.P. 66269
Tel: +52 (81) 8748 4146
Age range: G2–19 years
No. of pupils: 900
Curriculum: IBDP
Language instr: English, Spanish

Liceo de Monterrey – Centro Educativo
Col Sendero San Jeronimo, Monterrey, Nuevo Leon C.P. 64659
Tel: +1 8122 8900
Curriculum: IBDP, IBMYP
Language instr: English, Spanish

Liceo Federico Froebel de Oaxaca SC
Ajusco No 100, Colonia Volcanes, Oaxaca C.P. 68020
Tel: +52 951 5200 675
No. of pupils: 735
Curriculum: IBDP
Language instr: English, Spanish, French

Lomas Hill
Av. Veracruz 158, Cuajimalpa, Ciudad de México C.P. 05000
Tel: +52 55 5812 0818
Curriculum: IBPYP
Language instr: English, Spanish

Madison Campus Monterrey
Marsella #3055, Col. Alta Vista, Monterrey, Nuevo León C.P. 64840
Tel: +52 81 8359 0627
Age range: 2–15 years
Curriculum: IBMYP, IBPYP
Language instr: English, Spanish

Madison International School
Camino Real #100, Col. El Uro, Monterrey, Nuevo León C.P. 64986
Tel: +52 81 8218 7909
Age range: 1–15 years
No. of pupils: 837
Curriculum: IBMYP, IBPYP
Language instr: English, Spanish

Madison International School Campus Country-Mérida
Calle 24776 s/n, Chablekal, Merida, Yucatán C.P. 97300
Tel: +52 99 9611 9053
Curriculum: IBDP, IBMYP, IBPYP
Language instr: English, Spanish

Noordwijk International College
Blvd. del Mar #491, Fracc. Costa de Oro, Boca del Río, Veracruz C.P. 94299
Tel: +52 229 130 0714
Age range: 3–15
No. of pupils: 500
Curriculum: IBMYP, IBPYP
Language instr: English, Spanish

Nuevo Colegio Israelita de Monterrey
Preescolar y Primaria, Canadá #207, Col Vista Hermosa – CP 64620, Monterrey, NL C.P. 64620
Tel: +52 81 8346 9677
No. of pupils: 110

Orbis International School
Km 3.5 Carretera Aeropuerto #551, Colonia Rivera, Mexicali, Baja California C.P. 21220
Tel: +52 686 565 0877
Curriculum: IBPYP
Language instr: English

Pan American School – Campus Monterrey
Hidalgo No 656 Pte Col Centro, Apartado Postal 474, Monterrey C.P. 64000
Tel: +52 81 8342 0778
Age range: 2–15
No. of pupils: 554
Curriculum: USA

Peterson School – Cuajimalpa
Huizachito 80, Lomas de Vista Hermosa, Chajimalpa, Mexico City C.P. 05720
Tel: +52 55 5813 0114

Peterson School – Lomas
Monte Himalaya 615, Lomas de Chapultepec, Miguel Hidalgo, México D.F. C.P. 11000
Tel: +52 5520 2213
Age range: 17–19
Curriculum: IBDP
Language instr: Spanish

Peterson School – Pedregal
Rocío 142, Jardines del Pedregal, Álvaro Obregón, México D.F. C.P. 01900
Tel: +52 5568 3139

Peterson School Tlalpan
Carretera Federal a Cuernavaca, Km. 24 No. 6871, San Andrés Totoltepec, Tlalpan, México D.F. C.P. 14400
Tel: +52 55 5849 1885
Language instr: Spanish

Prepa UNI
Carretera Panamerican Km 269, Celaya, Guanajuato C.P. 38080
Tel: +52 461 61 39099
Curriculum: IBDP
Language instr: Spanish

Prepa UPAEP Angelópolis
Av. del Sol No. 5, Col. Concepción La Cruz, San Andrés Cholula, Puebla C.P. 72160
Tel: +52 222 225 2291
Age range: 14–19
Curriculum: IBDP, IBCP
Language instr: Spanish, English

Prepa UPAEP Cholula
Av. Forjadores No. 1804, Col Barrio de Jesús, San Pedro Cholula, Puebla C.P. 72760
Tel: +52 222 403 7373
Curriculum: IBDP, IBCP
Language instr: Spanish

Prepa UPAEP Huamantla
Carr. Lib. Carr. México-Veracruz Kilómetro 147.5, Santa Clara, Huamantla, Tlaxcala C.P. 90500
Tel: +52 247 472 2550
Curriculum: IBCP
Language instr: Spanish

Prepa UPAEP Lomas
Circuito Mario Molina No. 15, Lomas de Angelópolis, San Andrés Cholula, Puebla C.P. 72828
Tel: +52 (0)1 222 5822102
Curriculum: IBDP, IBCP
Language instr: English, Spanish

Prepa UPAEP Santiago
Av 9 Pte 1508, Barrio de Santiago, Puebla C.P. 72160
Tel: +52 222 246 8264
Curriculum: IBDP, IBCP
Language instr: Spanish

Prepa UPAEP Sur
Calle Independencia No. 6339, Col. Patrimonio, Puebla C.P. 72470
Tel: +52 222 233 1342
Curriculum: IBDP, IBCP
Language instr: Spanish

Prepa UPAEP Tehuacán
Boulevard Tehuacán San Marcos No. 1700, Col. El Humilladero, Tehuacán, Puebla
Tel: +52 238 383 7800
Curriculum: IBCP
Language instr: English, Spanish

Rootland School
Hortensia 6, Florida, Álvaro Obregón, Ciudad de México C.P. 01030
Tel: +52 55 2096 3660
Curriculum: IBPYP
Language instr: English, Spanish

San Roberto International School
Av Real San Agustín #4, Garza García, NL C.P. 66260
Tel: +52 81 8625 1500
Age range: 1–15
Language instr: English, Spanish

Tecnológico de Monterrey
Ave Eugenio Garza Sada 2501, Sur Col Tecnológico, Monterrey, NL C.P. 64849
Tel: +52 81 8358 2000

Tecnológico de Monterrey – Campus Cuernavaca
Autopista del Sol Km 104, Colonia Real del Puente, Xochitepec, Morelos, Cuernavaca C.P. 62790
Tel: +52 (77) 7362 0832
Language instr: Spanish

Tecnológico de Monterrey – Campus Puebla
Vía Atlixcáyotl 5718, Col Reserva Territorial Atlixcayotl, Puebla C.P. 72453
Age range: 15–18
No. of pupils: 1000
Language instr: Spanish, English

Tecnológico de Monterrey – Campus San Luis Potosí
Av Eugenio Garza Sada No 300, Fraccionamiento Lomas del Tecnológico, San Luis Potosi C.P. 78211
Tel: +52 44 4834 1000
Language instr: English

Tecnológico de Monterrey – PrepaTec Ciudad de México
Calle del Puente #222, Col. Ejidos de Huipulco, Tlalpan, Distrito Federal C.P. 14380
Tel: +52 (55) 5483 2110
Curriculum: IBDP
Language instr: Spanish

Tecnológico de Monterrey – PrepaTec Cumbres
Linces #1000, Col. Cumbres Elite, Monterrey, Nuevo León C.P. 64639
Tel: +52 (81) 8158 4622
Curriculum: IBDP
Language instr: Spanish, English

Tecnológico de Monterrey – PrepaTec Esmeralda
Fracc. Conjunto Urbano, Col. Bosque Esmeralda, Manzana 7 Lote 1 y 2, Atizapán de Zaragoza, Estado de México C.P. 52930
Tel: +52 (55) 5864 5370 (Ext:2903)
Age range: 15–19
No. of pupils: 600
Curriculum: IBDP
Language instr: Spanish

Tecnológico de Monterrey – PrepaTec Estado de México
Carretera Lago de Guadalupe, Km 3.5, Col. Margarita Maza de Juárez, Atizapán de Zaragoza, Estado de México C.P. 52926
Tel: +52 (55) 5864 5714
Curriculum: IBDP
Language instr: Spanish, English

Tecnológico de Monterrey – PrepaTec Eugenio Garza Lagüera
Topolobampo #4603, Valle de las Brisas, Monterrey, Nuevo León C.P. 647[illegible]0
Tel: +52 (81) 8155 449[illegible]
Age range: 15–18
Curriculum: IBDP, SAT
Language instr: Spanish

Tecnológico de Monterrey – PrepaTec Eugenio Garza Sada
Dinamarca #451 Sur Col Del Carmen, Monterrey, Nuevo León C.P. 647[illegible]0
Tel: +52 (81) 8151 426[illegible]
Curriculum: IBDP
Language instr: Spanish, English

Tecnológico de Monterrey – PrepaTec Metepec
Av. Las Torres 1957 Ote., San Salvador Tizatlalli Metepec C.P. 52172
Tel: +52 (722) 271 597[illegible]
Curriculum: IBDP
Language instr: Spanish

Tecnológico de Monterrey – PrepaTec Querétaro
Av. Epigmenio Gonzalez #500, Fracc. San Pablo, Santiago de Querétaro C.P. 76[illegible]30
Tel: +52 (442) 238 320[illegible]
Age range: 15–18
Curriculum: IBDP, SAT TOEFL
Language instr: Spanish

Tecnológico de Monterrey – PrepaTec Santa Catarina
Morones Prieto No 290 Pte., Col Jesús M. Garza, Santa Catarina, Nuevo León C.P. 66180
Tel: +52 (81) 8153 4045
Curriculum: IBDP
Language instr: English, Spanish

Tecnológico de Monterrey – PrepaTec Santa Fe
Av Carlos Lazo #100, Santa Fe, Delegación Alvaro Obregón C.P. 01389
Tel: +52 (55) 9177 8130
Curriculum: IBDP
Language instr: Spanish, English

Tecnológico de Monterrey – PrepaTec Valle Alto
Carretera Nacional #8002 Km. 267.7, Col. La Estanzuela, Monterrey, N.L C.P. 64986
Tel: +52 (81)8228 5310
Curriculum: IBDP
Language instr: Spanish, English

The American School Foundation, A.C.
Calle Sur 136-135, Colonia Las Americas, México D.F. C.P. 01120
Tel: +52 55 5227 4900
Age range: 3–18
No. of pupils: 2566 *B1324 G1242*
Curriculum: IBDP, IBMYP, IBPYP
Language instr: English

The American School of Tampico
Calle Hidalgo #100, Colonia Tancol, Tampico C.P. 89320
Tel: +52 833 2 27 20 80
Age range: 3–20
No. of pupils: 733
Curriculum: AP, USA

The Churchill School
Felipe Villanueva No. 24, Col. Guadalupe Inn, Mexico City
Tel: +52 55 50288800
Age range: 2–16
No. of pupils: *B547 G482*
Curriculum: IBMYP, IBPYP
Language instr: English, Spanish

The Edron Academy
Calz. Desierto de los Leones #5578, Col Olivar de Los Padres, Ciudad de México C.P. 1740
Tel: +52 55 5585 1920
Age range: 2–18 years
Curriculum: IBDP
Language instr: English, Spanish

Universidad de Monterrey Unidad Valle Alto
Carretera Nacionala Salida Valle Alto Km1, Colonia Valle Alto, Monterrey, NL C.P. 64989
Curriculum: IBDP, IBCP
Language instr: English, Spanish

University of Monterrey
Av. Ignacio Morones Prieto 4500, Pte., 66238, San Pedro Garza García, Nuevo León C.P. 66238
Tel: +52 81 8215 1010
Curriculum: IBDP, IBCP
Language instr: Spanish

Westhill Institute
Domingo Garcia Ramos No. 56, Col. Prados de la Montaña, Santa Fe, Cuajimalpa, Mexico City C.P. 05610
Tel: +52 55 8851 7000
Curriculum: IBDP, IBMYP, IBPYP
Language instr: English, Spanish, French

Winpenny School
José María Castorena 318, Colonia Cuajimalpa, México D. F. C.P. 05000
Tel: +52 55 8000 6100
Curriculum: IBDP
Language instr: Spanish

MONTSERRAT

St Augustine Primary
PO Box 192, Palm Loop
Tel: +1 664 491 4768

NICARAGUA

American Nicaraguan School
Frente al Club de Lomas de Montserrat, P.O. Box 2670, Managua
Tel: +505 2278 0029
Age range: 3–18
No. of pupils: 970
Curriculum: USA

Colegio Alemán Nicaragüense
Apartado 1636, Managua
Tel: +505 2265 8449
No. of pupils: 479
Curriculum: IBDP
Language instr: Spanish

Lincoln International Academy
Las Colinas Sur, Managua
Tel: +505 2276 3000

Notre Dame International School
Km 8.5 Carretera a Masaya, Managua
Tel: +505 2276 0353 54
Age range: 2–19
Curriculum: IBDP, IBMYP, IBPYP
Language instr: English

PUERTO RICO

Academia del Perpetuo Socorro
704 Calle Martí, Miramar, San Juan 907
Tel: +1 787 724 1447
Curriculum: USA

Caribbean School
Urb La Rambla, 1689 Calle Navarra, Ponce 00730-4043
Tel: +1 787 843 2048
Age range: 4–18
No. of pupils: 640
Curriculum: ACT, AP, SAT, TOEFL, USA

Commonwealth-Parkville School
PO BOX 70177, SAN JUAN, PR 00936-8177
Tel: +1 787 720 3992

Robinson School
5 Nairn Street, San Juan 00907
Tel: +1 787 999 4600
Curriculum: IBDP, IBMYP, IBPYP
Language instr: English

St John's School
1454 Ashford Avenue, San Juan 00907 1560
Tel: +1 787 728 5356

The Baldwin School of Puerto Rico
PO Box 1827, Bayamón 00960-1827
Tel: +1 787 720 2421
Age range: 3–18 years
No. of pupils: 820
Curriculum: ACT, AP, IBDP, IBMYP, IBPYP, SAT, USA
Language instr: English

SAINT LUCIA

International School of Saint Lucia
PO Box RB 2701, Rodney Bay, Gros Islet, Saint Lucia
Tel: +1 758 458 0989

TRINIDAD & TOBAGO

Maple Leaf International School
Alyce Heights Drive, Alyce Glen, Petit Valley
Tel: +1 868 632 9578
Age range: 4–19 years
No. of pupils: 300
Language instr: English

QSI International School of Trinidad
74 Long Circular Road, Port of Spain
Tel: +1 868 465 6198

The British Academy
23 Alexandra Street, St Clair, Port of Spain
Tel: +1 868 622 4285
Age range: 4–19
No. of pupils: 144 *B*85 *G*59 *VIth*23
Curriculum: UK, IGCSE, ALevs
Language instr: English

The International School of Port of Spain
1 International Drive, Westmoorings, Port of Spain
Tel: +1 868 633 4777
Age range: 4–19
No. of pupils: 452 *B*245 *G*207 *VIth*101
Curriculum: ACT, AP, IBMYP, IBPYP, SAT
Language instr: English

TURKS AND CAICOS ISLANDS

British West Indies Collegiate
PO Box 338, 51 Venetian Road, Providenciales TKCA 1ZZ
Tel: +1 649 941 3333

International School Turks and Caicos
P.O. Box 278, Leeward, Providenciales
Tel: +1 649 946 5523
Curriculum: UK

Providenciales Primary School
PO Box 329, Providenciales
Tel: +1 649 333 5638
Age range: 2–11
Curriculum: UK

The Ashcroft School
PO Box 278, Governor's Road, Leeward, Providenciales
Tel: +1 649 94 65523
Age range: 2–13
No. of pupils: 124

USA

Alabama

Cornerstone Schools of Alabama
118 55th Street North, Birmingham, Alabama AL 35212
Tel: +1 205 591 7600
Age range: 4–11
No. of pupils: 305
Curriculum: IBPYP
Language instr: English

Arizona

Desert Garden Montessori
5130 E. Warner Rd., Phoenix, Arizona AZ 85044
Tel: +1 480 496 9833
Curriculum: IBMYP
Language instr: English

International School of Arizona
9522 E. San Salvador Drive, Scottsdale, Arizona AZ 85258
Tel: +1 480 874 2326
Age range: 18 months–14 years
No. of pupils: 305
Curriculum: USA

International School of Tucson
1701 East Seneca Street, Tucson, Arizona AZ 85719
Tel: +1 520 406 0552
Age range: 6 months–14 years
No. of pupils: 230
Language instr: English

Maple Bear Tempe
1255 W. Elliot Road, Suite 20, Tempe, Arizona AZ 85284
Tel: +1 480 474 4455

Rancho Solano Preparatory School
9180 E. Via de Ventura, Scottsdale, Arizona AZ 85258
Tel: +1 480 646 8200
Age range: 4–18
Curriculum: IBDP
Language instr: English

Verde Valley School
3511 Verde Valley School Road, Sedona, Arizona AZ 86351
Tel: +1 928 284 2272
No. of pupils: 135
Curriculum: IBDP
Language instr: English

Arkansas

Mount Saint Mary Academy
3224 Kavanaugh Blvd, Little Rock, Arkansas AR 72205
Tel: +1 501 664 8006
Age range: G14–18
No. of pupils: 537
Language instr: English

California

Al-Arqam Islamic School & College Preparatory
6990 65th Street, Sacramento, California CA 95823
Tel: +1 916 391 3333
Curriculum: IBDP
Language instr: English

Alto International School
475 Pope St, Menlo Park, California CA 94025
Tel: +1 650 324 8617
Age range: 3–14
No. of pupils: 250
Curriculum: IBDP, IBMYP, IBPYP
Language instr: German, English

Cate School
1960 Cate Mesa Road, Carpinteria, California CA 93013
Tel: +1 805 684 4127
Language instr: English

Damien High School
2280 Damien Avenue, La Verne, California CA 91750
Tel: +1 909 596 1946
Age range: B13–19
No. of pupils: 922
Curriculum: IBDP, IBCP
Language instr: English

Ecole Bilingue de Berkeley
1009 Heinz Aveune, Berkeley, California CA 94710
Tel: +1 510 549 3867
Age range: 2–14
No. of pupils: 460
Curriculum: USA
Language instr: French, English

EF ACADEMY PASADENA
For further details see p. 265
1539 E Howard St., Pasadena, California CA 91104
Tel: +1 626 507 9223
Email: academy.admissions@ef.com
Website: www.efacademy.org
Head of School: Sally Mingarelli
Age range: 14–19 years
Fees: *Day* US$42,000 *FB* US$68,500
Curriculum: USA, IGCSE

Escuela Bilingüe Internacional
410 Alcatraz Avenue, Oakland, California CA 94609
Tel: +1 510 653 3324
Curriculum: IBMYP, IBPYP

Fairmont Private Schools – Anaheim Hills Campus
5300 E La Palma Avenue, Anaheim, California CA 92807
Tel: +1 714 693 3812

Fairmont Private Schools – Historic Anaheim Campus
1557 W. Mable Street, Anaheim, California CA 92805
Tel: +1 714 563 4050
Curriculum: IBMYP, IBPYP
Language instr: English

Fairmont Private Schools – North Tustin Campus
12421 Newport Avenue, North Tustin, California CA 92705
Tel: +1 714 832 4867

Fairmont Private Schools – Preparatory Academy
2200 West Sequoia Avenue, Anaheim, California CA 92801
Tel: +1 714 999 5055
Age range: 13–19
No. of pupils: 450
Curriculum: AP, IBDP, USA
Language instr: English

French American International School & International High School
150 Oak Street, San Francisco, California CA 94102-5812
Tel: +1 415 558 2000
Age range: 4–18
Curriculum: IBDP
Language instr: English

French-American School of Silicon Valley
1522 Lewiston Drive, Sunnyvale, California CA 94087
Tel: +1 408 746 0460
Curriculum: USA

GISSV German International School of Silicon Valley
Mountain View Campus, 310 Easy Street, Mountain View, California CA 94043
Tel: +1 650 254 0748

Granada Preparatory School
10400 Zelzah Avenue, Northridge, California CA 91326
Tel: +1 818 368 7254
Curriculum: IBMYP, IBPYP
Language instr: English

International Children's Academy
1046 South Robertson Blvd, Los Angeles, California CA 90035
Tel: +1 310 657 6798
Curriculum: IBPYP
Language instr: English

INTERNATIONAL SCHOOL OF LOS ANGELES
For further details see p. 268
1105 W. Riverside Drive, Burbank, California CA 91506
Tel: +1 626 695 5159
Email: admissions@lilaschool.com
Website: www.internationalschool.la
Head of School: Michael Maniska
Age range: 3–18 years
No. of pupils: 1040
Fees: *Day* $19,895–$25,725
Curriculum: ACT, AP, IBDP, FrenchBacc, SAT
Language instr: English, French

La Scuola International San Francisco
K-8 Campus, 735 Fell Street, San Francisco, California CA 94117
Tel: +1 415 551 0000
Curriculum: IBPYP

La Scuola International School
3250 18th Street, San Francisco, California CA 94110
Tel: +1 415 551 0000
Age range: 2–14 years
No. of pupils: 324
Curriculum: IBMYP, IBPYP
Language instr: English

LE LYCÉE FRANÇAIS DE LOS ANGELES
For further details see p. 270
3261 Overland Avenue, Los Angeles, California CA 90034
Tel: +1 310 836 3464
Email: generalinfo@LyceeLA.org
Website: www.lyceela.org
President: Clara-Lisa Kabbaz
Age range: 3 years 9 months–18 years
No. of pupils: 740 *B*320 *G*420
Fees: Day $23,000–$34,900
Curriculum: ACT, AP, National, FrenchBacc, SAT, USA
Language instr: English, French

Lycée Français de San Francisco
1201 Ortega Street, San Francisco, California CA 94122
Tel: +1 415 661 5232
Curriculum: FrenchBacc

Monte Vista Christian School
2 School Way, Watsonville, California CA 95076
Tel: +1 831 722 8178
Curriculum: IBDP
Language instr: English

New Covenant Academy
3119 W 6th Street, Los Angeles, California CA 90020
Tel: +1 213 487 5437
Age range: 6–19
No. of pupils: 137 *B*82 *G*55
Curriculum: ACT, IBDP, SAT, USA
Language instr: English

Pacific Rim International School
454 Peninsula Avenue, San Mateo, California CA 94401
Tel: +1 650 685 1881
Language instr: English

Quarry Lane School
6363 Tassajara Road, Dublin, California CA 94568
Tel: +1 925 829 8000
Curriculum: IBDP
Language instr: English

San Diego French-American School
6550 Soledad Mountain Road, La Jolla, California CA 92037
Tel: +1 858 456 2807
Age range: 2–13

San Gabriel Mission High School
254 South Santa Anita Street, San Gabriel, California CA 91776
Tel: +1 626 282 3181
Language instr: English

Santa Margarita Catholic High School
22062 Antonio Parkway, Rancho Santa Margarita, California CA 92688
Tel: +1 949 766 6000
Curriculum: IBDP
Language instr: English

Schools of the Sacred Heart
2222 Broadway, San Francisco, California CA 94115
Tel: +1 415 563 2900
Curriculum: IBDP
Language instr: English

Shu Ren International School
2125 Jefferson Avenue, Berkeley, California CA 94703
Tel: +1 510 841 8899
Curriculum: IBPYP
Language instr: English, Mandarin

Silicon Valley International School
151 Laura Lane, Palo Alto, California CA 94303
Tel: +1 650 251 8522
Age range: 3 1/2–14 years
Curriculum: USA
Language instr: English, Chinese

St. Francis of Assisi Elementary School
2500 K Street, Sacramento, California CA 95816
Tel: +1 916 442 5494
Curriculum: IBPYP
Language instr: English

St. Mary's School
7 Pursuit, Aliso Viejo, California CA 92656
Tel: +1 949 448 9027
Curriculum: IBMYP, IBPYP
Language instr: French

The Healdsburg School
33H Healdsburg Avenue, Healdsburg, California CA 95448
Tel: +1 707 433 4847
Curriculum: IBPYP
Language instr: English

THINK GLOBAL SCHOOL
For further details see p. 278
1460 Broadway #4027, New York, California NY 10036
Tel: +1 347 281 6855
Email: info@thinkglobalschool.org
Website: www.thinkglobalschool.com
Headteachers: Adnan Mackovic & Chelle Marshall
Age range: 15–18 years
No. of pupils: 60
Fees: $94,050

Valley Preparatory School
1605 Ford Street, Redlands, California CA 92373
Tel: +1 909 793 3063
Curriculum: IBPYP
Language instr: English, Spanish

Villanova Preparatory School
12096 N. Ventura Avenue, Ojai, California CA 93023
Tel: +1 805 646 1464
Curriculum: IBDP
Language instr: English

Vistamar School
737 Hawaii Street, El Segundo, California CA 90245
Tel: +1 310 643 7377
Age range: 13–19
No. of pupils: 176 *B*90 *G*86
Curriculum: USA
Language instr: English

Yew Chung International School of Silicon Valley
310 Easy Street, Mountain View, California CA 94043
Tel: +1 650 903 0986
Age range: 2–14 years
Curriculum: USA
Language instr: English, Mandarin

Colorado

Boulder Country Day School
4820 Nautilus Court North, Boulder, Colorado CO 80301
Tel: +1 303 527 4931
Curriculum: IBMYP
Language instr: English

Colorado International School
4100 E Iliff Ave, Denver, Colorado CO 80222
Tel: +1 303 759 5035
Language instr: English, French, German

Dos Rios Elementary School
2201 34th Street, Evans, Colorado CO 80620
Tel: +1 970 348 1309
Curriculum: IBPYP
Language instr: English

Fountain Valley School of Colorado
6155 Fountain Valley School Rd, Colorado Springs, Colorado CO 80911
Tel: +1 719 390 7035
Language instr: English

International School of Denver
7701 E. 1st Pl, Unit C, Denver, Colorado CO 80230
Tel: +1 303 340 3647
Age range: Preschool–8th Grade
No. of pupils: 730
Curriculum: IBMYP
Language instr: Chinese, English, French, Spanish

Mackintosh Academy Boulder
6717 S. Boulder Road, Boulder, Colorado CO 80303
Tel: +1 303 554 2011
Curriculum: IBMYP, IBPYP
Language instr: English

Mackintosh Academy Littleton
7018 S. Prince Street, Littleton, Colorado CO 80120
Tel: +1 303 794 6222
Curriculum: IBMYP, IBPYP
Language instr: English

Telluride Mountain School
Lawson Hill, 200 San Miguel River Dr., Telluride, Colorado CO 81435
Tel: +1 970 728 1969
Curriculum: IBDP
Language instr: English

Connecticut

Cheshire Academy
10 Main Street, Cheshire, Connecticut CT 06410
Tel: +1 203 272 5396
Curriculum: IBDP, National

Notre Dame High School
One Notre Dame Way, West Haven, Connecticut CT 06516
Tel: +1 203 933 1673
Curriculum: IBDP
Language instr: English, Spanish

The Hotchkiss School
11 Interlaken Road, Lakeville, Connecticut CT 06039-2141
Tel: +1 860 435 2591
Language instr: English

Whitby School
969 Lake Avenue, Greenwich, Connecticut CT 06831
Tel: +1 203 302 3900
Age range: 18 months–14 years
No. of pupils: 290
Curriculum: IBMYP, IBPYP
Language instr: English

Delaware

Wilmington Friends School
101 School Road, Wilmington, Delaware DE 19803
Tel: +1 302 576 2900
Age range: 2–19
Curriculum: AP, IBDP, SAT
Language instr: English

District of Columbia

Archbishop Carroll High School
4300 Harewood Road NE, Washington, District of Columbia DC 20017
Tel: +1 202 529 0900 Ext:135
No. of pupils: 545
Language instr: English

British International School of Washington
2001 Wisconsin Avenue NW, Washington, District of Columbia DC 20007
Tel: +1 202 829 3700
Age range: 2–18
No. of pupils: 450
Curriculum: IBDP, UK, IGCSE
Language instr: English

Creative Minds International Public Charter School
Sherman Building, 3700 N Capitol Street NW #217, Washington, District of Columbia DC 20011-8400
Tel: +1 202 588 0370
Curriculum: IPC

Washington International School
3100 Macomb Street NW, Washington, District of Columbia DC 20008
Tel: +1 202 243 1800
Age range: 4–18
Curriculum: IBDP, IBPYP
Language instr: English, French, Spanish, Dutch, Chinese

Whittle School & Studios – DC Campus
3007 Tilden St NW, Washington, District of Columbia DC 20008
Tel: +1 202 417 3615
Curriculum: IBDP
Language instr: English

Florida

Arthur I. Meyer Jewish Academy
5225 Hood Rd, Palm Beach Gardens, Florida FL 33418
Tel: +1 561 686 6520
Curriculum: IBMYP

Bhaktivedanta Academy
17414 NW 112th Blvd, Alachua, Florida FL 32615
Tel: +1 386 462 2886
Curriculum: IBMYP
Language instr: English

Boca Prep International School
10333 Diego Drive South, Boca Raton, Florida FL 33428
Tel: +1 561 852 1410
Curriculum: IBDP, IBMYP, IBPYP

Brandon Academy
801 Limona Road, Brandon, Florida FL 33510
Tel: +1 813 689 1952
Language instr: English

Cardinal Newman High School
512 Spencer Drive, West Palm Beach, Florida FL 33409
Tel: +1 561 683 6266
No. of pupils: 870
Curriculum: IBDP
Language instr: English

Carrollton School of the Sacred Heart
3747 Main Highway, Miami, Florida FL 33133
Tel: +1 305 446 5673
Curriculum: IBDP
Language instr: English

Carrollwood Day School
1515 W. Bearss Avenue, Tampa, Florida FL 33613
Tel: +1 813 920 2288
Age range: 2–18
Curriculum: IBDP, IBMYP, IBPYP
Language instr: English

Clearwater Central Catholic High School
2750 Haines Bayshore Road, Clearwater, Florida FL 33760
Tel: +1 727 531 1449
Curriculum: IBDP
Language instr: English

Corbett Preparatory School of IDS
12015 Orange Grove Drive, Tampa, Florida FL 33618
Tel: +1 813 961 3087
Curriculum: IBMYP, IBPYP
Language instr: English

Cornerstone Learning Community
2524 Hartsfield Road, Tallahassee, Florida FL 32303
Tel: +1 850 386 5550
Curriculum: IBMYP
Language instr: English

Creation Village Preparatory School
599 Celebration Place, Celebration, Florida FL 34747
Tel: +1 407 900 7708
Curriculum: IBPYP
Language instr: English

Gulliver Academy Middle School
12595 Red Road, Coral Gables, Florida FL 33156
Tel: +1 305 665 3593
Curriculum: IBMYP

Gulliver Preparatory School
6575 North Kendall Drive, Miami, Florida FL 33156
Tel: +1 305 666 6333
Age range: 2–18 years
No. of pupils: 2200
Curriculum: AP, IBDP
Language instr: English

International School of Broward – Charter School
3100 N. 75th Avenue, Hollywood, Florida FL 33024
Tel: +1 954 987 2026

New Gate School
5237 Ashton Road, Sarasota, Florida FL 34233
Tel: +1 941 922 4949
Age range: 2–18
No. of pupils: 175 B84 G91
Curriculum: IBDP, USA
Language instr: English

North Broward Preparatory School
7600 Lyons Road, Coconut Creek, Florida FL 33073
Tel: +1 954 247 0179
Age range: 3–18 years
Curriculum: ACT, AP, IBDP, SAT, USA
Language instr: English

Palmer Trinity School
7900 SW 176th Street, Miami, Florida FL 33157
Tel: +1 305 251 2230
Curriculum: IBDP
Language instr: English

Saint John Paul II Catholic School
4341 W Homosassa Trail, Lecanto, Florida FL 34461
Tel: +1 352 746 2020
Curriculum: IBMYP
Language instr: English

Scheck Hillel Community School
19000 NE 25th Avenue, North Miami Beach, Florida FL 33180
Tel: +1 305 931 2831

St Andrew's School
3900 Jog Road, Boca Raton, Florida FL 33434
Tel: +1 561 210 2000
Curriculum: IBDP, IBMYP, IBPYP
Language instr: English

St Ann Catholic School
324 North Olive Avenue, West Palm Beach, Florida FL 33401
Tel: +1 561 832 3676
Curriculum: IBMYP, IBPYP
Language instr: English

St John Vianney Catholic School
500 84th Avenue, St Pete Beach, Florida FL 33706
Tel: +1 727 360 1113
Age range: 3–12
Curriculum: IBMYP

St. Cecelia Interparochial Catholic School
1350 Court Street, Clearwater, Florida FL 33756
Tel: +1 727 461 1200
Curriculum: IBMYP, IBPYP
Language instr: English

St. Thomas the Apostle Catholic School
7303 S.W. 64th Street, Miami, Florida FL 33143
Tel: +1 305 661 8591
Age range: 2–14
No. of pupils: 512
Curriculum: USA
Language instr: English

THE BILTMORE SCHOOL
For further details see p. 277
1600 S. Red Road, Miami, Florida FL 33155
Tel: +1 305 266 4666
Email: info@biltmoreschool.com
Website: www.biltmoreschool.com
Principal: Gina C. Duarte-Romero
Age range: 1–14 years
No. of pupils: 200
Fees: US$9,800–US$20,800
Curriculum: IBPYP

The Discovery School
102 15th Street South, Jacksonville Beach, Florida FL 32250
Tel: +1 904 247 4577
Curriculum: IBPYP
Language instr: English

The Roig Academy
8000 SW 112 St, Miami, Florida FL 33156
Tel: +1 305 235 1313
Curriculum: IBPYP
Language instr: English, Spanish

Trinity Catholic School
706 E. Brevard Street Tallahassee, Florida FL 32308
Tel: +1 850 222 0444
Curriculum: IBMYP
Language instr: English, Spanish

Windermere Preparatory School
6189 Winter Garden Vineland Road, Windermere, Florida FL 34786
Tel: +1 407 905 7737
Age range: 3–18 years
No. of pupils: 1508
Curriculum: IBDP
Language instr: English

Georgia

Atlanta International School
2890 North Fulton Drive, Atlanta, Georgia GA 30305
Tel: +1 404 841 3840
Age range: 3–18 years
No. of pupils: 1319
Curriculum: IBDP, IBMYP, IBPYP
Language instr: English, Chinese, French, German and Spanish
CIS

Brandon Hall School
1701 Brandon Hall Drive, Atlanta, Georgia GA 30350
Tel: +1 770 394 8177
Curriculum: IBDP
Language instr: English

Endeavor International School
48 Perimeter Center East, Atlanta, Georgia GA 30346
Tel: +1 770 637 4737
Curriculum: IBMYP
Language instr: English, Spanish

High Meadows School
1055 Willeo Road, Roswell, Georgia GA 30188
Tel: +1 770 993 2940
Age range: 3–14
No. of pupils: 387
Curriculum: IBPYP
Language instr: English

Montessori Academy Sharon Springs
2830 Old Atlanta Road, Cumming, Georgia GA 30041
Tel: +1 770 205 6277
Curriculum: IBDP
Language instr: English, Spanish

Notre Dame Academy, GA
4635 River Green Parkway, Duluth, Georgia GA 30096
Tel: +1 678 387 9385
Age range: 2–18 years
Curriculum: AP, IBDP, IBMYP, IBPYP
Language instr: English

St Andrew's School
601 Penn Waller Road, Savannah, Georgia GA 31410
Tel: +1 912 897 4941
Age range: 3–18
Curriculum: IBDP
Language instr: English

Hawaii

Island Pacific Academy
909 Haumea Street, Kapolei, Hawaii HI 96707
Tel: +1 808 674 3523
Age range: 4–18
No. of pupils: *B250 G250*
Curriculum: IBDP
Language instr: English

Le Jardin Academy
917 Kalanianaole Highway, Kailua, Hawaii HI 96734
Tel: +1 808 261 0707
Age range: 3–17
No. of pupils: 800
Curriculum: IBDP, IBMYP, IBPYP, SAT
Language instr: English, French, Spanish, Japanese, Chinese

Mid-Pacific Institute
2445 Kaala Street, Honolulu, Hawaii HI 96822
Tel: +1 808 973 5020
Age range: 4–18
No. of pupils: 1500
Curriculum: IBDP, SAT, TOEFL
Language instr: English

Punahou School
1601 Punahou Street, Honolulu, Hawaii HI 96822-3336
Tel: +1 808 944 5711
Age range: 4–18 years
Curriculum: USA

Idaho

Riverstone International School
5521 Warm Springs Avenue, Boise, Idaho ID 83716
Tel: +1 208 424 5000
Age range: 5–19
No. of pupils: 330
Curriculum: AP, IBDP, IBMYP, IBPYP, SAT
Language instr: English

Illinois

Beacon Academy
622 Davis St., Evanston, Illinois IL 60201
Tel: +1 224 999 1177
Curriculum: IBDP
Language instr: English

BRITISH INTERNATIONAL SCHOOL OF CHICAGO, LINCOLN PARK
For further details see p. 262
814 & 821 W Eastman Street, Chicago, Illinois IL 60642
Tel: +1 773 907 5000
Email: admissions@bischicagolp.org
Website: www.bischicagolp.org
Principal: Mike Henderson
Age range: 15 months–11 years
No. of pupils: 575
Fees: *Day* $8,900–$32,950
Language instr: English
CIS

British International School of Chicago, South Loop
161 W. 9th Street, Chicago, Illinois IL 60605
Tel: +1 773 599 2472
Age range: 3–18
No. of pupils: 651
Curriculum: IBDP
Language instr: English

Daystar Academy
1550 S. State St., Chicago, Illinois IL 60605
Tel: +1 312 791 0001
Curriculum: IBDP, IBMYP, IBPYP
Language instr: English, Spanish

DePaul College Prep
3633 North California Avenue, Chicago, Illinois IL 60618
Tel: +1 773 539 3600
Curriculum: IBDP
Language instr: English

EFAC French-American School of Chicago
615 W Kemper Place, Chicago, Illinois IL 60614
Tel: +1 773 800 2728
Curriculum: FrenchBacc, USA

GEMS World Academy Chicago
350 E. South Water St., Chicago, Illinois IL 60601
Tel: +1 312 809 8900
Age range: 3–18 years
No. of pupils: 450
Curriculum: IBDP, IBMYP, IBPYP
Language instr: English

German International School Chicago
1447 West Montrose Ave, Chicago, Illinois IL 60613
Tel: +1 773 880 8812
Curriculum: IBPYP
Language instr: English

Josephinum Academy
1501 North Oakley Boulevard, Chicago, Illinois IL 60622
Tel: +1 773 276 1261
No. of pupils: 189 G189
Curriculum: ACT
Language instr: English

Lincoln Park High School
2001 North Orchard Street, Chicago, Illinois IL 60614
Tel: +1 773 534 8149
Age range: 13–19 years
No. of pupils: 2055
Curriculum: IBDP, IBMYP, IBCP
Language instr: English

Lycée Français de Chicago
1929 W Wilson Ave, Chicago, Illinois IL 60640
Tel: +1 773 665 0066
Age range: 2–18
No. of pupils: 820
Curriculum: IBDP, IBMYP, National, FrenchBacc
Language instr: English, French

St. Laurence High School
5556 West 77th Street, Burbank, Illinois IL 60459
Tel: +1 708 458 6900
Curriculum: IBDP
Language instr: English, Spanish

St. Matthias School
4910 N. Claremont Ave, Chicago, Illinois IL 60625
Tel: +1 773 784 0999
Curriculum: IBMYP, IBPYP
Language instr: English

Trinity College Preparatory High School
7574 West Division Street, River Forest, Illinois IL 60305
Tel: +1 708 771 8383
Curriculum: IBDP
Language instr: English

Indiana

Cathedral High School
5225 East 56th Street,
Indianapolis, Indiana IN 46226
Tel: +1 317 542 1481
Curriculum: IBDP
Language instr: English

Guerin Catholic High School
15300 Gray Road, Noblesville,
Indiana IN 46062
Tel: +1 317 582 0120
Curriculum: IBDP
Language instr: English

International School of Indiana
4330 N. Michigan Road,
Indianapolis, Indiana IN 46208
Tel: +1 317 923 1951
Age range: 3–18
No. of pupils: 600
Curriculum: AP, IBDP, IBMYP, IBPYP, SAT, USA
Language instr: English, French, Spanish, Mandarin

Kentucky

Sacred Heart Academy
3175 Lexington Road, Louisville,
Kentucky KY 40206
Tel: +1 502 897 6097
Age range: G14–18
Curriculum: ACT, AP, IBDP, IBMYP, SAT, USA
Language instr: English

Sacred Heart Model School
3107 Lexington Road, Louisville,
Kentucky KY 40206
Tel: +1 502 896 3931
Curriculum: IBMYP, IBPYP
Language instr: English

Louisiana

Audubon Charter School – Upper School
1111 Milan Street, New Orleans,
Louisiana LA 70115
Tel: +1 504 324 7110

Baton Rouge International School
5015 Auto Plex Drive, Baton
Rouge Louisiana LA 70809
Tel: +1 225 293 4338
Age range: 6 weeks–18 years
Curriculum: ACT, AP, IBDP, IBMYP, SAT, USA
Language instr: English, French, Spanish, Chinese, Portuguese

Kehoe-France Northshore
25 Patricia Drive, Covington,
Louisiana LA 70433
Tel: +1 985 892 4415
Age range: 8 weeks–13 years
Curriculum: IBPYP
Language instr: English

Kehoe-France School
720 Elise Avenue, Metairie,
Louisiana LA 70003
Tel: +1 504 733 0472
Curriculum: IBMYP, IBPYP
Language instr: English, Spanish

Maine

Academia Fórum
3 Canal Plaza, Suite 600,
Portland, Maine ME 04101
Tel: +1 207 553 2327
Language instr: Spanish

Foxcroft Academy
975 West Main Street, Dover-Foxcroft, Maine ME 04426
Tel: +1 207 564 8351
Age range: 14–18 years
No. of pupils: 420
Curriculum: IBDP
Language instr: English

Maryland

Archbishop Spalding High School
8080 New Cut Road, Severn,
Maryland MD 21144
Tel: +1 410 969 9105
Curriculum: IBDP
Language instr: English

German International School Washington D.C.
8617 Chateau Drive, Potomac,
Maryland MD 20854
Tel: +1 301 767 3800

Maryland International School
6135 Old Washington Road,
Elkridge, Maryland MD 21075
Tel: +1 410 220 3792
Age range: 6–18 years
No. of pupils: 200
Curriculum: IBDP, IBMYP, IBPYP
Language instr: English

Mercy High School Baltimore
1300 E. Northern Parkway,
Baltimore, Maryland MD 21239
Tel: +1 410 433 8880
Curriculum: IBMYP
Language instr: English, Spanish

Our Lady of Good Counsel High School
17301 Old Vic Boulevard,
Olney, Maryland MD 20832
Tel: +1 240 283 3200
Age range: 14–18 years
Curriculum: AP, IBDP, SAT
Language instr: English

ROCHAMBEAU, THE FRENCH INTERNATIONAL SCHOOL
For further details see p. 274
9600 Forest Rd, Bethesda,
Maryland MD 20814
Tel: +1 301 530 8260
Email: admissions@rochambeau.org
Website: www.rochambeau.org
Head of School: Xavier Jacquenet
Age range: 2–18 years
No. of pupils: 1150
Fees: US$23,640
Curriculum: IBDP, FrenchBacc, USA
Language instr: English, French

Saint James Academy
3100 Monkton Road, Monkton,
Maryland MD 21111
Tel: +1 410 771 4816
Age range: 5–14
No. of pupils: 296 *B151 G145*
Language instr: English

Sandy Spring Friends School
16923 Norwood Rd, Sandy
Spring, Maryland MD 20860
Tel: +1 301 774 7455
Age range: 3–18

Seneca Academy
15601 Germantown Road,
Darnestown, Maryland MD 20874
Tel: +1 301 869 3728
Age range: 2–12
Curriculum: IBPYP
Language instr: English

Springdale Preparatory School
1000 Green Valley Rd, New
Windsor, Maryland MD 21776
Tel: +1 443 671 0072
Curriculum: IBDP
Language instr: English

St. Francis of Assisi
3617 Harford Rd, Baltimore,
Maryland MD 21218
Tel: +1 410 467 1683
Curriculum: IBMYP
Language instr: English

St. Timothy's School
8400 Greenspring Ave,
Stevenson, Maryland MD 21153
Tel: +1 410 486 7400
No. of pupils: 200
Curriculum: IBDP, IBMYP
Language instr: English

Tarbiyah Academy
6785 Business Pky, Elkridge,
Maryland MD 21075
Tel: +1 844 827 2492
Curriculum: IBPYP
Language instr: English

The Academy of the Holy Cross
4920 Strathmore Avenue,
Kensington, Maryland MD 20895
Tel: +1 301 929 6459
Language instr: English

The Boys' School of St Paul's Parish
PO Box 8100, Brooklandville,
Maryland MD 21022-8100
Tel: +1 410 825 4400
Curriculum: IBDP
Language instr: English

The Calverton School
300 Calverton School Rd,
Huntingtown, Maryland MD 20639
Tel: +1 410 535 0216
Age range: 14–18
No. of pupils: 140 *B70 G70*
Curriculum: IBDP
Language instr: English

Massachusetts

British International School of Boston
416 Pond Street, Boston,
Massachusetts MA 02130
Tel: +1 617 522 2261
Age range: 2–18 years
No. of pupils: 445
Curriculum: IBDP, IPC, UK, IGCSE
Language instr: English

CATS Boston
2001 Washington St, Braintree,
Massachusetts MA 02184
Tel: +1 857 400 9700
Curriculum: USA

Chamberlain International School
1 Pleasant Street, PO
Box 778, Middleboro,
Massachusetts MA 02346
Tel: +1 508 946 9348
Age range: 11–22 years
Language instr: English

Deerfield Academy
7 Boyden Lane, P.O. Box 87, Deerfield, Massachusetts MA 01342
Tel: +1 413 772 0241
Age range: 14–19
No. of pupils: 650
Curriculum: AP, USA
Language instr: English

Eagle Hill School
242 Old Petersham Road, P.O. Box 116, Hardwick, Massachusetts MA 01037
Tel: +1 413 477 6000
Age range: 13–18
No. of pupils: 220
Curriculum: IBDP
Language instr: English

German International School Boston
57 Holton Street, Boston, Massachusetts MA 02134
Tel: +1 617 783 2600
Age range: 3–18
No. of pupils: 285
Language instr: English, German

International School of Boston
45 Matignon Road, Cambridge, Massachusetts MA 02140
Tel: +1 617 499 1451
Age range: 2–18 years
No. of pupils: 550
Curriculum: IBDP, FrenchBacc, USA
Language instr: English, French, Spanish

Notre Dame Academy, MA
1073 Main Street, Hingham, Massachusetts MA 02043-3996
Tel: +1 781 749 5930
Age range: G11–18 years
Language instr: English

Pope Francis Preparatory School
134 Springfield St, Chicopee, Massachusetts MA 01013
Tel: +1 413 331 2480
Language instr: English

Stoneleigh-Burnham School
574 Bernardston Road, Greenfield, Massachusetts MA 01301
Tel: +1 413 774 2711
Age range: G11–20
No. of pupils: 137
Curriculum: IBDP, USA
Language instr: English

The Newman School
247 Marlborough Street, Boston, Massachusetts MA 02116
Tel: +1 617 267 4530
Age range: 11–18 years
No. of pupils: 240
Curriculum: IBDP, IBMYP
Language instr: English

Michigan

Coit Creative Arts Academy
617 Coit Ave NE, Grand Rapids, Michigan MI 49503
Tel: +1 616 819 2390
Curriculum: IBPYP
Language instr: English

Detroit Country Day School
22305 West 13 Mile Road, Beverly Hills, Michigan MI 48025
Tel: +1 248 646 7717
Age range: 3–18 years
No. of pupils: 650
Curriculum: AP, IBDP, SAT
Language instr: English

French School of Detroit
Meadow Lake Center, 7100 Lindenmere Drive, Bloomfield Hills, Michigan MI 48301
Tel: +1 248 203 5703

Genesee Academy
9447 Corunna Road, Swartz Creek, Michigan MI 48473
Tel: +1 810 250 7557
Age range: 4–18
No. of pupils: 265 B127 G138
Curriculum: AP, IBMYP, SAT
Language instr: English

Huda School and Montessori
32220 Franklin Road, Franklin, Michigan MI 48025
Tel: +1 248 626 0900
Curriculum: IBMYP

Notre Dame Preparatory School & Marist Academy
1300 Giddings Road, Pontiac, Michigan MI 48340
Tel: +1 248 373 5300
Age range: 3–18
No. of pupils: 1081 B520 G561
Curriculum: ACT, AP, IBDP, IBMYP, IBPYP, SAT, USA

Minnesota

Annunciation Catholic School
525 W 54th St, Minneapolis, Minnesota MN 55419
Tel: +1 612 823 4394
Curriculum: IBPYP
Language instr: English

Rochester Arts and Sciences Academy
400 5th Avenue SW, Rochester, Minnesota MN 55902
Tel: +1 507 206 4646
Age range: 3–12
No. of pupils: 72
Curriculum: IBPYP, USA
Language instr: English

Rochester Montessori School
5099 7th Street NW, Rochester, Minnesota MN 55901
Tel: +1 507 288 8725
Curriculum: IBMYP

Saint John's Preparatory School
1857 Watertower Road, Collegeville, Minnesota MN 56321
Tel: +1 320 363 3315
Curriculum: IBDP
Language instr: English

The International School of Minnesota
6385 Beach Road, Eden Prairie, Minnesota MN 55344
Tel: +1 952 918 1800

Missouri

ATI St. Louis
3840 Washington Blvd., St. Louis, Missouri MO 63108
Tel: +1 314 884 1637
Curriculum: IBDP
Language instr: English

Montana

Missoula International School
1100 Harrison Street, Missoula, Montana MT 59802
Tel: +1 406 542 9924
Age range: 3–14
No. of pupils: 190
Curriculum: IBMYP, IBPYP
Language instr: Spanish, English

New Hampshire

New Hampton School
70 Main Street, New Hampton, New Hampshire NH 03256
Tel: +1 603 677 3401
Age range: 14–19 years
No. of pupils: 340
Curriculum: IBDP
Language instr: English

New Jersey

All Saints Episcopal Day School
707 Washington Street, Hoboken, New Jersey NJ 07030
Tel: +1 201 792 0736
Curriculum: IBMYP
Language instr: English

Donovan Catholic
711 Hooper Ave, Toms River, New Jersey NJ 08753
Tel: +1 732 349 8801
Curriculum: IBDP
Language instr: English

Learning Ladders
35 Hudson Street, Jersey City, New Jersey NJ 07302
Tel: +1 201 885 2960
Curriculum: IBPYP
Language instr: English

Newark Academy
91 South Orange Avenue, Livingston, New Jersey NJ 07039
Tel: +1 973 992 7000
Age range: 11–18
No. of pupils: 582
Curriculum: AP, IBDP
Language instr: English

Princeton Junior School
90 Fackler Road, Princeton, New Jersey NJ 08540
Tel: +1 609 924 8126
Curriculum: IBPYP
Language instr: English

Princeton Montessori School
487 Cherry Valley Road, Princeton, New Jersey NJ 08540
Tel: +1 609 924 4594
Curriculum: IBMYP
Language instr: English

Rutgers Preparatory School
1345 Easton Avenue, Somerset, New Jersey NJ 08873
Tel: +1 732 545 5600
Age range: 3–18
No. of pupils: 640
Curriculum: AP

Solomon Schechter Day School of Bergen County
275 McKinley Ave, New Milford, New Jersey NJ 07646
Tel: +1 201 262 9898
Curriculum: IBMYP
Language instr: English

St Dominic Academy
2572 Kennedy Boulevard, Jersey City, New Jersey NJ 07304
Tel: +1 201 434 5938
No. of pupils: 525
Curriculum: AP
Language instr: English

The Red Oaks School
340 Speedwell Ave., Morristown, New Jersey NJ 07960
Tel: +1 973 998 9424
Curriculum: IBMYP
Language instr: English

Waterfront Montessori
150 Warren St., Suite 108, Jersey City, New Jersey NJ 7302
Tel: +1 201 333 5600
Curriculum: IBMYP
Language instr: English

World of ABC
159 2nd St, Jersey City, New Jersey NJ 07302
Tel: +1 201 963 5555
Curriculum: IBPYP
Language instr: English

YingHua International School
25 Laurel Avenue, Kingston, New Jersey NJ 08528-0088
Tel: +1 609 375 8015
Age range: 18 months–13 years
No. of pupils: 118
Curriculum: IBPYP
Language instr: English, Chinese

New Mexico

New Mexico International School
8650 Alameda Blvd NE, Albuquerque, New Mexico NM 87122
Tel: +1 505 503 7670
Curriculum: IBPYP
Language instr: English

UWC-USA
State Rte 65, Montezuma, New Mexico NM 87731
Tel: +1 505 454 4252
Age range: 17–19
No. of pupils: 235
Curriculum: IBDP
Language instr: English

New York

Archbishop Walsh Academy
208 North 24th Street, Olean, New York NY 14760
Tel: +1 716 372 8122
Age range: 3–18 years
No. of pupils: 155
Curriculum: IBDP

Bishop Ludden Junior Senior High School
815 Fay Road, Syracuse, New York NY 13219
Tel: +1 315 468 2591
Curriculum: IBDP
Language instr: English

Brooklyn Friends School
375 Pearl Street, Brooklyn, New York, New York NY 11201
Tel: +1 718 852 1029
No. of pupils: 644
Curriculum: IBDP
Language instr: English

Buffalo Academy of the Sacred Heart
3860 Main Street, Buffalo, New York NY 14226
Tel: +1 716 834 2101
Curriculum: IBDP
Language instr: English

Convent of the Sacred Heart
1 East 91 Street, New York, New York NY 10128
Tel: +1 212 722 4745
Age range: G3–18
No. of pupils: 635

DWIGHT SCHOOL
For further details see p. 263
291 Central Park West, New York, New York NY 10024
Tel: +1 212 724 6360
Email: admissions@dwight.edu
Website: www.dwight.edu
Chancellor: Stephen H. Spahn
Age range: 2–18 years
No. of pupils: 920
Fees: *Day* US$56,250
Curriculum: ACT, IBDP, IBMYP, IBPYP, SAT, TOEFL
Language instr: English
CIS ECIS

EF ACADEMY NEW YORK
For further details see p. 264
582 Columbus Avenue, Thornwood, New York NY 10594
Tel: +1 914 495 6056
Email: academy.admissions@ef.com
Website: www.efacademy.org
Head of School: Vladimir D. Kuskovski
Age range: 14–19 years
Fees: *Day* US$42,000 *FB* US$65,500
Curriculum: IBDP, National
Language instr: English

French-American School of New York
320 East Boston Post Road, Mamaroneck, New York NY 10543
Tel: +1 914 250 0000
Age range: 3–18 years
No. of pupils: 725
Curriculum: AP, IBDP, National, FrenchBacc, SAT
Language instr: English, French

Hackley School
293 Benedict Ave, Tarrytown, New York NY 10591
Tel: +1 914 631 0128
Language instr: English
RS

International School of Brooklyn
477 Court Street, Brooklyn, New York, New York NY 11231
Tel: +1 718 369 3023
Age range: 3–14 years
No. of pupils: 358
Curriculum: IBMYP, IBPYP
Language instr: English, French, Spanish

La Scuola d'Italia Guglielmo Marconi
12 East 96th Street, New York, New York NY 10128
Tel: +1 212 369 3290
Age range: 2–18 years
No. of pupils: 125
Curriculum: IBDP
Language instr: English, Italian

Léman Manhattan Preparatory School
41 Broad Street, New York, New York NY 10004
Tel: +1 212 232 0266
Age range: 16 months–18 years
No. of pupils: 900
Curriculum: IBDP
Language instr: English

Lycée Français de New York
505 East 75th Street, New York, New York NY 10021
Tel: +1 212 439 3890
Age range: 4–17
No. of pupils: 1350
Curriculum: National, FrenchBacc
Language instr: French, English

Lyceum Kennedy French American School
225 East 43rd Street, New York, New York NY 10017
Tel: +1 212 681 1877
Age range: 3–18 years
No. of pupils: 300
Curriculum: IBDP
Language instr: French, English

Nord Anglia International School, New York
44 E 2nd St, New York, New York NY 10003
Tel: +1 212 600 2010
Age range: 2–14
Curriculum: IPC, UK

Pine Street School
25 Pine Street, New York, New York NY 10005
Tel: +1 212 235 2325
Age range: 2–9
No. of pupils: 150
Curriculum: IBPYP
Language instr: English, Spanish, Mandarin

Portledge School
355 Duck Pond Road, Locust Valley, New York NY 11560-2499
Tel: +1 516 750 3100
Curriculum: IBDP
Language instr: English

Saint Edmund Preparatory High School
2474 Ocean Avenue, Brooklyn, New York, New York NY 11229
Tel: +1 718 743 6100
Curriculum: IBDP
Language instr: English

The British International School of New York
20 Waterside Plaza, New York, New York NY 10010
Tel: +1 212 481 2700
Age range: 3–14
No. of pupils: 290
Curriculum: IBMYP, IBPYP, SAT, UK
Language instr: English
COB

The École
111 East 22nd Street, New York, New York NY 10010
Tel: +1 646 410 2238

United Nations International School
24-50 Franklin D Roosevelt Drive, New York, New York NY 10010
Tel: +1 212 684 7400
Age range: 5–18
No. of pupils: 1573 B763 G778
Curriculum: IBDP
Language instr: English
CIS ECIS

North Carolina

Charlotte Country Day School
1440 Carmel Road, Charlotte, North Carolina NC 28226
Tel: 0017049434500
Age range: 4–18
No. of pupils: 1634
Curriculum: AP, IBDP
Language instr: English

Hickory Day School
2535 21st Ave NE, Hickory, North Carolina NC 28601
Tel: +1 828 256 9492
Age range: 4–13
Curriculum: IBPYP
Language instr: English

Morganton Day School
305 West Concord Street, Morganton, North Carolina NC 28655
Tel: +1 828 437 6782
Age range: 4–13
No. of pupils: 100 *B45 G55*
Curriculum: IBPYP
Language instr: English

The British International School of Charlotte
7000 Endhaven Lane, Charlotte, North Carolina NC 28277
Tel: +1 704 341 3236
Age range: 1.5–18
No. of pupils: 187
Curriculum: IBDP, UK
(COB)

The Montessori School of Raleigh
408 Andrews Chapel Road, Durham, North Carolina NC 27703
Tel: +1 919 848 1545
Curriculum: IBDP
Language instr: English, Spanish

Ohio

Central Catholic High School
2550 Cherry Street, Toledo, Ohio OH 43608
Tel: +1 419 255 2280
Age range: 13–18
Language instr: English

Discovery School
855 Millsboro Rd, Mansfield, Ohio OH 44903
Tel: +1 419 756 8880
Curriculum: IBPYP
Language instr: English

Kent State University Child Development Center
775 Loop Rd., Kent, Ohio OH 44242
Tel: +1 330 672 2559
Age range: 18 months–6 years
No. of pupils: 150
Curriculum: IBPYP
Language instr: English

Notre Dame Academy, OH
3535 W Sylvania Avenue, Toledo, Ohio OH 43623
Tel: +1 419 475 9359
Curriculum: IBDP
Language instr: English

Purcell Marian High School
2935 Hackberry Street Cincinnati, Ohio OH 45206
Tel: +1 513 751 1230
Curriculum: IBDP
Language instr: English

St Edward High School
13500 Detroit Avenue, Lakewood, Ohio OH 44107
Tel: +1 216 221 3776
Age range: *B*14–18
No. of pupils: 945
Curriculum: IBDP, IBMYP
Language instr: English

Oregon

French American International School
8500 NW Johnson Street, Portland, Oregon OR 97229-6780
Tel: +1 503 292 7776
Curriculum: IBMYP, IBPYP
Language instr: English, French
(CIS) (ECIS)

German International School of Portland
3900 SW Murray Blvd, Beaverton, Oregon OR 97005
Tel: +1 503 626 9089
Curriculum: IBPYP
Language instr: German, English

Seven Peaks School
19660 SW Mountaineer Way, Bend, Oregon OR 97702
Tel: +1 541 382 7755
Curriculum: IBMYP, IBPYP
Language instr: English

The International School
025 SW Sherman Street, Portland, Oregon OR 97210
Tel: +1 503 226 2496
Age range: 3–11
Curriculum: IBPYP
Language instr: Chinese, Japanese, Spanish

Pennsylvania

French International School of Philadelphia EFIP
Upper School, 23 City Avenue, Bala Cynwyd, Pennsylvania PA 19004
Tel: +1 610 667 1284

George School
1690 Newtown Langhorne Rd, Newtown, Pennsylvania PA 18940-2414
Tel: +1 215 579 6500
Age range: 13–19 years
Curriculum: ACT, AP, IBDP, SAT
Language instr: English

Harrisburg Academy
10 Erford Road, Wormleysburg, Pennsylvania PA 17043
Tel: +1 717 763 7811
Age range: 3–18
No. of pupils: 315
Curriculum: AP, IBDP, IBPYP
Language instr: English

Mercyhurst Preparatory School
538 East Grandview Boulevard, Erie, Pennsylvania PA 16504
Tel: +1 814 824 2323
Age range: 13–18 years
No. of pupils: 425
Curriculum: ACT, IBDP, SAT, USA
Language instr: English

Westtown School
975 Westtown Rd, West Chester, Pennsylvania PA 19382
Tel: +1 610 399 0123
Language instr: English
(RS)

Rhode Island

Prout School
4640 Tower Hill Road, Wakefield, Rhode Island RI 02879
Tel: +1 401 789 9262
Age range: 14–18
No. of pupils: 647
Curriculum: IBDP
Language instr: English

St. Andrew's School (RI)
63 Federal Road, Barrington, Rhode Island RI 02806
Tel: +1 401 246 1230
Curriculum: IBDP, IBMYP
Language instr: English

The French American School of Rhode Island
75 John Street, Providence, Rhode Island RI 02906
Tel: +1 401 274 3325

South Carolina

Christ Church Episcopal School
245 Cavalier Drive, Greenville, South Carolina SC 29607
Tel: +1 864 299 1522
Age range: 5–19
No. of pupils: 1093
Curriculum: IBDP, IBPYP
Language instr: English

Christ Our King-Stella Maris School
1183 Russell Drive, Mt Pleasant, South Carolina SC 29464
Tel: +1 843 884 4721

Spartanburg Day School
1701 Skylyn Drive, Spartanburg, South Carolina SC 29307
Tel: +1 864 582 8380
No. of pupils: 500
Curriculum: IBPYP
Language instr: English

Tennessee

Lausanne Collegiate School
1381 West Massey Road, Memphis, Tennessee TN 38120
Tel: +1 901 474 1001
Curriculum: IBDP, IBMYP, IBPYP
Language instr: English

Texas

Alcuin School
6144 Churchill Way, Dallas, Texas TX 75230
Tel: +1 972 239 1745
Age range: 18 months–18 years
No. of pupils: 537 *B247 G290*
Curriculum: IBDP, IBMYP, SAT
Language instr: English

Austin Eco Bilingual School (Austin EBS) USA
8707 Mountain Crest Dr, Austin, Texas TX 78735
Tel: +1 512 299 5731
Curriculum: IBPYP
Language instr: English

Brighter Horizons Academy
3145 Medical Plaza Dr., Garland, Texas TX 75044
Tel: +1 972 675 2062
Curriculum: IBPYP
Language instr: English

British International School of Houston
2203 North Westgreen Boulevard, Katy, Texas TX 77449
Tel: +1 713 290 9025
Age range: 3–18
No. of pupils: 1200
Curriculum: IBDP, IBCP, UK, GCSE, IGCSE
Language instr: English
(COB)

CC Mason Elementary
1501 N. Lakeline Blvd, Cedar Park, Texas TX 78613
Tel: +1 512 570 5500
Curriculum: IBPYP
Language instr: English

Cunae International School LLC
5655 Creekside Forest Drive, Spring, Texas TX 77389
Tel: +1 281 516 3770
Curriculum: IBDP, IBPYP

Dallas International School
17811 Waterview Pkwy, Dallas, Texas TX 75252
Tel: +1 469 250 0001
Curriculum: IBDP, FrenchBacc, SAT
Language instr: English, French

Esprit International School
4890 W Panther Creek Dr, The Woodlands, Texas TX 77381
Tel: +1 281 298 9200
Curriculum: IBPYP
Language instr: English

International School of Texas
4402 Hudson Bend, Austin, Texas TX 78734
Tel: +1 512 351 3403
Curriculum: IBMYP, IBPYP
Language instr: English, Spanish

Lincoln Middle School
500 Mulberry Ave., El Paso, Texas TX 79932
Tel: +1 915 236 3400
Curriculum: IBMYP
Language instr: English, Spanish

Lycée International de Houston
15950 Park Row, Houston, Texas TX 77084
Tel: +1 832 474 1013
Curriculum: IBDP
Language instr: English, French

Magellan International School
7938 Great Northern Boulevard, Austin, Texas TX 78757
Tel: +1 512 782 2327
Age range: 3–14
No. of pupils: 465
Curriculum: IBMYP, IBPYP
Language instr: English, Spanish, Mandarin

St Paul's Episcopal Day School
517 Columbus Avenue, Waco, Texas TX 76701
Tel: +1 254 753 0246
No. of pupils: 160
Language instr: English

St. Stephens Episcopal School Houston
1800 Sul Ross Street, Houston, Texas TX 77098
Tel: +1 713 821 9100
Language instr: English

The Awty International School
7455 Awty School Lane, Houston, Texas TX 77055-7222
Tel: +1 713 686 4850
Age range: 3–18
No. of pupils: 1557 *VIth95*
Curriculum: IBDP, FrenchBacc
Language instr: English, French

The Post Oak School
4600 Bissonnet Street, Bellaire, Texas TX 77401
Tel: +1 713 661 6688
Age range: 14 months–18 years
No. of pupils: 502
Curriculum: IBDP
Language instr: English

THE VILLAGE SCHOOL
For further details see p. 280
13051 Whittington Drive, Houston, Texas TX 77077
Tel: +1 281 496 7900
Email: admissions@thevillageschool.com
Website: www.thevillageschool.com
Head of School: Bill Delbrugge
Age range: 2–18 years
No. of pupils: 1500
Fees: *Day* US$19,425–US$32,675 *FB* US$57,850–US$76,850
Curriculum: IBDP, USA
Language instr: English

The Westwood School
14340 Proton Road, Dallas, Texas TX 75244
Tel: +1 972 239 8598
Age range: 1–19
No. of pupils: 280
Curriculum: IBDP
Language instr: English

The Woodlands Preparatory School
27440 Kuykendahl Road, Tomball, Texas TX 77375
Tel: +1 281 516 0600
Curriculum: IBDP, IBMYP, IBPYP
Language instr: English

Westlake Academy
2600 J.T. Ottinger Road, Westlake, Texas TX 76262
Tel: +1 817 4905757
Age range: 5–18 years
No. of pupils: 879
Curriculum: ACT, AP, IBDP, IBMYP, IBPYP, SAT, USA
Language instr: English

Yorkshire Academy
14120 Memorial Drive, Houston, Texas TX 77079
Tel: +1 281 531 6088
Curriculum: USA

Vermont

Long Trail School
1045 Kirby Hollow Road, Dorset, Vermont VT 05251
Tel: +1 802 867 5717
Age range: 10–19
Curriculum: IBDP
Language instr: English

Virginia

Carlisle School
PO Box 5388, Martinsville, Virginia VA 24115
Tel: +1 276 632 7288
Age range: 3–19
No. of pupils: 430
Curriculum: AP, SAT
Language instr: English

K12 International Academy
2300 Corporate Park Drive, Herndon, Virginia VA 20171
Tel: +1 877 512 7748

King Abdullah Academy
2949 Education Dr, Herndon, Virginia VA 20171
Tel: +1 571 351 5520
Curriculum: IBDP, IBMYP, IBPYP
Language instr: Arabic, English

Mary Passage Middle School
400 Atkinson Way, Newport News, Virginia VA 23608
Tel: +1 757 886 7600
Language instr: English

Massanutten Military Academy
614 South Main Street, Woodstock, Virginia VA 22664
Tel: +1 540 459 2167
Language instr: English

Norfolk Academy
1585 Wesleyan Drive, Norfolk, Virginia VA 23502
Tel: +1 757 461 6236

Saint Mary's Catholic School
9501 Gayton Road, Richmond, Virginia VA 23229
Tel: +1 804 740 1048
No. of pupils: 140
Curriculum: IBMYP
Language instr: English

St Michael's Episcopal School
8706 Quaker Lane, Richmond, Virginia VA 23235
Tel: +1 804 272 3514
Age range: 11–14
No. of pupils: 138 *B64 G74*
Language instr: English

Strelitz International Academy
5000 Corporate Woods Driv, Suite 180, Virginia Beach, Virginia VA 23462
Tel: +1 757 424 4327
Curriculum: IBPYP
Language instr: English, Hebrew

The Hague School
739 Yarmouth St., Norfolk, Virginia VA 23510
Tel: +1 757 317 3033
Curriculum: IBDP
Language instr: English, French

Trinity Episcopal School
3850 Pittaway Road, Richmond, Virginia VA 23235
Tel: +1 804 272 5864
Age range: 13–18
No. of pupils: 503
Curriculum: AP, IBDP
Language instr: English

Trinity Lutheran School
6812 River Road, Newport News, Virginia VA 23607
Tel: +1 757 245 2576
Language instr: English

Williamsburg Christian Academy
101 School House Lane, Williamsburg, Virginia VA 23188
Tel: +1 757 220 1978
Curriculum: IBDP
Language instr: English, Spanish

Washington

Annie Wright Schools
827 N Tacoma Avenue, Tacoma, Washington WA 98403
Tel: +1 253 272 2216
Age range: 3–18 years
Curriculum: IBDP, IBMYP, IBPYP
Language instr: English

Bellevue Children's Academy
14600 NE 24th St., Bellevue, Washington WA 98007
Tel: +1 425 649 0791
Curriculum: IBPYP
Language instr: English

Forest Ridge School of the Sacred Heart
4800 139th Avenue SE, Bellevue, Washington WA 98006
Tel: +1 425 641 0700

French American School of Puget Sound
3795 East Mercer Way, Mercer Island, Washington WA 98040
Tel: +1 206 275 3533
Curriculum: IPC

Saint George's School
2929 W. Waikiki Road, Spokane, Washington WA 99208
Tel: +1 509 466 1636 Ext:331
Curriculum: IBDP
Language instr: English

Soundview School
6515 196th Street SW, Lynnwood, Washington WA 98036
Tel: +1 425 778 8572
Curriculum: IBMYP
Language instr: English

St. Luke School
17533 St Luke Place N, Shoreline, Washington WA 98133
Tel: +1 206 542 1133
Curriculum: IBMYP, IBPYP
Language instr: English

Washington Preparatory School
18323 Bothell-Everett Highway, Suite 220, Bothell, Washington WA 98012
Tel: +1 425 892 8669
Curriculum: IBDP
Language instr: English

West Sound Academy
16571 Creative Drive NE, Poulsbo, Washington WA 98370
Tel: +1 360 598 5954
Curriculum: IBDP

Willows Preparatory School
12280 NE Woodinville-Redmond Rd, Redmond, Washington WA 98052
Tel: +1 425 649 0791
Curriculum: IBDP, IBMYP
Language instr: English

Wisconsin

Catholic Memorial High School
601 East College Avenue, Waukesha, Wisconsin WI 53186
Tel: +1 262 542 7101
No. of pupils: 750
Curriculum: IBDP, IBCP
Language instr: English

Holy Family School
1204 S. Fisk Street, Green Bay, Wisconsin WI 54304
Tel: +1 920 494 1931
Curriculum: IBMYP
Language instr: English

Madison Country Day School
5606 River Road, Waunakee, Wisconsin WI 53597
Tel: +1 608 850 6000
Age range: 4–19
No. of pupils: 456
Curriculum: IBDP
Language instr: English

Notre Dame de la Baie Academy
610 Maryhill Drive, Green Bay, Wisconsin WI 54303
Tel: +1 920 429 6100
Age range: 14–18
No. of pupils: 731 *B*377 *G*354
Curriculum: ACT, IBDP, USA
Language instr: English

St. Joan Antida High School
1341 N. Cass Street, Milwaukee, Wisconsin WI 53202
Tel: +1 414 272 8423
Curriculum: IBCP
Language instr: English

Wauwatosa Catholic
1500 Wauwatosa Avenue, Wauwatosa, Wisconsin WI 53213
Tel: +1 414 258 9977
Curriculum: IBMYP, IBPYP
Language instr: English

Wyoming

Journeys School
700 Coyote Canyon Road, Jackson, Wyoming WY 83001
Tel: +1 307 733 3729
Age range: 4–18
No. of pupils: 160
Curriculum: IBDP
Language instr: English, Spanish

VIRGIN ISLANDS (US)

Antilles School
7280 Frenchman's Bay, St Thomas 802
Tel: +1 340 776 1600
Age range: 2–17/18
No. of pupils: 500
Curriculum: USA

Good Hope Country Day School
Rt 1 Box 6199, Kings Hill VI 00850
Tel: +1 340 778 1974

Virgin Islands Montessori School & Peter Gruber International Academy
6936 Vessup Lane, St Thomas VI 00802
Tel: +1 340 775 6360
Curriculum: IBDP, IBMYP
Language instr: English

International schools in South America

Schools ordered A–Z by Country

Key to directory

Country	**Whereford**
Name of school or college	**College Academy**
Indicates that this school has a profile	***For further details see p***
Address and contact number	Which Street, Whosville, Wherefordshire AB12 3CD **Tel:** 01000 000000
Head's name	**Head Master:** Dr A Person
Age range	**Age range:** 11–18
Number of pupils. B = boys G = girls VIth = sixth form	**No. of pupils:** 660 B330 G330 VIth 200
Fees per annum. Day = fees for day pupils. WB = fees for weekly boarders. FB = fees for full boarders.	**Fees:** Day £11,000 WB £16,000 FB £20,000
Curriculum	**Curriculum:** National, IBDP, ALevs
Language of instruction	**Language instr:** English, French
Memberships/Accreditation	(AISA) (COB) (EAR)

Key to icons

Key to symbols:

- Boys' school
- Girls' school
- Boarding accommodation

Member of:

- (AISA) Association of International Schools in Africa
- (CEE) Central and Eastern European Schools Association
- (EAR) East Asia Regional Council of Overseas Schools
- (ECIS) European Council of International Schools
- (RS) Round Square

Accreditation:

- (CIS) Council of International Schools
- (COB) Council of British International Schools

Please note: Schools are coeducational day schools unless otherwise indicated

ARGENTINA

Aberdare College
Av. Francia 1245, Bella Vista,
1661 San Miguel, Buenos Aires
Tel: +54 11 4666 8813
Curriculum: IGCSE

Academia Arguello
Avda Rafael Nunez 5675,
Arguello, 5021 Córdoba
Tel: +54 3543 421010/420387
Age range: 4–16
No. of pupils: 300
Curriculum: IGCSE

Asociación Cultural Pestalozzi
R Freire 1882, 1428 Ciudad
de Buenos Aires
Tel: +54 11 4555 3688
Age range: 2–18
No. of pupils: 346
Curriculum: IBDP
Language instr: Spanish, German

Asociación Escuelas Lincoln
Andres Ferreyra 4073, 1637
La Lucila, Buenos Aires
Tel: +54 11 4851 1700
Age range: 4–18
No. of pupils: 702 *B347 G355*
Curriculum: ACT, IBDP, SAT, USA
Language instr: English, Spanish

Austin Eco Bilingual School (Austin EBS) Argentina
Porto 463, Campana, Buenos Aires
Tel: +54 3489 462203/4
Curriculum: IBDP
Language instr: Spanish, English

Barker College
Mitre 131, 1832 Lomas de
Zamora, Buenos Aires
Tel: +54 11 4292 1107
Age range: 2–18
No. of pupils: 600
Curriculum: IGCSE, ALevs
Language instr: Spanish,
English, French

Bartolome Mitre Day School – Moreno
Padre Fahy and Miero, 1744
Moreno, Buenos Aires
Tel: +54 237 4623698

Bede's Grammar School
Alejandro Korn y Panama, 1667
Tortuguitas, Buenos Aires
Tel: +54 348 4477 355
Age range: 3–18
No. of pupils: 420
Curriculum: IGCSE

Belgrano Day School
Juramento 3035, 1428
Ciudad de Buenos Aires
Tel: +54 11 4781 6011
Age range: 2–18
No. of pupils: 1160 *B612 G548*
Curriculum: National,
UK, IGCSE, ALevs
Language instr: Spanish, English

Boston College (Childrens School)
Primario / EGB – Secundario,
Charcas 3949, 1425 Ciudad
de Buenos Aires
Tel: +54 11 4833 2607
Curriculum: National, UK, IGCSE

British School Cordoba-Cerro de las Rosas
Jose Roque Funes 1511, Córdoba
Tel: + 54 351 4812104

Buenos Aires International Christian Academy
1646 San Fernando, Buenos Aires
Tel: +54 11 4549 1300
Age range: 2–18
No. of pupils: 170
Curriculum: AP, USA

Cardinal Newman College
Eliseo Reclus 1133, 1609 Boulogne
Sur Mer, Buenos Aires
Tel: +54 11 4737 0042
Age range: 14–18
Curriculum: IGCSE

Caxton School (Escuela William Caxton)
José María Paz 3540, 1636
Olivos, Buenos Aires
Tel: +54 11 4799 6424

Chaltel College
Lucio Melendez 1617, 1611 Don
Torcuato, Buenos Aires
Tel: +54 11 4748 3153
Age range: 4–17
Curriculum: IGCSE

Colegio Alemán Córdoba
Recta Martinoli 6230 (Esq. Neper),
5021 Argüello, Córdoba
Tel: +54 35 4342 0834
Curriculum: IBDP
Language instr: Spanish

Colegio Arrayanes
Mateo Churich y Salvo s/n,
1619 Garín, Buenos Aires
Tel: +54 (0)348 4471283
Curriculum: National

Colegio Bayard
Castex 3348, Salguero, 2969
Ciudad de Buenos Aires
Tel: +54 11 4803 0902
Age range: 4–19
No. of pupils: 200
Curriculum: IGCSE

Colegio Bosque del Plata
Calle 501 e/ 28 y 30,
Gonnet, Buenos Aires
Tel: +54 (0)221 4845997

Colegio Carmen Arriola de Marin
Av del Libertador 17.115, 1642
San Isidro, Buenos Aires
Tel: +54 11 4743 0028

Colegio Confluencia
Dr. Luis Federico Leloir
210, 8300 Neuquén
Tel: +54 299 442 2417
Age range: 4–19
No. of pupils: 300
Curriculum: IGCSE

Colegio De La Salle
Ayacucho 665, 1025 Ciudad
de Buenos Aires
Tel: +54 011 4374 6449
No. of pupils: 286
Curriculum: IBDP
Language instr: Spanish

Colegio de Todos Los Santos
Thames 798, Villa Adelina,
1607 San Isidro, Buenos Aires
Tel: +54 114 766 3878
Age range: 2–18
No. of pupils: 700
Curriculum: IBDP
Language instr: Spanish, English

Colegio El Buen Ayre
Av. Uruguay 2820,
Beccar, Buenos Aires
Tel: +54 11 4723 0088
Curriculum: National, IGCSE

Colegio Esquiú
11 de Septiembre 1240, 1426
Ciudad de Buenos Aires
Tel: +54 11 4784 3222
Age range: 4–19
No. of pupils: 300
Curriculum: IGCSE

Colegio Franco Argentino
Lavalle 1067, Acassuso, 1641
San Isidro, Buenos Aires
Tel: +54 11 4792 4628
Language instr: Spanish

Colegio Lincoln
Olleros 2283, Belgrano,
Ciudad de Buenos Aires
Tel: +54 11 4772 0108
Age range: 2–18
No. of pupils: 800 *B400 G400 VIth35*
Curriculum: IBDP, National, UK
Language instr: Spanish, English

Colegio Maria Montessori
Segurola 949, Turdera, 1833
Ciudad de Buenos Aires
Tel: +54 11 4294 2068
Curriculum: National, UK

Colegio Mark Twain
José Roque Funes 1525,
5009 Córdoba
Tel: +543 514 830 664
Age range: 3–17
No. of pupils: *VIth25*
Curriculum: IBDP
Language instr: Spanish

Colegio Martin Y Omar
25 de Mayo 170, 1642 San
Isidro, Buenos Aires
Tel: +54 11 4743 6888
Age range: 4–19
No. of pupils: 500
Curriculum: IGCSE

Colegio Montessori de Luján
Mitre 1247, Lujan, Buenos Aires
Tel: +51 23 2343 3981
Curriculum: IBDP
Language instr: English, Spanish

Colegio Padre Luis Maria Etcheverry Boneo
Juncal 2131, 1125 Ciudad
de Buenos Aires
Tel: +54 11 4822 3687
Language instr: Spanish

Colegio Palermo Chico
Thames 2037/41, 1425
Ciudad de Buenos Aires
Tel: +54 114 774 3975
Curriculum: IBDP
Language instr: Spanish

Colegio Patris
Calle 146 entre 446 y Arroyo
Carnaval, City Bell, 1896
La Plata, Buenos Aires
Tel: +54 221 475 1091
Age range: 4–19
No. of pupils: 300
Curriculum: IGCSE

Colegio San Ignacio
Guardias Nacionales 1400,
5806 Río Cuarto, Córdoba
Tel: +54 (358) 464 8484/0802
Age range: 12–18
No. of pupils: 125 *B60 G65*
Curriculum: IBDP, IGCSE
Language instr: Spanish, English

Colegio San Jorge
Godoy Cruz, Pedro J Godoy
1191, 5547 Mendoza
Tel: +54 2 614 287 247
Curriculum: IBDP
Language instr: Spanish

Colegio San Marcos
Nivel Secundario, Jorge Miles 153,
1842 Monte Grande, Buenos Aires
Tel: +54 11 4296 3138
Curriculum: IBDP,
National, UK, IGCSE
Language instr: Spanish

Colegio San Pablo
25 de Mayo 430 E, 5400 San Juan
Tel: +54 264 422 9971
Age range: 5–19
No. of pupils: 475

Colegio San Patricio
Moreno y Las Higueritas, 4107 Yerba Buena, Tucumán
Tel: +54 381 4250 708
Curriculum: IBDP
Language instr: Spanish

Colegio San Patricio de Luján
Acceso Oeste 2145, Lujan, Buenos Aires
Tel: +54 23 2343 7998
Curriculum: IBDP
Language instr: Spanish

Colegio San Pedro Apostol
Av. Piamonte s/n, B. Chateau Carreras, 5016 Córdoba
Tel: +54 351 484 6584

Colegio Santa María
Coronel Suárez 453, 4400 Salta
Tel: +54 387 421 3127
Curriculum: IBDP
Language instr: Spanish
CIS

Colegio Tarbut
Rosales 3019, 1636 Olivos, Buenos Aires
Tel: +54 11 4794 3444
Curriculum: IBDP, IGCSE
Language instr: Spanish

Deutsche Schule Temperley
Av. Fernández 27, 1834 Temperley, Buenos Aires
Tel: +54 114244 2832
Curriculum: IBDP
Language instr: English, Spanish

Dover High School
San Martín y Ruta 26, 1623 Maschwitz, Buenos Aires
Tel: +54 93488 441106
Curriculum: IBDP
Language instr: English, Spanish

Escuela Goethe Rosario
España 440, 2000 Rosario, Santa Fe
Tel: +54 34 1426 3024
Age range: 2–18
No. of pupils: 80 *B*30 *G*50
Curriculum: IBDP
Language instr: Spanish

Escuela Privada Ranelagh
Avenida Eva Perón (ex Sevilla) 3842, 1886 Ranelagh, Buenos Aires
Tel: +54 11 4258 8509

Escula Argentina Modelo – Sede EAM / Sede NORTE
Riobamba 1059, Ciudad de Buenos Aires
Tel: + 54 11 4811 2705
Curriculum: National, IGCSE

Florida Day School
Gral. Justo José de Urquiza 2151, Florida, 1602 Ciudad de Buenos Aires
Tel: +54 11 4796 1122
Curriculum: National, IGCSE

Godspell College
Autopista Panamericana, KM 41 – Ramal Rilar, The Marigolds, 2600 Tortugitas, Buenos Aires
Tel: +54 2320 407676
Age range: 2–17
No. of pupils: 800
Curriculum: USA

Goethe Schule
Reclus 2250, 1609 Boulogne, Buenos Aires
Tel: +54 11 4513 7700

Holmberg Schule
Sarmiento 679, Quilmes, Buenos Aires
Tel: +54 11 4254 8583
Curriculum: IBDP
Language instr: German, Spanish

Hölters Schule Villa Ballester
Calle 65 No 5886, Ciudad de Buenos Aires
Tel: +54 11 4768 0480

Holy Trinity College
Gascón 544, 7600 Mar del Plata, Buenos Aires
Tel: +54 223 486 3471
Age range: 2–18
No. of pupils: 637 *B*328 *G*309
Curriculum: IBDP
Language instr: English, Spanish

Instituto Ballester
Calle 69 N° 5140 (ex San Martín 444), 1653 Villa Ballester, Buenos Aires
Tel: +54 11 4768 0760
No. of pupils: 1583
Curriculum: IBDP
Language instr: Spanish, German

Instituto Santa Brígida
Av Gaona 2068, 1416 Ciudad de Buenos Aires
Tel: +54 1 145 811 268
No. of pupils: *B*150 *G*141
Curriculum: IBDP
Language instr: Spanish

Instituto Wolfsohn
2972, AEB, Amenábar, 1429 Ciudad de Buenos Aires
Tel: +54 11 4545 6020
Curriculum: IBDP
Language instr: English, Spanish

Islands International School
Amenábar St. 1840, 1428 Ciudad de Buenos Aires
Tel: +54 11 4787 2294
Age range: 2–18 years
Curriculum: IBDP
Language instr: Spanish, English, Italian, Portuguese

Kindergarten Manantiales
Cabello 3735, 1425 Ciudad de Buenos Aires
Tel: +54 11 4806 3939
Age range: 4–11
No. of pupils: 200

Limerick Bilingual School
José Bonifacio 2560, Ciudad de Buenos Aires
Tel: +54 11 4612 3833
Curriculum: National, UK

Lomas High School
Lomas De Zamora, Buenos Aires
Tel: +54 11 4244 6555
Curriculum: IPC, IGCSE, ALevs

Lycée Franco-Argentin Jean Mermoz
Ramsay 2131, Ciudad de Buenos Aires
Tel: +54 11 47 81 16 00
Curriculum: FrenchBacc

Modern School
Enrique del Valle Iberlucea 3952, 1826 Remedios de Escalada, Buenos Aires
Tel: + 54 11 4241 2570
Curriculum: National, UK, IGCSE

New Model International School
El Salvador 3952, 1175 Ciudad de Buenos Aires
Tel: +54 11 4825 2900
Language instr: Spanish

Northern International School
Ruote 8 Km 61.5., 1633. Pilar, Buenos Aires
Tel: +54 2322 49 1208
Age range: 2–18 years
Curriculum: IBDP
Language instr: Spanish, English, Italian, Portuguese

Northlands School
Olivos Site: Roma 1248, Olivos, Buenos Aires
Tel: +54 11 4711 8400
Age range: 2–18 years
No. of pupils: 1828
Curriculum: IBDP, IBPYP, National, IGCSE
Language instr: English, Spanish

Northlands School Nordelta
Nordelta site: Av de los Colegios 590, Nordelta, Buenos Aires B1670NNN
Tel: +54 11 4871 2668/9
Curriculum: IBDP, IBPYP, National, IGCSE
Language instr: Spanish, English

Orange Day School
Av. San Martín 1651/7, 1657 Ramos Mejia, Buenos Aires
Tel: +54 11 4464 7014
Age range: 14–19
No. of pupils: 300
Curriculum: IBDP, IGCSE
Language instr: English, Spanish

Poplars School
Estrada 335, 9400 Río Gallegos, Santa Cruz
Tel: +54 29 6642 5703
Curriculum: IBDP
Language instr: English, Spanish

Quilmes High School
Rivadavia 460, 1878 Quilmes, Buenos Aires
Tel: +54 11 4253 0123
Age range: 1–18
No. of pupils: 900 *B*500 *G*400 *VIth*50
Curriculum: IGCSE, ALevs
Language instr: Spanish

Saint Alban's College, Lomas de Zamora
Ramon Falcon 250, 1832 Lomas de Zamora, Buenos Aires
Tel: +54 11 4244 8060

Saint Mary of the Hills School
Xul Solar 6650, 1646 San Fernando, Buenos Aires
Tel: +54 11 4714 0330
No. of pupils: 850
Curriculum: AP, IBDP, IPC, IGCSE
Language instr: Spanish, English

Saint Mary of the Hills School Sede Pilar
Ruta 25 y Caamaño, 1644 Pilar, Buenos Aires
Tel: +54 2304 458181
Curriculum: IBDP
Language instr: Spanish

Saint Matthews College
Roque Sáenz Peña 1855, 1636 Olivos, Buenos Aires
Tel: +54 11 4790 8211
Age range: 4–19
No. of pupils: 380
Curriculum: IGCSE, ALevs
Language instr: Spanish, English

Saint Patrick College
Av. Maipú 3187, Corrientes
Curriculum: IBDP
Language instr: English, Spanish

SGS Loma Verde Bilingual School
Leguizamo 1174, 1625 Belén de Escobar, Buenos Aires
Tel: +54 348 449 3375
Curriculum: National, IGCSE, ALevs

Southern International School
Freeway Buenos Aires – La Plata Km 34., 1884 Hudson, Buenos Aires
Tel: +54 11 4215 3636
Age range: 2–18 years
Curriculum: IBDP
Language instr: Spanish, English, Italian, Portuguese

St George's College
Guido 800, 1878 Quilmes, Buenos Aires
Tel: +54 (11) 4350 7900
Age range: 3–18
No. of pupils: 859 *B*451 *G*408 *VIth*49
Curriculum: IBDP, IBPYP, National, UK, IGCSE
Language instr: English, Spanish

St George's College North
Mosconi 3500 y Don Bosco s/n, 1613 Los Polvorines, Buenos Aires
Tel: +54 (11) 4663 2494
Age range: 2–18
No. of pupils: 640 *B*340 *G*300 *VIth*82
Curriculum: IBDP, IBPYP, National, IGCSE
Language instr: English, Spanish

St Lukes College
Miguel de Azcuénaga 2340, 1636 Olivos, Buenos Aires
Tel: +54 11 4799 5922
Age range: 2–18
No. of pupils: 600
Curriculum: UK, IGCSE

St Margarets School
Marsical Antonio Jose de Sucre 3668, 1430 Ciudad de Buenos Aires
Tel: +54 11 4551 2942
Age range: 4–18
No. of pupils: 300
Curriculum: IGCSE

St Mark's College
M. Alegre 325, 1842 Monte Grande, Buenos Aires
Tel: +54 11 4296 5045

St Mary's International College
Martin Garcia 1435/1236/1501, 1804 Ezeiza, Buenos Aires
Tel: +54 11 5075 0370
No. of pupils: 870
Curriculum: IBDP
Language instr: English, Spanish

St Matthew's College – Sede Fundadora
Moldes 1469, 1426 Ciudad de Buenos Aires
Tel: +54 11 4783 1110
Age range: 2–18
No. of pupils: 650
Curriculum: IBDP, National, IGCSE
Language instr: Spanish, English

St Matthew's College – Sede Norte
Caamano 493, 1631 Pilar, Buenos Aires
Tel: +54 230 4693600
Age range: 2–18
No. of pupils: 1365
Curriculum: IBDP, IGCSE
Language instr: English, Spanish

St Patrick's School
Nahuel Huapí 4134/40, 1430 Ciudad de Buenos Aires
Tel: +54 11 4545 7746
Age range: 4–19
No. of pupils: 800
Curriculum: UK

St Xavier's College
José Antonio Cabrera 5901, 1414 Ciudad de Buenos Aires
Tel: +54 114 777 5011/14
Curriculum: IBDP
Language instr: English

St. Andrew's Scots School
Roque Saenz Peña 601, 1636 Olivos, Buenos Aires
Tel: +54 11 4846 6500
Age range: 3–18
No. of pupils: 1866 *B*950 *G*916
Curriculum: IBDP, National, IGCSE
Language instr: English, Spanish

St. Catherine's Moorlands – Belgrano
Carbajal 3250, 1426 Ciudad de Buenos Aires
Tel: +54 11 4552 4353
Age range: 3–18
Curriculum: IBDP, IBMYP, National, UK
Language instr: English, Spanish

St. Catherine's Moorlands – Tortuguitas
Ruta Panamericana Km 38 Ramal Pilar, 1667 Tortuguitas, Buenos Aires
Tel: +54 348 463 9001/2
Age range: 3–18
Curriculum: IBMYP, National, UK, IGCSE
Language instr: English

St. John's School – Beccar
España 348/370, 1643 Beccar, Buenos Aires
Tel: +54 11 4513 4400
Curriculum: IBDP, IBPYP
Language instr: Spanish, English

St. John's School – Escobar
Av de los Colegios 385, 1625 Puertos Escobar, Buenos Aires
Tel: +54 03484 268118

St. John's School – Martínez
General Pueyrredón 1499, 1640 Martinez, Buenos Aires
Tel: +54 11 4580 3500
Age range: 6–16
No. of pupils: 1330
Curriculum: IGCSE

St. John's School – Pilar
Panamericana Km. 48.800, 1629 Pilar, Buenos Aires
Tel: +54 (0) 2304 667 667
Curriculum: IBDP, IBPYP
Language instr: English, Spanish

St. Nicholas' School
Guillermo Rawson 2625, 1636 Olivos, Buenos Aires
Tel: +54 11 4799 5254
Curriculum: National

St. Paul's College
Juan de Garay 950, 1686 Hurlingham, Buenos Aires
Tel: +54 11 4665 3309
Curriculum: IGCSE, ALevs

Sunrise School
Chacra 116 Colonia Lucinda, 8324 Cipolletti, Río Negro
Tel: +54 299 4786590
No. of pupils: 400
Curriculum: IBDP
Language instr: Spanish

Sworn College S.A. Moreno
Ruta 24 entre Gral. Savio y Puerto Madryn, Barrio Santa Ana, Francisco Alvarez, 1744 Moreno, Buenos Aires
Tel: +54 237 483 1552
Curriculum: IGCSE

Sworn Junior College
Viceroy del Pino 3299, 1426 Ciudad de Buenos Aires
Tel: +54 11 4552 2498
Age range: 14–19
No. of pupils: 1000
Curriculum: UK, ALevs

United High School
Montañeses 2434, 1428 Ciudad de Buenos Aires
Tel: +54 11 4783 3006
Curriculum: AICE, IGCSE

Villa Devoto School
Pedro Morán 4441, 1419 Ciudad de Buenos Aires
Tel: +54 114 501 9419
Curriculum: IBDP
Language instr: English, Spanish

Washington School
Avenida Federico Lacroze 2012, 1426 Ciudad de Buenos Aires
Tel: +54 11 4772 8131
Age range: 2–18
Curriculum: IBDP, IBPYP
Language instr: Spanish

Wellspring School
Las Camelias 3883, 1669 Del Viso, Ciudad de Buenos Aires
Tel: +54 (0)23 20 300100
Curriculum: AICE, IGCSE, ALevs

Woodville School
Av. Los Pioneros km 2,900, 8400 San Carlos de Bariloche, Río Negro
Tel: +54 2944 44 11 33
Age range: 16–18
No. of pupils: 169 *B*83 *G*86 *VIth*45
Curriculum: IBDP, IGCSE
Language instr: Spanish, English

BARBADOS

The Codrington School
St John BB 20008
Tel: +1 246 423 2570
Age range: 3–18
No. of pupils: 140 *B*80 *G*60
Curriculum: IBDP, IBMYP, IBPYP
Language instr: English

The Lester Vaughan School
Cane Garden
Tel: +1 246 535 6030
Age range: 11–17 years

BOLIVIA

American Cooperative School
c/o American Embassy, La Paz
Tel: +591 2 279 2302
Age range: 4–18

American International School of Bolivia
Casilla 5309, Cochabamba
Tel: +591 4 428 8577
Age range: 3–18
No. of pupils: 240
Curriculum: IBDP
Language instr: English

Cambridge College
Av. Banzer Carretera al norte, km 8 1/2 (frente a La Chonta), Santa Cruz
Tel: +591 3 343 4653
Age range: 3–18 years
No. of pupils: 1200

Cochabamba Co-Operative School
Avenida Circunvalacion, s/n Zona Mesadilla, Cochabamba
Tel: + 591 4 4490 605

Colegio Alemán Santa Cruz
Casilla 624, Av San Martin s/n, Santa Cruz
Tel: +591 3 3326820
Age range: 4–18
No. of pupils: 1400
Curriculum: IBDP
Language instr: Spanish

Deutsche Schule La Paz – Colegio Alemán 'Mariscal Braun'
Avenida Alexander # 100 Achumani, Casilla 605 – 4442, La Paz
Tel: +591 2 2710812

Highlands International School
Urbanizacion Valle Del Sol, Ex Fabrica de Ladrillos, Mallasilla, La Paz
Tel: +591 2745113
Curriculum: National, USA

Lycée Franco Bolivien Alcide d'Orbigny – La Paz
Av. Francia s/n, Achumani, Casilla postal 6547, La Paz
Tel: +591 2 2793370
Curriculum: FrenchBacc

Saint Andrew's School
Casilla 1679, Av Las Retamas s/n La Florida, La Paz
Tel: +591 22 79 24 84
Curriculum: IBDP, IBPYP
Language instr: English, Spanish

Santa Cruz Cooperative School
Barrio Las Palmas, Calle Barcelona #1, Santa Cruz 753
Tel: +591 3 353 0808
Age range: 3–18
Curriculum: AP, SAT

Santa Cruz International School
PO Box 4640, Santa Cruz de la Sierra, Santa Cruz 4640
Tel: +591 3 353 5035
Age range: 3–18
No. of pupils: 360
Curriculum: USA, ALevs

BRAZIL

ABA Global School
Av. Rosa e Silva, 1510, Aflitos, Recife, Pernambuco PE 52050-245
Tel: +55 81 3427 8800
Curriculum: IBPYP
Language instr: English

Amazon Valley Academy
Rodovia BR 316 – Km 3, Tv.Tenri, n132 Guanabara, Ananindeua, Pará PA 67113-120
Tel: +55 91 3245 2566
Age range: 4–18
No. of pupils: 89
Curriculum: ACT, SAT, USA
Language instr: English

American School of Brasilia
SGAS 605, Conjunto E, Lotes 34/37, Brasília DF 70200-650
Tel: +55 61 3442 9700
Age range: 3–19
No. of pupils: 569 *B262 G307*
Curriculum: IBDP, USA
Language instr: English

American School of Campinas – Escola Americana de Campinas
Rua Cajamar, #35, Campinas, São Paulo SP 13090-860
Tel: +55 19 21021006
Age range: 3–18
No. of pupils: 444 *B219 G225*
Curriculum: ACT, IBDP, IBPYP, SAT

American School of Recife
Street Sa e Souza, Boa Viagem, Recife, Pernambuco PE 51030-065
Tel: +55 81 3341 4716
Curriculum: USA
Language instr: English

Associação Educacional Luterana Bom Jesus / IELUSC
Rua Princesa Isabel, 438, Joinville, Santa Catarina SC 89201-270
Tel: +55 47 3026 8000
Curriculum: IBDP

Brasilia International School
SGAS 914 Conjunto C Lotes 67/68, Brasília DF 70390-140
Tel: +55 (61) 3346 1200
Age range: 3
Curriculum: USA

Centro Internacional de Educacao Integrada
Estrada do Pontal 2093, Recreio dos Bandeirantes, Rio de Janeiro RJ 22790-877
Tel: +55 21 2490 1673
Curriculum: IBDP, IBPYP
Language instr: English

Chapel School – The American International School of Brazil
Rua Vigário João de Pontes, 537, Chácara Flora, São Paulo SP 04748-000
Tel: +55 11 2101 7400
No. of pupils: 700
Curriculum: ACT, IBDP, SAT, TOEFL
Language instr: English

Colégio 7 de Setembro
R. Henriqueta Galeno, 1011, Dionísio Torres, Fortaleza, Ceará CE 60135-420
Tel: +55 85 4006 7777
Curriculum: IBDP
Language instr: English, Portuguese

Colégio Humboldt
Av. Engenheiro Alberto Kuhlmann, 525 – Jardim Ipanema (Zona Sul), São Paulo SP 04784-010
Tel: +55 11 5686 4055

Colégio Miguel de Cervantes
Avenida Jorge João Saad, 905, São Paulo, Morumbí SP 05618-001
Tel: +55 11 3779 1800
No. of pupils: 1500
Curriculum: IBDP
Language instr: Portuguese, Spanish, English

Colegio Positivo Internacional
Professor Pedro Viriato de Souza St 5300, Curitiba, Paraná PR 81280-330
Tel: +55 (41) 3335 3535
Age range: 3–17 years
No. of pupils: 917
Curriculum: IBDP, IBMYP, IBPYP
Language instr: Portuguese, English

Colegio Sao Luis
Av. Dr. Dante Pazzanese, 295, Vila Mariana, São Paulo SP 04012-180
Curriculum: IBDP
Language instr: English, Portuguese

Colégio Sidarta
Estrada Fernando Nobre, 1332, Granja Viana, Cotia, São Paulo SP 06705-490
Tel: +55 11 4612 2711

Colégio Soka do Brasil
Avenida Cursino, 362, Saúde SP 04132-000
Tel: +55 11 5060 3300
Curriculum: IBDP
Language instr: English, Portuguese

Colégio Suíço-Brasileiro de Curitiba
Rua Wanda dos Santos Mallmann, 537, Jardim Pinhais, Pinhais, Paraná PR 83323-400
Tel: +55 41 3525 9100
Curriculum: IBDP
Language instr: English

Coree International School
R. Gothard Kaesemodel 961, Anita Garibaldi, Joinville, Santa Catarina SC 89203-522
Tel: +55 47 3121 6700
Age range: 6–18
No. of pupils: 220
Curriculum: IBDP, IBPYP

Cultura Inglesa – Filial Cabral
Rua Moyses Marcondes 625, Cabral, Curitiba, Paraná PR 80030-410
Tel: +55 41 3254 7239
Age range: 4–18

Escola Alemã Corcovado
Rua São Clemente 388, Botafogo, Rio de Janeiro RJ 22260-000
Tel: +55 (21) 2528 0400

Escola Americana de Belo Horizonte
Av. Professor Mario Werneck, 3002, Bairro Buritis, Belo Horizonte, Minas Gerais MG 30575-180
Tel: +55 31 3378 6700
Age range: 3–18
No. of pupils: 180 *B95 G85*
Curriculum: IBMYP, IBPYP
Language instr: English, Portuguese

Escola Americana do Rio de Janeiro – Barra da Tijuca
Rua Colbert Coelho 155, Barra da Tijuca, Rio de Janeiro RJ 22793-313
Tel: +55 21 3747 2000
Curriculum: IBDP
Language instr: English

Escola Americana do Rio de Janeiro – Gávea
Estrada da Gávea 132, Gávea, Rio de Janeiro RJ 22451-263
Tel: +55 21 2125 9000
Age range: 3–18 years
No. of pupils: 1200
Curriculum: IBDP, National, USA
Language instr: English

Escola Beit Yaacov
Av Marques de Sao Vicente no 1748, Barra Funda, São Paulo SP 01139-002
Tel: +55 11 3611 0600
Curriculum: IBDP, IBPYP
Language instr: English

Escola Bilíngue Pueri Domus – Aclimação Campus
Rua Muniz de Sousa 1051, Aclimação, São Paulo SP 01534-020
Tel: +55 11 3478 7701
Curriculum: IBDP
Language instr: English, Portuguese

Escola Bilíngue Pueri Domus – Itaim Campus
Rua Itacema 214, Itaim Bibi, São Paulo SP 04530-050
Tel: +55 11 3078 6999
Curriculum: IBDP
Language instr: English, Portuguese

Escola Bilíngue Pueri Domus – Perdizes Campus
Rua Ministro Godói 1697, Perdizes, São Paulo SP 05015-001
Tel: +55 11 3803 4240
Curriculum: IBDP
Language instr: English, Portuguese

Escola Bilíngue Pueri Domus – Verbo Divino Campus
Rua Verbo Divino 993-A, Chacara Sto. Antonio, São Paulo SP 04719-001
Tel: +55 11 3512 2222
Curriculum: IBDP
Language instr: English, Portuguese

Escola Castanheiras
Alameda Castanheiras, 250, Res. Tres (Tambore), Santana de Parnaíba, São Paulo SP 06543-510
Tel: +55 114 152 4600
Curriculum: IBDP
Language instr: English

ESCOLA DO FUTURO – SÃO PAULO
For further details see p. 282
R. Dr. Francisco Pais 40, Cidade São Francisco, São Paulo SP 05352-120
Tel: +55 (11) 2168 4100
Email: visitas@escoladofuturo.com.br
Website: www.escoladofuturo.com.br
Headmaster: Ivonne Betsabé Muniz
Age range: 2–18 years
No. of pupils: 600

Escola Eleva – Barra da Tijuca
Av. José Silva de Azevedo Neto 309, Rio de Janeiro RJ 22740-361
Tel: +55 21 3094 5020
Curriculum: IBDP
Language instr: English, Portuguese

Escola Eleva – Botafogo
Rua General Severiano, 159, Botafogo, Rio de Janeiro RJ 22290-040
Tel: +55 21 4042 2492
Curriculum: IBDP
Language instr: English, Portuguese

Escola Francesa de Natal
Rua Pastor Gabino Brelaz, 1470 – Capim Macio, Natal RN 59082-010
Tel: +55 (84) 3217 4558

Escola Internacional de Alphaville
Av. Copacabana, 624, Cond. Empresarial 18 do Forte, Alphaville, Barueri SP 06472-001
Tel: +55 11 4134 6686
Curriculum: IBDP, IBPYP
Language instr: English

Escola Internacional Nova Geração
EING – Portaria de alunos, Rua Washington, 264, Vila Maia, Guarujá, São Paulo SP 11410-150
Tel: +55 (13) 3384-3009
Curriculum: National, USA

Escola Internacional UniSociesc Blumenau
Rua Pandiá Calógeras 272, Jardim Blumenau, Blumenau, Santa Catarina SC 89010-350
Tel: +55 47 2111 2966
Age range: 5–18 years
No. of pupils: 240
Curriculum: IBDP, IBPYP
Language instr: English, Portuguese

Escola Internacional UniSociesc Florianopolis
Rua Salvatina Feliciana dos Santos 525, Itacorubi, Florianópolis, Santa Catarina SC 88034-600
Tel: +55 48 3239 4757
Curriculum: IBDP, IBPYP
Language instr: English, Portuguese

Escola Lourenco Castanho
Rua Fiandeiras 77, Vila Olímpia, São Paulo SP 04545-000
Tel: +55 11 3047 0099
Age range: 15–18 years
No. of pupils: 300
Curriculum: IBDP
Language instr: English, Portuguese

Escola Nova
Rua Major Rubens Vaz, 392, Gávea, Rio de Janeiro RJ 22470-070
Tel: +55 21 3875 9899
Curriculum: IBDP
Language instr: English, Portuguese

Escola Suíço-Brasileira (ESB) by SIS Swiss International School
Rua Corrêa de Araújo 81, Barra da Tijuca, Rio de Janeiro RJ 22611-060
Tel: +55 21 33 89 20 89
Age range: 3–18 years
Curriculum: IBDP, IBMYP, IBPYP
Language instr: English, French, German, Portuguese

Escola Suíço-Brasileira de São Paulo
Rua Visconde de Porto Seguro 391, Alto da Boa Vista, São Paulo SP 04642-000
Tel: +55 11 5682 2140
Curriculum: IBDP, National
Language instr: German, English, Portuguese

GIS SP – The International School of São Paulo
Alameda dos Jurupis 485, Moema, São Paulo SP 04088-000
Tel: +55 11 3900 8931
Age range: 1.5–11 years
No. of pupils: 60
Curriculum: IBPYP
Language instr: English, Portuguese

Graded – The American School of São Paulo
Av. José Galante, 425, São Paulo SP 05642-000
Tel: +55 11 3747 4800
Age range: 2–18
No. of pupils: 1246
Curriculum: ACT, IBDP, SAT, USA
Language instr: English

International School of Curitiba
Ave. Eugenio Bertolli, 3900, Sta. Felicidade, Curitiba, Paraná PR 82410-530
Tel: +55 41 3525 7400
Age range: 3–19
No. of pupils: 681
Curriculum: IBDP, SAT, USA
Language instr: English

Land School
Av. Cardeal da Silva, No. 136, Federacao, Salvador, Bahia BA 40231-250
Tel: +55 71 3021 2550
Curriculum: IBMYP
Language instr: English, Portuguese

Lighthouse Ensino Bilíngue
Av. dos Expedicionários, 3548, Moradias Bom Jesus, Campo Largo, Paraná PR 83604-360
Tel: +55 (41) 3032 1222

Lycée Français François Mitterrand
SHIS QI 21 Bloco D, Lago Sul, Brasília DF 71655-580
Tel: +55 (61) 3246 9763
Curriculum: FrenchBacc

Lycée Pasteur (Lycée français de São Paulo / Unité Vergueiro)
Rua Vergueiro, 3799 – Vila Mariana, São Paulo SP 04101-300
Tel: +55 (11) 5904 7822
Curriculum: FrenchBacc

Pan American Christian Academy
Rua Cássio de Campos Nogueira, 393, São Paulo SP 04829-310
Tel: +55 11 5929 9500
Age range: 5–18
No. of pupils: 350
Curriculum: USA

Pan American School of Bahia
Av Ibirapitanga, Loteamento Patamares, s/n, Salvador, Bahia BH 41680-060
Tel: +55 71 3368 8400
Curriculum: IBDP, IBPYP

Pan American School of Porto Alegre
Av. João Obino 110, Petrópolis, Porto Alegre, Rio Grande do Sul RS 90470-150
Tel: +55 513 334 5866
Age range: 3–18
No. of pupils: 391 B191 G200
Curriculum: ACT, AP, IBMYP, IBPYP, National, SAT, USA
Language instr: English, Portuguese

PlayPen Escola Cidade Jardim
Praça Professor Américo de Moura, 101, São Paulo SP 05670-060
Tel: +55 1138 129122
Age range: 1–14
No. of pupils: 500
Curriculum: IPC, National
Language instr: English, Portuguese

Red House International School
Rua Engenheiro Edgar Egidio de Souza 444, Pacaembu SP 01233-020
Tel: +55 11 2309 7999
Curriculum: IBPYP
Language instr: English

Rio International School
Avenida Prefeito Dulcidio Cardoso, 4351, Barra da Tijuca, Rio de Janeiro RJ 22793-011
Tel: +55 (21) 97945 0088
Curriculum: USA

Saint Nicholas School
Av Eusébio Matoso 333, Pinheiros, São Paulo SP 05423-180
Tel: + 55 11 3465 9666
Curriculum: IBDP, IBPYP, IGCSE
Language instr: English

Sant'Anna International School
Av. Independência, 5588, Aquário, Vinhedo SP 13280-000
Tel: +55 19 3113 3777
Age range: 2–18
Curriculum: SAT, USA
Language instr: Portuguese

School of the Nations
SHIS QI 21 Área Especial Conjunto C1, Brasilia DF 71655-600
Tel: +55 61 3366 1800
Age range: 2–18 years
No. of pupils: 800
Curriculum: AP, USA
Language instr: English, Portuguese

SIS Swiss International School Brasília
SGA/SUL, Quadra 905, cj B, Brasília DF 70390-050
Tel: +55 61 34 43 41 45
Age range: 3–18 years
Curriculum: IBMYP, IBPYP
Language instr: English, Portuguese

Sphere International School
Av Anchieta, 908 – Jardim Nova Europa, Sao José dos Campos, São Paulo SP 12242-280
Tel: +55 11 9 7279 4340
Age range: 2–16 years
No. of pupils: 410
Curriculum: IBDP, IBMYP, IBPYP
Language instr: Portuguese, English

St Nicholas School – Alphaville Campus
Av. Honório Álvares Penteado, 5463, Tamboré, Santana de Parnaíba SP 06543-320
Tel: +55 11 3465 9658
Curriculum: IBMYP, IBPYP
Language instr: English, Portuguese

St. Francis College, Brazil
Rua Joaquim Antunes 678, Pinheiros, São Paulo SP 05415-001
Tel: +55 11 3728 8053
Age range: 3–18 years
No. of pupils: 850
Curriculum: IBDP, IBMYP, IBPYP, SAT, IGCSE
Language instr: English, Portuguese

ST. PAUL'S SCHOOL
For further details see p. 283
Rua Juquiá 166, Jardim Paulistano, São Paulo SP 01440-903
Tel: +55 11 3087 3399
Email: head@stpauls.br
Website: www.stpauls.br
Head Teacher: Titus Edge
Age range: 3–18 years
Curriculum: IBDP, UK, IGCSE
Language instr: English
COB

THE BRITISH COLLEGE OF BRAZIL
For further details see p. 286
Rua Álvares de Azevedo, 50, Chácara Flora, São Paulo SP 04671-040
Tel: +55 11 5547 3030
Email: info@britishcollegebrazil.org
Website: www.britishcollegebrazil.org
Headteacher: Nick West
Age range: 2–18 years
No. of pupils: 520
Curriculum: IBDP, UK, IGCSE
Language instr: English

The British School of Brasilia
EQS 708/907, Lote C, Asa Sul, Brasília DF 70390-079
Tel: +55 (61) 3248.3694
Curriculum: UK

THE BRITISH SCHOOL, RIO DE JANEIRO
For further details see p. 287
Rua Real Grandeza 99, Botafogo, Rio de Janeiro RJ 22281-030
Tel: +55 21 2539 2717
Email: edu@britishschool.g12.br
Website: www.britishschool.g12.br
Age range: 2–18 years
No. of pupils: 2234 B1037 G1197
Fees: Day R80,000
Curriculum: IBDP, IPC, National, UK, IGCSE
Language instr: English
CIS

The British School, Rio de Janeiro – Barra Site
Rua Mario Autuori, 100, Barra da Tijuca, RJ 22793
Tel: +55 21 3329 2854
Curriculum: IBDP

Valley International School
Av. Osvaldo Reis, 2000 Praia Brava, Itajai, Santa Catarina SC 88306-600
Tel: +55 47 3349 0969
Curriculum: IBPYP
Language instr: English, Portuguese

CHILE

Andrée English School
Avenida Principe de Gales 7605, La Reina, Santiago
Tel: +56 22 273 1027
Age range: 5–13
No. of pupils: 300

Antofagasta International School
Avenida Jaime Guzmán Errázuriz # 04300, Antofagasta
Tel: +56 55 694900
Language instr: English

Bradford School
Avada Luis Pateur 6335, Vitacura, Santiago
Tel: +56 (2) 29 12 31 40
Age range: 4–18
Curriculum: IBDP, UK

Caernarfon College
Fundo Mundo Nuevo, Ruta 68, Km. 65, Casablanca, Valparaíso
Tel: +56 (32) 2215 6193
Curriculum: IGCSE

Colegio Alemán Chicureo
Av. Alemania 170, Piedra Roja, Chicureo, Santiago
Tel: +56 223078962
Curriculum: IBMYP, IBPYP
Language instr: Spanish

Colegio Alemán de Concepción
Camino El Venado 1075, Andalué, San Pedro de la Paz, Concepción, Biobío
Tel: +56 41 2140000
No. of pupils: 1080
Curriculum: IBDP
Language instr: Spanish

Colegio Alemán de San Felipe de Aconcagua
60 CH N° 501 Panquehue, San Felipe, Valparaíso
Tel: +56 34 2 59 11 71
Age range: 3–17
No. of pupils: 343 B173 G170
Curriculum: IBDP
Language instr: Spanish

Colegio Alemán De Santiago
Nuestra Señora del Rosario 850, Las Condes, Santiago
Tel: +56 (2) 24246100

Colegio Alemán de Temuco
Avenida Holandesa 0855, Temuco, Araucanía
Tel: +56 45 963000
Curriculum: IBDP

Colegio Alemán de Valparaiso
Alvarez 2950, El Salto, Viña del Mar, Valparaíso
Tel: +56 32 216 1531
No. of pupils: 1252
Curriculum: IBDP
Language instr: Spanish

Colegio Alemán Los Angeles
Casilla 367, Av. Gabriela Mistral 1360 (ex 1751), Los Ángeles, Biobío
Tel: +56 43 2521111
Curriculum: IBDP

Colegio Alemán Puerto Varas
KM1, 4 Camino Ensenada, Puerto Varas, Los Lagos
Tel: +56 65 223 0450
Curriculum: IBPYP
Language instr: Spanish, German

Colegio Alemán St Thomas Morus
Avenida Pedro de Valdivia 320, Providencia, Santiago
Tel: +56 2 2729 1600
Curriculum: IBDP

Colegio Internacional SEK Chile
Avd Los Militares 6640, Las Condes, Santiago
Tel: +56 2 2127116
Curriculum: IBDP
Language instr: Spanish
ISA

Colegio Internacional SEK Pacifico
San Estanislao 50 Lomas de Montemar, Concón, Valparaíso
Tel: +56 32 2275700
Curriculum: IBDP, IBPYP
Language instr: English, Spanish
ISA

Colegio 'La Maisonnette'
Avda Luis Pasteur 6076, Vitacura, Santiago
Tel: +56 2 228162945
Curriculum: IBDP
Language instr: Spanish

Colegio Manquecura – Ciudad de Los Valles
Av. Del Canal 19877, Ruta 68, Pudahuel, Santiago
Tel: +56 2601 6025
Language instr: Spanish

Colegio Manquecura – Ciudad del Este
Avenida Diego Portales, Puente Alto, 07045 Santiago
Tel: +56 2267 1421
Language instr: Spanish

Colegio Manquecura – Valle lo Campino
Camino el Cerro, Quilicura, Santiago
Tel: +56 2249 0005
Language instr: Spanish

Colegio Pumahue – Chicuero
Camino Santa Elena 215, Santiago
Tel: +56 229 467 010
Language instr: Spanish

Colegio Pumahue – Curauma
Nudo Curauma 495, Valparaiso
Tel: +56 322 294 073
Language instr: Spanish

Colegio Pumahue – Huechuraba
Santa Rosa de Huechuraba 7201, Santiago
Tel: +56 227 210 080
Language instr: Spanish

Colegio Pumahue – Peñalolen
Av. Quilín 8200, Santiago
Tel: +56 222 988 412
Language instr: Spanish

Colegio Pumahue – Puerto Montt
Volcán Puntiagudo 1700, Puerto Montt, Los Lagos
Tel: +56 652 435 766
Language instr: Spanish

Colegio Pumahue – Temuco
Av. Martín Lutero 0200,
Temuco, Araucanía
Tel: +56 45 2 26 95 45
Language instr: Spanish

Craighouse School
Casilla 20 007, Correo 20., Santiago
Tel: +56 2 227560218
Age range: 3–18
No. of pupils: 1877
Curriculum: IBDP, IBMYP, IBPYP
Language instr: English, Spanish

Dunalastair Chicureo
Camino del Solar s/n,
Colina, Santiago
Tel: +56 22673 6097
No. of pupils: 1295 *B*648 *G*647
Language instr: English, Spanish

Dunalastair Las Condes
Av. Las Condes 11.931, Las
Condes, Santiago
Tel: +56 22495 6600
Age range: 3–18
No. of pupils: 1400
Curriculum: ALevs
Language instr: Spanish

Dunalastair Peñalolén
Av. Quilín 8411 Peñalolén, Santiago
Tel: +56 22592 0240

Instituto Alemán Carlos Anwandter
Los Laureles 050, Casilla
2-D, Valdivia, Los Ríos
Tel: +56 63 2471100
Curriculum: IBDP
Language instr: Spanish

Instituto Alemán de Osorno
Los Carreras 818, Osorno, Los Lagos
Tel: +56 64 233 1800/1805
Curriculum: IBDP, IBMYP, IBPYP
Language instr: Spanish

Instituto Alemán Puerto Montt
Bernardo Phillipi #350,
Sector Seminario, 5480000
Puerto Montt, Los Lagos
Tel: +56 65 2 252560
Curriculum: IBPYP
Language instr: Spanish

Instituto Chileno Britanico de Cultura
Santa Lucia 124, Santiago
Tel: +56 2 241 320 00
Age range: 6–19

International Preparatory School
PO Box 20015, Las
Condes, Santiago
Tel: +56 2 321 5800
Age range: 3–18
No. of pupils: 141 *B*83 *G*58
Curriculum: UK
COB

International School Nido de Aguilas
Av. El Rodeo 14200, Lo
Barnechea, Santiago
Tel: +56 2 2339 8100
Age range: 3–18 years
No. of pupils: 1600
Curriculum: ACT, IBDP, SAT, USA
Language instr: English, Spanish

Lincoln International Academy – Campus Lo Barnechea
Av. Las Condes 13.150, Lo
Barnechea, Santiago
Tel: +56 2 2 496 76 00
Age range: 3–18
No. of pupils: 486
Curriculum: USA

Lycée Antoine-de-Saint-Exupéry
Av. Luis Pasteur 5418,
Vitacura, Santiago
Tel: +56 2 28 27 82 00
Curriculum: FrenchBacc

Lycée Charles de Gaulle
Colo Colo 51, Concepción, Biobío
Tel: +56 41 262 7000

Lyceé Claude Gay
Las Quemas S/N Loteo
4A, Osorno, Los Lagos
Tel: +56 (64) 454 811

Lycée Jean d'Alembert
Avenida Las Perdices No 450,
Reñaca, Viña del Mar, Valparaíso
Tel: +56 32 251 2000

Mackay School
Vicuña Mackenna 700,
Viña del Mar, Valparaíso
Tel: +56 32 2386614
Age range: *B*4–18
No. of pupils: 880
Curriculum: IBDP, IBMYP,
IBPYP, National
Language instr: Spanish, English

Redland School
Camino El Alba 11357, Las
Condes, 7600022 Santiago
Tel: +56 2 29598500
Age range: 4–18
No. of pupils: 842 *B*420 *G*422
Curriculum: IBDP, IBMYP, IBPYP
Language instr: Spanish

Saint Gabriel's School
Avda Fco Bilbao 3070,
Providencia, Santiago
Tel: +56 22 462 5400
Age range: 4–18
Curriculum: IBDP, National, IGCSE
Language instr: English,
Spanish (5th-12th grade)

Santiago College
Av. Camino Los Trapenses 4007,
Lo Barnechea, Santiago
Tel: +56 2 27338800
Age range: 3 years 9
months–18 years
No. of pupils: 1970
Curriculum: IBDP, IBMYP, IBPYP
Language instr: Spanish, English
CIS ECIS

St John's School
Fundo el Venado, San Pedro de
la Paz, Concepción, Biobío
Tel: +56 41 2466440
Age range: 4–18
No. of pupils: 1348
Curriculum: IBDP, IBMYP,
IBPYP, National, IGCSE
Language instr: English, Spanish

St Margaret's British School For Girls
Casilla 392, Viña del
Mar, Valparaíso
Tel: +56 32 245 1700
Curriculum: IBDP
Language instr: Spanish, English

St Paul's School
Merced Oriente 54, Viña
del Mar, Valparaíso
Tel: (56 32) 314 2200
Curriculum: IBPYP
Language instr: English, Spanish

St Peter's School
Av. Libertad 575, Viña
del Mar, Valparaíso
Tel: +56 32 238 1400
Curriculum: UK

The American School
Michimahuida 301 Volcano,
Volcanoes Valle, Puerto
Montt, Los Lagos
Tel: +56 65 2383364
Age range: 4–18
Curriculum: SAT, USA

The Antofagasta British School
Pedro León Gallo 723, Antofagasta
Tel: +55 2 598931
Curriculum: IBDP, IBMYP, IBPYP
Language instr: English, Spanish

The British School – Punta Arenas
Waldo Seguel 454, Punta
Arenas, Magallanes
Tel: +56 61 2 22 33 81
Age range: 4–18
No. of pupils: 600
Curriculum: IBDP, IBMYP, IBPYP
Language instr: Spanish, English

The Grange School
Príncipe de Gales 6154,
La Reina, Santiago
Tel: +56 2 2598 1500
Age range: 4–18
Curriculum: National,
UK, IGCSE, ALevs
Language instr: English, Spanish

The Mayflower School
Avda Las Condes 12 167,
Las Condes, Santiago
Tel: +56 22 3523100
Age range: 4–18
Curriculum: IBDP, IBPYP, ALevs
Language instr: Spanish

The Wessex School
Granada 314-A, Vilumanque,
4081022 Concepción, Biobío
Tel: +56 41 238 7280
Age range: 3–18
No. of pupils: 695 *B*345 *G*350
Language instr: English
(Junior), Spanish (Senior)

Trebulco School
Camino Carampangue
550, Talagante, Santiago
Tel: +56 2 815 7550
Age range: 3–17
Language instr: English

Wenlock School
Casilla 27169, Correo 27, Santiago
Tel: +56 223631803
Age range: 3–18
No. of pupils: 780 *B*390 *G*390
Curriculum: IBDP,
National, UK, IGCSE
Language instr: Spanish

COLOMBIA

Altamira International School
Km 10 Autopista, Puerto, Atlántico
Tel: +57 (5) 385 35 77
Age range: 4–18
No. of pupils: 650
Curriculum: SAT, USA

Asociación Colegio Granadino
AA 2138, Manizales, Caldas
Tel: +57 (6) 874 57 74
Age range: 3–18
No. of pupils: 600 *B*295 *G*305
Language instr: English, Spanish

Aspaen Gimnasio Iragua
Av. Calle 170, No. 76-55, Barrio San
José de Bavaria, Bogotá, D.C.
Tel: +57 (1) 667 95 00
Curriculum: IBDP
Language instr: Spanish

Aspaen Liceo Tacuri
Callejon de la Viga Pance, Cll 22 and 23, Cali, Valle del Cauca
Tel: +57 (2) 555 75 02
Age range: 4–18
No. of pupils: 184

British International School
Apartado Aéreo 4368, Barranquilla, Atlántico
Tel: +57 (5) 359 92 43
Curriculum: IBDP, IBMYP
Language instr: English

Buckingham School
Cra 52 No 214 – 55, Bogotá, D.C.
Tel: +57 (1) 676 08 12
Age range: 3–17
Curriculum: IBDP, IBMYP, IBPYP, National
Language instr: English, Spanish

CAS Colombo American School
Carrera 73 No. 214-53, Bogotá, D.C.
Tel: +57 31 668 50 77
Curriculum: IBPYP
Language instr: English, Spanish

CIEDI – Colegio Internacional de Educación Integral
Km 3 vía Suba-Cota, Bogotá, D.C.
Tel: +57 (1) 683 06 04
Curriculum: IBDP, IBMYP, IBPYP
Language instr: Spanish, English

Colegio Abraham Lincoln
Av. Calle 170 # 65 31, Bogotá, D.C.
Tel: +57 (1) 742 31 66
Curriculum: IBDP
Language instr: Spanish

Colegio Albania
Calle 15 3-00, Campamento de Mushaisa, Cerrejón La Mina, La Guajira
Tel: +57 (5) 350 56 48
Curriculum: IBDP, IBMYP, IBPYP
Language instr: Spanish, English

Colegio Alemán
Autopista al Mar poste 89 Electricaribe, Baranquilla, Atlántico
Tel: +57 (5) 359 85 20
No. of pupils: 1000
Curriculum: IBDP
Language instr: Spanish

Colegio Americano
Carrera 89 No 4c-35B Melendez, Cali, Valle del Cauca
Tel: +57 (2) 332 58 40
Curriculum: USA

Colegio Andino – Deutsche Schule
Cra 51 No 218-85, Bogotá, D.C.
Tel: +57 (1) 668 42 50

Colegio Anglo-Colombiano
Apartado Aéreo 253393, Avenida 19 N° 152A-48, Santa Fé, Bogotá, D.C.
Tel: +57 (1) 259 57 00
Age range: 4–18
Curriculum: IBDP, IBMYP, IBPYP, National, UK
Language instr: Spanish, English

Colegio Bolivar
Calle. 5 #122-21, Cali, Valle del Cauca
Tel: +57 (2) 485 50 50
Curriculum: USA

Colegio Británico – The British School
Call 18 # 142-255 (Esquina), La Viga, Pance, Cali, Valle del Cauca
Tel: +57 (2) 555 75 45
Curriculum: IBDP

Colegio Británico de Cartagena
Anillo Vial Km. 12, Cartagena, Bolívar 130001
Tel: +57 5 693 0982 83 84
Curriculum: IBDP
Language instr: English, Spanish

Colegio Británico de Montería
Calle 65 No. 9-100, Montería
Tel: +57 3 227 71 82 91
Curriculum: IBPYP
Language instr: English, Spanish

Colegio Bureche
Troncal del Caribe Km2 vía Gaira, Santa Marta, Magdalena
Tel: +57 430 22 26
Curriculum: National, USA

Colegio Cambridge
Sede Cajicá, Kilómetro 2 Vía Cajicá, Chía Vereda El Canelón, Cajicá, Cundinamarca
Tel: +1 601 746 4737
Curriculum: IBDP
Language instr: English, Spanish

Colegio Canadiense
Carrera 51 # 97 Sur 137, Sector Sierra Morena, Itagüi, Antioquia
Tel: +57 (4) 279 88 48

Colegio Colombo Británico
Avenida La Maria 69 Pance, Pance, Cali, Valle del Cauca
Tel: +57 (2) 555 53 85
Age range: 2–18
No. of pupils: 1260 B634 G626
Curriculum: ACT, IBDP, IBMYP, IBPYP, National, SAT
Language instr: English, Spanish

Colegio Colombo Gales
Avenida Guaymaral, Costado sur Aeropuerto, Bogotá, D.C.
Tel: +57 (1) 668 49 10
No. of pupils: 808
Curriculum: IBDP, IBPYP

Colegio de Cambridge (Cambridge International School)
Vereda La Aurora, Municipio La Calera, Bogotá, D.C.
Tel: +57 (1) 593 18 90
Curriculum: IBDP
Language instr: Spanish

Colegio de Inglaterra – The English School
Calle 170 #15-68, Bogotá, D.C.
Tel: +57 (1) 676 77 00
Age range: 2–18 years
Curriculum: IBDP, IBMYP, IBPYP
Language instr: English, Spanish

Colegio Domingo Savio
Calle 24 Sur #24 f-16, Bogotá, D.C.
Tel: +57 366 61 63
Curriculum: IBMYP
Language instr: English, Spanish

Colegio Gran Bretaña
Carrera 51 No 215-20, Bogotá, D.C.
Tel: +57 (1) 676 03 91
Age range: 3–18
No. of pupils: 535 B265 G270
Curriculum: IBDP, IPC, National, UK, IGCSE
Language instr: English

Colegio Hacienda Los Alcaparros
Vía Bogotá La Calera, Vereda el Salitre, km 3, Bogotá, D.C.
Tel: +57 (1) 592 22 66
Age range: 3–18
Curriculum: USA
Language instr: English, Spanish, Portuguese

Colegio Helvetia
Calle 128 no 71A-91, Santa Fé, Bogotá, D.C.
Tel: +57 (1) 624 73 74
Age range: 4–19

Colegio Inglés de los Andes
Km 4 Vía Cali Puerto Tejada, Cali, Valle del Cauca
Tel: +57 550 43 11
Curriculum: UK, IGCSE

Colegio Internacional de Bogota
Carrera 49 no 202-85, Apartado Aereo 103314, Bogotá, D.C.
Tel: +57 (1) 676 22 00
Language instr: English

Colegio Internacional Los Cañaverales
Carrera 29 No 10-500, Arroyohonfo, Vía Dapa Km 1 Yumbo, Yumbo, Valle del Cauca
Tel: +57 (2) 658 28 18
Curriculum: IBDP
Language instr: English

Colegio Karl C. Parrish
Km. 2 Antigua Via a Puerto Colombia, Barranquilla, Atlántico
Tel: +57 (5) 359 89 29

Colegio Los Ángeles Tunja
Calle 73A No. 2-02 E, Altos de la Arboleda, Tunja, Boyacá
Tel: +57 304 380 8353
Curriculum: IBDP
Language instr: English, Spanish

Colegio Los Nogales
Calle 202 # 56 – 50, Bogotá, D.C.
Tel: +57 (1) 676 11 28
Age range: 4–18
No. of pupils: B451 G517
Curriculum: AP, National, SAT, USA
Language instr: English, Spanish

Colegio Los Tréboles
Vereda cerca de Piedra, Finca Santa Elena, Chía, Cundinamarca
Tel: +57 (1) 862 48 30
Age range: 4–18
No. of pupils: 250
Curriculum: IBDP
Language instr: Spanish

Colegio Marymount Barranquilla
Km. 5, Via a Sabanilla, Barranquilla, Atlántico
Tel: +57 (5) 388 50 20
Age range: 3–18
No. of pupils: 986
Curriculum: National
Language instr: Spanish, English

Colegio Mayor de los Andes
Kilómetro 3 vía Chía, Cajicá, Cundinamarca
Tel: +57 (1) 866 29 56
Curriculum: IBDP

Colegio Nueva Granada
Cra 2 Este # 70-20, Bogotá, D.C.
Tel: +57 (1) 212 35 11
Language instr: English

Colegio Nueva Inglaterra (New England School)
Calle 218, No. 50-60, Bogotá, D.C.
Tel: +57 (1) 676 07 88
Curriculum: IBDP
Language instr: Spanish

Colegio Panamericano
Calle 34 No. 8 -73 Cañaveral Alto, Floridablanca, Bucaramanga, Santander
Tel: +57 (7) 638 62 13
Curriculum: National

Colegio San Mateo
Calle 215 #50-24, Bogotá, D.C.
Tel: +57 1 676 08 85
Age range: 4–18 years
Language instr: English, Spanish

Colegio San Viator – Sede Bogotá
Autopista Norte 209-51, Bogotá, D.C.
Tel: +57 (1) 676 09 97
Curriculum: IBDP, IBMYP, IBPYP
Language instr: English

Colegio San Viator – Sede Tunja
Av Universitaria 62 – 100, Tunja, Boyacá
Curriculum: IBDP
Language instr: English, Spanish

Colegio Santa Francisca Romana
Calle 151 No. 16 – 40, Bogotá, D.C.
Tel: +57 1 580 44 44
Age range: 4–18 years
Curriculum: IBDP
Language instr: English, Spanish

Colegio Santa Maria
Carrera 11 #185B-17, Bogotá, D.C.
Tel: +57 (1) 671 44 40
Age range: G4–18
No. of pupils: 1000

Colegio Tilatá
Kilómetro 9 vía La Calera, Bogotá, D.C.
Tel: +57 (1) 592 14 14
Curriculum: IBDP, IBMYP, IBPYP

Deutsche Schule – Cali / Kolumbien
Avenida Gualí N° 31, Barrio Ciudad Jardín, Cali, Valle del Cauca
Tel: +57 (2) 685 89 00
Curriculum: IBDP
Language instr: German, Spanish

Deutsche Schule Medellín
Cra 61, No. 34-62, Itagüi, Antioquia
Tel: +57 (604) 2818811 (Ext:100)
Curriculum: IBDP
Language instr: Spanish

El Camino Academy
Calle 221 #52-30, Bogotá, D.C.
Tel: +57 (1) 742 23 30
Curriculum: National, USA

Fundacion Gimnasio Ingles de Armenia (GI SCHOOL)
KM.3 Via Armenia-Circasia, Salento, Quindío 630007
Tel: +57 6 749 51 11
Curriculum: IBDP, National, USA
Language instr: English, Spanish

Fundación Gimnasio Los Portales
Calle 212 No. 77- 20, Bogotá, D.C.
Tel: +57 (1) 676 40 55
Curriculum: IBDP, IBMYP, IBPYP
Language instr: English, Spanish

Fundacion Liceo Ingles (Pereira)
Km 5 Via Cerritos Entrada 17, Pereira, Risaralda
Tel: +57 (6) 320 55 63
Age range: 2–18
No. of pupils: 680
Curriculum: SAT, USA

Fundación Nuevo Marymount
Calle 169B, No 74A-02, Bogotá, D.C.
Tel: +57 (1) 669 90 77
Age range: G3–18
Curriculum: IBDP
Language instr: Spanish

GCB – Bilingüe Internacional
Costado Sur – Occidental Aeropuerto Guaymaral, Bogotá, D.C.
Tel: +57 1 668 39 99
Curriculum: IBDP
Language instr: English, Spanish

George Washington School
Apartado Aereo 2899, Cartagena, Bolívar
Tel: +57 (5) 665 31 36
Age range: 4–18
No. of pupils: 523 *B257 G266*
Curriculum: AP, SAT

Gimnasio Británico
Calle 21 No 9A-58, Avenida Chilacos, Chía, Cundinamarca
Tel: +57 (1) 861 50 84
Age range: 2–16
No. of pupils: 1500
Curriculum: IBDP
Language instr: Spanish, English, French

Gimnasio Campestre la Fontana
Km 4 Vereda El Amor, Vía Multf. Centauros, Villavicencio, Meta
Tel: +57 314 279 7928
Curriculum: IBDP
Language instr: English, Spanish

Gimnasio Campestre Los Cerezos
Vereda Canelón, Cajicá, Cundinamarca
Tel: +57 866 26 79
Curriculum: IBDP, IBPYP

Gimnasio Campestre San Rafael
Sede Campestre, Km 6 vía Siberia, Tenjo, Cundinamarca
Tel: +57 593 30 40
Curriculum: IBDP
Language instr: Spanish

Gimnasio Cantillana
Vereda La Mata, Menzuly Sector, Highway Piedecuesta, Floridablanca, Bucaramanga, Santander
Tel: +57 (7) 655 91 01
Curriculum: UK

Gimnasio Contemporaneo
Cra. 6 #29 Norte-648 a 29 Norte-1034, Salento, Quindío
Tel: +57 310 4322191
Curriculum: IBDP
Language instr: English, Spanish

Gimnasio de Los Cerros
Calle 119 N° 0-68, Usaquén, Santa Fé, Bogotá, D.C.
Tel: +57 (1) 657 60 00
Curriculum: IBDP
Language instr: Spanish

Gimnasio del Norte
Calle 207 N° 70 – 50, Bogotá, D.C.
Tel: +57 (1) 668 39 39
Curriculum: IBDP, IBMYP, IBPYP
Language instr: Spanish, English

Gimnasio El Hontanar
Cra. 76 No. 150-26, Bogotá, D.C.
Tel: +57 (1) 681 52 87
Curriculum: IBDP
Language instr: English, Spanish

Gimnasio Femenino
K7 #128-40, Bogotá, D.C.
Tel: +57 (1) 657 84 20
Age range: G4–19
No. of pupils: 600
Curriculum: IBDP, IBMYP, IBPYP
Language instr: Spanish, English

Gimnasio Fontana
Calle 221#108-20, Guaymaral, Bogotá, D.C.
Tel: +57 (1) 742 03 03 (Ext:122-123)
Age range: 4–18
No. of pupils: 922 *B465 G457*
Curriculum: National, TOEFL
Language instr: Spanish, English, French

Gimnasio Los Alcázares
Calle 63 Sur No 41-05 Sabaneta, Medellín, Antioquia
Tel: +57 (4) 305 40 00
Curriculum: IBDP
Language instr: Spanish

Gimnasio Los Pinares
Carrera 35 No. 9 sur 160, Medellín, Antioquia
Tel: +57 (4) 268 60 34
Curriculum: National, UK, IGCSE

Gimnasio Los Pinos
Calle 193 #38-20, Bogotá, D.C.
Tel: +57 1 670 00 08
Curriculum: IBPYP
Language instr: English, Spanish

Gimnasio Vermont
Cl 195 No 54-75, Bogotá, D.C.
Tel: +57 (1) 674 80 70
Age range: 4–18
No. of pupils: 1577
Curriculum: IBDP
Language instr: Spanish

International Berckley School
Km 5 – Vía al Mar, Poste 115, Barranquilla, Atlántico
Tel: +575 354 81 31
Curriculum: IBDP
Language instr: Spanish

Jardín Infantil Tía Nora y Liceo Los Alpes
Av 8 Norte, No. 66-05 Urbanización Menga, Cali, Valle del Cauca
Tel: +57 (2) 665 41 20
Curriculum: IBDP, IBMYP, IBPYP
Language instr: English, Spanish

KSI Bogotá
Calle 221 No 115-51, Bogotá, D.C.
Tel: +57 (1) 676 29 02
Age range: 4–18 years
No. of pupils: 229
Curriculum: IBDP, IBPYP
Language instr: English, Spanish

La Colina School
Km 9.5 Via La Calera Vda Salitre, Bogotá, D.C.
Tel: +57 (1) 439 13 74
Age range: 4–18
No. of pupils: 800
Curriculum: USA
Language instr: Spanish

La Sierra International School
KM 2.5 Vía Los Besotes Después, del Seminario Juan Pablo II, Valledupar, Cesar
Tel: +57 314 501 76 48
Curriculum: USA

Liceo Francés de Pereira
Kilometro 5 vía Armenia, Pereira, Risaralda
Tel: +57 (6) 315 23 55
Curriculum: National

Liceo Pino Verde
Vereda Los Planes kilometro, 5 Vía Cerritos Entrada 16, El Tigre, Pereira, Risaralda
Tel: +57 (6) 313 26 68
Curriculum: IBDP, IBPYP

Lycée Français Louis Pasteur
Calle 87 #7-77, Bogotá, D.C.
Tel: +57 (1) 796 50 40

Lycée français Paul-Valéry
Calle 50 N #4AN-56, Cali, Valle del Cauca
Tel: +57 (2) 485 58 50
Curriculum: National, FrenchBacc, UK

Marymount School – Medellín
Calle 7 No 25-64, Medellín, Antioquia
Tel: +57 (4) 266 15 55
Age range: G3–18
No. of pupils: 950
Curriculum: National
Language instr: Spanish, English

Montessori British School, Bogota
Calle 128 #72-80 Calatrava, Bogotá, D.C.
Tel: +57 (1) 652 85 85

Neil Armstrong School
Dir. Cr 44 Cl 14 El Buque, Villavicencio
Curriculum: IBDP
Language instr: English, Spanish

New Cambridge School Bucaramanga – Sede Cabecera
Cra. 39 No. 44-72, Bucaramanga, Santander
Tel: +57 7 638 61 52
Curriculum: IBDP, IGCSE, ALevs
Language instr: English, Spanish

New Cambridge School Bucaramanga – Sede Cañaveral
Calle 32 No. 22-140, Floridablanca, Bucaramanga, Santander
Tel: +57 7 638 61 52
Curriculum: IBDP
Language instr: English, Spanish

Nuevo Gimnasio School
Kilometro 1 Autopista, Villavicencio, Meta
Tel: +57 310 801 52 83
Curriculum: IBDP
Language instr: English, Spanish

The Columbus School
Vda. El Penasco, Envigado, Antioquia
Tel: +57 (4) 403 30 00
Curriculum: National, USA

The Victoria School
Calle 215 N° 50-60, Bogotá, D.C.
Tel: +57 (1) 676 15 03
Age range: 3–18
No. of pupils: 510
Curriculum: IBDP, IBMYP, IBPYP
Language instr: English, Spanish

Vermont School Medellín
Avenida Las Palmas Indiana Mall Km. 2 Vía La Fe, El Retiro, Antioquia
Tel: +57 (4) 520 60 60
Curriculum: IBDP
Language instr: English, Spanish

CURAÇAO

International School of Curaçao
PO Box 3090, Koninginnelaan z/n, Emmastad
Tel: +599 9 737 3633
Age range: 2–19
No. of pupils: 375
Curriculum: ACT, AP, IBDP, IBMYP, SAT, TOEFL, USA
Language instr: English

The Curacao American Preparatory School
Erosweg 69, Willemstad
Tel: +599 9 736 8674
Curriculum: USA

GUYANA

Georgetown International Academy
9-10 Delhi Street, Prashbad Nagar, Georgetown
Tel: +592 226 1595
Age range: 4–18
No. of pupils: 64 B31 G33
Curriculum: AP, SAT

HONDURAS

Academia Los Pinares
KM 10 El Hatillo, Apartado 3250, Tegucigalpa
Tel: + 504 2211 8231
No. of pupils: 729
Curriculum: USA

Albert Einstein International School
2 Calle, 11-12 Avenida NO, Los Andes #88, San Pedro Sula Cortes 21102
Tel: +504 2550 4622
Curriculum: National, USA

DelCampo School
P.O. Box 2100, Tegucigalpa
Tel: +504 2268 1820
Curriculum: USA

Discovery School
Zona El Molinón, Anillo Periférico, Salida a Valle de Angeles, Tegucigalpa
Tel: +504 2221 7790

Escuela Internacional Sampedrana
Col. Gracias a Dios, 500 metros arriba Blvd Hospital Catarino Rivas, San Pedro Sula
Tel: + 504 2540 2722
Age range: 4–18
Curriculum: USA

Happy Days School & Freedom High School
Km 2 carretera al Zapotal, San Pedro Sula
Tel: +504 2551 1501
Age range: 4–18
Curriculum: National, USA
Language instr: English, Spanish

Lycee Franco Hondurien
Col. las colinas, Boulevard francia calle principal, 11101 Tegucigalpa, Francisco Morazan
Tel: +504 2231 1472
Curriculum: FrenchBacc

Mazapan School
La Ceiba
Tel: +1 504 443 2716
Age range: 3–17
Curriculum: USA

The American School of Tegucigalpa
P.O. Box 2134, Tegucigalpa
Tel: +504 2276 8400
Age range: 3–18 years
No. of pupils: 1117
Curriculum: IBDP, USA
Language instr: English

PANAMA

Academia Internacional Arabe Panamena
Naciones Unidas Street, Colon
Tel: +507 474 071 3/4/5
Age range: 4–18
Language instr: English

Balboa Academy
Apartado 0843-02777, Panama
Tel: +507 302 0035
Age range: 3–18
Curriculum: USA
Language instr: English

Boston School International
Ave. Arnulfo Arias Madrid Building. #727, Balboa, Ancón, Panama City
Tel: +507 833 8888
Age range: 3–18
Curriculum: IBDP, IBPYP
Language instr: English

Caribbean International School
Box 0301 03289, Cristobel, Colon
Tel: +507 445 0933/0961
Age range: 3–18
No. of pupils: 672
Curriculum: AP, National, USA

Colegio Isaac Rabin
Edificio 130, Ciudad del Saber
Tel: +507 3170059
Curriculum: IBDP, IBMYP, IBPYP
Language instr: Spanish

International School of Panama
P.O. Box 0819-02588, Cerro Viento Rural, Panama City
Tel: +507 293 3000
Age range: 3–18
No. of pupils: 1262
Curriculum: ACT, IBDP, National, SAT, USA
Language instr: English

King's College, The British School of Panama
Edificio 518, Calle al Hospital, Clayton
Tel: +507 282 3300
Age range: 3–18 years
Curriculum: IBDP, UK, IGCSE, ALevs
Language instr: English, Spanish

METROPOLITAN SCHOOL OF PANAMA
For further details see p. 284
Green Valley, Panama Norte, Panama City
Tel: +507 317 1130
Email: admissions@themetropolitanschool.com
Website: www.themetropolitanschool.com
Headteacher: Daniel McKee
Age range: 3–18 years
No. of pupils: 755
Fees: Day $10,149–$20,169
Curriculum: IBDP, IBMYP, IBPYP, National
Language instr: English, Spanish

Oxford International School
74th East Street and Via España, Carrasquilla, Panama City
Tel: +507 308 7100
Age range: 4–18
No. of pupils: 1264
Language instr: English

Panama Preparatory School
Camino al nuevo Club de Golf, Brisas del Golf, Panama
Tel: +507 220 2520

SABIS International School – Costa Verde
Paseo de los Guayacanes y Av. Circunvalación, Costa Verde
Tel: +507 209 2606

The Oxford School
Edison Park, Via Simon Bolivar, Apartado 6-7247, El Dorado
Tel: +507 321 3800
Age range: 4–18

PARAGUAY

American School of Asunción
Avenida España 1175, PO Box 10093, Asunción
Tel: +595 21 236 4000
Age range: 4–18
No. of pupils: 640
Curriculum: National, USA

Asuncion Christian Academy
Avenida Santísimo Sacramento 1181, Casilla 1562, Asuncion 1209
Tel: +595 (21) 612-477
Curriculum: USA

Centro Educativo Arambé
Santísima Trinidad No 3.211, c/ Avda. Ita Ybaté (Zona Brítez Cue), Luque, Asunción
Tel: +595 21 694 662
Curriculum: IBDP
Language instr: Spanish

Colegio Goethe Asunción
Cnl Silva esq Tte Rochholl, Asuncion 232
Tel: +595 21 606860
Curriculum: IBDP

Colegio International SEK Paraguay
C/Mercedes Grau-Parques del Yacht y Golf Club, Asunción
Tel: +595 21 907650
Curriculum: IBDP
Language instr: Spanish

Colegio San Andrés
Avenue General Santos 567 Esp. Juan de Salazar, Asuncion
Tel: +595 21 221 647
Curriculum: UK, IGCSE, ALevs

Faith Christian School
Del Maestro 3471 c/ Soriano González, Barrio Herrera, Asunción
Tel: +595 21 620 5024
Curriculum: IBDP
Language instr: English, Spanish

Lycée Français d'Asunción Marcel Pagnol
Enrique Solano López 1139, Calle Concordia, Asuncion
Tel: 00 595 21 207083
Curriculum: FrenchBacc

Pan American International School
Calle América esq. 2da Capital de la República, Urb. Loma Merlo, Luque
Tel: +595 21 645 470
Age range: 4–18
No. of pupils: 200
Curriculum: USA

Santa Teresa de Jesús
Avda. Mcal. López 237 c/ Brasil, Asunción 927
Tel: +595 21 224683
Language instr: English

St Anne's School
Tte. Manuel Pino Gonzalez y Eulalio Facetti, Asunción
Tel: +595 21 295649
Age range: 4–18
No. of pupils: 600 *B*300 *G*300
Curriculum: IBDP
Language instr: English, Spanish

PERU

American School
Av. Larco Nro 288, Urb. San Andrés, Trujillo, La Libertad 13008
Tel: +51 44 612370
Curriculum: IBDP
Language instr: English, Spanish

Andino Cusco International School
Km 10.5 Carretera, Chinchero Distrito de Cachimayo, Cusco
Tel: +51 84 275135
Curriculum: IBDP, IBPYP
Language instr: English, Spanish

Cambridge College Lima
Av. Alemeda de los Molinos 728-730, La Encantada de Villa, Chorrillos, Lima 15067
Tel: +51 12 540107
Age range: 4–18 years
Curriculum: IBDP
Language instr: English, Spanish

Casuarinas International College
Av Jacarandá 391, Valle Hermoso, Monterrico, Santiago de Surco, Lima 15023
Tel: +51 13 444040
Age range: 4–17
No. of pupils: 881
Curriculum: IBDP, IBMYP, IBPYP, IBCP
Language instr: Spanish, English, French, Portuguese, Mandarin

Clemente Althaus
Prolongación Jirón Cuzco 360, San Miguel – Alt. Cdra. 12 Av. La Marina, Lima 15086
Tel: +51 14 194700
Curriculum: IBDP
Language instr: Spanish

Colegio Alpamayo
Calle Bucaramanga 145, Urb Mayorazgo, Lima 15026
Tel: +51 13 490111
Age range: *B*5–17
Curriculum: IBDP
Language instr: Spanish, English

Colegio Altair
Av. La Arboleda 385, Urb. Sirius, La Molina, Lima 15024
Tel: +51 13 650298
Age range: 2–18 years
No. of pupils: 900
Curriculum: IBDP, IBMYP, IBPYP
Language instr: Spanish, English

Colegio Champagnat
Paseo de la República 7930, Santiago de Surco, Lima 15049
Tel: +51 15 1905000
Curriculum: IBDP, IBMYP, IBPYP
Language instr: Spanish

Colegio Franklin Delano Roosevelt
Av. Las Palmeras 325, Camacho, Lima 15023
Tel: +51 14 350890
Age range: 3–18
No. of pupils: 1218 *B*687 *G*531
Curriculum: AP, IBDP, SAT
Language instr: English, Spanish

Colegio La Unión
Av. Cipriano Dulanto 1950, Pueblo Libre, Lima 15084
Tel: +51 12 610533
Curriculum: IBDP
Language instr: English

Colegio León Pinelo
Calle Maimónides 610 (ex Los Manzanos), San Isidro, Lima 15076
Tel: +51 12 183040
Age range: 3–17
Curriculum: IBDP, IBMYP, IBPYP, IGCSE
Language instr: Spanish

Colegio Los Álamos
Calle Estados Unidos 731, Jesús María, Lima 15701
Tel: +51 14 631044
Curriculum: IBDP

Colegio Magister
Calle Francisco de Cuéllar 686, Monterrico, Santiago de Surco, Lima
Tel: +51 14 363063
Age range: 3–17
Curriculum: IBDP, National, TOEFL
Language instr: Spanish

Colegio Mater Admirabilis
Av. Arica 898, San Miguel, Lima
Curriculum: IBMYP
Language instr: Spanish

Colegio Max Uhle
Av. Fernandini s/n, Sachaca, Arequipa 04013
Tel: +51 54 232921
No. of pupils: 1165
Curriculum: IBDP
Language instr: Spanish

Colegio Montealto
Los Eucaliptos 491, San Isidro, Lima
Tel: +51 441 2685
Curriculum: IBDP
Language instr: Spanish

Colegio Nuestra Señora del Pilar
Av. Virgen del Pilar 1711, Cercado, Arequipa
Tel: +51 54 226262
Curriculum: IBDP

Colegio Peruano – Alemán Reina del Mundo
Avenida Rinconada del Lago 675, La Molina, Lima
Tel: +51 14 792191
Age range: 2–17
No. of pupils: 771
Curriculum: IBDP
Language instr: Spanish

Colegio Peruano Alemán Beata Imelda
Carretera Central Km 29 s/n, Lurigancho-Chosica, Lima
Tel: +51 13 603119
Curriculum: IBDP

Colegio Peruano Británico
Av. Vía Láctea 445, Monterrico, Santiago de Surco, Lima 15023
Tel: +51 14 360151
Curriculum: IBDP
Language instr: Spanish, English

Colegio Peruano Norteamericano Abraham Lincoln
Av. José Antonio 475, Urb. Parque de Monterico, La Molina, Lima 15023
Tel: +51 16 174500
Age range: 3–17
Curriculum: IBDP, IBMYP, IBPYP, National
Language instr: Spanish, English

Colegio Pestalozzi (Colegio Suizo del Peru)
Casilla 18-1027, Aurora-Miraflores, Lima
Tel: +51 16 178600
Age range: 4–18
No. of pupils: 574 *B*282 *G*292
Curriculum: IBDP
Language instr: Spanish

Colegio Sagrados Corazones 'Recoleta'
Av. Circunvclación del Golf 368, La Molina, Lima 15023
Tel: +51 17 022500
Age range: 4–18 years
Curriculum: IBDP
Language instr: Spanish

Colegio Salcantay
Av. Pío XII 261, Monterrico, Santiago de Surco, Lima 15023
Tel: +51 14 359224
Curriculum: IBDP
Language instr: Spanish

Colegio San Agustín
Av. Javier Prado Este 980, Urb. El Palomar, San Isidro, Lima
Tel: +51 16 164242
Curriculum: IBDP, IBPYP

Colegio San Agustín de Chiclayo
Km. 8 Carretera Pimentel S/N, Pimentel, Chiclayo, Lambayeque
Tel: +51 74 208173
Age range: *B*4–17 *G*4–16
No. of pupils: *VIth*110
Curriculum: IBDP
Language instr: Spanish

Colegio San Ignacio de Recalde
Calle Géminis 251, San Borja, Lima 15037
Tel: +51 12 119430
Curriculum: IBDP, IBPYP
Language instr: English

Colegio San Pedro
Calle Hurón 409, Rinconada del Lago, La Molina, Lima 15026
Tel: +51 16 149500
Curriculum: IBDP
Language instr: English, Spanish

Colegio Santa Úrsula
Av. Nicolas de Rivera 132, San Isidro, Lima 15073
Tel: +51 12 027430
Curriculum: IBDP

Colegio Santísimo Nombre de Jesús
Urbanización Chacarilla del Estanque Calle Mayorazgo 176, San Borja, Lima
Tel: +51 13 721655
Curriculum: IBDP
Language instr: English, Spanish

Colegio Villa Caritas
Calle Hurón 409, Rinconada del Lago, La Molina, Lima 15026
Tel: +51 16 149500
Curriculum: IBDP
Language instr: English, Spanish

Colegio Virgen Inmaculada de Monterrico
Av. Morro Solar No. 110, Santiago de Surco, Lima 15039
Tel: +51 13 726499
Curriculum: IBDP
Language instr: English, Spanish

Collège André Malraux
Calle Batallón Concepción 245, Urb. Sta. Teresa, Santiago de Surco, Lima
Tel: +51 12 754937
Curriculum: IBDP
Language instr: English

Davy College
Av. Hoyos Rubio 2684, Cajamarca 06001
Tel: +51 76 367501
Age range: 2–18
No. of pupils: *B*359 *G*418 *VIth*8
Curriculum: IBDP
Language instr: Spanish, English

Euroamerican College
Fundo Casablanca, Pachacamac, Lima
Tel: +51 12 311617
Age range: 3–18
No. of pupils: 490 *B*245 *G*245
Curriculum: IBDP, IBPYP
Language instr: Spanish, English

Fleming College
Av América Sur 3701, Trujillo, La Libertad 13008
Tel: +51 44 284440
Age range: 2–18
No. of pupils: 600 *B*300 *G*300
Curriculum: IBDP, IBPYP, National, IGCSE
Language instr: Spanish, English

Hiram Bingham School
Av. Paseo la Castellana 919, Urbanización La Castellana, Santiago de Surco, Lima 15048
Tel: +51 12 719880
Age range: 3–17
No. of pupils: *B*337 *G*322
Curriculum: IBDP, IBMYP, IBPYP
Language instr: English, Spanish

IE Pedro Ruiz Gallo
Av. Cdra 2 S/N Costado de la Clinica Maison de Sante Chorrillos, Chorrillos, Lima
Tel: +51 16 802673
Curriculum: IBDP, IBMYP
Language instr: Spanish

Institución Educativa Particular San Antonio de Padua
Av. Estados Unidos 569, Jesús Maria, Lima
Tel: +51 16 143600
Curriculum: IBDP
Language instr: Spanish

Institución Educativa Privada Lord Byron
Calle Grande 250, Sr. de la Caña, Cayma, Arequipa
Tel: +51 54 255038
Curriculum: IBDP
Language instr: Spanish

Lord Byron School
Jr. Viña del Mar 375 – 379, Sol de la Molina, Lima 15026
Tel: +51 14 791717
Curriculum: IBDP, IBMYP, IBPYP
Language instr: English, Spanish

Lycée Franco-Péruvien
Jr. Morro Solar 550, Santiago de Surco, Lima 15039
Tel: +51 16 267800
Curriculum: FrenchBacc

Markham College
Calle Augusto Angulo 291, San Antonio, Miraflores, Lima 15048
Tel: +51 13 156750
Age range: 3–18 years
No. of pupils: 2100 *B*1200 *G*900
Curriculum: ACT, IBDP, SAT, IGCSE
Language instr: English, Spanish

Montessori International College
Maz. A Sub Lote 01A, Urb. Tecsup, Distrito Víctor Larco Herrera, Trujillo, La Libertad 13009
Tel: +51 44 340000
Curriculum: IBDP, IBPYP
Language instr: English, Spanish

Newton College
Av. Ricardo Elías Aparicio 240, Lima 15026
Tel: +51 12 079900
Age range: 2–18
Curriculum: IBDP, IBMYP, IBPYP
Language instr: English

San Francisco College
Urb. El Oasis II, Calle Costa del Sol Mz 'D' Lote 14, (Pista Camino a Huacachina), Ica 11004
Tel: +51 95 6298110
Curriculum: IBPYP
Language instr: Spanish

San Silvestre School
Av. Santa Cruz 1251, Miraflores, Lima 15074
Tel: +51 12 413334
Age range: *G*3–18
No. of pupils: 1180
Curriculum: IBDP
Language instr: English

St George's College – Sede Miraflores
Av. General Ernesto Montagne No.360, Miraflores, Lima 15048
Tel: +51 14 458147
Curriculum: IBDP, IBCP

Villa Alarife School
Jr. Alameda Don Augusto Mz. D Lt. 5, Urb. Los Huertos de Villa, Chorrillos, Lima 15067
Tel: +51 12 346969
Curriculum: IBDP

SURINAME

International Academy of Suriname
Lawtonlaan 20, Paramaribo
Tel: +597 499 461
Age range: 3–18
No. of pupils: 103
Curriculum: USA

URUGUAY

Colegio Stella Maris
Máximo Tajes 7357/7359, CP 11500 Montevideo 11500
Tel: +598 2 600 0702
Age range: 4–17
No. of pupils: 1086 *B*576 *G*510
Curriculum: IBDP, IGCSE
Language instr: Spanish, English

Escuela Integral Hebreo Uruguaya
Jose Benito Lamas 2835, Montevideo 11300
Tel: +598 2 708 1712
Curriculum: IBDP
Language instr: Spanish

Escuela y Liceo Elbio Fernandez
Maldonado 1381, Montevideo 11200
Tel: +598 2901 1254
Curriculum: IBDP, IBMYP
Language instr: English, Spanish

International College
Blvr Artigas y Avda del Mar, Punta del Este, Maldonado
Tel: +598 42 228 888
Curriculum: IBDP
Language instr: English, Spanish

St Brendan's School
Av Rivera 2314, Montevideo CP 11200
Tel: +598 2409 4939
Age range: 3–17
Curriculum: IBDP, IBMYP, IBPYP, IBCP
Language instr: English, Spanish

St Clare's College
California y los Médanos, Punta del Este, San Rafael 20000
Tel: +598 42 490200
Curriculum: IBDP, ALevs
Language instr: Spanish, English

St George's School
Juana Pereyra 1, Montevideo
Tel: +598 2613 5338
No. of pupils: 400 *B*200 G200
Curriculum: IGCSE

St Patrick's College
Camino Gigantes 2735,
Montevideo 12100
Tel: +598 2 601 3474
Age range: 3–18
Curriculum: IBMYP
Language instr: Spanish

The Anglo School
Sede Carrasco, Saldún de
Rodríguez 2195, Montevideo 11500
Tel: +598 2600 6452
Curriculum: National

The British Schools, Montevideo
Máximo Tajes 6400, esq
Havre, Montevideo 11500
Tel: +598 2 600 3421
Age range: 4–18
No. of pupils: *B*720 *G*750
Curriculum: IBDP, IBMYP, National
Language instr: English, Spanish
CIS

Uruguayan American School
Saldún de Rodríguez 2375,
Montevideo 11500
Tel: + (598) 2600 7681
Curriculum: IBDP
Language instr: English

Woodlands School
San Carlos de Bolivar s/n entre
Havre y Cooper, Montevideo 11500
Tel: +59 82 604 27 14
Curriculum: IBMYP, IGCSE
Language instr: Spanish

Woodside School
Mercedes y Louvre. Barrio
Cantegril, 20100 Punta
del Este, Maldonado
Tel: +598 4225 2552
Age range: 2–18
No. of pupils: 578 *B*295 *G*283
Curriculum: IBDP, National, UK, IGCSE, ALevs
Language instr: English, Spanish
ISA

VENEZUELA

CEIA School
Av José Antonio Anzoátegui
km 98, Anaco
Tel: +58 82 22683
Age range: 3–18
No. of pupils: 78
Curriculum: USA

Centro de Educación Valle Abierto
Calle Loma Azul, Urb San
Luis, El Cafetal, Caracas
Tel: +58 212 985 4552
Age range: 1–18
No. of pupils: *B*189 *G*151
Curriculum: National
Language instr: Spanish

Colegio Bellas Artes
Zulia, Av 3F, con calle 71,
Maracaibo, Zulia 4002
Tel: +58 0261 7911 175
No. of pupils: 897
Language instr: Spanish

Colegio Guayamuri
Av. Luisa Cáceres de Arismendi,
Atamo Norte, La Asunción
Tel: +58 295 2423048
Curriculum: IBDP
Language instr: English, Spanish

Colegio Humboldt
Prolongación Av. El Estanque
Urb. Ávila, Norte del
Country Club, Caracas
Tel: +58 212 5263 100

Colegio Integral El Avila
Centro de Artes Integradas,
Urb. Terrazas del Avila, La
Urbina Norte, Caracas 1073
Tel: +58 243.58.20
Curriculum: IBDP
Language instr: Spanish

Colegio Integral El Manglar
Carrera N°41 S/N Sector
Nueva Barcelona, Barcelona
6001, Anzoategui
Tel: +58 0281 317 21 70
Curriculum: IBDP
Language instr: English, Spanish

Colegio Internacional de Caracas
Calle Colegio, entre Los Samanes y
Las Minas de Baruta, Caracas 1080
Tel: +58 212 945 0444
Age range: 3–19 years
No. of pupils: 180
Curriculum: ACT, IBDP, IBMYP, SAT, USA
Language instr: English, Spanish

Colegio Los Campitos
Ruta C, Urbanización Los Campitos,
Prados del Este, Miranda
Tel: +58 212 977 1768
Curriculum: IBDP
Language instr: Spanish

Colegio Moral y Luces 'Herzl-Bialik'
Final Ave. Los Chorros, SEDE CLUB
HEBRAICA (Frente al INAM),
Los Chorros Caracas 1071
Tel: +58 212 273 6894/6807
Curriculum: IBDP

Escuela Bella Vista
67th Street between Av.
3D and 3E La Lago sector,
Macaracaibo, Zulia 4001
Tel: +58 261 794 0000
Curriculum: IBDP
Language instr: English

Escuela Campo Alegre
Final Calle La Cinta, Las
Mercedes, Caracas
Tel: +58 212 993 3922
Age range: 3–18
No. of pupils: 300 *B*153 *G*147
Curriculum: ACT, IBDP, SAT, USA
Language instr: English
CIS ECIS

Instituto Educacional Juan XXIII
Calle San Enrique No 85-
70, Trigal Centro, Valencia,
Estado Carabobo 2002
Tel: +58 241 8425732
Age range: 1–18
No. of pupils: 1500 *B*750 *G*750
Curriculum: IBDP, IBCP
Language instr: Spanish

International School of Monagas
Km 1 Carretera via a la Toscana,
Sector Costo Abajo, Maturin 6021
Tel: +58 291 315 0011
Age range: 3–19
No. of pupils: 243
Curriculum: SAT, USA

Le Lycée Français de Caracas – Colegio Francia
Avenida D Campo Claro,
Apartado 70151, Caracas
Tel: 00 58 212 237 5959
Curriculum: FrenchBacc

Liceo Los Robles
Urbanización el Doral Norte, Calle
34 esquina con Avenida, Fuerzas
Armadas, Mar, Estado Zulia 4002
Tel: +58 0261 7421833
Curriculum: IBDP
Language instr: Spanish

QSI International School of El Tigre
Escuela las Americas, El Tigre
Tel: +58 283 241 2005
Age range: 4–16
No. of pupils: 74
Curriculum: USA
Language instr: English

The British School Caracas
Transversal 9 Este Av. Luis Roche,
Quinta DAMI Urbanización
Altamira, Caracas
Tel: +58 212 627 1000
Age range: 3–18 years
Curriculum: IBDP, UK, IGCSE

Washington Academy
Calle C, Urb. Colinas de Valle
Arriba, Caracas 1080
Tel: +58 212 9757077
Age range: 4–18 years
No. of pupils: 520
Curriculum: IBDP, IBMYP
Language instr: Spanish, English

International school associations

THE ACCREDITING COMMISSION FOR SCHOOLS, WESTERN ASSOCIATION FOR SCHOOLS AND COLLEGES (ACS WASC)

ACS WASC works closely with the Office of Overseas Schools under the U.S. Department of State. ACS WASC provides assistance to schools worldwide, primarily in California, Hawaii, Guam, Asia, the Pacific Region, the Middle East, Africa, and Europe.

The Accrediting Commission for Schools, WASC, extends its services to over 5,000 public, independent, church-related, and proprietary Pre-K–12 and adult schools, works with 18 associations in joint accreditation processes, and collaborates with other organizations such as the California Department of Education (CDE).

ACS, WASC, Northern California Office, 533 Airport Boulevard, Suite 200, Burlingame, CA 94010-2009, USA
Tel: +1 650 696-1060
Email: mail@acswasc.org
Website: www.acswasc.org

THE ALLIANCE FOR INTERNATIONAL EDUCATION (AIE)

The Alliance for International Education is committed to promoting international learning in any context. Its aim is always to balance theoretical discourse and research with practical action. Its conferences and activities bring together mainstream international schools with universities, researchers, providers of curriculum, resources and training, and representatives from state and private educational systems who are keen to internationalise learning in their own schools. Besides its 'world conferences' the AIE supports regional initiatives in several parts of the world – and in line with its vision that international education should be available to every child, it operates as an open access, open source organization where there are no membership fees for becoming a partner or for accessing resources. For more information about the AIE, contact:

Email: vicki.aie.bath@gmail.com
Website: www.intedalliance.org

AMERICAN INTERNATIONAL SCHOOLS IN THE AMERICAS (AMISA)

AMISA, formerly the Associationof American Schools in South America, has 47 full member schools in 20 South American countries, namely: Argentina, Bolivia, Brazil, Chile, Cayman Islands, Colombia, Costa Rica, Curacao, Dominican Republic, Ecuador, Guatemala, Guyana, Honduras, Jamaica, Panama, Paraguay, Peru, Trinidad & Tobago, Uruguay and Venezuela. Its mission is to provide and promote programmes and services to their members, all of whom offer an American international education. AMISA's mission statement says their mission is to enhance the quality of education in American/international member schools.

Various services are provided for member schools including: a purchasing service; a recruiting fair in Central America and the Caribbean; four annual professional development conferences; a payroll processing service; awards to AMISA Heads; annual salary and benefits survey; and a quarterly newsletter.

AMISA member schools are all private institutions offering a mainly American curriculum; the language of instruction is English. Each of the schools combines US and host country courses of study, and many grant both host country and US diplomas. Some schools also offer the IB, Advanced Placement (AP) courses, and English as a Second Language (ESL).

AMISA schools who hold full membership are: elementary and/or secondary schools; have English as the primary language of instruction; are accredited by a recognised organization such as CIS or the IB; and agree to follow the principles, purposes and objectives of AMISA.

AASSA, 1931 NW 150 Avenue, Suite 263, Pembroke Pines, FL 33028, USA
Tel: +1 954 436 4034
Website: www.amisa.us

ASSOCIATION FOR THE ADVANCEMENT OF INTERNATIONAL EDUCATION (AAIE)

AAIE is a non-profit, membership-based international organization that partners with educational institutions and associations worldwide to exchange international ideas, resources and research that help develop and improve international education, to diversify and expand school leadership capacity.

Its mission global community that connects diverse people, ideas and resources, AAIE helps international educators lead with vision, wisdom, courage and integrity.

AAIE 15 Roszel Road
Princeton NJ 08540
Phone: +1 609-716-7441
www.aaie.org

ASSOCIATION OF AMERICAN SCHOOLS OF CENTRAL AMERICA (AASCA)

The Association of American Schools of Central America (AASCA) was formed to support and encourage academic, artistic, athletic and cultural interaction between international schools that offer a US type education in Central America. It believes that through the organization and sponsorship of these types of activities that all young people involved will be exposed to and benefit from the multicultural interaction. It is the desire of AASCA to promote a better understanding of multiculturalism among all races of young people through these events.

AASCA also supports the continuing education of its member teachers and administrators through facilitating workshops and conferences that focus on the latest educational ideas and teaching methods from the United States. AASCA aims to improve the quality of all education in the countries in which they reside and create a greater awareness and appreciation for cultural diversity through the programs they sponsor.

AASCA has schools in the following countries: Guatemala, El Salvador, Honduras, Nicaragua, Costa Rica and Panama. Any Central American school that provides a US curriculum is eligible to join this association.

President: Lilliana Jenkins (ljenkins@amschool.org)
Secretary: Adolfo González (adolfo@lincoln.edu.ni)
Website: www.aascaonline.net

ASSOCIATION OF BRITISH SCHOOLS IN CHILE (ABSCH)

Founded in 1977 with just seven schools, this association now has 22 member schools, in Santiago, Viña del Mar, Casablanca, Concepción, Punta Arenas and Antofagasta. Its schools offer education for pupils aged four to 18 and all schools are bilingual with similar aims and practices. It believes in ongoing training for teaching staff and its mission is to 'encourage and support member schools in its endeavour to provide an education of quality that reflects the best of British practice, in co-operation with one another, and with Chilean and British educational authorities'.

ABSCH, Apoquindo 7935, oficina 404 A, Las Condes, Santiago, Chile
Tel: +56 2 2121 953
Email: absoffice@absch.cl
Website: www.absch.cl

ASSOCIATION OF CHINA AND MONGOLIA INTERNATIONAL SCHOOLS (ACAMIS)

Founded to promote and support the building of international schools in China and Mongolia, ACAMIS now has a membership that includes more than 70 of the 150+ international schools operating within China, Hong Kong, Macao, Taiwan and Mongolia.

The association hosts various student activities, professional development workshops for teachers and networking opportunities for Heads of schools, and other educational personnel within member schools. There is an annual meeting for ACAMIS Heads.

The association's aims are: to widen and evolve the curriculum of ACAMIS schools; to encourage the professional development of staff within their schools; to facilitate communication between member schools; to promote understanding and international friendship; to co-operate with others pursuing the same objectives; to encourage student exchanges; to collaborate on professional development; and to support national and regional networking.

ACAMIS, 33 Wai Man Road, Sai Kung, Hong Kong
Email: eo@acamis.org
Website: www.acamis.org

ASSOCIATION OF COLOMBIAN-CARIBBEAN AMERICAN SCHOOLS (ACCAS)

ACCAS is one of the regional associations affiliated with the Tri-Association.

It has 27 schools offering an American education in the Colombian and Caribbean region. Its core values include: school improvement and ongoing staff development.

All member schools must be US accredited candidates for accreditation.

Currently it has schools in the Dominican Republic, Ecuador, Haiti, Jamaica and Colombia.

Tel: +57 311 403 4076
Website: www.tri-association.org

ASSOCIATION OF GERMAN INTERNATIONAL SCHOOLS (AGIS)

The Association of German International Schools (AGIS) represents and supports the educational and public interest of member schools and their communities by promoting and improving international education. It currently has 23 members.

AGIS, Bruchmeisterallee 6, 30169 Hannover, Germany
Tel: +49 0511 10532406
Email: julia@agis-schools.org
Website: www.agis-schools.org

ASSOCIATION OF INTERNATIONAL SCHOOLS IN AFRICA (AISA)

AISA represents international schools on the continent of Africa. Its schools range in size from 20 to 2000+ students. AISA schools tend to have an American or British-based curriculum; others have an eclectic mix but all have an international focus.

The association's goal is to serve the varying needs of its students, teachers and administrators. Its mission is to increase school effectiveness and inspire student learning by promoting communication, collaboration, and professional development.

AISA's objectives are: to enhance the quality

of learning by promoting effective practice; foster intercultural and international understanding; promote an appreciation and understanding of Africa; support professional development within member schools; collate, analyse, and distribute information to help guide member schools; enable collaboration and networking between members; and to develop and maintain partnerships with organisations and institutions that complement the association's values and mission.

AISA, PO Box 14103-00800, Nairobi, Kenya
Tel: +254 (0) 20 269 7442/8076067
Email: info@aisa.or.ke
Website: www.aisa.or.ke

ASSOCIATION OF AMERICAN SCHOOLS IN MEXICO (ASOMEX)

ASOMEX is a member of the Tri-Association (www.tri-association.org).

It was founded in 1957 and originally included eight American schools. Today, it is made up of 18 member schools throughout Mexico. These schools are private, non-profit establishments ranging in size from 42 to over 3000 students. It is committed to offering an American style curriculum, whilst meeting the criteria set down by the Mexican Secretariat of Education.

ASOMEX's main aims are: to develop a closer union of the American schools in Mexico; seek to resolve common problems of member schools; advance ideals and standards; assist member schools in establishing and maintaining high standards; encourage and enhance the multicultural/bilingual aspects of member schools; provide qualified consultants to teachers and administrators; select and procure quality educational materials and equipment; and develop communications and relations amongst member schools.

There are a wide variety of annual ASOMEX activities for members, including athletic tournaments, teacher and student workshops, model UN, and art and musical festivals.

Website: www.asomex.org

BRITISH ASSOCIATION OF INDEPENDENT SCHOOLS WITH INTERNATIONAL STUDENTS (BAISIS)

The British Association of Independent Schools with International Students (BAISIS) is a group of educational centres which provide a full academic curriculum in the United Kingdom to students from other countries.

Members are drawn from independent schools, study centres and colleges. Originally founded in 1997 by Bedford, Rossall, Sherborne and Taunton Schools, membership has grown steadily and today the association is an influential organisation which occupies, and speaks for, an important niche sector in international education in the UK.

The Association exists to provide help in the form of training, development, and mutual support to its members and for quality assurance purposes. This is achieved through regular meetings, training from inside and outside the Association and through a bespoke annual conference. All member institutions provide a supportive pastoral framework and quality academic environment for international students.The Association also represents the interests of schools and colleges with international students in the UK at the national level.

Website: www.baisis.org.uk

BRITISH SCHOOLS IN THE MIDDLE EAST (BSME)

BSME has more than 150 member schools and over 90 supporting members.

It provides a quality-assured network of schools helping Heads and Teachers share best practice and keep abreast of the latest educational developments. BSME runs its own Accreditation System, Annual Headteachers' Conferences and Continuing Professional Development (CPD) programme of conferences, courses and webinars.

All members schools are: an English Medium, essentially British Curriculum School in which the Principal/Head Teacher and the majority of teachers (apart from those teaching local languages) have qualifications recognised by the UK Department for Education.

Each year BSME holds a conference to discuss and learn about developments in UK education and school leadership and management issues.

BSEM, 12–14 Carlton Place, Southampton, Hampshire, SO15 2EA
Email: business@bsme.org.uk
Website: www.bsme.org.uk

CENTRAL & EASTERN EUROPEAN SCHOOLS ASSOCIATION (CEESA)

The Central & Eastern European Schools Association (CEESA) was founded as a result of the growth of American and International Schools in Central and Eastern Europe. In many cases, the schools were geographically isolated from each other and from the main stream of American and International Education.

CEESA was formed to broaden the horizons of schools and to promote professional growth. In addition to the CEESA Annual Conference in March, CEESA sponsors regional workshops, institutes and meetings to foster professionalism, scholarship, and a deeper understanding of improvements for leading, teaching and learning.

CEESA also sponsors student activities, focusing on a variety of academic and non-academic areas, and a full schedule of sports events.

Executive Director: Kathy Stetson
CEESA, Ul. Damira Tomljanovića 3, 10020, Zagreb, Croatia
Tel: +385 91 181 7921
Email: office@ceesa.org
Website: www.ceesa.org

COGNIA

Cognia, previously known as AdvancED, is a non-profit, non-partisan organization that conducts rigorous, on-site external reviews of Pre-K-12 schools and school systems to ensure that all learners realize their full potential.

Combining 'the knowledge and expertise of a research institute, the skills of a management consulting firm and the passion of a grassroots movement for educational change', Cognia serves as a partner to 36,000 schools and school systems across the United States and 70 other nations. Cognia was created through a 2006 merger of the Pre-K-12 divisions of the North Central Association Commission on Accreditation and School Improvement (NCA CASI) and the Southern Association of Colleges and Schools Council on Accreditation and School Improvement (SACS CASI) — and expanded through the addition of the Northwest Accreditation Commission (NWAC) in 2012.

Cognia, Alpharetta, GA 30009, USA
Tel: +1 888 413 3669
Website: www.cognia.org

COUNCIL OF BRITISH INTERNATIONAL SCHOOLS (COBIS)

COBIS is a membership association of British schools of quality worldwide and is committed to a stringent process of quality assurance for all its member schools.

Founded more than 30 years ago, it is governed by an elected board of Headteachers and Governors from member schools worldwide. COBIS hosts a range of conferences and professional development events for teachers, middle leaders, support staff throughout the year plus an annual conference in London in May for school leaders and Governors

COBIS represents its members with the British Government, educational bodies, the corporate sector and Ministries of Education worldwide. It is a member of the Independent Schools Council (ISC) of the United Kingdom.

CEO: Colin Bell (ceo@cobis.org.uk)
COBIS, 55-56 Russell Square, London WC1B 4HP
Tel: +44 (0) 20 3826 7190
Website: www.cobis.org.uk

COUNCIL OF INTERNATIONAL SCHOOLS (CIS)

CIS is a not-for-profit organisation committed to supporting its member schools and colleges in achieving and delivering the highest standards of international education.

CIS provides accreditation to schools, teacher and leader recruitment and best practice development. CIS Higher Education assists member colleges and universities in recruiting a diverse profile of qualified international students.

Executive Director: Jane Larsson
CIS, Schipholweg 113, 2316 XC Leiden, The Netherlands
Tel: +31 71 524 3300
Email: info@cois.org
Website: www.cois.org

EAST ASIA REGIONAL COUNCIL OF OVERSEAS SCHOOLS (EARCOS)

The East Asia Regional Council of Schools is an organization of 200 member schools in East Asia. These schools have a total of more than 164,022 pre-K to 12th grade students. EARCOS also has 144 associate members – textbook and software publishers and distributors, universities, financial planners, architectural firms, insurance companies, youth organizations, etc – and 23 individual members.

The Council has a vision that includes: developing collaborative educational partnerships worldwide; providing professional development opportunities for members; connecting schools, communities, and individuals through the use of technology; understanding, and access to broader educational opportunities; engaging all in learning activities that will promote friendship, understanding and global citizenship.

Executive Director: Dr. Edward Greene
EARCOS, Brentville subdivision, Barangay Mamplasan, Biñan, Laguna, 4024, Philippines
Tel: +63 (02) 8779-5147
Fax: +63 (49) 511 4694
Email: info@earcos.org
Website: www.earcos.org

ECIS

A network of schools and companies committed to promoting international education. Founded in 1965, ECIS is made up of regular member schools, affiliate members who provide services such as professional development for teachers, supporting members made up of commercial companies who supply/service the international schools market, and individual members.

Executive Director: Kam Chohan
ECIS, 24 Greville Street, London, EC1N 8SS, United Kingdom
Tel: +44 (0)20 7824 7040
Email: ecis@ecis.org
Website: www.ecis.org

FEDERATION OF BRITISH INTERNATIONAL SCHOOLS IN ASIA (FOBISIA)

FOBISIA is a regional federation of the leading British international schools in Asia. Member schools have to meet a range of quality standards in order to be accepted into the federation and to retain membership.

Additionally, affiliate membership of FOBISIA is open to reputable educational organisations and suppliers whose services and products are of interest to member schools.

FOBISIA hosts a range of student events including the FOBISIA Games, a music festival, drama festivals, gamelan festivals, community and environmental conferences, model united nations conferences, as well as a range of other events around the subject areas of maths, science, DT and English.

It also organises conferences and workshops where teachers from across the region can meet to share good practice, swap ideas and receive professional training from invited university lecturers and consultants from around the world.

Chief Operating Officer:
John Gwyn Jones MBE
39/4 Todsamon Clubhouse Building
M Fl, Soi Lasalle 39/1, Sukhumvit 105, Bangna
Bangkok, Thailand 10260
Tel: +66 82 574 1110
Website: www.fobisia.org

INTERNATIONAL SCHOOLS ASSOCIATION (ISA)

The ISA is based in Geneva, with offices in India and the USA, and was established in Paris in 1951 as an international organisation for the development of co-operation among its member schools and with all those interested in promoting international understanding.

The ISA was instrumental in the development of the International Baccalaureate Organization and in creating a programme for middle schools, which later developed into the IBMYP. It publishes Internationalism in Schools – a Self-Study Guide for schools and sponsors an annual 'Youth Encounter' for students from member and non-member schools. A biannual World Conference is organized around a theme dealing with international education and the association sponsors oral English examinations.

International Schools Association, 25 rue Schaub
CH 1202 Geneva, Switzerland
Email: info@isaschools.org
Website: www.isaschools.org

INTERNATIONAL SCHOOLS ASSOCIATION OF THAILAND (ISAT)

This association was established in 1994 principally to act as a link between its member international schools, the Ministry of Education and the Office of the Private Education Commission. It is now involved in the joint marketing of international education both in Thailand and overseas.

ISAT has over 75 schools offering a range of curricula: American, British and international systems. They are committed to the promotion of the Thai language and culture in international schools along with support for culture and sporting links between international schools in Thailand and worldwide. ISAT member schools are accredited by WASC, NEASC and CIS.

ISAT, 39/7 Soi Nichada Thani, Samakee Road, Pakkret,
Nonthaburi, Thailand 11120
Tel: +66 (0)2 960 4101
Email: isat@isat.or.th
Website: www.isat.or.th

MEDITERRANEAN ASSOCIATION OF INTERNATIONAL SCHOOLS (MAIS)

The Mediterranean Association of International Schools strives to improve the quality of education in its member schools. It promotes the professional development of faculty, administrators, and school board members, effective communication and interchange, and creates international understanding.

MAIS serves as a liaison between its 38 Member Schools, 30 Associate Member organizations as well as other regional, professional, and in-service organizations. Presently, MAIS is composed of schools from 16 different countries, including Austria, Cyprus, Egypt, France, Greece, Italy, Lebanon, Morocco, Oman, Portugal, Saudi Arabia, Spain, Tunisia, Turkey, United Arab Emirates and the United Kingdom. In addition, several associate members, such as schools outside the Mediterranean region, colleges, businesses, and interested individuals, support MAIS endeavors and have joined the organization.

Tel: +34 91 352 0678
Email: rohale@mais-web.org
Website: www.mais-web.org

MIDDLE STATES ASSOCIATION OF COLLEGES AND SCHOOLS

The MSA's Commissions on Elementary and Secondary Schools accredit early-childhood through post-secondary, non-degree granting public, private, faith-based educational institutions including special purpose schools, supplementary education centers, learning services providers, and distance education institutions.

Historically, MSA-CESS has operated in the mid-Atlantic region (Delaware, Maryland, New Jersey, New York, Pennsylvania, and the District of Columbia); with its cooperative partners, it has expanded its scope to include schools and institutions seeking accreditation throughout the United States. The Commissions also award accreditation to member institutions in more than 106 countries around the world.

The Commissions on Elementary and Secondary Schools are affiliated with the United States State Department's Office of Overseas Schools and provide accreditation services to American and international style schools attended by members of the US foreign service and US citizens working for non-government agencies and multi-national corporations. The Commission on Secondary Schools is also recognized by the U.S. Department of Education as a gatekeeper for eligibility for Title IV funding for post secondary non-degree granting institutions and distance education.

The Commissions on Elementary and Secondary Schools are founding members of the International Alliance of Accrediting Associations which includes the major regional, national and international accrediting agencies.

St. Leonard's Court 3819-33 Chestnut Street, Suite 310 |
Philadelphia, PA 19104-3171
Tel: +1 267-284-5000
Email: info@msa-cess.org
Website: www.msa-cess.org

NATIONAL ASSOCIATION OF BRITISH SCHOOLS IN SPAIN (NABSS)

The National Association of British Schools in Spain (NABSS) was founded in 1978 to promote, uphold and defend British education in Spain. The only schools permitted to be members of NABSS are those that are fully authorised British schools, recognised as such by the British Council and its official inspectorate.

NABSS insists on regular inspection of member schools, provides professional training for Heads and teachers and organises an annual conference with workshops.

The association aims to maintain contact with the British Council and the Spanish educational authorities as per the requirements of legislation referring to foreign schools in Spain.

NABSS's website lists all member schools. These schools follow the British National Curriculum and employ fully qualified staff. They range in age from early years to 16 and offer a broad selection of GCSE, AS and A level courses and generally administer UCAS entry to universities in the UK. Spanish authorities give full recognition to A levels and grant automatic access to Spanish universities for NABSS A level students.

NABSS, Calle de Ferraz, 85, 28008 Madrid, Spain
Tel: +34 91 550 0123
Email: nabss@acade.es
Website: www.nabss.org

NEAR EAST SOUTH ASIA COUNCIL OF OVERSEAS SCHOOLS (NESA)

NESA began informally in the early 1960s and has evolved into a world class organisation that serves more than 100 American international schools. The association promotes links between educators working in private, independent international schools in the Near East and South Asia region. Regular membership of the association is open to any American overseas or international overseas school located in the Near East South Asia geographical area, as long as they share the objectives and purposes of NESA and are accredited by a recognized agency.

NESA, Gravias 6, Aghia Paraskevia 153 42, Athens, Greece
Email: nesa@nesacenter.org
Website: www.nesacenter.org

NEW ENGLAND ASSOCIATION OF SCHOOLS AND COLLEGES (NEASC)

NEASC is an independent, voluntary, nonprofit membership organization which connects and serves over 1,500 public and independent schools, technical/career institutions, colleges and universities in New England plus International Schools in more than 65 nations worldwide. A globally recognized standard of excellence, NEASC Accreditation attests to a school's high quality and integrity. NEASC is comprised of four commissions which decide matters of accreditation in the context of research-driven standards reviewed by their membership.

NEASC, 3 Burlington Woods Drive, Suite 100, Burlington, MA 01803, USA
Tel: +1 781-425-7700
Email: info@neasc.org
Website: www.neasc.org

NORDIC NETWORK OF INTERNATIONAL SCHOOLS

Organisation that serves English speaking schools in the Nordic and Baltic regions. Originally founded by five international schools from Denmark, Norway and Sweden, it now offers membership to other schools in the region who provide an international education in English.

NNIS, c/o ISGR, Molinsgatan 6, 411 33 Göteborg, Sweden
Tel: +47 93 00 8648
Email: nordicnetworkonline@gmail.com
Website: www.nordicnetworkonline.net

ROUND SQUARE INTERNATIONAL SCHOOLS (RSIS)

Round Square is a world-wide association of schools on five continents. Students attending Round Square schools make a strong commitment, beyond academic excellence, to personal development and responsibility.

The Round Square approach promotes six IDEALS of learning: Internationalism, Democracy, Environment, Adventure, Leadership and Service. These are incorporated into the curriculum throughout all member schools.

Access to the Round Square network affords member schools the opportunity to arrange local and international student and teacher exchanges on a regular basis between their schools. Pupils also have the opportunity to participate in local and international community service projects and conferences

Tasks tackled through the community projects include building schools, classrooms and community centres; building clean water systems for remote hill-tribes or creating and maintaining trails in National Parks. Local materials are used, and teams always work with local people ensuring that they take ownership of the work once it has been completed

Round Square, First Floor, Morgan House, Madeira Walk, Windsor, SL4 1EP, United Kingdom
Website: www.roundsquare.org

SWISS GROUP OF INTERNATIONAL SCHOOLS (SGIS)

The Swiss Group of International Schools (SGIS) is a non-profit organization. It exists to: promote closer links between the teachers, administrators, and students of its member schools and professional development; provide opportunities for arranging educational, cultural and sporting activities; represent the concerns of Swiss international schools; and co-operate and maintain professional contacts with other regional and international educational bodies and associations.

Each year it holds conferences and workshops, promote inter-school sports competitions at all levels, and hold an AGM that all members are encouraged to attend.

Website: www.sgischools.com

THE TRI-ASSOCIATION – THE ASSOCIATION OF AMERICAN SCHOOLS OF CENTRAL AMERICA, COLOMBIA-CARIBBEAN AND MEXICO

Name of the joint association for AASCA, ACCAS and ASOMEX – see those entries for more information.

Executive Director:
Michael W. Adams, Ed.D.
2637 Ascot Dr., Florence, SC 29501, USA
Tel: +1 843 799 5754
Website: www.tri-association.org

Ministries of Education worldwide

Ministries of Education

Please note: every effort has been made to obtain information about all the Ministries of Education worldwide. However, some countries do not publish this information, others either do not have a specific education department or provide this information freely.

Most schools now refer to Years or Grades when talking about a specific age group. As a general guide the charts below outlines which Year/Grade denotes which age group.

UK SYSTEM

Year	Age
1	5-6
2	6-7
3	7-8
4	8-9
5	9-10
6	10-11
7	11-12
8	12-13
9	13-14
10	14-15
11	15-16
12	16-17
13	17-18

USA SYSTEM

Grade	Age
Preschool	
Pre-kindergarten	4-6
Elementary School	
Kindergarten	5-6
1st Grade	6-7
2nd Grade	7-8
3rd Grade	8-9
4th Grade	9-10
5th Grade	10-11
Middle School	
6th Grade	11-12
7th Grade	12-13
8th Grade	13-14
High School	
9th Grade – Freshman	14-15
10th Grade – Sophomore	15-16
11th Grade – Junior	16-17
12th Grade – Senior	17-18

ANGOLA

Angola Ministry of Education,
Avenue Comandante Gika, Luanda
Tel: +244 222 320 582
Primary school, ages 6-14
Secondary school, ages 14-19

ANTIGUA AND BARBUDA

Ministry of Education, Sports, Youth and Gender Affairs,
Government Office Complex, St John's, Antigua
Tel: +1 268 462 0192/3
Website: www.education.gov.ag
Primary school, ages 5-12
Secondary school, ages 12-16
Post-16 education available at three colleges

ARGENTINA

Ministry of Education, Pizzurno 935, Ciudad
Autónoma de Buenos Aires C1020ACA
Tel: +54 11 4129 1000
Website: www.argentina.gob.ar/educacion
Primary - Educación General Básica (EGB I), ages 6-8
Primary - Educación General Básica (EGB II), ages 9-11
Secondary - Educación General
Básica (EGB III), ages 12-14
Secondary - Polimodal, ages 15-17
Other: some areas of Argentina have different names and criteria for secondary education.

ARMENIA

The Ministry of Education, Science, Culture and Sports,
Vazgen Sargsyan 3, 0010 Yerevan
Tel: +374 (10) 52 6602
Website: https://escs.am/am
Elementary, ages 7-9
Basic secondary, ages 10-14
High school, ages 15-16
Post-16 education available in technical secondary colleges, universities

AUSTRALIA

Department of Education, Skills and Employment,
GPO Box 9880, Canberra, ACT 2601
Tel: +61 1300 566 046
Website: https://www.dese.gov.au
Compulsory education:

- Lower primary level education, ages 5-9
- Upper primary level education, ages 9-13
- Lower secondary phase education, ages 11-16
- Upper secondary level education, ages 16-18

Other: each state and territory in Australia has the responsibility for their own schools, including enrolment policies, curriculum content, course accreditation and certification, as well as the methods of assessment used.
Australia also has part-time, pre-schools, which are available for up to two years before the age of six. However, during the second pre-school year there is the option to go full-time; this year is known as the preparatory year.
Post-16 education in Australia is available in the form of secondary schools, technical or vocational colleges, senior colleges or rural training schools.

AUSTRIA

Federal Ministry of Education, Science and Research,
Minoritenplatz 5, A-1010 Vienna
Tel: +43 (0)1 53120 0
Website: https://www.bmbwf.gv.at/en
Pre-school, age 5
Primary, ages 6-9
Lower secondary, ages 10-13
Upper secondary, ages 14-17
Vocational, ages 14-18

AZERBAIJAN REPUBLIC

Ministry of Education, 49 Khatai Avenue, Baku, AZ-1008
Tel: +994 12 599 1155
Website: www.edu.gov.az
Primary, ages 6-10
Basic, ages 10-15
Secondary, ages 15-17

THE BAHAMAS

Ministry of Education, Thompson Boulevard, Nassau
Tel: +1 242 502 2700
Website: www.ministryofeducationbahamas.com
Nursery/kindergarten, ages 3-5
Primary, ages 5-11
Secondary, ages 12-15
Senior high school, ages 16-18

KINGDOM OF BAHRAIN

Ministry of Education, PO Box 43, Manama
Tel: +973 1727 8999
Website: www.moe.gov.bh
Primary, ages 6-11
Intermediate, 12-14
Secondary, ages 15-17
Other: state run schools tend to be single sex, whereas private education offers coeducational schools.

BANGLADESH

Ministry of Education, Building 6, Floor 17th & 18th, Bangladesh Secretariat, Dhaka-1000
Tel: +88 02 7167577
Website: www.moedu.gov.bd
Pre-primary, ages 3-6
Primary, ages 6-10
Secondary, ages 11-17

BARBADOS

Ministry of Education, Technological and Vocational Training, Elsie Payne Complex, St Michael, West Indies
Tel: +1 246 535 0600
Website: www.mes.gov.bb
Primary, ages 5-11
Secondary, ages 11-16
Other: some private secondary schools are government assisted.

REPUBLIC OF BELARUS

Ministry of Education, 9 Sovetskaya Street, 220010, Minsk
Tel: +375 (017) 327 47 36
Website: www.edu.gov.by
Primary, ages 6-10
Basic, ages 10-15
General secondary, ages 15-17
Specialised secondary, ages 15-19
Vocational secondary, ages 15-18
Other: secondary education lasts between two and four years, depending on which type the student enrols for.

BELGIUM

Flemish Ministry of Education and Training, Koning Albert II-laan 15, 1210 Brussels
Tel: +32 2 553 6601
Website: www.vlaanderen.be/en
Pre-primary, ages 2-6
Primary, ages 6-11
Secondary, ages 12-18
Other: VGO schools, which are privately owned and either religious (Catholic, Jewish etc) or method (Steiner, Freinet, Montessori); these schools are funded by the government.

BELIZE

Ministry of Education, Culture, Science & Technology, West Block Building 3rd Floor, Belmopan, Cayo
Tel: +501 822 2380/3315
Website: www.moe.gov.bz
Primary, ages 5-13
Secondary, ages 13-17
Other: Church-run schools. Secondary education in Belize is not free and students from many low-income families leave school before the age of 15.

BERMUDA

Ministry of Education, 14 Waller's Point Road St. David's DD 03, Bermuda
Tel: +1 (441) 278 3300
Website: www.moed.bm
Pre-school, ages 4-5
Primary, ages 5-11
Middle, ages 11-14
Secondary, ages 14-18

BHUTAN

Ministry of Education, PO Box 112, Thimphu
Tel: +975 32 53 25
Website: www.education.gov.bt
Primary, ages 6-12
Secondary, ages 12-16
Other: Monastic schools.

BOLIVIA

Ministry of Education, Avenida Arce No 2147, PO Box 3116, La Paz
Tel: +591 2244 2144
Website: www.minedu.gob.bo
Pre-primary, ages 4-6
Primary, ages 6-13
Secondary, ages 14-17

BOSNIA AND HERZEGOVINA

Federal Ministry of Education and Science, dr. Ante Starčevića bb., Sarajevo
Tel: +387 036 355 700
Website: www.fmon.gov.ba
Pre-school, ages 3-5
Elementary, ages 6-15
Secondary, ages 15-19

BOTSWANA

Ministry of Education and Skills Development, Private bag 005, Block 6 Building, Government Enclave, Gaborone
Tel: +267 365 5400
Website: www.gov.bw
Primary, ages 5-12
Junior secondary, ages 13-15
Senior secondary, ages 16-18

BRAZIL

Ministry of Education, Esplanada dos Ministeries, Bloeo L. Brasilia DF, 70047-900
Tel: +55 (61) 410 0444
Website: www.gov.br/mec/pt-br
Pre-school, ages 4-6
Fundamental, ages 7-14
Intermediate, ages 15-18

BRITISH VIRGIN ISLANDS

Ministry of Education, Culture, Youth Affairs, Fisheries and Agriculture, 33 Admin Drive, Wickhams Cay 1, Road Town, Tortola
Tel: +1 284 468 3701
Website: www.bvi.gov.vg/content/ministry-education-and-culture
Pre-primary, ages 3-5
Primary, ages 5-12
Secondary, ages 13-17

BRUNEI DARUSSALAM

Ministry of Education, Old Airport Road, Berakas BB3510
Tel: +673 2381133
Website: www.moe.gov.bn
Pre-school, age 5
Primary, ages 6-13
Secondary, ages 13-17

BULGARIA

Ministry of Education and Science, 2A Knyaz Dondukov Blvd, 1000 Sofia
Tel: +359 921 7799
Website: www.mon.bg
Primary, ages 7-10
Lower secondary, ages 10-14
Upper secondary, ages 15-19
Vocational secondary, ages 15-19
Professional secondary, ages 15-19
Other: time spent in secondary education depends on which secondary school is attended.

BURMA

Ministry of Education, Theinbyu Street, Botahtaung Township, Yangon
Tel: +95 1 503 141
Website: https://myanmar.gov.mm/en/ministry-of-education
Pre-school, ages 2-4
Kindergarten, age 5
Primary, ages 6-11
Middle, ages 12-16
Secondary, ages 17-19

CAMBODIA

Ministry of Education, Youth and Sport, 80 Norodom Blvd, Phnom Penh
Tel: +855 23 219 285
Website: www.moeys.gov.kh
Primary, ages 6-11
Secondary, ages 12-17

CAMEROON

Ministry of Education, Yaounde
Tel: +237 22 22 26 716
Website: www.minesec.gov.cm/en
Primary, ages 5-11
Secondary, ages 11-18
Other: primary schools are free but parents must pay for books and uniforms.

CANADA

New Brunswick Department of Education and Early Childhood Development, Place 2000, P.O. Box 6000 Fredericton, New Brunswick E3B 5H1
Tel: +1 506 453 3678
Website: www.gnb.ca/education

Newfoundland and Labrador Department of Education and Early Childhood Development, P.O. Box 8700, Confederation Building St. John's, Newfoundland and Labrador A1B 4J6
Tel: +1 709 729 5097
Website: https://www.gov.nl.ca/education

Northwest Territories Department of Education, Culture and Employment, P.O. Box 1320, Public Affairs Yellowknife, Northwest Territories X1A 2L9
Tel: + 1 867 920 6222
Website: www.ece.gov.nt.ca

Nova Scotia Department of Education and Early Childhood Development, P.O. Box 578, 2021 Brunwick Street, Halifax, Nova Scotia B3J 2S9
Tel: +1 902 424 5168
Website: https://beta.novascotia.ca/government/education-and-early-childhood-development

Nunavut Department of Education, P.O. Box 1000, Station 900 Iqaluit, Nunavut X0A 0H0
Tel: +1 867 975 5600
Website: www.gov.nu.ca/education

Ontario Ministry of Education, 900 Bay Street, 14th Floor, Mowat Block, Toronto, Ontario M7A 1L2
Tel: +1 416 325 2929
Website: https://www.ontario.ca/page/ministry-education

Prince Edward Island Department of Education and Lifelong Learning, 101-250 Water Street, Holman Centre Summerside, Prince Edward Island C1N 1B6
Tel: +1 902 438 4854
Website: https://www.princeedwardisland.ca/en/topic/education-and-lifelong-learning

Quebec - Ministère de l'Éducation et de l'Enseignement supérieur du Québec, 1035, rue De La Chevrotière, 28e étage, Québec, Quebec G1R 5A5
Tel: +1 418 643 7095
Website: www.education.gouv.qc.ca

Manitoba Department of Education and Training, 1181 Portage Avenue, Winnipeg, Manitoba R3G 0T3
Tel: +1 204 945 0746
Website: www.edu.gov.mb.ca

Alberta Education, 7th Floor, Commerce Place, 10155-102 Street Edmonton, Alberta T5J 4L5
Tel: +1 780 427 7219
Website: https://www.alberta.ca/education.aspx

Saskatchewan Ministry of Education, 6th Floor, 2220 College Avenue, Regina, Saskatchewan S4P 4V9
Tel: +1 306-787-6089
Website: www.saskatchewan.ca/government/government-structure/ministries/education

Yukon Department of Education, Box 2703 Whitehorse, Yukon Y1A 2C6
Tel: +1 867 667 5141
Website: https://yukon.ca/en/education-and-schools

British Columbia Ministry of Education, PO Box 9150, Stn Prov Govt Victoria, British Columbia V8W 9H1
Tel: +1 250 387 6121
Website: www.gov.bc.ca/bced

Primary education, ages 6-13, Grade 1-8.
Secondary education, ages 14-18, or Grade 9-12.
Each territory or province in Canada has control over their own School system. Most Local Authorities offer publicly-funded kindergarten classes from age five.

CAYMAN ISLANDS

Ministry of Education, Youth, Sports, Agriculture, and Lands, 5th Floor, Government Administration Building, 133 Elgin Avenue, George Town, Grand Cayman,
Tel: +1 345 244 2417
Website: www.education.gov.ky
Primary, ages 4-10
Secondary, ages 11-16

CHILE

Ministry of Education, Av. Libertador Bernardo O'Higgins, 1371 Santiago
Tel: +56 2 2406 6000
Website: www.mineduc.cl
Pre-school, ages up to 6
Primary, ages 6-13
Secondary, ages 13-18
Other: some private schools are subsidised by the government.

PR CHINA

Ministry of Education for PR of China, 37 Damucang Hutong, Xidan, Beijing 100816
Tel: +86 10 660 961 14
Website: www.moe.gov.cn
Pre-school or Kindergarten, ages 3-6
Elementary/primary school, ages 6-12
Junior middle school (secondary), ages 12-15
Senior middle school (secondary), ages 15-18

COLOMBIA

Ministry of Education, Calle 43 No 57-14, Bogota
Tel: +57 1222 2800
Website: www.mineducacion.gov.co
Primary, ages 6-11
Secondary (lower), ages 11-15
Secondary (vocational), ages 15-18
Other: there are non-profit schools that are not state run and do not charge fees they are largely funded by resources from outside Colombia from countries such as the US.

COOK ISLANDS

Ministry of Education, PO Box 97, Rarotonga, Cook Islands
Tel: +68 229 357
Website: www.education.gov.ck
Preschool, ages 3-5
Primary, ages 5-11
Secondary, ages 11-16

COSTA RICA

Ministry of Education, PO Box 10087-1000, San Jose
Tel: +506 2256 8132
Primary, ages 6-13
Secondary, ages 13-18
Other: Catholic schools

CROATIA

Ministry of Science and Education, Donje Svetice 38, 10000 Zagreb
Tel: +385 1 4569 000
Website: www.mzo.hr/en
Pre-school, ages 6m-6
Elementary, ages 6-14
Secondary, ages 14-18

CUBA

Ministry of Education of the Republic of Cuba, Calle 17 y O, Vedado, Havana, Cuba
Tel: +53 7832 8077
Website: www.mined.gob.cu
Primary, ages 6-11
Secondary, ages 12-15

CYPRUS

Ministry of Education, Culture, Sports and Youth, Corner of Kimonos and Thucydides, Acropolis, 1434 Nicosia
Tel: +357 2280 0600
Website: www.moec.gov.cy
Pre-school, ages 3-6
Primary, ages 6-12
Secondary, ages 12-18

CZECH REPUBLIC

Ministry of Education, Youth and Sport, Karmelitská 529/5, 118 12, Praha 1
Tel: +42 0234 811 111
Website: www.msmt.cz
Pre-school, ages 2-5
Primary, ages 6-11
Secondary, ages 12-16

DENMARK

Ministry of Children and Education, Frederiksholms Kanal 21, 1220 Copenhagen K
Tel: +45 3392 5000
Website: https://www.eng.uvm.dk
Primary school, grades 1-6, ages 7-12
Lower secondary, grades 7-10, ages 13-16
Upper secondary, ages 16-19, consists of either general education towards higher education or vocational/technical training.
Other: production schools, which are independent schools approved and partially funded by the Local Authority; they have representatives on their school board from the local employers.

DOMINICAN REPUBLIC

Ministry of Education, Avenida Máximo Gómez esq. Santiago, No. 02, Gazcue, Distrito Nacional
Tel: +1 809 688 9700
Website: http://education.gov.dm
Pre-school, ages 3-6
Elementary, ages 6-14
High School, ages 14-18

EGYPT

Ministry of Education, 12 El-Falaky Street, Cairo
Tel: +20 27963273
Website: www.moe.gov.eg
Kindergarten, ages 2-4
Primary, ages 4-10
Preparatory, ages 11-14
Secondary, ages 15-17

EL SALVADOR

Ministry of Education, Buildings A, Master Plan, Government Centre, Alameda Juan Pablo II & Calle Guadalupe, 503
Tel: +503 2537 2122
Website: www.mined.gob.sv
Pre-school, ages up to 6
Basic, ages 7-15
Middle, ages 15-18

EQUATORIAL GUINEA

Ministry of Education and Sciences
Website: www.guineaecuatorialpress.com
Preschool, ages 3-6
Primary, ages 6-12
Lower Secondary, ages 13-17
Upper Secondary, ages 17-19
Other: education in Equatorial Guinea is very basic and not enforced, particularly for females.

ESTONIA

Ministry of Education and Research, Munga Street 18, 50088 Tartu
Tel: +372 735 0222
Website: www.hm.ee
Preschool, ages 1-7
Basic, ages 7-16
General secondary, ages 16-19

ETHIOPIA

Ministry of Education, PO Box 1367, Addis Ababa
Tel: 00251 11 155 3133
Website: www.moe.gov.et
Elementary, ages 5-11
Junior elementary, ages 11-13
Senior secondary, ages 13-16

FIJI

Ministry of Education, Heritage and Arts, Marela House, Suva
Tel: +679 331 4477
Website: www.education.gov.fj
Pre-school/kindergarten, ages 3-5
Primary, ages 6-14
Secondary, ages 14-18
Other: church run schools.

FINLAND

Ministry of Education and Culture, PO Box 29, FI - 00023 Government
Tel: +358 2953 16001
Website: www.minedu.fi/en
Pre-primary, age 6
Primary or basic, ages 7-16
General upper secondary, ages 16-19
Other: most private schools follow the Finnish National Curriculum. However, Steiner schools and those offering education in languages other than Finnish, tend to follow their own curriculums.

FRANCE

Ministry of Education, 110 rue de Grenelle, 75357 Paris SP07
Tel: +33 01 5555 1080
Website: www.education.gouv.fr
Elementary school (école élémentaire), ages 6-11
Lower secondary school (college), ages 11-15
Lycée (general/technical or vocational) (lycée d'enseignement général et technologique, LEGT, or lycée professionnel, LP), ages 15-16
Other: the majority of the private fee-paying schools are Catholic schools. Some of these independent schools receive funding from the state to pay salaries and training costs and, in return, the schools must follow the same timetables and curriculum as the state schools. There are state-funded kindergartens available, for ages 2-6, called école maternelle or classe enfantine. There are also private pre-schools, which are fee paying. All pre-schools follow a National Curriculum. Post-16 education is covered by a lycée général et technologique, LEGT or a lycée d'enseignement professionnel, LP. Although the final year of compulsory state education (15-16 years old) usually takes place in a lycée.

GEORGIA

Ministry of Education, Science, Culture And Sport of Georgia, 0102 Tbilisi, Dimitri Uznadze N52
Tel: +995 32 2 200 220
Website: www.mes.gov.ge
Elementary, ages 6-12
Basic, ages 13-15
Secondary, ages 16-18

GERMANY

Federal Ministry of Education and Research
Tel: +49 228 99570
Website: www.bmbf.de/en
Each state controls its own school system.
Compulsory education:
Primary education, aged 6-10 (12 in Berlin and Brandenburg)
Lower secondary education, ages 10-16 (12-16)
Upper secondary education, ages 15-19
Other: private schools receive some government funding and are therefore subject to some state supervision. Kindergärten is available for children between the ages of 3-6. All such schools, whether state maintained or private, are supervised by the state. There is also a National Curriculum now for all pre-schools. Post-16 education is compulsory in Germany up to the age of 18; 19 in some areas.

GHANA

Ministry of Education, PO Box M45, Accra, Greater Accra
Tel: +233 302 683627
Website: www.moe.gov.gh
Kindergarten, ages 4-6
Primary, ages 6-11
Secondary, ages 12-15

GIBRALTAR

Ministry of Education, Suite 771 europort
Tel: +350 200 79336
Website: www.gibraltar.gov.gi
Pre-school, ages 3-4
Primary, ages 4-11
Secondary, ages 12-16

GREECE

Greek Ministry of Education, Research and Religious Affairs, Andrea Papandreou 37, Marousi 15180
Tel: +30 210 344 2000
Website: www.ypepth.gr
Kindergarten, ages 2.5-5
Primary (Dimotiko), ages 6-12
Middle School (Gymnasio), ages 12-15
Secondary (Lykeio), ages 15-17
Other: private schools are supervised by the Ministry of Education.

GRENADA

Ministry of Education and Human Resource Development, Botanical Gardens, Tanteen St George's, West Indies
Tel: +1 473 440 2737
Website: https://www.gov.gd/moe
Primary, ages 5-11
Secondary, ages 12-16

GUATEMALA

Ministry of Education, 6a calle 1-87 zona 10, 01010, Guatemala, CA
Tel: +502 2411 9595
Website: www.mineduc.gob.gt
Primary, ages 7-13
Middle, ages 13-16
Secondary, ages 16-18
Other: faith schools.

GUYANA

Ministry of Education, 26 Brickdam, Georgetown, 413722 Demerara – Mahaica
Tel: +592 223 7900
Website: www.education.gov.gy
Primary, ages 5-11
Secondary, ages 12-16

HONDURAS

Ministry of Education, 1a Avenida Entre 2a y 3a calle, Comayagüela, MDC
Tel: +504 2220 5583
Website: https://www.se.gob.hn
Primary, ages 6-12
Middle, ages 12-15
Secondary, ages 15-18

HONG KONG

Education Bureau, 15/F, Wu Chung House, 213 Queen's Road East, Wan Chai, Hong Kong (SAR)
Tel: +852 2891 0088
Website: www.edb.gov.hk/en
Kindergarten, ages 3-6
Primary, ages 6-12
Junior secondary, ages 12-15
Senior secondary, ages 15-17
Other: state schools are divided into three groups: government schools, subsidised schools (usually charities), and private schools run by organisations. Private, international schools tend to offer the IB. It is rare for an international student to take Hong Kong qualifications, particularly since they switched from the British to Chinese system.

HUNGARY

Ministry of National Resources, 1055 Budapest, Szalay u. 10-14
Tel: +36 1 795 1200
Website: http://www.nefmi.gov.hu/english
Pre-primary (Óvoda), ages 5-6
General school (Általános iskola), aged 6-14
General lower and upper secondary grammar school (Gimnázium), aged 10-19
Secondary or training school, ages 14-18
Other: for children aged 3-6 kindergarten is available and the final year is compulsory (for children aged 6). Post-16 education is compulsory in Hungary up to the age of 18.

ICELAND

The Ministry of Education, Science and Culture, Solvholsgata 4, 101 Reykjavik
Tel: +354 545 9500
Website: https://www.government.is/ministries/ministry-of-education-science-and-culture/
Pre-primary, ages 1-6
Compulsory schools, ages 6-16
Upper secondary, ages 16-20

INDIA

Ministry of Human Resource Development, Shastri Bhawan, New Delhi-110001
Tel: +91 11 2338 3936
Website: https://www.education.gov.in/hi
Primary, ages 6-14
Secondary, ages 14-18

INDONESIA

Ministry of Education, Culture, Research, and Technology, Jalan Jenderal Sudirman Senayan, Jakarta 10270
Tel: +62 21 5790 3020 ext. 2115
Website: www.kemdikbud.go.id
Kindergarten, ages 3-5
Elementary, ages 6-11
Middle school, ages 12-15
High school, ages 15-18

IRAN

Ministry of Education
Tel: +98 8889 4024 021
Website: www.medu.ir
Pre-school, age 5-6
Primary, ages 6-12
Lower Secondary, ages 12-16
Upper Secondary, ages 15-18

IRAQ

Ministry of Higher Education and Scientific Research
Pre-school, ages 4-5
Elementary, ages 6-11
Intermediate, ages 12-15
Secondary, ages 15-18

IRELAND

Department of Education and Skills, Marlborough Street, Dublin 1, D01 RC96
Tel: +353 1 8896 400
Website: www.education.ie
Primary level, ages 6-12
Second level (junior cycle), ages 12-16
Other: there are privately owned schools, usually by religious communities, which are state funded for the purposes of salaries and running costs. From the age of four, children can be enrolled in infant classes in primary schools. There is also a pre-school year for children aged from 39 months. Post-16 education for children aged 15-19 is called the second-level senior cycle and usually lasts two years. If they wish, students can opt for a further year of education, called a transition year, or undertake a two-year leaving certificate programme.

ISRAEL

Ministry of Education, Dvora Hanevia 2, Jerusalem 9510402
Tel: +972 1 800 25 00 25
Website: https://www.gov.il/en/departments/ministry_of_education
Kindergarten, ages 3-5
Primary, ages 6-12
Middle school, ages 12-15
High school, ages 15-18
Other: faith schools (Orthodox Jewish), and Arab schools.

ITALY

Ministry of Education, University and Research, Sede Viale Trastevere, 76A 00153 Roma
Tel: +39 065849 2377
Website: www.miur.gov.it
Primary education, ages 6-11
Lower secondary education, ages 11-14
Upper secondary education, ages 14-19
Other: there are private schools in Italy who are not bound by the same rules and who issue qualifications that are not legally recognised. Pre-schools/nurseries are available from the age of three. Upper secondary education is covered by the liceo classico, (general academic), liceo scientifico (sciencies), liceo artistico or istituti d'arte (art), and istituti professionali (technical/vocational).

JAMAICA

Ministry of Education, Youth and Information, 2a National Heroes Circle, Kingston 4
Tel: +1 876 922 14009
Website: www.moey.gov.jm
Early childhood, ages 3-5
Primary, ages 5-12
Secondary, ages 12-17
Other: independent education is strictly monitored and has its own department at the ministry: The Independent Schools Section. The schools are also required to be registered and regularly inspected.

JAPAN

Ministry of Education, Culture, Sports, Science and Technology (MEXT), 3-2-2 Kasumigaseki, Chiyoda-ku, Tokyo 100-8959
Tel: +81 03 5253 4111
Website: www.mext.go.jp/en
Kindergarten, ages 3-6
Elementary school, ages 6-12
Lower secondary school, ages 12-15
Upper secondary school, ages 15-18
Other: private schools receive public funding and they tend to follow the National Curriculum. The major difference between the state and private sectors are that the private schools tend to include religious education.

JORDAN

Ministry of Education, PO Box 1646, Amman
Tel: +962 6 5607 331
Website: www.moe.gov.jo
Basic, ages 6-16
Secondary/vocational, ages 16-18

KAZAKHSTAN

Ministry of Education and Science, 01000 Astana, Orenburgskaya St
Tel: +7 (7172) 74 23 62
Website: www.edu.gov.kz/en
Kindergarten, ages 5-6
Primary, ages 6-10
Basic, ages 10-15
General secondary, ages 15-17

KENYA

State Department of Education, Jogoo House B, Harambee Avenue, PO Box 30040-00100, Nairobi
Tel: +254 20 3318581
Website: www.education.go.ke
Preschool, age 5
Primary, ages 6-14
Secondary, ages 14-18

DEMOCRATIC PEOPLE'S REPUBLIC OF KOREA

Department of Education
Kindergarten, ages 4-6
Primary, ages 6-9
Senior middle school, ages 10-15

SOUTH KOREA
The Ministry of Education, Government Complex-Sejong, 408 Galmae-Ro, Sejong 30119,
Tel: +82 2 6222 6060
Website: www.english.moe.go.kr
Primary school, ages 7-12
Junior high school, ages 13-15
Senior high school, ages 16-18
Other: parents are expected to pay fees if their child goes to senior high school. Private fee-paying schools follow the National Curriculum. Kindergartens are available for children aged 4-6. They too follow a National Curriculum.

KOSOVO
Ministry of Education, Science and Technology, Rruga, Agim Ramadani, 10000 Prishtine
Tel: +381 038 213 327
Website: mashLrks-gov.net/en
Pre-school, age 5
Primary school, ages 6-11
Lower secondary, ages 12-15
Upper secondary, ages 16-18

KUWAIT
Ministry of Education, PO Box 7, Shuwaikh, Building No. 1, Al-Safat 13001
Website: www.moe.edu.kw
Tel: +965 483 5721
Primary, ages 6-11
Intermediate, ages 11-16
Secondary, ages 16-19

KYRGYZSTAN
Ministry of Education and Science, 720040 Biskek, Tynystanou St, 257, Bishkek
Tel: +996 312 62 05 19
Website: www.edu.gov.kg
Pre-school, ages 3-6
Primary, ages 6-10
Secondary, ages 10-15
High school, ages 15-17

LAO
Ministry of Education and Sports, (PO Box. 67 Free) Lan Xang Road No. 1, The Vientiane, Laos
Tel: +856 21 215 ̄61
Website: www.moes.edu.la
Primary, ages 6-10
Secondary, ages 11-17

LATVIA
Ministry of Education and Science, Valnu Street 2, Riga, LV-1050
Tel: +371 6722 6209
Website: www.izm.gov.lv/en/
Pre-school, ages up to 5
Primary, ages 5-7
Basic, ages 7-16
Secondary, ages 16-19

LEBANON
Center for Educational Research and Development, P.O. Box 55264 Dekwaneh, Beirut
Tel: +961 1 683 202
Website: www.crdp.org
Elementary, ages 6-11
Intermediate, ages 12-14
Secondary, ages 15-18

LESOTHO
Ministry of Education and Training, Constitution Rd, Maseru
Tel: +266 222 144 00
Website: www.education.org.ls
Pre-primary, up to age 6
Primary, ages 6-13
Secondary, ages 13-18

LIBYA
National Commission for Education, Science and Culture, PO Box 1091, Tripoli
Tel: +218 21 362 0602
Primary, ages 6-12
Secondary, ages 12-15
Specialised Secondary, ages 15-19

LITHUANIA
Ministry of Education, Science and Sport, A Volano str 2/1, LT-01516, Vilnius
Tel: +370 5219 1190
Website: https://www.smm.lt/
Primary, ages 6-11
Lower secondary, ages 10-17
Senior secondary, ages 16-19

LUXEMBOURG

Ministry of National Education, Children and Youth, 33, Rives de Clausen, L-2165
Tel: +352 2478 5100
Website: www.men.public.lu
Pre-elementary, ages 4-6
Primary, ages 6-12
Secondary, ages 12-19

MACAU

Ministry of Education, Public Information Centre – Rua do Campo, nos. 188-198, Vicky Plaza, 26 andar.
Tel: +853 8866 8866
Website: www.gov.mo/en/
Primary, ages 6-12
Secondary, ages 12-18
Other Macau does not have its own educational system at present. Different schools follow the Chinese, British and Portuguese systems and most schools are private or heavily subsidised schools. Therefore the years spent in each type of school will depend on which system the school follows. The Chinese and British schools have similar periods of attendance, the Portuguese schools tend to allow less time in primary, and more time in secondary and high school.

NORTH MACEDONIA

Ministry of Education and Science, ul. St. Cyril and Methodius no. 54, 1000 Skopje
Tel: +389 2 3117 896
Website: www.mon.gov.mk
Elementary, ages 7-15
General secondary, ages 15-19

MALAYSIA

Ministry of Education, No. 2, Menara 2, Jalan P5/6, Presint 5, Pusat Pentadbiran Kerajaan Persekutuan, 62200 Putrajaya,
Tel: +60 38 870 6000
Website: www.moe.gov.my
Pre-school, ages 4-6
Primary, ages 7-13
Secondary, ages 13-19

REPUBLIC OF THE MALDIVES

Ministry of Education, Boduthakurufaanu Magu, Malé
Tel: +960 332 3262
Website: www.moe.gov.mv
Primary, ages 5-10
Middle school, ages 11-15
Secondary, ages 15-17
Other: some private schools, called Makthab, are traditional Islamic schools.

MALI

Ministry of Education, Place de la Liberté, Bamako
Tel: +223 223 1036
Primary, ages 7-13
Secondary, ages 13-19

MALTA

Ministry of Education and Employment, Great Siege Road, Floriana, VLT2000
Tel: +356 2598 0000
Website: www.education.gov.mt
Pre-primary, ages 3-5
Primary, ages 5-11
Secondary, ages 11-16
Other: Malta also has Church schools.

MAURITIUS

Ministry of Education, Tertiary Education, Science and Technology
MITD House Pont Fer, Phoenix
Tel: +230 601 5200
Website: https://education.govmu.org
Pre-primary, ages 3-5
Primary, ages 5-11
Secondary, ages 12-18

MOLDOVA

Ministry of Education, Culture and Research, MD-2033, Chisinau mun., Great National Assembly Square 1
Tel: +373 22 22 76 20
Website: www.mecc.gov.md
Kindergarten, ages 3-6
Primary, ages 6-10
Gymnasium, ages 10-15
Lyceum, ages 15-18

MONACO

Education, Youth and Sports Direction, Lycée Technique, Avenue de l'Annonciade, MC – 98000
Tel: +377 9898 8305
Website: https://en.gouv.mc/Government-Institutions/The-Government/Ministry-of-Interior/Department-of-Education-Youth-and-Sport
Elementary school (école élémentaire), ages 6-11
Lower secondary school (college), ages 11-15
Lycée (general/technical or vocational) (lycée d'enseignement général et technologique, LEGT, or lycée professionnel, LP), ages 15-18
Other: the majority of the private fee-paying schools are Catholic schools. Some of these independent schools receive funding from the state to pay salaries and training costs and in return the schools must follow the same timetables and curriculum as the state schools. There are state-funded kindergartens available, for ages 3-6, called école maternelle or classe enfantine. There are also private pre-schools, which are fee paying. Post-16 education is covered by a lycée général et technologique, LEGT or a lycée d'enseignement professionnel, LP. Although the final year of compulsory state education (15-16 years old) usually takes place in a lycée.

MONTENEGRO

Ministry of Education and Science, Vaka Durovica, 81000 Podgorica
Tel: +382 20 410 100
Website: www.gov.me/en/mpnks
Elementary, ages 6-14
Secondary, ages 14-18

MOROCCO

Ministry of Education, Science, Culture and Sports, 29 Avenue d'Alger, 10000, Rabat
Tel: +212 5 3777 1822
Website: www.men.gov.ma
Pre-school, ages 4-6
Primary, ages 6-12
Secondary, ages 12-18
Other: Morocco has three systems of education: a continuation of the French system; Islamic; and technical, skills and vocational training.

MOZAMBIQUE

Ministry of Education, Avenida 24 de Julho, No 167, PO Box 34, Maputo
Tel: +258 21 490 677
Website: www.mined.gov.mz
Pre-primary, ages up to 6
Primary, ages 6-13
Secondary, ages 13-18
Other: missionary schools.

NAMIBIA

Ministry of Education, Arts and Culture, Government Office Park (Luther Street), Private Bag 13186, Windhoek
Tel: +264 61 293 3111
Website: www.moe.gov.na
Primary, ages 6-13
Secondary, ages 13-18

NEPAL

Department of Education, Sanothimi, Bhaktapur, Nepal
Tel: +977 1 4200340/390
Website: www.doe.gov.np
Pre-primary, ages 4-6
Primary, ages 6-11
Secondary, ages 11-18
Other: schools run by the local people that receive no grants or financial support.

NETHERLANDS

Ministry of Education, Culture and Science, Rijnstraat 50, 2515 XP The Hague
Tel: +31 (0)70 412 34 56
Website: www.government.nl/ministries/ministry-of-education-culture-and-science
Primary school, ages 4-12
Secondary school, ages 12-18
Other: private schools receive funding from the state and have to meet and maintain certain conditions to retain their funding, although they are allowed to set their own curriculum. Pre-school is available for children between 2.5 and 4, the cost is split between the parents and the government.

NEW ZEALAND

The Ministry of Education, PO Box 1666, Wellington 6140
Tel: +64 (04) 463 8000
Website: www.govt.nz/browse/education/
Primary school, ages 4-10
Middle school, ages 10-12, Forms 1-2.
Secondary school, ages 12-18, Forms 3-7.
Other: integrated schools: private schools that have been integrated into the state system and are therefore state funded. These are usually religious schools. Kindergarten/pre-school education is available for children ages 3-4.

NIGERIA

Federal Ministry of Education, Federal Secretarial Phase III, FCT, Abuja
Tel: +234 903 0009 912
Website: www.education.gov.ng
Basic, ages 6-12
Secondary, ages 12-18

NORWAY

Ministry of Education and Research, Postboks 8119 Dep, 0032 Oslo
Tel: +47 2224 9090
Website: www.regjeringen.no
Primary and lower secondary, ages 6-16
Upper secondary, ages 16-19

OMAN

Ministry of Education, PO Box 3, Muscat 113
Website: https://home.moe.gov.om
Tel: +968 24255552
Primary, ages 6-12
Preparatory, ages 12-15
Secondary, ages 15-18

PAKISTAN

Ministry of Federal Education and Professional Training
Tel: +92 51 92 11 622
Website: http://www.mofept.gov.pk
Pre-school, ages 3-5
Primary, ages 6-11
Middle, ages 11-14
High, ages 14-16
Intermediate, ages 16-18

PALAU

Ministry of Education, PO Box 6051, Koror
Tel: +680 767 2403
Website: www.palaumoe.net
Elementary, ages 6-12
Middle school, ages 13-15
High school, ages 15-19

PALESTINE

Ministry of Education and Higher Education
Tel: +970 22983200
Website: www.moehe.gov.ps
Pre-primary, ages 4-6
Primary, ages 7-15
Secondary, ages 15-18

PANAMA

Ministry of Education, PO Box 0816-04049, Villa Cárdenas, Ancón
Tel: +507 511 4400
Primary, ages 6-12
Middle school, ages 12-15
Secondary, ages 15-18

PARAGUAY

Ministry of Education and Sciences, Chile 849, Asunción
Tel: +595 21 452 440
Website: www.mec.gov.py
Pre-school, ages 3-6
Elementary, ages 6-15
High school, ages 15-18

PERU

Ministry of Education, Calle Del Comercio 193 San Borja, Lima - 15021
Tel: +51 1 615 5800
Website: www.gob.pe/minedu
Primary, ages 6-12
Secondary, ages 13-18

PHILIPPINES

Department of Education
Tel: +63 633 7208
Website: www.deped.gov.ph
Elementary, ages 4-12
Junior high, ages 12-16
Senior high, ages 16-18

POLAND
Ministry of National Education, al. J Ch Szucha 25, 00-918 Warsaw
Tel: +48 22 34 74 100
Website: www.gov.pl/web/edukacja
Kindergarten, ages 6-7
Primary, ages 7-15
Secondary, ages 15-19

PORTUGAL
Ministry of Education, Avenida 5 de Outubro, 107 1069-018, Lisboa
Tel: +351 217 811 800
Website: www.portugal.gov.pt
Pre-primary, ages 3-5
Basic, ages 6-14
Secondary, ages 15-17

PUERTO RICO
Department of Education, PO Box 190759, San Juan, PR 00919-0759
Tel: +787 759 2000
Website: www.de.pr.gov
Primary, ages 6-12
Intermediate, ages 12-15
High school, ages 15-18

QATAR
Ministry of Education
Website: www.edu.gov.qa
Elementary, ages 6-12
Preparatory, ages 13-15
Secondary, ages 16-18

ROMANIA
Ministry of National Education, Str Gen Berthelot 28-30, Sector 1, 010168, Bucharest
Tel: +40 21 405 6200
Website: www.edu.ro
Kindergarten, ages 3-6
Elementary, ages 6-14
High school, ages 15-19

RUSSIA
The Ministry of Education of the Russian Federation
Website: http://government.ru/en/department/390
Pre-school, ages up to 6 years
Primary school, ages 6-10
Middle school, ages 10-15
Secondary school, ages 15-17

RWANDA
Ministry of Education, PO Box 622, Kigali
Tel: +250 737 093 807
Website: www.mineduc.gov.rw
Primary, ages 6-12
Secondary, ages 12-18

SAUDI ARABIA
Ministry of Education, King Abdullah Road, Riyadh 12435
Tel: +966 11 4753 000
Website: www.moe.gov.sa
Kindergarten, ages 3-5
Primary, ages 6-12
Intermediate, ages 13-16
High school, ages 17-19

SENEGAL
Ministry of Education, Rue Alpha Hachamiyou TALL, BP 4025
Tel: +221 33 849 54 54
Primary, ages 7-12
Secondary, ages 13-19
Other: Islamic schools.

SERBIA
Ministry of Education, Science and Technological Development, 24 Nemanjina Street, Belgrade 11 000
Tel: +381 11 3613 734
Website: www.mpn.gov.rs
Pre-primary, age 6
Primary, ages 7-14
High school, ages 15-19

SEYCHELLES
Ministry of Education and Human Resource Development, Mont Fleuri, PO Box 48
Tel: +248 4283283
Website: www.education.gov.sc
Primary, ages 7-12
Secondary, ages 12-18

SIERRA LEONE
Ministry Of Basic And Senior Secondary Education, New England, Freetown, Sierra Leone
Website: https://mbsse.gov.sl
Primary, ages 6-12
Junior secondary, 12-15
Senior secondary, 15-18

SINGAPORE

Ministry of Education, 1 North Buona Vista Drive, Singapore 138675
Tel: +65 6872 2220
Website: www.moe.gov.sg
Primary school, ages 7-13
Secondary school, ages 14-17
Other: there are also government-aided schools (formerly privately owned by churches or other organisations), who receive most of their funding from the state. Kindergarten (ages 3-6) is also available. These are privately run establishments, which have to be registered with the Ministry of Education.

SLOVAKIA

Ministry of Education, Science, Research and Sport, Stromová 1, 813 30, Bratislava
Tel: +421 2593 74111
Website: www.minedu.sk
Nursery, ages 3-6
First stage, ages 6-10
Second stage (primary), ages 10-15
Secondary, ages 15-19

SLOVENIA

Ministry of Education, Science and Sport, Masarykova 16, SI-1000 Ljubljana
Tel: +386 1 400 52 00
Website: https://www.gov.si/drzavni-organi/ministrstva/ministrstvo-za-izobrazevanje-znanost-in-sport/
Pre-school, ages 1-6
Basic, ages 6-15
Secondary, ages 15-18

SOMALIA

Ministry of Education and Higher Education of Puntland
Website: www.moepuntland.com

Somaliland Ministry of Education and Science
Website: moe.govsomaliland.org

Early childhood, ages up to 6
Elementary, ages 6-10
Intermediate, ages 11-14
Secondary, ages 15-18

SOUTH AFRICA

Department of Basic Education, Sol Plaatje House, 222 Struben Street, Pretoria
Tel: +27 012 357 3000
Website: www.education.gov.za
Pre-primary, ages birth to 5
Reception, Grade R, ages 5-6
Primary, Grades 1-6, ages 7-12
Secondary, Grades 7-9, ages 12-15
Post secondary, Grades 10-12, ages 16-18
Other: South Africa runs a state school system that is unique. Schools are divided into five categories determined by the level of wealth in a particular area; the poorer schools are allocated larger funding than wealthier schools. Only the poorest state schools are completely free and entirely government funded, most charge some form of fee to top up their funding.

SPAIN

The Ministry of Education and Vocational Training, Calle de los Madrazo, 15 Madrid
Tel: +34 910 837 937
Website: www.educacionyfp.gob.es
Primary school, ages 6-12
Lower secondary school, ages 12-16
Other: there are also private schools that receive state funding and are therefore under the control of the state. Spain also offers pre-school education for children from birth to age six, which is free from the age of three. Post-16 education consists of either general upper secondary school or intermediate vocational training; both take place up to the age of 18. State colleges are free to students but parents are expected to pay for additional items such as meals, transport and various materials needed for their child's coursework.

SRI LANKA

Ministry of Education, Isurupaya, Pelawatta, Battaramulla
Tel: +94 112 785141 50
Website: www.moe.gov.lk
Primary, ages 6-11
Junior, ages 12-14
Senior secondary, ages 15-16
Post secondary, ages 17-18
Other: pirivenas (schools for Buddhist priests).

ST LUCIA

Ministry of Education, 4th Floor, Francis Compton Building, Waterfront Castries
Tel: +1 758 468 5202
Website: www.education.govt.lc
Preschools, ages 3-5
Primary, ages 5-13
Secondary, ages 13-18

SUDAN

Ministry of Education, PO Box 284, Sudan Khartoum, Alneel Avenue
Tel: +24 9122 838 009
Website: www.moe.gov.sd
Kindergarten, ages 3-5
Primary, ages 6-13
Secondary, ages 14-17

SWAZILAND

Ministry of Education and Training, PO Box 37, Lobamba
Tel: +268 241 62 407
Website: www.gov.sz
Early childhood care and development, ages up to 8
Primary, ages 6-13
Secondary, ages 14-19

SWEDEN

National Ministry of Education and Research, SE-103 33, Stockholm
Tel: +46 8 405 1000
Website: www.government.se
Other: independent schools receive grants from the NAE for each registered student, but they are essentially fee-paying. Compulsory education runs from age 6-16 and takes place in all-through schools, which are coeducational and non-selective. There are several varieties of pre-schools available for children from birth to ages seven. These are: Daghem (day nursery/pre-school), Familjedaghem (registered childminders), Deltidsgrupp (part-time group), Oppen förskola (pre-school/parent and toddler groups), and Förskoleklass (pre-school for ages 6-7). Post-16 is not compulsory but such education available is for students, should they want it, up to the age of 20.

SWITZERLAND

State Secretariat for Education, Research and Innovation SERI Einsteinstrasse 2, CH-3003 Bern
Tel: +41 58 462 21 29
Website: www.sbf.admin.ch
Pre-school/kindergarten, ages 4-6
Primary, ages 6-12
Secondary I, ages 12-16
Secondary II, ages 16-20
Other: tertiary education is either general or professional education. Professional education applies to universities or occupational qualifications; the latter tend to be supported/sponsored by the relevant association (medical, law, etc) who are also responsible for setting the examinations.

TAIWAN

Ministry of Education, No 5 Zhongshan S Road, Zhongzheng District, Taipei City 10051
Tel: +886 2773 66666
Website: english.moe.gov.tw
Preschool, ages 3-6
Primary, ages 6-12
Junior high, ages 12-15
Senior secondary, ages 15-18

TAJIKISTAN

Ministry of Education and Science, 734024, Dushanbe, Nisor Muhammad St, 13a
Tel: +992 3772 221 4605
Website: www.maorif.tj
Pre-school, ages 3-6
Primary, ages 7-11
Secondary, ages 11-18

TANZANIA

Ministry of Education, Science and Technology, PO Box 10, Dodoma
Tel: +255 26 296 3533
Website: www.moe.go.tz
Pre-primary, ages 3-4
Primary, ages 5-11
Secondary, ages 12-16

THAILAND

Ministry of Education, Bangkok 10300
Tel: +66 228 198 09
Website: www.en.moe.go.th
Pre-school, ages 4-6
Elementary, ages 7-12
Secondary, ages 13-18

TIMOR-LESTE

Ministry of Education
Website: www.moe.gov.tl

TRINIDAD AND TOBAGO

Ministry of Education, No 5 St Vincent Street, Port of Spain
Tel: +1 868 622 2181
Website: www.moe.gov.tt
Pre-school, ages 3-5
Primary, ages 5-11
Secondary, ages 12-16
Other religious schools.

TUNISIA

Ministry of Education, 3 Rue Asdrubal, 1002 Lafayette
Tel: +216 71 833 800
Website: www.education.gov.tn
Pre-school, ages 3-6
Primary, ages 6-12
Preparatory, ages 13-16
Secondary, ages 16-20

TURKEY

Ministry of National Education, Devlet Mahallesi, Atatürk Blv No 98, 06420 Çankaya/Ankara
Tel: +90 312 4132680
Website: www.meb.gov.tr
Pre-school, ages 3-6
Primary, ages 6-14
Secondary, ages 15-17

TURKS AND CAICOS ISLANDS

Department of Education (Zone I)
Mission Folly, Grand Turk
Tel: +1 649 9462319
Website: www.gov.tc/education
Primary, ages 5-11
Secondary, ages 12-16

UGANDA

Ministry of Education and Sports, PO Box 7063, Kampala
Tel: +256 414 259 338
Website: www.education.go.ug
Primary, ages 7-13
Secondary, ages 14-17

UK – ENGLAND

Department for Education, Piccadilly Gate, Store Street Manchester M1 2WD
Tel: 0370 000 2288
Website: https://www.gov.uk/government/organisations/department-for-education
Pre-school, ages 3-5
Primary/preparatory, ages 5-11 (or 13 in private preparatory schools)
Secondary/senior, ages 11-16
Sixth form, ages 16-18
Other: faith schools, free schools, and academies.

UK – NORTHERN IRELAND

Department of Education, Rathgael House, Balloo Road, Rathgill, Bangor, BT19 7PR
Tel: 028 9127 9279
Website: www.education-ni.gov.uk
Primary, ages 4-11
Secondary, ages 11-16
Sixth form, ages 16-18
Other: faith schools.

UK – SCOTLAND

Education and Skills, St Andrew's House, Regent Road, Edinburgh, EH1 3DG
Tel: 0300 244 4000
Website: www.gov.scot/education
Primary, ages 4-11
Secondary, ages 11-18
Other: faith schools.

UK – WALES

Department for Education and Skills, Cathays Park, Cardiff, CF10 3NQ
Tel: 0300 060 4400
Website: www.gov.wales/education-skills
Pre-school, ages 3-4
Primary/preparatory, ages 5-11 (or 13 in private preparatory schools)
Secondary/senior, ages 11-16
Sixth form, ages 16-18
Other: Welsh-speaking only schools.

UKRAINE

Ministry of Education and Science, 01135, Kyiv, prospect Peremohy, 10
Tel: +380 044 481 32 21
Website: www.mon.gov.ua
Primary, ages 6-10
Basic general secondary, ages 10-15
Complete general secondary, ages 15-18

UNITED ARAB EMIRATES

Ministry of Education
Tel: +971 8005 1115
Website: www.moe.gov.ae/English
Primary, ages 6-12
Middle, ages 12-15
Secondary, ages 15-18

UNITED STATES OF AMERICA

Department of Education, 400 Maryland Avenue, SW, Washington, DC 20202
Tel: +1 800 872 5327
Website: www.ed.gov
Pre-school, ages 4-5
Kindergarten, ages 5-6
Elementary, ages 6-11, 1st-5th grade
Middle/junior high, ages 11-14, 6th-8th grade
High school, ages 14-18, 9th-12th grade
Other: in high school, ninth graders are called 'freshmen', tenth graders 'sophomores', eleventh graders 'juniors' and twelfth graders 'seniors'.

VIRGIN ISLANDS

The Ministry of Education, Culture, Youth Affairs, Fisheries and Agriculture, 33 Admin Drive, Wickhams Cay 1, Road Town, Tortola
Tel: +1 284 468-3701
Website: http://www.bvi.gov.vg/content/ministry-education-and-culture
Junior high, ages 5-12
Senior high, ages 13-17

UZBEKISTAN

Ministry of Education, 120100, Syrdarya region, Gulistan city, Peoples' Friendship street, 30th building
Tel: +998 71 241 01 86
Website: www.uzedu.uz
Primary, ages 6-10
Secondary, ages 10-15
Upper secondary, ages 15-17

VENEZUELA

Ministry of Education
Preschool, ages up to 6
Primary, ages 6-11
Secondary, ages 11-17

VIETNAM

Ministry of Education and Training, 35 Dai Co Viet Street, Hanoi
Tel: +84 43869 5144
Website: en.moet.gov.vn
Pre-school, ages 3-6
Primary, ages 6-11
Lower secondary, ages 12-15
Upper secondary, ages 16-18

ZAMBIA

Ministry of General Education, PO Box 50093, Lusaka
Tel: +260 211 250 855
Website: www.moge.gov.zm
Primary, ages 6-13
Junior secondary, 13-15
Upper secondary, ages 15-18

ZIMBABWE

Ministry of Primary and Secondary Education, Head Office, PO Box CY 121, Causeway, Harare
Tel: +263 4 705153
Website: http://mopse.co.zw
Primary, ages 6-13
Secondary, ages 13-16
High schools, ages 17-19

Curricula, examinations and tests

INTERNATIONAL QUALIFICATIONS

Cambridge Advanced International Certificate of Education (AICE) Diploma

The Cambridge Advanced International Certificate of Education (AICE) Diploma prepares students for honours degree programmes. It is made up of individual Cambridge International Advanced Subsidiary (AS) Level and Advanced (A) Levels, and requires the study of subjects drawn from three curriculum areas within an international curriculum framework: mathematics and sciences; languages; and arts and humanities.

To achieve the Diploma, all learners also need to study and pass a compulsory core subject: Cambridge International AS Level Global Perspectives & Research. This is a cross-curricular skills-based course.

In order to receive a Cambridge AICE Diploma, a candidate must earn a minimum of seven credits (including Cambridge International AS Level Global Perspectives & Research), with at least one credit coming from each of the three curriculum areas. The remaining credits can come from any of the curriculum areas, including an optional group of interdisciplinary subjects (Group 4).

A Cambridge International AS Level is awarded one credit, and a Cambridge International A Level is awarded two credits.

Learners who pass the Cambridge International A Level in Global Perspectives & Research meet the compulsory requirement of the core group and also have one credit which may then be included in Group 4 to contribute to the overall requirement of seven credits.

Grading and points system

Cambridge International AS Level subjects – candidates are graded A to E.

Cambridge International A Level subjects – candidates are graded A* to E.

The Cambridge AICE Diploma is awarded on the basis of a points system:

Two credits study (A Levels)

Grade	Points
A*	140
A	120
B	100
C	80
D	60
E	40

One credit study (AS Levels)

Grade	Points
A	60
B	50
C	40
D	30
E	20

Candidates who meet the requirements will receive a Cambridge AICE Diploma at one of three levels – pass, merit or distinction – on the basis of their overall Cambridge AICE Diploma score:

Cambridge AICE Diploma with Distinction: awarded to students with a score of 360 points or above. The maximum Diploma score is 420 points.

Cambridge AICE Diploma with Merit: awarded to students with between 250 and 359 points.

Cambridge AICE Diploma at Pass level: awarded to students with between 140 and 249 points.

The maximum number of Cambridge AICE Diploma points is capped at 420.

Subjects

Group 1: Mathematics and sciences. Subjects available include biology, chemistry, computing, design and technology, environmental management, mathematics, physics and psychology.

Group 2: Languages. Subjects available include English language, Afrikaans, Chinese, Portuguese, Spanish, French, German, Urdu.

Group 3: Arts and humanities. Subjects available include accounting, art and design, business studies, economics, geography, history, English literature, French literature, Portuguese literature, Spanish literature, music, psychology, sociology.

Group 4: Interdisciplinary subjects (optional). Subjects include a general paper and thinking skills.

Core: Cambridge Global Perspectives. It is compulsory for all learners to study Cambridge International AS Level Global Perspectives & Research.

Website: www.cambridgeinternational.org/aice

Cambridge International AS & A Level

Cambridge International AS & A Level is an internationally benchmarked qualification, taught in over 130 countries worldwide. It is typically for learners aged 16 to 19 years who need advanced study to prepare for university. It was created specifically for an international audience and the content has been devised to suit the wide variety of schools worldwide and avoid any cultural bias.

Cambridge International A Level is typically a two-year course, and Cambridge International AS Level is typically one year. Some subjects can be started as a Cambridge International AS Level and extended to a Cambridge International A Level. Students can either follow a broad course of study, or specialise in one particular subject area.

Learners use Cambridge International AS & A Levels to gain places at leading universities worldwide, including the UK, Ireland, USA, Canada, Australia, New

Zealand, India, Singapore, Egypt, Jordan, South Africa, the Netherlands, Germany and Spain. In places such as the US and Canada, good grades in carefully chosen Cambridge International A Level subjects can result in up to one year of university course credit.

Assessment options:

Cambridge International AS & A Levels have a linear structure with exams at the end of the course. Students can choose from a range of assessment options:

Option 1: take Cambridge International AS Levels only. The Cambridge International AS Level syllabus content is half a Cambridge International A Level.

Option 2: staged assessment, which means taking the Cambridge International AS Level in one exam session and the Cambridge International A Level at a later session. However, this route is not possible in all subjects.

Option 3: take all Cambridge International A Level papers in the same examination session, usually at the end of the course.

Grades and subjects

Cambridge International A Levels are graded from A* to E. Cambridge International AS Levels are graded from A to E.

Subjects: available in 55 subjects including accounting, Afrikaans, Afrikaans – first language (AS only), Afrikaans language (AS only), applied information and communication technology, Arabic, Arabic language (AS only), art and design, biology, business, chemistry, Chinese, Chinese language (AS only), classical studies, computing, design and technology, design and textiles, digital media & design, divinity, economics, English language, English literature, environmental management, food studies, French, French language (AS only), French literature (AS only), general paper, geography, German, German language (AS only), Global Perspectives & Research, Hindi, Hindi language (AS only), Hindi literature (AS only), Hinduism, history, Islamic studies, Japanese language (AS only), English language and literature (AS only), law, Marathi, Marathi language (AS only), marine science, mathematics, further mathematics, media studies, music, physical education, physical science, physics, Portuguese, Portuguese language (AS only), Portuguese literature (AS only), psychology, sociology, Spanish, Spanish first language (AS only), Spanish language (AS only), Spanish literature (AS only), Tamil, Tamil language (AS only), Telugu, Telugu language (AS only), thinking skills, travel and tourism, Urdu, Urdu language (AS only).

Website: www.cambridgeinternational.org/alevel

Cambridge International Certificate of Education (ICE)

The Cambridge International Certificate of Education (ICE) is the group award of Cambridge IGCSE (see below). In order to be awarded a Cambridge ICE certificate, a student must obtain at least grade G in seven subjects from five subject groups. They must take two different languages and one subject from each of the other groups: humanities and social sciences, sciences, mathematics, and creative and professional. The seventh subject can be taken from any of the five subject groups. The certificates are awarded in the following levels:

Distinction – student must obtain grade A or above in five subjects and grade C or above in two further subjects.

Merit – student must obtain grade C or above in five subjects and grade F or above in two further subjects.

Pass – student must obtain grade G or above in seven subjects.

Cambridge IGCSE (Cambridge Upper Secondary)

Cambridge IGCSE is the world's most popular international qualification for 14 to16 year olds. It develops skills in creative thinking, enquiry and problem solving, in preparation for the next stage in a student's education. Cambridge IGCSE is taken in over 150 countries, and is widely recognised by employers and higher education institutions worldwide.

Cambridge IGCSE is graded from A*-G. In the UK, Cambridge IGCSE is accepted as equivalent to the GCSE. It can be used as preparation for Cambridge International A & AS Levels, UK A and AS levels, IB or AP and in some instances entry into university. Cambridge IGCSE First Language English and Cambridge IGCSE English Language qualifications are recognised by a significant number of UK universities as evidence of competence in the language for university entrance.

Subjects: available in over 70 subjects including accounting, Afrikaans – first language, Afrikaans – second language, agriculture, Arabic – first language, Arabic – foreign language, art and design, Baha Indonesia, Bangladesh studies, biology, business studies, chemistry, child development, Chinese – first language, Chinese – second language, Chinese (Mandarin) – foreign language, computer studies, Czech – first language, design and technology, development studies, drama, Dutch – first language, Dutch – foreign language, economics, English – additional language , English – first language, English – literature, English – second language, enterprise, environmental management, food and nutrition, French – first language, French – foreign language, geography, German – first language, German – foreign language, global perspectives, Greek – foreign language, Hindi as a second language, Italian – foreign language, history, India studies, Indonesian – foreign language, information and communication

technology, IsiZulu as a second language, Japanese – first language, Japanese – foreign language, Kazakh as a second language, Korean (first language), Latin, Malay – first language, Malay – foreign language, mathematics, mathematics – additional, international mathematics, music, Pakistan studies, physical education, physical science, physics, Portuguese – first language, Portuguese – foreign language, religious studies, Russian – first language, science – combined, sciences – co-ordinated (double), sociology, Spanish – first language, Spanish – foreign language, Spanish – literature, Thai – first language, travel and tourism, Turkish – first language, Urdu – second language, world literature.
Website: www.cambridgeinternational.org/igcse

Cambridge Primary

Cambridge Primary is typically for learners aged 5 to 11 years. It develops learner skills and understanding in 10 subjects: English as a first or second language, mathematics, science, art & design, digital literacy, music, physical education, Cambridge Global Perspectives and ICT. The flexible curriculum frameworks include optional assessment tools to help schools monitor learners' progress and give detailed feedback to parents. At the end of Cambridge Primary, schools can enter students for Cambridge Primary Checkpoint tests which are marked in Cambridge.
Website: www.cambridgeinternational.org/primary

Cambridge ICT Starters introduces learners, typically aged 5 to 14 years, to the key ICT applications they need to achieve computer literacy and to understand the impact of technology on our daily lives. It can be taught and assessed in English or Spanish.

Cambridge Lower Secondary

Cambridge Lower Secondary is typically for learners aged 11 to 14 years. It develops learner skills and understanding in 10 subjects: English, English as a second language, mathematics, science, art & design, digital literacy, music, physical education, Cambridge Global Perspectives and ICT, and includes assessment tools. At the end of Cambridge Lower Secondary, schools can enter students for Cambridge Lower Secondary Checkpoint tests which are marked in Cambridge and provide an external international benchmark for student performance.
Website: www.cambridgeinternational.org/lowersecondary

Edexcel International GCSEs

Pearson's Edexcel International GCSEs are academic qualifications aimed at learners aged 14 to 16. They're equivalent to a UK General Certificate of Secondary Education (GCSE), and are the main requirement for Level 3 studies, including progression to GCE AS or A levels, BTECs or employment. International GCSEs are linear qualifications, meaning that students take all of the exams at the end of the course. They are available at Level 1 and Level 2. There are currently more than 100,000 learners studying Edexcel International GCSEs, in countries throughout Asia, Africa, Europe, the Middle East and Latin America. Developed by subject specialists and reviewed regularly, many of Pearson's Edexcel International GCSEs include specific international content to make them relevant to students worldwide.

International GCSEs are offered in over 30 subjects. Subject areas include: Art and Design, Business & Economics, English, Humanities, Information and Communication Technology, Languages, Mathematics, Sciences. Note that the subject areas highlighted in bold are also available as part of the Edexcel Certificate qualification suite.

European Baccalaureate (EB)

Not to be confused with the International Baccalaureate (IB) or the French Baccalaureate, this certificate is available in European schools and recognised in all EU countries.

To obtain the baccalaureate, a student must obtain a minimum score of 50%, which is made up from: course-work, oral participation in class and tests (50%); five written examinations (35%) – mother-tongue, first foreign language and maths are compulsory for all candidates; three oral examinations (15%) – mother tongue and first foreign language are compulsory (history or geography may also be compulsory here, dependant on whether the candidate has taken a written examination in these subjects).

Subjects taught in different languages have the same syllabi, regardless of the language, and the same is valid for examinations – the content is simply translated into different languages. In case of languages, the syllabi vary, but nevertheless, they are harmonized and the examinations have to follow an agreed structure. The EB has been specifically designed to meet, at the very least, the minimum qualification requirements of each member state.

Study for the EB begins at nursery stage (age 4) and progresses through primary (age six) and on into secondary school (age 12).

Syllabus

Languages: Bulgarian, Czech, Danish, Dutch, English, Estonian, Finnish, Finnish as a second national language, French, Gaelic as other national language German, Greek, Hungarian, Italian, Latvian, Lithuanian, Maltese as other national language, Polish, Portuguese, Romanian, Slovak, Slovenian, Spanish, Swedish, Swedish for Finnish pupils.

Literary: art education, non-confessional ethics, geography, ancient Greek, history, human sciences, Latin, music, philosophy, physical education.

Sciences: biology, chemistry, economics, ICT, mathematics, physics.

For more information, contact:
Office of the Secretary-General of the European Schools
Rue de la Science 23, B-1040 Bruxelles
Tel: +32 2295 3745; Fax: +32 2298 6298
Website: www.eursc.eu

French Baccalaureate

The French Baccalauréat or 'le bac', is an academic qualification taken at the end of the lycée (secondary education), usually when the student is 18. It is the required qualification in France for those students wishing to carry on their studies at university. Students not wishing to go on to higher education can, in theory, opt out of taking the baccalaureate and those who do not have one can instead take the higher education entrance exam, which leads to its own diploma.

There are three main types of baccalaureate in France:

- the baccalauréat général (general);
- the baccalauréat professionnel (professional);
- the baccalauréat technologique (technological).

General Baccalaureate

The new bac général, introduced in 2021, includes six obligatory core subjects: French, history-geography, two foreign languages, sport, and a new subject called humanités scientifiques and numériques, which covers science and technology.

In the second year of lycée, students can choose three speciality subjects. In the third year, they continue with two speciality subjects.

Five exams, including an oral exam, will account for 60% of the overall mark. Continued assessment will account for 40% (of which 30% from set tests, and 10% from term grades).

Students will take the French exam (written and oral) at the end of the second year, as philosophy lessons replace French lessons in the final year. They will then sit the exam for each of the two speciality subjects immediately after the spring school holiday in the final year, and finally the philosophy and oral exam at the end of the summer term.

Option Internationale du Baccalauréat

This is an additional option to the general baccalaureate and offers further subjects. Extra exams are offered in literature, history and geography allowing a higher grade to be achieved towards the final baccalaureate mark. In general, this option is taken by students wishing to study at overseas universities.

Grades

Students need a total combined mark of 50% or above to pass their brévet and baccalauréat exams in France. Accreditations, known as mentions ('assez bien', 'bien', 'très bien'), are awarded for achieving certain percentage thresholds above the median.

The International Baccalaureate (IB)

The International Baccalaureate (IB) offers four challenging and high quality educational programmes for a worldwide community of schools, aiming to develop internationally minded people who, recognizing their common humanity and shared guardianship of the planet, help to create a better, more peaceful world.

The IB works with schools around the world (both state and privately funded) that share the commitment to international education to deliver these programmes.

Schools that have achieved the high standards required for authorization to offer one or more of the IB programmes are known as IB World Schools. There are over half a million students attending more than 5400 IB World Schools in 153 countries and this number is growing annually.

The Primary Years, Middle Years and Diploma Programmes share a common philosophy and common characteristics. They develop the whole student, helping students to grow intellectually, socially, aesthetically and culturally. They provide a broad and balanced education that includes science and the humanities, languages and mathematics, technology and the arts. The programmes teach students to think critically, and encourage them to draw connections between areas of knowledge and to use problem-solving techniques and concepts from many disciplines. They instil in students a sense of responsibility towards others and towards the environment. Lastly, and perhaps most importantly, the programmes give students an awareness and understanding of their own culture and of other cultures, values and ways of life.

A fourth programme called the IB Career Related Certificate (IBCC) became available to IB World Schools from September 2012.

All IB programmes include:

- a written curriculum or curriculum framework;
- student assessment appropriate to the age range;
- professional development and networking opportunities for teachers;
- support, authorization and programme evaluation for the school.

The IB Primary Years Programme

The IB Primary Years Programme (PYP), for students aged three to 12, focuses on the development of the whole child as an inquirer, both in the classroom and in the world outside. It is a framework consisting of five essential elements (concepts, knowledge, skills, attitude, action) and guided by six trans-disciplinary themes of global significance, explored using knowledge and skills derived from six subject areas (language, social studies, mathematics, science and technology, arts, and personal, social and physical education) with a powerful emphasis on inquiry-based learning.

The most significant and distinctive feature of the PYP is the six trans-disciplinary themes. These themes are about issues that have meaning for, and are important to, all of us. The programme offers a balance between learning about or through the subject areas, and learning beyond them. The six themes of global significance create a trans-disciplinary framework that allows students to 'step up' beyond the confines of learning within subject areas:

- Who we are.
- Where we are in place and time.
- How we express ourselves.
- How the world works.
- How we organize ourselves.
- Sharing the planet.

The PYP exhibition is the culminating activity of the programme. It requires students to analyse and propose solutions to real-world issues, drawing on what they have learned through the programme. Evidence of student development and records of PYP exhibitions are reviewed by the IB as part of the programme evaluation process.

Assessment is an important part of each unit of inquiry as it both enhances learning and provides opportunities for students to reflect on what they know, understand and can do. The teacher's feedback to the students provides the guidance, the tools and the incentive for them to become more competent, more skilful and better at understanding how to learn.

The IB Middle Years Programme (MYP)

The Middle Years Programme (MYP), for students aged 11 to 16, comprises eight subject groups:

- Language acquisition
- Language and literature
- Individuals and societies
- Sciences
- Mathematics
- Arts
- Physical and health education
- Design

The MYP requires at least 50 hours of teaching time for each subject group in each year of the programme. In years 4 and 5, students have the option to take courses from six of the eight subject groups within certain limits, to provide greater flexibility in meeting local requirements and individual student learning needs.

Each year, students in the MYP also engage in at least one collaboratively planned interdisciplinary unit that involves at least two subject groups.

MYP students also complete a long-term project, where they decide what they want to learn about, identify what they already know, discovering what they will need to know to complete the project, and create a proposal or criteria for completing it.

The MYP aims to help students develop their personal understanding, their emerging sense of self and their responsibility in their community.

The MYP allows schools to continue to meet state, provincial or national legal requirements for students with access needs. Schools must develop an inclusion/special educational needs (SEN) policy that explains assessment access arrangements, classroom accommodations and curriculum modification that meet individual student learning needs.

The IB Diploma Programme (IBDP)

The IB Diploma Programme, for students aged 16 to 19, is an academically challenging and motivating curriculum of international education that prepares students for success at university and in life beyond studies.

DP students choose at least one course from six subject groups, thus ensuring depth and breadth of knowledge and experience in languages, social studies, the experimental sciences, mathematics, and the arts. With more than 35 courses to choose from, students have the flexibility to further explore and learn subjects that meet their interest. Out of the six courses required, at least three and not more than four must be taken at higher level (240 teaching hours), the others at standard level (150 teaching hours). Students can take examinations in English, French or Spanish.

In addition, three unique components of the programme – the DP core – aim to broaden students' educational experience and challenge them to apply their knowledge and skills. The DP core – the extended essay (EE), theory of knowledge (TOK) and creativity, activity, service (CAS) – are compulsory and central to the philosophy of the programme.

The IB uses both external and internal assessment to measure student performance in the DP. Student results are determined by performance against set standards, not by each student's position in the overall rank order. DP assessment is unique in the way that it measures the extent to which students have mastered advanced academic skills not what they have memorized. DP assessment also encourages an international outlook and intercultural skills, wherever appropriate.

The IB diploma is awarded to students who gain at least 24 points out of a possible 45 points, subject to certain minimum levels of performance across the whole programme and to satisfactory participation in the creativity, activity, and service requirement.

Recognized and respected by leading universities globally, the DP encourages students to be knowledgeable, inquiring, caring and compassionate, and to develop intercultural understanding, open-mindedness and the attitudes necessary to respect and evaluate a range of viewpoints.

The IB Career Related Programme (IBCP)

The IB Career-related Programme, for students aged 16 to 19, offers an innovative educational framework that combines academic studies with career-related learning. Through the CP, students develop the competencies they need to succeed in the 21st century. More importantly, they have the opportunity to engage with a rigorous study programme that genuinely interests them while gaining transferable and lifelong skills that prepares them to pursue higher education, apprenticeships or direct employment.

CP students complete four core components – language development, personal and professional skills, service learning and a reflective project – in order to receive the International Baccalaureate Career-related Programme Certificate. Designed to enhance critical thinking and intercultural understanding, the CP core helps students develop the communication and personal skills, as well as intellectual habits required for lifelong learning.

Schools that choose to offer the CP can create their own distinctive version of the programme and select career pathways that suit their students and local community needs. The IB works with a variety of CRS providers around the world and schools seeking to develop career pathways with professional communities can benefit from our existing collaborations. All CRS providers undergo a rigorous curriculum evaluation to ensure that their courses align with the CP pedagogy and meet IB quality standards. The flexibility to meet the needs, backgrounds and contexts of learners allows CP schools to offer an education that is relevant and meaningful to their students.

Launched in 2012, there are more than 300 CP schools to date. Many schools with the IB Diploma Programme (DP) and the Middle Years Programme (MYP) have chosen the CP as an alternative IB pathway to offer students. CP schools often report that the programme has helped them raise student aspiration, increase student engagement and retention and encouraged learners to take responsibility for their own actions, helping them foster high levels of self-esteem through meaningful achievements.

For more information, visit: www.ibo.org

The International Early Years Curriculum (IEYC)

The International Early Years Curriculum is a research-based programme that incorporates international best practices in the developmental needs of 2-5 year olds, and can be easily extended to include older children in settings and countries where early years education goes beyond the age of five. It is also a perfect tool for the transition between early and formal education.

The IEYC is designed around eight learning principles, each conveying a belief considered essential to children's learning and development, and are intrinsically linked to a unique IEYC Process of Learning.

The IEYC Process of Learning

The IEYC Process of Learning provides a strong implementation structure, sequencing each unit. The process of learning captures children's natural curiosity as a starting point and, within an enabled environment, balances child-initiated and teacher-led learning. Each element of the Process of Learning is linked to the eight Learning Principles, ensuring the IEYC beliefs about children's learning and development are connected to all practices.

The IEYC Learning Strands

Underpinning all learning and development, are the IEYC Learning Strands:

- Independence and Interdependence
- Communicating
- Enquiring
- Healthy Living and Physical Wellbeing

Each unit has been carefully designed around a central theme, holistically linking all four Learning Strands to relevant and engaging activities that can be adapted and extended to meet individual needs.

For more details on the IEYC visit: fieldworkeducation.com/curriculums/early-years

The International Middle Years Curriculum (IMYC)

The International Middle Years Curriculum (IMYC) provides an enriching, engaging and rigorous learning experience for 11-14 year olds. It is practical for the school to deliver, and inspiring and relevant for students, preparing them well for the next stage in their learning.

The IMYC is a curriculum that makes meaning, connects learning and develops minds. It delivers rigorous and transformational knowledge, skills and understanding of all subjects, linking all learning to a conceptual theme. The IMYC creates a challenging, student-led learning environment preparing students well for iGCSE, A levels and IB Diploma.

Each IMYC unit guides students to make meaning of the conceptual theme through a personal and global perspective which they represent at the end of their unit learning through a media project. Within each IMYC unit there is a learning process designed to engage and inspire teenagers, helping them to become confident, independent learners.

IMYC member schools and students are part of a worldwide IMYC community through which they share learning experiences, ideas and resources.

The IMYC is part of Fieldwork Education which, since 1984, has been helping schools around the world to develop children's learning. For more information about the IMYC visit fieldworkeducation.com/curriculums/middle-years

The International Primary Curriculum (IPC)

The International Primary Curriculum (IPC) is one of the only comprehensive curricula in the world equally committed to improving learning and developing international mindedness. It focuses on developing knowledge, skills and understanding of subjects set within child-friendly, relevant, cross-curricular thematic units of work that are creative and challenging for children of all abilities. The IPC has over 140 different thematic units of learning; all modern-day topics appealing to all ages of primary children. This enables young children to remain motivated through the learning of science, geography, history and so on.

Within each theme, the IPC suggests many ideas for collaborative learning, for active learning, for learning outside the classroom, for role play, and for children learning from each other. The IPC's engaging approach also encourages parental involvement through a range of initiatives.

Each IPC unit incorporates most of the core subjects including science, history, geography, ICT, art and PE and provides opportunities to incorporate language arts and mathematics. Each subject then has a number of learning tasks to help teachers to help their children meet a range of learning goals set out in the curriculum. These learning goals are deliberately explicit, designed to make sure that teachers distinguish clearly between children's learning of knowledge, skills and understanding.

Each IPC unit has embedded within it learning-focused activities that help young children to start developing a global awareness and gain an increasing sense of the 'other'. Every unit creates opportunities to look at learning of the theme through a local perspective, a national perspective and an international perspective.

With schools in over 90 countries learning with the IPC, there are opportunities for children to share their local experiences related to an IPC unit with children in dramatically different environments.

Each IPC unit has a very structured yet flexible teaching framework providing teachers with a series of learning tasks. These are designed to achieve the learning goals through creative, meaningful and memorable learning activities that appeal to all learning styles and are relevant for all children of all abilities. However, the learning tasks are purely a guide and provide plenty of scope for creative teaching, personalisation to the class and locality, and development on the theme as well as linking with other schools learning with the IPC. With IPC member schools in countries as diverse as Swaziland, Malaysia, Qatar, and Japan, this sharing of learning opportunities ensures that no school, however remote, feels isolated.

The IPC is part of Fieldwork Education. For more information about the IPC visit fieldworkeducation.com/curriculums/primary-years

UK SYSTEM

What is Common Entrance?

The Common Entrance examinations are used in UK independent schools (and some independent schools overseas) for transfer from junior to senior schools at the ages of 11+ and 13+. They were first introduced in 1904 and are internationally recognised as being a rigorous form of assessment following a thorough course of study. The examinations are produced by the Independent Schools Examinations Board and backed by HMC (Headmasters' and Headmistresses' Conference), GSA (Girls' Schools Association), and IAPS (Independent Association of Prep Schools) which together represent the leading independent schools in the UK, and many overseas.

Common Entrance is not a public examination as, for example, GCSE, and candidates may normally be entered only in one of the following circumstances:

a) they have been offered a place at a senior school subject to their passing the examination, or

b) they are entered as a 'trial run', in which case the papers are marked by the junior school concerned. Candidates normally take the examination in their own junior or preparatory schools, either in the UK or overseas.

How does Common Entrance fit into the progression to GCSEs?

Rapid changes in education nationally and internationally have resulted in regular reviews of the syllabuses for all the Common Entrance examinations. Reviews of the National Curriculum, in particular, have brought about a number of changes, with the Board wishing to ensure that it continues to set high standards. It is also a guiding principle that Common Entrance should be part of the natural progression from 11-16, and not a diversion from it.

Common Entrance at 11+

At 11+, the examination consists of papers in English, mathematics and science. It is designed so that it can be taken by candidates either from independent preparatory schools or by candidates from schools in the maintained sector or overseas who have had no special preparation. The examination is normally taken in January for entrance to senior schools in the following September.

Common Entrance at 13+

At 13+, most candidates come from independent preparatory schools. The compulsory subjects are English, mathematics and science. Papers in French, geography, German, Classical Greek, history, Latin, religious studies and Spanish are also available and candidates usually offer as many subjects as they can. In most subjects, papers are available at more than one level to cater for candidates of different abilities. There are three examination sessions each year, with the majority of candidates sitting in the summer prior to entry to their senior schools in September.

Marking and grading

The papers are set centrally but the answers are marked by the senior school for which a candidate is entered. Mark schemes are provided by the Board but senior schools are free to set their own grade boundaries. Results are available within two weeks of the examinations taking place.

Pre-Testing and the ISEB Common Pre-Tests

A number of senior independent schools 'pre-test' pupils for entry, prior to them taking their main entrance examinations at a later date. Usually, these pre-tests take place when a pupil is in Year 6 or Year 7 of his or her junior school and will then be going on to sit Common Entrance in Year 8. The tests are designed to assess a pupil's academic potential and suitability for a particular senior school so that the child, the parents and the school know well in advance whether he/she is going to be offered a place at the school, subject to a satisfactory performance in the entrance examinations. The tests enable senior schools to manage their lists and help to ensure that pupils are not entered for examinations in which they are unlikely to be successful. In short, it reduces uncertainty for all concerned.

Pre-tests may be written specifically for the senior school for which the candidate is entered but a growing number of schools are choosing to use the Common Pre-Tests provided by the Independent Schools Examinations Board. These online tests are usually taken in the candidate's own junior school and one of their main advantages is that a pupil need sit the tests only once, with the results then made available to any senior school which wishes to use them. The multiple-choice tests cover verbal reasoning, non-verbal reasoning, English and mathematics, with the results standardised according to the pupil's age when they are taken. Further information is available on the ISEB website at www.iseb.co.uk.

Parents are advised to check the entrance requirements for senior schools to see if their child will be required to sit a pre-test.

Further information

Details of the Common Entrance examinations and how to register candidates are available on the ISEB website www.iseb.co.uk. Copies of past papers and a wide range of textbooks and other resources can be purchased from Galore Park Publishing Ltd at www.galorepark.co.uk. Support materials are also available from Hodder Education and other publishers; see the Resources section of the ISEB website for details.

Independent Schools Examinations Board
Endeavour House, Crow Arch Lane,
Ringwood, Hampshire BH24 1HP

Telephone: 01425 470555
Email: enquiries@iseb.co.uk
Web: www.iseb.co.uk

General Certificate of Secondary Education (GCSE)

What are the GCSE qualifications?

GCSE qualifications were first introduced in 1986 and are the principal means of assessment at Key Stage 4 across a range of academic subject areas. They command respect and have status not only in the UK but worldwide.

Main features of the GCSE

There are four unitary awarding organisations for GCSEs in England. WJEC and CCEA also offer GCSE qualifications in Wales and Northern Ireland. Each examining group designs its own specifications but they are required to conform to set criteria. For some aspects of the qualification system, the exam boards adopt common ways of working. When the exam boards work together in this way they generally do so through the Joint Council of Qualifications (JCQ). The award of a grade is intended to indicate that a candidate has met the required level of skills, knowledge and understanding.

New, reformed GCSEs have been introduced in recent years. New GCSEs in ancient languages (classical Greek, Latin), art and design, biology, chemistry, citizenship studies, combined science (double award), computer science, dance, drama, food preparation and nutrition, geography, history, modern foreign languages (French, German, Spanish), music, physics, physical education and religious studies were first taught in September 2016, with first results in summer 2018. Assessment in these reformed GCSEs consists primarily of formal examinations taken at the end of the student's two-year course. Other types of assessment, non-exam assessment (NEA), is used where there are skills and knowledge which cannot be assessed through exams. Ofqual have set the percentage of the total marks that will come from NEA.

The reformed GCSEs feature new and more demanding content, as required by the government and developed by the exam boards. Courses are designed for two years of study (linear assessment) and no longer divided into different modules.

Exams can only be split into 'foundation tier' and 'higher tier' if one exam paper does not give all students the opportunity to show their knowledge and their abilities. Such tiering is only available in maths, science and modern foreign languages; other subjects do not have tiers. Resit opportunities will only be available each November in English language and maths, and then only for students who have turned 16 by the 31st of August in the year of the November assessment.

New GCSEs taught from September 2017: ancient history, astronomy, business, classical civilisation, design and technology, economics, electronics, engineering, film studies, geology, media studies, psychology, sociology, statistics, other (minority) foreign languages e.g. Italian, Polish.

New GCSEs taught from September 2018: ancient languages (biblical Hebrew) and modern foreign languages (Gujarati, Persian, Portuguese, Turkish).

Grading

The basic principle that exam boards follow when setting grade boundaries is that if the group of students (the cohort) taking a qualification in one year is of similar ability to the cohort in the previous year then the overall results (outcomes) should be comparable.

The reformed exams taken in summer 2017 were the first to show a new grading system, with the A* to G grades being phased out.

The new grading system is 9 to 1, with 9 being the top grade. Ofqual says this allows greater differentiation between students. It expects that broadly the same proportion of students will achieve a grade 4 and above as currently achieve a grade C and above, that broadly the same proportion of students will achieve a grade 7 and above as currently achieve a grade A and above. There are three anchor points between the new grading system and the old one: the bottom of the new 1 grade is the same as the bottom of the old G grade, the bottom of the new 4 grade is the bottom of the old C grade, and the bottom of the 7 grade is the same as the bottom of the old A grade. Grade 9 will be set using the tailored approach formula in the first award.

Grades 2, 3, 5 and 6 will be awarded arithmetically so that the grade boundaries are equally spaced in terms of marks from neighbouring grades.

The government's definition of a 'strong pass' will be set at grade 5 for reformed GCSEs. A grade 4 – or 'standard pass' – will continue to be a level 2 achievement. The DfE does not expect employers, colleges or universities to raise the bar to a grade 5 if a grade 4 would meet their requirements.

Can anyone take GCSE qualifications?

GCSEs are intended mainly for 16-year-old pupils, but are open to anyone of any age, whether studying full-time or part-time at a school, college or privately. There are no formal entry requirements.

Students normally study up to ten subjects over a two-year period. Short course GCSEs are available in some subjects (including PE and religious studies) – these include half the content of a full GCSE, so two short course GCSEs are equivalent to one full GCSE.

The English Baccalaureate

The English Baccalaureate (EBacc) is a school performance measure. It allows people to see how many pupils get a grade C or above (current grading) in the core academic subjects at Key Stage 4 in any government-funded school. The DfE introduced the EBacc measure in 2010.

General Certificate of Education (GCE) Advanced level (A level)

Typically, A level qualifications are studied over a two-year period. There are no lower or upper age limits. Schools and colleges usually expect students aged 16-18 to have obtained grades A*-C (grade 5 in the new criteria) in five subjects at GCSE level before taking an advanced level course. This requirement may vary between centres and according to which specific subjects are to be studied. Mature students may be assessed on different criteria as to their suitability to embark on the course.

GCE Qualifications

Over the past few years, AS level and A level qualifications have been in a process of reform. New subjects have been introduced gradually, with the first wave taught from September 2015. Subjects that have not been reformed are no longer available for teaching.

GCE qualifications are available at two levels: the Advanced Subsidiary (AS), which is generally delivered over one year and is seen as half an A level; and the A level (GCE). Nearly 70 titles are available, covering a wide range of subject areas, including humanities, sciences, language, business, arts, mathematics and technology.

One of the major reforms is that AS level results no longer count towards an A level (they previously counted for 50%). The two qualifications are linear, with AS assessments typically taking place after one year and A levels after two.

New-style AS and A levels were first taught from September 2015 for: art and design, biology, business studies, chemistry, computer studies, economics, English language, English language and literature, English literature, history, physics, psychology, and sociology.

Subjects first taught from September 2016 include: ancient languages such as Latin or Greek, dance, drama (theatre studies), geography, modern languages such as Spanish or French, music, physical education, religious studies.

Those introduced for first teaching from September 2017: accounting, design and technology, music technology, history of art, environmental science, philosophy, maths, further maths, archaeology, accounting, electronics, ancient history, law, classical civilisation, film studies, media studies, politics, geology, statistics, Chinese, Italian, Russian. In 2018 Biblical Hebrew, Modern Hebrew & languages such as Bengali, Polish and Urdu were available for first teaching.

Some GCE AS and A levels, particularly the practical ones, contain a proportion of coursework. All GCE A levels that contain one or more types of assessment will have an element of synoptic assessment that tests students' understanding of the whole specification. GCE AS are graded A-E and A levels are graded A*-E.

Overall the amount of coursework at A level has been reduced in the reforms. In some subjects, such as the sciences, practical work will not contribute to the final A level but will be reported separately in a certificate of endorsement. In the sciences, students will do at least 12 practical activities, covering apparatus and techniques. Exam questions about practical work will make up at least 15% of the total marks for the qualification and students will be assessed on their knowledge, skills and understanding of practical work.

US SYSTEM

Programs and tests

The Advanced Placement Program (AP)

The coronavirus global pandemic has created new challenges for schools and students. Visit pages. collegeboard.org/collegeboard-covid-19-updates for more updates to support students and educators in continuing the AP journey, even if their school is closed.

The Advanced Placement (AP) program provides an opportunity for willing and academically prepared students to take rigorous, university-level courses that help them develop the skills necessary for success in university and their future careers. Over 3,800 universities in more than 60 countries recognize qualifying AP Exam scores in the admission process.

Students who succeed on AP Exams also have the opportunity to earn college credit and/or advanced placement, helping them to reduce tuition costs and offering more time and flexibility to double major, study abroad, complete an internship or graduate earlier.

AP courses are typically taught in secondary schools, and AP Exams measure a student's mastery of university-level course content. The program allows students to develop a global perspective, as well as skills such as critical thinking and problem solving. For each course, there is a standardized university-level exam that tests the skills and knowledge addressed in the course. AP Exams are administered in May of every year around the world, and are scored by College Board's AP Program. AP® Exams registration deadline is in mid-November and administered over two weeks in May of the following year. The mobile friendly digital resources and data support, AP Classroom, provides educators with free new instructional resources to help students master AP content and skills. In addition, the student performing data and educator professional development events empower educators to gain deep content knowledge to better guide their students. For more information, visit myap. collegeboard.org

AP courses and exams are designed by teams of experts to match the rigor of real university courses and exams. Because of this, a student's score on an AP Exam gives universities a globally recognized validation of their mastery of university-level content.

To find schools that offer AP around the world, visit: https://apcourseaudit.inflexion.org/ledger/ and begin the search by entering a country in the 'Ledger Search' area. The AP Course Ledger is the official record of schools with authorized courses that can use the AP designation.

AP Capstone

AP Capstone™ is an innovative diploma program that provides students with an opportunity to engage in rigorous scholarly practice of the core academic skills necessary for successful college completion.

AP Capstone is built on the foundation of two courses – AP Seminar and AP Research. These two AP Capstone courses, with their associated performance tasks, assessments, and application of research methodology, complement the rigor of AP courses and exams by equipping students with the power to analyze and evaluate information with accuracy and precision in order to craft and communicate evidence-based arguments.

Students who earn scores of 3 or higher in AP Seminar and AP Research and on four additional AP Exams of their choosing receive the AP Capstone Diploma™. This signifies their outstanding academic achievement and attainment of university-level academic and research skills. Students who earn scores of 3 or higher in both AP Seminar and AP Research but not on four additional AP Exams receive the AP Seminar and Research Certificate™.

AP Capstone was developed in response to feedback from higher education and is easily implemented, affordable, and flexible. It has the potential to differentiate and transform high schools and their students by elevating the learning environment through a challenging, university-level program with high standards of assessment.

For more information, visit collegeboard.org/ apcapstone or email apcapstone@collegeboard.org.

Advanced Placement International Diploma (APID)

The Advanced Placement International Diploma (APID) is a globally recognized credential for students who embrace an international outlook. The APID also challenges a student to display exceptional achievement across several disciplines. Universities worldwide utilize the APID in admissions.

The APID is available to students attending secondary schools outside the United States and to US resident students applying to universities outside the country. The APID is not a substitute for a high school diploma, but provides additional recognition of outstanding academic excellence.

In addition, for students attending schools within the United States to be eligible for the APID scholar award, they must send their official AP score report to a university outside the United States. For a list of universities outside the US that recognize AP, visit: international.collegeboard.org/students/ap/find-universities-recognize-ap

In order to earn the APID, students must earn scores of 3 or higher on five or more total AP Exams, based on the exam criteria requirements listed within each of the following content areas:

a) Two AP Exams from two different languages, either one selected from English and one from another world language OR two different world languages other than English: AP Chinese Language and Culture, AP English Language and Composition, AP English Literature and Composition, AP French Language and Culture, AP German Language and Culture, AP Spanish Language and Culture, AP Italian Language and Culture, and AP Japanese Language and Culture.
b) One AP Exam offering a global perspective: AP Art History, AP Comparative Government and Politics, AP Environmental Science, AP Human Geography, AP Macroeconomics and AP World History.
c) One AP Exam from the sciences or mathematics and computer science content areas: AP Biology, AP Calculus AB, AP Calculus BC, AP Chemistry, AP Computer Science A, AP Environmental Science, AP Physics C: Electricity and Magnetism, AP Physics C: Mechanics, AP Physics 1: Algebra-based, AP Physics 2: Algebra-based and AP Statistics.
d) One additional exam from among any content areas except English and world languages, excluding Latin. These include the content areas already described as well as AP Capstone, history and social science, and arts: AP Seminar, AP Research, AP Art History, AP European History, AP Latin, AP Macroeconomics, AP Microeconomics, AP Music Theory, AP Psychology, AP Studio Art: Drawing, AP Studio Art: 2-D Design, AP Studio Art: 3-D Design, AP US Government and Politics, AP US History and AP World History.

High School diploma

The American High School Diploma is a certificate awarded to students when they complete high school. Students generally study for the diploma for four years, from the 9th to 12th grade.

There is no national curriculum in the US, although states, school districts and national associations do recommend that certain standards are met and guidelines followed.

Each state sets the requirements for the high school diploma. Students are assessed throughout each semester with tests, exams, essays, homework assignments, classroom preparation, group work, projects and attendance, and given a final 'grade' for each course at the end of the semester.

Parents are sent a 'report card' with the grades achieved in each subject at the end of each quarter, semester or year. They will also ultimately receive a 'transcript' – an overview of their academic history, produced by the school – which will be requested by universities upon application.

Marks are given as letters (A+, A, B+ etc) or a percentage. These marks will result in a Grade Point Average (GPA). The grading system is not standardised across school districts. However, in general they are:

A grade – excellent level – 4 points
B grade – above average –3 points
C grade – average – 2 points
D grade – below average – 1 point
F – failure – 0 points (Note: a student that fails a required course must take it again.)

A student's high school GPA represents their accumulated grades throughout high school. It is calculated by adding the total of all points earned for each course, then dividing the total points by the total number of courses taken. Additional points may be awarded for extra work done in honors, AP or IB courses.

When applying for university, a student's GPA is taken into consideration and there are also admissions tests, such as the SAT and the ACT.

University admissions tests and programs

American College Testing (ACT)

The ACT test is a curriculum-based achievement test, meaning it measures what students have learned in school, and tests them on the knowledge and skills they should have prior to pursuing a college or career path.

The ACT is not an aptitude or IQ test, it is a standardized achievement test, used for admissions purposes, scholarship eligibility, course placement, remediation, and retention.

Composite scores range from one to 36; and each section test (English, math, reading, science) is also scored on a scale from 1–36. The composite score given to each student is the average of the four tests added together, rounded to the nearest whole number. Students taking the optional writing test can score from two to 12.

The ACT is offered in the US on seven national test dates in September, October, December, February, April, June and July. ACT testing is also administered internationally on five international test dates, and on school days in the US. in select states and school districts that pay for their students to test.

Contact ACT for further information or to register for a test, via their website: www.act.org.

See how ACT scores compare to SATs: www.act.org/content/dam/act/unsecured/documents/ACT-SAT-Concordance-Tables.pdf

College Level Examination Program (CLEP)

CLEP gives students of any age the opportunity to demonstrate college level achievement through a programme of exams in undergraduate college courses. It enables students to earn college credit for learning gained through independent study, advanced high school courses, non-credit courses, or professional development. Students can use the CLEP examinations to demonstrate learning and earn placement, credit or exemption from entry-level courses.

Exams are offered in 34 subjects within the following areas: composition and literature, foreign languages, history and social science, science and mathematics, business. There are more than 2900 colleges that grant credit and/or advanced standing for CLEP exams. The exams themselves are 90 minutes long and are mostly multiple choice, covering material taught in courses that most students take during their first two years of college. Most examinations are designed to correspond to one-semester courses; some, however, correspond to full year or two year courses.

The exams are administered at over 1700 US test centres and at several international sites. There are no national test dates; students can work with their individual test centre to schedule the CLEP exam when they are ready.

The American Council on Education (ACE) has developed a recommended credit granting score and number of semester hours of credit for each CLEP exam. Bear in mind that the amount of credit you receive for each CLEP exam you take and the score you have to achieve to get that credit or exemption is determined by the credit granting policy of your college or university.

SAT (USA)

The coronavirus global pandemic has created new challenges for schools and students. Visit pages. collegeboard.org/sat-covid-19-updates for most recent updates and newly added SAT Administrations dates globally.

The SAT® is taken by millions of students each year and helps them achieve their dreams of studying in the US and elsewhere. The SAT measures the skills that students develop in secondary school.

The SAT is designed to predict a student's likely academic performance at a particular college or university in their first year and beyond. The SAT covers content areas deemed critical for success in college and SAT performance data illustrate that success on the SAT is linked to the type and rigor of course work completed during high school.

Over four million students take the SAT each academic year via nearly 7,000 test centers in more than 180 countries and territories. SAT questions are prescreened on students from around the world to ensure fairness. Before any test question appears on a scored section of the SAT, it is included on one of the unscored test forms that are included in every SAT administration. By pretesting questions in this way, College Board researchers can be sure that each question is fair and valid for all students regardless of gender, race, ethnicity, country of origin or socio-economic status. The SAT is the only college entrance exam that prescreens test questions on a global population of test-takers. The SAT is currently offered five times a year outside the United States.

Dates for international test administrations, registrations requirements and deadlines can be found at: sat.org/international

The SAT Suite of Assessments

College Board announced in January 2022 that the SAT® Suite of Assessments will be delivered digitally. While the transition to digital will bring a number of student- and educator-friendly changes, many important features of the SAT Suite (SAT, PSAT/NMSQT®, PSAT™ 10, PSAT™ 8/9) will stay the same. The SAT Suite will continue to measure the knowledge and skills that students are learning in high school and that matter most for college and career readiness. The SAT will still be scored on a 1600 scale, and educators and students can continue to track growth across the SAT Suite of Assessments over time. The assessments will continue to be administered in a school or in a test center with a proctor present—not at home. Students will still have access to free practice resources on Khan Academy. And students taking the SAT Suite will continue to connect to scholarships.

The Digital SAT

Beginning in 2023, the SAT® Suite of Assessments will be delivered digitally. While the transition to digital will bring a number of student- and educator-friendly changes, many important features of the SAT Suite will stay the same.

- The SAT Suite (SAT, PSAT/NMSQT, PSAT 10, PSAT 8/9) will continue to measure the knowledge and skills that students are learning in high school and that matter most for college and career readiness.
- The SAT will still be scored on a 1600 scale, and educators and students can continue to track growth across the suite over time.

- Where the SAT is given isn't changing. The digital SAT will continue to be administered in a school or in a test center with a proctor present—not at home.
- Practice resources will be even more closely linked to the test day experience. Students will still have access to free practice resources on Khan Academy, plus new practice resources will be available directly on the digital testing application.
- Students will still connect directly to scholarships and the College Board National Recognition Programs.
- College Board will continue to support all students, including those who receive accommodations on test day.

College Board will make the transition from paper and pencil to digital at international test centers in spring of 2023 and at U.S. schools and test centers in spring of 2024.

- Most students who take the SAT for the first time do so in the spring of their junior year.
  - For students testing internationally, those in the class of 2024 will be the first to take the digital SAT.
  - In the U.S., students in the high school class of 2025 will be the first class to take the digital test.
- All students will take the digital PSAT 8/9 and PSAT/NMSQT starting in fall 2023, followed by the digital PSAT 10 in spring 2024.

What's Changing?

- The digital SAT Suite will be shorter, about two hours instead of three, with more time per question.
- Reading and Writing passages will be shorter, with one question tied to each.
  - College Board's intention is to create a test experience that is less stressful for all students, particularly English learners.
  - More than 80% of students who participated in the recent digital SAT pilot said the test experience was less stressful than the paper-and-pencil test.
- Students and educators will see scores in a matter of days: Students get the information they need to make key college decisions, and educators get the information they need to support students and inform instruction.

The digital SAT Suite will be more secure.

Currently, if one test form is compromised, it can mean canceling scores for whole groups of students. Going digital allows College Board to give every student a virtually unique test form, so it will be practically impossible to share answers.

The SAT will be more relevant for students

- Students are now doing more of their learning and testing digitally, and taking the SAT shouldn't be the exception.
  - A digital test means no more bubble sheets and no more #2 pencils.
  - Calculators will be allowed on the entire Math section. A graphing calculator and other tools will be built into the digital testing application, or students can bring their own calculator.
- Featuring many shorter Reading and Writing passages instead of a few long texts means students will see a wider range of topics that represent the works they read in college.
- The digital SAT will be a useful tool for more students as the digital SAT score reports will connect students to information and resources about local two-year college and workforce training programs.

Watch this video to learn more about the Digital SAT Suite of Assessments.

PSAT 8/9

PSAT™ 8/9 can be administered in the fall or spring of U.S.-equivalent eighth and/or ninth grade, depending on the goals of districts and schools. The test serves as a foundation for understanding student progress as they enter secondary school and ensuring that they are on target for being university and career ready by the time they leave secondary school

PSAT 10 and PSAT/NMSQT

Both exams cover the same content domain and serve as a "check-in" on student progress and pinpoint areas for focused practice. Students can take the PSAT/NMSQT in the fall of U.S.-equivalent tenth and/or eleventh grade (though only eleventh graders who are U.S. citizens are eligible for the National Merit Scholarship Program). Instead of delivering the PSAT/NMSQT to tenth graders in the fall, some schools may instead deliver the PSAT™ 10 in the spring.

Preliminary SAT/National Merit Scholarship Qualifying Test (PSAT/NMSQT ®)

The Preliminary SAT/National Merit Scholarship Qualifying Test (PSAT/NMSQT®) is a standardized test that measures the skills that students will need for higher education and careers after secondary school. Like the SAT, the digital PSAT/NMSQT measures the skills and knowledge that are essential for university readiness and success.

For more information visit: http://sat.org/digital

Student Search Service ®

The College Board's Student Search Service is a free, voluntary program that connects students with information about educational and financial aid opportunities from more than 1,500 eligible colleges and universities, and over 300 Million scholarship dollars and other educational programs.

When students take the SAT, PSAT/NMSQT, and PSAT 10, they're asked if they want to participate. Students can also opt in online at any time. By opting in, they give the College Board permission to share their names and limited information with colleges and scholarship programs looking for students like them.

Learn more about Student Search Service.

Index

Index

B

Index

C

Index

D

E

F

G

I

Index

J

K

L

Index

M

N

Q

R

S

Index

T

U

V

W

X

Y

Z